A BIBLIOGRAPHY OF
UNITED STATES–LATIN AMERICAN
RELATIONS SINCE 1810

A BIBLIOGRAPHY OF
UNITED STATES–
LATIN AMERICAN
RELATIONS SINCE 1810

A Selected List of Eleven Thousand Published References

WITHDRAWN
L. R. COLLEGE LIBRARY

Compiled and Edited by

DAVID F. TRASK
MICHAEL C. MEYER
ROGER R. TRASK

CARL A. RUDISILL LIBRARY
LENOIR RHYNE COLLEGE

UNIVERSITY OF NEBRASKA PRESS · LINCOLN

Publishers on the Plains

UNP

Copyright © 1968 by the University of Nebraska Press

All Rights Reserved

Library of Congress Catalog Card Number 67–14421

016.32773
T 69 b

65,351
March, 1969

Manufactured in the United States of America

Preface

The history of United States–Latin American relations is of vital concern to all who inhabit the Western Hemisphere, and it is of increasing importance elsewhere in the world. Given the significance of this field, it is surprising that no comprehensive bibliographical guide to its literature has heretofore been available in one volume. To be sure, interested investigators have been able to turn to a number of exceedingly useful bibliographical works dealing in part with the history of United States–Latin American relations. Among these are the classic work of Bemis and Griffin, *Guide to the Diplomatic History of the United States, 1775–1921* (item 335); the *Index to Latin American Periodical Literature, 1929–1960* (item 277); the four-volume set entitled *Foreign Affairs Bibliography* (item 56) made available by the Council on Foreign Relations; Humphreys' *Latin American History: A Guide to the Literature in English* (item 218); and the indispensable *Handbook of Latin American Studies* (item 208). Nevertheless, these works and comparable materials pose difficulties because they deal with other fields as well as hemispheric relations and are limited in their coverage by chronology, topic, organization, scope, and type of listing. Accordingly, any adequate bibliographical search has required the historical investigator to consult a large number of volumes not necessarily developed to meet his particular needs. For example, Bemis and Griffin do not survey the years after 1921, nor do they list materials published after 1935. The periodical *Index* lists only items from serial publications for the period 1929–1960, although supplements for more recent years are becoming available. *Foreign Affairs Bibliography* lists only books published during the period 1919–1962. Humphreys does not list material available in languages other than English. The *Handbook of Latin American Studies*, perhaps the most comprehensive in its coverage, now extends to some twenty-eight volumes covering publications since 1934.

Our objective as compilers has been to provide in one volume an extensive listing of published sources and authorities which both collates and expands the corpus of previous general lists of references for the history of United States–Latin American relations. This bibliography includes published materials of all kinds—books, articles, pamphlets, documents, and the like—in a wide variety of languages, particularly English, Spanish, Portuguese, French, German, Italian, Russian, and Japanese. We have not attempted to list unpublished materials, although we have cited a large number of guides to manuscript collections in Chapter I. The only exceptions to this rule are a large sampling of unpublished doctoral dissertations and a very small number of mimeographed items of particular significance. We make no claim to have incorporated all materials relevant to our subject, but we believe that no other work of comparable scope and convenience is now available.

Organization. The bibliography is organized in two main sections, which are supplemented by several specialized chapters. Chapters III–X provide a chronological survey of United States–Latin American relations from the beginning of the national independence movements in Latin America in 1810 until the present. The periodization adopted for this chronological survey is based on the conventional perspective of historians in the United States. Chapters XIII–XXIV offer a country-by-country survey. Each country's chapter is periodized according to the perspective of historians from that nation. In addition, Chapter I includes an extensive list of guides and aids; Chapter II covers general studies of the field and other useful works; Chapter XI surveys the course of the Pan American movement since 1889; and Chapter XII lists works relating to certain Latin American movements of a political, ideological, and cultural nature which have exerted considerable influence on the course of hemispheric relations—in particular, Pan Hispanism, Yankeephobia, and Aprismo. We have made no attempt to survey hemispheric relations with Spain prior to the independence movements or to cover relations with areas of the Western Hemisphere which have remained dependent on European nations or the United States, such as the British West Indies, the

Guianas, and Puerto Rico. We have attempted to make the work helpful to users with various perspectives and intentions, including those peculiar not only to students in the United States but to those of other countries. We believe that the country chapters are of particular utility to Latin American users.

Citation. Each item is cited in full only once, but cross references from the original citation are provided for other relevant sections of the bibliography. All citations are alphabetized by author (or by title if no author is given) within sections or subsections. The conventional English alphabet is used for this purpose. Names and words beginning with Spanish letters like *ll* and *ch* are not listed separately but are incorporated into the alphabetization as in English. The same practice is used for other languages. A typical citation for a book-length publication or pamphlet includes author, title, edition (if relevant), volumes (if relevant), place of publication, and year of publication. For example:

> 8702. Orellana, J. G. *Resumen Histórico del Ecuador.* 2d ed., 2 vols., Quito, 1948.

The citations for dissertations include author, title, university, and year accepted. For example:

> 2564. Van Aken, M. J. "Origins of the Pan-Hispanic Movement to 1866," U. of California Diss., 1956.

The citations for items from periodicals or other serial publications include author, title, symbol for publication, volume number, year of publication, and page numbers. For example:

> 7357. Olney, R. "Fortification of the Panama Canal," *AJIL* 5 (1911) 298–301.

A list of symbols for periodicals and serial publications appears at the beginning of the bibliography. There is also a separate list of other abbreviations used in citations. If additional information is needed to locate a given item, it is added to the basic form, e.g., the month of publication or the number of the publication.

Annotation. Annotations are included occasionally to provide additional publication data, to clarify content, or to identify the author or subject in instances where this information may be helpful to the user. No critical comments are made; annotations are entirely descriptive in nature. If a listing has been translated or is available in more than one place, this information is provided in the annotation. A clarification is given if the title is susceptible of diverse interpretation. For example:

> 3758. Lieuwen, E. *Arms and Politics in Latin America.* N.Y., 1960.
> Rev. ed. in pb., N.Y., 1963. Part I discusses the role of the military; Part II considers military aspects of United States–Latin American policy. The revised edition contains a new chapter on Cuba.

Cross References. Lists of cross references appear at the conclusion of sections and subsections. These inserts refer the searcher either to entire sections elsewhere in the bibliography where other relevant items appear, or to the numbers of individual citations which may prove useful. The cross references provide a necessary link between the chronological chapters (III–X) and the country chapters (XIII–XXIV). The full citation for cross-referenced items is listed in the place where the work makes its primary contribution.

Users of this bibliography will note that certain areas of interest have received much more attention in the past than others, e.g., United States–Mexican relations or the New Pan Americanism, whereas others, like United States–Costa Rican relations or United States–Paraguayan relations have been studied far less extensively. In the latter case, we have included general items which may be useful in the absence of specialized information. Our bibliography reflects the amount of labor expended on any given topic rather than the quality or depth of those labors. We leave to those who consult this work the task of rendering critical judgments and selecting from the available materials those items they wish to consult.

Despite rigorous efforts, we realize that our bibliography undoubtedly contains a certain number of errors and omissions. We ask that users inform us of any they note so that they might be corrected in the future. We will be satisfied with our compilation if it proves as helpful to its users as those imposing bibliographical works we have relied upon so heavily in the course of our own endeavor, especially those mentioned at the outset of this Preface, have been to us.

D. F. T.
M. C. M.
R. R. T.

Acknowledgments

A bibliographical work of this scope requires an unusual amount of assistance and encouragement. We are pleased to list those who contributed their interest and energies to the preparation of this volume. The responsibility for the final product, of course, rests with the joint compilers.

We are grateful to the research councils of the University of Nebraska, Macalester College, and Wesleyan University for financial assistance. We respectfully recognize the contributions of the libraries at Macalester College, the State University of New York at Stony Brook, Wesleyan University, the University of New Mexico, and the University of Nebraska.

Our research assistants were William Beezley, Robert Cherny, Allen Gerlach, Mark Gilderhus, Irving Goldmacher, Stephen Green, Holger Herwig, Susan Middleton, James Moore, Norman Rosenberg, Jeanne Schilling, John Sticken, the late Peter Tuttle, Linda Vollmar, and John C. Woodbury. Our typists were Barbara Brogin, Suzanne Broz, Catherine Chapman, Dorothy Forward, Dorothy Hay, Goldalee Meyer, Ann Olson, Charlene Staska, Elizabeth Trask, and Donna Weiss.

Colleagues who read parts of the manuscript and offered helpful suggestions included Albin T. Anderson, University of Nebraska; Winfield Burgraff, University of Missouri; Thomas M. Davies, Jr., University of New Mexico; Richard K. Debo, Simon Fraser University; Roberto Esquenazi-Mayo, University of Nebraska; José Ferrer, Southern Oregon College; Lawrence A. Gelfand, University of Iowa; Norman A. Graebner, University of Virginia; Leon Helguera, Vanderbilt University; Norman Marin, University of Southern California; Ernest R. May, Harvard University; Frederick M. Nunn, Portland State College; Stanley R. Ross, State University of New York at Stony Brook; Walter V. Scholes, University of Missouri; William Sherman, Colorado State University; Aurea B. Warren, University of Nebraska; and Dave Warren, University of Nebraska.

Finally, we offer our greatest thanks to our wives: Elizabeth Brooks Trask, Goldalee Kochman Meyer, and Dorothy Buettner Trask.

D. F. T.
M. C. M.
R. R. T.

Contents

Abbreviations

Ala.	Alabama	MIT	Massachusetts Institute of Technology
Arg.	Argentina	Mo.	Missouri
Ariz.	Arizona	N.C.	North Carolina
Aug.	August	N.d.	No date
B.A.	Buenos Aires	Nebr.	Nebraska
Calif.	California	New ed.	New edition
Cd.	Ciudad	N.J.	New Jersey
Colo.	Colorado	No.	Number
Comm.	Committee	Nov.	November
Comp.	Compiler	N.p.	No place
Cong.	Congress	N.s.	New series
Conn.	Connecticut	N.Y.	New York
C.R.	Costa Rica	NYU	New York University
D.C.	District of Columbia	O.	Ohio
Dec.	December	OAS	Organization of American States
Del.	Delaware	Oct.	October
D.F.	Distrito Federal	Okla.	Oklahoma
Diss.	Dissertation	Ore.	Oregon
Doc.	Document	O.s.	Old series
D.R.	Dominican Republic	Pa.	Pennsylvania
Ed.	Editor; edition	PAU	Pan American Union
Eng.	England; English	Pb.	Paperback
Ex.	Executive	Phil.	Philadelphia
Feb.	February	P.I.	Philippine Islands
Fla.	Florida	Port.	Portugal; Portuguese
Fr.	French	P.R.	Puerto Rico
Ga.	Georgia	Pseud.	Pseudonym
Ger.	Germany; German	Pt.	Part
Ia.	Iowa	Rept.	Report
IAS	Inter-American System	Rev. ed.	Revised edition
Ill.	Illinois	R.I.	Rhode Island
Ind.	Indiana	Rio	Rio de Janeiro
Jan.	January	Russ.	Russian
Kan.	Kansas	S.C.	South Carolina
Ky.	Kentucky	Sept.	September
L.A.	Los Angeles	Ser.	Series
La.	Louisiana	Sess.	Session
LN	League of Nations	So.	South
Mass.	Massachusetts	Sp.	Spanish
Md.	Maryland	Suppl.	Supplement
Me.	Maine	Tenn.	Tennessee
Mich.	Michigan	Trans.	Translator
Minn.	Minnesota	Tri.	Trimester

U.	University	USDW	United States Department of War
UCLA	University of California at Los Angeles	USIA	United States Information Agency
USC	United States Congress	USLC	United States Library of Congress
U.S.C.	University of Southern California	USNA	National Archives of the United States
USCH	United States Congress, House of Representatives	Va.	Virginia
		Ven.	Venezuela
USCS	United States Congress, Senate	Vol.	Volume
USDAG	United States Department of Agriculture	Vt.	Vermont
		Wash.	Washington
USDC	United States Department of Commerce	Wis.	Wisconsin
USDD	United States Department of Defense	WPA	Works Progress Administration
USDN	United States Department of the Navy	W. Va.	West Virginia
USDS	United States Department of State	Wyo.	Wyoming

Key to Journals and Other Serials

A *América*. Havana, Cuba.

AA *American Archivist*. Washington, D.C.

AAAPSS *Annals of the American Academy of Political and Social Science*. Philadelphia, Pa.

AACE *Anales de Academia de Ciencias Económicas*. B. A., Argentina.

AAHC *Anales de la Academia de la Historia de Cuba*. Havana, Cuba.

AAPSSPS *American Association of Political and Social Science Pamphlet Series*. Philadelphia, Pa.

ABAJ *American Bar Association Journal*. Chicago, Ill.

AC *Aconcagua*. B. A., Argentina.

ACE *Annals of Collective Economy*. Geneva, Switzerland.

AE *América Española*. Cartagena, Colombia.

AEA *Anuario de Estudios Americanos*. Seville, Spain.

AEE *Anales de Económica y Estadística*. Bogotá, Colombia.

AER *American Economic Review*. Ithaca, N.Y.

AERC *Anuario Estadístico de la República de Chile*. Santiago, Chile.

AF *American Federationist*. Washington, D.C.

AFCJS *Anales de la Facultad de Ciencias Jurídicas y Sociales*. Santiago, Chile.

AFS *Arnold Foundation Studies*. Dallas, Texas.

AFSJ *American Foreign Service Journal*. Washington, D.C.

AG *Agenda*. Oxford, England.

AGSJ *American Geographic Society Journal*. New York, N.Y.

AHA *Anuario de Historia Argentina*. B. A., Argentina.

AHAAR *Annual Report of the American Historical Association*. Washington, D.C.

AHE *American Heritage*. Montpelier, Vt.

AHI *Agricultural History*. Baltimore, Md.

AHQ *Alabama Historical Quarterly*. Montgomery, Ala.

AHR *American Historical Review*. Washington, D.C.

AIA *Agriculture in the Americas*. Washington, D.C.

AIDCICM *Academia Interamericana de Derecho Comparado e Internacional: Cursos Monográphicos*. Havana, Cuba.

AIGM *Anuario del Instituto Geográfico Militar*. B. A., Argentina.

AJ *Anales de Jurisprudencia*. Bogotá, Colombia.

AJES *American Journal of Economics and Sociology*. Lancaster, Pa.

AJHSP *American Jewish Historical Society Publications*. Baltimore, Md.

AJIL *American Journal of International Law*. New York, N.Y.

AJO *Arbitration Journal*. New York, N.Y.

AJS *American Journal of Sociology*. Chicago, Ill.

AJTM *American Journal of Tropical Medicine*. Baltimore, Md.

ALA *American Library Annual*. New York, N.Y.

ALR *American Law Review*. New York, N.Y.

ALRR *American Law Register and Review*. Philadelphia, Pa.

AM *Atlantic Monthly*. Boston, Mass.

AMA *Argentina en Marcha*. B. A., Argentina.

AME *American Mercury*. New York, N.Y.

AMER *Amerasia*. New York, N.Y.

AMEX *América*. Mexico, D.F.

AMNDJG *Anales del Museo Nacional David J. Guzmán*. San Salvador, El Salvador.

AMNM *Anales del Museo Nacional*. Mexico, D.F.

AMP *American Psychologist*. Washington, D.C.

AN *Antología*. Mexico, D.F.

ANH *Anhembi*. São Paulo, Brazil.

ANR *Antioch Review*. Yellow Springs, O.

AOAS *Annals of the Organization of American States*. Washington, D.C.

AP *Aussenpolitik*. Stuttgart, Germany.

APAU *Americas*. Washington, D.C.

APSP   *American Philosophical Society Proceedings.* Philadelphia, Pa.

APSR   *American Political Science Review.* Baltimore, Md.

AQ   *American Quarterly.* Philadelphia, Pa.

AQU   *Arizona Quarterly.* Tucson, Ariz.

AR   *American Review.* New York, N.Y.

ARE   *Alabama Review.* University, Ala.

ARHR   *Arizona Historical Review.* Phoenix, Ariz.

AS   *American Scholar.* New York, N.Y.

ASCDI   *Anuario de la Sociedad Cubana de Derecho Internacional.* Havana, Cuba.

ASCI   *Annals of Science.* London, England.

ASGHG   *Anales de la Sociedad de Geografía e Historia de Guatemala.* Guatemala City, Guatemala.

ASILP   *American Society of International Law Proceedings.* Washington, D.C.

ASO   *Acción Social.* Santiago, Chile.

AT   *Atlantic.* Boston, Mass.

AUC   *Anales de la Universidad de Cuenca.* Cuenca, Ecuador.

AUCE   *Anales de la Universidad Central del Ecuador.* Quito, Ecuador.

AUCH   *Anales de la Universidad de Chile.* Santiago, Chile.

AUCV   *Anales de la Universidad Central de Venezuela.* Caracas, Venezuela.

AUM   *Anales de la Universidad de Madrid.* Madrid, Spain.

AUSD   *Anales de la Universidad de Santo Domingo.* Cd. Trujillo, D.R.

AZ   *Archivalische Zeitschrift.* Stuttgart, Germany.

B   *Bolívar.* Bogotá, Colombia.

BACH   *Boletín de la Academia Chilena de la Historia.* Santiago, Chile.

BACPS   *Boletín de la Academia de Ciencias Políticas y Sociales.* Caracas, Venezuela.

BAGNDR *Boletín del Archivo General de la Nación.* Cd. Trujillo, D.R.

BAGNM   *Boletín del Archivo Nacional de la Nación.* Mexico, D.F.

BAHM   *Boletín del Archivo Histórico de Miraflores.* Caracas, Venezuela.

BANC   *Boletín del Archivo Nacional.* Havana, Cuba.

BANCC   *Boletín de la Academia Nacional de Ciencias.* Córdoba, Argentina.

BANDR   *Boletín del Archivo Nacional.* Cd. Trujillo, D.R.

BANH   *Boletín de la Academia Nacional de Historia.* Quito, Ecuador.

BANHC   *Boletín de la Academia Nacional de la Historia.* Caracas, Venezuela.

BAPH   *Boletín de Academia Panameña de la Historia.* Panama City, Panama.

BB   *Brazilian Business.* Rio de Janeiro, Brazil.

BBCV   *Boletín del Banco Central de Venezuela.* Caracas, Venezuela.

BBM   *Boletín Bibliográfico.* Mexico, D.F.

BBN   *Boletín de la Biblioteca Nacional.* Santiago, Chile.

BBNG   *Boletín de la Biblioteca Nacional.* Guatemala City, Guatemala.

BBNM   *Boletín de la Biblioteca Nacional.* Mexico, D.F.

BBP   *Boletín Bibliográfico.* Lima, Peru.

BCC   *Boletín de la Camara de Comercio.* Lima, Peru.

BCN   *Boletín del Centro Naval.* B. A., Argentina.

BH   *Behind the Headlines.* Toronto, Canada.

BHA   *Boletín de Historia y Antigüedades.* Bogotá, Colombia.

BHR   *Business History Review.* Boston, Mass.

BHS   *Bulletin of Hispanic Studies.* Liverpool, England.

BHSP   *Buffalo Historical Society Publications.* Buffalo, N.Y.

BI   *Bulletin Interparlementaire.* Geneva, Switzerland.

BIIH   *Boletín del Instituto de Investigaciones Históricas.* B. A., Argentina.

BILCDI *Boletín del Instituto de Legislación Comparada y Derecho Internacional.* Panama City, Panama.

BIP   *Boletín de Informaciones Petroleras.* B. A., Argentina.

BISER   *Bulletin of the Institute of Social and Economic Research.* Panama City, Panama.

BISUSSR *Bulletin of the Institute for the Study of the USSR.* Munich, Germany.

BITB   *Bulletin of the Inter-American Trade-Mark Bureau.* Havana, Cuba.

BM   *Banker's Magazine.* New York, N.Y.

BMRE   *Boletín del Ministerio de Relaciones Exteriores.* Montevideo, Uruguay.

BMREC   *Boletín del Ministerio de Relaciones Exteriores y Culto.* B. A., Argentina.

BMREE   *Boletín del Ministerio de Relaciones Exteriores.* Quito, Ecuador.

BMSA   *Boletín del Museo Social Argentino.* B. A., Argentina.

BMTIC *Boletim do Ministério do Trabalho, Indústria e Comércio.* Rio de Janeiro, Brazil.

BOL   *Bolivia.* New York, N.Y.

BOSRE *Boletín Oficial de la Secretaría de Relaciones Exteriores.* Mexico, D.F.

BPAU   *Bulletin of the Pan American Union.* Washington, D.C.

BR   *Brazil.* New York, N.Y.

BSAP   *Bibliographical Society of America Papers.* Chicago, Ill.

BSBDI *Boletim da Sociedade Brasileira do Direito Internacional.* Rio de Janeiro, Brazil.

BSCEH *Boletín de la Sociedad Chihuahuense de Estudios Históricos.* Chihuahua, Mexico.

BSGS   *Boletín de la Sociedad Geográfica " Sucre."* Sucre, Bolivia.

BSMGE *Boletín de la Sociedad Mexicana de Geografía y Estadística.* Mexico, D.F.

BTIE   *Boletín Trimestral de Información Económica.* Quito, Ecuador.

BUIC   *Boletín de la Unión Interamericana del Caribe.* Havana, Cuba.

C   *Chile.* New York, N.Y.

CA   *Cuadernos Americanos.* Mexico, D.F.

CAT   *Comments on Argentine Trade.* B. A., Argentina.

CC   *Cuba Contemporánea.* Havana, Cuba.

CCE   *Casa de Cultura Ecuatoriana.* Quito, Ecuador.

CCH   *Ceskoslovensky Casopis Historicky.* Prague, Czechoslovakia.

CDC   *Cuadernos Dominicanos de Cultura.* Cd. Trujillo, D.R.

CDILR *Cumulative Digest of International Law and Relations.* Washington, D.C.

CE   *Century.* New York, N.Y.

CEC   *Colombia Económica.* Bogotá, Colombia.

CECO   *Conjectura Econômica.* Rio de Janeiro, Brazil.

CEHA   *Contribuciones para el Estudio de la Historia de América: Homenaje al Dr. Emilio Ravignani.* B. A., Argentina.

CENAM *Centro-América.* Guatemala City, Guatemala.

CEST   *Cuadernos de Estudio.* Lima, Peru.

CEX   *Comercio Exterior.* Mexico, D.F.

CF   *Canadian Forum.* Toronto, Canada.

CH   *Current History.* New York, N.Y.

CHA   *Cuadernos de Historia y Arqueología.* Quito, Ecuador.

CHAM   *Cultura Hispanoamericana.* Madrid, Spain.

CHIR   *Catholic Historical Review.* Washington, D.C.

CHJ   *Cambridge Historical Journal.* Cambridge, England.

CHR   *Canadian Historical Review.* Toronto, Canada.

CHSP   *California Historical Society Papers.* San Francisco, Calif.

CHSQ   *California Historical Society Quarterly.* San Francisco, Calif.

CHSR   *Columbia Historical Society Review.* Washington, D.C.

CI   *Communist International.* New York, N.Y.

CIJ   *Commercial Intelligence Journal.* Ottawa, Canada.

CIN   *Comunitá Internazionale.* Rome, Italy.

CJ   *Cavalry Journal.* Washington, D.C.

CJE   *Canadian Journal of Economics and Political Science.* Toronto, Canada.

CL   *Clio: Revista Bimestre de la Academia Dominicana de la Historia.* Cd. Trujillo, D.R.

CLA   *Claridad.* B. A., Argentina.

CLEH   *Cuadernos Latinoamericanos de Economía Humana.* Montevideo, Uruguay.

CO   *Current Opinion.* New York, N.Y.

COL   *Colombia.* Bogotá, Colombia.

COM   *Commonweal.* New York, N.Y.

COMB   *Combate.* San José, C.R.

COMU   *El Comunista.* Havana, Cuba.

CP   *Cultura Política: Revista Mensal de Estudos Brasileiros.* Rio de Janeiro, Brazil.

CPA   *Commercial Pan America.* Washington, D.C.

CPS   *Ciencias Políticos y Sociales.* Mexico, D.F.

CQ   *Caribbean Quarterly.* Mona, Jamaica.

CR   *Contemporary Review.* London, England.

CRE   *Cresset.* Valparaiso, Ind.

CREV   *Cuba Review.* New York, N.Y.

CRI   *Criterio.* B. A., Argentina.

CS   *Caribbean Studies.* San Juan, P.R.

CSMP   *Colonial Society of Massachusetts Publications.* Boston, Mass.

CSO   *Cuba Socialista.* Havana, Cuba.

CT   *Commentary.* New York, N.Y.

CU   *Cuaderno Universitarius.* León, Nicaragua.

CUA	*Cuadernos.* Paris, France.
CUH	*Cuadernos Hispanoamericanos.* Madrid, Spain.
CUQ	*Columbia University Quarterly.* New York, N.Y.
CUTA	*Clark University Thesis Abstracts.* Worcester, Mass.
CV	*Cultura Venezolana.* Caracas, Venezuela.
D	*Dissent.* New York, N.Y.
DC	*Développement & Civilisations.* Paris, France.
DHR	*Duquesne Hispanic Review.* Pittsburgh, Pa.
DLJ	*Duke Law Journal.* Durham, N.C.
DNC	*DNC: Revista do Departmento Nacional do Café.* Rio de Janeiro, Brazil.
DO	*Diario Official.* San Salvador, El Salvador.
DOC	*Diario Official.* Bogotá, Colombia.
DR	*Democratic Review.* Washington, D.C.
DRCA	*Derecho: Revista de Colegio de Abogados.* Medellín, Colombia.
DRE	*Deutsche Revue.* Berlin, Germany.
DUIIM	*Deutschamerikanischen und Iberischen Instituts Mitteilungens.* Aachen, Germany.
E	*Events.* New York, N.Y.
EA	*Estudios Americanos.* Seville, Spain.
EAR	*Europa-Archiv.* Bonn, Germany.
EBLA	*Economic Bulletin for Latin America.* New York, N.Y. (UN).
EC	*Economica.* London, England.
ECA	*Estudio Centro Americano.* San Salvador, El Salvador.
ECO	*El Economista.* Mexico, D.F.
ECON	*Economist.* London, England.
ECR	*Economic Reports.* Washington, D.C. (USDC).
ED	*Estudios de Derecho.* Medellín, Colombia.
EDCC	*Economic Development and Cultural Change.* Chicago, Ill.
EG	*Europaische Gespräche.* Hamburg, Germany.
EH	*Economic History* (supplement to *Economic Journal*). London, England.
EHA	*Estudios Históricos Americanos: Homenaje a Silvio Zavala.* Mexico, D.F.
EHNM	*Ensayos Sobre la Historia del Nuevo Mundo.* Mexico, D.F.
EHR	*English Historical Review.* London, England.

EHRE	*Economic History Review.* London, England.
EI	*L'Esprit International.* Paris, France.
EM	*España Moderna.* Madrid, Spain.
EMA	*Engineering Magazine.* New York, N.Y.
EN	*Encounter.* London, England.
EO	*Est & Ouest.* Paris, France.
EPEFC	*Estudios Políticos, Económicos, Filosóficos, Culturales.* Montevideo, Uruguay.
ER	*Edinburgh Review.* London, England.
ERR	*Editorial Research Reports.* Washington, D.C.
ES	*Estadística.* Mexico, D.F.
ESC	*Estudios Sobre El Comunismo.* Santiago, Chile.
EST	*Estudios.* Santiago, Chile.
ESTA	*Estudios: Revista Argentina de Cultura Información y Documentación.* B. A., Argentina.
ESUS	*Estudios Sobre la Unión Soviética.* Munich, Germany.
ETHSP	*East Tennessee Historical Society Publications.* Knoxville, Tenn.
ETS	*Export Trade and Shipper.* New York, N.Y.
ETSS	*Economía, Trabajo y Seguridad Social.* Lima, Peru.
F	*Forum.* New York, N.Y.
FA	*Foreign Affairs.* New York, N.Y.
FAG	*Foreign Agriculture.* Washington, D.C.
FAM	*France-Amérique.* Paris, France.
FAV	*Fuerzas Armadas de Venezuela.* Caracas, Venezuela.
FCTCW	*For Commanders, This Changing World.* Washington, D.C.
FCW	*Foreign Commerce Weekly.* Washington, D.C.
FH	*Foro Hondureño.* Tegucigalpa, Honduras.
FHQ	*Florida Historical Quarterly.* Jacksonville, Fla.
FI	*Foro International.* Mexico, D.F.
FL	*Filosofía y Letras.* Mexico, D.F.
FLB	*Florida Library (Association) Bulletin.* Jacksonville, Fla.
FN	*Fortnightly.* London, England.
FOR	*Fortune.* New York, N.Y.
FPAB	*Foreign Policy Association Bulletin.* New York, N.Y.
FPAHS	*Foreign Policy Association Headline Series.* New York, N.Y.
FPAIS	*Foreign Policy Association Information Service.* New York, N.Y.

FPAP Foreign Policy Association Pamphlets. New York, N.Y.

FPAR Foreign Policy Association Reports. New York, N.Y.

FRBN Fénix: Revista de la Biblioteca Nacional. Lima, Peru.

FT Finis Terrae. Santiago, Chile.

FU Futuro. Mexico, D.F.

FW Free World. New York, N.Y.

G Galaxy. New York, N.Y.

GHQ Georgia Historical Quarterly. Savannah, Ga.

GJ Geographical Journal. London, England.

GL Grace Log. New York, N.Y.

GR Geographical Review. New York, N.Y.

GSPPW Grotius Society: Problems of Peace and War. London, England.

GST Grotius Society Transactions. London, England.

H Hispania. Greencastle, Ind.

HA Harper's Magazine. New York, N.Y.

HAHR Hispanic American Historical Review. Bloomington, Ind.

HAM Homenaje de la Universidad de Chile . . . a Domingo Amunátegui Solar. Santiago, Chile.

HBR Harvard Business Review. Boston, Mass.

HE Horizontes Económicos. B. A., Argentina.

HEQ History of Education Journal. Ann Arbor, Mich.

HER Harvard Educational Review. Cambridge, Mass.

HI History. London, England.

HID Hechos y Ideas. B. A., Argentina.

HIS Historian. Albuquerque, N.M.

HIST Historia. B. A., Argentina.

HK Hôgaku Kenkyû. Tokyo, Japan.

HL Historia. Lima, Peru.

HLAS Handbook of Latin American Studies. Gainesville, Fla.

HLQ Huntington Library Quarterly. San Marino, Calif.

HLR Harvard Law Review. Cambridge, Mass.

HM Historia Mexicana. Mexico, D.F.

HO Historical Outlook. Philadelphia, Pa.

HOR Horizontes. Ponce, P.R.

HSANZ Historical Studies: Australia and New Zealand. Melbourne, Australia.

HT History Today. London, England.

HTM History Teachers' Magazine. Philadelphia, Pa.

HUM Humanidades. La Plata, Argentina.

HV Historische Vierteljahrschrift. Leipzig, Germany.

HW Harper's Weekly. New York, N.Y.

I Iberica. Hamburg, Germany.

IA Inter-America. New York, N.Y.

IAA Ibero-Amerikanisches Archiv. Berlin, Germany.

IAF International Affairs. London, England.

IAQ Inter-American Quarterly. Washington, D.C.

IAR Istoricheskii Archiv. Leningrad, USSR.

IBR Inter-American Bibliographical Review. Washington, D.C.

IC International Conciliation. New York, N.Y.

IE Investigaciones Económicas. Mexico, D.F.

IEA Inter-American Economic Affairs. Washington, D.C.

IH Investigaciones Históricas. Mexico, D.F.

IJ International Journal. Toronto, Canada.

ILR International Labour Review. Geneva, Switzerland.

IM International Mind (L'Esprit International). Paris, France.

IN Independent. Boston, Mass.

INA Inter-American. Washington, D.C.

INAF Inter-American Affairs. Washington, D.C.

INAM Inter-America. New York, N.Y.

INS Insula. Madrid, Spain.

IO International Organization. Boston, Mass.

IP Ipna. Lima, Peru.

IR Ibero-Amerikanisches Rundschau. Hamburg, Germany.

IRB Inter-American Review of Bibliography (Revista Interamericana de Bibliografía). Washington, D.C.

ISSB International Social Science Bulletin. Paris, France.

J Jus. Mexico, D.F.

JA Journal of Air Law. Chicago, Ill.

JAGS Journal of the American Geographical Society. New York, N.Y.

JAHI Journal of American History. New Haven, Conn.

JB Journal of Business. Chicago, Ill.

JEH Journal of Economic History. New York, N.Y.

JFE   *Journal of Farm Economics.* Lancaster, Pa.

JG   *Journal of Geography.* Chicago, Ill.

JIA   *Journal of International Affairs.* New York, N.Y.

JIAS   *Journal of Inter-American Studies.* Gainesville, Fla.

JIR   *Journal of International Relations.* Worcester, Mass.

JISHS   *Journal of the Illinois State Historical Society.* Springfield, Ill.

JMH   *Journal of Modern History.* Chicago, Ill.

JMIH   *Journal of Mississippi History.* Jackson, Miss.

JNH   *Journal of Negro History.* Washington, D.C.

JP   *Journal of Politics.* Gainesville, Fla.

JPE   *Journal of Political Economy.* Chicago, Ill.

JPH   *Journal of Presbyterian History.* Philadelphia, Pa.

JQ   *Journalism Quarterly.* Urbana, Ill.

JR   *Juridical Review.* London, England.

JRD   *Journal of Race Development.* Worcester, Mass.

JRIIA   *Journal of the Royal Institute of International Affairs.* London, England.

JRUSI   *Journal of the Royal United Service Institute.* London, England.

JSH   *Journal of Southern History.* Baton Rouge, La.

JSHS   *James Sprunt Historical Studies.* Chapel Hill, N.C.

JUS   *La Justicia.* Mexico, D.F.

K   *Kollasuyo: Revista Mensual de Estudios Bolivianos.* La Paz, Bolivia.

L   *Lotería.* Panama City, Panama.

LARR   *Latin American Research Review.* Austin, Texas.

LE   *Lectura.* Mexico, D.F.

LEA   *Librarians, Editors, Authors.* Washington, D.C.

LH   *Labor History.* New York, N.Y.

LHQ   *Louisiana Historical Quarterly.* New Orleans, La.

LHSP   *Louisiana Historical Society Publications.* New Orleans, La.

LIP   *Lippincotts'.* Philadelphia, Pa.

LL   *Letras.* Lima, Peru.

LM   *Letras de México.* Mexico, D.F.

LMO   *Labour Monthly.* London, England.

LN   *League of Nations.* Boston, Mass.

LP   *Libro y Pueblo.* Mexico, D.F.

LQR   *London Quarterly Review.* London, England.

LQRE   *Law Quarterly Review.* London, England.

LSH   *Law Students' Helper.* Detroit, Mich.

M   *Mayo.* B. A., Argentina.

MA   *Mid-America.* Chicago, Ill.

MAF   *Military Affairs.* Washington, D.C.

MAG   *México Agrario.* Mexico, D.F.

MAH   *Magazine of American History.* Mount Vernon, N.Y.

MAL   *Michigan Alumnus.* Ann Arbor, Mich.

MAMH   *Memorias de la Academia Mexicana de la Historia.* Mexico, D.F.

MANHG   *Memoria de la Academia Nacional de Historia y Geografía.* Mexico, D.F.

MAP   *Monatshefte für Auswärtige Politik.* Hamburg, Germany.

MAR   *Mexican-American Review.* Mexico, D.F.

MCG   *Marine Corps Gazette.* New York, N.Y.

MCN   *Memoria de El Colegio Nacional.* Mexico, D.F.

MEMZ   *Mirovaia Ekonomika i Mezhdunarodnaia Zhizn'.* Moscow, USSR.

MEN   *Mensário.* Rio de Janeiro, Brazil.

MGG   *Mitteilungen der Geographischen Gesselschaft.* Hamburg, Germany.

MH   *Michigan History Magazine.* Lansing, Mich.

MHE   *Military Historian and Economist.* Cambridge, Mass.

MHM   *Maryland Historical Magazine.* Baltimore, Md.

MHR   *Missouri Historical Review.* Columbia, Mo.

MHSP   *Massachusetts Historical Society Proceedings.* Boston, Mass.

MJC   *Mensário do Jornal do Comercio.* Rio de Janeiro, Brazil.

MJPS   *Midwest Journal of Political Science.* Detroit, Mich.

ML   *Mexican Life.* Mexico, D.F.

MLI   *Mundo Libre.* Mexico, D.F.

MLR   *Minnesota Law Review.* Minneapolis, Minn.

MM   *Masses and Mainstream.* New York, N.Y.

MP   *Mercurio Peruano.* Lima, Peru.

MPCH   *Memoria del Primer Congreso de Historiadores de México y los Estados Unidos ... Septiembre de 1949.* Mexico, D.F.

MR   *Monthly Review.* New York, N.Y.
MRANC   *Memorias y Revista de la Academia Nacional de Ciencias.* Mexico, D.F.
MV   *El Mercado de Valores.* Mexico, D.F.
MVHR   *Mississippi Valley Historical Review.* Bloomington, Ind.
MVHPR   *Mississippi Valley Historical Association Proceedings.* N.p.
MZ   *Mezhdunarodnaia Zhizn'.* Moscow, USSR.

N   *Nation.* New York, N.Y.
NAR   *North American Review.* New York, N.Y.
NC   *Nineteenth Century.* London, England.
NCHR   *North Carolina Historical Review.* Raleigh, N.C.
ND   *Nueva Democracia.* New York, N.Y.
NEQ   *New England Quarterly.* Portland, Me.
NG   *National Geographic Magazine.* Washington, D.C.
NH   *Nebraska History.* Lincoln, Nebr.
NLGQ   *National Lawyers' Guild Quarterly.* Washington, D.C.
NMHR   *New Mexico Historical Review.* Albuquerque, N.M.
NNCL   *News Notes of the California Library.* Sacramento, Calif.
NNI   *Novaia i Noveishaia Istoriia.* Moscow, USSR.
NOS   *Nosotros.* B. A., Argentina.
NR   *New Republic.* New York, N.Y.
NRE   *Nouvelle Revue.* Paris, France.
NULR   *National University Law Review.* Washington, D.C.
NYH   *New York History.* Cooperstown, N.Y.

O   *Outlook.* New York, N.Y.
OD   *Oriente Dominicano.* Quito, Ecuador.
OEF   *O Observador Económico e Financeiro.* Rio de Janeiro, Brazil.
OHQ   *Oregon Historical Quarterly.* Salem, Ore.
OHTJ   *Ohio History Teachers' Journal.* Columbus, O.
OR   *Orbis.* Philadelphia, Pa.
OSSJ   *Ohio Social Science Journal.* Athens, O.

P   *Política.* Caracas, Venezuela.
PA   *Pan-América: Revista de Derecho Internacional Americano.* B. A., Argentina.
PAAM   *The Pan American.* New York, N.Y.
PAAS   *Proceedings of the American Antiquarian Society.* Worcester, Mass.

PAF   *Présence Africain: Revue Culturelle du Monde Noir.* Paris, France.
PAIM   *Problemas Agrícolas e Industriales de México.* Mexico, D.F.
PAM   *Pan American Magazine.* New York, N.Y.
PAPS   *Proceedings of the Academy of Political Science.* New York, N.Y.
PC   *Problems of Communism.* Washington, D.C.
PE   *Política y Espíritu.* Santiago, Chile.
PEASC   *Proceedings of the Eighth American Scientific Congress.* Washington, D.C.
PEC   *Política Económica.* B. A., Argentina.
PER   *Peruanidad.* Lima, Peru.
PESP   *Political, Economic, and Social Problems of the Latin-American Nations of Southern South America.* Austin, Texas.
PHR   *Pacific Historical Review.* Berkeley, Calif.
PI   *Política Internacional.* Madrid, Spain.
PIS   *Prepodavanie Istorii v Shkole.* Moscow, USSR.
PIWA   *Proceedings of the Institute of World Affairs.* Los Angeles, Calif.
PL   *Problemas de Latinoamérica.* Mexico, D.F.
PMH   *Pennsylvania Magazine of History and Biography.* Philadelphia, Pa.
PPAIGH *Proceedings of the Pan American Institute of Geography and History.* Washington, D.C.
PQ   *Political Quarterly.* London, England.
PR   *The Progressive.* Madison, Wis.
PSQ   *Political Science Quarterly.* New York, N.Y.
PSSHR   *Philippine Social Sciences and Humanities Review.* Manila, P.I.
PUL   *Publicación de la Universidad del Litoral.* Sante Fe, Argentina.

QDC   *Questions Diplomatiques et Colonieles.* Paris, France.
QJE   *Quarterly Journal of Economics.* Cambridge, Mass.
QJIR   *Quarterly Journal of Inter-American Relations.* Washington, D.C.
QR   *Quartermaster Review.* Washington, D.C.
QRC   *Quarterly Review of Commerce.* London, Ontario, Canada.
QRL   *Quarterly Review.* London, England.

R   *Revista*. B. A., Argentina.
RA   *Revista de América*. Bogotá, Colombia.
RABA   *Revista Americana de Buenos Aires*. B. A., Argentina.
RABL   *Revista de Academia Brasileira de Letras*. Rio de Janeiro, Brazil.
RABN   *Revista del Archivo y Biblioteca Nacionales*. Tegucigalpa, Honduras.
RABNY   *Record of the Association of the Bar of New York*. New York, N.Y.
RACP   *Revista Argentina de Ciencias Políticas*. B. A., Argentina.
RADI   *Revista Argentina de Derecho Internacional*. B. A., Argentina.
RAGDI   *Revista de la Asociación Guatemalteca de Derecho Internacional*. Guatemala City, Guatemala.
RAGHN   *Revista de la Academia de Geografía e Historia de Nicaragua*. Managua, Nicaragua.
RAL   *Revue de Amérique Latine*. Paris, France.
RAM   *Revista Americana*. Rio de Janeiro, Brazil.
RAMER   *Repertorio Americano*. San José, C.R.
RAN   *Revista de los Archivos Nacionales*. San José, C.R.
RARG   *La Revue Argentine*. Paris, France.
RB   *Revista Bolivariana*. Bogotá, Colombia.
RBA   *Revista Bancaria*. Mexico, D.F.
RBC   *Revista de Bibliografía Chilena*. Santiago, Chile.
RBCU   *Revista Bimestre Cubana*. Havana, Cuba.
RBIC   *Revista Bibliográphica Cubana*. Havana, Cuba.
RBN   *Revista de la Biblioteca Nacional*. San Salvador, El Salvador.
RBNA   *Revista de la Biblioteca Nacional*. B. A., Argentina.
RBNCU   *Revista de la Biblioteca Nacional*. Havana, Cuba.
RBPI   *Revista Brasileira de Política Internacional*. Rio de Janeiro, Brazil.
RBR   *Revista Brasiliense*. São Paulo, Brazil.
RBRC   *Revista del Banco de la República*. Bogotá, Colombia.
RBRI   *Revue Britannique*. Paris, France.
RC   *Revista Chilena*. Santiago, Chile.
RCAM   *El Reproductor Campechano*. Campeche, Mexico.
RCDI   *Revista Colombiana de Derecho Internacional*. Bogotá, Colombia.
RCE   *Revista de Ciencias Económicas*. B. A., Argentina.

RCHG   *Revista Chilena de Historia y Geografía*. Santiago, Chile.
RCHGC   *Revista del Centro de Estudios Históricos y Geográficos de Cuenca*. Cuenca, Ecuador.
RCJS   *Revista de Ciencias Jurídicas y Sociales*. Sante Fe, Argentina.
RCNE   *Revista do Conselho Nacional de Economia*. Rio de Janeiro, Brazil.
RDCC   *Revista de Derecho*. Concepción, Chile.
RDCP   *Revista de Derecho y Ciencias Políticas*. Lima, Peru.
RDCS   *Revista de Derecho y Ciencias Sociales*. Mexico, D.F.
RDCSP   *Revista de Derecho y Ciencias Sociales*. Asunción, Paraguay.
RDHL   *Revista de Derecho, Historia y Letras*. B. A., Argentina.
RDHLC   *Revista de Derecho, Historia y Letras*. Havana, Cuba.
RDI   *Revista de Derecho Internacional*. Havana, Cuba.
RDICD   *Revista de Derecho Internacional y Ciencias Diplomáticas*. Rosario, Argentina.
RDILC   *Revue de Droit Internacional et de Legislation Comparée*. Brussels, Belgium.
RDIP   *Revue de Droit International Privé*. Paris, France.
RDISDP   *Revue de Droit Internationale de Sciences Diplomatiques et Politiques*. Geneva, Switzerland.
RDJA   *Revista de Derecho, Jurisprudencia, y Administración*. Montevideo, Uruguay.
RDLH   *Revista de la Habana*. Havana, Cuba.
RDM   *Revue de Deux Mondes*. Paris, France.
RDP   *Revista de Derecho Público*. Tucumán, Argentina.
RE   *Revista de las Españas*. Madrid, Spain.
REA   *Revista de Economía Argentina*. B. A., Argentina.
REC   *Revista de Escuela de Contabilidad, Economía y Administración*. Monterrey, Mexico.
REDR   *Revista de Educación*. Cd. Trujillo, D.R.
REE   *Revista de Economía y Estadística*. Córdoba, Argentina.
REM   *Revista de Economía*. Mexico, D.F.
REMI   *Revista de la Escuela Militar*. Chorillos, Peru.
REP   *Revista de Estudios Políticos*. Madrid, Spain.
REPORT   *Reporter*. New York, N.Y.

RF   *Revista del Foro.* Lima, Peru.

RFCECP *Revista de la Facultad de Ciencias Económicas, Comerciales y Políticas.* Rosario, Argentina.

RFCJSG *Revista de Facultad de Ciencias Jurídicas y Sociales de Guatemala.* Guatemala City, Guatemala.

RFD   *Revista de la Facultad de Derecho.* Caracas, Venezuela.

RFDCS   *Revista de la Facultad de Derecho y Ciencias Sociales.* B. A., Argentina.

RFDM   *Revista de la Facultad de Derecho de México.* Mexico, D.F.

RFO   *Revista de Fomento.* Caracas, Venezuela.

RG   *Revue de Genève.* Geneva, Switzerland.

RGC   *Revista de Guardia Civil.* Guatemala City, Guatemala.

RGDIP   *Revue Générale de Droit International Public.* Paris, France.

RGDJ   *Revista General de Derecho y Jurisprudencia.* Mexico, D.F.

RGUA   *Revista de Guatemala.* Guatemala City, Guatemala.

RH   *Revista Histórica de la Universidad.* Montevideo, Uruguay.

RHA   *Revista de Historia de América.* Mexico, D.F.

RHC   *Revista de Historia.* Caracas, Venezuela.

RHD   *Revue d'Histoire Diplomatique.* Paris, France.

RHGM   *Revue d'Histoire de la Guerre Mondiale.* Paris, France.

RHI   *Revue Historique.* Paris, France.

RHIS   *Revista de Historia.* São Paulo, Brazil.

RHIST   *Revista Histórica.* Lima, Peru.

RHM   *Revista Hispánica Moderna.* New York, N.Y.

RHME   *Revista de Historia.* Mendoza, Argentina.

RHST   *Royal Historical Society Transactions.* London, England.

RI   *Revista Iberoamericana.* Mexico, D.F.

RIA   *Review of International Affairs.* Belgrade, Yugoslavia.

RIBEU   *Revista do Instituto Brasil-Estados Unidos.* Rio de Janeiro, Brazil.

RIC   *Revista de Imigração e Colonização.* Rio de Janeiro, Brazil.

RICS   *Revista Interamericana de Ciencias Sociales.* Washington, D.C.

RIH   *Rhode Island History.* Providence, R.I.

RIHGB   *Revista do Instituto Histórico e Geográfic Brasileiro.* Rio de Janeiro, Brazil.

RIHGSP *Revista do Instituto Histórico y Geográfico de São Paulo.* São Paulo, Brazil.

RIHGU   *Revista del Instituto Histórico y Geográfico del Uruguay.* Montevideo, Uruguay.

RIN   *Revista de Indias.* Madrid, Spain.

RISA   *Revue Internationale des Sciences Administratives.* Brussels, Belgium.

RISP   *Revista Industrial de São Paulo.* São Paulo, Brazil.

RIT   *Revista Internacional de Trabajo.* Geneva, Switzerland.

RJ   *Revista Jurídica.* Cochabamba, Bolivia.

RJA   *Revista Javeriana.* Bogotá, Colombia.

RJI   *Revista Jurídica Interamericana.* New Orleans, La.

RMA   *Revista del Museo del Atlántico.* Barranquilla, Colombia.

RMB   *Revista Marítima Brasileira.* Rio de Janeiro, Brazil.

RMDI   *Revista Mexicana de Derecho Internacional.* Mexico, D.F.

RMN   *Revista Militar y Naval.* Montevideo, Uruguay.

RMP   *Revista Militar del Perú.* Lima, Peru.

RMS   *Revista Mexicana de Sociología.* Mexico, D.F.

RNC   *Revista Nacional de Cultura.* Caracas, Venezuela.

RP   *Review of Politics.* Notre Dame, Indiana.

RPA   *Revue de Paris.* Paris, France.

RPAA   *Revista de Problemas Argentinos y Americanos.* La Plata, Argentina.

RPCC   *Revista Peruana de Ciencias Jurídicas.* Huancayo, Peru.

RPDI   *Revista Peruana de Derecho Internacional.* Lima, Peru.

RPL   *Revue Politique et Littéraire.* Paris, France.

RPP   *Revue Politique et Parliamentaire.* Paris, France.

RR   *Review of Reviews.* New York, N.Y.

RRO   *Revista Rotaria.* Chicago, Ill.

RRP   *Review of the River Plate.* B. A., Argentina.

RS   *Rural Sociology.* Ithaca, N.Y.

RSB   *Revista de la Sociedad Bolivariana.* Caracas, Venezuela.

RSHGH   *Revue de Societé d'Histoire et de Géographie d'Haiti.* Port-au-Prince, Haiti.

RSO   *Reforma Social.* Havana, Cuba.

RSP   *Revue des Sciences Politiques.* Paris, France.

RSPI   *Rivista di Studi Politici Internazionale.* Florence, Italy.

RSPU *Revista do Serviço Público.* Rio de Janeiro, Brazil.

RT *Round Table.* London, England.

RTIHGB *Revista Trimestral do Instituto Histórico e Geográfico Brasileiro.* Rio de Janeiro, Brazil.

RU *Revista Universitaria.* Lima, Peru.

RUA *Revista de la Universidad de los Andes.* Bogotá, Colombia.

RUCP *Revista de la Universidad Católica del Peru.* Lima, Peru.

RUCR *Revista de la Universidad de Costa Rica.* San José, C.R.

RUO *Revue de l' Université de Ottawa.* Ottawa, Canada.

RUY *Revista de la Universidad de Yucatán.* Mérida, Mexico.

RV *Revoliutsionnyi Vostok.* Moscow, USSR.

S *Scribner's.* New York, N.Y.

SAISR *SAIS Review.* Washington, D.C.

SAQ *South Atlantic Quarterly.* Durham, N.C.

SCHAP *South Carolina Historical Society Proceedings.* Charleston, S.C.

SCHSP *Southern California Historical Society Publications.* Los Angeles, Calif.

SCIHA *Segundo Congreso Internacional de Historia de América.* B. A., Argentina.

SCPQ *Society of California Pioneers Quarterly.* San Francisco, Calif.

SFQ *Southern Folklore Quarterly.* Jacksonville, Fla.

SG *Survey Graphic.* New York, N.Y.

SHAP *Southern History Association Publications.* Washington, D.C.

SHQ *Southwestern Historical Quarterly.* Austin, Texas.

SPSQ *Southwestern Political Science Quarterly.* Austin, Texas.

SPSSQ *Southwestern Political and Social Science Quarterly.* Austin, Texas.

SR *Southwest Review.* Dallas, Texas.

SRE *Social Research.* New York, N.Y.

SS *Science and Society.* New York, N.Y.

SSC *Social Science.* Winfield, Kan.

SSM *Social Sciences in Mexico.* Mexico, D.F.

SSSQ *Southwestern Social Science Quarterly.* Austin, Texas.

SSU *Studies in the Soviet Union.* Munich, Germany.

ST *Statsvetenskaplig Tidskrift.* Upsala, Sweden.

SUR *Sur.* B. A., Argentina.

SY *Schmollers Jahrbuch.* Leipzig, Germany.

T *Tradição.* Petrópolis, Brazil.

TA *The Americas.* Washington, D.C.

TE *El Trimestre Económico.* Mexico, D.F.

TF *Tierra Firme.* Madrid, Spain.

THAQ *Texas Historical Association Quarterly.* Austin, Texas.

THM *Tennessee Historical Magazine.* Nashville, Tenn.

TI *Tiempo.* Mexico, D.F.

TLR *Tulane Law Review.* New Orleans, La.

TPP *Tareas del Pensamiento Peruano.* Lima, Peru.

TQHGM *Tyler's Quarterly Historical and Genealogical Magazine.* Richmond, Va.

TSHAQ *Texas State Historical Association Quarterly.* Austin, Texas.

TU *Tribuna Universitaria.* Montevideo, Uruguay.

U *Universitas.* Bogotá, Colombia.

UA *Universidad de Antioquia.* Medellín, Colombia.

UCB *Universidad Católica Bolivariana.* Medellín, Colombia.

UCC *University of California Chronicles.* Berkeley, Calif.

UCS *University of Colorado Studies.* Boulder, Colo.

UH *Universidad de la Habana.* Havana, Cuba.

UHQ *Utah Historical Quarterly.* Salt Lake City, Utah.

UL *Ultra.* Havana, Cuba.

UM *University Magazine.* Montreal, Canada.

UNIV *Universidades.* B. A., Argentina.

UNR *United Nations Review.* New York, N.Y.

UPB *Universidad Pontificia Bolivariana.* Medellín, Colombia.

UQ *Ukrainian Quarterly.* New York, N.Y.

UR *Unpopular Review.* New York, N.Y.

USCHSRS *U.S. Catholic Historical Society, Records and Studies.* New York, N.Y.

USDSB *United States Department of State Bulletin.* Washington, D.C.

USLR *United States Law Review.* New York, N.Y.

USMDR *United States Magazine and Democratic Review.* Washington, D.C.

USNIP   *United States Naval Institute Proceedings.* Annapolis, Md.

V   *Völkerbund.* Geneva, Switzerland.
VAM   *Vassar Alumnae Magazine.* Poughkeepsie, N.Y.
VANSSSR *Vestnik Akademii Nauk SSSR.* Vladivostok, USSR.
VER   *Veritas.* B. A., Argentina.
VI   *Voprosy Istorii.* Moscow, USSR.
VIMK   *Vestnik Istorii Mirovoi Kul'tury.* Moscow, USSR.
VLR   *Virginia Law Review.* Charlottesville, Va.
VQR   *Virginia Quarterly Review.* Charlottesville, Va.
VS   *Vital Speeches of the Day.* Pelham, N.Y.

WA   *World Affairs.* Washington, D.C.
WAI   *World Affairs Interpreter.* Los Angeles, Calif.
WAP   *World Affairs Pamphlets.* New York, N.Y.
WMQ   *William and Mary Quarterly.* Williamsburg, Va.
WMR   *World Marxist Review.* Toronto, Canada.
WP   *World Politics.* New Haven, Conn.
WPFP   *World Peace Foundation Pamphlets.* Boston, Mass.

WPQ   *Western Political Quarterly.* Salt Lake City, Utah.
WR   *Wehrwissenschaftliche Rundschau.* Darmstadt, Germany.
WT   *World Today.* London, England.
WTHAYB *West Texas Historical Association Year Book.* Abilene, Texas.
WU   *World Unity.* New York, N.Y.
WW   *World's Work.* New York, N.Y.
WWE   *Wissen und Wehr.* Berlin, Germany.
WZHUB   *Wissenschaftliche Zeitschrift der Humboldt—Universität zu Berlin.* Berlin, Germany.

Y   *Yapeyú.* B. A., Argentina.
YLJ   *Yale Law Journal.* New Haven, Conn.
YR   *Yale Review.* New Haven, Conn.
YULG   *Yale University Library Guide.* New Haven, Conn.

ZG   *Zeitschrift für Geschichtswissenschaft.* Berlin, Germany.
ZGE   *Zeitschrift für Geopolitik.* Berlin, Germany.
ZIR   *Zeitschrift für Internationales Recht.* Leipzig, Germany.
ZP   *Zeitschrift für Politik.* Berlin, Germany.
ZV   *Zeitschrift für Völkerrecht.* Breslau, Germany.

Chapter I   Guides and Aids

A. BIBLIOGRAPHY

1. BIBLIOGRAPHY OF BIBLIOGRAPHIES

1. Arnim, M. *Internationale Personalbibliographie, 1800–1949.* 3 vols., Leipzig, 1950–1962.
   In progress. One of the most extensive works of its kind.

1a. Besterman, T. *A World Bibliography of Bibliographies and of Bibliographical Catalogues, Calendars, Abstracts, Digests, Indexes, and the Like.* 3d ed., 4 vols., Geneva, 1955–1956.
   Subject guide to bibliographies.

2. *Bibliographical Services Throughout the World.* Paris, 1951– .

3. *Bibliographic Index: A Cumulative Bibliography of Bibliographies, 1937– .* N.Y., 1938– .

4. Binnis, N. E. *An Introduction to Historical Bibliography.* London, 1953.

5. Bohatta, H., and W. Funke. *Internationale Bibliographie der Bibliographie.* Frankfurt am Main, 1939– .

6. Brunet, J. C. *Manuel du Libraire et de l'Amateur de Livres.* 5th ed., 6 vols., Paris, 1860–1865.

7. Caron, P., and M. Jaryc. *World List of Historical Periodicals and Bibliographies.* Oxford, 1939.

8. Collison, R. L. *Bibliographies, Subject and National: A Guide to Their Contents, Arrangement and Use.* N.Y., 1951.

9. Coulter, E. M., and M. Gerstenfeld. *Historical Bibliographies.* Berkeley, Calif., 1935.
   Somewhat dated but still useful.

10. Courtney, W. P. *Register of National Bibliography: With a Selection of the Chief Bibliographical Books and Articles Printed in Other Countries.* 3 vols., London, 1905–1912.

11. Herre, P. *Quellenkunde zur Weltgeschichte.* Leipzig, 1910.

11a. Heyl, L. *Current National Bibliographies: a List of Sources of Information Concerning Current Books of All Countries.* Rev. ed., Chicago, 1942.

12. *Index Bibliographicus: Directory of Current Periodical Abstracts and Bibliographies.* 4th ed., 2 vols., Paris, 1959– .

13. International Committee for Social Sciences Documentation. *Etude des Bibliographies Courantes des Publications Officielles Nationales: Guide Sommaire et Inventaire. A Study of Current Bibliographies of National Official Publications: Short Guide and Inventory.* Paris, 1958.

14. Jones, C. K. *A Bibliography of Latin American Bibliographies.* 2d ed., Wash., 1942.
   Chapters on each country.

15. ———. *Hispanic American Bibliographies: Including Collective Biographies, Histories of Literature and Selected General Works.* Baltimore, 1922.

16. Kaiser, J. B. *The National Bibliographies of the South American Republics: Preliminary List.* Boston, 1913.

17. PAU. Columbus Memorial Library. *Sources of Information for Books on Latin America: Magazines Containing Book Reviews, Library and Book Trade Journals.* 2d ed., Wash., 1930.

18. ———. ———. *Bibliographies Pertaining to Latin America in the Columbus Memorial Library of the Pan American Union.* Wash., 1928.

19. Pinto, O. *Le Bibliographie Nazionali.* Veilano, 1935.

20. Shores, L. *Basic Reference Sources: An Introduction to Materials and Methods.* Chicago, 1954.

20a. *Les Sources du Travail Bibliographique. Tome 1: Bibliographies Générales.* Geneva, 1950.

21. Taylor, A. *A History of the Bibliographies of Bibliographies.* New Brunswick, N.J., 1955.

22. Wilcox, J. K. *Bibliography of New Guides and Aids to Public Documents Use, 1953–1956.* N.Y., 1957.

23. Winchell, C. M. *Guide to Reference Books.* 7th ed., Chicago, 1951.
    Supplements 1–4, Chicago, 1954– . The leading United States bibliography of bibliographies.

2. General Bibliography

24. *Abridged Readers' Guide to Periodical Literature.* N.Y., 1936– .

25. *A.L.A. Catalog.* Chicago, 1926–
    Publication of the American Library Association.

26. *A.L.A. Index.* 2d ed., Chicago, 1901.
    Supplement, Chicago, 1914.

26a. Albion, R. G. *Naval and Maritime History: An Annotated Bibliography.* 3d ed., Mystic, Conn., 1963.

27. *American Book Publishing Record, 1960– .* N.Y., 1960–
    Issued monthly.

28. American Universities Field Staff. *A Select Bibliography: Asia, Africa, Eastern Europe, Latin America.* N.Y., 1960.
    Supplements, N.Y., 1961– .

29. *Annual Magazine Subject Index.* 41 vols. Boston, 1908–1949.
    Coverage from United States and British periodicals.

30. Aufricht, H. *Guide to League of Nations Publications: A Bibliographical Survey of the Work of the League 1920–1947.* N.Y., 1951.

31. *Ayer and Son's Directory of Newspapers and Periodicals . . . 1880– .* Phil., 1880– .

32. Benjamin, L. S. *Greenly's Guide to the World Press.* N.p., 1924.

32a. Boehm, E. H. (ed.). *Historical Abstracts, 1775–1945: Bibliography of the World's Periodical Literature.* N.Y., 1955–1959; Santa Barbara, Calif., 1960– .

33. ———, and A. Lalit.. *Historical Periodicals: An Annotated World List of Historical and Related Serial Publications.* Santa Barbara, Calif., 1961.
    The most recent and comprehensive work on the subject.

34. Boemer, K. *Handbuch der Weltpresse: Eine Darstellung des Zeitungswesens Aller Länder.* 3d ed., Leipzig, 1937.

35. *Book Review Digest, 1905– .* N.Y., 1905– .
    Contains references to reviews in professional journals.

36. *Books in Print: An Author-Title-Series Index to "The Publishers' Trade List Annual, 1948– ."* N.Y., 1948– .

37. British Museum. Department of Printed Books. *Catalogue of Printed Books.* 95 vols., London, 1881–1900.
    Supplement, 13 vols., London, 1905–1915. Reprinted in 68 vols., Ann Arbor, Mich., 1946–1950.

38. ———. ———. *General Catalogue of Printed Books.* London, 1931– .
    New edition of original, London, 1881–

39. ———. ———. *Subject Index of the Modern Works Added to the Library, 1881–1900.* 3 vols., London, 1902–1903.
    Supplements appear every five years.

40. *British Union Catalogue of Periodicals: A Record of the Periodicals of the World, from the 17th Century to the Present Day, in British Libraries.* London, 1955– .

41. Canadian Bibliographic Centre. *Canadian Graduate Theses in the Humanities and Social Sciences, 1921–1946.* Ottawa, 1951.

42. Childs, J. B. *Government Document Bibliography in the United States and Elsewhere.* 3d ed., Wash., 1942.

43. Clark, A. W. *Check List of Indexed Periodicals.* White Plains, N.Y., 1917.

44. Coggeshall, W. T. *The Newspaper Record, Containing a Complete List of Newspapers and Periodicals in the U.S., Canadas, and Great Britain.* Phil., 1856.

45. Craig, H., Jr. (comp.). *A Bibliography of Encyclopedias and Dictionaries Dealing with Military, Naval, and Maritime Affairs, 1626–1959.* Houston, Texas, 1962.

46. *Cumulative Book Index, 1898– .* N.Y., 1898–.
    Appears monthly. Lists all books published in English.

46a. Cushing, H. G., and A. V. Morris (eds.). *Nineteenth Century Readers' Guide to Periodical Literature, With Supplementary Indexing, 1900–1922.* 2 vols., N.Y., 1944.

47. Davis, E. P. *Periodicals of International Organizations.* Wash., 1950.

Second part lists Inter-American organizations.

48. *Dissertation Abstracts: A Guide to Dissertations and Monographs Available in Microfilm.* Ann Arbor, Mich., 1952– .
Formerly *Microfilm Abstracts*; see item 80.

49. *Doctoral Dissertations Accepted by American Universities.* N.Y., 1934– .

50. Dutcher, G. M., H. R. Shipman, *et al. A Guide to Historical Literature.* N.Y., 1931.
Lists bibliographies for major geographical areas of the world.

51. *Editor and Publisher.* N.Y., 1920– .
Annual international yearbook for publishing trade.

52. *El Libro Español: Revista Mensual.* Madrid, 1958– .

53. *Everett's Dictionary of the Principal Newspapers of the World.* N.p., 1881.

54. Eyre, S. *Eyre's Complete Newspaper and Periodical Guide, Containing All the Principal Papers Published in the World.* N.p., 1856.

55. Fessler, A. L., and S. J. Riccardi. *Current Newspapers: U.S. and Foreign: A Union List of Newspapers Available in the Libraries of the New York Metropolitan Area.* N.Y., 1957.

56. *Foreign Affairs Bibliography.* 4 vols., N.Y., 1933–1964.
Lists books by geographic regions.

57. Gregory, W. (ed.). *International Congresses and Conferences, 1840–1937: A Union List of Their Publications Available in Libraries of the United States and Canada.* N.Y., 1938.

58. ———. *List of Serial Publications of Foreign Governments, 1815–1931.* N.Y., 1932.

59. ———. *Union List of Serials in Libraries of the United States and Canada.* 2d ed., N.Y., 1943.
E. B. Titus is the editor of the 3d edition (N.Y., 1965).

60. Griffin, A. P. C. *List of References on International Arbitration.* Wash., 1908.

61. ———. *List of References on Recognition in International Law and Practice.* Wash., 1904.

62. *Guide to Microforms in Print, 1961– .* Wash., 1961.

63. Hale, R. W. *Guide to Photocopied His-*

torical Materials in the United States and Canada. Ithaca, N.Y., 1961.

64. Henry Adams History Club. *A Select Bibliography of History.* 3d ed., Cambridge, Mass., 1966.
Contains a short general section on Latin American history.

64a. Howe, G. F., *et al. The American Historical Association's Guide to Historical Literature.* N.Y., 1960.
A comprehensive work with extensive listings on Latin America.

65. Hubbard, H. P. *Hubbard's Newspaper and Bank Directory of the World.* 2 vols., New Haven, Conn., 1882–1884.

66. ———. *Right Hand Record and Newspaper Directory . . . . A Complete List of All American Newspapers and All the Leading Newspapers of the World.* New Haven, Conn., 1880.

67. *Indexed Periodicals.* Boston, 1953.

68. *Index to Book Reviews in the Humanities, 1960– .* Detroit, 1960– .

69. *Index to Legal Periodicals, 1908– .* N.Y., 1909– .

70. *International Bibliography of Economics, 1952– .* Paris, 1955– .

71. *International Bibliography of Historical Sciences, 1926– .* Paris, 1930– .
Books and periodical literature.

72. *International Bibliography of Political Science, 1952– .* Paris, 1953– .
Books, articles, and official publications.

73. *International Index to Periodicals.* N.Y., 1907– .
Title and coverage vary.

74. Kelly, J. *American Catalogue of Books Published in the United States from January, 1861, to January, 1871.* 2 vols., N.Y., 1866–1871.

74a. Kuehl, W. F. *Dissertations in History: An Index to Dissertations Completed in History Departments of United States and Canadian Universities, 1873–1960.* Lexington, Ky., 1965.

75. Larsen, K. *National Bibliographical Services, Their Creation and Operation.* Paris, 1953.

76. Linder, L. H. *The Rise of Current Complete National Bibliography.* N.Y., 1959.

77. *List of Doctoral Dissertations in History Now in Progress at Universities in the U.S.* Wash., 1909– .

Published irregularly by the American Historical Association.

78. *Masters Abstracts: Abstracts of Selected Masters Theses on Microfilm.* Ann Arbor, Mich., 1962– .

79. *Meulenhoff's International Catalogue of Periodicals.* 4th ed., Amsterdam, 1955.

80. *Microfilm Abstracts: A Collection of Abstracts of Doctoral Dissertations and Monographs Which are Available in Complete Form on Microfilm.* Ann Arbor, Mich., 1938–1951.
    See item 48.

81. Moor, C. C., and W. Chamberlin. *How to Use United Nations Documents.* N.Y., 1952.

81a. Myers, D. P. *Manual of Collections of Treaties and of Collections Relating to Treaties.* Cambridge, Mass., 1922.

82. *New Serial Titles: A Union List of Serials Commencing Publication After December 31, 1949.* Wash., 1954– .
    Issued monthly.

83. *New Serial Titles, 1950–1960.* 2 vols., Wash., 1961.

84. *New York Daily Tribune Index.* 31 vols., N.Y., 1876–1907.

85. *New York Times Index, 1913– .* N.Y., 1913– .
    Covers 1858– .

86. Palfrey, T. R., and H. E. Coleman, Jr. *Guide to Bibliographies of Theses, United States and Canada.* 2d ed., Chicago, 1940.

87. *Paperbound Books in Print.* N.Y., 1955– .

88. Paris. Bibliothèque Nationale. *Catalogue Général: des Livres Imprimés: Auteurs.* Paris, 1900– .

89. Peddie, R. A. *National Bibliographies: A Descriptive Catalogue of the Works Which Register the Books Published in Each Country.* London, 1912.

90. Pettengill, S. M. *Pettengill's Newspaper Directory . . . for 1878, Comprising a Complete List of the Newspapers Published in the United States and British America: Also the Prominent European and Australasian Newspapers.* N.Y., 1878.

91. Phelps, E. M., and E. E. Ball. *Periodicals of International Importance: A Selection of 600 Useful in Libraries Everywhere.* N.Y., 1926.

92. Philadelphia Bibliographical Center and

Union Library Catalogue. *Union List of Microfilms.* Rev. ed., Ann Arbor, Mich., 1951.

93. ———. *Union List of Microfilms, Cumulation 1949–1959.* 2 vols., Ann Arbor, Mich., 1961.
    Supplements item 92.

94. *Poole's Index to Periodical Literature, 1802–81.* Rev. ed., 2 vols., Boston, 1893.
    Supplements for January, 1882–January 1, 1907, 5 vols., Boston, 1887–1908. Covers nineteenth century.

95. *Publisher's Trade List Annual, 1873– .* N.Y., 1873– .

96. *Publishers' Weekly.* N.Y., 1872– .

97. *Readers' Guide to Periodical Literature, 1900– .* N.Y., 1905– .
    Published semi-monthly; frequent cumulations. Lists literature from popular periodicals.

98. Sánchez Belda, L. (ed.). *Bibliografía de Archivos Españoles y Archivística.* Madrid, 1963.

99. Schneider, G. *Handbuch der Bibliographie.* Leipzig, 1930.

100. *Sell's World Press.* N.p., 1901.
     Earlier editions exist.

101. *Serials of an International Character: Tentative List Prepared in the Columbia University Law Library.* N.Y., 1921.

102. Speekaert, G. P. *Select Bibliography on International Organization.* Brussels, 1965.

103. Stewart, J. D. *British Union Catalogue of Periodicals.* 4 vols., N.Y., 1955–1957.

104. *Subject Index to Periodicals, 1915– .* London, 1919– .

105. Szladits, C. *A Bibliography on Foreign and Comparative Law: Books and Articles in English.* N.Y., 1955.

106. *Tercentenary Handlist of English and Welsh Newspapers, Magazines and Reviews.* London, 1920.
     Covers 1620–1919.

107. *The Booklist, 1905– .* Chicago, 1905– .

108. *The British National Bibliography, 1950– .* London, 1950– .
     Weekly publication.

109. *The Cumulative Book Index.* N.Y., 1898– .

110. *The Newspaper Press Directory and Advertisers' Guide.* N.Y., 1846– .

111. Thomas, D. H., and L. M. Case (eds.). *Guide to the Diplomatic Archives of Western Europe.* Phil., 1959.

    Most comprehensive work of its kind.

112. Tilton, E. M. *A Union List of Publications in Opaque Microforms.* N.Y., 1959.

    Supplements available.

113. *Times Official Index.* London, 1907– .

    Indexes *Times* of London.

114. Ulrich, C. F. (ed.). *Periodicals Directory: A Classified Guide to a Selected List of Current Periodicals, Foreign and Domestic.* N.Y., 1932– . 8th ed., N.Y., 1956.

    Subject guide to periodicals rather than an index to individual articles.

115. U.N. *Checklist of United Nations Documents.* N.Y., 1949– .

116. UNESCO. *Guide des Centres Nationaux d'Information Bibliographique, Etabli Conformément aux Recommandations du Comité Consultatif International de Bibliographie.* Paris, 1953.

117. ———. *Repertorio de Publicaciones Periódicas Actuales Latinoamericanas. Directory of Current Latin American Periodicals. Répertoire des Périodiques en Cours Publiés en Amérique Latine.* Paris, 1958.

118. Union of International Associations. *Directory of Periodicals Published by International Organizations.* 2d ed., Brussels, 1959.

119. ———. *Ten Years of United Nations Publications, 1945 to 1955.* N.Y., 1955.

120. *United Nations Documents Index, 1950– .* N.Y., 1950– .

121. University of Colorado. Social Sciences Library. *History: A Selective and Annotated Bibliographical Guide.* Boulder, Colo., 1963.

    Compiled by L. R. Wyner.

122. *The U.S. Quarterly Book Review, 1945– .* Wash., 1945–1947. New Brunswick, N.J., 1947– .

123. USLC. *A Catalog of Books Represented by Library of Congress Printed Cards Issued to July 31, 1942.* 167 vols., Ann Arbor, Mich., 1942–1946.

    Supplemented by items 124–130.

124. ———. *A Catalog of Books Represented by Library of Congress Printed Cards: Supplement.* 42 vols., Ann Arbor, Mich., 1948.

125. ———. *A Check List of Foreign Newspapers in the Library of Congress.* Wash., 1929.

126. ———. *The Library of Congress Author Catalog 1948–1952.* 24 vols., Ann Arbor, Mich., 1953.

127. ———. *Library of Congress Catalog: A Cumulative List of Works Represented by Library of Congress Printed Cards: Books: Subjects 1950–1954.* 20 vols., Ann Arbor, Mich., 1955.

128. ———. *Library of Congress Catalog: A Cumulative List of Works Represented by Library of Congress Printed Cards: Books: Subjects 1955–1959.* 22 vols., Paterson, N.J., 1960.

129. ———. *The National Union Catalog: A Cumulative Author List Representing Library of Congress Printed Cards and Titles Reported by Other American Libraries: 1953–1957.* 28 vols., Ann Arbor, Mich., 1958.

130. ———. *The National Union Catalog: A Cumulative Author List Representing Library of Congress Cards and Titles Reported by Other American Libraries 1958–1962.* 54 vols., N.Y., 1963.

131. ———. *The National Union Catalog 1952–1955, Imprints: An Author List Representing Library of Congress Printed Cards and Titles Reported by Other American Libraries.* 30 vols., Ann Arbor, Mich., 1961.

132. ———. *The National Union Catalog of Manuscript Collections 1959–1961.* Ann Arbor, Mich., 1962.

133. ———. *The National Union Catalog of Manuscript Collections 1962.* Hampden, Conn., 1964.

134. ———. *List of American Doctoral Dissertations.* 26 vols., Wash., 1913–1940.

135. ———. *List of References on International American Conferences, 1826–1914.* Wash., 1917.

136. ———. *Postwar Foreign Newspapers: A Union List.* Wash., 1953.

137. ———. *Statistical Bulletins: An Annotated Bibliography of the General Statistical Bulletins of Major Political Subdivisions of the World.* Wash., 1954.

138. ———. *Statistical Yearbooks: An Annotated Bibliography of the General Statisti-*

cal Yearbooks of Major Political Sub-divisions of the World. Wash., 1953.

139. *Vertical File Index.* N.Y., 1935– .
Formerly *The Vertical File Service Catalog.* Lists pamphlets.

140. *Vertical File Service Catalog.* N.Y., 1932–1934.
Pamphlet index.

141. *William Thomas's Universal Newspaper & Periodical List.* N.p., 1863.

142. *Willing's Press Guide, 1874– .* London, 1874– .

3. LATIN AMERICA IN GENERAL

143. Akimova, N. A., *et al.* (comps.). *Strany Latinskoi Ameriki: Rekomendatel'nyi Uka-zatel' Literatury.* Moscow, 1962.
Countries of Latin America: A Recommended Guide to the Literature.

144. Alisky, M. *Latin American Journalism Bibliography.* Mexico, 1958.

144a. Al'perovich, M. S. "Issledovanie Problem Istorii Latinskoi Ameriki," *VAN-SSSR,* no. 12 (1964) 24–29.
"Research in the Problems of Latin American History."

144b. ———. "Izuchenie Istorii Latinskoi Ameriki v Sovetskom Soiuze," in *Latinskaia Amerika v Proshlom i Nastoiashchem.* N.p., 1960.
"The Study of Latin American History in the Soviet Union," in *Latin America Past and Present.*

144c. ———. "Izuchenie Istorii stran Latinskoi Ameriki," in *Sovetskaia Istoricheskaia Nauka ot XX k XXII S'ezdu KPSS: Istoriia Zapadnoi Evropy i Ameriki.* Moscow, 1963.
"The Study of the History of the Countries of Latin America," in *Soviet Historical Science from the Twentieth to the Twenty-second Congress of the CPSU: The History of Western Europe and America.*

145. "América en la Bibliografía Española: Reseñas Informativas," *AEA* 18 (1961) 765–819.

146. American Foreign Law Association. *Bibliographies of Foreign Law Series.* 11 vols., N.Y., 1926–1937.
Individual Latin American bibliographies listed in country sections.

147. American Library Association. *Biblio-grafía para Bibliotecas Universitarias. Bibliography of Works Recommended for Latin American University Libraries.* Chicago, 1958.
Published in English and Spanish.

148. Andrews, D. H. *Latin America: a Bibliography of Paperback Books.* Wash., 1964.

149. "Annotated Bibliography of the Principal Publications of the United Nations and Specialized Agencies Relating to Latin America," *ISSB* 4 (1952) 501–520.

150. *Anuario de la Prensa Española.* Madrid, 1943– .

150a. Archivo y Biblioteca de la Diputación de Vizcaya. *Catálogo de la Exposición Bibliográfica "Simón Bolívar."* Bilbao, Spain, 1960.

151. Babcock, C. E. (comp.). *Bibliographies Pertaining to Latin America in the Columbus Memorial Library of the Pan American Union.* Wash., 1928.
Mimeograph.

152. Bard, H. E. *South America: Brief Outline of Study Suggestions with Bibliography.* Boston, 1916.

153. Barringer, G. A. (ed.). *Catalogue de l'Histoire de l'Amérique.* 5 vols., Paris, 1903–1911.
Materials in the Bibliothèque Nationale.

154. Bayitch, S. A. *Latin America: A Bibliographical Guide to Economy, History, Law, Politics, and Society.* Coral Gables, Fla., 1961.

155. ———. *Latin-American Law: A Selective Bibliography of Works in English for Students' Use.* Coral Gables, Fla., 1954.

156. Bealer, L. W. "Some Recent Additions to the South American Collections in the University of California Libraries," *HAHR* 12 (1932) 103–106.

157. Behrendt, R. F. *Modern Latin America in Social Science Literature: A Selected, Annotated Bibliography of Books, Pamphlets, and Periodicals in English in the Fields of Economics, Politics, and Sociology of Latin America.* Albuquerque, N.M., 1949.

158. Beman, L. T. (comp.). *Selected Articles on Intervention in Latin America.* N.Y., 1928.

159. Bernstein, S. P. *Bibliography on Labor and Social Welfare in Latin America*. Wash., 1944.

160. *Bibliografía Española, 1958– *. Madrid, 1959– .

161. *Bibliografía Hispánica, 1942– *. Madrid, 1942– .

162. *Bibliografía Histórica de España e Hispanoamérica*. Barcelona, 1955– .

163. Biblioteca Benjamin Franklin. *Lista de Revistas y Otras Publicaciones en Serie que se Encuentran en la Biblioteca*. Mexico, 1944.

164. Blanksten, G. "Bibliography on Latin American Politics and Government," *IRB* 4 (1954) 191–216.

165. Boggs, R. S. *Bibliography of Latin American Folklore*. N.Y., 1940.

166. *Books About Latin America: 1800 Libros Sobre la América Latina*. N.Y., 1959.

167. "Books Recommended for Reading, Study, and Reference in the New Pan Americanism," *WPFP* 6, no. 2 (1916).

168. Boston Public Library. *A Selected List of Books on the Commercial Relations of South America, Principally with the United States*. Boston, 1918.

169. Brown, L. C. *Latin America: A Bibliography*. Kingsville, Texas, 1962.

169a. Buenos Aires. Biblioteca Nacional. *Catálogo de Manuscritos, Papeles de Gregorio Funes, Simón Bolívar, Antonio José de Sucre (1823–1828)*. B.A., 1939.

170. Bullejos, J. *Bibliografía Sobre Desarrollo Económico de los Países Subdesarrollados, América Latina y México (1940–1955)*. Mexico, 1957.

171. Burrus, E. J. "An Introduction to Bibliographical Tools in Spanish Archives and Manuscript Collections Relating to Hispanic America," *HAHR* 35 (1955) 443–483.

172. ———. "Research Opportunities in Italian Archives and Manuscript Collections for Students of Hispanic American History," *HAHR* 39 (1959) 428–463.

173. Butler, R. L. (ed.). *Guide to the Hispanic American Historical Review, 1918–1945*. Durham, N.C., 1950.

Covers vols. 1–25 of *HAHR*; see item 200.

174. ———. "The Latin American Manuscripts in the Royal Library at Copenhagen," *HLAS* 2 (1936) 482–487.

175. Castañeda, C. E., and J. A. Dabbs (eds.). *Guide to the Latin American Manuscripts in the University of Texas Library*. Cambridge, Mass., 1939.

176. *Catálogo General de la Librería Española e Hispanoamericana, 1901–1930*. 4 vols., Madrid, 1932–1944.

177. Chapman, C. E. *Catalogue of Materials in the Archivo General de Indias for the History of the Pacific Coast and the American Southwest*. Berkeley, Calif., 1919.

178. ———. "List of Books Referring to Caudillos in Hispanic America," *HAHR* 13 (1933) 143–146.

179. Childs, J. B. *Bibliography of Official Publications and the Administrative Systems in Latin America*. Wash., 1938.

179a. ———. "Caribbean and South American Treaty Matters: A Consideration of Sources," in Wilgus, *The Caribbean: Contemporary Trends*, pp. 257–286.

Discusses the treaty publications of all the countries. See item 6807.

180. ———. "Hispanic American Government Documents in the Library of Congress," *HAHR* 6 (1926) 131–141.

181. ———, and H. V. Besso (eds.). *A Guide to the Official Publications of the Other American Republics*. 19 vols., Wash., 1945–1948.

Various volumes are listed separately in the country sections.

182. Clagett, H. L., *et al*. *Guides to the Law and Legal Literature of Latin America*. 12 vols., Wash., 1943–1948.

Each volume listed separately in country sections.

182a. Cline, H. F. (ed.). *Latin American History: Essays on its Study and Teaching, 1898–1965*. 2 vols., Austin, Texas, 1967.

183. Cohen, B. "América Latina y las Publicaciones de las Naciones Unidas," *IRB* 1 (1951) 178–181.

184. Cole, G. W. *A Catalogue of Books Relating to the Discovery and Early History of North and South America Forming a Part of the Library of E. D. Church*. 5 vols., N.Y., 1907.

Reprinted, N.Y., 1951.

185. Colombo, C. "Fuentes Existentes en Madrid para la Historia Contemporánea de América Latina: Informe de una

Misión en Archivos Españoles," *RH*, 2d ser., 1 (1959) 153–180.

185a. Cosío Villegas, D. *Cuestiones Internacionales de México: Una Bibliografía.* Mexico, 1966.

Found in the *Archivo Histórico Diplomático Mexicano.* Coverage is much broader than the title indicates, as only half of the entries pertain explicitly to Mexico. See item 5517.

186. Cox, E. G. *A Reference Guide to the Literature of Travel, Including Voyages, Geographical Descriptions, Adventures, Shipwrecks and Expeditions: The New World.* Seattle, 1938.

186a. Cuba. Secretaría de Estado. *Catálogo de Obras de Derecho Internacional e Historia de América que el Gobierno Cubano Pone a Disposición, para su Consulta, de los Señores Delegados a la Sexta Conferencia Internacional Americana.* Havana, 1928.

186b. Deibel, U. "Die Lateinamerikanischen Freistaaten," *AZ* 5 (1929) 283–300.

Brief notes on Latin American archives.

187. Dillon, R. H. "Sutro Library's Resources in Latin Americana," *HAHR* 45 (1965) 267–274.

187a. ———. "The Sutro Library," *NNCL* 51 (1956) 338–352.

188. Domínguez Bordona, J. *Manuscritos de América.* Madrid, 1935.

189. Eberhardt, F. *Amerikaliteratur: Die Wichtigsten seit 1900 in Deutscher Sprache Erschienenen Werke über Amerika.* Leipzig, 1926.

190. Elías de Molíns, A. *Ensayo de una Bibliografía Literaria de España y América: Noticias de Obras y Estudios Relacionados con la Poesía, Teatro, Historia, Novela, Crítica Literaria, etc.* 2 vols., Madrid, 1902.

191. Esteve Barbá, F. "Los Manuscritos Americanos de la Biblioteca Pública de Toledo," *AUM* 3 (1934) 94–109.

191a. Ewing, W. S. *Guide to the Manuscript Collections in the William L. Clements Library,* 2d ed., Ann Arbor, Mich., 1953.

192. *Fichero Bibliográfico Hispanoamericano: Catálogo Trimestral de Toda Clase de Libros Publicados en las Américas en Español.* N.Y., 1961– .

193. Fisher, M. A. *Preliminary Guide to the Microfilm Collection in the Bancroft Library.* Berkeley, Calif., 1955.

194. Fletcher, W. H., and W. W. Lyman. *A Guide to Spanish-American Literature in Translation.* L.A., 1936.

195. Gavrilovic, S. "Hispanic American History Research Opportunities in Yugoslav Archives," *HAHR* 42 (1962) 37–50.

196. Gayangos, P. de. *Catalogue of the Manuscripts in the Spanish Language in the British Museum.* 4 vols., London, 1875–1893.

197. Geiger, M. J. *Calendar of Documents in the Santa Barbara Mission Archives.* Wash., 1947.

198. Gibson, C. *The Colonial Period in Latin American History.* Wash., 1958.

Publication 7 of the Service Center for Teachers of History.

199. ———, and B. Keen. "Trends of U.S. Studies in Latin American History," *AHR* 62 (July, 1957) 855–877.

200. ———, and E. V. Niemeyer (eds.). *Guide to the Hispanic American Historical Review, 1946–1955.* Durham, N.C., 1958.

Guide to vols. 26–35 of *HAHR*; see item 173.

201. Goldsmith, P. H. *A Brief Bibliography of Books in English, Spanish and Portuguese, Relating to the Republics Commonly Called Latin American, with Comments.* N.Y., 1915.

202. Gómez Canedo, L. *Los Archivos de la Historia de América.* Mexico, 1961– .

203. Grismer, R. L. *A Reference Index to Twelve Thousand Spanish American Authors: A Guide to the Literature of Spanish America.* N.Y., 1939.

204. ——— (ed.). *A New Bibliography of the Literatures of Spain and Spanish America, Including Many Studies on Anthropology, Archaeology, Art, Economics, Education, Geography, History, Law, Music, Philosophy, and Other Subjects.* Minneapolis, Minn., 1941– .

205. Gropp, A. E. *Union List of Latin American Newspapers in Libraries in the United States.* Wash., 1953.

Lists 5,000 titles. Arranged geographically by country.

206. Grubbs, H. A. "A Tentative Guide to Manuscript Material in Latin American Archives and Libraries," *HLAS* (1935) 219–230.

207. Gutiérrez del Cano, M. (ed.). *Catálogo de los Manuscritos Existentes en la Biblioteca Universitaria de Valencia*. 3 vols., Valencia, Spain, 1913.

208. *Handbook of Latin American Studies*. Cambridge, Mass., and Gainesville, Fla., 1936– .
The most comprehensive bibliographical guide to all types of Latin American publications.

209. Haring, C. H., *et al.* (eds.). *The Economic Literature of Latin America: A Tentative Bibliography*. 2 vols., Cambridge, Mass., 1935–1936.
More comprehensive than title implies.

210. Harrison, J. P. *Guide to Materials on Latin America in the National Archives*. Wash., 1961.

211. ———. "The Archives of United States Diplomatic and Consular Posts in Latin America," *HAHR* 33 (1953) 168–183.

212. Hebblethwaite, F. P. "A Bibliographical Survey of Pan Americanism," *IRB* 15 (1965) 324–334.

213. Hedrick, B. C. *Survey of Investigations in Progress in the Field of Latin American Studies*. Wash., 1959.

214. Hilton, R. (ed.). *Handbook of Hispanic Source Materials and Research Organizations in the U.S.* 2d ed., Stanford, Calif., 1956.
Description of collections.

214a. *Hispanic Author and Subject Catalogues*. Boston, 1966.

215. Hispanic Society of America. *Bibliographie Hispanique, 1905–1917*. 13 vols., N.Y., 1909–1917.

216. ———. *Catalogue of the Library of the Hispanic Society of America*. 10 vols., Boston, 1962.

217. Hoskins, H. L. *Guide to Latin-American History*. Boston, 1922.

218. Humphreys, R. A. *Latin American History: A Guide to the Literature in English*. London, 1958.
A much used work listing published materials for each country.

219. Hussey, R. D. (ed.). "Manuscript Hispanic Americana in the Harvard College Library," *HAHR* 17 (1937) 259–277.

219a. Ia-n, G. "Bibliograficheskii Ukazatel' Periodicheskoi i Ne-periodicheskoi Literatury o Stranakh Latinskoi Ameriki," *RV*, nos. 3–4 (1934) 346–364.
"A Bibliography of Periodical and Non-Periodical Literature on the Latin American Countries."

220. *Indice Histórico Español: Bibliografía Histórica de España e Hispanoamérica*. Barcelona, 1953– .

221. Institute of Latin American Studies. *Seventy-five Years of Latin American Research at the University of Texas: Masters Theses and Doctoral Dissertations, 1893–1958, and Publications of Latin American Interest, 1941–1958*. Austin, Texas, n.d.

222. Instituto Panamericano de Geografía e Historia. Comisión de Historia. *Guía de los Documentos Microfotografiados por la Unidad Móvil de Microfilm de la UNESCO*. Mexico, 1963.

222a. Inter-American Bibliographical and Library Association. *Proceedings of the First Convention of the Inter-American Bibliographical and Library Association*. N.Y., 1938.

222b. ———. *Proceedings of the Second Convention of the Inter-American Bibliographical and Library Association*. N.Y., 1939.

222c. ———. *Proceedings of the Third Convention of the Inter-American Bibliographical and Library Association*. N.Y., 1940.

223. Inter-American Institute of International Legal Studies. *Material de Referencia Sobre la Enseñanza del Derecho Internacional y Materias Afines en Latinoamérica y Canadá*. Wash., 1964.

223a. *Inter-American Review of Bibliography. Revista Interamericana de Bibliografía*. Wash., 1951– .
Supersedes *LEA*, Wash., 1949–1950, and *Pan American Bookshelf*, Wash., 1938–1948.

224. Inter-American Statistical Institute. *Bibliography of Selected Statistical Sources of the American Nations*. Wash., 1947.

225. International Bureau of the American Republics. *Newspaper Directory of Latin America*. Wash., 1892.

226. Jacquet, C. H. *Our Neighbors to the South: A Selected and Annotated Bibliography of English Titles on the Republics of Central*

and South America and the Caribbean, Including the Colonies, Territories, and Possessions of the United Kingdom, France, the Netherlands, and the United States. N.Y., 1954.

227.   Jones, T. B., E. A. Warburton, *et al. A Bibliography of South American Economic Affairs: Articles in Nineteenth Century Periodicals.* Minneapolis, Minn., 1955.

   Contains 9,939 entries on subjects such as agriculture, commerce, communications, finance, immigration, labor, mining, and transportation.

228.   Jones, W. K. *Latin American Writers in English Translation: A Tentative Bibliography.* Wash., 1944.

229.   Kantor, H. *A Bibliography of Unpublished Doctoral Dissertations and Masters' Theses Dealing with Governments, Politics, and International Relations of Latin America.* Gainesville, Fla., 1953.
   See item 281.

230.   Keniston, H. *List of Works for the Study of Hispanic-American History.* N.Y., 1920.

231.   ———. *Periodicals in American Libraries for the Study of the Hispanic Languages and Literatures.* N.Y., 1927.

   Does not include all periodicals found in the Library of Congress.

232.   Kidder, F. E., and A. D. Bushong (comps.). *Theses on Pan American Topics Prepared by Candidates for Doctoral Degrees in Universities and Colleges in the United States and Canada.* 4th ed., Wash., 1962.

233.   *La Prensa Ibero-Americana.* 3d ed., B.A., 1934.

234.   Lauerhass, L., Jr. *Communism in Latin America: A Bibliography.* L. A., 1962.

   Lists works published between 1945 and 1960.

235.   Leavitt, S. E. (ed.). *Revistas Hispanoamericanas: Indice Bibliográfico, 1843–1935.* Santiago, 1960.

236.   Leguizamon, J. A. *Bibliografía General de la Literatura Hispanoamericana.* B.A., 1954.

237.   *Libros en Venta en Hispanoamérica y España.* N.Y., 1964.

237a. Luquiens, F. B. (ed.). *Spanish American Literature in the Yale University Library: A Bibliography.* New Haven, Conn., 1939.

238.   Madrid. Biblioteca Nacional. Sección de Hispanoamérica. *Catálogo de Obras Iberoamericanas y Filipinas de la Biblioteca Nacional de Madrid.* Madrid, 1953– .

238a. ———. Universidad. *Catálogo de las Tesis Doctorales Manuscritas Existentes en la Universidad de Madrid.* Madrid, 1952.

238b. Marchant, A. (comp.). *Boundaries of the Latin American Republics: An Annotated List of Documents, 1493–1943.* Wash., 1944.

239.   Martin, T. P. "Transcripts, Facsimiles, and Manuscripts in the Spanish Language in the Library of Congress, 1929," *HAHR* 10 (1930) 243–246.

239a. Mikhailov, S. S. "Izuchenie Latinskoi Ameriki v Sovetskom Soiuze," *VI*, no. 4 (April, 1962) 98–106.
   "The Study of Latin America in the Soviet Union."

239b. ———. "Izuchenie Problem Latinskoi Ameriki," *VANSSSR*, no. 5 (1962) 54–59.
   "The Study of Latin American Problems."

239c. Millares Carlo, A. "La Bibliografía y las Bibliografías," *CA* 79, no. 1 (1955) 176–194.
   Lists general Latin American bibliographies.

240.   Morgan, D. L., and G. P. Hammond (eds.). *A Guide to the Manuscript Collections of the Bancroft Library.* Berkeley, Calif., 1963.

241.   Mörner, M. "Swedish Contributions to the Historical Bibliography of Latin America," *HAHR* 34 (1954) 393–398.

242.   Moscow. Akademiia Nauk SSSR. Institut Latinskoi Ameriki. *Latinskaia Amerika v Sovetskoi Pechati: Bibliografiia Knig i Zhurnal'nykh Statei na Russkom Iazyke o Sovremennom Politicheskom Polozhenii. Istorii, Ekonomike, i Kul'ture Stran Latinskoi Ameriki, 1946–1962.* Moscow, 1964.

   Latin America in Soviet Literature: Bibliography of Books and Articles in the Russian Language on Contemporary Politics. History, Economics and Culture of the Latin American Countries 1946–1962.

243.   National Education Association. *Latin American Backgrounds: A Bibliography of 497 References.* Wash., 1940.

244. New England Institute of Inter-American Affairs. *An Informal List of Books on Latin America for the General Reader and a Directory of Latin American Collections in New England Libraries.* Boston, 1943.

245. New York Public Library. *Dictionary Catalog of the History of the Americas Collection.* 28 vols., Boston, 1961.
    An extensive listing of catalog entries.

246. ———. *Latin American Periodicals Current in the Reference Department.* N.Y., 1920.

247. O'Halloran, T. P. *A Bibliography of South America.* B.A., 1912.

248. Okinshevich, L., and C. J. Gorokhoff. *Latin America in Soviet Writings, 1945–1958: A Bibliography.* Wash., 1959.
    Reflects the recent surge of Latin American interest in the USSR.

249. O'Leary, T. J. *Ethnographic Bibliography of South America.* New Haven, Conn., 1963.

250. Olivos, L. (comp.). "Publicaciones que Contienen Datos Bibliográficos Sobre las Ciencias Sociales en América Latina," *RICS,* 2d ser., 1 (1962) 407–414.

251. Ortega y Medina, J. A. *Historiografía Soviética Iberoamericanista, 1945–1960.* Mexico, 1961.

252. Oswald, J. G. "Contemporary Soviet Research on Latin America," *LARR* 1 (Spring, 1966) 77–96.

253. Owen, E. D. *Index to Publications and Articles on Latin America: Issued by the United States Bureau of Labor Statistics, 1902–1943.* Wash., 1945.

254. Palau y Dulcet, A. *Manual del Librero Hispano-Americano.* 7 vols., Barcelona, 1923–1927.
    2d ed., Barcelona, 1948– .

254a. Patterson, J. E. "Spanish and Spanish American Manuscripts in the Yale University Library," *YULG* 31, no. 3 (1957) 110–133.

255. PAU. *Bibliography on Public Administration in Latin America.* Wash., 1954.
    Subdivided by country and subject.

256. ———. *Bibliography of the Liberator, Simon Bolivar, Compiled in Commemoration of the One Hundred and Fiftieth Anniversary of the Birth of the Liberator on July 24, 1783.* Wash., 1933.

257. ———. *Books and Libraries in the Americas: Recommendations of Inter-American Conferences, 1947–1962. Libros y Bibliotecas en América: Recomendaciones de Conferencias Inter-Americanas, 1947–1962.* Wash., 1963.

258. ———. *Catalogue of Newspapers and Magazines in the Columbus Memorial Library of the Pan American Union.* Wash., 1931.

259. ———. *Catálogo de Publicaciones: Documentos Oficiales, OEA. Catalog of Publications: Official Records, OAS.* Wash., 1964.

260. ———. *Catalogue of Pan American Union Publications in English, Spanish, Portuguese, and French.* Wash., 1950.
    Guide to a number of valuable series published by the Pan American Union, including those on congresses and conferences, fine arts, foreign trade, law and treaties, and bibliography.

261. ———. *Catalogue of Publications and Official Records of the OAS. Catálogos de Publicaciones y Documentos Oficiales de la OEA.* Wash., 1961.

262. ———. *Current Latin American Periodicals Relating to Economic Subjects in the Library of the Pan American Union.* Wash., 1938.
    Mimeograph.

263. ———. *Current Periodicals Printed in English Relating Exclusively to Latin America Received in the Library.* Wash., 1939.

264. ———. *Education in Latin America: A Partial Bibliography.* Wash., 1958.

265. ———. *Fuentes de Información Sobre Libros de la América Latina: Revistas con Secciones de Crítica Literaria, Revistas Bibliografías y de Bibliotecas.* Wash., 1930.
    Mimeograph.

266. ———. *Latin American Journals Dealing with the Social Sciences and Auxiliary Disciplines.* Wash., 1941.

267. ———. *Latin American Newspapers (Other than Official) Received in the Library of the Pan American Union.* Wash., 1942.

268. ———. *Latin American University Journals and Serial Publications.* Wash., 1944.

268a. ———. *List of Books Accessioned and*

Periodical Articles Indexed in the Colum-bus Memorial Library. Wash., 1950– .

269. PAU. *Recent Trends in Inter-American Relations: A Bibliography.* Wash., 1939.

270. ———. *Repertorio de Publicaciones Perió-dicas Actuales Latinoamericanas.* Paris, 1958.

271. ———. *Selected List of Books (in English) on Latin America.* 5th ed., Wash., 1939.

272. ———. *A Selective List of Periodicals of General Interest Published in Latin America.* Wash., 1940.

273. ———. *Serie de los Documentos Oficiales de la Organización de los Estados Ameri-canos: Guía, Esquema y Cuadros Explica-tivos de Categorías.* Wash., 1961.

274. ———. Biblioteca Conmemorativa de Colón. *Bibliografía de las Conferencias Interamericanas.* Wash., 1954.

275. ———. ———. *Bibliografía Biblio-tecológica: Suplemento 1960–1962.* Wash., 1964.

276. ———. ———. *Books and Magazine Articles on Geography in the Columbus Memorial Library of the Pan American Union.* Wash., 1935.

277. ———. ———. *Index to Latin Ameri-can Periodical Literature, 1929–1960.* 8 vols., Boston, 1962.

Continued by *Index to Latin American Periodicals: Humanities and Social Scien-ces, 1961–* . Boston, 1962– .

277a. ———. ———. *List of Books Acces-sioned and Periodical Articles Indexed: 1950–* . Wash., 1950– .

A monthly.

278. ———. ———. *List of Latin American History and Description in the Columbus Memorial Library.* Wash., 1907.

Supplements, Wash., 1909–1914.

279. ———. Columbus Memorial Library. *A List of Literary and Cultural Maga-zines Received in the Columbus Memorial Library.* Wash., 1940.

280. ———. ———. *Selected List of Books and Magazine Articles on Inter-American Relations.* 2d ed., Wash., 1934.

281. ———. ———. *Theses on Pan American Topics Prepared by Candidates for Doc-toral Degrees in Universities and Colleges in the United States and Canada.* Wash., 1962.

See item 229.

282. Paz, J. *Catálogo de Manuscritos de América Existentes en la Biblioteca Nacional.* Madrid, 1933.

283. Peña y Cámara, J. M. de la. *Guía del Archivo del Indias de Sevilla.* Madrid, 1958.

284. Peraza Sarausa, F. *Bibliografías Sobre Publicaciones Oficiales de la América Latina.* Gainesville, Fla., 1964.

285. Polišenský, J. "Novější Práce k Dějinám Latinské Ameriky," *CCH* 11 (1963) 81–85.

"Recent Works on the History of Latin America."

286. Praesent, H. (comp.). *Ibero-Amerikan-ische Bibliographie.* Berlin, 1930– .

287. *Prensa Iberoamericana: Indice de las Publicaciones Periódicas Antiguas y Mod-ernas. Editadas en Lenguas Ibéricas, que Figuran en el Pabellón de Prensa Ibero-americana de la Exposición de Sevilla.* Madrid, 1929.

288. Programa Interamericano de Información Popular. *Three Preliminary Bibliogra-phies of Works Related to the Social Sciences in Latin America. Tres Biblio-grafías Preliminares de Obras Relaciona-das con las Ciencias Sociales en América Latina.* San José, C.R., 1962.

289. Quelle, O. *Verzeichnis Wissenschaftlicher Einrichtungen, Zeitschriften und Biblio-graphien der Ibero-Amerikanischen Kultur-welt.* Stuttgart, 1916.

Supplement in *DUIIM* 7 (1919) 47–71.

290. Reid, D. W., and J. T. Reid. "An Annotated Bibliography of Books on Spanish South America and the West Indies," *H* 20 (1937) 313–326.

291. Robertson, J. A. "The Oliveira Lima Collection of Hispanoamericana," *HAHR* 3 (1920) 78–83.

291a. Rohen y Gálvez, G. A. "Latin American Periodicals Dealing with Labor and Social Welfare," *HLAS* (1942) 449–479.

292. Sánchez Alonso, B. *Fuentes de la Historia Española e Hispanoamericana.* 3d ed., 3 vols., Madrid, 1952.

293. Sandoval, F. B. *Bibliografía General del Azúcar.* Mexico, 1954.

294. Spain. Ministerio de Educación Nacional. *Catálogo de Publicaciones: 1958.* Madrid, 1958.

295. Spell, L. M. *Research Materials for the Study of Latin America at the University of Texas.* Austin, 1954.

296. Steck, F. B. *A Tentative Guide to Historical Materials on the Spanish Borderlands.* Phil., 1943.

297. Stokes, W. S. *The Causes of Inter-American Misunderstandings: A Selected Bibliography.* Madison, Wis., 1957.

298. Strout, C. L. "Literary-Historical Treasures in the Thomas Gilcrease Institute of American History and Art," *HAHR* 43 (1963) 267–270.

299. Taylor, M. R. *Guide to Latin American Reference Materials, A Union List for Use in the Atlanta-Athens Area.* Atlanta, Ga., 1958.

300. Tereshtenko, V. J. (ed.). *Cooperation in Latin America: Part 1: Bibliographical Review of Literature.* N.Y., 1942.

301. Te Velde, J. C. *Modern Latin America: A Popular Bibliography.* Chicago, 1939.

302. Toro, J. del. *A Bibliography of the Collective Biography of Spanish America.* Rio Piedras, P.R., 1938.

303. Torres Lanzas, P. *Independencia de América, Fuentes para su Estudio, Catálogo de Documentos Conservados en el Archivo General de Indias de Sevilla.* 6 vols., Madrid, 1912.

304. Tudela, J. *Los Manuscritos de América en las Bibliotecas de España.* Madrid, 1954.

305. Twitchell, R. E. *The Spanish Archives of New Mexico.* 2 vols., Cedar Rapids, Ia., 1914.

306. Ulibarri, G. S. "Materials in the National Archives Relating to Latin America," *HLAS* 22 (1960) 334–336.

307. UN. *Latin America, 1935–1949: A Selected Bibliography.* N.Y., 1952.
Organized by topic and region.

308. UNESCO. Regional Center for the Western Hemisphere. *Guía de Museos de la América Latina.* Havana, 1963.

309. University of California (Berkeley). Bancroft Library. *Catalog of Printed Books.* 22 vols., Boston, 1964.

310. University of California Library. *Spain and Spanish America in the Libraries of the University of California: A Catalog of Books.* 2 vols., Berkeley, Calif., 1928–1930.

311. USDA. *Latin America: Hemispheric Partner: A Bibliographic Survey.* Wash., 1964.

312. USLC. *Latin American Periodicals Currently Received in the Library of Congress and the Library of the Department of Agriculture.* Wash., 1944.

313. ———. Law Library. Hispanic Law Division. *Index to Latin American Legislation, 1950–1960.* 2 vols., Boston, 1961.

314. USNA. *Materials in the National Archives Relating to the Countries on the West Coast of South America.* Wash., 1942.

314a. ———. *Materials Relating to Latin America in Records of Emergency War Agencies, 1917–1919, in the National Archives.* Wash., 1942.

315. U.S. Military Assistance Institute Library. *Suggested Reading List on Latin America.* Rev. ed., Arlington, Va., 1962.

316. Urban, P. "Los Estudios Iberoamericanos en la URSS," *ESUS* 2 (1962) 27–40.

317. Utrecht. Rijkuniversiteit. Bibliotheek. *España e Hispanoamérica: Catálogo de Libros Españoles y Publicaciones Extranjeras Sobre España e Hispanoamérica.* Utrecht, 1948.
Continued by supplements.

317a. Valle, R. H. "Bibliografía del Periodismo de América Española," *HLAS* (1941) 559–604.

318. Velázquez, M. del C. (comp.). *Guía Bibliográfica para la Enseñanza de la Historia Hispano-Americana.* Mexico, 1964.

319. Villalon-Galdames, A. "Una Introducción a la Bibliografía Jurídica Latinoamericana," U. of Michigan Diss., 1959.

320. Vindel, F. *Manual Gráfico-Descriptivo del Bibliófilo Hispano-Americano, 1475–1850.* 11 vols., Madrid, 1930–1931.
Supplement, Madrid, 1934.

321. Vivo, J. A. *Instituto Panamericano de Geografía e Historia: Catálogo de la Biblioteca.* Tacubaya, Mexico, 1940.
Covers 1930–1939.

322. Walford, A. J. "Latin Americana in British Libraries and Archives," *IRB* 1 (1951) 174–177.

323. Walne, P. "Guide to Sources for the History of Latin America, *British Volume,*" *HAHR* 44 (1964) 375–376.

324. Whitaker, A. P. *Latin American History Since 1825*. Wash., 1961.

Pamphlet issued by the Service Center for Teachers of History.

324a. *Widener Library Shelflist: Latin America and Latin American Periodicals*. 2 vols., Cambridge, Mass., 1966.

325. Wilgus, A. C. "Bibliography of Works in English on Hispanic American Civilization," *PAM* 44 (1931) 208–210.

325a. ———. *Histories and Historians of Hispanic America*. 2d ed., N.Y., 1942.

326. ———. *The Histories of Hispanic America: A Bibliographical Essay*. Wash., 1932.

326a. ———. "Some Bibliographies in English Dealing with Hispanic American History," *PAM* 43 (1930) 162–164.

327. ———. (comp.). *Source Materials and Special Collections Dealing with Latin American Libraries of the United States*. Wash., 1934.

328. Wise, M. M. *Latin American Periodicals Currently Received in the Library of Congress: Preliminary Edition*. Wash., 1941.

328a. Wish, J. R. *Economic Development in Latin America: An Annotated Bibliography*. N.Y., 1966.

Almost 7,000 entries. Primarily English language.

329. Zamora Lucas, F., and M. Casada. *Publicaciones Periódicas Existentes en la Biblioteca Nacional: Catálogo*. Madrid, 1952.

330. Zimmerman, I. *A Guide to Current Latin American Periodicals: Humanities and Social Sciences*. Gainesville, Fla., 1961.

Contains descriptive information on periodicals from the various Latin American countries.

I–A–3   cross references: 614, 1077–1148, 4365

4. UNITED STATES

331. *America: History and Life*. Santa Barbara, Calif., 1964–   .

Annotated bibliography of periodical literature relating to United States history.

331a. *The American Catalogue of Books, 1876–1910*. 9 vols., N.Y., 1876–1910.

331b. Ames, J. G. *Comprehensive Index to the Publications of the United States Government, 1881–1893*. 2 vols., Wash., 1905.

See also item 419.

332. Arnade, C. "A Guide to Spanish Florida Source Material," *FHQ* 35 (1957) 320–325.

333. Beer, W. *Checklist of American Periodicals, 1741–1800*. Worcester, Mass., 1923.

334. Beers, H. P. (ed.). *Bibliographies in American History: Guide to Materials for Research*. Rev. ed., N.Y., 1942.

Divided topically and chronologically. Descriptive rather than critical commentaries.

335. Bemis, S. F., and G. G. Griffin. *Guide to the Diplomatic History of the United States, 1775–1921*. Wash., 1935.

An annotated guide for all aspects of the history of American foreign relations to 1921.

336. Billington, R. A. *Guides to American History Manuscript Collections in Libraries of the United States*. N.Y., 1952.

337. Bolton, H. E. *Guide to Materials for the History of the United States in the Principal Archives of Mexico*. Wash., 1913.

337a. ———. "Material for Southwestern History in the Central Archives of Mexico," *AHR* 13 (1908) 510–527.

338. Bowker, J. W. (comp.). *A List of American Learned Journals Devoted to Humanistic and Social Studies*. Wash., n.d.

339. Boyd, A. M. *United States Government Publications*. 3d ed., N.Y., 1949.

Organized according to the government agency issuing the publication. The index constitutes a subject guide.

340. Bradley, P. *A Bibliography of the Monroe Doctrine, 1919–1929*. London, 1929.

341. Brayer, H. O. "Preliminary Guide to Indexed Newspapers in the United States, 1850–1900," *MVHR* 33 (1946) 237–258.

342. Brigham, C. S. *History and Bibliography of American Newspapers, 1690–1820*. 2 vols., Worcester, Mass., 1947.

Supplementary information in C. S. Brigham, *Additions and Corrections to History*. . . . Worcester, Mass., 1961.

343. Brown, E. S. *Manual of Government Publications, United States and Foreign*. N.Y., 1950.

344. Butler, R. L. *A Check List of Manuscripts in the Edward E. Ayer Collection*. Chicago, 1937.

345. Carman, H. J., and A. W. Thompson. *A Guide to the Principal Sources for American Civilization, 1800–1900, in the City of New York: Printed Materials.* N.Y., 1962.

346. Channing, E., *et al. Guide to the Study and Reading of American History.* Rev. ed., Boston, 1912.

346a. Columbia University. Oral History Research Office. *The Oral History Collection of Columbia University.* N.Y., 1964.

Guide to transcripts of oral history interviews.

347. Conover, H. F. (comp.). *A Guide to Bibliographic Tools for Research in Foreign Affairs.* 2d ed., Wash., 1958.

348. Crick, B. R., and M. Alman (eds.). *A Guide to Manuscripts Relating to America in Great Britain and Ireland.* London, 1961.

349. Dargan, M. *Guide to American Biography.* 2 vols., Albuquerque, N.M., 1947–1952.

350. DeConde, A. *New Interpretations in American Foreign Policy.* Rev. ed., Wash., 1961.

Pamphlet issued by the Service Center for Teachers of History.

351. District of Columbia. "A List of Newspapers Published in the District of Columbia, 1820–1850," *BSAP* 19 (1927) 43–65.

352. Downs, R. B. *American Library Resources: A Bibliographical Guide.* Chicago, 1951.

353. *Exposición de Libros Españoles Antiguos y Modernos Referentes a los Estados Unidos y de Obras de Autores Norteamericanos Traducidas y Publicadas en España.* Barcelona, 1956.

354. Ford, P. L. *Check-List of Bibliographies, Catalogues, Reference Lists, and Lists of Authorities of American Books and Subjects.* Brooklyn, 1889.

355. Fox, L. H. "New York City Newspapers, 1820–1850: A Bibliography," *BSAP* 21 (1927) 1–131.

356. Greely, A. W. *Public Documents of the Early Congresses.* Wash., 1897.

357. ———. *Public Documents of the First Fourteen Congresses, 1789–1817: Papers Relating to Early Congressional Documents.* Wash., 1900.

Supplement, Wash., 1904.

358. Hamer, P. M. (ed.). *A Guide to Archives and Manuscripts in the United States.* New Haven, Conn., 1961.

A comprehensive guide to manuscript holdings of leading United States archives.

359. Hammond, G. "Manuscript Collections in the Bancroft Library," *AA* 13 (January, 1950) 15–26.

360. Handlin, O., *et al. Harvard Guide to American History.* Cambridge, Mass., 1954.

Covers the period to 1952. Considerable listings for United States–Latin American relations.

361. Hart, A. B. *The Foundations of American Foreign Policy, with a Working Bibliography,* N.Y., 1901.

362. Hartwell, M. A. (ed.). *Checklist of United States Public Documents, 1789–1909.* 3d ed., Wash., 1911.

363. Hasse, A. R. *Index to United States Documents Relating to Foreign Affairs, 1828–1861.* 3 vols., Wash., 1914–1921.

363a. Helton, H. S. (comp.). *Preliminary Inventory of the Records of the Office of Inter-American Affairs.* Wash., 1952.

364. Hill, R. R. *Descriptive Catalogue of the Documents Relating to the History of the United States in the Papeles Procedentes de Cuba Deposited in the Archivo General de Indias at Seville.* Wash., 1916.

365. ———. "Sources of American History in Spanish Archives," *HAHR* 17 (1937) 538–545.

366. Hirshberg, H. S., and C. H. Melinat. *Subject Guide to United States Government Publications.* Chicago, 1947.

367. Johnson, W. D., and I. G. Mudge. *Special Collections of Libraries in the United States.* Wash., 1912.

368. Kaplan, L. *A Bibliography of American Autobiographies.* Madison, Wis., 1961.

369. Kenny, D. J. *The American Newspaper Directory and Record of the Press: Containing an Accurate List of all the Newspapers, Magazines, Reviews, Periodicals, etc., in the United States and British Provinces of North America.* N.Y., 1861.

370. Larned, J. *Literature of American History: A Bibliographical Guide in Which the Scope, Character, and Comparative Worth of Books in Selected Lists Is Set Forth in Brief Notes by Critics of Authority.* Boston, 1902.

Supplement for 1901–1902, Boston, 1902.

371. Leidy, W. P. *A Popular Guide to Government Publications.* N.Y., 1953.

Subject guide to 2,500 U.S. government publications.

372. Lowenstein, L. (comp.). *Government Resources Available for Foreign Affairs Research.* Wash., 1965.

373. Manning, M. M. "The East Florida Papers in the Library of Congress," *HAHR* 10 (1930) 392–397.

374. Marino Pérez, L. *Guide to the Materials for American History in Cuban Archives.* Wash., 1907.

375. Matthews, M. A. *The Department of State: With Supplement Covering Treaties Between the United States and Other Powers.* Wash., 1936.

376. Mavro, A. P. *Preliminary Inventory of the Records of Selected Foreign Service Posts.* Wash., 1953.

377. McCamy, J. L. *Government Publications for the Citizen.* N.Y., 1949.

378. McKee, T. H. *Reports of the Committee on Foreign Affairs, House of Representatives, from the Organization of the Committee, March 13, 1822, to the Close of the Forty-ninth Congress, 1887.* Wash., 1887.

379. ———. *Reports of the Committee on Foreign Relations, United States Senate, from the Organization of the Committee, December 10, 1816, to the Close of the Forty-ninth Congress, 1887.* Wash., 1887.

380. Merritt, T. C. *United States Government as a Publisher.* Chicago, 1943.

381. Meyer, H. H. B. *List of References on the Monroe Doctrine.* Wash., 1919.

382. Mott, F. L. *A History of American Magazines.* 4 vols., Cambridge, Mass., 1930–1957.

383. Mugridge, D. H. *American History and Civilization: A List of Guides and Annotated or Selected Bibliographies.* 2d ed., Wash., 1951.

384. ———, and B. P. McCrum. *A Guide to the Study of the United States of America: Representative Books Reflecting the Development of American Life and Thought.* Wash., 1960.

An extended annotated list of works on all aspects of the United States, including foreign relations.

385. *Newspapers in Libraries of Metropolitan Chicago: A Union List Prepared by the University of Chicago Libraries.* Chicago, 1931.

386. New York Public Library. *Checklist of Newspapers and Official Gazettes in the New York Public Library.* N.Y., 1915.

387. ———. *A Guide to the Reference Collections of the New York Public Library.* N.Y., 1941.

387a. ———. *Manuscript Collections in the New York Public Library.* N.Y., 1901.

388. PAU. Columbus Memorial Library. *Bibliography on the Monroe Doctrine.* Wash., 1924.

389. Paullin, C. O., and F. L. Paxson. *Guide to the Material in London Archives for the History of the United States Since 1783.* Wash., 1914.

390. Phelps, E. M. *Selected Articles on the Monroe Doctrine.* 2d ed., White Plains, N.Y., 1916.

391. Plischke, E. *American Foreign Relations.* N.p., 1955.

392. Poore, B. P. *A Descriptive Catalogue of the Government Publications of the United States, September 5, 1774–March 4, 1881, Compiled by Order of Congress.* Wash., 1885.

Contains abstracts of the included documents.

393. "Preliminary Check List of Floridiana, 1500–1865, in the Libraries of Florida," *FLB* 2, no. 2 (1930) 4–16.

394. *Publications of the Department of State: A Cumulative List from October 1, 1929.* Wash., 1941–

Quarterly.

395. Robertson, J. A. *List of Documents in Spanish Archives Relating to the History of the United States, Which Have Been Printed, or of Which Transcripts are Preserved in American Libraries.* Wash., 1910.

396. Roorbach, O. A. *Bibliotheca Americana, 1820–1861.* 4 vols., N.Y., 1852–1861.

397. Sabin, J. *Bibliotheca Americana: A Dictionary of Books Relating to America, From Its Discovery to the Present Time: Begun by Joseph Sabin, Continued by Wilberforce Eames and Completed by R. W. G. Vail for the Bibliographical Society of America.* 29 vols., N.Y., 1868–1936.

Sabin's original work was extended by Wilberforce Eames and R. W. G. Vail.

398. Schmeckebier, L. F., and R. B. Eastin. *Government Publications and Their Use.* Rev. ed., Wash., 1961.

399. Shaw, R. R., and R. H. Shoemaker. *American Bibliography: A Preliminary Checklist, 1801–* . N.Y., 1958– .

400. Shepherd, W. R. *Guide to the Materials for the History of the United States in Spanish Archives.* Wash., 1907.

401. Slade, W. A. *Foreign Relations of the United States: A Bibliographical List.* Wash., 1929.
Supplements, Wash., 1935–1940.

402. Summers, N. *List of Documents Relating to Special Agents of the Department of State, 1789–1906.* Wash., 1951.

403. Tompkins, D. C. *Materials for the Study of the Federal Government.* Chicago, 1948.

404. *The United States Catalog.* N.Y., 1900–1928.
All books published in the U.S. which were in print in 1928. Supplemented by item 46.

405. USCH. *Index to Congressional Committee Hearings in the Library of the United States House of Representatives Prior to January 1, 1951.* Wash., 1954.
Supplemental index (1949–1955), Wash., 1956.

405a. USCS. *Compilation of Reports of Committee on Foreign Relations, United States Senate, 1789–1901.* 8 vols., Wash., 1901.

406. ———. *Selected Bibliography on the Monroe Doctrine, with Special Reference to Its Modern Aspects* (76th Cong., 3d Sess., S. Doc. 303). Wash., 1941.

407. ———. Library. *Cumulative Index of Congressional Committee Hearings (Not Confidential in Character) from 74th Congress (Jan. 3, 1935) Through 85th Congress (Jan. 3, 1959) in the United States Senate Library.* Wash., 1959.

408. ———. ———. *Index of Congressional Committee Hearings (Not Confidential in Character) Prior to January 3, 1935 in the Senate Library.* Wash., 1935.

409. USDS. *Selected Publications and Materials Relating to the Foreign Policies of the United States.* 2d ed., Wash., 1948.

410. USLC. *Brief List of Books on History of Interventions in the United States.* Wash., 1917.

411. ———. *A Check List of American Newspapers in the Library of Congress, Comp. Under the Direction of A. G. Slauson.* Wash., 1901.

412. ———. *The Department of State: A Selected List of References.* Wash., 1946.
Supplement, Wash., 1946.

413. ———. *A List of References on the Diplomacy of the United States, 1789–1823.* Wash. 1924.

414. ———. *Newspapers on Microfilm.* 4th ed., Wash., 1961.

415. ———. Hispanic Foundation. *A Provisional Bibliography of the United States Books Translated into Spanish.* Wash., 1957.

416. ———. ———. *Spanish and Portuguese Translations of U.S. Books, 1955–1962: A Bibliography.* Wash., 1963.

417. ———. ———. *United States Books in Portuguese and Spanish.* Wash., 1963.

418. USNA. *List of National Archives Microfilm Publications, 1961.* Wash., 1961.
Rev. ed., Wash., 1965.

419. U.S. Superintendent of Documents. *Catalog of the Public Documents of Congress and of All Departments of the Government of the United States for the Period March 4, 1893–December 31, 1940.* Wash., 1896–1945.
This is a supplement to item 331b.

420. ———. *Selected United States Government Publications.* Wash., 1928– .

421. ———. *Tables of and Annotated Index to the Congressional Series of United States Public Documents (1817–1893).* Wash., 1902.

422. ———. *United States Government Publications: Monthly Catalog, 1895– .* Wash., 1895– .
A comprehensive listing.

423. Winsor, J. *Narrative and Critical History of America.* 8 vols., Boston, 1884–1889.
Includes thorough bibliographical information.

424. Wright, A. R. "Archival Sources for the Study of Wartime Relations of Latin America with the United States, 1917–1920: Illustrations of their Use," *IBR* 1 (Spring, 1941) 23–35.

Refers only to United States source material.

425. *Writings on American History, 1902– .* Princeton, N.J.; New Haven, Conn.; and Wash.; 1904– .
Various compilers. 1904–1905 not issued. Index for 1902–1940, Wash., 1956. Published yearly.

I–A–4 cross references: 780, 781, 786, 799, 1149–1187

5. ARGENTINA

426. Amaral, S. M. *Organización del Archivo, Guía de Clasificación, Precedida de Breves y Sencillas Instrucciones para la Confección del Catálogo Temático.* La Plata, Argentina, 1925.

427. Angelis, P. de. *Colección de Obras Impresas y Manuscritas, que Tratan Principalmente del Río de la Plata.* B.A., 1853.
Contains works printed in Argentina and Uruguay.

428. *Anuario Bibliográfico de la República Argentina: 1879–1887.* 9 vols., B.A., 1880–1888.
Descriptively annotated.

429. *Anuario Bibliográfico: Letras, Historia, Educación y Filosofía.* 4 vols., La Plata, Argentina, 1927–1930.

430. Argentina. Ministerio de Relaciones Exteriores y Culto. *Catálogo de la Biblioteca, Mapoteca y Archivo.* 3d ed., B.A., 1910.

431. Barager, J. "Historiography of the Río de la Plata Area," *HAHR* 39 (1959) 588–642.

432. Becco, H. J. "Bibliografía de Sarmiento," *HUM* 37, no. 2 (1961) 119–144.

433. Becú, T. *La Bibliografía en la República Argentina.* B.A., 1945.

434. *Bibliografía Argentina de Artes y Letras.* B.A., 1959– .
Quarterly.

435. Biblioteca del Congreso de la Nación. *Bibliografía de San Martín.* B.A., 1950.

436. Biedma, J. J. "Archivo General de la Nación," *RDHL* 51 (1915) 237–253.

437. Binayán, N. *Bibliografía de Bibliografías Argentinas.* B.A., 1919.

438. *Boletín Bibliográfico Argentino . . . 1937.* B.A., 1937– .

439. Borchard, E. M. *Guide to the Law and Legal Literature of Argentina, Brazil and Chile.* Wash., 1917.

440. Buenos Aires. Biblioteca Nacional. *Catálogo de las Revistas y Periódicos Existentes en la Biblioteca Nacional.* Rev. ed., B.A., 1923.

441. ———. ———. *Catálogo Metódico de la Biblioteca Nacional.* 6 vols., B.A., 1893–1925.

442. ———. ———. *Catálogo por Orden Cronológico de los Manuscritos Relativos a América Existentes en la Biblioteca Nacional de Buenos Aires.* 2 vols., B.A., 1905–1906.

443. ———. *Un Siglo de Periódicos en la Biblioteca Nacional (Políticos): Catálogo por Fechas, 1800–1899.* B.A., 1935.

444. ———. Universidad. Facultad de Ciencias Económicas. *Catálogo de la Sección Revistas, Diarios y Periódicos.* B.A., 1932.

445. Carbía, R. D. *Historia Crítica de la Historiografía Argentina, Desde sus Orígenes en el Siglo XVI.* Rev. ed., B.A., 1940.
An analytical evaluation of Argentine historical scholarship.

446. ———. *Los Historiógrafos Argentinos Menores: Su Clasificación Crítica.* B.A., 1923.

447. Childs, J. B. (ed.). *A Guide to the Official Publications of the Other American Republics. I. Argentina.* Wash., 1945.

448. Clagett, H. L. *A Guide to the Law and Legal Literature of Argentina, 1917–1946.* Wash., 1948.

449. Furlong Cardiff, G., *et al. Historia y Bibliografía de las Primeras Imprentas Rioplatenses, 1700–1850.* B.A., 1953– .
Three volumes through 1959.

450. ———, and A. R. Geoghegan. *Bibliografía de la Revolución de Mayo, 1810–1828.* B.A., 1960.

451. *Indice General del Archivo de la Cámara de Representantes de Buenos Aires.* N.p., n.d.
Covers 1820–1856.

452. Lamas, A. *Biblioteca del Río de la Plata: Colección de Obras, Documentos, y Noticias . . . para Servir a la Historia, Física, Política, y Literaria del Río de la Plata.* B.A., 1873.

453. La Plata. Universidad Nacional. Biblioteca. *Bibliografía de Sarmiento, con Prólogo de Ricardo Rojas: Trabajo Realizado por los Alumnos de Letras.* B.A., 1911.

454. ———. ———. ———. *Bibliografía Sobre Sarmiento (Piezas Bibliográficas Existentes en la Biblioteca Pública de la Universidad): Con una Nómina de las Obras de Sarmiento Pertenecientes a la Institución.* La Plata, Argentina, 1938.

455. ———. ———. ———. *Catálogo de la Biblioteca.* 2 vols., B.A., 1917–1918.

456. ———. ———. ———. *Catálogo de Periódicos Sudamericanos Existentes en la Biblioteca Pública de la Universidad (1791–1861), Publicación del Cincuentenario de la Biblioteca Pública de la Universidad y de la Ciudad de la Plata: Prólogo de Alberto Palcos.* La Plata, Argentina, 1934.

457. Masini, J. L. *Los Archivos Históricos de Mendoza: Historia, Organización, Contenido.* Mendoza, Argentina, 1959.

457a. Massa, N., and E. Quesada. *Catálogo Sistemático y Alfabético de la Colección de Obras Argentinas.* B.A., 1878.

458. Matijevic, N. *Bibliografía Bibliotecológica Argentina.* Bahia Blanca, Argentina, 1963.

459. Molina, R. *Misiones Argentinas en los Archivos Europeos.* Mexico, 1955.

460. Monsegur, S. J. *El Derecho Internacional Privado en la República Argentina: Apuntaciones Bibliográficas.* B.A., 1898.

461. Montt, L. *Noticias de las Publicaciones Hechas en Chile por Don Domingo F. Sarmiento (1841–1871).* Santiago, 1884.

461a. Quesada, H. C. (ed.). "Misiones Diplomáticas: Por Archivo General de la Nación," *SCIHA* 4 (1938) 36–63.

462. Quesada Zapiola, C. A. (comp.). *Catálogo de la Documentación Referente a las Relaciones Diplomáticas Entre Estados Unidos de América y la República Argentina, 1810–1830, Existente en el Archivo Nacional de los Estados Unidos de América, Sección Departamento de Estado.* B.A., 1948.

463. Robertson, J. A. "The Publications of the Instituto de Investigaciones Históricas de la Facultad de Filosofía y Letras," *HAHR* 10 (1930) 101–113.

464. Salas, C. I. *Bibliografía del General Don José de San Martín y de la Emancipación Sudamericana.* 5 vols., B.A., 1910.

Errores y Omisiones, B.A., 1912. Consists primarily of titles pertaining to San Martin's military activities.

465. Selva, M., *et al. Bibliografía General Argentina: Inventario Analítico-Crítico de Todas las Publicaciones Argentinas Desde el Origen de la Primera Imprenta en Río de la Plata, Hasta el Presente.* B.A., 1931– .

465a. Soria, G. "Biblioteca y Mapoteca Histórico-Geográfica de la República Argentina (1810–1828)," *AIGM* 5 (1922) 245–280.

466. Torre Revello, J. "El Archivo General de la Nación Argentina," *RHA,* no. 1 (1938) 41–52.

467. ———. *Los Archivos de la República Argentina.* Seville, 1925.

468. ———. *Bibliografía de las Islas Malvinas: Obras, Mapas y Documentos.* B.A., 1953.

469. ———. "La Biblioteca Nacional de la República Argentina," *RHA,* no. 2 (1938) 69–92.

470. ———. *Documentos Referentes a la Argentina en la Biblioteca Nacional y en el Depósito Hidrográfico de Madrid.* B.A., 1929.

471. ———. *Documentos Referentes a la Historia Argentina en la Real Academia de la Historia.* B.A., 1929.

472. ———. "Museo Mitre," *RHA,* no. 6 (1939) 97–115.

473. USLC. *Select List of References on Argentina.* Wash., 1913.

Additional references, Wash., 1919.

474. Zingoni, C. V. *El Archivo Histórico de la Provincia de Buenos Aires.* La Plata, Argentina, 1928.

474a. Zinny, A. *Bibliografía Histórica de las Provincias del Rio de la Plata, 1780–1821.* B.A., 1875.

475. ———. *Efemeridografía Argirometropolitana Hasta la Caída del Gobierno de Rosas.* B.A., 1869.

Surveys periodical literature of Buenos Aires from 1801 to 1852.

I–A–5 cross references: 1188–1218

6. BOLIVIA

476. American Foreign Law Association. *Bolivia.* N.Y., 1926.

477. Arnade, C. W. "A Selected Bibliography of Bolivian Social Sciences," *IRB* 8 (1958) 256–266.

478. Arnade, C. W. "The Historiography of Colonial and Modern Bolivia," *HAHR* 42 (1962) 333–384.

479. Bolivia. Congreso. Biblioteca. *Catálogo.* La Paz, 1915.

480. Childs, J. B. *A Guide to the Official Publications of the Other American Republics. II: Bolivia.* Wash., 1945.

481. Clagett, H. L. *A Guide to the Law and Legal Literature of Bolivia.* Wash., 1947.

482. Gutiérrez, J. R. *Datos para la Bibliografía Boliviana: Primera Sección.* La Paz, 1875.
    Supplement, La Paz, 1880.

483. Guttentag Tichauer, W. *Bibliografía Boliviana del Año 1962: Ensayo de Catalogación.* La Paz, 1963.

484. PAU. *Catalogue of Books, Pamphlets, Periodicals and Maps Relating to the Republic of Bolivia in the Columbus Memorial Library.* Wash., 1905.

485. René-Moreno, G. *Biblioteca Boliviana: Catálogo de la Sección de Libros i Folletos.* Santiago, 1879.
    Apéndice, Santiago, 1889. *Adiciones,* Santiago, 1899. Supplements, Santiago, 1900–1908.

486. ———. *Biblioteca Boliviana: Catálogo del Archivo de Mojos y Chiquitos.* Santiago, 1888.

487. ———. *Ensayo de una Bibliografía General de los Periódicos de Bolivia, 1825–1905.* Santiago, 1905.
    Lists over 1,400 periodicals and newspapers.

488. USLC. *List of References on Bolivia.* Wash., 1926.

489. Vázquez-Machicado, H. *Fuentes para la Historia Boliviana en los E.E. U.U.* Potosí, Bolivia, 1964.

490. Zengotita, J. de. "The National Archive and the National Library of Bolivia at Sucre," *HAHR* 29 (1949) 649–676.

I–A–6   cross references: 1219–1228

7. BRAZIL

491. Almeida, E. de Castro. *Inventário dos Documentos Relativos ao Brasil Existentes no archivo de Marinha e Ultramar, Organisado para a Bibliotheca Nacional do Rio de Janeiro por Eduardo de Castro e Almeida.* 6 vols., Rio, 1913–1921.

492. Anselmo, A. *Bibliografia das Bibliografias Portuguêsas.* Lisbon, 1923.

493. *Anuário Brasileiro de Literatura, 1937– .* Rio, 1937– .

494. Bezerra, A. *Bibliographia Histórica do Primeiro Reinado á Maioridade, 1822–1840.* Rio, 1930.

495. *Bibliografia Brasileira, 1940– .* Rio, 1947– .

495a. Boehrer, G. C. A. "Brazilian Historical Bibliography: Some Lacunae and Suggestions," *IRB* 11 (1961) 137–144.
    A useful discussion of bibliographical studies available to the scholar.

496. *Boletim Bibliográfico Brasileiro, 1952– .* Rio, 1953– .
    Bi-monthly.

497. *Boletim Internacional de Bibliografia Luso-Brasileira.* Lisbon, 1960– .
    Quarterly.

498. Brazil. Archivo Público Nacional. *Catálogo da Bibliotheca do Archivo Público Nacional.* Rio, 1901.

499. ———. *Elenço das Publicações e dos Documentos Originais ou em Reprodução Fotográfica com o Respectivo Relacionamento, Apresentados pelo Director do Arquivo Nacional da República dos Estados Unidos do Brasil em Execução da Parte do seu Programa de Colaboração com o Comité Brasileiro dos Centenários de Portugal.* Rio, 1942.

500. ———. Congresso. Senado. *Catálogo Alphabético, Bibliotheca do Senado Federal da República dos Estados Unidos do Brazil.* Rio, 1898.

501. ———. Ministério das Relações Exteriores. *Arquivo Histórico do Itamaraty. Parte 1: Correspondência.* Rio, 1952.
    Annotated Index of foreign office records from independence to 1930.

502. ———. ———. *Bibliografia de Historia do Brasil.* 4 vols., Rio, 1943–1946.

503. ———. ———. *Bibliografia de Joaquim Nabuco.* Rio, 1949.

504. ———. ———. *Indice-geral da Coleção de Atos Internacionais.* Rio, 1947.
    Covers 1918–1947.

505. ———. ———. *Lista de Publicações, 1826–1950.* Rio, 1950(?).

506. ———. ———. *Traduções de Autores Brasileiros e Livros Sôbre o Brasil, Escritos em Idiomas Estrangeiros.* Rio, 1960.

507. Burns, E. B. "A Bibliographical Essay on the Baron of Rio-Branco and His Ministry," *IRB* 14 (1964) 406–414.
Analysis of the literature on Brazilian foreign relations from 1902 to 1912.

508. Cabral, A. Valle. *Annaes da Imprensa Nacional do Rio de Janeiro de 1808 a 1822.* Rio, 1881.

508a. Cardozo, M. "A Guide to the Manuscripts in the Lima Library, the Catholic University of America, Washington, D.C.," *HLAS* (1940) 471–504.

509. Carmo, J. A. Pinto do. *Bibliografia de Capistrano de Abreu.* Rio, 1943.

510. Carvalho, O. de. *Bibliografia de Hemerografias.* São Paulo, 1956.
Mimeograph.

511. *Catálogo das Publicações Periódicas das Instituições Anexas e Complementares da Universidade de São Paulo.* São Paulo, 1953.

512. *Catálogo dos Manuscriptos da Bibliotheca Nacional.* Rio, 1904.

513. *Catálogo dos Manuscritos do Instituto Histórico e Geográfico Brasileiro, Existentes em 31 de Dezembro de 1883.* 2d ed., Rio, 1889.

514. Cutin, N. L. *Periódicos nas Bibliotecas Universitárias e Especializadas.* São Paulo, 1956.

515. De Noia, J. *A Guide to the Official Publications of the Other American Republics. III: Brazil.* Wash., 1948.

516. Duval, P. "Relação dos Documentos Navais Existentes no Instituto Histórico Brasileiro, Feita em 1942," *RMB* 66 (October, 1946) 295–315.

517. Esteves, A. *Catálogo dos Livros da Secção Histórica do Archivo Nacional.* 2 vols., Rio, 1913–1916.

518. Ferreira, C. A. *Inventário dos Manuscritos da Biblioteca da Ajuda Referentes à América do Sul.* Coimbra, Portugal, 1950.

518a. Fleiuss, M., *et al.* "Special Articles and Notes on Brazil," *HLAS* (1937) 444–501.

518b. Fonseca, E. N. da. "Panorama da Bibliografia Brasileira Corrente," *HLAS* 23 (1961) 401–406.

519. Galvão, B. F. Ramiz. *Catálogo da Exposição de História do Brazil Realizada pela Bibliotheca Nacional do Rio de Janeiro a 2 de Dezembro de 1881.* 2 vols., Rio, 1881.
Supplement, Rio, 1883.

520. Garraux, A. L. *Bibliographie Brésilienne: Catalogue des Ouvrages Français et Latins Relatifs au Brésil, 1500–1898.* 2d ed., Rio, 1962.
Arranged by author but contains subject index.

521. Gehse, H. *Die Deutsche Presse in Brasilien von 1852 bis zur Gegenwart: Ein Beitrag zur Geschichte und zum Aufgabenkreis Auslanddeutschen Zeitungswesens.* Münster, Ger., 1931.

522. Holmes, R. E. V. *Bibliographical and Historical Description of the Rarest Books in the Oliveira Lima Collection at the Catholic University of America.* Wash., 1927.

523. Instituto Brasileiro de Bibliografia e Documentação. *Bibliotecas Especializadas Brasileiras: Guia para Intercâmbio Bibliográfico.* Rio, 1962.

524. Instituto Histórico e Geográphico Brasileiro. *Catálogo da Biblioteca do Instituto Histórico e Geográphico Brazileiro.* Rio, 1860.

525. Instituto Rio Branco. *Catálogo da Coleção Visconde do Rio Branco.* 2 vols., Rio, 1950.

526. Jackson, W. V. *Library Guide for Brazilian Studies.* Pittsburgh, 1964.
Inventory of Brazilian holdings in United States libraries.

527. Lima, M. de Oliveira. *Relação dos Manuscriptos Portuguezes e Estrangeiros, de Interes para o Brazil, Existentes no Museu Britânnico de Londres.* Rio, 1903.

527a. *Luso-Brazilian Author and Subject Catalogues.* Boston, 1966.

528. Lyra, H. *Archivo Diplomático da Independência.* Rio, 1922.

529. Manchester, A. K. "Descriptive Bibliography of the Brazilian Section of the Duke University Library," *HAHR* 13 (1933) 238–266.

530. "Materials Relating to Brazil in the National Archives," *HAHR* 22 (1942) 521–528.

531. Medeiros, F. Sabóia de. *Precedentes Diplomáticos de 1889 a 1932.* Rio, 1940.
Index to the annual publication of the Ministry of Foreign Relations (Relatorio).

532. Melo, O. Braga. *Bibliografia de Joaquim Nabuco.* Rio, 1952.

533. Moraes, R. Borba de. *Bibliografia Brasiliana: A Bibliographical Essay on Rare*

Books About Brazil Published from 1504 to 1900 and Works of Brazilian Authors Published Abroad Before the Independence of Brazil in 1822. 2 vols., Rio, 1958.
Continued by *Série Bibliográfica de Estudos Brasileiros.* Rio, 1954– .

534. Moraes, R. Borba de, and W. Berrien. *Manual Bibliográfico de Estudos Brasileiros.* Rio, 1949.

535. Napoleão, A. *Os Arquivos Particulares do Itamarati.* Rio, 1940.
A guide to private collections in the archive.

536. Pereira, A. Baptista. *Ruy Barbosa, Catálogo das suas Obras.* Rio, 1929.

537. *Periódicos Brasileiros de Cultura.* Rio, 1956.

538. Phillips, P. L. *A List of Books, Magazine Articles, and Maps Relating to Brazil, 1800–1900.* Wash., 1901.

539. Pierson, D. *Survey of the Literature on Brazil of Sociological Significance Published up to 1940.* Cambridge, Mass., 1945.

540. Readers, G. (comp.). *Bibliographie Franco-Brésilienne, 1551–1957: Avec la Collaboration de Edson Nery da Fonseca.* Rio, 1960.

541. Reis, A. Simões dos. *Bibliografia das Bibliografias Brasileiras.* Rio, 1942.

542. Ricard, R. *Documents des Bibliothèques Espagnoles Relatifs au Brésil.* Coimbra, Portugal, 1924.

543. Richardson, I. L. (ed.). *Bibliografia Brasileira de Administração Pública e Assuntos Correlatos.* Rio, 1964.

544. Rio de Janeiro. Bibliotheca Municipal. *Catálogo da Bibliotheca Municipal (Publicação Official).* Rio, 1878.

545. –––––. Bibliotheca Nacional. *Boletim Bibliográfico.* Rio, 1951– .
Semi-annual publication.

546. –––––. –––––. *Catálogo da Collecção Salvador de Mendonça.* Rio, 1906.

547. –––––. Museu Nacional. *Archivos.* 36 vols., Rio, 1876–1934.

548. Rodrigues, J. C. *Bibliotheca Brasiliense: Catálogo Annotado dos Libros Sobre o Brasil e de Alguns Autografos e Manuscriptos Pertencentes a J. C. Rodrigues.* Rio, 1907.

549. Rodrigues, J. H. *As Fontes da História do Brasil na Europa.* Rio, 1950.

550. –––––. *História e Historiadores do Brasil.* São Paulo, 1965.

551. Ruas, F. Santos. *Fontes para a História da F.E.B. Ensaio.* Rio, 1958.

552. São Paulo. Universidad. Biblioteca Central. *Catálogo das Publicações Periódicas da Universidade de São Paulo.* São Paulo, 1951.
Mimeograph.

552a. Schwartz, S. B. "Francisco Adolfo de Varnhagen: Diplomat, Patriot, Historian," *HAHR* 47 (1967) 185–202.

553. Silva, I. F. da. *Diccionario Bibliográphico Portuguêz.* 22 vols., Lisbon, 1858–1923.

554. Sodré, N. Werneck. *O Que se Deve Ler para Conhecer o Brasil.* 2d ed., Rio, 1960.
A useful commentary on the books essential for a knowledge of Brazil.

555. Stein, S. J. "The Historiography of Brazil, 1808–1889," *HAHR* 40 (1960) 234–278.

556. Trübner, N. *Biblioteca Brazilica: Ancient and Modern Books Relating to the Empire and the Neighboring States.* London, 1879.

556a. USLC. *A List of Books on Brazil.* Wash., 1924.

556b. USNA. *Materials in the National Archives Relating to Brazil.* Wash., 1942.

556c. Varnhagen, F. A. de. *Sucinta Indicação de Alguns Manuscriptos Importantes Respectivos ao Brasil e a Portugal, Existentes no Museu Britânico em Londres e não Comprehendidos no Catálogo Figaniere, Publicado em Lisboa em 1853, ou Simples Aditamento ao Dito Catálogo.* Havana, 1863.

I–A–7   cross references: 439, 1229–1254

8. Central America and the Caribbean in General

557. Albanell, N., *et al.* (comps.). *Cuba, Dominican Republic, Haiti, and Puerto Rico: A Selected Bibliography on the Caribbean Area, Including Only Islands Which Are Members of the Organization of American States.* Gainesville, Fla., 1956.

557a. Arce Behrens, F. "Integración Centroamericana: Selección Bibliográfica," *FI* (April–June, 1966) 556–605.
Unannotated listing by country.

558. *Bibliografía de Centroamérica y del Caribe, 1956– .* Havana, 1958– .
Compiled under the direction of

Fermin Peraza and the *Agrupación Bibliográfica Cubana José Toribio Medina.*

559. Bonhilla Ruano, J. M. *Acontecimiento Bibliográfico: En Torno de la Obra; La Unión de Centro América de Alberto Herrarte.* Guatemala, 1956.

560. Childs, J. B. *The Memorias of the Republics of Central America and of the Antilles.* Wash., 1932.

561. *Current Caribbean Bibliography.* Port-of-Spain, Trinidad, 1951– .

562. Frank, J. C. *American Interoceanic Canals: A List of References in the New York Public Library.* N.Y., 1916.

563. Griffith, W. J. "The Historiography of Central America Since 1830," *HAHR* 40 (1960) 548–569.

564. Lounsbury, R. G. *Materials in the National Archives Relating to the Caribbean Region.* Wash., 1942.

565. Morrison, H. A., Jr. *List of Books and of Articles Relating to Inter-Oceanic Canal and Railway Routes.* Wash., 1900.

566. Munden, K., and F. L. Foor. *Materials in the National Archives Relating to Military Government of the United States in the Caribbean Area, 1898–1934.* Wash., 1934.

566a. Parker, F. D. "The Histories and Historians of Central America to 1850," U. of Illinois Diss., 1951.

567. Phillips, P. L. *A List of Books, Magazine Articles, and Maps Relating to Central America, Including the Republics of Costa Rica, Guatemala, Honduras, Nicaragua, and Salvador, 1800–1900.* Wash., 1902.

568. Schuster, E. *Guide to the Law and Legal Literature of Central American Republics.* N.Y., 1937.

569. Spain. Dirección General de Archivos y Bibliotecas de España. *Bibliografía de Centro América y del Caribe.* Madrid, 1958– .

570. U.S. Superintendent of Documents. *Bibliography of United States Public Documents Relating to Interoceanic Communication Across Nicaragua, Isthmus of Panama, Isthmus of Tehuantepec, etc.* Wash., 1899.

571. Wilson, C. M. *Books About Middle America: A Selected Bibliography.* N.Y., 1943.

571a. Zimmerman, I. "Central America: Bibliography, Indexes, Guides," in Wilgus, *The Caribbean: The Central American Area*, pp. 345–378. See item 6814.

I–A–8 *cross references: 784, 1254a–1260*

9. CHILE

572. Anales de la Universidad de Chile. *Indice Alfabético y Analítico de los Trabajos Publicados, 1843–1887.* Santiago, 1890.
Compiled by Eduardo Valenzuela y Guzmán.

573. ————. *Indice de los Trabajos Contenidos Desde 1888 Hasta 1899.* Santiago, 1900.

574. ————. *Indice General de los Anales de la Universidad de Chile, Dispuesto por Rigoroso Orden Alfabético de Materias y Apellidos, y Comprensivo de Trece Años, Desde 1843 Hasta 1855.* Santiago, 1856.

575. Anrique Reyes, N. *Bibliografía de los Principales Revistas i Periódicos de Chile.* Santiago, 1904.

576. ————, and L. I. Silva A. *Ensayo de una Bibliografía Histórica i Jeográfica de Chile: Obra Premiada con Medalla de Oro en el Certamen de la Universidad para Presentarla al Congreso Internacional de Ciencias Históricas i Jeográficas de Roma.* Santiago, 1902.

577. Benelli, A. *Bibliografía General de Vicuña Mackenna: Integrada con Trabajos de Ramón Briseño, Carlos Vicuña M. Guillermo Feliu Cruz y Eugenio Orrego Vicuña.* Santiago, 1940.

578. Briseño, R. *Estadística Bibliografía de la Literatura Chilena.* 2 vols., Santiago, 1862–1879.

579. *Boletín Catálogo de los Libros de Autores Nacionales.* Santiago, 1946.

580. Castillo, H. *La Literatura Chilena en los Estados Unidos.* Santiago, 1963.

581. *Catálogo Breve de la Biblioteca Americana que Obsequia a la Nacional de Santiago J. T. Medina: Manuscritos.* 3 vols., Santiago, 1928–1930.

582. *Catálogo Razonado de la Biblioteca Chileno-Americana de Don Ramón Briseño.* Santiago, 1874.

583. Chiappa, V. M. *Colección de Historiadores de Chile y Documentos Relativos a la*

Historia Nacional: Indice Bibliográfico. Santiago, 1931.

584. Chiappa, V. M. *Noticias Bibliográficas Sobre la Colección de Historiadores de Chile y Documentos Relativos a la Historia Nacional.* Santiago, 1905.

585. Chile. Congreso. Biblioteca. *Catálogo de la Biblioteca del Congreso Nacional, 1921–22.* Santiago, 1922.

586. Clagett, H. L. *A Guide to the Law and Legal Literature of Chile, 1917–1946.* Wash., 1947.

587. Donoso, R. "Aspectos de la Producción Histórica Chilena en los Ultimos Diez Años," *IRB* 1 (1951) 95–100.

588. Echeverría y Reyes, A. *Ensayo Bibliográfico Sobre la Revolución de 1891.* Santiago, 1894.

589. Encina, F. A. *La Literatura Histórica Chilena y el Concepto Actual de la Historia.* Santiago, 1935.

590. Griffin, C. C. "Francisco Encina and Revisionism in Chilean History," *HAHR* 37 (1957) 1–28.

591. Labarca H., A. "Chile and Its Books," *BPAU* 79 (1957) 567–573.

592. Laval, R. A. *Bibliografía de Bibliografías Chilenas.* Santiago, 1915.
"Suplemento y Adiciones," *RBC* (1929) 115–176.

593. Lindsay, S. "Catálogo de las Obras Publicadas en Chile Desde el Año 1812 Hasta el de 1858," *AERC* (1861) 144–156.

594. Lord, R. A. "Contribution Toward a Bibliography on the O'Higgins Family in America," *HAHR* 12 (1932) 107–138.
Spanish ed., *BBN* 6 (1935) 58–63, 74–79, 93–95, 106–111, 123–125.

595. Neuberger, O. *A Guide to the Official Publications of the Other American Republics: IV. Chile.* Wash., 1947.

596. Pereira Salas, E. *Bibliografía Chilena Sobre el "Gold Rush" en California.* Santiago, n.d.

597. Phillips, P. L. *A List of Books, Magazine Articles, and Maps Relating to Chile.* Wash., 1903.

598. Santiago de Chile. Biblioteca Nacional. *Anuario de la Prensa Chilena . . . 1886–1916.* 31 vols., Santiago, 1887–1927.

599. ———. ———. *Bibliografía General de Chile: Por Emilio Vaïsse.* 2 vols., Santiago, 1915–1918.

Suplemento y Adiciones, Santiago, 1930.

600. ———. ———. *Lista de las Publicaciones Periódicas Chilenas.* Santiago, 1937–1938.

601. *Servicio Bibliográfico Chileno, 1940– .* Santiago, 1940– .

602. Soto Cárdenas, A. *Misiones Chilenas en los Archivos Europeos.* Mexico, 1953.

603. Thayer Ojeda, T. "La Sección de Manuscritos de la Biblioteca Nacional de Chile," *HAHR* 4 (1921) 156–197.

604. Toribio Medina, J. *Bibliotheca Americana: Catálogo Breve de mi Colección de Libros Relativos a la América Latina, con un Ensayo de Bibliografía de Chile Durante el Período Colonial.* Santiago, 1888.

605. ———. *Indices de los Documentos Existentes en el Archivo del Ministerio del Interior.* Santiago, 1884.

606. Vial Correa, G. "La Nueva Bibliografía Sobre las Causas de la Independencia Nacional," *BACH* 27 (1960) 288–300.

607. Villalobos R., S. *Indice de la Colección de Historiadores y de Documentos Relativos a la Independencia de Chile.* Santiago, 1956.

608. Zamudio Z., J. *Fuentes Bibliográficas para el Estudio de la Vida y de la Epoca de Bernardo O'Higgins.* Santiago, 1946.

I–A–9 cross references: *439, 1261–1282*

10. COLOMBIA

609. American Foreign Law Association. *Colombia.* N.Y., 1926.

610. *Anuario Bibliográfico Colombiano, 1951– .* Bogotá, 1958– .

611. Backus, R. C., and P. J. Eder. *A Guide to the Law and Legal Literature of Colombia.* Wash., 1943.

612. *Biblioteca del Ex-Coronel Pineda, o Colección de las Publicaciones de la Imprenta en el Virreinato de Santa Fe i en las Repúblicas de Colombia i Nueva Granada, de 1774 a 1850, i de Varios Manuscritos Nacionales, e Impresos Estranjeros Relacionados con los Negocios de las Repúblicas Anteriores: Contemporáneos i Posteriores a la Revolución de 1810.* Bogotá, 1853.

613. Bogotá. Biblioteca Nacional. *Catálogo de las Obras Existentes en la Biblioteca Nacional.* 4 vols., Bogotá, 1855–1857.

614. ———. ———. *Catálogo de las Obras Hispanoamericanas Existentes en la Biblioteca Nacional de Bogotá*. Bogotá, 1897.

615. ———. ———. *Catálogo de Todos los Periódicos que Existen Desde su Fundación Hasta el Año de 1935, Inclusivo*. 2 vols., Bogotá, 1936.

616. ———. ———. *Catálogos de Periódicos y Libros de la Biblioteca Nacional*. Bogotá, 1914.

617. Childs, J. B. *Colombian Government Publications*. Wash., 1941.

618. Colombia. Congreso. Archivo del Congreso Nacional. *Indice Alfabético, 1819–1935*. Bogotá, 1936– .

619. Colombia. Ministerio de Relaciones Exteriores. *Catálogo de la Biblioteca de Información*. 2d ed., Bogotá, 1914.

620. Florén Lozano, L. *Obras de Referencia y Generales de la Bibliografía Colombiana*. Medellín, 1960.

620a. Gil, C., and M. M. Herrera. *Archivo Nacional. Indice del Archivo Colonial*. Vols. 1 and 2, Bogotá, 1935–1936.
     See also item 626a.

621. Giraldo Jaramillo, G. *Bibliografía de Bibliografías Colombianas*. 2d ed., Bogotá, 1960.

622. ———. *Bibliografía Colombiana de Viajes*. Bogotá, 1957.

623. ———. *Bibliografía Selecta de Nariño*. Bogotá, 1953.

624. Keen, B., *et al. Preliminary Bibliography of Colombia: Compiled from the Strategic Index of the Americas*. Wash., 1943.

625. Laverde Amaya, I. *Apuntes Sobre Bibliografía Colombiana*. Bogotá, 1882.

626. ———. *Bibliografía Colombiana*. Vol. 1, Bogotá, 1895.

626a. Ortega Ricaurte, E. *Archivo Nacional. Indices del Archivo Colonial*. Vols. 3 and 4, Bogotá, 1946.
     See also item 620a.

627. Otero D'Costa, E. "Noticias Bibliográficas Relativas a Obras Raras Escritas por Autores Ingleses Sobre Historia y Viajes por Colombia," *BHA* 30 (1943) 848–858.

628. Otero Muñoz, G. "Ensayo Sobre una Biobibliografía Colombiana," *BHA* 23 (1936) 169–176, 303–315, 418, 427, 498–507, 678.

629. ———. *Historia del Periodismo en Colombia*. Bogotá, 1936.

630. PAU. *Books and Magazine Articles in the Library of the Pan American Union on Relations Between the United States and Colombia*. Wash., 1924.

631. Peraza Sarausa, F., and J. T. Bohórquez C. *Publicaciones Oficiales Colombianas*. Gainesville, Fla., 1964.

632. Posada, E. *Bibliografía Bogotana*. 2 vols., Bogotá, 1917–1925.
     Covers 1738–1831.

633. Rodríguez, J. *Indice General de la Biblioteca del Congreso*. Bogotá, 1936.

634. USLC. *Select List of References on Colombia*. Wash., 1901.

635. Vergara y Velasco, F. J. *República de Colombia, Archivos Nacionales: Indice Analítico, Metódico y Descriptivo*. Bogotá, 1913.

I–A–10 cross references: 889, 890, 893, 1283–1295a

11. Costa Rica

636. *Anuario Bibliográfico Costarricense, 1956– . San José, C.R., 1958– .*
     Supersedes item 642.

637. Besso, H. V. *A Guide to the Official Publications of the Other American Republics: VI. Costa Rica*. Wash., 1947.

638. Dobles Segreda, L. *Indice Bibliográfico de Costa Rica*. 9 vols., San José, C.R., 1927–1936.
     Projected for 12 vols. The Comité Nacional de Bibliografía Adolfo Blen is preparing the final three volumes.

639. Fernández, L. *Indice General de los Documentos del Archivo de Cartago Anteriores al Año 1840*. 5 vols., San José, C.R., 1883–1898.

640. Lines, J. A. *Libros y Folletos Publicados en Costa Rica Durante los Años 1830–1849*. San José, C.R., 1944.
     Discusses 103 titles.

641. Meléndez, C. "Informaciones Bibliográficas Americanas: Costa Rica," *AEA* 18 (1961) 701–714.

642. San José, Costa Rica. Biblioteca Nacional. *Boletín Bibliográfico: Publicaciones Nacionales Correspondientes al Año 1935–1938– . San José, C.R., 1939–1955.*
     Superseded by item 636.

643. USLC. *List of References on Costa Rica*. Wash., 1923.

644. Universidad de Costa Rica. *Lista de Tesis de Grado Presentadas a la Universidad de Costa Rica Hasta 1957.* San Pedro, 1961. Supplement, San Pedro, 1962.

I–A–11   cross references: 1296–1299, 2480a

12. CUBA

645. *Anuario Bibliográfico Cubano: 1937–   .* Havana, 1938–   .

646. Becerra Bonet, B. *Indice de la Revista de la Facultad de Letras y Ciencias de la Universidad de la Habana.* Havana, 1955.

647. "Bibliografía Revolucionaria Cubana, Relativa a la Independencia, 1809–1830," in *Discursos Leídos en la Recepción Pública del Sr. Carlos M. Trelles y Govín, 1926.* Havana, 1926.

648. Bishop, C. M., and A. M. Marchant. *A Guide to the Law and Legal Literature of Cuba, the Dominican Republic, and Haiti.* Wash., 1944.

649. Childs, J. B. *A Guide to the Official Publications of the Other American Republics: VII. Cuba.* Wash., 1945.

650. Cuba. Archivo Nacional. *Inventario General del Archivo de la Delegación del Partido Revolucionario Cubano en Nueva York (1892–1898).* 2 vols., Havana, 1953–1955.

651. ——. Congreso. Cámara de Representantes. *Catálogo de las Obras Existentes en la Biblioteca.* Havana, 1905.

652. ——. ——. ——. *Catálogo de las Obras que Forman su Biblioteca: Derecho Internacional.* Havana, 1917.

653. ——. ——. ——. *Catálogo de las Obras que Forman su Biblioteca: Secciones de Hacienda Pública y de Comercio y Transporte.* Havana, 1913.

654. ——. ——. Senado. *Catálogo de las Obras Existentes en la Biblioteca, Año de 1916.* Havana, 1917.

655. *Directorio de Revistas y Periódicos de Cuba, 1942–   .* Havana, 1942–   .

656. Figarola Caneda, D. "Bibliografía Histórica Cubana," *AAHC* 8 (1926) 105–119.

657. González, M. P. *Fuentes para el Estudio de José Martí: Ensayo de Bibliografía Clasificada.* Havana, 1950.

658. Griffin, A. P. C. *List of Books Relating to Cuba.* Wash., 1898.

659. Harbron, J. D. "Cuba: Bibliography of a Revolution," *IJ* 18 (1963) 215–223.

660. Havana. Biblioteca Nacional. *Impresos Relativos a Cuba Editados en los Estados Unidos de Norteamérica.* Havana, 1956.

661. ——. ——. *Publicaciones Periódicas de Fechas más Recientes, que se Hallen a Disposición del Público en el Sala de Lectura.* Havana, 1908.

661a. Hellman, F. *List of References on the Platt Amendment.* Wash., 1934.

661b. Hitchman, J. H. "The Platt Amendment Revisited: A Bibliographical Survey," *TA* 23 (1967) 343–369. Contains text of the amendment and extensive commentary on secondary literature.

662. Iraizoz y de Villar, A. *Libros y Autores Cubanos.* Havana, 1956.

663. Munden, K. *Records of the Bureau of Insular Affairs Relating to the United States Military Government of Cuba, 1898–1902, and the United States Provisional Government of Cuba, 1906–1909: A List of Selected Files.* Wash., 1943.

664. Peraza Sarausa, F. *Bibliografías Cubanas.* Wash., 1954.

665. ——. *Bibliografía Martiana, 1853–1955.* Havana, 1956.

666. ——. "Martí: Los Libros y sus Libros," *IRB* 3 (1953) 245–251.

667. Pérez Cabrera, J. M. *Fundamentos de una Historia de la Historiografía Cubana.* Havana, 1959.

667a. ——. *Historiografía de Cuba.* Mexico, 1962. Covers only the period to 1898.

667b. Pomrenze, S. J. (comp.). *Materials in the National Archives Relating to Cuba.* Wash., 1948.

668. ——. "Materials Relativos a Cuba en los Archivos Nacionales de Estados Unidos," *RBCU* 62 (July, 1948) 5–22.

668a. Quesada, G. de. *Cuba.* Wash., 1905.

669. Raggi Ageo, C. M. *Bibliografía Político-Social Cubana.* Havana, 1940.

670. Reason, B., M. B. Mughisuddin, *et al. Cuba Since Castro: A Bibliography of Relevant Literature.* Wash., 1962.

670a. Remos, J. J. "Historiadores de Cuba," *RBNCU* 6 (January, 1955) 45–92.

670b. Smith, H. F. "A Bibliography of American Travellers' Books About Cuba Published Before 1900," *TA* 22 (1966) 404–412.

The books are arranged alphabetically by decade.

670c. Smith, R. F. "Twentieth Century Cuban Historiography," *HAHR* 44 (1964) 44–73.

671. Trelles y Govín, C. M. *Bibliografía Cubana del Siglo XIX.* 8 vols., Matanzas, 1911–1915.

672. ———. *Bibliografía Cubana del Siglo XX.* 2 vols., Matanzas, 1916–1917.
Covers 1900 to 1916.

673. ———. "Bibliografía de la Prensa Cubana (de 1704 a 1900) y de los Periódicos Publicados por Cubanos en el Extranjero," *RBIC* 2 (1938) 7–40, 81–114, 145–168, 209–268.

674. ———. *Bibliografía de la Segunda Guerra de Independencia Cubana y de la Hispano-Yankee.* Havana, 1902.
Covers 1895 to 1900.

675. ———. *Biblioteca Histórica Cubana.* 3 vols., Matanzas, 1922–1926.

676. ———. "Estudio de la Bibliografía Cubana Sobre la Doctrina de Monroe," *HAHR* 5 (1922) 99–115.

677. USLC. *Guantánamo Bay and Guantánamo Naval Station: A Brief List of References.* Wash., 1948.

678. ———. *A List of Books on the Spanish-American War, as They Relate to the Cuban Campaign, 1898.* Wash., 1900.
Supplements, Wash., 1930, 1942.

679. ———. *List of References on Annexation of Cuba.* Wash., 1912.

680. ———. *Select List of References on Cuba.* Wash., 1911.

681. ———. *A Selected List of References on Cuba.* Wash., 1934.

682. Vérez de Peraza, E. L. *José Martí: Compilación Bibliográfica de los Fondos que Posee la Biblioteca Pública Panamericana "Habana."* Havana, 1953.

I–A–12   cross references: 1300–1311, 7448

13. DOMINICAN REPUBLIC

683. Alfau Durán, V. "100 Notículas de Bibliografía Dominicana," *AUSD* 20 (January, 1955) 73–76.

684. American Foreign Law Association. *Dominican Republic.* N.Y., 1933.

685. *Anuario Bibliográfico Dominicano, 1946– .* Cd. Trujillo, 1947–

686. De Noia, J. *A Guide to the Official Publications of the Other American Republics: VIII. Dominican Republic.* Wash., 1947.

687. Dominican Republic. Archivo General de la Nación. "Fondos de la Anexión a España, 1861–1865: Catálogo," *BAGNDR* 19 (1956) 162–239, 260–337.

688. Florén Lozano, L. *Bibliografía de la Bibliografía Dominicana.* Cd. Trujillo, 1948.

688a. ———. "Contribuciones a la Bibliografía Dominicana," *REDR* 19, no. 91 (1943) 35–72; 19, no. 92 (1943) 51–68.

689. ———. "La Bibliografía Histórica en la República Dominicana," *CL* 19 (January, 1951) 47–52.

690. Hauch, C. C. "Fuentes en los Estados Unidos Relativas al Proyecto de Anexión de la República Dominicana, 1869–1871," *BAGNDR* 4 (1941) 183–187.

691. Lugo Lovatón, R. *Periódicos Dominicanos en el Archivo General de la Nación.* Cd. Trujillo, 1953.

692. Munden, K. *List of Records of the Bureau of Insular Affairs Relating to the Dominican Customs Receivership, 1905–1940.* Wash., 1943.

693. PAU. *Books and Magazine Articles in the Library of the Pan American Union on Relations Between the United States and Dominican Republic.* Wash., 1924.

694. ———. Division of Law and Treaties. *Selected Bibliography on Legal and Related Matters Affecting Business in the Dominican Republic.* Wash., 1953.

694a. Pomrenze, S. J. (comp.). *Materials in the National Archives Relating to the Dominican Republic.* Wash., 1948.

695. Rodríguez Demorizi, E. "Historia Diplomática Dominicana (Bibliografía)," in *Memoria del Secretario de Relaciones Exteriores de la República Dominicana, 1939* (pp. 325–417). Cd. Trujillo, 1940.

696. USLC. *List of Writings Relating to the Santo Domingo Question, 1904–1906.* Wash., 1906.
Additional References, Wash., 1914.

I–A–13   cross references: 648, 751, 752, 1312–1317

14. ECUADOR

697. Alvarado, R. *Indice de Traducciones Ecuatorianas.* Quito, 1954.

698. Arboleda R., G. *El Periodismo en el Ecuador.* Guayaquil, 1909.

699. Barrera, I. J. *Historiografía del Ecuador.* Mexico, 1956.

700. Chaves, A. *Fuentes Principales de la Bibliografía Ecuatoriana.* Quito, 1958.

701. Clagett, H. L. *A Guide to the Law and Legal Literature of Ecuador.* Wash., 1947.

702. De Noia, J. *A Guide to the Official Publications of the Other American Republics: IX. Ecuador.* Wash., 1947.

703. Ecuador. Ministerio de Educación Pública. *Exposición del Libro Ecuatoriano: Diez Años de Publicaciones Nacionales, 1930–1940.* Quito, 1940.

704. Pattee, R. "Libraries and Archives for Historical Research in Ecuador,' *HAHR* 19 (1939) 231–237.

705. Rolando, C. A. *Catálogo de la Bibliografía Nacional del Dr. Carlos A. Rolando.* Guayaquil, 1913.

706. ———. *Cronología del Periodismo Ecuatoriano.* Rev. ed., Guayaquil, 1934.

707. San Cristóval, E. *Bibliografía: La Controversia Limítrofe Entre el Perú y el Ecuador.* Lima, 1937.

708. Stols, A. A. M. *Historia de la Imprenta en el Ecuador de 1755 a 1830: Historia, Documentos Inéditos, Bibliografía, 1759–1830.* Quito, 1953.

709. Szaszdi, A. "The Historiography of the Republic of Ecuador," *HAHR* 44 (1964) 503–550.

710. USLC. *Ecuador and Paraguay: A Bibliographical List of Works in English in the Library of Congress.* Wash., 1927.

711. Vargas, J. M. *Misiones Ecuatorianas en Archivos Europeos.* Wash., 1956.

I–A–14   cross references: 1318–1328

15. EL SALVADOR

712. "Bibliografía Salvadoreña," *RBN* 1 (1948) 183–195; 2 (1948) 173–207.

713. *Bibliografía Salvadoreña: Lista Preliminar por Autores.* San Salvador, 1953.

714. De Noia, J. *A Guide to the Official Publications of the Other American Republics: X: El Salvador.* Wash., 1947.

715. Flores, R. H. *Catálogo de Tesis Doctorales de las Facultades de la Universidad de El Salvador.* San Salvador, 1960.

715a. Gallegos Valdés, L. "Dos Generaciones Literarias Salvadoreñas," *CENAM* 6, no. 21 (1960) 28–31.

716. García Villas, M. (ed.). *Lista Preliminar de la Bibliografía Salvadoreña de las Obras Existentes en la Biblioteca Nacional.* San Salvador, 1953.

717. *Nómina de las Obras Editadas en la Imprenta Nacional y Existentes en el Archivo de la Misma.* San Salvador, 1943.
    List of works published by the government printing office.

718. San Salvador. Biblioteca Nacional. *Catálogo Alfabético y por Materias de Todos los Libros que Contiene la Biblioteca Nacional de El Salvador, Formado por Rafael U. Palacios.* San Salvador, 1887.
    Apéndice, San Salvador, 1890.

719. ———. ———. *Catálogo de la Biblioteca Nacional Arreglado por Materias Según el Sistema "Dewey Decimal" por Rafael García Escobar.* 2 vols., San Salvador, 1930.

720. ———. ———. *Catálogo General Alfabético.* 3 vols., San Salvador, 1896–1897.

721. USLC. *List of References on Salvador.* Wash., 1923.

I–A–15   cross references: 1328a–1331

16. GUATEMALA

722. Batres Jáuregui, A. *Bibliografía Histórica Guatemalteca.* Guatemala, 1908.

723. Besso, H. V. *A Guide to the Official Publications of the Other American Republics: XI. Guatemala.* Wash., 1947.

724. "Bibliografía Sobre el General Justo Rufino Barrios," *BBNG* 4 (1935) 580–583.

725. Chávez Zelaya, E. (comp.). *Indice de Libros Escolares de Autores Guatemaltecos.* Guatemala, 1963.

726. Guatemala. Archivo General del Gobierno. *Indice de los Documentos Existentes en el Archivo.* 2 vols., Guatemala, 1937.

727. ———. Biblioteca Nacional. *Boletín.* Guatemala, 1932– .

728. ———. ———. *Catálogo.* Guatemala, 1932.

729. ————. Tipografía Nacional. *Catálogo General de Libros, Folletos y Revistas Editados en la Tipografía Nacional de Guatemala Desde 1892 Hasta 1943.* Guatemala, 1944.

Supplement for the years 1944 to 1953 was published in 1954.

730. *Indice Bibliográfico Guatemalteco, 1958– .* Guatemala, 1959– .

Two preliminary volumes appeared in 1951 and 1952.

731. Instituto Guatemalteco Americano. *Books About Guatemala: A Bibliography of Books in English and Spanish.* Guatemala, 1960.

731a. Lamadrid, L. "A Survey of the Historiography of Guatemala Since 1821," *TA* 8 (1951–1952) 189–202, 305–320.

The first part of the article (pp. 189–202) is devoted to the nineteenth century and the second part (pp. 305–320) to the twentieth century.

732. Pardo, J. *Indice de los Documentos Existentes en el Archivo General del Gobierno.* Guatemala, 1944.

733. Rey, J. A. "Revolution and Liberation: A Review of Recent Literature on the Guatemalan Situation," *HAHR* 38 (1958) 239–255.

734. USLC. *List of References on Guatemala.* Wash., 1923.

735. Valenzuela, G. *La Imprenta en Guatemala: Algunas Adiciones a la Obra que con Este Título Publicó en Santiago de Chile el Ilustre Literato Don José Toribio Medina.* Guatemala, 1933.

736. ————, and G. Valenzuela Reyna. *Bibliografía Guatemalteca.* 6 vols., Guatemala, 1961–1963.

737. Villacorta Calderón, J. A. *Bibliografía Guatemalteca.* Guatemala, 1944.

737a. ————. "Ensayo Sobre una Bibliografía Geográfico–Histórica de Guatemala," *ASGHG* 2 (1925) 99–111.

I–A–16   cross references: 1332–1335

17. Haiti

738. American Foreign Law Association. *Haiti.* N.Y., 1933.

739. Bissainthe, M. *Dictionnaire de Bibliographie Haitienne.* Wash., 1951.

740. Debien, G. *Les Sources Manuscrites de l'Histoire et de la Géographie de Saint-Domingue.* Port-au-Prince, 1935.

741. Duvivier, U. *Bibliografie Générale et Méthodique d'Haïti.* 2 vols., Port-au-Prince, 1941.

742. Franco, J. L. (comp.). *Documentos para la Historia de Haiti en el Archivo Nacional.* Havana, 1954.

743. Mintz, S. W., and V. Carroll (comps.). "A Selective Social Science Bibliography of the Republic of Haiti," *RICS* 2 (1963) 405–419.

744. Neuberger, O. *A Guide to the Official Publications of the Other American Republics: XII. Haiti.* Wash., 1947.

745. PAU. *Books and Magazine Articles in the Library of the Pan American Union on Relations Between the United States and Haiti.* Wash., 1924.

746. Pattee, R. "Haitian Notes," *HAHR* 16 (1936) 113–118.

747. Port-au-Prince, Haiti. Institution Saint-Louis de Gonzague. Bibliothèque Haïtienne des Frères. *Catalogue de la Bibliothèque Haïtienne des Frères de l'Instruction Chrétienne: The Catalogue of the Haitian Library of the Brothers of Christian Instruction.* Port-au-Prince, 1958.

748. Pressoir, C., *et al. Historiographie d'Haiti.* Mexico, 1953.

749. Toth, J., and W. A. Trembley. "The Alfred Nemours Collection of Haitian History: A Catalogue," *CS* 2 (October, 1962) 61–70.

750. USLC. *List of References on Haiti.* Wash., 1917.

751. ————. *List of References on Haiti and Santo Domingo.* Wash., 1921.

752. ————. *List of References on Relations Between the United States and Haiti and the Dominican Republic.* Wash., 1918. *Additional References,* Wash., 1919.

752a. Young, M. de. "Checklists for Archives and Private Collections in Haiti," *HLAS* 23 (1961) 406–408.

I–A–17   cross references: 648, 1336–1337

18. Honduras

753. Durón, J. F. *Indice de la Bibliografía Hondureña.* Tegucigalpa, 1946.

Lists over 3,000 entries.

754. Durón, J. F. *Repertorio Bibliográfico Hon-dureño.* Tegucigalpa, 1943.
Contains unpublished works not included in item 753.

755. Honduras. Biblioteca Nacional. *Catálogo Metódico de la Biblioteca Nacional.* Tegucigalpa, 1915.

756. Neuberger, O. *A Guide to the Official Publications of the Other American Republics: XIII. Honduras.* Wash., 1947.

757. *Nuevo Indice del Archivo de Tierras Custodiado en el Archivo Nacional: Indice de los Documentos y Expedientes que se Custodian en el Archivo Nacional.* 3d ed., Comayagüela, Honduras, 1927.

758. Sevillano Colom, F. (comp.). *Lista de Materiales Microfilmados.* Tegucigalpa, 1958.

759. USLC. *List of References on Honduras.* Wash., 1923.

759a. Valle, R. H. "Bibliografía Historiográfica de Honduras," *IRB* 2 (1952) 7–14.

759b. ———. "Bibliografía que Interesa a Honduras," *CENAM* 7 (1915) 530–534.

759c. ———. "Indice Bibliográfico Hondureño," *CENAM* 5 (1913) 583–587.

I–A–18   cross references: 1338–1339

19. MEXICO

760. Al'perovich, M. S. "Istoricheskaia Nauka v Meksike," *VI*, no. 8 (August, 1962) 198–202.
"Historical Science in Mexico."

760a. ———. "Istoriia Otnoshenii Mezhdu Meksikoi i SShA v Poslevoennoi Mekskanskoi Istoriografii," *VI*, no. 3 (1958) 171–183.
"The History of Mexican–U.S. Relations in Post-War Mexican Historiography."

760b. ———. "Sovremennaia Meksikanskaia Istoriografia Voiny za Nezavisimost'," *VI*, no. 2 (1961) 166–176.
"Contemporary Mexican Historiography on the War of Independence."

760c. Andrade, V. de P. *Noticia de los Periódicos que se Publicaron Durante el Siglo XIX Dentro y Fuera de la Capital.* Mexico, 1901.

761. *Anuario Bibliográfico Mexicano de 1940– .* Mexico, 1942– .

762. Arnade, C. W. "The Porfirio Díaz Papers of the William Clements Library," *HAHR* 33 (1953) 324–325.

763. Barker, E. C. "Report on the Bexar Archives," *AHAAR* 1 (1902) 357–363. Wash., 1903.

764. Barrett, E. C. *Baja California, 1535–1956: A Bibliography of Historical, Geographical and Scientific Literature Relating to the Peninsula of Baja California and to the Adjacent Islands in the Gulf of California and the Pacific Ocean.* L.A., 1957.

765. Bernal, I. *Bibliografía de Arqueología y Etnografía: Mesoamérica y Norte de México, 1514–1960.* Mexico, 1962.

766. Berroa, J. (comp.). *México Bibliográfico, 1957–1960: Catálogo General de Libros Impresos en México.* Mexico, 1961.

767. *Bibliografía Mexicana (1942–).* Mexico, 1944– .

768. Bogardus, E. S. *The Mexican Immigrant: An Annotated Bibliography.* L.A., 1929.

769. *Boletín Bibliográfico Mexicano: 1939– .* Mexico, 1939– .

770. Bopp, M. O. de. "Historiografía Mexicanista: Alemania, 1959," *HM* 10 (1960) 172–176.

771. California. State Library, Sacramento. Sutro Branch, San Francisco. *Catalogue of Mexican Pamphlets in the Sutro Collection.* San Francisco, 1939–1940.
Supplement (1605–1887), San Francisco, 1941; author index, San Francisco, 1941.

772. Carrasco Puente, R. *Bibliografía del Istmo Tehuantepec.* Mexico, 1948.

773. Carreño, A. M. "Documentos Relacionados con la Historia de México Existentes en la Nueva Biblioteca de Nueva York," *AMNM* 4 (1912) 489–504.

774. Carrera Stampa, M. *Archivalia Mexicana.* Mexico, 1952.

775. ———. "Mapas y Planos Relativos a México," *RI* 12 (1945) 153–198.
Guide to documents, many of which are relative to the Mexican War.

776. Castañeda, C. E., and J. A. Dabbs. *Calendar of the Manuel E. Gondra Manuscript Collection, The University of Texas Library.* Mexico, 1952.

777. Castillo, I. B. del. *Bibliografía de la Imprenta de la Cámara de Diputados para Servir a los Historiadores de la Epoca de*

Madero, Huerta y la Convención, 1912–1915. Mexico, 1918.

778. ———. *Bibliografía de la Revolución Mexicana de 1910–1916: Historia, Legislación, Literatura, Cuestiones Sociales, Políticas y Económicas Documentos, etc., Marzo de 1908 a Junio de 1916.* Mexico, 1918.

779. *Catálogo de la Exposición de Libros Mexicanos de Historia: Primer Congreso de Historiadores de México y de los Estados Unidos.* Mexico, 1949.

780. Chapman, C. E. *Catalogue of Materials in the Archivo General de Indias for the History of the Pacific Coast and the American Southwest.* Berkeley, Calif., 1919.

781. ———. "The Literature of California History," *SHQ* 12 (1919) 318–352.

782. Chávez, T. (comp.). *Notas para la Bibliografía de las Obras Editadas o Patrocinadas por la Universidad Nacional Autónoma de México: Contiene Además las Notas Bibliográficas de las Tesis Presentadas por los Graduados, Durante los Años de 1937 a 1942, y una Breve Noticia Histórica de la Universidad.* Mexico, 1943.

783. Clagett, H. L. *A Guide to the Law and Legal Literature of the Mexican States.* Wash., 1947.

784. Cortés Alonso, V. "Manuscripts Concerning Mexico and Central America in the Library of Congress, Washington, D.C.," *TA* 18 (1962) 255–296.

785. Cosío Villegas, D. *La Historiografía Política del México Moderno.* Mexico, 1953.

786. Cowan, R. E. *A Bibliography of the History of California and the Pacific West, 1510–1906, Together with the Text of John W. Dwinelle's Address on the Acquisition of California by the United States of America.* San Francisco, 1914.

787. Cumberland, C. C. "The United States–Mexican Border: A Selective Guide to the Literature of the Region," *RS* 25 (1960).

A supplement to *Rural Sociology.*

788. Dienst, A. "The New Orleans Newspaper Files of the Texas Revolutionary Period," *TSHAQ* 4 (1900) 140–151.

789. Estrada, G. *200 Notas de Bibliografía Mexicana.* Mexico, 1935.

790. ———. *Nuevas Notas de Bibliografía Mexicana.* Mexico, 1954.

791. Fernández de Córdoba, J. *Tesoros Biblio-gráficos de México en los Estados Unidos.* Mexico, 1959.

792. Franco, J. L. *Documentos para la Historia de México.* Havana, 1961.

Materials in the Cuban National Archives.

793. García, G. "Indice Alfabético de la 'Colección de Documentos para la Historia de la Guerra de Independencia de México, de 1808 a 1821': Formada por J. E. Hernández Dávalos," *AMNM* 4 (1907) 225–306.

794. ———. "Indice Alfabético de los 'Documentos para la Historia de México' Publicados en Cuatro Series por D. Manuel Orozco y Berra," *AMNM* 3 (1906) 523–540.

795. Gardiner, C. H. "Foreign Travelers' Accounts of Mexico, 1810–1910," *TA* 8 (1952) 321–351.

796. González, S. M. (comp.). *Algunas Fichas para una Bibliografía General de la Secretaría de la Defensa Nacional.* Mexico, 1943.

797. González y González, L., *et al. Fuentes de la Historia Contemporánea de México: Libros y Folletos.* 3 vols., Mexico, 1961–1962.

See also item 844a.

798. ———. "Nuevas Aventuras de la Bibliografía Mexicana," *HM* 10 (July, 1960) 14–53.

799. Greenwood, R. *California Imprints, 1833–1862: A Bibliography.* Los Gatos, Calif., 1961.

800. Guzmán y Raz Guzmán, J. *Bibliografía de la Independencia de México.* 3 vols., Mexico, 1937–1939.

801. ———. *Bibliografía de la Reforma, la Intervención y el Imperio.* 2 vols., Mexico, 1930–1931.

802. Haferkorn, H. E. *The War with Mexico, 1846–1848: A Select Bibliography.* Wash., 1914.

803. Harding, G. L. "A Census of California Spanish Imprints, 1833–1845," *CHSQ* 12 (1933) 125–136.

804. Harris, B. B. *United States Books on Mexico, 1935–1949.* Mexico, 1949.

805. Harrison, J. P. *Materials in the National Archives Relating to the Mexican States of Sonora, Sinaloa, and Baja California.* Wash., 1952.

806. Hernández Tapia, G. *Ensayo de una Bibliografía de la Intervención Europea en México en el Siglo XIX, 1861–1867.* Mexico, 1962.

807. Herrera Gómez, N., and S. M. J. González. *Apuntes para una Bibliografía Militar de México: 1536–1936.* Mexico, 1938.

808. Iguíniz, J. B. *Bibliografía Biográfica Mexicana.* Mexico, 1930.

809. Jones, C. K. "Bibliography of the Mexican Revolution," *HAHR* 2 (1919) 311–314.

810. ———. "The Mexican Secretariat of Foreign Relations and Bibliography," *BSAP* 19 (1927) 73–75.

811. Jones, R. C. *Mexicans in the United States: A Bibliography.* Wash., 1942.

812. Ker, A. M. *Mexican Government Publications: A Guide to the More Important Publications of the National Government of Mexico, 1821–1936.* Wash., 1940.

813. León, N. *Bibliografía Bibliográfica Mexicana: Primera Parte.* Mexico, 1923.

814. ——— (comp.). "El Instituto Bibliográfico Mexicano: Los Libros, los Bibliófilos y los Bibliógrafos Mexicanos," *BBNM* 14 (July, 1963) 17–55.

815. *List of Works in the New York Public Library Relating to Mexico.* N.Y., 1909.

816. "Lista de los Ramos que Comprenden el Archivo General de la Nación," *BAGNM* 1 (1930) 113–118.

817. Martínez, H. Pérez. "Una Bibliografía de México," *LP* 13 (1935) 28–39, 90–96, 147–154.

818. Massa Gil, B. *Bibliografía Sobre Migración de Trabajadores Mexicanos a los Estados Unidos.* Mexico, 1959.

818a. Mecham, J. L. "Northern Expansion of New Spain, 1522–1822: A Selected Descriptive Bibliographical List," *HAHR* 7 (1927) 233–276.

819. Mendoza López, M. *Catálogo de Publicaciones Periódicas Mexicanas.* Mexico, 1959.

820. Mexico. Biblioteca Nacional. *Catálogo Especial de las Obras Mexicanas o Sobre México.* Mexico, 1911.

821. ———. ———. *Catálogos de la Biblioteca Nacional de México.* Mexico, 1889–1908.

822. ———. Secretaría de Hacienda y Crédito Público. *Bibliografía, 1821–1942.* Mexico, 1943.

823. ———. Secretaría de la Economía Nacional. *Publicaciones Oficiales, Secretaría de la Economía Nacional, 1933–1942.* Mexico, 1943.

824. ———. Secretaría de Relaciones Exteriores. *Catálogo de las Publicaciones de la Secretaría.* Mexico, 1926.

825. ———. Universidad Nacional. Facultad de Filosofía y Letras. *Registro Bibliográfico.* Mexico, 1941– .

Indexes periodicals; annual supplement to *Revista Filosofía y Letras.*

826. Meyer, M. C. "Albert Bacon Fall's Mexican Papers: A Preliminary Investigation," *NMHR* 40 (1965) 165–174.

Examines the nature of the collection.

827. Millares Carlo, A. *Repertorio Bibliográfico de los Archivos Mexicanos y de los Europeos y Norteamericanos de Interés para la Historia de México: Nota Preliminar de Manuel Alcalá.* Mexico, 1959.

828. ———, and J. I. Mantecón. *Ensayo de una Bibliografía de Bibliografías Mexicanas: La Imprenta, el Libro, las Bibliotecas, etc.* Mexico, 1943.

829. ———. *Repertorio Bibliográfico de los Archivos Mexicanos y de las Colecciones Diplomáticas Fundamentales para la Historia de México.* Mexico, 1948.

830. Monroy, G. "El Archivo Histórico de Matías Romero," *HM* 8 (1958) 208–221.

831. Moore, E. R. *Bibliografía de Novelistas de la Revolución Mexicana.* Mexico, 1941.

832. Muro, L. *Historia Mexicana: Indice de sus Primeros Diez Años—Julio 1951–Junio 1961.* Mexico, 1961.

833. Murray, P. V. "La Historiografía Mexicana Sobre la Guerra de 1847," *RDCS* 21 (1948) 173–189.

834. New York Public Library. *List of Works in the New York Public Library Relating to Mexico.* N.Y., 1909.

835. Oswald, J. G. "La Revolución Mexicana en la Historiografía Soviética," *HM* 12 (1963) 340–357.

836. PAU. *Books and Magazine Articles in the Library of the Pan American Union on Relations Between the United States and Mexico.* Wash., 1924.

837. Patterson, J. E. *The Mexican War, 1846–1848: A Collection of Contemporary Materials Presented to the Yale University Library of Frederick W. Beinecke, 1909.* New Haven, Conn., 1960.
Reprinted from *University Library Gazette* 34 (1960) 93–123.

838. Potash, R. A. "The Historiography of Mexico Since 1821," *HAHR* 40 (1960) 383–424.

839. Priestley, H. I. "Mexican Literature on the Recent Revolution," *HAHR* 2 (1919) 286–311.

840. Raines, C. W. *A Bibliography of Texas: Being a Descriptive List of Books, Pamphlets, and Documents Relating to Texas in Print and Manuscript Since 1536, Including a Complete Collation of the Laws; With an Introductory Essay on the Materials of Early Texan History.* New ed., Austin, Texas, 1934.

841. Ramos, R. *Bibliografía de la Historia de México.* Mexico, 1956.
A compilation of 4,776 entries listed alphabetically by author. No subject index.

842. ———. *Bibliografía de la Revolución Mexicana.* 2d ed., 3 vols., Mexico, 1959–1960.

842a. *Recent Books in Mexico, 1954– .* Mexico, 1954– .
Bi-monthly review.

843. Ríos, E. E. "Indice Geográfico de Manuscritos que se Conservan en la Biblioteca Nacional," *IH* 1 (1938) 97–120, 211–240, 349–360.

843a. Rippy, J. F. "The Diplomatic Monographs of the Mexican Government," *HAHR* 10 (1930) 247–254.

843b. Ross, S. R. "Aportación Norteamericana a la Historiografía de la Revolución Mexicana," *HM* 10 (1960) 282–308.

844. ———. "Bibliography of Sources for Contemporary Mexican History," *HAHR* 39 (1959) 234–238.

844a. ——— (comp.). *Fuentes de la Historia Contemporánea de México. Periódicos y Revistas.* Mexico, 1965.
Companion volume to item 797.

845. Salado Alvarez, V. *Breve Noticia de Algunos Manuscritos de Interés Histórico para México, que se Encuentran en los Archivos y Bibliotecas de Wáshington.* Mexico, 1908.

846. Saldívar, G. *Bibliografía de la Secretaría de Relaciones Exteriores.* Mexico, 1943.

847. Saunders, L. *Spanish-speaking Americans and Mexican-Americans in the United States: A Selected Bibliography.* N.Y., 1944.

847a. Smith, J. H. "Sources for the History of the Mexican War, 1846–48," *MHE* 1 (1916) 18–32.

848. Streeter, T. W. *Bibliography of Texas, 1795–1845.* 4 vols., Cambridge, Mass., 1955–1960.

849. Torre Villar, E. de la. *Las Fuentes Francesas para la Historia de México y la Guerra de Intervención.* Mexico, 1962.

850. Toussaint, M. *Bibliografía Mexicana de Heredia.* Mexico, 1953.

851. Ulloa Ortíz, B. *La Revolución Mexicana a Través del Archivo de la Secretaría de Relaciones Exteriores.* Mexico, 1963.

852. ———. *Revolución Mexicana, 1910–1920.* Mexico, 1963.
A guide to the most important of the Revolutionary collections of the foreign relations archive.

853. United Nations Library (Mexico). *Guía Analítica de Publicaciones Periódicas.* Mexico, 1960.

854. USLC. *Brief List of References on the Recognition of the Government of Mexico by the United States.* Wash., 1923.

855. ———. *A List of Books in the English Language on Maximilian's Empire in Mexico.* Wash., 1924.

856. ———. *List of References on Intervention in Mexico by the United States.* Wash., 1920.

857. ———. *List of References on Mexicans in the United States.* Wash., 1920.

858. ———. *List of References on Mexico.* Wash., 1903.
Supplement, Wash., 1910; additional references, Wash., 1913, 1914, 1916, 1941.

859. ———. *List of References on the American Punitive Expedition into Mexico, 1916.* Wash., 1920.

860. ———. *List of References on the Present Situation in Mexico.* Wash., 1927.

861. ———. *List of References on the War with Mexico.* Wash., 1914.

862. USLC. *Mexican Labor in the United States: A Brief Bibliographical List.* Wash., 1928.

863. ———. *References to Speeches, etc., in the Congressional Record on Intervention in Mexico.* Wash., 1916.

864. ———. *Selected List of Books in the Library of Congress on Mexico.* Wash., 1919.

865. USDW. *Index of Publications, Articles and Maps Relating to Mexico in the War Department Library.* Wash., 1896.

866. Uribe de Fernández de Córdoba, S. "Bibliografía Histórica Mexicana," *HM* 6 (1957) 437–492.

867. Vance, J. T., and H. L. Clagett. *A Guide to the Law and Legal Literature of Mexico.* Wash., 1945.

868. Wagner, H. R. *Bibliography of Printed Works Relating to Those Portions of the United States Which Formerly Belonged to Mexico.* Santiago, 1917.

869. Wright, D. M. *A Guide to the Mariano Guadalupe Vallejo Documentos para la Historia de California, 1780–1875.* Berkeley, Calif., 1953.

I–A–19   cross references: 185a, 296, 1340–1364, 5778a, 6228, 6239

20. NICARAGUA

870. De Noia, J. *A Guide to the Official Publications of the Other American Republics: XIV. Nicaragua.* Wash., 1947.

871. *Indice de los Documentos que Comprende la "Sección de Tierras" y que Existen en Depósito en el Archivo General de Esta Ciudad.* 2 vols., Managua, 1900–1916.

872. Kalb, C. de. "A Bibliography of the Mosquito Coast of Nicaragua," *JAGS* 26 (1894) 241–248.

873. Managua. Biblioteca Americana de Nicaragua. *Bibliografía de Libros y Folletos Publicados en Nicaragua (en 1942, o Antes Según Fecha de Publicación), que se Encuentran en Algunas Bibliotecas Particulares de Nicaragua.* Managua, 1945.

Contains 2,663 entries found in six private libraries in Managua.

874. ———. *Bibliografía de Trabajos Publicados en Nicaragua . . . 1943– .* Managua, 1944– .

875. ———. *Una Lista de Artículos de Revista Sobre Nicaragua, Apareciendo en Importantes Revistas de los Estados Unidos Desde 1815 Hasta 1945.* Managua, 1945.

876. Minor, V. L. "A Brief Classified Bibliography Relating to the United States Intervention in Nicaragua," *HAHR* 11 (1931) 261–277.

877. Molina Argüello, C. "Bibliografía Historiográfica de Nicaragua," *IRB* 4 (1954) 9–22.

878. ———. *Misiones Nicaragüenses en Archivos Europeos.* Mexico, 1957.

879. Nicaragua. Biblioteca Nacional. *Catálogo General de los Libros de que Consta la Biblioteca Nacional de la República de Nicaragua.* Managua, 1882.
Rev. ed., Managua, 1900.

880. USLC. *List of References on Intervention in Nicaragua.* Wash., 1916.

881. ———. *List of References on the Nicaraguan Treaty.* Wash., 1916.

882. ———. *Recent References on Nicaragua (with Special Reference to Her Relations with the United States).* Wash., 1927.

883. ———. *Select List of References on Nicaraguan Canal.* Wash., 1906.

I–A–20   cross references: 1365, 2480a, 7051

21. PANAMA

884. Brown, A. D. *The Panama Canal and Panama Canal Zone: A Selected List of References.* Wash., 1943.

885. De Noia, J. *A Guide to the Official Publications of the Other American Republics: XV. Panama.* Wash., 1947.

886. Meyer, H. H. B. *List of References on the Panama Canal and the Panama Canal Zone.* Wash., 1919.

887. Panama (Ciudad). Biblioteca Nacional. *Bibliografía Panameña.* Panama, 1954.

888. Rhoads, J. B. (comp.). *Preliminary Inventory of Cartographic Records of the Panama Canal.* Wash., 1956.

888a. Susto, J. A. "Historia de las Historias de Panamá Escritas por Panameños," *RHA*, nos. 35–36 (1953) 77–103.

889. ———. *Introducción a la Bibliografía Panameña, 1619–1945: Prólogo de Rodrigo Miró.* Panama, 1946.

890. USLC. *List of References on Acquisition of the Panama Canal Zone by the United States.* Wash., 1917.

891.   ———. *List of References on the Influence of the Panama Canal on American Commerce.* Wash., 1906.

892.   ———. *List of References on the Panama Canal Tolls.* Rev. ed., Wash., 1921.

893.   ———. *List of References on the Revolution in Panama.* Wash., 1914. *Additional References*, Wash., 1915.

894.   ———. *List of References Relating to Labor on the Panama Canal.* Wash., 1906.

895.   ———. *Select List of Discussions on the Panama Canal Purchase, etc.* Wash., 1906.

896.   ———. *Select List of References on the International Status of the Panama Canal and Similar Waterways.* Wash., 1911.

897.   ———. *Select List of References on the Panama Canal.* 2d ed., Wash., 1910.

898.   ———. *Select List of References on the Panama Canal: Administration, Commercial Aspects, etc.* Wash., 1912.

899.   ———. *Select List of References on the Panama Canal in Its Commercial Aspects.* Wash., 1913.

900.   U.S. Superintendent of Documents. *Panama Canal and the Canal Zone: Public Documents for Sale by the Superintendent of Documents, Washington.* Wash., 1914.

I–A–21   cross references: 1366–1369

22. PARAGUAY

901.   Asunción. Biblioteca Nacional. *Bibliografía Paraguaya: Catálogo de la Biblioteca Paraguaya Solano López.* Asunción, 1906.

902.   Binayán, N. *Bibliografía de Bibliografías Paraguayas.* B.A., 1922.

903.   Brazil. Ministerio de Relaciones Exteriores. *Archivo Diplomático y Consular del Paraguay.* Asunción, 1908.

904.   Cardoso, E. *Historiografía del Paraguay.* Mexico, 1957.

905.   Childs, J. B. *A Guide to the Official Publications of the Other American Republics: XVI. Paraguay.* Wash., 1947.

906.   Clagett, H. L. *A Guide to the Law and Legal Literature of Paraguay.* Wash., 1947.

907.   Decoud, J. S. *A List of Books, Magazine Articles, and Maps Relating to Paraguay: Books, 1638–1903; Maps, 1599–1903.* Wash., 1904.

908.   Keen, B., and G. S. Métraux. *Preliminary Bibliography of Paraguay.* Wash., 1943.

909.   Pérez, J. F. *Los Archivos de la Asunción del Paraguay.* B.A., 1923.

910.   Sevillano Colom, F. "Lista del Contenido de los Volúmenes Microfilmados del Archivo Nacional de Asunción," *HAHR* 38 (1958) 60–120.

I–A–22   cross references: 710, 1370–1376

23. PERU

911.   *Anuario Bibliográfico Peruano, 1943– .* Lima, 1945– .

911a.   Basadre, J. "Recent Historical Tendencies in Peru," *HAHR* 12 (1932) 231–235.

912.   ———. *Report on Sources for National History of Peru.* Wash., 1960.

913.   Clagett, H. L. *A Guide to the Law and Legal Literature of Peru.* Wash., 1947.

914.   De Noia, J. *A Guide to the Official Publications of the Other American Republics: XVII. Peru.* Wash., 1949.

915.   Kantor, H. *Sources for the Study of the Peruvian Aprista Movement.* Gainesville, Fla., 1955.

916.   Lohmann Villena, G. "Actuales Tendencias de la Historiografía en el Perú," *IRB* 14 (1964) 371–390.

916a.   ———. "La Sección Manuscritos de la Biblioteca del Ministerio de Relaciones Exteriores del Perú," *HLAS* (1940) 518–522.

917.   Odriozola, M. "Catálogo de los Periódicos Nacionales Existentes en la Biblioteca Nacional," *BBP* 1 (1924) 170–179, 234–265.

917a.   Pareja y Paz Soldán, J., and J. C. Mariátegui A. "Para una Bibliografía Diplomática del Perú," *BBP* 23 (December, 1950) 235–262.

918.   Patterson, J. E. "Manuscripts Relating to Peru in the Yale University Library," *HAHR* 36 (1956) 244–256.

919.   Paz Soldán, M. F. *Biblioteca Peruana.* Lima, 1879.

920.   Pérez de Velasco, F. *Catálogo de la Biblioteca Peruana.* Lima, 1918.

921.   Peru. Congreso. Cámara de Senadores. *Catálogo de las Obras de la Biblioteca.* Lima, 1906.

922. Porras Barrenechea, R. *Fuentes Históricas Peruanas*. Lima, 1954.

923. Pret, C. A. *Bibliographie Péruvienne*. Paris, 1903.

924. *Primera Exposición de la Prensa Peruana*. Lima, 1941.

925. Prince, C. *La Biblioteca Peruana en la Exposición Universal de Paris de 1900*. Lima, 1900.

926. René-Moreno, G. *Biblioteca Peruana*. 2 vols., Santiago, 1896.

927. Rivera, R. O. "The Peruvian Collection of Duke University," *HAHR* 10 (1930) 255–256.

928. Rivera Serna, R. "Informaciones Bibliográficas Americanas: Perú," *AEA* 18 (1961) 729–740.

929. Saco, A. "Aprista Bibliography," *HAHR* 23 (1943) 555–585.

930. Schwab, F. *Bibliografía de Libros y Folletos Peruanos, 1940/1941–* . Lima, 1942– .

931. Tauro, A. *Bibliografía Peruana de Historia, 1940–1953*. Lima, 1953.

932. ———. *Guía de Estudios Históricos*. Lima, 1956.

933. Tumba Ortega, A. *Periódicos Nacionales del Siglo XIX, que Existen en la Biblioteca Central de la Universidad Nacional Mayor de San Marcos*. Lima, 1945.

934. Ugarteche, P., and J. P. Paz Soldán. *Al Servicio de una Bibliografía de Historia Internacional y Diplomática del Perú*. Lima, 1942.

935. Vargas Ugarte, R. *Biblioteca Peruana*. 6 vols., Lima, 1935–1949. Supplement, Lima, 1961.

936. ———. *Historia del Perú: Fuentes*. Lima, 1939.

937. ———. *Manual de Estudios Peruanistas*. Lima, 1952.

I–A–23 cross references: 707, 1377–1387

24. URUGUAY

938. American Foreign Law Association. *Uruguay*. N.Y., 1933.

939. *Anuario Bibliográfico Uruguayo, 1946–* Montevideo, 1947– .

940. Ardao, M. J., and A. C. de Castellanos (eds.). *Bibliografía de Artigas*. 2 vols., Montevideo, 1958.

941. Arredondo, H. "Bibliografía Uruguaya," *RIHGU* 6 (1929) 433–610. Supplements work of D. Estrada; see item 946.

942. Azarola Gil, L. E. *Fondos Documentales Relativos a la Historia del Uruguay Obrantes en los Archivos Extranjeros*. Madrid, 1930.

943. Bealer, L. W. "Contribution to a Bibliography on Artigas and the Beginnings of Uruguay, 1810–1820," *HAHR* 11 (1931) 108–134. Consists of printed materials available in United States collections.

944. Clagett, H. L. *A Guide to the Law and Legal Literature of Uruguay*. Wash., 1947.

945. De Noia, J., and G. Crevenna. *A Guide to the Official Publications of the Other American Republics: XVIII. Uruguay*. Wash., 1948.

946. Estrada, D. *Historia y Bibliografía de la Imprenta en Montevideo, 1810–1865*. Montevideo, 1912. Arranged by year of publication.

947. Fernández y Medina, B. *La Imprenta y la Prensa en el Uruguay Desde 1807 á 1900*. Montevideo, 1900.

948. Praderio, A. *Indice Cronológico de la Prensa Periódica del Uruguay, 1807–1852*. Montevideo, 1962.

949. Rela, W. *Contribución a la Bibliografía de la Literatura Uruguaya (1835–1962)*. Montevideo, 1963.

950. Speroni Vener, J. "La Bibliografía en el Uruguay," *IRB* 4 (1954) 35–42.

951. Zinny, A. *Historia de la Prensa Periódica de la República Oriental del Uruguay, 1807–1852*. B.A., 1883.

I–A–24 cross references: 1388–1395

25. VENEZUELA

952. Academia Nacional de la Historia. Biblioteca General. *Catálogos de las Bibliotecas Bolivariana y Mirandina de la Misma Institución: Trabajos Efectuados por E. Colina y D. Bonet de Sotillo bajo la Dirección J. A. Cova*. Caracas, 1957.

953. *Anuario Bibliográfico Venezolano, 1942–* . Caracas, 1944– .

954. Bonfanti, C., and E. Gómez M. *Fuentes*

Periódicas de Información Bibliográfica. Maracay, Venezuela, 1963.

955. Caracas. Biblioteca Nacional. *Catálogo de la Sección de Bibliografía Nacional.* Caracas, 1930.

956. ———. ———. *Catálogo de la Sección de Bibliografía Nacional: Obras de Autores Nacionales Impresas en el País o en el Extranjero y de Autores Extranjeros Impresas en el País.* Caracas, 1921.

957. ———. ———. *Libros Venezolanos: Catálogo de la Colección Donada por el Gobierno de los EE. UU. de Venezuela a la Biblioteca Nacional de Bogotá.* Caracas, 1945.

958. Carrera Damas, G. *Cuestiones de Historiografía Venezolana.* Caracas, 1964.

958a. ——— (ed.). *Historia de la Historiografía Venezolana: Textos para su Estudio.* Caracas, 1961.

959. Childs, J. B. "Venezuelan Government Publications: A Brief Survey of the Present Situation," *IBR* 3 (1943) 120–125.

960. Clagett, H. L. *A Guide to the Law and Legal Literature of Venezuela.* Wash., 1947.

961. Clavery, E. "Les Archives de Miranda à Caracas," *RAL* 17 (1929) 113–119.

962. De Villiers, J. A. J. *Chronological List of Printed Works Bearing upon the Boundary Arbitration Between British Guiana and Venezuela.* N.p., 1897.

963. Exposición Bibliográfica Bolivariana, Caracas, 1960. *Catálogo: Organizada en Ocasión del Primer Congreso Internacional de Sociedades Bolivarianas, por Pedro Grases, Caracas.* Caracas, 1962.

964. Franco, J. L. (comp.). *Documentos para la Historia de Venezuela Existentes en el Archivo Nacional de Cuba.* Havana, 1960.

965. Fundación John Boulton. *Sección Venezolana del Archivo de la Gran Colombia: Indice Sucinto.* Caracas, 1960.

966. García Chuecos, H. *Catálogo de Documentos Referentes a Historia de Venezuela y de América, Existentes en el Archivo Nacional de Washington.* Caracas, 1950.

967. ———. *Memoria Sobre el Archivo General de la Nación.* Caracas, 1951.

968. Grases, P. *Nuevos Temas de Bibliografía y Cultura Venezolanas.* Maracaibo, Venezuela, 1960.

969. ———. *Temas de Bibliografía y Cultura Venezolanas.* B.A., 1953.

970. Institute of Strategic Relations. *Tentative List of References on Venezuela.* New Haven, Conn., 1942.

971. Machado, J. E. *Lista de Algunos Periódicos que Vieron la Luz en Caracas de 1808 a 1900.* Caracas, 1929.

972. Neuberger, O. *A Guide to the Official Publications of the Other American Republics: XIX. Venezuela.* Wash., 1948.

973. Patrizi, L. G. "Documentos Relativos a Venezuela que se Conservan en The National Archives de Washington, 1835–1906," *BANHC* 32 (January, 1949) 81–98.

974. Pérez Vila, M. *Indice de los Documentos Contenidos en las Memorias del General Daniel Florencio O'Leary.* Caracas, 1957.

975. Pi Sunyer, C. "Catalogación de las Reproducciones en Microfilm de Documentos de Archivos Londinenses de Interés para la Historia Venezolana," *BANHC* 40 (April, 1957) 343–345.

976. Planchart, E. *Catálogo de la Exposición de Libros de Geografía y Historia de Venezuela.* Caracas, 1946.

976a. Robertson, W. S. "The Lost Archives of Miranda," *HAHR* 7 (1927) 229–232.

976b. Sánchez, M. S. "Bibliografía de Indices Bibliográficos Relativos a Venezuela," *HLAS* (1939) 428–442.

977. ———. *Bibliografía de las Ediciones Nacionales y de las Extranjeras Relativas a Venezuela Incompletas o Truncas.* Caracas, 1925.

978. ———. *Bibliografía de Obras Didácticas Publicadas en Venezuela o por Autores Venezolanos en el Extranjero.* Caracas, 1946.

979. ———. *Bibliografía Venezolanista: Contribución al Conocimiento de los Libros Extranjeros Relativos a Venezuela y sus Grandes Hombres.* Caracas, 1914.

980. ———. *Obras.* 2 vols., Caracas, 1964.
Reprint of *Bibliografía Venezolanista*, and also *Estudios Bibliográficos e Históricos.*

981. USLC. *List of Writings on the Venezuela Case, 1902–1903.* Wash., 1908.

982. ———. *Select List of Writings on the Venezuelan Boundary Dispute, 1895–1896.* Wash., 1912.

983. Venezuela. Universidad Central. *Catálogo de la Biblioteca de la Universidad de Caracas.* Caracas, 1875.

I–A–25   cross references: 1396–1401

B. OTHER GUIDES AND AIDS

1. GENERAL GUIDES AND AIDS

984. *The American Annual, 1923– .* N.Y., 1923– .

985. American Geographical Society of New York. *Current Geographical Publications, 1938– .* N.Y., 1938– .

986. *The Annual Register, 1758– .* London, 1758– .

987. *Annual Review of United Nations Affairs.* N.Y., 1949– .

988. *Appleton's Annual Encyclopedia, and Register of Important Events.* N.Y., 1862–1903.

989. Arnold-Baker, C., and A. Dent. *Everyman's Dictionary of Dates.* N.Y., 1954.

990. Baldwin, S. E. "List of Memorable International Conferences, Congresses or Associations of Official Representatives of Governments, Exclusive of Those Mainly Concerned in Dealing with the Results of a Particular War, 1826–1907," *AJIL* 1 (1907) 808–817.

991. ———. "List of the More Important International Congresses, Conferences or Associations of the Past Century, Composed of Private Individuals, 1826–1907," *AJIL* 1 (1907) 817–829.

992. *Bibliographie Cartographique Internationale, 1936– .* Paris, 1938– .

993. *Bibliographie Géographique Internationale, 1891– .* Paris, 1894.

994. *Biography Index: A Cumulative Index to Biographical Material in Books and Magazines.* N.Y., 1947– .

995. Boyd, A. *An Atlas of World Affairs.* 4th ed., N.Y., 1959.

996. *Britannica Book of the Year, 1938– .* Chicago, 1938– .

997. Burickson, S. (comp.). *Concise Dictionary of Contemporary History.* N.Y., 1959.

998. *Chambers's Biographical Dictionary.* New ed., N.Y., 1962.

999. *Chambers's Encyclopaedia.* London, 1859– .

1000. *Collier's Encyclopedia.* N.Y., 1950– .

1001. *Collier's Yearbook, 1939– .* N.Y., 1939– .

1002. Collocott, T. C., and J. O. Thorne (eds.). *Macmillan World Gazeteer and Geographical Dictionary.* N.Y., 1954.

1003. *Columbia Encyclopedia.* N.Y., 1935– .

1004. *Columbia-Lippincott Gazeteer of the World.* N.Y., 1952.

1005. *Current Biography: Who's Who and Why.* N.Y., 1940– .
   Issued monthly; annual yearbooks available.

1006. *Deadline Data on World Affairs.* N.Y., 1956– .

1007. De Ford, M. A. *Who Was When?* N.Y., 1951.

1008. *Dictionary of National Biography.* 63 vols., London, 1885–1901.
   Supplements available periodically to 1940. The English counterpart to item 1163.

1009. *Directory of Library Photo-duplication Services in the United States, Canada, and Mexico, 1962.* Chicago, 1962.

1010. *Documents on International Affairs, 1928– .* London, 1929– .

1011. *Elsevier's Lexicon of Archive Terminology: French, English, German, Spanish, Italian, Dutch.* Amsterdam, N.Y., 1964.

1012. *Encyclopaedia Britannica.* London and Chicago, 1768– .

1013. *Encyclopaedia Britannica World Atlas.* Chicago, 1942– .

1014. *Encyclopedia Americana.* N.Y., 1829– .

1014a. Esdail, A. *National Libraries of the World: Their History, Administration and Public Services.* 2d ed., London, 1957.

1015. *Facts on File: A Weekly Synopsis of World Events, 1940– .* N.Y., 1940– .

1016. Garollo, G. *Dizionario Biografico Universale.* 2 vols., Milan, 1907.

1017. *Geographisches Jahrbuch, 1866– .* Gotha, 1866– .

1018. Grimal, P. *Dictionnaire des Biographies.* 2 vols., Paris, 1958.

1019. Hammerton, J. A. (ed.). *Concise Universal Biography.* 2 vols., London, 1935.

1020. Harris, C. D. *An Annotated World List of Selected Current Geographical Serials in English.* Chicago, 1960.

1021. ———, and J. D. Fellman. *A Union List of Geographical Serials.* 2d ed., Chicago, 1950.

1022. Hefling, H., and E. Richards. *Index to Contemporary Biography and Criticism.* Rev. ed., Boston, 1934.

1023. Heilprin, A. (ed.). *Complete Pronouncing Gazeteer or Geographical Dictionary of the World.* Phil., 1931.

1024. Hirshberg, H. J. *Subject Guide to Reference Books.* Chicago, 1942.

1025. Hyamson, A. M. *A Dictionary of Universal Biography of All Ages and People.* 2d ed., N.Y., 1951.

1026. *Information Please Almanac, 1947–* N.Y., 1947– .

1027. *International Who's Who, 1935– .* London, 1935– .

1028. *International Year Book: A Compendium of the World's Progress, 1898–1902.* 5 vols., N.Y., 1899–1903.

1029. *International Yearbook and Statesmen's Who's Who.* London, 1953– .

1030. Ireland, N. O. *An Index to Indexes.* Boston, 1942.

1031. *Keesing's Contemporary Archives: Weekly Diary of World Events, 1931– .* London, 1931– .

1032. Keller, H. R. *The Dictionary of Dates.* N.Y., 1934.

1033. Langer, W. L. *An Encyclopedia of World History: Ancient, Medieval, and Modern, Chronologically Arranged.* Rev. ed., Boston, 1948.

1034. *Larousse de XXᵉ Siècle.* Paris, 1928– .

1035. Lawson, R. C. (ed.). *International Regional Organizations.* N.Y., 1962.

1036. Logasa, H. *Biography in Collections.* 3d ed., N.Y., 1940.

1037. Merrill, J. C. *A Handbook of the Foreign Press.* Baton Rouge, La., 1959.

1038. Mirkin, S. M. *When Did It Happen?* N.Y., 1956.

1039. Murphey, R. W. *How and Where to Look It Up: A Guide to Standard Sources of Information.* N.Y., 1958.

1040. *The New Century Encyclopedia of Names.* 3 vols., N.Y., 1954.

1040a. *New International Year Book, 1907– .* N.Y., 1908– .

1041. *Newspaper Press Directory: An Advertiser's Guide.* London, 1846– .

1042. *ORBIS: The Encyclopaedia of Extra-European Countries: Survey and Directory of Political, Industrial, Financial, Cultural, and Scientific Organisations in the* Continents of Africa, America, Asia, and Australasia. London, 1939–
Called *Europa Yearbook* after 1959.

1043. Palmer, R. R. *Atlas of World History.* Chicago, 1951.

1044. Phillips, L. B. *Dictionary of Biographical Reference.* Rev. ed., London, 1889.

1045. Phillips, P. L. *Checklist of Large-Scale Maps Published by Foreign Governments (Great Britain Excepted) in the Library of Congress.* Wash., 1904.

1046. *Political Handbook and Atlas of the World, 1927– .* N.Y., 1927– .

1047. Roberts, A. D. *Introduction to Reference Books.* 2d ed., London, 1951.

1048. Sabor, J. E. *Manual de Fuentes de Información: Obras de Referencia: Enciclopedias, Diccionarios, Bibliografías, Biografías, etc.* B.A., 1957.

1049. Schellenberg, T. R. *Archivos Modernos: Principios y Técnicos.* Havana, 1958.

1050. Sears, M. E. *Standard Catalog, Biography Section.* N.Y., 1927.
Supplement, N.Y., 1932.

1051. Seligman, E. R. A. (ed.). *Encyclopedia of the Social Sciences.* 15 vols., N.Y., 1930–1935.

1052. Shepherd, W. R. *Historical Atlas.* 7th ed., N.Y., 1929.

1053. *Statesman's Year-Book: Statistical and Historical Annual of the States of the World, 1864– .* London, 1864– .

1054. *Survey of International Affairs, 1920/23– .* London, 1925– .

1055. Thiele, W. *Official Map Publications: A Historical Sketch, and a Bibliographical Handbook of Current Maps and Mapping Services in the U.S., Canada, Latin America, France, Great Britain, Germany and Certain Other Countries.* Chicago, 1938.

1056. *Union of International Associations Yearbook of International Associations.* Brussels, 1950– .

1057. *United Nations Association Yearbook.* London, 1945– .

1058. *United Nations Documents and Official Records.* N.Y., 1954– .
In microprint.

1059. UN Statistical Office. *Demographic Yearbook: Annuaire Démographique.* N.Y., 1949– .

1060. ———. *Statistical Yearbook, 1948– .* N.Y., 1948– .

1061. U.S. Bureau of the Census. *Statistical Abstract of the United States, 1878–* . Wash., 1878– .

1062. USLC. *Biographical Sources for Foreign Countries.* Wash., 1944–1945.

1063. ———. *Library of Congress Catalog: A Cumulative List of Works Represented by Library of Congress Printed Cards: Maps and Atlases.* 3 vols., Wash., 1953–1955.

1064. ———. *List of Geographical Atlases in the Library.* 5 vols., Wash., 1909–1958.

1065. Vicens Vives, J., and L. Visitin (eds.). *Atlas Iberoamericano de Geografía Mundial.* B.A., 1957.

1066. Walford, A. J. *Guide to Reference Material.* London, 1959.

1067. Walsh, S. P. *General Encyclopedias in Print: A Comparative Analysis.* Newark, Del., 1965.

1068. *Webster's Biographical Dictionary: A Dictionary of Names of Noteworthy Persons with Pronunciations and Concise Biographies.* Springfield, Mass., 1957.

1069. *Webster's Geographical Dictionary: A Dictionary of Names and of Places with Historical Information and Pronunciations.* Rev. ed., Springfield, Mass., 1953.

1070. White, L. C. *International Non-Governmental Organizations.* New Brunswick, N.J., 1951.

1071. *The World Almanac, 1868–* . N.Y., 1868– .

1072. *World Biography, 1940–* . N.Y., 1940– .

1073. *World Diplomatic Directory and World Diplomatic Biography.* London, 1950– .

1074. Wright, J. K., and E. T. Platt. *Aids to Geographical Research: Bibliographies, Periodicals, Atlases, Gazeteers, and Other Reference Books.* 2d ed., N.Y., 1947.

1075. *Yearbook of the United Nations, 1946–1947.* N.Y., 1947– .

1076. *The Yearbook of World Affairs, 1947–* . N.Y., 1947– .

I–B–1 cross references: 24–142

2. LATIN AMERICA IN GENERAL

1077. Aiton, A. S., and J. L. Mecham. "The Archivo General de Indias," *HAHR* 4 (1921) 553–567.

1078. Almela Melia, J. *Guía de Personas que Cultivan la Historia de América.* Mexico, 1951.

1079. American Geographical Society. *A Catalogue of Maps of Hispanic America.* 4 vols., N.Y., 1933.

1080. ———. *Index to Map of Hispanic America, 1:1,000,000.* Wash., 1945. Edited by Earl P. Hanson.

1081. *Atlas America Latina: A Geographic, Economic and Commercial Atlas of Mexico, Central America, West Indies and South America, Presenting a Series of New Maps, Commercial Charts and Descriptive Data of the Twenty Latin American Republics.* N.Y., 1919.

1082. Babcock, C. E. (comp.). "The Libraries of Latin America, Compiled by the Pan American Union, Washington, D.C.," *ALA* (1918) 253–263.

1083. Balen, W. J. van. *Atlas van Zuid-Amerika.* Amsterdam, 1957.

1084. Beltrán, F. *Biblioteca Biobibliográfica: Catálogo de una Importante Colección de Libros y Folletos Españoles y Extranjeros Referentes a Bibliografía, Biografía, Bibliofilia, la Imprenta y sus Artes Auxiliares.* Madrid, 1927.

1084a. Beristain de Souza, J. M. *Biblioteca Hispano Americana Setentrional.* Amecameca, Mexico, 1883.

1085. Bosch García, C. *Guía a las Instituciones que Cultivan la Historia de América.* Mexico, 1949.

1086. Butland, G. J. *Latin America: A Regional Geography.* London, 1960.

1087. Calvo, C. (ed.). *Colección Histórica Completa de los Tratados . . . y Otros Actos Diplomáticos de Todos los Estados de la América Latina . . . Desde el Año de 1493 Hasta Nuestros Días.* 11 vols., Paris, 1862–1869.

    Includes treaties of colonial period.

1088. Carlson, F. A. *Geography of Latin America.* 3d ed., N.Y., 1952.

1088a. Cline, H. F. (comp.). *Historians of Latin America in the United States, 1965: Biobibliographies of 680 Specialists.* Durham, N.C., 1966.

    Coverage is more comprehensive for historians than item 1105a.

1089. Coleman, L. V. *Directory of Museums in South America.* Wash., 1929.

1089a. Conover, H. F. "Records of Current Publishing in Latin America," *HLAS* 22 (1960) 327–334.

1090. Cortés, José Domingo. *Diccionario Bio-gráfico Americano: Este Volumen Contiene los Nombres, con los Datos Biográficos i Enumeración de las Obras de Todas las Personas que se Han Ilustrado en las Letras, las Armas, las Ciencias, las Artes, en el Continente Americano.* Paris, 1875.

1091. Daniels, M. *The Seminars on the Acquisition of Latin American Library Materials: A Seven-Year Report, 1956–1962.* Wash., 1962.

1092. Dávila, V. *Diccionario Biográfico de Ilustres Próceres de la Independencia Suramericana.* 2 vols., Caracas, 1924–1926.

1093. Davis, H. E. *Latin American Leaders.* N.Y., 1949.

1094. Denis, P. *Amérique du Sud.* Paris, 1927.
A geography.

1095. *Diccionario Enciclopédico Abreviado.* 6th ed., 7 vols., Madrid, 1954–1955.

1096. *Diccionario Enciclopédico de las Américas: Geografía, Historia, Economía, Política, Literatura, Arte, Música, Deporte, Cine, Teatro, Etnografía, Fauna, Flora, Ciencias Generales.* B.A., 1947.

1097. *Diccionario Enciclopédico Hispano-Americano de Literatura, Ciencias, y Artes.* 2 vols., Barcelona, 1887–1910.

1098. *Enciclopedia Universal Ilustrada Europeo Americano.* 80 vols., Barcelona, 1935– .
Annual supplements.

1098a. *Encyclopédie de l'Amérique Latine: Politique, Economique, Culturelle.* Paris, 1954.

1099. Godoy, J. F. *Enciclopedia Biográfica de Contemporáneos.* Wash., 1898.

1100. Gropp, A. E. *Bibliografía Sobre las Bibliotecas Nacionales de los Países Latinoamericanos y sus Publicaciones.* Wash., 1960.
One section treats guides to the various national libraries and another treats their publications.

1101. Hanson, E. P. (ed.). *The New World Guides to the Latin American Republics.* 3d ed., 3 vols., N.Y., 1950.

1102. Hernández Millares, J. *Atlas del Nuevo Mundo.* Mexico, 1926.

1102a. Hill, R. R. "Impressions of Hispanic American Archives," *HAHR* 17 (1937) 538–545.
Spanish ed., *BANC* 37–38 (1938–1939) 12–19.

1103. ———— (ed.). *The National Archives of Latin America.* Cambridge, Mass., 1945.
Spanish ed., Havana, 1948. General descriptions of the collections.

1103a. ————. "The National Archives of Latin America," *HLAS* (1936) 433–442.

1104. Hilton, R. (ed.). *Who's Who in Latin America.* 3d ed., 7 vols., Stanford, Calif., 1945–1951.

1105. Hirschowicz, E. (ed.). *Contemporâneos Inter-Americanos.* Rio, 1949.
A "biobibliographical" handbook.

1105a. Hispanic Foundation. Library of Congress. *National Directory of Latin Americanists: Biobibliographies of 1,889 Specialists in the Social Sciences and Humanities.* Wash., 1966.
See also item 1088a.

1106. Hispanic Society of America. *A History of the Hispanic Society of America, Museum and Library, 1904–1954: With a Survey of the Collections.* N.Y., 1954.

1107. "Historical Societies in Mexico, Central and South America, Compiled by the Pan American Union," *HAHR* 8 (1928) 563–565.

1107a. Holmes, L. T. "An Atlas of Latin America," *FPAHS*, no. 100 (1953).

1108. Humphreys, R. A. "The Historiography of the Spanish American Revolutions," *HAHR* 36 (1956) 81–93.

1109. James, P. E. *Latin America.* 2d ed., N.Y., 1950.
A basic English-language geography.

1110. Jones, C. F. *South America.* N.Y., 1930.
A geography.

1111. Kossok, M. "Zum Stand der Sowjetischen Geschichtsschreibung über Lateinamerika," *ZG* 7 (1959) 426–441.

1111a. Labelle, Y., and A. Estrada (comps.). *Latin America in Maps, Charts, Tables: No. 1. Socio-Economic Data; No. 2. Socio-Religious Data.* 2 vols., Cuernavaca, 1963–1964.

1111b. Latin America Kyôkai. Tokyo. *Latin America Jiten.* Tokyo, 1964.
Latin American Handbook.

1111c. "The Library of South Americana of the University of Notre Dame," *HAHR* 2 (1919) 490–492.

1112. Martin, L., *et al.* "Hispanic American Map Exhibition at the Library of Congress: A Selection of Hispanic American

Maps Representative of Four Centuries of Historical, Diplomatic and Cartographic Progress in the Two Americas," *PPAIGH* (1935) 243–254.

1113. Martin, M. R., and G. H. Lovett. *An Encyclopedia of Latin-American History.* N.Y., 1956.

1114. Martin, P. A. (ed.). *Who's Who in Latin America: A Biographical Dictionary of the Outstanding Men and Women of Spanish America and Brazil.* 2d ed., Stanford, Calif., 1940.

Precedes the work by Hilton.

1115. Masters, R. D., *et al. Handbook of International Organizations in the Americas.* Wash., 1945.

1116. Mendoza L., G. *Situación Actual de los Archivos Latino-Americanos: Manual de Información Básica.* Wash., 1961.

1117. Migone, R. C., *et al. Inter-American Statistical Yearbook.* 2d ed., N.Y., 1942.

1118. Mitani, H. "Latin American Studies in Japan," *HLAS* 27 (1965) 457–463.

1119. Morse, R. M. "Language as a Key to Latin American Historiography," *TA* 11 (1955) 165–169.

1120. *The Pan American Yearbook: An Economic Handbook and Ready-Reference Directory of the Western Hemisphere, 1945.* N.Y., 1945.

1121. PAU. *Directory of Statistical Personnel in the American Nations.* Wash., 1955.

1121a. ———. *Guía de las Bibliotecas de la América Latina.* Wash., 1963.

1122. ———. *Manual of Inter-American Relations (Revised): A Systematic Classification of the Treaties, Conventions, Resolutions, Declarations, and Recommendations Adopted at Inter-American Conferences and Meetings of Consultation.* Rev. ed., Wash., 1956.

1123. ———. *Pan American Associations in the United States: A Directory with Supplementary Lists of the Other Associations, Inter-American and General.* 4th ed., Wash., 1962.

1124. Pearcy, G. E. *Names and Places in Latin America.* Wash., 1961.

1125. Pendle, G. *South America.* London, 1958.
One of the Oxford "visual geographies."

1126. Pillsbury, S. R. *The Western Hemisphere: An Exhibition . . . of Maps of the World and of America from 1492 to 1942.* N.Y., 1942.

1127. Platt, R. S. *Latin America, Countrysides and United Regions.* N.Y., 1942.

1128. *Quién Es Quién en Venezuela, Panamá, Ecuador, Colombia, con Datos Recopilados Hasta el 30 de Junio de 1952.* Bogotá, 1952.

1128a. *Resources Survey for Latin American Countries.* Wash., 1965.
Lists government agencies and private firms with Latin American operations.

1129. Rivera, R. O. *Preliminary List of Libraries in the Other American Republics.* Wash., 1942.

1130. Sabater, G. (ed.). *Diccionario Biográfico Español e Hispanoamericano.* Palma de Mallorca, Spain, 1950– .

1131. Sandvig, M. M., and L. Dudgeon. "The Library Program of the U.S. Information Agency in Latin America," *IRB* 5 (1955) 291–301.

1132. Schmieder, O. *Geografía de América.* Mexico, 1946.

1133. Shanahan, E. W. *South America: An Economic and Regional Geography.* 9th ed., London, 1953.

1134. Sievers, W. *Süd- und Mittelamerika.* Leipzig, 1914.
A geography.

1135. Smith, R. C. "The Hispanic Foundation in the Library of Congress," *HAHR* 19 (1939) 564–571.

1136. Spain. Dirección General de Archivos y Bibliotecas. *Guía de las Bibliotecas de Madrid.* Madrid, 1953.

1137. *The South American Handbook . . . Including Central America, Mexico and Cuba, 1924– .* London, 1924– .

1138. *Sutro Library Through the Centuries.* San Francisco, 1957.

1138a. Taeuber, I. B. *General Censuses and Vital Statistics in the Americas.* Wash., 1943.

1138b. Torre Revello, J. *El Archivo de Indias.* Paraná, Arg., 1939.

1139. UCLA. Center of Latin American Studies. *Master Directory for Latin America.* Los Angeles, 1965.

1140. ———. ———. *Statistical Abstract of Latin America.* Los Angeles, 1955– .

1141. USDC. *Guide to Foreign Business Directories.* Wash., 1955.

1142. Whitbeck, R. H., and F. E. Williams. *Economic Geography of South America.* 3d ed., N.Y., 1940.

1143. Wilcox, M., and G. E. Rines (eds.). *The Encyclopedia of Latin America.* N.Y., 1917.

1144. Wilgus, A. C. *An Atlas of Hispanic American History.* Wash., 1932.

1145. ———. "Index of Articles Relating to Hispanic America Published in the *Geographical Journal*, (vols. 1–84), 1893–1934, Inclusive," *HAHR* 19 (1939) 117–126.

1146. ———. *Latin America in Maps.* N.Y., 1943.

1147. ———. "List of Articles Relating to Hispanic America Published in the Periodicals of the American Geographical Society, 1852–1933, Inclusive," *HAHR* 14 (1934) 114–130.

1148. ———. *Maps Relating to Latin America in Books and Periodicals.* Wash., 1933.

I–B–2   cross references: 143–330, 1172, 1344, 4530

3. UNITED STATES

1149. Adams, J. T. (ed.). *Atlas of American History.* N.Y., 1943.

1150. ——— (ed.). *Dictionary of American History.* 6 vols., N.Y., 1940.
Supplement (1940–1960), N.Y., 1961.

1151. American Association for State and Local History. *Historical Societies in the United States and Canada.* Wash., 1944– .
Title varies in subsequent editions.

1152. Andrews, W. (ed.). *Concise Dictionary of American History.* N.Y., 1962.

1153. *Appleton's Cyclopaedia of American Biography.* 7 vols., N.Y., 1887–1900.

1154. Brown, R. H. *Historical Geography of the United States.* N.Y., 1948.

1155. Carruth, G. (ed.). *The Encyclopedia of American Facts and Dates.* 2d ed., N.Y., 1959.

1156. Downs, R. B. *Resources of New York City Libraries: A Survey of Facilities for Advanced Study and Research.* Chicago, 1942.

1157. ———. *Union Catalogs in the United States.* Chicago, 1942.

1158. *Foreign Service List.* Wash., 1837– .
Lists United States representatives abroad; title varies.

1159. Griffin, A. P. C. "Bibliography of American Historical Societies, the United States and the Dominion of Canada," *AHAAR* (1905). Wash., 1907.

1160. Hamer, P. M. *Guide to the Material in the National Archives.* 2d ed., Chicago, 1948.

1161. Hart, A. B., H. E. Bolton, and D. B. Matteson. *American History Atlas.* 2d ed., Wash., 1949.

1162. Jameson, J. F. *Dictionary of United States History.* Rev. ed., Phil., 1931.

1163. Johnson, A., and D. Malone (eds.). *Dictionary of American Biography.* 21 vols. and index, N.Y., 1928–1944.
Supplements, N.Y., 1935, 1958. Contains biographical sketches of famous Americans and cites useful references.

1164. Kane, J. N. *Facts About the Presidents: A Compilation of Biographical and Historical Data.* N.Y., 1959.

1165. Kiger, J. S. *American Learned Societies.* Wash., 1963.

1166. Kull, I. S., and N. M. Kull. *A Short Chronology of American History, 1492–1950.* New Brunswick, N.J., 1952.

1167. Lord, C. L., and E. H. Lord. *Historical Atlas of the United States.* N.Y., 1944.
Rev. ed., 1953.

1168. Martin, M., L. Gelber, and L. Leonard. *The New Dictionary of American History.* N.Y., 1952.

1169. Morris, R. B. (ed.). *Encyclopedia of American History.* Rev. ed., N.Y., 1961.

1170. *National Cyclopaedia of American Biography.* N.Y., 1892– .
Forty-two volumes had appeared through 1958.

1171. O'Neill, E. H. *Biography by Americans, 1658–1936: A Subject Bibliography.* Phil., 1939.

1172. PAU. *Pan-American Societies in the United States: A List with Supplementary Lists of Other Associations, Inter-American and General.* 2d ed., Wash., 1957.

1173. Paullin, C. O. *Atlas of the Historical Geography of the United States.* Wash., 1932.

1174. Preston, W. *American Biographies.* N.Y., 1940.

1175. USC. *Biographical Dictionary of the American Congress, 1774–1961.* Rev. ed., Wash., 1961.

1176. USDC. *Historical Statistics of the United States: Colonial Times to 1957.* Wash., 1961.

1176a. USDS. *Foreign Consular Offices in the United States.* Wash., 1932– .
Issued semi-annually.

1177. USDS. *Public Availability of Diplomatic Archives in the United States and Certain Foreign Countries.* Wash., 1961.

1178. ———. *Register.* Wash., 1869– .
Lists diplomatic representatives of the United States.

1179. *United States Government Organization Manual.* Wash., 1935– .

1180. USLC. *Library and Reference Facilities in the Area of the District of Columbia.* 3d ed., Wash., 1948.

1181. Van Tyne, C. H., and W. G. Leland. *Guide to the Archives of the Government of the United States in Washington.* Wash., 1904.

1182. Wasson, D. *American Agencies Interested in International Affairs.* 5th ed., N.Y., 1964.
Earlier editions by Ruth Savord.

1183. *White's Conspectus of American Biography: A Tabulated Record of American History and Biography.* 2d ed., N.Y., 1937.

1184. Wilcox, J. K. *United States Reference Publications.* Boston, 1931.
Supplement, Boston, 1932.

1185. Wish, H. *The American Historian.* N.Y., 1960.

1186. *Who Was Who in America.* Chicago, 1942– .
Vol. 1 covered 1897 to 1942; vol. 2 covered 1943 to 1950.

1187. *Who's Who in America.* Chicago, 1899– .
Issued biennially.

I–B–3   cross references: 331–425

4. ARGENTINA

1188. Aparicio, F. de, and H. A. Difrieri (eds.). *La Argentina: Suma de Geografía.* 9 vols., B.A., 1958–1963.

1189. *Apuntes Biográficos Contemporáneos.* Rosario, Argentina, 1878.
Forty biographical sketches.

1190. Ardissone, R. *Historia de los Hechos Geográficos de la Argentina.* B.A., 1958.

1191. Argentina. *Album Nacional: Galería de Hombres Públicos de Actualidad: Comprendiendo Poder Ejecutivo de la Nación, Parlamento, Ejército y Armada.* B.A., 1903.

1192. ———. Instituto Geográfico Militar. *Catálogo del Material Cartográfico.* B.A., 1927.

1193. Arnolds, A. *Geografía Económica Argentina.* B.A., 1963.

1194. Beltrán, J. G., and J. R. Beltrán. *Geografía de la Argentina.* B.A., 1920.

1195. Beorio, J. A. *Geografía de la Nación Argentina.* B.A., 1914.

1196. Buenos Aires. Biblioteca Nacional. *Catálogo de la Mapoteca.* B.A., 1942.

1196a. Cutolo, V. O. *Historiadores Argentinos y Americanos.* B.A., 1966.
Brief biographical data on some 2,000 scholars.

1197. Daus, F. A. *Geografía de la República Argentina.* 2 vols., B.A., 1958.

1198. Denis, P. *The Argentine Republic.* N.Y., 1911.
A geography.

1199. Fregeiro, C. L. *Vidas de Argentinos Ilustres.* Rev. ed., B.A., 1899.

1200. *Galería de Celebridades Argentinas: Biografías de los Personajes más Notables del Río de la Plata, por los Señores Bartolomé Mitre, Domingo F. Sarmiento, Juan M. Gutiérrez, Félix Frías, Luis Domínguez, General Ignacio Alvarez y Thomas, y Otros Más.* B.A., 1857.

1201. Gutiérrez, J. M. *Apuntes Biográficos de Escritores, Oradores, Hombres de Estado de la República Arjentina.* B.A., 1860.

1202. *Hombres de la Argentina: Diccionario Biográfico Contemporáneo.* 2d ed., B.A., 1946.

1203. Kühn, F. H. *Geografía de la Argentina.* 2d ed., Barcelona, 1941.

1204. Latzina, F. *Diccionario Geográfico Argentino, con Ampliaciones Enciclopedias Rioplatenses.* 3d ed., B.A., 1899.
A gazetteer.

1205. ———. *Geografía de la República Argentina.* B.A., 1890.

1206. Manito, O., and J. J. Noguera. *Geografía Física de las Américas y de la República Argentina.* B.A., 1938.

1207. Marrazzo, J. *Nuevo Diccionario Geográfico-Histórico de la República Argentina.* B.A., 1921.

1208. Momsen, R. P. *Argentina.* N.Y., 1960.
A geography.

1209. Muzzio, J. A. *Diccionario Histórico y Biográfico de la República Argentina.* 2 vols., B.A., 1920.

1210. Parker, W. B. *Argentines of Today.* 2 vols., B.A., 1920.

1211. Piccirilli, R., F. L. Romay, and L. Gianello (eds.). *Diccionario Histórico Argentino*. 6 vols., B.A., 1953–1954.

1212. Pinto, J. *Diccionario de la República Argentina: Histórico, Geográfico, Biográfico, Literario*. B.A., 1950.

1213. *Quién Es Quién en la Argentina: Biografías Contemporáneas*. 6th ed., B.A., 1955.

1214. Santillán, D. A. de (ed.). *Gran Enciclopedia Argentina*. 7 vols., B.A., 1956–1963.

1215. Scotto, J. A. *Notas Biográficas Publicadas en la Seccion Efemérides Americanas de "La Nación" en los Años 1907–1909*. 2 vols., B.A., 1912.

1216. Udaondo, E. *Diccionario Biográfico Argentino*. B.A., 1938.

1217. Urien, C. M., and E. Colombo. *Geografía Argentina*. B.A., 1901.

1218. Yarben, J. R. *Biografías Argentinas y Sud-Americanas*. 5 vols., B.A., 1938–1940.

I–B–4 cross references: *426–475, 1278, 4527*

5. BOLIVIA

1219. Aranzaes, N. *Diccionario Biográfico de La Paz*. La Paz, 1915.

1220. Cortes, J. D. *Galería de Hombres Célebres de Bolivia*. Santiago, 1869.

1221. Díaz, A. J. *Los Generales de Bolivia (Rasgos Biográficos), 1824–1925*. La Paz, 1929.

1222. *Diccionario Geográfico de la República de Bolivia*. 4 vols., La Paz, 1890–1894.

1223. Garza, P. de la. "Records of Current Publication in Bolivia, Ecuador, and Honduras," *HLAS* 23 (1961) 408–413.

1223a. Mendoza, J. *El Factor Geográfico en la Nacionalidad Boliviana*. Sucre, 1925.

1224. O'Connor d'Arlach, T. *Los Presidentes de Bolivia Desde 1825 Hasta 1912*. La Paz, 1912.

1225. Parker, W. B. *Bolivians of Today*. 2d ed., London, 1922.

1226. *Quién Es Quién en Bolivia*. La Paz, 1942.

1227. U.S. Office of Geography. *Bolivia: Official Standard Names Approved by the United States Board on Geographic Names*. Wash., 1955.

1228. Urquidi, J. M. *Bolivianas Ilustres: Prólogo de Ismael Vásquez*. 2 vols., La Paz, 1918.

I–B–5 cross references: *476–490, 1278*

6. BRAZIL

1229. Blake, A. V. do Sacramento. *Diccionário Bibliográphico Brazileiro*. 7 vols., Rio, 1883–1902.
Index, Rio, 1937.

1230. Brazil. Conselho Nacional de Geografia. *Atlas do Brasil: Geral e Regional*. Rio, 1959.

1231. ———. ———. *Geografia do Brasil: Roteiro de uma Viagem, Organizado por A. Teixeira Guerra e E. de Carvalho*. Rio, 1960.

1232. *Brazil Information Handbook*. N.Y., 1954– .

1233. Brazil. Ministério da Justiça e Negócios Interiores. *Catálogo dos Mapas Existentes na Biblioteca do Arquivo Nacional*. Rio, 1944.

1234. ———. Ministério dos Relações. *Catálogo da Mappoteca do Ministerio das Relações*. 2 vols., Rio, 1926–1929.

1235. Campos, R. Adalberto de. *Relações Diplomáticas do Brasil, Contendo os Nomes dos Representantes Diplomáticos do Brasil no Estrangeiro e os dos Representantes Diplomáticos dos Diversos Paizes no Rio de Janeiro de 1808 a 1912*. Rio, 1913.

1236. *Encyclopédia e Diccionário Internacional: Organizado e Redigido de Distinctos Homens de Sciência e de Lettras Brasileiros e Portuguêses*. 20 vols., Rio, 1933.

1237. *Grande Encyclopédia Portuguêsa e Brasileira*. 33 vols., Lisbon and Rio, 1936–1956.

1238. Guerra, A. Teixeira (ed.). *Geografia do Brasil*. Rio, 1959.

1239. Guimarães, A. *Diccionario Biobibliográphico Brasileiro de Diplomácia, Política Exterior e Direito Internacional*. Rio, 1938.

1240. Instituto Histórico e Geográphico Brasileiro. *Diccionario Histórico, Geográphico, Ethnográphico do Brasil*. Rio, 1944.

1241. Instituto Nacional do Livro. *Guia das Bibliotecas Brasileiras*. 2d ed., Rio, 1944.
Lists 1,328 libraries.

1241a. Levine, R. M. (ed.). *Brazil: Field Research Guide in the Social Sciences*. N.Y., 1966.

1242. Macedo, J. M. de. *Anno Biográphico Brazileiro*. 4 vols., Rio, 1876.

1243. ———. *Brasiliam Biográphicas Annual*. 3 vols., Rio, 1876.

1244. Oliveira, J. Teixeira de. *Diccionário Brasileiro de Datas Históricas*. 2d ed., Rio, 1950.

1245. Paranhos Filho, J. M. da Silva. *Efemerides Brasileiras*. 2d ed., Rio, 1938.

1246. Pinto, A. Moreira. *Apontamentos Para o Diccionario Geográphico do Brazil*. 3 vols., Rio, 1894–1899.

1247. Senna, N. Coelho de. *Serranos Illustres: Esboços Biográphicos*. Bello Horizonte, Brazil, 1905.

1248. Sisson, S. A. *Galeria dos Brasileiros Illustres (os Contemporaneos): Retratos dos Homens Mais Illustres do Brasil, na Política, Sciencias e Letras Desde a Guerra da Independencia até os Nossos Dias*. 2 vols., Rio, 1861.

1249. Silva, J. N. de Souza. *Brasileiros Célebres*. Rio, 1862.

1250. Silva, M. F. Dias da. *Diccionário Biográphico de Brasileiros Célebres nas Letras, Artes, Política, Philantrophia, Guerra, Diplomácia, Indústria, Sciencias e Caridade, Desde o Anno 1500 até Nossos Dias*. Rio, 1871.

1251. Sobrinho, J. F. Velho. *Diccionário Bio-Bibliográfico Brasileiro*. 2 vols., Rio, 1937–1940.

1252. USDS. Office of Research and Intelligence. *Some Brazilian Maps and Map Sources*. Wash., 1946.

1253. U.S. Office of Geography. *Brazil: Official Standard Names Approved by the United States Board on Geographic Names*. Wash., 1963.

1254. Vianna, H. "Atuais Tendências da Historiografia Brasileira," *IRB* 13 (1963) 30–59.

I–B–6   cross references: 491–556c

7. CENTRAL AMERICA AND THE CARIBBEAN IN GENERAL

1254a. Aguilar P., C. *Geografía de Centroamérica*. Tegucigalpa, 1944.

1255. Eyre, A. *A New Geography of the Caribbean*. London, 1962.

1256. Gropp, A. E. *Guide to Libraries and Archives in Central America and the West Indies, Panama, Bermuda and British Guiana*. New Orleans, 1941.
Contains information on private collections, book-binding, and book-selling.

1257. Hill, R. R. "Los Archivos Españoles y los Archivos del Caribe," *BUIC* (January, 1941) 15–26.

1258. Long, E. J. *Central America*. N.Y., 1959. A geography.

1259. MacPherson, J. *Caribbean Lands: A Geography of the West Indies*. London, 1963.

1260. Trembly, W. *Directory of Caribbean Scholars*. 2d ed., Rio Piedras, P.R., 1965.

I–B–7   cross references: 557–571a

8. CHILE

1261. Almeyda Arroyo, E. *Geografía de Chile*. Santiago, 1955.

1262. Amunátegui, M. L. *Ensayos Biográficos*. 4 vols., Santiago, 1893–1896.

1263. Campo, C. del. *Quién Es Quién en Chile*. Santiago, 1940.

1264. *Catálogo de los Planos i Cartas Hidrográficas i Topográficas que Existen en el Ministerio de Marina de la República de Chile*. Santiago, 1863.

1265. Chile. Congreso. Senado. *Manual del Senado que Contiene . . . la Composición de los Senados y el Origen Constitucional de Cada Uno, la Nómina de los Presidentes . . . y de los Ministros*. Santiago, 1929.

1265a. Cunill Grau, P. *Atlas Histórico de Chile*. Santiago, 1961.

1266. Desmadryl, N. *Galería Nacional, o Colección de Biografías y Retratos de Hombres Célebres de Chile, Escrita por los Principales Literatos del País*. 2 vols., Santiago, 1854–1861.

1267. *Diccionario Biográfico de Chile*. 5th ed., Santiago, 1944.

1268. Figueroa, P. P. *Diccionario Biográfico de Estranjeros en Chile*. Santiago, 1900.

1269. Figueroa, V. T. [Virgilio Talguino]. *Diccionario Histórico, Biográfico y Bibliográfico de Chile*. 5 vols., Santiago, 1925–1931.
Covers the period from 1800 to date of publication.

1270. Fuenzalida, E. A. *Galería Contemporánea de Hombres Notables de Chile (1850–1901)*. Valparaiso, 1901.

1271. García-Huidobro Guzmán, A. J. *Geografía de Chile*. Santiago, 1954.

1272. Keller, C. R. *Sinopsis Geográfico-Estadística de Chile*. Santiago, 1933.

1273. Larraín Zañartu, J. J. *Chile: Figuras Contemporáneas.* Santiago, 1882.

1274. Matta Vial, E. "Apuntes para un Diccionario Biográfico (Chileno)," *RCHG* 12 (1924) 300–532.

1275. McBride, G. M. *Chile: Land and Society.* N.Y., 1936.

1276. Parker, W. B. *Chileans of Today.* Santiago, 1920.

1277. Pinochet Ugarte, A. *Síntesis Geográfica de Chile.* Santiago, 1955.

1278. ———. *Síntesis Geográfica de Chile, Argentina, Bolivia y Perú.* Santiago, 1953.

1279. Pinto Durán, C. *Diccionario Personal de Chile.* Santiago, 1921.

1280. Risopatrón Sánchez, L. *Diccionario Geográfico de Chile.* Santiago, 1924.

1281. Suárez, J. B. *Rasgos Biográficos de Hombres Notables de Chile.* Santiago, 1863.

1282. Valencia Avaria, L. (comp.). *Anales de la República: Textos Constitucionales de Chile y Registros de los Ciudadanos que Han Integrado los Poderes Ejecutivo y Legislativo Desde 1810.* 2 vols., Santiago, 1951.

I–B–8   cross references: 572–608

9. Colombia

1283. Azpurúa, R. *Biografías de Hombres Notables de Hispano-América.* 4 vols., Caracas, 1877.

Figures of the independence movement and early national history, chiefly of Gran Colombia.

1283a. *Bosquejos Biográficos de los Personajes más Eminentes: Historia Condensada de la República.* N.Y., 1918.

1284. Codazzi, G. B. A. *Atlas Geográfico e Histórico de la República de Colombia.* Paris, 1889.

1285. Goez, R. C. *Geografía de Colombia.* Mexico, 1947.

1286. Gómez, E. J. *Diccionario Geográfico de Colombia.* Bogotá, 1953.

1287. Mejía Córdoba, J. *Geografía de Colombia.* Bogotá, 1945.

1288. Mesa Ortíz, R. M. *Colombianos Ilustres (Estudios y Biografías) con Juicio de la Academia Nacional de Historia.* 5 vols., Bogotá, 1916–1929.

1289. Monsalve Martínez, M. *Colombia: Posesiones Presidenciales, 1810–1954.* Bogotá, 1954.

Short biographies and extracts of presidential addresses.

1290. Moreno Mattos, A. *Directorio de Bibliotecas en Colombia.* Bogotá, 1959.

Lists 321 libraries.

1291. Mosquera, T. C. *Compendio de Geografía General Política, Física y Especial de los Estados Unidos de Colombia.* London, 1866.

1292. Ospina, J. *Diccionario Biográfico y Bibliográfico de Colombia.* 3 vols., Bogotá, 1927–1939.

1293. Perry, O., and A. Brugés Carmona (eds.). *Quién Es Quién en Colombia.* Rev. ed., Bogotá, 1961.

1294. Rivas, R. *Los Fundadores de Bogotá.* Bogotá, 1923.

1295. Samper, J. M. *Galería Nacional de Hombres Ilustres o Notables.* Vol. 1, Bogotá, 1879.

1295a. Zamora, M. M. *Guía de la República de Colombia.* Bogotá, 1907.

I–B–9   cross references: 609–635

10. Costa Rica

1296. Dobles Segreda, L. *Lista de Mapas Parciales o Totales de Costa Rica.* San José, C.R., 1928.

1297. Monge A., C. *Geografía Social y Humana de Costa Rica.* San José, C.R., 1942.

1298. Solórzano Calvo, F. *Indice Alfabético de Leyes y Acuerdos del Poder Legislativo.* San José, C.R., 1947.

1299. U.S. Office of Geography. *Costa Rica: Official Standard Names Approved by the United States Board on Geographic Names.* Wash., 1956.

I–B–10   cross references: 636–644

11. Cuba

1300. Alvarez Conde, J. *Historia de la Geografía de Cuba.* Havana, 1961.

1301. Calcagno, F. *Diccionario Biográfico Cubano.* N.Y., 1878.

1302. *Cuba en el Mano: Enciclopedia Popular Ilustrada.* Havana, 1940.

1303. *Libro de Cuba: Una Enciclopedia Literaria que Abarca las Artes, las Letras, las Ciencias, la Economía, la Política, la*

Historia, la Docencia y el Progreso General de la Nación Cubana. Havana, 1955.

1304. Llaverías, J. *Historia de los Archivos de Cuba.* Havana, 1912.

1305. Marrero y Artiles, L. *Geografía de Cuba.* Havana, 1950.

1306. Mossip, J. *Introducción a la Geografía de Cuba.* Havana, 1942.

1307. Parker, W. B. *Cubans of Today.* N.Y., 1919.

1308. Peraza Sarausa, F. *Directorio de Bibliotecas de Cuba, 1943– .* Havana, 1943– .

1309. Pezuela y Lobo, J. de la. *Diccionario Geográfico, Estadístico, Histórico, de la Isla de Cuba.* 4 vols., Madrid, 1863–1866.

1310. Suárez de Tangil y de Angulo, F. *Nobiliario Cubano: O, Las Grandes Familias Isleñas.* 2 vols., Madrid, 1929.

1311. U.S. Office of Geography. *Cuba: Official Standard Names Approved by the United States Board on Geographic Names.* Wash., 1957.

I–B–11   cross references: 645–682

12. DOMINICAN REPUBLIC

1312. Cucurullo, O. *Geografía de Santo Domingo.* Cd. Trujillo, 1956.

1313. García, J. G. *Rasgos Biográficos de Dominicanos Célebres.* Santo Domingo, 1875.

1314. Inchaustegui, J. M. *Geografía Descriptiva de la República Dominicana.* Cd. Trujillo, 1947.

1315. Martínez, R. *Hombres Dominicanos.* Cd. Trujillo, 1936.

1316. Peraza Sarausa, F., and A. del Valle. *Bibliotecas, Archivo y Museo de la República Dominicana.* Havana, 1941.

1317. Saint Juste, L. "Los Archivos de la República Dominicana," *BAGNDR* 28 (1959) 6–8.

I–B–12   cross references: 683–696

13. ECUADOR

1318. Arboleda R., G. *Diccionario Biográfico de la República del Ecuador.* Quito, 1910.

1319. Calle, M. J. *Biografías y Semblanzas.* Quito, 1920.

1320. Campos, F. *Galería Biográfica de Hombres Célebres Ecuatorianos.* Guayaquil, 1885.

1321. Ceballos, P. F. *Ecuatorianos Ilustres.* Quito, 1912.

1322. ———. *Geografía de la República del Ecuador.* Lima, 1888.

1323. Destruge, C. *Album Biográfico Ecuatoriano.* 5 vols., Guayaquil, 1903–1905.

1324. Pérez, J. *Rasgos Biográficos de Personas Notables de Guayaquil.* Guayaquil, 1906.

1325. Pérez Marchant, B. *Diccionario Biográfico del Ecuador.* Quito, 1928.

1326. Rumazo González, A. *Gobernantes del Ecuador (1830–1932).* La Paz, 1933.

1327. U.S. Office of Geography. *Ecuador: Official Standard Names Approved by the United States Board on Geographic Names.* Wash., 1957.

1328. Wolf, T. *Geografía y Geología del Ecuador.* Leipzig, 1892.

I–B–13   cross references: 697–711, 1223

14. EL SALVADOR

1328a. *Diccionario Histórico Enciclopédico de la República de El Salvador: Procesos por Infidencia Contra los Proceres Salvadoreños de la Independencia de Centro-América Desde 1811 Hasta 1818.* San Salvador, 1940.

1328b. El Salvador. Dirección General de Estadística y Censos. *Diccionario Geográfico de la República de El Salvador.* 3d ed., San Salvador, 1959.

1329. García, M. A. *Diccionario Histórico-Enciclopédico de la República de El Salvador.* 24 vols., San Salvador, 1927– 1955.

1330. Pérez Marchant, B. *Diccionario Biográfico de El Salvador.* San Salvador, 1937.

1331. U.S. Office of Geography. *El Salvador: Official Standard Names Approved by the United States Board on Geographic Names.* Wash., 1956.

15. GUATEMALA

1332. Guatemala. Dirección General de Cartografía. *Diccionario Geográfico de Guatemala.* 2 vols., Guatemala, 1961–1962.

1333. Peraza Sarausa, F. *Directorio de Bibliotecas de Guatemala.* Havana, 1946.

1334. Termer, F. "Zur Geographie der Republik Guatemala," *MGG* 44 (1936) 89–275; 47 (1941) 7–262.

1335. Valle Matheu, J. del. *Guía Sociogeográfica de Guatemala.* Guatemala, 1956.

I–B–14   cross references: 722–737a

16. Haiti

1336. Herskovits, M. J. *Life in a Haitian Valley.* N.Y., 1937.

1337. Oriol, R. B. *Aperçu sur la Géographie, la Cartographie et la Géodésie en Haiti.* Port-au-Prince, 1953.

17. Honduras

1338. Bonilla, M. *Diccionario Histórico-Geográfico de las Poblaciones de Honduras.* Tegucigalpa, 1945.

1339. Rubio Melhado, A. *Geografía General de la República de Honduras.* Tegucigalpa, 1953.

I–B–17 cross references: 753–759c, 1223

18. Mexico

1340. Acosta, F. J. *The Acosta Directory of the English Speaking Residents of the Republic of Mexico for 1910 . . . Including a Directory of the . . . Mining Companies, Plantations, Government Departments and Officials, Diplomatic Corps.* Mexico, 1910.

1341. Casasola, G. *Enciclopedia Histórica Ilustrada de México: 1825–1958.* Mexico, 1958.

1342. *Diccionario Enciclopédico U.T.E.H.A.* 10 vols., Mexico, 1950–1952.

1343. *Diccionario Porrua: De Historia, Biografía y Geografía de México.* Mexico, 1964.
    Supplement, Mexico, 1966.

1344. *Diccionario Universal de Historia y de Geographia: Obra Dada a Luz en España y Refundida y Aum. Considerablemente para su Publicación en México con Noticias Históricas, Geográficas, Estadísticas y Biográficas Sobre las Américas en General, y Especialmente Sobre la República Mexicana.* 10 vols., Mexico, 1853–1856.

1345. Gallo, E. L. *Hombres Ilustres Mexicanos: Biografías de los Personajes Notables Desde Antes de la Conquista Hasta Nuestros Días.* 4 vols., Mexico, 1873–1874.

1346. García Cubas, A. *Diccionario Geográfico, Histórico y Biográfico de los Estados Unidos Mexicanos.* 5 vols., Mexico, 1888–1891.

1347. Leduc, A., and L. Lara y Pardó. *Diccionario de Geografía, Historia y Biografía Mexicanas.* Mexico, 1910.

1348. Liebes, H., and J. Liebes. *Rand McNally Guide to Mexico.* Chicago, 1961.

1349. Mestre Ghiliazza, M. *Efemérides Biográficas (Defunciones-Nacimientos).* Mexico, 1945.

1350. Mexico. Departamento de Bibliotecas. *Directorio de Bibliotecas de la República Mexicana.* Mexico, 1962.

1351. ———. Dirección General de Geografía y Meteorología. *Bibliografía Geográfica de México.* Batalla, 1955.

1352. ———. Secretaría de Relaciones Exteriores. *Personas que Han Tenido a su Cargo la Secretaría de Relaciones Desde 1812 Hasta 1924.* Mexico, 1924.

1353. Morales Jiménez, A. *Hombres de la Revolución Mexicana: 50 Semblanzas Biográficas.* Mexico, 1960.

1354. Naranjo, F. *Diccionario Biográfico Revolucionario.* Mexico, 1935.

1355. Parsons, M. D., and R. A. Gordillo (comps.). *Directorio de Bibliotecas de la Ciudad de Mexico. Directory of Mexico City Libraries.* Mexico, 1958.

1356. Paz, I. *Los Hombres Prominentes de México. The Prominent Men of Mexico. Les Hommes Eminents du Mexique.* Mexico, 1888.

1357. ———. *México Actual: Galería de Contemporáneos.* Mexico, 1898.

1358. Peral, M. A. *Diccionario Biográfico Mexicano de 544 a 1944.* 2 vols., Mexico, 1944.

1359. Peraza Sarausa, F. *Directorio de Bibliotecas de México, 1946.* Havana, 1946.

1360. Rivera Cambas, M. *Los Gobernantes de México: Galería de Biografías y Retratos de los Virreyes, Emperadores, Presidentes y Otros Gobernantes que Ha Tenido México, Desde Don Hernando Cortés Hasta el C. Benito Juárez.* 2 vols., Mexico, 1872–1873.

1361. Sosa, F. *Biografías de Mexicanos Distinguidos.* Mexico, 1884.

1362. U.S. Office of Geography. *Mexico: Official Standard Names Approved by the United States Board on Geographic Names.* Wash., 1956.

1363. Vázquez Santa Ana, H. *Bosquejos Biográficos de Hombres Ilustres Nacionales.* Mexico, 1920.

1364. Villaseñor y Villaseñor, A. *Biografías de los Héroes y Caudillos de la Independencia.* 2 vols., Mexico, 1910.

I–B–18   cross references: 760–869

19. NICARAGUA

1365. U.S. Office of Geography. *Nicaragua: Official Standard Names Approved by the United States Board on Geographic Names.* Wash., 1956.

I–B–20   cross references: 870–883

20. PANAMA

1366. Aguilera, R. *Galería de Hombres Públicos del Istmo.* Panama, 1906.
1367. Mejía Robledo, A. *Quién Es Quién en Panamá: Diccionario Biográfico y Bibliográfico de Personalidades Actuales.* Medellín, 1949.
1368. Peraza Sarausa, F. *Directorio de Bibliotecas de Panama.* Havana, 1948.
1369. Rubio, A., and L. Guzmán. *Regiones Geográficas Panameñas.* Panama, 1957.

I–B–20   cross references: 884–900, 7294

21. PARAGUAY

1370. Capurro, A. *Geografía del Paraguay.* Asunción, 1957.
1371. Decoud, H. *Geografía de la República del Paraguay.* Leipzig, 1911.
1372. Paraguay. Ministerio de Relaciones Exteriores. *Lista de Ministros de Relaciones Exteriores del Paraguay Desde la Epoca de su Independencia.* Asunción, 1943.
1373. Parker, W. B. *Paraguayans of Today.* 2d ed., London, 1921.
1374. *Quién Es Quién en el Paraguay.* B.A., 1941– .
1375. U.S. Office of Geography. *Paraguay: Official Standard Names Approved by the United States Board on Geographic Names.* Wash., 1957.
1376. Zubizarreta, C. *Cien Vidas Paraguayas.* B.A., 1961.

I–B–21   cross references: 901–910

22. PERU

1377. Barreto V., C. A., and G. de la Fuente Chávez. *Diccionario Biográfico de Figuras Contemporáneas.* Lima, 1926–1928.

1378. Bustamente, C. *Geografía Humana del Peru.* Lima, 1931.
1378a. Chang Laos, C. *El Perú y sus Hombres a Través de la República: Reseña Histórica.* Lima, 1959.
   Brief biographical sketches of 150 men prominent in gaining Peru's independence.
1379. Cornejo Bouroncle, J. *Introducción a la Geografía Económica General de América y del Perú.* Cuzco, 1950.
1380. *Diccionario Biográfico del Perú.* Lima, 1944.
1381. Lavalle y Arias de Saavedra, J. A. *Galería de Retratos de los Gobernantes del Perú Independiente (1821–1871).* Barcelona, 1909.
1382. Mendiburu, M. de. *Diccionario Histórico-Biográfico del Perú.* 11 vols., Lima, 1931–1935.
1383. Pareja Paz Soldán, J. *Geografía del Perú.* 2 vols., Lima, 1950.
1384. Parker, W. B. *Peruvians of Today.* Lima, 1919.
1385. Paz-Soldán, J. P. *Diccionario Biográfico de Peruanos Contemporáneos.* Rev. ed., Lima, 1921.
1385a Paz Soldán, M. F. *Diccionario Geográfico Estadístico del Perú: Contiene Además la Etimología Aymara y Quechua de las Principales Poblaciones, Lagos, Rios, Cerros, etc.* Lima, 1887.
1386. *Pequeño Diccionario Histórico-Biográfico del Perú: Sucintas Biografías de Personajes Ilustres.* Lima, 1961.
1387. Stiglich, G. *Diccionario Geográfico del Perú.* 4 vols., Lima, 1922–1923.

I–B–22   cross references: 911–937

23. URUGUAY

1388. Araujo, O. *Diccionario Geográfico del Uruguay.* 2d ed., Montevideo, 1912.
1389. ———. *Diccionario Popular de Historia de la República O. del Uruguay.* 3 vols., Montevideo, 1901–1903.
1390. Demaría, I. *Rasgos Biográficos de Hombres Notables de la República Oriental del Uruguay.* 3 vols., Montevideo, 1879–1880.
1391. Fernández Saldaña, J. M. *Diccionario Uruguayo de Biografías, 1810–1940.* Montevideo, 1946.

1392. Jalabert, R. M., and R. Cabal. *Album Biográfico Ilustrado y Descripción Histórico-Geográfica de la República Oriental del Uruguay.* B.A., 1903.

1393. Parker, W. B. *Uruguayans of Today.* London, 1921.

1394. Scarone, A. *Uruguayos Contemporáneos: Nuevo Diccionario de Datos Biográficos y Bibliográficos.* Montevideo, 1937.

1395. ———. *Uruguayos Contemporáneos: Obra de Consulta Biográfica: Diccionario de Datos Referentes a Compatriotas . . . y de Algunos Extranjeros Desde Largo Tiempo Incorporados y Descollantes en Nuestra Vida Pública.* Montevideo, 1918.

I–B–23   cross references: 938–951

24. VENEZUELA

1396. Arraiz, A. *Geografía Física de Venezuela.* B.A., 1952.

1397. Cárdenas C., A. L. *Geografía Física de Venezuela.* Mérida, Venezuela, 1963.

1398. Cárdenas Ramírez, J., *et al. Diccionario Biográfico de Venezuela.* Madrid, 1953.

1399. Codazzi, G. B. A. *Atlas Físico y Político de la República de Venezuela.* Caracas, 1840.

1400. ———. *Resumen de la Geografía de Venezuela.* Paris, 1841.

1401. U.S. Office of Geography. *Venezuela: Official Standard Names Approved by the United States Board on Geographic Names.* Wash., 1961.

I–B–24   cross references: 952–983

Chapter II   Basic Works for the Study of
United States–Latin American Relations

A. SURVEYS AND INTERPRETATIONS OF LATIN AMERICAN HISTORY

1402. Akers, C. E. *A History of South America.* Rev. ed., N.Y., 1930.

1403. Bailey, H., and A. Nasatir. *Latin America: The Development of Its Civilization.* Englewood Cliffs, N.J., 1960.

1404. Bannon, J. F., and P. M. Dunne. *Latin America: An Historical Survey.* Milwaukee, 1947.

1405. Barbagelata, H. D. *Histoire de l'Amérique Espagnole.* Paris, 1936.

1406. Bayo, C. *Historia Moderna de la América Española.* Madrid, 1930.
    Survey from independence to date of publication.

1407. Beals, C. *America South.* Phil., 1937.
    Impressions.

1408. Bernstein, H. *Modern and Contemporary Latin America.* Phil., 1952.
    Covers Mexico, Argentina, Brazil, Chile, Colombia, and Peru.

1409. Bertrand, J. T. *Histoire de l'Amérique Espagnole.* 2 vols., Paris, 1929.

1409a. Bierck, H. A. (ed.). *Latin American Civilization: Readings and Essays.* Boston, 1967.

1410. Bryce, J. *South America: Observations and Impressions.* Rev. ed., N.Y., 1914.

1411. Carrancá y Trujillo, R. *La Evolución Política de Iberoamérica.* Madrid, 1925.

1412. Chapman, C. E. *Republican Hispanic America: A History,* N.Y., 1937.
    Contains a useful essay on sources.

1413. Chaunu, P. *Histoire de l'Amérique Latine.* Paris, 1949.

1414. Crawford, W. R. *A Century of Latin-American Thought.* Cambridge, Mass., 1944.
    Rev. pb. ed., N.Y., 1966.

1415. Crow, J. A. *The Epic of Latin America.* Garden City, N.Y., 1946.

1416. Dávila, C. G. *We of the Americas.* N.Y., 1949.
    Spanish ed., Santiago, 1950.

1417. Davis, H. E. *Latin American Social Thought: The History of Its Development Since Independence.* Wash., 1961.
    Translations of 38 Latin American thinkers.

1418. Dawson, T. C. *The South American Republics.* 2 vols., N.Y., 1903–1904.

1419. Deberle, A. J. *The History of Spanish America from Its Discovery to the Present.* London, 1899.

1420. Dozer, D. *Latin America: An Interpretive History.* N.Y., 1962.

1421. Duggan, S. P. H. *The Two Americas: An Interpretation.* N.Y., 1934.

1422. Fagg, J. E. *Latin America: A General History.* N.Y., 1963.

1423. Foster, W. Z. *Outline Political History of the Americas.* N.Y., 1951.
    Author was a leading United States Communist.

1424. Galíndez Suárez, J. de. *Iberoamérica: Su Evolución Política, Socio-Económica, Cultural e Internacional.* N.Y., 1954.

1425. Gandía, E. de. *Nueva Historia de América: Las Epocas de Libertad y Anti-libertad Desde la Independencia.* 2 vols., B.A., 1946.

1426. García Calderón, F. *Latin America: Its Rise and Progress.* London, 1913.

1427. Gleichen-Russwurm, A. von, and F. Wencker. *Die Entstehung Latein-Amerikas.* Hamburg, 1935.

1428. Hanke, L. *Modern Latin America: Continent in Ferment.* 2 vols., Princeton, N.J., 1959.
    First volume covers Mexico, the

Caribbean, Colombia, and Venezuela; second volume covers remaining South American countries. Summary histories and readings.

Rev. ed. Princeton, N.J., 1967.

1428a. *History of Latin American Civilization: Sources and Interpretations.* 2 vols., N.Y., 1967.

Vol. II covers the years since independence.

1429. Hernández Sánchez-Barba, M. *Las Tensiones Históricas Hispanoamericanos en el Siglo XX.* Madrid, 1961.

1430. Herring, H. *A History of Latin America.* 2d ed. rev., N.Y., 1965.

1431. Humphreys, R. A. *The Evolution of Modern Latin America.* N.Y., 1946.

1432. James, H. G., and P. A. Martin. *The Republics of Latin America.* N.Y., 1923.

1433. Jane, C. *Liberty and Despotism in Spanish America.* N.Y., 1929.

Spanish ed., B.A., 1942.

1434. Jones, T. B. *South America Rediscovered.* Minneapolis, 1949.

1435. ———, and W. D. Beatty. *An Introduction to Hispanic American History.* Rev. ed., N.Y., 1950.

1436. Keen, B. (ed.). *Readings in Latin American Civilization.* N.Y., 1955.

1437. Kirkpatrick, F. A. *Latin America: A Brief History.* Cambridge, 1938.

1438. Latin America Kyôkai. Tokyo. *Latin America No Rekishi.* Tokyo, 1964.

History of Latin America.

1439. Markov, W. *Lateinamerika Zwischen Emanzipation und Imperialismus: 1810–1960.* Berlin, 1961.

1440. Mecham, J. L. *Church and State in Latin America.* Chapel Hill, N.C., 1934.

1441. Moore, D. R. *A History of Latin America.* N.Y., 1938.

Spanish ed., B.A., 1945.

1442. Mörner, M. *Latinamerika: Kulturländernas Historia.* Stockholm, 1957.

Danish ed., Copenhagen, 1959.

1443. Munro, D. G. *The Latin American Republics.* 3d ed., N.Y., 1960.

1443a. Nakaya, K. *Latin America Shi.* Tokyo, 1964.

Latin American History.

1444. Opisso, A. *Historia de España y de las Repúblicas Latino-Americanas.* 25 vols., Barcelona, 19—(?).

1445. Ortega y Rubio, J. *Historia de América.* 3 vols., Madrid, 1917.

1446. Pattee, R. F. *Introducción a la Civilización Hispanoamericana.* Boston, 1945.

1447. Peck, A. M. *The Pageant of South American History.* Rev. ed., N.Y., 1958.

1448. Pendle, G. *A History of Latin America.* Baltimore, 1963.

1449. Pereyra, C. *Breve Historia de América.* Madrid, 1930, and Santiago, 1938.

Condensed version of the author's work in eight volumes.

1450. ———. *Historia de América Española.* 8 vols., Madrid, 1920–1926.

Country-by-country analysis.

1451. Petrov, F. N. (ed.). *Strany Latinskoi Ameriki.* Moscow, 1949.

The Countries of Latin America.

1452. Pierson, W. W. *Hispanic-American History: A Syllabus.* Rev. ed., Chapel Hill, N.C., 1926.

1452a. Revunenkov, V. G. *Istoriia Stran Latinskoi Ameriki v Noveishee Vremia.* Moscow, 1963.

A Contemporary History of the Countries of Latin America.

1453. Rippy, J. F. *Historical Evolution of Hispanic America.* 3d ed. rev., N.Y., 1945.

1454. ———. *Latin America: A Modern History.* Ann Arbor, Mich., 1958.

More emphasis on international relations than other survey texts.

1455. ———, and L. I. Perrigo. *Latin America: Its History and Culture.* N.Y., 1944.

1456. Robertson, W. S. *History of the Latin American Nations.* 3d ed. rev., N.Y., 1943.

1457. Rodríguez Larreta, A. *Orientación de la Política Internacional en América Latina.* 2 vols., Montevideo, 1938.

1458. Samhaber, E. *Sudamérica, Biografía de un Continente.* B.A., 1946.

1459. ———. *Südamerika: Gesicht, Geist, Geschichte.* Hamburg, 1939.

1460. Schoen, W. A. von. *Geschichte Mittel- und Südamerikas.* Munich, 1953.

1461. Schurz, W. L. *Latin America.* Rev. ed., N.Y., 1963.

Rev. pb. ed., N.Y., 1964.

1462. ———. *This New World: The Civilization of Latin America.* N.Y., 1954.

1463. Shepherd, W. R. *Central and South America*. London, 1914.

1464. ———. *The Hispanic Nations of the New World: A Chronicle of Our Southern Neighbors*. New Haven, Conn., 1919.

1465. Siegfried, A. *América Latina: Versión Castellana, Anotado, con Nuevos Datos Sobre la Realidad del Continente*. Santiago, 1935.

1466. Stark, H. *Modern Latin America*. Coral Gables, Fla., 1957.
Emphasis on economic development.

1467. Sweet, W. W. *A History of Latin America*. N.Y., 1929.
A pioneer effort.

1468. Tannenbaum, F. *Whither Latin America? An Introduction to Its Economic and Social Problems*. N.Y., 1934.

1469. Thomas, A. B. *Latin America: A History*. N.Y., 1956.

1470. Vol'skii, V. V., *et al.* (eds.). *Latinskaia Amerika v Proshlom i Nastoiashchem*. Moscow, 1960.
Latin America Past and Present.

1471. Webster, H. *History of Latin America*. Boston, 1924.

1472. Whitaker, A. P. *Nationalism in Latin America: Past and Present*. Gainesville, Fla., 1962.
Historical development of nationalism.

1473. ———. *The United States and South America: The Northern Republics*. Cambridge, Mass., 1948.
United States relations with Bolivia, Peru, Ecuador, Colombia, and Venezuela, 1822–1948.

1474. Wilgus, A. C. (ed.). *Argentina, Brazil and Chile Since Independence*. Wash., 1935.

1475. ———. *The Development of Hispanic America*. N.Y., 1941.

1476. ———. *A History of Hispanic America: A Text Handbook for College Students*. Wash., 1931.

1477. ———. *Modern Hispanic America*. Wash., 1933.

1478. ———. *South American Dictators During the First Century of Independence*. Wash., 1937.

1479. ———, and R. d'Eça. *Latin American History: A Summary of Political, Economic, Social, and Cultural Events from 1492 to the Present*. N.Y., 1963.

1480. Williams, M. W., *et al*. *The People and Politics of Latin America*. 4th ed., Boston, 1955.

1481. Worcester, D. E., and W. G. Schaeffer. *The Growth and Culture of Latin America*. N.Y., 1956.

B. HISTORIES OF GREATER AMERICA

1482. Baldwin, L. D. *The Story of the Americas: The Discovery, Settlement, and Development of the New World*. N.Y., 1943.

1483. Ballesteros Gaibros, M. *Historia de América*. Madrid, 1946.

1484. Ballesteros y Beretta, A. (ed.). *Historia de América y de los Pueblos Americanos*. Barcelona, 1936– .
Heavy emphasis on Spanish America.

1485. Bannon, J. F. *History of the Americas*. 2 vols., 2d ed., N.Y., 1963.

1486. Barros Arana, D. *Compendio de Historia de América*. 2 vols., Santiago, 1865.
One-volume ed., B.A., 1960.

1487. Bolton, H. E. *History of the Americas: A Syllabus with Maps*. Rev. ed., Boston, 1935.

1488. ———. *La Epopeya de la Máxima América*. Mexico, 1937.

1489. ———. *Wider Horizons of American History*. N.Y., 1939.

1490. Brooks, P. C. "Do the Americans Share a Common History?" *RHA* (1952) 75–83.
Supports the Bolton thesis.

1491. Caughey, J. W. *America Since 1763: A Survey of Its History*. Mexico, 1955.

1492. Cotterill, R. S. *A Short History of the Americas*. Rev. ed., N.Y., 1945.

1493. Davis, H. E. *The Americas in History*. N.Y., 1953.

1494. Delgado, J. *Introducción a la Historia de América*. Madrid, 1957.

1495. *Greater America: Essays in Honor of Herbert Eugene Bolton*. Berkeley, Calif., 1945.

1496. Griffin, C. C. *The National Period in the History of the New World: An Outline and Commentary*. Mexico, 1961.

1497. Guerrero C., J. N. *Historia de América*. Guatemala, 1962.

1498. Hanke, L. (ed.). *Do the Americas Have a Common History? A Critique of the Bolton Theory*. N.Y., 1964.
Readings pro and con.

1499. Harris, M. *Patterns of Race in the Americas.* N.Y., 1964.

1500. "Have the Americas a Common History?" *CHR* 23 (1942) 125–156.

1501. Hernández Sánchez-Barba, M. *Historia Universal de América.* 2 vols., Madrid, 1963.

1502. Holmes, V. L. *A History of the Americas.* 2 vols., N.Y., 1950–1964.

1503. Jaramillo Pérez, C. *Resumen de Historia de América.* Quito, 1950.

1504. Levene, R. (ed.). *Historia de América.* 14 vols., B.A., 1940–1941.

1505. Marbán Escobar, E. *Curso de Historia de América.* 2 vols., N.Y., 1963.

1506. McInnis, E., *et al. Ensayos Sobre la Historia del Nuevo Mundo.* Mexico, 1951.

1507. Mendoza, C. L. "La Idea de la Unidad de América," *RNC* 23 (1961) 133–155.

1508. Morales Padrón, F. *Historia de América.* 2 vols., Madrid, 1962.

1509. Navarro y Lamarca, C. *Compendio de la Historia General de América.* 2 vols., B.A., 1910–1913.

1510. O'Gorman, E. *Fundamentos de la Historia de América.* Mexico, 1942.

1511. ———. "Hegel y el Moderno Pan-americanismo," *UH* 4 (1939) 61–74.

1512. ———. *The Invention of America: An Inquiry into the Historical Nature of the New World and the Meaning of Its History.* Bloomington, Ind., 1961.

1513. Pan American Institute of Geography and History. Commission on History. *Programa de Historia de América: Introducciones y Comentarios.* Mexico, 1955.

1514. Posada, G. "La Idea de América en Vasconcelos," *HM* 47 (1963) 379–403.

1515. "The Problem of a General History of the Americas," *RHA* 34 (1952) 469–589.

1516. Rio, A. del. *El Mundo Hispánico y el Mundo Anglo-Sajón en América: Choque y Atracción de las Culturas.* B.A., 1960.

1517. Rippy, J. F. "The Western-Hemisphere Concept: Permanent or Fleeting?" *IEA* 10 (Spring, 1957) 3–21.

1518. Sánchez, L. A. *Historia General de América: Con Mapas e Ilustraciones.* 2 vols., Santiago, 1942.
         Aprista interpretation.

1519. Serrano y Sanz, M. *Compendio de Historia de América.* 2 vols., Barcelona, 1919–1921.

1520. Tannenbaum, F. *Slave and Citizen: The Negro in the Americas.* N.Y., 1946.
         Pb. ed., N.Y., 1965.

1521. Thompson, W. *Greater America: An Interpretation of Latin America in Relation to Anglo-Saxon America.* N.Y., 1932.

1522. Turner, R. E. "Comments on the Project of the History of America," in *Do the Americas Have a Common History?*, pp. 197–201.
         See item 1498.

1523. Wesley, C. H. (ed.). *The Negro in the Americas.* Wash., 1940.

1524. Whitaker, A. P. *The Western Hemisphere Idea: Its Rise and Decline.* Ithaca, N.Y., 1954.

1525. ———. "The Americas in the Atlantic Triangle," *EHNM* (1951) 69–95.

1526. Zavala, S. *Programa de Historia de América: Epoca Colonial.* 2 vols., Mexico, 1961.

II–B   *cross references: 423, 1717, 4431*

C. SURVEYS OF LATIN AMERICAN GOVERNMENT

1527. Alexander, R. *Latin American Politics and Government.* N.Y., 1965.

1528. Bishop, C. M. *The Constitutional Law of the Latin-American Republics.* Wash., 1942.

1529. Busey, J. L. *Latin America: Political Institutions and Processes.* N.Y., 1964.

1530. Christenson, A. N. (ed.). *The Evolution of Latin American Government.* N.Y., 1951.
         Series of readings.

1531. Davis, H. E. (ed.). *Government and Politics in Latin America.* N.Y., 1958.

1532. Edelmann, A. T. *Latin American Government and Politics.* Homewood, Ill., 1965.

1533. Fitzgibbon, R. H. (ed.). *The Constitutions of the Americas, as of January 1, 1948.* Chicago, 1948.
         Texts and explanatory notes.

1534. Gomez, R. A. *Government and Politics in Latin America.* Rev. ed., N.Y., 1963.

1535. Jorrín, M. *Governments of Latin America.* N.Y., 1953.

1536. MacDonald, A. F. *Latin American Politics and Government.* 2d ed., N.Y., 1954.

1537. Mecham, J. L. "Latin American Constitutions: Nominal and Real," *JP* 21 (1959) 258–275.

1538. Miranda Arenas, O. E. *El Jefe de Estado en las Constituciones Americanas*. Santiago, 1944.

1539. Muñoz, L. *Comentarios a las Constituciones Políticas de Iberoamérica*. 2 vols., Mexico, 1954.

1540. Needler, M. C. *Latin American Politics in Perspective*. Princeton, N.J., 1963.

1541. ———— (ed.). *Political Systems of Latin America*. Princeton, N.J., 1964.

1542. Pierson, W. W., and F. G. Gil. *Governments of Latin America*. N.Y., 1957.

1543. Rodríguez, J. I. *American Constitutions: A Compilation of the Political Constitutions of the Independent Nations of the New World*. 2 vols., Wash., 1945.

1544. Stokes, W. S. *Latin American Politics*. N.Y., 1959.

D. WORKS ON UNITED STATES FOREIGN RELATIONS

1. GENERAL HISTORIES

1545. Adams, R. G. *A History of the Foreign Policy of the United States*. N.Y., 1924.

1546. Bailey, T. A. *A Diplomatic History of the American People*. 7th ed., N.Y., 1964.

Stresses the role of public opinion in shaping the history of United States foreign relations.

1547. Bemis, S. F. *A Diplomatic History of the United States*. 5th ed., N.Y., 1965.

1548. ————. *A Short History of American Foreign Policy and Diplomacy*. N.Y., 1958.

1549. ————. *The United States as a World Power: A Diplomatic History, 1900–1955*. Rev. ed., N.Y., 1955.

1550. Blake, N. M., and O. T. Barck, Jr. *The United States in Its World Relations*. N.Y., 1960.

1551. Davids, J. *America and the World of Our Time: U.S. Diplomacy in the Twentieth Century*. N.Y., 1960.

1552. DeConde, A. *A History of American Foreign Policy*. N.Y., 1963.

1553. Divine, R. A. (ed.). *American Foreign Policy: A Documentary History*. N.Y., 1960.

1554. Dulles, F. R. *America's Rise to World Power, 1898–1954*. N.Y., 1954.

1555. Duroselle, J. B. *From Wilson to Roosevelt: Foreign Policy of the United States, 1913–1945*. Cambridge, Mass., 1963. French ed., Paris, 1960.

1556. Ellis, L. E. *A Short History of American Diplomacy*. N.Y., 1951. Adopts a topical approach.

1557. Ferrell, R. H. *American Diplomacy: A History*. N.Y., 1959.

1558. Fish, C. R. *American Diplomacy*. 4th ed., N.Y., 1923.

1559. García Mérou, M. *Historia de la Diplomacia Americana: Política Internacional de los Estados Unidos*. 2 vols., B.A., 1904.

1560. Latané, J. H. *A History of American Foreign Policy*. Rev. ed., Garden City, N.Y., 1934.

1561. Leopold, R. W. *The Growth of American Foreign Policy: A History*. N.Y., 1962.

Detailed chronological coverage begins with 1889.

1562. Perkins, D. *The Evolution of American Foreign Policy*. N.Y., 1948.

1563. Pratt, J. W. *A History of United States Foreign Policy*. 2d ed., N.Y., 1965.

1564. Sears, L. M. *A History of American Foreign Relations*. N.Y., 1936.

1565. Van Alstyne, R. W. *American Crisis Diplomacy: The Quest for Collective Security, 1918–1952*. Stanford, Calif., 1952.

1566. ————. *American Diplomacy in Action: A Series of Case Studies*. 2d ed., Stanford, Calif., 1947.

1567. Williams, W. A. (ed.). *The Shaping of American Diplomacy: Readings in American Foriegn Relations*. Chicago, 1956.

2. SPECIAL STUDIES AND INTERPRETATIONS

1568. Albion, R. G., and J. B. Pope. *Sea Lanes in Wartime: The American Experience, 1775–1942*. N.Y., 1942.

1569. Allen, H. C. *Great Britain and the United States: A History of Anglo-American Relations, 1783–1952*. N.Y., 1955.

1569a. Allix, A. *Les Fondements de la Politique Extérieure des Etats-Unis*. Paris, 1949.

1570.   Almond, G. A. *The American People and Foreign Policy.* N.Y., 1950.

       Analyzes attitudes toward foreign policy.

1570a. Anderson, G. L. *Issues and Conflicts: Studies in Twentieth Century American Diplomacy.* Lawrence, Kan., 1959.

       A series of essays by distinguished contributors.

1571.   Bailey, T. A. "America's Emergence as a World Power: The Myth and the Verity," *PHR* 30 (1961) 1–16.

1572.   ———. *The Man in the Street: The Impact of American Public Opinion on Foreign Policy.* N.Y., 1948.

1573.   Bartlett, R. J. *Power and Policy: Two Centuries of American Foreign Relations.* N.Y., 1963.

       A short interpretive work.

1574.   ———. *The Record of American Diplomacy: Documents and Readings in the History of American Foreign Relations.* 4th ed., N.Y., 1964.

       Intended for classroom use.

1574a. Beard, C. A. *The Idea of National Interest: An Analytical Study in American Foreign Policy.* N.Y., 1934.

       Pb. ed., Chicago, 1966.

1575.   Beloff, M. *Foreign Policy and the Democratic Process.* Baltimore, 1955.

1576.   Bemis, S. F., and R. F. Ferrell (eds.). *The American Secretaries of State and Their Diplomacy.* 13 vols., N.Y., 1927–1965.

       Chapters on each secretary of state by different contributors. Extended by book-length studies for those who have held office since 1929. The longer studies (Vols. XI–XIII) are under the editorship of Robert Ferrell.

1577.   Bigelow, J. *Breaches of Anglo-American Treaties.* N.Y., 1917.

1578.   Burns, E. M. *The American Idea of Mission: Concepts of National Purpose and Destiny.* New Brunswick, N.J., 1957.

1579.   Cole, T. *The Recognition Policy of the United States Since 1901.* Baton Rouge, La., 1928.

1580.   Curti, M. *American Philanthropy Abroad.* New Brunswick, N.J., 1963.

1581.   ———. *Peace or War: The American Struggle, 1636–1936.* N.Y., 1936.

1582.   ———, and K. Birr. *Prelude to Point Four: American Technical Missions Overseas, 1838–1938.* Madison, Wis., 1954.

1583.   Davis, F. *The Atlantic System: The Story of Anglo-American Control of the Seas.* N.Y., 1941.

1584.   Davis, G. T. *A Navy Second to None.* N.Y., 1940.

       A history of the modern American Navy.

1585.   DeConde, A. (ed.). *Isolation and Security.* Durham, N.C., 1957.

       A series of essays on recent United States foreign relations.

1586.   Dinagar, C. A. "Some Aspects of the Use of the Recognition of New Governments as an Instrument of United States Foreign Policy, 1900–1960," Columbia U. Diss., 1963.

1587.   Ellsworth, H. A. *One Hundred Eighty Landings of United States Marines, 1800–1934.* 2 vols., Wash., 1934.

1588.   Galpin, W. F. *Pioneering for Peace: A Study of American Peace Efforts to 1846.* Syracuse, N.Y., 1933.

1589.   Goebel, D. B. (ed.). *American Foreign Policy: A Documentary Survey, 1776–1960.* N.Y., 1961.

       Intended for classroom use.

1590.   Goebel, J., Jr. *The Recognition Policy of the United States.* N.Y., 1915.

1591.   Graber, D. A. *Crisis Diplomacy: A History of U.S. Intervention Policies and Practices.* Wash., 1959.

1592.   Graebner, N. A. (ed.). *An Uncertain Tradition: American Secretaries of State in the Twentieth Century.* N.Y., 1961.

       Essays on secretaries of state from Hay to Dulles.

1593.   ———. *Ideas and Diplomacy: Readings in the Intellectual Tradition of American Foreign Policy.* N.Y., 1964.

1594.   Graham, M. W. *American Diplomacy in the International Community.* Baltimore, 1946.

1595.   Haas, W. H. (ed.). *The American Empire: A Study of the Outlying Territories of the United States.* Chicago, 1940.

1596.   Hackworth, G. H. *Digest of International Law.* 8 vols., Wash., 1940–1944.

       Coverage from 1906 to date of publication. Supplements item 1614.

1597.   Halle, L. J. *Dream and Reality: Aspects of American Foreign Policy.* N.Y., 1959.

1598. Hill, C. E. *Leading American Treaties.* N.Y., 1922.

1599. Huntington, S. M. *The Soldier and the State: The Theory and Politics of Civil-Military Relations.* Cambridge, Mass., 1957.

1600. Hyde, C. C. *International Law, Chiefly as Interpreted and Applied by the United States.* 2 vols., Boston, 1922.

1601. Johnson, E. R., *et al. History of Domestic and Foreign Commerce of the United States.* 2 vols., Wash., 1915.

1602. Johnson, W. *1600 Pennsylvania Avenue: Presidents and People, 1929–1959.* Boston, 1960.

1603. Joseph, F. M. (ed.). *As Others See Us: The United States Through Foreign Eyes.* Princeton, N.J., 1959.

1604. Kennan, G. F. *American Diplomacy, 1900–1950.* Chicago, 1951.
Spirited "power realist" interpretation.

1605. ———. *Realities of American Foreign Policy.* Princeton, N.J., 1954.

1606. Kohn, H. *American Nationalism: An Interpretative Essay.* N.Y., 1957.

1607. Marshall, C. B. *The Limits of Foreign Policy.* N.Y., 1954.
Stresses restrictions on national freedom of action.

1608. Martin, C. E. *The Policy of the United States as Regards Intervention.* N.Y., 1921.

1609. May, E. R. (ed.). *The Ultimate Decision: The President as Commander in Chief.* N.Y., 1960.
Studies of wartime presidencies.

1610. Merk, F. *Manifest Destiny and Mission in American History: A Reinterpretation.* N.Y., 1963.
Emphasis on Mexico and the Caribbean area.

1611. Metcalf, C. H. *A History of the United States Marine Corps.* N.Y., 1939.

1612. Millis, W. *Arms and Men.* N.Y., 1956.
Historical interpretation of United States military policy.

1613. ———, *et al. Arms and the State: Civil-Military Elements in National Policy.* N.Y., 1958.

1614. Moore, J. B. *A Digest of International Law, as Embodied in Diplomatic Discussions, Treaties, and Other International Agreements, International Awards, the Decisions of Municipal Courts, and Writings of Jurists, and Especially in Documents, Published and Unpublished, Issued by Presidents and Secretaries of State of the United States, the Opinions of Attorneys-General, and the Decisions of Courts, Federal and State.* 8 vols., Wash., 1906.

1615. ———. *History and Digest of the International Arbitrations to Which the United States Has Been a Party, Together with Appendices Containing the Treaties Relating to Such Arbitrations, and Historical and Legal Notes.* 6 vols., Wash., 1898.

1616. ———. *The United States and International Arbitration.* Richmond, Va., 1896.

1617. Morgenthau, H. J. *In Defense of the National Interest.* N.Y., 1951.
Enphasizes importance of power as against legal and moral factors in conduct of international relations.

1618. Mowat, R. B. *The Diplomatic Relations of Great Britain and the United States.* N.Y., 1925.

1619. Offutt, M. *The Protection of Citizens Abroad by the Armed Forces of the United States.* Baltimore, 1928.

1620. Osgood, R. E. *Ideals and Self-Interest in America's Foreign Relations: The Great Transformation of the Twentieth Century.* Chicago, 1953.
A "power realist" interpretation.

1621. Patterson, R. S. (comp.). *The Secretaries of State: Portraits and Biographical Sketches.* Wash., 1956.

1622. Paullin, C. O. *Diplomatic Negotiations of American Naval Officers, 1778–1883.* Baltimore, 1912.

1623. Perkins, D. *America's Quest for Peace.* Bloomington, Ind., 1962.

1624. ———. *The American Approach to Foreign Policy.* Cambridge, Mass., 1952.
Critique of "power realism."

1625. Perkins, W. T. "American Policy in the Government of Its Dependent Areas: A Study of the Policy of the United States Toward the Inhabitants of Its Territories and Insular Possessions," Fletcher School of Law and Diplomacy Diss., 1949.

1626. Potter, D. M. *People of Plenty.* Chicago, 1954.
Stresses importance of affluence in shaping United States history.

1627. Pratt, J. W. *America's Colonial Experiment: How the U.S. Gained, Governed and in Part Gave Away a Colonial Empire.* N.Y., 1950.

1628. ———. "The Origin of 'Manifest Destiny,'" *AHR* 32 (1927) 795–798.

1629. Rappaport, A. (ed.). *Issues in American Diplomacy.* 2 vols., N.Y., 1965.
Reprints of articles on crucial topics.

1630. Roseboom, E. H. *A History of Presidential Elections.* N.Y., 1957.

1631. Schuyler, E. *American Diplomacy and the Furtherance of Commerce.* N.Y., 1895.

1632. Setser, V. G. *The Commercial Reciprocity Policy of the U.S.* Phil., 1937.

1633. Smith, D. (ed.). *Major Problems in American Diplomatic History: Documents and Readings.* N.Y., 1964.
Reprints of articles on important issues.

1634. Sprout, H., and M. Sprout. *The Rise of American Naval Power, 1776–1918.* 3d ed., Princeton, N.J., 1944.

1635. Tannenbaum, F. *The American Tradition in Foreign Policy.* Norman, Okla., 1955.
Criticizes "power realism" and calls for international federalism.

1636. Tate, M. *The Disarmament Illusion: The Movement for a Limitation of Armaments to 1907.* N.Y., 1942.
See also item 1703.

1637. Taussig, F. W. *Tariff History of the U.S.* 8th ed., N.Y., 1931.

1638. Thayer, C. W. *Diplomat.* N.Y., 1959.
Informal treatment of United States diplomatic functions.

1639. Thompson, K. W. *American Diplomacy and Emergent Patterns.* N.Y., 1962.

1640. ———. *Political Realism and the Crisis of World Politics: An American Approach to Foreign Policy.* Princeton, N.J., 1960.

1641. USCH. Committee on Foreign Affairs. *Expropriation of American-owned Property by Foreign Governments in the Twentieth Century: Report, Prepared by the Legislative Reference Service* (88th Cong., 1st Sess., Comm. Print). Wash., 1963.

1642. Vagts, A. *Defense and Diplomacy: The Soldier and the Conduct of Foreign Relations.* N.Y., 1956.
An extensive survey of the interaction between the military and the makers of foreign policy.

1643. Van Alstyne, R. W. *The Rising American Empire.* N.Y., 1960.

1644. Van Deusen, G. G., and R. W. Wade (eds.). *Foreign Policy and the American Spirit: Essays by Dexter Perkins.* Ithaca, N.Y., 1957.

1645. Van Hoogstrate, D. J. *American Foreign Policy, Realists and Idealists: A Catholic Interpretation.* St. Louis, Mo., 1960.

1646. Vevier, C. "American Continentalism: An Idea of Expansion, 1845–1910," *AHR* 65 (1960) 323–335.

1647. Weinberg, A. K. *Manifest Destiny: A Study of Nationalist Expansionism in American History.* Baltimore, 1935.

1648. Williams, W. A. *The Tragedy of American Diplomacy.* Rev. pb. ed. N.Y., 1962.
Stresses domestic preoccupation with commercial expansion overseas as a key factor in determining the course of United States policy.

1649. Wolfers, A., and L. W. Martin (eds.). *The Anglo-American Tradition in Foreign Affairs.* New Haven, Conn., 1956.

3. The Conduct of Foreign Relations

1650. American Assembly. *The Representation of the United States Abroad: Background Papers Prepared for the Use of Participants and the Final Report of the Ninth Assembly, Arden House, Harriman Campus of Columbia University, Harriman, New York, May 3–6, 1956.* N.Y., 1956.

1651. Barnes, W., and J. H. Morgan. *The Foreign Service of the United States: Origins, Development, and Functions.* Wash., 1961.

1652. Blix, H. *Treaty-Making Power.* N.Y., 1960.

1653. Bradshaw, M. E. "Congress and Foreign Policy Since 1900," *AAAPSS* 289 (1953) 40–48.

1654. Butler, C. H. *The Treaty-Making Power of the United States.* 2 vols., N.Y., 1902.

1655. Byrd, E. M., Jr. *Treaties and Executive Agreements in the United States.* The Hague, 1960.

1656. Cardozo, M. H. *Diplomats in International Cooperation: Stepchildren of the Foreign Service.* Ithaca, N.Y., 1962.

1657. Carroll, H. N. *The House of Representatives and Foreign Affairs.* Pittsburgh, 1958.

1658.   Cheever, D. S., and H. F. Haviland, Jr. *American Foreign Policy and the Separation of Powers.* Cambridge, Mass., 1952.

1659.   Childs, J. R. *American Foreign Service.* N.Y., 1948.
        Treats the organization and functions of the foreign service.

1660.   Cohen, B. C. *The Influence of Non-Governmental Groups on Foreign Policy-Making.* Boston, 1959.

1661.   Cohen, B. V. "The Evolving Role of Congress in Foreign Affairs," *PAPS* 92 (1948) 211–216.

1662.   Cooper, R. M. *American Consultation in World Affairs.* N.Y., 1934.
        Considers contacts with peace-keeping organizations.

1663.   Corwin, E. S. *The President, Office and Powers: 1787–1957.* 4th ed., N.Y., 1957.

1664.   ———. *The President's Control of Foreign Relations.* Princeton, N.J., 1917.

1665.   Crabb, C. V. *Bipartisan Foreign Policy: Myth or Reality?* Evanston, Ill., 1957.

1666.   Crandall, S. B. *Treaties: Their Making and Enforcement.* 2d ed., N.Y., 1916.

1667.   Dahl, R. A. *Congress and Foreign Policy.* New Haven, Conn., 1949.

1668.   Dangerfield, R. J. *In Defense of the Senate: A Study in Treaty Making.* Norman, Okla., 1933.

1669.   DeConde, A. *The American Secretary of State: An Interpretation.* N.Y., 1962.

1670.   Dennison, E. E. *The Senate Foreign Relations Committee.* London, 1942.
        See also item 1673.

1671.   Dickey, J. S. "Our Treaty Procedure Versus Our Foreign Policies," *FA* 25 (1947) 357–377.

1672.   Elder, R. E. *The Policy Machine: The Department of State and American Policy.* Syracuse, N.Y., 1960.

1673.   Farnsworth, D. N. *The Senate Committee on Foreign Relations.* Urbana, Ill., 1961.
        See also item 1670.

1674.   Fleming, D. F. *The Treaty Veto of the American Senate.* N.Y., 1930.

1675.   Griffin, A. P. C. *Ratification of Treaties: Methods and Procedure in Foreign Countries Relative to the Ratification of Treaties* (66th Cong., 1st Sess., S. Doc. 26). Wash., 1919.

1676.   Hayden, R. *The Senate and Treaties 1789–1817: The Development of the Treaty-Making Functions of the U.S. Senate During Their Formative Period.* N.Y., 1920.

1677.   Haynes, G. H. *The Senate of the U.S.: Its History and Practice.* 2 vols., Boston, 1938.

1678.   Hershey, A. S. *Diplomatic Agents and Immunities.* Wash., 1919.

1679.   Hickey, J. "The Role of Congress in Foreign Policy," *IEA* 14 (Spring, 1961) 67–89.

1680.   Hill, N. L. *Mr. Secretary of State.* N.Y., 1963.
        Discusses the role and functions of the secretary.

1681.   Holt, W. S. *Treaties Defeated by the Senate: A Study of the Struggle Between President and Senate over the Conduct of Foreign Relations.* Baltimore, 1933.

1682.   Hulen, B. D. *Inside the Department of State.* N.Y., 1939.

1683.   Hunt, G. *The Department of State of the United States: Its History and Functions.* New Haven, Conn., 1914.

1684.   Ilchman, W. F. *Professional Diplomacy in the United States, 1779–1939.* Chicago, 1961.

1685.   Jackson, H. M. (ed.). *The National Security Council.* N.Y., 1965.

1686.   ———. *The Secretary of State and the Ambassador.* N.Y., 1964.

1687.   Jewell, M. E. *Senatorial Politics and Foreign Policy.* Lexington, Ky., 1962.
        Covers period 1947–1960.

1688.   Jones, C. L. *The Consular Service of the United States, Its History and Activities.* Phil., 1906.

1689.   Lay, T. C. *The Foreign Service of the United States.* N.Y., 1928.

1690.   Liska, G. *The New Statecraft: Foreign Aid in American Foreign Policy.* Chicago, 1960.

1690a. MacMahon, A. W. *Administration in Foreign Affairs.* University, Ala., 1953.

1691.   McCamy, J. L. *Conduct of the New Diplomacy.* N.Y., 1964.

1692.   ———. *The Administration of American Foreign Affairs.* N.Y., 1960.

1693.   McClure, W. *International Executive Agreements.* N.Y., 1941.
        Considers the device frequently used as an alternative to a formal treaty.

1693a. McKenna, J. C. *Diplomatic Protest in Foreign Policy.* Chicago, 1962.

Examines some U.S. diplomatic protests on vital issues between 1900 and 1935.

1694. Plischke, E. *Summit Diplomacy: Personal Diplomacy of the President of the United States.* College Park, Md., 1958.

1695. Price, D. K. (ed.). *The Secretary of State.* Englewood Cliffs, N.J., 1960.

1696. Robinson, J. A. *Congress and Foreign Policy-Making: A Study in Legislative Influence and Initiative.* Homewood, Ill., 1962.

1697. Sapin, B. M., and R. C. Snyder. *The Role of the Military in American Foreign Policy.* N.Y., 1954.

1698. Schurz, W. L. *American Foreign Affairs: A Guide to International Affairs.* N.Y., 1959.

1699. Spaulding, E. W. *Ambassadors Ordinary and Extraordinary.* Wash., 1961.

1700. Steiner, Z. S. *The State Department and The Foreign Service: The Wriston Report —Four Years Later.* Princeton, N.J., 1958.

Considers reorganization of the State Department.

1701. Stuart, G. H. *American Diplomatic and Consular Practice.* 2d ed., N.Y., 1952.

1702. ———. *The Department of State: A History of Its Organization, Procedure and Personnel.* N.Y., 1949.

1703. Tate, M. *The United States and Armaments.* Cambridge, Mass., 1948.

See also item 1636.

1704. Warren, S. *The President as World Leader.* Phil., 1964.

1705. Westerfield, H. B. *Foreign Policy and Party Politics: Pearl Harbor to Korea.* New Haven, Conn., 1955.

1706. ———. *The Instruments of America's Foreign Policy.* N.Y., 1963.

1707. Wriston, H. M. *Executive Agents in American Foreign Relations.* Baltimore, 1929.

II–D–3 cross references: 2113a

4. DOCUMENTARY COLLECTIONS

1708. *American State Papers. Class I. Foreign Relations.* 6 vols., Wash., 1832–1859.

Assembles diplomatic correspondence, together with presidential messages, reports of the Secretary of State, and other relevant material.

1709. *Annals of Congress, 1789–1824.* 42 vols., Wash., 1834–1856.

Records of debates.

1710. Benton, T. H. *Abridgment of the Debates of Congress from 1789 to 1856.* 16 vols., N.Y., 1857–1861.

1711. ———. *Thirty Years' View: Or a History of the Working of the American Government, 1820–1850.* 2 vols., N.Y., 1854–1856.

1712. *Congressional Globe, 1833–1873.* 109 vols., Wash., 1834–1873.

Record of debates.

1713. *Congressional Record.* Wash., 1873–

Record of debates.

1714. Davenport, F. G. (ed.). *European Treaties Bearing on the History of the United States and Its Dependencies.* 4 vols., Wash., 1917–1937.

1715. *Documents on American Foreign Relations, 1938–* . N.Y., 1939– .

An annual volume of current documents.

1716. Donnan, E. *Documents Illustrative of the History of the Slave Trade to America.* 4 vols., Wash., 1930–1935.

1717. Flournoy, R. W., and M. O. Hudson (eds.). *A Collection of Nationality Laws of Various Countries, as Contained in Constitutions, Statutes and Treaties.* N.Y., 1929.

1718. LN. *Treaty Series.* 205 vols., London, 1920–1946.

1719. Malloy, W. M., et al. (eds.). *Treaties, Conventions, International Acts, Protocols, and Agreements Between the United States and Other Powers, 1776–1937.* 4 vols., Wash., 1910–1938.

1720. Miller, D. H. *Treaties and Other International Acts of the United States of America.* 8 vols., Wash., 1931–1948.

Covers treaties to 1863.

1721. PAU. Legal Division. *Inter-American Treaties and Conventions: Signatures, Ratifications, and Deposits, with Explanatory Notes.* 2d ed., Wash., 1957.

Status of inter-American treaties as of June, 1957.

1722. *Register of Debates in Congress (1824–1837).* 29 vols., Wash., 1825–1837.

1723. Richardson, J. D., *et al.* (comps.). *A Compilation of the Messages and Papers of the Presidents, with Additions . . . to 1922.* 20 vols., N.Y., n.d.

1724. Sparks, J. (ed.). *Diplomatic Correspondence of the United States of America.* 7 vols., Wash., 1834.

1725. *The U.S. in World Affairs, 1931– .* N.Y., 1932– .
   Annual policy review.

1725a. USCS. *Journal of the Executive Proceedings of the Senate of the United States of America.* 32 vols., Wash., 1828–1909.

1726. ———. *Treaties and Conventions Concluded Between the United States of America and Other Powers* (48th Cong., 2d Sess., S. Doc. 47). Wash., 1889.

1727. ———. *Treaty Reservations: A Compilation of Reservations Made to Treaties and Conventions by the Senate of the United States* (66th Cong., 1st Sess., S. Doc. 148). Wash., 1919.

1728. USDS. *American Foreign Policy: Current Documents.* Wash., 1956– .
   An annual cumulation of important state papers.

1729. ———. *Papers Relating to the Foreign Relations of the U.S., 1861– .* Wash., 1862– .
   Basic collection of diplomatic correspondence. Title varies. *General Index* is available for period 1861–1899 (Wash., 1902) and for 1900–1918 (Wash., 1941).

1730. ———. *U.S. Treaties and Other International Agreements, 1950– .* Wash., 1952– .

1731. WPA. *Historical Records Survey: Presidential Executive Orders.* 2 vols., N.Y., 1944.

II–D–4   cross references: 1733, 1860, 2102

E. UNITED STATES–LATIN AMERICAN RELATIONS: COMPREHENSIVE WORKS

1732. Bemis, S. F. *The Latin American Policy of the United States: An Historical Interpretation.* N.Y., 1943.
   Spanish ed., Mexico, 1944.

1733. Cárdenas y Echarte, R. de. *La Política de los Estados Unidos en el Continente Americano.* Havana, 1921.

1734. Gantenbein, J. W. (ed.). *The Evolution of our Latin-American Policy: A Documentary Record.* N.Y., 1950.

1735. Guerra y Sánchez, R. *La Expansión Territorial de los Estados Unidos a Expensas de España y de los Países Hispanoamericanos.* Havana, 1935.

1736. Guilaine, L. *L'Amérique Latine et l'Imperialisme Américain.* Paris, 1928.

1737. Humphreys, R. A. "Britain, the United States, and Latin America," *NC* 145 (1949) 44–50.
   Covers 1823–1948.

1738. Ibarguren, C. *De Monroe a la Buena Vecindad.* B.A., 1946.
   Critical of United States imperialism.

1739. Kimpen, E. *Die Ausbreitungspolitik der Vereinigten Staaten von Amerika.* Stuttgart, 1923.

1740. Latané, J. H. *The Diplomatic Relations of the United States and Spanish America.* Baltimore, 1899.

1741. ———. *The United States and Latin America.* N.Y., 1920.
   Surveys diplomatic relations since independence movements.

1742. Lieuwen, E. *United States Policy in Latin America: A Short History.* N.Y., 1965.
   Emphasis on the post–World War II period.

1743. Mecham, J. L. *A Survey of United States–Latin American Relations.* Boston, 1965.
   The most recent general survey. Includes country chapters as well as a chronological survey.

1744. Perkins, D. *The United States and Latin America.* Baton Rouge, La., 1961.
   An interpretive account by the historian of the Monroe Doctrine.

1745. Rippy, J. F. *Latin America in World Politics.* 3d ed., N.Y., 1938.

1746. Robertson, W. S. *Hispanic-American Relations with the United States.* N.Y., 1923.

1747. Stuart, G. H. *Latin America and the United States.* 5th ed., N.Y., 1955.

1748. USDS. *Our Southern Partners: The Story of Our Latin American Relations.* Wash., 1954.
   Broad official interpretation.

1749. Whitaker, A. P. "From Dollar Diplomacy

to the Good Neighbor Policy," *IEA* 4 (1951) 12–19.
Covers 1903–1950.

1750. Williamson, R. de V. *Culture and Policy: The United States and the Hispanic World*. Knoxville, Tenn., 1949.

F. UNITED STATES–LATIN AMERICAN RELATIONS: SPECIAL STUDIES

1751. Caruso, J. A. "The Pan American Railway," *HAHR* 31 (1951), 608–639.

1752. Galíndez, J. de. "Vaivenes de la Política Hispano-Americano de los Estados Unidos," *CA* 15, no. 3 (1956) 7–16.

1753. Geisler, R. A. "Measures for Military Collaboration Between the U.S. and Latin America: The Record, 1826–1951," Columbia U. Diss., 1955.

1754. Grigulevich, I. R. "Ideologicheskaia Expansiia SSHA v Latinskoi Amerike," *NNI* (1965) 60–68.
"Ideological Expansion of the U.S. in Latin America."

1755. Harter, D. "Contributions of U.S. Diplomacy in Latin America to Hemispheric Solidarity," U. of Iowa Diss., 1942.

1756. Holt, W. S. "The United States and the Defense of the Western Hemisphere, 1815–1940," *PHR* 10 (1941) 29–38.

1757. Inman, S. G. *Latin America: Its Place in World Life*. Rev. ed., N.Y., 1942.

1758. Ireland, G. *Boundaries, Possessions, and Conflicts in Central and North America and the Caribbean*. Cambridge, Mass., 1941.
Treatise on boundary disputes and their adjustments.

1759. ———. *Boundaries, Possessions and Conflicts in South America*. Cambridge, Mass., 1938.
Covers 26 incidents.

1760. Newton, W. P. "Aviation in the Relations of the United States and Latin America, 1916–1929," U. of Alabama Diss., 1964.

1761. Pantoja, D. de. *Los Estados Unidos y la América del Sur: Los Yankees Pintados por sí Mismos*. B.A., 1893.
Pseudonym for V. G. Quesada.

1762. Redfield, A. H. "Our Petroleum Diplomacy in Latin America," American U. Diss., 1942.

1763. Turlington, E. W. "The Control of Foreign Relations Under the Constitutions of the American Republics," *AIDCICM* 4 (1954) 193–247.

1764. Whitaker, A. P. "The United States in Latin America Since 1865," *CH* 28 (1955) 154–159.

1765. Wright, T. P. "Free Elections in the Latin American Policy of the United States," *PSQ* 74 (1959) 89–112.
Covers 1900–1933.

II–F cross references: 2894, 4535

G. GENERAL WORKS ON THE MONROE DOCTRINE

1766. Alvarado Garaicoa, T. *El Imperialismo y la Democracia a Través de la Doctrina Monroe*. Guayaquil, 1946.

1767. Alvarez, A. *The Monroe Doctrine: Its Importance in the International Life of the States of the New World*. N.Y., 1924.

1768. Barcía Trelles, C. *Doctrina de Monroe y Cooperación Internacional*. Madrid, 1931.

1769. Bewes, W. A. "The Monroe Doctrine and Entangling Alliances," *GST* 13 (1928) 1–29.

1770. Bolkhovitinov, N. N. *Doktrina Monro: Proischozhdenie i Kharakter*. Moscow, 1959.
The Monroe Doctrine: Its Origin and Character. Contends that the doctrine has always been a guise for U.S. imperialism.

1770a. "The Centenary of the Monroe Doctrine: Addresses Delivered at the Sessions Commemorative of the Centenary of the Monroe Doctrine, Philadelphia, Pa., Nov. 30th and Dec. 1st, 1923," *AAAPSS* suppl. (1924).

1771. Cleland, R. G. *One Hundred Years of the Monroe Doctrine*. Los Angeles, 1923.

1772. Correa Villa, E. "Doctrina de Monroe," *ED* (1940) 333–348.

1773. Delle Piane, A. L. *Doctrina de Monroe*. Montevideo, 1930.

1774. Dmytryshyn, B., and J. L. Gilmore. "The Monroe Doctrine: A Soviet View," *BISUSSR* 11 (1964) 3–14.

1775. Donovan, F. *Mr. Monroe's Message: The Story of the Monroe Doctrine*. N.Y., 1963.

1776. Dunn, L. C. "The United States Navy and 104 Years of the Monroe Doctrine," *USNIP* 54 (1928) 1067–1079.

1777. Fabela, I. *Las Doctrinas de Monroe y Drago*. Mexico, 1957.
Emphasis is on the Monroe Doctrine rather than on the Drago Doctrine.

1778. Gómez Robledo, A. *Epopeya del Monroismo*. Mexico, 1940.

1779.ʹ Hart, A. B. *Monroe Doctrine: An Interpretation*. Boston, 1916.

1780. Henderson, D. C., Jr. "A Comparative Study of the Application of the Monroe Doctrine in Two Selected Instances," Michigan State U. Diss., 1964.
Compares the Spanish interference in Chile (1863–1866) and the French intervention in Mexico (1862–1867).

1781. Izaga, L. *La Doctrina de Monroe: Su Origen y Principales Faces de su Evolución*. Madrid, 1929.

1782. Jobim, D. *O Cicla da Doutrina de Monroe*. Rio, 1955.

1783.ʹ Kohler, C. (comp.). *The Monroe Doctrine: A Complete History*. Rev. ed., N.Y., 1922.

1784. Kraus, H. "Die Monroe-Doktrin," in *Ihren Beziehungen zur Amerikanischen Diplomatie und zum Völkerrecht*. Berlin, 1913.

1785.ʹ Laasch, M. H. A. "Implementation of the Monroe Doctrine," Princeton U. Diss., 1943.

1786. Lodge, H. C. *One Hundred Years of the Monroe Doctrine* (68th Cong., 1st Sess., S. Doc. 8). Wash., 1923.

1787. Logan, J. A., Jr. *No Transfer: An American Security Principle*. New Haven, Conn., 1961.
A detailed study of the no-transfer aspect of the Monroe Doctrine.

1788.ʹ Manning, C. A. "The Meaning of the Monroe Doctrine," *UQ* 18 (1962) 246–254.

1789. Marchiori, C. *Gli Stati Uniti dall' Isolamento all' Intervento Nella Guerra Mondiale*. Pavia, 1932.

1790. Nerval, G. *Autopsy of the Monroe Doctrine*. N.Y., 1934.
Pseudonym of Raúl Díez de Medina.

1791. Nieto Navia, R. *La Doctrina de Monroe: Presencia Histórica*. Bogotá, 1962.

1792. Peña, D. de la. *La Doctrina de Monroe*. Bogotá, 1949.

1793.ʹ Pena, H. V. de. "Latin America and the Monroe Doctrine," American U. Diss., 1924.

1794.ʹ Perkins, D. *A History of the Monroe Doctrine*. New ed., Boston, 1955.
Originally entitled *Hands Off*.

1795. Quesada, E. *La Doctrina Monroe: Su Evolución Histórica*. B.A., 1920.

1796.ʹ Reddaway, W. F. *The Monroe Doctrine*. 3d ed., N.Y., 1924.

1797. Reynolds, T. H. *Economic Aspects of the Monroe Doctrine*. Nashville, Tenn., 1938.

1798. Roa, J. *Los Estados Unidos y Europa en Hispano América: Interpretación Política y Económica de la Doctrina Monroe, 1823–1933*. Havana, 1935.

1799. Robertson, W. S. "Hispanic American Appreciations of the Monroe Doctrine," *HAHR* 3 (1920) 1–16.

1800.ʹ Scudder, E. S. *The Monroe Doctrine and World Peace*. London, 1939.

1801. Sociedade Brasileira de Direito Internacional. *The Monroe Doctrine Centenary: Addresses Delivered at the Brazilian Society of International Law's Solemn Session, on December 2, 1923, in Commemoration of the First Centenary of President James Monroe's Declaration of Principles*. Rio, 1924.

1802. Thomas, D. Y. *One Hundred Years of the Monroe Doctrine, 1823–1923*. N.Y., 1923.

1803. Whitridge, A. "The Monroe Doctrine," *HT* 6 (1956) 376–386.

1804.ʹ Wilbur, W. A. (ed.). *The Monroe Doctrine*. Boston, 1965.
Documentary extracts and interpretations.

II–G cross references:

a) For origins of the Monroe Doctrine, see items 1989–2053.

b) For European violations of the Monroe Doctrine during the nineteenth century, see items 2150–2348.

c) For the status of the Monroe Doctrine during the imperialist era, see items 2947a–2983.

d) For the Monroe Doctrine and World War I, see items 3113–3127.

e) For the status of the Monroe Doctrine from 1921 to 1938, see items 3243–3260.

f) For the Monroe Doctrine and World War II, see items 3547–3555.

g) For the relationship of the Monroe Doctrine to the Inter-American system, see items 4507–4519.

h) See also items 2060a, 2063, 2066, 2068, 2069, 2073, 2077, 2081, 2086, 2090, 2093, 2100, 2103, 2108, 2116, 2117, 2118, 2121, 2129, 2130, 2132, 2137, 2139, 2140, 3872.

Chapter III   The United States and the Period of
Latin American Independence

A. GENERAL WORKS

1805. Abbey, K. T. "La Influencia del Movimiento de Independencia Norteamericana Sobre la Política Colonial Española," *SCIHA* 2 (1938) 7–17.

1806. Academia Nacional de la Historia. Caracas. *El Movimiento Emancipador de Hispanoamérica: Actas y Ponencias.* 3 vols., Caracas, 1961.

1807. Adams, C. F. (ed.). *The Memoirs of John Quincy Adams.* 12 vols., Phil., 1874–1877.

1808. Adams, H. *History of the United States of America During the Administrations of Jefferson and Madison.* 9 vols., N.Y., 1889–1909.

1808a. Adams, J. Q. *Writings.* 7 vols., N.Y., 1913–1917.
    Edited by W. C. Ford.

1809. Aguirre Elorriaga, M. *El Abate de Pradt en la Emancipación Hispanoamericana, 1800–1830.* 2d ed., B.A., 1946.

1809a. Al'perovich, M. S. "Ob Osvoboditel'noi Voine Ispanskikh Kolonii v Amerike (1810–1826)," *VI*, no. 11 (November, 1956) 52–71.
    "Regarding the Liberation War of the Spanish Colonies in America (1810–1826)."

1810. Altamira y Crevea, R. *Resumen Histórico de la Independencia de América Española.* B.A., 1910.

1811. Amunátegui Solar, D. *La Emancipación de Hispanoamérica.* Santiago, 1936.

1812. Arnade, C. W., *et al.*, "Causes of Spanish American Independence," *JIAS* 2 (1960) 125–144.

1813. Auchmuty, J. J. *The United States Government and Latin American Independence, 1810–1830.* London, 1937.

1814. Beals, C. *Eagles of the Andes: South American Struggles for Independence.* Phil., 1963.

1815. Bemis, S. F. *John Quincy Adams.* 2 vols., N.Y., 1949–1956.

1816. Bernstein, H. "Las Primeras Relaciones Entre New England y el Mundo Hispánico, 1700–1815," *RHM* 5 (1938)1–17.

1817. *Biblioteca Ayacucho.* 63 vols., Madrid, n.d.
    Basic documentary collection.

1818. Bierck, H. A., Jr. "Una Vista a Estados Unidos Proyectada por Simón Bolívar en 1815," *BANHC* 45 (1962) 105–113.

1819. Bornholdt, L. A. "Baltimore as a Port of Propaganda for South American Independence," Yale U. Diss., 1945.

1820. Bowers, C. G. "Thomas Jefferson and South America," *BPAU* 77 (1943) 183–191.

1821. Brackenridge, H. M. *South America: A Letter on the Present State of that Country, to James Monroe, President of the United States.* Wash., 1817.

1822. ———. *Voyage to South America Performed by Order of the American Government in the Years 1817 and 1818.* 2 vols., Baltimore, 1819.

1823. Brant, I. *James Madison.* 6 vols., Indianapolis, 1941–1961.

1824. Brown, V. L. "Contraband Trade: A Factor in the Decline of Spain's Empire in America," *HAHR* 8 (1928) 178–189.

1825. Bulnes, G. *Nacimiento de las Repúblicas Americanas.* 2 vols., B.A., 1927.

1826. Busaniche, J. L. *Bolívar Visto por sus Contemporáneos.* Mexico, 1960.

1827. Calvo, C. *Anales Históricos de la Revolución de la América Latina.* 5 vols., Paris, 1864–1867.

1828. Chandler, C. L. *Inter-American Acquaintances.* 2d ed., Sewanee, Tenn., 1915.

1829. ———. "United States Commerce with Latin America at the Promulgation of the Monroe Doctrine," *QJE* 38 (1923) 466–487.

Provides statistical data prior to 1823.

1830. Cuervo Márquez, L. *Independencia de las Colonias Hispano-Americanas: Participación de la Gran Bretaña y de los Estados Unidos: Legión Británica.* 2 vols., Bogotá, 1938.

1831. Dangerfield, G. *The Era of Good Feelings.* N.Y., 1952.

General study of Monroe era.

1832. Delgado, J. *La Independencia Hispanoamericana.* Madrid, 1960.

1833. Donoso, R. "Antecedentes de la Emancipación Hispano-Americana," *CA* (January, 1961) 179–218.

1834. Encina, F. A. *El Imperio Hispano Hacia 1810 y la Génesis de su Emancipación.* Santiago, 1957.

1835. Fernández Almagro, M. *La Emancipación de América y su Reflejo en la Conciencia Española.* 2d ed., Madrid, 1957.

1836. Fiallos Gil, M. "Influencia de la Revolución de los Estados Unidos de Norteamérica Sobre las Ideas Políticas de Hispanoamérica," *CU* 18 (1961) 3–11.

1837. Ford, P. L. (ed.). *The Writings of Thomas Jefferson.* 10 vols., N.Y., 1895–1899.

1838. Gandía, E. de. *Conspiraciones y Revoluciones de la Independencia Americana: Movimientos Precursores.* B.A., 1960.

1839. ———. *La Independencia Americana.* B.A., 1961.

1839a. ———. "Política de los EE. UU. Durante la Guerra de Independencia Iberoamericana," *ND* 35, no. 4 (1955) 14–18.

1840. García Samudio, N. *La Independencia de Hispanoamérica.* Mexico, 1945.

Emphasizes the role of foreign powers in the independence movement.

1840a. Gilman, D. C. *James Monroe.* Rev. ed., Boston, 1898.

1841. Graham, G. S., and R. A. Humphreys. *The Navy and South America, 1807–1823: Correspondence of the Commanders-in-Chief on the South American Station.* London, 1962.

1842. Griffin, C. C. "Economic and Social Aspects of the Era of Spanish-American Independence," *HAHR* 29 (1949) 170–187.

1843. ———. "La Opinión Pública Norteamericana y la Independencia de Hispanoamérica, 1810–1822," *BANHC* 24 (1941) 7–29.

1844. ———. *Los Temas Sociales y Económicos en la Epoca de la Independencia.* Caracas, 1962.

1845. ———. "Privateering from Baltimore During the Spanish-American Wars of Independence," *MHM* 25 (1940) 1–25.

1846. ———. *The United States and the Disruption of the Spanish Empire, 1810–1822.* N.Y., 1937.

Stresses U.S. relations with Spain during the period of L.A. independence.

1847. Hall, B. *Extracts from a Journal Written on the Coasts of Chile, Peru, and Mexico in the Years 1820, 1821, 1822.* 2 vols., Edinburgh, 1824.

1847a. Hamilton, S. M. (ed.). *The Writings of James Monroe.* 7 vols., N.Y., 1898–1903.

1848. Hasbrouck, A. *Foreign Legionaries in the Liberation of Spanish South America.* N.Y., 1928.

1849. Hudson, J. E. "The United States and Latin American Independence, 1776–1812," Tulane U. Diss., 1965.

1850. Humphreys, R. A. (ed.). *British Consular Reports on the Trade and Politics of Latin America, 1824–1826.* London, 1940.

1851. ———. "Economic Aspects of the Fall of the Spanish American Empire," *RHM* 30 (1950) 450–456.

1852. ———. *La Marina Real Británica y la Liberación de Sudamérica.* Caracas, 1962.

1853. ———. "The Fall of the Spanish American Empire," *HI*, n.s., 37 (1952) 213–227.

1854. ———, and J. Lynch. *The Origins of the Latin American Revolutions.* N.Y., 1966.

Selected readings.

1855. Hunt, G. (ed.). *The Writings of James Madison.* 8 vols., N.Y., 1908.

1856. Jefferson, T. *The Writings of Thomas Jefferson.* 20 vols., Wash., 1905.

1857. Kaufmann, W. W. *British Policy and the Independence of Latin America, 1804–1828.* New Haven, Conn., 1951.

1857a. LaFeber, W. (ed.). *John Quincy Adams and American Continental Empire: Letters, Papers, and Speeches.* Chicago, 1965.

A convenient paperback collection.

1858.   Lansing, M. *Liberators and Heroes of South America*. Boston, 1940.

1858a. Lavrov, N. M., *et al.* (eds.). *Voina za Nezavisimost' v Latinskoi Amerike (1810–1826)*. Moscow, 1964.
        The Wars of Independence in Latin America (1810–1826).

1859.   Levene, R. *El Mundo de las Ideas y la Revolución Hispanoamericana de 1810*. Santiago, 1956.

1860.   Lewin, B. *Los Movimientos de Emancipación en Hispanoamérica y la Independencia de Estados Unidos*. B.A., 1952.

1861.   Malagón, J. (ed.). *Las Actas de Independencia de América*. Wash., 1954.
        The texts of the declarations of independence.

1862.   Manning, W. R. (ed.). *Diplomatic Correspondence of the United States Concerning the Independence of the Latin-American Nations*. 3 vols., N.Y., 1925.
        Documents arranged chronologically within each country.

1863.   McNally, B. C. "Coverage and Attitudes of the United States Press Relative to the Independence Movements in the Spanish Americas, 1810–1825," St. Louis U. Diss., 1949.

1863a. Mikhailov, S. S., *et al.* (eds.). *Osvoboditel'noe Dvizhenie v Latinskoi Amerike*. Moscow, 1964.
        The Liberation Movement in Latin America.

1864.   Mitre, B. *Historia de San Martín y de la Emancipación Sudamericana*. 2d ed. rev., 4 vols., B.A., 1890.
        Condensed translation by W. Pilling, London, 1893.

1865.   Moses, B. *South America on the Eve of Emancipation*. N.Y., 1908.

1866.   ———. *Spain's Declining Power in South America, 1730–1806*. Berkeley, Calif., 1919.

1867.   ———. *The Intellectual Background of the Revolution in South America, 1810–1824*. N.Y., 1926.

1867a. Nevins, A. (ed.). *The Diary of John Quincy Adams, 1794–1845: American Political, Social and Intellectual Life*. N.Y., 1928.
        Abridged.

1868.   Nichols, R. F. "Trade Relations and the Establishment of the United States Consulates in Spanish America, 1779–1809," *HAHR* 13 (1933) 289–313.

1869.   Pine, J. C. "The Role of United States Special Agents in the Development of a Spanish American Policy, 1810–1822," U. of Colorado Diss., 1955.

1870.   Poinsett, J. R. *Exposición de la Conducta Política de los Estados Unidos, para con las Nuevas Repúblicas de América*. Mexico, 1827.

1871.   Potter, K. "The Hispanic-American Policy of John Quincy Adams, 1817–1825," U. of California Diss., 1934.

1871a. Rasmussen, W. D. "Diplomats and Plant Collectors: The South American Commission, 1817–1818," *AHI* 29 (1955) 22–31.

1872.   Reeves, J. S. *The Napoleonic Exiles in America, a Study in American Diplomatic History, 1815–1819*. Baltimore, 1905.

1872.   Renaut, F. P. "La Politique des Etats-Unis dans l'Amérique du Nord Espagnole sous le Règne de Joseph Bonaparte, 1808–1814," *RSP* 39 (1918) 76–93.

1873a. Rippy, J. F. *Rivalry of the United States and Great Britain over Latin America, 1808–1830*. Baltimore, 1929.

1874.   Robertson, W. S. "The Beginnings of Spanish-American Diplomacy," in *Essays in American History Dedicated to Frederick Jackson Turner* (pp. 231–267). N.Y., 1910.

1875.   ———. *France and Latin American Independence*. Baltimore, 1939.

1876.   ———. *Rise of the Spanish-American Republics as Told in the Lives of Their Liberators*. N.Y., 1918.
        Pb. ed. N.Y., 1961.

1876a. ———. "Russia and the Emancipation of Spanish America, 1816–1826," *HAHR* 21 (1941) 196–221.

1877.   Rodríguez Beteta, V. *Ideologías de la Independencia*. Paris, 1926.
        Deals with Central America.

1878.   Romero, M. "The United States and the Liberation of the Spanish-American Colonies," *NAR* 165 (1897) 70–86.

1878a. Shur, L. A. *Rossiia i Latinskaia Amerika: Ocherki Politicheskikh, Ekonomicheskikh i Kul'turnykh Otnoshenii*. Moscow, 1964.
        Russia and Latin America: Essays in Their Political, Economic and Cultural Relations.

1878b. Slezkin, L. I. *Rossiia i Voina za Neza-visimost' v Ispanskoi Amerike.* Moscow, 1964.
   Russia and the War of Independence in Spanish America.

1879. Solnick, B. B. "American Opinion Concerning the Spanish American Wars of Independence: 1808–1824," New York U. Diss., 1960.

1880. *Spanish America and the United States, or Views on the Actual Commerce of the United States with the Spanish Colonies.* Phil., 1818.
   Anonymous account by a Philadelphia merchant.

1881. Stewart, W. "The South American Commission, 1817–1818," *HAHR* 9 (1929) 31–59.

1882. *Strictures on a Voyage to South America as Indited by the "Secretary to the (Late) Mission" to the La Plata.* Baltimore, 1820.
   Anonymous attack on H. M. Brackenridge, secretary of a mission to South America, 1817–1818.

1883. Tanner, E. C. "South American Ports in the Foreign Commerce of Providence [R.I.]: 1800–1830," *RIH* 16 (1957) 65–78.

1884. Torrente, M. *Historia de la Revolución Hispano-Americana.* 3 vols., Madrid, 1830.
   Reflects the Spanish point of view.

1885. Torre Villar, E. de la. "Dos Proyectos para la Independencia de Hispanoamérica: James Workman y Aaron Burr," *RHA* 49 (1960) 1–83.

1886. Urrutia, F. J. *Páginas de Historia Diplomática: Los Estados Unidos de América y las Repúblicas Hispanoamericanas de 1810 á 1830.* Bogotá, 1917.

1887. USCH. *Message from the President . . . November 17, 1818* (15th Cong., 2d Sess., H. Doc. 2). Wash., 1818.
   Reports of C. A. Rodney and J. Graham on their mission to South America, 1817–1818.

1888. Webster, C. (ed.). *Britain and the Independence of Latin America, 1812–1830: Select Documents from the Foreign Office Archives.* 2 vols., London, 1938.
   Spanish ed., 2 vols., B.A., 1944.

1889. Whitaker, A. P. "El Concepto de la América Latina en la Mentalidad Norteamericana, 1815–1823," *RUCP* 9 (1941) 296–308.

1890. ———. "La Marina de Guerra Norteamericana y las Guerras de Independencia Hispano-americanas, 1815–1823," *RUCP* 10 (1942) 39–48.
   U.S. naval policy regarding independence.

1891. ———. *The United States and the Independence of Latin America, 1800–1830.* Baltimore, 1941.
   Pb. ed., N.Y., 1964.

1892. Wilgus, A. C. "Some Activities of United States Citizens in the South American Wars of Independence, 1808–1824," *LHQ* 14 (1931) 182–203.

1893. ———. "Some Notes on Spanish American Patriot Activity Along the Atlantic Seaboard, 1816–1822," *NCHR* 4 (1927) 172–181.

1894. ———. "Spanish American Patriot Activity Along the Gulf Coast of the United States, 1811–1822," *LHQ* 8 (1925) 193–215.

1895. Yepes, J. M. "Influencias Internacionales en la Emancipación Hispanoamericana," *U* (1960) 33–50.

1896. Zimmerman, A. F. "Spain and Its Colonies, 1808–1820," *HAHR* 11 (1931) 439–463.

III–A cross references:

a) For works treating the influence of the United States in independence movements of particular countries, see the country chapters (XIII–XXIV)

b) See also items 1622, 1993, 2009, 2539, 7439, 7456, 8831, 9349

B. ACQUISITION OF EAST AND WEST FLORIDA

1897. Arthur, S. C. *The Story of the West Florida Rebellion.* St. Francisville, La., 1935.

1898. Bolkhovitinov, N. N. "Prisoedinenie Floridy Soedinennymi Shtatami," *NNI* (1959) 110–119.
   "The Annexation of Florida by the United States."

1899. Brevard, C. M. *A History of Florida from*

the Treaty of 1763 to Our Own Times. Deland, Fla., 1924.

1900. Burns, F. P. "West Florida and the Louisiana Purchase: An Examination into the Question of Whether It Was Included in the Territory Ceded by the Treaty of 1803," *LHQ* 15 (1932) 391–416.

1901. Chatelain, V. E. *The Defenses of Spanish Florida, 1565–1763.* Wash., 1941.

1902. Cox, I. J. "General Wilkinson and his Later Intrigues with the Spaniards," *AHR* 19 (1914) 794–812.

1903. ———. "Hispanic American Phases of the Burr 'Conspiracy,'" *HAHR* 12 (1932) 145–175.

1904. ———. "The American Intervention in West Florida," *AHR* 27 (1912) 290–311.

1905. ———. "The Border Missions of General George Mathews," *MVHR* 12 (1925) 309–333.
   Mathews captured East Florida from the Spanish but the action was repudiated by President Madison.

1906. ———. *The West Florida Controversy, 1798–1813: A Study in American Diplomacy.* Baltimore, 1918.

1907. Davis, T. F. "Elotchaway, East Florida, 1814," *FHQ* 8 (1930) 143–155.
   An account of the Mathews expedition.

1908. ———. *MacGregor's Invasion of Florida, 1817: Together with an Account of His Successors, Irwin, Hubbard and Aury on Amelia Island, East Florida.* Jacksonville, Fla., 1928.
   Concerns the filibustering expedition which captured Fernandina.

1909. ———. "United States Troops in Spanish East Florida, 1812–1813," *FHQ* 9 (1930) 3–23, 96–116, 135–155, 259–278.

1910. Favrot, H. L. "The West Florida Revolution," *LHSP* 1 (1895–1896).
   Deals with the Baton Rouge revolution of 1810.

1911. Faye, S. "British and Spanish Fortifications of Pensacola, 1781–1821," *FHQ* 20 (1942) 277–292.

1912. Fuller, H. B. *The Purchase of Florida: Its History and Diplomacy.* Cleveland, 1906.

1913. Hyde de Neuville, J. G. *Mémoires et Souvenirs.* 3 vols., Paris, 1890–1892.
   Abridged English ed. (2 vols.), London, 1913.

1914. James, M. *Andrew Jackson, the Border Captain.* Indianapolis, Ind., 1933.

1915. Kaplan, L. S. "Jefferson, the Napoleonic Wars and the Balance of Power," *WMQ* 3d ser., 14 (1957) 196–217.
   Jefferson's attempt to obtain the Floridas.

1916. Kendall, J. S. (ed.). "Documents Concerning the Florida Revolution, 1810," *LHQ* 17 (1934) 80–95, 306–314, 474–501.

1917. Kinnaird, L. (ed.). *Spain in the Mississippi Valley, 1765–1794: Translations of Materials from the Spanish Archives in the Bancroft Library.* 3 vols., Wash., 1946–1949.

1918. Latour, A. L. *Historical Memoir of the War in West Florida and Louisiana in 1814–15.* 2 vols., Phil., 1816.

1919. Leonhard, J. W. "An Original Letter on the West Florida Revolution of 1810," *LHQ* 18 (1935) 354–362.

1920. McQueen, R. A. "Andrew Jackson and the Acquisition of the Floridas," U. of Pittsburgh Diss., 1942.

1921. *Observations on the Conduct of Our Executive Toward Spain.* N.p., 1812.
   Written anonymously by Luis de Onís.

1922. Ogg, F. A., and D. Rowland. "The American Intervention in West Florida," *MVHRP* 4 (1912) 47–58.
   Justifies American intervention of 1810.

1923. Patrick, R. W. *Florida Fiasco: Rampant Rebels on the Georgia-Florida Border, 1810–1815.* Athens, Ga., 1954.

1924. Phinney, A. H. "First Spanish-American War," *FHQ* 4 (1926) 114–129.
   Treats the attempted seizure of St. Augustine by Americans in 1812.

1925. Podgett, J. A. "Constitution of the West Florida Republic," *LHQ* 20 (1937) 590–605.

1926. Pratt, J. W. *Expansionists of 1812.* N.Y., 1925.

1927. Rowland, D. (ed.). *Official Letter Books of W. C. C. Claiborne, 1801–1816.* 6 vols., Jackson, Miss., 1917.
   Deals with West Florida.

1928. *Secret Statutes of the United States: A Memorandum, by David Hunter Miller, Special Assistant in the Dept. of State.* Wash., 1918.
   Congressional discussions of 1811–1813.

1929. Serrano y Sanz, M. *Documentos Históricos de la Florida y la Luisiana.* Madrid, 1912.

1930. Stenberg, R. R. "Jackson's 'Rhea Letter' Hoax," *JSH* 2 (1936) 480–496.

Treats the letter supposedly received by Andrew Jackson from President Monroe (delivered through Congressman Rhea) authorizing the capture of all of East Florida.

1931. ———. "The Boundaries of the Louisiana Purchase," *HAHR* 14 (1934) 32–64.

1932. Tanner, H. H. *Zespedes in East Florida, 1784–1790.* Coral Gables, Fla., 1963.

1933. Vaughan, B. *Remarks on a Dangerous Mistake as to the Eastern Boundary of Louisiana.* Boston, 1814.

1934. Vignoles, C. B. *The History of the Floridas, 1497–1821.* Brooklyn, 1824.

1935. Villa-Urrutia, W. R. de. *Fernán-Núñez, el Embajador.* Madrid, 1931.

Discusses José García de León y Pizarro, Spanish minister.

1936. Warren, H. G. "Pensacola and the Filibusters, 1816–1817," *LHQ* 21 (1938) 806–822.

1937. "West Florida and Its Attempt on Mobile, 1810–1811," *AHR* 2 (1897) 699–705.

Five letters.

1938. Whitaker, A. P. (ed.). *Documents Relating to the Commercial Policy of Spain in the Floridas with Incidental Reference to Louisiana.* Deland, Fla., 1931.

Covers 1778–1808.

1939. ———. *The Mississippi Question, 1795–1803.* N.Y., 1934.

1940. Wyllys, R. K. "The East Florida Revolution of 1812–1814," *HAHR* 9 (1929) 415–445.

1941. Young, H. "A Topographical Memoir on East and West Florida with Itineraries of General Jackson's Army, 1818," *FHQ* 13 (1935) 129–164.

III–B cross references: 1823, 1853, 2062

C. ADAMS–ONÍS (TRANSCONTINENTAL) TREATY

1942. Bécker, J. "La Cesión de las Floridas," *EM* 240 (1908) 41–70.

1943. Brooks, P. C. *Diplomacy and the Borderlands: The Adams–Onís Treaty of 1819.* Berkeley, Calif., 1939.

1944. ———. "Pichardo's Treatise and the Adams–Onís Treaty," *HAHR* 15 (1935) 94–99.

1945. ———. "The Pacific Coast's First International Boundary Delineation, 1816–1819," *PHR* 3 (1934) 62–79.

1946. Callava, J. *Manifiesto Sobre las Tropelías y Bejaciones que Cometió el Gobernador Americano de Panzacola* [sic] ... *Contra* ... *Nombrado Papa la Entrega de Florida Occidental a los Estados Unidos.* Havana, 1821.

1947. Catterall, R. C. H. "A French Diplomat and the Treaty with Spain, 1819," *AHR* 11 (1906) 495–496.

The diplomat was G. Hyde de Neuville.

1948. Clark, B. C. *John Quincy Adams, "Old Man Eloquent."* Boston, 1932.

1949. Collier, C. B. *Spain and the United States: The Treaty of 1819: To the Senate and House of Representatives: Spain Calls upon the United States for the Fulfillment of the Ninth Article of the Said Treaty.* Wash., 1880.

1950. Curry, J. L. M. "The Acquisition of Florida," *MAH* 19 (1888) 286–301.

1951. Dewhurst, W. W. "Disputes Between the United States and Spain over Florida Settled by the Treaty of 1819," in *Proceedings of the Fifteenth Annual Session of the Florida State Bar Association, Orlando, Florida, June 14th, 15th, and 16th, 1922* (pp. 103–118).

1952. Fuller, H. B. *The Purchase of Florida: Its History and Diplomacy.* Cleveland, 1906.

1953. Hackett, C. W. "Tratado de Pichardo Sobre los Límites de Luisiana y Tejas: Su Olvido y su Significado," *BSMGE* 59 (1944) 455–471.

1954. ———, *et al.* (eds.). *Pichardo's Treatise on the Limits of Louisiana and Texas.* 4 vols., Austin, Texas, 1931–1946.

1955. Hackett, F. W. *The Meade Claim.* Wash., 1910.

Deals with Spanish ratification of the Treaty of 1819.

1956. "Letter of William Wirt, 1819," *AHR* 25 (1920) 692–695.

Concerns ratification of the Adams–Onís Treaty.

1957. Lockey, J. B. "The Florida Intrigues of José Alvarez de Toledo," *FHQ* 12 (1934) 145–178.

1958. MacGregor, G., and J. Skinner. "Letters Relating to MacGregor's Attempted Conquest of East Florida, 1817," *FHQ* 5 (1926) 54–57.

1959. Marshall, T. M. *A History of the Western Boundary of the Louisiana Purchase, 1819–1841.* Berkeley, Calif., 1914.

1960. *Memorias de la Vida del Exmo. Señor D. José García de León y Pizarro Escritas por el Mismo.* 3 vols., Madrid, 1894–1897.
    Spanish Minister of State at time of the treaty.

1961. *Memorial of Major General Andrew Jackson, March 6, 1820, Printed by Order of the Senate* (16th Cong., 1st Sess., S. Doc. 73). Wash., 1820.

1962. *Monroe's Messages on Florida.* Boston, 1902.
    Old South Leaflet No. 129.

1963. *Narrative of a Voyage to the Spanish Main (1819) in the Ship "Two Friends": The Occupation of Amelia Island by McGregor, etc., Sketches of the Province of East Florida and Anecdotes Illustrative of the Habit and Manners of the Seminole Indians, with an Appendix Containing a Detail of the Seminole War and the Execution of Arbuthnot and Ambrister.* London, 1819.

1964. Onís, L. de. *Memoria Sobre las Negociaciones Entre España y los Estados Unidos que Dieron Motivo al Tratado de 1819.* 2 vols., Madrid, 1820.
    English ed., Baltimore, 1821.

1965. Patrick, R. W. *Florida Under Five Flags.* 3d ed., Gainsville, Fla., 1960.

1966. Rattenberry, J. F. "Remarks on the Cession of the Floridas to the United States of America, and on the Necessity of Acquiring the Island of Cuba by Great Britain," in *The Pamphleteer* (London) 15 (1819) 261–280.

1967. Thomas, A. D. "The Yellowstone River, James Long and Spanish Reaction to American Intrusion into Spanish Dominions, 1818–1819," *NMHR* 4 (1929) 164–177.

1968. USCH. *Message from the President ... Transmitting a Report of the Secretary of State, with the Documents Relative to a Misunderstanding Between Andrew Jackson and Elijius Fromentin, Judge of a Court Therein: Also the Correspondence Between the Secretary of State and the Minister of Spain, on Certain Proceedings in that Territory & c.c.* (17th Cong., 1st Sess., H. Doc. 42). Wash., 1822.

1969. Van Ness, W. P. *Concise Narrative of General Jackson's First Invasion of Florida.* N.Y., 1827.

1970. Webster, D. "Acquisition of the Floridas," *MHSP* 11 (1871) 329–330.

1971. Wyllys, R. K. "The Filibusters of Amelia Island," *GHQ* 12 (1928) 297–325.

III–C cross references: 1815, 1846, 1908, 1911, 1934

D. RECOGNITION OF LATIN AMERICAN INDEPENDENCE

1972. Anduaga, J. de. "A Spanish Protest Against the United States' Recognition of Latin-American Independence," *JAHI* 8 (1912) 411–415.

1973. Clay, H. *Works: Comprising His Life, Correspondence, and Speeches.* 7 vols., N.Y., 1897.
    Edited by C. Colton.

1974. Hoskins, H. L. "The Hispanic American Policy of Henry Clay, 1816–1828," *HAHR* 7 (1927) 460–478.

1975. Lanning, J. T. "Great Britain and Spanish Recognition of the Hispanic American States," *HAHR* 10 (1930) 429–456.

1976. Lindley, L. C. "Some Aspects of the Foreign Policy of Henry Clay," *CUTA* (1929) 117–120. Worcester, Mass., 1930.

1977. Mayo, B. *Henry Clay: Spokesman of the New West.* Boston, 1937.

1978. Paxson, F. L. *The Independence of the South American Republics: A Study in Recognition and Foreign Policy.* Phil., 1916.

1979. Planas-Suárez, S. *Notas Históricas y Diplomáticas: El Reconocimiento de la Independencia Hispanoamericana y el Proyecto de Confederación de la Independencia de las Naciones del Estadista Portugués Silvestre Pinheiro Ferreira.* B.A., 1961.

1980. Pradt, D. de Fourt. *Europe and America in 1821: With an Examination of the Plan Laid Before the Cortes of Spain for the Recognition of the Independence of South America.* 2 vols., London, 1822.

1981. Robertson, W. S. "Documents Concerning the Consular Service of the United States in Latin America, with Introductory Note," *MVHR* 2 (1916) 561–568.

1982. ———. "The First Legations of the United States in Latin America," *MVHR* 2 (1915) 183–212.

1983. ———. "Metternich's Attitude Toward Revolutions in Latin America," *HAHR* 21 (1941) 538–558.

1984. ———. "The Recognition of the Hispanic American Nations by the United States," *HAHR* 1 (1918) 239–269.

1985. ———. "The Recognition of the Spanish Colonies by the Motherland," *HAHR* 1 (1918) 70–91.

1986. ———. "The United States and Spain in 1822," *AHR* 20 (1915) 781–800.

1987. Schurz, C. *Henry Clay*. 2 vols., Boston, 1896.

1988. Van Deusen, G. G. *The Life of Henry Clay*. Boston, 1937.

III–D cross references:

a) For works pertaining to United States recognition of particular countries, see the appropriate country chapters (XIII–XXIV).

b) For works on the general question of recognition in international law, see items 4557–4565.

c) See also item 2006.

E. ORIGINS OF THE MONROE DOCTRINE, 1815–1823

1989. Arbeláez Urdaneta, C. "El Verdadero Origen de la Doctrina Monroe," *América Habana* 11 (September, 1941) 14–17.

1990. Bagot, J. *George Canning and His Friends, Containing Hitherto Unpublished Letters, Jeux d'Esprit, Etc.* 2 vols., London, 1909.

1991. Bornholdt, L. "The Abbé de Pradt and the Monroe Doctrine," *AHR* 24 (1944) 201–221.

1922. ———. *Baltimore and Early Panamericanism: A Study in the Background of the Monroe Doctrine*. Northampton, Mass., 1949.

1993. Chandler, C. L. "United States Commerce with Latin America at the Promulgation of the Monroe Doctrine," *QJE* 38 (1924) 466–486.

1994. Chateaubriand, V. de. *Congrès de Vérone*. 2 vols., 2d ed., Paris, 1838.
   English ed., 2 vols., London, 1838.

1995. ———. *Oeuvres Complètes*. 12 vols., Paris, 1865–1873.

1996. Cline, M. A. *The American Attitude Toward the Greek War of Independence, 1821–1828*. Atlanta, 1930.

1997. Craven, W. R., Jr. "The Risk of the Monroe Doctrine (1823–1824)," *HAHR* 7 (1941) 320–333.

1998. Cresson, W. P. "Chateaubriand and the Monroe Doctrine," *NAR* 227 (1923) 475–487.

1999. ———. *Diplomatic Portraits: Europe and the Monroe Doctrine One Hundred Years Ago*. Boston, 1923.

1999a. ———. *The Holy Alliance: The European Background of the Monroe Doctrine*. N.Y., 1922.

2000. Davis, T. B., Jr. "Carlos de Alvear and James Monroe: New Light on the Origin of the Monroe Doctrine," *HAHR* 23 (1943) 632–649.

2001. Ford, W. C. "John Quincy Adams and the Monroe Doctrine," *AHR* 7 (1902) 28–52.

2002. ———. *John Quincy Adams: His Connection with the Monroe Doctrine*. Cambridge, Mass., 1902.

2003. ———. "Some Original Documents on the Genesis of the Monroe Doctrine," *MHSP* 15, 2d ser. (1902) 373–436.

2004. Hamilton, S. M. (ed.). *The Hamilton Facsimiles in the National Archives Relating to American History: Part I. The Monroe Doctrine: Its Origin and Intent*. N.Y., 1896.
   Monroe's correspondence with Jefferson and Madison.

2005. Heinz, G. *Die Beziehungen Zwischen Russland, England und Nordamerika im Jahre 1823: Beiträge zur Genesis der Monroedoktrin*. Berlin, 1911.
   Emphasizes Cuba as a key issue in Anglo-American rivalry.

2006. Iriarte, T. de. *Memorias: Rivadavia, Monroe y la Guerra Argentino-Brasileña*. B.A., 1945.

2006a. Kossok, M. *Im Schatten der Heiligen Allianz: Deutschland und Lateinamerika, 1815–1830*. Berlin, 1964.

2007. Lawson, L. A. *The Relation of British*

Policy to the Declaration of the Monroe Doctrine. N.Y., 1922.

2008. Lloyd, E. M. "Canning and Spanish America," *RHST* 18, n.s. (1904) 77–105.

2009. Lockey, J. B. (ed.). "An Early Pan-American Scheme," *PHR* 2 (1933) 439–447.

    Proposal of William Shaler to Secretary of State James Monroe in 1812.

2010. Lovat-Fraser, J. A. "President James Monroe and His Doctrine," *LQR* 4, 6th ser. (1935) 372–381.

2011. MacCorkle, W. A. *The Personal Genesis of the Monroe Doctrine.* N.Y., 1923.

2012. Manning, C. A. *Russian Influence on Early America.* N.Y., 1953.

2013. Marriott, J. A. R. *George Canning and His Times: A Political Study.* London, 1903.

2014. Mazour, A. G. "The Russian-American and Anglo-Russian Conventions, 1824–1825: An Interpretation," *PHR* 14 (1945) 303–310.

2015. McGee, G. W. "The Monroe Doctrine—A Stopgap Measure," *MVHR* 38 (1951) 233–250.

2016. Moore, R. W. "President Monroe and His Message of December 2, 1823," *TQHGM* 5 (1924) 145–164.

2017. Morison, S. E. "The Origin of the Monroe Doctrine, 1775–1823," *EC* 4 (1924) 27–51.

2018. Perkins, B. "The Suppressed Dispatch of H. U. Addington, Washington, November 3, 1823," *HAHR* 37 (1957) 480–485.

    Addington was the British chargé in Washington.

2019. Perkins, D. "Europe, Spanish America, and the Monroe Doctrine," *AHR* 27 (1922) 207–218.

2020. ———. *The Monroe Doctrine, 1823–1826.* Cambridge, Mass., 1927.

2021. ———. "Russia and the Spanish Colonies, 1817–1818," *AHR* 28 (1923) 656–672.

2022. Petrie, C. *George Canning.* London, 1930.

2023. Phillips, W. A. *The Confederation of Europe: A Study of the European Alliance, 1813–1823.* London, 1920.

2024. Polovtsov, A. A. *Correspondance Diplomatique des Ambassadeurs et Ministères de Russie en France et de France en Russie.* 3 vols., Paris, 1902–1907.

2025. Powell, J. H. *Richard Rush, Republican Diplomat: 1780–1859.* Phil., 1942.

2026. Pritchett, J. P. "Selkirk's Views on British Policy Toward the Spanish American Colonies, 1806," *CHR* 24 (1943) 381–396.

2027. "Protocols of Conferences of Representatives of the Allied Powers Respecting Spanish America, 1824–1825," *AHR* 22 (1917) 596–616.

2028. Rippy, J. F. "Latin America and the British Investment 'Boom' of the 1820's," *JMH* 19 (1947) 122–129.

2029. Robertson, W. S. "The Monroe Doctrine Abroad in 1823–24," *APSR* 6 (1912) 545–563.

2030. Rush, B. *The Court of London from 1819 to 1825.* London, 1873.

2031. Rush, R. (ed.). *Memoranda of a Residence at the Court of London.* Phil., 1833.

2032. Salit, C. H. "La Política de no Intervención de Canning en la América Española," *BIIH* 11 (1932) 432–457.

2033. Schellenberg, T. R. "Jeffersonian Origins of the Monroe Doctrine," *HAHR* 14 (1934) 1–32.

2034. ———. "The European Background of the Monroe Doctrine, 1818 to 1823," U. of Pennsylvania Diss., 1934.

2035. Schweide, I. B. "La Diplomacia de la Santa Alianza y la Independencia Hispanoamericana," *TF* 2 (1936) 5–21.

2036. "Some Unedited Letters of Chateaubriand Printed as the 'Supplement au Congrès de Vérone,'" *RPL* 50 (1912) 513–518.

2037. Stapleton, E. J. (ed.). *Some Official Correspondence of Lord Canning.* 2 vols., London, 1887.

2038. Tatum, E. H. *The United States and Europe, 1815–1823.* Berkeley, Calif., 1936.

2039. Temperley, H. W. V. "Documents Illustrating the Reception and Interpretation of the Monroe Doctrine in Europe, 1823–4," *EHR* 39 (1924) 590–593.

2040. ———. *The Foreign Policy of Canning, 1822–1827: England, the Neo-Holy Alliance, and the New World.* London, 1925.

The standard treatment of the European background to the Monroe Doctrine.

2041. ———. "The Instructions to Donzelot, Governor of Martinique, 17 December, 1823," *EHR* 4 (1926) 583–585.

2042. ———. "French Designs on Spanish America in 1820–5," *EHR* 40 (1925) 34–53.

2043. ———. *Life of Canning.* London, 1905.

2044. Thomas, B. P. *Russo-American Relations, 1815–1867.* Baltimore, 1930.

2045. USCS. *Promulgation of the Monroe Doctrine: Proceedings of the International Centennial Celebration of the Promulgation of the Monroe Doctrine Held at Richmond, Va., December 2–4, 1923* (69th Cong., 1st Sess., S. Doc. 125). Wash., 1924.

2046. Vasconcelos, J. *Bolivarismo y Monroísmo.* Santiago, 1937.

2047. Villanueva, C. A. *La Monarquía en América.* 4 vols., Paris, 1912–1913.

2048. ———. *La Santa Alianza.* Paris, 1912.

2049. Villèle, J. de. *Mémoires et Correspondance.* 5 vols., Paris, 1888–1890.

2050. Webster, C. K. "Castlereagh and the Spanish Colonies, 1: 1815–1818," *EHR* 27 (1912) 78–95.

2051. ———. "Castlereagh and the Spanish Colonies, 2: 1818–1822," *EHR* 30 (1915) 631–645.

2052. ———. *The Foreign Policy of Castlereagh, 1815–1822.* London, 1925.

2053. Whitaker, A. P. "Los Orígenes de la Doctrina Monroe," *MP* 23 (1941) 677–688.

III–E cross references: 1807, 1808a, 1815, 1823, 1829, 1831, 1837, 1840a, 1847a, 1849, 1854, 1855, 1856, 1867a, 1871, 1873, 1876a, 1886, 1888, 1974, 2027, 2121, 2140, 2578, 9588

Chapter IV United States–Latin American
Relations, 1823–1895

A. GENERAL WORKS, BIOGRAPHIES, AND SPECIAL STUDIES

2054. Adams, E. D. *Great Britain and the American Civil War*. 2 vols., N.Y., 1925.

2055. Alexander, H. *The American Talleyrand: The Career and Contemporaries of Martin Van Buren*. N.Y., 1935.

2056. Americus. *Spain, Cuba, and the United States: Recognition and the Monroe Doctrine*. N.Y., 1870.

Pseudonym of V. W. Kingsley. Book opposes intervention.

2057. Armstrong, W. M. *E. L. Godkin and American Foreign Policy, 1865–1900*. N.Y., 1957.

Godkin was a journalist who often took sharp issue on foreign policy matters with the Hearst and Pulitzer newspapers.

2058. Bancroft, F. *The Life of William H. Seward*. 2 vols., N.Y., 1900.

2059. ———. "Seward's Ideas of Territorial Expansion," *NAR* 167 (1898) 79–89.

Secretary of State, 1861–1869.

2060. Barral-Montferrat, H. D. *De Monroë à Roosevelt, 1823–1905*. Paris, 1905.

2060a. ———. "La Doctrine de Monroë et les Evolutions Successives de la Politique Etrangère des Etats-Unis (1823–1903)," *RHD* 17 (1903) 594–619.

2061. Barrows, C. L. *William M. Evarts: Lawyer, Diplomat, Statesman*. Chapel Hill, N.C., 1941.

Secretary of State under Hayes (1877–1881).

2062. Bassett, J. S. *The Life of Andrew Jackson*. 2 vols., Garden City, N.Y., 1911.

2063. Beaumarchais, M. D. de. *La Doctrine de Monroë: L'Evolution de la Politique des Etats-Unis au XIX Siècle*. 2d ed., Paris, 1898.

2063a. Blaine, J. G. *Foreign Policy of the Garfield Administration: Peace Congress of the Two Americas*. Chicago, 1882.

2064. Blumenthal, H. *A Reappraisal of Franco-American Relations, 1830–1871*. Chapel Hill, N.C., 1959.

2065. Bowers, C. *The Party Battles of the Jackson Period*. Boston, 1922.

2065a. Calhoun, J. C. *The Papers of John C. Calhoun*. 2 vols., Columbia, S.C., 1959–1963.

Edited by R. L. Meriwether and W. E. Hemphill.

2066. Callahan, J. M. "Statements, Interpretations, and Applications of the Monroe Doctrine and of More or Less Allied Doctrines from 1845 to 1870," *ASILP* (1914) 59–105.

2067. Calvo, A. *Política Americana*. B.A., 1886.

2068. Caylus, E. *Doctrine Monroë*. Paris, 1865.

2069. Céspedes, J. M. *La Doctrina de Monroe*. Havana, 1893.

2070. Chitwood, O. P. *John Tyler: Champion of the Old South*. N.Y., 1939.

2070a. Cleaves, F. *Old Tippecanoe: William Henry Harrison and His Time*. N.Y., 1939.

2071. Cleveland, G. *Presidential Problems*. N.Y., 1904.

2072. Coit, M. L. *John C. Calhoun, American Portrait*. Boston, 1950.

Secretary of State, 1844–1845.

2072a. Comegys, J. P. *Memoir of John M. Clayton*. Wilmington, Del., 1882.

2073. Crichfield, G. W. *American Supremacy: The Rise and Progress of the Latin American Republics and Their Relations to the*

United States Under the Monroe Doctrine.
2 vols., N.Y., 1908.

2074. Curtis, W. E. *Trade and Transportation
Between the United States and Spanish
America.* Wash., 1889.

2075. Dodd, W. E. *Robert J. Walker, Imperialist.* Chicago, 1914.
Walker was a mid-century expansionist
and was in President Polk's cabinet.

2076. Dozer, D. M. "Anti-Expansionism During the Johnson Administration," *PHR*
12 (1943) 253–275.

2076a. ———. "Anti-Imperialism in the United
States, 1865–1895," Harvard U. Diss.,
1936.

2076b. Dulebohn, G. R. *Principles of Foreign
Policy Under the Cleveland Administration.* Phil., 1941.

2077. Dustin, H. *The Monroe Doctrine up to
Date: With a Life of President Monroe,
from the Press of the Illustrated American.*
N.Y., 1896.

2078. Dyer, B. *The Public Career of Edward M.
Evarts.* Berkeley, Calif., 1933.

2079. Eaton, C. *Henry Clay and the Art of
American Politics.* Boston, 1957.

2080. Eckenrode, H. J. *Rutherford B. Hayes:
Statesman of Reunion.* N.Y., 1930.

2081. Edgington, T. B. *The Monroe Doctrine.*
Boston, 1905.

2082. Eustis, F. A. *Augustus Hemenway, 1805–
1876: Builder of the United States Trade
with the West Coast of South America.*
Salem, Mass., 1955.

2083. Everett, A. H. *America: Or a General
Survey of the Political Situation of the
Several Powers of the Western Continent,
with Conjectures on Their Future Prospects.*
Phil., 1827.

2084. Ferris, N. L. "The Relations of the
United States with South America
During the American Civil War," *HAHR*
21 (1941) 51–78.

2085. Foster, J. W. *Diplomatic Memoirs.* 2 vols.,
N.Y., 1919.
Secretary of State, 1892–1893.

2086. Francis, G. F. *The Monroe Doctrine: A
Concise History of Its Origins and Growth.*
Boston, 1885.

2087. Garland, A. *South American Conflicts and
the United States.* Lima, 1900.

2088. Grant, U. S. *The Personal Memoirs of
U. S. Grant.* 2 vols., N.Y., 1885–1886.

2089. Gresham, M. *Life of Walter Quintin
Gresham, 1832–1895.* 2 vols., Chicago,
1919.
Secretary of State, 1893–1895.

2090. Grotius. *A Review of the Monroe Doctrine
and the American Theory of the Panama
Canal.* Wash., 1882.
Pseudonym of B. Darneille and J.
Darneille.

2091. Hamilton, G. *Biography of James G.
Blaine.* Norwich, Conn., 1895.
Pseudonym of M. A. Dodge.

2092. Hamilton, H. *Zachary Taylor: Soldier in
the White House.* Indianapolis, 1951.

2093. Hart, A. B., and E. Channing (eds.).
*Extracts from Official Declarations of the
United States Embodying the Monroe
Doctrine, 1789–1891.* N.Y., 1892.

2094. Hesseltine, W. B. *Ulysses S. Grant,
Politician.* N.Y., 1935.

2095. Holst, H. E. von. *John C. Calhoun.*
Boston, 1882.

2096. Howe, G. F. *Chester A. Arthur: A
Quarter Century of Machine Politics.*
N.Y., 1934.

2097. James, M. *Andrew Jackson: Portrait of a
President.* Indianapolis, 1937.

2097a. ———. *The Raven: A Biography of Sam
Houston (1793–1863).* Indianapolis, 1929.

2098. Jordan, D., and E. J. Pratt. *Europe and the
American Civil War.* N.Y., 1931.

2099. King, C. S. "Horace Mann's Influence on
South American Libraries," *HEQ* 1
(1961) 16–26.

2099a. Klein, P. S. *President James Buchanan.*
University Park, Pa., 1962.

2099b. LaFeber, W. "Grant No. 2915, Penrose
Fund (1961): An Analysis of American
Foreign Policy (1860–1898)," in *American
Philosophical Society Yearbook.* Phil., 1962.

2099c. ———. *The New Empire: An Interpretation of American Expansion, 1860–
1898.* Ithaca, N.Y., 1963.

2100. Leavitt, J. *The Monroe Doctrine.* N.Y.,
1863.

2101. Lincoln, A. *Collected Works.* 9 vols.,
New Brunswick, N.J., 1953–1955.
Edited by R. P. Basler.

2102. Manning, W. R. (ed.). *The Diplomatic
Correspondence of the United States:
Inter-American Affairs, 1831–1860.* 12
vols., Wash., 1932–1939.

2103. ———. "Statements, Interpretations,

and Applications of the Monroe Doctrine, etc., 1823–1845," *ASILP* (1914) 34–59.

2103a. Marchant, A. "Britain and the United States in Latin America Before 1865," *CH* 28 (1955) 145–147.

2103b. McCormac, E. I. *James K. Polk, A Political Biography*. Berkeley, Calif., 1922.

2104. McCoy, C. A. *Polk and the Presidency*. Austin, Texas, 1960.

2104a. McElroy, R. *Grover Cleveland, The Man and the Statesman: An Authorized Biography*. 2 vols., N.Y., 1923.

2105. McLemore, R. A. *Franco-American Diplomatic Relations, 1816–1836*. Baton Rouge, La., 1941.

2106. Meade, R. D. *Judah P. Benjamin, Confederate Statesman*. N.Y., 1943.
    Secretary of State for the Confederacy.

2107. Monaghan, J. *Diplomat in Carpet Slippers: Abraham Lincoln Deals with Foreign Affairs*. Indianapolis, 1945.

2107a. "The Monroe Doctrine," *NAR* 82 (1856) 478–512.
    A critique.

2107b. Moore, J. B. "A Great Secretary of State: William L. Marcy," *PSQ* 30 (1915) 377–396.
    Secretary of State, 1853–1857.

2108. ———. *The Monroe Doctrine: Its Origin and Meaning*. N.Y., 1895.

2109. ——— (ed.). *The Works of James Buchanan*. 12 vols., Phil., 1908–1911.

2110. Morgan, R. J. *A Whig Embattled: The Presidency Under John Tyler*. Lincoln, Nebr., 1954.

2111. Muzzey, D. S. *James G. Blaine, A Political Idol of Other Days*. N.Y., 1934.
    Secretary of State, 1889–1892.

2112. Nevins, A. *Grover Cleveland: A Study in Courage*. N.Y., 1933.

2112a. ———. *Hamilton Fish: The Inner History of the Grant Administration*. N.Y., 1936.
    Secretary of State, 1869–1877.

2112b. ——— (ed.). *Letters of Grover Cleveland, 1850–1908*. N.Y., 1933.

2113. ——— (ed.). *Polk: The Diary of a President, 1845–1849, Covering the Mexican War, the Acquisition of Oregon, and the Conquest of California and the Southwest*. London, 1929.

2113a. Nichols, J. P. "The United States Congress and Imperialism, 1861–1897," *JEH* 21 (1961) 526–538.

2114. Nichols, R. F. *Franklin Pierce: Young Hickory of the Granite Hills*. Phil., 1931.

2115. Owsley, F. L. *King Cotton Diplomacy: Foreign Relations of the Confederate States*. Chicago, 1931.

2116. Perkins, D. *The Monroe Doctrine, 1826–1867*. Baltimore, 1933.

2117. ———. *The Monroe Doctrine, 1867–1907*. Baltimore, 1937.

2118. Pétin, H. *Les Etats-Unis et la Doctrine Monroë*. Paris, 1900.
    Opposes intervention.

2119. Pierson, W. W. "Alberdi's Views on the Monroe Doctrine," *HAHR* 3 (1920) 362–374.

2120. Plesur, M. "America Looking Outward: The Years from Hayes to Harrison," *HIS* 22 (1960) 280–295.

2120a. Pletcher, D. M. *The Awkward Years: American Foreign Relations Under Garfield and Arthur*. Columbia, Mo., 1961.

2121. Portell Vilá, H. "Cubí y [Mariano] Soler y el Presidente Monroe," *RBCU* 29, no. 3 (1932) 327–331.
    Concerns first translation of Monroe Doctrine into Spanish.

2122. Pratt, E. J. "Spanish Opinion of the North American Civil War," *HAHR* 10 (1930) 14–25.

2123. Pratt, J. W. "John L. O'Sullivan and Manifest Destiny," *NYH* 14 (1933) 213–232.

2124. "Protocols of Conferences of Representatives of the Allied Powers Respecting Spanish America, 1824–1825," *AHA* 22 (1917) 595–616.

2124a. Quaife, M. M. (ed.). *Diary of James K. Polk During His Presidency, 1845 to 1849*. 4 vols., Chicago, 1910.

2125. Randall, J. G. *Lincoln the President*. 4 vols., N.Y., 1945–1955.

2126. Rayback, R. J. *Millard Fillmore: Biography of a President*. Buffalo, 1959.

2127. Rebello, C. *Compañía Oceánica Telegráfica Internacional Entre los Estados Unidos y la Isla de Cuba y Otras Islas Occidentales, Panamá y Sud-América*. Bogotá, 1867.

2128. Reeves, J. S. *American Diplomacy Under Tyler and Polk*. Baltimore, 1907.

2129.   Reid, W. *The Monroe Doctrine, the Polk Doctrine, and the Doctrine of Anarchism.* N.Y., 1903.
        Analysis of Polk's policy.

2130.   Robertson, W. S. "South America and the Monroe Doctrine, 1824–1828," *PSQ* 30 (1915) 82–105.

2131.   Russell, C. E. *Blaine of Maine: His Life and Times.* N.Y., 1931.

2132.   Salas, I. *La Doctrina Monroe Es un Principio del Derecho de Gentes, Reconocido y Aceptado en Europa y América.* Mexico, 1896.

2133.   Sievers, H. J. *Benjamin Harrison.* N.Y., 1960.

2134.   Smith, E. B. *Magnificent Missourian: The Life of Thomas Hart Benton.* Phil., 1958.

2135.   Smith, J. P. *The Republican Expansionists of the Early Reconstruction Era.* Chicago, 1933.
        Deals with Caribbean adventures.

2136.   Smith, T. C. "Expansion after the Civil War, 1865–1871," *PSQ* 16 (1901) 412–463.

2137.   Solar, A. del. *La Doctrina de Monroe y la América Latina: Conferencia Leída en el Ateneo el 20 de Junio de 1898.* B.A., 1898.

2137a. Spencer, I. D. *The Victor and the Spoils: A Life of William L. Marcy.* Providence, R.I., 1959.

2138.   Tansill, C. C. *The Foreign Policy of Thomas F. Bayard, 1885–1897.* N.Y., 1940.
        Secretary of State, 1885–1889.

2139.   Temperley, H. W. V. "Canning and the Conferences of the Four Allied Governments in Paris, 1823–1826," *AHR* 30 (1924) 16–43.

2140.   Tucker, G. F. *The Monroe Doctrine: A Concise History of Its Origin and Growth.* Boston, 1885.

2141.   Tyler, A. F. *The Foreign Policy of James G. Blaine.* Minneapolis, Minn., 1927.

2142.   Tyrner-Tyrnauer, A. R. *Lincoln and the Emperors.* N.Y., 1962.

2143.   Urién, C. M. *El Derecho de Intervenir y la Doctrina de Monroe.* B.A., 1898.

2144.   Van Deusen, G. G. *The Jacksonian Era, 1828–1848.* N.Y., 1959.

2145.   Volwiler, A. T. "Harrison, Blaine, and American Foreign Policy, 1889–1893," *APSP* 69 (1938) 637–648.

2146.   ———. *The Correspondence Between Benjamin Harrison and James G. Blaine, 1882–1893.* Phil., 1940.

2147.   Wilgus, A. C. "Official Expression of Manifest Destiny Sentiment Concerning Hispanic America, 1848–1871," *LHQ* 15 (1932) 486–506.

2148.   Williams, C. R. (ed.). *Diary and Letters of Rutherford Birchard Hayes.* 5 vols., Columbus, O., 1922–1926.

2149.   Wiltse, C. M. *John C. Calhoun.* 3 vols., Indianapolis, 1944–1951.

IV–A cross references:

   a)   For works pertaining to the Washington Conference of 1889 see items 4902a–4916a

   b)   See also 2500, 2503, 2513, 2948, 2951, 6670, 6677, 6683, 7891, 7894, 9985

B. EUROPEAN VIOLATIONS OF THE MONROE DOCTRINE

1. FRANCE AND GREAT BRITAIN IN THE LA PLATA, 1838–1850

2150.   Angelis, P. de. *De la Conducta de los Agentes de la Francia Durante el Bloqueo del Río de la Plata.* B.A., 1839.

2151.   Bergee, P. *Los Blocus de Buenos Aires por l'Escadre Française, en 1838.* B.A., 1938.

2152.   Beverina, J. *Las Invasiones Inglesas al Río de la Plata.* 2 vols., B.A., 1939.

2153.   Braconnay, C. M. *La Legión Francesa en la Defensa de Montevideo.* Montevideo, 1943.

2154.   Brossard, A. de. *Considérations Historiques et Politiques sur les Républiques de la Plata dans Leurs Rapports avec la France et l'Angleterre.* Paris, 1850.
        French point of view, by a participant.

2155.   Busaniche, J. L. "Nuevas Comprobaciones Sobre la Misión Cullen (1838)," *HUM* 25 (1936) 315–342.
        Cullen was the Deputy Governor of Sante Fé who attempted to convince Rosas to strike an accord with the French.

2156.   Bustamante, J. L. *Los Cinco Errores Capitales de la Intervención Anglo-Francesa en El Plata.* B.A., 1942.

2157.   Cady, J. F. *Foreign Intervention in the Rio de la Plata, 1838–50: A Study of French, British, and American Policy in Relations to the Dictator Juan Manuel Rosas.* Phil., 1929.

2158. Caillet-Bois, T. *Los Marinos Durante la Dictadura (1841–1851)*. B.A., 1935.

2159. Colli, N. S. *Rosas a Través de la Intervención Francesa en el Río de la Plata Durante Años 1838 a 1840*. B.A., 1948.

2160. *Correspondencia Sostenida Entre el Excmo. Gobierno de Buenos Aires Encargado de las Relaciones Exteriores de la Confederación Argentina y el Sr. Juan B. Nicolson, Capitán Comandante de las Fuerzas Navales de los Estados Unidos Sobre la Costa del Brazil y Río de la Plata, Sobre la Questión Promovida por los ss. Argentes de la Francia*. B.A., 1839.

2161. Cushing, C. "English and French Intervention in the Río de la Plata," *USMDR* 18 (1846) 163–184.

2162. Drago, M. J. *El Bloqueo Francés de 1838 en el Río de la Plata*. B.A., 1948.

2163. Duprey, J. *Un Fils de Napoleon Ier dans les Pays de la Plata, sous la Dictature de Juan Manuel de Rosas: La Mission du Comte Alexandre Colonna Valewski en Argentine et en Uruguay (1847)*. Montevideo, 1937.

2164. Gandía, E. de. "Los Bloqueos en el Río de la Plata y la Política Extranjera," *UPB* 18 (October, 1952) 94–106.

2165. "Intervención Europea en el Río de la Plata," *RBNA* 6 (1942) 414–433.
         Observations of Valentín Alcina, 1844–1849.

2166. "Intervención Europea en El Río de La Plata," *RBNA* 8 (1943) 223–240.
         Covers 1849–1850.

2167. Iriarte, T. de. *Memorias: La Tiranía de Rosas y el Bloqueo Francés*. B.A., 1948.

2168. Lavalle Cobo, J. "El Nacionalismo de Rosas," *AHA* (1940) 631–650.
         Discusses the Falkland Islands and the French blockade.

2169. Mackinnon, L. B. *La Escuadra Anglo-Francesa en el Paraná, 1846*. B.A., 1957.

2170. Muñoz Azpiri, J. L. *Rosas Frente al Imperio Inglés: Historia Intima de un Triunfo Argentino*. B.A., 1960.

2171. Nowell, C. E. "The British Invasion of Rio de la Plata," U. of California Diss., 1932.

2172. Oribe, M. *Manifiesto Sobre la Infamia, Alevosía, y Perfidia con que el Contra-Almirante Francés Mr. Leblanc, y Demás Agentes de la Francia Residentes en Montevideo Han Hostilizado y Sostenido a la Tiranía del Rebelde F. Rivera al Estado Oriental del Uruguay*. B.A., 1838.
         French ed., 1839.

2173. Pereira, A. N. *La Invasión Inglesa en el Río de la Plata*. Montevideo, 1877.

2174. Pereyra, C. *Rosas y Thiers: La Diplomacia Europea en el Río de la Plata, 1838–1850*. Madrid, 1919.

2175. Puentes, G. A. *La Intervención Francesa en el Río de la Plata: Federales, Unitarios y Románticos*. B.A., 1958.

2176. Ratto, H. E. *Los Comodoros Británicos de Estación en el Plata, 1810–1852*. B.A., 1946.

2177. ———. "Diplomáticos y Marinos en el Plata," *BCR* 58 (1940) 679–693, 813–826; 59 (1940) 1–20, 99–215, 459–483, 635–649.

IV–B–1 cross references: 2182b, 9583, 9586, 9594, 9597, 9600

2. THE PASTRY WAR (MEXICO), 1838

2177a. Arista, M. *Manifiesto que Hace á sus Conciudadanos el General Mariano Arista, Sobre las Circunstancias Ocurridas en su Prisión y Libertad por las Tropas Francesas*. Mexico, 1839.

2178. Blanchard, P., and A. Dauzats. *San Juan de Ulúa ou Relation de l'Expédition Française au Mexique sous les Ordres de M. le Contre-Amiral Baudin: Suivi de Notes et Documents, et d'um Aperçu Géneral sur l'Etat Actuel de Texas, par M. E. Maissin*. Paris, 1839.

2178a. Cuevas, L. G. *Exposición del Ministro que la Suscribe Sobre las Diferencias con Francia*. Mexico, 1839.

2178b. Escalada, I. *Manifiesto que Sobre la Capitulación de Tampico, el 4 de Junio de 1839, Escribe el que en Aquella Fecha se Hallaba Mandando la Plaza*. Mexico, 1839.

2178c. France. Legation. Mexico. *El Ultimatum Remitido por S.E. el Sr. Baron Deffaudis, Ministro Plenipotenciario de Francia, al Gobierno Megicano. . . .* Mexico, 1838.

2178d. [Lanuza, P. J.] *Vindicación del General Manuel Rincón ante el Consejo de Guerra que lo Juzgó en 7 y 8 de Febrero del Corriente Año, por los Acontecimientos*

Desgraciados de Ulloa y Veracruz en los Días 27 y 28 de Noviembre de 1838. Mexico, 1840.

2179. Maissin, E. *The French in Mexico and Texas, 1838–1839.* Salado, Texas, 1961.

2179a. Mexico. Ministerio de Relaciones Exteriores. *Documentos Relativos a las Conferencias en Jalapa, entre el Ministro de Relaciones Exteriores Plenipotenciario de la República, y el Contra-Almirante Plenipotenciario de Francia, Sobre el Arreglo de las Diferencias Entre Ambas Naciones.* Mexico, 1838.

2179b. ———. Presidente, 1839–1841 (Bustamante). *Manifiesto que el Ciudadano Anastasio Bustamante Dirige a sus Compatriotas como General en Gefe del Ejército de Operaciones Sobre Tamaulipas y Demás Departamentos de Oriente (Septiembre 20 de 1839).* Mexico, 1839.

2179c. Peña y Reyes, A. de la (comp.). *La Primera Guerra Entre México y Francia.* Mexico, 1927.

2180. Putman, J. F. "Fear of European Intervention in Mexico, 1808–1861," U. of California Diss., 1936.

2181. Robertson, W. S. "French Intervention in Mexico in 1838," *HAHR* 24 (1944) 222–252.

2182. Torre Villar, E. de la (ed.). *Correspondencia Diplomática Franco-Mexicana (1808–1839).* Mexico, 1957– .

2182a. Urrea, J. *Protesta de José Urrea, Contra la Violación de las Capitulaciones de Tampico y Tuspam.* Mexico, 1839.

2182b. USDS. *Report of the Secretary . . . on the Subject of the Blockades of the Mexican Coast and the Rio de la Plata, February 22, 1839* (25th Cong., 3d Sess., H. Ex. Doc. 211). Wash., 1839.

3. British Incursions on the Mosquito Coast

2183. Gámez, J. D. *Historia de la Costa de Mosquitos, Hasta 1894, en Relación con la Conquista Española, los Piratas y Corsarios en las Costas Centra-Americanas, los Avances y Protectorado del Gobierno Inglés en la Misma Costa y la Famosa Cuestión Inglesa con Nicaragua, Honduras y El Salvador.* Managua, 1939.

2184. Henderson, G. B. "German Colonial Projects on the Mosquito Coast, 1844–8," *EHR* 59 (1944) 257–271.

2185. Hooker, R. M. *La Reincorporación de la Mosquitia Desde el Punto de Vista del Derecho Internacional y Patrio.* Managua, 1945.

2185a. "Intrigas del Gral. Juan José Flores, Ex-Presidente de Ecuador, con el Encargado del Negocios Inglés Contra la Unión de Centro América y Los Intereses Territoriales Centroamericanos," *RAGHN* 10 (October, 1948) 182–188.

2186. Rodríguez Beteta, V. *La Política Inglesa en Centro America Durante el Siglo XIX.* Guatemala, 1963.

2187. Squier, E. G. "British Encroachments and Aggressions in Central America: The Mosquito Question," *AR* 6 (1850) 188–203, 235–268.

2188. Travis, I. D. *British Rule in Central America, or a Sketch of Mosquito History.* Ann Arbor, Mich., 1895.

2189. Van Aken, M. "British Policy Considerations in Central America Before 1850," *HAHR* 42 (1962) 54–59.

4. Spanish Reconquest of Santo Domingo, 1861–1865

2190. Alfau Durán, V. "Weyler en Santo Domingo," *CL* 23 (1955) 138–141.

2191. Bona, F. de. *Cuba, Santo Domingo, y Puerto Rico.* Madrid, 1861.

2192. *Documentos Relativos á la Cuestión de Santo Domingo, Remitidos al Congreso de los Diputados por el Ministerio de la Guerra.* Madrid, 1865.
Documents for 1864.

2193. Ferrer de Couto, J. *Reincorporación de Santo Domingo á España: Breves Consideraciones Sobre Este Acontecimiento.* Madrid, 1861.

2194. Gandara y Navarro, J. de la. *Anexión y Guerra de Santo Domingo.* 2 vols., Madrid, 1884.

2195. Hauch, C. C. "Attitudes of Foreign Governments Towards the Spanish Reoccupation of the Dominican Republic," *HAHR* 27 (1947) 247–268.

2196. ———. "Attitudes of Foreign Governments Towards the Spanish Reoccupation of the Dominican Republic," U. of Chicago Diss., 1943.

2197. López de la Vega, J. *La Cuestión de Santo Domingo.* Madrid, 1865.

2198. Martín y Oñate, C. *España y Santo Domingo*. Toledo, 1864.

2199. Rodríguez Demorizi, E. *Antecedentes de la Anexión a España*. Cd. Trujillo, 1955.

2200. ———. *Diarios de la Guerra Dominico-Española de 1863–1865*. Santo Domingo, 1963.

2201. ———. *Relaciones Dominico-Españolas (1844–1859)*. Cd. Trujillo, 1955.

2202. Yuengling, D. G. *The Spanish Annexation of the Dominican Republic*. Pottsville, Pa., 1940.

5. ATTEMPTED RECONQUEST OF CHILE AND PERU, 1863–1866

2203. Amunátegui, M. L., and G. Víctor. *La Reconquista Española*. Santiago, 1912.

2203a. Belgrano, M. "España y el Conflicto del Pacífico, 1864–1867," *CEHA* (1941) 515–549.

2204. Cárdenas, V. *Ojeada Sobre la Cuestión Española*. Lima, 1864.

2205. Carvallo, M. "Una Misión Diplomática en Europa, 1860–1867," *BACH* 15 (1948) 101–137.
    Letters referring to Spanish intervention in Peru and Chile.

2206. Cerruti, F. E. *Peru y España: De los Acontecimientos que Precedieron y Siguieron a la Toma de las Islas de Chincha*. Lima, 1864.

2207. Chile. *Discurso de su Excelencia Presidente de la República en la Apertura del Congreso Nacional de 1884*. Santiago, 1864.
    President Pérez states official Chilean policy.

2208. ———. Ministerio de Relaciones Exteriores. *Contra Manifiesto del Ministro de Relaciones Exteriores de Chile Sobre la Presente Guerra Entre la República y España*. Santiago, 1865.
    English ed., Wash., 1866.

2209. ———. ———. *Memoria que el Ministro de Estado en el Departamento de Relaciones Exteriores Presenta al Congreso Nacional de 1863*. Santiago, 1863.

2210. ———. ———. *Memoria que el Ministro de Estado en el Departamento de Relaciones Exteriores Presenta al Congreso Nacional de 1867*. Santiago, 1867.

2211. ———. ———. *Documentos Relativos á la Mediación de la Francia i la Gran-Bretaña i de los Estados-Unidos en la Guerra Entre las Repúblicas Aliadas del Pacífico i la España*. Santiago, 1867.

2212. Courcelle-Seneuil, J. G. *Agresión de España Contra Chile*. Santiago, 1866.
    French ed., Paris, 1866.

2213. Davis, W. C. *The Last Conquistadores: The Spanish Intervention in Peru and Chile, 1863–1866*. Athens, Ga., 1950.

2214. Edwards Bello, J. *El Bombardeo de Valparaíso y su Epoca*. Santiago, 1934.

2215. Great Britain. Foreign Office. *Papers Relating to the Seizure of the Chincha Islands by a Spanish Squadron*. London, 1864.

2216. Grez Pérez, C. E. *Los Intentos de Unión Hispano-Americana y la Guerra de España en el Pacífico*. Santiago, 1928.

2217. Hardy, O. "When the Monroe Doctrine Was Forgotten," *C* 8 (1930) 115–119, 143–145.
    Discusses refusal of the United States to assist Chile, 1865–1866.

2218. Hunter, D. J. *Chile, the United States and Spain*. N.Y., 1866.

2219. Lisson, C. *La República en el Perú y la Cuestión Peruano-Española*. Lima, 1865.

2220. Matta, M. A. *Documentos para un Capítulo de la Historia Diplomática de Chile en su Ultima Guerra con España*. Santiago, 1872.
    Author was Chilean chargé d'affaires in Bogotá and Caracas at the time of the Spanish interventions.

2221. Novo y Colson, P. de. *Historia de la Guerra de España en el Pacífico*. Madrid, 1882.

2222. Peru. Ministerio de Relaciones Exteriores. *Correspondencia Diplomática Relativa a la Cuestión Española*. Lima, 1867.

2223. ———. ———. *Cuestión Entre el Perú y la España*. Lima, 1864.

2224. ———. ———. *Documentos Relativos a la Cuestión Española*. Lima, 1866.

2225. Pons Muzzo, G. "El Conflicto Entre el Perú y España, 1864–1866," U. of Lima Diss., 1939.

2226. Ramírez, J. M. *Apresamiento del "Paquete de Maule."* Valparaiso, 1868.

2227. Ribeyro, J. A. *Perú y España: Exposición de Algunos Puntos Importantes de la*

Situación Actual Entre los Dos Países.
Lima, 1865.

2228. *The Bombardment of Valparaiso, Rear-Admiral Denman, Mr. Layard and the British Community of Valparaiso.* Liverpool, 1866.

2229. *The Question Between Chile and Spain.* N.Y., 1865.
    Published by the Chilean legation.

2230. Urrea, J. C. *Una Página Gloriosa para la Historia del Perú o el 2 de Mayo de 1866.* 2d ed., Lima, 1866.

2231. Vicuña, P. F. *Guerra Inevitable Entre la América i la Europa.* Valparaiso, 1866.

2232. Vicuña Mackenna, B. *Historia de la Guerra de Chile con España, 1863–1866.* Santiago, 1883.

IV–B–5 cross references: 1780

6. FRENCH INTERVENTION IN MEXICO, 1862–1867

2233. Acevedo, J. P. de. *Europa y México, 1861–1862.* Havana, 1935.

2234. Algara, I. *La Corte de Maximiliano.* Mexico, 1938.

2234a. Alvensleben, M. von. *With Maximilian in Mexico. From the Notebook of a Mexican Officer.* London, 1867.

2235. Anderson, W. M. *An American in Maximilian's Mexico, 1865–1866.* San Marino, Calif., 1959.
    Diary of a United States engineer who settled in Mexico after the Civil War.

2235a. Argüelles, J. A. *Breves Apuntes para la Historia de la Intervención en México.* Havana, 1863.

2236. Bancroft, F. "The French in Mexico and the Monroe Doctrine," *PSQ* 11 (1896) 30–43.

2236a. Basch, S. S. von. *Maxmiliano de Mexico.* Madrid, 1943.

2237. Belen'kii, A. B. *Razgrom Meksikanskim Narodom Inostrannoi Interventsii, 1861–1867.* Moscow, 1960.
    Defeat of Foreign Intervention by the Mexican People, 1861–1867.

2238. Benjamin, R. L. "Marcus Otterbourg, United States Minister to Mexico in 1867," *AJHSP*, no. 32 (1931) 65–94.

2239. Blanchot, C. *Mémoires: l'Intervention Française au Mexique.* 3 vols., Paris, 1911.

2240. Blasio, J. L. *Maximiliano Intimo. El Emperador Maximiliano y su Corte: Memorias de un Secretario Particular.* Paris, 1905.
    English ed., New Haven, Conn., 1934.

2241. Blumberg, A. "A Swedish Diplomat in Mexico, 1864," *HAHR* 45 (1965) 275–286.

2242. ———. "United States and the Role of Belgium in Mexico, 1863–1867," *HIS* 26 (1964) 206–277.

2243. Brown, R. B. "Guns over the Border: American Aid to the Juárez Government During the French Intervention," U. of Michigan Diss., 1951.

2244. Burner, W. J. "Napoleon III and Intervention in Mexico," *OSSJ* 4 (1932) 18–23.

2245. Caillet-Bois, R. R. "Argentina y la Intervención Europea en México en 1862," *HM* 12 (1963) 522–594.

2246. Callahan, J. M. *Evolution of Seward's Mexican Policy.* Morgantown, W.Va., 1909.

2247. Case, L. M. (ed.). *French Opinion on the United States and Mexico, 1860–1867.* N.Y., 1936.

2248. Casper, H. W. *American Attitudes Toward the Rise of Napoleon III.* Wash., 1947.

2249. Castañeda Batres, O. (comp.). *La Convención de Londres.* Mexico, 1962.

2250. ———. *Francisco Zarco ante la Intervención Francesca y el Imperio (1863–1864).* Mexico, 1958.

2251. Chevalier, M. *La France, le Mexique et les Etats Confédérés.* Paris, 1863.
    English ed., N.Y., 1863.

2252. ———. *L'Expédition du Mexique.* Paris, 1862.

2253. *Circulares y otros Publicaciones Hechas por la Legación Mexicana en Washington, Durante la Guerra de Intervención, 1862–1867.* 2 vols., Mexico, 1868.

2254. Clapp, M. *Forgotten First Citizen: John Bigelow.* Boston, 1947.
    Consular official in France during the Mexican intervention.

2255. *Correspondencia de la Legación Mexicana en los Estados Unidos de América, Sobre los Contratos Celebrados por Don Juan Bustamente, 1862–1863.* Mexico, 1869.

2256. *Correspondencia de la Legación Mexicana en Washington con el Ministerio de Relaciones Exteriores de la República y el Departamento de Estado de los Estados Unidos, Sobre la Captura, Juicio y Ejecución de Don Fernando Maximiliano de Hapsburgo.* 2 vols., Mexico, 1868.

2257. *Correspondencia Entre la Legación de la República Mexicana en Washington, el Departamento de Estado de los Estados Unidos de América y el Gobierno de México, con Relación a la Exportación de Armas y Municiones de Guerra de los Estados Unidos para Puertos de Naciones Beligerantes.* 2d ed., Mexico, 1867.

2258. *Correspondencia Official de la Legación Mexicana en Washington con el Ministerio de Relaciones Exteriores de la República y el Departamento de Estado de Washington, Sobre la Conducta de D. Jésus G. Ortega, 1865–1866.* Mexico, 1869.

2259. Corti, E. C. *Maximilian and Charlotte of Mexico.* 2 vols., N.Y., 1928.
German ed., 2 vols., Zurich, 1924.

2260. Dabbs, J. A. *The French Army in Mexico, 1861–1867.* The Hague, 1963.

2261. Delamare, G. *L'Empire Oublié.* Paris, 1935.

2262. Domenech, E. *Histoire du Mexique: Juárez et Maximilien: Correspondance Inédite des Présidents, Ministères et Généraux Almonte, Santa Anna, Gutiérrez, Miramón, Márquez, Mejías, Woll, etc., de Juárez, de l'Empereur Maximilien et de l'Impératrice Charlotte.* 3d ed., 3 vols., Brussels, 1868.

2263. Duniway, C. A. "Reasons for the Withdrawal of the French from Mexico," *AHAAR* (1902). Wash., 1903.

2264. Fabela, I. "La Doctrina Monroe y la Segunda Intervención Francesa en México," *CA* 16 (September, 1957) 201–214.
Contends that the United States refused to enforce the doctrine in any way.

2265. Foster, J. W. "Maximilian and His Mexican Empire," *CHSR* 14 (1911) 184–202.

2266. Frazer, R. W. "Latin American Projects to Aid Mexico During the French Intervention," *HAHR* 28 (1948) 377–388.

2267. ———. "Maximilian's Propaganda Activities in the United States, 1865–1866," *HAHR* 24 (1944) 4–29.

2268. ———. "Trade Between California and the Belligerent Powers During the French Intervention in Mexico," *PHR* 15 (1946) 390–399.

2269. Frías y Soto, H. *Juárez Glorificado y la Intervención y el Imperio, ante la Verdad Histórica: Refutando con Documentos la Obra del Señor Francisco Bulnes Intitulada El Verdadero Juárez.* Mexico, 1957.

2270. ———. *México y los Estados Unidos Durante la Intervención Francesa.* Mexico, 1901.

2271. Fuentes Díaz, V. *La Intervención Europea en México, 1861–1862.* Mexico, 1962.

2272. Fuentes Mares, J. *Juárez y el Imperio.* Mexico, 1963.

2273. ———. *Juárez y la Intervención.* Mexico, 1962.

2274. ———. "Washington, París y el Imperio Mexicano," *HM* 13 (1963) 244–271.

2275. García, G. (ed.). *Correspondencia Secreta de los Principales Intervencionistas Mexicanos, 1860–1862.* 3 vols., Mexico, 1905–1907.

2276. Gaulot, P. *La Vérité sur l'Expédition du Mexique.* 3 vols., Paris, 1889–1890.

2277. Gerrity, F. X. "American Editorial Opinion of the French Intervention in Mexico, 1861–1867," Georgetown U. Diss., 1952.

2278. Gilbert, B. F. "French Warships on the Mexican West Coast, 1861–1866," *PHR* 24 (1955) 25–38.

2279. Goldwert, M. "Matías Romero and Congressional Opposition to Seward's Policy Toward the French Intervention in Mexico," *TA* 12 (1965) 22–40.

2279a. Gooch, G. P. "The Second Empire: The Mexican Fiasco," *CR* 193 (April, 1958) 187–191; 193 (May, 1958) 244–248.

2280. Grajales, G. "Intervención Francesa y el Segundo Imperio," *HM* 13 (1963) 284–316.

2281. Gutiérrez de Estrada, J. M. *México y el Archiduque Fernando Maximiliano de Austria.* Paris, 1862.

2282. Hanna, A. J., and K. A. Hanna. "The Immigration Movement of the Intervention and Empire as Seen Through the Mexican Press," *HAHR* 27 (1947) 220–246.

2283. Hanna, K. A. "The Roles of the South in the French Intervention in Mexico," *JSH* 20 (1954) 3–21.

2284. Hanstein, O. von. *Kaiser Maximilian von Mexiko*. Leipzig, 1935.

2285. Harding, B. *Phantom Crown: The Story of Maximilian and Carlota of Mexico*. N.Y., 1939.

2286. Hellwald, F. von. *Maximilian I, Kaiser von Mexico: Sein Leben, Wirken und Sein Tod, Nebst Einem Abriss der Geschichte des Kaiserreichs*. 2 vols., Vienna, 1869.

2287. Hernández Rodríguez, R. "Comonfort y la Intervención Francesa," *HM* 13 (1963) 59–75.

2288. Hidalgo, J. M. *Apuntes para Escribir la Historia de los Proyectos de Monarquía en México Desde el Reinado de Carlos III Hasta la Instalación del Emperador Maximiliano*. Paris, 1868.

2289. Hobson, J. A. "Matías Romero and the Monroe Doctrine in the French Invasion of Mexico: 1862–1867," U. of Chicago Diss., 1961.

2290. Hoskins, H. L. "French View of the Monroe Doctrine and the Mexican Expedition," *HAHR* 4 (1921) 677–689.

2291. Huart, M. R. d'Artois d'. *Maximilien d'Autriche Empereur du Mexique*. Paris, 1935.

2292. Hyde, H. M. *Mexican Empire: The History of Maximilian and Carlota of Mexico*. London, 1946.

2293. Iglesias Calderón, F. *El Egoísmo Norte-Americano Durante la Intervención Francesa*. Mexico, 1905.

2294. Jay, J. *Mr. Jay's Letter on the Recent Relinquishment of the Monroe Doctrine*. N.Y., 1863.

2295. Kingsley, V. W. *French Intervention in America, or A Review of la France, le Mexique, et les Etats-Confédérés*. N.Y., 1863.

2296. Lally, F. E. *French Opposition to the Mexican Policy of the Second Empire*. Baltimore, 1931.

2297. LeFèvre, E. *Documentos Oficiales Recogidos en la Secretaría Privada de Maximiliano: Historia de la Intervención Francesa en Méjico*. 2 vols., Brussels, 1869.

2298. León Toral, J. de. *Historia Militar: La Intervención Francesa en México*. Mexico, 1962.

2299. Malloy, G. W. "The U.S. and the French Intervention in Mexico, 1861–1867," U. of California Diss., 1937.

2300. Martin, P. F. *Maximilian in Mexico: The Story of the French Intervention (1861–1867)*. N.Y., 1914.

2301. Mazade, C. de. "L'Expédition du Mexique et la Politique Française," *RDM* 48, 2d. ser. (1863) 675–706.

2302. McCornack, R. B. "James Watson Webb and French Withdrawal from Mexico," *HAHR* 31 (1951) 274–286.

2303. Mercier de Lacombe, H. *Le Mexique et les Etats-Unis*. 2d ed., Paris, 1863.

2304. *Mexico and the Monroe Doctrine*. N.Y., 1865.

2305. Miller, R. R. "The American Legion of Honor in Mexico," *PHR* 30 (1961) 229–241.
      About U.S. Civil War veterans fighting in Mexico.

2306. Monroy, G. "Una Misión Amarga," *HM* 8 (1959) 524–528.
      Letters from Juan Antonio de la Fuente in Europe to Matías Romero, 1861–1862.

2307. Moreau, H. *La Politique Française en Amérique—1861–1864*. Paris, 1864.
      Urges French withdrawal.

2308. Moreno, D. *Los Intereses Económicos en la Intervención Francesa*. Mexico, 1962.

2309. Musser, J. *The Establishment of Maximilian's Empire in Mexico*. Menasha, Wis., 1918.

2310. Parker, F. J. *The Mexican Empire and the American Union*. Boston, 1865.
      Urges recognition of Maximilian.

2311. Paula de Arrangóiz, F. de. *Apuntes para la Historia del Segundo Imperio Mexicano*. Madrid, 1869.

2312. Peña y Reyes, A. de la. *Comentarios de Francisco Zarco Sobre la Intervención Francesa (1861–1863)*. Mexico, 1929.

2313. ———. *La Labor Diplomática de D. Manuel María de Zamacona como Secretario de Relaciones Exteriores*. Mexico, 1928.
      Mexico's Secretary for Foreign Relations, July 13, 1861, to November 26, 1861.

2314. Pennette, M., and J. Castaingt. "La Legión Extranjera en la Intervención Francesa," *HM* 12 (1962) 229–273.

2315. Pérez de Acevedo, J. *Europa y México, 1861–1862*. Havana, 1935.

2316. *Periodismo Mexicano ante la Intervención Francesa: Hemerografía, 1861–1863*. Mexico, 1962.

2317. *Periodismo Mexicano ante la Intervención Francesa: La Prensa Liberal Frente a la Intervención y el Imperio*. Mexico, 1962.

2318. Rangel Gaspar, E. *La Intervención Francesa en México: Consideraciones Sobre la Soberanía Nacional y la no Intervención*. Mexico, 1963.

2319. *Responsabilidades Contraídes por el Gobierno Nacional de México con los Estados Unidos, en Virtud de los Contratos Celebrados por su Agentes, 1864–1867*. Mexico, 1867.

2320. Robertson, W. S. "The Tripartite Treaty of London," *HAHR* 20 (1940) 167–189.

   A treaty signed by France, Great Britain, and Spain.

2321. Romero, M. *Comisionados de la República Mexicana en los Estados Unidos, Dos Notas del Señor Romero á Mr. Seward*. Baltimore, 1867.

   Minister of the Mexican Republic to Washington during the French intervention, 1861–1867.

2322. ———. *Contratos Hechos en los Estados-Unidos por los Comisionados del Gobierno de México Durante los Años de 1865 y 1866*. Mexico, 1868.

2323. ——— (ed.). *Correspondencia de la Legación Mexicana Durante la Intervención Extranjera*. 10 vols., Mexico, 1870–1892.

2324. ———. *Historia de las Intrigas Europeas que Ocasionaron la Intervención Francesa en México: Nota del Sr. Romero a Mr. Seward, el 2 de Octubre de 1862*. Mexico, 1868.

2325. ———. *The Situation of Mexico*. N.Y., 1863.

   Speech delivered in New York in December, 1863.

2326. Schefer, C. *Los Orígenes de la Intervención Francesa en México, 1858–1862*. Mexico, 1963.

2327. Sheridan, P. J. "The Committee of Mexican Bondholders and European

Intervention in 1861," *MA* 42 (1960) 18–29.

2328. Solana y Gutiérrez, M. *Maximiliano de Hapsburgo*. Mexico, 1939.

2329. Sonolot, L. "L'Agonie de l'Empire du Mexique, d'après des Lettres et des Notes Inédités du Général Castelnau," *RPA* 39 (1927) 590–625, 862–898.

2330. Suckau, H. de. *Deux Interventions en Amérique: Mexique et Honduras*. Paris, 1869.

2331. Tavera, E. S. Ritter von. *Geschichte der Regierung des Kaisers Maximilian I, und die Französische Intervention in Mexiko*. 2 vols., Vienna, 1903.

2332. USCH. *Message on Affairs in Mexico: Pres. Abraham Lincoln, Apr. 15, 1862* (37th Cong., 2d Sess., H. Ex. Doc. 100). Wash., 1862.

2333. ———. *Message on Condition of Mexico: Pres. A. Lincoln, Feb. 7, 1863* (37th Cong., 3d Sess., H. Ex. Doc. 54). Wash., 1863.

2333a. ———. *Message on the Evacuation of Mexico: Pres. Andrew Johnson, Apr. 23, 1866* (39th Cong., 1st Sess., H. Ex. Doc. 93). Wash., 1866.

2333b. ———. *Message Relating to Mexican Affairs: Pres. Andrew Johnson, March 20, 1866* (39th Cong., 1st Sess., H. Ex. Doc. 73). Wash., 1866.

2334. Villarello Vélez, I. *La Opinión Francesa Sobre la Intervención en México*. Mexico, 1963.

2335. Weber, F. G. "Bismark's Man in Mexico: Anton von Magnus and the End of Maximilian's Empire," *HAHR* 46 (1966) 53–65.

2336. West, W. R. *Contemporary French Opinion on the American Civil War*. Baltimore, 1924.

2337. White, E. B. *American Opinion of France*. N.Y., 1927.

IV–B–6 cross references:

a) For general accounts of the period, see items 5845–5930.

b) See also items 1780, 2059, 2098, 2115, 2125, 2180, 5868.

7. OTHER VIOLATIONS

2337a. Arboleya, J. de. *España y Méjico: Compendio de Historia Internacional*. 2 vols., Havana, 1861–1862.

2338. Delgado, J. *España y México en el Siglo XIX.* 3 vols., Madrid, 1950.

2339. Destruge, C. *La Expedición Flores—Proyecto de Monarquía Americana, 1846–1847.* Guayaquil, 1906.

2340. Flores Magón, E. *Combatimos la Tiranía: Un Pionero Revolucionario Mexicano Cuenta su Historia a Samuel Kaplan.* Mexico, 1958.
      Treats Spanish attempted reconquest of Mexico in 1829.

2341. García Chuecos, H. (ed.). "Proyecto de Reconquista para España de las Provincias Libres de Venezuela," *BANHC* 44 (1961) 82–155.
      Covers 1826–1829.

2342. Haskins, R. W. "Juan José Flores and the Proposed Expedition Against Ecuador, 1846–1847," *HAHR* 27 (1947) 467–495.

2343. Howe, G. F. "García Moreno's Efforts to Unite Ecuador and France," *HAHR* 16 (1936) 257–262.

2343a. Luthin, R. H. "St. Bartholomew: Sweden's Colonial and Diplomatic Venture in the Caribbean," *HAHR* 14 (1934) 307–324.
      Treats Sweden's attempted violation of the doctrine in 1877.

2343b. Malagón-Barceló, J. *et al. Relaciones Diplomáticas Hispano-Mexicanas, 1839–1898.* 2 vols., Mexico, 1949–1952.

2344. Mariluz Urquijo, J. M. *Los Proyectos Españoles para Reconquistar el Río de la Plata (1820–1833).* B.A., 1958.

2344a. Menéndez, C. R. (ed.). *El Proyecto Expansionista de Inglaterra en Yucatán en 1849.* Mérida, 1939.

2345. "Reclamaciones Francesas: El Caso de la 'Jeanne Amalie': Archivo de Félix Frías," *RBNA* 10 (1944) 232–242.
      Letters of Frías in 1858 relating to French claims.

2346. Robertson, W. S. "An Early Threat of Intervention by Force in South America," *HAHR* 23 (1943) 611–631.
      Franco-Colombian dispute during the 1830's.

2347. ———. "García Moreno's Dream of a European Protectorate," in *Contribuciones para el Estudio de la Historia de América.* B.A., 1941.

2348. "The Islands of the Gulf of Honduras: Their Seizure and Organization as a British Colony," *DR* 31 (1852) 544–552.

IV–B–7 cross references: 2020, 2052, 2064, 2093, 2116, 7460

C. TRANS-ISTHMIAN DIPLOMACY, 1823–1895

1. GENERAL WORKS

2349. Allen, C. "The Career of Félix Belly in Connection with the Canal Project in Central America," U. of Minnesota Diss., 1950.
      Belly was a French promoter.

2349a. ———. "Félix Belly: Nicaraguan Canal Promoter," *HAHR* 37 (1957) 46–59.

2350. Bonilla Lara, A. *Los Estados Unidos y los Canales Interoceánicos de América.* Santiago, 1929.

2351. Du Val, M. P. *Cádiz to Cathay: The Story of the Long Diplomatic Struggle for the Panama Canal.* 2d ed., Stanford, Calif., 1947.

2352. Fernández MacGregor, G. *El Istmo de Tehuantepec y los Estados Unidos.* Mexico, 1954.
      Emphasizes the nineteenth century, but carries the story to 1937.

2353. Hart, A. B. *Extracts from Official Papers Relating to the Isthmian Canal, 1515–1909.* N.Y., 1910.

2354. Hill, R. R. "The Nicaraguan Canal Idea to 1913," *HAHR* 28 (1948) 197–211.

2355. Huberich, C. H. *The Trans-Isthmian Canal: A Study in American Diplomatic History.* Austin, Texas, 1904.
      Covers 1825 to 1904.

2356. Jinesta, R. *El Canal de Nicaragua: Su Historia, Base Internacional y Participación de Costa Rica.* San José, C.R., 1958.

2357. ———. *Derechos de Costa Rica en el Canal de Nicaragua.* San José, C.R., 1936.

2358. Johnson, W. F. *Four Centuries of the Panama Canal.* N.Y., 1906.

2359. Keasbey, L. M. *The Early Diplomatic History of the Nicaragua Canal.* Newark, N.J., 1890.

2360. Keasbey, L. M. *The Nicaragua Canal and the Monroe Doctrine: A Political History of the Isthmus Transit, with Special Reference to the Nicaragua Canal Project and the Attitude of the United States Government Thereto.* N.Y., 1896.

2361. Mack, G. *The Land Divided: A History of the Panama Canal and Other Isthmian Canal Projects.* N.Y., 1944.

2362. March, J. J. *El Mito del Darién.* Mexico, 1960.

2363. Mathews, S. T. "The Nicaragua Canal Controversy: The Struggle for an American-Constructed and Controlled Transitway," Johns Hopkins U. Diss., 1949.

2364. Pierson, W. W. "The Political Influences of an Inter-Oceanic Canal, 1826–1926," *HAHR* 6 (1926) 205–231.

2365. Sáenz, V. *Nuestras Vías Interoceánicas: Tehuántepec, Nicaragua, Panamá.* Mexico, 1957.

2365a. Scheips, P. J. "Gabriel Lafond and Ambrose W. Thompson: Neglected Isthmian Promoters," *HAHR* 36 (1956) 211–228.
      Discusses the Chiriqui region.

2366. Tascher, H. "American Foreign Policy Relative to the Selection of the Trans-Isthmian Canal Route," U. of Illinois Diss., 1933.

2367. Whiteley, J. G. "The Diplomacy of the United States in Regard to Central American Canals," *NAR* 165 (1897) 364–378.

2368. Williams, M. W. *Anglo-American Isthmian Diplomacy, 1815–1915.* Wash., 1916.

IV–C–1   cross references: 2103, 2186, 5871

2. TRANS-ISTHMIAN DIPLOMACY, 1823–1850

2369. Arosemena, J. *Examen Sobre la Franca Comunicación Entre los dos Océanos.* Bogotá, 1846.

2370. Behrendt, R. F. "Aspectos Sociales y Económicos del Istmo de Panamá Durante la Epoca del Tráfico Interoceánico Primitivo, 1519–1848," *RMS* 5, no. 1 (1943) 49–61.

2371. Belknap, G. E. (ed.). "Letters of Bancroft and Buchanan on the Clayton-Bulwer Treaty, 1849–1850," *AHR* 5 (1899) 95–102.

2372. Bourne, K. "The Clayton-Bulwer Treaty and the Decline of British Opposition to the Territorial Expansion of the United States, 1857–1860," *JMH* 33 (1961) 287–291.

2373. "Canal de Nicaragua," *RAN* 2 (1938) 329–357.

2374. Carrington, J. *The Passage of the Isthmus or Practical Hints to Persons About to Cross the Isthmus of Panama.* N.Y., 1849,

2375. Chase, P. P. "On the Panama Route During the Gold Rush to California," *CSMP* 27 (1932) 235–256.

2376. Childs, O. W. *Report of the Survey of a Route for the Proposed Nicaragua Ship-Canal.* N.Y., 1852.

2377. Colby, C. M. "Diplomacy of the Quarter Deck," *AJIL* 8 (1914) 443–476.
      Activities of naval officers concerning the treaty of 1846 with Nueva Granada.

2378. *Compilation of Executive Documents and Diplomatic Correspondence Relative to a Trans-Isthmian Canal in Central America: With Specific Reference to the Treaty of 1846 Between the United States and New Granada (U.S. of Colombia) and the "Clayton-Bulwer" Treaty of 1850.* 3 vols., N.Y., 1905.

2379. Cullen, E. *The Isthmus of Darien Ship Canal.* London, 1852.

2380. Dénain, A. *Ensayo Sobre los Intereses Políticos y Commerciales del Istmo de Panamá Considerandoles Bajo el Punto de Vista de la Nueva Granada.* Panama, 1844.
      French ed., Paris, 1845.

2380a. Folkman, D. I. "Westward via Nicaragua: The United States and the Nicaraguan Route, 1826–1869." U. of Utah Diss., 1966.

2381. Garella, M. N. *Project d'un Canal de Jonction de l'Océan Pacifique et de l'Océan Atlantique à Travers l'Isthme de Panama.* Paris, 1845.

2382. Hazeltine, M. W. "The Clayton-Bulwer Treaty," *NAR* 165 (1897) 452–459.

2383. Hickson, G. F. "Palmerston and the Clayton-Bulwer Treaty," *CHJ* 3 (1931) 295–303.

2384. Howe, G. F. "The Clayton-Bulwer Treaty," *AHR* 42 (1937) 484–490.

2385. Hughes, G. W. *Letter in Answer to the*

Hon. John M. Clayton on Inter-Marine Communications. Wash., 1850.

2386.   Keasbey, L. M. *The Terms and Tenor of the Clayton-Bulwer Treaty.* Phil., 1899.

2387.   Liot, W. B. *Panama, Nicaragua and Tehuantepec.* London, 1849.

2388.   Lockey, J. B. "A Neglected Aspect of Isthmian Diplomacy," *AHR* 41 (1936) 295–305.
        The treaty of 1846 with New Granada.

2389.   Naylor, R. A. "The British Role in Central America Prior to the Clayton-Bulwer Treaty of 1850," *HAHR* 40 (1960) 361–382.

2390.   Richards, E. W. "Louis Napoleon and Central America," *JMH* 34 (1962) 178–184.
        Nicaraguan canal interest in the 1840's.

2391.   Rodrigues, M. U. "The 'Prometheus' and the Clayton-Bulwer Treaty," *JMH* 36 (1964) 260–278.

2392.   Snow, F. "Legal Rights Under the Clayton-Bulwer Treaty," *HLR* 3 (1899) 53–73.

2393.   Travis, I. D. *The History of the Clayton-Bulwer Treaty.* Ann Arbor, Mich., 1900.

2394.   USCS. *The Clayton-Bulwer Treaty and the Monroe Doctrine: A Letter from the Secretary of State to the Minister of the United States at London, Dated May 8, 1882* (47th Cong., 1st Sess., S. Doc. 194). Wash., 1882.

2395.   Van Alstyne, R. W. "The Central American Policy of Lord Palmerston, 1846–1848," *HAHR* 16 (1936) 339–359.

2396.   Wheelright, W. *Observations on the Isthmus of Panama.* London, 1844.

2397.   Williams, M. W. (ed.). "Letters of E. George Squier to John M. Clayton, 1849–50," *HAHR* 1 (1918) 426–434.

IV–C–2 cross references: 2072a, 2189, 6693, 7040a, 8275

3. Trans-Isthmian Diplomacy, 1851–1870

2397a. Arroniz, J. J. *Tratado MacLane.* Orizaba, 1860.

2398.   Belly, M. F. *Canal Interocéanique de Nicaragua.* Paris, 1869.

2399.   Berbusse, E. J. "The Origins of the McLane-Ocampo Treaty of 1859," *TA* 14 (1958) 223–245.

2400.   Bidwell, C. T. *The Isthmus of Panama.* London, 1865.

2401.   Bionne, M. H. *La Question du Percement de l'Isthme de Panama Devant un Congrès International.* Paris, 1864.

2402.   Bolaños, P. "Napoleón III y el Nicaragüense Licenciado Don Francisco Castellón," *RAN* 14 (1950) 274–281.

2403.   Colombia. *Documentos Relativos al Canal Interoceánico.* Bogotá, 1870.

2404.   Cudmore, P. *Buchanan's Conspiracy: The Nicaragua Canal and Reciprocity.* N.Y., 1892.

2405.   Cue Canovas, A. *El Tratado McLane-Ocampo: Juárez, los Estados Unidos y Europa.* 2d ed., Mexico, 1959.

2406.   Debayle, L. "Historia del Canal de Nicaragua," *RAGHN* 9 (December, 1947) 89–99.
        Concerns Squier.

2407.   Galindo, A. *El Tratado de 14 de Enero para la Escavación del Canal de Darién.* Bogotá, 1869.

2408.   Kelley, F. M. *The Union of the Oceans by Ship-Canal Without Locks via the Atrato Valley.* N.Y., 1859.

2409.   Kemble, J. R. "The Genesis of the Pacific Mail Steamship Company," *CHSQ* 13 (1934) 240–254.

2410.   ———. *The Panama Route: 1848–1869.* Berkeley, Calif., 1943.

2411.   Kirkpatrick, R. Z. "Strain's Panama Expedition," *USNIP* 51 (1935) 1128–1135.
        Strain was in charge of the expedition of 1853–1854 to map the Isthmus of Darien for canal construction.
        See also item 2426.

2412.   Larrainzar, M. *Análisis del Dictamen de la Comisión de Negocios Estrangeros del Senado de los Estados Unidos Sobre el Negocio de Tehuantepec.* N.Y., 1852.
        English ed., N.Y., 1952.

2413.   ———. *La Cuestión de Tehuantepec: Contiene dos Notas del Enviado Extraordinario y Ministro Plenipotenciario de la República Mexicana en Washington, y Algunos Artículos que Sobre Esta Materia se Han Publicado.* N.Y., 1852.

2414.   Martín, C. *Canal Interoceánico: Informe*

*para Segundo Debate del Tratado Cele-
brado en 1870.* Bogotá, 1870.

Author was Colombian minister to the
United States, 1872–1876.

2415.   Mexico. Cámara de Diputados. *Documentos Relativos á la Apertura de una Vía
de Comunicación Inter-oceánica por el
Istmo Tehuantepec.* Mexico, 1852.

2416.   ———. Ministro de Relaciones (Ex-
teriores). *A Memorial Setting Forth the
. . . Reasons . . . of the Government of . . .
Mexico for Not Recognizing the Validity
of the Privilege Granted to D. José
Garay, for Opening a Way of Communica-
tions Between the Atlantic and Pacific
Oceans by the Isthmus of Tehuantepec. . . .*
Mexico, 1852.

2417.   ———. Senado. *Dictamen de la Comisión
Especial de Tehuantepec del Senado,
Encargada de Examinar las Varias
Resoluciones Dictadas con Motivo del
Privilegio Exclusivo Concedido á D. José
Garay.* Mexico, 1851.

2418.   Moore, J. P. "Correspondence of Pierre
Soulé: The Louisiana Tehuantepec
Company," *HAHR* 32 (1952) 59–72.

2418a. Murray, P. *Tres Norteamericanos y su
Participación en el Desarrollo del Tratado
McLane-Ocampo, 1856–1860.* Guadala-
jara, 1946.

2419.   Otis, F. N. *History of the Panama Railroad; and of the Pacific Mail Steamship
Company.* N.Y., 1867.

2420.   "Our Foreign Relations. Central America
—The Crampton and Webster Project,"
DR 31 (1852) 337–352.

2421.   Payno, M., *et al. Cuestión de Tehuantepec.*
Mexico, 1851.

2422.   Ramírez, J. F. *Memorias, Negociaciones y
Documentos, para Servir á la Historia de
las Diferencias que Han Suscitado Entre
México y los Estados Unidos, los Tenedores
del Antiguo Privilegio, Concedido para la
Comunicación de los Mares Atlántico y
Pacífico, por el Istmo de Tehuantepec.*
Mexico, 1853.

2423.   Rippy, J. F. "Diplomacy of the United
States and Mexico Regarding the Isthmus
of Tehuantepec, 1848–1860," *MVHR* 6
(1920) 503–532.

2424.   Romero, M. *The Tehuantepec Isthmus
Railway.* Wash., 1894.

2425.   Squier, E. G. *Nicaragua . . . and the*

Proposed Inter-Oceanic Canal. N.Y.,
1852.

2426.   Strain, I. C. *A Paper on the History and
Prospect of Interoceanic Communication
by the American Isthmus.* N.Y., 1856.

See also item 2411.

2427.   Van Alstyne, R. W. (ed.). "Anglo-
American Relations, 1853–1857," *AHR*
42 (1937) 491–500.

2427a. ———. "British Diplomacy and the
Clayton-Bulwer Treaty, 1850–60,"
JMH 11 (1939) 149–183.

2428.   Villaseñor y Villaseñor, A. *Antón Liz-
ardo: El Tratado MacLane-Ocampo: El
Brindis del Desierto.* Mexico, 1962.

2429.   Williams, J. J. *The Isthmus of Tehuantepec.* N.Y., 1852.

IV–C–3 cross references: 2380a, 5856, 5873, 5896

4. TRANS-ISTHMIAN DIPLOMACY, 1871–1895

2430.   Ammen, D. *The American Interoceanic
Ship Canal Question.* Phil., 1880.

2431.   ———. *The Errors and Fallacies of the
Interoceanic Canal Question.* N.Y., 1886.

2432.   Arosemena, J. *The Panama Canal in the
Light of American Interests.* Wash., 1880.

2433.   Atkins, T. B. *The Interoceanic Canal
Across Nicaragua and the Attitude Toward
It of the Government of the United States,
Presented by the Nicaraguan Canal
Company.* N.Y., 1890.

2434.   Benard, E. *Nicaragua and the Interoceanic
Canal.* Wash., 1874.

Benard was the Nicaraguan minister
to the United States.

2435.   Bigelow, J. *The Panama Canal.* N.Y.,
1886.

2436.   Colquhoun, A. R. *The Key of the Pacific:
The Nicaraguan Canal.* N.Y., 1898.

2437.   Deschanel, P. E. L. *La Politique Française en Océanie à Propos du Canal de
Panama.* Paris, 1884.

2438.   Goodwin, J. M. *The Panama Ship Canal
and Interoceanic Ship Railway.* Cleveland,
1880.

2439.   Gorgorza, A. de. *Tracé d'un Canal Inter-
océanique sans Ecluses à Travers le
Territoire du Darién, Etats-Unis de
Colombie.* Paris, 1876 (?).

2440.   Johnson, E. R. "The Nicaraguan Canal
and the Economic Development of the
United States," *AAAPSS* (1896) 38–48.

2441. Mahan, A. T. *The Interest of America in Sea Power*. Boston, 1897.

2442. ———. "The Isthmus and Sea Power," *AT* 62 (1893) 459–473.

2443. Manson, N. J. *The Nicaragua Canal: Corporate Construction and Control Against the Policy and Business Interests of the United States*. San Francisco, 1892.

2444. Nimmo, J., Jr. *The Proposed American Interoceanic Canal in Its Commercial Aspects*. Wash., 1880.

2445. Peralto, M. M. de. *Canal Interoceánico de Nicaragua y Costa Rica*. Brussels, 1887.

2446. Pletcher, D. M. "General William S. Rosecrans and the Mexican Transcontinental Railroad Project," *MVHR* 38 (1952) 657–678.

2447. Reclus, A. *Exploraciones a los Istmos de Panamá y Darién en 1876, 1877 y 1878*. Panama, 1958.

2448. Reed, T. B. "The Nicaraguan Canal," *NAR* 168 (1899) 552–562.

2449. Rippy, J. F. "Justo Rufino Barrios and the Nicaraguan Canal," *HAHR* 20 (1940) 190–197.

2450. Rodrigues, J. C. *The Panama Canal: Its History, Its Political Aspects, and Financial Difficulties*. London, 1885.

2451. Scheips, P. J. "United States Commercial Pressures for a Nicaragua Canal in the 1890's," *TA* 20 (1964) 333–358.

2452. Smith, J. L. *Interoceanic Canal: Practicability of the Different Routes, and Questionable Nature of the Interest of the United States in a Canal*. Louisville, Ky., 1880.

2453. Stadden, C. M. "The Latest Aspects of the Nicaragua Canal Project," *NAR* 167 (1898) 698–709.

2454. USCS. *Correspondence Touching the Construction of a Ship-Canal Through Nicaragua* (49th Cong., 2d Sess., S. Doc. 50). Wash., 1887.

2454a. ———. *Documents Relating to Interoceanic Canals* (55th Cong., 2d Sess., S. Doc. 26). Wash., 1898.

2454b. Villacrés Moscoso, J. W. "El Ecuador Apoya Fervorosamente el Proyecto Francés del Trazo del Canal de Panamá," *CHA* 9 (1960) 55–73.

2455. Webb, W. H. *Monroe Doctrine and Control of the Isthmian Canal, Nicaragua*. N.Y., 1881.

2456. Williams, A. *The Interoceanic Canal and the Monroe Doctrine*. N.Y., 1880.

2457. Wyse, L. N. B. *Le Canal de Panama*. Paris, 1886.

2458. ———. *Canal Interocéanique de Panama: Mission de 1890–91 en Colombie*. Paris, 1891.

IV–C–4 cross references: 2061, 2090

D. FILIBUSTERING EXPEDITIONS

2459. Allen, M. P. *William Walker, Filibuster*. N.Y., 1932.

2460. Bass, J. M. *William Walker*. Nashville, 1898.

2461. Bemis, S. F. *La Crisis de los Filibusteros: Abraham Lincoln y el Proyectado Compromiso Crittendem* [sic]. Havana, 1956.

2462. Calvo, J. B. *La Campaña Nacional Contra los Filibusteros en 1856 y 1857*. San José, C.R., 1909.

2463. Cañas, J. J. "General Don Ramón Belloso," *AMNDJG* (1957) 25–28, 61–66.

Central American commander against Walker in 1856.

2464. Carr, A. Z. *The World and William Walker*. N.Y., 1963.

2465. Chamorro, P. J. *El Ultimo Filibustero*. Managua, 1933.

Historical novel about William Walker.

2466. Costa Rica. Comisión de Investigación Histórica de la Campaña de 1856–1857. *Crónicas y Comentarios*. San José, C.R., 1956.

2467. ———. ———. *Documentos Relativos a la Guerra Contra los Filibusteros*. San José, C.R., 1956.

2468. ———. ———. *Proclamas y Mensajes*. San José, C.R., 1954.

2469. Curtis, R. E. "The Law of Hostile Military Expeditions as Applied by the United States," *AJIL* 8 (1914) 1–37, 224–255.

2470. Davis, R. H. *Real Soldiers of Fortune*. N.Y., 1906.

Contains accounts of filibusters.

2471. Deutsch, H. B. "Cronología de William Walker," *RAN* 25 (1961) 5–44.

2471a. Esquivel Molina, M. "Un Caso de Panamericanismo Práctico: La Solidaridad

Continental en 1856," *RAN* 20, nos. 1–6 (1956) 143–147.
Discusses assistance against Walker.

2472. Exquemelin, A. O. *Historia de los Aventureros-Filibusteros y Bucaneros de América*. Cd. Trujillo, 1953.

2473. Fabela, I. "El Filibusterismo Americano en Centro América," *RMDI* 3 (1921) 1–57.

2474. Feipel, L. N. "The Navy and Filibustering in the Fifties," *USNIP* 44 (1918) 767–780, 1009–1029, 1219–1240, 1527–1545, 1827–1848, 2063–2085.

2475. Greene, L. *The Filibuster: The Career of William Walker*. Indianapolis, 1937.

2476. "La Contribución de Honduras a la Guerra de los Filibusteros," *RABN* 24 (1946) 523–532.

2477. Lamb, D. I. *The Incurable Filibuster: Adventures of Colonel Dean Ivan Lamb*. N.Y., 1934.

2478. Masis Rojas, T. *Breve Introducción para el Estudio de la Guerra Contra los Filibusteros, 1856–57*. San José, C.R., 1956.

2479. Mayes, G. *Campaña Nacional Centroamericana Contra los Filibusteros en Nicaragua, 1856–1956*. Tegucigalpa, 1956.

2480. Meléndez Ch., C. *Ideario Político de Walker*. San José, C.R., 1956.

2480a. Molina de Lines, M. "Apuntes para una Bibliografía Sobre la Campaña Filibustera de 1856–7 de Costa Rica y Nicaragua (Publicada Fuera de Costa Rica)," *RHA* 40 (1955) 601–610.

2481. Montúfar, L. *Walker en Centro-América*. 2 vols., Guatemala, 1887.

2482. Nicaise, A. *Les Filibustiers Américains: Walker et l'Amérique Centrale*. Paris, 1861.

2483. Nichols, R. F. *Advance Agents of American Destiny*. Phil., 1956.

2484. Obregón Loria, R. *La Campaña del Tránsito, 1856–1857*. San José, C.R., 1956.

2484a. "Reclamos Presentados por Ciudadanos Norteamericanos Residentes en Nicaragua en 1856 al Gobierno de Costa Rica," *RAN* 21, nos. 1–6 (1957) 168–184.

2484b. "Reclamos Presentados por Ciudadanos Norteamericanos Residentes en Nicaragua en 1856 al Gobierno de Costa Rica Intervención de Don Luis Molina,

1860–63," *RAN* 21, nos. 7–12 (1957) 233–238.
Walker claims.

2485. Roche, J. J. *The Story of the Filibusters*. London, 1891.

2486. Rodríguez Betata, V. "Trascendencia de la Guerra Nacional de Centro América Contra William Walker y sus Filibusteros," *ASGHG* 30 (January, 1957) 7–92.

2487. Rodríguez Porras, A. *Juan Rafael Mora Porras y la Guerra Contra los Filibusteros*. San José, C.R., 1955.
The author published a slightly revised version under the title *By-Ways of War: The Story of the Filibusters*. Boston, 1901.

2488. Rollins, C. *William Walker*. Managua, 1945.
Translated into Spanish and published in book form by Guillermo Figueroa from a series of articles which appeared originally in the *San Francisco Chronicle* in 1909.

2489. Scroggs, W. O. *Filibusters and Financiers: The Story of William Walker and His Associates*. N.Y., 1916.

2489a. ———. "William Walker's Designs on Cuba," *MVHR* 1 (1914) 198–211.

2490. Soto V., M. A. *Guerra Nacional de Centroamérica*. Guatemala, 1957.

2491. Urban, C. S. "The Abortive Quitman Filibustering Expedition, 1853–1855," *JMIH* 18 (1956) 175–196.

2492. Walker, W. *The War in Nicaragua*. Mobile, Ala., 1860.

2493. Wells, W. V. *Walker's Expedition to Nicaragua: A History of the Central American War and the Sonora and Kinney Expeditions, Including All the Recent Diplomatic Correspondence*. N.Y., 1856.
Spanish ed., *RAN* 20, nos. 1–6 (1956) 149–184; 20, nos. 7–12 (1956) 292–358; 21, nos. 1–6 (1957) 122–167.

IV–D cross references:

a) For filibustering in Cuba, see items 2761, 2771, 7441, 7446, 7449, 7452, 7457, 7462, 7464, 7471, 7472, 7473, 7478, 7480.

b) For filibustering in Mexico, see items 5848, 5854, 5855, 5855a, 5860, 5867, 5902, 5926, 5928, 5989.

c) For filibustering in Nicaragua, see items 7037, 7038, 7039, 7040, 7045, 7046,

7050, 7052, 7054, 7057, 7058, 7059, 7062, 7064, 7065.

d) See also items 2006, 2103, 2546.

E. OLNEY COROLLARY OF 1895

2494. Blake, N. M. "Background of Cleveland's Venezuelan Policy," *AHR* 47 (1942) 259–277.

2495. Boutwell, G. S. *The Venezuelan Question and the Monroe Doctrine.* Wash., 1896.

2496. Bryce, J. "British Feeling on the Venezuelan Question," *NAR* 162 (1896) 145–153.

2497. Cecil, G. *Life of Robert, Marquis of Salisbury.* 4 vols., London, 1921–1932.

2498. Daly, C. P. *Is the Monroe Doctrine Involved in the Controversy Between Venezuela and Great Britain?* N.Y., 1896.

2499. Hazeltine, M. W. "The United States and the Late Lord Salisbury," *NAR* 177 (1903) 720–724.

2500. James, H. *Richard Olney (1835–1917) and His Public Service: With Documents, Including Unpublished Diplomatic Correspondence.* Boston, 1923.

Secretary of state under Cleveland, 1895–1897.

2501. LaFeber, W. "The American Business Community and Cleveland's Venezuelan Message," *BHR* 34 (1960) 393–402.

2502. ———. "The Background of Cleveland's Venezuelan Policy: A Reinterpretation," *AHR* 66 (1961) 947–967.

2503. ———. "The Latin American Policy of the Second Cleveland Administration," U. of Wisconsin Diss., 1959.

2504. Lodge, H. C. "England, Venezuela, and the Monroe Doctrine," *NAR* 160 (1895) 651–658.

2505. Low, S. "The Olney Doctrine and America's New Foreign Policy," *NC* 40 (1896) 849–860.

2506. Miller, C. R. "The Monroe Doctrine in the Venezuela Dispute: How That Controversy Paved the Way for the Panama Canal," *CE* 86 (1913) 750–764.

2506a. Moore, J. B. "The Monroe Doctrine," *PSQ* 11 (1896) 1–29.

2507. Núñez, E. B. *Tres Momentos en la Controversia de Límites de Guayana: Cleveland y la Doctrina Monroe.* Caracas, 1945.

2508. Rippy, J. F. "Some Contemporary Mexican Reactions to Cleveland's Venezuelan Message," *PSQ* 39 (1924) 280–292.

2509. Scruggs, W. L. *The Venezuelan Question: British Aggressions in Venezuela, or the Monroe Doctrine on Trial: Lord Salisbury's Mistakes: Fallacies of the British "Blue Book" on the Disputed Boundary.* Atlanta, 1896.

2510. Sloan, J. A. "Anglo-American Relations and the Venezuelan Boundary Dispute," U. of Chicago Diss., 1934.

2511. ———. "Anglo-American Relations and the Venezuelan Boundary Dispute," *HAHR* 18 (1938) 486–506.

2512. Smith, T. C. "Secretary Olney's Real Credit in the Venezuelan Affair," *MHSP* 65 (1933) 112–147.

2513. Summers, F. P. (ed.). *The Cabinet Diary of William L. Wilson, 1896–1897.* Chapel Hill, N.C., 1957.

Wilson was President Cleveland's postmaster-general.

2514. Venezuela. Ministerio de Relaciones Exteriores. *Memorandum del Ministerio de Relaciones Exteriores Acerca de la Nota de Lord Salisbury al Señor Olney, Fechada a 26 de Noviembre de 1895, y Relativa á la Cuestión de los Límites de Venezuela con la Guyana Británica.* Caracas, 1896.

2515. Young, G. B. "Intervention Under the Monroe Doctrine: The Olney Corollary," *PSQ* 57 (1942) 247–280.

IV–E cross references:

a) For works on the Venezuelan–British Guiana dispute, see items 8562–8605a.

b) See also items 2076a, 2076b, 2104a, 2112, 2112b, 2143, 2630.

F. THE OLD PAN AMERICANISM

1. FORMULATION OF THE CONCEPT

2516. Alba, P. de. "Panamericanismo Clarividente y Generoso de Bolívar," *RB* 3 (1938) 289–293.

2517. Arias, H. "The International Policy of Bolivar," *IA* 2 (October, 1918) 7–13.

2518. Bellegarde, D. "Alexandre Pétion, a Pioneer of Pan Americanism," *BPAU* 77 (1943) 245–252.

Haitian President, 1808–1818.

2519. Bernstein, H. *Origins of Inter-American Interest, 1700–1812.* Phil., 1945.

2520. Bierck, H. A., Jr. *Vida Pública de Don Pedro Gual.* Caracas, 1947.
Foreign Minister of Gran Colombia who had Pan American ideas in the 1820's.

2521. Blanco, J. E. "Razonamientos Sobre el Panamericanismo," *RMA* (March, 1944) 61–133.

2522. Bolívar, S. *El Pensamiento Político del Libertador.* Bogotá, 1953.

2523. Bumgartner, L. E. "José Cecilio del Valle's Dream of a Latin American Federation," *JIAS* 5 (January, 1963) 103–106.

2524. Carcovich, L. *Portales y la Política Internacional Hispanoamericana.* Santiago, 1937.

2525. Chew, B. *A Sketch of the Politics, Relations, and Statistics of the Western World, and of Those Characteristics of European Policy Which Most Immediately Affect Its Interests: Intended to Demonstrate the Necessity of a Grand American Confederation and Alliance.* Phil., 1827.

2526. Cuevas Cancino, F. *Bolívar: El Ideal Panamericano del Libertador.* Mexico, 1951.

2527. Davis, H. E. "Juan Bautista Alberdi—Americanist," *JIAS* 4 (1962) 53–65.

2528. Egaña, J. "Proyecto de una Reunión General," in *Escritos Inéditos y Dispersos.* Santiago, 1949.

2529. Eyzaguirre, J. "Proyectos Chilenos de la Unión Americana (1810–1829)," *RNC* 23 (1961) 156–167.

2530. Finot, E. *Bolívar Pacifista.* N.Y., 1936.

2531. ———. "El Panamericanismo de Bolívar," *RSB* 3 (July, 1941) 70–78.

2532. Grisanti, A. *Miranda: Precursor del Congreso de Panamá y del Panamericanismo: El Convenio de París de 1797: Origen del Derecho Internacional Hispanoamericano.* Caracas, 1954.

2533. Guerra Iñíguez, D. *El Pensamiento Internacional de Bolívar.* Caracas, 1955.

2534. Hernández de Alba, G. "Origen de la Doctrina Panamericana de la Confederación," *RHA* 22 (1946) 367–398.
Southern South American contributions to development of Pan Americanism early in the nineteenth century.

2535. Huntley, F. C. "Trade of the Thirteen Colonies with the Foreign Caribbean Area," U. of California Diss., 1949.

2536. Lecuna, V. *Relaciones Diplomáticas de Bolívar con Chile y Buenos Aires.* 2 vols., Caracas, 1954.

2537. Levene, R. "El Panamericanismo de Bolívar y San Martín," *RIN* (1940) 242–251.

2538. Leyton Rodríguez, R. *Valle, Padre del Panamericanismo.* Guatemala, 1955.
About José Cecilio de Valle.

2539. Lockey, J. B. *Pan-Americanism: Its Beginnings.* N.Y., 1920.
Spanish ed., Caracas, 1927. Covers 1741–1825.

2540. Lyra, H. "Pan Americanism in Brazil Prior to the Declaration of Monroe," *IA* 3 (December, 1919) 67–78.

2541. MacKenzie, M. *Los Ideales de Bolívar en el Derecho Internacional Americano.* Bogotá, 1955.

2542. Martínez, E. N. "Bolívar y la Bella Norteamericana Jeanette Hart," *BHA* 31 (1944) 361–362, 1106–1133.

2543. Méndez Pereira, O. *Bolívar y las Relaciones Interamericanas.* Panama, 1960.

2544. Mendoza, C. L. "Los Antecedentes del Pan-Americanismo en Hispano-América, la Doctrina Bolivariana," *BANHC* (1934) 118–128.

2545. Monteagudo, B. *Ensayo Sobre la Necesidad de una Federación Jeneral Entre los Estados Hispano-Americanos, y Plan de su Organización.* Lima, 1825.

2546. Moore, J. B. "Henry Clay and Pan-Americanism," *CUQ* 17 (1915) 346–362.

2547. Núñez, E. "Franklin en Hispano-América," *CA* 15 (July, 1956) 155–168.

2548. Olascoaga, L. "El Panamericanismo Nació en Sudamérica," *A* 5 (February, 1940) 25–27.
Traces Pan Americanism to Bolívar and San Martín.

2549. Ordóñez Espinosa, H. "El Panamericanismo y la Gran Colombia," *AUC* 6 (1950) 61–85.

2549a. Palacios, A. L. "Bolívar y Alberdi: Comunidad Regional Iberoamericana," *CA* 14, no. 4 (1955) 170–218.
Contrasts ideas of Bolívar and Alberdi.

2550. Parra-Pérez, C. *Bolívar: A Contribution*

to the Study of His Political Ideas. Pittsburgh, 1935.

2551. Parra Valbuena, J. de los Santos. *Bolívar, Internacionalista.* Madrid, 1932.

2552. Pérez Concha, J. *Bolívar Internacionalista.* Quito, 1939.

2553. Quesada, E. *El Panamericanismo Bolivariano.* B.A., 1927.

2554. Reyes, C. "Panamericanismo: Monroe y Alberdi," *RDHL* 59 (1918) 496–512.

2555. Rivas, R. "Bolívar Internacionalista," *BHA* 25 (1938) 664–698.

2555a. Rodríguez-Alcala, H. "Francisco Romero, Filósofo de América," *CA* 75, no. 3 (1954) 132–143.

Biographical sketch and analysis of philosophic ideas of Francisco Romero, professor of philosophy at the University of Buenos Aires, who visualized the unity of all America.

2556. Roig de Leuchsenring, E. "Bolívar y la Fraternidad Americana," *RBCU* 51 (1943) 184–198.

2557. Rojas, A. "Don Pedro Gual y los Orígenes del Panamericanismo," *RNC* 14 (1953) 169–175.

2558. Santovenia, E. S. *Lincoln: El Precurso de la Buena Vecindad.* Havana, 1951.

2559. Sodre, A. "Jefferson, Dom João VI e o Panamericanismo," *T* (January, 1948) 4–12.

2560. Stimson, F. S. "The Beginnings of American Hispanism, 1770–1830," *H* 37 (1954) 482–489.

2561. Stuart, G. H. "Simón Bolívar's Project for a League of Nations," *SPSQ* 7 (1926) 238–252.

2562. Torres Caicedo, J. M. *Unión Latino-Americana: Pensamiento de Bolívar para Formar una Liga Americana: Su Origen y sus Desarrollos.* Paris, 1865.

2563. Urrutia, F. J. *El Ideal Internacional de Bolívar.* Quito, 1911.

2564. Van Aken, M. J. "Origins of the Pan-Hispanic Movement to 1866," U. of California Diss., 1956.

IV–F–1 cross references: 1816, 1859, 2009, 4456, 9556

2. CONGRESS OF PANAMA, 1826

2565. Arragon, R. F. "The Panama Congress of 1826," Harvard U. Diss., 1923.

2566. Bolívar, S. *Un Pensamiento Sobre el Congreso de Panamá.* Wash., 1916.

2567. Brice, A. F. "Bolívar y el Congreso de Panamá," *RSB* 21 (1962) 60–64.

2568. Castañeda, C. E. "The First Pan-American Congress," *NAR* 223 (1926) 248–255.

2569. Castillero R., E. J. "Intimidades del Congreso de Panamá de 1826," *L* 6 (1961) 70–93.

2570. ———. "Origen y Labores del Primer Congreso Interamericano de Panamá en 1826," *L* 1 (December, 1956) 10–17.

2571. Centeno, F. "El Congreso de Panamá y la Diplomacia Armada de Bolívar," *RDHL* 53 (1912) 507–515; 54 (1913) 42–68, 189–223, 358–368, 523–554.

2572. Cleven, N. A. N. "The First Panama Mission and the Congress of the United States," *JNH* 13 (1928) 225–254.

2573. Collings, H. T. "The Congress of Bolívar," *HAHR* 6 (1926) 194–198.

2574. "Documentación Inédita del Congreso de Panamá (1826)," *BAPH* 5 (1937) 281–382.

2575. "El Congreso de Panamá de 1826," *CHAM* 9 (July, 1920) 5–10.

2576. Escudero Guzmán, J. "Las Actas Extraviadas del Congreso de Panamá de 1826," *AFCJS* 10 (January, 1944) 65–78.

2577. Hackett, C. W. "The Development of John Quincy Adams' Policy with Respect to an American Confederation and the Panama Congress, 1822–1825," *HAHR* 8 (1928) 496–526.

2578. Johnson, G. G. "The Monroe Doctrine and the Panama Congress," *JSHS* 19, no. 2 (1927) 53–73.

2579. López, J. "La Doctrina de Monroe y el Congreso de Panamá," *RSO* (1916) 353–384.

2580. Lozano y Lozano, F. *Bolívar, el Congreso de Panamá y la Solidaridad Americana.* Bogotá, 1948.

2581. Mendoza López, V. *El Congreso de Bolívar y el Panamericanismo.* B.A., 1926.

2582. O'Leary, D. F. *El Congreso Internacional de Panamá en 1826: Desgobierno y Anarquía de la Gran Colombia.* Madrid, 1920.

2583. Otero, L. A. *El Congreso Internacional de Panamá en 1826.* Bogotá, 1906.

2584. PAU. *Sesión Conmemorativa del Congreso de Panamá de 1826.* Panama, 1956.

2585. Peña y Reyes, A. de la. *El Congreso de Panamá y Algunos Otros Proyectos de Unión Hispano-Americano.* Mexico, 1926. In *Archivo Histórico Diplomático Mexicano.*

2585a. Peru. Ministerio de Relaciones Exteriores. *El Congreso de Panamá de 1826: Documentación Inédita.* Lima, 1942.

2586. Porras Barrenechea, R. (ed.). *El Congreso de Panamá (1826).* Lima, 1930. In *Archivo Diplomático Peruano.*

2587. Pradt, D. de Fourt. *Congrès de Panama.* Paris, 1825.

2588. Rein, A. "Zur Geschichte des Panama-Kongresses 1826," *I* 5 (July, 1926) 113–117.

2589. Reinhold, F. L. "New Research on the First Pan-American Congress Held at Panama in 1826," *HAHR* 18 (1938) 342–363.

2590. Robledo, A. "The Congress of Bolivar in Panama, June 1826," *BPAU* 60 (1926) 588–593.

2591. Rodríguez Cerna, J. *Centro-América en el Congreso de Bolívar.* 2d ed., Guatemala, 1956.

2591a. Sanders, R. "Congressional Reaction in the United States to the Panama Congress of 1826," *TA* (1954) 141–154.

2592. Schoonhaven, J., and C. T. de Jong. "The Dutch Observer at the Congress of Panama," *HAHR* 36 (1956) 28–37.

2593. Scott, J. B. "The Larger Significance of the Bolivar Congress," *BPAU* 60 (1926) 571–577.

2594. *Spanish America: Observations on the Instructions Given by the President of the United States of America to the Representatives of That Republic at the Congress Held at Panama in 1826: On the Conduct of Mr. Poinsett, Minister of the United States in Mexico: And Generally on Our Relations with Spanish America: With a Copy of the Instructions.* London, 1829.

2595. USCS. *The Congress of 1826, at Panama, and Subsequent Movements Toward a Conference of American Nations* (51st Cong., 1st Sess., S. Doc. 232). Wash., 1890.

2596. ———. *The Executive Proceedings of the Senate of the United States, on the Subject of the Mission to the Congress of Panama,* *Together with the Messages and Documents Relating Thereto* (19th Cong., 1st Sess., S. Doc. 68). Wash., 1826.

2597. Velarde, F., and F. J. Escobar. *El Congreso de Panamá en 1826.* Panama, 1922.

2598. Zubieta, P. A. *Congresos de Panamá y Tacubaya.* Bogotá, 1912.

IV–F–2   cross references: 1862, 2006a, 2020, 2516, 4435, 5583, 8203, 8211, 8236

3. ATTEMPTS AT ORGANIZATION, 1826–1889

2599. Accioly, H. P. P. *Raízes ou Causas Históricas do Pan-Americanismo.* Rio, 1953.

2600. Alberdi, J. B. *Memoria Sobre la Conveniencia i Objetos de un Congreso General Americano.* Santiago, 1844.

2601. Andrade, O. de Souza. *Joaquim Nabuco e o Pan-Americanismo.* São Paulo, 1950.

2602. Aranda, R. (ed.). *Congresos y Conferencias Internacionales en que Ha Tomado Parte el Perú.* 4 vols., Lima, 1909–1913.

2603. Barrenechea y Raygada, O. *Congresos y Conferencias Internacionales Celebrados en Lima, 1847–1894.* B.A., 1947.

2604. ———. "Los Estadistas Peruanos, Herederos de la Tradición Bolivariana, y los Congresos Internacionales Americanos Reunidos en Lima: Don Manuel Bartolomé Ferreyros y de la Mata," *BHA* 28 (1941) 600–607.

2605. Bastert, R. H. "Diplomatic Reversal: Frelinghuysen's Opposition to Blaine's Pan-American Policy in 1882," *MVHR* 42 (1956) 653–671.

2606. ———. "A New Approach to the Origins of Blaine's Pan American Policy," *HAHR* 39 (1959) 375–402.

2607. Burr, R. N. *The Stillborn Panama Congress: Power Politics and Chilean-Colombian Relations During the War of the Pacific.* Berkeley, Calif., 1962.

2608. Calderón Cousiño, A. *Short Diplomatic History of Chilean-Peruvian Relations, 1819–1879.* Santiago, 1920.

2609. *Congresos Americanos de Lima.* 2 vols., Lima, 1940. In *Archivo Diplomático del Perú.*

2610. Frazer, R. W. "The Role of the Lima Congress, 1864–1865, in the Development of Pan Americanism," *HAHR* 29 (1949) 319–348.

2611. Gomes, L. S. *Joaquim Nabuco e o Pan-Americanismo*. Rio, 1950.

2612. González Vigil, F. de P. *Paz Perpetua en América o Federación Americana*. Bogotá, 1856.

2613. Lastarria, J. F., *et al.*, (eds.). *Colección de Ensayos i Documentos Relativos a la Unión i Confederación de los Pueblos Hispano-Americanos*. 2 vols., Santiago, 1862–1867.

2614. López Barber, L. R. *Panamericanismo, 1826–1889*. B.A., 1936.

2615. Magnet, A. *Orígenes y Antecedentes del Panamericanismo*. Santiago, 1945.
         Covers 1826–1889.

2616. Marcus, E. A. "Chile and Hispanic-American Solidarity, 1830–1865," *TA* 9 (1952) 177–200.

2617. Matienzo, J. N. "La Política Americana de Alberdi," *RACP* 1 (1910) 1–42.

2618. Nuermberger, G. A. "The Continental Treaties of 1856: An American Union 'Exclusive of the United States,'" *HAHR* 20 (1940) 32–55.

2619. Palcos, A. *The Pan-American Ideals of Sarmiento*. B.A., 1938.

2620. Portell Vilá, H. "Un Esfuerzo Panamericano en Favor de la Independencia de Cuba, 1872–1875," *BHA* 26 (1939) 216–227.
         About Colombian effort to gain support for Cuba and frustration of its effort by Hamilton Fish.

2621. Ruiz Moreno (h.), I. *El Pensamiento Internacional de Alberdi*. B.A., 1945.

2622. Varas Velásquez, M. (ed.). *Correspondencia de Don Antonio Varas con El Almirante Manuel Blanco Encalada Sobre su Misión en Europa, 1853–1857*. Santiago, 1919.

IV–F–3   cross references:

a) For works on the general concept of Pan Americanism, many of which treat the period before 1889, see items 4385–4506.

b) For works treating Pan Hispanism, as opposed to Pan Americanism, see items 5313–5384.

c) See also items 2063a, 2103, 2120a, 2203a, 2215, 2260, 2558, 2562, 2564, 2595, 2598, 4435, 4487.

Chapter V   The Spanish-American War, 1895–1900

A. GENERAL WORKS, BIOGRAPHIES, AND SPECIAL STUDIES

2623. Azcárate, P. de. "La Guerra de Hispano-Americana de 1898 (Estudio de Historia Diplomática)," *CHE* (1960) 201–209.

2624. Beer, T. *Hanna*. N.Y., 1929.
Influential senator during the McKinley and Roosevelt administrations.

2625. Benoist, C. *L'Espagne, Cuba et les Etats-Unis*. Paris, 1898.

2626. Campbell, A. "The Spanish-American War," *HT* 8 (1958) 239–247.

2627. Chadwick, F. E. *The Relations of the United States and Spain: The Spanish-American War*. 2 vols., N.Y., 1911.

2628. Croly, H. *Marcus Alonzo Hanna*. N.Y., 1912.
Senator from Ohio and close adviser of President McKinley.

2629. Dawes, C. G. *A Journal of the McKinley Years*. Chicago, 1950.

2629a. Didapp, J. P. *España en la Guerra: Estudio Histórico-Crítico del Conflicto Ibérico-Americano*. Puebla, Mexico, 1898.

2630. Faulkner, H. U. *Politics, Reform, and Expansion, 1890–1900*. N.Y., 1959.
General study of the decade in United States history.

2631. Ferrara, O. *The Last Spanish War: Revelations in "Diplomacy."* N.Y., 1937.

2631a. Fité, V. *Las Desdichas de la Patria: Nuestra Decadencia.—Insurrecciones de Cuba y Filipinas.—Guerra y Censura Militar.—Pérdidas y· Responsabilidades. —Exposiciones á S.M. la Reina Regente.— Patriotismo.—Nuestra Regeneración*. Madrid, 1899.

2631b. García, G. (comp.). *Notables Documentos que Pueden Servir para la Historia de la Guerra Provocada por los Estados Unidos de Norte América Contra España en 1898*. Guayaquil (?), 1898 (?).

2631c. Gardner, L. C. (ed.). *A Different Frontier: Selected Readings in the Foundations of American Economic Expansion*. Chicago, 1966.
A collection of readings on the intellectual rationale for economic imperialism at the turn of the century.

2632. Gómez, M. *En la Guerra y en la Paz: Episodios Históricos de la Revolución por la Independencia y Consideraciones Acerca de la República Cordial "Cuique Sum."* Havana, 1939.

2633. Guerrero, R. *Crónica de la Guerra de Cuba (y de la Rebelión de Filipinas, 1895–97)*. 5 vols., Barcelona, 1895–1897.

2633a. Iglesia y Santos, A. de la. *Cuba para los Cubanos: Folleto Político*. Havana, 1898.

2634. Latané, J. H. "Intervention of the U.S. in Cuba," *NAR* 166 (1898) 350–361.

2635. Lee, F., and J. Wheeler. *Cuba's Struggle Against Spain, with the Causes of American Intervention and a Full Account of the Spanish-American War, Including the Peace Negotiations*. N.Y., 1899.

2636. Leech, M. *In the Days of McKinley*. N.Y., 1959.
General study of the President.

2637. Leuchtenburg, W. E. "The Needless War with Spain," *AHE* 8 (February, 1957) 32–41, 95.

2638. Marburg, T. *Political Papers*. Baltimore, 1898.
Covers the Spanish-American War and the Venezuelan boundary dispute.

2639. Martínez Arango, F. *Cronología Crítica de la Guerra Hispano-Cubanoamericana*. 2d ed., Santiago de Cuba, 1960.

2640. May, E. R. *Imperial Democracy: The Emergence of the United States as a Great Power*. N.Y., 1961.
General study of wartime diplomacy.

2641. Medel, J. A. *The Spanish-American War and Its Results*. Havana, 1932.

2641a. Mendoza y Vizcaino, E. *Historia de la Guerra Hispano-Americana.* 3d ed., Mexico, 1902.

2642. Millis, W. *The Martial Spirit: A Study of Our War with Spain.* N.Y., 1931.
Covers the period 1895–1899.

2643. Miró Quesada, A. *La Intervención Americana en Cuba.* Lima, 1898.

2644. Moore, J. B. *McKinley as a Diplomatist: Speech Before the Ohio Society of Washington, D.C., on McKinley's Birthday, Jan. 29, 1914.* Wash., 1914.

2645. Morales y Morales, V. *Iniciadores y Primeros Mártires de la Revolución Cubana.* 3 vols., Havana, 1931.

2646. Morgan, H. W. *America's Road to Empire: The War with Spain and Overseas Expansion.* N.Y., 1965.

2647. ———. *William McKinley and His America.* Syracuse, N.Y., 1963.

2648. O'Connor, N. L. "The Spanish-American War: A Re-Evaluation," *SS* 22 (1958) 129–143.

2649. Olcott, C. *The Life of William McKinley.* 2 vols., Boston, 1916.

2650. Parker, R. H. "Imperialism and the Liberation of Cuba (1868–1898)," U. of Texas Diss., 1935.

2650a. Pérez Rioja, A. *La Invasión Norte Americana en Cuba.* Havana, 1898.

2650b. ———. *Narraciones de un Testigo: La Invasión Norte Americana en Cuba.* Havana, 1898.

2651. Pérez y Soto, J. B. *Causas y Consecuencias, Antecedentes Diplomáticos y Efectos de la Guerra Hispano-Americana.* San Juan, P.R., 1922.

2651a. Peterson, C. F. *Spansk-Amerikanska Kriget.* Chicago, 1899.

2652. Portell Vilá, H. *Historia de la Guerra de Cuba y los Estados Unidos Contra España.* Havana, 1949.

2653. Pratt, J. W. *Expansionists of 1898: The Acquisition of Hawaii and the Spanish Islands.* Baltimore, 1936.
Pb. ed., Chicago, 1964. Emphasizes the role of business groups in foreign policy formulation.

2654. Pritchett, H. S. "Some Recollections of President McKinley and the Cuban Intervention," *NAR* 189 (1909) 397–403.

2655. Quint, H. H. "American Socialists and the Spanish-American War," *AQ* 10 (1958) 131–141.

2656. Rhodes, J. F. *The McKinley and Roosevelt Administrations, 1897–1909.* N.Y., 1922.

2657. Roig de Leuchsenring, E. *Cuba no Debe su Independencia a los Estados Unidos.* 3d ed., Havana, 1960.

2658. ———. *La Guerra Cubano-Hispano-americana Fué Ganada por el Lugarteniente General del Ejército Libertador Calixto García Iñíguez.* Havana, 1955.

2659. ———. *Por su Propio Esfuerzo Conquistó el Pueblo Cubano su Independencia.* Havana, 1957.

2660. Rubens, H. *Liberty: The Story of Cuba.* N.Y., 1932.
By New York legal adviser to the Cuban *juntas* in the 1890's.

2661. Slezkin, L. I. *Ispano-Amerikanskaia Voina 1898 Goda.* Moscow, 1956.
The Spanish-American War of 1898. A general study of the origin, character, and significance of the war.

2662. Spielman, W. C. *William McKinley: Stalwart Republican.* N.Y., 1954.

2663. Torriente y Peraza, C. de la. *Calixto García Cooperó con las Fuerzas Armadas de los EE. UU. en 1898, Cumpliendo Ordenes del Gobierno Cubano.* Havana, 1952.

2664. USCH. *Relations of the United States and Spain by Reason of Warfare in the Island of Cuba* (55th Cong., 2d Sess., H. Doc. 405). Wash., 1898.

2665. USDS. *Correspondence Relating to the War with Spain, Including the Philippine Expedition, and the China Relief Expedition.* 3 vols., Wash., 1902.

2666. ———. *Proclamations and Decrees During the War with Spain.* Wash., 1899.

2667. ———. *Spanish Diplomatic Correspondence and Documents, 1896–1900, Presented to Cortes by Minister of State.* Wash., 1905.

2668. USDW. *Correspondence Relating to the War with Spain.* 2 vols., Wash., 1902.

2669. Vagts, A. "Der Spanische-Amerikanische Krieg," *EG* 3 (1925) 626–650.

2670. Varona Guerrero, M. *La Guerra de la Independencia de Cuba, 1895–1898.* 3 vols., Havana, 1946.

2671. Viallate, A. *Essais d'Histoire Diplomatique Américaine: le Développement*

Territorial des Etats-Unis: le Canal Interocéanique: la Guerre Hispano-Américaine. Paris, 1905.

2672. Villanueva, H. A. "The Diplomacy of the Spanish-American War," UCLA Diss., 1941.

2673. ———. "Diplomacy of the Spanish-American War," *PSSHR* 14 (1949) 135–182, 303–306, 429–468; 15 (1950) 3–44, 103–162, 305–331.

2674. Vladimirov, L. S. *Diplomatiia S. Sh. Ameriki v Period Amerikanoispanskoi Voiny 1898 Goda*. Moscow, 1957.
The Diplomacy of the United States During the Period of the Spanish-American War of 1898. Sp. ed., Moscow, 1958.

2675. Weigle, R. D. "The Sugar Interests and American Diplomacy in Hawaii and Cuba, 1893–1903," Yale U. Diss., 1939.

2676. Wilkerson, M. M. *Public Opinion and the Spanish-American War: A Study in War Propaganda*. Baton Rouge, La., 1932.

V–A cross references: 2754, 2764, 2765, 2878, 7428, 7549, 7555, 7556

B. BACKGROUND OF THE CONFLICT, 1868–1898

2677. Acheson, S. "Joseph W. Bailey and the Spanish War," *SR* 17 (1932) 142–160.
About minority leader of USCH during the war.

2678. Appel, J. C. "The Unionization of Florida Cigarmakers and the Coming of the War with Spain," *HAHR* 36 (1956) 38–49.

2679. Arias, A. *José Martí*. Quito, 1954.

2680. Armas y Céspedes, J. de. *Position of the United States on the Cuban Question*. N.Y., 1872.

2681. Atkins, E. F. *Sixty Years in Cuba: Reminiscences*. Cambridge, Mass., 1926.
Memoirs of an anti-interventionist planter in Cuba.

2682. Auxier, G. W. "Middle Western Newspapers and the Spanish-American War, 1895–1898," *MVHR* 26 (1940) 523–534.

2683. ———. "The Cuban Question as Reflected in the Editorial Columns of Middle Western Newspapers, 1895–1898," Ohio State U. Diss., 1941.

2684. ———. "The Propaganda Activities of the Cuban Junta in Precipitating the Spanish-American War, 1895–1898," *HAHR* 19 (1939) 268–305.

2685. Baeza Flores, A. *Vida de José Martí: El Hombre Intimo y el Hombre Público*. Havana, 1954.

2686. Bartlett, C. J. "British Reaction to the Cuban Insurrection of 1868–1878," *HAHR* 37 (1957) 296–312.

2687. Bécker, J. *De los Derechos de las Naciones y del Principio de Intervención: La Neutralidad y la Beligerancia: España y los Estados Unidos*. Madrid, 1895.

2688. Bertel, C. T. "Hojas del Diario de Un Filibustero: La Expedición 'Comodoro' en Junio, 1896," *RBCU* 35 (1935) 226–236.

2689. Boromé, J. A. "Antonio Maceo," *CQ* 3 (1954) 237–240.

2690. Butler, C. H. *The Voice of the Nation: The President Is Right*. N.Y., 1898.

2690a. Candamo, V. G. *Weyler: La Insurrección de Cuba: La Guerra Hispano-Yankee*. Puerto Rico, 1897.

2691. Carlisle, C. *Reports to E. Dupuy de Lome, Spanish Minister*. 2 vols., Wash., 1896–1897.
Concerns neutrality laws of the United States.

2692. Carlson, O., and E. S. Bates. *Hearst: Lord of San Simeon*. N.Y., 1936.
Biography of a "yellow journalist."

2693. Córdova, R. de. "The 'Virginius' Incident and Cuba," *NC* 60 (1906) 976–985.

2694. Cortina, J. M. *Néstor Leonelo Carbonell*. Havana, 1950.
Organizer of the Tampa Junta.

2695. Cuba. Archivo Nacional. *Antonio Maceo: Documentos para su Vida: Homenaje del Archivo Nacional de Cuba al Lugarteniente General del Ejército Libertador en el Centenario de su Nacimiento, 1845–1945*. Havana, 1945.

2696. ———. ———. *Correspondencia Diplomática de la Delegación Cubana en Nueva York Durante la Guerra de Independencia de 1895 a 1898*. 5 vols., Havana, 1943–1946.

2697. Cuban League of the United States. *The Present Condition of Affairs in Cuba: A Report*. N.Y., 1877.

2698. Cuban Society of Judicial and Economic

Studies. *Cuban Opinion on the President's [Cleveland's] Message.* N.Y., 1896.

2699. Curtis, G. T. *The Case of the Virginius, Considered with Reference to the Law of Self-Defense.* N.Y., 1874.

2700. Davis, R. H. *Cuba in War Time.* N.Y., 1897.

2701. Detter, R. A. "The Cuban Junta and Michigan: 1895–1898," *MH* 48 (1964) 35–46.

2702. "Documentos de la Revolución de 1868 a 1876 Comprados por el Archivo Nacional," *BANC* 53–54 (1956) 104–196.

2703. Ellis, E. *Henry Moore Teller: Defender of the West.* Caldwell, Idaho, 1941.

2704. Ellmore, W. S. "Diplomatic Background of the Spanish-American War: The Cuban Question," Georgetown U. Diss., 1956.

2705. "Expediente Promovido por Nuestro Cónsul en Nueva Orleans Acerca de la Barca Americana 'Venus,'" *BANC* 20 (1921) 139–155.

2706. "Expediente Relativo á la Salida de New York de los Hermanos Sanguilí, para Nueva Orleans y Cayo-Hueso, y de los Actos Ejecutados por Estos y Otros Insurrectos para Organizar Expediciones Filibusteras (1877)," *BANC* 20 (1921) 117–138.

2707. Farrell, J. T. "Archbishop Ireland and Manifest Destiny," *CHIR* 33 (1947) 269–301.
Concerns activities of a United States clergyman.

2708. Fernández-Rúa, J. L. *1898: Cuba y Filipinas.* Madrid, 1954.

2709. Flack, H. E. *Spanish-American Diplomatic Relations Preceding the War of 1898.* Baltimore, 1906.

2710. Franco, J. L. *Antonio Maceo: Apuntes para una Historia de su Vida.* 3 vols., Havana, 1951–1957.

2711. ———. *Ruta de Antonio Maceo en el Caribe.* Havana, 1961.

2712. Gay Calbó, E. "Las Crónicas de la Guerra de Cuba," *RBNCU*, 2d ser., 6 (April, 1955) 79–94.

2713. Gil Munilla, O. "Cuba, Problema Español, 1891–1898," *AEA* 9 (1953) 481–512.
Efforts of Spain to placate Cuba.

2714. Gómez, J. G. "La Cuestión de Cuba en 1884," *RBNCU* 5, 2d ser., (January, 1954) 9–15.

2715. Gómez Toro, B. *La Famosa Expedición Gómez–Martí (1895): Un Eslabón Perdido en su Cadena de Vicisitudes.* Havana, 1953.

2716. González, M. P. *José Martí, Epic Chronicler of the United States in the Eighties.* Chapel Hill, N.C., 1953.

2717. González y Torres, P. *The "Virginius" Case, as Reviewed in England and Regarded by the New York Herald.* N.Y., 1874.

2718. Gray, R. B. *José Martí, Cuban Patriot.* Gainesville, Fla., 1962.

2719. Guerra y Sánchez, R. *Guerra de los Diez Años, 1868–1878.* 2 vols., Havana, 1950–1952.

2719a. Guiteras, J. *The United States and Cuba: A Review of the Documents Relating to the Intervention of the United States in the Affairs of the Spanish-American Colonies.* Phil., 1895.

2720. Gullason, T. A. "Stephen Crane's Private War on Yellow Journalism," *HLQ* 22 (1959) 201–208.

2721. Hacker, L. M. "The Holy War of 1898," *AM* 21 (1930) 316–326.
Spanish ed., *RBCU* 46 (1940) 397–413.

2722. ———. "The Incendiary Mahan: A Biography," *S* 95 (1934) 263–268, 311–320.

2723. Harding, L. A. *The Preliminary Diplomacy of the Spanish-American War.* Indianapolis, 1912.

2724. Hengelmüller, Baron von. "Die Diplomatische Vorgeschichte des Krieges der Vereinigten Staaten Gegen Spanien," *DRE* 41 (1916) 93–107, 164–179.
The Austrian Ambassador to the United States at the time.

2725. Heredia, N. *Crónicas de la Guerra de Cuba: Reproducción de la Primera Edición de "El Figaro" Hecho en 1895 y 1896, en Dos Cuadernos.* Havana, 1957.

2726. Hershey, A. S. "Intervention and the Recognition of Cuban Independence," *AAAPSS* 11 (1898) 353–380.

2726a. Holman, D. A. "The Destruction of the *Maine*, February 15, 1898," *MAL* 60 (1954) 147–160.

2726b. *La Independencia de Cuba en Relación con*

CARL A. RUDISILL LIBRARY
LENOIR RHYNE COLLEGE

el *Criterio Americano y los Intereses Mexicanos: Colección de Notables Artículos Sobre Esta Cuestión de Distinguidos Escritores Mexicanos.* Mexico, 1897.

Articles by Francisco Bulnes and others.

2727. Infiesta, R. *El Pensamiento Político de Martí.* Havana, 1953.

2728. Jiménez de la Romera, W. *Cuba no se Vende.* Madrid, 1870.

Spanish opposition to purchase by the United States.

2729. *La Anexión de Cuba y los Estados Unidos: Polémica Entre . . . Juan Bellido de Luna y Enrique Trujillo.* N.Y., 1892.

2730. Labra y Cadrana, R. M. de. *La Cuestión de Cuba en 1897.* Madrid, 1897.

Spanish opposition to government policy.

2731. LaFeber, W. "A Note on the 'Mercantilistic Imperialism' of Alfred Thayer Mahan," *MVHR* 48 (1962) 674–685.

2732. Latané, J. H. "The Diplomacy of the United States in Regard to Cuba," *AHAAR* (1897) 217–278. Wash., 1898.

2733. Lizaso, F. *Martí: Martyr of Cuban Independence.* Albuquerque, N.M., 1953.

2734. Lodge, H. C. "Our Duty to Cuba," *F* 21 (1896) 278–287.

2735. Low, A. M. "Unwritten Chapter in American Diplomacy: War with Spain," *CR* 78 (1900) 83–93.

2736. Lundberg, F. *Imperial Hearst.* N.Y., 1936.

Study of a "yellow journalist."

2737. Mañach, J. *Martí, el Apóstol.* Madrid, 1933.

English ed., N.Y., 1950.

2738. Márquez Sterling, C. *Nueva y Humana Visión de Martí.* Havana, 1953.

2739. Márquez Sterling, M. *La Diplomacia en Nuestra Historia.* Havana, 1909.

2740. Martí, J. *Cuba y los Estados Unidos.* N.Y., 1889.

A short pamphlet.

2741. ———. *Obras Completas.* 2 vols., Havana, 1946.

2742. ———. *Obras Completas de José Martí.* 2 vols., Paris, 1926.

2743. ———. *Obras Completas de José Martí.* 74 vols., Havana, 1936–1953.

2744. ———. *Obras Completas de Martí.* 8 vols., Havana, 1918–1920.

2745. ———. *Obras del Maestro.* 16 vols., Havana, 1900–1933.

2746. Mason, G. *Remember the Maine.* N.Y., 1939.

2747. McKee, D. L. "Samuel Gompers, the A. F. of L., and Imperialism, 1895–1900," *HIS* 21 (1959) 187–199.

2748. Melville, G. W. "The Destruction of the Battleship 'Maine,'" *NAR* 193 (1911) 831–849.

2749. Meriwether, W. S. "Remembering the 'Maine,'" *USNIP* 74 (1948) 549–556.

2750. Monner Sans, R. *España y Norteamérica: La Guerra Actual, Antecedentes y Consideraciones.* B.A., 1898.

2751. Moore, J. B. "The Question of Cuban Belligerency," *F* 21 (1896) 288–300.

2752. Moreno, C. G. *José Martí, Ciudadano de América.* B.A., 1953.

2753. Moret y Prendergast, S. "La Insurrección de Cuba ante los Estados Unidos," *EM* 7, no. 78 (1896) 46–72, and no. 79 (1896) 42–61.

2754. Morgan, J. T. *Belligerent Rights in Cuba.* Wash., 1897.

By a senator from Alabama.

2755. Offner, J. L. "President McKinley and the Origins of the Spanish-American War," Pennsylvania State U. Diss., 1957.

2756. Older, C. M. *William Randolph Hearst.* N.Y., 1936.

2757. Ponte Domínguez, F. J. *Historia de la Guerra de los Diez Años.* 2 vols., Havana, 1944–1958.

2758. Portell Vilá, H. *Martí, Diplomático.* Havana, n.d.

2759. Pratt, J. W. "American Business and the Spanish-American War," *HAHR* 14 (1934) 163–201.

2760. ———. "The 'Large Policy' of 1898," *MVHR* 19 (1932) 219–242.

2761. Proctor, S. "Filibustering Aboard the *Three Friends,*" *MA* 38 (1956) 84–100.

Filibustering from Florida in the period 1895 to 1898.

2762. Puleston, W. D. *Mahan: The Life and Work of Captain Alfred Thayer Mahan.* New Haven, Conn., 1939.

2763. Quesada y Miranda, G. de. *Martí, Hombre.* Havana, 1940.

2764. Roig de Leuchsenring, E. *1895 y 1898: Dos Guerras Cubanas: Ensayo de Revaloración.* Havana, 1945.

2765. ———. *La Guerra Libertadora Cubana de los Treinta Años, 1868–1898: Razón de su Victoria.* Havana, 1952.

2766. ———. *El Internacionalismo Antiimperialista en la Obra Político-Revolucionario de José Martí.* Havana, 1935.

2767. ———. *Martí, Antiimperialista.* 2d. ed. rev., Havana, 1961.

2768. ———. *Máximo Gómez, el Libertador de Cuba y el Primer Ciudadano de la República.* Havana, 1959.

2769. ——— (ed.). *La Revolución de Martí, 24 de Febrero de 1895.* Havana, 1941.

2770. ———. *Trece Conclusiones Fundamentales Sobre la Guerra Libertadora Cubana de 1895.* Mexico, 1945.

2771. Ruiz de León, J. *Los Filibusteros en Madrid y el Apresamiento del "Virginius."* Madrid, 1874.

2771a. Santos, J. N. *España, Cuba, Estados Unidos: Reformas que se Imponen.* Madrid, 1897.

2772. Santovenia y Echaide, E. S. *Martí, Hombre de Estado.* Havana, 1953.

2773. Serra y Montalvo, R. *Ensayos Políticos.* N.Y., 1896.
By a member of the Cuban junta.

2774. Sigsbee, C. D. *The "Maine."* N.Y., 1899.

2775. Spain. Ministerio de Estado. *Documentos Parlamentarios Preparados para Ser Presentados a las Cortes en la Legislatura de 1886: Negociaciones con los Estados Unidos de América Sobre la Interpretación del Convenio Comercial del 13 de Febrero de 1884.* Madrid, 1886.

2776. Swanberg, W. A. *Citizen Hearst.* N.Y., 1961.
Biography of a "yellow journalist."

2777. Tejera, D. V. "Autonomistas y Anexionistas," *RBCU* 47 (1941) 367–380.

2777a. True, M. M. "Revolutionaries in Exile: The Cuban Revolutionary Party, 1891–1898," U. of Virginia Diss., 1965.

2778. USCH. *Final Report on Removing Wreck of Battleship Maine from Harbor of Habana, Cuba* (63d Cong., 2d Sess., H. Doc. 480). Wash., 1914.

2779. USCS. *Correspondence of the Department of State Between November 5, 1875, and the Date of the Pacification of Cuba in 1878, Relating to the Subject of Mediation or Intervention by the United States in the Affairs of Cuba* (54th Cong., 1st Sess., S. Ex. Doc. 213). Wash., 1897.

2780. ———. *Report of the Committee on Foreign Relations, United States Senate, Relative to Affairs in Cuba, Apr. 13, 1898* (55th Cong., 2d Sess., S. Rept. 885). Wash., 1898.

2781. ———. *Report of the Naval Court of Inquiry upon the Destruction of the Battleship "Maine" in Havana Harbor, February 15, 1898, Together with the Testimony Taken Before the Court, 1898* (55th Cong., 2d Sess., S. Doc. 207). Wash., 1898.

2782. ———. *The Terms and Conditions Under Which the Surrender of the Cuban Insurgents Has Been Made, and in Relation to the Future Policy of Spain in the Government of Cuba, 1878* (45th Cong., 2d Sess., S. Ex. Doc. 79). Wash., 1879.

2782a. Valera y Alcalá Galiano, J. *Los Estados Unidos Contra España, por un Optimista.* Madrid, 1896.

2783. Viallate, A. "Les Preliminaires de la Guerre Hispano-Américaine et l'Annexion des Philippines," *RHI* 82 (1903) 242–291.

2784. Vitier, M. *Martí: Estudio Integral: Premio del Centenario.* Havana, 1954.

2785. Weems, J. E. *The Fate of the Maine.* N.Y., 1958.

2786. Whitney, E. B. "The Cuban Revolt and the Constitution," *YR* o.s. 7 (1898) 8–23.

2787. Wisan, J. E. *The Cuban Crisis as Reflected in the New York Press (1895–1898).* N.Y., 1934.
Discusses the role of newspapers in promoting the war.

2788. Younger, E. *John A. Kasson: Politics and Diplomacy from Lincoln to McKinley.* Iowa City, Ia., 1955.
About an influential politician of the times who held expansionist views.

2789. Zaragoza, J. *Las Insurrecciones de Cuba.* 2 vols., Madrid, 1872–1873.

V–B cross references:

a) For general works on the United States and Spanish Cuba, see items 7438–7499.

b) See also items 2056, 2076a, 2099b, 2099c, 2113a.

C. CONDUCT OF THE WAR, 1898

2790.   Alger, R. A. *The Spanish-American War.*
        N.Y., 1901.
        A justification by McKinley's secretary
        of war in 1898.

2791.   Azoy, A. C. M. *Charge! The Story of the
        Battle of San Juan Hill.* N.Y., 1961.

2792.   ———. *Signal 250! The Sea Fight off
        Santiago.* N.Y., 1964.

2792a. Bergés, R. *Cuba y Santo Domingo:
        Apuntes de la Guerra de Cuba de Mi
        Diario en Campaña, 1895–96–97–98.*
        Havana, 1906.

2792b. Boza, B. *Mi Diario de la Guerra, Desde
        Baire Hasta la Intervención Americana.*
        2 vols., Havana, 1900–1904.

2792c. Casasús, J. J. E. *La Invasión: Sus Ante-
        cedentes, sus Factores, su Finalidad:
        Estudio Crítico-Militar.* Havana, 1950.

2792d. Cervera y Topete, P. *Views of Admiral
        Cervera Regarding the Spanish Navy in
        the Late War: November, 1898.* Wash.,
        1898.

2793.   Davis, R. H. *Cuba and Porto Rico Cam-
        paigns.* N.Y., 1898.

2794.   Foraker, J. B. "Our War with Spain: Its
        Justice and Necessity," *F* 25 (1898)
        385–395.

2795.   Freidel, F. *The Splendid Little War.*
        Boston, 1959.
        Pb. ed., N.Y., 1962.

2795a. Gómez Núñez, S. *La Guerra Hispano-
        Americana: El Bloqueo y la Defensa de las
        Costas.* Madrid, 1899.

2796.   Goode, W. A. M. *With Sampson Through
        the War.* N.Y., 1899.

2797.   Lodge, H. C. *The War with Spain.*
        N.Y., 1899.

2798.   Long, J. D. *America of Yesterday, as
        Reflected in the Journal of John D. Long.*
        Boston, 1923.
        Journal of the Secretary of the Navy in
        1898.

2799.   Luce, S. B. "The Spanish-American
        War," *NAR* 194 (1911) 612–627.

2800.   Müller y Tejeiro, J. *Battles and Capitu-
        lation of Santiago de Cuba.* Wash.,
        1898.
        By Lieutenant José Müller y Tejeiro.
        Part of the author's *Combates y Capitu-
        lación de Santiago de Cuba.*

2801.   Reyno Cossio, R. E. *Estudios Histórico-*

*Militares Sobre la Guerra de Indepen-
dencia de Cuba.* Havana, 1954.

2802.   Sargent, H. H. *The Campaign of Santiago
        de Cuba.* 3 vols., Chicago, 1907.

2803.   Schley, W. S. *Forty-Five Years Under the
        Flag.* N.Y., 1904.

2804.   Spears, J. R. *Our Navy in the War with
        Spain.* N.Y., 1899.

2805.   Titherington, R. H. *A History of the
        Spanish-American War of 1898.* N.Y.,
        1900.

2806.   Wilson, H. W. *The Downfall of Spain:
        Naval History of the Spanish-American
        War.* London, 1902.

2807.   Zobrist, B. K. "How Victor Lawson's
        Newspapers Covered the Cuban War of
        1898," *JQ* 38 (1961) 323–331.

V–C cross references: *7618a, 9408*

D. EUROPEAN INTERESTS

2808.   Bailey, T. A. "Dewey and the Germans
        at Manila Bay," *AHR* 45 (1939) 59–81.

2809.   Blake, N. M. "England and the U.S.,
        1897–1898," in D. E. Lee and G. E.
        McReynolds (eds.). *Essays in History and
        International Relations in Honor of George
        Hubbard Blakeslee.* Worcester, Mass.,
        1949.

2810.   Campbell, A. E. *Great Britain and the
        United States, 1895–1903.* London, 1960.

2811.   Campbell, C. S., Jr. *Anglo-American
        Understanding, 1898–1903.* Baltimore,
        1957.

2812.   Ferguson, J. H. *American Diplomacy and
        the Boer War.* Phil., 1939.

2813.   Ferrara, O. *Tentativas de Intervención
        Europea en América, 1896–1898.* Havana,
        1933.
        English ed., N.Y., 1937.

2814.   Findlay, J. V. *Some of the International
        Aspects of the Cuban Question.* Baltimore,
        1898.

2815.   Gelber, L. M. *The Rise of Anglo-
        American Friendship: A Study in World
        Politics, 1898–1906.* N.Y., 1938.

2816.   Labra y Cadrana, R. M. de. *Aspecto
        Internacional de la Cuestión de Cuba.*
        Madrid, 1900.

2817.   *La Question de Cuba: Ce que l'Europe Doit
        Penser, par un Européen.* Vienna, 1896.

2817a. *Les Intérêts de l'Europe dans la Question*

Cubaine, par un Diplomate Européen. N.p., 1896.

2818. McMinn, J. H. "The Attitude of the English Press Toward the U.S. During the Spanish-American War," Ohio State U. Diss., 1939.

2819. Neale, R. G. "British-American Relations During the Spanish-American War: Some Problems," *HSANZ* 6 (November, 1953) 72-89.

2820. Quintana, J. *Indice de Extranjeros en el Ejército Libertador de Cuba.* Havana, 1953.
Covers 1895 to 1898.

2821. Reuter, B. A. *Anglo-American Relations During the Spanish-American War.* N.Y., 1924.

2822. Rippy, J. F. "The European Powers and the Spanish-American War," *JSHS* 19 (1927) 22-52.

2823. Sears, L. M. "French Opinion of the Spanish-American War," *HAHR* 7 (1927) 25-44.

2824. Seed, G. "British Reactions to American Imperialism Reflected in Journals of Opinion, 1889-1900," *PSQ* 73 (1958) 254-272.

2825. Shippee, L. B. "Germany and the Spanish-American War," *AHR* 30 (1925) 754-777.

2826. Spain. Ministro de Estado. *Disposiciones de España y los Estados Unidos Referentes a la Guerra y Declaraciones de Neutralidad.* Madrid, 1898.

2827. Vagts, A. *Deutschland und die Vereinigten Staaten in der Weltpolitik, 1890-1906.* 2 vols., N.Y., 1935.

2828. White, A. D. *Autobiography of Andrew Dickson White.* 2 vols., N.Y., 1905.
The U.S. Ambassador to Germany during the war.

V-D   cross references: 3085-3092, 7544

E. LEGAL ASPECTS

2829. Amador y Carrandi, E. *La Guerra Hispano-Americana ante el Derecho Internacional.* Madrid, 1900.

2830. Becerra, R. *Cuestión Palpitante: Un Poco de Historia á Propósito de la Independencia de Cuba y Puerto Rico, y la Doctrina Monroe y la Intervención Norteamericana en Cuba.* Caracas, 1898.

2831. Benton, E. J. *International Law and the Diplomacy of the Spanish-American War.* Baltimore, 1908.

2832. Deming, W. C. *How a Letter of a Country Lawyer Became International Law.* Cheyenne, Wyo., 1923.
Refers to advice of a Wyoming lawyer at the time of McKinley's war message.

2833. Desjardins, A. "La Guerre Hispano-Américaine et le Droit des Gens," *RDM* 147 (1898) 518-549.

2834. Lebraud, E. *La Guerre Hispano-Américaine et le Droit des Gens.* Paris, 1904.

2835. LeFur, L. *Etude sur la Guerre Hispano-Américaine de 1898, Envisagée au Point de Vue du Droit International Public.* Paris, 1899.

2836. Moore, J. B. "International Law in the War with Spain," *RR* 19 (1899) 563-568.

2837. ———. "Maritime Law in the War with Spain," *PSQ* 15 (1900) 399-425.

2838. Olivart, M. de. *Del Reconocimiento de Beligerancia y sus Efectos Inmediatos.* Madrid, 1895.

2839. ———. "Le Différend entre l'Espagne et les Etats-Unis au Sujet de la Question Cubaine," *RGDIP* 4 (1897) 577-620; 5 (1898) 358-422, 499-555; 7 (1900) 541-629; 9 (1902) 161-202.

2839a. Stoerk, F. *El Derecho Internacional Americano: Estudio Doctrinal y Crítico.* Madrid, 1898.

2839b. Vargas Machuca, J. de. *Cuba y los Estados Unidos: Estudio Vulgar Acerca de las Cuestiones Pendientes con el Gobierno de la Unión Federal bajo el Punto de Vista del Derecho Positivo Americano.* Madrid, 1898.

V-E   cross references: 2843, 2845

F. PARIS PEACE SETTLEMENT

2840. Chetwood, J. *Manila, or Monroe Doctrine?* N.Y., 1898.

2841. Coletta, P. E. "Bryan, McKinley, and the Treaty of Paris," *PHR* 26 (1957) 131-146.

2842. ———. "McKinley, the Peace Negotiations, and the Acquisition of the Philippines," *PHR* 30 (1961) 341-350.

2843. Crandall, S. B. "Principles of International Law Applied by the Spanish

Treaty Claims Commission," *AJIL* 4 (1910) 806–822.

2844. France. Ministère des Affaires Etrangères. *Documents Diplomatiques: Négociations pour la Paix Entre l'Espagne et les Etats-Unis, 1898*. Paris, 1898.

2845. Gonzáles Benard, J. M. *Proceso Histórico del Tratado de París de 10 Diciembre de 1898, con Algunas Ideas de Derecho Internacional Público*. Valencia, 1903.

2846. Iznaga, F. "Ecos del Tratado de París: La Deuda Colonial," *CC* 13 (1917) 214–280.

2847. Labra y Cadrana, R. M. de. *El Tratado de París de 1898*. Madrid, 1899.

2848. *Le Traité de Paix Entre l'Espagne et les Etats-Unis*. N.p., 1898(?).

2849. Montero Ríos, E. *El Tratado de París*. Madrid, 1904.
    The author was a delegate of Spain in Paris.

2850. Morgan, H. W. *Making Peace with Spain: The Diary of Whitelaw Reid, September–December, 1898*. Austin, Texas, 1965.
    Reid was one of the peace commissioners.

2851. Morgan, J. T. "What Shall We Do with the Conquered Islands?" *NAR* 166 (1898) 641–649.

2851a. Murphy, J. T., Jr. "A History of American Diplomacy at the Paris Peace Conference of 1898," American U. Diss., 1965.

2852. Reid, W. *Some Consequences of the Last Treaty of Paris, Advances in International Law and Changes in National Policy*. London, 1899.

2853. ———. *The Treaty of Paris: Some Speeches on Its Policy and Scope*. N.Y., 1899.

2854. Rippy, J. F. "Enthusiasms of 1898," *SAQ* 37 (1938) 139–149.
    Concerns United States justifications for expansion.

2855. Spain. Ministro de Estado. *Conferencia de París y Tratado de Paz de 10 de Diciembre de 1898: Documentos Presentados á las Cortes en la Legislatura de 1898, por el Ministro de Estado*. Madrid, 1899.

2856. ———. *Negociaciones Diplomáticas Desde el Principio de la Guerra con los Estados Unidos Hasta la Firma del Protocolo de Washington y Gestiones Practicadas para su Complimiento*. Madrid, 1898.

2857. Spanish Treaty Claims Commission. *Final Report, May 2, 1910*. Wash., 1910.

2858. Taylor, H. "The Spanish Treaty Claims," *NAR* 182 (1906) 738–746.
    By the United States minister to Spain.

2859. ———. "The Work of the Peace Commission," *NAR* 167 (1898) 744–751.

2860. USCS. *A Treaty of Peace Between the United States and Spain, Signed at the City of Paris, on December 10, 1898* (55th Cong., 3d Sess., S. Doc. 62). Wash., 1899.

2861. ———. *Papers Relating to the Treaty with Spain* (56th Cong., 2d Sess., S. Doc. 148). Wash., 1901.

2862. USDW. *Report on Legal Status of Islands Acquired During the War with Spain*. Wash., 1900.

2863. Webster, S. "Revelations of a Senate Document," *NAR* 172 (1901) 867–881.
    Refers to S. Doc. 148 of 56th Cong., 2d Sess.; see item 2861.

G. AFTEREFFECT: THE IMPERIALIST DEBATE

2864. Adams, B. "The Spanish War and the Equilibrium of the World," *F* 25 (1898) 641–651.

2865. Bailey, T. A. "Was the Presidential Election of 1900 a Mandate on Imperialism?" *MVHR* 24 (1937) 43–52.

2866. Barnes, A. M. "American Intervention in Cuba and Annexation of the Philippines, an Analysis of the Public Discussion," Cornell U. Diss., 1948.

2867. Baron, H. "Anti-Imperialism and the Democrats," *SS* 21 (1957) 222–239.

2868. Boutwell, G. S. *The President's Policy: War and Conquest Abroad*. Chicago, 1900.
    By a president of the Anti-Imperialist League.

2869. Bowers, C. G. *Beveridge and the Progressive Era*. Boston, 1932.

2870. Brown, R. C. "Goldwin Smith and Anti-Imperialism," *CHR* 43 (1962) 93–105.
    Indicates that Canada generally approved of the Spanish-American War.

2871. Bryan, W. J. "The Issue in the Presidential Campaign," *NAR* 170 (1900) 753–771.

2872. Carnegie, A. "Americanism *versus* Imperialism," *NAR* 168 (1899) 1–13, 362–372.

2873. ———. *Autobiography of Andrew Carnegie*. Boston, 1920.

2873a. Cuban-American League. *Questions and Results of the War with Spain: American Editorial Opinion Presented by the Cuban-American League in Newspaper Clippings for Preservation in the Library Americana.* 3 vols., n.p., 1898.

2874. Gibson, W. M. "Mark Twain and Howells: Anti-Imperialists," *NEQ* 20 (1947) 435–470.

2875. Giddings, F. H. "Imperialism?" *PSQ* 139 (1898) 585–605.

2876. Gillett, F. H. *George Frisbie Hoar*. Boston and N.Y., 1934.

  Hoar was an anti-imperialist senator. See also item 2883.

2877. Glad, P. W. *The Trumpet Soundeth: William Jennings Bryan and His Democracy, 1896–1912*. Lincoln, Nebr., 1960.

2878. Greene, T. P. (ed.). *American Imperialism in 1898*. N.Y., 1955.

2879. Harrington, F. H. "Literary Aspects of American Anti-Imperialism, 1898–1902," *NEQ* 10 (1937) 650–667.

2880. ———. "The Anti-Imperialist Movement in the United States, 1898–1900," *MVHR* 22 (1935) 211–230.

2881. Hazeltine, M. W. "What Is to Be Done with Cuba?" *NAR* 167 (1898) 318–325.

2882. Hendrick, B. J. *The Life of Andrew Carnegie*. 2 vols., Garden City, N.Y., 1932.

2883. Hoar, G. F. *Autobiography of Seventy Years*. 2 vols., N.Y., 1903.

  Memoirs of an anti-imperialist senator from Massachusetts.

2884. Lasch, C. "The Anti-Imperialists, the Philippines, and the Inequality of Man," *JSH* 24 (1958) 319–331.

2885. Mahan, A. T. *Lessons of the War with Spain*. Boston, 1899.

  Concentrates on problems of defense.

2886. Morgan, J. T. *Cuba: El Método Seguro y Justo para el Arreglo de la Cuestión Cubana (por el Senador John T. Morgan)*. N.p., 1901.

2887. Schurz, C. *American Imperialism*. Chicago, 1899.

2888. ———. *The Policy of Imperialism*. Chicago, 1899.

2889. ———. "Thoughts on American Imperialism," *CE* 56 (1898) 781–788.

2890. Sillen, S. "Dooley, Twain, and Imperialism," *MM* 1 (1948) 6–13.

2891. Williams, W. A. "Brooks Adams and American Expansion," *NEQ* 25 (1952) 217–232.

V–G cross references: 2631c, 2676, 2747, 2854, 2906, 2925, 2944, 2947, 3048, 6720, 7529, 7596, 7597, 7600

Chapter VI   The Imperial Era and Latin America, 1900–1921

A. GENERAL WORKS AND INTERPRETATIONS

2892. Barrett, J. "The United States and Latin America," *NAR* 183 (1906) 474–483.
By the U.S. Minister to Colombia.

2893. Bigelow, J. *American Policy: The Western Hemisphere and Its Relation to the Eastern.* N.Y., 1914.

2894. Billman, C. J. "Backgrounds and Policies of Selected United States Diplomats to Latin America, 1898–1938," Tulane U. Diss., 1955.

2895. Blakeslee, G. H. "Our Relations with South America and How to Improve Them," *IC*, no. 76 (1914).

2896. Brown, P. M. "American Diplomacy in Central America," *APSR* 6 suppl. (1912) 152–163.

2897. ———. "American Intervention in Central America," *JRD* 4 (1914) 409–426.

2898. Bryan, W. J., and M. B. Bryan. *The Memoirs of William Jennings Bryan.* Chicago, 1925.

2899. Callcott, W. H. *The Caribbean Policy of the United States, 1890–1920.* Baltimore, 1942.

2900. Carabello Sotolongo, F. *El Imperialismo Norteamericano.* Havana, 1914.

2901. Cárdenas y Echarte, R. de. "La Preponderancia de los Estados Unidos en el Mar Caribe," *CC* 25 (1921) 221–237.
English ed., *IA* 4 (1921) 275–284.

2902. Coolidge, A. C. *The United States as a World Power.* N.Y., 1908.

2903. Cox, I. J. "'Yankee Imperialism' and Spanish-American Solidarity: A Colombian Interpretation," *HAHR* 4 (1921) 256–265.

2904. Crokaert, J. *La Méditerranée Américaine: L'Expansion des Etats-Unis dans la Mer des Antilles.* Paris, 1927.

2905. Dennis, A. L. P. *Adventures in American Diplomacy, 1896–1906.* N.Y., 1928.

2906. Diez, W. E. "Opposition in the United States to American Diplomacy in the Caribbean, 1898–1932," U. of Chicago Diss., 1946.

2907. Drascher, W. *Das Vordringen der Vereinigten Staaten im Westindischen Mittelmeergebiet: Eine Studie über die Entwicklung und die Methoden des Amerikanischen Imperialismus.* Hamburg, 1918.

2908. Dulles, F. R. *The Imperial Years.* N.Y., 1956.

2909. Eister, A. W. *The United States and the A.B.C. Powers, 1889–1906.* Dallas, 1950.

2910. Fabela, I. *Los Estados Unidos Contra la Libertad: Estudios de Historia Diplomática Americana.* Barcelona, 1921.
Covers U.S. relations with Cuba, the Philippines, Panama, Nicaragua, and the Dominican Republic.

2911. Faulkner, H. U. *The Decline of Laissez-Faire, 1897–1917.* N.Y., 1951.

2912. ———. *The Quest for Social Justice, 1898–1914.* N.Y., 1931.
General study of the Progressive Era in U.S. history.

2913. Fish, C. R. *The Path of Empire: A Chronicle of the United States as a World Power.* New Haven, Conn., 1919.

2914. Garraty, J. A. *Henry Cabot Lodge.* N.Y., 1953.

2915. Ghiraldo, A. *Yanquilandia Bárbara: La Lucha Contra el Imperialismo.* Madrid, 1929.

2916. Gondra, C. *Los Estados Unidos y las Naciones Americanas.* B.A., 1918.

2917. González Arrili, B. *El Futuro de América.* Barcelona, 1928.

2918. Grenville, J. A. S. "Diplomacy and War Plans in the United States, 1890–1917," *RHST* 11 (1961) 1–21.

2919. Guerra y Sánchez, R. *La Expansión Territorial de los Estados Unidos a Expensas de España y de los Paises Hispanoamericanos.* Havana, 1935.

2920. Hays, S. P. *The Response to Industrialism, 1885–1914.* Chicago, 1957.

2921. Jones, C. L. *The Caribbean Since 1900.* N.Y., 1936.

2922. ———, et al. *The United States and the Caribbean.* Chicago, 1929.

2923. Kennedy, P. W. "The Concept of Racial Superiority and United States Imperialism, 1890–1910," St. Louis U. Diss., 1963.

2924. Lane, J. C. "Leonard Wood and the Shaping of American Defense Policy, 1900–1920," U. of Georgia Diss., 1963.

2925. Langer, W. *The Diplomacy of Imperialism, 1890–1902.* 2 vols., N.Y., 1935.

2926. Latané, J. H. *America as a World Power, 1897–1907.* N.Y., 1907.

2927. Leuchtenberg, W. E. "Progressivism and Imperialism: The Progressive Movement and American Foreign Policy, 1898–1916," *MVHR* 39 (1952) 483–504.

2928. Livermore, S. W. "Battleship Diplomacy in South America: 1905–1925," *JMH* 16 (1944) 31–48.
   Concerns competition for naval armaments.

2929. McKibbin, D. B. "Percival Farquhar: American Promoter in Latin America, 1900–1914," U. of Chicago Diss., 1950.

2930. Moore, J. B. *The Collected Papers of John Bassett Moore.* 7 vols., New Haven, Conn., 1944.

2931. Muñóz, I. *La Verdad Sobre los Gringos.* Mexico, 1927.
   4th ed., Mexico, 1961.

2932. Munro, D. G. *Intervention and Dollar Diplomacy in the Caribbean, 1900–1921.* Princeton, N.J., 1964.

2933. Nearing, S. *The American Empire.* N.Y., 1921.

2934. ———, and J. Freeman. *Dollar Diplomacy: A Study in American Imperialism.* N.Y., 1925.

   Emphasizes the Central American-Caribbean area.

2935. Nevins, A. *Henry White.* N.Y., 1930.
   White was an influential United States diplomatist.

2936. Ogg, F. A. *National Progress, 1907–1917.* N.Y., 1918.
   A general history of the period in United States history.

2937. Pratt, J. W. *America's Colonial Experiment: How the U.S. Gained, Governed and in Part Gave Away a Colonial Empire.* Englewood Cliffs, N.J., 1950.
   Examines colonial policies of the United States.

2938. Rippy, J. F. *The Caribbean Danger Zone.* N.Y., 1940.

2939. Roosevelt, T. *Colonial Policies of the U.S.* N.Y., 1937.
   By the son of the President.

2940. Sands, W. F. *Our Jungle Diplomacy.* Chapel Hill, N.C., 1944.
   Treats Mexico, Guatemala, Panama, and Ecuador in the period 1904 to 1912.

2941. Straus, O. S. *Under Four Administrations.* Boston, 1922.
   Memoirs of an important public servant during the period 1900–1921.

2942. Sullivan, M. *Our Times: The United States, 1900–1925.* 6 vols., N.Y., 1926–1935.
   A general history of the era.

2943. Thorton, E. W. "The Emergence of a New American Colonial Policy, 1898–1902," U. of Iowa Diss., 1934.

2944. Tompkins, E. B. "The Great Debate: Anti-Imperialism in the United States, 1890–1920," U. of Pennsylvania Diss., 1963.

2945. Upton, E. *The Military Policy of the United States.* Wash., 1916.

2946. Welles, S. "Is America Imperialistic?" *AM* 134 (1924) 412–423.

2947. Weston, R. F. "The Influence of Racial Assumptions on American Imperialism, 1893–1946," Syracuse U. Diss., 1964.

VI–A cross references:

a) Many of the general works on United States relations with the Central American–Caribbean area also treat the subject of imperialism. See items 6706–6818.

b) See also items 1587, 1591, 1608, 1611, 1736, 2631c, 2722, 2731, 2762, 2869, 3193, 3297.

B. THE MONROE DOCTRINE AND INTERVENTION

2947a. Alvarez, A. "La Doctrina de Monroe y la América Latina," *RACP* 1 (1911) 613–624.
> Treats the Roosevelt Corollary.

2948. Antokoletz, D. *La Doctrine de Monroe et l'Amérique Latine.* Paris, 1905.

2949. Argentina. Ministerio de Relaciones Exteriores. *La Doctrine de Monroe: Note Diplomatique du Gouvernement Argentina à son Représentant à Washington, en Date du 29 Décembre 1902: Lettre-Circulaire de M. Carlos Calvo à Quelques-uns de ses Collègues de l'Institut de France et de l'Institut de Droit International.* Paris, 1903.

2949a. Bidau, E. L. *Las Doctrinas de Monroe y Drago.* B.A., 1906.

2950. Bingham, H. "Latin America and the Monroe Doctrine," *YR* 3 (1914) 656–672.

2951. ———. *The Monroe Doctrine: An Obsolete Shibboleth.* New Haven, Conn., 1913.
> For Latin-American commentary on this work, see item 2981.

2952. Blakeslee, G. H. "A New Basis Needed for the Monroe Doctrine," *NAR* 198 (1913) 779–789.

2953. Capella y Pons, F. *Monroïsmo? Notes-études sur la Politique Continentale Américaine, à l'Egard de l'Europe.* Paris, 1913.

2953a. Castro-Ruiz, C. "The Monroe Doctrine and the Government of Chile," *APSR* 11 (1917) 231–238.

2954. Chamberlin, E. K. "The Japanese Scare at Magdalena Bay," *PHR* 24 (1955) 354–360.

2955. Chapman, C. E. "A Monroe Doctrine Divided," *PSQ* 37 (1922) 75–82.

2956. ———. "New Corollaries of the Monroe Doctrine, with Especial Reference to the Relations of the United States with Cuba," *UCC* 33 (1931) 161–189.
> Deals with the Roosevelt and Wilson Corollaries.

2956a. Drago, L. M. "La Doctrine de Monroe —Une Note Diplomatique du Gouvernement Argentin—Consultations et Axis," *RDISDP* 35 (1903) 597–623.

2957. Dunning, J. C. *Die Neuesten Anwendungen der Monroedoktrin.* Borna-Leipzig, 1908.

2958. Fiallos, E. C. *La Doctrina de Monroe Juzgada por un Centro Americano.* Tegucigalpa, 1907.

2959. García Calderón, F. "La Doctrina Monroe y la América Latina," *CC* 6 (1914) 151–169.
> English ed., *AM* 113 (1914) 305–315.

2960. Knox, P. C. *The Monroe Doctrine and Some Incidental Obligations in the Zone of the Caribbean.* N.Y., 1912.

2961. "Is the Monroe Doctrine a Bar to Civilization?" *NAR* 176 (1903) 518–529.

2962. Laferriére, J. "La Résolution Lodge et la Doctrine Monroe," *RGDIP* 20 (1913) 549–574.

2963. Loomis, F. B. *The Position of the United States on the American Continent: Some Phases of the Monroe Doctrine.* Phil., 1903.
> Author was Assistant Secretary of State.

2964. Marburg, T. "A Modified Monroe Doctrine," *SAQ* 10 (1911) 227–231.

2965. Miller, A. E. "The Monroe Doctrine from an English Standpoint," *NAR* 176 (1903) 728–733.
> Supports the Monroe Doctrine.

2966. Peña, C. M. de. "La Doctrina Americanista de Monroe: Opiniones de Distinguidos Estadistas Sobre su Justicia y Significación," *BMRE* 2 (1914) 1038–1077.

2967. Penfield, F. C. "Practical Phases of Caribbean Domination," *NAR* 178 (1904) 75–85.

2968. Pereyra, C. *La Doctrina de Monroe: El Destino Manifiesto y el Imperialismo.* Mexico, 1908.

2969. ———. *El Mito de Monroe.* B. A., 1959.
> Originally published in Madrid, 1914.

2970. Perry, E. "Central America and the Monroe Doctrine," *HAHR* 3 (1920) 407–408.

2971. Rapallo, E. S. "The New Monroe Doctrine," *NAR* 180 (1905) 386–601.

2972. Rippy, J. F. "Antecedents of the Roosevelt Corollary of the Monroe Doctrine," *PHR* 9 (1940) 267–279.

2973. ———. "The British Bondholders and the Roosevelt Corollary of the Monroe Doctrine," *PSQ* 49 (1934) 195–206.

2974. Rollin, L. *El Imperio de una Sombra.* Madrid, 1930.

2975. Root, E. "Real Monroe Doctrine," *AJIL* 8 (1914) 427–442.

2976. Scruggs, W. L. "The Monroe Doctrine— Its Origin and Import," *NAR* 176 (1903) 185–199.
  By a former minister to Venezuela and Colombia.

2977. Shepherd, W. R. "New Light on the Monroe Doctrine," *PSQ* 31 (1916) 578–589.

2978. Sherrill, C. H. *Modernizing the Monroe Doctrine.* Boston, 1916.

2979. "The Present Status of the Monroe Doctrine," *AAAPSS* 54 (1914) 1–333.

2980. Thomas, D. Y. "The Monroe Doctrine from Roosevelt to Roosevelt," *SAQ* 34 (1935) 117–136.

2981. Uribe Uribe, R. *The Monroe Doctrine: An Obsolet* [sic] *Shibboleth by Hiram Bingham.* Bogotá, 1914.
  Comment on the book by Bingham. See item 2951.

2982. Wellman, W. "Shall the Monroe Doctrine Be Modified?" *NAR* 173 (1901) 832–844.

2983. Zeballos, E. S. "La Diplomatie des Etats-Unis dans l'Amérique du Sud," *RPP* 104 (1920) 328–346.
  Author was Argentine minister of foreign affairs.

VI–B   cross references:

a) See the general works on the Monroe Doctrine for additional information on this subject. See items 1766–1804.

b) See also items 1777, 2117, 2984a, 3031, 3259, 4600.

C. THE ROOSEVELT AND TAFT ADMINISTRATIONS, 1901–1913

2984. Adams, H. *The Education of Henry Adams.* N.Y., 1931.

2984a. Bailey, T. A. "The Lodge Corollary to the Monroe Doctrine," *PSQ* 48 (1933) 220–239.

2985. Beale, H. K. *Theodore Roosevelt and the Rise of America to World Power.* Baltimore, 1956.
  Pb. ed., N.Y., 1962.

2986. Bishop, J. B. *Theodore Roosevelt and His Time, Shown in His Own Letters.* 2 vols., N.Y., 1920.

2986a. Blake, N. M. "Ambassadors at the Court of Theodore Roosevelt," *MVHR* 42 (1955) 179–206.

2987. Blum, J. M. *The Republican Roosevelt.* Cambridge, Mass., 1954.

2988. Burton, D. H. "Theodore Roosevelt: Confident Imperialist," *RP* 23 (1961) 356–377.

2989. Butt, A. *Taft and Roosevelt: The Intimate Letters of Archie Butt.* N.Y., 1930.
  By a confidant of the President.

2990. Croly, H. *Willard Straight.* N.Y., 1924.
  About a "dollar diplomatist."

2991. Cummins, L. "The Origin and Development of Elihu Root's Latin American Diplomacy," U. of California Diss., 1964.

2992. Davis, J. "The Latin American Policy of Elihu Root," U. of Illinois Diss., 1957.

2993. Dennett, T. *John Hay: From Poetry to Politics.* N.Y., 1933.
  Secretary of state, 1898 to 1905.

2994. Dozer, D. M. "Secretary of State Elihu Root and Consular Reorganization," *MVHR* 29 (1942) 339–350.

2995. Einstein, L. D. *Roosevelt: His Mind in Action.* Boston and N.Y., 1930.

2996. Ellis, E. *Mr. Dooley's America: A Life of Finley Peter Dunne.* N.Y., 1941.

2996a. Evans, R. D. *An Admiral's Log: Being Continued Recollections of Naval Life.* N.Y., 1910.
  Commander of the Great White Fleet which sailed around the world in 1907–1908.

2997. Finch, G. A. "Elihu Root's Contribution to Pan Americanism," *BPAU* 79 (1945) 63–73.

2998. Fowler, D. C. *John Coit Spooner: Defender of Presidents.* N.Y., 1961.
  Spooner was a Republican senator from Wisconsin.

2999. Goldman, E. F. *Charles G. Bonaparte.* Baltimore, 1943.
  Influential progressive adviser to Roosevelt.

3000. Hale, W. B. "With the Knox Mission in Central America," *WW* 24 (1912) 179–193.

3001. Hall, R. G., Jr. "American Imperialism in Central America During the Taft-Knox Administration," Harvard U. Diss., 1948.

3002. Harbaugh, W. H. *Power and Responsibility: The Life and Times of Theodore Roosevelt.* N.Y., 1961.

3003. Hay, J. *Letters of John Hay and Extracts from Diary.* 3 vols., Wash., 1908.

3004. Hechler, K. W. *Insurgency: Personalities and Politics of the Taft Era.* N.Y., 1940.

3005. Hill, H. C. *Roosevelt and the Caribbean.* Chicago, 1927.

3006. Huntington Wilson, F. M. *Memoirs of an Ex-Diplomat.* Boston, 1945.
Important State Department figure under Roosevelt and Taft.

3007. Jessup, P. C. *Elihu Root.* 2 vols., N.Y., 1938.
Secretary of State, 1905–1909.

3008. Kennedy, P. C. "La Follette's Imperialist Flirtation," *PHR* 29 (1960) 131–144.
Progressive Republican senator from Wisconsin.

3009. Knox, P. C. *Speeches Incident to the Visit of Philander Chase Knox to the Countries of the Caribbean.* Wash., 1913.

3010. Leopold, R. W. *Elihu Root and the Conservative Tradition.* Boston, 1954.

3011. Lodge, H. C. (ed.). *Selections from the Correspondence of Theodore Roosevelt and Henry Cabot Lodge, 1884–1918.* 2 vols., N.Y., 1925.

3012. Megaree, R. "The Diplomacy of John Bassett Moore: Realism in American Foreign Policy," Northwestern U. Diss., 1963.

3013. Morison, E. E. (ed.). *The Letters of Theodore Roosevelt.* 8 vols., Cambridge, Mass., 1951–1954.

3014. Mowry, G. E. *The Era of Theodore Roosevelt, 1900–1912.* N.Y., 1958.
Pb. ed., N.Y., 1962.

3015. ———. *Roosevelt and the Progressive Movement.* Madison, Wis., 1946.

3016. O'Gara, G. C. *Theodore Roosevelt and the Rise of the Modern Navy.* Princeton, N.J., 1943.

3017. Okuneva, M. A. "Proiskhozhdenie i Kharakter Latinoamerikanskoi Doktriny Teodora Ruzvel'ta," *NNI* 5 (1961) 52–64.
"The Origin and Character of Theodore Roosevelt's Latin American Doctrine."

3018. Pringle, H. F. *The Life and Times of William Howard Taft.* 2 vols., N.Y., 1939.

3019. ———. *Theodore Roosevelt, a Biography.* N.Y., 1931.

3020. Radke, A. C., Jr. "John Tyler Morgan, an Expansionist Senator, 1877–1907," U. of Washington Diss., 1953.
Morgan was a senator from Alabama.

3021. Roosevelt, T. *The New Nationalism.* N.Y., 1910.

3022. ———. *Theodore Roosevelt: An Autobiography.* N.Y., 1916.

3023. ———. *Works.* 24 vols., N.Y., 1923–1926.

3024. Root, E. *Addresses on International Subjects.* Cambridge, Mass., 1916.

3025. ———. *Latin America and the United States.* Cambridge, Mass., 1917.

3026. ———. *Men and Policies.* Cambridge, Mass., 1924.

3027. ———. *The Military and Colonial Policy of the U.S.* Cambridge, Mass., 1916.

3028. ———. *Miscellaneous Addresses.* Cambridge, Mass., 1917.

3029. ———. *Speeches Incident to the Visit of Secretary Root to South America, July 4 to September 30, 1906.* Wash., 1906.

3030. Scott, J. B. "Elihu Root, His Latin American Policy," *BPAU* 71 (1937) 296–304.

3031. Taft, W. H. "The Monroe Doctrine," *IN* 76 (1913) 530–540.

3032. Thayer, W. R. *The Life and Letters of John Hay.* 2 vols., Boston, 1915.

3033. ———. *Theodore Roosevelt: An Intimate Biography.* Boston, 1919.

3034. Walters, E. *Joseph Benson Foraker.* Columbus, O., 1948.
Republican senator from Ohio.

3035. Zeballos, E. S. "Theodore Roosevelt y la Política Internacional Americana," *RDHL* 46 (1913) 545–604.

VI–C   cross references:

a) For works treating the role of President Theodore Roosevelt's administration in separating Panama from Colombia, see items 8290–8382.

b) For works on the Mexico City Conference of 1901, see items 4917–4926; for the Rio de Janeiro Conference of 1906, see items 4927–4935; for the Buenos Aires Conference of 1910, see items 4936–4944.

c) For works on the Central American Peace Conference of 1907, held in Washington, D.C., see items 5128–5135.

d) See also items 2624, 2628, 2656, 2873, 2877, 2882, 2891, 2909, 6724, 6987, 7197, 7586, 8082, 8612b, 8615.

D. WILSON'S ADMINISTRATION, 1913–1921

3036. Adler, S. "Bryan and Wilsonian Caribbean Penetration," *HAHR* 20 (1940) 198–226.

3037. Bacon, R. *For Better Relations with Our Latin American Neighbors: A Journey to South America.* Wash., 1915.
Spanish ed., Wash., 1915.

3038. Bailey, T. A. *Wilson and the Peacemakers.* N.Y., 1947.
Study of peacemaking after World War I.

3039. Baker, G. W., Jr. "The Caribbean Policy of Woodrow Wilson, 1913–1917," U. of Colorado Diss., 1961.

3040. Baker, R. S. *Woodrow Wilson, Life and Letters.* 8 vols., Garden City, N.Y., 1927–1939.

3041. ———, and W. E. Dodd (eds.). *The Public Papers of Woodrow Wilson.* 6 vols., N.Y., 1925–1927.

3042. Bard, H. E. *Intellectual and Cultural Relations Between the United States and the Other Republics of America.* Wash., 1914.

3043. Bell, H. C. F. *Woodrow Wilson and the People.* Garden City, N.Y., 1945.

3044. Blum, J. M. *Joe Tumulty and the Wilson Era.* Boston, 1951.
Tumulty was Wilson's private secretary.

3045. ———. *Woodrow Wilson and the Politics of Morality.* Boston, 1956.

3046. Bonilla, P. *Wilson Doctrine: How the Speech of President Wilson at Mobile, Ala., Has Been Interpreted by Latin American Countries.* N.Y., 1914.

3047. Buehrig, E. H. (ed.). *Wilson's Foreign Policy in Perspective.* Bloomington, Ind., 1957.
Symposium papers.

3047a. ———. *Woodrow Wilson and the Balance of Power.* Bloomington, Ind., 1955.

3048. Coletta, P. E. "Bryan, Anti-Imperialism and Missionary Diplomacy," *NH* 44 (1963) 167–187.

3049. ——— (ed.). "Bryan Briefs Lansing," *PHR* 27 (1958) 383–396.
Stresses Latin America.

3050. Cronon, E. D. (ed.). *The Cabinet Diaries of Josephus Daniels, 1913–1921.* Lincoln, Nebr., 1963.
Secretary of the navy.

3051. Curti, M. E. *Bryan and World Peace.* Northampton, Mass., 1931.
An anti-imperialist interpretation.

3052. Daniels, J. *The Wilson Era: Years of Peace, 1910–1917.* Chapel Hill, N.C., 1944.

3053. Dudden, A. P. (ed.). *Woodrow Wilson and the World of Today.* Phil., 1957.
Symposium on Wilson.

3054. Garraty, J. A. *Woodrow Wilson.* N.Y., 1956.

3055. George, A. L., and J. L. George. *Woodrow Wilson and Colonel House.* N.Y., 1956.

3056. Gil, E. *Evolución del Panamericanismo: El Credo de Wilson y el Panamericanismo.* B.A., 1933.

3057. Hendrick, B. J. *The Life and Letters of Walter Hines Page.* 3 vols., Garden City, N.Y., 1924–1926.
United States ambassador to Great Britain.

3058. Hibben, P. *The Peerless Leader.* N.Y., 1929.
Concerns W. J. Bryan.

3059. Houston, D. F. *Eight Years with Wilson's Cabinet.* 2 vols., Garden City, N.Y., 1926.
By the secretary of agriculture in Wilson's administration.

3060. Kerney, J. *The Political Education of Woodrow Wilson.* N.Y., 1926.

3061. Lane, A. W., and L. Wall (eds.). *The Letters of Franklin K. Lane.* Boston, 1922.
Lane was secretary of the interior in Wilson's cabinet.

3062. Lansing, R. *War Memoirs of Robert Lansing, Secretary of State*. Indianapolis, 1935.

3063. Latham, E. (ed.). *The Philosophy and Policies of Woodrow Wilson*. Chicago, 1958.

3064. Link, A. S. "The Higher Realism of Woodrow Wilson," *JPH* 41 (1963) 1–13.

3065. ———. *La Política de los Estados Unidos en América Latina, 1913–1916*. Mexico, 1960.
Selections from Link's extensive writings on Wilson translated into Spanish.

3066. ———. *Wilson: Campaigns for Progressivism and Peace, 1916–1917*. Princeton, N.J., 1965.

3067. ———. *Wilson: Confusions and Crises, 1915–1916*. Princeton, N.J., 1964.

3068. ———. *Wilson: The New Freedom*. Princeton, N.J., 1956.

3069. ———. *Wilson: The Struggle for Neutrality, 1914–1915*. Princeton, N.J., 1960.

3070. ———. *Wilson the Diplomatist*. Baltimore, 1957.

3071. ———. *Woodrow Wilson and the Progressive Era, 1910–1917*. N.Y., 1954.

3072. Long, J. C. *Bryan: The Great Commoner*. N.Y., 1928.

3072a. Myers, D. P. "The New Pan Americanism," *WPFP* 6, nos. 1–2 (1916); 7, no. 1 (1917).
Three-part series considers various aspects of President Wilson's policies, and especially Mexican and Central American affairs.

3073. Notter, H. *The Origins of the Foreign Policy of Woodrow Wilson*. Baltimore, 1937.

3073a. Osborn, G. C. "Woodrow Wilson Visits Mobile, October 27, 1913," *AHQ* 19 (1957) 157–169.

3073b. Phillips, W. *Ventures in Diplomacy*. London, 1955.
By an official in the U.S. Department of State.

3074. Schoenrich, O. *Former Senator Burton's Trip to South America, 1915*. Wash., 1915.
Senator Theodore Elijah Burton was a Republican from Ohio.

3075. Scott, J. B. (ed.). *President Wilson's Foreign Policy: Messages, Addresses, Papers*. N.Y., 1918.

3076. Seymour, C. (ed.). *The Intimate Papers of Colonel House*. 4 vols., Boston, 1926–1928.

3077. Smith, D. M. "Bainbridge Colby and the Good Neighbor Policy, 1920–1921," *MVHR* 50 (1963) 56–78.
Colby was secretary of state, 1920–1921. He is credited with initiating a softer Latin American policy.

3078. ———. *Robert Lansing and American Neutrality, 1914–1917*. Berkeley, Calif., 1958.

3079. Walworth, A. W. *Woodrow Wilson: American Prophet*. 2 vols., N.Y., 1958.

3080. Werner, M. R. *Bryan*. N.Y., 1929.

3081. Williams, W. C. *William Jennings Bryan*. N.Y., 1936.

3082. Wilson, W. *United States and Latin America*. Wash., 1913.

3083. Woolsey, L. H. "Robert Lansing's Record as Secretary of State," *CH* 29 (1928) 384–396.
Secretary of state, 1915–1920.

VI–D cross references:

a) For material relating specifically to World War I, see Chapter VII.

b) See also items 2898, 2899, 3006, 6185, 6855, 6979, 7075a, 7078, 7079, 7091, 7224, 7241, 7311a, 7504, 7508, 7908, 7909.

E. EUROPEAN INTRUSIONS AND THE UNITED STATES RESPONSE

3084. Bonsal, S. "Greater Germany in South America," *NAR* 176 (1903) 58–67.

3085. Dugdale, E. T. S. (ed.). *German Diplomatic Documents, 1871–1914*. 4 vols., London, 1929.
Excerpts from *Die Grosse Politik*. See item 3089.

3086. Harrison, A. *The Pan-Germanic Doctrine*. London, 1904.

3087. Heindel, R. H. *The American Impact on Great Britain, 1898–1914: A Study of the U.S. in World History*. Phil., 1940.

3088. Keim, J. *Forty Years of German-American Political Relations*. Phil., 1919.

3089. Lepsius, J., *et al.* (eds.). *Die Grosse Politik der Europäischen Kabinette, 1871–1914*. 40 vols., Berlin, 1922–1927.

3090. Schieber, C. E. *The Transformation of*

American Sentiment Toward Germany, 1870–1914. Boston, 1923.

3091.   Shepherd, W. R. *The Attitude of the United States Toward the Retention by European Nations of Colonies In and Around the Caribbean.* N.Y., 1917.

3092.   Sternburg, S. von. "The Phantom Peril of German Emigration and South American Settlements," *NAR* 182 (1906) 641–650.

VI–E   cross references: 2810, 2811, 2815, 2827, 3104, 3105, 3177, 6180a

F. ECONOMIC RELATIONS IN THE IMPERIALIST ERA

3092a.   Barrett, J. "Latin America as a Field for United States Capital and Enterprise," *BM* 74 (1907) 920–926.

3093.   ———. *The United States and Latin America: Some Special Phases Not Commonly Considered or Understood of the Commercial and General Relations of the United States with Her Sister American Republics.* Wash., 1917.

3094.   Kepner, C. D., and J. H. Southill. *The Banana Empire: A Case Study in Economic Imperialism.* N.Y., 1936.

3095.   Kinley, D. "The Promotion of Trade with South America," *AER* 1 (1911) 50–71.

3096.   Klein, J. "Economic Rivalries in Latin America," *FA* 3 (1924) 236–243.

3097.   Lewis, B. G. "Our Trade Relations with Latin America," *JPE* 14 (1906) 602–613.

3098.   Rowe, L. S. "Our Trade Relations with South America," *NAR* 184 (1907) 513–519.

3099.   Shepherd, W. R. "Our South American Trade," *PSQ* 24 (1909) 667–693.

3100.   "The Relation of Government to Foreign Investment," *AAAPSS* 68 (1916) 298–311.

3101.   Tower, W. S. "Buying South American Goods as a Factor in Selling to South America," *JPE* 24 (1916) 897–902.

3102.   Willis, H. P. "Transportation and Competition in South American Markets," *AER* 2 (1912) 814–833.

VI–F   cross references: 1582, 2631c, 2929, 2934, 2973, 3203

Chapter VII   Latin America and World War I

A. GENERAL WORKS

3103. Barroetaveña, F. A. *Alemania Contra el Mundo.* B.A., 1916.

3103a. Bott, E. J. J. *El Comercio Entre los Estados Unidos y la América Latina Durante la Gran Guerra.* B.A., 1919.

3103b. ———. *Una Evolución Trascendental de la Vida Internacional en América.* B.A., 1918.

3103c. Cox Méndez, R. *A Través de la Europa en Guerra.* Santiago, 1916.

3104. Halsey, F. M. *Investments in Latin America and the British West Indies.* Wash., 1918.

3105. ———. *Railway Expansion in Latin America.* N.Y., 1916.

3106. Haring, C. H. *The Germans in South America: A Contribution to the Economic History of the World War.* N.Y., 1920.

3107. Kirkpatrick, F. A. *South America and the War.* Cambridge, Mass., 1918.

3107a. Maitrot, C. A. E. X. *La France et les Républiques Sud-Américaines.* Paris, 1920.

3108. Martin, P. A. *Latin America and the War.* Baltimore, 1925.

3109. Michel, P. H. "L'Amérique Espagnole et la Guerre," *RHGM* 8 (1930) 352–371; 9 (1931) 28–54.

3110. ———. *L'Hispanisme dans les Républiques Espagnoles d'Amérique Pendant la Guerre de 1914–1918: Etude d'Esprit Public.* Paris, 1931.

3111. Paxson, F. L. *American Democracy and the World War.* 3 vols., Boston, 1936–1948.
   Covers the period 1913–1923.

3112. Wagner, E. R. *L'Allemagne et l'Amérique Latine.* Paris, 1918.

VII–A cross references: 2928, 3040, 3041, 3043, 3045, 3047, 3054, 3055, 3062, 3070, 3073, 3076, 3079

B. THE MONROE DOCTRINE AND THE WAR

3113. Barrett, J. "What the War Has Done to the Monroe Doctrine," *CO* 65 (1918) 291–293.

3114. Becker, C. "The Monroe Doctrine and the War," *HTM* 9 (1918) 87–90.

3115. Bonn, M. J. "Germany and the Monroe Doctrine," *AAAPSS* 66 (1916) 102–105.

3116. Brito, O. N. *O Monroismo e a Sua Nova Phase.* Rio, 1918.

3117. Hall, A. B. *The Monroe Doctrine and the Great War.* Chicago, 1920.

3117a. Hart, A. B. "Shall We Defend the Monroe Doctrine?" *NAR* 202 (1915) 681–692.

3118. Hasenclever, A. *Die Bedeutung der Monroedoktrin für die Amerikanische Politik der Gegenwart.* Halle, Germany, 1918.

3119. Latané, J. H. "The Monroe Doctrine and the American Policy of Isolation in Relation to a Just and Durable Peace," *AAAPSS* 72 (1917) 100–109.

3120. McChesney, M. "Latin America and the Monroe Doctrine," *UR* 9 (January, 1918) 97–111.

3121. Munro, D. G. "Pan Americanism and the War," *NAR* 208 (1918) 710–721.

3122. Plum, H. G. *The Monroe Doctrine and the War.* Iowa City, Ia., 1918.

3123. Roig de Leuchsenring, E. "La Doctrina de Monroe y el Pacto de la Liga de las Naciones," *CC* 25 (1921) 11–12.

3124. Sáenz Peña, R. "Los Estados Unidos en Sud-América: La Doctrina de Monroe y su Evolución," in *Escritos y Discursos.* 2 vols., B.A., 1914–1915.

3125. Taft, W. H. *The United States and Peace.* N.Y., 1914.
   Defends the Monroe Doctrine.

3126. Wilson, G. G. "The Monroe Doctrine

After the War," *LN* 1 (1918) 253–305.

3127. ———. *The Monroe Doctrine and the Program of the League to Enforce Peace.* Boston, 1916.
World Peace Foundation pamphlet.

VII–B   cross references: 1768

C. NEUTRALITY AND BELLIGERENCY, 1914–1918

3128. Bailey, T. A. *The Policy of the United States Toward the Neutrals, 1917–1918.* Baltimore, 1942.

3129. Barrett, J. "Practical Pan-Americanism," *NAR* 202 (1915) 413–423.

3129a. Bernstorff, J. H. *Memoirs of Count Bernstorff.* N.Y., 1936.

3129b. ———. *My Three Years in America.* N.Y., 1920.
German ambassador to the United States.

3130. Gelfand, L. E. *The Inquiry: American Preparation for Peace, 1917–1919.* New Haven, Conn., 1963.

3131. Jones, J. P., and P. M. Hollister. *The German Secret Service in America, 1914–1918.* Boston, 1918.

3132. Mock, J. R. "The Creel Committee in Latin America," *HAHR* 22 (1942) 262–279.

3133. ———, and C. Larson. *Words That Won the War: The Story of the Committee on Public Information, 1917–1919.* Princeton, N.J., 1939.

3134. "The New Pan Americanism," *WPFP* 6, nos. 1–2 (1916); 7, no. 1 (1917).

3135. Olney, R. "Our Latin-American Policy," *NAR* 203 (1916) 185–193.

3136. Seymour, C. *American Diplomacy During the World War.* Baltimore, 1934.

3137. Sherrill, C. H. "The Strengthening of Latin America," *NAR* 203 (1916) 388–396.

3138. Tansill, C. C. *The Purchase of the Danish West Indies.* Baltimore, 1932.

3139. Trask, D. F. *The United States in the Supreme War Council: American War Aims and Inter-Allied Strategy, 1917–1918.* Middletown, Conn., 1961.

3140. USCS. *Note of German Secretary of Foreign Affairs* (64th Cong., 1st Sess., S. Doc. 728). Wash., 1917.
The Zimmerman Note.

3141. Usher, R. G. *Pan-Americanism: A Forecast of the Inevitable Clash Between the United States and Europe's Victor.* N.Y., 1915.

3142. Zárate, R. *España y América: Proyecciones y Problemas Derivados de la Guerra.* Madrid, 1917.

VII–C   cross references: 3036, 3047a, 3067, 3069, 3071, 3078, 6180a, 7540

D. LATIN AMERICAN RESPONSES TO WORLD WAR I

3143. Abranches, D. de. *A Allemanha e a Paz: Appello ao Presidente da Câmara dos Deputados no Congresso Nacional do Brasil.* São Paulo, 1917.

3144. Alvarez, A. *La Grande Guerre Européenne et la Neutralité du Chili.* Paris, 1915.

3145. Bagaglia, A. C. R. *Poder Maritimo nas Duas Guerras Mundiais (1914–1918—1939–1945).* Rio, 1953.

3146. Baum, L. "German Political Designs with Reference to Brazil," *HAHR* 2 (1919) 586–99.

3147. Bautista de Lavalle, J. *El Perú y la Gran Guerra.* Lima, 1919.

3148. Bopp, M. O. de. "El Periodismo Alemán en México," *HM* 9 (1960) 558–570.

3149. Boyle, A. (ed.). *Brazilian Green Book, Consisting of Diplomatic Documents Relating to Brazil's Attitude with Regard to the European War, 1914–1917, as Issued by the Brazilian Ministry for Foreign Affairs.* London, 1918.
Authorized English edition.

3150. Brazil. Ministerio das Relações Exteriores. *Guerra da Europa: Documentos Diplomáticos. Attitude do Brasil, 1914–1917.* 2 vols., Rio, 1917–1918.

3151. Etchepareborda, R. "Hipólito Yrigoyen y el Conflicto Bélico," *M* 1 (May, 1960) 65–86.

3152. Gallardo Nieto, G. *Neutralidad de Chile ante la Guerra Europea.* Santiago, 1917.

3153. Katz, F. *Deutschland, Diaz und die Mexikanische Revolution: Die Deutsche Politik in Mexiko, 1870–1920.* Berlin, 1964.

3154. Königk, G. *Die Politik Brasiliens Wahrend des Weltkrieges und die Stellung des Brasilianischen Deutschtums.* Hamburg, 1935.

3155. *Le Chili Germanophile.* Cahors, France, 1919.

3156. Manero, A. *México y la Solidaridad Americana.* Madrid, 1918.

3157. Mathieu, B. "The Neutrality of Chile During the European War," *AJIL* 14 (1920) 319–342.

3158. Menocal, M. G. "Cuba's Part in the World War," *CH* 9 (1918) 315–318.

3159. Mock, J. R., and C. Larson, "Activities of the Mexico Section of the Creel Committee, 1917–1918," *JQ* 16 (1939) 136–150.

3160. Otero de la Torre, I. *Verdades y Mentiras de la Cuestión Internacional.* Mexico, 1917.

3161. Primelles, L. *Crónica Cubana, 1915–1918: La Reelección de Menocal y la Revolución de 1917: La Danza de los Millones: La Primera Guerra Mundial.* Havana, 1955.

3162. Robertson, W. S. "Argentina's Attitude to the War," *N* 14 (1917) 208–209.

3163. Robinson, W. L. "A Marinha Brasileira na Guerra Mundial," *RMB* 56 (January, 1937) 585–600.

3164. Rocuant y Figueroa, E. *La Neutralité du Chili.* Santiago, 1919.

3165. Rowe, L. S. *Early Effects of the European War upon the Finance, Commerce and Industry of Chile.* N.Y., 1918.

3166. ———. *Early Effects of the War upon the Finance, Commerce, and Industry of Peru.* N.Y., 1920.

3167. Schatzky, B. "La Neutralité du Chili Pendant la Guerre Mondiale," *RHGM* 14 (1936) 123–144.

3168. Silva Vildósola, C. *Le Chili et la Guerre.* Paris, 1917.

3169. ———. *La Guerra Mundial Vista por un Chileno.* Santiago, 1916.

3170. Smith, L. B., *et al. The Economic Position of Argentina During the War.* Wash., 1920.

3171. Soto Rojas, S. *Los Alemanes en Chile, 1541–1917: Progreso y Servicios que les Debe la República.* Valparaiso, 1917.

3172. Tuchman, B. *The Zimmermann Telegram.* N.Y., 1958.

3173. Uruguay. Ministerio de Relaciones Exteriores. *Disposiciones Sobre Neutralidad (1914–1915).* Montevideo, 1915.

3173a. USDS. Bureau of Foreign and Domestic Commerce. *The Economic Position of Argentina During the War.* Wash., 1920.

3174. Valdés-Roig, L. *El Comercio Exterior de Cuba y la Guerra Mundial.* Havana, 1920.

3175. Vial Solar, J. *Conversaciones Sobre la Guerra.* Santiago, 1917.

3176. ———, *et al. Las Repúblicas Sudamericanas, Chile, Argentina y Uruguay ante la Guerra.* Santiago, 1917.

3177. Wright, A. R. "German Interest in Panama's Piñas Bay, 1910–1938," *JMH* 27 (1955) 61–65.

Chapter VIII   From Imperialism to the
Good Neighbor Policy, 1921–1938

A. GENERAL WORKS AND INTERPRETATIONS

3178. Adler, S. *The Isolationist Impulse: Its Twentieth-Century Reaction.* N.Y., 1957.
Study of United States policy between the two World Wars, with special reference to domestic influences.

3179. ———. *The Uncertain Giant, 1921–1941.* N.Y., 1966.
General history.

3179a. Araquistaín, L. *El Peligro Yanqui.* 2d ed., Valencia, Spain, 1924(?).

3179b. Barcia Trelles, C. *El Imperialismo del Petróleo y la Paz Mundial.* Valladolid, 1925.

3179c. ———. *La Política Exterior Norteamericana de la Postguerra.* Valladolid, 1924.

3180. Belaúnde y Díez Canseco, R. *Por la Unidad de América: Recopilación de Discursos y Proyectos, 1931–1941.* Lima, 1944.
Collections of letters, speeches, and other writings on various inter-American subjects.

3180a. Benítez, C. *El Peligro Ruso y la América Latina.* Caracas, 1932.

3181. Bernard, L. L. "What Our Latin-American Neighbors Think of Us," *HO* 19 (1928) 363–367.

3182. Blanco-Fombona, H. *Crímenes del Imperialismo Norteamericano.* Mexico, 1927.

3183. Buell, R. L. "The Future of American Imperialism," *YR,* no. 15, n.s. (1925) 13–29.

3184. ———. "The United States and Central American Stability," *FPAR* 7 (1931).

3185. Carr, E. H. *The Twenty Years' Crisis, 1919–1939: An Introduction to the Study of International Relations.* London, 1946.

3185a. Dávila, C. G. *North American Imperialism.* N.Y., 1930.

3186. Dozer, D. M. *Are We Good Neighbors? Three Decades of Inter-American Relations, 1930–1960.* Gainesville, Fla., 1959.

3186a. Edwards Bello, J. *El Nacionalismo Continental.* Madrid, 1927.

3187. Faulkner, H. U. *From Versailles to the New Deal.* New Haven, Conn., 1950.

3188. Fitzgibbon, R. H. *The Role of Latin America in World Politics.* Berkeley, Calif., 1938.

3189. Fleming, D. F. *The United States and World Organization, 1920–1933.* N.Y., 1938.

3189a. Goldschmidt, A. *Die Dritte Eroberung Amerikas.* Berlin, 1929.

3190. Haring, C. H. *South American Progress.* Cambridge, Mass., 1934.

3191. Johnson, C. O. *Borah of Idaho.* N.Y., 1936.
Chairman of Senate Foreign Relations Committee in the 1920's.

3192. Mitchell, B. *Depression Decade: From New Era to New Deal, 1929–1941.* N.Y., 1947.

3192a. Nevins, A. *The United States in a Chaotic World.* New Haven, Conn., 1950.
Surveys period 1918–1933.

3193. ———, and L. M. Hacker (eds.). *The United States and Its Place in World Affairs, 1918–1943.* Boston, 1943.

3194. Newton, W. P. "Aviation in the Relations of the United States and Latin America, 1916–1929," U. of Alabama Diss., 1964.

3194a. ———. "International Aviation Rivalry in Latin America, 1919–1927," *JIAS* 7 (July, 1965) 345–356.

3195. Normano, J. F. "Changes in Latin American Attitudes," *FA* 11 (1932) 161–172.

3196. Normano, J. F. *The Struggle for South America: Economy and Ideology.* Boston, 1931.

3197. Palacios, A. L. *Nuestra América y el Imperialismo Yanqui.* Madrid, 1930.

3198. Poblete Troncoso, M. *Problemas Sociales y Económicas de América Latina.* Santiago, 1936.
       Problems of the interwar period.

3199. "Recent Aspects of Our Relations with Latin America," *AAAPSS* 138 (1928) 54–81.
       Collection of writings by academic figures and diplomats.

3200. Rippy, J. F. "Letting Go of Latin America," *E* 2 (1937) 110–118.

3201. Roemer, H. "Strukturwandel der Nord-amerikanischen Ibero-Amerika-Politik, 1928–1934," *IAA* 8 (1935) 231–259.

3201a. Rollin, L. *Sous le Signe de Monroe.* Paris, 1930.

3201b. Shannon, D. A. *Between the Wars: America, 1919–1941.* Boston, 1965.

3202. Slezkin, L. I. *Politika Soiedinnionykh Shtatov Ameriki v Iuzhnoi Amerike (1929–1933).* Moscow, 1956.
       The Diplomacy of the United States in South America (1929–1933).

3203. Soule, G. *Prosperity Decade, 1917–1929.* N.Y., 1947.
       Economic history.

3204. Sprout, H., and M. Sprout. *Toward a New Order of Sea Power: American Naval Policy and the World Scene, 1918–1922.* Princeton, N.J., 1943.
       Treats the Washington Naval Conference.

3205. "Unsettled Boundary Disputes in Latin America," *FPAIS* 5, no. 26 (1930).

3206. Wambaugh, S. *Plebiscites Since the World War, with a Collection of Official Documents.* 2 vols., Wash., 1933.

3207. Watt, D. C. "American Strategic Interests and Anxieties in the West Indies," *JRUSI* 108 (1963) 224–232.
       Covers 1918–1960.

3208. Williams, B. H. *Economic Foreign Policy of the United States.* N.Y., 1929.

3209. Williams, W. A. "Latin America: Laboratory of American Foreign Policy in the Nineteen-Twenties," *IEA* 11 (Autumn, 1957) 3–30.

3209a. Woolsey, L. H. "Boundary Disputes in Latin America," *AJIL* 25 (1931) 324–333.

VIII–A cross references: *158, 1555, 1733, 1736, 1757, 1760, 2894, 2947, 5411*

B. LATIN AMERICA AND THE LEAGUE OF NATIONS

3210. Alvarez, A. *La Réforme du Part de la Société des Naciones sur des Bases Continentales et Régionales.* Paris, 1926.

3211. Argentina. Ministerio de Relaciones Exteriores y Culto. *La República Argentina ante la Liga las Naciones.* B.A., 1922.

3212. Barros Borgoño, L. *La Liga de las Naciones.* Santiago, 1920.

3213. Bolivia. Ministerio de Relaciones Exteriores. *El Mandato de la Liga de las Naciones al A.B.C.P.* La Paz, 1933.

3214. Carrasco, J. *Bolivia's Case for the League of Nations.* London, 1920.
       French ed., Paris, 1921; Spanish ed., Lima, 1920.

3215. Díaz Cisneros, C. *La Doctrina ante la Liga de las Naciones.* B.A., 1922.

3216. ———. *La Liga de Naciones y la Actitud Argentina.* B.A., 1921.

3217. Draghicescu, D. *América y la Liga de las Naciones.* Mexico, 1937.

3218. Duggan, S. P. "Latin America, the League, and the United States," *FA* 12 (1934) 281–293.

3219. Edwards, A. *La América Latina y la Liga de las Naciones.* Santiago, 1937.

3219a. ———. "Latin America and the League of Nations," *JRIIA* 8 (1929) 134–153.

3219b. Ferrara, O. "La Doctrina de Monroe y la Liga de las Naciones," *RSO* 13 (April, 1919) 308–312.

3220. Galeano, V. B. *L'Amérique Latine, les Etats-Unis et la Société des Nations.* Paris, 1927.

3221. García González, A. *La Doctrina Monroe y el Pacto de la Sociedad de las Naciones.* Mexico, 1931.

3222. Guiral Moreno, E. *La Liga de las Naciones: Sus Antecedentes, Fines y Propósitos: Organización Funcionamiento: Algunos de los Resultados Obtenidos: La Cooperación de Cuba.* Havana, 1935.

3223. Hockett, H. C. "The Monroe Doctrine and the League of Nations," *OHTJ*, no. 13 (1919) 45–55.

3224. Hudson, M. O. "Afghanistan, Ecuador and the Soviet Union in the League of Nations," *AJIL* 29 (1935) 109–116.

3225. Kelchner, W. H. *Latin American Relations with the League of Nations*. Boston, 1930.
A comprehensive analysis of Latin American participation.

3226. ———. "The Relations of the Union of American Republics to World Organization," *USDSB* 2 (1940) 57–63.

3226a. Latané, J. H. "The League of Nations and the Monroe Doctrine," *WW* 37 (1919) 441–444.

3227. LN. Assembly. First Committee. *Relations Between the League of Nations and the Pan-American Union*. Geneva, 1935.
Report submitted by the first committee to the assembly.

3228. ———. Chaco Commission. *Dispute Between Bolivia and Paraguay*. Geneva, 1934.

3229. Macedo-Soares, J. C. de. *Brazil and the League of Nations*. Paris, 1928.

3230. Miller, D. H. *The Drafting of the Covenant*. 2 vols., N.Y., 1928.

3231. Pérez Guerrero, M. *Les Relations des Etats de l'Amérique-Latine avec la Société des Nations*. Paris, 1936.

3232. Planas-Suárez, S. *La Sociedad de las Naciones del Tratado de Versailles: Una Institución Inútil y Peligrosa para Iberoamérica*. Barcelona, 1958.

3233. Pogue, F. C. "The Monroe Doctrine and the League of Nations," Clark U. Diss., 1939.

3234. Poincaré, R. *La Cuestión del Pacífico y la Liga de las Naciones*. Paris, 1921.

3235. Quijano, A. *La Liga de las Naciones*. Bogotá, 1919.

3236. Sivori, J. B. *La Liga de las Naciones, Su Origen y la Obra Realizada en la República Argentina*. B.A., 1928.

3237. Spencer, J. H. "The Monroe Doctrine and the League Covenant," *AJIL* 30 (1936) 400–413.

3237a. Tello, M. "Algunos Aspectos de la Participación de México en la Sociedad de las Naciones," *FI* 6 (1965–1966) 358–383.

3238. Van Leisen, H. *L'Amérique Latine à la Société des Nations*. Geneva, 1934.

3239. Walters, F. P. *A History of the League of Nations*. 2 vols., London, 1952.

3240. Wilson, A. T. "The Monroe Doctrine and Latin-American States," *ER* 249 (1929) 247–259.

3241. ———, and P. da Silva. *Commentaire Théorique et Pratique du Pacte de la Société des Nations et des Statuts de l'Union Panaméricaine*. Paris, 1935.

3242. Yepes, J. M. "Collaboration de l'Union Panaméricaine avec la Société des Nations," *RDISDP* 12 (1934) 295–300.

C. THE MONROE DOCTRINE AND THE CHANGING IMAGE

3243. Bingham, H. "The Future of the Monroe Doctrine," *JIR* 10 (1920) 392–403.

3244. Cambon, J. "La Doctrine de Monroe en 1928," *RDM* 47 (September, 1928) 90–101.

3245. Catt, C. C. *The Monroe Doctrine and Our Latin-American Relations, Discussed by Mrs. Carrie Chapman Catt and Judge Otto Schoenrich: Excerpts from Stenographic Report of a Luncheon Meeting at the Hotel Astor, New York, Dec. 15, 1923*. N.Y., 1923.

3246. Clark, J. R. *Memorandum on the Monroe Doctrine*. Wash., 1930.

3247. Cooke, C. W. "An Expanding Doctrine," *O* 135 (1923) 539–541.

3248. Corwin, E. S. "The Monroe Doctrine," *NAR* 218 (1923) 721–735.

3249. Garner, J. W. "The Recrudescence of the Monroe Doctrine," *PSQ* 45 (1930) 231–258.

3250. Herring, H. "Exit the Monroe Doctrine," *HA* 174 (1937) 449–458.

3251. Hughes, C. E. *The Centenary of the Monroe Doctrine*. Wash., 1923.

3252. ———. "The Monroe Doctrine After 100 Years," *CH* 19 (October, 1923) 102–113.

3253. ———. *Observations on the Monroe Doctrine*. Wash., 1923.
Reprinted in *AJIL* 17 (1923) 611–628.

3254. Inman, S. G. "The Monroe Doctrine as an Obsolete Principle," *CH* 26 (1927) 875–881.

3255. Lenoir, J. J. "The Monroe Doctrine and International Law: 1933–1941," *JP* 4 (1942) 47–67.

3256. Mahoney, T. H. *The Monroe Doctrine: The Vital Necessity of Its Continued Maintenance.* Boston(?), 1921.
Published by the Knights of Columbus Historical Commission.

3257. Moore, J. B. "The Monroe Doctrine," *AAAPSS* 96 (1921) 31–33.

3258. Roemer, H. "Das Clarksche Memorandum über die Monroe-Doktrin: Sinn und Auswirkung," *ZP* 20 (1930) 590–606.

3259. Shepherd, W. R. "The Monroe Doctrine Reconsidered," *PSQ* 39 (1924) 35–66.

3260. Ulloa Sotomayor, A. "La Doctrina de Monroe," *RU* 17 (1923) 8–28.
Attacks the Monroe Doctrine as not compatible with Pan Americanism.

VIII–C   cross references: 2980, 3123, 3219b, 3221, 3223, 3226a, 3240

D. THE HARDING, COOLIDGE, AND HOOVER ADMINISTRATIONS: BACKGROUND TO THE GOOD NEIGHBOR POLICY, 1921–1933

3261. Adams, S. H. *Incredible Era: The Life and Times of Warren Gamaliel Harding.* Boston, 1939.

3262. Beals, C. "Can the U.S.A. Flout Spanish-American Sentiment?" *AS* 1 (1932) 433–442.

3263. Blakeslee, G. H. *The Recent Foreign Policy of the United States: Problems in American Cooperation with Other Powers.* N.Y., 1925.

3264. Brandes, J. *Herbert Hoover and Economic Diplomacy: Department of Commerce Policy, 1921–1928.* Pittsburgh, 1962.

3265. Bryn-Jones, D. *Frank B. Kellogg: A Biography.* N.Y., 1937.

3266. Buell, R. L. "Changes in Our Latin American Policy," *AAAPSS* 156 (1931) 126–132.

3267. ———. "New Latin American Policy," *F* 81 (1929) 113–118.

3268. ———. "The United States and Central American Revolutions," *FPAR* 7 (1931) 187–204.

3269. ———. "The United States and Latin America," *FPAIS* 3 (January, 1928) 77–94.
A special supplement.

3270. Capdevila, A. *América: Nuestras Relaciones ante los Estados Unidos: Para los Horizontes de América, Desde Buenos Aires, Ciudad Fuerte.* B.A., 1926.

3271. Carter, J. *Conquest: America's Painless Imperialism.* N.Y., 1928.

3272. Cleven, N. A. N. "Mr. Hoover Concludes Good-Will Mission in South America," *CH* 29 (1929) 852–855.

3273. ———. "President-Elect Hoover's Visit to South America," *CH* 29 (1929) 683–685.

3274. Collings, H. T. "Importance of Our Relations with Latin America," *AAAPSS* 156 (1931) 133–135.

3275. Coolidge, C. *The Autobiography of Calvin Coolidge.* N.Y., 1929.

3276. Cumberland, W. W. "Our Economic Policy Toward Latin America," *AAAPSS* 156 (1930) 167–168.

3277. Current, R. N. *Secretary Stimson: A Study in Statecraft.* New Brunswick, N.J., 1954.
Secretary of State, 1929–1933.

3278. Davis, N. H. "Wanted: A Consistent Latin American Policy," *FA* 9 (1931) 547–568.

3279. DeConde, A. "Herbert Hoover's Good Will Tour," *HIS* 12 (1950) 167–181.

3280. ———. *Herbert Hoover's Latin American Policy.* Stanford, Calif., 1951.
Suggests that the Good Neighbor policy began with the Hoover administration.

3281. Ellis, L. E. *Frank B. Kellogg and American Foreign Relations, 1925–1929.* New Brunswick, N.J., 1961.

3282. Feis, H. *The Diplomacy of the Dollar: First Era, 1919–1932.* Baltimore, 1950.

3283. Ferrell, R. H. *American Diplomacy in the Great Depression: Hoover-Stimson Foreign Policy, 1929–1933.* New Haven, Conn., 1957.

3284. ———. *Frank B. Kellogg: Henry L. Stimson.* N.Y., 1963.
The eleventh volume of *The American Secretaries of State and Their Diplomacy.*

3284a. ———. *Peace in Their Time: The Origins of the Kellogg-Briand Pact.* New Haven, Conn., 1952.

3285. Fuess, C. M. *Calvin Coolidge.* Boston, 1940.

3286. Gutiérrez, E. "Hoover-Yrigoyen-Leguía," *AC* 2 (December, 1928) 11–14.

3287. Hart, A. B. "United States and Latin American Dictatorships," *CH* 31 (1930) 744–746.

3288. Hernández-Usera, R. *Semillas a Voleo*. Madrid, 1925.
Series of essays, several of which treat United States influence in the Caribbean area.

3289. Hicks, J. D. *Republican Ascendancy, 1921–1933*. N.Y., 1960.
General history of the United States for the period 1921–1933.

3290. Hoover, H. *Addresses Delivered During the Visit of Herbert Hoover, President-elect of the United States, to Central and South America, November–December, 1928*. Wash., 1929.

3291. ———. *The Memoirs of Herbert Hoover: The Cabinet and the Presidency, 1920–1933*. N.Y., 1952.

3292. ———. *The Memoirs of Herbert Hoover: The Great Depression, 1929–1941*. N.Y., 1952.

3293. ———. *The New Day*. 2d ed., Stanford, Calif., 1929.
Speeches during the campaign of 1928.

3294. Hughes, C. E. *Our Relations to the Nations of the Western Hemisphere*. Princeton, N. J., 1928.
Secretary of state, 1921 to 1925, presents the official United States view.

3295. ———. *Pan-American Peace Plans*. New Haven, Conn., 1929.

3296. ———. *The Pathway of Peace*. N.Y., 1925.
Addresses, 1920–1924, by Harding's secretary of state.

3297. Inman, S. G. "Imperialistic America," *AM* 134 (July, 1924) 107–116.

3298. Jiménez Montellano, B. *Fundamentos Jurídicos de la Solidaridad Americana*. Mexico, 1948.
Traces the initiation of the Good Neighbor Policy to the Coolidge administration, 1923 to 1929.

3299. Kellogg, F. B. *Some Foreign Policies of the United States*. N.Y., 1926.
By the Secretary of State from 1925 to 1929.

3300. ———. *Some Objectives of American Foreign Policy*. Wash., 1926.

3301. Lyons, E. *Herbert Hoover*. Garden City, N.Y., 1964.

3302. Mann, L. B. "Foreign Reactions to the American Tariff Act," *FPAIS* 6 (1930) 261–278.

3303. McKenna, M. C. *Borah*. Ann Arbor, Mich., 1961.
Concerns the chairman of the Senate Foreign Relations Committee during the 1920's.

3304. McMahon, J. L. *Recent Changes in the Recognition Policy of the United States*. Wash., 1933.

3305. Morison, E. E. *Turmoil and Tradition: A Study of the Life and Times of Henry L. Stimson*. Boston, 1960.

3306. Myers, W. S. *The Foreign Policies of Herbert Hoover, 1929–1933*. N.Y., 1940.

3307. ———, and W. H. Newton. *The Hoover Administration: A Documented Narrative*. N.Y., 1936.

3308. ——— (ed.). *The State Papers and Other Public Writings of Herbert Hoover*. 2 vols., Garden City, N.Y., 1934.

3309. Navarrete, G. "The Latin American Policy of Charles Evans Hughes, 1921–1925," U. of California Diss., 1964.

3310. Norton, H. D. "New Avenues of Cultural Approach Between the Nations of America," *BPAU* 66 (1932) 77–87.

3311. Norton, H. K. "The Ethics of Imperialism," *WW* 51 (1926) 321–328.

3312. Perkins, D. *Charles Evans Hughes and American Democratic Statesmanship*. Boston, 1956.

3313. Pusey, M. J. *Charles Evans Hughes*. 2 vols., N.Y., 1951.

3314. Rippy, J. F. "The Significance of the Pan American Movement," *SAQ* 30 (1931) 280–289.

3315. Schriftgiesser, K. *This Was Normalcy*. Boston, 1948.
Treats the Harding administration.

3316. Scroggs, W. O. "The American Investments in Latin America," *FA* 10 (1932) 502–504.

3317. Simonds, F. H. "Hoover South Americanus," *RR* 79 (February, 1929) 60–70.

3318. Stimson, H. L. "Bases of American Foreign Policy During the Past Four Years," *FA* 11 (1933) 383–396.

3319. ———. *The United States and the Other American Republics: A Discussion of Recent Events*. Wash., 1931.

3320. Stimson, H. L., and M. Bundy. *On Active Service in Peace and War*. N.Y., 1948.
Memoir-biography of Stimson.

3321. Sullivan, M. "President Hoover in International Relations," *YR* 19 (1929) 219–232.

3322. ———. "With Hoover in Latin America," *RR* 29 (February, 1929) 53–57.

3322a. Sutherland, W. R. *A Debate Handbook on the United States and the Protection of Capital Invested in Central and Latin America: A Collection of Essays and Addresses Concerning Our Economic, Political, and Military Developments Under the Monroe Doctrine and Our Caribbean Policy*. Lexington, Ky., 1928.

3322b. Taussig, F. W. "The Tariff Act of 1922," *QJE* 37 (1922) 1–28.

3323. Tessan, F. de. *Le Président Hoover et la Politique Américaine*. Paris, 1931.

3324. Thurston, W. C. "Relations with Our Latin American Neighbors," *AAAPSS* 156 (1931) 116–125.

3325. Traphagen, J. C. "The Inter-American Diplomacy of Frank B. Kellogg," U. of Minnesota Diss., 1956.

3326. Warren, H. G. *Herbert Hoover and the Great Depression*. N.Y., 1959.

3327. White, W. A. *A Puritan in Babylon: The Story of Calvin Coolidge*. N.Y., 1938.

3328. Wilbur, R. L., and A. M. Hyde. *The Hoover Policies*. N.Y., 1937.
The authors were members of Hoover's cabinet.

3329. Wilgus, A. C. "'Imperialism' in the Relations of the United States to Hispanic America," *PAM* 44 (1931) 363–368.

3329a. Williams, M. W. "Latin Fears and Yankee Favors," *AME* 13 (1928) 320–325.

3329b. Williams, W. A. "The Legend of Isolationism in the 1920's," *SS* 18 (1954) 1–20.

VIII–D   cross references:

a) For works on the Santiago Conference of 1923, see items 4945–4954; for the Havana Conference of 1928, see items 4955–4975b.

b) For works on the second Conference on Central American Affairs (Washington, 1922–1923), see items 5136–5143; for

works on the Conference on Conciliation and Arbitration (Washington, 1928–1929), see items 5144–5149.

c) See also items 1760, 3246, 3258.

E. FRANKLIN D. ROOSEVELT AND THE GOOD NEIGHBOR POLICY, 1933–1938

3330. Alvarado Garaicoa, T. *La Doctrina Internacional de Franklin D. Roosevelt*. Guayaquil, 1947.
Sympathetic appreciation of the Good Neighbor Policy.

3331. Argentina. Ministerio de Justicia e Instrucción. *Política de Buena Vecindad*. Sante Fe, Argentina, 1945.
Speeches by Josué Gollán, Ambassador Spruille Braden, and Cortez Plá.

3332. Beals, C. "A Self-Sufficient Latin America," *YR* 24 (1935) 479–497.

3333. ———. *The Coming Struggle for Latin America*. Phil., 1938.

3334. Beard, C. A. *American Foreign Policy in the Making, 1932–1940*. New Haven, Conn., 1946.
A "revisionist" study.

3334a. Beckett, G. *The Reciprocal Trade Agreements Program*. N.Y., 1941.

3335. Blum, J. M. *From the Morgenthau Diaries: Years of Crisis, 1928–1938*. Boston, 1959.
Morgenthau was secretary of the treasury in Roosevelt's cabinet.

3336. Burns, J. M. *Roosevelt: The Lion and the Fox*. N.Y., 1956.

3337. Callorda, P. E. *En Diplomacia*. Lima, 1939.
Comments on Latin America by an Ecuadorian diplomat.

3338. Castro, A. "Sobre la Relación Entre Ambas Américas," *RI* 2 (April, 1940) 25–34.

3339. Cole, W. S. *Senator Gerald P. Nye and American Foreign Relations*. Minneapolis, 1962.
Isolationist senator from North Dakota.

3340. Coleman, G. C. "The Good Neighbor Policy of F. D. Roosevelt, with Special Reference to Three Inter-American Conferences, 1933–1938," U. of Iowa Diss., 1951.

3341. Cox, C. M. *En Torno al Imperialismo*. Lima, 1933.

3342. Cronon, E. D. "Interpreting the New Good Neighbor Policy: the Cuban Crisis of 1933," *HAHR* 39 (1959) 538–567.

3343. ———. *Josephus Daniels in Mexico*. Madison, Wis., 1960.

3344. Cuevas Cancino, F. M. *Roosevelt y la Buena Vecindad*. Mexico, 1954.

3345. Daniels, J. *Shirt-Sleeve Diplomat*. Chapel Hill, N.C., 1947.

3346. Dennis, L. "What Price Good Neighbor?" *AME* 45, no. 178 (1938) 150–158.

3347. Duggan, L. "Our Relations with the Other American Republics," *AAAPSS* 198 (1938) 128–132.

3348. Dulles, F. R., and G. E. Ridinger. "The Anti-Colonial Policies of Franklin D. Roosevelt," *PSQ* 70 (1955) 1–18.

3349. Einaudi, M. *The Roosevelt Revolution*. N.Y., 1959.

3350. Ellis, L. E. "Dwight Morrow and the Mexican Revolution," *HAHR* 38 (1958) 482–505.

3351. Freidel, F. B. *Franklin D. Roosevelt*. Boston, 1952–1956.
   Three volumes have appeared of a projected six-volume biography.

3352. Funk, W. (ed.). *Roosevelt's Foreign Policy, 1933–1941*. N.Y., 1942.

3353. García Robles, A. *Le Panaméricanisme et la Politique de Bon Voisinage*. Paris, 1938.
   Spanish ed., Mexico, 1940.

3354. Goetz, D., and V. Fry. "The Good Neighbors: The Story of the Two Americas," *FPAHS* 17 (1939).

3355. González, J. V. *Política Internacional*. B.A., 1934.
   Considers United States–Latin American relations.

3356. Greer, T. H. *What Roosevelt Thought*. East Lansing, Mich., 1958.

3357. Guerrant, E. O. *Roosevelt's Good Neighbor Policy*. Albuquerque, N.M., 1950.

3358. Gunther, J. *Roosevelt in Retrospect*. N.Y., 1950.

3359. Hinton, H. B. *Cordell Hull*. Garden City, N.Y., 1942.
   Secretary of state, 1933 to 1944.

3360. Hoover, H. *Addresses upon the American Road, 1933–1938*. N.Y., 1938.

3361. ———. *The Challenge to Liberty*. N.Y., 1934.

3362. Hull, C. *The Memoirs of Cordell Hull*. 2 vols., N.Y., 1948.

3363. Inman, S. G. "Building an Inter-American Neighborhood," *WAP*, no. 20 (1937).

3364. Kilpatrick, C. (ed.). *Roosevelt and Daniels: A Friendship in Politics*. Chapel Hill, N.C., 1952.

3365. Leuchtenburg, W. E. *Franklin D. Roosevelt and the New Deal, 1932–1940*. N.Y., 1963.

3366. Lyautey, P. *Survol des Amériques*. Paris, 1937.

3367. MacLeish, A. "El Arte de Ser Buen Vecino," *RI* (September, 1940) 268–275.

3368. Mathews, J. M. "Roosevelt's Latin American Policy," *APSR* 29 (1935) 805–820.

3369. Mora Valverde, M. *Nuestra Soberanía Frente al Departamento de Estado*. San José, C.R., 1940.
   A Costa Rican Communist's comments on the Good Neighbor Policy.

3370. Morineau, O. *The Good Neighbor*. Mexico, 1938.

3371. Nevins, A. *The New Deal and World Affairs: A Chronicle of International Affairs, 1933–1945*. New Haven, Conn., 1950.

3372. Orrego Vicuña, E. *Los Problemas de la Unificación Americana*. Santiago, 1933.

3373. Perkins, D. *The New Age of Franklin D. Roosevelt, 1932–1945*. Chicago, 1957.

3374. Perkins, F. *The Roosevelt I Knew*. N.Y., 1946.
   By the secretary of labor under F.D.R.

3375. Piñero, N. *Problemas Internacionales*. B.A., 1936.
   Stresses Pan American questions.

3376. Popper, D. H. "Latin American Policy of the Roosevelt Administration," *FPAR* 10 (1934–1935) 270–281.

3377. Pratt, J. W. *Cordell Hull: 1933–1944*. 2 vols., N.Y., 1964.

3378. Ramírez, H. *El Gran Amanecer (al Margen del Desarrollo Continental de América)*. Caracas, 1935.

3379. Rauch, B. *The History of the New Deal, 1933–1938*. N.Y., 1944.
   Brief summary of the period.

3380. Robinson, E. E. *The Roosevelt Leadership, 1933–1945.* Phil., 1955.

3381. Rollins, A. B., Jr. (ed.). *Franklin D. Roosevelt and the Age of Action.* N.Y., 1960.
    Contains documentary materials.

3382. ———. *Roosevelt and Howe.* N.Y., 1962.
    On Roosevelt's relationship with a close adviser.

3383. Roosevelt, E. *Selected Speeches, Messages, Press Conferences and Letters.* N.Y., 1957.

3384. ———. *This I Remember.* N.Y., 1949.
    Memoirs of the President's wife.

3385. ———. *This Is My Story.* N.Y., 1937.

3386. Roosevelt, Elliott (ed.). *F.D.R.: His Personal Letters.* 4 vols., N.Y., 1947–1950.

3387. Roosevelt, F. D. *Public Papers and Addresses.* 13 vols., N.Y., 1938–1950.
    Edited by S. I. Rosenman.

3388. Roosevelt, N. *Wanted: Good Neighbors: The Need for Closer Ties with Latin America.* N.Y., 1939.

3389. Rosenman, S. I. *Working with Roosevelt.* N.Y., 1952.

3390. Saavedra Lamas, C. *Por la Paz de las Américas.* B.A., 1937.

3391. Schlesinger, A. M., Jr. *The Age of Roosevelt.* Boston, 1957–
    Three volumes of this work are available to date.

3392. Scott, J. B. "The Good Neighbor Policy," *AJIL* 30 (1936) 287–290.

3393. Sherwood, R. E. *Roosevelt and Hopkins: An Intimate History.* Rev. ed., N.Y., 1950.

3394. Sierra, M. J. "De Monroe a Roosevelt," *CA* 1 (January, 1942) 17–32.

3395. Timmons, B. N. *Garner of Texas.* N.Y., 1948.
    Treats Roosevelt's vice-president, 1933–1941.

3396. Tugwell, R. G. *The Democratic Roosevelt.* Garden City, N.Y., 1957.

3397. Vasconcelos, J. *Hispano-américa Frente a los Nacionalismos Agresivos de Europa y Estados Unidos.* La Plata, 1934.

3398. Vega, J. de la. *El Buen Vecino.* Bogotá, 1944.
    Extremely critical view of the Good Neighbor policy by a member of the Colombian senate.

3399. Welles, S. *The Roosevelt Administration and Its Dealings with the Republics of the Western Hemisphere.* Wash., 1935.

3400. ———. *Two Years of the "Good Neighbor" Policy.* Wash., 1935.

3401. Wood, B. "The Department of State and the Non-National Interest: The Cases of Argentine Meat and Paraguayan Tea," *IEA* 15 (1961) 3–32.

3402. ———. *The Making of the Good Neighbor Policy.* N.Y., 1961.
    Covers 1926–1943.

VIII–E   cross references:

a) For accounts of the seventh Inter-American Conference at Montevideo (1933), see items 4976–5012b; for the eighth Inter-American Conference at Lima (1938), see items 5013–5063.

b) For the special Conference on the Maintenance of Peace at Buenos Aires (1936), see items 5150–5181h.

c) See also items 1757, 3073b, 3450, 3454, 3483, 3814, 7320, 7598, 7615, 9120, 10163.

F. INTER-AMERICAN TRADE AND COMMERCE, 1921–1938

3403. Beckett, G. "Effect of the Reciprocal Trade Agreements upon the Foreign Trade of the United States," *QJE* 55 (1940) 80–94.

3404. ———. "The Problem of Reclassification in the Reciprocal Trade Agreements," *JPE* 48 (1940) 199–209.

3405. Bellegarde, D. "Inter-American Economic Policy," *AAAPSS* 150 (1930) 186–191.

3406. Berglund, A. "The Tariff Act of 1922," *AER* 13 (1923) 14–33.

3407. Bidwell, P. W. *Tariff Policy of the U.S.: A Study of Recent Experience.* N.Y., 1933.

3408. Blair, C. P. *Fluctuations in United States Imports from Brazil, Colombia, Chile, and Mexico, 1919–1954.* Austin, Texas, 1959.

3409. Bratter, H. M. "Foreign Exchange Control in Latin America," *FPAR* 14, no. 23 (1939).

3409a. Carus, C. D. "The Hull Trade Policies with Latin America," *PIWA* 15 (1938) 77–79.

3409b. "Casa Grace," *FOR* 12 (1935) 94–101.

Concerns the activities of W. R. Grace and Company, active in Latin America since 1884.

3409c. Chamberlin, S. F. "American Investments in Argentina, Brazil, and Chile," New York U. Diss., 1935.

3409d. Cooper, C. S. *Latin America: Men and Markets*. Boston, 1927.

3409e. Culbertson, W. S. *Reciprocity: A National Policy for Foreign Trade*. N.Y., 1937.

The author was a vice-chairman of the U.S. Tariff Commission. He supports the reciprocal trade agreements.

3409f. Elsassor, E. O. "The Export-Import Bank and Latin America, 1934–1945," U. of Chicago Diss., 1955.

3410. Gideonse, H. D. "The Relation of American Foreign-Trade Policy to New Deal Domestic Policy," *AER* 30 (1940) 87–97.

3411. Jones, C. F. *Commerce of South America*. Boston, 1928.

3412. Jones, J. M., Jr. *Tariff Retaliation: Repercussions of the Hawley-Smoot Bill*. Phil., 1934.

3413. Kreider, C. "The Effect of American Trade Agreements on Third Countries: Retrospect," *AER* 31 (1941) 780–793.

3414. Larkin, J. D. *Trade Agreements*. N.Y., 1940.

A defense of the Trade Agreements Act.

3415. Lee, T. F. *Latin American Problems: Their Relation to Our Investors' Billions*. N.Y., 1932.

3416. Mathy, L. G. "The Industrialization of the West Coast of South America and the Good Neighbor Policy," U. of Illinois Diss., 1946.

3417. Minelli, P. M. *Las Inversiones Internacionales en América Latina*. B.A., 1938.

3418. Morales, M. "Política Económica de los Estados Unidos en la América Latina," *FI* 4 (1964) 397–428.

Surveys 1933 to 1964.

3419. Pearson, J. C. *The Reciprocal Trade Agreements Program*. Wash., 1942.

3420. Phelps, D. M. "Industrial Expansion in Temperate South America," *AER* 25 (1935) 273–282.

3421. ———. *Migration of Industry to South America*. N.Y., 1936.

3422. Quesada, E. *Die Wirtschaftsbeziehungen Zwischen Latein-Amerika und der Vereinigten Staaten*. Leipzig, 1931.

3423. Raleigh, W. A., Jr. "The Reciprocal Trade Agreements Program in Latin America," *CPA* 11 (January, 1942) 1–25.

3424. Rippy, J. F. "A Bond-Selling Extravaganza of the 1920's," *JB* 23 (1950) 238–247.

About Latin American bonds sold in the United States, 1920–1930.

3425. Sayre, F. B. *The Way Forward: The American Trade Agreements Program*. N.Y., 1939.

3426. ———. *The Protection of American Export Trade*. Chicago, 1940.

Deals with trade agreements.

3427. Tasca, H. J. *The Reciprocal Trade Policy of the United States*. Phil., 1938.

3428. Trueblood, H. J. "Trade Rivalries in Latin America," *FPAR* 13, no. 13 (1937).

3429. Welles, S., and A. Stevenson. "Reciprocal Trade Agreements," *IC*, no. 390 (1943).

3430. Wertenbaker, C. C. *A New Doctrine for the Americas*. N.Y., 1941.

On the Good Neighbor Policy. The author was a foreign-news editor for *Time*.

3431. Winkler, M. "Investments of United States Capital in Latin America," *WPFP* 11, no. 6 (1928).

3432. Wood, B. "External Restraints in the Good Neighbor Policy," *IEA* 16 (Autumn, 1962) 3-24.

3433. Wythe, G. "Pan Americanism: Economic and Cultural," *SR* 22 (1937) 114–130.

VIII–E   cross references: 3334a

Chapter IX Latin America and World War II

A. GENERAL WORKS AND SPECIAL STUDIES

3434. Antonioletti, M. "América Latina Frente a Estados Unidos y Europa," *ASO* 12 (April, 1941) 34–41.

3435. Barnhart, E. N. "Citizenship and Political Tests in Latin American Republics in World War II," *HAHR* 42 (1962) 297–332.

3436. Catalán U., J. L. *Solidaridad Americana.* Guatemala, 1944.

3437. Chase, A. *Falange: The Axis Secret Army in the Americas.* N.Y., 1943.

3438. Fernández Artucio, H. *The Nazi Underground in South America.* N.Y., 1942. Spanish ed., Mexico, 1943.

3439. Fox, A. B. *The Power of Small States: Diplomacy in World War II.* Chicago, 1959.

3440. Furniss, E. S., Jr. "American Wartime Objectives in Latin America," *WP* 2 (1950) 373–388.

3441. Muniz, J. C. "El Momento de América," *RBCU* 51 (1943) 321–335.

3442. Quintanilla, L. *A Latin American Speaks.* N.Y., 1943. By a former Mexican ambassador to the United States.

3443. Range, W. *Franklin D. Roosevelt's World Order.* Athens, Ga., 1959.

3444. Rowe, L. S. "The Mission of the Americas in World Affairs," *AAAPSS* 222 (1942) 74–79.

3445. Snell, J. L. *Illusion and Necessity: The Diplomacy of Total War, 1939–1945.* Boston, 1963.

3446. USCS. Committee on Foreign Relations. *A Decade of American Foreign Policy: Basic Documents, 1941–1949, Prepared at the Request of the Senate Committee on Foreign Relations by the Staff of the Committee and the Department of State* (81st Cong., 1st Sess., S. Doc. 123). Wash., 1950.

3447. Welles, S. *The Time for Decision.* N.Y., 1944.

3448. Whitaker, A. P. (ed.). *Inter-American Affairs: An Annual Survey.* 5 vols., N.Y., 1942–1946.

IX–A cross references:

a) For general works on the response of the inter-American system to World War II, see items 4729–4751.

b) See also items 3145, 3186, 3356, 3362, 3373, 3377, 3380, 3387, 3389, 3607, 5344.

B. BACKGROUND OF WORLD WAR II AND THE PERIOD OF UNITED STATES NEUTRALITY, 1937–1941

3449. Aikman, D. *The All-American Front.* N.Y., 1940. Despite the title, the author recognizes the dangers inherent in considering Latin America as a single unit.

3450. Alfaro, R. J. *Commentary on Pan American Problems.* Cambridge, Mass., 1938. Three lectures, also published in Spanish.

3451. *América ante la Crisis Mundial.* Havana, 1943. Report of a symposium held in Havana in November, 1941.

3452. Barreda Laos, F. *Hispano América en Guerra?* B.A., 1941.

3453. Beals, C. *Pan America.* Boston, 1940.

3454. ———. *The Coming Struggle for Latin America.* Phil., 1938. The struggle will be with totalitarianism.

3455. ———. "Swastika over the Andes," *HA* 177 (1938) 176–186.

3456. ———. "Totalitarian Inroads in Latin America," *FA* 17 (1938) 78–89.

3457. Beard, C. A. *President Roosevelt and the Coming of the War, 1941.* New Haven, Conn., 1948.

3458. Behrendt, R. F. *Fascist Penetration in Latin America.* Wash., 1941.

3459. ———. "Foreign Influence in Latin America," *AAAPSS* 204 (1939) 1–8.

3460. Bemis, S. F. "The New Holy Alliance Crosses the Ocean," *QJIR* 1, no. 1 (1939) 18–24.

3461. Bernal de León, J. *La Quinta Columna en el Continente Americano.* Mexico, 1940(?).

3462. Bidwell, P. W. "Latin America, Germany and the Hull Treaties," *FA* 17 (1938) 374–390.

3463. Bradley, P. "European War and the Americas," *QJIR* 1, no. 4 (1939) 5–20.
Favors continued neutrality for the Western Hemisphere.

3464. Contreras Labarca, C. *América Latina Invadida por el Fascismo.* Santiago, 1938.

3465. Crow, C. *Meet the South Americans.* N.Y., 1948.

3466. Cunningham, W. R. "Design for an Inter-American Union," *IAQ* 2, no. 3 (1940) 5–15.

3467. Cusano, A. M. *Sud América bajo la Amenaza Soviética.* Montevideo, 1936.
Series of articles on the communist threat to South America.

3468. Divine, R. A. *The Illusion of Neutrality.* Chicago, 1962.
History of United States neutrality prior to World War II.

3469. ———. *The Reluctant Belligerent: American Entry into World War II.* N.Y., 1965.

3470. Drummond, D. F. *The Passing of American Neutrality, 1937–1941.* Ann Arbor, Mich., 1955.

3471. Fabela, I. *Neutralidad: Estudio Histórico, Jurídico y Político: La Sociedad de las Naciones y el Continente Americano ante la Guerra de 1939–1940.* Mexico, 1940.

3472. Giúdici, E. *Hitler Conquista América.* B.A., 1938.

3473. Gunther, J. *Inside Latin America.* N.Y., 1941.

3474. Haas, H. *The Battle for South America.* Wash., 1941.

3475. Haring, C. H. "Is There a Fascist Danger in South America?" *QJIR* 1, no. 1 (1939) 7–17.

3476. Hass, J. A. de. *Building Our Fences in Latin America.* N.Y., 1941.

3477. Henry, H. M. "The Nazi Threat to the Western Hemisphere," *SAQ* 39 (1940) 367–384.

3478. Herring, H. C. *Good Neighbors.* New Haven, Conn., 1941.
Concentrates heavily on Argentina, Brazil, and Chile.

3479. ———. "Making Friends with Latin America," *HA* 179 (1938) 360–375.

3480. Hessler, W. H. "Is South America Hedging on the War?" *IAQ* 3 (July, 1941) 5–12.

3481. Ibero-Amerikanisches Institut. *Alemania y el Mundo Ibero-Americano.* Berlin, 1939.
An attempt by German Reich officials to improve relations.

3482. Ingrey, N. A. "Fascism in South America," *CR* 15 (1938) 218–228.

3483. Inman, S. G. "Democracy Versus the Totalitarian State in Latin America," *AAPSSPS*, no. 7 (1938).

3484. Jaramillo Alvarado, P. *El Régimen Totalitario en América: Tres Ensayos Políticos.* Quito, 1962.
Anti-fascist lectures given in 1937–1939.

3485. Langer, W. L., and S. E. Gleason. *The Challenge to Isolation, 1937–1940.* N.Y., 1952.

3486. ———, and ———. *The Undeclared War, 1940–1941.* N.Y., 1953.

3487. Lauro, F. di. "L'Imperialismo Americano," in *Problem d'Oriente Imperialismo Americano.* Milan, 1939.

3488. Laves, W. H. C. (ed.). *Inter-American Solidarity.* Chicago, 1941.
Published lecture series.

3489. MacDonald, N. P. "The 'Axis' in South America," *FN* 145, n.s. (1939) 336–343.

3490. ———. *Hitler over Latin America.* London, 1940.
Country-by-country analysis.

3491. Magalháes, S. de. *Contra o Hitlerismo: Pela Integridad das Nações Americanas.* Rio, 1938.

3492. Marx, F. M. "The Dilemma of Fraternity," *QJIR* 1, no. 2 (1939) 62–70.

3493. McCulloch, J. I. B. *Challenge to the Americas.* N.Y., 1940.

3494. McCulloch, J. I. B. "Latin America and the Hemisphere Front," *YR* 30, n.s. (1940) 291–308.

3495. *The Meaning of War to the Americas.* Berkeley, Calif., 1941.

A lecture series published under the auspices of the University of California International Relations Committee.

3496. Méndez Calzada, E. "L'Amérique Ibérique et la Guerre de Hitler," *RPA* 46 (1939) 699–709.

3497. Murillo, G. *La Victoria de Alemania y la Situación de la América Latina.* Mexico, 1941.

3498. Myers, S. D., Jr. *America and the World Crisis: Proceedings of the Sixth Annual Conference, Institute of Public Affairs.* Dallas, 1939.

3499. Naft, S. "Fascism and Communism in South America," *FPAR* 13 (1937) 230–242.

3500. Nerval, G. "Europe Versus the United States in Latin America," *FA* 15 (1937) 636–645.

3501. PAU. Division of Law and Treaties. *Bilateral Treaty Developments in Latin America, 1942–1952.* Wash., 1953.

3502. Platt, R. S. "Latin America in World Affairs," *JG* 40 (1941) 321–330.

3503. "Protest of the American Republics to the Belligerent Countries," *BPAU* 74 (1940) 403–408.

Concerns the *Graf Spee* incident.

3504. Rangel Couto, H. *La Democracia y el Comunismo en América.* Mexico, 1939.

3505. Rauch, B. *Roosevelt: From Munich to Pearl Harbor.* N.Y., 1950.

3506. Rippy, J. F. "Why Worry About Latin America?" *E* 3 (February, 1938) 106–111.

3507. Rizzuto, F. A., Jr. *Anatomía de los Problemas Americanos.* B.A., 1941.

The author was the editor of the Argentine review *Veritas*.

3508. Roberts, B. A. "U.S. Propaganda Warfare in Latin America, 1938–1942," U. of S. California Diss., 1944.

3509. Sayán de Vidaurre, A. *Por la Cooperación Interamericana.* 5th ed., B.A., 1942.

3510. Schnake, O. *América y la Guerra.* Santiago, 1941.

3511. Schoenemann, F. *Die Aggressive Wirtschaftspolitik der Vereinigten Staaten in Südamerika und die Stellung Deutschlands.* Stuttgart, 1940.

3512. Seone, M. *Nuestra América y la Guerra.* Santiago, 1940.

3513. Spivak, J. L. *Secret Armies: The New Technique of Nazi Warfare.* N.Y., 1939.

3514. Strausz-Hupé, R. *Axis America: Hitler Plans Our Future.* N.Y., 1941.

3515. Suárez, B. *Problemas de América.* San Juan, P.R., 1941.

3516. Tejera, A. *Penetración Nazi en América Latina.* Montevideo, 1938.

3517. Whitaker, J. T. *Americas to the South.* N.Y., 1939.

3518. Woody, T. B., and P. M. Minelli. "Are the Americas Ready Economically and Politically to Defend Their Sovereignty and Integrity?" *VQR* 16 (1940) 35–44.

3519. Ybarra, T. R. *America Faces South.* N.Y., 1939.

3520. Zamora, J. C. "El Momento Político Europeo y su Trascendencia para América," *A* 1, no. 5 (1939) 1–5.

Concerns Nazi penetration.

IX–B   cross references:

a) For information concerning the first and second Consultative Conferences at Panama (1939) and Havana (1940), see items 5189a–5229.

b) See also items 1756, 2938, 3398, 3682, 3697, 5229, 10098.

C. THE PERIOD OF BELLIGERENCY, 1941–1945

3521. Aguiar, R. J. *Hacia la Comunidad Democrática Americana.* Montevideo, 1943.

3522. Alekseyev, V. *Fashistskaya Ugroza Latinskoy Amerike.* Moscow, 1942.

The Fascist Threat to Latin America. Discusses rightest activity in Latin America.

3523. Anderson, H. D., and S. K. Bailey. "O Nosso Hemisfério e a Paz do Povo," *RIBEU* 2 (May, 1944) 144–148.

This article originally appeared in English in the *Free World* (December, 1942).

3524. Aufricht-Ruda, H. "The Pan-American System and the United Nations," *SR* 10 (1943) 417–435.

3525. Brescia Camagni, A. "La Penetración Nazi-Facista en el Continente," *A* 13 (February, 1942) 62–66.

3526. Carr, P. "South America and the United Nations," *FW* 3 (1942) 66–69.

3527. Dean, V. *Latin America and the War.* London, 1942.

3528. Hall, M., and W. Peck. "Wings for the Trojan Horse," *FA* 19 (1941) 347–369. Discusses Axis airlines.

3529. Manger, W. *The United States and Latin America: A Survey of Recent Changes in the Relations of the United States with the Other American Republics.* Wash., 1943.

3530. ———. *The War and the Americas.* Rev. ed., Wash., 1944.

3531. Manross, L. M. *Development of the Good Neighbor Policy, January, 1942, to July, 1945.* Wash., 1945.

3532. Martínez-López, R. "Continental Solidarity," *SR* 29 (1944) 481–491.

3533. Normano, J. F., and A. Gerbi. *The Japanese in South America.* N.Y., 1943.

3534. Popper, D. H. "America's Alternative to Imperialism," *AMER* 6 (1942) 225–232.

3535. ———. "Hemisphere Solidarity in the War Crisis," *FPAR* 17 (1942) 50–63.

3536. ———. "South America and the Pacific War," *AMER* 5 (1942) 536–541.

3537. Reynolds, T. H. (ed.). *The Progress of Pan-Americanism.* Wash., 1943.

3538. Río, P. del. *Lo Que Debe Ser el Pan-americanismo: El Continente ante la Guerra y su Organización para la Paz.* Havana, 1942.

3539. Rodríguez, H. "La Solidaridad Americana," *RDLH* 1 (November, 1942) 296–301.

3540. Smith, G. *American Diplomacy During the Second World War, 1941–1945.* N.Y., 1965.

3541. Vergara, O. S. *América y la Guerra: Sensacional Discurso.* Santiago, 1941.

3542. Volkov, A. *Latinskaia Amerika v Borbye Protiv Gitlerisma.* Moscow, 1942. *Latin America in the Struggle Against Hitlerism.*

3543. Walker, R. L. *E. R. Stettinius, Jr.* N.Y., 1965. U.S. Secretary of State, 1944–1945.

3544. Welles, S. "La Política de Buena Vecindad," *RDLH* 5 (September, 1944) 35–48.

3545. ———. *Seven Decisions That Shaped History.* N.Y., 1960.

3546. White, J. W. "El Nazismo en América," *RA* 1 (February, 1945) 222–228.

IX–C   cross references:

a) For works dealing with the third Consultative Conference at Rio de Janeiro (1942), see items 5216–5229.

b) For works dealing with the Conference on Problems of War and Peace at Mexico City (1945), see items 5230–5255a.

D. THE MONROE DOCTRINE AND WORLD WAR II

3547. Ballón Benavides, F. "La Doctrina de América," *K* 2 (June, 1938) 44–51.

3548. Jessup, P. C. "The Monroe Doctrine in 1940," *AJIL* 34 (1940) 704–711.

3549. Kirk, G. *The Monroe Doctrine Today.* N.Y., 1941.

3550. Perkins, D. "Bringing the Monroe Doctrine up to Date," *FA* 20 (1942) 253–265.

3551. ———. "The Monroe Doctrine Today." *YR* 30 (1941) 686–702.

3552. Rippy, J. F. *America and the Strife of Europe.* Chicago, 1938.

3553. Showman, R. K., and L. S. Judson. *The Monroe Doctrine and the Growth of Western Hemisphere Solidarity.* N.Y., 1941.

3554. Verdaguer, R. "¿Debe Mantenerse en Todo su Vigor la Doctrina de Monroe?" *A* 1 (January, 1939) 13–18.

3555. Wilcox, F. O. "The Monroe Doctrine and World War II," *APSR* 17 (1942) 433–453.

E. ECONOMIC RELATIONS DURING THE WAR

3556. Alarcón, M. A. "La Guerra y el Comercio de Exportación de Productos Agropecuarios de Latino-América," *ES* 1 (March, 1943) 119–131.

3557. Behrendt, R. F., *et al. The Economic Defense of the Western Hemisphere: A Study in Conflicts.* Wash., 1941.

3558. Bellegarde, D. "Organización de la Solidaridad Económica Interamericana," *AUSD* 6 (January, 1942) 85–96.

3559. Bidwell, P. W. *Economic Defense of Latin America*. Boston, 1941.
  Spanish ed., Mexico, 1942.

3560. ———. "El Dorado Beckons," *FA* 18 (1940) 324–336.
  Effect of the European war on Latin American trade.

3561. ———. "Good Neighbors in the War, and After," *FA* 21 (1943) 524–534.

3562. Bliss, C. A. "Our Trade to South America," *HBR* 20 (1941) 107–115.

3563. Brand, D. D. "Latin America as a Source of Strategic Materials," in *Proceedings of the Conference on Latin America in Social and Economic Transition*. Albuquerque, N.M., 1943.

3564. Brossard, E. B. "The Effect of the War on Trade in the Americas," *BPAU* 76 (1942) 661–667.

3565. Camp, R. J. de. "Railroads of the Americas Do War Duty," *FCW* 16, no. 3 (1944) 5–7, 34, 36–39.

3566. Carson, J. S. "New Approaches in Inter-American Commercial Relations," *AAAPSS* 204 (1939) 66–71.

3567. Chalmers, H. "Wartime Controls and Stimuli upon the Foreign Trade of Latin America," *FCW* 11, no. 4 (1943) 3–5, 37.

3568. Clark, L. B. "Competing for Latin American Markets," *AAAPSS* 21 (1940) 165–172.

3569. Culbertson, W. S. "Economic Defense of the Americas," *AAAPSS* 211 (1940) 186–196.

3570. DeWilde, J. C. "Economic Projects for Hemisphere Development," *FPAR* 17 (1942) 298–306.

3571. ———. "Wartime Economic Cooperation in the Americas," *FPAR* 17 (1942) 286–295.

3572. Diebold, W., Jr. *New Directions in Our Trade Policy*. N.Y., 1941.

3573. Dietrich, E. B. *Economic Relations of the U.S. and Latin America*. Wash., 1941.

3574. Domke, M. *Western Hemisphere: Control over Enemy Property: A Comparative Study*. Durham, N.C., 1945.

3575. "Export-Import Bank Loans to Latin America," *FPAR* 17 (1941–1942) 82–93.

3576. Feuerlein, W., and E. Hannan. *Dollars in Latin America*. N.Y., 1941.

Discusses Latin American economic nationalism.

3577. Forsling, C. L. *The Role of Western Hemisphere Forests in the War and Reconstruction Following the War*. Mexico, 1944.

3578. Gerard, C. "Comércio Inter-Americano," *OEF* 6 (January, 1942) 101–106.

3579. Goldner, B. B. "Latin America's Strategic Metals and Their Relationship to the United States War Program," *CPA* 11 (March, 1942) 26–49.

3580. Haas, J. A. de. "Buying Latin American Loyalty," *HBR* 19 (1941) 298–310.

3581. Hanson, S. G. "Problems of an Inter-American Economy," *QJIR* 1, no. 1 (1939) 58–68.

3582. Harris, S. E. (ed.). *Economic Problems of Latin America*. N.Y., 1944.
  Divided into two major sections. The first section considers general economic problems and the second presents a country-by-country analysis.

3583. ———. "Price Control as a Hemisphere Problem," *MAR* 11 (July, 1943) 42–43.

3584. Haussmann, F. "Latin American Oil in War and Peace," *FA* 21 (1943) 354–361.

3585. Henius, F. *Latin American Trade*. N.Y., 1941.
  Suggestions for ways of increasing Western Hemisphere trade.

3586. Hessel, M. S. H., *et al. Strategic Materials in Hemisphere Defense*. N.Y., 1942.

3587. Hickman, C. A. "Economic Implications and Repercussions of Possible Development of Western Hemisphere Sources of Strategic Raw Materials," U. of Iowa Diss., 1942.

3588. Horne, B. C. "La Agricultura y la Economía en el Continente Americano," *RPAA* (July, 1943) 49–52.

3589. Institute of International Finance. *European War and Trade of the United States with Latin America*. N.Y., 1940.

3590. Lloyd, J. W. *Pan American Trade: With Special Reference to Fruits and Vegetables*. Danville, Ill., 1942.

3591. McClintock, J. C. "Food for the Americas," *FCW* 10, no. 8 (1943) 3–5, 11.

3592. Moran, W. T. "Our Latin American Trade Faces Financial Difficulties," *AAAPSS* 211 (1940) 173–179.

3593. Olson, P. R., and C. A. Hickman. *Pan-American Economics*. N.Y., 1943.

Discusses internal economic problems as well as trade relations with the United States.

3594. Patterson, G. "The Export-Import Bank," *QJE* 58 (November, 1943) 65–90.

3595. PAU. Division of Economic Information. "Economic Wartime Measures in Brazil and Colombia," *CPA* (September, 1940) 268–276.

3596. Pérez-Constanzé, F. *Política Económica Sudamericana ante la Guerra Europea*. B.A., 1940(?).

3597. Phelps, D. M. (ed.). *Economic Relations with Latin America: Proceedings of a Conference Held as a Part of the Institute of Latin American Studies, Ann Arbor, August 11–12, 1939*. Ann Arbor, Mich., 1940.

3598. Rasmussen, W. D. "Agriculture in War," *AIA* 3 (June, 1943) 103–106.

3598a. Raushenbush, J. "Look at Latin America," *FPAHS*, no. 27 (1940).

3599. Rippy, J. F. "South America's Foreign Trade and Hemisphere Defense," *JB* 14 (1941) 89–98.

3600. Thomas, E. P. "Inter-American Trade Problems," *AAAPSS* 204 (1939) 147–154.

3601. Trueblood, H. J. "Economic Defense of the Americas," *FPAR* 16 (1940) 126–136.

3602. ———. "Raw Material Resources of Latin America," *FPAR* 15 (1939) 114–128.

3603. ———. "War and United States–Latin American Trade," *FPAR* 15 (1939) 218–228.

3604. United States Tariff Commission. *Latin America as a Source of Strategic and Other Essential Materials*. Wash., 1941.

3605. Villaseñor Angeles, E. *Ensayos Interamericanos*. Mexico, 1944.

Author was the director of the Banco de México. The essays are primarily economic in nature.

3606. Williams, F. E. "Economic Diversification in Latin America," *AAAPSS* 211 (1940) 147–154.

IX–E cross references: 3408, 3409f, 3418, 3615, 3639, 3699, 3706, 3707, 3708, 3801, 3817, 3835

F. HEMISPHERE DEFENSE

3607. Conn, S., and B. Fairchild. *The Western Hemisphere: The Framework of Hemisphere Defense*. Wash., 1960.

3608. Baldwin, H. W. "Our New Long Shadow," *FA* 17 (1939) 465–476.

Deals with defense problems.

3609. ———. *United We Stand! Defense of the Western Hemisphere*. N.Y., 1941.

3610. Bidwell, P. W. "Self-Containment and Hemisphere Defense," *AAAPSS* 218 (1941) 175–185.

3611. Chéradame, A. *Defense of the Americas*. Garden City, N.Y., 1941.

3612. Eliot, G. F. "Defending America," *WAP*, no. 4 (1939).

3613. Foreman, C., and J. Raushenbush. *Total Defense*. N.Y., 1940.

On hemisphere defense.

3614. Garland, J. V. *War and the Americas*. N.Y., 1941.

3615. Hansen, A. H. "Hemisphere Solidarity: Some Economic and Strategic Considerations," *FA* 19 (1940) 12–21.

3616. Hartley, L. *Our Maginot Line*. N.Y., 1939.

3617. Johnson, L. "Hemisphere Defense," *AM* 166 (July, 1940) 1–7.

3618. MacLeish, A. F., and C. Reynolds. *Strategy of the Americas*. N.Y., 1941.

3619. Mecham, J. L. "Defense of the Americas: The Recent Trend Toward Cooperation," *SR* 26 (Winter, 1941) 211–222.

3620. Méndez Pereira, O. "Significance of Hispanic American Defense of the Continent," *PHR* 10 (March, 1941) 39–45.

3621. Nichols, E. R. (comp.). *Western Hemisphere Defense*. N.Y., 1941.

3622. Rippy, J. F. *South America and Hemispheric Defense*. Baton Rouge, La., 1941.

3623. Santos, E. "Mis Conferencias con el Presidente Roosevelt y los Planes de Organización Militar Interamericana," *RA* 10 (April, 1947) 3–14.

By the President of Colombia, 1938–1942.

3624. Sprout, H. *America's Problem of National Defense*. Princeton, N.J., 1939.

3625. ———. "Strategic Considerations of Hemisphere Defense," *QJIR* 1, no. 4 (1939) 21–29.

3626.   Staley, E. "The Myth of the Continents," *FA* 19 (1941) 481–494.

3627.   Stefansson, V. "What Is the Western Hemisphere?" *PA* 19 (1941) 343–347.

IX–F   cross references:

 a) For arrangements made at the Consultative Conferences held at Panama (1939), Havana (1940), and Rio de Janeiro (1942), see items 5189a–5229.

 b) For information concerning the Conference on War and Peace at Mexico City (1945), see items 5230–5255a.

 c) See also items 3557, 3559, 3569, 3599, 3601, 3667.

G. MEXICO AND WORLD WAR II

3627a. Amador, A. C. *México en la Contienda Mundial.* Mexico, 1943.

3628.   Avila Camacho, M. *Discurso en el Día de las Américas 14 de Abril, 1941.* Mexico, 1942.
  By the President of Mexico, 1940–1946.

3629.   ———. *The International Policy, 1943–1944.* Mexico, 1944.

3630.   ———. *Mexico and the War in the Pacific.* Mexico, 1941.

3631.   ———. *México ante la Situación International.* Mexico, 1941.

3632.   ———. *México: Cooperación las Naciones Aliadas.* Mexico, 1944.

3633.   ———. *Un Año de Política Internacional Mexicana, 1941–1942.* Mexico, 1942.

3634.   Beteta, R. *Las Repercusiones de la Guerra en el Comercio Exterior de México.* Mexico, 1942.

3635.   Carillo, A. *Mexico and the Fascist Menace.* Mexico, 1940.

3636.   Etheridge, M. "Speech of Foreign Secretary Ezequiel Padilla in the Mexican Senate, March 7, 1941: The Economic Consequences of a Hitler Victory," *IC*, no. 370 (1941).

3637.   Gurza, J. *Cuadros Sinópticos Sobre la Guerra: La Actitud de México.* Mexico, 1942.

3638.   Halperin, M. "Mexico Shifts Her Foreign Policy," *FA* 19 (1940) 207–221.

3639.   Hediger, E. S. "Impact of War on Mexico's Economy," *FPAR* 19 (1943) 78–87.

3640.   Lombardo Toledano, V. *La Alianza Histórica Entre los Pueblos de México y de los Estados Unidos.* Mexico, 1942.
  By Mexico's most famous Marxist.

3641.   ———. *Como Actuan los Nazis en México.* Mexico, 1941.

3642.   Mexico. *Comité Nacional Anti-Nazifascista.* Mexico, 1944.

3643.   "Mexico: One Year at War," *FOR* 28 (August, 1943) 120–121, 151–152, 154, 156, 158, 160, 162.

3644.   Partido de la Revolución Mexicana. *México en Guerra.* Mexico, 1942.

3645.   Scroggs, W. O. "Mexican Anxieties," *FA* 18 (1940) 266–280.

3646.   Villaseñor, E. "La Economía de Guerra en México," *IE* 3, no. 1 (1943) 7–33.

IX–G   cross references: 6293

H. CENTRAL AMERICAN–CARIBBEAN REGION AND WORLD WAR II

3647.   Alfaro, R. J. *Los Acuerdos Entre Panamá y los Estados Unidos.* Panama, 1943.

3648.   Arévalo, J. J. *Escritos Políticos.* Guatemala, 1945.

3649.   Cruz, A. *Una Voz de Alerta Frente a la Amenaza del Falangismo en Cuba.* Havana, 1940.

3650.   Díaz Versón, S. *El Nazismo en Cuba.* Havana, 1944.

3651.   Eyre, J. K., Jr. "Martinique, A Key Point in Hemisphere Defense," *IAQ* 3 (October, 1941) 82–88.

3652.   Harding, J., and J. A. E. Orloski. "Dominican Republic Tackles War Problems," *FCW* 10, no. 3 (1943) 6–9, 26–28.

3653.   Lourié, I. *Haiti: The Ally of the Democracies.* Port-au-Prince, 1942.

3654.   McLean, E. R. "The Caribbean: An American Lake," *USNIP* 67 (1941) 947–960.

3655.   Merlos, S. R. *Centro-América en el Conflicto.* San Salvador, 1942.

3656.   Moran, C. "The Evolution of Caribbean Strategy," *USNIP* 68 (1942) 365–373.

3657.   "Nottebohm Case," *AJIL* 49 (1955) 390–403.
  Concerns German property in Guatemala during World War II.

3658. Ortiz y Fernández, F. *Italia y Cuba.* 4th ed., Havana, 1944.

3659. Scott, W. H. H. "War's Effect on Panama's Economy," *FCW* 11, no. 13 (1943) 15–19, 44–45.

3660. Smith, C. A. "Martinique in World War II," *USNIP* 81 (1955) 169–174.

3661. Stark, H. N. "War Bolsters Haiti's Economy," *FCW* 9, no. 11 (1942) 4–8, 38–40.

3662. ———. "War Poses Problems for British West Indies," *FCW* 9, no. 12 (1942) 8–12, 34–36.

3663. Torriente y Peraza, C. de la. "Cuba, America and the War," *FA* 19 (1940) 145–155.

3664. ———. *Libertad y Democracia.* Havana, 1941.
       On Cuban politics and World War II.

3665. USDA. Anglo-American Caribbean Commission. *The Caribbean Islands and the War.* Wash., 1943.

3666. Vargas Gómez, A. "La Isla de Cuba Frente a la Guerra Europea," *UL* 11 (April, 1942) 420–429.

3667. Wright, A. R. "Defense Sites Negotiation Between the United States and Panama, 1936–1948," *USDSB* 27 (1952) 212–217.

I. SPANISH SOUTH AMERICA AND WORLD WAR II

3668. Argentina. *Situación del Agregado Cultural de la Embajada Alemana, Octubre de 1942.* B.A., 1942.

3669. ———. Cámara de Diputados. Comisión Investigadora de Actividades Antiargentinas. *Un Centro de Actividades Anti-Argentina.* B.A., 1942.

3670. Arze, J. A. *Bolivia bajo el Terrorismo Nazifascista: Un Llamado a la Ciudadanía Boliviana y a la Conciencia Democrática Internacional. Para Reforzar la Acción de la Unión Democrática Boliviana.* Lima, 1945.

3671. Ballivián Calderón, R. "América ante el Conflicto Europeo," *K* 3 (May, 1941) 69–80.

3672. Bianchi, M. *Chile and Great Britain, Twelve Addresses.* London, 1944.
       By the Chilean ambassador to Great Britain.

3673. Bradford, S. E. *The Battle for Buenos Aires.* N.Y., 1943.
       Journalist's account of nazi activity in Argentina.

3674. Bravo, M. *Proposiciones Sobre la Defensa Nacional.* B.A., 1940.

3675. Brena, T. G., and J. V. Iturbide. *Alta Traición en el Uruguay.* Montevideo, 1940.
       Nazi activity in Uruguay.

3676. Campos, A. R. *Un Episodio de la Segunda Guerra Mundial en Aguas Territoriales de la República Oriental del Uruguay.* Montevideo, 1952.
       Author was Uruguayan minister of national defense during the *Graf Spee* incident.

3677. Creydt Abelenda, O. "El Paraguay bajo la Amenaza Fascista," *FU*, no. 28 (1938).

3678. Dickmann, E. *La Infiltración Nazi-Fascista en la Argentina.* B.A., 1939.

3679. "Fascist Trends in Chile," *FOR* 17, no. 5 (1938) 74–95.

3680. Fernández Artucio, H. *Nazis en el Uruguay.* B.A., 1940.

3681. Ghioldi, R. *La Política Exterior Argentina.* Montevideo, 1944.
       A Communist's view of the Farrell-Perón foreign policy.

3682. *La Guerra Mundial y la Política Internacional de Colombia.* Bogotá, 1941.

3683. Hilton, S. E. "Argentine Neutrality, September, 1939–June, 1940: A Re-Examination," *TA* 22 (January, 1966) 227–257.

3684. "The International Position of Argentina: Correspondence Between the Secretary of State and the Argentine Foreign Minister," *USDSB* 9 (1943) 159–166.

3685. Kelly, H. W., and D. [Smith] Kelly. *Dancing Diplomats.* Albuquerque, N.M., 1950.
       Report of United States vice-consul in Iquitos, Peru, during World War II.

3686. Loewenstein, K. "Legislation Against Subversive Activities in Argentina," *HLR* 56 (1943) 1261–1306.

3687. Martínez de la Torre, R. *Fascistas y Pro-Nazis: Apuntes para Interpretación Marxista de Historia del Perú.* Lima, 1941.

3688. Mendoza, J. C. *La Argentina y la Swástica.* B.A., 1941.

3689. Moreno Quintana, L. M. "La Economía Argentina Frente a la Guerra," *RCE* 30 (May, 1942) 383–389.

3690. Plaza A., E. *La Contribución de Venezuela al Panamericanismo Durante el Período 1939–1943.* Caracas, 1945.

3691. Repetto, N. *Política Internacional.* B.A., 1943.
Socialist criticism of President Castillo of Argentina.

3692. Rudolph, W. E. "Argentine Trade Under Wartime Conditions," *GR* 34 (1944) 311–316.

3693. Ruiz-Guiñazú, A. *La Argentina ante sí Misma.* B.A., 1942.
Proto-fascist recommendations for the Argentine revolution.

3694. Ruiz-Guiñazú, E. *La Política Argentina y el Futuro de América.* B.A., 1944.
President Castillo's foreign minister defends Argentine foreign policy from 1941 to 1943.

3695. Santander, S. *Nazismo en Argentina: La Conquista del Ejército.* Montevideo, 1946.
Treats fascist inroads into the Argentine army.

3696. ———. *Técnica de Una Traición: Juan Perón y Eva Duarte, Agentes del Nazismo en la Argentina.* 2d ed., Montevideo, 1953.

3697. Schneider, A. "Argentinien: Neutralität und Blockade: Handelspolitik im Zeichen des Krieges," *IR* 5 (September, 1939) 158–159.

3698. Setaro, R. M. *Argentina: Fascist Headquarters.* N.Y., 1944.
Issued by the Council for Pan American Democracy.

3699. ———. "The Argentine Fly in the International Ointment," *HM* 189 (August, 1944) 203–209.
Stresses the economic situation.

3700. Silveyra, C. M. *La Cuestión Nazi en la Argentina.* B.A., 1939.

3701. Tomic R., R. *Chile y la Guerra.* Santiago, 1942.

3702. Uruguay. Ministerio de Relaciones Exteriores. *Antecedentes Relativos al Hundimiento del Acorazado "Admiral Graf Spee" y la Internación del Barco Mercante "Tacoma."* Montevideo, 1940.

3703. Venezuela. Congreso Nacional. *La "Quinta Columna" en Venezuela: Informe Sobre Actividades Antinacionales Presentado al Congreso Nacional el 13 de Julio de 1942 por la Minoría Unificada.* Caracas, 1942.

3704. Vergara, O. S. *Chile y la Guerra: Hacia una Democracia Dirigida: Discurso del Ministro de Fomento.* Santiago, 1941.

3705. Vivero, L. de. *Avance del Imperialismo Fascista en el Perú.* Mexico, 1938.

3706. "War's Effect on Venezuela's Economy," *FCW* 9, no. 4 (1942) 4–7, 38–39.

3707. Zeidenfelt, A. "Transportation in the Caribbean During World War II," *IEA* 4 (Winter, 1950) 75–96.

3708. Zulaga, Z. J. A. "El Comercio Exterior Colombiano, Antes y Durante los Primeros Siete Meses de Guerra Europea," *AEE* 3 (August, 1940) 16–29.

IX–I   *cross references: 3595, 4746, 4848, 4861, 5229, 5234, 5248, 9484, 9764, 9804*

J. BRAZIL AND WORLD WAR II

3709. Barros, J. de. "A Diplomácia Brasileira e a Guerra," *CP* 3, no. 31 (1943) 65–76.

3710. ———. "A Diplomácia Brasileira e a Defesa da América," *CP* 3, no. 34 (1943) 107–111.

3711. Brazil. Ministerio das Relações Exteriores. *O Brazil e a Segunda Guerra Mundial.* 2 vols., Rio, 1944.
Documentary collection.

3712. Carneiro, V. T. Diniz. *Histórico: A Participação do Brasil na 2ª Guerra Mundial.* Rio, 1947.

3713. Castello Branco, M. T. *O Brasil na II Grande Guerra.* Rio, 1960.

3714. Delegacia da Ordem Política e Social de Santa Catarina. *O Punhal Nazista no Coração do Brasil.* Florianopolis, 1944.
Pro-Nazi activity in Santa Catarina.

3715. Dorland, A. G. "Brazil and a 'German Menace' in South America," *QRC* 5 (1938) 117–127.

3716. Ganzert, F. W. "The Brazilian Attitude Toward Hemispheric Unity," *BR* (February, 1941) 8–10, 22–26.

3716a. Klein, L. R. "The American Invasion of Brazil," *PAAM* (February, 1946) 45–48.
Concerns improvement of relations after the influx of American troops.

3717.   Maack, R. "The Germans of South Brazil: A German View," *QJIR* 1, no. 3 (1939) 5–23.

3718.   Martins, M. *Hitler Guerreia o Brasil Ha Dez Anos.* Curitiba, 1942(?).
        Nazi activity in the state of Paraná.

3719.   Moraes, J. B. Mascarenhas de. *A. F. E. B. Pelo seu Comandante.* São Paulo, 1947.
        About the Brazilian expeditionary force in Italy during World War II.

3720.   Motta Lima, P., and J. Barboza Mello. *El Nazismo en el Brasil: Proceso del Estado Corporativo.* B.A., 1938.

3721.   "O Brasil na Guerra," *OEF* 7 (September, 1942) 41–57.
        Brazil's contributions in World Wars I and II.

3722.   Perdigão, L. F. *Missão de Guerra: Os Expedicionários de FAB na Guerra Européia.* Rio, 1958.

3723.   Py, A. da Silva. *A Quinta Coluna no Brasil: A Conspiração Nazista no Rio Grande do Sul.* Porto Alegre, 1942.

3724.   Silveira, A. *O Sexto Regimento de Infantaria Expedicionário.* 2d ed., Rio, 1947.
        Treats Brazilian forces in World War II.

IX–J   cross references: 3595, 4734, 10098

Chapter X The United States and Latin America
Since World War II

A. GENERAL WORKS AND SPECIAL STUDIES

3725. Adams, R. N., and C. C. Cumberland. *U.S. University Cooperation in Latin America*. East Lansing, Mich., 1960.
>An examination of thirteen cooperative university programs.

3726. Alexander, R. J. *Prophets of the Revolution: Profiles of Latin American Leaders*. N.Y., 1962.
>Short biographies of leaders in Latin America, including Juan Perón, Rómulo Betancourt, and Fidel Castro.

3727. ———. *Today's Latin America*. Garden City, N.J., 1962.
>An institutional survey stressing changing conditions in the postwar period.

3728. Arciniegas, G. *The State of Latin America*. N.Y., 1952.
>By Colombia's famous liberal intellectual.

3728a. Bailey, N. A. (ed.). *Latin America: Politics, Economics, and Hemispheric Security*. N.Y., 1965.

3729. Beals, C. *Latin America: World in Revolution*. London, 1963.

3730. Benton, W. *The Voice of Latin America*. N.Y., 1961.
>Spanish ed., Mexico, 1963. The author, a senator from Connecticut (1949–1953), prepared the work after an extensive tour of the area.

3731. Berle, A. A., Jr. *Latin America: Diplomacy and Reality*. N.Y., 1962.
>By an ex-ambassador to Brazil and a Latin American adviser to the Kennedy administration.

3732. Campos, R. de Oliveira. "Relações Estados Unidos-América Latina: Uma Interpretação," *RBPI* 2 (December, 1959) 24–40.

3733. Carleton, W. G. *The Revolution in American Foreign Policy: Its Global Range*. N.Y., 1963.

3734. Carnero Checa, G. *El Aguila Rampante: El Imperialismo Yanqui Sobre América Latina*. Mexico, 1956.
>A general indictment of United States policy in Latin America.

3735. Clark, G. *The Coming Explosion in Latin America*. N.Y., 1962.
>A journalistic interpretation.

3736. Danilevich, M. V., and A. F. Shul'govskii (eds.). *Problemy Sovremennoi Latinskoi Ameriki*. Moscow, 1959.
>*Problems of Contemporary Latin America*. Treats Latin American resistance to United States interference.

3737. Dizard, W. P. *The Strategy of Truth: The Story of the U.S. Information Service*. Wash., 1961.

3738. Duggan, L. *The Americas: The Search for Hemisphere Security*. N.Y., 1949.
>By a State Department official who was partially responsible for the formulation of the Good Neighbor policy.

3739. Eisenhower, M. S. *The Wine is Bitter: The United States and Latin America*. N.Y., 1963.
>By a brother of the President.

3740. Fabela, I. *Buena y Mala Vecindad*. Mexico, 1958.
>Collection of essays generally critical of U.S. policy in the postwar period.

3741. Fraga Iribane, M. "Tendencias Políticas de Hispanoamérica Después de la Segunda Guerra Mundial," *EA* 20 (1960) 105–130.

3742. Fuentes, C. "América Latina—Estados Unidos," *P* (August, 1960) 51–72.
>By a Mexican Marxist intellectual.

3743. ———, et al. *Whither Latin America?* N.Y., 1963.

3744. Gabaldón, J. R. *En Defensa de la Paz y de la América Latina.* Caracas, 1957.

3745. Gatzke, H. W. *The Present in Perspective.* 2d ed., Chicago, 1961.
General survey of international affairs since World War II.

3746. *Gegenwartsprobleme Lateinamerikas.* Berlin, 1961.

3747. Gil, F. G. "Cuatro Tendencias en la Política Latino-Americana," *JIAS* 1 (1959) 459–476.

3748. Gonionskii, S. A. *Latinskaia Amerika i SShA: Ocherki Istorii Diplomaticheskykh Otnoshenii, 1939–1959.* Moscow, 1960.
Latin America and the USA: Essays on the History of Diplomatic Relations, 1939–1959.

3749. González, J. E. (trans.). *Los Estados Unidos y la América Latina: Conferencia del Caribe.* San Juan, P.R., 1960.
Published proceedings of the sixteenth American Assembly Conference, held in the fall of 1959.

3750. Graebner, N. A. *Cold War Diplomacy: American Foreign Policy, 1945–1960.* Princeton, N.J., 1962.

3751. Grechev, M. A. *Imperialisticheskaia Ekspansiia SShA v Stranakh Latinskoi Ameriki Posle Vtoroi Mirovoi Voiny.* Moscow, 1954.
United States Imperialistic Expansion in Latin America Following the Second World War. Attack on U.S. investments in Latin America.

3752. Guggenheim, H. F. *Hemisphere Integration Now.* Gainesville, Fla., 1951.
The former ambassador to Cuba calls for reduced tariff barriers and a new military alliance between the United States and Latin America.

3752a. Gunther, J. *Inside South America.* N.Y., 1967.

3753. Hauser, P. M. (ed.). *Urbanization in Latin America.* N.Y., 1961.

3754. Hirschman, A. O. "Las Relaciones de Estados Unidos con Latinoamérica," *CUA* (January, 1962) 37–46.

3755. Johnson, K. F. "Urbanization and Political Change in Latin America," UCLA Diss., 1963.

3756. Jorrín, M. *Political Instability in Latin America.* Albuquerque, N M., 1953.
A pamphlet.

3757. *Latinoamérica más allá de sus Fronteras.* San José, C.R., 1960.
Compiled by the editors of *Combate.*

3758. Lieuwen, E. *Arms and Politics in Latin America.* N.Y., 1960.
Rev. ed. in pb., N.Y., 1963. Part I discusses the role of the military; Part II considers military aspects of United States–Latin American policy. The revised edition contains a new chapter on Cuba.

3759. Lima, A. A. "Os Estados Unidos e América Latina," *RBPI* 4 (March, 1961) 17–28.

3760. Maier, J., and R. W. Weatherhead (eds.). *Politics of Change in Latin America.* N.Y., 1964.

3761. Manger, W. (ed.). *The Two Americas: Dialogue on Progress and Problems.* N.Y., 1965.
Essays by Wayne Morse, José Figueres, Alberto Lleras Camargo, Arthur P. Whitaker, Felipe Herrera, and Arturo Morales-Carrión.

3762. Matthews, H. L. (ed.). *The United States and Latin America.* 2d ed., Englewood Cliffs, N.J., 1963.
Papers presented to the American Assembly.

3763. Nehemkis, P. *Latin America: Myth and Reality.* N.Y., 1964

3764. Pflaum, I. P. *Arena of Decision: Latin America in Crisis.* Englewood Cliffs, N.J., 1964.

3765. Plaza Lasso, G. *Problems of Democracy in Latin America.* Chapel Hill, N.C., 1955.

3766. Porter, C. O., and R. J. Alexander. *The Struggle for Democracy in Latin America.* N.Y., 1961.

3767. Quintanilla, L. "Panamericanismo e Internacionalismo," *H* 30 (1947) 175–182.
By the Mexican ambassador to the United States.

3768. Reitzel, W., et al. *United States Foreign Policy, 1945–1955.* Wash., 1956.

3769. Riemens, H. *L'Europe Devant l'Amérique Latine.* The Hague, 1962.

3770. Rio, A. del. *Responsible Freedom in the Americas.* Garden City, N.Y., 1955.

3771. Sáenz, V. *Nuestra América en la Cruz: Siete Prólogos, Varias Apologías y Otros Apuntes*. Mexico, 1960.
    Critical of U.S. policy in Latin America.

3772. Silvert, K. H. "Nationalism in Latin America," *AAAPSS* 334 (1961) 1–9.

3773. Spanier, J. *American Foreign Policy Since World War II*. Rev. ed., N.Y., 1965.

3774. Stephens, O. *Facts to a Candid World: America's Overseas Information Program*. Stanford, Calif., 1955.

3775. Szulc, T. *Latin America*. N.Y., 1966.
    The most recent work by the Latin American correspondent of the *New York Times*.

3776. ———. *The Winds of Revolution: Latin America Today and Tomorrow*. N.Y., 1963.

3777. ———. *Twilight of the Tyrants*. N.Y., 1959.
    Concerns the overthrow of five South American dictators: Vargas of Brazil, Perón of Argentina, Odría of Peru, Rojas Pinilla of Colombia, and Pérez Jiménez of Venezuela.

3778. Tannenbaum, F. "The Political Dilemma in Latin America," *FA* 38 (1960) 497–515.

3779. ———. *Ten Keys to Latin America*. N.Y., 1962.
    An institutional approach, with a concluding section on the impact of the Cuban revolution.

3780. ———. "The United States and Latin America," *PSQ* 76 (1961) 161–180.

3781. Tomlinson, E. *Look Southward, Uncle: A New Look at the Other 175,000,000 Americans*. N.Y., 1959.
    A plea for greater interest in the area.

3782. USCS. Committee on Foreign Relations. *United States–Latin American Relations: Post World War II Political Developments in Latin America* (86th Cong., 1st Sess.). Wash., 1959.
    Prepared for USCS by the University of New Mexico School of Inter-American Affairs.

3783. USDS. *American Foreign Policy: Current Documents 1956–* . Wash., 1959–

3784. Vanger, M. I. "Latin America in Perspective," *YR* 48, n.s. (1958) 229–243.

3785. Vial Correa, G. "El Torno al Panamericanismo," *EST* 16 (December, 1948) 3–35.
    Condemnation of U.S. racism and imperialism.

3786. Villoldo, P. A. *Latin American Resentment*. N.Y., 1959.
    Critical analysis by a Cuban lawyer.

3787. Waiss, O. *Nacionalismo y Socialismo en América Latina*. Santiago, 1954.

3788. Whitaker, A. P. *Nationalism in Latin America: Past and Present*. Gainesville, Fla., 1962.

3789. Wythe, G. *The United States and Inter-American Relations: A Contemporary Appraisal*. Gainesville, Fla., 1964.

3790. Ycaza Tigerino, J. C. *Sociología de la Política Hispanoamericana*. Madrid, 1950.

X–A cross references:

a) For post-World War II consultative conferences, see items 5270–5312.

b) For the Conference on Maintenance of Continental Peace and Security at Rio de Janeiro (1947), consult items 5256–5269.

c) For the ninth Inter-American Conference at Bogotá (1948), see items 5064–5104; for the tenth Inter-American Conference at Caracas (1954), see items 5104a–5127a.

d) See also items 3186, 3446, 5441.

B. EARLY POSTWAR PROJECTIONS

3791. Alvarez, A. *Después de la Guerra: La Vida Internacional, Social e Intelectual*. B.A., 1943.

3792. Arrús, O. F. "Las Proyecciones Económicas Latino-Americanas en la Post-Guerra," *A* 27 (October, 1945) 7–12.

3793. Arze, J. A. "El Papel de América Latina en la Reconstrución de Postguerra," *RJ* 6 (September, 1944) 34–43.

3794. Avila Camacho, M. *Los Problemas de la Guerra y la Preparación de la Paz: Una América Libre, Fuerte y Culta, Inestimable Promesa para el Mundo*. Mexico, 1945.

3795. Barclay, W. C. *Greater Good Neighbor Policy*. Chicago, 1945.

3796. Behrendt, R. F. "Inter-American Economy and Post-War Reconstruction," *WA* 106 (March, 1943) 53–58.

3797. ———. "Problemas y Orientaciones Socio-Económicas para la Post-Guerra," *ECO* 13 (August, 1945) 15–22.

3798. ———. "Cooperación Económica Interamericana: Un Resumen de Problemas Básicos, Desarrollos Recientes y Perspectivas Futuras," *BISER* 1 (February, 1944) 35–120.

3799. Butler, G. H. *Inter-American Relations After World War II.* Wash., 1945.

3800. Carrillo Flores, A. *El Nacionalismo de los Países Latinoamericanos en la Post-Guerra.* Mexico, 1945.

3801. Carson, J. S. "The Post-War Significance of Our Loans and Investments in Latin America," *ETS* 47, no. 17 (1943) 3–5, 16, 18–19.

3802. Chediak, N. "Los Problemas de la Post-Guerra," *RDI* 22 (September, 1943) 125–135.

3803. Cosío Villegas, D., *et al. La Post-Guerra.* Mexico, 1944.

3804. Eguiguren, L. A. *La Creación de la Democracia de Postguerra.* Lima, 1944.
  Ten brief studies in pamphlet form.

3805. Fitzgibbon, R. H. (ed.). "Latin America Looks to the Future," *APSR* 39 (1945) 481–547.

3806. Flores López, S. *Problemas Americanos de la Post-Guerra.* Managua, 1944.
  The author was a Nicaraguan lawyer.

3807. Hanke, L. "Friendship Now with Latin America," *VQR* 22 (1946) 498–518.

3808. Herring, H. *America and the Americas: An Appraisal and a Forecast.* Claremont, Calif., 1944.

3809. Humphreys, R. A. "Latin America and the Post War World," *AG* 2 (February, 1943) 80–92.

3810. Inman, S. G. "Some Latin American Views on Post-War Reconstruction," *FPAR* 20 (1944) 1–11.

3811. Latham, H. L. *Post-War Problems Discussed in Latin America During the Second World War.* Chicago, 1944.

3812. Lerena Acevedo, A. *Los Problemas de la Post-Guerra.* Montevideo, 1944.

3813. Lombardo Toldedano, V. *The CTAL, The War and the Postwar.* Mexico, 1945.
  By the Mexican labor leader and Marxist.

3814. Márquez Padilla, T. *Consideraciones Sobre la Interpretación Mexicana de la Política del Buen Vecino.* Mexico, 1944.
  An optimistic projection.

3815. Medina Echavarría, J. *Consideraciones Sobre el Tema de la Paz.* Mexico, 1945.

3816. Morineau, O. "Aportación de la América Latina al Mundo de la Post-Guerra," *CA* 13 (January, 1944) 14–30.

3817. Munro, D. G. "Comércio Interamericano no Após-Guerra," *BMTIC* 11 (December, 1944) 187–198.

3818. Notter, H. *Postwar Foreign Policy Preparation, 1939–1945.* Wash., 1949.

3819. Padilla, E. *América Después de la Victoria.* Mexico, 1944.

3820. ———. *Free Men of America.* Chicago, 1943.

3821. PAU. Governing Board. *Pan American Postwar Organization: Observations and Suggestions of the Executive Committee on Postwar Problems: With a Report and Project of Coordinated Agreement for the Maintenance of Peace Prepared by the Inter-American Juridical Committee.* Wash., 1944.

3822. ———. Inter-American Juridical Committee. *Preliminary Recommendation on Post War Problems: Submitted to the Governments of the American Republics by the Governing Board of the Pan American Union.* Wash., 1942.

3823. Picón-Salas, M. *On Being Good Neighbors.* Wash., 1944.

3824. "Post War Problems," *BPAU* 77 (1943) 212–224.

3825. Prewett, V. *The Americas and Tomorrow.* N.Y., 1944.

3826. Privitera, J. F. *The Latin American Front.* Milwaukee, 1945.
  Contains a series of suggestions for improving United States–Latin American relations in the postwar period.

3827. "Recomendaciones Interamericanas Sobre la Planificación de la Postguerra," *RIT* 27 (February, 1943) 241–244.

3828. Sánchez, L. A. "Latin America in the Post-War World," *ML* 20 (July, 1944) 15–16, 63–68.

3829. Shaw, A. E. "Esperanzas y Temores de la Post-Guerra," *AACE* 2, 2d ser. (1944) 237–249.

3830. Smith, R. S. "Latin America in the Post-War World," *FCW* 16, no. 4 (1944) 3–5, 41–42.

3831. Soule, G. H., D. Efron, N. T. Ness, *et al. Latin America in the Future World.* N.Y., 1945.

3832. Tannenbaum, F. "The Future of the Inter-American System." *PAPS* 21 (1945) 415–420.

3833. Torriente, C. de la. "Las Conversaciones Sobre la Organización de la Paz y la Seguridad en la Post-Guerra," *RDI* 23 (December, 1944) 115–123.

3834. ———. "Organización Internacional de la Paz en la Post-Guerra," *RDI* 23 (September, 1944) 39–52.

3835. Trueblood, H. J. "New Directions for Postwar Trade," *INA* 3 (October, 1944) 10–13, 46.

3836. Valle, R. H. "América Latina en el Mundo de la Post-Guerra," *CA* 15 (May, 1944) 7–17.

3836a. Vejar Vásquez, O. "La Organización Interamericana en la Post-Guerra," *BILCDI*, no. 2 (1946) 37–44.

3837. Wallich, H. C. "The Outlook for Latin America," *HBR* 23 (Autumn, 1944) 65–78.

3838. Whitaker, A. P. "Latin America and Postwar Organization," *AAAPSS* 240 (1945) 109–115.

X–B   cross references: 4159, 4774, 5222, 5255, 5478, 6343, 6349, 7985, 9770, 10136

C. THE TRUMAN AND EISENHOWER ADMINISTRATIONS, 1945–1961

3839. Acheson, D. *Power and Diplomacy.* Cambridge, Mass., 1958.
  U.S. Secretary of State, 1949 to 1953.

3840. ———. *Sketches from Life of Men I Have Known.* N.Y., 1961.

3841. ———. *Strengthening the Forces of Freedom: Selected Speeches and Statements of Secretary of State Acheson, February, 1949, to April, 1950.* 2 vols., Wash., 1950.

3842. Adams, S. *Firsthand Report: The Story of the Eisenhower Administration.* N.Y., 1961.
  By the special assistant to the President.

3842a. Arandia, T. de. "La Reunión Presidencial Americana en Panamá," *PI* (July, 1956) 131–140.

3843. Arciniegas, G. "Estados Unidos y América Latina," *CUA* (July, 1960) 14–18.

3844. ———. "Una Reacción Constructiva," *CUA* (September, 1958) 82–85.
  Concerns the Nixon visit.

3845. Arismendi, R. *Para un Prontuario del Dólar: (Al Margen del Plan Truman).* Montevideo, 1947.

3846. Arizona Assembly. *The United States and Latin America.* Tucson, 1960.

3847. Barber, W. F. "Our Inter-American Policy," *WAI* 21 (April, 1950) 12–25.

3848. Barkley, A. W. *That Reminds Me—.* Garden City, N.Y., 1954.
  Memoirs of Truman's vice-president.

3849. Beal, J. R. *John Foster Dulles.* N.Y., 1957.

3850. Benson, E. T. *Cross Fire: The Eight Years with Eisenhower.* Garden City, N.Y., 1962.

3851. Berding, A. H. *Dulles on Diplomacy.* N.Y., 1965.

3852. Brookings Institution. *Major Problems of U.S. Foreign Policy.* 7 vols., Wash., 1947–1954.
  Useful annual series but was discontinued in 1954.

3853. Brown, S. G. *Conscience in Politics: Adlai E. Stevenson in the 1950's.* Syracuse, N.Y., 1961.

3854. Bundy, M. (ed.). *The Pattern of Responsibility.* Boston, 1952.
  Edition of Secretary of State Dean Acheson's statements.

3855. Byrnes, J. F. *All in One Lifetime.* N.Y., 1958.
  Autobiography of the secretary of state, 1945–1947.

3856. ———. *Speaking Frankly.* N.Y., 1947.

3857. Cabot, J. M. *Toward Our Common American Destiny.* Medford, Mass., 1955.
  Speeches and public statements of the assistant secretary of state for inter-American affairs, 1953–1954.

3858. Childs, M. W. *Eisenhower: Captive Hero: A Critical Study of the General and the President.* N.Y., 1958.

3859. Connally, T., and A. Steinberg. *My Name is Tom Connally.* N.Y., 1954.

Memoirs of the chairman of the Senate Foreign Relations Committee.

3860. Cook, T. I., and M. Moos. *Power Through Purpose*. Baltimore, 1954.

3861. Costa, L. *Uma Nova Política para as Américas*. São Paulo, 1960.

3862. Curry, J. *James F. Byrnes*. N.Y., 1965.

3863. Daniels, J. *The Man of Independence*. Phil., 1950.
Biography of President Harry Truman.

3863a. Davis, H. E. "A New Look at Latin American Relations," *WA* 122 (Summer, 1959) 48–52.

3864. Donovan, R. J. *Eisenhower: The Inside Story*. N.Y., 1956.

3865. Drummond, R., and G. Coblentz. *Duel at the Brink: John Foster Dulles' Command of American Power*. N.Y., 1960.

3865a. Dulles, E. L. *John Foster Dulles: The Last Year*. N.Y., 1963.

3866. Eisenhower, D. D. *The White House Years*. 2 vols., Garden City, N.Y., 1963–1965.
Eisenhower's memoirs of his Presidency.

3867. Eisenhower, M. S. "United States–Latin American Relations: Report to the President," *USDSB* 29 (1953) 695–717.

3868. ———. "United States–Latin American Relations, 1953–1958: Report to the President," *USDSB* 40 (1959) 89–105.

3869. Finletter, T. K. *Foreign Policy: The Next Phase, the 1960's*. 2d ed., N.Y., 1960.

3870. "Foreign Policies in Latin America," *CH* 28 (1955) 129–191.
Entire issue is devoted to Latin American relations with the outside world.

3871. Frei, E. "Current Trends and Prospects in Latin America," *JIA* 12 (1958) 107–117.

3872. Frondizzi, R. A. "La Doctrina de Monroe y la Tesis de Truman," *CA* 39 (May, 1948) 7–19.

3873. González, H. "The House Investigation of the Nixon Incident," *IEA* 12 (Autumn, 1958) 53–81.

3874. Goold-Adams, R. *John Foster Dulles: A Reappraisal*. N.Y., 1962.

3875. Graebner, N. A. *The New Isolationism*. N.Y., 1956.

3876. Gunther, J. *Eisenhower: The Man and the Symbol*. N.Y., 1952.

3877. Hanson, S. G. "The End of the Good-Partner Policy," *IEA* 14 (Summer, 1960) 65–92.

3878. Heller, D., and D. Heller. *John Foster Dulles: Soldier for Peace*. N.Y., 1960.

3879. Holland, H. F. *Objectives of U.S. Foreign Policy in Latin America*. Wash., 1955.

3880. Hughes, E. J. *The Ordeal of Power: A Political Memoir of the Eisenhower Years*. N.Y., 1963.

3881. Josephs, R. *Latin America: Continent in Crisis*. N.Y., 1948.

3882. Koenig, L. W. (ed.). *The Truman Administration: Its Principles and Practice*. N.Y., 1956.

3882a. Luzardo, R. *Episodes of the Americas*. Caracas, 1962.

3882b. MacDonald, N. P. "Latin America and the United States," *QRL* 297 (April, 1959) 219–231.
Emphasis is on economic relations.

3883. Martin, J. B. *Adlai Stevenson*. N.Y., 1952.

3883a. Matthews, H. L. "The United States and Latin America," *IAF* 37 (1960) 9–18.

3884. Mazo, E. *Richard Nixon: A Political and Personal Portrait*. N.Y., 1959.

3885. McCloy, J. J. *The Challenge to American Foreign Policy*. Cambridge, Mass., 1953.

3886. Meyer, K. E. (ed.). *Fulbright of Arkansas*. Wash., 1963.
Collection of speeches of the senator from Arkansas and chairman of the Senate Foreign Relations Committee.

3887. Millis, W. (ed.). *The Forrestal Diaries*. N.Y., 1951.
The first secretary of defense.

3887a. Nitze, P. H. *United States Foreign Policy, 1945–1955*. N.Y., 1956.
Included in *FPAHS*.

3888. Nixon, R. *Six Crises*. Garden City, N.Y., 1962.
One of the crises was the South American visit.

3889. Palmer, T. W., Jr. *Search for a Latin American Policy*. Gainesville, Fla., 1957.

3890. Pusey, M. J. *Eisenhower the President*. N.Y., 1956.
Appraisal of the first Eisenhower administration.

3891. "Report on Latin America," *CH* 32 (1957) 1–256.

3892. Rovere, R. H. *Affairs of State: The Eisenhower Years*. N.Y., 1956.

3893. Rubottom, R. R., Jr. "Basic Principles Governing United States Relations with Latin America," *USDSB* 38 (1958) 608–614.

3894. ———. "Toward Better Understanding Between the United States and Latin America," *AAAPSS* 330 (1960) 116–123.

3895. ———. "The United States and Latin America: A Maturing Relationship," *USDSB* 42 (1960) 519–523.

3896. ———. "The Vice President's Visit to South America in Perspective," *USDSB* 38 (1958) 1104–1109.

3897. Sánchez, L. A. "El Vicepresidente Nixon en América Latina," *CUA* (September, 1958) 75–81.

3898. Sánchez Camacho, B. *El Problema Colonial de América*. Mexico, 1950.
    The author believes that the Good Neighbor policy deteriorated after World War II.

3899. Smith, M. *A President's Odyssey*. N.Y., 1961.
    Concerns President Eisenhower's tours in 1959–1960.

3900. Sulzberger, C. L. *What's Wrong with U.S. Foreign Policy?* N.Y., 1959.

3901. Szulc, T. *New Trends in Latin America*. N.Y., 1960.
    In *FPAHS* collection.

3902. Thorning, J. F. "Latin American Reaction to the Korean Situation," *WA* 114 (Spring, 1951) 14–16.

3903. Truman, H. S. *Memoirs*. 2 vols., Garden City, N.Y., 1955–1956.

3904. ———. *Mr. Citizen*. N.Y., 1960.
    Post-presidential views of Harry Truman.

3905. ———. *Truman Speaks*. N.Y., 1960.

3906. USCH. Committee on Appropriations. *A Review of United States Government Operations in Latin America, by Allen J. Ellender* (86th Cong., 1st Sess., H. Doc. 13). Wash., 1959.

3907. ———. House Committee on Foreign Affairs. *Hearings Before the Sub-Committee on Inter-American Affairs: A Review of the Relations of the U.S. and Other American Republics* (85th Cong., 2d Sess.). Wash., 1958.

3908. ———. ———. *Report on United States Relations with Latin America by the Subcommittee on Inter-American Affairs* (86th Cong., 1st Sess.). Wash., 1959.

3908a. USCS. Committee on Foreign Relations. *American Republics Cooperation Act and other Subjects: Hearings* (86th Cong., 2d Sess.). Wash., 1960.

3909. ———. ———. *Latin America: Venezuela, Brazil, Peru, Bolivia, and Panama: Report of George D. Aiken on a Study Mission* (86th Cong., 2d Sess.). Wash., 1960.

3909a. ———. ———. *South America: Argentina, Bolivia, Brazil, Chile, Colombia, and Venezuela: Report of Wayne Morse on a Study Mission* (86th Cong., 2d Sess.). Wash., 1960.

3909b. ———. ———. *South America: Report of Senator Theodore Francis Green on a Study Mission* (83d Cong., 2d Sess.). Wash., 1954.

3910. ———. ———. *Study Mission in the Caribbean and Northern South America: Report of Senator Homer E. Capehart to the Committee on Foreign Relations, April 1, 1960* (86th Cong., 2d Sess.). Wash., 1960.

3911. ———. ———. Subcommittee on American Republics Affairs. *United States–Latin American Relations* (86th Cong., 2d Sess., S. Doc. 125). Wash., 1960.

3912. USDS. *American Foreign Policy, 1950–1955: Basic Documents*. 2 vols., Wash., 1957.

3913. ———. *Objectives of U.S. Foreign Policy in Latin America*. Wash., 1955.

3914. ———. *Our Foreign Policy in Latin America*. Wash., 1953.

3915. ———. *Report to the President, United States–Latin American Relations: by Milton S. Eisenhower*. Wash., 1959.

3916. U.S. General Services Administration. *Public Papers of the Presidents of the United States: Dwight D. Eisenhower, 1953–1961*. 8 vols., Wash., 1955–1961.

3917. ———. *Public Papers of the Presidents of the U.S.: Harry S. Truman, 1945–1953*. 9 vols., Wash., 1961.

3918. Vandenberg, A. H., Jr., and J. A. Morris (eds.). *The Private Papers of Senator Vandenberg*. Boston, 1952.

The papers of the Republican senator from Michigan.

3919.   Van Dusen, H. P. (ed.). *The Spiritual Legacy of John Foster Dulles*. Phil., 1960.

3920.   Welles, S. *Where Are We Heading?* N.Y., 1946.

3921.   White, W. S. *The Taft Story*. N.Y., 1954. Concerns Senator Robert A. Taft, the Republican from Ohio.

X–C   cross references:

a) For various inter-American conferences, consult items 5064–5127a, 5230–5286b.

b) See also items 3501, 3972, 4646, 5395, 5410, 9814.

D. THE KENNEDY ADMINISTRATION, 1961–1963

3922.   Alexander, R. J. "New Directions: The United States and Latin America," *CH* 42 (February, 1962) 65–70.

3923.   Burns, J. M. *John Kennedy: A Political Profile*. 2d ed., N.Y., 1961.

3924.   Chilcote, R. H. *The Press in Latin America, Spain, and Portugal: A Summary of Recent Developments*. Stanford, Calif., 1963.

3924a. Federal Reserve System. Board of Governors. *United States Policies and Latin American Progress, Remarks of J. L. Robertson, Member of Board of Governors of Federal Reserve System, Before National and State Bank Divisions of American Bankers' Association*. Wash., 1962.

3925.   Grace, J. P. *It Is Not Too Late in Latin America: Proposals for Action Now*. N.Y., 1961.

3925a. Griffin, C. C. "On the Present Discontents in Latin America," *VAM* 84 (February, 1963) 12–16.

3926.   Humphrey, H. H. "U.S. Policy in Latin America," *FA* 42 (1964) 585–601.

3927.   Kantor, H. "La Administración Kennedy y sus Relaciones con Latinoamérica," *CUA* (September, 1962) 12–17.

3928.   Kennedy, J. F. *The Strategy of Peace*. N.Y., 1960.

3929.   ———. *To Turn the Tide*. N.Y., 1962.

3929a. Kertesz, S. D. (ed.). *American Foreign Policy in a New Era*. Notre Dame, Ind., 1961.

3930.   McClellan, G. S. (ed.). *U.S. Policy in Latin America*. N.Y., 1963.

3931.   Morales M., M. "Tendencias y Virajes de la Política Norteamericana en América Latina," *FI* 4 (1963) 213–242.

3932.   Rubottom, R. R., Jr. "The Goals of United States Policy in Latin America," *AAAPSS* 342 (1962) 30–41.

3933.   Sánchez Sarto, M. "John F. Kennedy, el Presidente para una Era Nueva," *CUA* (January, 1961) 28–48.

3934.   Schlesinger, A. M., Jr. *A Thousand Days: John F. Kennedy in the White House*. N.Y., 1965.

3935.   Seers, D. "Latin America and U.S. Foreign Policy," *PQ* 34 (April, 1963) 200–210.

3935a. Sorensen, T. C. *Kennedy*. N.Y., 1965.

3936.   USCH. *Special Report on Latin America: United States Activities in Mexico, Panama, Peru, Chile, Argentina, Brazil, and Venezuela* (87th Cong., 2d Sess., Comm. Print). Wash., 1962.

3936a. ———. Committee on Armed Services. *Report to Accompany H.R. 7811, Authorizing Sale or Loan of Naval Vessels to Friendly Latin American Countries* (89th Cong., 1st Sess.). Wash., 1965.

3937.   ———. Committee on Foreign Affairs. *Regional and Other Documents Concerning United States Relations with Latin America* (89th Cong., 2d Sess., Comm. Print). Wash., 1962.

3937a. ———. ———. *Special Study Mission to Latin America: Peru, Ecuador, Colombia, Panama, Costa Rica* (87th Cong., H. Doc. 223). Wash., 1963.

3938.   ———. ———. *Special Study Mission to Latin America: Venezuela, Brazil, Argentina, Chile, Bolivia, Panama. Report by Armistead I. Selden, Jr., and Dante B. Fascell* (87th Cong., 1st Sess., Comm. Print). Wash., 1961.

3939.   USCS. Committee on Appropriations. *Latin America and United States Policies: Report of Senator Mike Mansfield on a Study Mission to Latin America* (87th Cong., 2d Sess., S. Doc. 82). Wash., 1962.

3940.   ———. ———. *Study Mission to South America, Nov.–Dec., 1961: Report of Senators Gale W. McGee, Frank E. Moss, Clair Engle, and Stephen M. Young* (87th

Cong., 2d Sess., S. Doc. 91). Wash., 1962.

3940a. USCS. Committee on Foreign Relations. *Latin America: Report by Senator Bourke B. Hickenlooper* (87th Cong., 1st Sess.). Wash., 1961.

3940b. USDS. *Democracy vs. Dictators in Latin America, How can We Help? Based on Address by Thomas C. Mann.* Wash., 1964.

3940c. ———. *State Dept. Activities, 1963: Latin America.* Wash., 1963.

3941. U.S. General Services Administration. *Public Papers of the Presidents of the U.S.: John F. Kennedy, 1961–1963.* 3 vols., Wash., 1962–1964.

3941a. ———. *Public Papers of the Presidents: Lyndon B. Johnson, 1963–1964.* 2 vols., Wash., 1965.

3942. White, T. H. *The Making of the President, 1960.* N.Y., 1961.

X–D   cross references:

a) For the eighth Consultative Conference at Punta del Este (1962), see 5287–5311.

b) For works on the Alliance for Progress, see items 4096–41471.

c) For works on the Peace Corps, see items 4148–4153.

d) See also item 3886.

E. HEMISPHERIC DEFENSE AND COLLECTIVE SECURITY

3942a. Alba, V. *El Militarismo: Ensayo Sobre un Fenómeno Político Social Ibero-Americano.* Mexico, 1959.

3943. Amorim Sánchez, F. "El Clima de Guerra y el Pacto Militar Interamericano," *I* (December, 1947) 57–73.

3944. Anaya, R. "La Defensa Continental y la Unidad Latinoamericana," *RJ* 8 (June, 1946) 119–124.

3944a. Candioti, L. A. "La Unidad de los Países Hispanoamericanos ante la Defensa Nacional," *RCJS* 16 (1954) 105–118.

3945. Center for International Studies (M.I.T.). *Regional Arms Control Arrangements for Developing Areas: Arms and Arms Control in Latin America, the Middle East, and Africa.* Cambridge, Mass., 1964.

3946. Fitzgibbon, R. H. "What Price Latin American Armies?" *VQR* 36 (1960) 517–532.

3947. Francis, M. J. "Attitudes of the United States Government Toward Collective Military Arrangements with Latin America, 1945–1960," U. of Virginia Diss., 1963.

3948. ———. "Military Aid to Latin America in the U.S. Congress," *JIAS* 6 (1964) 389–404.

3949. Furniss, E. S., Jr. "The Place of Latin America in the Security Policy of the U.S.," Yale U. Diss., 1947.

3950. García Robles, A. *La Desnuclearización de la América Latina.* Mexico, 1965.

3950a. Glick, E. B. "The Feasibility of Arms Control and Disarmament in Latin America," *OR* 9 (1965) 743–759.

3951. Gómez Robledo, A. *La Seguridad Colectiva en el Continente Americano.* Mexico, 1960.

3951a. Hanley, P. T. "The Inter-American Defense Board," Stanford U. Diss., 1965.
Concludes that the board has been strengthened in recent years.

3952. Harlow, A. M. "The Inter-American Defense Board," *USNIP* 73 (1947) 191–200.

3953. Holmes, O. "Army Challenge in Latin America," *FPAR* 25 (1949) 166–175.

3953a. Hovey, H. A. *United States Military Assistance: A Study of Policies and Practices.* N.Y., 1965.
Covers the period since 1950 and has one section on Latin America.

3954. Johnson, J. J. *The Military and Society in Latin America.* Stanford, Calif., 1964.
Pb. ed., Stanford, Calif., 1965.

3955. ——— (ed.). *The Role of the Military in Underdeveloped Countries.* Princeton, N.J., 1962.

3956. Kagawa, T. "Raten Amerika ni Okeru Guntai no Seijiteki Yakuwari," *HK* 34 (1961) 258–280.
"The Political Role of the Army in Latin America."

3957. Kunz, J. L. "The Idea of 'Collective Security' in Pan American Developments," *WPQ* 6 (1953) 658–679.

3957a. "La América Latina ante la Amenaza Atómica," *PL* 4, no. 14 (1957).

3958. Larco Herrera, R. *Por la Ruta de la Confederación Americana.* Lima, 1948.

3959. Lieuwen, E. *Generals vs. Presidents: Neomilitarism in Latin America.* N.Y., 1964.

Analyzes the series of military coups since the publication of *Arms and Politics*. See item 3758.

3960. Loveiko, G. "Dela Pentagona na 'Zadniem Dvore,'" *MZ* 4 (1961) 65–73.
"The Activities of the Pentagon in the Backyard."

3961. Mason, B. D. (ed.). *The Political-Military Defense of Latin America.* Tempe, Ariz., 1963.

3962. Maúrtua, M. F. "La Legislación Americana de Emergencia y la Defensa Continental," *IP* 6 (May, 1946) 3–12.

3963. McAlister, L. N. "Civil-Military Relations in Latin America," *JIAS* 3 (1961) 341–350.

3964. McArdle, C. *The Role of Military Assistance in the Problem of Arms Control: The Middle East, Latin America, and Africa.* Cambridge, Mass., 1964.

3964a. Mountain, M. J. "United States Military Assistance in the Caribbean Area," in Wilgus, *The Caribbean: Current United States Relations,* pp. 182–192.
Covers the period 1950–1965. See item 6807a.

3965. Pablo Pardo, L. M. de. "La Posición Geográfica de la Argentina como Factor de su Política Exterior," *RFDCS* 4 (January, 1949) 205–215.

3966. Pellicer Silva, O. *El Problema de la Seguridad Colectiva de las Relaciones Inter-Americanas.* Mexico, 1958.

3967. Rich, S. G., Jr. "Inter-American Machinery for Collective Security," Stanford U. Diss., 1949.

3968. Rubottom, R. R., Jr. "The Mutual Security Program in Latin America," *USDSB* 42 (1960) 623–629.

3969. USCH. Committee on Foreign Affairs. *Inter-American Military Cooperation Act: Hearings* (79th Cong., 2d Sess.). Wash., 1946.

3970. ———. ———. *Inter-American Military Cooperation Act: Hearings* (80th Cong., 1st Sess.). Wash., 1947.

3970a. USCS. Committee on Foreign Relations. *Control and Reduction of Armaments, Disarmament and Security in Latin America* (85th Cong., 1st Sess., Comm. Print). Wash., 1957.

3970b. USDA. *Latin America, Hemispheric Partner: Biographic Survey.* Wash., 1964.

3971. USDA. *Military Assistance to Latin America.* Wash., 1953.

3971a. Wilson, L. C. "The Principle of Non-Intervention in Recent Inter-American Relations: The Challenge of Anti-Democratic Regimes," U. of Maryland Diss., 1964.

3972. Winters, J. A. "Eisenhower—'Good Partner' of Latin American Dictators: A Critical Study of United States Hemispheric Defense Policy," U. of Chicago Diss., 1963.

3973. Wolfers, A. (ed.). *Alliance Policy in the Cold War.* Baltimore, 1959.

3974. Wyckoff, T. "The Role of the Military in Contemporary Latin American Politics," *WPQ* 13 (1960) 745–763.

3974a. ———. "Tres Modalidades del Militarismo Latinoamericano," *COMB* 2 (September, 1960) 7–15.

X–E cross references:

a) For works on the Rio Pact (1947), see items 5256–5269.

b) For works on the ninth Inter-American Conference at Bogotá (1948) and the tenth Inter-American Conference at Caracas (1954), see items 5064–5127a.

c) For consultative conferences, see items 5270–5312.

d) For collective hemispheric action against Cuba, see items 5311a–5312; for collective action against the Dominican Republic, see items 7994a–8004a.

e) See also items 3758, 3990, 4249, 4352, 4815, 4828, 5242.

F. COLD WAR AND SOCIAL REVOLUTION IN LATIN AMERICA

3975. Adams, M. (ed.). *Latin America: Evolution or Explosion?* N.Y., 1963.
Essays by Galo Plaza, José Figueres, Lincoln Gordon, Chester Bowles, and others.

3976. Adams, R. N., *et al. Social Change in Latin America Today: Its Implications for United States Policy.* N.Y., 1961.

3977. Alexander, R. J. "Nationalism, Latin America's Predominant Ideology," *JIA* 15 (1961) 108–114.

3977a. Al'perovich, M. S. "Pod'em Natsional'no-osvoboditel'nogo i Demokraticheskogo

Dvizheniia v Latinskoi Amerike Posle Vtoroi Mirovoi Voiny," *PIS* no. 4 (1959).

"The Rising National Liberation and Democratic Movement in Latin America After the Second World War."

3978. Antonio, W. V., d', and F. B. Pike. *Religion, Revolution, and Reform: New Forces for Change in Latin America*. N.Y., 1964.

3979. Aptheker, H. *American Foreign Policy and the Cold War*. N.Y., 1962.

3980. Arévalo, J. J. *Anti-Communism in Latin America*. N.Y., 1964.

Spanish ed., B.A., 1959. By the ex-President of Guatemala.

3980a. Avarina, V. I., and M. V. Danilevich (eds.). *Natsional'no-osvoboditel'noe Dvizhenie v Latinskoi Amerike na Sovremennom Etape*. Moscow, 1961.

The Present Stage of the National Liberation Movement in Latin America.

3981. Barreda y Laos, F. *Segunda Emancipación de América Hispana*. B.A., 1947.

Peruvian diplomat calls for positive policy in Latin America vis-à-vis the United States.

3982. Berle, A. A., Jr. *The Cold War in Latin America*. Storrs, Conn., 1961.

3983. Betancourt, R. *Que Debiera Hacer Estados Unidos por América Latina: Francas Opiniones del Presidente Betancourt en Declaraciones a la Revista, "Life."* Caracas, 1960.

3984. Burr, R. N. (ed.). "Latin America's Nationalistic Revolutions," *AAAPSS* 334 (1961) 1–147.

The entire issue is devoted to Latin America.

3985. Campos, R. de Oliveira. "Sôbre o Conceito de Neutralismo," *RBPI* 4 (September, 1961) 5–12.

3986. Carnoy, A. *Democracia Sí: A Way to Win the Cold War*. N.Y., 1962.

3987. Carranza, C. P. *El Mundo del Futuro: ¿Capitalismo Norte-Americano o Comunismo Ruso?* B.A., 1948.

3988. Castro Delgado, E. *S. O. S. al Mundo Libre*. Mexico, 1961.

3989. Chávarri Porpeta, R. "Vecindad y Enemistad de los Estados Unidos y Iberoamérica," *REP* 116 (March, 1961) 149–172.

3990. Christopher, H. A. "The Political Behavior of the Military in Latin America," Northwestern U. Diss., 1964.

3991. Coerr, W. R. de. *Forces of Change in Latin America*. Wash., 1961.

3992. Cosío Villegas, D. *Change in Latin America: The Mexican and Cuban Revolutions*. Lincoln, Nebr., 1961.

3993. ———. "Rusia, Estados Unidos y la América Hispánica," *PE* 3 (February, 1948) 223–231.

3994. Daniels, W. M. (ed.). *Latin America in the Cold War*. N.Y., 1952.

A collection of journalistic appraisals.

3995. Danilevich, M. V. *Rabochii Klass v Osvoboditel'nom Dvizhenii Narodov Latinskoi Ameriki*. Moscow, 1962.

The Working Class in the Liberation Movement of the Nations of Latin America.

3996. Dozer, D. M. "Roots of Revolution in Latin America," *FA* 27 (1949) 274–288.

3997. Fitzgibbon, R. H. "Dictatorship and Democracy in Latin America," *IAF* 36 (1960) 48–57.

3998. Form, W. H., and A. A. Blum (eds.). *Industrial Relations and Social Change in Latin America*. N.Y., 1965.

3999. Funes, R. *Mito Democracia y Comunismo*. B.A., 1961.

4000. Galíndez Suárez, J. "Revolución Socio-Económica en Iberoamérica," *CA* 13, no. 2 (1954) 7–18.

4001. Gaos, J. "Los Estados Unidos y la Revolución de América Latina," *CA* 123 (July, 1962) 7–17.

4002. Gerassi, J. *The Great Fear: The Reconquest of Latin America by Latin Americans*. N.Y., 1963.

Pb. ed., N.Y., 1965.

4003. Gillin, J. P. "Changing Depths in Latin America," *JIAS* 2 (1960) 379–389.

4004. Gómez Hurtado, A. *La Revolución en América*. Bogotá, 1959.

4004a. Gonionskii, S. A. *Ocherki Noveishei Istorii Stran Latinskoi Ameriki*. Moscow, 1964.

Essays on the Contemporary History of Latin American Countries.

4005. Gravina, A. D. *La Sonrisa del "Buen" Vecino*. Montevideo, 1960.

Attacks United States policy in the cold war.

4005a. Guber, A. A. *Bor'ba za Edinyi Rabochii i Antiimperialisticheskii Front v Stranakh Latinskoi Ameriki.* Moscow, 1963.
The *Struggle for a Common Workers' and Anti-Imperialist Front in the Countries of Latin America.*

4006. Hamuy, E., D. Salcedo, and O. Sepúlveda. *El Primer Satélite Artificial: Sus Efectos en la Opinión Pública.* Santiago, 1958.

4007. Harbron, J. D. "Crisis and Change in Latin America," *BH* 20, no. 2 (1960).

4008. Houtart, F., and E. Pin. *The Church and the Latin American Revolution.* N.Y., 1965.
By two Catholic sociologists.

4008a. Inter-American Development Bank. *Institutional Reforms and Social Development Trends in Latin America.* Wash., 1963.

4009. Johnson, J. J. (ed.). *Continuity and Change in Latin America.* Stanford, Calif., 1964.

4010. ———. *Political Change in Latin America: The Emergence of the Middle Sectors.* Stanford, Calif., 1958.

4011. ———. "Whither the Latin American Middle Sectors?" *VQR* 37 (1961) 508–521.

4012. Justo, L. *Estrategia Revolucionaria: Lucha por La Unidad y por la Liberación Nacional y Social de la América Latina.* B.A., 1957.
Author also publishes under the pseudonym Quebracha.

4013. Kalugin, G. A. *Latinskaia Amerika v Agressivnych Planach Imperialistov SShA.* Moscow, 1952.
Latin America in U.S. Imperialists' Plans for Aggression.

4014. Lens, S. "The Dilemma in Latin America," *PR* 26 (June, 1962) 24–29.

4015. Linares Quintana, S. V. "The Etiology of Revolution in Latin America," *WPQ* 4 (1951) 254–267.

4016. Lodge, G. C. "Revolution in Latin America," *FA* 44 (1966) 173–197.

4017. MacEoin, G. *Latin America: The Eleventh Hour.* N.Y., 1962.
Calls for a positive U.S. response to the social revolution.

4017a. Madariaga, S. de. *Latin America Between the Eagle and the Bear.* N.Y., 1962.

4018. Madden, C. H., and L. Rall. *Latin America: Reform or Revolution.* N.p., 1963.

4019. Milk, R. G. "Agrarian Reform and Economic Progress in Latin America," Iowa State U. Diss., 1959.

4019a. Mills, C. W., *et al.* "Izquierda, Subdesarrollo y Guerra Fría: Un Coloquio Sobre Cuestiones Fundamentales," *CA* 110 (May, 1960) 53–69.

4020. Mora, J. A. "Will Latin America Continue to Adhere to the West?" *AAAPSS* 336 (1961) 98–105.

4021. Obyden, K. M. *Kuba v Bor'bie za Svobodu i Nezavisimost'.* Moscow, 1959.
Cuba in the Struggle for Freedom and Independence.

4022. Pike, F. B. "Can We Slow Our Loss of Latin America?" *IEA* 15 (Summer, 1961) 3–29.

4023. ——— (ed.). *Freedom and Reform in Latin America.* Notre Dame, Ind., 1959.
A series of essays which explore the compatibility of freedom and reform.

4024. Powelson, J. P. *Latin America: Today's Economic and Social Revolution.* N.Y., 1964.

4025. Ravines, E. *América Latina: Un Continente en Erupción.* 3d ed., Havana, 1960.

4025a. Rubinshtein, M. I. R. (ed.). *Narody Latinskoi Ameriki v Borbie Protiv Amerikanskogo Imperializma.* Moscow, 1951.
Peoples of Latin America in the Struggle Against American Imperialism.

4026. Schmitt, K., and D. D. Burks. *Evolution or Chaos: Dynamics of Latin American Government and Politics.* N.Y., 1963.

4027. Shapiro, S. *Invisible Latin America.* Boston, 1963.

4028. Silvert, K. H. *The Conflict Society: Reaction and Revolution in Latin America.* New Orleans, 1961.
A series of interpretive essays.

4029. Smith, R. F. "Latin America, the United States, and Revolutions," *JIAS* 4 (1962) 89–104.

4030. Stark, H. *Social and Economic Frontiers in Latin America.* Dubuque, Ia., 1961.

4031. Suñol, J. C. *Latinoamérica en Revolución.* San José, C.R., 1960.

4032. Teichert, P. C. M. "Latin America and the Socio-Economic Impact of the Cuban Revolution," *JIAS* 4 (1962) 105–120.

4033. TePaske, J. J., and S. N. Fisher. *Explosive Forces in Latin America*. Columbus, O., 1964.

4034. Thomas, A. B. "Latin American Nationalism and the United States," *JIAS* 7 (1965) 5–14.

4035. Tomlinson, E. *Battle for the Hemisphere: Democracy Versus Totalitarianism in the Other Hemisphere*. N.Y., 1947.

 Calls for the United States not to support totalitarian regimes, either of the left or the right.

4036. Toynbee, A. J. *America and the World Revolution and Other Lectures*. N.Y., 1962.

4037. Urrea, B. *Una Opinión Mexicana Sobre el Conflicto Mundial*. Mexico, 1951.

4037a. USCS. Committee on Foreign Relations. *United States Foreign Policy: Economic, Social, and Political Change in the Underdeveloped Countries and Its Implications for United States Policy* (86th Cong., 2d Sess.). Wash., 1960.

4037b. USDD. Armed Forces Information and Education Office. "Making the World Safe for Diversity," *FCTCW* 4, nos. 4–5 (1964).

4038. Véliz, C. (ed.). *Obstacles to Change in Latin America*. N.Y., 1965.

4039. Whitaker, A. P. *Anticolonialism in Latin America*. Phil., 1956.

4040. ———. "Protracted Conflict in Latin America," *OR* 6 (1962) 301–310.

4041. Wilgus, A. C. "The Chemistry of Political Change in Latin America," *AAAPSS* 342 (1962) 42–53.

4042. Yrarrázaval Concha, E. *América Latina en la Guerra Fría*. Santiago, 1959.

4043. Zea, L. "Latinoamérica y la Guerra Fría," *CA* 19 (January, 1960) 7–17.

X–F cross references:

 a) For the Punte del Este Conference (1962), see items 5287–5311.

 b) For the Alliance for Progress, see 4096–41471.

 c) See also items 3758, 3764, 3787, 4236, 4356, 6337, 6371, 8474, 8484, 8486, 8669, 9777, 10097, 10174, 10176.

G. COMMUNISM IN LATIN AMERICA

4044.! Alba, V. "Communism and Nationalism in Latin America," *PC* 8 (September, 1958) 24–31.

4045. ———. *Esquema Histórico del Comunismo en Iberoamérica*. 3d ed., Mexico, 1960.

 Revision of *Historia del Comunismo en América Latina*. Mexico, 1954.

4046. ———. *Historia del Frente Popular: Análisis de una Táctica Política*. Mexico, 1959.

4047. ———. *La América Latina y los Congresos del Partido Comunista Ruso*. San José, C.R., 1958(?).

4048. Alexander, R. J. *Communism in Latin America*. New Brunswick, N.J., 1957.

 The first comprehensive English-language treatment.

4049. Allen, R. L. *Soviet Influence in Latin America: The Role of Economic Relations*. Wash., 1959.

 A pre-Castro analysis emphasizing trade and commerce.

4050. Alvarez, J. "Orientaciones: La Nueva Estrategia Comunista en la América Latina," *RJA* 22 (1944) 257–261.

4051. ———. "Tácticas Comunistas en América Latina," *RJA* 21 (1944) 73–81.

4052. Andres, N. *La Política Nacional del Trotskismo en América Latina*. B.A., 1949.

4053. Basaldúa, P. de. *La Garra Comunista en América Latina*. B.A., 1962.

 Country-by-country analysis of communist activities.

4054. Beals, C. "The Soviet Wooing of Latin America," *HA* 189 (1944) 210–218.

4055. Blasier, S. C. "The Cuban and Chilean Communist Parties, Instruments of Soviet Policy (1935–1948)," Columbia U. Diss., 1955.

4056.! Brandenburg, F. R. "Communism and Security in Latin America," *YR* 46, n.s. (1957) 413–424.

4057. Burnett, B. G. "Communist Strategy in the Latin American Labor Movement," *SSC* 35 (1960) 105–113.

4058. Clark, R. J. "Latin American Economic Relations with the Soviet Bloc," Indiana U. Diss., 1963.

4059. Congreso Continental Anticomunista. *IV Congreso Continental Anticomunista, 12 a 16 de Octubre de 1958: Antigua, Guatemala*. Guatemala, 1961.

4060. Congreso Contra la Infiltración Soviética en América Latina. *Memoria del Primer Congreso Contra la Soviética en América Latina*. Mexico, 1955.

4061. ———. *Memoria del Segundo Congreso Contra la Soviética en América Latina.* Mexico, 1956.

4062. Dillon, D. *International Communism and Latin America: Perspectives and Prospects.* Gainesville, Fla., 1962.
In the Latin American monograph series of the U. of Florida.

4063. Donovan, J. *Red Machete: Communist Infiltration in the Americas.* Indianapolis, 1962.

4064. Dubois, J. *Operation America: The Communist Conspiracy in Latin America.* N.Y., 1963.
By the late Latin American correspondent of the *Chicago Tribune.*

4065. Ebon, M. *World Communism Today.* N.Y., 1948.
Section 4 pertains to the Western Hemisphere.

4065a. Efimov, A. V., *et al.* (eds.). *Natsii Latinskoi Ameriki.* Moscow, 1964.
Nations of Latin America.

4066. Elliott, J. R. *The Appeal of Communism in the Underdeveloped Nations.* Dubuque, Ia., 1962.

4066a. Glovinsky, E. "The Economic Relations of the USSR with Latin America," *SSU* 1 (1962) 64–79.

4067. González Rodríguez, A. *Comunismo y Democracia: Con un Estudio Preliminar de Luis David Cruz Ocampo.* Santiago, 1951.

4068. Haupt, W. "Moskaus Griff nach Lateinamerika," *WR* 10 (1960) 349–362.

4069. Hillekamps, C. H. "Verstärkte Aktivität der Sowjets in Südamerika," *AP* 11 (1960) 396–405.

4070. Instituto de Estudios Políticos. *El Comunismo en la América Hispana.* Madrid, 1961.

4071. Kalvoda, J. "Communist Strategy in Latin America," *YR* 50, n.s. (1960) 32–41.

4071a. Lazitch, B. "El Comunismo Latino-Americano y el Conflicto Moscu-Pekin," *EO* 2, no. 33 (1963) 4–10.

4072. Martillo, T. "Politika SShA v Latinskoi Amerike 1959–1961 Godov," *MEMZ* 3 (1962) 50–64.
"Latin American Policy of the USA, 1959–1961."

4073. Murillo Rubiera, F. "La Acción de la Unión Soviética Sobre las Repúblicas Americanas," *CUH* 28 (1956) 155–164.

4074. Nardone, B. *Peligro Rojo en América Latina.* Montevideo, 1961.

4075. Owen, C. F. "U.S. and Soviet Relations with Underdeveloped Countries: Latin America—A Case Study," *IEA* 14 (Winter, 1960) 85–116.

4076. Page, C. A. "Communism and the Labor Movements of Latin America," *VQR* 31 (1955) 373–382.

4077. Pelypenko, A. *Infiltración Comunista en las Iglesias Cristianas de América.* B.A., 1961.

4078. Poppino, R. *International Communism in Latin America: A History of the Movement, 1917–1963.* N.Y., 1964.

4079. Ravines, E. *The Yenan Way: The Kremlin's Penetration of South America.* N.Y. 1951.
The author at one time was an organizer of the Chilean Communist party.

4080. Ray, P. A. *South Wind Red: Our Hemispheric Crisis.* Chicago, 1962.
From the conservative point of view.

4081. Rienffer, K. *Comunistas Españoles en América.* Madrid, 1953.

4082. Ross, S. *Communism in Latin America.* N.Y., 1947.
News Background Report No. 19.

4083. Rubottom, R. R., Jr. *Communism in the Americas.* Wash., 1958.

4084. ———. *International Communism in Latin America.* Wash., 1960.

4085. Santa Pinter, J. J. "Soviet Diplomacy and Communist Penetration in Spanish America," *UQ* 15 (1959) 66–79.

4086. Scotti, E. J. "Infiltración Comunista en América y Argentina," *ESTA* 48 (May, 1959) 212–216.

4087. Seguí González, L. *Política Migratoria e Infiltración Totalitaria en América.* Montevideo, 1947.

4088. Silva Cabrera, L. *La Herida Roja de América.* 2 vols., Cd. Trujillo, 1959.

4089. Suárez, A. *Los Comunistas y los Problemas del Mundo Contemporáneo.* Montevideo, 1961.
A publication of the Uruguayan Communist party.

4090. "The Reds in Latin America," *RT* 53 (1962) 7–18.
Brief analysis of the movement since World War I.

4091.   USCH. Select Committee on Communist Infiltration. *Report of the Subcommittee to Investigate Communist Aggression in Latin America* (78th Cong., 2d Sess.). Wash., 1954.

4091a.   ————. Committee on Foreign Affairs. Subcommittee on Inter-American Affairs. *The Communist Threat in Latin America: Hearings* (86th Cong., 2d Sess.). Wash., 1960.

4091b.   USCS. Committee on Foreign Relations. *United States–Latin American Relations: Soviet Bloc Latin American Activities and Their Implications for the United States Foreign Policy* (86th Cong., 2d Sess.). Wash., 1960.

4091c.   ————. Committee on the Judiciary. *Communist Problems in Latin America, Report by Olin D. Johnston* (85th Cong., 1st Sess.). Wash., 1957.

4092.   ————. ————. *Communist Threat to the United States Through the Caribbean: Hearing Before the Subcommittee to Investigate the Administration of the Internal Security Act and other Internal Security Laws . . . Parts 1–9, July 14, 1959–Aug. 30, 1960* (86th Cong., 1st Sess.). Wash., 1959–1960.

4093.   ————. ————. *Cuban Aftermath: Red Seeds Blow South. Implications for the United States of the Latin American Conference for National Sovereignty and Economic Emancipation and Peace, Testimony of Dr. Joseph F. Thorning* (87th Cong., 1st Sess.). Wash., 1961.

4093a.   ————. ————. *Red Chinese Infiltration into Latin America: Hearings* (89th Cong., 1st Sess.). Wash., 1965.

4094.   USIA. *Communist Propaganda Activities in Latin America in 1961.* Wash., 1962.

4095.   Whitaker, A. P. "Our Reaction to Communist Infiltration in Latin America," *AAAPSS* 330 (1960) 103–115.

X–G   cross references:

a) For pertinent studies on Mexican communism, see items 6611–6629.

b) For the pledge of unity against communist penetration of the hemisphere at the fourth Consultative Conference (Washington, 1951), see items 5270–5280.

c) For the anti-communist resolution adopted at the Caracas Conference (1954), see items 5104a–5127a.

d) For communist penetration of Guatemala, see items 6864–6868, 6871–6874, 6876, 6879–6882, 6885, 6887, 6891, 6895–6897, 6900, 6902–6903, 6906, 6908, 6911–6912, 6914, 6917, 6920, 6923, 6925.

e) See also items 3180a, 3467, 4096a, 4813, 5064a, 7214, 7218, 7674, 7944, 7950, 7983, 8400, 8713, 8946a, 8947, 8950a, 9004, 9008, 9012, 9167, 9168, 9181a, 9441, 9446, 9447, 9456, 9462, 9465a, 9467, 9468, 9469, 9472, 9472a, 9475, 9481, 9528, 9722, 9723, 9807, 10093, 10099, 10120a, 10122, 10158.

H. THE ALLIANCE FOR PROGRESS

4096.   Aguirre, J. M. "La Alianza para el Progreso: La Confianza, Factor Decisivo," *CUA* (January, 1962) 55–57.

4096a.   Alba, V. *Alliance Without Allies: The Mythology of Progress in Latin America.* N.Y., 1965.

4097.   ————. "Obstáculos y Posibilidades," *CUA* (April, 1962) 43–50.

4097a.   Allende Posse, J. "La Alianza para el Progresso, o Sea, la Aplicación de la Carta de Punta del Este," *BCN* 80 (July, 1962) 368–402.

4098.   Birou, A. "Les Déboires de l'Alliance pour le Progrès," *DC* (1963) 64–79.

4099.   Brazil. Comissão Nacional de Pecuária de Leite. Presidencia. *Operação Pan-Americana.* 2 vols., Rio, 1959–1960.

4100.   ————. Ministerio das Relações Exteriores. *Artigos e Entrevistas Sobre a Operação Pan-Americana.* Rio, 1960.

4100a.   Canelas O., A. *Radiografia de la Alianza para el Atraso.* La Paz, 1963.

Takes the view that the Alliance is bound to end in failure.

4101.   Castellano, P. "Dificultades y Problemas de la Alianza para el Progreso," *LE* 153 (1963) 61–64.

4102.   ————. "La 'Alianza para el Progreso' Después de la Conferencia de Punta del Este," *LE* 146 (1962) 118–122.

4103.   Centro para el Desarrollo Económico y Social de América Latina. *La Alianza para el Progreso y el Desarrollo Social de América Latina: Sinopsis del Informe Preliminar.* Santiago, 1963.

4104. Committee for Economic Development. *Cooperation for Progress in Latin America.* N.Y., 1961.

4105. Consejo Interamericano Económico y Social. *La Marcha de la Alianza para el Progreso, 1961–1962.* Wash., 1963.

4106. Costa, L. *Uma Nova Política para as Américas: Doutrina Kubitschek e OPA.* São Paulo, 1960.

4107. Diniz, H. "A 'Aliança para o Progresso' e a Realidade Nacional," *RBR* (March, 1962) 12–17, and (July, 1962) 37–48.

4108. Dreier, J. C. (ed.). *The Alliance for Progress: Problems and Perspectives.* Baltimore, 1962.
   Portuguese ed., Rio, 1963.

4109. Ecuador. Junta Nacional de Planificación y Coordinación Económica. *Memorandum que el Gobierno del Ecuador Presenta al Banco Interamericano de Desarrollo: Medidas que Ha Adoptado y Proyecta Establecer el Gobierno del Ecuador en Cumplimiento de las Obligaciones Emanadas del Acta de Bogotá y la Carta de Punta del Este.* Quito, 1961.

4110. Flores, E. *Land Reform and the Alliance for Progress.* Princeton, N.J., 1963.

4110a. Frei Montalva, E. "The Alliance that Lost its Way," *FA* 45 (1967) 436–448.

4111. Freyre, J. "Perspectivas Económicas," *CUA* (April, 1962) 35–42.

4112. Friedenberg, D. M. "Can the Alliance for Progress Work?" *CT* 34 (1962) 93–101.

4113. Frondizi, A. "Argentina and the 'Alliance for Progress' Objectives," *RRP* 130 (October, 1961) 39–41.

4114. Gordon, L. *A New Deal for Latin America: The Alliance for Progress.* Cambridge, Mass., 1963.
   By the U.S. ambassador to Brazil, and subsequently the assistant secretary of state for inter-American affairs.

4115. Hanson, S. G. "The First Year: Economic," *IEA* 16 (Summer, 1962) 3–22.
   This entire issue of the *IEA* is devoted to the Alliance.

4116. Herrera Lane, F. *The Economic Aspects of the Alliance for Progress: Address Delivered at the Colloquium on Latin America Presented by the Summer School and the Latin America Studies Program of George-town University, June 27, 1962.* Wash., 1962.

4117. Hickey, J. "The First Year: Business," *IEA* 16 (Summer, 1962) 49–72.

4117a. Inter-American Economic and Social Council. Special Meeting at the Ministerial Level. Punta del Este, Uruguay, 1961. *Ideario y Planificación de la Alianza para el Progreso: Carta de Punta del Este, Punta del Este, Agosto de 1961.* Montevideo, 1962.

4117b. International Development Agency. *Alliance for Progress, American Partnership.* Wash., 1965.

4117c. ———. *Alliance for Progress, Its Program and Goals.* Wash., 1963.

4117d. ———. *Alliance Reaches Turning Point, by President Lyndon B. Johnson, Address to Ambassadors of Latin American Nations.* Wash., 1964.

4118. ———. *Report to Inter-American Economic and Social Council, Presented by the Government of the United States, Alliance for Progress, 1963.* Wash., 1963.

4119. Jinesta, R., and J. C. Suñol. *La Operación Panamericana: América con Vocación de Liderazgo.* San José, C.R., 1960.

4119a. Joint Publications Research Service. *Venezuelan Comments on Alliance for Progress.* Wash., 1962.

4120. Kennedy, J. F. "Alianza para Progreso," *USDSB* 44 (1961) 471–478.

4121. Krause, W. *The United States and Latin America: The Alliance for Progress Program.* Austin, Texas, 1963.

4122. Lleras Camargo, A. "The Alliance for Progress: Aims, Distortions, Obstacles," *FA* 42 (1963) 25–37.

4123. Mallo, J. "Su Verdadera Significación," *CUA* (April, 1962) 29–34.

4124. Manger, W. (ed.). *The Alliance for Progress: A Critical Appraisal.* Wash., 1963.

4125. Marchant, R. "Un Año de Alianza para el Progreso," *CUA* (September, 1962) 3–11.

4126. Maritano, N., and A. H. Obaid. *An Alliance for Progress: The Challenge and the Problem.* Minneapolis, 1963.

4127. May, E. R. "The Alliance for Progress in Historical Perspective," *FA* 41 (1963) 757–774.

4128. McCabe, M. "The Alliance for Progress

and the Cooperative Movement," *HOR* 5 (April, 1962) 48–55.

4129. Meléndez López, A. "Toynbee y la Alianza para el Progreso," *CUA* (November, 1962) 40–48.

4130. Morales Carrión, A. "Fundamentos Ideológicos de la Alianza para el Progreso," *JIAS* 6 (1964) 123–129.

4131. Moscoso, T. "A Decisive Moment of History: Success Depends Primarily on Latin American Countries Themselves," *VS* 28 (1962) 333–336.
By Kennedy's top Alliance official.

4131a. National Advisory Council on International Monetary and Financial Problems. *Letter from Secretary of the Treasury Transmitting Report on Activities During Period Jan. 1–June 30, 1964* (89th Cong.). Wash., 1965.

4131b. ———. *Semiannual Report of National Advisory Council on International Monetary and Financial Problems, Letter from the Secretary of the Treasury Transmitting Report on Activities During the Period July 1–Dec. 31, 1964* (89th Cong.). Wash., 1965.

4131c. Nystrom, J. W. *The Alliance for Progress: Key to Latin America's Development.* Princeton, N.J., 1966.

4132. PAU. *Alliance for Progress: Official Documents Emanating from the Special Meeting of the Inter-American Economic and Social Council, Held in Punta del Este, Uruguay, Aug. 5–17, 1961.* Wash.,1961.

4133. ———. *The Alliance for Progress: Its First Year, 1961–1962.* Wash., 1963.

4134. ———. *Primer Año de Aplicación de la Alianza para el Progreso: Informe Presentado por el Gobierno de Chile.* Wash., 1962.

4135. ———. Inter-American Economic and Social Council. *The Alliance for Progress: Its Second Year, 1962–1963: Second Report on the Progress of Economic and Social Development in Latin America and Prospects for the Future.* Wash., 1963.
Available in Spanish and Portuguese.

4136. Pinto, P. F. "O Café e a Aliança para o Progresso," *RBR* (November, 1961) 78–93.

4137. "Progress of the Alliance," *APAU* 14 (June, 1962) 3–10.

4138. Rauschenbush, S. *The Challenge to the Alliance for Progress.* Wash., 1962.

4139. Rippy, J. F. "Vague Plans and Huge Expenditures for the Solution of Hemispheric Problems," *IEA* 14 (Autumn, 1960) 55–70.

4140. Scott, J. *How Much Progress? Alianza para el Progreso.* N.Y., 1963.

4141. Silva, C. A. de Souza e. "Operação Pan Americana: Antecedentes e Perspectivas," *RBPI* 3 (March, 1960) 41–59.

4142. Trías, V. *El Plan Kennedy y la Revolución Latinoamericana.* Montevideo, 1961.
A very critical appraisal.

4143. Upton, T. G. "Operação Pan Americana, O Catalizador Oculto?" *RBPI* 4 (June, 1961) 58–69.

4144. Urquidi, V. L. "Latinoamérica ante la Alianza para el Progreso," *FI* 2 (1962) 369–390.

4145. ———. "Two Years of the Alliance for Progress," *IEA* 17 (Spring, 1964) 21–35.

4146. USCH. Committee on Appropriations. *Inter-American Programs for 1961, Denial of 1962 Budget Information* (87th Cong., 1st Sess.). Wash., 1961.

4146a. ———. ———. *Inter-American Social and Economic Cooperation Program and Chilean Reconstruction and Rehabilitation Program: Hearings* (87th Cong., 1st Sess.). Wash., 1961.

4146b. ———. Committee on Foreign Affairs. *Report of 1st Annual Review of Alliance for Progress, by the Inter-American Economic and Social Council, OAS* (87th Cong., 2d Sess.). Wash., 1962.

4146c. ———. ———. *American Republics Cooperation Act: Hearings* (86th Cong., 2d Sess.). Wash., 1960.

4147. USCS. Committee on Foreign Relations. *United States–Latin American Relations: Some Observations on the Operation of the Alliance for Progress: The First Six Months: A Study Prepared for the Subcommittee on American Republics Affairs* (87th Cong., 2d Sess.). Wash., 1962.

4147a. ———. ———. *Report on Alliance for Progress, 1963, by Hubert H. Humphrey to Committee on Appropriations and Committee on Foreign Relations* (88th Cong.). Wash., 1963.

4147b. USDAG. *Agriculture and Alliance for Progress, Address by Orville L. Freeman at Conference of Alliance for Progress Ambassadors and Aid Directors.* Wash., 1964.

4147c. USDS. *Alliance for Progress, Based on Address by Thomas C. Mann, Assistant Secretary of State for Inter-American Affairs.* Wash., 1964.

4147d. ———. *Alliance for Progress, Road Map to New Achievements, by Adlai E. Stevenson.* Wash., 1961.

4147e. ———. *American Republics Establish Alliance for Progress.* Wash., 1961.

4147f. ———. *Financing of Assistance Under Alliance for Progress, Agreement Between United States and Pan American Union, Modifying and Supplementing Agreement of Nov. 29, 1961.* Wash., 1964.

4147g. ———. *President Kennedy's Inter-American Program for Social Progress, Questions and Answers.* Wash., 1961.

4147h. ———. *Social Implications of Act of Bogotá, by Lester D. Mallory.* Wash., 1961.

4147i. ———. *Social Progress Trust Fund Agreement, Between United States and Inter-American Development Bank.* Wash., 1961.

4147j. ———. *Third Anniversary of Alliance for Progress, by President Lyndon B. Johnson, Made at Pan American Union.* Wash., 1964.

4147k. USDD. Armed Forces Information and Education Office. "Alliance for Progress, Program for Peoples of the Americas," *FCTCW* 1, no. 6 (1961).

4147l. ———. ———. "Future of Alliance for Progress," *FCTCW* 2, no. 17 (1963).

X–H   cross references:

a) For the planning of the Alliance for Progress at the Punta del Este Conference, see items 5287–5311.

b) See also items 4236, 4282, 4360, 6352, 7169, 8668, 9250, 10131.

I. THE PEACE CORPS IN LATIN AMERICA

4148. Adams, V. *The Peace Corps in Action.* Chicago, 1964.

4149. Albertson, M. L., *et al. New Frontiers for American Youth: Perspective on the Peace Corps.* Wash., 1961.

4150. Brooks, R., and E. Brooks. *The Barrios of Manta: A Personal Account of the Peace Corps in Ecuador.* N.Y., 1965.

4150a. Envenwembi, O. *Peace-Corpism.* N.Y., 1962.

4150b. Haverstock, N.A. "Volunteers for Progress: Peace Corps in Latin America," *APAU* 15 (July, 1963) 2–10.

4151. Hayes, S. P. *An International Peace Corps: The Promise and Problems.* Wash., 1961.

4151a. Madow, P. (ed.). *The Peace Corps.* N.Y., 1964.
    Published in *The Reference Shelf*, vol. 32, no. 2.

4151b. McGuire, E. *The Peace Corps, Kindlers of the Spark.* N.Y., 1966.

4151c. Oklahoma University. Extension Division. *Peace Corps, Peru: Rural Community Action and Agriculture, September 25–December 19, 1964. Syllabus.* Norman, Okla., 1964.

4151d. ———. ———. *Peace Corps Project: El Salvador, Costa Rica Training Program Syllabus, June 15–August 24, 1963.* Norman, Okla., 1963.

4151e. Parmer, J. N. (ed.). "The Peace Corps," *AAAPSS* 365 (May, 1966).

4152. Shriver, S. *Point of the Lance.* N.Y., 1964.
    By the first director of the Peace Corps.

4152a. Sullivan, G. *The Story of the Peace Corps.* N.Y., 1964.

4152b. University of Nebraska. *Peace Corps Training Program. Colombia Project 12.* Lincoln, Nebraska, 1963.
    Mimeographed syllabus for agricultural development.

4152c. University of New Mexico. *Syllabus, Peace Corps Training Program: Brazil III.* Albuquerque, N.M., 1963.
    Mimeographed.

4152d. ———. *Syllabus, Peace Corps Training Program: Brazil IV.* Albuquerque, N.M., 1963.
    Mimeographed.

4152e. ———. *Syllabus, Peace Corps Training Program: Colombia Educational Television.* Albuquerque, N.M., 1963.
    Mimeographed.

4152f. ———. *Syllabus, Peace Corps Training Program: Colombia, RCA.* Albuquerque, N.M., 1963.
    Mimeographed syllabus for rural community action.

4152g. University of New Mexico. *Syllabus, Peace Corps Training Program: Colombia VIII*. Albuquerque, N.M., 1963.
    Mimeographed syllabus for health and community development.

4152h. USCH. Committee on Foreign Affairs. *Amending the Peace Corps Act: Report* (87th Cong., 2d Sess.). Wash., 1962.

4152i. ———. ———. *Peace Corps Act Amendments: Hearings* (87th Cong., 2d Sess.). Wash., 1962.

4152j. ———. ———. *Peace Corps Activities in Latin America and the Caribbean: Hearing Before Subcommittee on Inter-American Affairs* (87th Cong., 1st Sess.). Wash., 1965.

4152k. ———. ———. *To Amend Further the Peace Corps Act: Hearings* (88th Cong., 2d Sess.). Wash., 1964.

4152l. ———. ———. *To Amend the Peace Corps Act: Hearings, Oct. 15–16, 1963* (88th Cong., 1st Sess.). Wash., 1963.

4152m. USCS. Committee on Foreign Relations. *Peace Corps Act Amendment: Hearings* (87th Cong., 2d Sess.). Wash., 1962.

4152n. U.S. Peace Corps, Division of Public Information. *The Peace Corps Bibliography, March, 1961–March, 1965*. Wash., 1965.

4153. Wingenbach, C. E. *The Peace Corps: Who, How, and Where*. N.Y., 1961.

J. LATIN AMERICA AND THE UNITED NATIONS

4154. Aguirre, A. (ed.). *Uruguay and the United Nations*. N.Y., 1958.

4155. Aldunate Phillips, R. *3000 Delegados en San Francisco*. Santiago, 1946.

4156. Aparicio Urrutia, C. "América y las Naciones Unidas," *CA* 13 (1954) 243–245.

4157. Bohórquez Ramírez, R. *La Conferencia de San Francisco*. Potosí, Bolivia, 1946.

4158. Brazil. Ministerio das Relações Exteriores. *Relatório de Delegação do Brasil a Conferencia das Nações Unidas para a Organização Internacional*. Rio, 1946.

4159. Bustamante y Rivero, J. L. "La Conferencia Inter-Americana de Abogados de 1943 y la Organización Mundial de Post-Guerra," *RPCC* 1 (1945) 1–18.

4160. Castañeda, J. *Mexico and the United Nations*. N.Y., 1958.

4161. Chile. Ministerio de Relaciones Exteriores. *Chile y la Conferencia de San Francisco: Antecedentes y Documentos Relativos a la Conferencia de San Francisco de California Sobre Organización Internacional y la Carta de las Naciones Unidas*. Santiago, 1945.

4162. ———. ———. *Política Internacional de Chile: Exposición del Ministro de Relaciones Exteriores, Raul Juliet Gómez, ante el Senado de la República*. Santiago, 1947.
    Concerns the veto power in the Security Council.

4163. Cornelius, W. G. "Latin American Patterns of Voting in the United Nations," Columbia U. Diss., 1956.

4164. ———. "The 'Latin-American Bloc' in the United Nations," *JIAS* 3 (1961) 419–435.
    Indicates that there really is no such thing as a Latin American bloc.

4165. Corral, J. S. del. "Problemas Relativos a la Organización de las Naciones Unidas," *RCDI* 1 (1947) 21–37.

4166. Crespo, J. B. *La Conferencia de San Francisco y la Seguridad de los Pueblos*. B.A., 1946.

4167. Delgadillo Schulze, J. A. *La Organización de las Naciones Unidas*. Potosí, Bolivia, 1946.

4168. Eichelberger, C. M. *UN: The First Twenty Years*. N.Y., 1965.

4169. Fuselli, A. *Ecos de la Conferencia de San Francisco*. B.A., 1945.

4170. Glick, E. B. *Latin America and the Palestine Problem*. N.Y., 1958.

4171. Gomes, H. de Souza. "A Ação do Brasil, em Dez Anos, nas Nações Unidas," *BSBDI* 11 (1955) 35–43.

4172. Gonzales, F. S. "Mexico and the United Nations," UCLA Diss., 1953.

4173. Hanson, S. G. "Case Study in Futility: United Nations Economic Commission for Latin America," *IEA* 2 (Autumn, 1948) 81–99.

4174. ———. "Preliminary Report to the United Nations Economic and Social Council on an Economic Commission for Latin America," *IEA* 1 (December, 1947) 99–101.

4175. Harley, J. E. "Latin America and the United Nations," *WAI* 18 (1947) 137–147.

4176. Hohmann, J. E. "The Latin American Voting Bloc in the United Nations," *WA* 154 (1951) 38–40.

4177. Houston, J. A. *Latin American Participation in the United Nations*. N.Y., 1953.

4178. ———. *Latin America in the United Nations*. N.Y., 1956.
Comprehensive coverage to date of publication.

4179. Hovet, T., Jr. *Bloc Politics in the United Nations*. Cambridge, Mass., 1960.

4180. Hunt, J. B. "The Entrance of Brazil into the United Nations," U. of Utah Diss., 1952.

4181. Kidder, F. E. *Latin America and UNESCO: The First Five Years*. Gainesville, Fla., 1960.

4182. Maúrtua, M. F. "El Grupo Latino-americano en las Naciones Unidas y Algunos Problemas Jurídicos," *RPDI* 16 (1956) 10–43.

4183. Mexico. Secretaría de Relaciones Exteriores. *Discursos y Declaraciones del Licenciado Luis Padilla Nervo, como Secretario de Relaciones Exteriores o como Jefe de la Delegación Mexicana ante la Organización de las Naciones Unidas*. Mexico, 1958.

4184. ———. *Opinión de la Secretaría de Relaciones Exteriores de México Sobre el Proyecto de Dumbarton Oaks, para la Creación de una Organización Internacional General*. Mexico, 1944.

4185. Neal, M. "United Nations Programs in Haiti," *IC*, no. 468 (1951).

4186. Panama. Presidente. *Derechos y Deberes de los Estados: Anteproyecto de Declaración Internacional que Somete, el Gobierno de Panamá a la Consideración de la Asamblea General de las Naciones Unidas*. Panama, 1946.

4187. Plaza, G. "Latin America's Contribution to the United Nations Organization," *IC*, no. 419 (1946) 150–157.

4188. Regules, D. "Posición del Uruguay Frente a la Carta de las Naciones Unidas," *RDJA* 44 (March, 1946) 65–78.

4189. Riaño Juame, R. "Presencia de Cuba en la ONU," *RDI* 28 (September, 1949) 47–53.

4190. Sandifer, D. V. "Regional Aspects of the Dumbarton Oaks Proposals," *USDSB* 12 (1945) 145–147.

4191. UN. Office of Public Information. *The United Nations and Latin America: A Collection of Basic Information Material About the Work of the United Nations and the Related Agencies in Latin America*. N.Y., 1961.

4192. Venezuela. Ministerio de Relaciones Exteriores. *Venezuela en las Naciones Unidas*. Caracas, 1963.

4193. Viera Méndez, L. "La Obra de las Naciones Unidas: A Través de sus Organismos Specializados y su Proyección a la República de Honduras," *FH* 25 (1956–1957) 22–40.

4194. Volpe, A. E. "Latin America at San Francisco: The Aims, Attitudes, and Accomplishments of Latin America at the U.N. Conference on International Organization, San Francisco, April 25–June 26, 1945," Stanford U. Diss., 1950.

4195. Walls, F. W. "The Activities of Selected United Nations Specialized Agencies with Particular Reference to Field Projects in Mexico," U. of Washington Diss., 1958.

4195a. Whitaker, A. P. "Role of Latin America in Relation to Current Trends in International Organization," *APSR* 39 (1945) 500–511.

4196. Woltz, C. C. "Bloc Voting in the U.N., 1946–1951," New York U. Diss., 1957.

X–J cross references:

a) For works referring to the inter-American system and the United Nations, see items 4752–4786.

b) See also items 4981, 7411, 7721, 7952, 9046.

K. ECONOMIC RELATIONS

1. GENERAL WORKS AND SPECIAL STUDIES

4197. Alexander, R. J. *Labor Movements in Latin America*. London, 1947.

4198. ———. "Labor and Inter-American Relations," *AAAPSS* 334 (1961) 41–53.

4199. ———. *Organized Labor in Latin America*. N.Y., 1965.

4199a. Avarina, V. I., and M. V. Danilevich (eds.). *Ekonomicheskie Problemy Stran Latinskoi Ameriki.* Moscow, 1963.
Economic Problems of the Countries of Latin America.

4200. Behrendt, R. F. W. *Inter-American Economic Relations: Problems and Prospects.* N.Y., 1948.

4201. Belaúnde, V. A. "The Economic Basis of Politics in Latin America," *AAAPSS* 342 (1962) 54–58.

4202. Benham, F. C., and H. A. Holley. *A Short Introduction to the Economy of Latin America.* N.Y., 1960.

4203. Brandenburg, F. R. *The Development of Latin American Private Enterprise: A Report.* Wash., 1964.

4204. Carneiro, O. A. Dias. "Interêsses Políticos e Econômicos dos Estados Unidos na América Latina," *RBPI* 1 (December, 1958) 49–75.

4205. Carrillo Flores, A. "Cooperación Económica Inter-Americana," *FI* 1 (1960) 1–13.

4206. Chamisso, X. de. *Une Politique Economique d'Hémisphère.* Paris, 1953.

4207. Costanzo, G. A. *Programas de Estabilización Económica en América Latina.* Mexico, 1961.

4208. Dorfman, A. "Latin American Economic Problems and International Cooperation," *ILR* 58 (1948) 601–624.

4209. Drucker, P. R. "A Plan for Revolution in Latin America," *HA* 223 (July, 1961) 31–38.

4210. Gnazzo, E., and R. González Casal. *Integración Económica de América Latina.* Montevideo, 1960.

4211. Gordon, W. C. *The Economy of Latin America.* N.Y., 1950.
A comprehensive general survey.

4212. ———. *The Political Economy of Latin America.* N.Y., 1965.

4213. Grace, J. P., Jr. *An Economic Program for the Americas.* Wash., 1954.

4214. Grove, D. L. *Las Fluctuaciones Económicas en Estados Unidos y América Latina.* Mexico, 1959.

4214a. Herrera Lane, F. *Economic Integration and Political Reintegration: Statement by the President of the Inter-American Development Bank at the Conference on Tensions of Development in the Western Hemisphere, at Salvador, Bahia, Brazil, August 6, 1962.* Wash., 1962.

4215. Hirschman, A. O. *Journeys Toward Progress: Studies of Economic Policy-Making in Latin America.* N.Y., 1963.

4216. ——— (ed.). *Latin American Issues: Essays and Comments.* N.Y., 1963.

4217. Holmes, O. "Latin America and the United States—Problems of Economic Readjustment," *FPAR* 23 (1947–1948) 262–273.

4218. Illanes Benítez, F. *El Sistema Económica Interamericano: Problemas y Posibilidades.* Santiago, 1963.

4219. Inter-American Institute of International Legal Studies. *Instrumentos Relativos a la Integración Económica en América Latina.* Wash., 1964.

4220. *Latin America's Merging Market: The Challenge of Economic Integration.* N.Y., 1964.

4221. Lewis, G. K. *United States Foreign Economic Policy: Potential Obstacles to Latin American Economic Growth.* Wichita, Kan., 1960.

4221a. Mejía-Ricart, M. A. *Crisis of Small States in the Present Economic World.* London, 1960.

4222. Mikesell, R. F. *U.S. Economic Policy and International Relations.* N.Y., 1952.

4223. Moncada Sánchez, J. A. "La Integración Económica Latinoamericana," *BTIE* 12 (April, 1960) 66–83.

4224. OAS. Comité Coordinador de Asistencia Técnica. *Programa de Cooperación Técnica de la Organización de los Estados Americanos, Aprobado por el Consejo Interamericano Económico y Social, 31 de Enero de 1952.* Wash., 1952.

4225. ———. Council. *Final Report of the Secretary General of the OAS on the Third Meeting of the Special Committee to Study the Formulation of New Measures for Economic Cooperation.* Wash., 1960.

4226. ———. ———. *New Measures for Economic Cooperation: Report and Documents, First Meeting, Washington, D.C., November 17–December 12, 1958.* Wash., 1959.

4227. ———. ———. *Resolutions Based on the Draft Resolutions Presented by the Special Committee to Study the Formulation of New Measures for Economic Cooperation at*

Its Second Meeting (CECE/II), Buenos Aires, Argentina, April 27 to May 8, 1959. Wash., 1959.

4228.   ———. ———. *Special Committee to Study the Formulation of New Measures for Economic Cooperation ("Committee of 21"): Latin American Experience with Commodity Agreements (Working Paper Prepared by the Secretariat, Submitted in Relation to Point III of the Brazilian Aide-Mémoire of February 23, 1960).* Wash., 1960.

4229.   Ossio Sanjinés, L. *Integración Económica Defensa de la Soberanía de los Estados Latino-Americanos y Motor de su Industrialización.* Potosí, Bolivia, 1960.

4230.   PAU. *The Effects of the European Economic Community on the Latin American Economies.* Wash., 1963.

4231.   ———. Division of Economic Research. *Fiscal Receipts, Expenditures, Budgets and Public Debt of the Latin American Republics.* Wash., 1956.

4232.   Polit, G. "Variaciones Sobre el Tema de la Buena Vecindad," *CA* 29 (September, 1946) 24–42.
        Extremely critical of the early postwar economic policy of the United States.

4233.   Rippy, J. F. *Globe and Hemisphere: Latin America's Place in the Post-War Foreign Relations of the U.S.* Chicago, 1958.
        Examines reasons for Latin American resentment in the postwar period.

4233a. Romanova, Z. I. *Ekonomicheskaia Ekspansiia SShA v Latinskoi Amerike.* Moscow, 1963.
        Economic Expansion of the U.S.A. in Latin America.

4233b. ———. *Problemy Ekonomicheskoi Integratsii v Latinskoi Amerike.* Moscow, 1965.
        Problems of Economic Integration in Latin America.

4234.   Salzman, O. H., Jr. "Technical Cooperation in the Organization of American States," *WA* 120 (Spring, 1957) 17–21.

4235.   Sosa-Rodríguez, R. *Les Problèmes Structurels des Relations Economiques Internationales de l'Amérique Latine.* Geneva, 1963.

4236.   Toynbee, A. J. *The Economy of the Western Hemisphere.* N.Y., 1962.
        Three lectures delivered by Professor Toynbee at the University of Puerto Rico.

4237.   U.N. Department of Economic Affairs. Economic Commission for Latin America. Secretariat. *Economic Survey of Latin America: 1949.* N.Y., 1951.

4237a. ———. ———. *Multilateral Economic Cooperation in Latin America: Text and Documents.* Paris, 1962.

4238.   U.S. Bureau of Foreign and Domestic Commerce. Foreign Agricultural Service. *Notes on the Agricultural Economies of the 20 Latin American Republics.* Wash., 1959.

4239.   United States. Foreign Operations Administration. *Report on the Economic Situation in Latin America, Prepared for the International Development Advisory Board.* Wash., 1954.

4240.   Urquidi, V. L. *Viabilidad Económica de América Latina.* Mexico, 1962.

4240a. USCH. Joint Economic Committee. *Economic Policies and Programs in South America* (87th Cong., 2d Sess.). Wash., 1962.

4240b. USCS. Committee on Foreign Relations. *United States and Latin American Policies Affecting Their Economic Relations, by National Planning Association* (86th Cong., 2d Sess.). Wash., 1960.

4240c. Vol'skii, V. V. *Latinskaia Amerika, Neft' i Nezavisimost'.* Moscow, 1964.
        Latin America: Oil and Independence.

4241.   Warren, H. G. (ed.). "Economic Diplomacy with Latin America: A Symposium Presented at the Annual Convention of the Mississippi Valley Historical Association, Cincinnati, April 19–21, 1951," *IEA* 4 (Spring, 1951) 3–47.

4242.   Wionczek, M. S. (ed.). *Integración de la América Latina.* Mexico, 1964.

4243.   Withers, W. *The Economic Crisis in Latin America.* N.Y., 1964.

4244.   Woytinsky, W. S. *The U.S. and Latin America's Economy.* N.Y., 1958.

4245.   Wythe, G. "The United States and the Latin-American Economy," *JIAS* 3 (1961) 451–468.

X–K–1   cross references: 209, 328a, 3418, 4019

2. Economic Development

4246.   Broide, J. *Banco Interamericano de Desarrollo: Sus Antecedentes y Creación.* Wash., 1961.

4247. "Economic Growth and Social Policy in Latin America," *ILR* 84 (July, 1958) 50–74.

4248. Ellis, H. S., and H. C. Wallich (eds.). *Economic Development for Latin America.* N.Y., 1961.
Series of papers prepared for the meeting of the International Economic Association at Rio in 1957.

4249. Facio, G. J. "O Desarmamento como Fator de Desenvolvimento Econômico na América Latina," *RBPI* 1 (June, 1958) 29–44.

4250. Frigerio, R. *Cuba or Argentina: Two Alternatives to a Common Problem: Underdevelopment.* Wash., 1961.

4251. Frankenhoff, C. A. "The Prebisch Thesis: A Theory of Industrialism for Latin America," *JIAS* 4 (1962) 185–206.

4252. Greffier, M. E. *La Acción del Capital Extranjero en el Desarrollo Económico de la América Latina.* B.A., 1945.
A call for heavy foreign investment in Latin America.

4253. Hanson, S. G. *Economic Development in Latin America.* Wash., 1951.

4254. Herrera Lane, F. *El Banco Interamericano de Desarrollo: Origen y Perspectivas.* Wash., 1960.

4255. Hughlett, L. J. (ed.). *Industrialization of Latin America.* N.Y., 1946.

4255a. Institute of International Studies and Overseas Administration. University of Oregon. *United States–Latin American Relations: Problems of Latin American Economic Development. A Study Prepared at Request of Subcommittee on American Republics Affairs of the Committee on Foreign Relations, U.S. Senate, by the University of Oregon* (86th Cong., 2d Sess.). Wash., 1960.

4256. Inter-American Development Bank. *Institutional Reforms and Social Development Trends in Latin America.* Wash., 1963.

4257. ———. *Round Table on Europe's Role in Latin American Development: Inter-American Development Bank, Third Meeting of the Board of Governors, April 24, 1962, Buenos Aires, Argentina.* Wash., 1962.

4258. ———. *Round Table on Private Enterprise and the Development of Latin America: Inter-American Development Bank, Third Meeting of the Board of Governors, April 25, 1962, Buenos Aires, Argentina.* Wash., 1962.

4259. International Bank for Reconstruction and Development. *The World Bank in Latin America: A Summary of Activities.* Wash., 1960.

4260. ———. *The World Bank Group in the Americas: A Summary of Activities.* Wash., 1963.

4261. International Economic Association. *Economic Development for Latin America: Proceedings of a Conference Held by the International Economic Association.* N.Y., 1961.

4261a. "Latin American Economy: Regional Commission Outlines Development Program," *UNR* 8 (June, 1961) 28–30.

4262. Leite, C. "Banco Interamericano de Desenvolvimiento," *RBPI* 2 (June, 1959) 26–43.

4263. Mende, T. *The Inter-American Development Bank.* Wash., 1964.

4264. PAU. *Organizaciones Internacionales que Operan en el Campo Relacionado con el Desarrollo Agrícola, la Reforma Agraria y la Vida Rural en América Latina.* Wash., 1964.

4265. Poblete Troncoso, M. *Standard de Vida y Desarrollo Económico-Social.* Santiago, 1956.

4266. Prebisch, R. "El Desarrollo Económico de la América Latina y Algunos de sus Principales Problemas," *TE* 16 (1949) 347–431.

4267. ———. "El Desarrollo Económico de la América Latina y sus Principales Problemas," *REA* 48 (1949) 211–221, 254–266.

4268. ———. *Hacia una Dinámica del Desarrollo Latinoamericano.* Mexico, 1963.

4269. Ranis, G. (ed.). *The United States and the Developing Economies.* N.Y., 1964.

4270. Rippy, J. F. *Latin America and the Industrial Age.* 2d ed., N.Y., 1947.

4270a. Tamagna, F. M., and G. B. Wolfe. "A Financial System for Economic Development: Problems and Prospects in Central America," *JIAS* 6 (October, 1964) 463–468.

4271. Teichert, P. C. M. "Analysis of Real Growth and Wealth in the Latin American Republics," *JIAS* 1 (1959) 173–202.

4272. ———. *Economic Policy Revolution and Industrialization in Latin America.* University, Miss., 1959.
Spanish ed., Mexico, 1961.

4273. ———. *The General Background of Latin America: A Syllabus for an Economics Class in Latin American Resources and Development.* University, Miss., 1961.

4274. U.N. Department of Public Information. *The Economic Growth of the Twenty Republics: The Work of the Economic Commission for Latin America.* 3d ed., N.Y., 1956.

4275. ———. Economic Commission for Latin America. *The Economic Development of Latin America in the Postwar Period.* 2 vols., Santiago, 1963.

4276. ———. Economic Commission for Latin America and Food and Agriculture Organization. *Joint Report: The Selective Expansion of Agricultural Production in Latin America.* N.Y., 1957.

4277. USCS. Subcommittee on American Republics Affairs. *Problems of Latin-American Economic Development, Prepared by the Institute of International Studies and Overseas Administration of the University of Oregon* (86th Cong., 2d Sess., S. Doc. 125). Wash., 1960.

4278. Wythe, G. *Industry in Latin America.* 2d ed., N.Y., 1949.
Spanish ed., Mexico, 1947.

3. FOREIGN ASSISTANCE

4279. Acierto [pseudonym]. "A Marshall Plan for Latin America," *IEA* 1 (September, 1947) 3–20.

4280. Advisory Committee on Voluntary Foreign Aid. *Guide to Technical Assistance Services of United States Voluntary Agencies Abroad, 1949–1951, Latin America, Africa, Near East, and Far East.* Wash., 1952.

4281. Amuzegar, J. "Point Four: Performance and Prospect," *PSQ* 73 (1958) 530–546.

4282. Andreis, M. *Gli Stati Uniti e i Paesi Sottosviluppati: Forme e Problemi dell' Assistenza Economica da Truman a Kennedy.* Turin, Italy, 1962.
Discusses motivations of United States aid programs.

4283. Behrman, D. *When the Mountains Move: Technical Assistance and the Changing Face of Latin America.* Paris, 1954.

4283a. Beltrán, P. G. "Foreign Loans and Politics in Latin America," *FA* 34 (1956) 297–304.

4284. Bingham, J. B. *Shirt-Sleeve Diplomacy: Point 4 in Action.* N.Y., 1954.
By the deputy administrator of the Point Four Program.

4284a. Blanksten, G. I. "Technical Assistance and the Political Instability of Latin America," *EDCC* 2 (1954) 350–356.

4285. Brown W. A., Jr., and R. Opie. *American Foreign Assistance.* Wash., 1953.

4286. Commerce Committee for the Alliance for Progress. *Proposals to Improve the Flow of U.S. Private Investment to Latin America: Report.* Wash., 1963.

4287. Chilton, W. L. "The Choice of Technology for United States Direct Investment in Latin American Manufacturing Industry and Its Implications for Economic Development," Columbia U. Diss., 1952.

4288. Daniels, W. M. (ed.). *The Point Four Program.* N.Y., 1951.

4289. Doyle, G. A. "The 'Point Four' Program: Its Position in the History of International Investments and a Consideration of the Economics of Brazil and Venezuela," Fordham U. Diss., 1951.

4290. Espy, W. *Bold New Program.* N.Y., 1950.
Discusses the Point Four Program.

4291. Gary, H. C. "The United States and Point Four Problems," *FPAR* 26 (1950–1951) 94–105.

4292. Glick, P. H. *The Administration of Technical Assistance: Growth in the Americas.* Chicago, 1957.
Analyzes United States programs as well as programs of the UN and the OAS.

4293. Gordon, W. C. "From Reciprocal Trade to Point IV," *IEA* 4 (Spring, 1951) 20–29.

4294. Hanson, S. G. "Latin America and the Point Four Program," *AAAPSS* 268 (1950) 66–74.

4294a. Joint Publications Research Service. *Bolivian Comments on U.S. Aid and Freer Trade in Latin America.* Wash., 1962.

4295. Maddox, J. G. *Technical Assistance by Religious Agencies in Latin America.* Chicago, 1956.

4296. ———, and H. R. Tolley. *Technical Cooperation in Latin America: Case Studies of Training Through Technical Cooperation: With a Statement by the NPA Special Policy Committee on Technical Cooperation.* Wash., 1957.

4297. Mosher, A. T. *Technical Cooperation in Latin-American Agriculture.* Chicago, 1957.

4298. National Planning Association. *Technical Cooperation in Latin America: Recommendations for the Future, by the NPA Special Policy Committee on Technical Cooperation.* Wash., 1956.

4299. Patterson, E. M. (ed.). "Formulating a Point Four Program," *AAAPSS* 270 (July, 1950) 1–211.

4300. Peffer, N. "The Prospect for Point Four," *VQR* 29 (1953) 369–380.

4301. Rippy, J. F. "Contributions of the U.S. Government to Latin America, Fiscal Year 1956," *IEA* 9 (Autumn, 1955) 87–96.

4302. ———. "Foreign Aid and the Problem of Non-Intervention," *IEA* 11 (Winter, 1957) 23–47.

4303. ———. "U.S. Aid to Latin America," *JIAS* 1 (1959) 83–96.

4304. ———. "U.S. Post-War Aid to Latin America: An Exhibit of Incomplete Official Accounting," *IEA* 14 (Spring, 1961) 57–65.

4305. Sanz, C. *El Plan Marshall y América-Latina.* Santiago, 1954.

4306. Sharp, W. R. *International Technical Assistance.* Chicago, 1952.

4307. Simonsen, R. "O Plano Marshall e a América Latina," *BMTIC* 13 (February, 1948) 89–99.

4308. ———. "O Plano Marshall e um Novo Criterio em Face das Relações Internacionais," *RISP* 4 (April, 1948). An unnumbered supplement.

4309. Teaf, H. M., Jr., and P. G. Franck (eds.). *Hands Across Frontiers: Case Studies in Technical Cooperation.* Ithaca, N.Y., 1955.

4310. USCH. Committee on Foreign Affairs. *Point Four, Background and Program* (81st Cong., 1st Sess.). Wash., 1949.

4311. ———. Committee on Government Operations. *United States Aid Operations in Latin America: Hearings Before a Subcommittee of the Committee on Government Operations, House of Representatives* (87th Cong., 1st Sess.). Wash., 1963.

4312. ———. ———. *United States Technical Assistance and Related Activities in Latin America: Hearings Before a Subcommittee of the Committee on Government Operations* (84th Cong., 1st Sess.). Wash., 1956.

4313. ———. Joint Economic Committee. *Economic Developments in South America: Hearings Before the Subcommittee on Inter-American Economic Relationships of the Joint Economic Committee, Congress of the United States* (87th Cong., 2d Sess.). Wash., 1962.

4314. ———. ———. *Economic Policies and Programs in South America* (87th Cong., 2d Sess.). Wash., 1962.

4315. ———. ———. *Economic Policies and Programs in Middle America: A Report . . . by Representative Martha W. Griffiths* (88th Cong., 1st Sess.). Wash., 1963.

4316. ———. ———. *Private Investment in Latin America: Report of Subcommittee on Inter-American Economic Relationships* (86th Cong., 2d Sess.). Wash., 1964.

4316a. USCS. Committee on Foreign Relations. *Development of Technical Assistance Programs: Background Information and Documents* (83d Cong., 2d Sess., Comm. Print). Wash., 1954.

4316b. ———. ———. *Study of Technical Assistance Programs* (84th Cong., 1st Sess.). Wash., 1955.

4316c. ———. ———. *Technical Assistance and Related Programs* (84th Cong., 2d Sess., S. Rept. 1956). Wash., 1956.

4316d. ———. ———. *Technical Assistance: Final Report of Committee on Foreign Relations* (85th Cong.). Wash., 1957.

4316e. ———. ———. *Technical Assistance Programs: Hearings* (84th Cong., 2d Sess.). Wash., 1956.

4316f. USDC. *Proposals to Improve Flow of U.S. Private Investment to Latin America, Report of Commerce Committee for Alliance for Progress.* Wash., 1963.

4316g. ———. Business Economics Office. *U.S. Investments in Latin American Economy:*

By Samuel Pizer and Frederick Cutler. Wash., 1957.

4317. USDS. *Point Four.* Wash., 1950.

4318. ———. *Point Four, Cooperative Program for Aid in the Development of Economically Under-Developed Areas.* Wash., 1949.

4319. ———. *The "Point Four" Program: Progress Reports.* Wash., 1949.

4319a. ———. *Protocol to Social Progress Trust Fund, Agreement Between United States and Inter-American Development Bank.* Wash., 1964.

4320. Warren, H. G. "Economic Aid for Latin America," *IEA* 5 (Spring, 1952) 92–108.

X–K–3 cross references: 3908, 3969, 3970, 3971, 5414a, 6790, 9047, 10116, 10117, 10186, 10203

4. Trade, Commerce, and Foreign Investment

4321. Acierto [pseudonym]. "The Economics of the Good Neighbor Policy: Dollar Bonds and Dollar Loans," *IEA* 4 (Autumn, 1950) 3–26; 4 (Summer, 1950) 3–34.

4322. Alexander, R. J. "Trade Policies in Latin America," *CH* 43 (August, 1962) 77–81.

4323. Arey, H. *History of Operations and Policies of Export-Import Bank of Washington.* Wash., 1953.

4324. *Aspectos Monetarios de las Economías Latinaoamericanas, 1956– .* Mexico, 1957–
Annual surveys.

4325. Auten, J. H. "Adjusted Terms of Trade for Latin America," *IEA* 13 (Spring, 1960) 3–11.

4325a. Baerresen, D. W., *et al. Latin American Trade Patterns.* Wash., 1965.

4326. Barnes, W. S., *et al. Tax Policy on U.S. Investments in Latin America: Symposium Conducted by the Tax Institute Incorporated (Now Tax Institute of America), Oct. 25–26, 1962.* Princeton, N.J., 1963.

4327. Bilbija Z., G. "American Long-Term Investment Abroad and the Export of Capital Goods: Latin American Experience, 1944–1956," U. of Chicago Diss., 1958.

4327a. Business International Corporation. *Latin America's Merging Market.* N.Y., 1964.

4328. Carson, J. S. "Latin American Foreign Trade Characteristics," *AAAPSS* 211 (1940) 155–163.

4329. Conference on Legal Problems of Trade and Investment in Latin America. *United States Trade and Investment in Latin America: Proceedings of the Conference on Legal Problems of Trade and Investment in Latin America, Held at Columbia U. School of Law, March, 1963.* N.Y., 1963.

4330. Cortes Rodrígues, H. *Las Inversiones Extranjeras en Hispanoamérica.* Madrid, 1953.

4331. Delwart, L. O. *The Future of Latin American Exports to the United States: 1965 and 1970.* Wash., 1960.

4332. Dyer, J. M. *United States–Latin American Trade and Financial Relations.* Coral Gables, Fla., 1961.

4332a. Felix, D. "United States Investment in Latin America: Problems and Prospects," *JIA* 14 (1960) 140–151.

4333. Fuentes Irurozqui, M. *El Bloque Económico Iberoamericano (Punto de Vista de un Español).* Madrid, 1953.

4334. Herrero-Beaumont, R. H. *Relaciones Comerciales Entre Hispanoamérica y América Sajona.* Madrid, 1953.

4335. Horn, P. V., and H. E. Bice. *Latin-American Trade and Economics.* N.Y., 1949.

4335a. International Economic Consultants. *United States–Latin American Relations: Commodity Problems in Latin America. A Study Prepared at the Request of the Subcommittee on American Republics Affairs of the Committee on Foreign Relations, United States Senate (86th Cong., 1st Sess.).* Wash., 1959.

4335b. Ivovich, E. "Latin America's Position in Relation to World Changes in Trade Policy," *EBLA* 7 (February, 1962) 53–72.

4336. Johnson, L. L. *The Course of U.S. Private Investment in Latin America Since the Rise of Castro.* Santa Monica, Calif., 1964.

4337. Letiche, J. M. *Reciprocal Trade Agreements in the World Economy.* N.Y., 1948.

4337a. Lower, M. D., *et al. Some Aspects of Latin American Trade Policies.* Austin, Texas, 1964.

4337b. Madden, C. H. (ed.). *Exporting to Latin America.* Bethlehem, Pa., 1963.

4338. Martin, B. L. "Problems of United States Direct Private Investment in Latin America," U. of Cincinnati Diss., 1963.

4339. Mikesell, R. F. *Foreign Investments in Latin America.* Wash., 1955.

4340. ———. *Liberalization of Inter–Latin American Trade.* Wash., 1957.

4341. ——— (ed.). *U.S. Private and Government Investment Abroad.* Eugene, Ore., 1962.

4342. Moody, W. I. *United States Trade and Investment in Latin America.* N.Y., 1963. A mimeographed work.

4343. Motten, C. G., *et al. Latin America: Development Programming and United States Investments.* Phil., 1956.

4344. PAU. *Foreign Investments in Latin America: Measure for Their Expansion.* Wash., 1954.

4345. Postweiler, R. A. "Problems Concerning the Supply and Demand for Direct U.S. Private Investment in Latin America for the Years 1957–1965," U. of Wisconsin Diss., 1959.

4346. Randle, C. L. "United States Trade with Latin America," U. of Kentucky Diss., 1947.

4347. Rippy, J. F. "Public Policy and the Foreign Investor in Latin America," *IEA* 4 (Spring, 1951) 30–36.

4348. Shearer, J. C. *High-Level Manpower in Overseas Subsidiaries: Experience in Brazil and Mexico.* Princeton, N.J., 1960.

4349. Steele, E., Jr., "Sources of Development Funds for Latin America with Reference to the Proposed Inter-American Bank for Economic Development," U. of Iowa Diss., 1957.

4350. U.N. *Foreign Capital in Latin America.* N.Y., 1955.

4351. ———. Economic Commission for Latin America. *Acontecimientos y Tendencias Recientes en el Intercambio de América Latina con la Comunidad Económica Europea: Documento Preparado por la Secretaría Ejecutiva.* Santiago, 1962.

4352. ———. ———. *Effects of United States Defense Program on Trade with Latin America.* N.Y., 1951.

4353. ———. ———. *External Financing in the Economic Development of Latin America.* Mar del Plata, Argentina, 1963.

4354. ———. ———. *Foreign Private Investment in the Latin American Free-Trade Area.* N.Y., 1961.

4355. ———. ———. *Inter-Latin American Trade: Current Problems.* N.Y., 1957.

4356. ———. ———. *Las Inversiones Privadas Extranjeras en le Zona Latinoamericana de Libre Comercio: Informe del Grupo Consultor Designado Conjuntamente por la Comisión Económica de América Latina y la Organización de los Estados Americanos.* N.Y., 1960.

4357. ———. ———. *Study of Inter–Latin American Trade.* N.Y., 1957.

4358. ———. ———. Department of Economic Affairs. Economic Commission for Latin America. *United States Capacity to Absorb Latin American Products.* Mexico, 1951.

4359. ———. Secretariat. *United States Income Taxation of Private United States Investment in Latin America: Description of the United States System and Some of Its Implications.* N.Y., 1953.

4359a. USC. Joint Economic Committee. Subcommittee on Inter-American Economic Relationships. *Private Investment in Latin America: Hearings* (88th Cong., 2d Sess.). Wash., 1964.

4359b. ———. ———. ———. *Private Investment in Latin America: Report* (88th Cong., 2d Sess.). Wash., 1964.

4359c. USCH. Committee on Ways and Means. *Foreign Trade Policy. Compendium of Papers on United States Foreign Trade Policy* (85th Cong., 1st Sess., H. Doc. 209). Wash., 1958.

4359d. USCS. *Study of Latin American Countries: Interim Report. A Study of the Operations in Latin American Countries of the Export-Import Bank and the International Bank and Their Relationship to the Expansion of International Trade* (83d Cong., 1st Sess.). Wash., 1954.

4359e. ———. Committee on Foreign Relations. *Commodity Problems in Latin America, by International Economics Consultants, Inc.* (86th Cong., 1st Sess.). Wash., 1959.

4359f. ———. ———. *United States Business and Labor in Latin America, by University of Chicago Research Center in Economic Development and Cultural Change* (86th Cong., 2d Sess.). Wash., 1960.

4359g. USDAG. Economic Research Service. *Foreign Agricultural Economics: U.S. Farm Exports Hit Record in 1960–61, Only Latin American Purchases Fall.* Wash., 1962.

4359h. ———. Foreign Agricultural Service. *New Developments Affecting Trade Among Americas, Speech Notes of Max Meyers, Administrator, Foreign Agricultural Service.* Wash., 1960.

4359i. ———. ———. *U.S. Agricultural Trade with Latin America.* Wash., 1959.

4360. USDC. *Proposals to Improve the Flow of U.S. Private Investment to Latin America.* Wash., 1963.
Report of the Commerce Committee for the Alliance for Progress.

4361. ———. *U.S. Investments in the Latin American Economy.* Wash., 1957.

4361a. ———. *United States Trade with 19 Latin American Republics, 1959–1963.* Wash., 1964.

4361b. ———. Foreign Commerce Bureau. *Trade of United States with Latin America, Annual 1956 and 1957, Quarterly April, 1957–June, 1958.* Wash., 1958.

4361c. ———. ———. *Trade of United States with Latin America, 1956, and Comparisons with 1952–1955: Prepared by Muriel S. Moore.* Wash., 1957.

4361d. ———. ———. *Trade of United States with Latin America, Years 1956–58, and Half Years July, 1957–Dec., 1958.* Wash., 1959.

4361e. ———. International Program Bureau. *Trade of U.S. with Latin America, 1959–61, and Half Years July–Dec., 1960–61.* Wash., 1962.

4361f. U.S. General Accounting Office. *Additional Interest Costs to United States Because of Premature Releases of Funds to Social Progress Trust Fund Administered by Inter-American Development Bank; Treasury Department and Agency for International Development; by Comptroller of the United States.* Wash., 1964.

4362. Urquidi, V. L. "The Montevideo Treaty: A Comment on Mr. Sumberg's Views," *IEA* 14 (Autumn, 1960) 19–27.
See item 4378.

4363. Vial Grez, A. *Comercio Exterior Latino Americano.* Santiago, 1951.

4363a. Wilkinson, J. R. *Latin America and the European Economic Community.* Denver, 1965.

X–K–4   cross references: *3408, 4058, 5414a*

5. LATIN AMERICAN COMMON MARKET

4364. Association of the Bar of the City of New York. Committee on Foreign Law. *Economic Integration in Latin America: The Central American Program of Economic Integration and the Latin American Free-Trade Association: A Report.* N.Y., 1962.

4365. Banco de México. Departmento de Investigaciones Industriales. *Información del Mercado Común y Bibliografía Preliminar Sobre Actividades Económicas de los Países Latinoamericanos.* Mexico, 1960.

4366. Campos Salas, O. "La Zona de Libre Comercio de América Latina," *CEX* 10 (March, 1960) 140–141.

4366a. Chile. Cámara de Comercio. *La Asociación Latino-Americana de Libre Comercio: Tratado de Montevideo.* Santiago, 1962.

4366b. Committee on Foreign Law. "Economic Integration in Latin America: The Central American Program of Economic Integration and the Latin American Free Trade Association: A Report by the Committee on Foreign Law," *RABNY* 17 suppl. (June, 1962).

4367. Dell, S. S. *Problemas de un Mercado Común en América Latina.* Mexico, 1959.
The author was a member of the Economic Commission for Latin America.

4367a. "El Mercado Común Latinoamericano," *CEX* 9 (May, 1959) 258–261.

4367b. "En Camino de la Integración: La Asociación Latinoamericana de Libre Comercio," *CEX* suppl. (September, 1962).

4367c. Estéves, V. R. "Desarrollo del Mercado Común Latinoamericano," *TE* 26 (July, 1959) 398–409.

4367d. Feder, E. "Some Reflections on Latin America's 'Common Market,'" *AJES* 20 (1961) 433–442.

4368. Flammang, R. A. "The Common Market Movement in Latin America," U. of Iowa Diss., 1962.

4369. *Fundamentos, Objectivos e Bases do Mercado Regional Latino-Americano.* San Salvador, 1958.

4369a. García Reynoso, P. "Dos Conferencias Sobre el Mercado Común Latinoamericano," *TE* 26 (October, 1959) 541–560.

4369b. ———. "El Mercado Común Latino Americano," *RBA* 7 (July, 1959) 284–290.

4369c. Garrido Torres, J. "The Latin-American Free Trade Zone," *JIAS* 2 (1960) 421–428.

4369d. Giffin, K. B. "The Potential Benefits of Latin American Integration," *IEA* 17 (Spring, 1964) 3–20.

4369e. Huelin, D. "A Free Trade Area in South America," *WT* 16 (February, 1960) 79–88.

4369f. Javits, J. K. "Last Chance for a Common Market," *FA* 45 (1967) 449–462.

4370. Maschke, A. Mercado Común para os Países do Continente Americano," *RCNE* 5 (November, 1956) 48–53.

4371. Massad, C., and J. Strasma. *La Zona de Libre Comercio en América Latina: Algunos Problemas por Resolver.* Santiago, 1961.

4371a. "Mercado Común Latinoamericano: Recomendaciones Sobre Estructuras y Normas," *MV* 19, no. 9 (1959) 97–98.

4371b. Pimienta, I. "Posibilidades Actuales para un Mercado Común Latinoamericana," *CLEH* 4, no. 10 (1961) 43–70.

4372. Plaza Lasso, G. "For a Regional Market in Latin America," *FA* 37 (1959) 607–616.

4372a. Prebisch, R. "El Mercado Común Latinoamericano," *CEX* 9 (September, 1959) 509–513.

4373. ———. "Joint Responsibilities for Latin American Progress," *FA* 39 (1964) 622–633.

4373a. "Proyecto de Acuerdo de Zona de Libre Comercio en la Parte Meridional de América Latina," *CEX* 9 (May, 1959) 262–265.

4374. Rizzuto, F. A., Jr. *Necesidad e Idea del Mercado Común Latinoamericano: Disertación.* B.A., 1961.

4375. Sedwitz, W. J. "A Common Market for Latin America?" *CH* 43 (July, 1962) 1–10.

4376. Serpulanda, E. A., Jr. "The Contribution of the Latin American Free Trade Association to Latin American Welfare: A Preliminary Survey Applying the Theory of Economic Integration," U. of Texas Diss., 1964.

4376a. Shonfield, A. "Latin American Integration: A New Phase," *WT* 21 (1965) 460–469.

4377. Sostin Weinstein, N. *El Mercado Común Latinoamericano.* Santiago, 1961.

4378. Sumberg, T. A. "Free Trade Zone in Latin America," *IEA* 14 (Summer, 1960) 51–64.

4379. Torres, J. G. "Porque um Mercado Regional Latino-Americano?" *RBPI* 1 (June, 1958) 74–121.

4379a. "Tres Conferencias Sobre Mercado Común Latinoamericano," *CEX* 9 (November, 1959) 641–652.

4380. UN. Economic Commission for Latin America. *The Latin American Common Market.* N.Y., 1959.

4381. United States Tariff Commission. *The Latin American Free Trade Association.* Wash., 1962.

4382. Urquidi, V. L. *Trayectoria del Mercado Común Latino-Americano.* Mexico, 1960. English ed., *Free Trade and Economic Integration in Latin America: The Evolution of a Common Market Policy.* Berkeley, Calif., 1962.

4382a. Valencia, L. E. "Mercado Común Democrático," *COMB* 10 (May, 1960) 7–17.

4383. Wehner, F. *Die Lateinamerikanische Freihandelsvereinigung.* Hamburg, 1965.

4384. Wionczek, M. S. "Latin American Free Trade Association," *IC*, no. 551 (1965).

4384a. ——— (ed.). *Latin American Economic Integration.* N.Y., 1966.

X–K–5 cross references: 4223, 4229, 4233b, 4242, 4354, 4355, 4356, 4357, 5438, 6764, 6766, 6770, 6775, 6785, 6789, 6790, 6797, 6798, 6799, 9021

Chapter XI   The New Pan Americanism Since 1889

A. GENERAL ACCOUNTS AND INTERPRETATIONS

4385. Abadia Valencia, M. *La Sociedad de las Naciones de América*. Bogotá, 1947.

4386. Alba, P. de. *Breve Reseña Histórica del Movimiento Panamericanista*. Mexico, 1940.

A summary treatment.

4387. ————. *De Bolívar a Roosevelt: Democracia y Unidad de América*. Mexico, 1949.

4388. Alfaro, R. J. "A Half Century of Pan Americanism," *BPAU* 74 (1940) 214–231.

4389. ————. *Panorama Internacional de América*. Cambridge, Mass., 1938.

4390. ————. "Toward an American Association of Nations," *QJIR* 1 (1939) 25–36.

4391. Alvarado Garaicoa, T. *La Trascendencia de las Reuniones Interamericanas*. Guayaquil, 1949.

A study of Pan American conferences from the 1920's until the time of publication.

4392. Alvarez, A. *El Derecho Internacional del Porvenir*. Madrid, 1917.

4392a. ————. "La Panaméricanisme et la Politíque Internationale de l'Amérique," *RG* (March, 1923) 257–282.

English ed., *IA* 7 (December, 1923) 69–88.

4393. Amados, M. *Por una Convivencia Internacional*. B.A., 1954.

4394. "An Appraisal of the Inter-American System: A Symposium," *IEA* 2, no. 4 (1949) 45–95.

4395. Antiasov, M. V. *Sovremennyi Panamerikanizm: Proiskhozhdenie i Sushchnast' Doktrin Panamerikanskoi Solidarnosti*. Moscow, 1960.

Present-day Pan Americanism: The

Origin and Nature of the Doctrine of Pan American Solidarity.

4396. Ball, M. M. *The Problem of Inter-American Organization*. Stanford, Calif., 1944.

4397. Barros Hurtado, C. *América: Penurias de su Libertad*. B.A., 1950.

A series of essays.

4398. Berner, H. *Die Panamerikanischen Friedenssicherungsverträge*. Berlin, 1938.

Although the author begins with a discussion of the old Pan Americanism, his chief concern is the fifteen-year period prior to publication.

4399. Bernstein, H. *Making an Inter-American Mind*. Gainesville, Fla., 1961.

4400. Blanco, J. E. "Razonamientos Sobre el Panamericanismo," *RMA* (March, 1945) 209–290.

4401. Brum, B. *The Peace of America*. Montevideo, 1924.

4402. Büchi, R. *Die Geschichte der Panamerikanischen Bewegung*. Breslau, 1914.

4403. Burr, R. N., and R. D. Hussey (eds.). *Documents on Inter-American Cooperation*. 2 vols., Phil., 1955.

Reprints sixty-eight documents for the period 1810–1948.

4404. Caicedo Castilla, J. J. *El Panamericanismo*. B.A., 1961.

A scholarly study by a prominent Colombian internationalist.

4405. Carbonell, N. *Las Conferencias Internacionales Americanas*. Havana, 1928.

4406. Casey, C. B. "The Disposition of Political Proposals by the Various Pan American Conferences, 1889–1928," U. of Texas Diss., 1931.

4407. Castillo, A. del. *Antecedentes del Panamericanismo: Panamá, del Congreso de 1826 a la Reunión de Presidentes Americanos, 1956*. Bogotá, 1956.

4408. Chaumette, M. *Considérations Historiques*

sur l'Ideal Pan-Américain. Port-au-Prince, 1937.

4408a. Cline, H. F. "The Inter-American System," *CH* 28 (1955) 177–184.

4409. Corominas, E. V. *Historia de las Conferencias Interamericanas: Desde el Congreso de Panamá Hasta la Conferencia Interamericana de Caracas en 1954.* B.A., 1959.

4410. Cronin, W. F. "Some Basic Concepts of Inter-American Organization," Harvard U. Diss. (2 vols.), 1949.

4411. Cruchaga Tocornal, M. "Las Conferencias Pan-Americanas," *RCHG* 11 (June, 1927) 7–26.

4412. ———. "Les Conferences Panaméricaines, de 1889 à 1928: Le Bilan des Faits et Resultats," *RGDIP*, 3d ser., 3 (1929) 88–107.

4413. Cuevas Cancino, F. M. *Del Congreso de Panamá a la Conferencia de Caracas, 1826–1954: El Genio de Bolívar a Través de la Historia de las Relaciones Interamericanas.* 2 vols., Caracas, 1955.

4414. Dunker, H. J. *Die Interamerikanischen Beziehungen und der Gedanke der Gleichberechtigten Partnerschaft.* Hamburg, 1957.

4415. Dupuy, R. J. *Le Nouveau Panaméricanisme: L'Evolution de Système Inter-Américain vers le Fédéralisme.* Paris, 1956.

4416. Facio, G. J. "Impulso Democrático al Sistema Interamericano," *COMB* 2 (May, 1960) 48–56.

4417. Fenwick, C. G. *The Inter-American Regional System.* N.Y., 1949.
Three lectures stressing history of the movement, legal status, and the relationship of the system to the world organization.

4418. ———. "The Inter-American Regional System," *JIA* 9 (1955) 93–100.

4419. ———. "The Inter-American Regional System: Seventy-Five Years of Progress," *IRB* 15 (1965) 319–323.

4420. Fernández y Medina, B. *La Política Internacional en América (Pasado—Presente—Futuro).* Valladolid, Spain, 1928.
Uruguayan opposes continuation of the system.

4421. Ferrara, O. *El Panamericanismo y la Opinión Europea.* Paris, 1930.

4422. Fessen, F. "Die Ökonomische Grundlage der Panamerikanischen Idee," *SY* 52, no. 5 (1928) 79–112.

4423. Finlayson, C. "Confederation of the Americas," *COM* 38 (1943) 339–341.

4424. Frei, E. "Tendências e Perspectivas Interamericanas," *RBPI* 2 (March, 1959) 5–19.
By the Christian Democratic President of Chile.

4425. Fried, A. H. *Pan-Amerika: Entwicklung, Umfang und Bedeutung der Zwischenstaatlichen Organisation in Amerika (1810–1916).* 2d ed., Zurich, 1918.

4426. Gallardo Nieto, G. *Panamericanismo.* Santiago, 1941.
A collection of newspaper articles spanning a thirty-year period.

4427. Gálvez Sarmiento, L. A. *Education for Inter-Americanism.* Notre Dame, Ind., 1950.

4428. García, J. C. "La Evolución del Panamericanismo," *ED* (April, 1940) 125–139.

4429. García Calderón, F. "El Panamericanismo: Su Pasado y su Porvenir," *CC* 12 (1916) 126–178.
Expounds the thesis that the United States has used the inter-American system for its own selfish reasons.

4430. Godoy, J. F. *Las Conferencias Panamericanas: Breve Reseña de los Trabajos y Resultados de la Primera, Segunda, Tercera, Cuarta, y Quinta Conferencias Panamericanas y Preparativos para la Sexta.* Mexico, 1927.

4431. Gómez Robledo, A. *Idea y Experiencia de América.* Mexico, 1948.
Emphasizes intellectual history of the American idea.

4432. Gómez Ruiz, L. E. "Del Congreso de Panamá a la Conferencia de Caracas, 1826–1953," *RSB* 12, no. 35 (July, 1952) 131–140.

4433. Green, P. L. *Pan American Progress.* N.Y., 1942.

4434. Guani, A. *La Solidarité Internationale dans l'Amérique Latine.* Paris, 1926.

4435. Hernández Solís, L. "El Pan-Americanismo," *BACPS* 10 (January, 1945) 35–98.

4436. ———. *El Panamericanismo, Una Moderna Interpretación.* Mexico, 1944.

4437. Hiller, H. E. "The Development of an Inter-American Peace System," U. of Minnesota Diss., 1962.

4438. Howard, J. A., Jr. "The Public Inter-American Conferences, 1889–1939," U. of S. Calif. Diss., 1939.

4439. Inman, S. G. *Inter-American Conferences, 1826–1954: History and Problems*. Wash., 1965.

A conference by conference examination.

4440. ———. "Pan American Conferences and Their Results," *SPSQ* 4 (1923) 238–266.

4441. ———. *Problems in Pan Americanism*. New ed., N.Y., 1925.

4442. Johannesson, F. *Det Panamerikanska Problemet, 1826–1920, en Studie i Modern Politik*. Norrköping, 1922.

4443. Kelchner, W. *Department of State List of Inter-American Conferences, 1826–1933: Chronological and Classified List, Prepared by Warren Kelchner*. Wash., 1933.

4444. Latorre y Setién, G. *El Panamericanismo y el Porvenir de la América Española*. Madrid, 1924.

4445. Linares Fleytas, A. "Nacimiento y Desarrollo del Panamericanismo," *PA* 1 (November, 1946) 49–57.

4446. Lleras Camargo, A. *El Sistema Regional Americano*. Bogotá, 1947.

4447. Lockey, J. B. *Essays in Pan-Americanism*. Berkeley, Calif., 1939.

Nine essays treating the history of the movement.

4447a. ———. "Pan-Americanism and Imperialism," *AJIL* 32 (1938) 233–243.

4448. Manger, W. "The Evolution of International American Conferences," *BPAU* 67 (1933) 769–780.

4449. ———. *Inter-American Highlights, 1890–1940*. Wash., 1940.

4450. Martínez, R. A. *De Bolívar a Dulles: El Panamericanismo: Doctrina y Práctica Imperialista*. Mexico, 1959.

Indictment of United States domination of the hemisphere through the inter-American system.

4451. Mecham, J. L. *The United States and Inter-American Security, 1889–1960*. Austin, Texas, 1961.

4452. Mello, A. de Toledo Bandeira. *O Espírito do Pan-Americanismo*. Rio, 1956.

4453. Miller, C. G. *Un Estado Federal Interamericano*. Mexico, 1952.

4454. Moreno Quintana, L. M. *El Sistema Internacional Americano*. 2 vols., B.A., 1925–1926.

4455. ———. "Pan Americanism and the Pan American Conferences," *IA* 8 (1925) 429–444.

4455a. Navarro Andrade, U. *Unión de las Naciones Americanas: La Política del Buen Vecino Sustituye la Doctrina Monroe por el Panamericanismo de Bolívar*. Quito, 1949.

4456. Nuermberger, G. A. "Multilateral Diplomacy Among the American States: The Conference and Congress Phase, 1826–1906," Duke U. Diss., 1935.

4457. Ordóñez Fetzer, M. T. *Panamericanismo*. Guatemala, 1943.

4458. Orlando, A. *Pan-Americanismo*. Rio, 1906.

4459. Padilla, E. "The Meaning of Pan-Americanism," *FA* 32 (1954) 270–281.

4460. *PAU. The Basic Principles of the Inter-American System*. Wash., 1943.

4461. ———. *Conferencias Internacionales Americanas, 1889–1936*. Wash., 1938.

4462. ———. *Conferencias Internacionales Americanas, Primer Suplemento, 1938–1942*. Wash., 1943.

4463. ———. *Conferencias Internacionales Americanas, Segundo Suplemento, 1945–1954*. Wash., 1956.

4464. ———. *Historical Evolution of Inter-American Cooperation*. Wash., 1942.

4465. ———. *The Inter-American System*. Wash., 1947.

4466. ———. *The Inter-American System: Its Evolution and Role Today*. Wash., 1963.

4467. ———. *Pan Americanism: Its Meaning and Significance*. 2 vols., Wash., 1933.

4467a. ———. Department of International Law. *Manual of Inter-American Relations*. Rev. ed., Wash., 1956.

4468. Pépin, E. *La Panaméricanisme*. Paris, 1938.

4469. Pezet, F. A. *Pan-American Cooperation in Pan-American Affairs*. Baltimore, 1917.

4470. Planas-Suárez, S. *Cuestiones Internacionales y Políticas*. B.A., 1962.

4471. ———. *Política Internacional y Panamericanismo Ideal*. B.A., 1959.

4472. ———. *La Solidaridad Americana:*

Historia y Crítica de la Epoca Presente.
Caracas, 1945.

4473. Quesada, E. "La Evolución del Pan-americanismo," *R* 41 (1919) 289–358.

4474. Quintanilla, L. *Pan Americanism and Democracy.* Boston, 1952.
Spanish ed., Mexico, 1952.

4475. Richarz-Simons, I. "Chronik der Inter-amerikanischen Rechtsbeziehungen," *IAA* 4 (1931) 544–557.

4476. Río, P. del. *Lo que Deber Ser el Pan-americanismo: El Continente ante la Guerra y su Organización para la Paz.* Havana, 1942.

4477. Rippy, J. F. "The Significance of the Pan-American Movement," *SAQ* 30 (1931) 280–289.

4478. Robertson de Otayza, E. M. *Organismos Internacionales: La Evolución Histórica de las Relaciones Interamericanas: Aspecto Histórico, Objectivos, Estructura y Funcionamiento de los Grandes Organismos Internacionales.* Lima, 1958.

4479. Sansón-Terán, J. *El Interamericanismo en Marcha: De Bolívar y Monroe al Roosevelt-ianismo.* Wash., 1949.
An historical analysis containing documentary extracts.

4480. Scott, J. B. "The Ideals of Pan-Americanism," *WA* 98 (1935) 87–91.

4481. ——— (ed.). *The International Conferences of American States, 1889–1928: A Collection of the Conventions, Recommendations, Resolutions, Reports, and Motions Adopted by the First Six International Conferences of the American States, and Documents Relating to the Organization of the Conferences.* N.Y., 1931.
Special ed., Wash., 1938.

4482. ———. *The International Conferences of American States: First Supplement, 1933–1940.* Wash., 1940.

4483. Simkins, F. B. "Latin-American Opinion of Pan-Americanism," *SAQ* 22 (1923) 216–227.

4484. Smith, A. C. "The Bases of International Organization in the Americas," U. of Minnesota Diss., 1945.

4485. Stanford, H. K. "The Need for an Inter-American Approach," *JIAS* 7 (1965) 1–4.

4486. Tannenbaum, F. "An American Com-

monwealth of Nations," *FA* 22 (1944) 577–588.

4487. Torres Bodet, J. "Trayectoria Histórica del Panamericanismo Desde Panamá (1826) Hasta Bogotá (1948)," *Y* (January, 1948) 85–94.

4488. Travis, M. B. "Evolution of the Inter-American Peace Structure," U. of Chicago Diss., 1948.

4489. Turlington, E. "The General Principles of Inter-American Organization," *PEASC* 10 (1943) 149–152.

4490. Ulloa, A. "Principios Generales de Organización Interamericana: Nueva Organización de la Unión Panamericana," *PEASC* 10 (1943) 141–147.

4491. Uribe Vargas, D. *Panamericanismo Democrático: Bases para una Transformación del Sistema Continental.* Bogotá, 1958.

4492. Urquidi, J. M. "El Panamericanismo: Sus Bases, Principios y Fines: Cómo Cabe Conceptuarlo y que Debe Esperarse de El," *PEASC* 10 (1943) 161–173.

4493. Urrutia, F. J. *Les Conférences Pan-Américaines.* Paris, 1924.
Summary of the conferences until time of publication.

4494. USDS. *Our Southern Partners, Story of Inter-American Cooperation.* Wash., 1962.

4495. ———. *Sovereignty and Independence in the New World: Comments on the Inter-American System.* Wash., 1948.

4496. Viallate, A. "Les Etats-Unis et le Pan-américanisme," *RDM* 51, 5th ser. (1909) 419–445.

4497. "What the Latin American Republics Think of the Pan-American Conferences," *NG* 27 (1906) 474–479.

4498. Whitaker, A. P. *Development of American Regionalism.* N.Y., 1951.

4499. ———. *The Western Hemisphere Idea: Its Rise and Decline.* Ithaca, N.Y., 1954.
Pb. ed., 1965.

4500. Wilgus, A. C. "Pan-Americanism: Its Origin and Development," *PAM* 44 (1931) 252–259.

4501. Woods, K. F. "Samuel Guy Inman—His Role in the Evolution of Inter-American Cooperation," American U. Diss., 1962.

4502. Wyatt, D. D. "The Development of the Concept of Americanism, 1885–1910," Stanford U. Diss., 1936.

4503. Yepes, J. M. *Del Congreso de Panamá a la Conferencia de Caracas, 1826–1954: El Genio de Bolívar a Través de la Historia de las Relaciones Interamericanas.* 2 vols., Caracas, 1955.

4504. ———. *Estudios Internacionales.* Bogotá, 1929.

4505. ———. *Le Panaméricainisme au Point de Vue Historique, Juridique et Politique.* Paris, 1936.

4506. ———. *La Solidarité Continentale Américaine: Ses Origines et Son Avenir.* Brussels, 1936.

XI–A   cross references: 1416, 1596, 1600, 1614, 1743, 3056, 3186, 3488, 3509, 3537, 3789, 3957, 4884, 5501, 9659

B. THE INTER-AMERICAN SYSTEM AND THE MONROE DOCTRINE

4507. Alvarez, A. "The New Monroe Doctrine and American Public Law," *MLR* 2 (1918) 357–366.

4508. Bailey, T. A. "A Multilateral Monroe Doctrine," *PIWA* 15 (1938) 474–476.

4509. Calderón, I. "The Pan-American Union and the Monroe Doctrine," *JIR* 10 (1919) 133–137.

4510. Castle, W. R., Jr. "The Monroe Doctrine and Pan Americanism," *AAAPSS* 204 (1939) 111–118.

4511. Estrada, G. *La Doctrina de Monroe y el Fracaso de una Conferencia Panamericana en México.* Mexico, 1937.

    Deals with abortive conference of 1896 called by President Alfaro of Ecuador.

4512. Fenwick, C. G. "The Monroe Doctrine and the Declaration of Lima," *AJIL* 3 (1939) 257–268.

4513. Klein, J. "The Monroe Doctrine as a Regional Understanding," *BPAU* 52 (1921) 139–144.

4514. Lima, M. de Oliveira. *Pan-Americanismo (Monroe–Bolívar–Roosevelt).* Rio, 1907.

4515. López, J. "Monroísmo y Pan-Americanismo," *CC* 10 (1916) 329–343.

4516. Reno, W. L. "The Monroe Doctrine in Inter-American Diplomatic Relations," U. of California Diss., 1935.

4517. Tardieu, A. "La Doctrine de Monroë et le Panaméricanisme," in *Les Questions Actuelles de Politique Etrangère dans l'Amérique du Nord.* Paris, 1911.

4518. Teyssaire, J. "La Doctrine de Monroë et le Pan-Américanisme," *RPP* 137 (1928) 87–100.

4519. Yepes, J. M. *La Véritable Doctrine de Monroe et les Conséquences de la Conférence de Buenos-Ayres.* Paris, 1937.

XI–B   cross references: 4942, 5028

C. INTER-AMERICAN JURISPRUDENCE

1. GENERAL WORKS

4520. Albertini, L. E. *Derecho Diplomático en sus Aplicaciones Especiales a las Repúblicas Americanas.* 2d ed., Paris, 1909.

4521. Alvarez, A. *Le Droit International Américain, son Fondement: Sa Nature d'après l'Histoire Diplomatique des Etats du Nouveau Monde et Leur Vie Politique et Economique.* Paris, 1910.

4522. ———. "Latin America and International Law," *AJIL* 3 (1909) 269–354.

4523. Antokoletz, D. *Tratado de Derecho Internacional Público en Tiempo de Paz.* 2 vols., B.A., 1924–1925.

4524. Bustamante y Sirvén, A. S. de. "America and International Law," *BPAU* 68 (1934) 158–165.

4525. Carlos, G. *Derecho Internacional Teórico y Práctico de Europa y América.* 2 vols., Paris, 1868.

4526. Ceretti, C. *Panamericanesimo e Diritto Internazionale.* Milan, 1939.

4527. Chavarri, A. *Derecho Civil Internacional Argentino.* B.A., 1935.

4528. Cock Arango, A. *Derecho Internacional Americano.* Bogotá, 1948.

4529. Cruchaga Tocornal, M. *Nociones de Derecho Internacional.* Santiago, 1902.

4530. DeVries, H. P., and J. Rodríguez-Novas. *The Law of the Americas: An Introduction to the Legal System of the American Republics.* N.Y., 1965.

4531. Drago, L. M. *Discursos y Escritos.* 3 vols., B.A., 1938.

4532. Eder, P. J. *A Comparative Survey of Anglo-American and Latin-American Law.* N.Y., 1950.

    Includes ninety pages of bibliography.

4533. Fugger Kirchberg-Weissenhorn, C. *Der Panamerikanismus und das Amerikanische Völkerrecht.* Munich, 1931.

4534. Gallardo, R. *Estudios de Derecho Constitucional Americano Comparado.* Madrid, 1961.

4535. Garland, A. *Derecho Internacional Americano: Los Conflictos Sud Americanos en Relación con los Estados Unidos.* 2 vols., B.A., 1914.

4536. Gottberg, O. von. *Die Entwicklung Eines Amerikanischen Völkerrechts: Beiträge zur Geschichte der Panamerikanischen Bewegung.* Königsberg, Germany, 1928.

4537. Henríquez, H. *Origen y Evolución del Derecho Internacional Americano.* Cd. Trujillo, 1948.

4538. Inter-American Juridical Committee. *Contribución del Continente Americano a los Principios del Derecho Internacional que Rigen la Responsabilidad del Estado.* Wash., 1962.

4539. Jacobini, H. B. *A Study of the Philosophy of International Law as Seen in the Works of Latin-American Writers.* The Hague, 1954.

4540. Korovin, E. A. (ed.). *Voprosy Mezhdunarodnogo Prva i Teorii i Praktike SShA.* Moscow, 1957.
Problems of International Law in Theory and Practice in the U.S.A.

4541. Kunz, J. L. *Latin-American Philosophy of Law in the Twentieth Century.* N.Y., 1950.

4542. Meyer-Lindenberg, H. *El Procedimiento Interamericano para Consolidar la Paz.* Bogotá, 1941.

4543. Parraguez Acevedo, R. *Aspectos Jurídicos del Antiguo y del Nuevo Panamericanismo.* Santiago, 1947.

4544. Planas-Suárez, S. *Estudios de Derecho Internacional: Las Intervenciones, Reclamaciones de Extranjeros, Denegación de Justicia, el Recurso Diplomático, Nacionalidad y Naturalización.* B.A., 1959.

4545. Pradier-Foderé, P. *Traité de Droit International Public, Européen et Américain.* 7 vols., Paris, 1885–1894.

4546. Puig, J. C. *Les Principes du Droit International Public Américain.* Paris, 1954.

4547. Recaséns Siches, L., *et al. Latin-American Legal Philosophy.* Cambridge, Mass., 1948.

4548. Ronning, C. N. *Law and Politics in Inter-American Diplomacy.* N.Y., 1963.

4549. Seijas, R. F. *El Derecho Internacional Hispano-Americano, Público y Privado.* 6 vols., Caracas, 1884–1885.

4550. Urrutia, F. J. *Un Comentario a la Declaración de los Derechos de las Naciones Hecha por el Instituto del Derecho Internacional Americano, Edición Oficial.* Bogotá, 1917.

4551. ——. *Le Continent Américain et le Droit International.* Paris, 1928.

4552. Valladão, H. *Démocratisation et Socialisation du Droit International: L'Impact Latino-Américain et Afro-Asiatique.* Paris, 1962.

4553. Vance, J. T. *The Background of Hispanic-American Law.* Wash., 1937.

4554. Yepes, J. M. *El Panamericanismo y el Derecho Internacional.* Bogotá, 1930.

4555. ——. *La Contribution de l'Amérique Latine au Développement du Droit International Public et Privé.* Paris, 1931.

4556. ——. *Philosophie du Panaméricanisme et Organisation de la Paix: Le Droit Panaméricain.* Neuchâtel, Switzerland, 1945.

XI–C–1   cross references: 3298, 5323

2. RECOGNITION

4557. Bollini Shaw, C. *El Reconocimiento en el Derecho Internacional Público.* B.A., 1936.

4558. Fenwick, C. G. "Recognition of *de facto* Governments: Is There a Basis for Inter-American Collective Action?" *AJIL* 58 (1964) 109–113.

4559. Gutiérrez, A. O. *La Doctrina de Noreconocimiento de la Conquista en América.* Rio, 1938.

4560. Hervey, J. G. *The Legal Aspects of Recognition in International Law as Interpreted by the Courts of the United States.* Phil., 1928.

4561. Kahle, L. G. "Deviations from the *de facto* Principle in the Latin-American Recognition Policy of the U.S.," U. of Texas Diss., 1951.

4562. Latrille Urriola, F. *El Reconocimiento de los Gobiernos de Facto como Institución Jurídica y su Evolución en América.* Santiago, 1947.

4563. Lauterpacht, H. *Recognition in International Law.* Cambridge, Mass., 1947.

4564. Neumann, W. L. *Recognition of Governments in the Americas*. Wash., 1947.

4565. PAU. *Conocimiento y Desconocimiento de América*. 2d ed., Wash., 1958.

XI–C–2   cross references: 1579, 1586, 1590, 3304, 4812, 5539, 6168, 6707, 6754, 7108, 7223b, 7224, 7241, 8946b.

3. EXILE AND ASYLUM

4566. *El Asilado "Silencioso": Antología del Caso Haya de la Torre*. Mexico, 1954.
   A collection of articles treating the famous case of Victor Raúl Haya de la Torre.

4567. Caldwell, R. G. "Exile as an Institution," *PSQ* 58 (1943) 239–262.

4568. Castillo y Bahena, R. del. *El Asilo Diplomático*. Mexico, 1951.

4569. Colombia. Ministerio de Relaciones Exteriores. *Documentos Relativos al Asilo del Sr. Victor R. Haya de la Torre en la Embajada de Colombia en Lima*. Bogotá, 1950.

4570. ———. ———. *La Opinión Americana y el Derecho de Asilo: Plebiscito Internacional en Favor de las Tesis Colombianas: Suplemento a "Noticias de Colombia."* Bogotá, 1951.

4571. Evans, A. E. "The Colombian-Peruvian Asylum Case: The Practice of Diplomatic Asylum," *APSR* 46 (1952) 142–157.

4572. Inter-American Juridical Committee. *Novos Artigos Sobre Asilo Diplomático*. Wash., 1960.

4573. Luque Angel, E. *El Derecho de Asilo*. Bogotá, 1959.

4574. Moreno Quintana, L. M. *Derecho de Asilo*. B.A., 1952.

4575. Muñoz, M. del V. *El Derecho de Asilo Eclesiástico en el Reino de Chile*. Santiago, 1952(?).

4576. Parra, F. J. *El Derecho de Asilo*. Lima, 1936.

4577. Planas-Suárez, S. *El Asilo Diplomático*. B.A., 1953.

4578. Plaza Martínez, J. J. *El Asilo Diplomático*. Mexico, 1952.

4579. Ronning, C. N. "The Legal Status of the Institution of Diplomatic Asylum in Latin America as Determined by Practice and Conventions," U. of Minnesota Diss., 1958.

4580. Torres García, F. *El Asilo ante el Derecho Internacional Americano*. Mexico, 1955.

4581. Ungerer, W. *Das Diplomatische Asyl in Deutschen Vertretungen Lateinamerikas*. Hamburg, 1955.

4582. Urrutia Aparicio, C. *Diplomatic Asylum in Latin America*. Guatemala, 1960.

4583. Ursúa, F. A. *El Asilo Diplomático*. Mexico, 1952.
   Discusses the decision of the International Court of Justice in the Haya de la Torre case.

4584. Viteri Lafronte, H. "El Asilo y el Caso Haya de la Torre," *CCE* 4 (January–December, 1951) 47–121.

4585. Zárate, L. C. *El Asilo en el Derecho Internacional Americano: Con un Apéndice de la Corte Internacional de Justicia y de Anexos de la Cancillería de Colombia*. Bogotá, 1957.

XI–C–3   cross references: 8125

4. CODIFICATION OF INTERNATIONAL LAW

4586. Alvarez, A. *La Codificación del Derecho Internacional en América: Trabajos de la Tercera Comisión de la Asamblea de Jurisconsultos Reunida en Santiago de Chile*. Santiago, 1925.

4587. ———. *Considérationes Générales sur la Codification du Droit International: Mémorial Presenté a la 2ème Commission de Juristes Réunié a Rio de Janeiro le 18 Avril 1927*. Rio, 1927.

4588. ———. *Le Continent Américain et la Codification du Droit International: Une Nouvelle "Ecole" du Droit des Gens*. Paris, 1938.

4589. Bishop, C. M. *Legal Codes of the Latin American Republics*. Wash., 1942.

4590. Eça, R. d'. "The Codification of International Law in the Americas," *WA* 98 (1935) 94–101.

4591. Maúrtua, V. M. *Páginas Diplomáticas: I. La Codificación Americana del Derecho Internacional*. Lima, 1940.

4592. Octavio, R. "L'Amérique et la Codification du Droit International Privé," *RDISDP* 4 (1930) 492–521.

4593. Scott, J. B. "The Gradual and Progressive Codification of International Law," *BPAU* 61 (1927) 849–870.

4594. Yepes, J. M. *La Codificación del Derecho Internacional Americano*. Bogotá, 1927.

XI–C–4   cross references: 4958

5. INTERVENTION AND NONINTERVENTION

4595. Aguirre, E., and F. Harris. *La no Intervención y la Quiebra de la Soberanía Nacional*. Mexico, 1946.

4596. Alvarado Garaicoa, T. *Los Principios Internacionales de no Intervención y Autodeterminación*. The Hague, 1962.

4597. Arangua Rivas, C. J. *La Intervención: Doctrinas de Monroe, Drago y Tobar*. Santiago, 1952.

4597a. Arroyo Rivera, A. *La No-Intervención en el Derecho Internacional Americano*. Mexico, 1952.

4598. Baldwin, E. F. "Three South Americans and Their Doctrines," *O* 87 (1907) 118–123.
    Concerns Triana, Barbosa, and Drago.

4599. Ball, M. M. "Issue for the Americas: Nonintervention vs. Human Rights and the Preservation of Democratic Institutions," *IO* 15 (Winter, 1961) 21–37.

4600. Bowen, H. W. "Monroe, Calvo, and Drago Doctrines," *IN* 42 (1907) 902–904.

4601. Bream, C. G. "Intervention Short of Armed Force in Latin America," U. of Chicago Diss., 1942.

4602. Bustamante y Sirvén, A. S. de, and C. de la Torriente. "Opiniones Sobre la Intervención-Colectiva," *RDLH* 7 (December, 1945) 308–310.

4603. Bustos García, R. *Nociones Sobre la Intervención*. Santiago, 1944.

4604. Cuyer, R. E. "Consideraciones Sobre la Doctrina Rodríguez Larreta," *RADI* 10 (May, 1947) 121–150.

4605. Díaz Doin, G. "La Organización de Estados Americanos y la no Intervención," *CA* 19 (May, 1960) 73–88.

4606. Drago, L. M. *Cobro Coercitivo de Deudas Públicas*. B.A., 1906.

4607. ———. "State Loans in Their Relation to International Law," *AJIL* 1 (1907) 692–726.

4608. "El Principio de no Intervención y la Nota Uruguaya," *PA* 1 (February, 1946) 7–14.

4609. Fabela, I. *Intervención*. Mexico, 1959.

4610. Feller, A. H. "Some Observations on the Calvo Clause," *AJIL* 5 (1933) 461–468.

4611. Fenn, P. "México, la no Intervención y la Autodeterminación en el Caso de Cuba," *FI* 4 (1963) 1–19.

4612. Fernández Larraín, S. "América y el Principio de no Intervención," *REP* 18 (1947) 89–128.

4613. García Santos, R. *La Doctrina Drago*. Mexico, 1948.

4614. Gómez Valle, S. *La no Intervención en los Estados Americanos*. Mexico, 1949.

4614a. Guerra Iñiguez, D. "El Principio de la no Intervención en América," *RFD* 14 (February, 1958) 9–40.

4615. Guillén Atienza, L. *El Principio Internacional de no Intervención y las Doctrinas Americanas*. Santiago, 1949.

4615a. Gutiérrez, C. J. "Neutralidad e Intervención," *RUCR* 14 (November, 1956) 9–61.

4616. Guzmán Carrasco, M. A. *No Intervención y Protección Internacional de los Derechos Humanos*. Quito, 1963.

4617. Guzmán Vial, M. *La Intervención y la no Intervención, Planteamiento Doctrinario*. Santiago, 1948.

4618. Herrera Soto, R. "La Doctrina Drago: En Pos de la Paz," *B* (September, 1952) 495–520.

4619. Hershey, A. S. "Calvo and Drago Doctrines," *AJIL* 1 (1907) 26–45.

4620. Hodges, H. G. *The Doctrine of Intervention*. Princeton, N.J., 1915.

4621. Jiménez y Núñez, V. *La Doctrina Drago y la Política Internacional*. Madrid, 1927.

4622. Kennedy, C. "The Drago Doctrine," *NAR* 185 (1907) 614–622.

4623. ———. "Forcible Collection of Contract Debts," *ASILP* 1 (1908) 100–122.

4624. León de Elías, A. *El Principio de la no Intervención y su Influencia en el Desarrollo del Derecho Internacional Americano*. Mexico, 1946.

4625. Lépervanche Parparcén, R. *Intervencionismo: Dos Cartas Sobre la "Doctrina Betancourt" o Doctrina Tobar Revivida*. Caracas, 1963.

4626. López Jiménez, R. *El Principio de no Intervención en América y la Nota Uruguaya*. B.A., 1947.
    A heavily documented study.

4627. Moreno Rodríguez, R. *La Doctrina*

Drago y sus Proyecciones en la Vida Internacional. Córdoba, Argentina, 1960.

4628. Moulin, H. A. *La Doctrine de Drago.* Paris, 1908.

4629. Nettles, H. E. "The Drago Doctrine in International Law and Politics," *HAHR* 8 (1928) 204–223.

4630. Pérez Triana, S. *La Doctrina Drago: Colección de Documentos.* London, 1908.

4631. Roa González, L. *La Doctrina Estrada.* Mexico, 1952.

4631a. Rodríguez Larreta, E. "El Derecho a la Intervención Colectiva," *COMB* 2 (July, 1959) 23–26.

4632. Ronning, C. N. "Intervention, International Law, and the Inter-American System," *JIAS* 3 (1961) 249–271.
Surveys the period 1928–1960.

4633. Ruda Villarreal, I. A. *La no Intervención en el Derecho Internacional Americano.* Mexico, 1948.

4634. Saavedra Lamas, C. G. de. "La Propuesta Uruguaya Frente a la Realidad Americana," *PA* 1 (March, 1946) 30–38.
Supports the Rodríguez Larreta Doctrine.

4635. ———. *Luis María Drago: Su Obra, Proyecciones y Trascendencia.* B.A., 1943.

4636. Sánchez Viamonte, C. "Intervencionismo," *CA* (May, 1959) 28–42.

4637. Scott, G. W. "International Law and the Drago Doctrine," *NAR* 183 (1906) 602–610.

4638. Shapiro, H. H. "The U.S. and the Principle of Absolute Nonintervention in Latin America with Particular Reference to Mexico," U. of Pennsylvania Diss., 1949.

4639. Shea, D. R. *The Calvo Clause: A Problem of Inter-American and International Law and Diplomacy.* Minneapolis, 1955.

4640. Stowell, E. C. *Intervention in International Law.* Wash., 1921.

4640a. Summers, L. N. "The Calvo Clause," *VLR* 19 (1933) 459–484.

4641. Tello, M. "No Intervención, Autodeterminación, y Naciones Unidas," *FI* 2 (1962) 346–350.

4642. Terrazas Sánchez, X. *El Principio de la no Intervención.* Mexico, 1955.

4643. Thomas, A. V. W., and A. J. Thomas, Jr. *Non-Intervention: The Law and Its Import in the Americas.* Dallas, 1956.

Spanish ed., B.A., 1959. A technical legalistic discussion.

4644. Torriente, C. de la. "El Principio de no Intervención y la Nota Uruguaya," *RDLH* 7 (December, 1945) 303–307.

4645. Vivote, A. N. *La Doctrina Drago.* B.A., 1911.

4646. Welles, S. "Intervention and Interventions," *FA* 26 (1947) 116–133.

4647. ———. "La Proposición Uruguaya," *RDLH* 7 (December, 1945) 299–302.
On the Rodríguez Larreta Memorandum.

4648. Whitaker, A. P. "Inter-American Intervention," *CH* 10 (March, 1946) 206–211.
Analysis of the Rodríguez Larreta Doctrine.

4649. Wilson, L. C. *The Principle of Non-Intervention in Recent Inter-American Relations: The Challenge of Anti-Democratic Regimes.* College Park, Md., 1964.

4650. Zárate, C. L. *La no Intervención ante el Derecho Americano.* N.p., 1963.

XI–C–5 cross references:

a) For the initial qualified endorsement of nonintervention by the United States at the Montevideo conference (1933), see items 4976–5012a; for a more comprehensive endorsement of the principle at the Buenos Aires Conference (1936), see items 5150–5181h.

b) For the Venezuelan debt controversy of 1902–1903, which involved the forced collection of debts by European countries, see items 8605b–8627.

c) For the heyday of interventionism, consult appropriate sections of Chapter VI; for the decline of interventionism, consult appropriate sections of Chapter VIII.

d) For post–World War II intervention in Guatemala, see various citations among items 6847b–6925; for Cuba, see items 7696a–7852; for the Dominican Republic, see items 7994a–8004a.

e) See also items 1608, 2143, 2687, 2949, 2949a, 2956a, 2957a, 4302, 4791, 4801, 4824, 4836, 4963, 4966, 5114, 5294, 7598.

6. ARBITRATION, MEDIATION, AND CONCILIATION

4651. *Algunos Datos Sobre Tratados de Arbitraje y Buenos Oficios Celebrados por las Naciones de América.* Mexico, 1901.

4652. Cáceres, J. R. "Datos Sobre el Arbitraje en América," *PEASC* 10 (1943) 263–291.

4653. Cardon, R. L. *La Solución Pacífica de Controversias Internacionales en el Sistema Americano*. B.A., 1954.

4654. Fenwick, C. G. "Inter-American Regional Procedures for the Settlement of Disputes," *IO* 10 (1956) 12–21.

4655. Gérardin, E. "La Question de l'Arbitrage aux Conférences Panaméricaines," *RSP* 30 (1913) 241–260.

4656. Gil Borges, E. *Conciliación y Arbitraje*. Caracas, 1936.

4657. Guerra Iñíguez, D. *El Arbitraje de las Disputas Internacionales en América, Según las Provisiones de los Tratados (Estudio Comparativo)*. Caracas, 1956.

4658. Hudson, M. O. "The Inter-American Treaties of Pacific Settlement," *FA* 15 (1936) 165–178.
    Treats the Gondra Treaty of 1923, the Arbitration Treaty of 1929, and the Saavedra Lamas Treaty of 1933.

4659. Kellor, F. *American Arbitration: Its History, Functions and Achievements*. N.Y., 1948.

4660. Lagos Valenzuela, E. *El Arbitraje Internacional en América*. Santiago, 1938.

4661. Manning, W. R. (ed.). *Arbitration Treaties Among the American Nations to the Close of the Year 1910*. N.Y., 1924.

4662. Martínez Méndez, N. *El Arbitraje Obligatorio ante los Congresos Panamericanos*. Santiago, 1910.

4663. Maúrtua, A. *La Idea Panamericana y la Cuestión del Arbitraje: Estudio Histórico a Propósito del Congreso de México*. Lima, 1901.

4664. Maúrtua, V. M. *Conciliation and Arbitration in America*. Wash., 1931.

4665. Murdock, J. O. "Arbitration and Conciliation in Pan America," *AJIL* 23 (1929) 273–291.

4666. Myers, D. P. "Acceptance of General Treaty of Inter-American Arbitration," *AJIL* 30 (1936) 57–62.

4667. Quesada, G. de. *Arbitration in Latin America*. Rotterdam, 1907.

4668. Robinson, M. *Arbitration and the Hague Peace Conferences, 1899 and 1907*. Phil., 1936.

4669. Taylor, H. "International Arbitration and the Panamerican Conference," *NAR* 174 (1902) 303–314.

4670. Toro, G. *Notas Sobre Arbitraje Internacional en las Repúblicas Latino-Americanas*. Santiago, 1898.

4671. Urrutia, F. J. *La Evolución del Principio de Arbitraje en América*. Madrid, 1920.

XI–C–6 cross references:

a) Proceedings associated with various Latin American boundary disputes are listed in appropriate country chapters (XIII–XXIV).

b) For works on the Washington Conference on Conciliation and Arbitration (1928–1929), see items 5144–5149.

c) For works on the attempted A.B.C. mediation of the United States–Mexican dispute of 1914–1916, see items 6205–6225.

d) See also items 1615, 1616, 4778, 4790, 4902b, 4966, 9062a, 9495.

7. SPECIAL ASPECTS

4672. Accioly, H. "O Barão do Rio-Branco e a 2ª Conferencia da Haia," *RIHGB* 187 (April, 1945) 61–104.

4673. Auguste, B. B. L. *The Continental Shelf: The Practice and Policy of the Latin American States with Special Reference to Chile, Ecuador, and Peru: A Study in International Relations*. Geneva, 1960.

4673a. Ayala, E. "El Uti-Possidetis en América," *RDCSP* 6, nos. 20–22 (1932) 5–35.

4674. Azcárraga Bustamente, L. de. *La Plataforma Submarina y el Derecho Internacional*. Madrid, 1952.

4675. Barbosa, R. *A Conferência de Haia: Dois Autógrafos do Arquivo da Casa de Rui Barbosa*. Rio, 1952.

4676. Baxter, R. R. *The Law of International Waterways*. Cambridge, Mass., 1964.

4677. Bayitch, S. A. *Interamerican Law of Fisheries: An Introduction with Documents*. N.Y., 1957.

4678. Berenguer, F. *El Hispano-Americanismo Estudiado Desde el Punto de Vista del Derecho Internacional y el Problema Territorial de América*. Havana, 1918.

4679. Celis y Vega, S. *Consideraciones Sobre Algunos Problemas Jurídicos que Surgen en el Régimen de los Canales Interoceánicos*. Mexico, 1962.

4680. Checa Drouet, B. *La Doctrina Americana del Uti Possidetis de 1810 (Un Estudio de Derecho Público Americano)*. Lima, 1936.

4681. Choate, J. H. *The Two Hague Conferences*. Princeton, N.J., 1913.

4682. Colegio de Abogados de México. *El Pensamiento Jurídico de México en el Derecho Internacional*. Mexico, 1960.

4683. Cruchaga Tocornal, M. "Andres Bello, A Great Contributor to International Law," *BPAU* 66 (1932) 673–676.

4684. Culbertson, W. S. "Protection of Business Enterprise in the Americas," *AAAPSS* 204 (1939) 169–174.

4685. Davis, C. D. *The United States and the First Hague Conference*. Ithaca, N.Y., 1962.

4686. Esquivel Obregón, T. *Latin American Commercial Law*. N.Y., 1921.

4687. Gil Borges, E. *Notas Sobre la Estructura Técnica de los Tratados Multilaterales Interamericanas*. Caracas, 1936.

4688. Gómez Reinoso, T. "El Tribunal de Justicia Interamericana y las Conferencias Panamericanas," *RDI* 44 (September, 1943) 119–124.

4689. Holls, F. W. *The Peace Conference at the Hague, and Its Bearings on International Law and Policy*. N.Y., 1900.

4690. Hull, W. I. *The United States and Latin America at The Hague*. N.Y., 1911.

4691. Inter-American Council of Jurists. *Etude sur les Délits Politiques*. Wash., 1960.

4692. Inter-American Juridical Committee. *Draft Convention on Territorial Waters and Related Questions*. Wash., 1952.

4693. Jessup, P. C., and F. Deák. *Neutrality, Its History, Economics and Law*. 4 vols., N.Y., 1935–1936.

4693a. Kunz, J. L., and R. D. Hayton. "Buenos Aires 'Jornadas de Derecho Internacional,' " *AJIL* 56 (1962) 743–747.
Concerns symposium held in Buenos Aires by representatives of several professional organizations of international law.

4693b. Ladas, S. P. *The International Protection of Trademarks by the American Republics*. Cambridge, Mass., 1929.

4694. Langer, R. *Seizure of Territory: The Stimson Doctrine and Related Principles in Legal Theory and Diplomatic Practice*. Princeton, N.J., 1947.

4695. Lawrence, T. J. *International Problems and Hague Conferences*. London, 1908.

4696. Loureiro, P. *El "Uti Possidetis Juris" de 1810 y el Derecho Internacional Americano*. Rio, 1935.

4697. Maciel, A. B. *Extradição Internacional*. Rio, 1957.

4698. Moreno Quintana, L. M., and C. M. Bollini Shaw. "La Política Internacional," *RFDCS* 4 (1949) 1107–1147, 1475–1508.

4699. Nunes, R. *As Duas Conferências de Haia*. Rio, 1958.

4700. PAU. *Documentos y Notas Sobre Privilegios e Immunidades con Referencia Especial a la Organización de los Estados Americanos*. Wash., 1960.

4701. Sánchez de Bustamante y Sirvén, A. *The World Court*. N.Y., 1925.

4702. Sá Vianna, M. A. de S. *De la Non-Existence d'Un Droit International Américain*. Rio, 1912.

4703. Scott, J. B. *The Hague Peace Conferences of 1899 and 1907*. 2 vols., Baltimore, 1909.

4704. ———. *The Work of the Second Hague Conference*. N.Y., 1908.

4705. Sosa-Rodríguez, C. *Le Droit Fluvial International et les Fleuves de l'Amérique Latine*. Paris, 1935.

4706. Yepes, J. M. "Estudio Jurídico del Anteproyecto de Declaración de Derechos y Deberes de los Estados Americanos," *RCDI* 1 (July, 1947) 94–119.

4707. York, B. V. "International Air Law in the American Republics," *JA* 3 (1932) 411–444.

4707a. Young, R. "Pan American Discussions on Offshore Claims," *AJIL* 50 (1956) 909–916.

XI–C–7 cross references: 1600, 3255, 4869, 4920, 4952, 4961, 4975a, 5023, 5044, 5323, 6722, 6727, 7310, 7366, 7730, 7732, 7754, 7766, 7790, 7792, 7850, 8338, 8613, 9452

D. PAN AMERICAN UNION

4708. Baquero Lazcano, E. *La Unión Panamericana, Actual Secretaría de la O.E.A.: Origen, Evolución, y Régimen Actual*. Córdoba, 1956.

4709. Barrett, J. *The Pan American Union.* Baltimore, 1911.

4710. Casey, C. B. "The Creation and Development of the Pan American Union," *HAHR* 13 (1933) 437–456.

4711. Kelchner, W. H. *Fundación y Desarrollo de la Unión Panamericana.* Wash., 1931.

4712. Kull, R. I. "The Pan American Union: An International Secretariat," *AG* 2 (May, 1943) 114–123.

4713. Lane, G. B., Jr. "The Role of John Barrett in the Development of the Pan American Union, 1907–1920," American U. Diss., 1963.

4714. Manger, W. "The Pan-American Union at the Sixth International Conference of American States," *AJIL* 22 (1928) 764–775.

4715. Messina Matos, M. *La Unión Panamericana en el Sistema de Paz Continental.* Cd. Trujillo, 1946.

4716. "Pan-American Union and Pan-American Conferences," *V* 8 (December, 1938) 57–72.

4717. PAU. *The Pan American Union, Formerly Known as the International Bureau of American Republics: Its Organization and Purpose, Its Building, Its History, Its Activities, Its Field. L. S. Rowe, Director.* Wash., 1929(?).

4718. ———. *Para toda América: La Unión Panamericana, Historia y Acción.* Wash., 1944.

4719. ———. *Report on the Activities of the Pan American Union, 1938–1948: Submitted by the Director General . . . to the Member Governments in Accordance with the Resolution of the Fifth International Conference of American States.* Wash., 1948.

4720. Reid, W. A. *Story of the Pan American Union: Its Origin and Its Services to the Republics of the Western World.* Phil., 1924.

4721. Rowe, L. *The Founding and Development of the Pan American Union.* Wash., 1930.

4722. ———. "L'Oeuvre de l'Union Panaméricaine Depuis 1928," *EI* 5 (1931) 245–259.

4723. ———. "La Unión Panamericana y las Conferencias Panamericanas," *RABA* 16 (April, 1940) 107–116.

4724. ———. *The Pan American Union and the Pan American Conferences: The Pan American Union, 1890–1940.* Wash., 1940.

4725. ———. *The Pan American Union in Pan American Affairs.* Wash., 1931.

4726. Sanders, W. *International Law and International Peace in the Americas: Fiftieth Anniversary of the Pan American Union, 1890 to April 14, 1940.* Wash., 1940.

4727. "La Unión Panamericana, 1890–1940," *RABA* 16 (April, 1940) 117–131.

4728. Yturbide, A. de. "The Proposed Pan American Union," *NAR* 174 (1902) 201–211.

XI–D cross references: *4509, 4992.*

E. THE INTER-AMERICAN SYSTEM AND WORLD WAR II

4729. Abalo, J. L. *La Gran Crisis y la Necesidad de una Confederación Panamericana.* Havana, 1940.

4730. Berle, A. A., Jr. "Peace Without Empire," *SG* 30 (March, 1941) 103–109.

4731. Carrancá y Trujillo, R. *Panamericanismo y Democracia: Conferencia en la Sala de Conferencias del Teatro de Bellas Artes de México el 4 de Marzo de 1941.* Mexico, 1942.

4732. Dale, A. W. *Western Hemisphere Alliance.* 2 vols., Omaha, 1940.

4733. Duggan, S. "The Western Hemisphere as a Haven of Peace," *FA* 18 (1940) 601–614.

4733a. Franceschi, G. J. "Panamericanismo y Guerra," *CRI* 14 (May, 1941) 29–32.

4734. Grande, H. "A Doutrina do Panamericanismo Bélico e o Brasil," *CP* 5 (January, 1945) 26–42.

4735. Green, P. L. *Pan American Progress.* N.Y., 1942.

4736. Hansen, A. H. "La Solidaridad del Hemisferio Americano," *BMSA* (November, 1941) 425–437.

4737. Henry, H. M. "Western Hemisphere Accord," *SAQ* 41 (1942) 239–253.

4738. Humphrey, J. P. "Pan America in the World Order," *CF* 21 (October, 1941) 199–202.

4739. James, E. K. "A New Pan Americanism," *ANR* 2 (1942) 361–387.

4740. Leme, E. *Conceito Atual do Panamericanismo*. São Paulo, 1941.

4741. Loewenstein, K. "Pan Americanism in Action: Committee for Political Defense," *CH* 5 (November, 1943) 229–236.

4742. Olch, I. "Pan-Americanism and Naval Policy," *USNIP* 67 (1941) 1527–1532.

4743. Padilla, E., M. de Pimentel Brandão, and J. L. Chouhy Terra. *The Political Defense of the Americas*. Mexico, 1943.

4744. Planas-Suárez, S. "Una Crisis del Pan-Americanismo," *BACPS* 10 (January, 1945) 1–19.

4745. Rippy, J. F. "The New Pan Americanism and the Fascist Threat," in R. E. McNicoll and J. R. Owre, *University of Miami Hispanic-American Studies: Lectures Delivered at the Hispanic-American Institute*. Coral Gables, Fla., 1939.

4746. Sayán de Vidaurre, A. *Réplica a las Antidemócratas y Antipanamericanistas*. B.A., 1943.

4747. Trueblood, H. J. "Progress of Pan-American Cooperation," *FPAR* 15 (February, 1940) 286–300.

4748. Villarroel, R. *El Día de las Américas y el Ideal de la Solidaridad Mundial*. 2d ed., Santa Fe, Argentina, 1941.

4749. Whitaker, A. P. "Our Pan American Policy and the Post-War World," *HER* (1943) 285–300.

4750. ———. "Politics and Diplomacy: The United States and Latin America," *INAF* 3 (1943) 6–49.

4751. Yepes, J. M. "Le Nouveau Panaméricanisme et la Seconde Guerre Mondiale," *RGDIP* 18 (1946) 79–111.

XI–E cross references:

a) For works on the Panama Conference (1939), see items 5189a–5201; for the Havana Conference (1940), see items 5202–5215; for the Rio Conference (1942), see items 5216–5229; for the Chapultepec Conference (1945), see items 5230–5255a.

b) See also items 3538, 3832, 4423, 4844, 4862.

F. THE INTER-AMERICAN SYSTEM AND THE UNITED NATIONS

4752. Accioly, H. "As Nações Unidas e as Organizações Regionais," *RBPI* 2 (June, 1959) 5–25.

4752a. Aguilar Navarro, M. "El Panamericanismo y el Pacto del Atlántico," *EA* 1 (1949) 729–755.

4753. Angel Campa, M. "La Conferencia de San Francisco," *RDI* 24 (September, 1945) 57–61.

4754. Aranha, O. "Regional Systems and the Future of the U.N.," *FA* 26 (1948) 415–420.

4755. Ball, M. M., "The Inter-American System and the United Nations," *WA* 12 (1946) 48–61.

4755a. ———. "Inter-American and World Organization," *CH* 10 (1946) 1–7.

4755b. Bebr, G. "Regional Organizations: A United Nations Problem," *AJIL* 49 (1955) 166–184.

4756. Belaúnde, V. A. *La Conferencia de San Francisco*. Lima, 1945.

4756a. Blackmer, H. M., II. *United States Policy and the Inter-American Peace System*. Paris, 1952.

4757. Boeckel, F. B. *Pan American Principles Fundamental to World Cooperation*. Wash., 1944.

4758. Calzada Flores, M. *La Organización Interamericana Dentro de la Organización Mundial*. Mexico, 1949.

4759. Canyes, M. *The Organization of American States and the United Nations*. 3d ed., Wash., 1955.
   Spanish ed., Wash., 1953. Compares and contrasts the two charters.

4760. Castañeda, J. "Conflictos de Competencia Entre las Naciones Unidas y la Organización de Estados Americanos," *FI* 6 (1965–1966) 303–322.

4761. Claret De Voogd, L. *La OEA, y las Naciones Unidas: Contribución de la Organización de los Estados Americanos al Afianzamiento de las Naciones Unidas*. B.A., 1956.

4762. Claude, I. F. "OAS, the UN, and the US," *IC*, no. 547 (1963).

4763. Cuevas Cancino, F. "Práctica en las Relaciones Entre la Organización de los Estados Americanos y las Naciones Unidas," *RFDM* 4 (January, 1954) 63–77.

4764. Fenwick, C. G. "Continental Solidarity and International Organization," *FW* 2 (1942) 317–319.
   Believes that a world-wide organization

is not a substitute for the inter-American system.

4765. Fenwick, C. G. "The Organization of American States and the United Nations," *WA* 117 (Fall, 1954) 75–76.

4766. Furniss, E. S., Jr. "The United States, the Inter-American System and the United Nations," *PSQ* 65 (1950) 415–430.

4766a. Goodrich, L. M. "Regionalism and the United Nations," *JIA* 3 (Spring, 1949) 5–20.

4767. Hadley, P. E. "The Organization of American States: A Regional System Within the United Nations," *WAI* 22 (April, 1951) 31–43.

4768. Humphreys, R. A. "The Pan American System and the United Nations," *IAF* 22 (1946) 75–84.

4769. Kunz, J. L. "Individual and Collective Self-Defense in Article 51 of the Charter of the United Nations," *AJIL* 41 (1947) 872–879.

4770. ———. "The Inter-American System and the United Nations Organization," *AJIL* 39 (1945) 758–767.

4771. Lleras Camargo, A. "The Pan American Union and the United Nations," *BPAU* 81 (1948) 587–590.

4772. Marinho, I. P. *O Funcionamento do Sistema Interamericano Dentro do Sistema Mundial.* Rio, 1959.

4773. Mecham, J. L. "The Integration of the Inter-American Security System into the United Nations," *JP* 9 (1947) 178–196.

4774. Medina y Sobrado, P. G. de. "La Post-Guerra y la Organización Internacional de Dumbarton Oaks," *RDI* 24 (March, 1945) 72–86.

4774a. Padelford, N. J. "Regional Organization and the United Nations," *IO* 8 (1954) 203–216.

4775. Padilla, E. "The American System and the World Organization," *FA* 24 (1945) 99–107.

Author was head of the Mexican delegation to the San Francisco conference.

4776. PAU. *Agreement Between the OAS and the International Labor Organization.* Wash., 1951.

4777. ———. *Agreement Between UNESCO and the OAS.* Wash., 1951.

4778. Prada Jaimes, L. M. *Paralelo Entre la ONU y la OEA: Solución Pacífica de las Controversias.* Bogotá, 1960.

4778a. Reid, H. D. "Regionalism Under the United Nations Charter," *IC*, no. 419 (1946) 120–127.

4779. Rockefeller, N. "The Inter-American System and the United Nations," *PAPS* 22 (January, 1947) 12–19.

4780. Rowe, L. S. "The Americas and the World Order," *BPAU* 78 (1944) 60–63.

4781. ———. "Regional Arrangements and the United Nations," *BPAU* 79 (1945) 429–433.

4782. ———. "The Relation of the Pan American Union to the United Nations, 1945," *BPAU* 81 (1947) 258–259.

4783. Sharp, W. R. "The Inter-American System and the United Nations," *FA* 23 (1945) 450–464.

4784. Sierra, M. J. "Unidad Interamericana," *CA* 12, no. 1 (1953) 64–70.

Argues that the United Nations should not weaken the inter-American system.

4785. "United Nations Security Council Rejects Cuban Call for Opinion of World Court on OAS Action," *USDSB* 46 (1962) 684–694.

4786. Wiencke Gualtieri, E. *La Función Regional de la Organización de los Estados Americanos y su Importancia.* Mexico, 1962.

XI–F cross references:

a) For early views on the relationship between the inter-American system and world organization, see works on the Chapultepec Conference (1945), items 5230–5255a.

b) See also items 3524, 4166, 4181, 4417, 5067.

G. THE ORGANIZATION OF AMERICAN STATES (OAS)

4787. Alba, V. "¿Futuro o Pasado de la O.E.A.?" *CUA* 49 (June, 1961) 81–84.

4787a. Artiles Jérez, H. *Organización de los Estados Americanos.* León, Nicaragua, 1954.

4788. Calvocoressi, P. "The Organization of American States," in *Survey of International Affairs, 1947–1948.* London, 1952.

4788a. Carrión, B. "Oración Funebre por la OEA," *CA* (July, 1965) 19–35.

4789. Corominas, E. V. *La Práctica del Hispano-americanismo*. Madrid, 1952.

4789a. Costa, S. C. da. "O Panamericanismo e os Modernos Pactos Regionais," *RTIHGB* 233 (October, 1956) 159–172.

4789b. Davis, H. E. "The Charter of the Organization of the American States," *WPQ* 1 (1948) 439–448.

4790. Deshazo, E. A. "The Peaceful Settlement of Disputes in the Inter-American System Since World War II," Indiana U. Diss., 1957.

4791. Díaz Doin, G. "La Organización de Estados Americanos y la no Intervención," *CA* (May, 1960) 73–88.

4791a. Dreier, J. C. "The OAS and the Cuban Crisis," *SAISR* 5 (Winter, 1961) 3–8.

4792. ———. *The Organization of American States and the Hemisphere Crisis*. N.Y., 1962.
The author served as a United States representative on the council of the OAS for ten years.

4793. ———. "The Organization of American States and United States Policy," *IO* 17 (Winter, 1963) 36–53.

4794. Fenwick, C. G. "The Organization of American States," *AJIL* 59 (1965) 315–320.

4795. ———. *The Organization of American States: The Inter-American Regional System*. Wash., 1963.

4796. Fernández-Shaw y Baldasano, F. G. *La Organización de los Estados Americanos (OEA): Una Nueva Visión de América*. 2d ed., Madrid, 1963.

4797. "First Special Inter-American Conference: Act of Washington (Text)," *AJIL* 59 (1965) 719–721.
Established procedures for the admission of new members.

4798. Fitzgibbon, R. H. "The Organization of American States: Time of Ordeal," *OR* 5 (Spring, 1961) 74–86.

4799. Furniss, E. S., Jr. "The Inter-American System and Recent Caribbean Disputes," *IO* 4 (1950) 585–597.

4800. Gvozdarev, B. I. *Organizatsiia Amerikanskikh Gosudarstv*. Moscow, 1960.
Organization of American States.

4801. Hickey, J. "Blackmail, Mendicancy and Intervention: Latin America's Conception

of the Good Neighbor Policy," *IEA* 12 (Summer, 1958) 43–82.

4802. Hoyo Algara, F. del. *Estudio de la Organización de los Estados Americanos*. Mexico, 1952.

4803. Inter-American Juridical Committee. *Opinion on the Scope of the Powers of the Council of the Organization of American States*. Wash., 1961.

4804. Kiser, M. *Organization of American States: A Handbook for Use in Schools, Colleges and Adult Study Groups*. 4th ed., Wash., 1955.

4805. Lleras Camargo, A. "The Inter-American System Today," *AAAPSS* 282 (1952) 97–103.

4806. ———. *The Organization of American States: An Example for the World*. Lewisburg, Pa., 1954.

4807. Manger, W. *Pan America in Crisis*. Wash., 1961.
Manger was at one time assistant secretary-general.

4808. Mello Franco, A. A. de. *Pela Solidariedade Continental*. Rio, 1953.

4809. Mora, J. A. "The Organization of American States," *IO* 14 (1960) 514–523.

4809a. Morgan, G. G. "The Organization of American States: A Problem of Administrative Reorganization," *RISA* 18 (1952) 501–529.

4810. OAS. *Annals, 1949– .* Wash., 1952– .

4811. ———. Council. *Regulations of the Council of the Organization of American States*. Wash., 1954.

4812. ———. Inter-American Council of Jurists. *Report and Draft Convention on Recognition of De Facto Governments*. Wash., 1950.

4813. ———. Special Consultative Committee on Security Against the Subversive Action of International Communism. *Initial General Report, 1962*. Wash., 1962.

4814. PAU. *Applications of the Inter-American Treaty of Reciprocal Assistance, 1948–1956: With a Discussion of the Inter-American System of Peace and Security and Its Operation Within the World*. Wash., 1957.

4815. ———. *Inter-American Treaty of Reciprocal Assistance Applications*. 2 vols., Wash., 1964.
Spanish ed., 2 vols., Wash., 1964.

4816.   PAU. *A Organização dos Estados Americanos: Sua Estructura e Funcionamento*. Wash., 1960.

4817.   ———. *The Organization of American States, 1954–1959: Report Submitted by the Pan American Union to the Eleventh Inter-American Conference*. Wash., 1959.
Official review of activities from the tenth conference to the time of publication.

4818.   ———. Division of Law and Treaties. *Documents and Notes on Privileges and Immunities with Special Reference to the Organization of American States*. Wash., 1953.

4819.   Rich, S. G., Jr. *Inter-American Machinery for Collective Security*. Stanford, Calif., 1949.

4820.   Rodríguez, A., A. "La Conferencia de la OEA," *FI* 5 (1965) 547–575.
Discusses the various meetings in the 1960's.

4821.   Rogué Alcócer, L. "The Organization of American States with Special Reference to Problems of International Administration," American U. Diss., 1953.

4822.   Rubottom, R. R., Jr. "Inter-American Progress Through the Organization of American States," *USDSB* 40 (1959) 659–665.

4822a.   Sanders, W. "The Organization of American States on Its 69th Anniversary," *RJI* 1 (July, 1959) 417–432.

4822b.   Scheman, L. R. "Admission of States to the OAS," *AJIL* 58 (1964) 968–974.

4822c.   Slater, J. N. "The Role of the Organization of American States in United States Foreign Policy, 1947–1963," Princeton U. Diss., 1965.

4823.   Stoetzer, O. C. *Panamerika, Idee und Wirklichkeit: Die Organisation der Amerikanischen Staaten*. Hamburg, 1964.
English ed., N.Y., 1965.

4824.   Thomas, A. J., Jr. "The Organization of American States and Subversive Intervention," *ASILP* (1961) 19–24.

4825.   Thomas, A. V. W., and A. J. Thomas, Jr. *The Organization of American States*. Dallas, 1963.

4826.   Travis, M. B., Jr. "The Organization of American States: A Guide to the Future," *WPQ* 10 (1957) 491–512.

4826a.   USCS. Committee on Foreign Relations.

Organization of American States, by George I. Blanksten, Harold Guetzkow and John N. Plank, Northwestern University (86th Cong., 1st Sess., Comm. Print). Wash., 1959.

4827.   USDA. *Inter-American Efforts to Relieve International Tensions in the Western Hemisphere, 1959–1960*. Wash., 1962.

4828.   ———. *Peace in the Americas: A Résumé of Measures Undertaken Through the Organization of American States to Preserve the Peace, with Relevant Documents*. Wash., 1950.

4829.   Whitaker, A. P. "Development of American Regionalism: The Organization of American States," *IC*, no. 469 (1951).

4830.   Zanotti, I. *Organização dos Estados Americanos*. Rio, 1948.
A general description.

XI–G   cross references:

a)   For the creation of the OAS at Bogotá in 1948, see items 5064–5104.

b)   See also items 4234, 4700, 4841, 7995c.

H. NATIONAL AND REGIONAL RELATIONS WITH THE INTER-AMERICAN SYSTEM

1. Mexico

4831.   Castañeda, J. *México y el Orden Internacional*. Mexico, 1956.

4831a.   ———. "Pan Americanism and Regionalism: A Mexican View," *IO* 10 (August, 1956) 373–389.

4831b.   ———. "Pan-Americanismo: Posição de México," *RBPI* 1 (September, 1958) 5–41.

4832.   Corominas, E. V. *México-Cuba y la OEA*. B.A., 1965.

4833.   Domínguez Ferman, S. *Principios Constitucionales: Fundamento de la Actuación de México en la OEA*. Mexico, 1963.

4834.   López Mateos, A. "México ante la OEA, y las Naciones Unidas," *RUY* 1 (September, 1959) 9–20.

4835.   Padilla Nervo, L. *Discursos y Declaraciones Sobre Política Internacional ante la OAS, 1948–1958*. Mexico, 1958.

4835a.   Pellicer de Brody, O. "México en la OEA," *FI* 6 (1965–1966) 288–302.

4836. Rubio García, L. "Méjico, la no Intervención, y el Sistema Interamericano," *CUH* 169 (1964) 71–85.

XI–H–1 cross references: 3156, 4906, 4922, 4967, 4995, 4996, 5001, 5003, 5004, 5034, 5074, 5088, 5112, 5119, 5120, 5282.

2. THE CENTRAL AMERICAN–CARIBBEAN REGION

4837. Alvarez Pedroso, A. "Cuba y la Comunidad Americana de Naciones," *A* 22 (April, 1944) 74–78.

4838. Capó Rodríguez, P. "Porto Rico y el Panamericanismo," *CC* 13 (1917) 155–162.

4839. Chaumette, M. G. *Le Panaméricanisme à Travers l'Histoire d'Haïti*. Port-au-Prince, 1944.

4840. Cuba. Ministerio de Relaciones Exteriores. *Cuba en la OEA: VI e VII Reuniones de Consulta de Ministros de Relaciones Exteriores, San José, C.R., 16 al 29 de Agosto de 1960*. Havana, 1960.

4841. Godoy, G. *El Caso Cubano y la Organización de Estados Americanos*. Madrid, 1961.

4842. Guatemala. Secretaría de Relaciones Exteriores. *Aporte de Guatemala a la Solidaridad y Cooperación Interamericanas*. Guatemala, 1942.

4843. Honduras. Comisión Hondureña de Cooperación Intelectual. *El Pensamiento Panamericanista de los Próceres Centroamericanos Nacidos en Honduras*. Tegucigalpa, 1944(?).

4844. Márquez Camacho, R. *La Doctrina Márquez: Por la Solidaridad de los Pueblos Libres de la América*. Havana, 1940.
    A Cuban plan to end U.S. domination of IAS.

4845. Mendoza, J. L. (comp.). *Pactos Multilaterales Centroamericanos y Regionales*. Guatemala, 1960.

4846. Urist, M. D. "An Analysis of the Participation of Guatemala in the Pan-American Conferences: 1889–1933," U. of S. California Diss., 1958(?).

4847. Urrutia Aparicio, C. "Guatemalan Withdrawal from the Organization of Central American States," *AJIL* 48 (1945) 145–148.

XI–H–2 cross references:
a) For the expulsion of Cuba from the inter-American system, see items 5287–5311.
b) See also items 2520, 2538, 4832, 4981, 5007, 5070, 5111, 5152, 5163, 5174, 5175, 5273, 5292b.

3. SPANISH SOUTH AMERICA

4848. Andreozzi, M. *La República Argentina y los Problemas de la Solidaridad Americana*. B.A., 1942.

4849. Ciasullo, A. L. *El Uruguay y la Solidaridad Interamericano*. Montevideo, 1952.

4850. Ecuador. Departamento de Actos y Organismos Internacionales. *Relación de Tratados y Convenciones Panamericanos Firmados por el Ecuador*. Quito, 1947.

4851. ————. Ministro de Relaciones Exteriores. *La Liga de Naciones Americanas: Postulados Ecuatorianos*. Quito, 1936.

4852. Filippo, V. *Confabulación Contra la Argentina*. B.A., 1944.

4853. Frondizi, A. "Ha Sonado para la América la Hora de la Ley, del Derecho y de la Colaboración Entre las Naciones que la Integran," *JUS* 28 (November, 1958) 15–25.

4854. García de la Parra, P. *Colombia en las Conferencias Panamericanas*. Bogotá, 1926.

4855. Hazelton, A. W. *Eloy Alfaro, Apostle of Pan Americanism*. Forest Hills, N.Y., 1943.
    Spanish ed., Chicago, 1944.

4856. Iturralde Chinel, L. de. *De Ginebra a la Defensa Continental*. B.A., 1947.

4857. Jáuregui Rosquellas, A. "Panamericanismo," *BSGS* 40 (May, 1944) 38–41.
    Concerns Bolivia and the inter-American system.

4858. Kinnaird, L. B. "Argentina and the Pacific Settlement of International Disputes," U. of California Diss., 1934.

4859. Miró Quesada G., A. "Actuación del Perú en las Conferencias Internacionales Americanas," *RF* 27 (1940) 99–120, 507–540.

4860. Moreno Quintana, L. M. "Argentina y la Defensa Continental," *RFDCS* 6 (January, 1951) 11–24.

4861. Phillips, H. A. *Argentina, Pivot of Pan American Peace*. N.Y., 1944.

4862. Rada, J. J. "La Política Diplomática del Perú y el Panamericanismo," *RPDI* 3 (1943) 389–402.

4863. Smith, O. E. "Argentina and the Program of Hemispheric Solidarity," U. of Chicago Diss., 1950.

4864. Ulloa Sotomayor, A. *Congresos Americanos de Lima.* 2 vols., Lima, 1938.

4865. Velásquez Toro, J. "El Banco Interamericano y sus Repercusiones en Colombia," *UA* 10 (March, 1940) 111–121.

4866. Villacrés Moscoso, J. W. *La Política Económica Internacional de los Estados Hispanoamericanos: Iniciativas y Contribución del Ecuador.* Guayaquil, 1955.

4867. White, J. W. "Uruguay, Bulwark of Pan Americanism," *INA* 1 (November, 1942) 10–14.

4868. Yepes, J. M. "La Política Internacional de Colombia y el Panamericanismo," *RCDI* 1 (July, 1947) 38–60.

XI–H–3   cross references: 2524, 2527, 2528, 2529, 2534, 2602, 2603, 2616, 2617, 3690, 4109, 4908, 4918, 4930, 4948, 4957, 4971, 4991, 4994, 5014, 5016, 5085, 5105, 5189b, 5221, 5234, 5235, 5240, 5248, 5259, 5272, 5293, 9175, 9659.

4. BRAZIL

4869. Accioly, H. "Le Brésil et la Doctrine de 'l'Uti Possidetus,'" *RDISDP* 15 (1935) 36–45.

4870. Aranha, O. "El Panamericanismo en el Desenvolvimiento Histórico-Político del Brasil," *A* 18 (April, 1943) 19–24.

4871. Gomes, A. "Vocação Continental da América e Tradição Americanista do Brasil," *RIHGSP* 52 (1956) 37–63.

4872. Lôbo, H. *O Pan-Americanismo e o Brasil.* São Paulo, 1939.

4873. Maul, C. *As Fontes Brasileiras do Panamericanismo.* Rio, 1941.

4874. Medeiros, J. P. de. "Aspectos de Panamericanismo e uma Tradição da Política Brasileira," *CP* 3 (January, 1943) 31–36.

4875. Neel, V. P. "Major Contributions of Brazil to the Theory and Practice of International Organization and Procedure from 1889–1949," American U. Diss., 1951.

4876. Oliveira, B. de. "O Panamericanismo do Brasil," *CP* 2 (February, 1942) 94–100.

XI–H–4   cross references: 2540, 2601, 2611, 3716, 5025, 5292, 5299, 9878

5. CANADA

4876a. Anglin, D. G. "United States Opposition to Canadian Membership in the Pan American Union," *IO* 15 (Winter, 1961) 1–20.

4877. Brebner, J. B. "Canada's Choice in Foreign Affairs," *QJIR* 1, no. 12 (1939) 50–57.

4878. Brown, G. W. *Canada and the Americas.* Toronto, 1953.

4879. "Canada and Pan Americanism," *QJIR* 1 (October, 1939) 30–34.

4880. Corbett, P. E. "Canada in the Western Hemisphere," *FA* 19 (1941) 778–789.

4881. Crawford, H. D. "Should Canada Join Pan-America?" *NAR* 248 (1939) 219–233.

4881a. Fenwick, C. G. "Canada and the Monroe Doctrine," *AJIL* 32 (1938) 782–785.

4882. ———. "The Question of Canadian Participation in Inter-American Conferences," *AJIL* 31 (1937) 473–476.

4883. Harbron, J. D. *Canada and the Organization of American States.* Wash., 1963.

4884. Humphrey, J. P. *The Inter-American System: A Canadian View.* Toronto, 1942.

4885. Jaffin, G. *New World Constitutional Harmony: A Pan-Americadian Panorama.* N.Y., 1942.

4886. Johnson, J. E. (comp.). *Canada and the Western Hemisphere.* N.Y., 1944.
   A series of some 30 articles.

4887. Lazcano Mazón, A. M. "Armonía Constitucional del Nuevo Mundo: Panorama Panamericandeinse," *RDI* 44 (September, 1943) 7–42.

4888. Massey, V. "Canada and the Inter-American System," *FA* 26 (1948) 693–700.
   Opposes Canadian membership.

4889. Miller, E. H. "El Canadá y la Unión Panamericana," *MLI* 5 (August, 1948) 33-43.

4890. Morin, J. Y. *Thoughts on Canada and the Inter-American System.* Dallas, Texas, 1954.

4891. Nicholson, N. L. *Canada in the American Community.* Princeton, N.J., 1963.

4892. Podea, I. S. "Pan American Sentiment in

French Canada," *IJ* 3 (1948) 334–349.

4893. Roussin, M. *Le Canada et le Système Interaméricain*. Ottawa, 1959.

The author suggests that Canada would have joined the system except for opposition from the United States.

4894. ———. "Evolution of the Canadian Attitude Towards the Inter-American System," *AJIL* 47 (1953) 296–300.

4895. ———. "Inter-Americanism for Canada?" *WA* 122 (Fall, 1959) 74–76.

4896. Rubio García, L. "Canadá y el Sistema Interamericano," *EA* 7 (February, 1954) 63–69.

4897. Sage, W. N. "The Historical Peculiarities of Canada with Regard to Hemisphere Defense," *PHR* 10 (1941) 15–27.

4898. Santos Muñoz, P. "Posibilidad de la Incorporación de Canadá a la Unión Panamericana," *RADI* (October, 1943) 332–346.

4899. Sébilleau, P. *Le Canada et la Doctrine de Monroe*. Paris, 1937.

4900. Seward, F. H. *Canada and the Americas: Report of a Round Table of the Fourth Annual Conference of the Canadian Institute of International Affairs, Hamilton, Ontario, May, 1937*. Toronto, 1937.

4901. ———, and A. M. Marnlay. *Canada and the Pan American System*. Toronto, 1948.

4902. Trotter, R. G. "More on Canada and Pan Americanism," *IAQ* 2 (January, 1940) 5–10.

XI–H–5   cross references: 4738

I. REGULAR INTER–AMERICAN CONFERENCES

1. WASHINGTON, 1889

4902a. *Actas del Congreso Internacional Americano, 1889–1890*. Wash., 1890.

4902b. Alfonso, J. *El Arbitraje Internacional en la Conferencia Americana de Washington*. Santiago, 1892.

4902c. Calderón, I. *El Congreso de Washington y su Misión*. Iquique, Chile, 1889.

4902d. Curtis, W. E. *Trade and Transportation Between the United States and Latin America*. Wash., 1890.

4903. Eisenhower, D. D. "Commemorating the First Inter-American Conference," *BPAU* 35 (1956) 219–221.

4904. Inman, S. G. "James G. Blaine and the Pan American Movement," *HAHR* 5 (1922) 662–708.

4905. K. W. "First Conference Scrapbook, 1889–1890," *APAU* 6 (February, 1954) 20–23.

4906. Kaiser, C. "México en la Primera Conferencia Panamericana," *HM* 11 (July, 1961) 56–78.

The two Mexican delegates were Matías Romero and Enrique Mexía.

4907. Martínez Méndez, N. *El Congreso Internacional Americano en Washington*. Santiago, 1892.

The author was in the Chilean ministry of foreign relations.

4908. McGann, T. F. "Argentina at the First Pan American Conference," *IEA* 1 (September, 1947) 21–53.

Discusses rivalry between the United States and Argentina.

4909. *Minutes of the International American Conference*. Wash., 1890.

Official records of the Washington Conference.

4910. O'Rourke, C. A. *Congreso Internacional Americano: Paseo de los Delegados: Objeto del Congreso*. N.Y., 1890.

4911. Phillips, E. *El Congreso Internacional Americano de Washington*. Santiago, 1890.

4912. Prince, A. *Le Congrès des Trois Amériques, 1889–1890*. Paris, 1891.

4912a. *Reports and Recommendations*. Wash., 1890.

For the first International Conference of American States.

4913. *Reports of Committees and Discussions Thereon*. 4 vols., Wash., 1890.

4914. Romero, M. *La Conferencia Internacional Americana*. Mexico, 1890.

By one of the Mexican delegates.

4914a. Saenz Peña, R. *La Zollverein Americaine*. Sceaux, 1890.

4915. Varigny, C. de. "J. G. Blaine et le Congrès des 3 Amériques," *RDM* 95, 3d ser. (1890) 433–462.

Interprets the congress as a means by which the United States can cultivate Latin American markets.

4916. Wilgus, A. C. "James G. Blaine and the Pan-American Movement," *HAHR* 5 (1922) 662–708.

XI–I–1   cross references:

a) For accounts of the role of Secretary of State James G. Blaine, see items 2091, 2111, 2131, 2141, 2145, 2146.

b) See also items 2063a, 2081, 2120a, 2547, 2605, 2606.

2. Mexico City, 1901

4916a. *Actas y Documentos.* Mexico, 1902.

4917. Alvarez, A. *L'Histoire Diplomatique des Républiques Américaines et la Conférence de México.* Paris, 1902.

4918. Argentina. *Informe que la Delegación de la República Argentina Presenta a la Segunda Conferencia Pan-Americana.* Mexico, 1901.

4919. *Crónica Social, 1901.* Mexico, 1902(?).

4920. *La Adhesión de la Segunda Conferencia Internacional Americana a las Convenciones de la Haya.* Mexico, 1902.

4921. Martínez, M. *Segunda Conferencia Internacional Americana Tenida en Méjico (1901–1902).* Santiago, 1902.
    Author was the Chilean envoy to Washington in the early 1880's.

4922. Mexico. *Report Which the Mexican Delegation Submits to the Second Pan-American Conference.* Mexico, 1901.

4923. *Minutes and Documents.* Mexico, 1902.
    Spanish ed., *Actas y Documentos de la Segunda Conferencia Pan-Americana.* Mexico, 1901–1902.

4924. Noel, J. V. *History of the Second Pan American Congress.* Baltimore, 1902.

4925. *Recomendaciones, Resoluciones, Convenciones y Tratados.* Mexico, 1902.

4926. Wilgus, A. C. "The Second International American Conference at Mexico City," *HAHR* 11 (1931) 27–68.

XI–I–2   cross references: 4663

3. Rio de Janeiro, 1906

4927. *Actas Authénticas: Debates: Annexos.* Rio, 1906.

4928. *Actas: Resoluciones: Documentos.* Rio, 1907.

4929. Baseevant, J. *La Conférence de Rio de Janeiro de 1906 et l'Union Internationale des Républiques Américaines.* Paris, 1908.

4930. *Memoria de la Delegación de la República Argentina Presentada a la Tercera Conferencia Internacional Americana Reunida en Rio de Janeiro, Julio y Agosto de 1906.* Rio, 1906.

4931. Reinsch, P. S. "The Third International Conference of American States," *APSR* 1 (1907) 187–199.

4932. Root, E. *Speeches Incident to the Visit of Senator Root to South America, July 4 to September 30, 1906.* Wash., 1906.

4933. "The Pan-American Conferences and Their Significance," *AAAPSS* suppl. (May, 1906).

4934. Vicuña Subercaseaux, B. *Los Congresos Pan-Americanos.* 2d ed., Santiago, 1910.
    Chilean delegate at Rio describes the conference.

4935. Wilgus, A. C. "The Third International American Conference at Rio de Janeiro, 1906," *HAHR* 12 (1932) 420–456.

4. Buenos Aires, 1910

4936. *Annexes, Resolutions, and Conventions.* B.A., 1911.

4937. Chile. Ministerio de Relaciones Exteriores. *La Conferencia Panamericana de Buenos Aires: Informe Presentado por los Delegados Plenipotenciarios de Chile en la Cuarta Conferencia Internacional Americana, Reunida en Buenos Aires, Desde el 12 de Julio Hasta el 27 de Agosto de 1910.* Santiago, 1911.

4938. *Daily Account of Sessions.* B.A., 1911.

4938a. La Valle, J. B. *El Programa de la IV Conferencia Pan-Americana, Buenos Aires, 1910.* Lima, 1909.

4939. Lugo, A. *La Cuarta Conferencia Internacional Americana.* Seville, Spain, 1912.

4940. PAU. *Tratados y Convenciones Suscritos en la Cuarta Conferencia Internacional Americana, Buenos Aires, 12 de Julio–30 Agosto de 1910.* Wash., 1948.

4941. Pôrto, L. de A. N. "A Quarta Conferência Internacional Americana," *CP* 4 (January, 1944) 131–136.

4942. ———. "Um Episódio da Doutrina de Monroe: A Formula Nabuco na 4ª Conferência Internacional Americana," *CP* 3 (June, 1943) 39–42.

4943. Reinsch, P. S. "The Fourth International Conference of American Republics," *AJIL* 4 (1910) 777–793.

4944. White, H. "The Fourth International Conference of American States," *AAAPSS* 37 (1911) 585–593.

5. SANTIAGO, 1923

4945. *Actas de las Sesiones de las Comisiones de la Conferencia.* Santiago, n.d.

4945a. Alessandri, A. *Discurso en la de Instalación de la V Conferencia Internacional Americana.* Santiago, 1923.

4946. Alvarez, A. La Vᵉ. *Conférence Panaméricaine et la Société des Nations.* Paris, 1924(?).
    Reprinted from *Révue des Sciences Politiques.*

4947. Galeano, V. B. "The Gondra Treaty," *GSPPW* 15 (1930) 1–9.

4948. *Informe de la Delegación de Chile.* Santiago, 1923.

4949. Inman, S. G. *Hacia la Solidaridad Americana.* Madrid, 1924.

4950. Márquez Sterling, M. *El Panamericanismo: Acuerdos y Orientaciones de la Quinta Conferencia Internacional Americana, Reunida en Santiago de Chile.* Havana, 1923.

4951. PAU. *Treaties and Conventions Signed at the Fifth International Conference of American States, Santiago, Chile, March 28–May 3, 1923.* Wash., 1949.

4952. Rodriguez Alves, J. de P. "El Tratado Gondra," *RADI* 1, no. 3 (1930) 165–183.
    The treaty to avoid or prevent conflicts between the American states (named after Dr. Manuel Gondra of Paraguay) was adopted at the Santiago Conference.

4953. USDA. *Report of Delegates of United States to Fifth International Conference of American States Held at Santiago, Chile, March 25–May 3, 1923, with Appendices.* Wash., 1924.

4954. *Verbatim Record of the Plenary Sessions of the Fifth International Conference of American States.* 2 vols., Santiago, 1923–1925.

XI–1–5   cross references: 4719, 9253

6. HAVANA, 1928

4955. *Acta Final.* Havana, 1928.

4956. Alvarez, A. *Le Panaméricanisme et la VI Conférence Panaméricaine.* Paris, 1928.

4957. Amezaga, J. J. de. "La Participación del Uruguay en la VI Conferencia Internacional Americana Reunión en la Ciudad Habana en 1928: Informe del Presidente de la Delegación," *BMRE* 6, no. 5 (1928) 386–435.

4958. Bustamante y Sirvén, A. S. de. *Le Code de Droit International Privé et la Sixième Conférence Panaméricaine.* Paris, 1929.

4959. Cuba, República de. *Diario de la Sexta Conferencia Internacional Americana.* Havana, 1928.

4960. Ferrara y Marino, O. "The Significance of the Recent Pan American Conference at Havana," *AAAPSS* 138 (1928) 57–65.

4961. Garner, J. W. "The Pan American Convention on Maritime Neutrality," *AJIL* 26 (1932) 574–579.

4962. González Roa, F. "La Convención Panamericana Sobre Deberes y de Hechos de los Estados en Caso de Luchas Civiles," *RGDJ* 1 (1930) 519–537.

4963. Guerrero, J. "La Question de l'Intervention a la VIᵉ Conférence Panaméricaine," *RGDIP* 36 (1929) 40–51.
    The United States refused to endorse nonaggression at the Havana Conference.

4964. "La VI Conferencia Panamericana, La Unión Pan-Americana," *RDCSP* 3 (January, 1930) 49–53.

4965. Manger, W. "Making Effective the Conclusions of the Sixth International Conference of American States," *BPAU* 64 (1930) 232–237.

4966. Maúrtua, V. M. *Intervención, Conciliación, Arbitraje en las Conferencias de la Habana, 1928 y Washington, 1929.* Havana, n.d.

4967. Mexico. Secretaría de Relaciones Exteriores. *La Participación de México en la Sexta Conferencia Internacional Americana: Informe General de la Delegación de México.* Mexico, 1928.

4968. Oría y Sentíes, E. de. *El VI Congreso Panamericano.* Mexico, 1928.

4969. PAU. *Treaties and Conventions.* Wash., 1950.

4970. ———. *Address of President Coolidge Before Pan American Conference, Havana, Cuba, Jan. 16, 1928.* Wash., 1928.

4971. Ruíz Moreno, J. "Rôle et Action de

l'Argentine à la Sixième Conférence Panaméricaine," *RGDIP* 36 (1929) 73–87.

4972. Scott, J. B. "The Sixth International Conference of American States, Held at Havana, January 16–February 20, 1928," *IC*, no. 241 (June, 1928).

4973. Sibert, M. "Etude de Deux Aspects Primordiaux," *RGDIP* 36 (1929) 52–72.

4974. "The Sixth Pan-American Conference," *FPAIS* 4 (1928) 50–58, 188–222.

4974a. USCH. Foreign Affairs Committee. *Sixth International Conference of American States, Habana, Cuba: Hearings* (70th Cong., 1st Sess.). Wash., 1928.

4975. USDS. *Report of Delegates of United States to 6th International Conference of American States Held at Havana, Cuba, Jan. 16–Feb. 20, 1928, with Appendices.* Wash., 1928.

4975a. Weiss, R. "La Convention Panaméricaine de la Havana sur le Droit d'Auteur," *RDIP* 27, 2d tri. (1932) 372–375.

XI–I–6   cross references: 3295, 4714

7. MONTEVIDEO, 1933

4975b. *Actas y Antecedentes, Primera a Novena Comisiones.* Montevideo, 1933.

4976. Antuña, J. G. "Ante la VII Conferencia Internacional Americana: Discurso en la Sesión Solemne en Honor de los Delegados," *RDI* 25, no. 49 (1934) 123–134.

4976a. Aris, J. T. *La Bandera de América.* Salto, 1935.

4977. Buell, R. L. "The Montevideo Conference and the Latin American Policy of the United States," *FPAR* 9, no. 19 (1933–1934) 210–221.

4978. Dávila, C. "The Montevideo Conference: Antecedents and Accomplishments," *IC*, no. 300 (May, 1934).

4979. Doyle, H. G. "The Conference at Montevideo," *CH* 39 (1934) 466–470.

4980. Eça, R. d'. "The Convention on the Teaching of History Signed at the Seventh Pan American Conference," *WA* 97 (1934) 109–113.

4981. Esquenazi-Mayo, R. *Ensayos y Apuntes. Part I: Cuba Internacional.* Havana, 1956.

4982. *Final Act.* Montevideo, 1934(?).

4983. Giúdici, E. "Los EE. UU. en la VII Conferencia Panamericana: La N.I.R.A. y su Espansión en el Exterióor," *CLA* 12, no. 272 (1933) 9–12.

4984. Gruening, E. H. "A New Deal for Latin America?" *CH* 39 (1933) 270–275.

4985. ———. "Pan-Americanism Reborn," *CH* 39 (1934) 529–534.
A sequel to item 4984.

4986. Haring, C. H. "Recent Pan American Achievements," *BPAU* 70 (1936) 78–84.

4987. Heath, D. R. "The Montevideo Conference," *AFSJ* 9 (1934) 47–50.

4988. "Informe del Sr. Presidente de la Delegación," *BMREE* (January, 1934) 32–37.
Report of the delegation from Ecuador.

4989. Inman, S. G. "Emerging America," *WA* 97 (1934) 167–172.
Optimistic appraisal of the Montevideo Conference.

4990. "Intellectual Cooperation in the Americas: The Action of the Seventh International Conference of American States," *BPAU* 68 (1934) 177–183.

4991. López, A. "La 7ª Conferencia Internacional Americana: El Jefe de la Delegación de Colombia Pronunció Discurso Sobre la Política Panamericana," *RBRC* (December, 1933) 427–430.

4992. Manger, W. "The Pan American Union and the Conclusions of the Seventh International Conference of American States," *BPAU* 69 (1935) 77–94.

4993. ———. "The Seventh International Conference of American States," *BPAU* 68 (1934) 271–283.

4994. "México en la VII Conferencia Panamericana: Labor de la Delegación Proposiciones Presentados por México: Extractos de los Discursos del Presidente de la Delegación Dr. Puig Casauranc," *BOSRE* 6 (December, 1933) 7–40.

4995. Mexico. Secretaría de Relaciones Exteriores. *Séptima Conferencia Internacional Americana, Memorial General y Actuación de la Delegación de México.* 3 vols., Mexico, 1934.

4996. *Minutes and Antecedents with General Index.* Montevideo, 1933.

4997. PAU. Governing Board. "Program and Regulation of the Seventh International

Conference of American States," *BPAU* 67 (1933) 549–557.

4998. ———. ———. "Program of the Seventh International Conference of American States," *BPAU* 66 (1932) 89–91.

4999. ———. *Treaties and Conventions Signed at the 7th International Conference of American States, Montevideo, Uruguay, December 3–26, 1933*. Wash., 1952.

5000. Pando, A. "La VII Conferencia Panamericana," *RE* (January, 1934) 68–71.

5000a. Pérez Duarte, C. *La Unión Económica Panamericana*. Montevideo, 1933.

5001. "La Posición de México en Montevideo en Materiales Económicas en General," *BOSRE* 62 (January, 1934) 7–21.

5002. "Postponement of the Seventh International Conference of American States," *BPAU* 66 (1932) 388–389.

5003. Puig Casauranc, J. M. *Algo Sobre la Posición de México en Montevideo*. Mexico, 1934.

5004. ———. "Declaraciones del Dr. Puig Casauranc, Sec. de Relaciones Exteriores y Presidente de la Delegación de México a la 7ª Conferencia Panamericana," *BOSRE* (October, 1933) 11–13.

5005. Rowe, L. S. "Foreword: The Seventh International Conference of American States," *BPAU* 68 (1934) 153–157.

5006. Scott, J. B. "Seventh International Conference of American States," *AJIL* 28 (1934) 219–230.

5007. "Séptima Conferencia Internacional Americana," *DO* (May 4, 1934) 915–936.
Report of the delegation from El Salvador.

5008. "La Séptima Conferencia Internacional Pan-Americana de Montevideo Informe: Proposición Acerca de los Bancos Centrales Sud-Americanos," *BCC* (December, 1933) 716–717.

5009. Thomson, C. A. "The Seventh Pan-American Conference: Montevideo," *FPAR* 10 (1934–1935) 86–97.

5009a. "U.S. Commercial Policy and the Montevideo Program," *CPA*, no. 32 (January, 1935).

5010. USDS. *Report of the Delegates of the United States of America to the Seventh International Conference of American States, Montevideo, Uruguay, December 3–26, 1933*. Wash., 1934.

5011. ———. *Seventh International Conference of American States, Montevideo-Uruguay, December 3–26, 1933: Final Act, Including the Conventions and Additional Protocol Adopted by the Conference*. Wash., 1934.

5011a. Villard, H. S. "Sailing Down to Montevideo," *AFSJ* 10 (January, 1934) 12–14.

5012. Wolfe, G. B. "The Montevideo Conference, 1933: Reactions of North and South American Press to Foreign Policy of the United States," Fletcher School of Law and Diplomacy Diss., 1960.

5012a. Wright, H. "The Montevideo Conference and Organization for Peace," *WA* 97 (June, 1934) 100–103.

XI–I–7   cross references: 3340, 3359, 3362, 3377

8. LIMA, 1938

5012b. *Actas de las Sesiones Plenarias*. 2 vols., Lima, 1938.

5013. Alfaro, R. J. "Significación Internacional de la Conferencia de Lima," *RDI* 35 (June, 1939) 153–162.
Author was the Provisional President of Panama, 1931–1932, and a delegate to the conference.

5014. Antuña, J. G. *El Uruguay, en Ginebra y en Lima: En el Senado de la República*. Montevideo, 1939.

5015. Arantes, A. "O Panamericanismo e suas Realizações no Conferência de Lima," *MJC* 3 (1939) 739–746.
Author was in the Brazilian delegation.

5016. Argentina. Ministerio de Relaciones Exteriores y Culto. División de Asuntos Jurídicos. *La República Argentina en la Octava Conferencia Internacional Americana Reunida en Lima del 9 al 27 de Diciembre de 1938*. B.A., 1939.

5017. Bacher, E. L. "Economic and Export Trade Subjects at the Pan-American Conference," *ETS* 38, no. 14 (1938) 11–13.

5018. Belaúnde, V. A. "La Conferencia Panamericana de Lima," *RUCP* 7 (April, 1939) 26–30.

5019. ———. "La VIII Conferencia Panamericana," *MP* 21, no. 146 (1939) 47–57.

5020. Beltraneja, L. "La Octava Conferencia Americana," *RFCJSG*, no. 4 (1939) 430–436.

5021. Berle, A. A., Jr. "After Lima," *YR* 28 (1939) 449–471.

5022. Berner, H. *Die Panamerikanischen Friedenssicherungsverträge*. Berlin, 1938.

5023. Borchard, E. "The 'Committee of Experts' at the Lima Conference," *AJIL* 33 (1939) 269–282.

5024. Butler, G. H. "The Lima Conference," *AFSJ* 16 (April, 1939) 187–189, 220.

5024a. Carbajal, F. "América y la Conferencia de Lima," *RRO* 12 (March, 1939) 4–6.

5025. Carson, J. S. "Brazil at the Lima Conference," *BR* 11 (February, 1939) 6–7.

5026. Castillo Nájera, F. *Discurso Pronunciado en la Octava Conferencia Internacional Americana Celebrada en Lima, Perú, en Sesión Plenaria Efectuada el Viernes 16 de Diciembre de 1938*. Mexico, 1939.

5027. Chamber of Commerce of the United States. *Economic Topics of the Eighth Pan-American Conference*. Wash., 1938.

5028. Colby, B. "The Lima Conference and the Monroe Doctrine," *ABAJ* 25 (March, 1939) 210–214.

5029. Colombia. Ministerio de Relaciones Exteriores. *Proyecto de Tratado Sobre la Creación de una Asociación de Naciones Americanas y Exposición de Motivos*. Bogotá, 1938.

5030. Cox, G. H. "Lima and Inter-American Solidarity," *WA* 102 (March, 1939) 26–41.

5031. *Diario de la VIII Conferencia Internacional Americana*. Lima, 1938.

5032. "Eighth International Conference of American States," *IC* 349 (April, 1939).

5033. Fenwick, C. G. "Lima Conference, in Relation to World Peace," *AAAPSS* 204 (1939) 119–125.

5033a. Grand, A. "Pan American Peace: Results Obtained at Lima," *AM* 163 (March, 1939) 385–389.

5034. *Informe de la Delegación de México a la Octava Conferencia Internacional Americana, Reunida en Lima, Peru, de 9 al 27 de Diciembre de 1938*. Mexico, 1940.

5035. Inman, S. G. (ed.). "The Lima Conference and the Future of Pan Americanism: Addresses at a Conference Sponsored by the Wharton School of the University of Pennsylvania, March 10 and 11, 1939," *AAAPSS* 204 (1939) 129–174.

5036. ———. "The Lima Conference and the Totalitarian Issue," *AAAPSS* 204 (1939) 9–16.

5037. *Final Act*. Lima, 1938.

5038. League of Nations Association. Latin American Committee. *The Lima Conference and World Peace*. N.Y., 1938.

5039. Ludewig, C. K. "Commercial Policy and the Lima Conference," *CPA* (February, 1939) 1–9.

5040. Macedonio Urquidi, J. "Ecos de la VIII Conferencia Panamericana: Breves Observaciones al Proyecto Concerniente a la Corte Interamericana de Justicia Internacional, Presentado por la Delegación Argentina," *RJ* (February, 1939) 79–81.

5041. McCulloch, J. I. B. "Lima Conference Results," *E* 5 (1939) 96–103.

5042. McSpadden, G. E. "Cultural Aspects of the Conference in Lima," *H* 22 (May, 1939) 159–164.

5043. Mencia y de Armas, A. "Comentarios y Sugestiones Sobre el Tema 8 de la VIII Conferencia Panamericana," *RDI* 34, no. 67 (1938) 81–138.

5044. Oficina Interamericana de Marcas. "Report Which the Inter-American Trademark Bureau, of Havana, Presents to the Eighth International American Conference in Relation to the Protection on Industrial Property in America," *BITB* 6 (October, 1938) 51–58.

5045. Orrego, A. "La Conferencia Pan-Americana de Lima," *CLA* 18 (February, 1939).

5046. PAU. *Eighth International Conference of American States, Lima, Peru, December 9–27, 1938: Report of the Results of the Conference*. Wash., 1939.

5047. ———. *Eighth International Conference of American States, Lima, Peru, December 1938: Report of the Committee on the Relations of the Pan-American Organs to Other Entities and on the Functions of the Pan-American Union to Be Submitted to* the Eighth International Conference of American States. Wash., 1938.

5048. ———. Special Handbook for the Use of Delegates. Wash., 1938.

5049. Pepin, E. "La Conférence de Lima et l'Avenir du Pan-Américanisme," FAM n.s., 30 (January, 1939) 11–15.

5050. Ravines, E. Ante la Octava Conferencia Panamericana. Santiago, 1938.

5051. Rheinbaben, W. von. "Die Panamerikanische Konferenz in Lima," MAP 5 (1939) 138–150, 251–262.

5052. Rowe, L. S. "The Eighth International Conference of American States," BPAU 73 (1939) 121–128.

5053. ———. "The Larger Significance of the Lima Conference," AAAPSS 204 (1939) 137–140.

5054. Schneider, A. "Streiflichter auf Pan-Amerikanismus und die Konferenz von Lima," IR 4 (January, 1939) 275–277.

5055. Secretaría de Prensa y Propaganda del Partido Aprista Peruano. VIII Conferencia Panamericana: Informe Acerca de la Realidad Peruana. N.p., 1938.

5056. Stuart, G. H. "The Eighth International Conference of American States," WAI 10 (April, 1939) 9–14.

5057. Tavara, M. M. "Les Travaux de la Conférence," FAM 30, n.s. (January, 1939) 6–11.

5058. Thomson, C. A. "Results of the Lima Conference," FPAR 15 (March, 1939) 1–8.

5059. Tomlinson, E. "The Meaning of Lima: Secretary Hull's Handling of the Argentine Problem Was the Highspot of the Conference," CH 49 (February, 1939) 37–41.

5060. Tracy, D. W. "Eighth International Conference of American States," AF 46 (March, 1939) 284–287.

5061. USDS. Report of the Delegation of the United States of America to the Eighth International Conference of American States, Lima, Peru, Dec. 9–27, 1938. Wash., 1941.

5061a. Villalobos Domínguez, C. "La Conferencia de Lima," NOS 4 (January, 1939) 38–50.

5062. Yepes, J. M. "La Conférence Panaméricaine de Lima," FAM 30, n.s. (January, 1939) 1–5.

5063. White, J. W. "The New Pan-Americanism," QJIR 1, no. 22 (1939) 31–36.

XI–I–8 cross references:

a) For the establishment of emergency procedures, see items 5181i–5189.

b) See also items 3340, 3388, 4512, 5451, 5477.

9. BOGOTÁ, 1948

5064. "Acta Final de la Conferencia de Bogotá," MLI 5 (August, 1948) 3–18; 5 (September, 1948) 3–15; 5 (October, 1948) 35–48.

5064a. Arango Vélez, C. Comunismo y Democracia: Texto y Comentario de la Moción Anti-Comunista Aprobada por la IX Conferencia Pan-Americana de Bogotá. Bogotá, 1948.

5064b. Armour, N. "Achievements of the Bogotá Conference," USDSB 18 (1948) 714–715.

5064c. ———. "Economic Aspects of the Bogotá Conference," USDSB 17 (1947) 1214–1218.

5065. Brigard Silva, C. de. La Neuvième Conférence Internationale Américaine de Bogotá, 1948. Paris, 1948.

5066. Caceres, J. R. "Lectura Acerca de la Novena Conferencia Interamericana," VER 18, no. 210 (1948) 1020–1023.

5067. Canyes, M. S. "The Ninth International Conference of American States," BPAU 81 (1947) 351–360.

5068. Chalmers, H. "The Economic Agreement of Bogotá: An Inter-American Milestone," FCW 31, no. 11 (1948) 5–6.

5068a. Colección Cronológica de Documentos. 5 vols., Wash., 1946-1948.

5069. Colombia. Ministerio de Relaciones Exteriores. Actas y Documentos. 7 vols., Bogotá, 1953.

5069a. "La Conferencia de Bogotá: Argentina y Estados Unidos Fijan Posiciones," HID 13 (March, 1948) 21–36.

5069b. Córdova, R. "Los Problemas Políticos y Jurídicos en la Conferencia de Bogotá," MANHG 4, no. 7 (1948) 9–25.

5069c. Cuevas Cancino, F. "The Bogotá Conference and Recent Developments in Pan-American Relations: A Mexican View," IAF 24 (1948) 524–533.

5070. Deambrosis Martins, C. *La Conferencia de Bogotá y la Posición de Guatemala.* Guatemala, 1948.

5071. Duggan, L. "Lo que Falta a la IX CIA: Las Relaciones Culturales," *RA* (April, 1948) 136–140.

5071a. Ernst, H. *Die Interamerikanischen Konferenzen von Rio de Janeiro und Bogota.* Mainz, N.d.

5072. Fenwick, C. G. "The Ninth International Conference of American States," *AJIL* 42 (1948) 553–567.

5073. ———. "The Pact of Bogotá and Other Juridical Decisions of the Ninth Conference," *BPAU* 82 (1948) 421–435.

5074. Fernández MacGregor, G. "México en Bogotá," *MLI* 5 (June, 1948) 30–31.

5075. Furniss, E. S., Jr. "Recent Changes in the Inter-American System," *IO* 2 (1948) 455–468.

5076. Hadley, P. E. "Ninth International Conference of American States, Bogotá, Colombia, March 30–May 2, 1948," *WAI* 19 (Summer, 1948) 181–193.

5077. Haya de la Torre, V. R. "La Próxima Conferencia Interamericana," *RA* (March, 1948) 353–355.

5078. Inman, S. G. "Failure at Bogotá," *WA* 2, n.s. (1948) 429–433.

5079. ———. "Pan-American and U.S. Issues at Bogotá," *SG* 37 (April, 1948) 208–212.

5080. Kunz, J. L. "The Bogotá Charter of the Organization of the American States," *AJIL* 42 (1948) 568–589.

5081. Lleras Camargo, A. "The Bogotá Conference," *BPAU* 82 (1948) 301–311.

5082. ———. "La Conferencia de Bogotá," *RGC* 4 (July, 1948) 64, 67–70.

5083. ———. "Conferencia Pronunciada en la Unión Panamericana," *DRCA* 9 (1950) 113–125.

5084. Lockwood, J. E. "The Economic Agreement of Bogotá," *AJIL* 42 (1948) 611–620.

5085. Lozano y Lozano, C. "Colombia en la IX Conferencia," *CEC* 7 (April, 1948) 483–485.

5086. Manross, L. M. *The Bogotá Conference.* Wash., 1949.

5087. Martínez Moreno, R. S. *América, en Bogotá: Novena Conferencia Internacional Americana: Documentos Suscritos, Im-presiones Generales, la Revolución de Abril.* Tucumán, 1948.

5088. Mexico. Secretaría de Relaciones Exteriores. Departamento de Información para el Extranjero. *México en la IX Conferencia Internacional Americana, Bogotá, 30 de Marzo–2 de Mayo de 1948.* Mexico, 1948.

5089. "Novena Conferencia Internacional Americana," *BMREC* 3 (April, 1948) 5–183.

5090. PAU. *Final Act.* Wash., 1948.

5091. ———. *Program and Regulations.* Wash., 1947.

5092. Piccirilli, R. "La Novena Conferencia Internacional Americana," *RDICD* 1 (April, 1949) 9–58.

5093. Regules, D. *La Lucha por la Justicia y por el Derecho: Apuntes Sobre la IX Conferencia Panamericana Reunida en Bogotá Durante el Mes de Abril de 1948.* Montevideo, 1949.
    Author was chairman of the Uruguayan delegation.

5094. "Report on the Ninth International Conference of American States," *AOAS* 1, no. 1 (1949) 1–75.

5094a. Rosa, P. de la. "La Conferencia de Bogotá," *BMREC* 3 (August, 1948) 65–83.

5095. ———. "La Conferencia Panamericana de Bogotá," *Y* 58 (January, 1949) 17–33.

5096. Sanin Cano, B. "Bogotá y la Novena Conferencia," *RA* (April, 1948) 1–5.

5096a. Szulc, T. "Ninth Conference of the Americas," *PAAM* 9 (May, 1948) 5–9.

5097. Torres Bodet, J. "The Ninth International Conference of American States," *SSM* 1, no. 4 (1948) 1–12.

5098. Turlington, E. "The Pact of Bogotá," *AJIL* 42 (1948) 608–611.

5099. USDA. *Ninth International Conference of American States, Bogotá, Colombia, March 30–May 2, 1948: Report of the Delegation of the United States of America with Related Documents.* Wash., 1948.

5100. Whitaker, A. P. "Rio and Bogotá: Pan American Perspective," *IEA* 1 (December, 1947) 23–44.

5101. Ycaza Tigerino, J. "Crisis del Panamericanismo en la IX Conferencia Interamericana," *CUH* (May, 1948) 479–492.

5102. Yepes, J. M. "La Conférence Pan-américaine de Bogotá, et le Droit International Américain," *RGDIP* 20 (1949) 17–88.

5103. ———. "La Conferencia de Bogotá y los Progresos del Panamericanismo," *RIN* (March, 1948) 355–404.

5104. Zuleta, L. de. "La Conferencia de Bogotá: América y el Mundo," *RA* (April, 1948) 103–106.

XI–I–9   cross references: 5263, 9842, 9853

10. CARACAS, 1954

5104a. *Actas y Documentos*. 6 vols., Wash., 1956.

5105. Argentina. Ministerio de Relaciones Exteriores. *Argentina en la X Conferencia Interamericana*. B.A., 1954.

5106. Betancourt, R. "La Conferencia de Caracas, Hora Crítica del Panamericanismo," *CUA* 7 (July, 1954) 64–68.

5107. ———. "La Opinión Continental Frente a la X Conferencia Interamericana," *CA* 71 (September, 1953) 7–37.

5108. Bowdler, W. G. "Report on the Tenth Inter-American Conference," *BPAU* 30 (1954) 634–639.

5109. Caicedo Castilla, J. J. "La Comité Juridique de Rio de Janeiro et la Préparation de la Prochaine Conférence Panaméricaine de Caracas," *RGDIP* 24 (1953) 40–54.

5110. Castañeda, J. "El Panamericanismo y la Conferencia de Caracas," *IE* 14, no. 3 (1954) 373–384.

5110a. Compton, G. C. "Prologue to the Tenth Conference," *APAU* 6 (February, 1954) 3–5, 35.

5111. Durón, J. F. "Honduras y la Décima Conferencia Interamericana," *HR* 12 (April, 1954) 8–11.

5112. Fabela, I. *La Conferencia de Caracas y la Actitud Anticomunista de México*. Mexico, 1954.

5113. Fenwick, C. G. "The Coming Inter-American Conference at Caracas," *WA* 116 (Winter, 1953) 115–117.

5114. ———. "Intervention at the Caracas Conference," *AJIL* 48 (1954) 451–453.

5115. ———. "The Tenth Inter-American Conference at Caracas," *AJIL* 48 (1954) 136–140, 464–469.

5116. Ganzert, F. W. "The Caracas Conference," *WA* 117 (Summer, 1954) 44–46.

5117. Hadley, P. E. "The Caracas Conference," *WAI* 25 (Summer, 1954) 123–139.

5118. Lleras Camargo, A. "Tenth Conference Report," *APAU* 6 (May, 1954) 3–5, 41–43.

5119. Mexico. Secretaría de Relaciones Exteriores. *México en la X Conferencia Interamericana*. 2 vols., Mexico, 1959.

5119a. Otárola Aqueveque, H. "Algunos Comentarios Sobre la 'Declaración de Solidaridad para la Preservación de la Integridad Política de los Estados Americanos Contra la Intervención del Comunismo Internacional,' de la Décima Conferencia Interamericana," *RDCC* 24 (April, 1956) 172–191.

5120. Padilla Nervo, L. "México en Caracas," *CA* 75 (May, 1954) 45–56.

5121. PAU. *Organization of American States, 10th Inter-American Conference, Caracas, Venezuela, 1954: Documents*. Wash., 1954.

5122. ———. *Relatório da União Pan-Americana Sôbre a Conferência*. Wash., 1955.

5123. Roussin, M. "Caracas, Mars 1954," *RUO* 24 (October, 1954) 421–431.

5124. Ruiz, B. F. "La Xª Conferencia Interamericana," *RAGDI* 1 (January, 1954) 165–167.

5125. Samper, D. *La X Conferencia Interamericana de Caracas ante los Pueblos del Continente*. Bogotá, 1954.

5125a. Secretaría General de la Décima Conferencia Interamericana. *Acta Final*. Caracas, 1954.

5126. Stebbins, J. H. "Conference at Caracas," *GL* 29 (May, 1954) 2–4.

5127. USDS. *Tenth Inter-American Conference, Caracas, Venezuela, March 1–28, 1954: Report of the Delegation of the United States of America, with Related Documents*. Wash., 1955.

5127a. Vergara Donoao, G. "La Conferencia de Caracas," *FT* 1, no. 1 (1954) 5–19.

XI–I–10   cross references:

For studies on John F. Dulles see items 3849, 3851, 3865, 3874, 3878, 3919.

J. SPECIAL AND CONSULTATIVE CONFERENCES

1. CENTRAL AMERICAN PEACE CONFERENCE— WASHINGTON, 1907

5128. Anderson, L. "Peace Conference of Central America," *AJIL* 2 (1908) 144–151.

5129. Central American Peace Conference. *Actas y Documentos.* Wash., 1907.

5130. Buchanan, W. I. *The Central American Peace Conference, Held at Washington, D.C., 1907.* Wash., 1908.

5131. *Conferencia de Paz Centroamericana, 20 de Diciembre de 1907.* San José, C.R., 1907.

5132. *Documentos Relativos a la Conferencia de Paz Centroamericana: Tratados y Convenciones Concluidos por los Delegados de las Cinco Repúblicas de Centro América.* San Salvador, 1908.

5133. Martínez Moreno, A. *La Conferencia de Washington de 1907 y la Corte de Justicia Centroamericana.* San Salvador, 1957.

5134. Rey, F. *La Unión Centro-Americana: Estudio Relativo a las Instituciones Creadas en Washington por la Conferencia de Paz Centro-Americana de 1907.* Guatemala, 1911.

5135. Scott, J. B. "The Central American Peace Conference of 1907," *AJIL* 2 (1908) 121–143.

2. SECOND CONFERENCE ON CENTRAL AMERICAN AFFAIRS—WASHINGTON, 1922–1923

5136. "Central American Conference, Inaugural Session, December, 1922," *BPAU* 56 (1923) 1–12.

5137. "Closing Session," *BPAU* 56 (1923) 217–229.

5138. *Conferencia Sobre Asuntos Centroamericanos: Manual Especial para el Uso de los Delegados.* Wash., 1922.

5139. Nicaragua. Secretaría de Relaciones Exteriores. *Memoria de Relaciones Exteriores Presentada al Congreso Nacional por el Señor Ministro Ingeniero Don José Andrés Urtecho, 1923.* Managua, 1924.

5140. Perry, E. "Central American Union," *HAHR* 5 (1922) 30–51.
    Summarizes the 1922 conference.

5141. Scott, J. B. "The Central American

Conference," *AJIL* 17 (1923) 313–319.

5142. "The Conference on Central American Affairs, Held in Washington, D.C., from December 4, 1922, to February 7, 1923: Texts of Treaties, Conventions, and Protocols Adopted, with an Introduction by Dr. Leo S. Rowe," *IC*, no. 189 (1923).

5143. USDS. *Conference on Central American Affairs, Washington, Dec. 4, 1922–Feb. 7, 1923.* Wash., 1923.

3. CONFERENCE ON CONCILIATION AND ARBITRATION —WASHINGTON, 1928–1929

5144. Hughes, C. E. "Pan-American Peace," *YR* 18, n.s. (1929) 646–668.

5145. Oliveira, P. M. "El Tratado General de Arbitraje Interamericano de Wáshington," *RDCP* 3, no. 1 (1939) 3–34.

5146. *Proceedings of the International Conference of American States on Conciliation and Arbitration.* Wash., 1929.

5147. Scott, J. B. "The Pan American Conference on Conciliation and Arbitration," *AJIL* 23 (1929) 143–152.

5148. Stone, W. T. "The Pan American Arbitration Treaty," *FPAIS* 5 (1929) 313–326.

5149. USDS. *General Convention of Inter-American Conciliation.* Wash., 1929.
    Text of the agreement.

XI-J-3   cross references: 4966

4. CONFERENCE ON MAINTENANCE OF PEACE— BUENOS AIRES, 1936

5150. Accioly, H. *Relatório Sôbre os Trabalhos da 1ª, 2ª, 4ª Commissões da Conferência Interamericana de Consolidação da Paz Reunida em Buenos Aires em Dezembro de 1936 Apresentado a s. Ex. o Sr. Dr. Mario de Pimentel Brandão, Ministro de Estado das Relações Exteriores, por Hildebrando Accioly, Delegado do Brasil.* Rio, 1937.

5150a. Alfaro, R. J. *El Problema de la Paz en Buenos Aires.* Wash., 1936.

5150b. Borge, E. *Buenos Oficios y Mediación: Conferencia Interamericana de la Paz, Buenos Aires, 1936.* León, Nicaragua, 1938.

5151. *Conferencia Interamericana de Consolidación de la Paz: Diario de Sesiones (Versiones Taquigráficas).* B.A., 1937.

5152. *Conferencia Inter-Americana de Consolidación de la Paz: Informe de la Delegación de El Salvador.* San Salvador, 1937.

5153. Cortina, J. M. *América y el Destino del Hombre.* Havana, 1938.
Summary of the conference.

5154. Cox, G. H. "Buenos Aires Host to Inter-American Congress," *WA* 99 (December, 1936) 238–246.

5154a. *Diario de la Conferencia Interamericana de Consolidación de la Paz.* B.A., 1936.

5155. Diez de Medina, R. "The Buenos Aires Conference Reinterpreted," *WA* 100 (September, 1937) 151–159.

5156. "Economic Aspects of the Buenos Aires Conference," *CPA* (February, 1937).

5157. Etcheverry, E. "Derecho Internacional Americano, por Nuevos Conceptos Políticos y Económicos," *BIP* 13 (May, 1936) 17–20.

5158. Fenwick, C. G. "The Buenos Aires Peace Conference, 1936," *FPAR* 13 (1937) 90–100.

5159. ———. "Inter-American Conference for Maintenance of Peace," *AJIL* 31 (1937) 201–225.

5159a. *Final Act of the Inter-American Conference for the Maintenance of Peace.* B.A., 1936.

5160. Henríquez, H. *La Liga de Naciones Americanas: Prefacio de Joaquín Balaguer.* Cd. Trujillo, 1956.

5161. Henríquez Ureña, M. *La Liga de Naciones Americanas y la Conferencia de Buenos Aires: Discursos ante la Asamblea: Rectificaciones al Dr. Saavedra Lamas: Antecedentes, Proyectos, Documentos.* N.Y., 1937.

5162. Herring, H. "Toward Pan American Peace," *CH* 44 (April, 1936) 75–77.

5163. Honduras. Secretaría de Relaciones Exteriores. *Conferencia Interamericana de Consolidación de la Paz.* Tegucigalpa, 1937.

5164. Hull, C. "The Results and Significance of the Buenos Aires Conference," *FA* 15 suppl., no. 3 (1937).

5165. Inman, S. G. "An Appraisal of the Buenos Aires Conference," *WA* 100 (March, 1937) 50–54.

5166. ———. *The Inter-American Conference for the Maintenance of Peace.* Phil., 1936.

5167. "Inter-American Conference for the Maintenance of Peace," *AJIL* 31 (1937) 201–225.

5167a. "The Inter-American Conference for the Maintenance of Peace," *IC*, no. 328 (1937) 198–289.

5168. "Inter-American Conference for the Maintenance of Peace: Text of Mr. Hull's Address at the Closing Session, and of Main Articles of Treaties and Conventions," *BPAU* 71 (1937) 87–109.

5169. Jessup, P. C. "Inter-American Conference for the Maintenance of Peace," *AJIL* 31 (1937) 85–91.

5169a. Kain, R. S. "Peace and the Americas, the Aims and the Problems of the Pan American Conference," *CH* 45 (December, 1936) 57–61.

5170. McKelvey, R. G. "Achievements of the Buenos Aires Conference," *PIWA* 15 (1938) 69–72.

5171. Méndez Calzada, E. "La Conférence Pan-Américaine de la Paix," *RARG* 2 (1936) 1–10.

5172. México. Delegación a la Conferencia Interamericana de Consolidación de la Paz. *Informe de la Delegación de México a la Conferencia Interamericana de Consolidación de la Paz, Reunida en Buenos Aires.* Mexico, 1938.

5173. Nerval, G. "The Buenos Aires Conference Reinterpreted," *WA* 100 (1937) 151–159.

5174. Nicaragua. *Memorandum Preparado por la Delegación Nicaragüense que Representará a la República en la Conferencia Interamericana de Consolidación de la Paz.* Managua, 1936.

5175. Prats-Ramírez, F. *La República Dominicana en la Conferencia de Buenos Aires.* Cd. Trujillo, 1937.

5176. Rippy, J. F. "The Buenos Aires Peace Conference of 1936," *SAQ* 36 (1937) 171–179.

5177. ———. "The Conference of Buenos Aires: A Retrospective View," *WA* 100 (March, 1937) 46–49.

5178. Saavedra Lamas, C. *La Conferencia Inter-Americana de Consolidación de la Paz.* B.A., 1938.

5179. *Special Handbook for the Use of Delegates.* Baltimore, 1936.

5180. Stowell, E. C. "President Roosevelt's Proposal of an Extraordinary Pan American Conference," *AJIL* 30 (1936) 270–273.

5181. USDS. *Report of the Delegation of the United States of America to the Inter-American Conference for the Maintenance of Peace, Buenos Aires, Argentina, December 1–23, 1936.* Wash., 1937.

5181a. ———. *Results and Significance of Buenos Aires Conference, Address by Cordell Hull, Secretary of State, Before the Council on Foreign Relations.* Wash., 1937.

5181b. Welles, S. *The Accomplishments of the Inter-American Conference for the Maintenance of Peace. Address . . . Before the People's Mandate to Government to End Wars. New York City, February 4, 1937.* Wash., 1937.

5181c. ———. "The New Era in Pan American Relations," *FA* 15 (1937) 443–454.

5181d. ———. "Results of the South American Conference," *PAPS* 17 (1937) 297–308.

5181e. Yepes, J. M. *La Conception Américaine de la Paix et la Conférence de Buenos-Ayres.* Paris, 1937.

5181f. ———. "La Conférence Panaméricaine pour la Consolidation de la Paix et la Nouveau Panaméricanisme," *RDILC* 18 (1937) 476–544, 745–785.

5181g. ———. "The League of American Nations," *BI* 16 (June, 1936) 91–104.

5181h. ———. "Pax Americana: The New Pan Americanism and the Pan American Peace Conference Convoked by President Franklin D. Roosevelt," *WA* 99 (1936) 80–86.

XI–J–4   cross references: 3340, 4519, 9107

5. ESTABLISHMENT OF EMERGENCY PROCEDURES

5181i. Caisullo, A. L. *El Sistema Consultivo Panamericano: Su Estructura, su Naturaleza, su Aplicación, sus Consecuencias.* Montevideo, 1947.

5181j. Canyes, M. *Las Reuniones de Consulta: Origen, Desarrollo y Papel que Desempeñan en las Relaciones Interamericanas.* 3d ed., Wash., 1962.

5182. Carbajal, C. "Espíritu de las Conferencias Panamericas de Lima, Panamá y La Habana," *RMN* 2d sem. (1941) 17–26.

5183. Cravioto González, J. *El Panamericanismo a Través de las Tres Reuniones de Consulta Entre los Ministros de Relaciones Exteriores de las Repúblicas Americanas.* Mexico, 1943.

5184. Morales Morales, M. *Aspectos Políticos del Sistema Interamericano: Las Reuniones de Cancilleres.* Mexico, 1961.

5185. PAU. *Medidas Adoptadas por la Unión Panamericana para Llevar a Efecto las Resoluciones Aprobadas por la Octava Conferencia Internacional Americana y Ciertas Convenciones y Resoluciones de Otras Conferencias Interamericanas.* Wash., 1942.

5186. ———. *Medidas Adoptadas por la Unión Panamericana para Llevar a Efecto las Resoluciones Aprobadas por la Octava Conferencia Internacional Americana y las Tres Reuniones de Consulta de los Ministros de Relaciones Exteriores de las Repúblicas Americanas.* Wash., 1943.

5187. ———. *Perfeccionamiento y Coordinación de los Instrumentos Interamericanos de Paz: Resolución 15 de la Octava Conferencia Internacional Americana.* 5 vols., Wash., 1940.

5187a. ———. *Report on the Results of the [Lima] Conference.* Wash., 1939.

5188. ———. *Steps Taken by the Pan American Union in Fulfillment of the Resolutions Adopted at the Eighth International Conference of American States and Other Interamerican Conferences.* Wash., 1940.

5189. Staines Flores, M. J. *El Sistema de Consulta en las Relaciones Interamericanas.* Mexico, 1956.

XI–J–5   cross references: For works on the Lima Conference (1938), see items 5013–5063.

6. FIRST CONSULTATIVE CONFERENCE—PANAMA, 1939

5189a. *Acta Final de la Reunión de Consulta Entre los Ministros de Relaciones Exteriores de las Repúblicas Americanas en Panamá.* Panama, 1939.

5189b. Argentina. Ministerio de Relaciones Exteriores y Culto. *Reuniones de Consulta Entre Ministros de Relaciones Exteriores de las Repúblicas Americanas: Panamá, 23 de Septiembre al 3 de Octubre de 1939:*

la Habana, 21 al 30 de Junio de 1940: Participación Argentina. B.A., 1941.

5190.   Arias, H., Jr. "A Collective Neutrality Front for the Americas," *IAQ* 2 (January, 1940) 59–67.

5191.   Arosemena, J. D. *Discurso Pronunciado por el Presidente de la República de Panamá, . . . en la Sesión Inaugural de la Reunión Consultiva de los Ministros de Relaciones Exteriores de las Repúblicas Americanas.* Panama, 1939.

5192.   Betancur, C. "La Conferencia de Panamá," *RJA* 12 (November, 1939) 284–288.

5193.   Brown, P. M. "Protective Jurisdiction," *AJIL* 34 (1940) 112–116.

5194.   "Consultative Meeting of Foreign Ministers of the American Republics," *IC*, no. 356 (September, 1939).

5195.   "Consultative Meeting of Foreign Ministers of the American Republics: Final Act of the Meeting" *USDSB* 1 (1939) 321–334.

5196.   Fenwick, C. G. "The Declaration of Panama," *AJIL* 34 (1940) 116–119.

5197.   PAU. Inter-American Neutrality Committee. *Recommendation on the Security Zone Created by the Declaration of Panama Submitted to the Governments, Members of the Pan American Union.* Wash., 1940.

5198.   *La Reunión de Consulta Entre las Ministros de Relaciones Exteriores de las Repúblicas Americanas (Panamá, 23 de Septiembre–3 de Octubre de 1939): Informe de la Delegación de Bolivia.* La Paz, 1939.

5199.   Rowe, L. S. "Meeting of the Ministers of Foreign Affairs of the American Republics, Panama, Sept. 23–Oct. 3," *BPAU* 73 (1939) 609–620.

5200.   Sanders, W. "Consultation Among the American Republics: The Panama Meeting," *WA* 102 (December, 1939) 231–234.

5201.   USDS. *Report of the Delegate of the United States of America to the Meeting of the Foreign Ministers of the American Republics Held at Panama, September 23–October 3, 1939.* Wash., 1940.

7. SECOND CONSULTATIVE CONFERENCE—HAVANA, 1940

5202.   *Acta Final de la II Reunión de Consulta Entre los Ministros de Relaciones Exteri-* *ores de las Repúblicas Americanas: Suscrita en la Habana el Día Treinta de Julio de Mil Novecientos Cuarenta.* Rio, 1942.

5203.   Dozer, D. M. "Certain Backgrounds and Results of the Havana Conference," *WA* 103 (September, 1940) 164–171.

5204.   Ducassi Mendieta, F. *El Desempleo en la Economía: Oportunidad de la Conferencia de los Estados de América en la Habana.* Matanzas, Cuba, 1939.

5205.   "The Havana Conference," *FOR* 22 (September, 1940) 74–76, 141–151.

5206.   Melo, L. *Panamericanismo y la Reunión de la Habana: Publicación Dispuesta en Homenaje al Dr. Leopoldo Melo con Motivo de su Destacada Actuación en la Presidencia de la Delegación Argentina a la II Reunión Consultiva de Ministros de Relaciones Exteriores y sus Representantes Realizada en la Habana.* B.A., 1940.

5207.   Obermeyer, C. *The Havana Conference.* N.Y., 1940.

5208.   PAU. *Report on the Second Meeting of the Ministers of Foreign Affairs of the American Republics.* Wash., 1940.

5209.   *Reunión de Consulta Entre los Ministros de Relaciones Exteriores, de las Repúblicas Americanas, Segunda, la Habana, 1940: Diario de Sessiones.* Havana, 1940.

5210.   Stowell, E. C. "The Habana Conference and Inter-American Cooperation," *AJIL* 35 (1941) 123–131.
         Contains texts of Cordell Hull's speeches.

5211.   Trueblood, H. J. "The Havana Conference of 1940," *FPAR* 16 (1940–1941) 158–165.

5212.   USCS. *Provisional Administration of European Colonies and Possessions in the Americas, Message from the President of the United States Transmitting a Convention Entitled "Convention on the Provisional Administration of European Colonies and Possessions in the Americas," Signed at Habana on July 30, 1940* (76th Cong., 3d Sess.). Wash., 1940.

5213.   USDS. *Achievements of the Second Meeting of the Foreign Ministers of the American Republics: Statement of the Honorable Cordell Hull, Secretary of State, at the Close of the Meeting, Havana, July 30, 1940.* Wash., 1940.

5214. USDS. *Meeting of Ministers of Foreign Affairs of American Republics. Second Meeting . . . Havana, July 21–30, 1940, Report of the Secretary of State.* Wash., 1941.

5215. ————. *Report on the Second Meeting of the Ministers of Foreign Affairs of the American Republics, Havana, July 21–30, 1940: Submitted to the Governing Board of the Pan American Union by the General Director.* Wash., 1940.

XI–J–7   cross references: 3493, 5189b

8. THIRD CONSULTATIVE CONFERENCE—RIO DE JANEIRO, 1942

5216. *Ato Final da Terceira Reunião de Consulta dos Ministros das Relações Exteriores das Repúblicas Americanas.* Rio, 1942.

5217. Ayala, S. F. *El Tratado del Sacrificio: (Protocolo de Rio de Janeiro, 29 de Enero de 1942): Conferencia.* Santiago, 1942.

5218. Carnegie Endowment for International Peace. Division of Intercourse and Education. "Third Meeting of Ministers of Foreign Affairs of the American Republics, Rio de Janeiro, January 15–28, 1942: Text of Final Act with Introduction by the Hon. Sumner Welles," *IC*, no. 378 (March, 1942).

5219. Fenwick, C. G. "The Third Meeting of Ministers of Foreign Affairs at Rio de Janeiro," *AJIL* 36 (1942) 169–203.

5220. Gallardo N., G. *La Conferencia de Rio de Janeiro de 1942.* Santiago, 1942.

5221. Humphrey, J. P. "Argentina's Diplomatic Victory," *CF* 21 (March, 1942) 362–364.

5222. Latin American Juridical Committee. "Preliminary Recommendations on Postwar Problems: Formulated at the Request of the Third Meeting of Ministers of Foreign Affairs of the American Republics, Rio de Janeiro, January, 1942," *IC*, no. 387 (February, 1943).

5223. PAU. *Report on the Third Meeting of the Ministers of Foreign Affairs of the American Republics.* Wash., 1942.

5224. Popper, D. H. "The Rio de Janeiro Conference of 1942," *FPAR* 17 (April, 1942) 26–35.

5225. Rio, P. del. "La Reunión de Rio de Janeiro y sus Consecuencias para la Unidad Continental," *A* 13 (February, 1942) 1–6.

5226. "Reunião das Nações Americanas," *OEF* 6 (February, 1942) 9–19, 65–71.

5227. Sierra, M. J. "La Conferencia de Rio de Janeiro," *CA* 2 (March, 1942) 46–49.

5228. USDS. *Final Act of the Third Meeting of Ministers of Foreign Affairs. . . .* Wash., 1942.

5229. Varsi, T. *La Neutralidad Argentina ante la Guerra Mundial.* 2d rev. ed., Rosario, Argentina, 1943.

XI–J–8   cross references: 3444

9. CONFERENCE ON PROBLEMS OF WAR AND PEACE—MEXICO CITY (CHAPULTEPEC), 1945

5230. *Acta Final de la Conferencia Interamericana Sobre Problemas de la Guerra y de la Paz, Febrero–Marzo, 1945.* Mexico, 1945.

5231. *Actas de las Conferencias de Chapultepec y San Francisco.* B.A., 1945.

5232. Alfaro, R. J. "La Conferencia de México de 1945," *PA* 1 (August, 1946) 26–39.

5232a. ————. *Asociación de las Naciones Americanas: Estudio Acerca de la Organización de las Repúblicas de América como Comunidad Jurídica de Carácter Regional, y Proyecto de Pacto Constitutivo, Arreglado a las Estipulaciones de la Carta de las Naciones Unidas y las Recomendaciones de la Resolución 9 de la Conferencia de México Sobre Problemas de la Guerra y de la Paz.* Panama, 1946.

5233. Argentina. Ministerio del Interior. *La Política Internacional de la Nación Argentina: Absoluta Identidad de su Tradición y sus Principios con los Sustentados en el Acto de Chapultepec, la Declaración de México, la Declaración de las Naciones Unidas y la Carta del Atlántico.* B.A., 1946.
  Compiled by Carlos A. Silva. Defense of Argentina's relationship to the inter-American system.

5234. Argentine Embassy (U.S.A.). *Report of the Position of Argentina in Reference to the Conference on the Problems of War and Peace Held in Mexico, 1945, and Other Declarations of the United Nations.* 3 vols. in one, Wash., 1945.

5235. Bernstein C., E. "Compromisos Militares Contraídos por Chile en Chapultepec y San Francisco," *PE* 1 (February, 1946) 53–56.

5236. Canyes, M. S. "The Inter-American System and the Conference of Chapultepec," *AJIL* 39 (1945) 504–517.

5237. Cárdenas, R. F. "Aspectos Económicos de la Conferencia de Chapultepec," *IE* 5, no. 1 (1945) 81–94.

5238. Cosío Villegas, D. "La Conferencia de Chapultepec," *CA* 21 (May, 1945) 13–45.

5239. *Diario de la Conferencia Interamericana Sobre Problemas de la Guerra y de la Paz.* Mexico, 1945.

5240. Ecuador. Ministerio de Relaciones Exteriores. *La Cancillería Ecuatoriana y la Conferencia Interamericana de México Sobre los Problemas de la Guerra y de la Paz.* Quito, 1945.

5240a. Enríquez, L. "A Latin Looks at Chapultepec," *INA* 4 (April, 1945) 16–17.

5241. Francis, M. J. "The United States and the Act of Chapultepec," *SSSQ* 45 (December, 1964) 249–257.

5242. Holmes, O. "The Mexico City Conference and Regional Security," *FPAR* 21, no. 4 (1945) 42–49.

5243. Kunz, J. L. "The Inter-American Conference on Problems of War and Peace at Mexico City and the Problems of the Reorganization of the Inter-American System," *AJIL* 39 (1945) 527–533.

5244. Martínez Hague, C. "La Conferencia Panamericana de México," *PER* 5 (November, 1945) 1173–1185.

5245. Munro, D. G. "The Mexico City Conference and the Inter-American System," *USDSB* 12 (1945) 525–530.

5245a. Pruneda, A. "La Conferencia de Chapultepec y su Trascendencia Social," *BSMGE* 60 (May, 1945) 437–450.

5245b. *Resolution XXX on the Establishment of a General International Organization and Annexed Documents.* Mexico, 1945.

5246. Rosenzweig-Díaz A., A. de. *El Acta de Chapultepec.* Mexico, 1946.

5247. Rowe, L. S. "The Inter-American Conference on Problems of War and Peace," *BPAU* 79 (1945) 249–259.

5248. Schweide, I. B. *El Gobierno Argentino ante la Conferencia de Chapultepec, un Informe Dirigido al Canciller Enrique*

Ruíz Guiñazú y una Carta Abierta al Coronel Juan D. Perón. Mexico, 1945.

5249. Sierra, M. J. "La Conferencia de Secretarios de Relaciones Celebrada en México," *CA* 20 (March, 1945) 50–64.

Defense of Argentina's relationship to the inter-American system.

5250. Urquidi, V. L. "Problemas Económicos Planteados en la Conferencia de Chapultepec," *BBCV* 4 (April, 1945) 32–40.

5251. USDS. *Inter-American Relations After World War II.* Wash., 1945.

5252. ———. *Report of the Delegation of the United States of America to the Inter-American Conference on Problems of War and Peace, Mexico City, Mexico, February 21–March 8, 1945.* Wash., 1946.

5253. Uruguay. *Conferencia Interamericana Sobre Problemas de la Guerra y de la Paz, Mexico-Chapultepec, 21 de Febrero–8 de Marzo de 1945.* Montevideo, 1946.

5254. Vehila, R. *Los Principios Sociales de la Conferencia de Chapultepec.* Montevideo, 1945.

5255. Vejar Vázquez, O. "La Organización Interamericana en la Postguerra," *MLI* 3 (September, 1944) 23–27.

5255a. Vidal Guardiola, M. "La Conferencia de Chapultepec y el Futuro Económico de la América Latina," *RCAM* 3 (May, 1945) 38–47.

XI-J-9 cross references: 3821

10. CONFERENCE ON MAINTENANCE OF CONTINENTAL PEACE AND SECURITY— RIO DE JANEIRO, 1947

5256. Brazil. Ministerio das Relações Exteriores. *Discursos na Sessão Inaugural da 15 de Agôsto da 1947.* Rio, 1947.

5257. Caicedo Castilla, J. J. *La Conferencia de Petrópolis y el Tratado Interamericano de Asistencia Recíproca Firmado en Rio de Janeiro en 1947.* São Paulo, 1949.

5258. Corominas, E. V. *Paz y Seguridad Americana.* B.A., 1950.

Author was a member of the Argentine delegation to the Rio conference.

5259. *El Ecuador en la Conferencia de Petrópolis.* Quito, 1947.

5260. Finch, G. A. "The Inter-American Defense Treaty," *AJIL* 41 (1947) 863–866.

5261. Gómez Robledo, A. "El Tratado de Río," *FI* 1 (July, 1960) 47–81.

5262. Hadley, P. E. "The Inter-American Defense Conference," *WAI* 18 (Autumn, 1947) 264–272.

5263. Hermann, E. *Die Interamerikanischen Konferenzen von Rio de Janeiro (15. August-2. September 1947) und Bogotá (30. Mars-2. Mai 1948).* Mainz, 1950(?).

5264. Kunz, J. L. "The Inter-American Treaty of Reciprocal Assistance," *AJIL* 42 (1948) 111–120.

5264a. Lee, H. E. "Rio Conference," *PAAM* 8 (October, 1947) 4–8.

5265. PAU. *Consulta Sobre los Puntos Principales del Tratado que se Firmará en Rio de Janeiro.* Wash., 1947.

5266. ———. *Inter-American Conference for the Maintenance of Continental Peace and Security, Rio, 1946.* Wash., 1946.

5267. ———. "The Inter-American Conference for the Maintenance of Continental Peace and Security," *BPAU* 81 (1947) 527–542.

5267a. Roncella, N. "Los Pactos de Rio de Janeiro y del Atlántico Norte, Baluartes del Mundo Democrático," *RDP* 2 (December, 1950) 205–232.

5268. Salas Elgart, P. F. *El Tratado Interamericano de Asistencia Recíproca de Rio de Janeiro, 1947.* Santiago, 1962.

5269. USDS. *Inter-American Conference for the Maintenance of Continental Peace and Security.* Wash., 1948.

11. FOURTH CONSULTATIVE CONFERENCE— WASHINGTON, 1951

5270. *Actas y Documentos.* Wash., 1951.

5271. Bassols, N. "Veinte Ratones y un Gato, o la Conferencia de Washington," *RGUA* 2 (July, 1951) 5–18.

5271a. Dreier, J. C. *Taking Stock of Inter-American Relations.* Wash., 1951.

5272. Ecuador. Ministerio de Relaciones Exteriores. *Reunión de Consulta de Ministros de Relaciones Exteriores, 4ª Washington, 1951: El Gobierno del Sr. Galo Plaza: Informe Sobre los Resultados de la Reunión y de las Labores de la Delegación Ecuatoriana.* Quito, 1951.

5273. Guatemala. Ministerio de Educación Pública. *Guatemala ante América. La Verdad Sobre la Cuarta Reunión de Consulta de Cancilleres Americanos.* Guatemala, 1951.

5274. *Informe Sobre los Resultados de la Reunión y de las Labores de la Delegación Ecuatoriana: Anexo no. 1 a la Memoria Anual del Señor Ministro de Relaciones Exteriores.* Quito, 1951.

5275. Kunz, J. L. "Fourth Meeting of Consultation of Ministers of Foreign Affairs of American States," *AJIL* 45 (1951) 743–744.

5276. PAU. *Documents 1–168: Index.* Wash., 1951.

5277. ———. *Final Act.* Wash., 1951.

5278. ———. *Proceedings.* Wash., 1951.

5279. USCH. Committee on Expenditures in the Executive Departments. *United States Relations with International Organizations: Fourth Meeting of Consultation of Foreign Ministers of the American Republics* (82d Cong., 1st Sess., H. Rept. 210). Wash., 1951.

5280. USDS. *Fourth Meeting of Consultation of Ministers of Foreign Affairs of American States, Washington, D.C., March 26–April 7, 1951: Report of the Secretary of State.* Wash., 1953.

12. FIFTH CONSULTATIVE CONFERENCE— SANTIAGO, 1959

5280a. *Actas y Documentos.* Wash., 1961.

5281. Herter, C. R. "Foreign Ministers of American Republics Discuss Tensions in Caribbean Area," *USDSB* 41 (1959) 299–306.

5282. Inter-American Council of Jurists. *Opinion on the Legal Aspects of the Draft Declaration on Nonintervention Presented by the Mexican Delegation: Prepared in Accordance with Resolution V of the Fifth Meeting of Consultation of Ministers of Foreign Affairs.* Wash., 1961.

5283. PAU. *Quinta Reunión de Consulta de Ministros de Relaciones Exteriores, Santiago de Chile.* Wash., 1961.

13. SIXTH AND SEVENTH CONSULTATIVE CONFERENCES—SAN JOSÉ, C.R., 1960

5283a. *Actas y Documentos.* Wash., 1961.

5284. Fabela, I. "La Sexta y Séptima Conferencias de Cancilleres ante el Derecho

Positivo Internacional," *CA* (November, 1960) 9–27.

5285. PAU. *Informe de la Comisión Inter-americana de Paz a la Séptima Reunión de Consulta de Ministros de Relaciones Exteriores, San José, Costa Rica, Agosto de 1960.* Wash., 1960.

5286. ———. *Séptima Reunión de Consulta de Ministros de Relaciones Exteriores: Actas y Documentos.* Wash., 1961.

5286a. Rippy, J. F., and A. Tischendorf. "The San José Conference of American Foreign Ministers," *IEA* 14 (Winter, 1960) 59–72.

5286b. "San José Doctrine," *ECON* 196 (1960) 869–870.

XI–J–13   cross references: 4840

14. EIGHTH CONSULTATIVE CONFERENCE—PUNTA DEL ESTE, 1962

5287. *Actas y Documentos: Punta del Este, Uruguay, del 5 al 17 de Agosto de 1961.* Wash., 1962.

5288. "American Republics Unite to Halt Spread of Communism in Western Hemisphere," *USDSB* 46 (1962) 270–284.

5289. Barreda y Laos, F. *Punta del Este, Conferencia de la O.E.A.: VIII Reunión de Consulta de Ministros de Relaciones Exteriores: Expulsión de Cuba.* Lima, 1962.

5290. Bernstein Carabantes, E. "Punta del Este y las Erróneas Interpretaciones de un Tratado," *FI* 2 (1962) 518–534.

5291. Blanco, E. J. *De Playa Girón a Punta del Este.* B.A., 1962.

5292. Brazil. Ministerio das Relações Exteriores. *Brasil em Punta del Este.* Rio, 1962.

5292a. Corominas, E. V. *Cuba en Punta del Este.* B.A., 1962.

5292b. "Eighth Meeting of Consultation," *APAU* 14 (March, 1962) 2–7.

5293. Falcón Briceño, M. *Posición de Venezuela.* Wash., 1962.

5294. Fenwick, C. G. "The Issue at Punta del Este: Non-Intervention v. Collective Security," *AJIL* 56 (1962) 469–474.

5295. *Final Act.* Wash., 1962.

5295a. García Reynoso, P. "La Carta de Punta del Este, Planeación Económica," *CEX* 11 (December, 1962) 726–729.

5296. Hanson, S. G. "Failure at Punta del Este," *IEA* 15 (Spring, 1962) 29–45.

5297. Inter-American Economic and Social Council. *Ideario y Planificación de la Alianza para el Progreso: Carta de Punta del Este, Punta del Este, Agosto de 1961.* Montevideo, 1962.

5298. Inter-American Peace Committee. *Report of the Inter-American Peace Committee to the Eighth Meeting of Consultation of Ministers of Foreign Affairs, 1962.* Wash., 1962.

5299. Lima, A. "A Posição do Brasil em Punta del Este," *RBPI* 17 (March, 1962) 5–16.

5299a. Meek, G. "Eighth Meeting of Consultation," *APAU* 14 (March, 1962) 2–7.

5300. Morrison, D. S. *Latin American Mission: An Adventure in Hemisphere Diplomacy.* N.Y., 1965.
    Author was the U.S. ambassador to the OAS, 1961–1963.

5301. OAS Council. *Acta de la Sesión Extraordinaria Celebrada el 4 de Diciembre de 1961.* Wash., 1962.
    Minutes of the OAS meeting which decided to convoke the Punta del Este Conference.

5302. ———. ———. *Antecedentes Relacionados con la Convocatoria de la Reunión.* Wash., 1962.

5303. PAU. *Alliance for Progress: Official Documents Emanating from the Special Meeting of the Inter-American Economic and Social Council at the Ministerial Level, Held at Punta del Este, Uruguay, August 5–17, 1961.* Wash., 1961.

5304. ———. *Informe de la Comisión Interamericana de Paz a la Octava Reunión de Consulta de Ministros de Relaciones Exteriores, 1962.* Wash., 1962.

5305. ———. *Octava Reunión de Consulta de Ministros de Relaciones Exteriores: Actas y Documentos.* Wash., 1963.

5306. Ronning, C. N. *Punta del Este: The Limits of Collective Security in a Troubled Hemisphere.* N.Y., 1963.

5307. Rusk, D. "Report to the Nation on the Punta del Este Conference," *USDSB* 46 (1962) 267–269.
    By the U.S. Secretary of State.

5308. Scheyven, R. *De Punta del Este a la Habana: América Latina y el Mundo.* Santiago, 1962.

5309.   Smith, A. C. "Future of the OAS: Significance of Punta del Este Conference," *WT* 18 (March, 1962) 112–120.

5309a. "Special Meeting of the Inter-American Economic and Social Council at the Ministerial Level," *ILR* 85 (January, 1962) 51–57.

5310.   USCS. Committee on Foreign Relations. *Punta del Este Conference, January 1962: Report of Senators Wayne Morse and Bourke Hickenlooper to the Committee on Foreign Relations. March 1962* (87th Cong., 2d Sess., Comm. Print). Wash., 1962.

5311.   Zárate, C. L. *Conferencia de Cancilleres en Punta del Este.* N.p., 1963.

XI–J–14   cross references:

a) For specialized materials relating to the Alliance for Progress, see items 4096–41471.

b) See also item 10175.

15. NINTH CONSULTATIVE CONFERENCE— WASHINGTON, 1964

5311a. "Ninth Meeting of Consultation: OAS Foreign Ministers Vote Measures Against Cuba; Concerning Rio Treaty, with Resolution and Excerpts from Governmental Statements," *APAU* 16 (September, 1961) 1–10.

5311b. PAU. *Novena Reunión de Consulta de Ministros de Relaciones Exteriores: Documentos de la Reunión.* Wash., 1964.

5312.   Rodríguez, A. A. "La Conferencia de la OEA. ¿Reunión de Cancilleres o Mascarada Internacional?" *FI* 5 (1965) 547–575.

Chapter XII   Pan Hispanism, Yankeephobia, and Aprismo

A. PAN HISPANISM

5313. Adams, N. B. *The Heritage of Spain.* N.Y., 1943.

5314. Altamira, R. *Cuestiones Hispano-Americanas.* Madrid, 1900.

5315. Amadeo, M. *Por una Convivencia Internacional: Bases para una Comunidad Hispánica de Naciones.* Madrid, 1956.

5316. Antuña, J. G. *El Nuevo Acento.* B.A., 1935.

5317. Astigueta, F. B. "Solidaridad Americana," U. of Buenos Aires Diss., 1885.

5318. Atria R., M., R. Barahona, *et al. Hacia una Cultura Ibero-Americana.* Santiago, 1944.
    Three Hispanist essays.

5319. Bardina, J. *Leyenda Perjudicial: La Supuesta Inferioridad de los Españoles.* Santiago, 1918.

5320. Barón Castro, R. *Españolismo y Antiespañolismo en la América Hispana.* Madrid, 1945.

5321. Balseiro, J. A. *Expresión de Hispanoamérica.* San Juan, P.R., 1963.

5322. Belaúnde, V. A. "Peruanidad e Hispanidad," *MP* 23 (1941) 485–498.

5323. Berenguer, F. *El Hispano-Americanismo: Estudiado Desde el Punto de Vista del Derecho Internacional y el Problema Territorial de América.* Havana, 1928.

5324. Briceño-Iragorry, M. *El Fariseísmo Bolivariano y la Anti-América: Temas Sobre Hispanoamericanismo y Panamericanismo.* Madrid, 1953.

5324a. Bristol, W. B. "Hispanidad in South America," *FA* 21 (1943) 312–321.

5325. ———. "Hispanidad in South America, 1936–1945," U. of Pennsylvania Diss., 1947.

5326. Bustamante y Rivero, J. L. "Panamericanismo e Iberoamericanismo," *AEA* 8 (1951) 323–397.

Recognizes the validity of both approaches.

5326a. Conty, A. "L'Ibero-Americanisme et le Panaméricanisme," *IM* 3 (April, 1929) 181–197.

5327. Cortes Medina, H. *Ibero-Americanismo y Pan-Americanismo: Hacia una Verdadera Comprensión Americana.* Mexico, 1943.

5328. Daly, R. W. "An Examination of Manuel Ugarte's Contribution to *Hispanoamericanismo*," Loyola U. Diss., 1949.

5329. Deakin, F. B., "Spain and Hispano-Americanism," *CR* 125 (1924) 616–623.

5330. Diffie, B. W. "The Ideology of Hispanidad," *HAHR* 23 (1943) 457–482.

5331. Ednesor, A. *Apuntes para el Hispano-Americanismo.* Montevideo, 1925.

5332. Englekirk, J. E. "El Hispanoamericanismo y la Generación del 98," *RI* 2 (1940) 321–351.
    Evaluations by various Spanish intellectuals.

5332a. Esquivel Obregón, T. *Influencia de España y los Estados Unidos Sobre México (Ensayos de Sociología Hispano-Americana).* Madrid, 1918.

5333. Fernández-Shaw, F. G. "Hispanoamericanismo," *REP* 66 (September, 1959) 163–190.

5334. Foster, G. M. *Culture and Conquest: America's Spanish Heritage.* N.Y., 1960.

5335. Foulché-Delbosc, R., and L. Barrau-Dihigo. *Manuel de l'Hispanisant.* 2 vols., N.Y., 1920–1925.

5336. García, C. *El Problema Ibero-Americano.* Cádiz, 1926.
    Calls for a strengthening of cultural and economic ties between Spain and Spanish America.

5337. García Robles, A. "Latinoamericanismo y Panamericanismo," *MLI* 1 (December, 1942) 31–36; 2 (January, 1943) 39–43.

5337a. Gigerba y Gali, E. *El Panamericanismo y el Panhispanismo*. Havana, 1916.

5338. Gómez, J. F. *La Solidaridad Latina en América*. Havana, 1897.

5339. Gutiérrez-Solana, V. *Hispanoamericanismo Práctico*. Madrid, 1925.

5340. Hamilton D., C. "Hispanoamericanismo, Indoamericanismo, Interamericanismo y Realidad," *AFCJS* 10 (1944) 177–187.

5341. Hernández-Usera, R. *De América y de España, Problemas y Orientaciones*. Madrid, 1922.

    An attempt to reconcile Pan Hispanism and Pan Americanism.

5342. Icaza Tigerino, J. "El Nacionalismo Hispanoamericano y sus Problemas," *REP* 57 (July, 1956) 157–173.

5343. Ingenieros, J. *Por la Unión Latino Americana*. B.A., 1922.

5344. Jústiz del Valle, T. "Hispanidad Nazi-fascista," *RDLH* 3 (February, 1944) 574–580.

5345. Lira, O. *Hispanidad y Mestizaje y Otros Ensayos*. Madrid, 1952.

5346. ———. *La Vida en Torno*. Santiago, 1949.

5347. Lira Urquieta, P. *Temas Hispano-Americanos*. Santiago, 1942.

5348. Madariaga, S. de. "Alberdi, Precursor," *SUR* 5, no. 10 (1935) 32–53; 5, no. 11 (1935) 48–49.

    Alberdi reviewed as the precursor of Panhispanism.

5349. Maeztu, R. de. *Defensa de la Hispanidad*. 3d ed., Valladolid, 1938.

5350. Magariño, S., and R. Puigdollers. *Pan-hispanismo, su Trascendencia Histórica, Política y Social: Obra Premiada en el Concurso Hispano Antillano de 1925*. Barcelona, 1926.

5351. Martín Artajo, A. D. *Hacia la Comunidad Hispánica de Naciones: Discursos del Excmo. Señor Ministro de Asuntos Exteriores*. Madrid, 1956.

5351a. Nenclares, F. C. "Hispanismo y His-panidad," *CA* (May, 1942) 43–55.

5352. Onís, J. de. "Pan-Hispanism," *IRB* 13 (1963) 428–432.

    Takes issue with the Van Aken work (item 5378). Onís views Pan Hispanism as more significant culturally than politically.

5353. Otero, G. A. *Sociología del Nacionalismo en Hispano-América*. Quito, 1947.

5354. Pérez, D. *Presencia Universal de España: Historia de la Cultura Hispánica en España y en América*. Mexico, 1960.

5355. Pico, C. E. *Hacia la Hispanidad*. B.A., 1943.

5356. Piga, A. *Humanismo y Espíritu Nacionalista*. Santiago, 1927.

5357. Plá, J. *La Misión Internacional de la Raza Hispánica*. Madrid, 1928.

5358. Puyo Delgado, C. "Panamericanismo y Latinoamericanismo," *COL* I (June, 1944) 297–300.

5359. Quesada, E. *Nuestra Raza*. B.A., 1900.

5360. Ravignani, E. "Nuevos Aspectos de Iberoamericanismo," *A* 22 (April, 1944) 9–13.

5361. Recabarren, S. *Latinoamérica y Imperialismo*. Santiago, 1949.

5362. ———. *Progreso y Destino Cultural Latino-Americano*. Santiago, 1950.

    Latin American unity is viewed as a counterbalance to United States imperialism.

5363. ———. *La Solidaridad Continental*. Santiago, 1951.

5364. Restrepo, D. "Panamericanismo e His-panoamericanismo," *RJA* 11 (April, 1939) 156–160.

5365. Riesco, G. *El Destino de la Argentina*. B.A., 1944.

5366. Rippy, J. F. "Pan-Hispanic Propaganda in Hispanic America," *PSQ* 37 (1922) 389–414.

5367. Schück, W. "Wurzel und Gegenwarts-gestalt des Pan-Iberoamerikanismus," *ZP* 29 (1929) 316–329.

5368. Silva, J. F. V. *Reparto de América Española y Pan-Hispanismo*. Madrid, 1918.

5369. Southworth, H. R. "The Spanish Phalanx and Latin America," *FA* 18 (1939) 148–152.

    Pan Hispanism under the Franco regime.

5370. Suárez, C. *La Des-Unión Hispano-Americana*. Barcelona, 1919.

5371. ———. *La Verdad Desnuda*. Madrid, 1924.

5372. Suárez Somoano, J. *Ibero América, Nuestro Ideal*. Havana, 1930.

5372a. Teyssier, E. *América Indo-Hispana y Yanquilandia*. Mexico, 1941.

5373. Thomas, D. Y. "Pan-Americanism and

Pan-Hispanism," *NAR* 217 (1923) 327–333.

5374. Turner, E. H. S. "Hispanism in the Life and Works of Manuel Gálvez," U. of Washington Diss., 1958.

Gálvez was an Argentine social critic who wrote extensively in the early twentieth century.

5375. Ugarte, M. *Mi Campaña Hispanoamericana*. Barcelona, 1922.

5376. Urrutia Ibáñez, L. *Federación Iberoamericana*. Santiago, 1942.

5377. Valdés, E. B. *Anhelo y Visión de España*. Santiago, 1958.

5378. Van Aken, M. J. *Pan-Hispanism: Its Origin and Development to 1866*. Berkeley, Calif., 1959.

5379. Vasconcelos, J. *La Raza Cósmica*. Paris, n.d.

5380. Vega, J. *La Tierra del Provenir*. Santiago, 1941.

5381. Vergara, M. *La Unidad de la Raza Hispana*. Madrid, 1925.

5382. Viteri, M. H. *For a Federated Latin America*. N.Y., 1965.

5383. Zavala, I. M. "Hacia una Teoría de 'Espanoamérica': Hispanoamérica en Unamuno, ¿Realidad o Ficción?" *IRB* 15 (1965) 347–354.

5383a. Zubritskii, I. A. "Latinidad i Ego Sushchnost," *VIMK* 25 (January, 1961) 116.

"The Meaning of Latinidad."

5384. Zurano Muñoz, E. *Alianza Hispano-Americana*. Madrid, 1926.

XII–A cross references:

a) Latin American attempts at union are considered in items 2599–2622.

b) See also items 2545, 2560, 2562, 3110.

B. YANKEEPHOBIA: APPRAISALS

5385. Albarran Puente, G. *El Pensamiento de José Enrique Rodó*. Madrid, 1953.

5386. Beals, C., B. Oliver, *et al. What the South Americans Think of Us*. N.Y., 1945.

5387. Berrien, W. J. "Rodó: Biografía y Estudio Crítico," U. of California Diss., 1937.

5388. Botelho Gonsálvez, R. *Reflexiones Sobre el Cincuentenario del Ariel de Rodó*. La Paz, 1950.

5388a. Burner, W. J. "The Attitudes of Contemporary South American Authors Toward the United States," Ohio State U. Diss., 1930.

5389. Cestero, T. M. "Rufino Blanco Fombona," *CA* (January, 1946) 269–281.

5389a. Chapman, A. *The Spanish American Reception of United States Fiction, 1920–1940*. Berkeley, Calif., 1966.

North American authors were not widely read.

5390. Chapman, M. P. "Yankeephobia: An Analysis of the Anti-U.S. Bias of Certain Spanish South American Intellectuals," Stanford U. Diss., 1950.

Covers the period 1898–1928.

5391. Dunn, W. E. "The Post-War Attitude of Hispanic America Toward the United States," *HAHR* 3 (1920) 173–183.

5392. Esquenazi-Mayo, R. "El Interamericanismo de Darío," *INS* 22 (July-August, 1967) 10-13.

Demonstrates that Darío's famous "Ode to Roosevelt" portrays only one aspect of his inter-American views.

5393. ———. "Revaloración de Rodó," in *Actas del Primer Congreso Internacional de Hispanistas*. Oxford, 1964.

5394. Galbán, J. S. "Apreciaciones Contemporáneas Hispanoamericanas de los Estados Unidos," U. of Virginia Diss., 1931.

5395. Galíndez, J. de. "Anti-American Sentiment in Latin America," *JIA* 9 (1955) 24–32.

5396. González-Blanco, A. *Escritores Representativos de América*. Madrid, 1917.

5397. Griffith, W. J. "Juan Galindo, Central American Chauvinist," *HAHR* 40 (1960) 25–52.

5398. Haring, C. H. *South America Looks at the United States*. N.Y., 1928.

5399. Henríquez Ureña, M. *Rodó y Rubén Darío*. Havana, 1918.

5400. Henríquez-Ureña, P. *Literary Currents in Hispanic America*. Cambridge, Mass., 1945.

5401. ———. *La Obra de José Enrique Rodó*. Mexico, 1910.

5402. Luebke, F. C. "Yankeephobia in Latin America," *CRE* 28, no. 11 (1965) 8–13.

5403. Merrill, J. C. *Gringo: The American as*

Seen by Mexican Journalists. Gainesville, Fla., 1963.

5404. Monticone, C. R. "Rufino Blanco-Fombona: The Man and His Work," U. of Pittsburgh Diss., 1931.

5405. Normano, J. F. "Changes in Latin American Attitudes," *FA* 11 (1932) 161–172.

5406. Onís, J. de. *Los Estados Unidos Vistos por Escritores Hispanoamericanos.* Madrid, 1956.
   English ed., N.Y., 1952.

5407. Pérez Petit, V. *Rodó, Su Vida, Su Obra.* Montevideo, 1918.

5408. Perry, E. "Anti-American Propaganda in Hispanic America," *HAHR* 3 (1920) 17–40.

5409. Radler, D. H. *El Gringo: The Yankee Image in Latin America.* Phil., 1962.

5410. Ramírez Novoa, E. *América Latina y Estados Unidos: Las Aventuras de Mr. Nixon en Latinoamérica.* Lima, 1958.

5411. Reynolds, T. H. (ed.). *As Our Neighbors See Us.* Stillwater, Okla., 1940.
   Collection of articles by leading Latin Americans.

5412. Rice, W. F. "The Ideology of José Enrique Rodó," Northwestern U. Diss., 1930.

5412a. Rippy, J. F. "Literary Yankee-Phobia in Latin America," *JIR* 12 (1922) 350–371, 524–538.

5413. Stokes, W. S. "Economic Anti-Americanism in Latin America," *IEA* 11 (Winter, 1957) 3–22.

5414. Urist, H. E. "Some Aspects of the 'Yanqui' in the Literature of Hispanic America," U. of California Diss., 1947.

5414a. Vernon, R. (ed.). *How Latin America Views the U.S. Investor.* N.Y., 1965.

5415. Waldo, T. "Why Latin America Distrusts Us," *HA* 217 (November, 1958) 83–92.

5416. Washington, S. W. *A Study of the Causes of Hostility Toward the United States in Latin America.* Wash., 1956–1957.

5416a. Whitaker, A. P. "Yankeephobia: The United States and Latin America," *CH* 42 (January, 1962) 15–19.

XII–B cross references: 1414, 5328, 6336, 9460, 9461a, 9480a, 9480b, 9481a, 9649, 9826

C. YANKEEPHOBIA: MANIFESTATIONS

5417. Arévalo, J. J. *The Shark and the Sardines.* N.Y., 1961.
   The "shark" is the United States and the "sardines" are Latin America. By the former president of Guatemala.

5418. Arguello, A. *La Garra Yanqui.* Ahuachapan, El Salvador, 1934.

5419. Blanco-Fombona, H. *Crímenes del Imperialismo Norteamericano.* Mexico, 1927.

5420. ———. *En las Garras del Aguila: Crímenes de los Yanquis en Santo Domingo.* Mexico, 1921.

5421. Blanco-Fombona, R. "Historia del Ogro Yanqui y de la Caperucita Isleña," *NOS* 37 (February, 1921) 137–143.

5422. ———. *La Evolución Política y Social de Hispano-America.* Madrid, 1911.
   By the Venezuelan diplomat and literary critic.

5423. Brandão, O. "O Brasil, Explorado e Oprimido," *RBR* 40 (1962) 181–193.

5424. Castillo Ibarra, C. *Un Siglo de Imperialismo Yanqui, 1856–1956.* Mexico, 1957.

5425. Edwards Bello, J. *El Nacionalismo Continental: Ensayos Políticos Sociales.* Santiago, 1935.

5426. Enamorado Cuesta, J. *El Imperialismo Yanqui y la Revolución en el Caribe.* San Juan, P.R., 1936.

5427. Encina, D. *Fuera el Imperialismo y sus Agentes.* Mexico, 1940.

5428. Faleroni, A. D. "El Panamericanismo Es la Voz Diplomática del Imperialismo Yanqui," *CLA* 14, no. 288 (1935).

5429. Fernández MacGregor, G. *En la Era de la Mala Vecindad.* Mexico, 1960.

5430. Guillén, A. *El Imperialismo del Dolár: América Latina: Revolución o Alienación.* B.A., 1962.

5431. Henríquez, E. A. *Episodios Imperialistas.* Cd. Trujillo, 1959.
   Examples, taken primarily from the nineteenth century.

5432. "Imperialismo y Buena Vecindad," *CA* 35 (September, 1947) 64–88.
   Opinions by Jesús Silva Herzog, Fernando Ortíz, and Daniel Cosío Villegas.

5433. Lagarrique, J. E. *La Religión de la Humanidad.* Santiago, 1884.

5434. Merlos, S. R. *América Latina ante el Peligro*. San José, C.R., 1914.

5435. Oliveres, R. *El Imperialismo Yanqui en América: La Dominación Política y Económica del Continente*. B.A., 1952.

5436. Osegueda, R. *Operación Centroamérica $$ OK $$*. Santiago, 1958.

5437. Peralta, J. *La Esclavitud de la América Latina*. Cuenca, Ecuador, 1960.
    Reprint of a work originally written in 1927 by a former minister of foreign relations in Ecuador.

5438. Rodríguez, R. R. *Latino América: Víctima del Dollar*. Caracas, 1958.

5439. Saenz, V. *Hispano América Contra el Coloniaje*. Mexico, 1949.

5440. Santelices, A. *El Imperialismo Yanqui y su Influencia en Chile*. Santiago, 1926.

5441. Selser, G. *Diplomacia, Garrote y Dólares en América Latina*. B.A., 1962.

5442. Ugarte, M. *El Porvenir de la América Latina: La Raza y la Integridad Territorial: La Organización*. Valencia, 1911.
    By the Argentine novelist and propagandist who coined the phrase "el coloso del norte."

5443. ———. *La Patria Grande*. Madrid, 1924.

5444. ———. *The Destiny of a Continent*. N.Y., 1925.
    Spanish ed., Madrid, 1923.

5445. Vargas Vila, J. M. *Ante los Bárbaros*. Barcelona, 1917.
    Author was a Colombian novelist and intellectual.

XII–C   cross references: 1738, 2137, 2293, 2910, 2915, 2931, 2968, 2969, 3182, 3740, 4609, 5342, 5375, 5768, 6614, 7536, 8355, 9424, 10072, 10202

D. APRISMO

5446. Alexander, R. J. "The Latin American Aprista Parties," *PQ* 20 (1949) 236–247.

5447. Baeza Flores, A. *Haya de la Torre y la Revolución Constructiva de las Américas*. B.A., 1962.

5448. Bazán, A. *Biografía de José Carlos Mariátegui*. Santiago, 1939.

5448a. Beals, C. "Aprismo: The Rise of Haya de la Torre," *FA* 13 (1935) 236–246.

5449. Bernaschina, M. de. *Mi Entrevista con Víctor Raúl Haya de la Torre*. Panama, 1940.

5549a. Chang-Rodríguez, E. "Aprismo and the New Peruvian Administration," *JIAS* 4 (1962) 426–431.

5450. ———. *La Literatura Política de Gonzalez Prada, Mariátegui y Haya de la Torre*. Mexico, 1957.

5451. Comité Aprista de México. *El Aprismo Frente a la VIII Conferencia Panamericana*. Mexico, 1938.

5452. ———. *El Perú bajo el Oprobio*. Mexico, 1938.

5453. Comité Aprista de Montevideo. *Defendiendo las Libertades en América*. Montevideo, 1936.

5454. Comité Aprista de Santiago. *Mensaje a Haya de la Torre de los Apristas Desterrados en Chile*. Santiago, 1936.

5455. Cossío del Pomar, F. *Haya de la Torre: El Indoamericano*. Rev. ed. Lima, 1946.
    This is an expansion of the original edition of 1939.

5456. ———. *Víctor Raúl: Biografía de Haya de la Torre*. Mexico, 1961– .
    First volume of a projected multivolume study.

5457. Cox, C. M. *Ideas Económicas del Aprismo*. Lima, 1934.

5457a. Fletcher, W. G. "Aprismo Today—An Explanation and a Critique," *IAQ* (October, 1941) 14–20.

5458. Gonzáles, T. *Haya de la Torre: Trayectoria de una Ideología*. Caracas, 1958.
    An analysis of Haya's political thought.

5459. González-Prada, M. *Horas de Lucha*. Callao, 1924.

5459a. ———. *Prosa Menuda*. B.A., 1941.

5460. Haya de la Torre, V. R. *¿A Dónde Va Indoamérica?* Santiago, 1935.

5461. ———. *El Anti-Imperialismo y la Apra*. Santiago, 1936.

5461a. ———. "El Apra: Treinta Años Después," *COMB* (March, 1962) 49–62.

5462. ———. *Construyendo el Aprismo*. B.A., 1933.

5463. ———. *Dos Documentos Comprobatorios de la Dirección Comunista del Apra*. Lima, 1932.

5464. ———. *Enfoque Aprista de Imperialismo, Antiimperialismo y Marxismo*. Mexico, 1955.

5465. ———. *Excombatientes y Desocupados*. Santiago, 1936.

5466. ———. *Haya de la Torre Responde al*

General Benavides. Incahuasi, Peru, 1938.

5467. González-Prada, M. *Ideario y Acción Aprista.* B.A., 1930.

5468. ———. *Instructiva Secreta a Haya de la Torre.* Santiago, 1933.

5469. ———. *Manifesto a la Nación.* Panama, 1932.

5470. ———. *Pensamiento Político.* 5 vols. Lima, 1961.

5471. ———. *El Plan del Aprismo.* Ecuador, 1932.

5472. ———. *Política Aprista.* Lima, 1933.

5473. ———. *Por la Emancipación de la América Latina.* B.A., 1927.

5473a. ———. "Sobre la 'Historia del Comunismo en América' y una Rectificación," *CA* 14, no. 4 (1955) 14–26.
Discusses separate development of Aprismo.

5474. ———. *Teoría y Táctica del Aprismo.* Lima, 1931.

5475. ———. *Treinta Años de Aprismo.* Mexico, 1956.
Covers 1924–1942.

5476. ———. *Vibrante Mensaje de Haya de la Torre: El Lider Aprista Habla Nuevamente para Colombia.* Incahuasi, Peru, 1936.

5477. ———. *La VIII Conferencia Panamericana ¿Otra Comedia? Frente Norte Indoamericano Contra la Internacional Negra Fascista.* Santiago, 1938.

5478. ———. *Y Después de la Guerra¿ Qué?* Lima, 1946.

5479. ———, and J. Ingenieros. *Teoría y Táctica de la Juventud Anti-Imperialista.* B.A., 1928.

5480. Kantor, H. "Aprismo: Peru's Indigenous Political Theory," *SAQ* 53 (January, 1954) 1–9.

5481. ———. *The Ideology and Program of the Peruvian Aprista Movement.* Berkeley, Calif., 1953.
Rev. ed., N.Y., 1966.

5482. Mariátegui, J. C. *Siete Ensayos de Interpretación de la Realidad Peruana.* Lima, 1938.

5483. Martínez de la Torre, R. E. *Páginas Anti-Apristas: Apuntes para una Interpretación Marxista de Historia Social del Perú.* Lima, 1933.

5484. McNicoll, R. E. "Intellectual Origins of Aprismo," *HAHR* 23 (1943) 424–440.

5484a. Mejía Valera, M. "El Pensamiento Filosófico de Manuel González Prada," *CA* 71 (1953) 122–135.

5485. Meneses, R. *Aprismo Femenino Peruano.* Lima, 1934.

5486. ———. *Por el Apra.* Lima, 1933.

5487. Muñiz, P. E. *Penetración Imperialista.* Santiago, 1935.

5488. ———, and C. Showing. *Lo Que Es el Aprismo.* Bogotá, 1933.

5489. Partido Aprista Cubano. *El Aprismo ante la Realidad Cubane: Manifiesto a la Nación.* Havana, 1934.

5490. ———. *Cartilla Aprista.* Santiago de Cuba, 1936.

5491. Partido Aprista Peruano. *Aspectos Importantes del Aprismo: Preguntas y Respuestas.* Lima, 1933.

5492. ———. *Autopsia de la Finanzas de Benavides.* Lima, 1939.

5493. ———. *Brigada de Organización: Organización Vertical del Partido Aprista Peruano.* Santiago, 1937.

5494. ———. *Catolicismo y Aprismo: Dúplica al Folleto de Propaganda Anti-Aprista Titulado: ¿Aprista o Católico?* Lima, 1934.

5495. ———. *Circular Aprista No. 1: Preguntas y Respuestas: Lo Que Todo Hijo del Pueblo Debe Saber.* N.p., n.d.

5496. ———. *Manifiesto a la Nación por el Comité Ejecutivo Nacional. ¿Por Qué y Cómo Se Ataca al Aprismo?* Lima, n.d.
A two-part pamphlet. One part was written by Antenor Orrego and the other by Haya de la Torre.

5497. ———. *El Proceso de Haya de la Torre.* Guayaquil, 1933.

5498. ———. *Programa Mínimo o Plan de Acción Inmediata, Dictado por el Primer Congreso Nacional del Partido, Reunido en Lima, en 1931.* Lima, 1931.

5499. ———. *El Verdadero Plan de la Alianza Popular Revolucionaria Americana.* Lima, n.d.

5500. Portal, M. *El Partido Aprista Frente al Momento Actual.* Lima, n.d.

5501. Ramírez Novoa, E. *La Farsa del Panamericanismo y la Unidad Indoamericana.* B.A., 1955.
A Peruvian Aprista criticizes United States policy in the hemisphere.

5502. ———. *Monroísmo y Bolivarismo en América Latina.* B.A., 1957.

The two concepts are considered antithetical.

5503. Saco, A. *Síntesis Aprista.* Lima, 1934.

5504. ———, and G. Vegas León. *¡ Partidos de Frente Unico para Indo-América!* Mexico, 1938.

5505. Sánchez, L. A. *Aprismo y Religión.* Lima, 1933(?).

5506. ———. *Cuestiones Fundamentales del Aprismo.* Lima, 1933.

5507. ———. *Don Manuel: Vie de Manuel González-Prada—Un Precurseur Sud-Américain.* Paris, 1931.

5508. ———. *Elementos del Aprismo: Carta a una Indoamericana.* Quito, 1932.

5509. ———. *Haya de la Torre y el Apra: Crónica de un Hombre y un Partido.* Santiago, 1955.

Sympathetic biographical treatment.

5510. ———. "Indoamérica Versus Pan-américa," *ND* 20 (June, 1939) 18–20.

5511. ———. *Raúl Haya de la Torre o el Político: Crónica de una Vida sin Tregua.* Santiago, 1934.

5512. Secretariado Nacional de Cooperativas del P.A.P. *Páginas de Divulgación Aprista.* Lima, 1933.

5513. Seminario Económico del Comité Aprista de Buenos Aires. *Autopsia del Presupuesto Civilista.* B.A., 1936.

5514. Seoane, M. *Las Calumnias Contra el Aprismo.* B.A., 1932.

5515. Vargas, J. *Aprismo y Marxismo.* B.A., 1936.

5515a. Villagómez Yépez, J. *Indoamericanismo y Panamericanismo.* Quito, 1940.

XII–D cross references: 1518, 5055, 5077, 8835, 8955a

Chapter XIII   The United States and Mexico

A. GENERAL WORKS AND SPECIAL STUDIES

5516. Adams, P. L. "The American Struggle for a Preeminent Position in Mexico, 1822–1876," Ohio State U. Diss., 1951.

5516a. Al'perovich, M. S., and N. M. Lavrov (eds.). *Ocherki Novoi i Noveishei Istorii Meksiki, 1810–1945*. Moscow, 1960.
> Essays in the Modern and Contemporary History of Mexico, 1810–1945.

5517. *Archivo Histórico Diplomático Mexicano*. 1st ser., 40 vols., Mexico, 1923–1940; 2d ser., Mexico, 1943–   .
> A major documentary collection; especially relevant volumes are listed separately.

5518. Bancroft, H. H. *History of California*. 7 vols., San Francisco, 1884–1890.

5519. ———. *History of Mexico*. 6 vols., San Francisco, 1883–1888.
> Covers from the sixteenth century to the date of publication.

5519a. Bosch García, C. (ed.). *Material para la Historia Diplomática de México*. Mexico, 1957.
> Covers United States–Mexican relations to 1867.

5520. Bravo Ugarte, J. *Historia de México*. 2d ed., 4 vols., Mexico, 1959.

5521. Callahan, J. M. *American Foreign Policy in Mexican Relations*. N.Y., 1932.

5522. Callcott, W. H. *Liberalism in Mexico, 1857–1929*. Stanford, Calif., 1931.
> Covers 1857 to time of publication. Sequel to item 5603.

5523. Carreño, A. M. *La Diplomacia Extraordinaria Entre México y Estados Unidos, 1789–1947*. 2 vols., Mexico, 1951.

5524. ———. *México y los Estados Unidos de América: Apuntaciones para la Historia del Acrecentamiento Territorial de los Estados Unidos a Costa de México Desde la Epoca Colonial Hasta Nuestros Días*. Mexico, 1922.

5525. Chávez Orozco, L. *Historia Económica y Social de México*. Mexico, 1938.

5526. Cline, H. F. *The United States and Mexico*. Rev. ed., N.Y., 1963.

5527. Corwin, H. *These Are the Mexicans*. N.Y., 1947.

5528. Cue Canovas, A. *Historia Política de México*. Mexico, 1957.

5529. Cuevas, M. *Historia de la Nación Mexicana*. 2d ed., 2 vols., Mexico, 1952–1953.
> A Catholic interpretation.

5530. Dunn, F. S. *The Diplomatic Protection of Americans in Mexico*. N.Y., 1933.
> Covers the period since Mexican independence.

5531. Elguero, J. *España en los Destinos de México*. Mexico, 1929.

5532. Esquivel Obregón, T. "Factors in the Historical Evolution of Mexico," *HAHR* 2 (1919) 135–172.

5533. Estrada, G. (ed.). *Un Siglo de Relaciones Internacionales de México a Través de los Mensajes Presidenciales*. Mexico, 1935.
> Volume 39 of the *Archivo Histórico*. See item 5517.

5534. *Funcionarios de la Secretaría de Relaciones Exteriores Desde el Año 1821 a 1940*. Mexico, 1940.

5534a. García, G., and C. Pereyra (eds.). *Documentos Inéditos ó muy Raros para la Historia de México*. 36 vols., Mexico, 1905–1911.

5535. García Cantú, G. "Las Dos Políticas Exteriores de México," *CA* 106 (September, 1959) 41–55.
> One policy is of submission to external pressures; the other is independent exertion.

5536. Gruening, E. *Mexico and Its Heritage*. N.Y., 1928.

5537. James, D. *Mexico and the Americans*. N.Y., 1963.

5538. Lemert, B. F., and R. V. Lemert. "The United States and Mexico," *JG* 34 (1935) 261–266.

5539. MacCorkle, S. A. *American Policy of Recognition Towards Mexico*. Baltimore, 1933.

5540. McCaleb, W. F. *The Public Finances of Mexico*. N.Y., 1922.
    Covers from independence to date of publication.

5541. McHenry, J. P. *A Short History of Mexico*. Garden City, N.Y., 1962.

5541a. Mexico. Secretaría de Relaciones Exteriores. *Breves Apuntes para Uso de los Miembros del Cuerpo Diplomático y Consular Mexicano*. Mexico, 1923.

5542. Parkes, H. B. *A History of Mexico*. 3d A much used one-volume survey. ed., Boston, 1960.

5543. Plenn, J. H. *Mexico Marches*. Indianapolis, 1939.

5544. Priestley, H. I. *The Mexican Nation, a History*. N.Y., 1923.
    The first comprehensive English-language treatment.

5545. Rabasa, E. *La Evolución Histórica de México*. Mexico, 1920.

5546. Reyes Heroles, J. *El Liberalismo Mexicano*. 3 vols., Mexico, 1957–1961.

5547. Rippy, J. F. *The United States and Mexico*. Rev. ed., N.Y., 1931.

5548. Riva Palacio, V. (ed.). *México a Través de los Siglos*. 5 vols., Mexico, 1887–1889.

5549. Romero, M. *Tabla Sinóptica de los Tratados y Convenciones que Han Negociado los Estados Unidos Mexicanos con las Naciones Extranjeras*. Tabasco, 1859.

5550. Schlarman, J. H. *Mexico: Land of Volcanoes*. Milwaukee, 1950.
    A conservative, pro-clerical interpretation.

5551. Sheremet'ev, I. K. *Gosudarstvennyi Kapitalizm v Meksike*. Moscow, 1963.
    State Capitalism in Mexico.

5552. Simpson, L. B. *Many Mexicos*. 3d ed., Berkeley, Calif., 1952.
    Emphasis is on the colonial period.

5553. Starr, F. *Mexico and the United States: A Story of Revolution, Intervention, and War*. Chicago, 1914.
    More an internal history than the title indicates.
    Emphasis is on the period since 1910.

5554. Strode, H. *Timeless Mexico*. N.Y., 1944.
    Survey from Cortés to Avila Camacho.

5555. Teja Zabre, A. *Guide to the History of Mexico*. Mexico, 1935.

5556. ———. *Historia de México*. 2d ed., Mexico, 1948.

5557. Vasconcelos, J. *Breve Historia de México*. Madrid, 1952.

5558. Veríssimo, E. *Mexico*. N.Y., 1960.
    Impressions rather than history.

5559. Zamacois, N. de. *Historia de Méjico Desde sus Tiempos más Remotos Hasta Nuestros Días*. 18 vols., Mexico, 1877–1882.
    Vols. 19 to 23 continued by F. G. Cosmes (Barcelona and Mexico, 1901–1903).

XIII–A cross references:

For works on Mexico and the inter-American system, see items 4831–4836.

B. THE UNITED STATES AND MEXICAN INDEPENDENCE

5560. Alamán, L. *Historia de Méjico, Desde los Primeros Movimientos que Prepararon su Independencia en el Año de 1808 Hasta la Epoca Presente*. 5 vols., Mexico, 1850–1852.
    From the conservative point of view.

5560a. Al'perovich, M. S. "Rol' Narodnykh Mass v Voine za Nezavisimost' Meksiki," *NNI*, no. 5 (1960) 52–63.
    "The Role of the Popular Masses in the Mexican War of Independence."

5560b. ———. *Voina za Nezavisimost' Meksiki (1810–1824)*. Moscow, 1964.
    The Mexican War of Independence (1810–1824).

5561. Bulnes, F. *La Guerra de Independencia: Hidalgo-Iturbide*. Mexico, 1910.

5562. Bustamante, C. M. de. *Cuadro Histórico de la Revolución Mexicana*. 6 vols., Mexico, 1843.
    The second volume treats the Mina expedition.

5563. Castillo Ledón, L. *Hidalgo: La Vida del Héroe*. 2 vols., Mexico, 1948.

5564. Chavarri, J. N. *Historia de la Guerra de Independencia de 1810 a 1821 en Conmemoración al 150° Aniversario*. Mexico, 1960.

5565. Chávez, E. A. *Agustín de Iturbide.* Mexico, 1957.

5566. Cox, I. J. "Monroe and the Early Mexican Revolutionary Agents," *AHAAR* 1 (1911) 199–215.

5566a. Espoz y Mina, F. *A Short Extract from the Life of General Mina.* London, 1825.

5567. Fabela, I. *Los Precursores de la Diplomacia Mexicana.* Mexico, 1926.

5568. Fisher, L. E. "American Influence upon the Movement for Mexican Independence," *MVHR* 13 (1932) 463–478.

5569. ———. *The Background of the Revolution for Mexican Independence.* Boston, 1934.

5570. García, G. (ed.). *Documentos Históricos Mexicanos: Obra Conmemorativa del Primer Centenario de la Independencia de México.* 6 vols., Mexico, 1910.

5571. ———. *El Plan de Independencia de la Nueva España en 1808.* Mexico, 1903.

5572. Garrett, J. K. *Green Flag over Texas.* N.Y., 1939.

5573. ———. "The War of Independence in Texas, 1811–1813," U. of California Diss., 1935.

5574. "La Guerra de Independencia: Expedición de Mina," *BAGNM* 20 (July, 1949) 365–377.

5574a. Hamill, H. M. *The Hidalgo Revolt: Prelude to Mexican Independence.* Gainesville, Fla., 1966.

5575. Hernández y Dávalos, J. E. *Colección de Documentos para la Historia de la Guerra de Independencia de México de 1808 a 1821.* 6 vols., Mexico, 1877–1882. New ed., N.Y., 1967.

5576. Márquez Montiel, J. *Datos Raros Sobre Caudillos de la Independencia.* Mexico, 1963.

5577. McCaleb, W. F. "The First Period of the Gutiérrez-Magee Expedition," *THAQ* 4 (1901) 218–229. Filibuster against Mexico, 1811–1812.

5578. Navarro y Rodrigo, C. *Vida de Agustín de Iturbide: Memorias de Agustín de Iturbide.* Madrid, 1919.

5578a. Ramos Pedrueza, R. *Francisco Javier Mina, Combatiente Clasista en Europa y América.* Mexico, 1937.

5579. Rippy, J. F. "Britain's Role in the Early Relations of the United States and Mexico," *HAHR* 7 (1927) 2–24.

5580. Robertson, W. S. *Iturbide of Mexico.* Durham, N.C., 1952.

5581. Robinson, W. D. *Memoirs of the Mexican Revolution: Including a Narrative of the Expedition of General Xavier Mina.* Phil., 1820.

5582. Rydjord, J. *Foreign Interest in the Independence of New Spain.* Durham, N.C., 1935.

5583. Santibáñez, E. (ed.). *La Diplomacia Mexicana.* 3 vols., Mexico, 1910–1913. Covers only through 1825.

5584. Smith, R. S. "Shipping in the Port of Vera Cruz, 1790–1821," *HAHR* 23 (1943) 5–20.

5585. Timmons, W. *Morelos of Mexico: Priest, Soldier, Statesman.* El Paso, Texas, 1963.

5586. Trelles y Govín, C. M. "Un Precursor de la Independencia de Cuba: Don José Alvarez de Toledo," in *Discursos Leídos en la Recepción Pública del Sr. Carlos M. Trelles y Govín.* Havana, 1926.

5587. Van Arsdale, E. V. "A Consideration of the Policy of the U.S. Toward the Movements for Independence in the Spanish Colonies, with an Account of the Mina Expedition to Mexico, 1816–1817," U. of S. California Diss., 1938.

5588. Warren, H. G. "Documents Relating to the Establishment of Privateers at Galveston, 1816–1817," *LHQ* 21 (1938) 1086–1109.

5589. ———. "The Origin of General Mina's Invasion of Mexico," *SHQ* 42 (1938) 1–20.

5590. ———. *The Sword Was Their Passport: A History of American Filibustering During the Mexican Revolution.* Baton Rouge, La., 1943.

5591. ———. "Xavier Mina's Invasion of Mexico," *HAHR* 23 (1943) 52–76.

5591a. Walker, H. P. (ed.). "William McLaine's Narrative of the Magee-Gutiérrez Expedition, 1812–1813," *SHQ* 66 (1962–1963) 234–251, 457–479, 569–588.

5592. West, E. H. (ed.). "Diary of José Gutiérrez de Lara, 1811–1812," *AHR* 34 (1928) 55–77. Mexican emissary to Washington.

5593. Zavala, L. de. *Ensayo Histórico de las Revoluciones de México Desde 1808 Hasta 1830.* 2 vols., Paris, 1831–1832.

XIII–B   cross references: 9326a

C. UNITED STATES–MEXICAN RELATIONS, 1821–1836

5594. Alamán, L. *Defensa del Ex-Ministro de Relaciones D. Lucas Alamán, en la Causa Formada Contra él y Contra los Ex-Ministros de Guerra y Justicia del Vice-Presidente D. Anastasio Bustamente.* Mexico, 1834.

5595. Alessio Robles, V. (ed.). *La Correspondencia de Agustín de Iturbide Después de la Proclamación de Plan de Iguala.* 2 vols., Mexico, 1945.

5596. Alvarez, J. R. "Los Primeros Contactos Diplomáticos de México," *HM* 3 (July, 1953) 87–101.

Description of early Mexican relations with the United States, Peru, Colombia, and Spain.

5597. Baur, J. E. "The Evolution of a Mexican Foreign Trade Policy, 1821–1828," *TA* 19 (1962–1963) 225–261.

5598. Bidwell, R. L. "The First Mexican Navy, 1821–1830," U. of Virginia Diss., 1960.

5599. Bolton, H. E. "General James Wilkinson as Advisor to Emperor Iturbide," *HAHR* 1 (1918) 163–180.

5600. ———— (ed.). "The Iturbide Revolution in the Californias," *HAHR* 2 (1919) 188–242.

5601. Bosch García, C. *Historia de las Relaciones Entre México y los Estados Unidos, 1819–1848.* Mexico, 1961.

5602. ————. *Problemas Diplomáticos del México Independiente.* Mexico, 1947.

Covers the period from 1811 to 1836.

5603. Callcott, W. H. *Church and State in Mexico, 1822–1857.* Durham, N.C., 1926.

See also item 5522.

5604. Feliú Cruz, G. "Comprobaciones Históricas: Poinsett en Méjico y en Chile," *RCHG* 12 (1928) 37–46.

5604a. Flaccus, E. W. "Commodore David Porter and the Mexican Navy," *HAHR* 34 (1954) 365–373.

5605. Fuentes Mares, J. *Poinsett: Historia de una Gran Intriga.* Mexico, 1951.

Poinsett was the first U.S. minister to Mexico.

5606. ————. *Santa Anna: Aurora y Ocaso de un Comediante.* Mexico, 1956.

5607. Gardiner, C. H. (ed.). *Mexico, 1825–1828: The Journal and Correspondence of Edward Thornton Tayloe.* Chapel Hill, N.C., 1959.

Tayloe was Poinsett's secretary.

5608. ————. "The Role of Guadalupe Victoria in Mexican Foreign Relations," *RHA*, no. 26 (1948) 379–392.

First President of Mexico, 1824–1828.

5609. Gómez, F. V. *Guadalupe Victoria, Primer Presidente de México.* Mexico, 1952.

5610. Hawgood, J. A. "The Pattern of Yankee Infiltration in Mexican Alta California, 1821–1846," *PHR* 27 (1958) 27–37.

5611. Knapp, F. A., Jr. "John Quincy Adams, ¿Defensor de México? *HM* 7 (July, 1957) 116–123.

5612. Lay, B. *The Lives of Ellis P. Bean.* Austin, Texas, 1960.

Bean led an unsuccessful filibustering expedition to Mexico and subsequently served in the revolutionary army under Morelos.

5613. Manning, W. R. *Early Diplomatic Relations Between the United States and Mexico.* Baltimore, 1916.

5614. María Tornel, J. *Manifestación del C. José María Tornel.* Mexico, 1833.

Mexican Minister to the United States, 1830–1831.

5615. McElhannon, J. C. "Foreign Relations of Imperial Mexico, 1821–1823," U. of Texas Diss., 1951.

5615a. ————. "Imperial Mexico and Texas, 1821–1823," *SHQ* 53 (1949) 117–150.

5615b. Morton, O. "The Life of General Don Manuel de Mier y Terán as It Affected Texas-Mexican Relations, 1821–1852," U. of Texas Diss., 1939.

5616. Parton, D. M. *The Diplomatic Career of Joel Roberts Poinsett.* Wash., 1934.

5617. Poinsett, J. R. *Notes on Mexico, Made in the Autumn of 1822.* Phil., 1824.

Spanish ed., Mexico, 1950.

5618. Potash, R. A. *El Banco de Avío de México: El Fomento de la Industria, 1821–1846.* Mexico, 1959.

5619. Puga y Acal, M. "Poinsett en Méjico y en Chile," *RCHG* (1927) 43–58.

5620. Putnam, H. E. *Joel Roberts Poinsett: A Political Biography.* Wash., 1935.

5621. Rippy, J. F. *Joel R. Poinsett, Versatile American.* Durham, N.C., 1935.

5622. Rivera Cambas, M. *Antonio López de Santa Anna*. Mexico, 1959.

5623. Rives, G. L. *The United States and Mexico, 1821–1848: A History of the Relations Between the Two Countries from the Independence of Mexico to the Close of the War with the United States*. 2 vols., N.Y., 1913.

5624. Salit, C. R. "Anglo-American Rivalry in Mexico, 1823–1830," *RHA*, no. 16 (1943) 65–84.

5624a. Smith, J. H. "Poinsett's Career in Mexico," *PAAS* 24 (1914) 77–92.

5624b. Spell, L. M. "Gorostiza and Texas," *HAHR* 37 (1957) 425–462.
A Mexican minister to the United States in 1836.

5625. Sprague, W. F. *Vicente Guerrero, Mexican Liberator: A Study in Patriotism*. Chicago, 1939.
Second President of Mexico.

5626. Stillé, C. J. "The Life and Services of Joel R. Poinsett," *PMH* 12 (1888) 129–164, 257–303.

5627. Suárez y Navarro, J. *Historia de México y del General Antonio López de Santa-Anna*. Mexico, 1850.

5628. Thompson, W. *Recollections of Mexico*. London, 1846.

5629. True, C. A. "British Loans to the Mexican Government, 1822–1832," *SSSQ* 17 (1937) 353–362.

5630. Ulibarri, R. O. "American Interest in the Spanish-Mexican Southwest, 1803–1848," Utah U. Diss., 1963.

5631. Ward, H. G. *Mexico in 1827*. 2 vols., London, 1828.
Ward was the British minister in Mexico and rival of Poinsett.

XIII–C cross references: 2340, 5560, 5565, 5578, 5580, 5583, 5593, 5888, 9316, 9326a

D. THE TEXAS ISSUE, 1836–1845

5632. Adams, E. D. (ed.). *British Diplomatic Correspondence Concerning the Republic of Texas, 1838–1846*. Austin, Texas, 1918.

5633. ———. *British Interests and Activities in Texas, 1838–1846*. Baltimore, 1910.

5634. Alamán, L. *Iniciativa de Ley Proponiendo al Gobierno las Medidas que se Debían Tomar para la Seguridad del Estado de Tejas y Conservar la Integridad del Territorio Mexicano de Cuyo Proyecto Emanó la Ley de 6 Abril de 1830*. Mexico, 1946.

5635. Alessio Robles, V. *Coahuila y Texas Desde la Consumación de la Independencia Hasta el Tratado de Paz de Guadalupe Hidalgo*. 2 vols. Mexico, 1945.

5636. Almada, F. R. "Documentos Sobre Santa Anna," *BSCEH* 10 (January, 1957) 10–14; 10 (April, 1957) 13–15.
Concerns Santa Anna's Texas campaign.

5637. Ashford, G. "Jacksonian Liberalism and Spanish Law in Early Texas," *SHQ* 57 (July, 1953) 1–37.

5638. Austin, S. F. *Exposición al Público Sobre los Asuntos de Texas por . . . y las Siete Guerras por Texas*. Mexico, 1959.

5639. Bacarisse, C. A. "The Union of Coahuila and Texas," *SHQ* 61 (1958) 341–349.

5640. Bancroft, H. H. *History of the North Mexican States and Texas*. 2 vols., San Francisco, 1884–1889.

5641. Barker, E. C. "The Annexation of Texas," *SHQ* 50 (July, 1946) 49–74.

5642. ——— (ed.). *The Austin Papers*. 4 vols., Wash., D.C., and Austin, Texas, 1924–1928.

5643. ———. "The Influence of Slavery in the Colonization of Texas," *MVHR* 11 (1924) 3–36.

5644. ———. *The Life of Stephen F. Austin, Founder of Texas, 1793–1836: A Chapter in the Westward Movement of the Anglo-American People*. Nashville, 1925.

5645. ———. *Mexico and Texas, 1821–1835*. Dallas, 1928.

5646. ———. "Notes on the Colonization of Texas," *SHQ* 27 (1923) 108–119.

5647. ———. "President Jackson and the Texas Revolution," *AHR* 12 (1907) 788–809.

5648. ———. "The United States and Mexico, 1835–1837," *MVHR* 1 (1914) 3–30.

5648a. Berge, D. E. "Mexican Response to United States Expansionism, 1841–1848." U. of California Diss., 1965.

5649. Binkley, W. C. *Official Correspondence of the Texan Revolution, 1835–1836*. 2 vols., N.Y., 1936.
A basic documentary collection.

5650. ———. *The Expansionist Movement in Texas, 1836–1850*. Berkeley, Calif., 1925.

5651. ———. *The Texas Revolution*. Baton Rouge, La., 1952.

5651a. Bosch García, C. "Dos Diplomáticos y un Problema," *HM* 2 (July, 1952) 46–55.
Deals with negotiations of 1843–1845 concerning Texas.

5652. Boucher, C. S. "The Annexation of Texas and the Bluffton Movement in South Carolina," *MVHR* 6 (1919) 3–33.

5653. *Breve Reseña Histórica de los Principales Acontecimientos Ocurridos con Motivo de la Rebelión de la Colonia de Tejas y Guerra con los Estados-Unidos de Norte América*. Mexico, 1941.

5654. Brown, A. H. "The Consular Service of the Republic of Texas," *SHQ* 33 (1930) 184–230, 299–314.

5655. Callcott, W. H. *Santa Anna: The Story of an Enigma Who Once Was Mexico*. Norman, Okla., 1936.

5656. Carroll, B. H. *Die Annexion von Texas: Ein Beitrag zur Geschichte der Monroe-Doktrin*. Berlin, 1904.

5657. Castañeda, C. E. *Our Catholic Heritage in Texas, 1519–1936*. 6 vols., Austin, Texas, 1936–1950.
See especially vol. 6.

5658. ——— (trans.). *The Mexican Side of the Texas Revolution (1836) by the Chief Mexican Participants: General Antonio López de Santa Anna, D. Ramón Martínez Caro, General Vicente Filisola, General José Urrea, General José María Tornel*. Dallas, 1928.

5659. Chase, M. K. *Négociations de la République du Texas en Europe, 1837–1845*. Paris, 1932.

5660. Cleaves, W. S. "Lorenzo de Zavala in Texas," *SHQ* 36 (1932) 29–40.

5661. *Correspondencia Entre los Señores J. N. Almonte, Arrangoiz, Consul de N. Orleans a los Sres. Pedro Fernández del Castillo y Joaquín Velásquez de León, Sobre Texas y los E.E. U.U., 1841–1843*. Mexico, 1949.

5662. *Correspondencia que Ha Mediado Entre la Legación Extraordinaria de México y el Departamento de Estado de los Estados Unidos, Sobre el Paso del Sabina por las Tropas que Mandaba el General Gaines*. Mexico, 1837.
Correspondence of the Mexican Minister, M. E. de Gorostiza, with USDS. English ed., Wash., 1837.

5663. Cotner, T. E. *The Military and Political Career of José Joaquín de Herrera, 1792–1854*. Austin, Texas, 1949.
President of Mexico, 1844–1845.

5664. Cox, I. J. "The Southwest Boundary of Texas," *TSHAQ* 6 (1902) 81–102.

5665. Crane, R. C. "Santa Anna and the Aftermath of San Jacinto," *WTHAYB* 11 (1935) 56–61.

5666. Day, D., and H. H. Ullom (eds.). *The Autobiography of Sam Houston*. Norman, Okla., 1954.

5667. Estep, R. "Lorenzo de Zavala and the Texas Revolution," *SHQ* 57 (January, 1954) 322–335.

5668. Estrada, G. (ed.). *Joaquín Moreno, Diario de un Escribiente de Legación*. Mexico, 1925.
Volume 16 of the *Archivo Histórico Diplomático Mexicano*. See item 5517.

5669. *Exposiciones Dirigidas al Supremo Gobierno por D. Tadeo Ortíz, Relativas á la Seguridad de los Límites de Esta República Mandadas Imprimir por Acuerdo de la Cámara de Diputados*. Mexico, 1841.

5670. Filisola, V. *Memorias para la Historia de la Guerra de Tejas*. 2 vols., Mexico, 1848–1849.

5671. Flores D., J. (comp.). *Lorenzo de Zavala y su Misión Diplomática en Francia, 1834–1835*. Mexico, 1951.
In *Archivo Histórico Diplomático Mexicano*, 2d ser., vol. 8. See item 5517.

5672. Friend, L. *Sam Houston, The Great Designer*. Austin, Texas, 1954.

5673. Gailey, H. A., Jr. "Sam Houston and the Texas War Fever, March to August, 1842," *SHQ* 42 (July, 1958) 29–44.

5674. Gambrell, H. *Anson Jones, The Last President of Texas*. Garden City, N.Y., 1948.

5675. Garrison, G. P. (ed.). *Diplomatic Correspondence of the Republic of Texas*. 3 vols., Wash., 1908–1911.
Found in the *AHAAR* for 1907–1908.

5676. ———. "The First Stage of the Movement for the Annexation of Texas," *AHR* 10 (1904) 72–96.

5677. Gibson, G. R. *Journal of a Soldier Under Kearny and Doniphan, 1846–1847*. Glendale, Calif., 1935.

5678. Gorostiza, M. E. de. *Dictamen Leído el 3*

de 1840 en el Consejo de Gobierno Sobre le Cuestión de Tejas. Mexico, 1844.

5679. Greer, J. K. "The Committee on the Texas Declaration of Independence," *SHQ* 30 (1927) 239–251; 31 (1927) 33–39, 130–149.

5680. Gulick, C. A., and K. Elliot (eds.). *The Papers of Mirabeau Buonaparte Lamar.* 6 vols., Austin, Texas, 1921–1927.

5681. Harris, H. W. "Almonte's Inspection of Texas in 1834," *SHQ* 4 (1938) 195–211.

5682. Harrison, H. V. "Los Federalistas de 1839–40 y sus Tanteos Diplomáticos en Texas," *HM* 6 (January, 1957) 321–349.

5683. Hatcher, M. A. *The Opening of Texas to Foreign Settlement, 1801–1821.* Austin, Texas, 1927.

5684. Hogan, W. R. *The Texas Republic.* Norman, Okla., 1946.

5685. Houston, S. "The Annexation of Texas," *TSHAQ* 1 (1897) 79–86.

5686. Howren, A. "Causes and Origin of the [Colonization] Decree of April 6, 1830," *SHQ* 16 (1913) 378–422.

5686a. Hutchinson, C. A. "Mexican Federalists in New Orleans and the Texas Revolution," *LHQ* 39 (1956) 1–47.
    The Mexican federalists gave aid to the Texans.

5687. Jones, A. *Memoranda and Official Correspondence Relating to the Republic of Texas, Its History and Annexation, Including a Brief Autobiography of the Author.* N.Y., 1859.

5688. Jordan, H. D. "A Politician of Expansion: Robert J. Walker," *MVHR* 19 (1932) 362–381.

5689. *Journal of the Proceedings of the General Council of the Republic of Texas, Held at San Felipe de Austin, November 14th, 1835.* Houston, 1839.

5690. *Journals of the Consultation Held at San Felipe de Austin, October 16, 1835.* Houston, 1838.

5691. Kennedy, W. *Texas: The Rise, Progress and Prospects of the Republic of Texas.* 2 vols., London, 1841.

5692. Lane, W. P. *The Adventures and Recollections of General Walter P. Lane, a San Jacinto Veteran.* Marshall, Texas, 1928.

5693. López de Santa Anna, A. *Mi Historia Militar y Política, 1810–1874: Memorias Inéditas.* Mexico, 1905.

5694. Lowrie, S. H. *Culture Conflict in Texas, 1821–1835.* N.Y., 1932.

5695. Martínez Caro, R. *Verdadera Idea de la Primera Campaña de Tejas y Sucesos Ocurridos Después de la Acción de San Jacinto.* Mexico, 1837.

5696. McClendon, R. E. "Daniel Webster and Mexican Relations: The Santa Fe Prisoners," *SHQ* 36 (1933) 288–311.
    Webster was secretary of state from 1841 to 1843.

5697. McLemore, R. A. "The Influence of French Diplomatic Policy on the Annexation of Texas," *SHQ* 43 (1939) 342–347.

5698. María Tornel, J. *Tejas y los Estados Unidos de América, en sus Relaciones con la República Mexicana.* Mexico, 1837.

5699. Marshall, T. M. "Diplomatic Relations of Texas and the United States, 1839–1843," *TSHAQ* 15 (1912) 267–293.

5699a. Merk, F. "A Safety Valve Thesis and Texan Annexation," *MVHR* 49 (1962) 413–436.

5700. Middleton, A. L. "Donelson's Mission to Texas in Behalf of Annexation," *SHQ* 14 (1920–1921) 247–249.

5701. ———. "Studies Relating to the Annexation of Texas by the United States," U. of Texas Diss., 1938.

5702. Minge, W. A. "Frontier Problems in New Mexico Preceding the Mexican War, 1840–1846," U. of New Mexico Diss., 1965.

5703. Muñóz, R. F. *Santa Ana: El que Todo lo Ganó y Todo lo Perdió.* Madrid, 1935.

5704. Nance, J. M. *After San Jacinto.* Austin, Texas, 1963.
    Treats Texas-Mexican relations after Santa Anna's defeat.

5705. Newell, C. *History of the Revolution in Texas, Particularly of the War of 1835 and '36, Together with the Latest Geographical, Topographical and Statistical Accounts of the Country from the Most Authentic Sources, Also an Appendix.* Austin, Texas, 1935.

5706. Núñez Ortega, G. "Diario de un Prisionero de la Guerra de Texas," *BAGNM* 4 (1933) 833–879.

5707. Peña, J. E. de la. *La Rebelión de Texas: Manuscrito Inédito de 1836 por un Oficial de Santa Anna.* Mexico, 1955.

5708. Peña y Reyes, A. de la (ed.). *Don Manuel Eduardo de Gorostiza y la Cuestión de Texas: Documentos Históricos.* Mexico, 1924.

In *Archivo Histórico Diplomático Mexicano*, vol. 8. See item 5517.

5709. Pereyra, C. *Tejas: La Primera Desmembración de Méjico.* Madrid, 1917(?).

5710. Pichardo, J. A. *Pichardo's Treatise on the Limits of Louisiana and Texas ... to Disprove the Claim of the United States That Texas Was Included in the Louisiana Purchase.* 4 vols., Austin, Texas, 1931–1941.

5710a. Pitchford, L. C., Jr. "The Diplomatic Representatives from the United States to Mexico from 1836 to 1848," U. of Colorado Diss., 1965.

Examines the attitudes of Wilson Shannon, John Slidell, Powhatan Ellis, Waddy Thompson, and Nicholas P. Trist.

5711. Presley, J. "Santa Anna in Texas: A Mexican Viewpoint," *SHQ* 42 (1959) 489–512.

Studies the 1836 campaign.

5711a. Pugh, N. M. "Contemporary Comments on Texas, 1844–1847," *SHQ* 62 (1959) 367–370.

5712. Rather, E. Z. "Recognition of the Republic of Texas by the United States," *TSHAQ* 13 (1910) 155–255.

5713. Red, W. S. *The Texas Colonists and Religion, 1821–1836: A Centennial Tribute to the Texas Patriots Who Shed Their Blood That We Might Enjoy Civil and Religious Liberty.* Austin, Texas, 1924.

5714. Richardson, R. N. "Framing the Constitution of the Republic of Texas," *SHQ* 31 (1928) 191–220.

5714a. Salado Alvarez, V. "La Independencia de Tejas y la Esclavitud," *RSO* 8 (August, 1916) 46–61.

5715. Sánchez Navarro, C. *La Guerra de Texas.* Mexico, 1938.

5716. Schmitz, J. W. *Texan Statecraft, 1836–1845.* San Antonio, Texas, 1941.

5717. ———. *Texas Culture, 1836–1846: In the Days of the Republic.* San Antonio, Texas, 1960.

5718. Seymour, F. W. *Sam Houston, Patriot.* N.Y., 1930.

5719. Shuffler, R. H. "The Signing of Texas' Declaration of Independence: Myth and Record," *SHQ* 65 (1962) 310–332.

5720. Siegel, S. *A Political History of the Texas Republic, 1836–1845.* Austin, Texas, 1956.

5721. Smith, J. H. *The Annexation of Texas.* 2 vols., N.Y., 1911.

5722. ———. "La República de Rio Grande," *AHR* 25 (1920) 660–675.

5723. Smith, R. C. "James W. Fannin, Jr., in the Texas Revolution," *SHQ* 23 (1920) 79–90, 171–203, 271–284.

5724. Smither, H. (ed.). *Journals of the Fourth Congress of the Republic of Texas, 1839–1840.* 3 vols., Austin, Texas, 1931(?).

5724a. Spellman, L. U. (ed.). "Letters of the 'Dawson' Men from Perote Prison, Mexico, 1842–1843," *SHQ* 38 (1935) 246–249.

5725. Steen, R. W. "Analysis of the Work of the General Council, Provisional Government of Texas, 1835–1836," *SHQ* 41 (1938) 225–240, 324–348; 42 (1938) 29–54.

5726. Stenberg, R. R. "Jackson, Anthony Butler and Texas," *SHQ* 13 (1932) 264–286.

5727. ———. "President Polk and the Annexation of Texas," *SSSQ* 14 (1934) 332–356.

5728. ———. "The Texas Schemes of Jackson and Houston, 1829–1836," *SSSQ* 15 (1934) 229–250.

5729. Strickland, R. H. "Anglo-American Activities in Northeastern Texas, 1803–1845," U. of Texas Diss., 1937.

5730. Tyler, J. "Tyler and the Texas Question," *TQHGM* 12 (1932) 235–237.

5731. Valadés, J. C. *Santa Anna y la Guerra de Texas.* Mexico, 1936.

5732. Vigness, D. M. "A Texas Expedition into Mexico, 1840," *SHQ* 42 (1958) 18–28.

5733. ———. "Relations of the Republic of Texas and the Republic of the Rio Grande," *SHQ* 57 (1954) 312–321.

5734. Ward, F. E. "The Lower Brazos Region of Texas, 1820–1845," U. of Texas Diss., 1962.

5735. Webb, W. P. "The Last Treaty of the Republic of Texas," *SHQ* 25 (1922) 151–173.

5736. Wharton, C. R. *El Presidente: A Sketch of the Life of General Santa Anna.* Houston, 1924.

5737. Williams, A. M. *Sam Houston and the War of Independence in Texas*. Boston, 1893.

5738. Winkler, E. W. *Secret Journals of the Senate, Republic of Texas, 1836–1845*. Austin, Texas, 1911.

5739. Winston, J. E. "The Attitude of the Newspapers of the United States Towards Texan Independence," *MVHRP* 8 (1916) 160–175.

5740. ————. "The Mississippi Whigs and the Annexation of Texas," *SHQ* 29 (1926) 161–180.

5741. ————. "New Orleans Newspapers and the Texas Question, 1835–1837," *SHQ* 36 (1932) 109–129.

5742. ————. "Notes on Commercial Relations Between New Orleans and Texan Ports, 1838–1839," *SHQ* 34 (1930) 91–105.

5743. ————. "Texas Annexation Sentiment in Mississippi, 1835–1844," *SHQ* 33 (1919) 1–19.

5744. Wisehart, M. K. *Sam Houston, American Giant*. Wash., 1962.

5745. Worley, J. L. "The Diplomatic Relations of England and the Republic of Texas," *TSHAQ* 9 (1905) 1–40.

XIII–D cross references:

a) For works on the Pastry War (1838), see items 2177a–2182b.

b) See also items 2070, 2097a, 2110, 5560, 5601, 5606, 5615a, 5615b, 5622, 5623, 5624b, 5627, 5630, 5810, 5888.

E. THE MEXICAN WAR, 1846–1848

5746. Abel, A. H. (ed.). *The Official Correspondence of James S. Calhoun While Indian Agent at Santa Fe and Superintendent of Indian Affairs in New Mexico (1849–1852)*. Wash., 1915.

5747. Alcaraz, R., *et al. Apuntes para la Historia de la Guerra Entre México y los Estados Unidos*. Mexico, 1952.

5748. ————. *The Other Side: Or Notes for the History of the War Between Mexico and the U.S.* N.Y., 1850.

5749. *Apuntes Históricos Sobre los Acontecimientos Notables de la Guerra Entre México y los Estados Unidos del Norte*. Mexico, 1945.

5750. *Apuntes para la Historia de la Guerra Entre México y los Estados Unidos*. Mexico, 1848.

5751. Armond, L. de. "Justo Sierra O'Reilly and Yucatecan–United States Relations, 1847–1848," *HAHR* 31 (1951) 420–436.

5751a. Barton, H. W. "Five Texas Frontier Companies During the Mexican War," *SHQ* 66 (1962) 17–30.

5752. Bauer, K. J., "United States Naval Operations During the Mexican War," Indiana U. Diss., 1953.

5753. ————. "The Veracruz Expedition of 1847," *MAF* 20 (1956) 162–169.

5754. Betts, J. L. "The U.S. Navy in the Mexican War," U. of Chicago Diss., 1955.

5755. Bill, A. H. *Rehearsal for Conflict: The War with Mexico, 1846–1848*. N.Y., 1947.

5756. Bloom, J. P. "With the American Army into Mexico, 1846–1848," Emory U. Diss., 1956.

5757. Bosch García, C. "Antecedentes Históricos del Principio de no Intervención en Torno a la Guerra de 1847," *CPS* 8 (January, 1962) 15–25.

5758. Boucher, C. S. "In re That Aggressive Slavocracy," *MVHR* 8 (1921) 13–79.

5759. Bourne, E. G. "The Proposed Absorption of Mexico in 1847–1848," *AHAAR* (1899). Wash., 1900.

5760. ————. "The United States and Mexico, 1847–1848," *AHR* 5 (1900) 491–502.

5761. Brent, R. A. "Reaction in the U.S. to Nicholas Trist's Mission to Mexico, 1847–1848," *RHA*, nos. 35–36 (1953) 105–118.

5762. Brooke, G. M., Jr. "The Vest Pocket War of Commodore Jones," *PHR* 31 (1962) 217–233. Seized Monterey in 1842.

5763. Bustamante, C. M. de. *El Nuevo Bernal Díaz del Castillo: O Sea, Historia de la Invasión de los Anglo-Americanos en México*. 2 vols. in one, Mexico, 1949.

5764. Castañeda, C. E. "Relations of General Scott with Santa Anna," *HAHR* 29 (1949) 455–473.

5765. Castillo Nájera, F. *Invasión Norteamericana: Efectivos y Estado de los Ejércitos*

Beligerantes, Consideraciones Sobre la Campaña. Mexico, 1947.

5766. ———. "La Invasión Norteamericana en México, 1847–1848," *MRANC* 56 (1948) 265–331.

5767. Chamberlin, E. K. "Nicholas Trist and Baja California," *PHR* 32 (1963) 49–63.
Concludes that Trist should not be held responsible for the failure to obtain Baja California.

5768. Chaney, H. C. "The Mexican–United States War as Seen by Mexican Intellectuals, 1846–1956," Stanford U. Diss., 1959.

5769. Clarke, D. L. *Stephen Watts Kearny, Soldier of the West.* Norman, Okla., 1961.

5770. *Comunicación Circular que el Exmo. Sr. D. Manuel de la Peña y Peña, Estendió en el Año de 1845 como Ministro de Relaciones, para Dirigirla á los Gobiernos y Asambleas, Departamentales, Sobre la Cuestión de Paz o Guerra, Según el Estado que Guardaban en Aquella Epoca.* Querétaro, Mexico, 1848.

5771. Curti, M. E. "Pacifist Propaganda and the Treaty of Guadalupe Hidalgo," *AHR* 33 (1928) 593–598.

5772. Davies, T. M., Jr. "Assessments During the Mexican War: An Exercise in Futility," *NMHR* 41 (1966) 197–216.
Establishes that U.S. assessment policy was a failure.

5773. De Voto, B. A. *The Year of Decision, 1846.* Boston, 1943.
Much broader coverage than title indicates.

5774. Downey, F., and P. M. Angle. *Texas and the War with Mexico.* N.Y., 1961.

5775. Downey, J. T. *The Cruise of the Portsmouth, 1845–1847: A Sailor's View of the Naval Conquest of California.* New Haven, Conn., 1958.

5776. Echanove Trujillo, C. *La Vida Pasional e Inquieta de Don Crecencio Rejón.* Mexico, 1941.
Secretary of foreign relations at the time of the Mexican War.

5777. Edwards, J. N. "Shelby's Expedition to Mexico: An Unwritten Leaf of the War," *MHR* 19 (1925) 438–471.

5778. Elliott, C. W. *Winfield Scott, The Soldier and the Man.* N.Y., 1937.

5778a. Esquenazi-Mayo, R. "Historiografiá de la Guerra Entre México y los EE. UU.," *DHR* 2 (Winter, 1962) 34–77.

5779. Fuentes Díaz, V. *La Intervención Norteamericana en México, 1847.* Mexico, 1947.

5780. Fuller, J. D. P. "Slavery Propaganda During the Mexican War," *SHQ* 38 (1935) 235–245.

5781. ———. *The Movement for the Acquisition of All Mexico, 1846–48.* Baltimore, 1936.

5782. ———. "The Slavery Question and the Movement to Acquire Mexico, 1846–1848," *MVHR* 21 (1934) 31–48.

5783. Fulmore, Z. T. "The Annexation of Texas and the Mexican War," *TSHAQ* 5 (1901) 28–48.

5784. Gallatin, A. *Peace with Mexico.* N.Y., 1847.

5785. Gerhard, P. "Baja California in the Mexican War, 1846–1848," *PHR* 14 (1945) 418–424.

5786. Going, C. B. *David Wilmot, Free-Soiler (1814–1868): A Biography of the Great Advocate of the Wilmot Proviso.* N.Y., 1924.

5787. Boldin, G. "Business Sentiment and the Mexican War, with Particular Emphasis on the New York Businessman," *NYH* 33 (1952) 54–70.

5788. Gómez, M. R. "Sobre Justo Sierra O'Reilly," *HM* 3 (January, 1954) 309–327.

5789. Goodwin, C. *John Charles Fremont: An Explanation of His Career.* Stanford, Calif., 1930.

5790. Graebner, N. A. "American Interest in California, 1845," *PHR* 22 (1953) 13–28.

5791. ———. *Empire on the Pacific: A Study in American Continental Expansion.* N.Y., 1955.

5792. ———. "James K. Polk's Wartime Expansionist Policy," *ETHSP*, no. 23 (1951) 32–45.

5793. ———. "Party Politics and the Trist Mission," *JSH* 19 (1953) 137–156.

5794. ———. "The Treaty of Guadalupe Hidalgo: Its Background and Formation." U. of Chicago Diss., 1950.

5795. ———. "United States Gulf Commerce with Mexico, 1822–1848," *IEA* 5, no. 1 (1951) 36–51.

5796. Hale, C. A. "The War with the United

States and the Crisis in Mexican Thought," *TA* 14 (1957) 153–173.

Analysis of contemporary Mexican reaction.

5797. Hammond, G. P. (ed.). *The Larkin Papers: Personal Business, and Official Correspondence of Thomas Oliver Larkin, Merchant and U.S. Consul in California.* 5 vols., Berkeley, Calif., 1951– .

5798. ———— (ed.). *The Treaty of Guadalupe Hidalgo, February Second, 1848.* Berkeley, Calif., 1949.

5799. Henry, R. S. *The Story of the Mexican War.* Indianapolis, 1950.

5800. Hicks, R. S. "Diplomatic Relations with Mexico During the Administration of James K. Polk," *SCHSP* 12, pt. 2 (1922) 5–17.

5801. Jay, W. *A Review of the Causes and Consequences of the Mexican War.* Boston, 1849.

Spanish ed., Mexico, 1948. Blames Polk for precipitating the conflict.

5802. Kearney, T. "The Mexican War and the Conquest of California: Stockton or Kearney Conqueror and First Governor?" *CHSQ* 8 (1929) 251–261.

5803. Kelsey, R. W. *The United States Consulate in California.* Berkeley, Calif., 1910.

5804. Klein, J. "The Making of the Treaty of Guadalupe Hidalgo, on February 2, 1848," *UCC* 7 (1905) 247–318.

5805. Kohl, C. C. *Claims as a Cause of the Mexican War.* N.Y., 1914.

5805a. Lavender, D. *Climax at Buena Vista: The American Campaigns in Northeastern Mexico, 1846-47.* N.Y., 1966.

5806. Leggett, A. "An Important Letter: Aaron Leggett to William Marcy, October 16, 1845," *CHSQ* 9 (1932) 33–34.

Discusses a possible British intervention in California.

5807. Lamoine Villacaña, E. *Crónica de la Ocupación de México por el Ejército de los Estados Unidos.* Mexico, 1950.

5808. Lewis, L. *Captain Sam Grant.* Boston, 1950.

Experiences of U. S. Grant in Mexico.

5809. Livermore, A. *Revisión de la Guerra Entre México y los Estados Unidos.* Mexico, 1948.

United States anti-expansionist argument. Trans. from Eng. ed., Boston, 1850.

5810. Luelmo, J. *Los Antiesclavistas Norteamericanos: La Cuestión de Texas y la Guerra con México.* Mexico, 1947.

5810a. Mayo, B. "Apostle of Manifest Destiny (Anthony Butler)," *AME* 18 (1929) 420–426.

5811. McCornack, R. B. "The San Patricio Deserters in the Mexican War," *TA* 8 (1951) 131–142.

5812. McElroy, R. M. *The Winning of the Far West: A History of the Regaining of Texas, of the Mexican War, and the Oregon Question.* N.Y., 1914.

5813. McEniry, B. M. "American Catholics in the War with Mexico," Catholic U. Diss., 1937.

5814. *Memoria de la Primera Secretaría de Estado y del Despacho de Relaciones Interiores y Exteriores de los Estados Unidos Mexicanos, 1846.* Mexico, 1846.

5815. Menéndez, C. R. (ed.). *La Célebre Misión del Doctor Don Justo Sierra O'Reilly a los Estados Unidos de Norteamérica en 1847 y 1848.* Mérida, 1945.

5816. Nevins, A. *Fremont: Pathmaker of the West.* N.Y., 1939.

5817. Nicolau d'Olwer, L. "Santa Anna y la Invasión por Bermúdez de Castro," *HM* 4 (1954) 47–65.

Spanish Minister's observations on the Mexican War.

5818. Owen, C. H. *The Justice of the Mexican War.* N.Y., 1908.

5819. Peña y Reyes, A. de la. *Algunos Documentos Sobre el Tratado de Guadalupe y la Situación de México Durante la Invasión Americana.* Mexico, 1930.

5820. Ramírez, J. F. *Mexico During the War with the United States.* Columbia, Mo., 1950.

5821. Rejón, M. C. *Observaciones del Diputado Saliente Manuel Crecencio Rejón, Contra los Tratados de Paz, Firmados en la Ciudad de Guadalupe el 2 del Próximo Pasado Febrero, Precididas de la Parte Histórica Relativa a la Cuestión Originaria.* Querétaro, 1848.

5822. Ripley, R. S. *The War with Mexico.* 2 vols., N.Y., 1849.

5823. Rives, G. L. "Mexican Diplomacy on

the Eve of the War with the United States," *AHR* 18 (1913) 275–294.

5824. Roa Bárcena, J. M. *Recuerdos de la Invasión Norteamericana, 1846–1848.* 3 vols., Mexico, 1947.

5825. Ruiz, R. E. *The Mexican War: Was It Manifest Destiny?* N.Y., 1963.

Short extracts taken from major historical works.

5826. Scott, L. M. "Oregon, Texas and California, 1846," *OHQ* 36 (1935) 154–162.

5827. Sears, L. M. "Nicholas P. Trist: A Diplomat with Ideals," *MVHR* 11 (1924) 85–98.

5828. ———. "Slidell and Buchanan," *AHR* 27 (1922) 709–730.

5829. ———. "Slidell's Mission to Mexico," *SAQ* 12 (1913) 12–26.

5830. Singletary, O. A. *The Mexican War.* Chicago, 1960.

Emphasis is on the military aspects of the war.

5831. Smith, J. H. "American Rule in Mexico," *AHR* 23 (1918) 287–302.

Deals with the occupation at the time of the Mexican War.

5832. ———. "Great Britain and Our War of 1846–1848," *MHSP* 47 (1914) 451–462.

5833. ——— (ed.). "Letters of General Antonio López de Santa Anna Relating to the War Between the United States and Mexico, 1846–48," *AHAAR* (1917) 355–431. Wash., 1920.

5834. ———. *The War with Mexico.* 2 vols., N.Y., 1919.

Reprinted, Gloucester, Mass., 1963.

5835. Smith, R. A. "Contrabando en la Guerra con Estados Unidos," *HM* 11 (January, 1962) 361–381.

5836. ———. "Indians in American-Mexican Relations Before the War of 1846," *HAHR* 43 (1963) 34–64.

5837. Spell, L. M. "The Anglo-Saxon Press in Mexico, 1846–1848," *AHR* 38 (1932) 20–31.

5838. Stenberg, R. R. "The Failure of Polk's Mexican War Intrigue of 1845," *PHR* 4 (1935) 39–68.

5839. Stephenson, N. W. *Texas and the Mexican War: A Chronicle of the Winning of the Southwest.* New Haven, Conn., 1921.

5840. USCH. *Correspondence Regarding the Treaty of Guadalupe Hidalgo* (30th cong., 1st sess., H. Ex. Doc. 50). Wash., 1849.

5841. Van Winkle, H. L. "The Treaty of Guadalupe Hidalgo," *SCPQ* 2, no. 1 (1925) 46–56.

5842. Wallace, E. S. "Deserters in the Mexican War," *HAHR* 15 (1935) 374–383.

5843. Williams, M. W. "Secessionist Diplomacy of Yucatan," *HAHR* 9 (1929) 132–143.

Discusses sentiment during the Mexican War.

5844. Wright, D. M. "A Yankee in Mexican California: Abel Stearns, 1798–1848," Claremont Graduate School Diss., 1955.

XIII–E cross references: 2092, 2103b, 2104, 2113, 2128, 5601, 5603, 5610, 5623, 5710a

F. UNITED STATES–MEXICAN RELATIONS, 1848–1876

5845. Abbott, G. D. *Mexico and the United States: Their Mutual Relations and Common Interests.* N.Y., 1869.

5846. Bartlett, J. R. *Personal Narrative of Explorations and Incidents in Texas, New Mexico, California, Sonora, and Chihuahua, Connected with the United States and Mexican Boundary Commission During the Years 1850, '51, '52, and '53.* Chicago, 1965.

Reprint of 1854 edition.

5847. Blanco Moheno, R. *Juárez: Ante Dios y ante los Hombres.* Mexico, 1959.

5848. Bridges, C. A. "The Knights of the Golden Circle: A Filibustering Fantasy," *SHQ* 44 (1941) 287–302.

5849. ———. "Southward Expansion Projects, 1848–1861," U. of Texas Diss., 1940.

5850. Broussard, R. F. "Ignacio Comonfort: His Contributions to the Mexican Reform, 1855–1857," U. of Texas Diss., 1959.

5851. Caldwell, E. M. "The War of 'La Reforma' in Mexico, 1858–1861," U. of Texas Diss., 1935.

5852. Callahan, J. M. "The Mexican Policy of Southern Leaders Under Buchanan's Administration," *AHAAR* (1910) 125–161. Wash., 1912.

5853. Carrillo Flores, A. "A Propósito de Lincoln y Matías Romero," *HM* 11 (April, 1962) 631–632.

5854. Chamberlin, E. K. "Baja California After Walker: The Zerman Enterprise," *HAHR* 34 (1954) 175–189.

Chamberlin concludes that Zerman was not a filibuster.

5855. Clarke, J. M. "Antonio Meléndrez, Nemesis of William Walker in Baja California," *CHSQ* 12 (1933) 318–322.

5855a. Cleland, R. G. (ed.). "Bandini's Account of William Walker's Invasion of Lower California," *HLQ* 7 (1944) 152–166.

The Bandini account was written in 1854 and treats Walker's activities from the time of his landing at Ensenada.

5856. Cleven, N. A. N. "The Corwin-Doblado Treaty, April 6, 1862," *HAHR* 17 (1937) 499–506.

Attempt to revise the MacLane-Ocampo Treaty. Corwin was appointed minister to Mexico in 1861.

5857. Coffey, F. A. "Some General Aspects of the Gadsden Treaty," *NMHR* 8 (1933) 145–164.

5858. Cosío Villegas, D. (ed.). *Historia Moderna de México*. 8 vols., Mexico, 1955– .

A monumental collaborative effort. The first three volumes are pertinent to this section.

5859. Cosío Villegas, E. (ed.). *Diario Personal de Matías Romero, 1855–1865*. Mexico, 1960.

5860. Crenshaw, O. "The Knights of the Golden Circle: The Career of George Bickley," *AHR* 47 (1941) 23–50.

Treats Bickley's scheme to annex Mexico to the United States in 1859.

5861. *Cuestión Americana: Negocios Diplomáticos con los Estados Unidos: Notas y Documentos Relativos*. Guadalajara, 1878.

Correspondence of the Mexican secretary of foreign relations to the Mexican minister in Washington.

5862. Delaney, R. W. "Matamoros, Port for Texas During the Civil War," *SHQ* 58 (1955) 473–587.

5863. Durham, M. L. "The American Expansionist Movement Toward Mexico, 1848–1862," Fletcher School of Law and Diplomacy Diss., 1962.

5864. Ellison, S. J. "An Anglo-American Plan for the Colonization of Mexico," *SSSQ* 16 (1935) 42–52.

Dr. William Gwin's proposal to found a Confederate colony in Mexico in 1865.

5865. Fernández MacGregor, G. (ed.). "Conspiración Santanista en 1868," *BAGNM* 15 (January, 1944) 3–51.

5866. Foix, P. *Juárez*. Mexico, 1949.

5867. Forbes, R. H. *Crabb's Filibustering Expedition into Sonora, 1857: An Historical Account with Map, Illustrations and Bibliography*. Tucson, Ariz., 1952.

5868. Fuentes Mares, J. *Juárez y los Estados Unidos*. Mexico, 1960.

5869. ———. "La Misión de Mr. Pickett," *HM* 11 (April, 1962) 487–518.

Concerns Confederate agent in Mexico.

5870. Garber, P. N. *The Gadsden Treaty*. Phil., 1923.

5871. Glick, E. B. "The Tehuantepec Railroad: Mexico's White Elephant," *PHR* 22 (1953) 373–382.

Examines the reasons for the failure of the project.

5872. Goetzmann, W. H. "The United States–Mexican Boundary Survey, 1848–1853," *SHQ* 42 (1958) 164–190.

5873. Gómez Robledo, A. "Nuestros Problemas Istmicos," *HM* 5 (1955) 92–98.

Summarizes interest of the United States in an inter-oceanic route, culminating in the McLane–Ocampo Treaty.

5874. Griggs, G. *History of Mesilla Valley: Or the Gadsden Purchase, Known in Mexico as the Treaty of Mesilla*. Las Cruces, N.M., 1930.

5875. Harmon, G. D. "Confederate Migration to Mexico," *HAHR* 17 (1937) 458–487.

5876. Iturribarria, J. F. "El 'Diario' de Don Matías Romero," *HM* 11 (January, 1962) 382–415.

5877. Johnson, R. A. *The Mexican Revolution of Ayutla, 1854–1855*. Rock Island, Ill., 1939.

5878. ———. "Santa Anna's Last Dictatorship, 1853–1855," *SHQ* 41 (1938) 281–311.

5879. Juárez, B. P. *Textos Políticos*. Mexico, 1944.

Collection of Juárez speeches, edited by A. Henestrosa.

5880. Kaiser, C. C. "John Watson Foster:

United States Minister to Mexico, 1873–1880," American U. Diss., 1954.

5881. Kearny, R. E. "The Magdalena Bubble," *PHR* 4 (1935) 25–38.

Treats a colonizing attempt on Magdalena Bay, 1866 to 1871.

5882. Knapp, F. A., Jr. *The Life of Sebastián Lerdo de Tejada, 1823–1889: A Study of Influence and Obscurity*. Austin, Texas, 1951.

5883. ———. "A New Source on the Confederate Exodus to Mexico: The Two Republics," *JSH* 19 (1953) 364–373.

5884. ———. "Precursors of American Investment in Mexican Railroads," *PHR* 21 (1952) 43–64.

5885. Lesley, L. B. "The International Boundary Survey from San Diego to the Gila River, 1849–1850," *CHSQ* 9 (1930) 3–15.

5886. ———. "The Negotiation of the Gadsden Treaty," *SHQ* 27 (1923) 1–26.

5887. Macmillan, D. S., and B. Plomley. "An American Surveyor in Mexico, 1837–1860," *NMHR* 34 (1959) 1–8.

5888. Maisel, J. M. "The Origin and Development of Mexican Antipathy Toward the South, 1821–1867," U. of Texas Diss., 1955.

5889. McCornack, R. B. "Juárez y la Armada Norteamericana," *HM* 6 (April, 1957) 493–509.

5890. ———. "Los Estados Confederados y México," *HM* 4 (January, 1955) 337–352.

5891. McPherson, H. M. "The Plan of William McKendree Gwin for a Colony in North Mexico, 1863–1865," *PHR* 2 (1933) 357–386.

5892. *Memoranda y Notas Relativas Cambiadas Entre el Ministerio de Relaciones Exteriores y el Ministro Plenipotenciario de los Estados Unidos*. Mexico, 1877.

5893. Miller, R. R. "Matías Romero: Mexican Minister to the United States During the Juárez-Maximilian Era," *HAHR* 45 (1965) 228–245.

5894. ———. "Mexican Secret Agents in the United States, 1861–1867," U. of California Diss., 1960.

5895. ———. "Plácido Vega: A Mexican Secret Agent in the United States, 1864–

1866," *TA* 19 (October, 1962) 137–148.

5896. Niosi, J. J. "The McLane Mission to Mexico, 1859–1860," New York U. Diss., 1954.

5897. Pickett, J. T. "Letter from Colonel John T. Pickett, of the Southern Confederacy, to Señor Don Manuel de Zamacona, Minister of Foreign Affairs, Mexico," *HAHR* 2 (1919) 611–617.

5898. Pletcher, D. M. "The Building of the Mexican Railway," *HAHR* 30 (1950) 26–62.

The Veracruz–Mexico City railroad.

5899. ———. "México Campo de Inversiones Norteamericanas, 1867–1880," *HM* 2 (April, 1953) 564–574.

5900. ———. "A Prospecting Expedition Across Central Mexico, 1856–1857," *PHR* 21 (1952) 21–41

5901. Reyes, R. *Benito Juárez, Ensayo Sobre un Carácter*. Madrid, 1936

5902. Rippy, J. F. "Anglo–American Filibusters and the Gadsden Treaty," *HAHR* 5 (1922) 155–180.

5903. ———. "Border Troubles Along the Rio Grande, 1848–1860," *SHQ* 23 (1919) 91–111.

5904. ———. "The Boundary of New Mexico and the Gadsden Treaty," *HAHR* 4 (1921) 715–742.

5905. ———. "The Indians of the Southwest in the Diplomacy of the United States and Mexico, 1848–1853," *HAHR* 2 (1919) 363–396.

5906. ———. "Mexican Projects of the Confederates," *SHQ* 22 (1919) 291–317.

5907. ———. "The Negotiation of the Gadsden Treaty," *SHQ* 27 (1923) 1–26.

5908. ———. "A Ray of Light on the Gadsden Treaty," *SHQ* 24 (1921) 235–242.

5909. Rister, C. C. "Carlota: Confederate Colony in Mexico," *JSH* 11 (1945) 33–50.

5910. Roeder, R. *Juárez and His Mexico*. 2 vols., N.Y., 1947.

5911. Rolle, A. F. *The Lost Cause: The Confederate Exodus to Mexico*. Norman, Okla., 1965.

5912. Ross, S. R. "Prólogo a un Prólogo a las Memorias de Lerdo," *HM* 10 (July, 1960) 110–146.

5913. Salmerón, C. *Las Grandes Traiciones de Juárez, a Través de sus Tratados con*

Inglaterra, Francia, España y Estados Unidos. 2d ed., Mexico, 1962.

5914. Scholes, W. V. *Mexican Politics During the Juárez Regime, 1855–1872.* Columbia, Mo., 1957.

5915. Shearer, E. C. "Border Diplomatic Relations Between the U.S. and Mexico, 1848–1860," U. of Texas Diss., 1940.

5916. ———. "The Callahan Expedition, 1855," *SHQ* 54 (1951) 430–451.

5917. Sierra O'Reilly, J. *Diario de Nuestro Viaje a los Estados Unidos.* Mexico, 1938.

5918. ———. *Juárez, su Obra y su Tiempo.* Mexico, 1948.

5919. ———. *Segundo Libro del Diario de mi Viaje a los Estados Unidos: La Pretendida Cesión de la Península de Yucatán a un Gobierno Extranjero.* Mexico, 1953.

5920. Smart, C. A. *Viva Juárez! A Biography.* Phil., 1963.

5921. Tamayo, J. (ed.). *Benito Juárez, Documentos, Discursos y Correspondencia.* 2 vols., Mexico, 1964.

5922. Torrea, J. M. "Sebastián Lerdo de Tejada," *MANHG* 2, no. 2 (1946) 28–40.

5923. Valadés, J. C. *El Pensamiento Político de Benito Juárez.* Mexico, 1957.

5924. Wilson, H. L. "President Buchanan's Proposed Intervention in Mexico," *AHR* 5 (1900) 687–701.

5925. Wyllys, R. K. "An Expansionist [Thomas Sprague] in Baja California, 1855," *PHR* 1 (1932) 477–482.
   A letter from a United States commercial agent.

5926. ———. *The French in Sonora (1850–1854): The Story of French Adventurers from California into Mexico.* Berkeley, Calif., 1932.

5927. ———. "The Republic of Lower California, 1853–1854," *PHR* 2 (1933) 194–213.

5928. ——— (ed.). "William Walker's Invasion of Sonora, 1854," *ARHR* 6 (1935) 61–67.

5929. Yáñez, A. "Santa Anna y la Guerra con Estados Unidos," *FL* 14 (July, 1947) 133–160.

5930. Zarco, F. *Historia del Congreso Extraordinario Constituyente, 1856–1857: Estudio Preliminar de Antonio Martínez Báez.* Mexico, 1956.

XIII–F   cross references:

a) For works relating to the McLane–Ocampo Treaty and other questions concerning transit rights across the Isthmus of Tehuantepec, see items 2352, 2400, 2406, 2413, 2414, 2416, 2417, 2418, 2422, 2423, 2424, 2428, 2429, 2446, 5963.

b) For works relating to the French intervention of 1862–1867, see items 2233–2337a.

c) See also items 5603, 5693, 9989.

G. THE UNITED STATES AND THE DÍAZ DICTATORSHIP, 1876–1910

5931. Aguirre, M. J. *Cananea: Las Garras del Imperialismo en las Entrañas de México.* Mexico, 1959.
   Discusses the mining interests and landholdings of Colonel William C. Greene.

5932. Amaya Topete, J. (trans.). *Combatimos la Tiranía: Un Pionero Revolucionario Mexicano Cuenta su Historia a Samuel Kaplan.* Mexico, 1958.
   Treats the activities of Enrique Flores Magón.

5933. Anaya Ibarra, P. M. *Precursores de la Revolución Mexicana.* Mexico, 1955.

5934. Anderson, [Relyea] P. S. *Diplomatic Relations Between the United States and Mexico Under Porfirio Díaz, 1876–1910.* Northampton, Mass., 1924.

5935. *Archivo del General Porfirio Díaz: Memorias y Documentos.* 29 vols., Mexico, 1947–1960.

5936. Barrera Fuentes, F. *Historia de la Revolución Mexicana: La Etapa Precursora.* Mexico, 1955.

5937. Beals, C. *Porfirio Díaz, Dictator of Mexico.* Phil., 1932.

5938. Brown, L. C. "The Mexican Liberals and Their Struggle Against the Díaz Dictatorship: 1900–1906," *AN* (1956) 317–362.
   Concentrates on the activities of the Flores Magón brothers in the United States.

5939. *Caya Arenas y Otras Islas Guaneras en los Mares de Campeche y Yucatán: Correspondencia Entre los Gobiernos de México y los Estados Unidos de América Acerca del Dominio Sobre Dichas Islas.* Mexico, 1895.

5940. Conant, C. A. *The Banking System of Mexico*. Wash., 1910.

5941. Coolsen, M. G. "British Interest in Mexico, 1900–1926," U. of Illinois Diss., 1943.

5942. *Correspondencia Diplomática Cambiada Entre el Gobierno de los Estados Unidos Mexicanos y los de Varias Potencias Extranjeras*. 6 vols., Mexico, 1882–1892.

5943. *Correspondencia Diplomática Relativa a las Invasiones del Territorio Mexicano, por Fuerzas de los Estados Unidos de 1873 a 1877*. Mexico, 1878.

5944. Cosío Villegas, D. *Estados Unidos Contra Porfirio Díaz*. Mexico, 1956.
Eng. ed., Lincoln, Nebr., 1964.

5945. Creelman, J. *Díaz, Master of Mexico*. N.Y., 1916.

5946. ———. *Entrevista Díaz-Creelman*. Mexico, 1963.

5947. Crimmins, M. L. "Colonel Buell's Expedition into Mexico in 1880," *NMHR* 10 (1935) 133–142.

5948. Cue Canovas, A. *Ricardo Flores Magón, la Baja California y los Estados Unidos*. Mexico, 1957.

5949. Cumberland, C. C. "Precursors of the Mexican Revolution of 1910," *HAHR* 22 (1942) 344–356.

5950. Davids, J. "American Political and Economic Penetration of Mexico, 1877–1920," Georgetown U. Diss., 1947.

5951. Díaz Dufoo, C. *Les Finances du Mexique, 1892–1911: Limantour, l'Homme et l'Oeuvre*. Paris, 1926.

5952. El Colegio de México. *Comercio Exterior de México, 1877–1911: Estadísticas Económicas del Porfiriato*. Mexico, 1960.

5953. Espinosa de los Reyes, J. *Relaciones Económicas Entre México y Estados Unidos, 1870–1910*. Mexico, 1951.

5954. Estrada, G. (ed.). *Las Memorias Diplomáticas de Mr. Foster Sobre México*. Mexico, 1929.
Foster was the United States minister to Mexico, 1873–1880.

5955. *Exposición de la Secretaría de Hacienda de los Estados-Unidos Mexicanos de 15 de Enero de 1879 Sobre la Condición Actual de México, y el Aumento del Comercio con los Estados Unidos*. Mexico, 1879.

5956. Flandrau, C. M. *Viva Mexico*. N.Y., 1937.
Pb. ed., Urbana, Ill., 1964. Impressions of a United States citizen residing on a coffee hacienda.

5957. Flores Magón, R., and J. Flores Magón. *Batalla a la Dictadura*. Mexico, 1948.

5958. Gamboa, F. *Mi Diario*. Mexico, 1938.

5959. García Granados, R. *Historia de México Desde la Restauración de la República en 1867 Hasta la Caída de Huerta*. 2 vols., Mexico, 1956.

5960. García Naranjo, N. *Porfirio Díaz*. San Antonio, Texas, 1930.

5961. Gillett, J. R. *Six Years with the Texas Rangers, 1875–1881*. 2d ed., New Haven, Conn., 1963.

5962. Gilmore, N. R. "Mexico and the Spanish–American War," *HAHR* 43 (1963) 511–525.

5963. Glick, E. B. *Straddling the Isthmus of Tehuantepec*. Gainesville, Fla., 1959.
A study of the interoceanic railroad.

5964. González Navarro, M. *La Colonización en México, 1877–1910*. Mexico, 1960.
The only genuinely successful colonists were the United States Mormons in Chihuahua.

5965. ——— (comp.). *Estadísticas Sociales del Porfiriato, 1877–1910*. Mexico, 1956.

5966. ———. "La Huelga de Río Blanco," *HM* 6 (April, 1957) 510–533.
Concerns the strike in the textile industry in the state of Veracruz.

5966a. ———. "La Política Colonizadora del Porfiriato," *EHA* (1953) 183–239.

5967. González Ramírez, M. (ed.). *La Huelga de Cananea*. Mexico, 1956.
Treats the 1906 strike against the United States-owned Greene Consolidated Copper Company.

5968. Gregg, R. D. *The Influence of Border Troubles on Relations Between the United States and Mexico, 1876–1910*. Baltimore, 1937.

5969. Gutiérrez Santos, D. *Historia Militar de México, 1876–1914*. Mexico, 1955.

5970. Hackett, C. W. *The Recognition of the Díaz Government by the United States*. Austin, Texas, 1924.

5971. Hardy, B. C. "The Mormon Colonies of Northern Mexico: A History, 1885–1912," Wayne State U. Diss., 1963.

5972. Hardy, O. "Ulysses S. Grant, President

of the Mexican Southern Railroad," *PHR* 24 (1955) 111–120.

5973. Iturribarria, J. F. "Gamboa, Admirador y Crítico de Díaz," *HM* 8 (April, 1959) 474–498.

5974. Jenkins, M. E. "Ricardo Flores Magón and the Mexican Liberal Party, 1900–1922," U. of New Mexico Diss., 1953.

5975. Kaiser, C. C. "J. W. Foster y el Desarrollo Económico de México," *HM* 7 (July, 1957) 60–79.
A study of the United States minister's encouragement of investment in Mexico.

5976. Knapp, F. A., Jr. "A Note on General Escobedo in Texas," *SHQ* 15 (1952) 394–401.

5977. Lewis, W. R. "The Hayes Administration and Mexico," *SHQ* 24 (1920) 140–153.

5978. López Portillo y Rojas, J. *Elevación y Caída de Porfirio Díaz*. Mexico, 1921.

5979. Mata, L. I. *Filomeno Mata, su Vida y su Labor: Ensayo Biográfico*. Mexico, 1945.

5980. McCornack, R. B. "Porfirio Díaz en la Frontera Texana, 1875–1877," *HM* 5 (1956) 373–410.

5981. Morales, V., and M. Caballero. *El Señor Root en México: Crónica de la Visita Hecha en Octubre de 1907*. Mexico, 1908.

5982. Pletcher, D. M. "The Development of Railroads in Sonora," *IEA* 1, no. 4 (1948) 3–45.

5982a. ———. "The Fall of Silver in Mexico 1870–1910, and Its Effect on American Investments," *JEH* 18 (March, 1958) 33–35.

5983. ———. "Mexico Opens the Door to American Capital, 1877–1880," *TA* 16 (July, 1959) 1–14.

5983a. ———. *Rails, Mines and Progress: Seven American Promoters in Mexico. 1867–1911*. Ithaca, N.Y., 1958.

5984. Purcell, A. *Frontier Mexico, 1875–1894: Letters of William L. Purcell*. San Antonio, Texas, 1963.

5985. Reyes, B. *El General Porfirio Díaz*. Mexico, 1960.
Eulogistic biography.

5986. Reynolds, A. W. "The Alabama Negro Colony in Mexico, 1894–1896," *ARE* 5 (October, 1952) 243–268.

5986a. Rodríguez, R. *La Condición Jurídica de los Extranjeros en México Durante la*

Administración del General Porfirio Díaz. Mexico, 1903.

5987. Roehl, C. "Porfirio Díaz in the Press of the U.S.," U. of Chicago Diss., 1953.

5988. Rolin, A. "L'Affaire Cutting: Conflit Entre les Etats-Unis de L'Amérique du Nord et le Mexique en 1886," *RDISDP* 20 (1888) 559–577.

5989. Rolle, A. F. "Futile Filibustering in Baja California, 1888–1890," *PHR* 20 (1951) 159–166.

5990. Romero, M. *Artículos Sobre México, Publicadas en los Estados Unidos de América por Matías Romero en 1891–1892*. Mexico, 1892.

5991. ———. "Cartas de Don Matías Romero a Don José Alfonso, 1890–1896," *RCHG* 123 (1954–1955[?]) 143–167.

5992. ———. *Mexico and the United States*. N.Y., 1898.

5993. ———. "Mr. Blaine and the Boundary Question Between Mexico and Guatemala," *AGSJ* 29 (1897) 281–330.

5994. ———. *Reciprocidad Comercial Entre México y los Estados Unidos*. Mexico, 1890.

5995. ———. "Settlement of the Mexico-Guatemala Boundary Question, 1882," *AGSJ* 29 (1897) 123–159.

5996. Rosenzweig Hernández, F. "Las Exportaciones Mexicanas de 1877 a 1911," *HM* 9 (January, 1960) 394–413.

5997. Saner, R. E. L. "When President Diaz Sought Recognition: Similarity of Conditions Imperiling Mexican–American Relations in Hayes Administration and International Difficulties Preceding Obregon's Election," *ABAJ* 6 (1920) 195–197.

5998. Schiff, W. "German Military Penetration into Mexico During the Late Díaz Period," *HAHR* 39 (1959) 568–579.
The Germans refused to push very hard for fear of antagonizing the United States.

5999. Schmitt, K. M. "Evolution of Mexican Thought on Church–State Relations, 1876–1911," U. of Pennsylvania Diss., 1954.
1949," Ohio State U. Diss., 1950.

6000. Solis Camara, F. *Biographical Sketch of Señor Lic. Joaquín D. Casasús, Ambassador of Mexico to the United States*. N.Y., 1905.

6001. Sollano Ramos, A. *El Sistema Monetario Mexicano de 1877 a 1911*. Mexico, 1961.

6002. Taracena, A. *Porfirio Díaz*. Mexico, 1960.

6003. Tischendorf, A. P. *Great Britain and Mexico in the Era of Porfirio Díaz*. Durham, N.C., 1961.

6004. Turner, E. D. *Ricardo Flores Magón y el Partido Liberal Mexicano*. Michoacán, 1960.

6005. Turner, J. K. *Barbarous Mexico*. Chicago, 1911.

6006. USCH. *Reports from the Secretaries of State and War in Reference to Mexican Border Troubles, November 13, 1877* (45th Cong., 1st Sess.., H. Ex. Doc. 13). Wash., 1877.

6007. ———. *Report and Accompanying Documents of the Committee on Foreign Affairs on the Relation of the United States with Mexico, Apr., 1878* (45th Cong., 2d Sess., H. Rept. 701). Wash., 1878.

6008. Valadés, J. C. *El Porfirismo: Historia de un Régimen*. 2 vols., Mexico, 1941–1948.

XIII–G cross references: 2085, 2508, 5867, 5871, 5880, 6070, 6751

H. THE UNITED STATES AND THE MEXICAN REVOLUTION, 1910–1940

1. General Accounts and Special Studies

6009. Alessio Robles, M. *Historia Política de la Revolución*. 3d ed., Mexico, 1946.
    Covers the period from the outbreak of the revolution to the fall of Calles.

6010. ———. *Ideales de la Revolución*. Mexico 1935.

6011. Al'perovich, M. S., and B. T. Rudenko. *Meksikanskaia Revoliutsiia 1910–1917 gg. i Politika SShA*. Moscow, 1958.
    The Mexican Revolution, 1910–1917, and the Policy of the U.S.A. Spanish ed., Mexico, 1960.

6012. Amaya, J. G. *Los Gobiernos de Obregón, Calles y Regimenes "Peleles" Derivados del Callismo: Tercera Epoca, 1920 a 1935*. Mexico, 1947.
    See also items 6087 and 6146.

6013. Beteta, R. *Pensamiento y Dinámica de la Revolución Mexicana*. 2d ed., Mexico, 1951.

6014. Blasco Ibáñez, V. *Mexico in Revolution*. N.Y., 1920.

6014a. Braddy, H. "Running Contraband on the Rio Grande," *SFQ* 25 (1961) 101–112.
    Treats smuggling from the early revolution to the date of publication.

6015. Brenner, A., and G. R. Leighton. *The Wind That Swept Mexico: The History of the Mexican Revolution, 1910–1942*. N.Y., 1943.
    A pictorial history with short explanatory texts.

6016. Calzadíaz Barrera, A. *Hechos Reales de la Revolución*. 3 vols., Mexico, 1961–1965.

6017. Casasola, G. *Historia Gráfica de la Revolución Mexicana, 1900–1960*. 4 vols., Mexico, 1960.
    A new edition of the older seven-volume set.

6018. Chamberlain, E. K. "Mexican Colonization versus American Interests in Lower California," *PHR* 20 (1951) 43–55.
    Treats U.S. investments in the period 1920–1950.

6019. Clark, M. R. *Organized Labor in Mexico*. Chapel Hill, N.C., 1934.

6020. Cline, H. F. "Mexico: A Matured Latin American Revolution, 1910–1960," *AAAPSS* 334 (1961) 84–94.

6021. Creel, G. *The People Next Door: An Interpretive History of Mexico and the Mexicans*. N.Y., 1926.

6022. De Bekker, L. J. *The Plot Against Mexico*. N.Y., 1919.
    An anti-interventionist tract.

6023. Dillon, E. J. *Mexico on the Verge*. N.Y., 1921.
    Emotional survey of Mexico's international relations.

6024. Dios Bojórquez, J. de. *Forjadores de la Revolución Mexicana*. Mexico, 1960.

6025. ———. *Hombres y Aspectos de México*. Mexico, 1963.

6026. Dopp, L. H. "A Summary of the Relations of the United States and Mexico Since 1919," *WA* 98 (1935) 186–191.

6027. Dulles, J. W. F. *Yesterday in Mexico: A Chronicle of the Revolution, 1919–1936*. Austin, Texas, 1961.

By a son of John Foster Dulles, who worked as a mining engineer in Mexico. Based on meticulous research.

6028. Espinosa de los Reyes, J. "Las Relaciones Económicas Entre México y los Estados Unidos en el Siglo XX," *MPCH* (1950) 103–114.

6029. Esquivel Obregón, T. *México y los Estados Unidos ante el Derecho Internacional*. Mexico, 1926.

Covers the period 1823 to 1925 but of greatest value for relations during the first fifteen years of the Revolution.

6030. Fabela, I. (ed.). *Documentos Históricos de la Revolución Mexicana*. 12 vols., Mexico, 1960– .

A significant documentary collection, edited by the Comisión de Investigaciones Históricas de la Revolución Mexicana. Projected for 23 volumes.

6031. ——. *Historia Diplomática de la Revolución Mexicana*. 2 vols., Mexico, 1959.

6032. ——. "Las Relaciones Entre los Estados Unidos de Norteamérica y México," *MLI* 2 (January, 1943) 7–16.

6033. García Formentí, A. *Problemas de México y del Mundo*. Mexico, 1939.

6034. González-Blanco, P. *Una Experiencia Política: Las Memorias del Lic. Portes Gil*. Mexico, 1945.

6035. González Garza, F. *La Revolución Mexicana*. Mexico, 1936.

6036. ——. *México y los Estados Unidos de América a la Luz de las Nuevas Ideas Internacionales*. Mexico, 1943.

6036a. González Ramírez, M. "La Política Internacional de la Revolución Mexicana," *CA* 14 (July, 1955) 27–48.

6037. ——. *La Revolución Social de México: Las Ideas—la Violencia*. Mexico, 1960.

6038. Guzmán Esparza, R. (ed.). *Memorias de Don Adolfo de la Huerta Según su Propio Dictado*. Mexico, 1957.

6039. Hackett, C. W. "The Mexican Revolution and the United States, 1910–1926," *WPFP* 9, no. 5 (1927) 339–346.

6040. Heiliger, E. M. "La Revolución Mexicana en la Prensa de Lengua Inglesa, 1910–1952," *HM* 3 (January, 1954) 451–472.

6041. Herring, H., and H. Weinstock (eds.). *Renascent Mexico*. N.Y., 1935.

6042. Hicks, W. T. "Economic Effects of the Nationalization of Foreign Property in Mexico Between 1917 and 1931," Northwestern U. Diss., 1935.

6043. Jones, C. L. *Mexico and Its Reconstruction*. N.Y., 1922.

Analysis of the revolution after the first ten years.

6044. King, R. E. *Tempest over Mexico*. Boston, 1935.

Impressions by a woman rancher.

6045. Lacuraín y Oslo, L. *La Segunda Intervención Americana*. Mexico, 1957.

An attack on United States policy in the revolution.

6046. Lieuwen, E. "Curbing Militarism in Mexico," *NMHR* 33 (October, 1958) 257–276.

6047. Mancisidor, J. *Historia de la Revolución Mexicana*. Mexico, 1958.

6047a. Mazin Cervantes, M. *La Revolución Extraviada*. Mexico, 1935.

6048. Mena P., M. A., and A. Obregón. *Historia Militar y Política 1912–1929*. Mexico, 1960.

6049. *México Cincuenta Años de Revolución*. 4 vols., Mexico, 1960–1962.

Vol. 1, *La Economía*; Vol. 2, *La Vida Social*; Vol. 3, *La Política*; Vol. 4, *La Cultura*.

6050. Mexico. Secretaría de Relaciones Exteriores. *Las Relaciones Internacionales de México, 1935–1956 a Través de los Mensajes Presidenciales*. Mexico, 1957.

6051. Morales Jiménez, A. *Historia de la Revolución Mexicana*. Mexico, 1951.

6052. Muñoz, I. *Verdad y Mito de la Revolución Mexicana, Relatada por un Protagonista*. 4 vols., Mexico, 1960–1964.

Anti-revolutionary and anti-United States anecdotal history.

6053. Muñoz y Pérez, D. "Precursores de la Revolución: Enrique Flores Magón," *BBM*, no. 175 (April, 1960) 1, 7.

6054. Pani, A. J. *Apuntes Autobiográficos*. 2d ed., 2 vols., Mexico, 1950.

6055. Pérez Verdía, L. *La Revolución Mexicana, 1910–1937*. Guadalajara, 1938.

6056. Phillips, R. B. "José Vasconcelos and the Mexican Revolution of 1910," Stanford U. Diss., 1953.

6057. Portes Gil, E. *Quince Años de Política Mexicana*. Mexico, 1941.

6058. Priestley, H. I. "The Relations of the

United States and Mexico Since 1910," *UCC* 22 (1920) 47–60.

6059. Quintanilla, L. "La Política Internacional de la Revolución Mexicana," *FI* 5 (July, 1964) 1–26.

Summarizes the major international doctrines of the revolution.

6060. Ramírez Plancarte, F. *La Revolución Mexicana: Interpretación Independiente.* Mexico, 1948.

A detailed survey.

6061. Romero Flores, J. *Anales Históricos de la Revolución Mexicana.* 5 vols., Mexico, 1939–1940.

6062. Ross, E. A. *The Social Revolution in Mexico.* N.Y., 1923.

6063. Sáenz, A. *La Política Internacional de la Revolución: Estudios y Documentos.* Mexico, 1961.

A comprehensive analysis centering primarily on United States relations with Mexico during the revolution.

6064. Sáenz, M., and H. I. Priestley. *Some Mexican Problems.* Chicago, 1926.

6065. Sánchez Azcona, J. *Apuntes para la Historia de la Revolución Mexicana.* Mexico, 1961.

6066. Silva Herzog, J. *El Agrarismo Mexicano y la Reforma Agraria: Exposición y Crítica.* Mexico, 1959.

6067. ———. *Breve Historia de la Revolución Mexicana.* 2 vols., Mexico, 1960.

Reproduces important documents and adds textual commentary. Coverage limited primarily to 1910–1920.

6068. ———. *Un Esayo Sobre la Revolución Mexicana.* Mexico, 1946.

An interpretive study.

6069. Simpson, E. N. *The Ejido: Mexico's Way Out.* Chapel Hill, N.C., 1937.

6070. Simpson, J. W. "The International Economic Position of Mexico, 1900–1949," Ohio State U. Diss., 1950.

6071. Smith, L. M. *American Relations with Mexico.* Oklahoma City, Okla., 1924.

6072. Tannenbaum, F. "The Anvil of American Foreign Policy," *PSQ* 63 (1948) 501–527.

6073. ———. *The Mexican Agrarian Revolution.* N.Y., 1929.

6074. ———. *Mexico: The Struggle for Peace and Bread.* N.Y., 1950.

A basic institutional study. The last chapter treats United States–Mexican relations.

6075. ———. *Peace by Revolution: An Interpretation of Mexico.* N.Y., 1933.

6076. Taracena, A. *Mi Vida y el Vértigo de la Revolución.* Mexico, 1936.

6077. ———. *La Verdadera Revolución Mexicana.* 12 vols., Mexico, 1960–1963.

A narrative chronicle with day-by-day coverage.

6078. Teja Zabre, A. *Panorama Histórico de la Revolución Mexicana.* Mexico, 1939.

6079. Turlington, E. W. *Mexico and Her Foreign Creditors.* N.Y., 1930.

6080. Vasconcelos, J. *El Desastre.* 2 vols., Mexico, 1937.

6081. ———. *La Tormenta.* 5th ed., Mexico, 1937.

6082. ———. *Ulises Criollo.* 7th ed., Mexico, 1937.

6083. Vera Estañol, J. *La Revolución Mexicana: Orígenes y Resultados.* Mexico, 1957.

An anti-revolutionary account. Author was a minister during the Díaz regime.

6084. Whetten, N. L. *Rural Mexico.* Chicago, 1948.

XIII–H–1 cross references: 3408, 4638, 5950, 5974, 6479

2. UNITED STATES–MEXICAN RELATIONS, 1910–1913

6085. Aguirre Benavides, A. *Madero el Inmaculado: Historia de la Revolución de 1910.* Mexico, 1962.

6086. Al'perovich, M. S. "Imperialisticheskaia Politika SShA v Meksike v 1913–1914 gg.," *VI*, no. 5 (May, 1950) 100–114.

"The Imperialistic Policy of the U.S.A. in Mexico, 1913–1914."

6087. Amaya, J. G. *Madero y los Auténticos Revolucionarios de 1910, Hasta la Decena Trágica y Fin del General Pascual Orozco: Primera Etapa, 1900–1913.* Mexico, 1946.

Companion volume to items 6012 and 6146.

6088. Arenas Guzmán, D. *La Consumación del Crimen.* Mexico, 1935.

6089. Berbusse, E. J. "Neutrality Diplomacy of the United States and Mexico, 1910–1911," *TA* 12 (1956) 265–283.

6090. Blaisdell, L. L. "The Consul in a Crisis:

Lower California, 1911," *MA* 37 (July, 1955) 131–139.

The consul was in Ensenada.

6091. Blaisdell, L. L. *The Desert Revolution: Baja California, 1911.* Madison, Wis., 1962.

Concludes that United States filibustering expeditions in Baja California were not an integral part of the Flores Magón radical movement.

6092. ———. "Henry Lane Wilson and the Overthrow of Madero," *SSSQ* 43 (1962) 126–135.

6093. Breceda, A. *México Revolucionario.* 2 vols., Mexico, 1920–1941.

The second volume covers the period 1910 to 1914.

6094. Busey, J. L. "Don Victoriano Huerta y la Prensa Yanqui," *HM* 4 (April, 1955) 582–594.

6095. Butterfield, D. "The Situation in Mexico," *NAR* 196 (1912) 649–664.

6095a. Cadenhead, I. E., Jr. "The American Socialists and the Mexican Revolution of 1910," *SSSQ* 43 (1962) 103–117.

6096. Christiansen, P. W. "Pascual Orozco: Chihuahua Rebel: Episodes in the Mexican Revolution, 1910–1915," *NMHR* 36 (April, 1961) 97–120.

First English-language summary of Orozco's revolutionary career.

6096a. Coker, W. S. "United States–British Diplomacy over Mexico, 1913," U. of Oklahoma Diss., 1965.

6097. Committee of the American Colony. *Facts Submitted by the Committee of the American Colony to President Wilson and Secretary of State Bryan Relative to the Mexican Situation and the Record of the Hon. Henry Lane Wilson Therewith.* N.p., 1913.

6098. Cosío Villegas, D. "Sobre Henry Lane Wilson," *MCN* 4, no. 4 (1961) 39–55.

6099. Cue Canovas, A. *Ricardo Flores Magón, la Baja California y los Estados Unidos.* Mexico, 1957.

6100. Cumberland, C. C. *Mexican Revolution: Genesis Under Madero.* Austin, Texas, 1952.

One of the two standard English biographies. See also item 6128.

6101. Didapp, J. P. *Los Estados Unidos y Nuestros Conflictos Internos.* Mexico, 1913.

6102. Doblado, M. *Huerta y el Fantasma del Norte.* Mexico, 1913.

6103. Ferrer de Mendiolea, G. *Vida de Francisco I. Madero.* Mexico, 1945.

6104. Flores D., J. "Carlos Pereyra y el Embajador Wilson," *HM* 8 (July, 1958) 95–121.

6104a. García Naranjo, N. *Memorias.* 7 vols., Monterrey, n.d.

Volumes VI and VII treat the Madero and Huerta periods.

6105. Gerhard, P. "The Socialist Invasion of Baja California, 1911," *PHR* 15 (1946) 295–304.

6106. Guzmán, M. L. "Henry Lane Wilson: Un Embajador Malvado," *CA* (July, 1963) 203–210.

6107. Harrison, J. P. "Henry Lane Wilson, el Trágico de la Decena," *HM* 6 (January, 1957) 374–405.

6108. Lara y Pardó, L. *Match de Dictadores.* Mexico, 1942.

Covers United States relations with Mexico during the Huerta and Carranza administrations.

6109. List Arzubide, G. *El México de 1910: El Maderismo.* Mexico, 1963.

6110. Mancisidor, J. "El Huertismo," *HM* 3 (July, 1953) 34–51.

6111. Márquez Sterling, M. *Los Ultimos Días del Presidente Madero: Mi Gestión Diplomática en México.* Havana, 1917. Rev. ed., Mexico, 1958.

Cuban minister to Mexico under Madero is extremely critical of United States policy.

6112. Masingill, E. F. "The Diplomatic Career of Henry Lane Wilson in Latin America," Louisiana State U. Diss., 1957.

6113. Meyer, M. C. *Mexican Rebel: Pascual Orozco and the Mexican Revolution, 1910–1915.* Lincoln, Nebr., 1967.

6114. Moreno, D. A. *Francisco I. Madero: José Ma. Pino Suárez: El Crimen de la Embajada.* Mexico, 1960.

6114a. Murray, R. H. "Huerta and the Two Wilsons," *HW* 62 (March–April, 1916) 301–303, 341–342, 364–365, 402–404, 434–436, 466–469.

6115. Niemeyer, E. V. "The Public Career of General Bernardo Reyes," U. of Texas Diss., 1958.

Sympathetic biographical coverage.

6116. Ortíz Rubio, P. *La Revolución de 1910: Apuntes Históricos*. 2d ed., Mexico, 1937.

6117. O'Shaughnessy, E. *A Diplomat's Wife in Mexico: Letters from the American Embassy at Mexico City, Covering the Dramatic Period Between October 8, 1913, and the Breaking Off of Diplomatic Relations on April 23, 1914, Together with an Account of the Occupation of Vera Cruz*. N.Y., 1916.

Author was the wife of the American chargé in Mexico City from 1912 to 1914.

6118. ———. *Diplomatic Days*. N.Y., 1917.

6119. Pereyra, C. *Las Dos Supercherías Diplomáticas Norteamericanas*. Madrid, 1916.

Author was a Mexican chargé in the U.S. in 1911.

6120. Prida, R. *La Culpa de Lane Wilson, Embajador de los E.U.A., en la Tragedia Mexicana de 1913*. Mexico, 1962.

Author contends that the American ambassador was at least indirectly responsible for the assassination of Madero and Pino Suárez.

6121. Rausch, G. R., Jr. "Victoriano Huerta: A Political Biography," U. of Illinois Diss., 1960.

6122. Reed, J. *Insurgent Mexico*. N.Y., 1914.

6123. Río Govea, M. del. "Reminiscencias Históricas: La Caída del Presidente Francisco I. Madero, la Decena Trágica y sus Consecuencias Políticas," *MANHG* 15 (1959) 5–35.

6124. Rittenhouse, F. O. "Emiliano Zapata and the Suriano Rebellion: A Phase of the Agrarian Revolution in Mexico, 1910–1920," Ohio State U. Diss., 1948.

6125. Roemer, H. G. *Amerikanische Interessen- und Prinzipien-Politik in Mexiko, 1910–1914: Ein Beitrag zur Kritik des Wilsonismus*. Hamburg, 1929.

6126. Rojas, L. M. *La Culpa de Henry Lane Wilson en el Gran Desastre de México*. Mexico, 1928.

6127. ———. *México Pide Justicia i Yo Acuso al Embajador Lane Wilson ,..!* Mexico, 1926.

6128. Ross, S. R. *Francisco I. Madero: Apostle of Mexican Democracy*. N.Y., 1955.

Spanish ed., Mexico, 1957. Standard biographical treatment.

6129. Rowe, L. S. "The Mexican Revolution," *PSQ* 27 (1912) 281–297.

6130. Rudenko, B. T. *México en Vísperas de la Revolución Democrático-Burguesa de 1910–1917*. Mexico, 1958.

6131. Sánchez Azcona, J. *La Etapa Maderista de la Revolución*. Mexico, 1960.

6132. Schulz, E. E. *El Porvenir de México y México y Sus Relaciones con los Estados Unidos*. Mexico, 1914.

6133. Sherman, W. L., and R. E. Greenleaf. *Victoriano Huerta: A Reappraisal*. Mexico, 1960.

The authors view Huerta in a more favorable light. Contains useful commentaries on secondary material.

6134. Stephenson, G. M. *John Lind of Minnesota*. Minneapolis, 1935.

Emphasizes Lind's diplomatic mission to Mexico.

6135. Taracena, A. *Madero, el Héroe Cívico*. Mexico, 1946.

6136. ———. *Madero: Víctima del Imperialismo Yanqui*. Mexico, 1960.

6137. ———. *Madero: Vida del Hombre y del Político*. Mexico, 1937.

6138. Thord-Gray, I. *Gringo Rebel, Mexico 1913–1914*. Coral Gables, Fla., 1960.

Memoirs of a U.S. citizen who fought with Villa, Carranza, and Obregón.

6139. Torrea, J. M. *La Decena Trágica: Apuntes para la Historia del Ejército Mexicano: La Asonada Militar de 1913*. 2 vols., Mexico, 1960.

6140. Travesi, G. G. *La Revolución de México y el Imperialismo Yanqui*. Barcelona, 1914.

6141. Turner, T. G. *Bullets, Bottles, and Gardenias*. Dallas, 1935.

Reminiscences of a journalist of various Mexican revolutionaries.

6142. Ulloa, B. "Las Relaciones México-Norteamericanas, 1910–1911," *HM* 14 (1965) 25–46.

6142a. USCS. *Affairs in Mexico: Brief in Support of Senate Resolution of April 20, 1911, Relative to Intervention in Affairs in Mexico* (62d Cong., 1st Sess., S. Doc. 25). Wash., 1911.

6143. Valadés, J. C. *Imaginación y Realidad de Francisco I. Madero*. 2 vols., Mexico, 1960.

6144. Vela González, F. "La Quincena Trágica

de 1913," *HM* 12 (January, 1963) 440–453.

6145. Wilson, H. L. *Diplomatic Episodes in Mexico, Belgium, and Chile.* Garden City, N.Y., 1927.

The Ambassador's apologia.

XIII–H–2 cross references: 5959, 5969, 5971, 6195a

3. UNITED STATES–MEXICAN RELATIONS, 1914–1920

6146. Amaya, J. G. *Venustiano Carranza, Caudillo Constitucionalista: Segunda Etapa, Febrero de 1913 a Mayo de 1920.* Mexico, 1947.

Companion volume to items 6012 and 6087.

6147. Barragán Rodríguez, J. B. *Historia del Ejército y de la Revolución Constitucionalista.* 2 vols., Mexico, 1946.

The author was Carranza's chief of staff.

6148. Barron, C. W. *The Mexican Problem.* Boston, 1917.

6149. Bulnes, F. *The Whole Truth About Mexico: President Wilson's Responsibility.* N.Y., 1916.

6150. Burns, J. T. *El Pulpo.* Madrid, 1921.

6151. Calero, M. *The Mexican Policy of President Woodrow Wilson as It Appears to a Mexican.* N.Y., 1916.

Spanish ed., Madrid, 1916. A condemnation of Wilson's Mexican policy.

6152. Carreño, A. M. *El Chamizal y el Presidente Norteamericano Woodrow Wilson.* Mexico, n.d.

6153. Clendenen, C. C. *The United States and Pancho Villa: A Study in Unconventional Diplomacy.* Ithaca, N.Y., 1961.

6154. Cuevas Cancino, F. "El Presidente Wilson y México," *HM* 6 (July, 1957) 157–160.

6155. Cumberland, C. C. "Border Raids in the Lower Rio Grande Valley, 1915," *SHQ* 57 (January, 1954) 285–311.

6156. ———. "The Jenkins Case and Mexican–American Relations," *HAHR* 31 (1951) 586–607.

Concerns the United States consul in Puebla captured by the revolutionists in 1919 and subsequently arrested by the Carranza government.

6157. Dunn, H. H. *The Crimson Jester: Zapata of Mexico.* N.Y., 1933.

6158. Esquivel Obregón, T. *La Influencia de España y los Estados Unidos Sobre México.* Mexico, 1918.

6159. Ewing, F. F., Jr. "Carranza's Foreign Relations: An Experiment in Nationalism," U. of Texas Diss., 1952.

6160. Fabela, I. *Arengas Revolucionarias: Discursos y Artículos Políticos.* Madrid, 1916.

6161. Fernández-MacGregor, G. *Artículos Publicados en la Revista Mexicana de Derecho Internacional, Referentes a la Investigación Hecha por el Subcomité Senatorial de los Estados-Unidos Acerca de los Daños y Perjuicios Sufridos por Ciudadanos Norteamericanos Durante la Revolución Mexicana, y Conclusiones de Dicha Investigación.* Mexico, 1921.

Mexican appraisals of the Fall Committee investigation. See also items 826 and 6175.

6162. Galindo, H. *La Doctrina Carranza y el Acercamiento Indo-Latino.* Mexico, 1919.

6163. Gibbon, T. E. *Mexico Under Carranza.* N.Y., 1919.

An anti-Carranza polemic.

6164. González Roa, F. *El Aspecto Agrario de la Revolución Mexicana.* Mexico, 1919.

6165. Guzmán, R. *El Intervencionismo de Mr. Wilson en México.* New Orleans, 1915.

6166. Inman, S. G. *Intervention in Mexico.* N.Y., 1919.

6167. Junco, A. *Carranza y los Orígenes de su Rebelión.* Mexico, 1935.

6168. Kahle, L. G. "Robert Lansing and the Recognition of Venustiano Carranza," *HAHR* 38 (1958) 353–372.

6169. Kemmerer, E. W. *Inflation and Revolution: Mexico's Experience of 1912–1917.* Princeton, N.J., 1940.

6170. Kestenbaum, J. L. "The Question of Intervention in Mexico, 1913–1917," Northwestern U. Diss., 1963.

6171. Lane, F. K. *The President's Mexican Policy, Presented in an Authorized Interview by Secretary of the Interior, Franklin K. Lane.* N.Y., 1916.

6172. Lansing, R. *Remarks of Robert Lansing, Secretary of State of the United States, at a Luncheon to the American–Mexican Joint Commission at the Hotel Biltmore, New*

York City, September 4, 1916. Wash., 1916.

6173. Lemke, W. *Crimes Against Mexico.* Minneapolis, 1915.

6174. Lopez de Roux, M. E. "Relaciones Mexicano-Norteamericanas, 1917–1918," *HM* 14 (January, 1965) 445–468.

6174a. Lopez-Portillo y Weber, J. "Como Perdió Carranza el Apoyo de Estados Unidos y como se Relacionó Esto con la Proposición que a México Presentó Alemania en 1917," *MAMH* 19, no. 1 (1960) 19–34.

6175. Lou, D. W. "Fall Committee: An Investigation of Mexican Affairs," Indiana U. Diss., 1963.

6176. Lowry, P. H. "The Mexican Policy of Woodrow Wilson," Yale U. Diss., 1949.

6177. Luquín, E. *La Política Internacional de la Revolución Constitucionalista.* Mexico, 1957.

6178. Mena Brito, B. *Carranza, sus Amigos, sus Enemigos.* Mexico, 1935.

6179. Mexican-American Peace Committee. *The Mexican-American League.* N.Y., 1916.

6180. Mexico. Secretaría de Relaciones Exteriores. *Labor Internacional de la Revolución Constitucionalista de México: Libro Rojo.* Mexico, 1960.

Originally published in 1918.

6180a. Meyer, M. C. "The Mexican-German Conspiracy of 1915," *TA* 23 (1966) 76–89.

Argues that fear of German activity helps to explain Wilson's recognition policy.

6181. Morris, H. *Our Mexican Muddle.* Chicago, 1916.

6182. O'Shaughnessy, E. *Intimate Pages of Mexican History.* N.Y., 1920.

For Mrs. O'Shaughnessy's other works, see items 6117 and 6118.

6183. Palacios, P. *Emiliano Zapata: Datos Biográfico-Históricos.* Mexico, 1960.

6184. Palavicini, F. F. *Historia de la Constitución de 1917.* 2 vols., Mexico, 1938.

The author was a member of the constituent assembly which met in Querétaro.

6185. Pereyra, C. *El Crimen de Woodrow Wilson: Su Contubernio con Villa: Sus Atentados en Santo Domingo: Su Régimen Corruptor en Nicaragua: Los Dos Polos de la Diplomacia Yanqui: La Hipocresía y el Miedo.* Madrid, 1917.

6186. Pletcher, D. M. "An American Mining Company in the Mexican Revolutions of 1911–1920," *JMH* 20 (1949) 19–26.

Concerns the Chicago Exploration Company.

6187. Priestley, H. I. "The Carranza Débâcle," *UCC* 22 (July, 1920) 3–17.

6188. Quirk, R. E. *The Mexican Revolution, 1914–1915: The Convention of Aguascalientes.* Bloomington, Ind., 1960.

Pb. ed., N.Y., 1963. The basic monograph for the convention.

6189. Ramírez Plancarte, F. *La Ciudad de México Durante la Revolución Constitucionalista.* Mexico, 1940.

6190. Rausch, G. J., Jr. "The Exile and Death of Victoriano Huerta," *HAHR* 42 (1962) 133–151.

6191. Rebolledo, M. *México y Estados Unidos.* Mexico, 1917.

6192. Rossiter, W. M. "Mexican-American Relations, 1913–1920: A Reappraisal," U. of Chicago Diss., 1953.

6192a. Santana Bravo, J. *El Problema del Reconocimiento del Gobierno de D. Venustiano Carranza.* Mexico, 1963.

6193. Schulz, E. E. *Por la Patria y por la Raza: El Porvenir de México y sus Relaciones con Estados Unidos.* Mexico, 1914.

6194. Singer, J. *Die Mexicanischen Finanzen und Wilsons Panamerikanische Politik.* Berlin, 1914.

6195. Taracena, A. *Venustiano Carranza.* Mexico, 1963.

6195a. Teitelbaum, L. M. *Woodrow Wilson and the Mexican Revolution (1913–1916): A History of United States–Mexican Relations from the Murder of Madero Until Villa's Provocation Across the Border.* N.Y., 1967.

A detailed account based upon United States documents.

6196. Turner, J. K. *Hands Off Mexico.* N.Y., 1920.

6197. USCS. *Investigation of Mexican Affairs: Preliminary Report and Hearings of the Committee on Foreign Relations, United States Senate, Pursuant to S. Res. 106, Directing the Committee on Foreign Relations to Investigate the Matter of*

Outrages on Citizens of the United States in Mexico (66th Cong., 2d Sess., S. Doc. 285). 2 vols., Wash., 1920.

6198. Urquizo, F. L. *Páginas de la Revolución.* Mexico, 1956.

6199. Vera Estañol, J. *Carranza and His Bolshevik Regime.* Los Angeles, 1920.
Conservative stricture of the Carranza administration.

6200. Whitney, C. *What's the Matter with Mexico?* N.Y., 1916.

6201. Williams, I. J. *The Menace of Mexico: Remarks Before the League of Free Nations Association, December 20, 1919, New York City.* N.Y., 1920.

6202. Wilson, W. *The Mexican Question.* Wash., 1916.

6203. Wyeth, J. A. "The United States and Mexico," *NAR* 202 (1915) 76–79.

6204. Zayas Enríquez, R. de. *El Caso México y la Política del Presidente Wilson.* Mexico, 1914.
English ed., N.Y., 1914.

XIII–H–3   cross references:

a) For more general accounts of President Wilson's Latin American policy, see items 3036–3083.

b) See also items 3153, 3159, 3160, 5999, 6108, 6113, 6117, 6118, 6124, 6130, 6134, 6141, 6439a.

4. TAMPICO, VERACRUZ, AND THE ABC MEDIATION

6205. Alducía, R. (comp.). *La Revolución Constitucionalista, los Estados Unidos y el "ABC": Recopilación de Documentos y Artículos Notables Referentes a la Intromisión de Elementos Extranjeros en los Asuntos Exteriores de México y la Patriótica Actitud Asumida por el C. Primer Jefe Venustiano Carranza.* Mexico, 1916.

6206. Almada, F. R. "Carranza y el Atentado de Veracruz," *BSCEH* 10 (July, 1957) 1–4.

6207. Ballivián, A. *Los Designios de Bolívar, la Doctrina Monroe y la Mediación Sudamericana en el Niagara.* N.Y., 1914.

6208. Becu, C. A. *El "ABC" y su Concepto Político y Jurídico.* B.A., 1915.

6209. Cumberland, C. C. "Huerta y Carranza ante la Ocupación de Veracruz," *HM* 6 (April, 1957) 534–547.

6210. Domenech, R. *Méjico y el Imperialismo Norte Americano.* B.A., 1914.

6211. Donnell, G. R. "United States Intervention in Mexico, 1914," U. of Texas Diss., 1951.

6212. Ecuador. Ministerio de Relaciones Exteriores. *La Mediación Latino-Americana en el Conflicto Entre los Estados Unidos y México: La Iniciativa del Ecuador.* Quito, 1916.

6213. Fernández MacGregor, G. "Federico Gamboa como Diplomático," *LM* 2, no. 10 (1939) 7.
Gamboa was Huerta's secretary of foreign relations at the time of the Tampico incident.

6214. Garza Treviño, C. de la. *Wilson y Huerta, Tampico y Veracruz: Ensayo de Divulgación Histórica.* Mexico, 1933.

6215. Gaxiola, J. *La Frontera de la Raza: Hispano-América, los Estados Unidos, la Diplomacia de Venustiano Carranza, la Sociedad Internacional Americana.* Madrid, 1917.

6216. Hinckley, T. C. "Wilson, Huerta, and the Twenty-one Gun Salute," *HIS* 22 (1960) 197–206.

6217. "International Relations of the United States," *AAAPSS* 54 (1914).

6218. Mallén, F. *Los Estados Unidos de Norte América y las Repúblicas del Sur, Reflexiones Sugeridas por la Insinceridad de los Directores Políticos del Gran Pueblo del Norte, con Motivo del Llamado Incidente de Tampico.* Panama, 1914.

6219. Palomares, J. N. *La Invasión Yanqui en 1914.* Mexico, 1940.

6220. Quirk, R. E. *An Affair of Honor: Woodrow Wilson and the Occupation of Vera Cruz.* N.Y., 1962.

6221. Russell, T. H. *Mexico in Peace and War.* Chicago, 1914.

6222. Severance, F. H. "The Peace Conference at Niagara Falls in 1914," *BHSP* 18 (1914) 1–75.

6223. Slayden, J. L. "The A.B.C. Mediation," *AJIL* 9 (1915) 147–152.

6224. Torrea, J. M. "El Desembarco de Americanos en Veracruz en 1914," *BSMGE* 42 (October, 1930) 429–433.

6225. Webster, A. "Woodrow Wilson's Mexican Policy: March 3, 1913, to April 21, 1914," U. of Chicago Diss., 1963.

XIII–H–4   cross references:

a) Many of the general works on United States–Mexican relations for this period treat these topics. See items 6146–6204.

b) For works on the Wilson administration see items 3036–3083.

c) See also item 9495.

5. THE COLUMBUS RAID AND PERSHING'S PUNITIVE EXPEDITION

6226. Braddy, H. *Cock of the Walk: The Legend of Pancho Villa.* Albuquerque, N.M., 1955.

6227. ——. *Pancho Villa at Columbus: The Raid of 1916.* El Paso, Texas, 1965.
Examines and offers conclusions on the numerous controversies concerning the attack.

6227a. ——. *Pershing's Mission in Mexico.* El Paso, Texas, 1966.
Reconstructs the chronology of the punitive expedition.

6228. Brandt, N. "Pancho Villa: The Making of a Public Legend," *TA* 21 (1964) 146–162.
Useful for the commentaries on the secondary literature.

6229. Calzadíaz Barrera, A. *Villa Contra Todo y . . . en Pos de la Venganza Sobre Columbus, N.M.* Mexico, 1960.

6230. Camín, A. *Pancho Villa.* Madrid, 1935.

6231. Campobello, N. *Apuntes Sobre la Vida Militar de Francisco Villa.* Mexico, 1940.

6232. Carranza, A. S. *La Expedición Punitiva.* Mexico, 1936.

6233. Ceja Reyes, V. *Cabalgando con Villa.* Mexico, 1961.

6234. Cervantes, F. *Francisco Villa y la Revolución.* Mexico, 1960.

6235. Dallam, S. F. "The Punitive Expedition of 1916: Some Problems and Experiences of a Troop Commander," *CJ* 36 (1927) 382–398.

6236. Dromundo, B. *Francisco Villa y la "Adelita."* Durango, 1936.

6237. Elser, F. B. "General Pershing's Mexican Campaign," *CE* 94 (February, 1920) 433–447.

6238. Foix, P. *Pancho Villa.* Mexico, 1950.
A popular biography.

6239. Fogelquist, D. F. "The Figure of Pancho Villa in the Literature of the Mexican Revolution," U. of Wisconsin Diss., 1941.

6240. Guzmán, M. L. *Memorias de Pancho Villa: Campos de Batalla.* 2 vols., Mexico, 1939–1940.
English ed., Austin, Texas, 1965.

6241. Harris, L. A. *Pancho Villa and the Columbus Raid.* El Paso, Texas, 1949.

6242. Herrera, C. *Francisco Villa ante la Historia.* Mexico, 1939.

6242a. Hines, C. W. *The Mexican Punitive Expedition of 1916.* San Antonio, Texas, 1962.

6243. Johnson, R. B. "The Punitive Expedition: A Military, Diplomatic, and Political History of Pershing's Chase After Pancho Villa, 1916–1917," U. of S. California Diss., 1964.

6244. Mahoney, T. "The Columbus Raid," *SR* 17 (1932) 161–171.

6245. Muñoz, R. F. *Vorwärts mit Pancho Villa! Erzählung aus Mexikos Geschichte der Gegenwart . . .: Berechtigte Ubersetzung. Einführung und Nachwort von Georg H. Neuendorff.* Leipzig, 1935.

6246. Mexico. *Nota Enviada por el Gobierno Constitucionalista, al de la Casa Blanca con Motivo de las Incursiones de Tropas Americanas en Territorio Mexicano.* Mexico, 1916.
Written by Candido Aguilar.

6247. O'Connor, R. *Black Jack Pershing.* Garden City, N.Y., 1961.

6248. Pinchon, E. *Viva Villa! A Recovery of the Real Pancho Villa.* N.Y., 1933.

6249. Porter, J. A. "The Punitive Expedition," *QR* 12, no. 4 (1933) 19–30.

6250. Puente, R. *Villa en Pie.* Mexico, 1937.

6251. ——. *Villa: Sus Auténticas Memorias.* Los Angeles, 1931.

6252. Rippy, J. F. "Some Precedents of the Pershing Expedition into Mexico," *SHQ* 24 (1921) 292–316.

6253. Salinas Carranza, A. *La Expedición Punitiva.* Mexico, 1936.

6254. Schuster, E. O. *Pancho Villa's Shadow: The True Story of Mexico's Robin Hood as Told by His Interpreter.* N.Y., 1947.

6255. Tomkins, F. *Chasing Villa: The Story Behind the Story of Pershing's Expedition into Mexico.* Harrisburg, Pa., 1934.
By a participant.

6256.   Toulmin, H. A., Jr. *With Pershing in Mexico*. Harrisburg, Pa., 1935.
        Author was on the punitive expedition.

6257.   Wolff, L. "Black Jack's Mexican Goose Chase," *AHE* 13 (1962) 22–27, 100–106.

XIII–H–5   cross references:

Many of the general works on United States–Mexican relations for this period treat these topics. See items 6146–6204.

I. UNITED STATES–MEXICAN RELATIONS, 1920–1940

6258.   Alessio Robles, M. *La Cena de las Burlas*. Mexico, 1939.
        Critical of the United States and the Calles regime.

6259.   Alessio Robles, V. *Los Tratados de Bucareli*. Mexico, 1937.
        Concerns the agreements reached in 1923 by the Obregón and Harding administrations. The author was a Mexican senator at the time the agreements were concluded.

6260.   Alvear Acevedo, C. *Lázaro Cárdenas: El Hombre y el Mito*. Mexico, 1961.

6261.   Anguiano Equihua, V. *Lázaro Cárdenas: Su Feudo y la Política Nacional*. Mexico, 1951.
        A criticism of the Cárdenas administration.

6262.   Barrera, C. *Obregón: Estampas de un Caudillo*. Mexico, 1957.

6263.   Baz, E. *Refutación que se Hace al Informe Rendido al Departamento de Estado de las Estados Unidos, por el Comité Senatorial*. Mexico, 1921.

6264.   Beals, C. "Cardenas Organizes Capitalism," *CH* 46 (1937) 47–54.

6265.   ———. *Mexico: An Interpretation*. N.Y., 1923.
        Sympathetic to the Obregón administration.

6266.   Bell, J. D. "Attitudes of Selected Groups in the U.S. Toward Mexico, 1930–1940," U. of Chicago Diss., 1941.

6267.   Beteta, R. "Mexico's Foreign Relations," *AAAPSS* 208 (March, 1940) 170–180.

6268.   Brown, J. W. *Modern Mexico and Its Problems*. London, 1927.
        Emphasis on the Mexican labor movement but some commentary on relations with the United States.

6269.   Brown, L. C. "General Lázaro Cárdenas and Mexican Presidential Politics, 1933–1940: A Study in the Acquisition and Manipulation of Political Power," U. of Texas Diss., 1964.

6270.   Brown, P. M. "Mexico and the Monroe Doctrine," *AJIL* 26 (1932) 117–121.

6271.   Calles, P. E. *Mexico Before the World*. N.Y., 1927.
        Collection of Calles' speeches and papers.

6272.   Cárdenas, L. *Declaraciones y Mensajes del C. Presidente de la República*. Mexico, 1940.

6273.   ———. *Seis Años de Gobierno al Servicio de México, 1934–40*. Mexico, 1940.
        Cárdenas' annual messages to congress.

6274.   Castillo Nájera, F. *Una Voz de México en el Extranjero: Discursos y Alocuciones*. Mexico, 1936.

6275.   Ceniceros, J. A. *Mexico's Attitude in Its International Relations*. Mexico, 1935.
        The author was an under-secretary of foreign relations.

6276.   Chaverri Matamoros, A. *El Verdadero Calles*. Mexico, 1933.

6277.   Confederación de Trabajadores de México.
        CTM, 1936–1941. Mexico, 1942(?).

6278.   Cuesta Soto, F. *Los Tratados de Bucareli Contra la Revolución*. Mexico, 1937.

6279.   Daniels, J. *Shirt-Sleeve Diplomat*. Chapel Hill, N.C., 1947.
        Autobiographical reminiscences. Spanish ed., Mexico, 1949.

6280.   Dillon, E. J. *President Obregón: A World Reformer*. Boston, 1923.

6281.   Foix, P. *Cárdenas*. 2d ed., Mexico, 1956.
        A sympathetic biography.

6282.   Frank, W. "Cárdenas of Mexico," *FA* 18 (1939) 91–101.

6283.   Gaxiola, F. J., Jr. *El Presidente Rodríguez, 1932–1934*. Mexico, 1938.

6284.   Gómez Robledo, A. *Los Convenios de Bucareli ante el Derecho Internacional*. Mexico, 1938.
        English ed., Mexico, 1940. Attacks the Obregón administration for concluding the agreements.

6285. González Ramírez, M. *Los Llamados Tratados de Bucareli: México y los Estados Unidos en las Convenciones Internacionales de 1923*. Mexico, 1939.

6286. ———. *Política Diplomática del Presidente Obregón*. Hermosillo, 1950.

6287. Green, A. B. *The Present Crises in Our Relations with Mexico*. N.Y., 1927.

6288. Halperin, M. "Under the Lid in Mexico," *CH* 41 (1935) 166–171.

6289. Hay, E. *Discursos Pronunciados en su Carácter de Secretario de Relaciones Exteriores, 1936–1940*. Mexico, 1940.

6290. Herring, H. "Cárdenas Triumphant in Mexico," *CH* 42 (1935) 636–638.

6291. Howland, H. H. *Dwight Whitney Morrow*. N.Y., 1930.
Biography of the United States ambassador.

6291a. Hutton, G. D. "The New-Old Crisis in Mexico," *FA* 16 (1938) 626–639.

6292. Jones, C. L. "The Good Neighbor Policy and Mexican Relations," *WA* 12, no. 1 (1938) 44–48.

6293. Kirk, B. *Covering the Mexican Front: The Battle of Europe Versus America*. Norman, Okla., 1942.
A journalistic account.

6294. Ladd, E. F. *Our Duty to Mexico: Recognition of Mexican Government*. Wash., 1922.

6295. León, L. L. "El Presidente Calles," *HM* 10 (October, 1960) 320–331.

6296. López Gutiérrez, M. E. *Procedimientos Diplomáticos del Régimen Obregonista: Antecedentes y Proyecciones*. Mexico, 1959.

6297. Manero Suárez, A., and J. Paniagua Arredondo. *Los Tratados de Bucareli: Traición y Sangre Sobre México*. 2 vols., Mexico, 1958.
An extremely anti-Obregón interpretation.

6298. Meehan, T. F. "Archbishop Hughes and Mexico," *USCHSRS* 19 (1929) 33–40.

6299. Méndez de Cuenca, L. *Alvaro Obregón*. Hermosillo, n.d.

6300. Mendoza, S. *La Doctrina Cárdenas: Texto, Antecedentes, Comentarios*. Mexico, 1939.

6301. Mexico. Secretaría de Relaciones Exteriores. *La Cuestión Internacional Mexicano-Americana, Durante el Gobierno del Gral. Don Alvaro Obregón*. 3d ed., Mexico, 1949.
Documents for the years 1921–1923.

6302. Morrison, J. L. "Josephus Daniels, Simpático," *JIAS* 5 (April, 1963) 277–289.

6302a. Morrow, E. R. *The Mexican Years: Leaves from the Diary of Elizabeth Cutter Morrow*. N.Y., 1953.

6303. Myers, S. D., Jr. (ed.). *Mexico and the United States*. Dallas, 1938.

6304. Nathan, P. "México en la Epoca de Cárdenas," *PAIM* 7 (1955) 17–262.

6305. ———. "Mexico Under Cárdenas," U. of Chicago Diss., 1953.

6306. Nicolson, H. G. *Dwight Morrow*. N.Y., 1935.

6307. Oberlitner, T. B. "The U.S. and Mexico, 1921–1932," Stanford U. Diss., 1950.

6308. Pani, A. J. *Las Conferencias de Bucareli*. Mexico, 1953.

6309. ———. *La Política Hacendaria y la Revolución*. Mexico, 1926.
Covers the years 1923–1926.

6310. *Proceedings of the United States–Mexican Commission Convened at Mexico City, May 14, 1923*. Wash., 1925.

6311. Rippy, J. F., et al. *American Policies Abroad: Mexico*. Chicago, 1928.

6312. Ross, S. R. "Dwight Morrow and the Mexican Revolution," *HAHR* 38 (1958) 506–528.
Argues that although Morrow might have slowed down the progress of the Revolution temporarily, in the last analysis he accelerated its development.

6313. ———. "Dwight W. Morrow, Ambassador to Mexico," *TA* 14 (January, 1958) 273–289.

6314. Sherwell, G. B. *Mexico's Capacity to Pay: A General Analysis of the Present International Economic Position of Mexico*. Wash., 1929.

6315. Stevens, G. et al. "The Issue in Mexico," *FPAP* no. 38 (1925–1926).

6316. Thomson, C. A. "Mexico's Challenge to Foreign Capital," *FPAR* 13 (1937) 126–136.

6317. Townsend, W. C. *Lázaro Cárdenas, Mexican Democrat*. Ann Arbor, Mich., 1952.

6318. Trujillo, R. *Adolfo de la Huerta y los Tratados de Bucareli*. Mexico, 1957.

6319. USCS. Committee on Foreign Relations. *Relations with Mexico . . . Opposing Sending of Armed Forces of United States into Mexico or Mobilizing Thereof in Territory of Waters Adjacent Thereto While Congress Is Not in Session* (69th Cong., 2d Sess.). Wash., 1927.

6320. Walling, W. E. *The Mexican Question.* N.Y., 1927.

6321. Weyl, N., and S. Weyl. *The Reconquest of Mexico: The Years of Lázaro Cárdenas.* N.Y., 1939.

6322. Whitaker, A. P. (ed.). "Mexico Today," *AAAPSS* 208 (March, 1940) 1–186.

6323. Woolsey, L. H. "Shooting of Two Mexican Students," *AJIL* 25 (1931) 514–516.

XIII–I   cross references:

a) For United States–Mexican relations during World War II, see items 3627a–3646.

b) See also items 3343, 3345, 3350, 3364, 3814.

J. UNITED STATES–MEXICAN RELATIONS SINCE 1940

6324. Alemán, M. *Discursos Pronunciado con Motivo de la Visita que Hizo a los Estados Unidos de Norteamérica.* Mexico, 1947.
President of Mexico, 1946–1952.

6325. ———. *Juntos Hemos de Vivir y Juntos Habremos de Prosperar.* Mexico, 1947.
Speeches by Alemán and Truman during Truman's 1947 Mexican visit.

6326. Banco de México. *Inversiones Extranjeras, 1940–1961.* Mexico, 1962.

6327. Brandenburg, F. R. *The Making of Modern Mexico.* Englewood Cliffs, N.J., 1964.

6328. Call, T. C. *The Mexican Venture: From Political to Industrial Revolution in Mexico.* N.Y., 1953.

6328a. Carrillo Flores, A. "La Política Exterior de México," *FI* 6 (1965–1966) 233–246.

6329. ———. "Mexico Forges Ahead," *FA* 36 (1958) 491–503.

6330. Castañeda, J. *Mexico y el Orden Internacional.* Mexico, 1956.

6331. ———. "Revolution and Foreign Policy: Mexico's Experience," *PSQ* 78 (1963) 391–417.

6332. Castellanos, F. X. *México, Estados Unidos de América, Cinco Años (1950–1954) de Comercio Exterior.* Mexico, 1955.

6333. ———. *Comercio Exterior de México con los Estados Unidos de América, 1950–1961.* Mexico, 1962.

6333a. Chayet Volchansky, I. *El Régimen Aduanal México-Norteamericano.* Mexico, 1961.
Concerns customs administration in both countries.

6334. Cline, H. F. *Mexico, Revolution to Evolution, 1940–1960.* N.Y., 1962.
A comprehensive interdisciplinary study.

6335. ———. "Mexico, Fidelismo and the United States," *OR* 5 (Summer, 1961) 152–165.

6336. Cosío Villegas, D. "México y Estados Unidos," *CA* 36 (November, 1947) 7–27.

6336a. Crow, J. A. *Mexico Today.* N.Y., 1957.

6337. Engel, J. F. "Mexican Reaction to United States Cuban Policy, 1959–1963," U. of Virginia Diss., 1964.

6338. Fayerweather, J. "Las Inversiones de Estados Unidos de América en México," *REC* 8 (January, 1956) 1–34.

6339. ———. "Las Inversiones en México Desde el Punto de Vista de los Hombres de Negocios de los Estados Unidos," *RBA* 3 (November, 1955) 348–355.

6340. ———. "Papel Que Representan las Inversiones de los Estados Unidos en el Desarrollo Económico de México," *RBA* 3, no. 5 (1955) 302–309.

6341. García Reynoso, P. "El Comercio Exterior de México y los Grupos Económicos Regionales," *CEX* 12 (December, 1962) 809–812.

6342. ———. "Veinticinco Años de Política Mexicana de Comercio Exterior y sus Resultados," *CEX* 12 (July, 1962) 406–409.

6343. García Robles, A. *México en la Postguerra.* Mexico, 1944.

6344. Gill, M. [pseudonym of C. M. Velasco Gil]. *Nuestros Buenos Vecinos.* Havana, 1960.
Title is misleading; book contends that Mexico is controlled by the Wall Street financiers.

6345. Glade, W. P., Jr., and C. W. Anderson.

The Political Economy of Mexico: Two Studies. Madison, Wis., 1963.

6346. González de León, A. "México en la Colectividad Internacional," *COMB* 13 (November, 1960) 105–108.

Advocates that Mexico take an independent position in the cold war.

6347. "Good Neighbors Meet: President Alemán and President Truman Exchange Visits," *BPAU* 81 (1947) 287–297.

6347a. Graham, D. L. "The United States and Mexico: A Reluctant Merger," *YR* 43, n.s. (1953) 235–245.

6348. Hanke, L. "México Avanza Exforzadamente," *RNC* 32 (May, 1960) 24–55.

6349. Hill, R. G. *Post-War Problems of Mexico.* N.Y., 1944.

6349a. Holmes, H. A., and L. Thomas." Mexico: Land of Great Experiments," *FPAHS* no. 94 (1952).

6350. James, D. *How to Invest and Live in Mexico.* Mexico, 1960.

6351. ———. *Where Mexico Stands: Thoughts and Ideas of President Adolfo López Mateos.* Mexico, 1960.

6352. Kemnitzer, W. J. "México en la Alianza para el Progreso," *FI* 4 (1963) 41–59.

6353. Lavín, J. D. *Inversiones Extranjeras: Análisis, Experiencias y Orientaciones para la Conducta Mexicana.* Mexico, 1954.

6354. López Mateos, A. *Pensamiento Político del Lic. Adolfo López Mateos.* Mexico, 1958.

President of Mexico, 1958 to 1964.

6355. ———. *Presencia Internacional de Adolfo López Mateos.* Mexico, 1963.

6356. María y Campos, A. de. *Un Ciudadano: Cómo Es y Cómo Piensa Adolfo López Mateos.* 2d ed., Mexico, 1958.

6357. Martínez del Río, R. *Miguel Alemán, ¿Otro Presidente, o un Presidente como Muchos Otros?* Mexico, 1948.

6358. Mexico. Departamento del Distrito Federal. *México en la Postguerra.* 3 vols., Mexico, 1944.

6359. ———. Secretaría de Relaciones Exteriores. *La Política Internacional de México, 1952–1956.* Mexico, 1957.

6360. Migone, A. F. "A Fief for Mexico: Colonel Greene's Empire Ends," *SR* 44 (1959) 332–339.

Concerns the expropriation of Greene's Cananea property in 1958.

6361. Orona y Tovar, J. *Miguel Alemán.* Culiacán, 1951.

Sympathetic biography of the Mexican President.

6362. Ortíz Mena, R., *et al. El Desarrollo Económico de México y su Capacidad para Absorber Capital del Exterior.* Mexico, 1953.

6363. Padilla, E. *Our International Policy.* Mexico, 1945.

6364. Padilla Zazueta, H. *El Desarrollo Económico, el Comercio Exterior y la Regulación de las Importaciones del Sector Público.* Mexico, 1961.

6365. Pelissier, R. F. "American Business Managers and Technicians in Mexican Business," *IEA* 7 (Winter, 1953) 73–79.

6366. ———. "The Contribution of Certain American Business Firms to the Development of Mexico Since World War II," American U. Diss., 1958.

6367. ———. "Intensifications of Competition in Mexico Through the Entry of American Private Enterprise," *IEA* 7 (Autumn, 1953) 30–91.

6368. Ponce, B. *Adolfo Ruiz Cortines: Ensayo para una Biografía Política.* Mexico, 1952.

President of Mexico, 1952–1958.

6369. Randall, L. R. *The Process of Economic Development in Mexico from 1940–1959.* N.Y., 1962.

6370. Ross, S. R. (ed.). *Is the Mexican Revolution Dead?* N.Y., 1966.

Series of readings debating both sides of the question.

6371. ———. "Mexico: Cool Revolution and Cold War," *CH* (February, 1963) 89–94, 116–117.

6372. ———. "Mexico: Golden Anniversary of the Revolution," *CH* 38 (March, 1960) 150–154.

6373. Ruiz Cortines, A. *El Gobierno de Ruiz Cortines.* Mexico, 1957.

6373a. Schmitter, P. C., and E. B. Haas. *Mexico and Latin American Economic Integration.* Berkeley, Calif., 1964.

6374. Scott, R. E. *Mexican Government in Transition.* Urbana, Ill., 1959.

Pb. rev. ed., Urban, Ill., 1964.

6375. Shifrin, E. *Ekspansiia Amerikanskogo Imperializma v Meksike Posle Vtoroi Mirovoi Voiny.* Moscow, 1952.

Expansion of American Imperialism in Mexico After World War II.

6376. Tannenbaum, F. "Reflections on the Mexican Revolution," *JIA* 9 (1955) 37–46.

6377. Torres Manzo, C. "Mexico y el GATT," *IE* 22, 3d tri. (1962) 679–690.

6378. Tucker, W. P. *The Mexican Government Today.* Minneapolis, 1957.

6379. USDC. Bureau of Foreign Commerce. *Investment in Mexico, Conditions and Outlook for United States Investors.* Wash., 1956.

6380. Vargas MacDonald, A. *Cartas de un Mexicano al Presidente Kennedy.* Mexico, 1962.

6381. Vernon, R. *The Dilemma of Mexico's Development.* Cambridge, Mass., 1963.

6382. ——— (ed.). *Public Policy and Private Enterprise in Mexico.* Cambridge, Mass., 1964.
Four essays.

6383. Werlin, J. S. "Mexican Opinion of Us," *SAQ* 43 (1944) 233–247.

6484. Wilgus, A. C. (ed.). *The Caribbean: Mexico Today.* Gainesville, Fla., 1964.

6385. Wise, G. S. *El México de Alemán.* Mexico, 1952.

6386. Wood, R. *Sears, Roebuck de México, S.A.* Wash., 1953.

6387. Wright Quesada, G. *El Comercio Exterior y el Desarrollo Económico de México.* Mexico, 1961.

6388. Wylie, K. *Mexico as a Market and Competitor for U.S. Agricultural Products.* Wash., 1957.

XIII–J cross references:

a) For United States–Mexican relations during World War II, see items 3627a–3646.

b) See also items 4037, 4160, 4172, 4184, 4348, 4611, 4831a, 4831b, 4832, 4834, 5069c, 5403, 6028, 6050, 6443, 6597, 7735.

K. SPECIAL ASPECTS OF UNITED STATES–MEXICAN RELATIONS

1. OIL CONTROVERSIES

6389. Allen, H. J. *The Mexican Confiscations: Together with a Careful Survey of the Present Revolutionary Trends in Mexico.* Topeka, Kans., 1938.

6389a. Arellano Belloc, F. *La Exclusividad del Estado en el Manejo de sus Recursos Petroleros.* Mexico, 1958.

6390. Armstrong, T. R. *The Trader's Interest in the Mexican Policy Toward Foreign Investments.* N.Y., 1938.

6391. ———. "Various Aspects of the Mexican Oil Confiscation," *WA* 101 (1938) 179–184.

6392. Bach, F., and M. de la Peña. *México y Su Petróleo: Síntesis Histórica.* Mexico, 1938.

6393. Bassols Batalla, N. *Diez Años de la Cuestión Petrolera.* Mexico, 1960.

6394. Bermúdez, A. J. *Doce Años al Servicio de la Industria Petrolera Mexicana.* Mexico, 1960.

6395. ———. *The Mexican National Petroleum Industry: A Case Study in Nationalization.* Stanford, Calif., 1963.
The author was in charge of PEMEX from 1946 to 1958.

6396. Boracres, P. *El Petróleo Mexicano . . . ¿Es "Cosa Robada"?* Mexico, 1939.

6397. Botella Asensi, J. *La Expropiación en el Derecho Mexicano.* Mexico, 1941.
Contends that the expropriation law violated the Constitution of 1917.

6398. Cárdenas, L. *Discurso del c. Presidente de la República, Pronunciado en Tuxtla Gutiérrez, Chiapas, el 17 de Marzo de 1940, con Motivo del Segundo Aniversario de la Expropiación Petrolera.* Mexico, 1940.

6399. ———. *Messages to the Mexican Nation on the Oil Question.* Mexico, 1938.

6400. Carrillo, A. *The Mexican People and the Oil Companies.* Mexico, 1938.

6401. Castillo, E. L. *La Cuestión del Petróleo.* Mexico, n.d.

6402. Castillo Nájera, F. *El Petróleo en la Industria Moderna: Las Companías Petroleras y los Gobiernos de México.* Mexico, 1949.

6403. Clark, J. R., Jr. "The Oil Settlement with Mexico," *FA* 6 (1928) 600–614.
Discusses the agreement between Morrow and Calles.

6404. Coleman, G. C. "The 'Good Neighbor' Tested, 1938," *SSSQ* 33 (December, 1952) 216–227.

6405. "Correspondence Between the United States and Mexico Regarding Mexico's Expropriation of Agrarian Properties

Owned by American Citizens," *IC*, no. 345 (1938) 521–528.

6406. Crawford, H. P. "Expropriation of Petroleum Companies in Mexico," *TLR* 12 (1938) 495–508.

6406a. Cuéllar, A. B. *Expropriación y Crisis en México*. Mexico, 1940.

6407. Culbertson, W. S. "Foreign Interests in Mexico," *IAF* 17 (1938) 769–787.

6408. Davis, H. E. "Mexican Petroleum Taxes," *HAHR* 12 (1932) 405–419.

6409. Denny, L. *We Fight for Oil*. N.Y., 1928.

6410. Díaz Dufoo, C. *La Cuestión del Petróleo*. Mexico, 1921.

6411. *Expropriation: A Factual Study of the Causes, Methods and Effects of Political Domination in Industry in Mexico*. N.Y., 1938.

6412. Gaither, R. B. *Expropriation in Mexico, the Facts and the Law*. N.Y., 1940.
   The expropriations are considered illegal.

6413. ———. "Mexican Expropriation of Oil Properties," *USLR* 72 (1938) 322–336.

6413a. Garcia Rangel, R. *El Problema Nacional Petrolera*. Mexico, 1939.

6414. González Aparicio, E. *Nuestro Petróleo*. Mexico, 1938.

6415. González Ramírez, M. *El Petróleo Mexicano: La Expropiación Petrolera ante el Derecho Internacional*. Mexico, 1941.

6416. Gordon, W. C. *The Expropriation of Foreign-Owned Property in Mexico*. Wash., 1941.

6417. Hurley, P. J. *The Struggle for the Mexican Oil: Statement by Attorney for the "Consolidated Oil Corporation" Made Before the Railways Commission of the State of Texas*. Mexico, 1940.

6418. Kunz, J. L. *The Mexican Expropriations*. N.Y., 1940.

6419. "La Industria Petrolera Mexicana y los Capitales Extranjeros—Polémica," *PAIM* 9 (January, 1957) 209–240.

6420. Lang, F. "The Struggle Over Oil in Mexico," *CI* 15 (1938) 664–669.

6421. Lavín, J. D. *Petróleo: Pasado, Presente y Futuro de una Industria Mexicana*. Mexico, 1950.
   A defense of the expropriations.

6422. Lerin, M. "México Dueño de su Petróleo," *AMEX* 1 (September, 1940) 51–54.

6423. Lombardo Toledano, V. "El Pueblo de México y las Compañías Petroleras," *FU* (February, 1938) 20–24.

6424. López Portillo y Weber, J. "Nacimiento de la Industria del Petróleo en México," *MAMH* 18 (October, 1959) 352–382.

6425. MacMahon, A. W., and W. R. Dittmar. "The Mexican Oil Industry Since Expropriation," *PSQ* 57 (1942) 28–50, 161–189.

6426. March, J. J. "Mexico and Oil," *LMO* 21 (March, 1939) 171–177.

6427. McConnell, B. M. *Mexico at the Bar of Public Opinion: A Survey of Editorial Opinion in Newspapers of the Western Hemisphere*. N.Y., 1939.

6428. McMahon, W. E. "As the Companies See It," *SR* 23 (1938) 404–416.

6429. ———. *Mexico's Expropriation of American Oil Properties: An Address Before the Institute of Public Affairs*. Dallas, 1938.

6430. ———. (ed.). *Two Strikes and Out*. Garden City, N.Y., 1939.
   The case for the oil companies.

6431. Mendoza, S. *Why Mexico Expropriates*. Mexico, 1939.

6431a. Menéndez, G. A. *Doheny el Cruel: Episodios de la Sangrienta Lucha por el Petróleo Mexicano*. Mexico, 1958.

6432. *Mexican Petroleum*. N.Y., 1922.

6433. Mexico. *Mexico's Oil: A Compilation of Official Documents in the Conflict of Economic Order in the Petroleum Industry, with an Introduction Summarizing Its Causes and Consequences*. Mexico, 1940.

6434. ———. *The True Facts About the Expropriation of the Oil Companies' Properties in Mexico*. Mexico, 1940.

6435. ———. Secretaría de Educación Pública. *Sobre el Petróleo de México*. Mexico, 1938.

6436. ———. Secretaría de Relaciones Exteriores. *Notas Diplomáticos Cruzadas Entre los Gobiernos de México y de Gran Bretaña con Motivo de la Expropiación de la Industria Petrolera*. Mexico, 1938.

6437. ———. ———. *Segunda Nota Diplomática del Gobierno de Gran Bretaña y Contestación Producida por el Gobierno de México con Motivo de la Expropiación de la Industria Petrolera*. Mexico, 1938.

6438. ———. ———. *Tercera Nota Diplo-*

mática del Gobierno de Gran Bretaña y Contestación Producida por el Gobierno de México con Motivo de la Expropiación de la Industria Petrolera. Mexico, 1938.

6439. Mexico. Secretaría de Relaciones Exteriores. *Tribunales Extranjeros Reconocen el Indiscutible Derecho con que México Expropió los Intereses Petroleros: Documentación Relacionada con los Incidentes Surgidos.* Mexico, 1940.

6439a. Meyer Cosío, L. "El Conflicto Petrolero Entre México y los Estados Unidos (1917–1920)," *FI* 6 (April–June, 1966) 425–465.

6440. Molina Enríquez, A. "Mexico's Defense: Action in Agrarian Reforms and Expropriation of Oil Lands," *AM* 163 (1939) 378–384.

6440a. Muñoz, I. *La Tragedia del Petróleo.* Mexico, 1938.

6441. O'Connor, H. "Mexican Oil: A Study of Nationalization," *MR* 4 (December, 1952) 263–274.

6442. Person, H. S. *Mexican Oil: Symbol of Recent Trends in International Relations.* N.Y., 1942.
Considers the background to the indemnification agreement.

6443. Powell, J. R. *The Mexican Petroleum Industry, 1938–1950.* Berkeley, Calif., 1956

6444. ———. "Some Financial Aspects of the Mexican Petroleum Industry, 1938–1950," *IEA* 6 (Winter, 1952) 14–31.

6445. Priestley, H. I. "The Contemporary Program of Nationalization in Mexico," *PHR* 8 (1939) 59–75.

6446. Rabasa, O. *Decision Rendered by the Supreme Court of Mexico in the Oil Expropriation Case.* Mexico, 1940.

6447. ———. *Estudio Constitucional Sobre la Expropiación Decretada Contra las Compañias Petroleras en México.* Mexico, 1938.

6448. Richberg, D. R. *The Mexican Oil Seizure.* N.Y., 1939.

6449. Rippy, M. "Oil and the Mexican Revolution," U. of Texas Diss., 1950.

6449a. Ritter, H. *Kampf um Ol in Mexico.* Leipzig, 1942.

6450. Rivera P. C., J. *Necesidad Jurídica de la Expropiación Petrolera, Conferencia Sustentada ante el Sindicato de Trabajadores del Departamento Autónomo de Prensa y Publicidad.* Mexico, 1938.

6451. Scroggs, W. O. "Mexico's Oil in World Politics," *FA* 17 (1938) 172–175.

6452. Serocold, J. *Oil in Mexico.* London, 1938.
British criticism of expropriation.

6453. Shul'govskii, A. F. "Natsionalizatsiia Neftianoi Promyshlennosti V Meksike," *NNI* (1960) 68–85.
"The Nationalization of the Oil Industry in Mexico."

6454. Silva Herzog, J. "La Cuestión del Petróleo en México," *TE* 7 (April, 1940) 1–74.

6455. ———. *La Expropiación del Petróleo en México.* Mexico, 1963.

6456. ———. "Mexico and the Oil Companies," *ACE* 15 (January, 1939) 55–69.

6457. ———. "Mexico's Case in the Oil Controversy: Correspondence Between the United States and Mexico," *IC*, no. 345 (December, 1938).

6458. ———. "Mexico's Stand on Oil," *SR* 23 (1938) 392–403.

6459. ———. *Petróleo Mexicano: Historia de un Problema.* Mexico, 1941.

6460. Sousa, M., and E. González Aparicio. *Dos Conferencias Sobre el Problema Petrolero.* Mexico, 1938.

6461. Standard Oil Company of New Jersey. *Confiscation or Expropriation? Mexico's Seizure of the Foreign Owned Oil Industry.* N.Y., 1940.

6462. ———. *Empty Promises.* N.Y., 1940.

6463. ———. *The Fine Art of Squeezing.* N.Y., 1940.

6464. ———. *Mexico Labor Controversy, 1936–1938.* N.Y., 1939.

6465. ———. *Present Status of the Mexican Oil Expropriations.* N.Y., 1940.

6466. ———. *The Reply to Mexico.* N.Y., 1940.

6467. ———. *The Solution for the Mexican Confiscation.* N.Y., 1940.

6468. ———. *They Took What They Wanted.* N.Y., 1939.

6469. ———. *Whose Oil Is It: The Question of Subsoil Rights in Mexico.* N.Y., 1939.

6470. Stocking, G. W. "Mexican Expropriation: The Mexican Oil Problem," *IC*, no. 345 (December, 1938).

6471. ———. "The Mexican Oil Problem," *AFS* 6, no. 4 (Spring, 1938).

6472. Thomson, C. A. "The Mexican Oil Dispute," *FPAR* 14 (1938) 122–132.

6473. ———. "Mexico's Challenge to Foreign Capital," *FPAR* 13 (1937) 126–136.

6474. Townsend, W. C. *The Truth About Mexico's Oil*. Mexico, 1940.

6475. USDS. *Compensation for American-Owned Lands Expropriated in Mexico*. Wash., 1939.

6476. ———. "Expropriation of American-Owned Oil Properties in Mexico: Statement by Acting Secretary Welles," *USDSB* 1 (1939) 131–132.

6477. ———. *Standard Oil Company: Details of Justice: A Memorandum on the Decision of the Mexican Supreme Court of Dec. 2, 1939: The Full Text of the Decision*. Wash., 1940.

6478. Universidad Obrera de México. *El Conflicto del Petróleo en México, 1937–1938*. Mexico, 1938.

6479. Vagts, A. *Mexico, Europa und Amerika*. Berlin, 1928.

6480. Villegas Mora, J. *Petróleo, Sangre y Justicia*. Mexico, 1939.

6481. Watt, J. R. "The Expropriation of Foreign-Owned Property in Mexico," *AER* 33 (1943) 149–151.

6482. Waugh, E. *Robbery Under Law: The Mexican Object Lesson*. London, 1939.

6483. Weinfeld, A. C. "The Mexican Oil Expropriations," *NLGQ* 1 (1938) 367–399; 2 (1938) 32–46.

6484. Wild, P. S., Jr. "International Law and Mexican Oil," *QJIR* 1, no. 2 (1939) 5–21.
    Spanish ed., *TE* 7, no. 2 (1940) 271–290.

6485. Woolsey, L. H. "Expropriation of Oil Properties by Mexico," *AJIL* 32 (1938) 519–526.

6486. Young, P. P. "Mexican Oil and American Diplomacy," U. of Texas Diss., 1934.

XIII–K–1 cross references: 3343, 6023, 6042

2. CLAIMS SETTLEMENTS

6487. *Benjamin Weil Contra México. Número 447. Petición de Revisión*. Mexico, 1877.

6487a. Beus, J. G. de. *The Jurisprudence of the General Claims Commission, United States and Mexico Under the Convention of Sept. 8, 1923*. The Hague, 1938.

6488. Bishop, C. M. "Procedure Under the General Claims Protocol Between the United States and Mexico of April 24, 1930," *CDILR* 4, nos. 10–11 (1935).

6489. Briggs, H. W. "The Settlement of Mexican Claims Act of 1942," *AJIL* 37 (1943) 222–232.

6490. *Case of Mexico upon the Newly Discovered Evidence of Fraud and Perjury in the Claims of Benjamin Weil and La Abra Silver Mining Company*. Wash., 1878.

6491. *Claim of Benjamin Weil No. 447 vs. Mexico: Award by the Umpire of the United States and Mexican Claims Commission*. Mexico, 1877.

6492. *Claim of "La Abra Mining Co." vs. Mexico, No. 489: Award by the United States and Mexican Claims Commission and Motion for Rehearing*. Mexico, 1877.

6493. Comisión Especial de Reclamaciones Entre México y E. Unidos. *Sentencia en los Casos de Santa Isabel, Cornelia J. Pringle et al. y Otros Reclamantes*. Mexico, 1926.

6494. Coxe, R. S. *Review of the Relations Between the United States and Mexico, and of the Claims of Citizens of the United States Against Mexico*. N.Y., 1846.

6495. Currey, J. *Treaty of Guadalupe Hidalgo and Private Land Claims and Titles Existing in California at the Date of the Treaty*. San Francisco, 1891.

6496. De Beus, J. G. *The Jurisprudence of the General Claims Commission, United States and Mexico, Under the Convention of September 8, 1923*. The Hague, 1938.

6497. Desverine, R. E. *Claims Against Mexico*. N.Y., 1922.

6498. *Documento Núm. 7: Anexo a la Memoria del Secretario de Estado y del Despacho de Relaciones Exteriores, Fechada el 10 de Diciembre de 1877*. Mexico, 1877(?).

6499. Elorduy, A. *Casos de Santa Isabel*. Mexico, 1927.

6500. Feller, A. H. *The Mexican Claims Commission*. N.Y., 1935.
    A comprehensive study of the work of the Claims Commission from 1923 to 1934.

6501. McClendon, R. E. "The Weil and La Abra Claims Against Mexico," *HAHR* 19 (1939) 31–54.

6502. McKernan, L. W. "Special Mexican Claims from 1910 to 1920," *AJIL* 32 (1938) 457–466.

6503. *Opinión del Comisionado Manuel M. de Zamacona en el Caso de la Compañía Minera de la "Abra," Contra México, No. 489.* Wash., 1875.

6504. *Opinión del Comisionado Manuel M. de Zamacona en el Caso de Thadeus Amat, Obispo de Monterey y Joseph S. Alemany, Arzobispo de San Francisco, Contra México, No. 493.* Wash., 1875.

6505. *Opiniones del Comisionado de México en Noventa y dos Casos de la Espedición Zerman y Algunas Constancias Documentales Relativas a los Casos, Signed M. de Zamacona.* Wash., 1875.

6506. Palacio, F. G. *Claims of Mexican Citizens Against the United States for Indian Depredation, Being the Opinion of the Mexican Commissioner in the Joint Claims Commission Under the Convention of July 4, 1868, between Mexico and the United States.* Wash., 1871.

6506a. Peña y Reyes, A. de la. *La Insubsistencia de una Convención de Reclamaciones.* Mexico, 1928.

6507. Rodríguez, J. I. *La Comisión Mixta de Reclamaciones Mexicanas y Americanas Establecida Conforme al Tratado de 4 Julio de 1868 Entre México y los Estados Unidos: Historia de sus Trabajos y Procedimientos y Exposición Metódica de los Principios Establecidos en sus Decisiones.* Mexico, 1873.

6508. *Sinopsis Histórica de la Comisión Mixta de Reclamaciones Entre México y los Estados Unidos.* Mexico, 1876.

6508a. Siqueiros Prieto, J. L. *Las Reclamaciones Internacionales por Intereses Extranjeros en Sociedades Mexicanos.* Mexico, 1947.

6509. Thorpe, G. C. "The Mexican Problem Solved," *NAR* 220 (1924) 51–62.
Treats both the general and the special claims commissions.

6509a. USCH. Committee on Foreign Affairs. *Mexican Claims: General Mexican Claims Commission: Hearings, June 20, 1939, on S. 326 for the Payment of Awards and Appraisals Heretofore Made in Favor of Citizens of the United States on Claims Presented Under the General Claims Convention of September 8, 1923. United States and Mexico* (76th Cong., 1st Sess.). Wash., 1939.

6510. USCS. *Claims on the Part of Citizens of the United States and Mexico Under the Convention of July 4, 1868, Between the United States and Mexico* (44th Cong., 2d Sess., S. Exec. Doc. 31). Wash., 1877.

6511. ———. *Claims Against Mexico for the Destruction of Life and Property of American Citizens in That Country, August 1, 1919* (66th Cong., 1st Sess., S. Doc. 67). Wash., 1919.

6512. ———. *Claims of American Citizens Against Mexico ... May 20, 1919* (66th Cong., 1st Sess., S. Doc. 1). Wash., 1919.

6513. ———. Committee on Foreign Relations. *Claims of American Nationals Against Mexico: Hearings* (77th Cong., 2d Sess.). Wash., 1942.

6514. United States and Mexican Claims Commission, 1869–1876. *Dictamen del Comisionado Mexicano, y Otros Documentos, Relativo a la Cuestión Sobre Reclamaciones Contra el Gobierno de los Estados Unidos de América, por Depredaciones de Indios Bárbaros.* Wash., 1872.

6515. ———. *Reclamaciones de Indemnización por Depredaciones de los Indios: Dictamen del Sr. D. Francisco Gómez Palacio.* Mexico, 1872.

6516. United States and Mexico Claims Commission. *Opinions of Commissioners Under the Convention Concluded September 8, 1923, Between the United States and Mexico: February 4, 1926, to July 23, 1927.* Wash., 1927.

6517. United States Special Mexican Claims Commission. *Report to the Secretary of State with Decisions Showing the Reasons for the Allowance or Disallowance of the Claims.* Wash., 1948.

6518. ———. "General Principles Applied by the Commission in the Decision on Claims," *AJIL* 32 (1938) 858–869.

6519. Woolsey, L. H. "Settlement of Claims Between the United States and Mexico," *AJIL* 30 (1936) 92–102.

XIII–K-·2   *cross references: 5856*

3. PIOUS FUND

6520. *Diplomatic Correspondence Between the United States and Mexico Relative to the Pious Fund of the Californias, Prepared for Use of the Permanent Court of Arbitration in Case of United States vs. Mexico.* Wash., 1902.

6521. Doyle, J. T. "History of the 'Pious Fund' of California," *CHSP* 1, pt. 1 (1887) 41–60.

6522. McDonald, W. E. "The Pious Fund of the Californias," *CHIR* 19 (1934) 427–436.

6522a. Mexico. Cámara de Diputados. *Tejas y el Fondo Piadoso de las Californias.* Mexico, 1937.

6523. *Reclamación del Gobierno de los Estados Unidos de América Contra México Respecto del Fondo Piadoso de las Californias: Documentos Principales Relativos.* Mexico, 1903.

6524. *Recueil des Actes et Protocoles Concernant le Litige du "Fonds Pieux des Californies," Soumis au Tribunal d'Arbitrage Constitué en Vertu du Traité Conclu à Washington le 22 Mai 1902 Entre les Etats-Unis d'Amérique et les Etats-Unis Mexicains.* The Hague, 1902.

6525. *Report of Jackson H. Ralston, Agent of the United States and Counsel, in Matter of Pious Fund . . . with Pleadings, Appendix Exhibits, Briefs, and Record of Proceedings.* Wash., 1902.

6525a. Rodríguez de San Miguel, J. N. (ed.). *Documentos Relativos al Piadoso Fondo de Misiones para Conversión y Civilizacion de las Numerosas Tribus Bárbaras de la Antigua y Nueva California.* Mexico, 1845.

6526. *The Case of the Pious Fund of the Californias: Replication of the United States of America, with Exhibits.* The Hague, 1902.

6527. *Transcript of Record of Proceedings Before Mexican and American Mixed Claims Commission (1869–1876) with Relation to the Pious Fund of the Californias, Being Claim 493, American Docket, and Entitled Thaddeus Amat, Bishop of Monterey, Joseph S. Alemany, Archbishop of San Francisco, vs. Mexico.* Wash., 1902.

6527a. Villaseñor y Villaseñor, A. *Reclamaciones a México por los Fondos de Californias.* Mexico, 1902.

6528. Weber, F. J. "The Pious Fund of the Californias," *HAHR* 43 (1963) 78–94.

XIII–K–3 cross references: 6504

4. BOUNDARY AND WATER CONTROVERSIES

6529. *Argument Submitted by the Government of the United Mexican States to the Honorable Arbitral Tribunal and to the Agent of the Government of the United States of America.* Mexico, 1911.
Official Mexican documents concerning the Chamizal case.

6530. Berdeja Galeana, S. *El Tratado de Aguas Internacionales Celebrado Entre México y los Estados Unidos, el 3 de Febrero de 1944 y Convención de 21 de Mayo de 1906.* Mexico, 1948.

6531. *Boundary Between the United States and Mexico, as Surveyed and Marked by the International Boundary Commission, Under the Convention of July 29th, 1882.* Wash., 1899.

6532. Castañeda Alatorre, F. *El Tratado de 1906 Celebrado Entre México y los Estados Unidos de Norteamérica Sobre la Distribución de las Aguas del Río Bravo, en el Valle de Juárez, Chih.: Su Historia y Crítica: Y Estudio Sobre el Derecho de México para Utilizar las Aguas del Río Bravo en el Propio Valle en Juárez, Chih., México.* Mexico, 1944.

6533. Chamizal Arbitration. *Argument of the United States of America.* Wash., 1911.

6534. ———. *Minutes of the Meetings of the International Boundary Commission, June 10 and 15, 1911, Containing the Award in the Chamizal Case.* Wash., 1911.

6535. ———. *The Case of the United States of America.* Wash., 1911.

6536. ———. *The Case of the United States of America: Appendix.* 2 vols., Wash., 1911.

6537. ———. *The Countercase of the United States.* Wash., 1911.

6538. "The Chamizal Arbitration Between the United States and Mexico," *AJIL* 5 (1911) 782–833.

6539. Davies, T. M., Jr. "The Rio Grande Treaty of 1933: A Prelude to Settlement," *NMHR* 40 (1965) 277–292.

6540. Eckert, J. C. G. "International Law in United States–Mexican Boundary Relations," U. of Texas Diss., 1939.

6541. Escoto Ochoa, H. *Integración y Desintegración de Nuestra Frontera Norte.* Mexico, 1945.

6542. Esquivel Obregón, T. "El Tratado de Aguas Pendiente Entre México y Estados Unidos," *J* 14 (May, 1945) 283–305.

6543. Gregory, G. G. "El Chamizal: A Boundary Problem Between the United States and Mexico," U. of Texas Diss., 1937.

6544. ———. *The Chamizal Settlement: A View from El Paso*. El Paso, Texas, 1963.

6545. Hundley, N., Jr. *Dividing the Waters: A Century of Controversy Between the United States and Mexico*. Berkeley, Calif., 1966.

6546. ———. "The Colorado Waters Dispute," *FA* 42 (1964) 495–500.

6547. International Boundary Commission. *Proceedings . . . American Section: Joint Report of Consulting Engineers on Field Operations of 1910–1911*. Wash., 1913.

6548. ———. *Proceedings of the International Boundary Commission, United States and Mexico: Elimination of Bancos Under Convention of March 20, 1905: El Paso–Juarez Valley*. Wash., 1931.

6549. ———. *Proceedings of the International (Water) Boundary Commission, United States and Mexico, Treaties of 1884 and 1889: Equitable Distribution of the Waters of the Rio Grande*. 2 vols., Wash., 1903.

6550. ———. *Report of the Boundary Commission upon the Survey and Remarking of the Boundary Between the United States and Mexico West of the Rio Grande, 1891 to 1896*. Wash., 1898.

6551. Liss, S. *A Century of Disagreement: The Chamizal Conflict, 1864–1964*. Wash., 1965.

6551a. Macías, P. C. *El Chamizal: Territorio de México en Poder de los Estados Unidos*. Mexico, 1961.

6552. *Memoria de la Sección Mexicana de la Comisión Internacional de Límites Entre México y los Estados Unidos que Restableció los Monumentos de El Paso al Pacífico*. N.Y., 1901.

6553. *Memoria Documentada del Juicio de Arbitraje del Chamizal Celebrado en Virtud de la Convención de Junio 24 de 1910*. 3 vols., Mexico, 1911.

6554. Mendoza, S. *El Chamizal: Un Drama Jurídico e Histórico*. Mexico, 1963.

6555. Mexico. Secretaría de Relaciones Exteriores. *El Tratado de Aguas Internacionales Celebrado Entre México y los Estados Unidos el 3 de Febrero de 1944: Antecedentes, Consideraciones y Resoluciones del Problema de las Aguas Internacionales*. Mexico, 1947.

6556. Peters, D. W. "The Rio Grande Boundary Dispute in American Diplomacy," *SHQ* 54 (1951) 412–429.
Covers the period since 1884.

6557. *Proceedings of the International Boundary Commission, United States and Mexico, American Section: Elimination of Bancos, Treaty of 1905 (First and Second Series, No. 1–89)*. 2 vols., Wash., 1910–1912.

6558. Reinhardt, G. F. "Rectification of the Rio Grande in the El Paso–Juarez Valley," *AJIL* 31 (1937) 44–51.

6559. *Reply Which the Government of the United Mexican States Submits*. Mexico, 1911.

6560. Riquelme Inda, J. "El Problema del Agua en la Región Mexicana del Colorado, B.C.," *BSMGE* 60 (July, 1945) 509–523.

6561. Sepúlveda, C. "Historia y Problemas de los Límites de México," *HM* 8 (1958) 1–34, 145–174.
Analysis of boundary controversies with both Guatemala and the United States.

6562. Tamayo, J. L. "Las Aguas Internacionales del Norte de México y el Tratado de 1944," *TE* 12 (October, 1945) 466–487.

6563. Timm, C. A. *The International Boundary Commission: United States and Mexico*. Austin, Texas, 1941.
Treats the organization and operation of the commission.

6564. ———. "Some International Problems Arising from Water Diversion on the United States Mexican Boundary," *SSSQ* 13 (1932) 1–15.

6565. ———. "Some Observations on the Nature and Work of the International Boundary Commission," *SSSQ* 15 (1935) 271–297.

6566. USCH. Committee on Foreign Affairs. *Compliance with the Convention on Chamizal: Hearings* (88th Cong., 2d Sess.). Wash., 1964.

6567. ———. ———. *Compliance with Convention on the Chamizal: Report* (88th Cong., 2d Sess.). Wash., 1964.

6567a. USCS. *Report of the Boundary Commission upon the Survey and Remarking of the Boundary Between the United States and Mexico . . . West of the Rio Grande, 1891 to 1896* (55th Cong., 2d Sess., S. Doc. 247). Wash., 1898.

6568. ———. Committee on Foreign Relations. *Convention with Mexico for Solution of the Problem of the Chamizal: Hearings Before the Committee of Foreign Relations* (88th Cong., 1st Sess.). Wash., 1963.

6569. Vargas Siva, J. A. *El Caso del Chamizal: Sus Peculiaridades Jurídicas.* Mexico, 1963.

XIII–K–4 cross references: 5872, 5885, 5903, 5905, 5915, 5968, 6006, 6152

5. CONTROVERSIES OVER THE RELIGIOUS ISSUE

6570. Báez Camargo, G., and K. G. Grubb. *Religion in the Republic of Mexico.* N.Y., 1935.

6571. Balderrama, L. C. *El Clero y el Gobierno de México.* 2 vols., Mexico, 1927.
Reflects the government's view.

6572. Cronon, E. D. "American Catholics and Mexican Anticlericalism, 1933–1936," *MVHR* 45 (1958) 201–230.

6573. Divinnie, L. la. *Les Phases de la Persécution au Mexique.* Paris, 1929.
From the church point of view.

6573a. Ellis, L. E. "Dwight Morrow and the Church-State Controversy in Mexico," *HAHR* 38 (1958) 482–505.

6574. Galarza, E. *The Roman Catholic Church as a Factor in the Political and Social History of Mexico.* Sacramento, Calif., 1928.
An indictment of the church.

6575. Hilton, S. E. "The Church-State Dispute over Education in Mexico from Carranza to Cárdenas," *TA* 21 (1964) 163–183.

6576. James, E. K. "Church and State in Mexico," *FPAR* 11 (1935) 106–116.

6577. Jones, C. L. "Roots of Mexican Church Conflict," *FA* 14 (1935) 135–145.

6578. Kelley, F. C. *Blood-Drenched Altars: Mexican Study and Comment.* Milwaukee, 1935.
Author was a Roman Catholic bishop in the United States.

6579. ———. "Mexico Persecutes the Church," *F* 94 (1935) 212–216.

6580. Larin, N. S. *Bor'ba Tserkvi s Gosudarstvom v Meksike (Vosstanie 'Kristeros' v 1926–1929 gg.).* Moscow, 1965.
The Struggle of Church and State in Mexico (The Cristero Rebellion of 1926–1929).

6581. Lippmann, W. "Church and State in Mexico: The American Mediation," *FA* 8 (1930) 186–207.

6582. MacFarlan, C. S. *Chaos in Mexico.* N.Y., 1935.
Concludes that anti-clericalism degenerated into anti-Catholicism.

6583. Moctezuma, A. P. *El Conflicto Religioso de 1926: Sus Orígenes, su Desarrollo, su Solución.* 2d ed., 2 vols., Mexico, 1960.

6584. Navarrete, F. *Sí Hay Persecución Religiosa en México.* San Francisco, 1935.

6585. Parsons, W. *Mexican Martyrdom.* N.Y., 1936.

6586. Pérez Lugo, J. (comp.). *La Cuestión Religiosa en México.* Mexico, 1927.
Collection of laws and other documentation to support the position of the government.

6587. Portes Gil, E. *The Conflict Between Civil Power and the Clergy.* Mexico, 1935.

6588. Quirk, R. E., Jr. "The Mexican Revolution and the Catholic Church, 1910–1929: An Ideological Study," Harvard U. Diss., 1951.

6589. Rice, E. A. *The Diplomatic Relations Between the United States and Mexico, as Affected by the Struggle for Religious Liberty in Mexico, 1925–1929.* Wash., 1959.

6590. Ríus Facius, A. *Méjico Cristero.* Mexico, 1960.

6591. Toro, A. *La Iglesia y el Estado en México.* Mexico, 1927.

XIII–K–5 cross references: 3350, 5813, 6291, 6298, 6306, 6312, 6313

6. MEXICAN IMMIGRATION TO THE UNITED STATES AND THE BRACERO QUESTION

6592. Beals, R. L., and N. D. Humphrey. *No Frontier to Learning: The Mexican Student in the United States.* Minneapolis, 1957.
Examines the influences of United States education on Mexican students.

6593. Bogardus, E. S. *The Mexican in the United States.* Los Angeles, 1934.

6594. Carney, J. P. "Postwar Mexican Migration, 1945–1955, with Particular Reference to the Policies and Practices of the U.S. Concerning Its Control," U. of S. California Diss., 1957.

6595. Coalson, G. O. "Mexican Contract Labor in American Agriculture," *SSSQ* 33 (1952) 228–238.

6596. Copp, N. G. "Wetbacks and Braceros: Mexican Migrant Laborers and American Immigration Policy, 1930–1960," Boston U. Diss., 1960.

6597. Elac, J. C. "The Employment of Mexican Workers in U.S. Agriculture, 1900–1960: A Binational Economic Analysis," UCLA Diss., 1961.

6598. Gallardo, L. L. "An Evaluation of United States Department of Labor Policy Regarding Wages Paid Mexican Nationals: Michigan Pickles, a Case Study," U. of California Diss., 1962.

6599. Gamio, M. *Mexican Immigration to the United States.* Chicago, 1930.

6600. Hancock, R. H. *The Role of the Bracero in the Economic and Cultural Dynamics of Mexico.* Stanford, Calif., 1959.

6600a. Hidalgo, E. *La Protección de Mexicanos en los Estados Unidos.* Mexico, 1940.

6600b. Kibbe, P. R. *Latin Americans in Texas.* Albuquerque, N.M., 1946.
Examines the problems of the Mexican minority in Texas.

6601. Lipschultz, R. J. "American Attitudes Towards Mexican Immigration, 1924–1952," U. of Chicago Diss., 1962.

6602. Lyon, R. M. "The Legal Status of American and Mexican Migratory Farm Labor: An Analysis of U.S. Farm Labor Legislation, Policy and Administration," Cornell U. Diss., 1954.

6603. Martinez, J. R. "Mexican Emigration to the U.S., 1910–1930," U. of California Diss., 1956.

6604. Sabghir, I. H. "Mexican Contract Labor in the U.S., 1948–1953: A Political and Economic Analysis," Harvard U. Diss., 1956.

6605. Scruggs, O. M. "The Bracero Program Under the Farm Security Administration, 1942–1943," *LH* 3 (1962) 149–168.

6606. ———. "Evolution of the Mexican Farm Labor Agreement of 1942," *AHI* 34 (1960) 140–149.

6607. ———. "A History of Mexican Agricultural Labor in the U.S., 1942–1954," Harvard U. Diss., 1958.

6608. ———. "The United States, Mexico and the Wetbacks, 1942–1947," *PHR* 30 (1961) 149–164.

6609. Taylor, P. *Mexican Labor in the United States.* Los Angeles, 1929.

6610. Tomasek, R. D. "The Political and Economic Implications of Mexican Labor in the United States Under the Non-Quota System, Contract Labor Program, and Wetback Movement," U. of Michigan Diss., 1958.

6610a. USCH. Committee on Agriculture. Subcommittee on Equipment Supplies and Manpower. *Mexican Farm Labor Program* (87th Cong., 2d Sess.). Wash., 1962.

7. COMMUNISM

6611. Barclay, H. W. ¿*Cómo Progresa el Comunismo en Méjico?* Caracas, 1939.

6612. Bernstein, H. "Marxismo en México, 1917–1925," *HM* 7 (1958) 497–516.

6613. Claraval, B. *Cuando Fuí Comunista.* Mexico, 1944.
Analysis by a former party member.

6614. Encina, D. *Liberemos a México del Yugo Imperialista.* Mexico, 1954(?).
By the head of the Mexican Communist party.

6615. Fiorini, M. "El Comunismo en México," *ESC* 5 (January, 1957) 71–77.

6616. García Trevino, R. "Crisis del Comunismo Mexicano," *EO* 1, no. 20 (1963) 4–8.

6617. ———. *La Ingerencia Rusa en México (y Sudamérica): Pruebas y Testimonios.* Mexico, 1959.
Examines the attitude of the Mexican Communist party toward major governmental decisions during the revolutionary period.

6618. González, T., and E. Lozarda. *Nuestro Lugar Está en el Partido Comunista.* Mexico, 1961.

6619. Herman, D. L. "The Comintern and the Development of Communism in Mexico," U. of Michigan Diss., 1964.

6620. Manzanilla, A. *El Comunismo en México*

    y el Archivo de Carrillo Puerto. 2d ed., Mexico, 1955.

6621.   *Materiales del Comité del D.F. para su Discusión en el XIII Congreso del Partido Comunista Mexicano.* Mexico, 1959.

6622.   Partido Comunista de México. *La Nueva Política del Partido Comunista de México.* Mexico, 1936.

6623.   ————. *Primer Congreso Extraordinario.* Mexico, 1940.

6624.   ————. *Resolución Sobre la Situación Actual a las Tareas del Partido.* Mexico, 1927.

6625.   Sánchez Salazar, L. A., and J. Gorkin. *Así Asesinaron a Trotski.* Santiago, 1950.

6626.   Schmitt, K. *Communism in Mexico: A Study in Political Frustration.* Austin, Texas, 1965.

6627.   Terrazas, M. *Hacia un Nuevo Programa del Partido Comunista Mexicano.* Mexico, 1954(?).

6628.   Treviño, R. *El Espionaje Comunista y la Evolución Doctrinaria del Movimiento Obrero en México.* Mexico, 1952.

6629.   Washington, S. W. "Mexican Resistance to Communism," *FA* 36 (1958) 504–515.

Chapter XIV The United States and the Central American–Caribbean Region

A. GENERAL WORKS

6630. Adams, R. N. *Cultural Surveys of Panama —Nicaragua — Guatemala — El Salvador—Honduras*. Wash., 1957.
An anthropological survey.

6631. Arciniegas, G. *Caribbean: Sea of the New World*. N.Y., 1946.

6632. Ashworth, J. "The Development of a United States Caribbean Policy Distinct from the Monroe Doctrine (1789–1909)," *CUTA* 2 (1930) 99–101.

6633. Auburn, C. V. *L'Amérique Centrale*. 2d ed., Paris, 1962.
Historical survey.

6634. Balink, A. *My Paradise Is Hell: The Story of the Caribbean*. N.Y., 1948.
Episodic history.

6635. Barón Castro, R. "El Centroamericano como Sujeto Histórico," *RIN* 19 (January, 1959) 17–34.

6636. Crowther, S. *The Romance and Rise of the American Tropics*. N.Y., 1929.
Brief historical sketch.

6637. Deerr, N. *The History of Sugar*. 2 vols., London, 1949.

6638. El Salvador. Secretaría de Información de la Presidencia de la República. *Política de Cordialidad Centro-Americana: Honduras y El Salvador en un Común Destino*. San Salvador, 1950.

6639. Facio B., R. *La Federación de Centroamérica: Sus Antecedentes, su Vida y su Disolución*. San José, C.R., 1960.

6639a. ———. "La Federación Centroaméricana," *RAN* 3 (1939) 266–318.

6640. ———. *Trayectoria y Crisis de la Federación Centroamericana*. San José, C.R., 1949.

6641. Fortier, A., and J. R. Ficklen. *Central America and Mexico*. Phil., 1907.

6642. Gómez Carillo, A. *Compendio de la Historia de la América Central*. Guatemala, 1906.

6643. Herrarte, A. (comp.). *Documentos de la Unión Centroamericana*. Guatemala, 1957.
Documents relating to attempted union for the period 1821–1951.

6644. ———. *La Unión de Centroamérica: Tragedia y Esperanza: Ensayo Político-Social Sobre la Realidad de Centroamérica*. Guatemala, 1955.
A call for federation.

6645. Kalijarvi, T. V. *Central America: Land of Lords and Lizards*. Princeton, N.J., 1962.

6646. Karnes, T. L. *The Failure of Union: Central America, 1824–1960*. Chapel Hill, N.C., 1961.
Traces early attempts at political union and recent attempts at economic union.

6647. Lardé y Arthés, E. *Historia de Centroamérica*. 4th ed., San Salvador, 1936.

6648. López, F. M. *Centro América Esparcida: El Tema de su Unidad*. Guatemala, 1958.

6649. López Villamil, H. *Política Internacional en Centro América*. León, Nicaragua, 1946.

6650. Matá Gavidia, J. *Anotaciones de Historia Patria Centro-Américana*. Guatemala, 1953.

6651. Marure, A. *Bosquejo Histórico de las Revoluciones de Centroamérica*. 2 vols., Guatemala, 1960.

6652. Mellman, H. G. "The American Policy of Intervention in the Caribbean," U. of Illinois Diss., 1940.

6653. Mendieta, S. *Alrededor del Problema Unionista de Centro-America*. 2 vols., Barcelona, 1934.
A review of attempts at unification with special consideration of the Nicaraguan policy.

6653a. Mendoza, J. L. (comp.) *Pactos Multi-*

laterales Centroamericanos y Regionales. Guatemala, 1960.

A compilation of treaties.

6654. Moreno, L. *Historia de las Relaciones Interestatuales de Centro-América.* Madrid, 1928.

Comprehensive study of the period between independence and the date of publication.

6655. Munro, D. G. *The Five Republics of Central America: Their Political and Economic Development and Their Relation with the United States.* N.Y., 1918.

6656. Parker, F. D. *The Central American Republic.* N.Y., 1964.

Historical survey with useful historiographical commentaries.

6657. Parry, J. H., and P. M. Sherlock. *A Short History of the West Indies.* N.Y., 1956.

6658. Peck, A. M. *The Pageant of Middle American History.* N.Y., 1947.

A popular history of the Central American republics and Mexico.

6659. Perkins, D. *The United States and the Caribbean.* Cambridge, Mass., 1947.

Rev. ed., Cambridge, Mass., 1966.

6660. Proudfoot, M. M. *Britain and the United States in the Caribbean: A Comparative Study in Methods of Development.* N.Y., 1954.

6661. Roberts, W. A. *The Caribbean: The Story of Our Sea of Destiny.* Indianapolis, 1940.

6662. Rodríguez, M. *Central America.* Englewood Cliffs, N.J.

6662a. Roemer, H. "Der Karibische Raum in der Weltpolitik," *ZGE* 12 (1935) 545–554.

6663. Royal Institute of International Affairs. *The British Caribbean: A Brief Political and Economic Survey.* Oxford, 1957.

6664. Slade, W. F. *The Federation of Central America.* Worcester, Mass., 1917.

6665. Thompson, W. *Rainbow Countries of Central America.* N.Y., 1926.

6666. Vallejo, A. R. *Historia Documentada de los Límites Entre la República de Honduras y las de Nicaragua, El Salvador y Guatemala.* 12 vols., Tegucigalpa, 1905–1926.

6667. Weitzel, G. T. "The United States and Central America: Policy of Clay and Knox," *AAAPSS* 132 (1927) 115–126.

Author was the United States minister to Nicaragua from 1912 to 1913.

6668. Williams, E. E. *The Negro in the Caribbean.* London, 1945.

Scholarly discussion by the prime minister of Trinidad and Tobago.

6669. Young, J. P. *Central American Currency and Finance.* Princeton, N.J., 1925.

XIV–A cross references:

a) For works dealing with canal diplomacy in Central America, see items 2349–2458.

b) For works on the Central American–Caribbean region and the inter-American system, see items 4837–4847.

c) See also item 1758.

B. THE UNITED STATES AND THE CENTRAL AMERICAN–CARIBBEAN REGION DURING THE NINETEENTH CENTURY

6670. Andrews, W. *The Vanderbilt Legend.* N.Y., 1941.

6671. Arce, M. J. *Memoria del General Manuel José Arce, Primer Presidente de Centro América: Comentada por Modesto Barrios: Breves Indicaciones Sobre la Reorganisación de Centro América y Documentos Inéditos Relacionados con la Incorporación de la Provincia de Sonsonate al Estado de El Salvador.* San Salvador, 1947.

6672. Bancroft, H. H. *History of Central America.* 3 vols., San Francisco, 1882–1887.

6673. Bumgartner, L. E. *José del Valle of Central America.* Durham, N.C., 1963.

6674. Bunce, K. W. "American Interests in the Caribbean Islands, 1783–1850," Ohio State U. Diss., 1939.

6675. Chamberlain, R. S. *Francisco Morazán, Champion of Central American Federation.* Miami, 1950.

6676. Chamorro, P. J. *Historia de la Federación de la América Central, 1823–1840.* Madrid, 1951.

6677. Croffut, W. A. *The Vanderbilts and the Story of Their Fortune.* N.Y., 1882.

6678. Crowell, J. H. "Central American Relations of the United States, 1869–1877," Fletcher School of Law and Diplomacy Diss., 1959.

6679. Cuadra Ch., P. J. "La Nacionalidad Centro Americana y la Guerra del 63," *RAGHN* 10 (October, 1950) 101–132.

6680. Dunn, H. *Guatimala* [sic], *or, the United*

Provinces of Central America, in 1827–1828. N.Y., 1828.

6681. Fields, H. B. "The Central-American Federation, 1826–1839: A Political Study," U. of Chicago Diss., 1942.

6682. Jackson, H. F. "The Technological Development of Central America, 1823–1913," U. of Chicago Diss., 1948.

6683. Lane, W. J. *Commodore Vanderbilt*. N.Y., 1942.

6684. "La Unión Centroamericana en 1846," *RAN* 9 (July, 1945) 402–413.

6685. Lockey, J. B. "Diplomatic Futility," *HAHR* 10 (1930) 265–294.

United States relations with Central America prior to 1849.

6686. Martz, J. D. *Justo Rufino Barrios and Central American Union*. Gainesville, Fla., 1963.

6687. Marure, A. *Bosquejo Histórico de las Revoluciones de Centro América Desde 1811 Hasta 1834*. 2 vols., Guatemala, 1877–1888.

6688. Mejía Nieto, A. *Morazán Presidente de la Desaparecida República Centroamericana*. B.A., 1947.

6689. Montes, A. H. *Morazán y la Federación Centroamericana*. Mexico, 1958.

6690. Montúfar y Rivera Maestre, L. *Reseña Histórica de Centro-América*. 7 vols., Guatemala, 1878–1887.

Covers the period to 1860 from the liberal point of view.

6691. "Mr. E. G. Squier, Chargé d'Affaires, Central America," *AR* 6 (October, 1850) 345–352.

6692. Parker, F. D. *José Cecilio del Valle and the Establishment of the Central American Confederation*. Tegucigalpa, 1954.

6693. Rodríguez, M. *A Palmerstonian Diplomat in Central America: Frederick Chatfield, Esq*. Tuscon, Ariz., 1964.

Chatfield was the British agent in Central America from 1834 to 1852.

6694. Smith, R. S. "Financing the Central American Federation, 1821–1838," *HAHR* 43 (1963) 483–510.

6695. Sparks, D. "Central America and Its Diplomatic Relations with the U.S., 1860–1893," Duke U. Diss., 1934.

6696. Squier, E. G. *Notes on Central America: Particularly the States of Honduras and San Salvador*. N.Y., 1855.

6697. ———. "Our Foreign Relations: Central America—the Crampton and Webster Project," *DR* 31 (October, 1952) 337–352.

6698. ———. *The States of Central America*. N.Y., 1858.

6699. ———. *Travels in Central America*. 2 vols., N.Y., 1853.

6700. Stanger, F. M. "The Struggle for Nationality in Central America, 1810–1825," U. of California Diss., 1930.

6701. Stansifer, C. L. "The Central American Career of E. George Squier," Tulane U. Diss., 1959.

6702. Valdés Oliva, A. *Caminos y Luchas por la Independencia*. Guatemala, 1956.

6703. Valle, J. del, and J. del Valle Matheu (eds.). *Obras de José Cecilio del Valle*. 2 vols., Guatemala, 1929–1930.

6704. Valle, R. H. "George Ephraim Squier," *HAHR* 5 (1922) 777–789.

6705. Zuñiga Huete, A. *Morazán: Un Representativo de la Democracia Americana*. Mexico, 1947.

XIV–B   cross references:

a) For general accounts of filibustering during the nineteenth century, see items 2459–2493.

b) For general works on canal diplomacy in Central America, see items 2349–2368. For 1823–1850, see items 2369–2397a; for 1851–1870, see items 2398–2429; for 1871–1900, see items 2430–2458.

c) For British incursions on the Mosquito Coast see items 2183–2189.

d) See also item 1877.

C. THE UNITED STATES AND THE CENTRAL AMERICAN–CARIBBEAN REGION, 1900–1940

6706. Adams, F. U. *Conquest of the Tropics: The Story of the Creative Enterprises Conducted by the United Fruit Company*. N.Y., 1914.

6707. Anderson, C. P. "Our Policy of Non-Recognition in Central America," *AJIL* 25 (1931) 298–301.

6708. Anquizola, G. A. "Fifty Years of Isthmian-American Relations: An Analysis of the Causes Jeopardizing Isthmian-American Friendship," Indiana U. Diss., 1954.

6709. Araquistain, L. *La Agonía Antillana: El Imperialismo Yanqui en el Mar Caribe.* Madrid, 1928.

6710. Beals, C. *Banana Gold.* Phil., 1932.

6711. Blakeslee, G. H. (ed.). *Mexico and the Caribbean.* N.Y., 1920.
Series of articles on domestic affairs and international relations.

6712. Bonsal, S. *The American Mediterranean.* N.Y., 1913.

6713. Buell, R. L. "The Central Americas," *FPAP*, no. 69 (1930–1931).

6714. ———. "Union or Disunion in Central America," *FA* 11 (1933) 478–490.

6715. ———. "The United States and Central American Revolutions," *FPAR* 7 (1931–1932) 187–205.

6716. ———. "The United States and Central American Stability," *FPAR* 7 (1931–1932) 161–187.

6717. Callcott, W. H. *The Caribbean Policy of the United States, 1890–1920.* Baltimore, 1942.

6718. Campa y Caraveda, M. A. *Política Regional del Caribe.* Havana, 1944.

6719. Cestero, J. M. *Estados Unidos y las Antillas.* Madrid, 1931.

6720. Diez, W. E. "Opposition in the U.S. to American Diplomacy in the Caribbean, 1898–1932," U. of Chicago Diss., 1946.

6721. Emerson, E. "The Unrest in Central America," *IN* 67 (1909) 1286–1291.

6722. Eyma, J. *La Cour de Justice Centre-Américaine.* Paris, 1928.

6723. Gay Calbó, E. "Centroamérica Intervenida," *CC* 32 (1923) 126–137.

6724. Hall, R. G., Jr. "American Imperialism in Central America During the Taft-Knox Administration," Harvard U. Diss., 1948.

6725. Hopkins, J. A. H., and A. Melinda. *Machine-Gun Diplomacy.* N.Y., 1928.

6726. Howland, C. P. *American Relations in the Caribbean: A Preliminary Issue of Section I of the Annual Survey of American Foreign Relations, 1929.* New Haven, Conn., 1929.

6727. Hudson, M. O. "The Central American Court of Justice," *AJIL* 26 (1932) 759–786.

6728. Jones, C. L. *Caribbean Backgrounds and Prospects.* N.Y., 1931.
Considerable emphasis on United States' interests in the area.

6729. ———. *The Caribbean Interests of the United States.* N.Y., 1916.

6730. ———. *The Caribbean Since 1900.* N.Y., 1936.

6731. ———. "Loan Controls in the Caribbean," *HAHR* 14 (1934) 141–162.

6732. ———. "Oil on the Caribbean and Elsewhere," *NAR* 202 (1915) 536–543.

6733. ———, et al. *The United States and the Caribbean.* Chicago, 1929.

6734. Kepner, C. D., Jr. *Social Aspects of the Banana Industry.* N.Y., 1936.
Studies the results of fruit-company activity.

6735. ———, and J. H. Soothill. *The Banana Empire.* N.Y., 1953.
Spanish ed., Havana, 1961.

6736. Key, H. *Kaffee, Zucker und Bananen.* Munich, 1929.
A study of economic imperialism.

6737. Marvaud, A. "La Paix dans le Centre-Amérique," *QDC* 25 (1908) 691–712.

6738. Miller, H. G. *The Isthmian Highway: A Review of the Problems of the Caribbean.* N.Y., 1929.

6739. Mitchell, H. *Europe in the Caribbean: The Policies of Great Britain, France and the Netherlands Towards Their West Indian Territories in the Twentieth Century.* Stanford, Calif., 1963.

6740. Morales Padrón, F. "Estados Unidos en el Caribe," *EA* 21 (1961) 169–181.

6741. Munro, D. G. "Relations Between Central America and the United States," *IC*, no. 296 (1934) 22–30.

6742. ———. *The United States and the Caribbean Area.* Boston, 1934.

6743. Norton, H. K. "American Imperialism in the Indies," *WW* 51 (December, 1925) 210–218.

6744. ———. "Self-Determination in the West Indies," *WW* 51 (November, 1925) 77–84.

6745. Popper, D. H. "Progress of American Tariff Bargaining," *FPAR* 11 (1935) 58–68.
Treats trade negotiations with Cuba, Haiti, El Salvador, Guatemala, and Nicaragua.

6746. Rippy, J. F. "Fundamental Factors in Our Policy with Reference to the Gulf and Caribbean Area," *WA* 97 (1934) 173–175.

6747. Sáenz, A. *La Situación Bananera en los Países del Caribe*. San José, C.R., 1928.

6748. Sáenz, V. *Norteamericanización de Centro América*. San José, C.R., 1925.

6749. ———. *Rompiendo Cadenas: Las del Imperialismo en Centro América y en Otras Repúblicas del Continente*. 2d ed., Mexico, 1951.

    The chains to be broken are those which the United States uses to bind Central America politically and economically.

6750. Salin, J. *L'Evolution du Contrôle des Etats-Unis en Amérique Centrale et Caraibe*. Lyons, France, 1937.

6751. Scholes, W. V. "Los Estados Unidos, México, y América Central en 1909," *HM* 10 (1961) 613–627.

6752. Silva, J. "El Banco Central Inter-americano," *TI* 1 (January, 1940) 7–12.

6753. ———. "La Política Económica en América y la Creación de un Banco Central Inter-Americano," *REE* 2 (1940) 465–478.

6754. Stewart, M. E. "The Recognition Policy of the U.S. in Central America Since 1907," Clark U. Diss., 1933.

6755. Thompson, W. "The Doctrine of the 'Special Interest' of the United States in the Region of the Caribbean Sea," *AAAPSS* 132 (1927) 153–159.

6756. Villard, O. G. "Rights of Small Nations in America: The Republics of the Caribbean," *AAAPSS* 95 (1917) 165–171.

6757. Wilgus, A. C. (ed.). *The Caribbean Area*. Wash., 1934.

6758. Zubok, L. I. *Imperialisticheskaia Politika SShA v Stranakh Karaibskogo Basseina, 1900–1939*. Moscow, 1948.

    The Imperialistic Policy of the United States in the Countries of the Caribbean, 1900–1939.

XIV–C   cross references:

  a) For works on the Central American Peace Conference held in Washington (1907), see items 5128–5135.

  b) For works on the second Conference on Central American Affairs held in Washington (1922–1923), see items 5136–5143.

  c) See also items 2896, 2897, 2899, 2901, 2904, 2905, 2906, 2910, 2915, 2921, 2932, 2934, 2938, 2960, 2967, 2970, 3000, 3005, 3036, 3039, 3091, 3228, 3268, 3605, 6682.

D. THE UNITED STATES AND THE CENTRAL AMERICAN–CARIBBEAN REGION SINCE 1940

6759. Anderson, C. W. "Political Ideology and the Revolution of Rising Expectations in Central America: 1944–1958," U. of Wisconsin Diss., 1960.

6760. ———. "Politics and Development Policy in Central America," *MJPS* 5 (1961) 232–250.

6761. Bayo, A. *Tempestad en el Caribe*. Mexico, 1950.

6762. Blanshard, P. *Democracy and Empire in the Caribbean: A Contemporary Review*. N.Y., 1947.

    By an official of the Caribbean Commission.

6763. Bough, J. A. "The Caribbean Commission," *IO* 3 (1949) 643–655.

6764. Busey, J. L. "Central American Union: The Latest Attempt," *WPQ* 14 (1961) 49–63.

6765. "Central America's Post-War Exports to the United States," *EBLA* 5 (October, 1960) 24–56.

6766. Cochrane, J. D. "Political Aspects of the Formation and Functioning of the Central American Program of Economic Integration," U. of Iowa Diss., 1964.

6767. Corominas, E. V. *En las Areas Políticas del Caribe*. B.A., 1952.

6768. Coto Romero, R. *Visión de Centro América*. San Salvador, 1946.

    Believes that Central America should endeavor to free itself from United States influence.

6769. Ducoff, L. J. *Human Resources of Central America, Panama and Mexico, 1950–80, in Relation to Some Aspects of Economic Development*. N.Y., 1960.

6770. Duncan, J. "Demographic Factors and Economic Integration in Central America," *JIAS* 5 (October, 1963) 533–543.

6771. Etienne, F. *La Commission des Caraibes*. Paris, 1952.

Treats the organization and development of the Caribbean Commission.

6772. Fenwick, C. G. "The Meeting of Presidents at Panama," *AJIL* 51 (1957) 83–87.

The text of the Declaration of Panama is included.

6773. Fox, A. B. *Freedom and Welfare in the Caribbean: A Colonial Dilemma.* N.Y., 1949.

A comparison of United States and British policy in Caribbean possessions.

6774. Frazier, E. F., and E. Williams (eds.). *The Economic Future of the Caribbean.* Wash., 1944.

A collection of twelve papers.

6775. Gigax, W. R. "The Central American Common Market," *IEA* 16 (Autumn, 1962) 59–77.

6776. Guatemala. Ministerio de Relaciones Exteriores. *Actas Taquigráficas de las Sesiones Plenarias de la Primera Reunión de Ministros de Relaciones Exteriores de las Repúblicas Centroamericanas.* Guatemala, 1955.

6777. ———. ———. *Opinión Centroamericano a Propósito del Libro Belice, Tierra Irredenta.* Guatemala, 1944.

6778. Hanke, L. (ed.). *Mexico and the Caribbean.* Princeton, N.J., 1959.

Summary history and short readings.

6779. Jones, J. M. "Caribbean Laboratory: Study of New Mechanisms for International Collaboration," *FOR* 29 (February, 1944) 122–127, 256, 258.

6780. Krehm, W. *Democracia y Tiranías en el Caribe.* Mexico, 1949.

6781. LaBarge, R. A. "The Impact of the United Fruit Company on the Economic Development of Isthmian America, 1946–1956," Duke U. Diss., 1960.

6782. Martz, J. D. *Central America: The Crisis and the Challenge.* Chapel Hill, N.C., 1959.

6783. May, S., and G. Plaza. *The United Fruit Company in Latin America.* Wash., 1958.

6784. Murkland, H. B. "The Complicated Caribbean," *CH* 18 (January, 1950) 8–11.

6785. Organización de Estados Centoamericanos. *Primer Seminario de Integración Económica Centroamericana.* Guatemala, 1959.

6786. ———. *Primera Reunión de Ministros de Relaciones Exteriores de las Repúblicas Centroamericanas, 17 de Agosto de 1955.* Guatemala, 1956(?).

6787. ———. *Reunión de Ministros de Relaciones Exteriores de Centroamérica: Acta Final Celebrada en la Ciudad de la Antigua, Guatemala, del 17 al 24 de Agosto de 1955.* Guatemala, 1955.

6788. Padelford, N. J. "Cooperation in the Central American Region: The Organization of Central American States," *IO* 11 (Winter, 1957) 41–54.

6789. Pincus, J. *The Central American Common Market.* Mexico, 1962.

6790. ———. *Historical Background and Objectives of the Central American Common Market.* Tegucigalpa, 1962.

6791. Pollan, A. A. *The United Fruit Company and Middle America.* N.Y., 1943(?).

6792. Poole, B. L. *The Caribbean Commission: Background of Cooperation in the West Indies.* Columbia, S.C., 1951.

6793. Rickards, C. *Caribbean Power.* London, 1963.

Journalist's account of the islands and mainland republics. Best for the English-speaking areas.

6794. Sáenz, V. *Centro América en Pie.* Mexico, 1944.

6795. Stockdale, F. "The Work of the Caribbean Commission," *IAF* 23 (1947) 213–220.

6796. UN. Economic Commission for Latin America. *Analysis and Prospects of Inter-Central American Trade.* Bogotá, 1955.

6797. ———. ———. *Cuestiones Fiscales, de Político Comercial y Metodológicas Relacionadas con la Formación del Mercado Común Centroamericano.* N.Y., 1959.

6798. ———. ———. *Examen Preliminar de las Posibilidades de Desarrollo Industrial Integrado en Centroamérica.* Santiago, 1963.

6799. ———. ———. *Informe del Comité de Cooperación Económica del Istmo Centroamericano, 3 de Septiembre de 1959 a 13 de Diciembre de 1960.* Mexico, 1961.

6800. ———. ———. Committee on Economic Cooperation in Central America. *Compendio Estadístico Centroamericano.* Mexico, 1957.

6800a. USCS. Committee on Commerce. *Second Transisthmian Canal: Hearings* (88th Cong., 2d Sess.). Wash., 1964.

6801. USDC. Bureau of Foreign Commerce. *Investment in Central America: Basic Information for United States Businessmen.* Wash., 1957.

6802. Valle, R. H. *Historia de las Ideas Contemporáneas en Centro-América.* Mexico, 1960.

6803. Wilgus, A. C. (ed.). *The Caribbean at Mid-Century.* Gainesville, Fla., 1951.

6804. ——— (ed.). *The Caribbean: British, Dutch, French, United States.* Gainesville, Fla., 1958.

6805. ——— (ed.). *The Caribbean: Contemporary Education.* Gainesville, Fla., 1960.

6806. ——— (ed.). *The Caribbean: Contemporary International Relations.* Gainesville, Fla., 1957.

6807. ——— (ed.). *The Caribbean: Contemporary Trends.* Gainesville, Fla., 1953.

6807a. ——— (ed.). *The Caribbean: Current United States Relations.* Gainesville, Fla., 1966.
Essays on diplomatic, economic, and cultural relations.

6808. ——— (ed.). *The Caribbean: Its Culture.* Gainesville, Fla., 1955.

6809. ——— (ed.). *The Caribbean: Its Economy.* Gainesville, Fla., 1954.

6810. ——— (ed.). *The Caribbean: Its Health Problems.* Gainesville, Fla., 1965.

6811. ——— (ed.). *The Caribbean: Its Political Problems.* Gainesville, Fla., 1956.

6812. ——— (ed.). *The Caribbean: Natural Resources.* Gainesville, Fla., 1959.

6813. ——— (ed.). *The Caribbean: Peoples, Problems, and Prospects.* Gainesville, Fla., 1952.

6814. ——— (ed.). *The Caribbean: The Central American Area.* Gainesville, Fla., 1961.

6815. Wilson, C. M. *Challenge and Opportunity: Central America.* N.Y., 1941.

6816. ———. *Empire in Green and Gold.* N.Y., 1947.
Favorable to the United Fruit Company.

6817. Wylie, K. *Central America as a Market and Competitor for U.S. Agriculture.* Wash., 1957.

6818. Zea González, E. "Reflexiones Sobre la Unión de Centro-América," *RGUA* 4 (April, 1946) 52–61.

XIV–D   cross references:

a) For works on this area relating to World War II, see items 3647–3667.

b) See also items 3707, 3964a, 4364, 6739.

E. THE UNITED STATES AND GUATEMALA

1. United States–Guatemalan Relations: General Works and Special Studies

6819. Fergusson, E. *Guatemala.* N.Y., 1937.

6820. Holleran, M. P. *Church and State in Guatemala.* N.Y., 1949.

6821. Jensen, A. E. *Guatemala: A Historical Survey.* N.Y., 1955.

6822. Jones, C. L. *Guatemala, Past and Present.* Minneapolis, 1940.

6823. Kelsey, V., and L. de Jongh Osborne. *Four Keys to Guatemala.* N.Y., 1939.

6824. Mendoza, J. L. (comp.). *Tratados y Convenciones Internacionales Vigentes para Guatemala.* Guatemala, 1958.

6825. Moreno, L. *Derecho Consular Guatemalteco.* Guatemala, 1946.

6826. Mosk, S. A. "The Coffee Economy of Guatemala, 1850–1918: Development and Signs of Instability," *IEA* 9 (Winter, 1955) 6–20.

6827. Muñoz, J., and A. B. Ward. *Guatemala: Ancient and Modern.* N.Y., 1940.

6828. Rodríguez Cerna, J. (comp.). *Colección de Tratados de Guatemala.* 3 vols., Guatemala, 1939–1944.
The first volume lists treaties with other Central American countries; the second with other countries in the hemisphere; and the third treats inter-American agreements to which Guatemala is a party.

6829. ———. *Nuestro Derecho Internacional: Sinopsis de Tratados y Anotaciones Históricas, 1821–1937.* Guatemala, 1938.

6830. Rosenthal, M. *Guatemala, The Story of an Emergent Latin American Democracy.* N.Y., 1962.

6831. Sensabaugh, L. F. "American Interest in the Mexican-Guatemalan Boundary Dispute," Johns Hopkins U. Diss., 1928.

6832. Valenzuela Reyna, G. *Guatemala y sus Gobernantes, 1821–1958: Recopilación.* Guatemala, 1959.

6833. Villacorta Calderón, J. A. *Historia de la República de Guatemala, 1821–1921.* Guatemala, 1960.

6834. Whetten, N. L. *Guatemala: The Land and the People.* New Haven, Conn., 1961.

2. UNITED STATES–GUATEMALAN RELATIONS: NINETEENTH CENTURY

6835. Barker, C. A. (ed.). *Memoirs of Elisha Oscar Crosby: Reminiscences of California and Guatemala from 1849 to 1864.* San Marino, Calif., 1945.

6836. Beck, W. A. "American Policy in Guatemala, 1839–1900," Ohio State U. Diss., 1954.

6837. Brigham, W. T. *Guatemala: The Land of the Quetzal.* London, 1887.

6838. Burgess, P. *Justo Rufino Barrios: A Biography.* Phil., 1926.
President of Guatemala, 1873–1885.

6839. Chapman, M. P. "The Mission of Elisha O. Crosby to Guatemala, 1861–1864," *PHR* 24 (1955) 275–286.

6840. ———. "The Mission of Lansing Bond Mizner to Central America," *HIS* 19 (1957) 385–401.
Blaine's minister was in Guatemala from 1889 to 1890.

6841. Maudslay, A. C., and A. P. Maudslay. *A Glimpse at Guatemala.* London, 1899.

6842. Moorhead, M. L. "Rafael Carrera of Guatemala: His Life and Times," U. of California Diss., 1943.
Carrera was President of Guatemala from 1854 to 1865.

6843. Raine, A. *Eagle of Guatemala, Justo Rufino Barrios, 1835–1885.* N.Y., 1947.

6843a. Rippy, J. F. "Justo Rufino Barrios," in A. C. Wilgus (ed.). *Hispanic American Essays.* Chapel Hill, N.C., 1943.

6844. ———. "Relations of the United States and Guatemala During the Epoch of Justo Rufino Barrios," *HAHR* 22 (1942) 595–605.

6845. Rubio, C. D. *Biografía del General Justo Rufino Barrios, Reformador de Guatemala.* Guatemala, 1935.

6846. Thompson, G. A. *Narrative of an Official Visit to Guatemala from Mexico.* London, 1829.

6847. Williford, M. "The Reform Program of Dr. Mariano Gálvez, Chief-of-State of Guatemala, 1831–1838," Tulane U. Diss., 1963.

6847a. Woodward, R. L., Jr. "Guatemalan Cotton and the American Civil War," *IEA* 18, no. 3 (1965) 87–94.

XIV–E–2 cross references: 5993, 5995

3. UNITED STATES–GUATEMALAN RELATIONS: TWENTIETH CENTURY

6847b. Adams, R. N. "Social Change in Guatemala and U.S. Policy," in Adams, *et al. Social Change in Latin America Today,* 231–284.
See item 3976.

6848. Adler, J. H., *et al. Public Finance and Economic Development in Guatemala.* Stanford, Calif., 1952.

6849. Alvarez Elizondo, P. *El Presidente Arévalo y el Retorno a Bolívar.* Mexico, 1947.
Sympathetic biographical treatment.

6850. Arévalo, J. J. *Discursos en la Presidencia, 1945–1947.*
A collection of Arévalo's speeches.

6851. ———. *Escritos Políticos.* 2d ed., Guatemala, 1946.

6852. ———. *Escritos Políticos y Discursos.* Havana, 1953.

6853. ———. *Guatemala, la Democracia y el Imperio.* Mexico, 1954.

6854. Arrocha, A. *Juan José Arévalo, Pensador Contemporáneo.* Mexico, 1962.

6855. Baker, G. W., Jr. "The Woodrow Wilson Administration and Guatemalan Relations," *HIS* 27 (1965) 155–169.

6856. Barrington and Company (New York). *Industrial Development of Guatemala.* N.Y., 1962.
Special study prepared for the government of Guatemala and the United States Operations Mission to Guatemala.

6857. Bauer Paíz, A. *Como Opera el Capital Yanqui en Centroamérica: El Caso de Guatemala.* Mexico, 1956.
A denunciation of the United Fruit Company.

6858. Bishop, E. W. "The Guatemalan Labor Movement, 1944–1959," U. of Wisconsin Diss., 1959.

6859. Britnell, G. E. "Factors in the Economic

Development of Guatemala," *AER* 43 (May, 1953) 104–114.

6860. Britnell, G. E. "Problems of Economic and Social Change in Guatemala," *CJE* 17 (1951) 468–481.

6860a. Brown, H. L. "Points for Exporters to Guatemala," *CIJ* 52 (1935) 103–110.

6861. Burbank, A. *Guatemala Profile.* N.Y., 1939.

6862. Bush, A. C. *Organized Labor in Guatemala, 1944–1949.* Hamilton, N.Y., 1950.

6863. Cardoza y Aragón, L. "Guatemala y el Imperio Bananero," *CA* 74 (March, 1954) 19–45.
Treats United Fruit Company's activities.

6864. ———. *La Revolución Guatemalteca.* Mexico, 1955.

6865. Castellanos, J. H. R. "Caída del Comunismo en Guatemala," *ECA* (October, 1954) 519–525.

6866. Castello, J. *Así Cayó la Democracia en Guatemala: La Guerra de la United Fruit.* Havana, 1961.

6867. Castillo Armas, C. *La Realidad de un Mensaje: Pláticas Presidenciales.* Guatemala, 1957.
A series of Castillo Armas' speeches as President of Guatemala, 1954–1957.

6868. Castro, J. *Bombas y Dólares Sobre Guatemala.* Montevideo, 1954.

6869. Coronado Lira, L. *Escritos Políticos Totalitarismo Espiritualista: Tres Panoramas y un Caso de Nacionalidad.* Alajuela, C.R., 1946.
Indictment of the Arévalo administration by a Guatemalan exile.

6870. Guatemala. Departamento de Publicidad de la Presidencia de la República. *Cruceros Británicos Amenazan a Guatemala: Mensajes Enviados al Gobierno de la República Expresando Solidaridad y Simpatía con Oportunidad de la Presencia de Grandes Barcos de Guerra Ingleses en Aguas de Belice.* Guatemala, 1948.

6871. Cumberland, C. C. "Guatemala: Labor and the Communists," *CH* 24 (March, 1953) 143–148.

6872. Díaz Rozzotto, J. *El Carácter de la Revolución Guatemalteca: Ocaso de la Revolución Democrático-Burguesa Corriente.* Mexico, 1958.

6873. Dion, M. B. *Las Ideas Sociales y Políticas de Arévalo.* Mexico, 1958.

6874. Dulles, J. F. *Intervention of International Communism in Guatemala.* Wash., 1954.
Text of a radio and television address on June 30, 1954, by the secretary of state.

6875. El Salvador. Secretaría de Información. *De la Neutralidad Vigilante a la Mediación con Guatemala.* San Salvador, 1954.

6876. Fenwick, C. G. "Jurisdictional Questions Involved in the Guatemalan Revolution," *AJIL* 48 (1954) 597–602.

6877. Frei, E. *Las Relaciones con los Estados Unidos y el Caso Guatemala.* Santiago, 1944.
The leader of the Chilean Christian Democrats expresses concern over United States policy.

6878. Galich, M. *Del Pánico al Ataque.* Guatemala, 1949.

6879. ———. *¿Por Qué Lucha Guatemala? Arévalo y Arbenz, Dos Hombres Contra un Imperio.* B.A., 1956.
Author was Arbenz' secretary of foreign relations.

6880. Gandarias, L. de (ed.). *Democracia, la Mejor Arma Contra el Comunismo.* Guatemala, 1957.

6881. García, L. G. *Las Luchas Revolucionarias de la Nueva Guatemala.* Mexico, 1952.

6882. Geiger, T. *Communism Versus Progress in Guatemala.* Wash., 1953.
Spanish ed., Wash., 1953.

6883. Gillin, J., and K. H. Silvert. "Ambiguities in Guatemala," *FA* 34 (1956) 469–482.

6883a. Gómez Robles, J. *A Statement of the Laws of Guatemala in Matters Affecting Business.* Wash., 1961.

6884. Grant, D. "Guatemala and United States Foreign Policy," *JIA* 9 (1955) 64–72.

6885. Great Britain. Foreign Office. *Report on Events Leading Up to and Arising Out of the Change of Regime in Guatemala, 1954.* London, 1954.

6886. Guatemala. *Discursos del Doctor Juan José Arévalo y del Teniente Coronel Jacobo Arbenz Guzmán en el Acto de Transmisión de la Presidencia de la República, 15 de Marzo de 1951.* Guatemala, 1951.

6887. ———. Secretaría de Divulgación Cultura y Turismo. *Así se Gestó la Liberación.* Guatemala, 1956.

Collected documents on the overthrow of Arbenz.

6888. Hildebrand, J. R. "Latin-American Economic Development, Land Reform, and U.S. Aid with Special Reference to Guatemala," *JIAS* 4 (1962) 351–361.

6889. Inman, S. G. *A New Day in Guatemala: A Study of the Present Social Revolution.* Wilton, Conn., 1951.

6890. International Bank for Reconstruction and Development. *The Economic Development of Guatemala: Report of a Mission Sponsored by the International Bank for Reconstruction and Development in Collaboration with the Government of Guatemala.* Wash., 1951.

6891. James, D. *Red Design for the Americas: Guatemalan Prelude.* N.Y., 1954.

Spanish ed., Mexico, 1955.

6892. Katz, F. "Der Sturz der Demokratischen Regierung in Guatemala im Jahre 1954," *WZHUB* 9 (1959–1960) 45–52.

6893. LaBarge, R. A. *Impact of the United Fruit Company on the Economic Development of Guatemala, 1946–1954.* New Orleans, 1960.

6894. León Aragón, O. de. *Los Contratos de la United Fruit Company y las Compañías Muelleras en Guatemala.* Guatemala, 1950.

6894a. *El Libro Negro del Comunismo en Guatemala.* Mexico, 1954.

Published by the Misión Permanente of the Congreso Contra la Intervención Soviética en América Latina.

6895. López Villatoro, M. *Por los Fueros de la Verdad Histórica: Una Voz de la Patria Escarnecida, Guatemala, ante la Diatriba de Uno de Sus Hijos Renegados.* Guatemala, 1956.

6896. ———. *¿Por Qué Fué Derrotado el Comunismo en Guatemala?* Guatemala, 195?

6897. Martz, J. D. *Communist Infiltration in Guatemala.* N.Y., 1956.

6898. Mejía, M. *Juan José Arévalo o el Humanismo en la Presidencia.* Guatemala, 1951.

6899. ———. *El Movimiento Obrero en la Revolución de Octubre.* Guatemala, 1949.

6900. Monroe, K. "Guatemala: What the Reds Left Behind," *HA* 211 (July, 1955) 60–65.

6901. Muñoz Meany, E. *El Hombre y la Encrucijada.* Guatemala, 1950.

Collected speeches of the Guatemalan foreign minister.

6902. Nájera Farfán, M. E. *Los Estafadores de la Democracia: Hombres y Hechos en Guatemala.* B.A., 1956.

Critical appraisal of the Arévalo administration.

6903. Newbold, S. [pseudonym]. "Receptivity to Communist-Fomented Agitation in Rural Guatemala," *EDCC* 5 (July, 1957) 338–361.

6904. Ordóñez Arguello, A. (ed.). *Arévalo Visto por América.* Guatemala, 1951.

6905. Osegueda, R. *Operación Guatemala $$ OK $$.* Mexico, 1955.

6906. Partido Guatemalteco del Trabajo. Comisión Política. *La Intervención Norteamericana y el Derrocamiento del Régimen Democrático.* Guatemala, 1955.

6907. Payne, W. A. "Guatemala: A Challenge and an Opportunity," *WA* 116 (Summer, 1953) 38–41.

6907a. Pellecer, C. M. *Renuncia al Comunismo.* Mexico, 1963.

6908. Pike, F. B. "Guatemala, the United States, and Communism in the Americas," *RP* 17 (1955) 232–261.

6908a. Raygada, J. *Democracia en Guatemala, 20 de Octubre de 1944–15 de Marzo de 1951.* Guatemala, 1951.

6909. Ruiz Franco, A. *Hambre y Miseria: Fermentos de Lucha.* Guatemala, 1950.

6910. Salazar, C. *La Muerte del Gral. Regalado: La Campaña de 1906.* Guatemala, 1956.

6911. Samayoa Chinchilla, C. *El Quetzal no Es Rojo.* Guatemala, 1956.

6912. Schneider, R. M. *Communism in Guatemala: 1944–1954.* N.Y., 1958.

6913. Silvert, K. H. *A Study in Government: Guatemala, National and Local Government Since 1944.* 3 vols., New Orleans, 1954.

6914. Simons, C. E. "El Comunismo en Guatemala," *ESC* 2 (September, 1954) 96–102.

6915. Suslow, L. A. *Aspects of Social Reforms in Guatemala, 1944–1949.* Hamilton, N.Y., 1949.

6916. Taylor, P. B. "The Guatemala Affair: A

Critique of United States Foreign Policy," *APSR* 50 (1956) 787–806.

6917. Toriello Garrido, G. *La Batalla de Guatemala*. Mexico, 1955.

Guatemalan minister during the Arbenz administration.

6918. UN. Economic and Social Council. Economic Commission for Latin America. *Economic Development of Guatemala*. Mexico, 1951.

6919. USCH. Committee on Foreign Affairs. *Report of the Special Study Mission to Guatemala, Washington, D.C.* (85th Cong., 1st Sess., H. Rept. 207). Wash., 1957.

6920. USDS. *A Case History of Communist Penetration: Guatemala*. Wash., 1957.

6921. ———. Office of Public Services. *Guatemala, Fact Sheet: Aid in Action*. Wash., 1961.

6922. United States Tariff Commission. *Economic Controls and Commercial Policy in Guatemala*. Wash., 1947.

6923. Valle Matheu, J. del. *La Verdad Sobre el "Caso de Guatemala."* Guatemala, 1956.

6924. Whitaker, A. P. "Guatemala, OAS and U.S.," *FPAB* 33 (September, 1954) 4–7.

6924a. Woodward, R. L., Jr. "Octubre: Communist Appeal to the Urban Labor Force of Guatemala, 1950–1953," *JIAS* 4 (July, 1962) 363–374.

6925. Ydígoras Fuentes, M., with M. Rosenthal. *My War with Communism*. Englewood Cliffs, N.J., 1963.

The president of Guatemala from 1958 to 1963 discusses Castroite agitation in his country.

XIV–E–3 cross references:

a) For the arbitration of the Guatemalan boundary dispute with Honduras, see items 7016–7027.

b) See also items 7218, 10037.

4. THE ANGLO-GUATEMALAN (BELICE) DISPUTE

6926. Aguilar, S. "Arbitraje Sobre Belice," *ASGHG* 16 (1940) 442–483.

6927. Aguirre Godoy, M. "Sobre la Cuestión de Belice," *RFCJSG* (April, 1949) 59–72.

6928. Alvarado, R. *La Cuestión de Belice*. Quito, 1948.

6929. Alvarez Lejarza, E. "Belice Es Tierra de Guatemala," *ASGHG* 17 (1941) 52–61.

6929a. Anderson, L. "Estudio Jurídico Acerca de la Controversia Entre Guatemala y la Gran Bretaña Relativa a la Convención de 30 de Abril de 1859 Sobre Asuntos Territoriales," *RDI*, no. 70 (1939) 163–231.

The Guatemalan point of view.

6930. Asturias, F. *Belice*. 2d ed., Guatemala, 1941.

6931. Bianchi, W. J. *Belize: The Controversy Between Guatemala and Great Britain over the Territory of British Honduras in Central America*. N.Y., 1959.

6932. Bloomfield, L. M. *The British Honduras–Guatemalan Dispute*. Toronto, 1953.

6933. Burdon, J. A. (ed.). *Archives of British Honduras*. 3 vols., London, 1931–1935.

6934. Caiger, S. L. *British Honduras, Past and Present*. London, 1951.

6935. Castellanos Sánchez, M. *La Cuestión de Belice*. Mexico, 1897.

6936. Clegern, W. M. "The International Role of British Honduras, 1859–1900," U. of California Diss., 1960.

6937. ———. "New Light on the Belize Dispute," *AJIL* 52 (1958) 280–297.

6938. Cravioto, A. *La Paz de América: Guatemala y Belice*. Mexico, 1943.

The author, a Mexican, argues for the return of Belice to Guatemala.

6939. Fabela, I. *Belice, Defensa de los Derechos de México*. Mexico, 1944.

States the Mexican claims to British Honduras.

6940. Gall, F. *Belice, Tierra Nuestra*. Guatemala, 1962.

6941. Gálvez, G. S. *El Caso de Belice a la Luz de la Historia y el Derecho Internacional*. Guatemala, 1941.

6942. García Bauer, C. "Beliza: Problema de América," *RBPI* 4 (March, 1961) 37–60.

6943. ———. *La Controversia Sobre el Territorio de Belice y el Procedimiento "ex-aequo et bono."* Guatemala, 1958.

A legalistic analysis.

6944. Giannini, A. "La Questione del Territorio di Belice," *RSPI* 27 (1960) 183–206.

6945. Giles, B. W. "The Belize Question: A Problem of Anti-Colonialism in the New World," Yale U. Diss., 1956.

6946. González-Blanco, P. *El Problema de Belice y sus Alivios*. Mexico, 1950.

6947. Guatemala. Ministerio de Relaciones Exteriores. *Belice Pertenece a Guatemala: La Propaganda Británica Tergiversa la Historia*. Guatemala, 1947.

6948. ———. ———. *El Caso de Belice ante la Conciencia de América*. Guatemala, 1948.

6949. ———. ———. *La Controversia Sobre Belice Durante el Año de 1946*. Guatemala, 1948.

6950. ———. ———. *Puntos Capitales que Sostiene el Gobierno de Guatemala en la Controversia Anglo-Guatemalteca para Reivindicar el Territorio de Belice*. Guatemala, 1950.

6951. ———. ———. *White Book: Controversy Between Guatemala and Great Britain Relative to the Convention of 1859 on Territorial Matters*. Guatemala, 1938.

6952. Humphreys, R. A. "The Anglo-Guatemalan Dispute," *IAF* 24 (July, 1948) 387–404.

6953. ———. *The Diplomatic History of British Honduras, 1638–1901*. London, 1961.

6954. Hurtado Aguilar, L. A. *Belice Es de Guatemala: Tratados, Situación Jurídica, Actuaciones, Opiniones*. Guatemala, 1958.

6955. Juárez Muñoz, J. F. "Belice Es Nuestro," *RFCJSG* 2 (1939) 557–561.

6956. Kunz, J. L. "Guatemala vs. Great Britain: In re Belice," *AJIL* 40 (1946) 383–390.
    Contains a commentary on sources.

6957. López, F. M. *Quiebra y Reintegración del Derecho de Gentes: Gibraltar, Belice, Las Malvinas*. Guatemala, 1958(?).

6958. López Jiménez, R. *Belice, Tierra Irredenta*. Mexico, 1943.

6959. Marín, R. "El Rapto de Belice a Guatemala, Problema de América," *RFCJSG* 6 (July, 1958) 21–62.

6960. ———. *Los Tres Bombas de Tiempo en América Latina*. 2d ed., Guatemala, 1959.

6961. Martínez Alomía, S. "Belice," *RCAM* 3 (May, 1945) 141–173; 4 (July, 1945) 127–179; 5 (September, 1945) 121–143.

6962. Martínez Palafox, L. *La Cuestión de Belice, Relación Documental*. Mexico, 1944.

6963. Mendoza, J. L. *Inglaterra y sus Pactos Sobre Belice: Guatemala Tiene Derecho a Revindicar el Territorio Integro de Belice*. Guatemala, 1942.
    English ed., Guatemala, 1946.

6964. Pasos, G. *Belice: Patrimonio de Guatemala*. Granada, 1944.

6965. Pérez Trejo, G. A. (ed.). *Documentos Sobre Belice o Balice*. Mexico, 1958.
    Documents supporting the Mexican claim.

6966. Prato y Beltrán, A. *Visión Actual de Belice*. Mexico, 1958.

6967. Rodríguez Beteta, V. *El Libro de Guatemala Grande: Petín-Belice*. 2 vols., Guatemala, 1951.

6968. Santiso Gálvez, G. *El Caso de Belice a la Luz de la Historia y el Derecho Internacional: La Condición Resolutoria Tácita por Incumplimiento en los Tratados Internacionales*. Guatemala, 1941.

6969. Sharpe, R. *British Honduras: Report of an Inquiry Held by Sir Reginald Sharpe into Allegations of Contacts Between the People's United Party and Guatemala*. London, 1954.

6970. Smith, R. E., and A. Goubaud Carrera. *Opinion of the Geographical and Historical Society of Guatemala on Guatemala's Right to British Honduras*. 2d ed., Guatemala, 1939.

6971. Termer, F. "Guatemala und Britisch-Honduras: Ein Landstreit," *IAA* 14 (April, 1940) 44–67.

6972. Urrutia Aparicio, C. *Juridical Aspects of the Anglo-Guatemalan Controversy: In re Belize*. Wash., 1951.

6973. Vela, D. *Nuestro Belice*. Guatemala, 1939.

6974. Villaseñor y Villaseñor, A. *La Cuestión de Belice*. Mexico, 1894.

6975. Waddell, D. A. G. "As Honduras Británicas e a Reivindição Guatemalteca," *RBPI* 4 (September, 1961) 55–71.

6976. ———. *British Honduras*. N.Y., 1961.

6977. ———. "More on the Belize Question," *HAHR* 40 (1960) 230–233.

XIV–E–4 cross references:

For the nineteenth-century background of the Belice controversy, see items 2183–2189.

F. THE UNITED STATES AND HONDURAS

1. GENERAL WORKS AND SPECIAL STUDIES

6978. Anderson, C. P. *Nicaragua-Honduras Boundary Mediation.* N.p., 1920.
Anderson was the counsel for Nicaragua.

6979. Baker, G. W., Jr. "Ideas and Realities in the Wilson Administration's Relations with Honduras," *TA* 21 (July, 1964) 3–19.

6980. Banco Central de Honduras. *Historia Financiera de Honduras: Informes de las Misiones.* Tegucigalpa, 1957.

6981. Bones, Q. A. *Geografía e Historia de Honduras.* Choluteca, 1927.

6982. Bradley, D. H. "Honduras Faces Its 'Unsold Bananas' Problem," *FCW* 11, no. 1 (1943) 5–8, 34.

6983. Canales Salazar, F. *Derechos Territoriales de la República de Honduras Sobre Honduras Británica o Belice, Islas del Cisne y Costas de los Indios Mosquitos.* Mexico, 1946.

6984. Cecil, C. *Honduras: The Land of Great Depths.* Chicago, 1890.
Discusses U.S. capital investment in Honduras.

6985. Checchi, V., and Associates. *Honduras: A Problem in Economic Development.* N.Y., 1959.
An analysis of problems and suggested solutions.

6986. Córdova, S. "The Meaning of the Monroe Doctrine to Honduras," *AAAPSS* suppl. 111 (1924) 32–33.

6987. Deutsch, H. B. *The Incredible Yanqui: The Career of Lee Christmas.* London, 1931.
Discusses the attempt to make Honduras a protectorate.

6988. Durón y Gamero, R. E. *Bosquejo Histórico de Honduras.* 2d ed., Tegucigalpa, 1956.

6989. ———. *Historia de Honduras Desde la Independencia Hasta Nuestros Días.* Tegucigalpa, 1956– .
First volume of a multi-volume project.

6990. ———. "José Cecilio de Valle, Foremost Figure in Honduran History," *BPAU* 69 (1935) 38–45.

6991. Fitzroy, R. *Report of Captain Robert Fitzroy, R.N., to the Earl of Clarendon on the Proposed Honduras Interoceanic Railway.* London, 1856.

6992. Herrán, V. *Documentos Oficiales Sobre los Empréstitos de Honduras.* Paris, 1884.

6993. *Homenaje a la Memoria del General Don Luis Molina en el LXXIII Aniversario de su Nacimiento.* Guatemala, 1909.
The Honduran minister to the U.S., 1860–1867.

6994. Honduras. *Tratados Internacionales: Período Colonial, República Federal de Centro América y Tratados Bilaterales con Costa Rica.* Tegucigalpa, 1954.

6995. *Índice de los Tratados Celebrados por Honduras.* Tegucigalpa, 1935.

6996. Johnson, W. E. "The Honduras-Nicaragua Boundary Dispute, 1957–1963: The Peaceful Settlement of an International Conflict," U. of Denver Diss., 1964.

6997. López Pineda, J. *Democracia y Redentorismo.* Managua, 1942.

6998. ———. *El General Morazán: Ensayo Biográfico.* Tegucigalpa, 1944.

6999. Mayes, G. *Honduras en la Independencia de Centro América y Anexión a México.* Tegucigalpa, 1956.

7000. Rodríguez González, S. "The Neutrality of Honduras and the Question of the Gulf of Fonseca," *AJIL* 10 (1916) 509–542.

7001. Rosenberger, D. G. "An Examination of the Perpetuation of Southern U.S. Institutions in British Honduras by a Colony of Ex-Confederates," New York U. Diss., 1958.

7002. Ross, D. F. "The Economic Development of Honduras," Harvard U. Diss., 1956.

7003. Somarriba-Salazar, J. *Les Limites Entre le Nicaragua et le Honduras.* Leiden, The Netherlands, 1962.

7004. Somberg, S. I. "A Program for Fostering the Economic Growth and Development of the Republic of Honduras Through Investments in Forestry," Duke U. Diss., 1962.

7005. Squier, E. G. *Apuntamientos Sobre Centro-América, Particularmente Sobre los Estados de Honduras y San Salvador.* Paris, 1856.

7006. ———. *Honduras: Descriptive, Historical, and Statistical.* London, 1870.

7007.   ———. *Honduras Interoceanic Railway: With Appendix Containing Report of Admiral Fitzroy, the Charter, Treaties, etc.* London, 1857.

7008.   ———. *Preliminary Notes to a Report on the Proposed Honduras Interoceanic Railway.* N.Y., 1854.

7009.   Stansifer, C. L. "E. George Squier and the Honduras Interoceanic Railroad Project," *HAHR* 46 (1966) 1–27.

7010.   Stokes, W. S. *Honduras: An Area Study in Government.* Madison, Wis., 1950.

7011.   ———. "Honduras: Problems and Prospects," *CH* (January, 1966) 22–26.

7012.   United States Tariff Commission. *Economic Controls and Commercial Policy in Honduras.* Wash., 1947.

7013.   Vallejo, A. R. *Compendio de la Historia Social y Política de Honduras.* 2 vols., Tegucigalpa, 1882–1883.

7014.   Wells, N. V. *Explorations and Adventures in Honduras.* N.Y., 1857.

7015.   Wright, T. P., Jr. "Honduras: A Case Study of United States Support of Free Elections in Central America," *HAHR* 40 (1960) 212–223.

XIV–F–1   cross references: 2476, 4193, 6696, 7148

2. The Honduran–Guatemalan Boundary Dispute

7016.   Castro Serrano, C. *Nuestra Cuestión de Límites con Guatemala.* Tegucigalpa, 1927.

7017.   Comisión Interamericana de Paz. *Informe Sobre la Controversia Entre Guatemala, Honduras, y Nicaragua.* Wash., 1954.

7018.   Fisher, F. C. "The Arbitration of the Guatemalan-Honduran Boundary Dispute," *AJIL* 27 (1933) 403–427.

7019.   *Fronteras de Honduras, Límites con Guatemala.* 3 vols., Tegucigalpa, 1929–1930.

7020.   Furnes Cerrato, M. *La Cuestión de Límites Entre Honduras y Guatemala.* San Salvador, 1928.

7021.   Guatemala. *Arbitraje de Límites Entre Guatemala y Honduras: Alegato Presentada por Guatemala ante el Tribunal de Arbitraje Integrado por el Honorable Charles Evans Hughes, Presidente de la Corte Suprema de Justicia de los Estados Unidos de América, Honorable Luis Castro Ureña, de Costa Rica, y Honorable Emilio Bello Codesido, de Chile, bajo las Estipulaciones de Tratado de 16 Julio de 1930.* Wash., 1932.

7022.   ———. *Guatemala-Honduras Boundary Arbitration: The Counter Case of Guatemala Submitted to the Arbitral Tribunal Composed of the Hon. Charles Evans Hughes, Chief Justice of the United States of America; Hon. Luis Castro Ureña, from Costa Rica; Hon. Emilio Bello Codesido, from Chile. Under Treaty of July 16, 1930.* 2 vols., Wash., 1932.

7023.   ———. Ministry of Foreign Affairs. *The Boundary Dispute Between Guatemala and Honduras.* Guatemala, 1928.

7024.   Medardo Zúniga, V. *La Cuestión de Límites.* Tegucigalpa, 1927.

7025.   *Mediation of the Honduran-Guatemalan Boundary Question.* 2 vols., Wash., 1919–1920.

7026.   Platt, R. R. "The Guatemala-Honduras Boundary Dispute," *FA* 7 (1929) 323–326.

7027.   Special Boundary Tribunal. *Guatemala-Honduras Boundary Arbitration: Opinion and Award.* Wash., 1933.

XIV–F–2   cross references: 6666

G. THE UNITED STATES AND NICARAGUA

1. United States–Nicaraguan Relations: General Works and Special Studies

7028.   Alvarez, E. *Las Constituciones de Nicaragua (Exposición, Crítica y Textos).* Madrid, 1958.

7029.   ———. *Ensayo Histórico Sobre el Derecho Constitucional de Nicaragua.* Managua, 1936.
       Contains texts of various constitutions.

7030.   Barquero, S. L. *Gobernantes de Nicaragua, 1825–1947.* 2d ed., Managua, 1945.

7031.   Cabrales, L. A. *Sinopsis de la República de Nicaragua.* Managua, 1937.

7032.   Castellón, H. A. *Historia Patria Elemental para las Escuelas de Nicaragua.* Managua, 1940.

7033.   Denig, J. L. "The Proposed Nicaragua

Canal," *USNIP* 65 (1939) 1012–1024.
Covers the period from independence to 1939.

7034. Imberg, K. E. *Der Nikaraguakanal: Eine Historischdiplomatische Studie*. Berlin, 1920.

7035. Medina, A. *Efermérides Nicaraguenses, 1502–1941*. Managua, 1945.

7036. Sánchez, R. *Panorama Político de Nicaragua, 1821–1940*. Managua(?), 1941(?).

XIV–G–1   cross references: 6653

2. UNITED STATES–NICARAGUAN RELATIONS: NINETEENTH CENTURY

7037. Alemán Bolaños, G. *Centenario de la Guerra Nacional de Nicaragua Contra Walker*. Guatemala, 1956.

7038. Alfaro, O. *El Filibustero Walker en Nicaragua*. Panama, 1932.

7039. Alvarez, M. A. *Los Filibusteros en Nicaragua, 1855–1856–1857*. Managua, 1944.

7040. "Apuntamientos de Don Jacinto García Relativos a la Campaña Contra los Filibusteros de Nicaragua," *RAN* 4 (March, 1940) 216–226.

7040a. Atlantic and Pacific Canal Company. *Terms of the Contract Between the State of Nicaragua and the Company*. N.Y., 1849.

7041. Ayón, T. *Historia de Nicaragua*. 3 vols., Managua, 1882–1889.

7042. Castrillo Gámez, M. *Estudios Históricos de Nicaragua*. Managua, 1947.

7043. "Documentos en los Cuales se Refieren a los Sucesos Ocurridos en Bluefields, República de Nicaragua, en el Año de 1894," *RAGHN* 8 (August, 1946) 49–68.

7044. *Documents and Correspondence Between the Republic of Nicaragua and the Representatives of the German Empire, the United States and England, in Regard to the Eisenstuck Affair, During the Years 1876, '77, and '78*. N.Y., 1878.

7045. Doubleday, C. W. *Reminiscences of the "Filibuster" War in Nicaragua*. N.Y., 1886.
Doubleday was a British national who served in Walker's army.

7046. Dueñas Van Severen, J. R. *La Invasión Filibustera de Nicaragua y la Guerra Nacional*. 2d ed., San Salvador, 1962.

7047. Escobar, E. *Biografía del General Don Pedro Joaquín Chamorro, 1818–1890*. Managua, 1935.

7048. Gámez, J. D. *Historia de Nicaragua*. Managua, 1889.
2d ed., Madrid, 1955. Coverage to 1860.

7049. Guzmán, H. *The Case of the Republic of Nicaragua*. Wash., 1888.

7050. Jamison, J. C. *With Walker in Nicaragua*. Columbia, Mo., 1909.

7051. Lévy, P. *Notas Geográficas y Económicas Sobre la República de Nicaragua, y una Exposición Completa de la Cuestión del Canal Interoceánio y la de Inmigración con una Lista Bibliográfica, la Más Completa Hasta el Día de Todos los Libros y Mapas Relativos a la América Central en General y a Nicaragua en Particular*. Paris, 1873.

7052. Lucas, D. B. *Nicaragua: War of the Filibusters*. Richmond, Va., 1896.

7053. Morrow, R. L. "A Conflict Between the Commercial Interests of the United States and Its Foreign Policy," *HAHR* 10 (1930) 2–13.
Refers to the United States and Nicaragua during the 1890's.

7054. Pérez, J. *Memorias para la Historia de la Revolución de Nicaragua y de la Guerra Nacional Contra los Filibusteros, 1854 a 1857*. 2 vols., Managua, 1865–1873.

7055. Portas, B. *Compendio de la Historia de Nicaragua*. Managua, 1918.
Covers the years 1492–1893.

7056. Ramos, M. A. *Reseña Histórica de Nicaragua, Desde el Descubrimiento Hasta la Invasión de Walker: Combate de San Jacinto*. Tegucigalpa, 1956.

7057. Ratterman, E. (Callaghan). "A Short Sketch of My Life for the Last Four Years in Nicaragua," *THM* 1 (1915) 315–330.
Author was a woman filibuster.

7058. Scroggs, W. O. (ed.). "Walker-Heiss Papers: Some Diplomatic Correspondence of the Walker Regime in Nicaragua," *THM* 1 (1915) 331–345.

7059. ———. "William Walker and the Stromberg Corporation in Nicaragua," *AHR* 10 (1904) 792–812.

7060. Squier, E. G. *Nicaragua*. N.Y., 1860.

7061. ———. *Nicaragua, Its People, Scenery, Monuments, and the Proposed Nicaraguan Canal*. 2 vols., N.Y., 1852.

7062. Stewart, W. F. *Last of the Filibusters*. Sacramento, Calif., 1857.

7063. Stout, P. F. *Nicaragua: Past, Present and Future*. Phil., 1859.
Author was the United States vice consul.

7064. Torre Villar, E. de la. *La Batalla de San Jacinto, Nicaragua, 1856*. Mexico, 1957.

7065. Walker, W. *The War in Nicaragua*. Mobile, Alabama, 1860.

XIV–G–2   cross references:

a) For accounts of filibustering, and particularly of William Walker, see items 2459–2493.

b) For works pertaining to the proposed Nicaraguan canal, see items 2350, 2354, 2356, 2359, 2360, 2363, 2365, 2373, 2376, 2380a, 2387a, 2390, 2398, 2403, 2404, 2406, 2425, 2433, 2434, 2436, 2440, 2443, 2445, 2448, 2449, 2451, 2453, 2454, 2455.

c) See also items 7252, 7495a.

3. UNITED STATES–NICARAGUAN RELATIONS: TWENTIETH CENTURY

7066. Alemán Bolaños, G. *Cómo Ganó Nicaragua su Segunda Independencia*. Managua, 1944.

7067. ———. *Un Lombrosiano: Somoza, 1939–1944*. Guatemala, 1945.
Volume 2 is entitled *Los Pobres Diablos* (Guatemala, 1947).

7068. ———. *El País de los Irredentos, Diciembre de 1927*. Guatemala, 1927.
Extremely critical of United States policy.

7069. ———. *Sandino, El Libertador: La Epopeya, la Paz, el Invasor, la Muerte*. Mexico, 1952.
Sandino led guerrilla opposition against the United States Marines in the period 1928–1933. He was murdered by the Guardia Nacional in 1934.

7070. ———. *Sandino: Estudio Completo del Héroe de las Segovias*. Mexico, 1932.
Sympathetic treatment.

7071. Alexander, A. *Sandino*. Santiago, 1937.

7072. Allen, J. C. *La Situación de Nicaragua*. Managua, 1921.
The central thesis is that Nicaragua was being controlled from Wall Street.

7073. Alvarado García, E. *La Base Naval en el Golfo de Fonseca ante el Derecho Internacional*. Tegucigalpa, 1931.

7074. Alvarez Lejarza, M. *Impresiones y Recuerdos de la Revolución de 1909 a 1910*. Granada, Nicaragua, 1941.

7075. Anderson, C. P. *The Disturbing Influence in Central America of the Nicaraguan Canal Treaty*. Wash., 1917.

7075a. Anderson, R. M. "The Bryan-Chamorro Treaty," *SCHAP* (1932) 3–12.

7076. Aquino, E. *Datos Biográficos del Excelentísimo Señor Presidente de la República de Nicaragua, General de División, A. Somoza*. Managua, 1938.
Somoza, the head of the Guardia Nacional established by the United States, controlled Nicaragua from 1937 until his assassination in 1956.

7077. ———. *La Personalidad Política del General José Santos Zelaya*. Managua, 1944.
Zelaya controlled the country from 1893 to 1909, when the United States supported an anti-Zelaya revolution.

7077a. Arana, C. *Compilación de Contratos Celebrados con los Banqueros de Nueva York, con el Ethelburga Syndicate de Londres y con el Banco Nacional de Nicaragua, Inc.* 3 vols., Managua, 1928–1929.

7078. Bailey, T. A. "Interest in a Nicaraguan Canal, 1903–1931," *HAHR* 16 (1936) 2–28.
Discusses the Bryan-Chamorro Treaty.

7079. Baker, G. W., Jr. "The Wilson Administration and Nicaragua, 1913–1921," *TA* 22 (1966) 339–376.

7080. Barcenas Menses, J. *Las Conferencias del "Denver": Actas Auténticas de las Sesiones con Introducción y Ligeros Comentarios*. Managua, 1926.

7081. Bayle, L. de. *Les Emprunts Extérieurs et la Réforme Monétaire de la République de Nicaragua*. Paris, 1927.

7082. Baylen, J. O. "American Intervention in Nicaragua, 1909–33: An Appraisal of Objectives and Results," *SSSQ* 35 (September, 1954) 128–154.

7083. ———. "Sandino: Death and Aftermath," *MA* 36 (April, 1954) 116–139.
Emphasizes the years 1926 to 1934.

7084. ———. "Sandino: Patriot or Bandit?" *HAHR* 31 (1951) 394–419.

7085. Beaulac, W. L. *Career Ambassador.* N.Y., 1951.

7086. Belausteguigoitia, R. de. *Con Sandino en Nicaragua: La Hora de la Paz.* Madrid, 1934.

7087. Blaños, P. *The Economical Situation of Nicaragua: Intervention of North America and Its Results, the Procedures of the Government of Adolfo Diaz.* New Orleans, 1916.

7088. Borge González, E. "Nicaragua por Dentro: Una Dictadura con el Beneplácito del Departamento de Estado," *COMB* 1 (March, 1959) 33–42.

Suggests that the United States must bear the responsibility for the Somoza dictatorship because of the establishment of the Guardia Nacional.

7089. Briones Torres, I. "Angustia y Esperanza de Nicaragua," *COMB* 3 (July, 1961) 44–50.

Contends that the Nicaraguan communists are allies of the Somozas.

7090. Brooks, C. T. "War in Nicaragua," *MCG* 17, no. 4 (1933) 45–48.

7091. Brownback, P. E. "The Acquisition of the Nicaragua Canal Route: The Bryan-Chamorro Treaty," U. of Pennsylvania Diss., 1952.

7092. Buell, R. L. "American Supervision of Elections in Nicaragua," *FPAIS* 6 (1930) 385–402.

7093. ———. "Reconstruction in Nicaragua," *FPAIS* 6 (1930) 315–343.

7094. Calderón Ramírez, S. *Ultimos Días de Sandino.* Mexico, 1934.

7095. Campos Ponce, X. *Los Yanquis y Sandino.* Mexico, 1962.

7096. Cantarero, L. A. "The Economic Development of Nicaragua, 1920–1947," U. of Iowa Diss., 1949.

7097. Cardenal, L. G. *Mi Rebelión: La Dictadura de los Somoza.* Mexico, 1961.

A scathing denunciation.

7098. Carlson, E. F. "The Guardia Nacional de Nicaragua," *MCG* 21 (August, 1937) 7–20.

7099. Castillo Ibarra, C. *Los Judas de Sandino.* Mexico, 1945.

7100. Chamorro Cardenal, P. J. *Estirpe Sangrienta: Los Somozas.* B.A., 1959.

Author was the editor of the anti-Somoza *La Prensa.* He was arrested and exiled by the dictator.

7101. ———. *Orígenes de la Intervención Americana en Nicaragua.* Managua, 1951.

7102. Conant, C. A. "Our Mission in Nicaragua," *NAR* 196 (1912) 63–71.

7103. "Conditions in Nicaragua," *MCG* 17 (November, 1932) 88–93.

7104. Cordero Reyes, M. *Nicaragua bajo el Régimen de Somoza, a los Gobiernos y Pueblos de América.* San Salvador, 1944.

Also published in English.

7105. Cox, I. J. "Nicaragua and the United States, 1909–1927," *WPFP* 10, no. 7 (1927).

7106. Cramer, F. *Our Neighbor Nicaragua.* N.Y., 1929.

7107. Cuadra Chamorro, P. J. *Motivos Sobre el Tratado Chamorro-Bryan: Editoriales de El Diario Nicaragüense.* Managua, 1950.

7108. Cuadra Pasos, C. *Recognition of Governments, Case of Nicaragua.* Wash., 1926.

7109. Cumberland, W. W. *Nicaragua, an Economic and Financial Survey.* Wash., 1928.

7110. Cummins, L. *Quijote on a Burro: Sandino and the Marines, a Study in the Formulation of Foreign Policy.* Mexico, 1958.

A sympathetic treatment.

7111. DeBayle, L. *La Cooperación Financiera de los Estados Unidos en Nicaragua.* Managua, 1943.

7112. Dennis, L. "Nicaragua: In Again, Out Again," *FA* 9 (1931) 496–500.

7113. Denny, H. N. *Dollars for Bullets: The Story of American Rule in Nicaragua.* N.Y., 1929.

Denny was a *New York Times* reporter in Nicaragua in the late 1920's.

7114. Dodds, H. W. "American Supervision of the Nicaraguan Election," *FA* 7 (1929) 488–496.

7115. ———. "The United States and Nicaragua," *AAAPSS* 132 (1927) 134–141.

7115a. *The Economic Development of Nicaragua: Report of a Mission Organized by the International Bank for Reconstruction and Development at the Request of the Government of Nicaragua.* Baltimore, 1953.

7115b. Fisher, G. J. B. "Diplomatic Aspects of the Nicaragua Canal," *USNIP* 56 (1930) 381–386.

7116. Frazier, C. E., Jr. "The Dawn of Nationalism and Its Consequences in Nicaragua," U. of Texas Diss., 1958.

7117. Frente Unitario Nicaragüense. *Intervención Sangrienta: Nicaragua y su Pueblo.* Caracas, 1961.

7118. Goldwert, M. *The Constabulary in the Dominican Republic and Nicaragua: Progeny and Legacy of United States Intervention.* Gainesville, Fla., 1962.

7119. Goméz, J. D. *General José Santos Zelaya, 1854–1919.* Managua, 1941.

7120. Gray, J. A. "The Second Nicaraguan Campaign," *MCG* 17 (February, 1933) 36–41.

7121. Greer, V. L. "Charles Evans Hughes and Nicaragua, 1921–1925," U. of New Mexico Diss., 1954.

7122. ———. "State Department Policy in Regard to the Nicaraguan Election of 1924," *HAHR* 34 (1954) 445–467.

7123. Hackett, C. W. "The Death of Sandino," *CH* 40 (1934) 78–80.

7124. ———. "A Review of Our Policy in Nicaragua," *CH* 29 (1928) 285–288.

7125. Hall, M. S. *Nicaragua y el Imperialismo Norteamericano.* B.A., 1928.

7125a. Ham, C. "Americanizing Nicaragua," *RR* 53 (February, 1916) 185–191.

7126. Hill, R. R. *Fiscal Intervention in Nicaragua.* N.Y., 1933.

Hill was a member of the High Commission in Nicaragua during the second intervention. Covers the Knox-Castillo Convention of 1911.

7127. ———. "Marinos Americanos en Nicaragua," *RAN* 7 (January, 1943) 20–34.

7128. ———. "The Nicaraguan Canal Idea to 1913," *HAHR* 28 (1948) 197–211.

7129. Hooker, R. M. "The Nicaraguan Intervention and Its Results," *WU* 4 (1929) 196–300.

7130. Huete Abella, R. *Los Banqueros y la Intervención en Nicaragua.* Managua, 1931.

7130a. Jones, C. L. "Nicaragua and the Crisis," *WA* 96 (September, 1933) 170–182.

7131. Kamman, W. "A Search for Stability: United States Diplomacy Toward Nicaragua, 1925–1933," Indiana U. Diss., 1962.

7132. Larin, N. S. "Iz Istorii Osvoboditelnoi Borby Naroda Nikaragua Protiv Vooru-

zhennoi Interventsee SShA v 1927–1933 Godakn," *VI* 8 (1961) 86–96.

History of the Struggle for Liberation of the People of Nicaragua Against the Armed Intervention of the United States, 1927–1933.

7132a. López, J. *The Conquest of Nicaragua by the United States: Letter to President Taft.* N.Y., 1913.

7133. López Bravo, F. *Somoza.* Managua, 1949.

7134. Macaulay, N. W., Jr. *The Sandino Affair.* Chicago, 1967.

7135. Maraboto, E. *Sandino ante el Coloso.* Veracruz, 1929.

7136. McClellan, E. N. "Supervising Nicaraguan Elections, 1928," *USNIP* 59 (1933) 33–38.

7137. McDevitt, J. R. "American-Nicaraguan Relations, 1909–1916," Georgetown U. Diss., 1954.

7138. Miranda, J. *El Ocaso del Tirano Somoza.* San José, C.R., 1949.

7139. Moncada, J. M. *Estados Unidos en Nicaragua.* Managua, 1942.

7140. Montiel Arguello, A. *Incidentes Diplomáticos.* Managua, 1955.

7141. Munro, D. G. "Dollar Diplomacy in Nicaragua, 1909–1913," *HAHR* 38 (1958) 209–234.

7142. ———. "The Establishment of Peace in Nicaragua," *FA* 11 (1933) 696–705.

7143. Murillo, A. *Sufragio Libre en Nicaragua.* Managua, 1924.

7144. Nicaragua. Administration of Customs. *Report of the Collector-General of Customs ...and the Statistics of the Commerce (1920–1926).* Managua, 1921–1927.

Provides revenues, expenditures, and foreign-commerce statistics.

7145. ———. Alta Comisión. *Report of the High Commission.* 5 vols., Managua, 1919–1925.

Reports of the commission to the President of Nicaragua and the U.S. secretary of state for the years 1919–1925.

7146. ———. Ministerio de Relaciones Exteriores. *Memoria Presentada al Congreso Nacional por el Señor Ministro del Ramo, Don Diego M. Chamorro, 1916.* 2 vols., Managua, 1917.

7147. ———. *Memoria Presentada al Congreso Nacional por el Subsecretario Encargardo* del Despacho, Don Humberto Pasos D., 1920. 3 vols., Managua, 1921.

7148. Nicaragua. Administration of Customs. *Discursos Pronunciados en el Momento Inaugural de las Conferencias de Mediación de San José de Costa Rica el Día Martes 9 de Noviembre, 1937.* Managua, 1937.

Concerns efforts of the United States, Venezuela, and Costa Rica to mediate the Nicaragua-Honduras boundary dispute.

7149. ———. ———. *Realidad Política de Nicaragua.* Managua, 1948.

Diplomatic dispatches for 1947–1948.

7150. ———. Presidente. *An Important Document: Message of Adolfo Díaz, President of Nicaragua, Central America, to the National Assembly at Managua Concerning Conventions with the United States of America.* Managua, 1911.

7151. Nogales y Méndez, R. de. *The Looting of Nicaragua.* N.Y., 1928.

7152. Osomo Fonseca, H. *La Revolución Liberal Constitucionalista de 1926.* Managua, 1958.

7153. Penfield, W. S. "Emiliano Chamorro, Nicaragua's Dictator," *CH* 24 (1926) 345–350.

7154. Playter, H. *Nicaragua: Commercial and Economic Survey.* Wash., 1927.

7155. Powell, A. "Relations Between the United States and Nicaragua, 1898–1916," *HAHR* 8 (1928) 43–64.

7156. ———. "Relations Between the U.S. and Nicaragua, 1898–1925," U. of Texas Diss., 1929.

7157. Quijano, C. *Nicaragua: Ensayo Sobre el Imperialismo de los Estados Unidos.* Paris, 1928.

7158. Reisinger, H. C. "La Palabra del Gringo! Leadership of the Nicaraguan National Guard," *USNIP* 56 (1935) 215–221.

7159. Robleto, H. *Los Estrangulados.* Madrid, 1933.

Condemnation of United States policy by a Spaniard.

7160. ———. "Nicaragua," *CA* 120 (January, 1962) 30–51.

United States–Nicaraguan relations in the 1960's.

7161. Rodríguez G., S. *El Golfo de Fonseca en el Derecho Público Centroamericano: la Doctrina Meléndez.* San Salvador, 1917.

7162. ———. *El Golfo de Fonseca y el Tratado Bryan-Chamorro Celebrado Entre los Estados Unidos de Norte América y Nicaragua: Doctrina Meléndez.* San Salvador, 1917.

7163. Romero, R. *Sandino y los Yanquis.* Mexico, 1961.

7164. ———. *Somoza, Asesino de Sandino.* Mexico, 1959.

7165. Russell, W. "Diplomatic Relations Between the U.S. and Nicaragua, 1920–1933," U. of Chicago Diss., 1953.

7166. Salvatierra, S. *Sandino: O, la Tragedia de un Pueblo.* Madrid, 1934.

7167. Sandino, A. C. *Los Grandes Documentos de la Campaña Libertadora de Sandino en el 14 Aniversario de la Muerte Cruenta del Héroe, Acaicida el 21 de Febrero de 1934.* San Salvador, 1948.

7168. ———. *Manifiesto a los Pueblos de la Tierra y en Particular de Nicaragua.* Managua, 1933.

7169. Schick, R. *Nicaragua y la Alianza para el Progreso.* Managua, 1963.

7170. Schoenrich, O. "The Nicaraguan Mixed Claims Commission," *AJIL* 9 (1915) 858–869.

Summary of the commission's work by one of the members.

7171. Selser, G. *Sandino, General de Hombres Libres.* 2 vols., B. A., 1959.

Eulogistic biographical treatment.

7172. Selva, M. de la. *Nicaragua (Ensayo Biográfico Político Sobre Sandino).* Mexico, 1954.

7173. Sequeira, D. M. *Emission et Amortissement des Emprunts Extérieurs de la République du Nicaragua.* Paris, 1931.

Covers the period 1900–1920.

7174. Smith, J. C., *et al. A Review of the Organization and Operations of the Guardia Nacional de Nicaragua, by the Direction of the Major General Commandant of the United States Marine Corps.* N.p., n.d.

7175. Solórzano, I. *La Guardia Nacional de Nicaragua: Su Trayectoria Incógnita, 1927–1944.* Granada, 1944.

Author also published under the pseudonym of Ildo Sol.

7176. Somoza, A. *El Verdadero Sandino o el Calvario de las Segovias.* Managua, 1936.

7177. Soto Hall, M. *Nicaragua y el Imperialismo Norteamericano: Contraste Entre la Insolencia Norteamericana y la Vergonzosa*

Tolerancia de los Gobiernos de la América Latina. B.A., 1928.

7178. / Stimson, H. L. *American Policy in Nicaragua*. N.Y., 1927.

7179. Tijerino, T. *El Tratado Chamorro-Bryan y sus Proyecciones en la América Central*. Managua, 1935.

7180. Tweedy, M. *This is Nicaragua*. Ipswich, 1953.

7181. "The United States and the Nicaraguan Canal," *FPAIS* 4 (1928–1929) 106–126.

7182. "United States Policy in Nicaragua: A Review of American Policy Since 1909," *FPAIS* 2, no. 24 (1927).

7183. USCH. Foreign Affairs Committee. *Conditions in Nicaragua and Mexico: Hearings* (69th Cong., 2d Sess.). Wash., 1927.

7184. USCS. *Operation of Naval Service in Nicaragua, May 4, 1927–April 16, 1928* (70th Cong., 1st Sess., S. Doc. 86). Wash., 1928.

7185. ———. Committee on Foreign Relations. *Foreign Loans ... Hearings Pursuant to S. Con. Res. 15, Relative to Engaging Responsibility of the Government in Financial Arrangements Between Its Citizens and Sovereign Foreign Governments* (69th Cong., 2d Sess.). Wash., 1927.

7186. ———. ———. *Nicaraguan Affairs: Hearings Before a Subcommittee of the Committee on Foreign Relations, United States Senate, Sixty-second Congress, Second Session ... to Investigate as to the Alleged Invasion of Nicaragua by Armed Sailors and Marines of the United States (El Paso, Texas, Oct. 8, 1912)* (62d Cong., 2d Sess.). Wash., 1912.

7187. ———. ———. *Use of the United States Navy in Nicaragua: Hearings* (70th Cong., 1st Sess.). Wash., 1928.

7188. USDC. *Nicaragua: A Review of Commerce and Industries, 1918–1923*. Wash., 1924.

7189. USDS. *The United States and Nicaragua: A Survey of Relations from 1909 to 1932*. Wash., 1932.

Contains the Dawson pacts, the Knox-Castrillo Convention, the Bryan-Chamorro Treaty, and the U.S.-Costa Rican agreement of Feb. 1, 1923.

7190. ———. *United States Marines in Nicaragua*. Wash., 1931.

7191. United States Tariff Commission. *Economic Controls and Commercial Policy in Nicaragua*. Wash., 1947.

7192. Urcuyo Gallegos, G. *El Tratado Bryan-Chamorro*. Mexico, 1949.

7193. Urtecho, J. *Reflexiones Sobre la Historia de Nicaragua de Gainza a Somoza*. 2 vols., n.p., 1962.

7194. Weitzel, G. T. *American Policy in Nicaragua: Memorandum on the Convention Between the United States and Nicaragua Relative to an Interoceanic Canal and Naval Station in the Gulf of Fonseca, Signed at Managua, in Nicaragua, on February 8, 1913* (64th Cong., 1st Sess., S. Doc. 334). Wash., 1916.

Spanish ed., Granada, Nicaragua, 1916.

7195. ———. *Nicaragua and the Bryan-Chamorro Treaty*. Wash., 1927.

Former U.S. minister to Nicaragua justifies State Department policy.

7196. Wilson, L. C. "The Nicaraguan Canal Project," *PAM* 42 (November, 1929) 169–174.

Also discusses United States–Costa Rican protocol of 1933.

7197. Zelaya, J. S. *Refutation of the Statement of President Taft*. Paris, 1911.

Denunciation of U.S. intervention.

7198. ———. *La Revolución de Nicaragua y los Estados Unidos*. Madrid, 1910.

XIV–G–3 cross references: 3305, 3320, 6978, 6996, 7003, 7200, 7203, 7220, 7230, 7233a, 7531

H. THE UNITED STATES AND EL SALVADOR

7199. *Argument: United States vs. Salvador*. Wash., 1902.

Treats the claims of the Salvador Commercial Company and the arbitration of 1902. See also item 7217.

7200. Corte de Justicia Centro-Americana. *The Republic of San Salvador Against the Republic of Nicaragua. Opinion and Decision of the Court*. Wash., 1917.

7201. Coyner, M. S. *El Salvador: Its Agriculture and Trade*. Wash., 1963.

7202. Cuencia, A. *El Salvador, una Democracia Cafelatera*. Mexico, 1962.

7203. *Demanda del Gobierno de El Salvador Contra el Gobierno de Nicaragua ante la Corte de Justicia Centro-Americana, 1916*. San Salvador, 1916.

7204. El Salvador. *Tratados, Convenciones y Acuerdos Internacionales Vigentes en El Salvador, 1865–1929*. San Salvador, 1938.

7205. ———. Ministerio de Hacienda. *La Política Económica Internacional y la Cláusula de la Nación mas Favorecida*. San Salvador, 1939.

7206. ———. Presidente. *Cartas Políticas Cruzadas Entre los Presidentes de El Salvador y de los Estados Unidos*. San Salvador, 1918.

7207. Figeac, J. *Recordatorio Histórico de la República de El Salvador*. San Salvador, 1938.
   Treats through the nineteenth century.

7208. Gallardo, M. A. (comp.). *Papeles Históricos*. San Salvador, 1954.

7209. García, M. A. *Diccionario Histórico-Enciclopédico de la República de El Salvador*. 24 vols., San Salvador, 1927–1955.

7210. Gavidia, F. *Historia Moderna de El Salvador*. 2d ed., San Salvador, 1958.

7211. Larde y Larín, J. *El Salvador: Historia de sus Pueblos, Villas y Ciudades*. San Salvador, 1957.

7212. ———. *Guía Histórica de El Salvador*. San Salvador, 1958.

7213. Martin, P. F. *Salvador of the Twentieth Century*. N.Y., 1911.

7214. Méndez, J. *Los Sucesos Comunistos en El Salvador*. San Salvador, 1935.

7215. Nathan Associates (Washington, D.C.). *Investment and Industrial Development in El Salvador: A Report for the International Cooperation Administration*. Wash., 1961.

7216. Osborne, L. de J. *Four Keys to El Salvador*. N.Y., 1956.

7217. *Report in the Case of Salvador Commercial Company vs. Salvador*. Wash., 1901.
   See also item 7199.

7218. Schlesinger, J. *Revolución Comunista*. Guatemala, 1946.
   Treats the uprising of 1932 in El Salvador.

7219. Solorzano, A. *A Propósito de la Interpretación del Gobierno de El Salvador al de los Estados Unidos Sobre la Doctrina de Monroe*. Managua, 1920.

7220. Thomson, C. A. "The Caribbean Situa-tion: Nicaragua and Salvador," *FPAR* 9 (1933) 142–148.

7221. UN. Food and Agriculture Organization. *Coffee in Latin America: Productivity Problems and Future Prospects: Colombia and El Salvador*. N.Y., 1958.

7222. United States Tariff Commission. *Economic Controls and Commercial Policy in El Salvador*. Wash., 1947.

7223. Vanni, M. *Salvador*. Rome, n.d.

7223a. *Voto del Magistrado por Nicaragua, Dr. Daniel Gutiérrez Navas: El Salvador versus Nicaragua . . . Marzo de 1917*. San José, C.R., 1917.

7223b. Woolsey, L. H. "Recognition of the Government of El Salvador," *AJIL* 28 (1934) 325–329.

XIV–H   cross references: 4151d, 6696, 7005

I. THE UNITED STATES AND COSTA RICA

1. UNITED STATES–COSTA RICAN RELATIONS: GENERAL WORKS AND SPECIAL STUDIES

7224. Baker, G. W., Jr. "Woodrow Wilson's Use of the Non-Recognition Policy in Costa Rica," *TA* (July, 1965) 3–21.

7225. Biesanz, J., and M. Biesanz. *Costa Rican Life*. N.Y., 1944.

7226. Busey, J. L. *Notes on Costa Rican Democracy*. Boulder, Colo., 1962.

7227. ———. "The Presidents of Costa Rica," *TA* 18 (July, 1961) 55–70.

7228. Castro Esquivel, A. *José Figueres Ferrer: El Hombre y su Obra: Ensayo de una Biografía*. San José, C.R., 1955.

7228a. Chacón Trejos, G. *Maquiavelo: Maquiavelismo del Presidente Ricardo Jiménez: Maquiavelismo del Presidente Alfredo González*. San José, C.R., 1935.

7229. *Colección de Tratados de la República de Costa Rica*. San José, C.R., 1896.

7230. Corte de Justicia Centro-Americana. *Decision and Opinion of the Court on the Complaint of the Republic of Costa Rica Against the Republic of Nicaragua, Growing out of a Convention Entered into by the Republic of Nicaragua with the United States of America for the Sale of the San Juan River and Other Matters*. Wash., 1916.

7231. Costa Rica. Congreso Constitucional. *Documentos Relativos al Proyecto de Contrato Petrolero Pinto-Greulich.* San José, C.R., 1920.

7232. ———. Secretaría de Relaciones Exteriores. *Colección de Tratados: Contiene Solamente los Tratados Vigentes en la Fecha del 30 de Diciembre de 1907.* San José, C.R., 1907.

7233. *Costa Rica Before the Central American Court of Justice.* Wash., 1916.

7233a. *Demanda de la República de Costa Rica Contra la de Nicaragua, ante la Corte de Justicia Centroamericana, con Motivo de una Convención Firmada por la Segunda con la República de los Estados Unidos de América, por la Venta del Río San Juan, y Otros Objetos.* San José, C.R., 1916.

7234. Facio, R. *Estudio Sobre Economía Costarricense.* San José, C.R., 1942.

7235. Fernández Guardia, R. *Colección de Documentos para la Historia de Costa Rica.* Vols. 1–3, San José, C.R., 1881–1883; vols. 4–5, Paris, 1886; vols. 6–10, Barcelona, 1907.

7236. Fernández Montúfar, J. *Historia Ferrovial de Costa Rica.* San José, C.R., 1935.

7237. *Fertile Lands of Friendship. The Florida–Costa Rican Experiment in International Agricultural Cooperation.* Gainesville, Fla., 1962.

7238. Froneck, M. Z. "Diplomatic Relations Between U.S. and Costa Rica, 1823–1882," Fordham U. Diss., 1959.

7239. González, L. F. *Biografía del Lic. Cleto González Víquez en Conmemoración del Centenario de su Nacimiento, 1858–Octubre–1958.* San José, C.R., 1958.
President of Costa Rica.

7240. ———. *Historia de la Influencia Extranjera en el Desenvolvimiento Educacional y Científico de Costa Rica.* San José, C.R., 1921.

7241. González Flores, A. *Manifiesto a mis Compatriotas, Noviembre de 1919.* San José, C.R., 1919.
Treats Wilson's recognition policy toward Costa Rica.

7242. ———. *El Petróleo y la Política en Costa Rica.* San José, C.R., 1920.

7243. Hoben, K. H. "The Out-of-Country Experience of Costa Ricans Sponsored by the United States Technical Co-operation Agencies, 1952–1956: A Study of Technical Cooperation Training," American U. Diss., 1961.

7244. Houk, R. J. "The Development of Foreign Trade and Communication in Costa Rica to the Construction of the First Railway," *TA* 10 (October, 1953) 197–209.

7245. Iglesias, F. M. (ed.). *Documentos Relativos a la Independencia.* 3 vols., San José, C.R., 1899–1901.

7246. Jinesta, R. *El Canal de Nicaragua y los Intereses de Costa Rica en la Magna Obra.* San José, C.R., 1964.

7247. Jones, C. L. *Costa Rica and Civilization in the Caribbean.* Madison, Wis., 1935.

7247a. ———. "The Costa Rica Attitude Toward the U.S.," *WA* 96 (March, 1933) 41–43.

7248. Kantor, H. *The Costa Rican Election of 1953: A Case Study.* Gainesville, Fla., 1958.

7249. López, J. *La Caída del Gobierno Constitucional en Costa Rica.* N.Y., 1919.
Discusses the overthrow of Alfredo González Flores (1913–1917).

7250. May, S., *et al. Costa Rica: A Study in Economic Development.* N.Y., 1952.

7250a. Merz, C. *El Comercio Internacional de la República de Costa Rica.* San José, C.R., 1929.

7251. Molina, F. *Der Freistaat Costa Rica in Mittel-Amerika und Seine Wichtigkeit für den Welthandel, den Ackerbau und die Kolonisation nach Französischen des F.M.* Berlin, 1850.

7252. ———. *Memoir on the Boundary Question Pending Between the Republic of Costa Rica and the State of Nicaragua.* Wash., 1851.

7253. Monge Alfaro, C. *Historia de Costa Rica.* San José, C.R., 1959.

7254. Montero Barrantes, F. *Elementos de Historia de Costa Rica.* 2 vols., San José, C.R., 1892–1894.
Coverage to 1890.

7255. Obregón Loría, R. "Nuestras Relaciones Internacionales a Mediados del Siglo XIX," *RUCR* 14 (November, 1956) 63–140.
Costa Rican foreign policy from 1836 to 1860.

7256. Peralta, H. G. *Las Constituciones de Costa Rica*. Madrid, 1962.

7257. ———. *Don José María de Peralta*. San José, C.R., 1956.

7258. Peralta, M. M. de. *Costa Rica y Costa de Mosquitos*. Paris, 1898.

7259. *Proceso de la Restauración: O, la Intervención Americana en Costa Rica*. San José, C.R., 1922.

7260. Quarta, O. *Costa Rica*. Rome, 1925.

7261. Rippy, J. F. "Relations of the United States and Costa Rica During the Guardia Era," *BPAU* 77 (1943) 61–68.
       Covers the period 1870 to 1889.

7262. Rojas Corrales, R. *El Tratado Chamorro-Weitzel ante Centro-América y ante el Derecho Internacional*. San José, C.R., 1914.

7262a. Romero G., M. *Estudio Sobre las Posibilidades de Inversión en Costa Rica*. San José, C.R., 1961.

7363. Sáenz, A. *Contratos y Actuaciones de las Compañías del Ferrocarril de Costa Rica, la Northern Railway Co. y la United Fruit Co., en Costa Rica*. San José, C.R., 1929.

7264. Soley Güell, T. *Historia Económica y Hacendaria de Costa Rica*. 2 vols., San José, C.R., 1947–1949.
       Analyzes Costa Rica's finances from colonial times to 1940.

7265. Stewart, W. *Keith and Costa Rica: A Biographical Study of Minor Cooper Keith*. Albuquerque, N.M., 1964.
       Keith built the railroad from Limón to the Meseta Central.

7266. United States Tariff Commission. *Economic Controls and Commercial Policy in Costa Rica*. Wash., 1949.

7267. "U.S.–Costa Rican Cooperative Program," *BPAU* 77 (1943) 299–330.

7267a. Valentine, L. G. *The Case of Costa Rica*. N.Y., 1919.

7268. Vargas Coto, J. *Biografía del Lic. Ricardo Jiménez Oreamuno*. San José, C.R., 1959.
       Three-term President of Costa Rica (1910, 1924, and 1932).

7269. Zelaya, R. *Minor C. Keith: Contestación a los Señores Villafranca*. San José, C.R., 1913.

7270. Zeledon, M. T. "Reseña Histórica del Régimen Constitucional de Costa Rica," *RAN* 5 (July, 1941) 422–440.

XIV–I–1   cross references: 2356, 2357, 2445, 3369, 4151d, 7189, 7196

2. The Costa Rican Boundary Dispute with Colombia and Panama

7271. Anderson, C. P. *Synopsis of Case and Argument for Costa Rica in Reply*. Wash., 1914.

7272. Barrantes F., M. *La Frontera Entre Costa Rica y Panamá*. San José, C.R., 1959.

7273. Borda, F. de P. *Límites de Colombia con Costa Rica*. Bogotá, 1896.

7274. *Controversia de Límites Entre Panamá y Costa Rica*. Panama, 1914.

7275. *Fallo Arbitral del Chief Justice de los Estados Unidos de América en la Controversia de Límites de las Repúblicas de Costa Rica y Panamá*. San José, C.R., 1914.

7276. Molina, F. *Costa Rica y Nueva Granada, Examen de la Cuestión de Límites*. Wash., 1852.
       English ed., Wash., 1853.

7277. Moret y Prendergast, S., and V. Santamaría de Paredes. *Dictamen Sobre la Cuestión de Límites Entre las Repúblicas de Costa Rica y de Panamá*. San José, C.R., 1942.

7278. ———, and ———. *Opinion Concerning the Question of Boundaries, Given at the Request of Costa Rica*. Wash., 1913.

7279. Matamoros, L. *Report of the Consulting Engineer of Costa Rica*. Wash., 1913.

7280. Moore, J. B. *Costa Rica–Panama Arbitration: Memorandum on Uti Possidetis*. Roslyn, Va., 1913.

7281. Peralta, M. M. de. *Historia de Jurisdicción Territorial de Costa Rica*. Madrid, 1891.

7282. ———. *Límites de Costa Rica y Colombia*. Madrid, 1890.

7282a. Pereira Jiménez, B. "Historia de la Controversia de Límites Entre Panamá y Costa Rica," *L* 7 (September, 1962) 7–125.

7283. Poincaré, R. *Cuestión de Límites Entre Colombia y Costa Rica*. Seville, 1899.

7284. Porras, B. *Límites Entre Panamá y Costa Rica, Primera Exposición*. Wash., 1911.

7285. Sensabaugh, L. F. "The Attitude of the United States Toward the Colombia–Costa Rica Arbitral Proceedings," *HAHR* 19 (1939) 16–30.

J. THE UNITED STATES AND PANAMA

1. UNITED STATES–PANAMANIAN RELATIONS: GENERAL WORKS AND SPECIAL STUDIES

7286. Alba C., M. M. *Cronología de los Gobernantes de Panamá, 1510–1932.* Panama, 1935.

7287. Alfaro, R. J. *Medio Siglo de Relaciones Entre Panamá y los Estados Unidos.* Panama, 1953.

7288. Arce, H. J., and E. J. Castillero R. *Guía Histórica de Panamá.* 2d ed., Panama, 1943.

7289. Arosemena G., D. (comp.). *Documentary Diplomatic History of the Panama Canal.* Panama, 1961.

7290. Bastista Ballesteros, I. *El Drama de Panamá y América: Nuestras Relaciones con los E.E. U.U.* Panama, 1961.

7291. Biesanz, J., and M. Biesanz. *The People of Panama.* N.Y., 1955.

7291a. Cameron, D. H. "Panama's Unusual Guest: The Canal Zone in United States–Panamanian Relations," Columbia U. Diss., 1965.
    Explores the possibility of the internationalization of the canal.

7292. Castillero Pimentel, E. *Panamá y los Estados Unidos.* Panama, 1953.
    New ed., Panama, 1964.

7293. ———. *Política Exterior de Panamá: Los Objetivos de Nuestra Política Exterior, los Instrumentos o Medios para Lograrlos y las Bases Generales del Nuevo Tratado que Debe la República de Panamá con los Estados Unidos de América.* Panama, 1961.

7294. Castillero Reyes, E. J. *Galería de Presidentes de Panamá.* Panama, 1936.

7295. ———. *Historia de la Comunicación Interoceánica y de su Influencia en la Formación y en el Desarrollo de la Entidad Nacional Panameña.* Panama, 1939.

7296. ———. *Panamá: Breve Historia de la República.* B.A., 1939.

7297. Ealy, L. O. *The Republic of Panama in World Affairs, 1903–1950.* Phil., 1951.
    A history of Panamanian foreign relations.

7298. García Ruiz, R. *El Canal de Panamá, una Epopeya de Nuestro Siglo: Síntesis Histórico-Geográfica.* Mexico, 1945.

7298a. Harding, E. *The Untold Story of Panama.* N.Y., 1959.
    Conservative indictment of Panamanian radicalism, published by Robert Welch, Inc.

7299. King H., T. *El Problema de la Soberanía en las Relaciones Entre Panamá y los Estados Unidos de América.* Panama, 1961.

7300. Meléndez, P. *Panamá y el Canal: Un Breve Ensayo Sobre los Problemas que a la Nacionalidad Panameña Ha Presentado y Sigue Presentando la Construcción y Administración del Canal.* Panama, 1961.

7301. Miró, R. (ed.). *Panamá: 50 Años de República.* Panama, 1953.
    A collection of essays.

7302. Moral Pérez, C. R. "The Sovereignty and Jurisdiction of the Republic of Panama over the Panama Canal Zone," New York U. Diss., 1948.

7303. Padelford, N. J. *The Panama Canal in Peace and War.* N.Y., 1942.

7304. Panama. Junta Nacional del Cincuentenario. *Documentos Fundamentales para la Historia de la Nación Panameña.* Panama, 1953.

7305. ———. *Historia de Panamá: Texto Ceñido a los Programas Vigentes para Uso de los Colegios Oficiales y Particulares de la República.* Panama, 1961.

7306. Seemann, B. C. *Historia del Istmo de Panamá.* Panama, 1959.

7307. Tate, M. D. "Partnerschaft an Panama-Kanal? Ursachen und Entwicklung der Gegensätze Zwischen Panama und den Vereinigten Staaten," *EAR* 19 (1964) 53–63.
    Reviews United States relations with Panama from 1903 to 1963.

7307a. Turner, D. H. *Tratado Fatal: Tres Ensayos y una Demanda.* Mexico, 1964.
    Author is a Panamanian politician and journalist.

XIV–J–1 cross references:

a) For canal projects and canal diplomacy during the nineteenth century, see items 2349–2458.

b) For studies pertaining to the role of the United States in Panama's separation from Colombia, see items 8290–8382.

2. UNITED STATES–PANAMANIAN RELATIONS,
   1903–1940

7308. Abbot, W. J. *Panama and the Canal.*
       N.Y., 1914.

7309. Anderson, C. P. *Panama Canal Tolls: An
       Address on the Issues Between the United
       States and Great Britain in Regard to
       Panama Canal Tolls, as Raised in the
       Recent Diplomatic Correspondence* (63d
       Cong., 1st Sess., S. Doc. 32). Wash.,
       1913.

7310. Arias, H. *The Panama Canal: A Study in
       International Law and Diplomacy.* Lon-
       don, 1911.
           Spanish ed., Panama, 1957.

7311. Arosemena, P. *Escritos.* 2 vols., Panama,
       1930.

7311a. Baker, G. W., Jr. "The Wilson Admin-
       istration and Panama, 1913–1921,"
       JIAS 8 (1966) 279–293.

7311b. Barrow, R. M. "The First Panama
       Crisis, 1904," *CS* 5 (1966) 12–27.

7312. Behrendt, R. F. "Panama's Foreign
       Trade," *IAQ* 2 (January, 1940)11–31.

7313. Bennett, I. E. *History of the Panama
       Canal: Its Construction and Builders.*
       Wash., 1915.

7314. Bishop, J. B., and F. Bishop. *Goethals:
       Genius of the Panama Canal, a Biography.*
       N.Y., 1930.
           Biography of one of the engineers who
       built the canal.

7315. Borchard, E. "United States–Panama
       Claims Arbitration," *AJIL* 29 (1935)
       99–104.

7316. Buell, R. L. "Panama and the United
       States," *FPAR* 7 (1932) 409–426.

7316a. Bunau-Varilla, P. *Le Détroit de Panama:
       Documents Relatifs à la Solution Parfaite
       du Problème de Panama* (*Détroit Libre,
       Large et Profond*): *Ces Documents Ren-
       ferment des Détails sur la Solution Très
       Imparfaite Adoptée par les Etats-Unis
       (Canal à Ecluses) et sur les Mauvais
       Résultats des Trois Premières Années de
       Travaux du Gouvernement Américain.*
       Paris, 1907.

7317. Butte, G. C. *Great Britain and the Pana-
       ma Canal.* Heidelberg, 1913.

7318. Colquhoun, A. R. "The Panama Canal
       Tolls, A British View," *NAR* 196 (1912)
       513–522.

7319. Consentini, F. *Los Tratados y las Con-
       venciones de la "Zona del Canal de Pana-
       má."* Panama, 1927.

7320. Crespo, J. D. *La Moneda Panameña y el
       Nuevo Tratado del Canal.* Panama, 1936.
           Critical of Franklin Roosevelt's modi-
       fication of the 1903 treaty.

7321. Curtis, W. J. *The History of the Purchase
       by the United States of the Panama Canal,
       the Manner of Payment and the Distribu-
       tion of the Proceeds of Sale.* Birmingham,
       Ala., 1909.

7322. Davis, G. W. "Fortification at Panama,"
       AJIL 3 (1909) 885–908.

7323. Dimock, M. E. *Government Operated
       Enterprises in the Panama Canal Zone.*
       Chicago, 1934.

7324. Dulles, J. F. *The Panama Canal Con-
       troversy Between Great Britain and the
       United States.* N.Y.(?), 1913.

7325. Enock, C. R. *The Panama Canal: Its
       Past, Present, and Future.* London, 1914.

7326. Finch, G. A. "The Panama–United
       States Claims Commission," *AJIL* 27
       (1933) 750–752.
           Concerns the commission established in
       1926.

7327. Freehoff, J. C. *America and the Canal
       Title.* N.Y., 1916.

7328. Gibson, J. M. *Physician to the World:
       The Life of General William C. Gorgas.*
       Durham, N.C., 1950.

7329. Goethals, G. W. *Government of the Canal
       Zone.* Princeton, N.J., 1915.
           By the canal's engineer.

7330. Gorgas, W. C. *Sanitation in Panama.*
       N.Y., 1915.

7331. Gram, G. W. W. "The International
       Interest in the Settlement of the Panama
       Canal Toll Question," *ASILP* 7 (1913)
       41–52.

7332. Haines, P. C. "Neutralization of the
       Panama Canal," *AJIL* 3 (1909) 354–
       394.

7333. Herring, H. "Nationalism in Panama,"
       CH 42 (1935) 414–415.

7333a. Hershey, A. S. "Should the Panama Canal
       Tolls Controversy Be Arbitrated?" *IC*,
       no. 63 (1913).

7334. Howard, H. N. *Military Government in
       the Panama Canal Zone.* Norman, Okla.,
       1931.

7335. Huebner, G. G. "Economic Aspects of

the Panama Canal," *AER* 5 (1915) 816–829.

7336. Hutchinson, L. *The Panama Canal and International Trade Competition.* N.Y., 1915.

7336a. "International Use of Straits and Canals, with Especial Reference to the Panama Canal," *ASILP* 7 (1913).

7337. Johnson, E. R. "Panama Canal Traffic and Tolls," *NAR* 196 (1912) 174–182.

7337a. Kaufmann, W. "Das Panama-Kanal-gesetz der Vereinigten Staaten vom 24. August 1912 und das Völkerrecht," *ZV* 6 (1912) 407–435.
French ed., *RDISDP*, 2d ser., 14 (1912) 581–613.

7338. Kennedy, C. "The Canal Fortifications and the Treaty," *AJIL* 5 (1911) 620–638.

7339. ———. "Neutralization and Equal Terms," *ASILP* 7 (1913) 27–50.

7340. Knapp, H. S. "The Panama Canal in International Law," *USNIP* 39 (1913) 95–126.

7341. ———. "The Real Status of the Panama Canal as Regards Neutralization," *AJIL* 4 (1910) 314–358.

7342. Knowland, J. R. (comp.). *Panama Canal Tolls.* Wash., 1913.
Collection of documentary extracts supporting the United States position.

7342a. Langley, L. D. "The United States and Panama, 1933–1941: A Study in Strategy and Diplomacy," U. of Kansas Diss., 1965.

7343. Latané, J. H. "The Panama Canal Act and the British Protest," *AJIL* 7 (1913) 17–26.

7343a. Lee, W. S. *The Strength to Move a Mountain.* N.Y., 1958.

7343b. Lehmann, R. "Der Panamakanal: Seine Geschichte, die Befestigungs- und die Gebührenfrage," *ZIR* 23 (1913) 46–102.

7344. Lindsay, F. *Panama and the Canal Title.* Boston, 1912.

7345. ———. *Panama and the Canal Today,* Boston, 1926.

7346. Loewel, P. *Le Canal de Panama.* Paris. 1913.

7347. Mahan, A. T. "Fortify the Panama Canal," *NAR* 193 (1911) 331–339.

7348. ———. "The Panama Canal and Sea Power in the Pacific," *CE* 82 (1911) 240–248.

7349. ———. "The Panama Canal and the Distribution of the Fleet," *NAR* 200 (1914) 406–417.

7350. McCain, W. D. *The United States and the Republic of Panama.* Durham, N.C., 1937.
Covers 1903 to date of publication.

7351. Méndez Pereira, O. *Antología del Canal de Panamá: Bodas de Plata, 1914–1939.* Panama, 1939.

7352. Miller, H. G. *The Panama Canal Tolls Controversy: Or a Statement of the Reasons for the Adoption and Maintenance of the Traditional American Policy in the Management of the Panama Canal.* Boston, 1914.

7353. Müller-Heymer, P. *Der Panamakanal in der Politik der Vereinigten Staaten: Eine Völkerrechtspolitische Studie.* Berlin, 1909.

7354. Nesbitt, W. *The Panama Canal and Its Treaty Obligations.* Toronto, 1912 (?).

7355. Nixon, L. *The Canal Tolls and American Shipping.* N.Y., 1914.

7356. ———. "Does the Expression 'All Nations' in Article 3 of the Hay-Pauncefote Treaty Include the United States?" *ASILP* 7 (1913) 101–126.

7357. Olney, R. "Fortification of the Panama Canal," *AJIL* 5 (1911) 298–301.

7358. ———. *Panama Canal Tolls and the Hay-Pauncefote Treaty* (63d Cong., 1st Sess., S. Doc 33). Wash., 1913.

7359. Oppenheim, L. *The Panama Canal Conflict Between Great Britain and the United States of America.* Cambridge, 1913.

7360. Panamá. Instituto Nacional. *Documentos Históricos Sobre la Independencia del Istmo de Panamá.* Panama, 1930.

7361. Parrish, S. L. *The Hay-Pauncefote Treaty and the Panama Canal.* N.Y., 1913.

7361a. Pepper, C. M. *Panama to Patagonia: The Isthmian Canal and the West Coast Countries of South America.* Chicago, 1906.

7362. Phelps, E. M. (comp.). *Selected Articles on Panama Canal Tolls.* Minneapolis, 1913.

7363. Porras, B., and F. Filos. *Estudio Sobre el Tratado del Canal.* Panama, 1920.

7364. Richards, H. E. *The Panama Canal Controversy.* Oxford, 1913.

7365. Rivera Reyes, J. "El Tratado del Canal de Panamá," *CL* 4 (1936) 46–54.

7366. Roa y Uriarte, A. *El Canal de Panamá y el Derecho Internacional*. Havana, 1926.

7366a. Root, E. "The Obligations of the United States as to Panama Canal Tolls," *WPFP* 3, no. 3 (1913).

7367. Rousseau, H. H. *The Isthmian Canal*. Wash., 1910.

7368. Scott, W. R. *The Americans in Panama*. N.Y., 1912.

7369. Siler, J. F. "Major-General William Crawford Gorgas," *AJTM* 2 (1922) 161–171.

7370. Smith, D. H. *The Panama Canal: Its History, Activities and Organization*. Baltimore, 1927.

7371. Stockton, C. H. "Panama Canal Tolls," *USNIP* 38 (1912) 493–499.

7372. Talley, G. A. *The Panama Canal, Tolls and Treaties*. Wash., 1916.

7373. Tower, C. "The Treaty Obligations of the United States Relating to the Panama Canal," *APSP* 52 (1913) 234–242.

7374. Travernier, E. *Etude du Canal Interocéanique de l'Amérique Centrale au Point de Vue Diplomatique, Juridique et Economique*. Paris, 1908.

7375. USCS. *Correspondence in Regard to the Relations of the United States with Colombia and Panama* (60th Cong., 2d Sess., S. Doc. 542). Wash., 1908.

7376. ———. *Diplomatic History of the Panama Canal: Correspondence Relating to the Negotiation and Application of Certain Treaties on the Subject of the Construction of an Interoceanic Canal, and Accompanying Papers* (63d Cong., 2d Sess., S. Doc. 474). Wash., 1914.

7377. ———. *Great Britain and Panama Canal, Study of Tolls Question* (63d Cong., 1st Sess., S. Doc. 19). Wash., 1913.

7378. ———. *Panama Canal Tolls, Instruction of Secretary of State of Jan. 17, 1913, to American Charge d'Affaires at London, and British Notes* (63d Cong., 1st Sess., S. Doc. 11). Wash., 1913.

7379. ———. Interoceanic Canals Committee. *Panama Canal Tolls: Hearings on S. 8114 to Prevent Discrimination in Panama Canal Tolls* (63d Cong., 2d Sess., S. Doc. 450). Wash., 1914.

7380. ———. ———. *Panama Canal Tolls: Hearings on H.R. 14385* (63d Cong., 2d Sess.). Wash., 1914.

7381. Vásquez Cobo, A. *Pro Patria: Cuestiones Internacionales con los Estados Unidos y Panamá*. Panama, 1910.

7382. Vélez, R. P. *Asuntos de Panamá*. Bogotá, 1909.

7383. Verrill, A. H. *Panama, Past and Present*. N.Y., 1921.

7384. Wambaugh, E. "Exemption from Panama Tolls," *AJIL* 7 (1913) 233–244.

7385. ———. "The Right to Fortify the Panama Canal," *AJIL* 5 (1911) 615–619.

7386. Westerman, G. W. *Carlos Antonio Mendoza, Father of Panama's Independence Act*. Panama, 1956.

Mendoza was the third President of independent Panama.

7387. White, T. R., and C. Tower. *Our Duty Concerning Panama Tolls*. Boston, 1913.

7388. Woolsey, L. H. "The New Treaties Between the United States and Panama," *AJIL* 31 (1937) 297–300.

XIV–J–2   cross references:

a) For a discussion of the boundary arbitration between Panama and Costa Rica, see items 7271–7285.

b) See also items 3177, 3667, 7521, 7609, 8303, 8308, 8323, 8346, 8371, 8374.

3. UNITED STATES–PANAMANIAN RELATIONS SINCE 1940

7389. Arosemena Arias, C. "Una Visión Sociológica de Nuestras Relaciones con los Estados Unidos," *L* 2 (March, 1957) 10–18.

7390. Biesanz, J., and L. M. Smith. "Panamanian Politics," *JP* 14 (1952) 386–402.

7391. ———, and ———. "Race Relations in Panama and the Canal Zone," *AJS* 57 (1951) 7–14.

7392. Chiari Remón, R. F. "Nuestras Relaciones con Estados Unidos: Carta del Presidente Chiari, Sep., 1961," *L* 6 (December, 1951) 15–19.

7393. Dubois, J. *Danger over Panama*. Indianapolis, 1964.

Defense of United States' Panama policy.

7394. Du Val, M. P. "Isthmian Canal Policy—

An Evaluation," *USNIP* 81 (1955) 263–276.

7394a. Fenwick, C. G. "Treaty Between the United States and Panama," *WA* 118, no. 3 (1955) 70–72.

Treaty of 1955 explained.

7395. Goytía, V. F. *La Función Geográfica del Istmo.* Panama, 1947.

7396. Metford, J. C. J. "The Background in Panama," *IAF* 40 (April, 1964) 277–286.

Background to the 1964 riots in the Canal Zone.

7397. Minger, R. E. "Panama, the Canal Zone, and Titular Sovereignty," *WPQ* 14 (1961) 544–554.

7398. Morgan Morales, A. "Panamá y los EE. UU.," *L* 5 (October, 1960) 42–51.

7399. Ortega, G. *Panamá.* Havana, 1961.

7400. Pippin, L. L. "The Challenge in Panama," *CH* 50 (January, 1966) 1–7.

7401. ———. "The Remón Era: An Analysis of a Decade of Events in Panama, 1947–1957," Stanford U. Diss., 1965.

7402. Reyes Testa, B. "Nuestra Relaciones con Estados Unidos: Nuestra Bandera y Nuestra Soberanía en la Zona del Canal," *L* 5 (July, 1960) 73–81.

7403. Rippy, J. F. "The United States and Panama: The High Cost of Appeasement," *IEA* 17 (Spring, 1964) 87–94.

7403a. Russo Berguido, A. *Panamá, Nación Mártir.* Panama, 1964.

Nationalistic treatment of the riots in January, 1964.

7404. Sáenz, V. "Mesa Redonda Sobre los Canales Interoceánicos: Repercusión de la Crisis del Canal de Suéz en Nuestros Istmos," *L* 2 (August, 1957) 34–45.

7404a. Stuart, G. "Should the Panama Canal Be Internationalized?" in Wilgus, *The Caribbean: Contemporary International Relations,* pp. 39–50.

See item 6806.

7405. Tate, M. D. "The Panama Canal and Political Partnership," *JP* 25 (1963) 119–138.

7406. Travis, M. B., and J. T. Watkins. "Control of the Panama Canal: An Obsolete Shibboleth?" *FA* 37 (1959) 407–418.

7407. Turner Morales, D. *Estructura Económica de Panamá.* Mexico, 1958.

7408. USCH. Committee on Foreign Affairs. *United States Relations with Panama: Hearings* (86th Cong., 2d Sess.). Wash., 1960.

7408a. ———. ———. *United States Relations with Panama: Report* (86th Cong., 2d Sess., H. Rept. 2218). Wash., 1960.

7409. USDA. *Special Warfare Area Handbook for Panama: Prepared by Foreign Areas Studies Division, Special Operations Research Office, The American University, Washington, D.C.* Wash., 1962.

7409a. USDD. Armed Forces Information and Education Office. "United States and Panama," *FCTCW* 3, no. 15 (1964).

7410. Venin, V. M. *Panama i Panamskii Kanal.* Moscow, 1951.

Panama and the Panama Canal.

7411. Westerman, G. W. "La Otra Versión de las Relaciones Entre Panamá y los Estados Unidos," *L* 5 (June, 1960) 90–106.

Speech by the Panamanian delegate to the U.N.

XIV–J–3 cross references: 4186, 7290

K. THE UNITED STATES AND CUBA

1. UNITED STATES–CUBAN RELATIONS: GENERAL WORKS AND SPECIAL STUDIES

7412. Barreras, A. *Textos de las Constituciones de Cuba, 1812–1940.* Havana, 1940.

7413. Barrero Pérez, J. G. *La Cubanía Aniquilada por la Enmienda Platt.* Sancti Spíritus, Cuba, 1959.

Cuba's social ills are attributed to colonialism in general and Plattism in particular.

7414. Carbonell, J. M. (ed.). *Evolución de la Cultura Cubana, 1508–1920.* 18 vols., Havana, 1928.

7415. Castellanos G., G. *Motivos de Cayo Hueso.* Havana, 1936.

Discusses emigration of Cuban revolutionaries to the United States.

7416. Chapman, C. E. *A History of the Cuban Republic: A Study in Hispanic American Politics.* N.Y., 1927.

7416a. Concheso, A. *Cuba en la Vida Internacional.* Jena, 1935.

7417. Cuba. Ministerio de Estado. *Política de*

Comercio Exterior: Tratados, Convenios y Arreglos Comerciales Celebrados por la República de Cuba Desde 1902 a 1948. Havana, 1949.

Not limited to treaties in force at time of publication.

7418. Fergusson, E. *Cuba.* N.Y., 1946.

7419. Foner, P. S. *A History of Cuba and Its Relations with the United States.* 2 vols., N.Y., 1962–1963.

Vol. I covers the period 1492–1845; vol. II covers 1845–1895.

7420. Fonseca, M. A. *Compendio de Historia de Cuba.* Havana, 1939.

7421. Guerra y Sánchez, R., *et al.* (eds.). *Historia de la Nación Cubana.* 10 vols., Havana, 1952.

A collaborative effort. The last three volumes cover the twentieth century to the date of publication.

7422. ———. *Manual de Historia de Cuba.* Havana, 1938.

7423. ———. *Sugar and Society in the Caribbean.* New Haven, Conn., 1964.

7424. Gutiérrez y Sánchez, G. *El Desarrollo Económico de Cuba.* Havana, 1952.

7424a. Infiesta, R. *Historia Constitucional de Cuba.* Havana, 1942.

7425. Johnson, W. F. *The History of Cuba.* 5 vols., N.Y., 1920.

7426. Leiva, E., and E. Marbán. *Curso de Historia de Cuba.* 2d ed., 2 vols., Havana, 1943.

7426a. MacGaffey, W., and C. R. Barnett. *Twentieth Century Cuba: The Background of the Castro Revolution.* Garden City, N.Y., 1965.

Originally published as *Cuba* in vol. 10 of the "Survey of World Culture" series (New Haven, Conn., 1962).

7426b. Maris, G. L. "Some Aspects of International Law in United States–Cuban Relations: 1898–1964," Duke U. Diss., 1965.

7427. Márquez Sterling, C. *Historia de Cuba, Desde Colón Hasta Castro.* N.Y., 1963.

7428. Portell Vilá, H. *Historia de Cuba en sus Relaciones con los Estados Unidos y España.* 4 vols., Havana, 1936–1941.

The most comprehensive coverage of the subject.

7429. Roig de Leuchsenring, E. (ed.). *Curso de Introducción a la Historia de Cuba.* Havana, 1938.

7430. Smith, R. F. (ed.). *Background to Revolution: The Development of Modern Cuba.* N.Y., 1966.

Series of readings by United States and Cuban historians.

7431. ———. *The United States and Cuba: Business and Diplomacy, 1917–1960.* N.Y., 1960.

7432. ———. (ed.). *What Happened in Cuba? A Documentary History.* N.Y., 1963.

7433. Torriente y Peraza, C. de la. *Cuba en la Vida Internacional: Discursos.* 2 vols., Havana, 1922.

7434. Wallich, H. C. *Monetary Problems of an Export Economy: The Cuban Experience, 1914–1947.* Cambridge, 1950.

7435. Whitridge, A. "Cuba's Role in American History," *HT* 11 (1961) 309–315, 373–379.

7436. Wolf, H. A. "The United States Sugar Policy and Its Impact upon Cuba: A Reappraisal," U. of Michigan Diss., 1958.

7437. Wright, T. P., Jr. "United States Electoral Intervention in Cuba," *IEA* 13 (Winter, 1959) 50–71.

XIV–K–1   cross references:

For references on the Spanish-American War, see items 2623–2891.

2. THE UNITED STATES AND SPANISH CUBA TO 1898

7438. Aimes, H. H. S. *A History of Slavery in Cuba, 1511–1868.* N.Y., 1907.

7439. Bécker, J. *Historia de las Relaciones Exteriores de la España Durante el Siglo XIX.* 3 vols., Madrid, 1924–1926.

7440. Belmont, P. "La Question Cubaine en 1852–56: Un Duel à Madrid," *RHD* 49 (1935) 235–241.

7441. Caldwell, R. G. *The López Expeditions to Cuba, 1848–1851.* Princeton, N.J., 1915.

7442. Callahan, J. M. "Cuba and Anglo-American Relations (1819–1829)," *AHAAR* (1897) 195–215. Wash., 1898.

7443. ———. *Cuba and International Relations: A Historical Study in American Diplomacy.* Baltimore, 1899.

7444. Campuzano, J. F. *Remedio Radical para su Situación, la de Cuba y Puerto Rico.* Madrid, 1865.

7445. Canning, G. "Canning and Cuba, 1812," *SHAP* 11 (1907) 1–5.

7446. *Colección de los Partes y Otros Documentos Publicados en la Gaceta Oficial de la Gavilla de Piratas Capitaneada por el Traidor Narciso López.* Havana, 1851.

7447. Concha, J. de la. *Memorias Sobre el Estado Político, Gobierno, y Administración de la Isla Cuba.* Madrid, 1853.

7448. Corbitt, D. C. "Cuban Revisionist Interpretations of Cuba's Struggle for Independence," *HAHR* 43 (1963) 395–404.

7449. ———. "The Junta de Fomento of Havana and the López Expeditions," *HAHR* 17 (1937) 339–346.

7450. "Correspondencia Reservada de los Cónsules de España en los Estados Unidos de América con el Gobernador y Capitán General de la Isla de Cuba," *BANC* 27 (1928) 129–273.

7451. Curti, M. E. "Young America," *AHR* 32 (1926) 34–55.
On expansionist sentiment during the 1850's.

7452. Delaplain, S. *A Thrilling and Exciting Account of the Sufferings and Horrible Tortures Inflicted on Mortimer Bowers and Miss Sophia Delaplain, by the Spanish Authorities, for a Supposed Participation with Gen. López in the Invasion of Cuba: Together with the Plan of Campaign of López.* Charleston, S.C., 1851.

7453. Ettinger, A. A. *The Mission to Spain of Pierre Soulé, 1853–1855: A Study in the Cuban Diplomacy of the United States.* New Haven, Conn., 1932.

7454. ———. "The Proposed Anglo-Franco-American Treaty of 1852 to Guarantee Cuba to Spain," *RHST*, 4th ser., 12 (1930) 149–186.

7455. Everett, E. *Correspondence on the Proposed Tripartite Convention Relative to Cuba.* Boston, 1853.

7455a. Ferrer Canales, J. "Martí y Puerto Rico," *CA* 14, no. 2 (1955) 141–169.
Martí sought to free Puerto Rico, as well as Cuba, from Spain.

7456. Franco, J. L. *Política Continental Americana de España en Cuba, 1812–1830.* Havana, 1947.
Discusses Spanish use of the island to quell the independence movements in the remainder of Spanish America.

7457. Freret, W. *Correspondence Between the Treasury Department, etc., in Relation to the Cuba Expedition, and William Freret, Late Collector.* New Orleans, 1851.

7457a. Ganniers, A. de. "Les Négociations Secrètes Relatives à Cuba, de 1822 à 1898 (d'après des Documents Inédites)," *NRE* 116 (1899) 48–65, 232–252.

7458. Garrigó, R. E. *Historia Documentada de la Conspiración de los Soles y Rayos de Bolívar.* 2 vols., Havana, 1929.
Concerns revolutionary movements in the 1850's.

7459. González, D. *Historia Documentada de los Movimientos Revolucionarios por la Independencia de Cuba de 1852 a 1867.* Havana, 1939– .

7460. Gooch, B. D. "Belgium and the Prospective Sale of Cuba in 1837," *HAHR* 39 (1959) 413–427.

7461. Guiteras, P. J. *Historia de la Isla de Cuba.* 3 vols., Havana, 1927–1928.
First published in New York, 1865–1866.

7462. Hardy, R. *The History and Adventures of the Cuban Expedition.* Cincinnati, 1850.

7463. Henderson, G. B. "Southern Designs on Cuba, 1854–1857, and Some European Opinions," *JSH* 5 (1939) 371–385.

7464. Hume, E. E. "Colonel Theodore O'Hara and Cuban Independence," *BPAU* 71 (1937) 363–367.
Treats the Narciso López expedition.

7465. Janes, H. L. "The Black Warrior Affair," *AHR* 12 (1907) 280–298.

7466. Jones, A. *Cuba in 1851.* N.Y., 1851.

7467. "La Question de Cuba, Jugée au Point de Vue Américaine," *RBRI* 22 (1854) 257–290.

7468. Leard, R. B. "Bonds of Destiny: The U.S. and Cuba, 1848–1861," Brown U. Diss., 1954.

7469. "López's Expeditions to Cuba, 1850–51: Betrayal of the 'Cleopatra,' 1851," *SHAP* 10 (1906) 345–362.

7469a. McCadden, J. J. "The New York–to–Cuba Axis of Father Varela," *TA* 20 (1964) 376–392.
Discusses an early Cuban refugee.

7470. Moore, J. P. "Pierre Soulé, Southern Expansionist and Promoter," *JSH* 21 (1955) 203–223.

7471. O.D.D.O. *The History of the Late Expedition to Cuba*. New Orleans, 1850.
Pseudonym of J. C. Davis.

7472. "Papeles Inéditos Relativos a las Expediciones del General Narciso López (1845–1852)," *BANC* 16 (1917) 256–283, 373–437; 17 (1917) 67–91.

7473. Pérez Rioja, A. *Los Yankees en Cuba*. Havana, 1897.

7474. Pezuela y Lobo, J. de la. *Historia de la Isla de Cuba*. 4 vols., Madrid, 1868–1878.

7475. Philippo, J. M. *The United States and Cuba*. London, 1857.

7476. Piñeyro, E. *Biografías Americanas*. Paris, 1906.
See pages 77–195 for an account of José Morales Lemus, Cuban agent in the United States, 1868–1869.

7477. Portell Vilá, H. "El Gobierno de Polk y las Conspiraciones Cubanas de 1848," *UH* (January, 1938) 112–145.

7478. ———. *Narciso López y su Epoca*. 3 vols., Havana, 1930–1958.
Argues forcefully that López was not simply a filibusterer.

7479. ———. "Primeras Relaciones Entre Cuba y los Estados Unidos," *UH* 2, no. 7 (1935) 21–47.
Covers the period 1776–1784.

7480. Quisenberry, A. C. *López's Expeditions to Cuba, 1850 and 1851*. Louisville, Ky., 1906.

7481. Rauch, B. *American Interest in Cuba, 1848–1855*. N.Y., 1948.

7482. Reineke, J. A., Jr. "The Diplomatic Career of Pierre Soulé," *LHQ* 15 (1932) 283–329.

7483. Rodríguez, J. I. *Estudio Histórico Sobre el Origen, Desenvolvimiento y Manifestaciones Prácticas de la Idea de la Anexión de la Isla de Cuba á los Estados Unidos de América*. Havana, 1900.
Covers 1776–1898.

7484. Roig de Leuchsenring, E. *Cuba y los Estados Unidos, 1805–1898: Historia Documentada de la Actitud Disímil del Estado y del Pueblo Norteamericano en Relación con la Independencia de Cuba*. Havana, 1949.

7485. Saco, J. A. *Contra la Anexión*. Havana, 1928.

7486. Santovenia, E. S. *Armonías y Conflictos en Torno a Cuba*. Mexico, 1956.
Concentrates on nineteenth-century diplomatic history.

7487. ———. *El Presidente Polk y Cuba*. Havana, 1935.

7488. Spain. *Negociaciones Diplomáticas Encaminadas á Garantizar á España la Posesión de la Isla de Cuba, de 1825 á 1853*. Madrid, 1853 (?).

7489. Taylor, J. G. *The United States and Cuba: Eight Years of Change and Travel*. London, 1851.

7490. *The Ostend Manifesto, 1854*. N.Y., 1892. *American History Leaflet No. 2*.

7491. Torrente, M. *Política Ultramarina que Abraza Todos los Puntos Referentes á las Relaciones de Españas con los Estados Unidos, con la Inglaterra, y las Antillas*. Madrid, 1854.

7492. Trescot, W. H. "The Cuban Debate," *DR*, n.s., 2 (1852) 433–456.

7493. ———. *A Few Thoughts on the Foreign Policy of the United States*. Charleston, S.C., 1849.

7494. ———. "The Late Cuba State Trials," *DR* 1, n.s. (1852) 307–319.

7495. Urban, C. S. "The Africanization of Cuba Scare, 1853–1855," *HAHR* 37 (1957) 29–45.

7495a. ———. "The Ideology of Southern Imperialism: New Orleans and the Caribbean, 1845–1860," *LHQ* 39 (1956) 48–73.
Southern interest in expansion into Cuba and Nicaragua.

7496. USCH. *Message on Relations with Spain: President F. Pierce* (33d Cong., 2d Sess., H. Ex. Doc. 93). Wash., 1855.
Discusses the Ostend Manifesto and *Black Warrior* case.

7497. Valle, A. del. "Esclavitud y Anexionismo en Cuba," *RBCU* 55 (January, 1945) 29–41.

7498. Varona, J. E. *De la Colonia a la República*. Havana, 1919.

7499. Webster, S. "Mr. Marcy, the Cuban Question and the Ostend Manifesto," *PSQ* 8 (1893) 1–32.

XIV–K–2   cross references:

a) For the background of the Spanish-American War, see items 2677–2789.

b) See also items 1966, 2005, 2103, 2107b, 2137a, 2191, 7419, 7428, 7541a, 7581.

3. UNITED STATES–CUBAN RELATIONS, 1898–1934

7500. Alvarez del Real, E. *Patrias Opacas y Caudillos Fulgurantes*. Havana, 1942.
Concerns the last years of the Machado dictatorship.

7501. Armas y Cárdenas, J. de. *Duty of the United States in Cuba*. Havana, 1906.
Collection of Cuban newspaper articles.

7502. Atkins, E. F. "Cuba's Imminent Bankruptcy," *NAR* 173 (1901) 768–773.

7503. ———. "Tariff Relations with Cuba—Actual and Desirable," *AAAPSS* 32 (1908) 321–329.

7504. Baker, G. "The Wilson Administration and Cuba, 1913–1921," *MA* 46 (1964) 48–63.
One of the series of articles by Baker concerning the Wilson administration's Latin American policy.

7505. Barbarrosa, E. *El Proceso de la República, Análisis de la Situación Política y Económica de Cuba bajo el Gobierno Presidencial de Tomás Estrada Palma y José Miguel Gómez*. Havana, 1911.

7506. Beals, C. *The Crime of Cuba*. Phil., 1934.
Extremely critical of United States policy.

7507. Beveridge, A. J. "Cuba and Congress," *NAR* 172 (1901) 535–550.
Analysis of the U.S. senator from Indiana.

7508. Blanck, W. de. "Wilson—Cuba," *CC* 19 (March, 1919) 264–275.

7508a. Boeckel, R. M. "Cuban-American Relations," *ERR* (1930) 437–460.

7509. Brooks, S. "Cuba and the Cuban Question," *NAR* 196 (1912) 52–62.

7510. Bryce, J. "Some Reflections on the State of Cuba," *NAR* 174 (1902) 445–456.

7511. Buell, R. L. "Cuba and the Platt Amendment," *FPAIS* 5, no. 3 (1929–1930) 37–62.

7512. ———. *Cuba y la Enmienda Platt*. Havana, 1934.

7513. ———. "The Caribbean Situation: Cuba and Haiti," *FPAR* 9, no. 8 (1933–1934) 82–93.

7514. Buttari Gaunaurd, J. *Boceto Crítico*
Histórico: Obra Escrita en Cuatro Etapas. Havana, 1954.
Covers from the Platt Amendment to the Machado administration.

7515. Cabarrocas, J. M. "Cuba y los Estados Unidos," *CC* 8 (June, 1915) 135–153.

7516. Camacho, P. D. *Estrada Palma, el Gobernante Honrado*. Havana, 1938.

7517. Cararallo Setelengo, F. *El Imperialismo Norte Americano*. Havana, 1914.

7518. Carballal, R. Z. *Estudio Sobre la Administración del General José M. Gómez, 1909–1913*. Havana, 1915.

7519. Carbonell, M. A. *El Peligro del Águila*. Havana, 1922.

7520. Cárdenas y Echarte, R. de. *Cuba no Puede Invocarse en Testimonio del Imperialismo Norteamericano*. Havana, 1917.

7521. Carrera y Jústiz, F. *Orientaciones Necesarias: Cuba y Panamá*. Havana, 1911.
Sympathetic toward the United States.

7521a. Casuso, E. *Política Cubana y Sistema Americano*. Havana, 1902.
Early conservative censure of the Platt Amendment.

7522. Collazo, E. *Cuba: Intervenida*. Havana, 1910.

7523. ———. *Los Americanos en Cuba*. 2 vols., Havana, 1905.

7524. Conant, C. A. "Our Duty in Cuba," *NAR* 185 (1907) 141–146.

7525. Coolidge, L. A. *An Old-Fashioned Senator: Orville H. Platt, of Connecticut: The Story of a Life Unselfishly Devoted to the Public Service*. N.Y., 1910.

7526. Cruz, C. M. de la. *Proceso Histórico del Machadato*. Havana, 1935.
Condemnation of the Machado dictatorship.

7527. Cuba. Convención Constituyente. *Opinión Sobre las Relaciones Entre Cuba y los Estados Unidos*. Havana, 1901.

7528. Cummins, L. "The Formulation of the Platt Amendment," *TA* 23 (1967) 370–389.
Treats authorship and intent.

7529. Currier, C. W. "Why Cuba Should Be Independent," *F* 30 (October, 1900) 139–146.

7530. Fabre-Luce, A. *Révolution à Cuba*. Paris, 1934.

7531. Ferrara y Marino, O. "El Gobierno de Washington y las Elecciones en Cuba y

Nicaragua," *RSO* 19 (January, 1921) 28–35.

7532. Figueras, F. *La Intervención y su Política.* Havana, 1906.

7533. Fitzgibbon, R. H. *Cuba and the United States, 1900–1935.* Menasha, Wis., 1935.

7534. Forbes-Lindsay, C. H. A., and N. O. Winter. *Cuba and Her People of Today.* 2d ed., Boston, 1928.

7535. Funcie, J. E. "American Misgovernment of Cuba," *NAR* 170 (1900) 284–294.

7536. Gandarilla, J. C. *Contra el Yanqui: Obra de Protesta Contra la Enmienda Platt y Contra la Absorción y el Maquiavelismo Norteamericano.* Havana, 1913.

7537. Garrigó, R. E. *La Convulsión Cubana.* Havana, 1906.

7538. Gay Calbó, E. "Génesis de la Enmienda Platt," *CC* 41 (May, 1926) 47–63.
Views the amendment against the background of 19th century United States expansionism.

7539. ———. "Cuba No Es un Estado Cliente," *CC* 38 (June, 1925) 109–120.

7540. Gilbean, V. H., Jr. "Relations of Cuba with the U.S., 1916–1921," U. of North Carolina Diss., 1954.

7541. Gómez, F. G. *El Burguesito Recién Pescado.* Havana, 1951.
Concerns the Machado administration.

7541a. Greer, H. E., Jr. "History of Southern Baptist Mission Work in Cuba, 1886–1916," U. of Alabama Diss., 1965.

7542. Gruening, E. "Cuba Under the Machado Regime," *CH* 34 (1931) 214–219.

7542a. Guber, A. A. "Agresiia SShA na Kube," *IAR* 7 (1961) 33–54.
"Aggression by the U.S.A. Against Cuba." Covers 1898–1912.

7542b. Guerra y Sánchez, R. *Cuba en la Vida Internacional.* Havana, 1923.

7543. ———. "El General Leonardo Wood y la Instrucción Pública en Cuba," *CC* 23 (July, 1920) 193–217.

7544. ———. *En el Camino de la Independencia: Estudio Histórico Sobre la Rivalidad de los Estados Unidos y la Gran Bretaña en sus Relaciones con la Independencia de Cuba, con un Apéndice Titulado de Monroe a Platt.* Havana, 1930.

7545. Guggenheim, H. F. "Amending the Platt Amendment," *FA* 12 (1934) 448–457.

7546. ———. *The United States and Cuba: A Study in International Relations.* N.Y., 1934.

7547. Guiral Moreno, M. "La Intromisión de los Extranjeros en Nuestros Asuntos Domésticos," *CC* 7 (February, 1915) 137–156.

7548. Gutiérrez y Sánchez, G. *Necesidad de Adoptar una Política Exterior Definida.* Havana, 1926.

7549. Hagedorn, H. *Leonard Wood, 1860–1927: A Biography.* 2 vols., N.Y., 1931.

7550. Healy, D. F. *The United States in Cuba, 1898–1902.* Madison, Wis., 1963.

7551. Heinl, R. D. "How We Got Guantanamo," *AHE* 13 (1962) 18–21, 94–97.

7552. Hernández Portela, R. *Diplomacia de Acción y de Emoción.* B.A., 1939.

7553. Hevia, A. (comp.). *Colección de Artículos y Documentos Referentes á la Condición Actual de Cuba.* Havana, 1908.

7553a. ———. "General Leonard Wood and Public Instruction in Cuba," *INAM* 4 (October, 1920) 3–16.

7554. Hitchman, J. H. "Leonard Wood and the Cuban Question, 1898–1902," U. of California Diss., 1965.

7555. Hobbs, W. H. *Leonard Wood, Administrator, Soldier, and Citizen.* N.Y., 1920.

7556. Hoome, J. G. *The Life of Leonard Wood.* N.Y., 1920.

7557. Iznaga, R. *Tres Años de República, 1902–1905.* Havana, 1905.

7558. Jackman, F. U. "America's Cuban Policy During the Period of the Machado Regime," Catholic U. Diss., 1964.

7559. Jenks, L. H. "La Influencia de los Intereses Americanos en Cuba," *RBCU* 35 (1935) 237–248.

7560. ———. *Our Cuban Colony: A Study in Sugar.* N.Y., 1928.
Very critical of United States policy. Spanish ed., Madrid, 1929.

7561. Jones, C. L. "The Cuban Situation and Our Treaty Relations," *AER* 22 (1932) 112–113.

7562. Knox, D. W. "An Adventure in Diplomacy," *USNIP* 52 (1926) 273–287.
Concerns the revolt of Alfredo Zayas in 1917.

7563. Lliteras, J. A. "Relations Between Cuba

and the United States," *IC*, no. 296 (1934) 5–21.

Covers the first three decades of the twentieth century.

7564. Lloyd, R. *Twentieth Century Impressions of Cuba*. London, 1913.

7565. Lockmiller, D. A. "Agriculture in Cuba During the Second United States Intervention, 1906–1909," *AHI* 11 (1937) 181–188.

7566. ———. "The Advisory Law Commission of Cuba," *HAHR* 17 (1937) 2–30.

7567. ———. "La Base Legal de la Intervención de los Estados Unidos en Cuba en 1906," *RBCU* 38 (September, 1936) 268–281.

7568. ———. *Enoch H. Crowder, Soldier, Lawyer, and Statesman*. Columbia, Mo., 1955.
The Ambassador to Cuba after World War I.

7569. ———. *Magoon in Cuba: A History of the Second Intervention, 1906–1909*. Chapel Hill, N.C., 1938.
A sympathetic biography.

7570. ———. "The Settlement of the Church Property Question in Cuba," *HAHR* 17 (1937) 488–498.

7571. López, J. "La Intervención en Cuba," *RSO* 19 (February, 1921) 103–116.

7572. López Hidalgo, A. V. *Cuba y la Enmienda Platt*. Havana, 1921.

7573. Lugo-Viña, R. de. *Un Internacionalista Representativo*. Paris, 1924.
Studies the career of Cosme de la Torriente.

7574. Machado y Ortega, L. *La Enmienda Platt*. Havana, 1922.

7575. ———, *et al.* "Peticiones a los Estados Unidos por el Azúcar de Cuba," *RBCU* 24 (January, 1929) 50–96.

7575a. Magoon, C. E. *Report of Provisional Administration from October 13th, 1906, to December 1st, 1907*. Havana, 1908.

7575b. ———. *Report of Provisional Administration from December 1, 1907, to December 1, 1908*. Havana, 1909.

7575c. Marino Pérez, L. "Cuba and the United States: Their Economic Relations," *INAM* 5 (August, 1922) 358–361.

7576. ———. "The Reciprocity Agreement with Cuba," *CREV* 24 (April, 1926) 11–18.

7576a. ———. "Las Relaciones Económicas Entre Cuba y los Estados Unidos," *CC* 28 (April, 1922) 264–270.

7577. Márquez Sterling, M. *Las Conferencias del Shoreham: El Cesarismo en Cuba*. Mexico, 1933.

7578. ———. *La Política Exterior y la Política Nacional del Presidente Machado*. Havana, 1926.
Pamphlet reprinted from *El Heraldo de Cuba*.

7579. ———. *Proceso Histórico de la Enmienda Platt, 1897–1934*. Havana, 1941.

7580. Martínez Ortiz, R. *Cuba: Los Primeros Años de Independencia*. 2 vols., Havana, 1911–1912.
3d ed., 2 vols., Paris, 1929.

7581. Maura y Nodarse, A. "Relaciones Políticas Entre Cuba y los Estados Unidos," *CC* 35 (1924) 101–128, 189–208.

7582. Maxey, E. "Legal Aspects of Our Intervention in Cuba," *LSH* 14 (October, 1906) 301–302.

7582a. ———. "The Policy of the United States Toward Cuba," *ALR* 43 (March, 1909) 266–281.

7583. Mederos, T. B. *La Enmienda Platt: Como la Consideramos para el Presente y Porvenir de Cuba*. Havana, 1901.

7583a. Merrifield, R. B. "The Magazine Press and Cuba, 1906–1933," *MA* 34 (1952) 233–253.

7584. Meyer, L. J. "Relations Between the U.S. and Cuba from 1895–1917," Clark U. Diss., 1928.

7585. ———. "The United States and the Cuban Revolution of 1917," *HAHR* 10 (1930) 138–166.

7586. Minger, R. E. "William H. Taft and the United States Intervention in Cuba in 1906," *HAHR* 41 (1961) 75–89.

7587. Muñoz, A. *United States and Cuba in Their Commercial Relations*. Phil., 1899.

7588. Navas, J. *Cuba y los Estados Unidos: Boceto Histórico Sobre el Eco de la Causa Cubana en la Gran Nación Vecina*. Havana, 1916.

7589. Ortiz y Fernández, F. *Las Actuales Responsabilidades Políticas y la "Nota" Americana*. Havana, 1919.

7590. ———. "Cuba's Title to the Isle of Pines," *CREV* 23 (December, 1924) 14–20.

7591. Ortiz y Fernández, F. "Las Relaciones Económicas Entre los Estados Unidos y Cuba," *RBCU* 22 (July, 1927) 574–584.

7592. ———. *Las Responsabilidades de los Estados Unidos en los Males de Cuba.* Wash., 1932.

7593. Pavey, F. D. "The Independence of Cuba," *NAR* 172 (1901) 403–415.

7594. Peralta, V. M. de. *Conmonitorio de Intervención a Intervención.* Havana, 1907.

7595. Peraza, C. G. *Machado: Crímenes y Horrores de un Régimen.* Havana, 1933.

7596. Platt, O. H. "Cuba's Claim upon the U.S.," *NAR* 175 (1902) 145–151.

7597. ———. "Our Relation to the People of Cuba and Porto Rico," *AAAPSS* 18 (1901) 145–159.
    Justifies the Amendment on grounds of United States self interest.

7598. Portell Vilá, H. *El Convenio de no Intervención de Montevideo y la Intervención Norteamericana en Cuba.* Havana, 1935.
    Suggests that the Good Neighbor policy was not being implemented in Cuba.

7599. Porter, R. P. "The Future of Cuba," *NAR* 168 (1899) 418–423.

7600. ———. *Report on the Commercial and Industrial Condition of the Island of Cuba.* Wash., 1898.

7601. Primelles, L. *Crónica Cubana, 1919–1922: Zayas y Crowder: Fin de la Danza de los Millones y Reajuste.* Havana, 1958.

7602. Quesada y Miranda, G. de. *En Cuba Libre: Historia Documentada y Anecdótica del Machadato.* Havana, 1938.

7603. Quincy, J. "Political Aspect of Cuba's Economic Distress," *NAR* 174 (1902) 12–19.

7604. Randolph, G. F. *Law and Policy of Annexation, With Special Reference to the Philippines: Together with Observations on the Status of Cuba.* N.Y., 1901.

7605. Roa, J. *Los Estados Unidos y Europa en Cuba y en Hispano América: Dictadura vs. Democracia.* Havana, 1939.

7606. Robinson, A. G. *Cuba and the Intervention.* N.Y., 1905.
    Treats the military government.

7607. Rodríguez Altunaga, R. "Cuba's Case for the Repeal of the Platt Amendment," *CH* 26 (September, 1927) 925–927.

7608. Rodríguez Lendián, E. "Algunas Con-

sider4aciones Sobre la Enmienda Platt," *RMDI* 1 (March, 1919) 81–93.

7609. ———. *Los Estados Unidos, Cuba y el Canal de Panamá.* Havana, 1909.

7610. Roig de Leuchsenring, E. *Análisis y Consecuencias de la Intervención Norteamericana en los Asuntos Interiores de Cuba.* Havana, 1923.

7611. ———. "La Enmienda Platt, su Interpretación Primitiva y sus Aplicaciones Posteriores," *ASCDI* 5 (1922) 323–462.

7612. ———. "La Ingerencia Norteamericana en los Asuntos Interiores de Cuba," *CC* 30 (September, 1922) 36–61.

7613. ———. *El Intervencionismo, Mal de Males de Cuba Republicana.* San José, C.R., 1931.

7614. ———. *El Presidente McKinley y el Gobernador Wood, Máximos Enemigos de Cuba Libre.* Havana, 1960.

7615. ———. "El Tratado Permanente de 1903 y su Arbitraria Modificación—No Abrogación—por Norteamérica en 1934," *RBCU* 39 (1937) 389–403.

7616. Runcie, J. E. "American Misgovernment of Cuba," *NAR* 170 (1900) 284–294.

7617. Sanguily, M. "La Anexión de Cuba a los Estados Unidos," *CC* 37 (March, 1925) 249–262.

7618. ———. "Sobre la Génesis de la Enmienda Platt," *CC* 30 (October, 1922) 119–127.

7618a. Santovenia y Echaide, E. S. *Theodore Roosevelt y la Soberanía de Cuba.* Havana, 1958.

7619. Schweyer, A. L. *Como Cayó el Presidente Machado.* 2d ed., Havana, 1938.

7620. Scott, J. B. "The Attitude of the United States Toward Political Disturbances in Cuba," *AJIL* 11 (1917) 419–423.
    Concerns the revolt of 1917.

7621. ———. *Cuba, la América Latina, los Estados Unidos.* Havana, 1926.

7622. ——— (ed.). *The Recommendations of Habana Concerning International Organization, Adopted by the American Institute of International Law at Habana, January 23, 1917.* N.Y., 1917.

7623. Slaughter, J. W. *The United States and Cuba, A Dangerous Policy.* N.Y., n.d.
    A short pamphlet treating events immediately before the revolution of 1917.

7624. Smith, R. F. "American Business Interests and Cuban-American Relations: 1919–1933," U. of Wisconsin Diss., 1958.

The subject is developed to 1960 in item 7431.

7625. Sotolongo, G. *La Verdad Internacional de Cuba*. Havana, 1928.

7626. Strode, H. *The Pageant of Cuba*. N.Y., 1934.

7627. Stuart, G. H. *Cuba and Its International Relations*. N.Y., 1923.

7628. "The Origin and Purpose of the Platt Amendment," *AJIL* 8 (1914) 585–591.

7629. Thomson, C. A. "The Cuban Revolution: Fall of Machado," *FPAR* 11 (1935–1936) 250–261.

7630. Tingley, D. F. "The Cuban Diary of Edwin M. Lacey," *JISHS* 56 (1953) 20–35.

A diary treating the United States military occupation.

7631. Torriente, C. de la. *Cuarenta Años de mi Vida, 1898–1938*. Havana, 1939.

7632. ———. *La Enmienda Platt y el Tratado Permanente*. Havana, 1930.

7633. ———. "The Platt Amendment," *FA* (1930) 364–378.

7634. ———. "Las Relaciones de la República de Cuba y los Estados Unidos de América Conforme al Tratado Permanente," *RDHLC* 75 (1923) 321–350.

7635. Torriente y Peraza, E. de la. *Cuba y los Estados Unidos*. Havana, 1929.

7636. Trelles y Govín, C. M. *El Progreso (1902 a 1905) a y Retroceso (1906 a 1922) de la República de Cuba*. Havana, 1923.

7637. United States Tariff Commission. *The Effects of the Cuban Reciprocity Treaty of 1902*. Wash., 1929.

7637a. USCH. Committee on Ways and Means. *Reciprocity with Cuba: Hearings* (57th Cong., 1st Sess.). Wash., 1902.

7637b. ———. ———. *Reciprocity with Cuba: Report* (57th Cong., 1st Sess., Misc. H. Rept. 1276). Wash., 1902.

7637c. USCS. *The Ethics of the Fight for Cuban Reciprocity* (57th Cong., 1st Sess., S. Doc. 434). Wash., 1902.

7638. USDW. *Acts of Congress, Treaties, Proclamations ... Relating to Non-Contiguous Territory, Cuba and Santo Domingo*. Wash., 1907.

Later editions appeared in 1909, 1912, and 1914.

7639. ———. *Cuban Pacification: Report of Secretary of War and Assistant Secretary of State, Dec. 11, 1906*. Wash., 1907.

7640. ———. Adjutant General of the Army. *Civil Report of Major General John R. Brooke, Military Governor, Island of Cuba*. Wash., 1900.

7641. ———. ———. *Civil Report of Brigadier General Leonard Wood, Military Governor of Cuba, for the Period from December 20, 1899, to December 31, 1900*. 12 vols., Wash., 1901.

7642. ———. ———. *Civil Report of Brigadier General Leonard Wood, Military Governor of Cuba, for the Period from January 1 to December 31, 1901*. 15 vols., Wash., 1902.

7643. ———. ———. *Civil Report of Brigadier General Leonard Wood, Military Governor of Cuba for the Period from January 1 to May 20, 1902*. Wash., 1902.

7644. Varona, E. J. "El Imperialismo Yankee en Cuba," *RAMER* 3 (1922) 309–311.

7645. Velasco, C. de. "La Unica Interpretación Racional de la Enmienda Platt," *CC* 14 (August, 1917) 341–355.

7646. Verrill, A. H. *Cuba of Today*. N.Y., 1931.

7647. Whitcomb, A. *La Situation Internationale de Cuba*. Paris, 1905.

7648. Willis, H. P. "Reciprocity with Cuba," *AAAPSS* 22 (1903) 129–147.

7649. Wood, E. F. *Leonard Wood, Conservator of Americanism: A Biography*. N.Y., 1920.

7650. Wood, L. "The Existing Conditions and Needs in Cuba," *NAR* 168 (1899) 593–601.

7651. Wright, P. G. *The Cuban Situation and Our Treaty Relations*. Wash., 1931.

7652. ———. *Sugar in Relation to the Tariff*. N.Y., 1924.

7653. Zaydín, R., and M. Márquez Sterling. *La Soberanía de Cuba ante las Conferencias de la Paz*. Havana, 1919 (?).

XIV–K–3 cross references:

a) For works on the Spanish-American War, see Chapter V.

b) See also items 2651, 2675, 2681, 2785, 2886, 2956, 3158, 3161, 3174, 3222, 3342, 7437.

7654. Basseur, C. A. *El Derecho de Soberanía Sobre la Isla de Pinos.* Panama, 1925.

7655. Clapp, M. E. "Have We Mislaid a Valuable Possession?" *NAR* 190 (1909) 330–337.

7656. Colby, E. "The Isle of Pines Controversy," *BPAU* 58 (1924) 971–976.

7657. Frost, J. D. "Cuban-American Relations Concerning the Isle of Pines," *HAHR* 11 (1931) 336–350.

7658. Hevia, A. "Los Derechos de Cuba Sobre la Isla de Pinos," *CC* 34 (1924) 177–203, 285–303.

7659. *In Re Treaty of Isle of Pines: An Appeal to the United States Senate, by American Citizens.* N.p., 1923 (?).

7660. Quesada, G. de. *Los Derechos de Cuba á la Isla de Pinos.* Havana, 1909.
English ed., "Cuba's Claims to the Isle of Pines," *NAR* 190 (1909) 594–604.

7661. Rodríguez Lendián, E. *La Isla de Pinos, Según el Tratado de París.* Havana, 1913.

7662. Scott, J. B. "La Isla de Pinos y la Solidaridad Panamericana," *RDLH* 4 (1944) 300–309.

7663. ———. "The Isle of Pines," *AJIL* 17 (1923) 100–104.

7664. Sociedad Cubana de Derecho Internacional. *Statements and Documents Relative to the Isle of Pines Treaty Between the United States and Cuba, Published by the Cuban Society of International Law.* Wash., 1925.

7665. Torriente, C. de la. "Examination of the Facts and Questions: Isle of Pines Treaty Between the United States and Cuba," *RDISDP* 3 (1925) 201–218.

7666. ———. "Los Derechos de Cuba Sobre la Isla de Pinos," *RDLH* 6 (March, 1945) 72–77.

7667. ———. *Mi Misión en Washington: La Soberanía de la Isla de Pinos, 1923–1925.* Havana, 1952.

7668. USCS. *Adjustment of the Title to Isle of Pines, 1906* (59th Cong., 1st Sess., S. Doc. 205). Wash., 1906.

7669. ———. *Isle of Pines: Papers Relating to the Adjustment of Titles to the Ownership of the Isle of Pines* (64th Cong., 2d Sess., S. Doc. 166). Wash., 1924.

7669a. Wright, I. A. *Isle of Pines.* Havana, 1910.

5. United States–Cuban Relations, 1934–1958

7670. Batista y Zaldívar, F. *Cuba, su Política Interna y sus Relaciones Exteriores.* Havana, 1939.

7671. ———. *Ideario de Batista.* Havana, 1940.
Selection of Batista's speeches and writings.

7672. ———. *Piedras y Leyes.* Mexico, 1961.
Batista's own defense of his record.

7673. ———. *Revolución Social o Política Reformista.* Havana, 1944.

7674. Blasier, S. C. "The Cuban and Chilean Communist Parties, Instruments of Soviet Policy, 1935–1948," Columbia U. Diss., 1955.

7675. Buell, R. L. (ed.). *Problems of the New Cuba.* N.Y., 1935.
Report of the Commission on Cuban Affairs, appointed at the request of the Cuban government.

7676. Cabús, J. D. *Batista: Pensamiento y Acción: Reportaje Histórica . . . 1933–1944.* Havana, 1944.

7677. Calderío, F. *Los Fundamentos de Socialismo en Cuba.* Rev. ed., Havana, 1960.
Author also uses the pseudonym of Blas Roca.

7677a. Campa, M. A. *Un Año de Política Exterior Cubana, 1939–1940.* Havana, 1941.

7678. Caraballo, I. *Batista: Una Vida sin Tregua.* Havana, 1944.
A sympathetic biography.

7679. Chester, E. A. *A Sergeant Named Batista.* N.Y., 1954.

7680. Gatría, J. "Los Tratados de Reciprocidad Entre Cuba y los Estados Unidos de Norte América," *A* 9 (January, 1941) 59–65.

7681. Grau San Martín, R. *La Revolución Cubana ante América.* Mexico, 1936.
By the two-time President of Cuba.

7682. Lorenzo, R. *El Empleo en Cuba.* Havana, 1955.

7683. Newman, P. C. *Cuba Before Castro: An Economic Appraisal.* Ridgewood, N.J., 1965.

7683a. Peso, J. del. "El Tratado de Reciprocidad Comercial," *COMU* (February, 1940) 284–296.

7684. Phillips, R. H. *Cuba: Island of Paradox.* N.Y., 1959.
By a *New York Times* correspondent in Havana.

7685. *Report on Cuba.* Wash., 1951.
A report prepared by a special mission of the International Bank for Reconstruction and Development.

7686. Rivero Agüero, A. *Itinerario de un Ideal.* Havana, 1958.
A series of articles defending Batista.

7687. Rodríguez Morejón, G. *Grau San Martín.* Havana, 1944.
Sympathetic treatment.

7688. *Some Facts Regarding the Development and Operation of the United Fruit Company Sugar Properties in the Republic of Cuba.* Preston, Cuba, 1944.
A publication of the United Fruit Company.

7689. Stokes, W. S. "The Cuban Parliamentary System in Action, 1940–47," *JP* 11 (1949) 335–364.

7690. ———. "'The Cuban Revolution' and the Presidential Elections of 1948," *HAHR* 31 (1951) 37–79.

7690a. Thomson, C. A. "The Cuban Revolution: Reform and Reaction," *FPAR* 11, no. 22 (1936).

7691. USDC. Bureau of Foreign Commerce. *Investment in Cuba: Basic Information for United States Businessmen.* Wash., 1956.

7692. United States Tariff Commission. *Economic Controls and Commercial Policy in Cuba.* Wash., 1946.

7693. Vega Cobiellas, U. *Batista y Cuba: Crónica Política y Realizaciones.* Havana, 1955.
Eulogistic analysis.

7694. ———. *El General Fulgencio Batista y la Sucesión Presidencial.* Havana, 1957.

7695. ———. *La Personalidad y la Obra del General Fulgencio Batista Zaldívar, Presidente de la República de Cuba.* Havana, 1943.

7696. ———. *Los Doctores Ramón Grau San Martín y Carlos Saladrigas Zayas.* Havana, 1944.

XIV–K–5   cross references: 4055, 7827

6. United States–Cuban Relations Since 1958

7696a. Abel, E. *The Missile Crisis.* Phil., 1966.
Pb. ed., Phil., 1966.

7697. Acuña, J. A. *Cuba: Revolución Traicionada.* Montevideo, 1962.

7698. Alford, N. H., Jr. "The Cuban Quarantine of 1962: An Inquiry into Paradox and Persuasion," *AJIL* 4 (1964) 35–73.

7699. Allemann, F. R. *Fidel Castro: Die Revolution der Bärte.* Hamburg, 1961.

7700. Allende, S. *Cuba, un Camino.* Santiago, Chile, 1960.

7701. Almansur Haddad, J. *Revolução Cubana e Revolução Brasileira.* Rio, 1961.

7702. Argüedas, S. *Cuba no Es una Isla.* Mexico, 1961.

7702a. ———. "¿Donde Está el Che Guevara?" *CA* 26 (1966) 67–89.

7703. Armas Medina, F. de. "Guantánamo, Bastión del Caribe," *EA* 21 (May, 1961) 255–278.

7704. Arnault, J. *Cuba et le Marxisme.* Paris, 1962.
A French Communist's appraisal.

7705. Arvelo, P. *Revolución de los Barbudos.* Caracas, 1961.
Pro-Castro analysis.

7706. Baciu, S. *Cortina de Ferro Sôbre Cuba.* Rio, 1961.

7707. Baran, P. A. *Reflections on the Cuban Revolution.* N.Y., 1961.

7708. Bartos, R. E. *The Soviet Penetration of Cuba.* Oberammergau, Germany, 1962.

7709. Batista y Zaldívar, F. *Cuba Betrayed.* N.Y., 1962.

7710. ———. *Respuesta* .... Mexico, 1960.

7711. Benítez, F. *La Batalla de Cuba: Seguido Fisonomía de Cuba por Enrique González Pedrero.* Mexico, 1960.
A sympathetic treatment of Castro by a Mexican historian.

7712. Berle, A. A., Jr. "The Cuban Crisis," *FA* 39 (1960) 40–55.

7713. Bernhard, G., and A. Etchepare. *Reportage a Cuba.* Montevideo, 1961.

7714. Brennan, R. *Castro, Cuba, and Justice.* Garden City, N.Y., 1959.
A romanticized sympathetic biography.

7715. Burks, D. D. "Cuba Under Castro," *FPAHS*, no. 165 (1964).

7716. ———. "Cuba Seven Years After," *CH* 50 (January, 1966) 38–44.

7717. ———. "The Future of Castroism," *CH* 44 (February, 1963) 78–83, 116.

7718. Cabús, J. D. *Castro ante la Historia.* Mexico, 1963.

7719. Casa de las Américas. *Cuba: Transformación del Hombre.* 2d ed., Havana, 1961.
    A collection of articles generally
favorable to the revolution.

7720. *Castro, el Anticristo de la Sierra Maestra:
9 Opiniones Profesionales.* Cd. Trujillo,
1960.

7720a. Castro, F. "A Combatir al Enemigo en
Todos los Frentes," *CSO* 3 (April, 1963)
1–24.

7721. ———. *Cuatro Horas Antiimperialistas
en la ONU.* Lima, 1961.

7722. ———. *Discurso de Clausura ante el
Congreso de Mujeres de Toda América.*
Peking, 1963.

7723. ———. *Discurso Pronunciado en el Gran
Mitin de Masas en Celebración del IV
Aniversario de la Victoria de la Revolución
Cubana.* Peking, 1963.

7724. ———. *Discursos del Dr. Fidel Castro,
Comandante en Jefe del Ejército Rebelde,
26 de Julio y Primer Ministro del Gobierno Revolucionario.* Havana, 1959.
    A collection of Castro's speeches im-
mediately following the overthrow of
Batista.

7725. ———. *Documentos: Declaración de la
Habana: Discurso en la O.N.U.* Havana,
1961.

7726. ———. *Historia de la Invasión a Cuba.*
Lima, 1961.

7727. ———. *History Will Absolve Me.* N.Y.,
1961.
    Text of the speech originally read in
Castro's trial after the failure of the
Moncada attack.

7728. ———. *Pensamiento Político, Económico
y Social de Fidel Castro.* Havana, 1959.

7728a. ———. "Un Pueblo Así Es un Pueblo
Invencible!" *CSO* 2 (December, 1962)
7–32.

7729. Casuso, T. *Cuba and Castro.* N.Y., 1961.
    By a former Castro supporter and
Cuban delegate to the United Nations.

7730. Chayes, A. "Law and the Quarantine of
Cuba," *FA* 41 (1963) 550–557.

7731. Chichkov, V. M. *Zaria nad Kuboi.*
Moscow, 1960.
    Sunrise over Cuba. By a *Pravda* corre-
spondent.

7732. Christol, C. Q., and C. R. Davis. "Maritime Quarantine: The Naval Interdiction
of Offensive Weapons and Associated

Material to Cuba, 1962," *AJIL* 57
(1963) 525–545.

7733. *Conjura Contra Cuba en Caimanera.*
Havana, 1961.
    An attack on alleged C.I.A. activities in
Guantánamo.

7734. Conte Agüero, L. *Los Dos Rostros de Fidel
Castro.* Mexico, 1960.
    A former supporter of Castro attacks
the regime.

7735. Cosío Villegas, D. *Change in Latin
America: The Mexican and Cuban
Revolutions.* Lincoln, Nebr., 1961.

7736. *Cuba: Ejemplo Revolucionario de Latino-
América.* Lima, 1961.
    Collection of articles, mainly from *La
Prensa Latina,* the official Cuban press
agency.

7737. Cuba. Ministerio de Relaciones Exteriores. Departamento de Relaciones
Públicas. *Una Nueva Diplomacia*: Havana, 1959.

7738. ———. Secretaría de Estado. *Cuba
Replies to the U.S.A. Note: In Defense of
National Sovereignty.* Havana, 1959.

7739. Daniel, J., and J. G. Hubbell. *Strike in
the West: The Complete Story of the Cuban
Crisis.* N.Y., 1963.

7740. Dewart, L. *Christianity and Revolution:
The Lesson of Cuba.* N.Y., 1963.

7741. Dorticos Torrado, O. *Committed to Our
Own Principles.* Havana, 1962.

7742. ———. *Cuba Is a Sovereign Nation by Its
Own Right, Not by Any Grant.* Havana,
1960.

7743. Draper, T. "Castro and Communism:
A Detailed Account of the Background
and Consequences of the Missile Crisis in
Cuba," *REPORT* 28, no. 2 (1963)
35–48.

7744. ———. *Castroism: Theory and Practice.*
N.Y., 1965.
    Consists of three essays.

7745. ———. "Castro's Cuba: A Revolution
Betrayed," *EN* 16 (March, 1961) 6–23.

7746. ———. *Castro's Revolution: Myths and
Realities.* N.Y., 1962.
    Articles originally published in *En-
counter* and the *New Leader.*

7747. ———. *Cuba and U.S. Policy.* N.Y.,
1961.

7748. ———. *Cuba—Uma Revolução Traída?*
Rio, 1961.

7748a. ———. "El Comunismo de Castro," *CUA* 58 (March, 1962) 19–38.

7749. Dubois, J. *Fidel Castro: Rebel-Liberator or Dictator?* Indianapolis, 1959.
Sympathetic treatment by a *Chicago Tribune* correspondent who subsequently changed his mind.

7750. Dumont, R. *Cuba: Socialisme et Développement.* Paris, 1964.

7751. Efimov, A. V., and I. R. Grigulevich (eds.). *Kuba: Istorikoetnograficheskie Ocherki.* Moscow, 1961.
Cuba: Ethno-Historical Essays.

7751a. ———, *et al.* (eds.). *Piat' Let Kubanskoi Revoliutsii.* Moscow, 1963.
Five Years of the Cuban Revolution.

7752. Fabela, I. *El Caso de Cuba.* Mexico, 1960.

7753. Federación Estudiantil Universitaria. *Carta Abierta a los Estudiantes Norteamericanos.* Havana, 1960.

7754. Fenwick, C. G. "The Quarantine Against Cuba: Legal or Illegal?" *AJIL* 57 (1963) 588–592.

7755. Ferraris, A. *Cuba en la Problemática Internacional.* B.A., 1965.

7756. *Fidel Castro Denounces Sectarianism: Speech of March 26, 1962.* Havana, 1962.

7757. Fitzgibbon, R. H. "The Revolution Next Door: Cuba," *AAAPSS* 334 (1961) 113–122.

7758. Franco, V. *The Morning After: A French Journalist's Impressions of Cuba Under Castro.* N.Y., 1963.
Disillusioned observations of a journalist who visited Cuba in 1961.

7759. Frank, W. *Cuba: Prophetic Island.* N.Y., 1961.
Spanish ed., B.A., 1961.

7760. Free, L. A. *Attitudes of the Cuban People Toward the Castro Regime in the Late Spring of 1960.* Princeton, N.J., 1960.

7761. Friedmann, G. *Signal d'une Troisième Voi?* Paris, 1961.

7762. Frondizi, S. *La Revolución Cubana: Su Significación Histórica.* Montevideo, 1960.

7763. Gilly, A. *Inside the Cuban Revolution.* N.Y., 1964.
Impressions of an Argentine journalist.

7764. Gironella, J. M. *On China and Cuba.* Notre Dame, Ind., 1963.

7765. González Pedrero, E. "La Caída de Otra Dictadura," *CA* 18 (March, 1959) 25–35.
Concerns the overthrow of Batista.

7766. Granfelt, H. "Sjöblockad Som Politiskt Vapen," *ST* 66 (1963) 380–399.
"The Naval Blockade as a Political Weapon."

7767. Grignon-Dumoulin, J. (ed.). *Fidel Castro Parle: La Révolution Cubaine par les Textes.* Paris, 1961.

7768. Grupo Cubano de Investigaciones Económicas. *Un Estudio Sobre Cuba.* Coral Gables, Fla., 1963.

7769. Guevara, C. *Ché Guevara on Guerilla Warfare.* N.Y., 1961.

7769a. ———. "Cuba and the 'Kennedy Plan,'" *WMR* 5 (February, 1962) 33–39.

7770. Harbron, J. D. "Castro in the Americas," *BH* 21, no. 3 (1961).

7771. Horelick, A. L. *The Cuban Missile Crisis: An Analysis of Soviet Calculations and Behavior.* Santa Monica, Calif., 1963.

7772. Huberman, L., and P. M. Sweezy. *Cuba: Anatomy of a Revolution.* 2d ed., N.Y., 1961.
The authors, who spent three weeks in Cuba in March, 1960, suggest that the Cuban revolution was in reality a peasant revolution.

7773. Hulsey, R. H. "The Cuban Revolution: Its Impact on American Foreign Policy," *JIAS* 14 (1960) 158–174.

7774. James, D. *Cuba: The First Soviet Satellite in the Americas.* N.Y., 1961.
Based primarily on interviews with exiles from the Castro regime.

7775. Johnson, H., *et al. The Bay of Pigs: The Leaders' Story of Brigade 2506.* N.Y., 1964.

7776. Julien, C. *La Revolución Cubana.* Montevideo, 1961.

7777. Kling, M. "Cuba: A Case Study of a Successful Attempt to Seize Political Power by the Application of Unconventional Warfare," *AAAPSS* 341 (1962) 42–52.

7777a. Komeyama, A. *Cuba no Kokumei: Chū—Nanbei no Kinô to Kojô.* Tokyo, 1944.
Cuban Revolution: Central and South America Today.

7778. Ladrón de Guevara, M. *Adiós al Cañaveral: Diario de una Mujer en Cuba.* 2d ed., B.A., 1962.

7779. Lamont, C. *The Crime Against Cuba.* N.Y., 1961.

7780. Lantz, B. *Castro's Kuba.* Stockholm, 1962.

7781. Larson, D. L. *The Cuban Crisis of 1962: Selected Documents and Chronology.* Boston, 1963.

Ninety-four documents, including the exchange of letters between President Kennedy and Chairman Khrushchev.

7782. Light, R. E., and C. Marzani. *Cuba versus CIA.* N.Y., 1961.

7782a. Lockwood, L. *Castro's Cuba, Cuba's Fidel.* N.Y., 1967.

7782b. López-Fresquet, R. *My Fourteen Months with Castro.* Cleveland, 1966.

By the Cuban minister of the treasury from January, 1959, to March, 1960. Subsequently he chose exile.

7783. Lowenthal, R. "Los Estados Unidos, Cuba y la Unión Soviética," *CUA* 68 (January, 1963) 27–36.

7784. Mallin, J. *Fortress Cuba: Russia's American Base.* Chicago, 1965.

7784a. Mañach, J. "La Revolución Cubana y sus Perspectivas," *CUA* 35 (March, 1959) 3–9.

7785. Martino, J. *I Was Castro's Prisoner: An American Tells His Story.* N.Y., 1963.

7786. Massó, J. L. *Cuba: 17 de Abril.* Mexico, 1962.

7787. Matthews, H. L. *Cuba.* N.Y., 1964.

By the *New York Times* correspondent who first publicized Castro's activities in the Sierra Maestra.

7788. ———. *The Cuban Story.* N.Y., 1961.

7789. Matos, A. *Cuba: A Revolução na América.* Rio, 1961.

7790. McDougal, M. S. "The Soviet-Cuban Quarantine and Self-Defense," *AJIL* 57 (1963) 597–603.

7791. McWhinney, E. "Coexistence of the Cuban Crisis and Cold War International Law," *IJ* 18 (1962–1963) 67–74.

7792. Meeker, L. C. "Defensive Quarantine and the Law," *AJIL* 57 (1963) 515–524.

7793. Meyer, K. E., and T. Szulc. *The Cuban Invasion: The Chronicle of a Disaster.* N.Y., 1962.

Discussion of the Bay of Pigs invasion of April, 1961.

7794. Mikoyan, A. I. *Mikoyan in Cuba: Full Texts of the Speeches Made by . . . First Vice-Chairman of the USSR on His Tour of Cuba Feb. 4–13, 1960.* N.Y., 1960.

7795. Miller, W. *90 Miles from Home: The Face of Cuba Today.* Boston, 1961.

7796. Mills, C. W. *Listen, Yankee: The Revolution in Cuba.* N.Y., 1960.

Author presents what he believes to be "the voice of the Cuban revolutionary."

7797. Monahan, J., and K. O. Gilmore. *The Great Deception: The Inside Story of How the Kremlin Took Over Cuba.* N.Y., 1963.

Spanish ed., Mexico, 1963.

7798. Morray, J. P. *The Second Revolution in Cuba.* N.Y., 1962.

7799. Murkland, H. B. "Cuba: The Evolution of Revolution," *CH* 38 (March, 1960) 129–133.

7799a. *The Ninth Anniversary of the 26th of July.* Havana, 1962.

7800. North, J. *Cuba: Hope of a Hemisphere.* N.Y., 1961.

7801. O'Connor, J. "On Cuban Political Economy," *PSQ* 79 (1964) 223–247.

7802. Osherov, G. *Fidel Kastro.* Vilnius, U.S.S.R., 1961.

7803. Otero Echeverría, R. *Reportaje a una Revolución: De Batista a Fidel Castro.* Santiago, 1959.

7804. Pachter, H. M. *Collision Course: The Cuban Missile Crisis and Coexistence.* N.Y., 1963.

7805. Palacios, A. L. *Una Revolución Auténtica en Nuestra América.* Mexico, 1960.

7806. PAU. Inter-American Commission on Human Rights. *Report on the Situation of Political Prisoners and Their Relatives in Cuba, Approved by the Inter-American Commission on Human Rights in the Thirteenth Meeting of Its Sixth Session.* Wash., 1963.

7807. Pardo Llada, J. *Memorias de la Sierra Maestra.* Havana, 1960.

7808. Partan, D. G. "The Cuban Quarantine: Some Implications for Self-Defense," *DLJ* (Autumn, 1963) 696–721.

7809. Pflaum, I. P. *Tragic Island: How Communism Came to Cuba.* Englewood Cliffs, N.J., 1961.

7810. Phillips, R. H. *The Cuban Dilemma.* N.Y., 1962.

Covers 1959 to 1962.

7811. Quijada G., F. *Cuba bajo el Terror*

(*Observaciones de un Periodista en Mission Diplomática*). Caracas, 1962.

7811a. Rauf, M. A., Jr. *Cuban Journal.* N.Y., 1964.
Impressions of a United States journalist.

7811b. Razumovich, N. N. *Gosudarstvennye Preobrazovaniia Revoliutsionnoi Kuby.* Moscow, 1964.
The State Transformation of Revolutionary Cuba.

7812. "Responsibility of Cuban Government for Increased International Tensions in the Hemisphere," *USDSB* 43 (1960) 314–346.

7813. Rivero, N. *Castro's Cuba: An American Dilemma.* Wash., 1962.
Author held diplomatic posts under Batista and Castro. He became disillusioned with both.

7814. Roa, R. *Cuba Tiene la Razón.* San José, C.R., 1960.

7815. Roca, B. [pseudonym for F. Calderío]. *Balance de la Labor del Partido Desde la Ultima Asamblea Nacional y el Desarrollo de la Revolución.* Havana, 1960.

7816. ———. *The Cuban Revolution: A Report to the Eighth National Congress of the Popular Socialist Party of Cuba.* N.Y., 1961.

7816a. ———. "The Cuban Revolution in Action," *WMR* 2 (August, 1959) 16–22.

7817. ———. "New Stage in the Cuban Revolution," *WMR* 4 (October, 1961) 3–10.

7817a. ———. "Sobre la Revolución Cubana," *EPEFC* 4 (September, 1959) 32–45.

7817b. ———. *El Socialismo Cubano y la Revolución de Fidel.* Lima, 1961.

7818. Rodríguez Morejón, G. *Fidel Castro: Biografía.* Havana, 1959.

7819. Rusk, D. "Task of the OAS," *VS* 30 (1964) 665–667.

7820. Sartre, J.-P. *Sartre on Cuba.* N.Y., 1961.
The French existentialist philosopher wrote this sympathetic account after a visit of several weeks. Spanish ed., Havana, 1960.

7820a. Sauvage, L. "Fidel Castro y Herbert Matthews o el Caso del Historiador Amoroso," *CUA* 57 (February, 1962) 57–62.

7821. Schneider, R. M. "Five Years of Cuban Revolution," *CH* 46 (January, 1964) 26–33.

7822. Seers, D. (ed.). *Cuba: The Economic and Social Revolution.* Chapel Hill, N.C., 1964.

7823. Shapiro, S. "Cuba: A Dissenting Report," *NR* 143, nos. 11–12 (1960) 8–26.

7824. Sierra, D. *Algo Rojo Cayó en el Caribe: Notas Sobre la Revolución de Cuba.* B.A., 1961.

7825. Smith, E. E. T. *The Fourth Floor: An Account of the Castro Communist Revolution.* N.Y., 1962.
Spanish ed., Mexico, 1963. Smith was the United States ambassador to Cuba when Castro came to power.

7826. Soria, G. *Cuba à l'Heure Castro.* Paris, 1961.

7827. Souchy, A. *Testimonios Sobre la Revolución Cubana.* B.A., 1960.

7828. Stecchini, L. "Cuba's Revolt—An Historical Appraisal," *D* 6 (1959) 129–133.

7829. Stein, E. C. *Cuba, Castro and Communism.* N.Y., 1962.
Anti-Castro interpretation.

7829a. Suárez Feliú, N. "La Actual Política Internacional," *CUA* suppl., 47 (March, 1961) 31–35.

7830. Synnestvedt, S. "Red Drive in Cuba," *CH* 45 (October, 1963) 216–222.

7831. Taber, R. *M—26: Biography of a Revolution.* N.Y., 1961.
Favorable appraisal of the revolution.

7832. Tang, P. S. H., and J. Maloney. *The Chinese Communist Impact on Cuba.* Chestnut Hill, Mass., 1962.

7833. Tanner, H. *Counter-Revolutionary Agent: Diary of the Events Which Occurred in Cuba Between January and July, 1961.* London, 1962.

7834. Urrutia Lleó, M. *Fidel Castro & Company, Inc.: Communist Tyranny in Cuba.* N.Y., 1964.
Author was Cuba's provisional President for six months under Castro, but subsequently split with Castro.

7835. *USDA. Special Warfare Area Handook for Cuba.* Wash., 1961.

7836. USDD. Armed Forces Information and Education Office. "Cuban Crisis," *FCTCW* 2, no. 20 (1962).

7836a. ———. ———. "Cuba, Questions and Answers," *FCTCW* 2, no. 10 (1962).

7836b. USDD. Armed Forces Information and Education Office. "U.S. Policy Toward Cuba," *FCTCW* 3, no. 24 (1964).

7837. USDS. *Cuba.* Wash., 1961.

7838. USCH. Committee on Foreign Affairs. *Castro-Communist Subversion in the Western Hemisphere: Hearings Before the Subcommittee on Inter-American Affairs* (88th Cong., 1st Sess.). Wash., 1963.

7839. ———. ———. *Castro-Communist Subversion in the Western Hemisphere: Report of the Subcommittee on Inter-American Affairs* (88th Cong., 1st Sess., H. Rept. 195). Wash., 1963.

7839a. ———. ———. *Communist Threat in Latin America, Hearings Before Subcommittee on Inter-American Affairs* (86th Cong., 2d Sess.). Wash., 1960.

7840. ———. Committee on Interstate and Foreign Commerce. *Trade with Cuba: Hearings* (87th Cong., 1st Sess.). Wash., 1961.

7841. USCS. Committee on Foreign Relations. *Events in U.S.–Cuban Relations: A Chronology, 1957–1963, Prepared by the Department of State* (88th Cong., 1st Sess.). Wash., 1963.

7842. ———. Committee on Foreign Relations and the Committee on Armed Services. *Situation in Cuba: Hearing* (87th Cong., 2d Sess.). Wash., 1962.

7843. ———. ———. *Situation in Cuba: Report* (88th Cong., 2d Sess.). Wash., 1962.

7844. ———. Committee on the Judiciary. *Cuba as a Base for Subversion in America: Study, Subcommittee to Investigate the Administration of the Internal Security Act* (88th Cong., 1st Sess.). Wash., 1963.

7845. USDS. *Cuba, Latin America, and Communism, by Edwin M. Martin, Assistant Secretary of State for Inter-American Affairs.* Wash., 1963.

7845a. ———. *U.S. Charges of Soviet Military Buildup in Cuba, Statements by Adlai E. Stevenson on Oct. 23 and 25, 1962, in U.N.* Wash., 1962.

7846. Vargas Echeverría, J. M. *Revolución Cubana, Despertar Latino Americano: Notas de un Viaje a Cuba.* Bogotá, 1961.
    Favorable to the revolution.

7847. Weyl, N. *Red Star over Cuba: The Russian Assault on the Western Hemisphere.* N.Y., 1960.
    A passionate condemnation.

7848. Wilkerson, L. *Fidel Castro's Political Programs from Reformism to "Marxism-Leninism."* Gainesville, Fla., 1966.

7849. Williams, W. A. *The United States, Cuba, and Castro.* N.Y., 1962.
    Supports the revolution enthusiastically.

7850. Wilson, L. C. "International Law and the United States Cuban Quarantine of 1962," *JIAS* 7 (October, 1965) 485–492.

7851. Wright, Q. "Intervention and Cuba in 1961," *ASILP* (1961) 2–19.

7852. Zeitlin, M., and R. Scheer. *Cuba: Tragedy in Our Hemisphere.* N.Y., 1963.

XIV–K–6   cross references:
  a) For the expulsion of Cuba from the OAS, see items 5287–5311.
  b) See also items 4250, 4611, 4785, 4791a, 4840, 4841, 6335, 6337, 10135.

L. THE UNITED STATES AND THE DOMINICAN REPUBLIC (SANTO DOMINGO)

1. UNITED STATES–DOMINICAN RELATIONS: GENERAL WORKS AND SPECIAL STUDIES

7853. Alfau Durán, V. "Presidentes de la República Dominicana, 1844–1952," *CL* 16 (July, 1948) 97–105.

7854. Despradel, A. *Historia Diplomática Dominicana.* Cd. Trujillo, 1940.

7855. Henríquez, M. C. *Historia de Santo Domingo.* Cd. Trujillo, 1938.

7856. Hoepelman, V. *Nuestra Vida Exterior: Notas Sobre Historia Diplomática Dominicana, 1844–1950.* Cd. Trujillo, 1951.

7857. Jiménez Grullón, J. I. *La República Dominicana: Análisis de su Pasado y de su Presente.* Havana, 1940.

7858. MacMichael, D. C. "The United States and the Dominican Republic, 1871–1940: A Cycle in Caribbean Diplomacy," U. of Oregon Diss., 1964.

7859. Marrero Aristy, R. *La República Dominicana: Origen y Destino del Pueblo Cristiano más Antiguo de América.* 2 vols., Cd. Trujillo, 1958–1959.
    Vol. 1 treats prehistory to the 1860's; vol. 2 treats the period from the 1860's to date of publication.

7860. Mejía, L. F. *De Lilís a Trujillo: Historia Contemporánea de la República Dominicana.* Caracas, 1944.

Covers the years 1889–1930.

7861. Mejía Ricart, G. A. *Historia de Santo Domingo.* 3 vols., Cd. Trujillo, 1948–1950.

7862. Rodman, S. *Quisqueya: A History of the Dominican Republic.* Seattle, 1964.

7862a. Rodríguez Demorizi, E. *Apuntes y Documentos.* Cd. Trujillo, 1957.

A compilation of articles and documents on various subjects and aspects of Dominican history, originally published from 1954 to 1956 in *Clío.*

7862b. ———. *Documentos para la Historia de la República Dominicana.* 3 vols., Cd. Trujillo, 1944–1959.

7863. Schoenrich, O. *Santo Domingo: A Country with a Future.* N.Y., 1918.

7864. Welles, S. *Naboth's Vineyard: The Dominican Republic, 1844–1924.* 2 vols., N.Y., 1928.

Detailed analysis with diplomatic emphasis.

2. UNITED STATES–DOMINICAN RELATIONS: INDEPENDENCE TO 1905

7865. Brown, J. *The History and Present Condition of St. Domingo.* 2 vols., Phil., 1837.

7866. Cabrera Leiva, G. "Aventura Olvidada: Migración de Negros de E.U. a la Española, a Principios del Siglo XIX," *APAU* 4 (July, 1952) 16–19, 47.

7867. Dozer, D. M. "Anti-Expansionism During the Johnson Administration," *PHR* 12 (1943) 253–275.

7868. Duin, E. C. "Dominican-American Relations, 1897–1907," Georgetown U. Diss., 1955.

7869. García, J. G. *Colección de los Tratados Internacionales Celebrados por la República Dominicana Desde su Creación Hasta Nuestros Días.* Santo Domingo, 1896.

Expanded version originally published in 1882.

7870. ———. *Compendio de la Historia de Santo Domingo.* 3d ed., 3 vols. Santo Domingo, 1896.

7871. Hazard, S. *Santo Domingo, Past and Present, with a Glance at Hayti.* N.Y., 1873.

The author toured the island with the commission sent by President Grant.

7872. Keim, D. R. *San Domingo.* Phil., 1870.

7873. Luperón, G. *Notas Autobiográficas y Apuntes Históricos Sobre la República Dominicana.* 2 vols., Ponce, 1896.

7874. Monte y Tejada, A. del. *Historia de Santo Domingo.* 4 vols., Santo Domingo, 1890–1892.

7875. "Partes Sobre la Salida de la Fragata Americana 'Albany,'" *BANC* 29, no. 1–6 (1930) 99–101.

7876. Perkins, D. *La Cuestión de Santo Domingo, 1849–1865.* Cd. Trujillo, 1956.

7877. Porter, D. D. "Secret Missions to San Domingo," *NAR* 128 (1879) 616–630.

7878. Rodríguez Demorizi, E. *Documentos para la Historia de la República Dominicana.* 2 vols., Santiago, D.R., 1944–1947.

7879. Tansill, C. C. *The United States and Santo Domingo, 1798–1873: A Chapter in Caribbean Diplomacy.* Baltimore, 1938.

7880. Treudley, M. *The United States and Santo Domingo, 1789–1866.* Worcester, Mass., 1916.

7881. Troncoso, J. M. "Notas para la Historia de las Finanzas de la República Dominicana, 1844–1901," *BANDR* 2 (1939) 341–365.

7882. USCH. *Dominican Republic . . . Report of Captain George B. McClellan upon the Dominican Republic, in the Year 1854* (41st Cong., 3d Sess., H. Exec. Doc. 43). Wash., 1871.

XIV–L–2   cross references:

a) For works treating the short-lived Spanish reconquest (1861–1865), see items 2190–2202.

3. ATTEMPTED UNITED STATES ANNEXATION (1871)

7883. Americus [pseudonym for V. W. Kingsley (?)]. "The Annexation of St. Domingo," *G* 11 (1871) 410–421.

7884. *Annexation of San Domingo.* N.Y., 1870.

7885. *Breve Refutación del Informe de los Comisionados de Santo Domingo, Dedicada al Pueblo de los Estados Unidos.* Curaçao, 1871.

Anti-annexation sentiment.

7886. Cazneau, W. L. *To the American Press:*

The Dominican Negotiacions [sic]: *I. Samana as a Naval Station. II. Samana as a Free Port. III. Samana and Annexation.* Santo Domingo, 1870.

Author was a special United States agent in the Dominican Republic in 1854.

7887. Cox, J. D. "How Judge Hoar Ceased to Be Attorney General," *AM* 76 (1895) 162–173.

7888. Hargrave, H. "The Dominican Republic and Annexation," *LIP* 6 (1870) 200–210.

7889. Howe, S. G. *Letters on the Proposed Annexation of Santo Domingo, in Answer to Certain Charges in the Newspapers.* Boston, 1871.

7890. Montllor, J. J. "Oposición Dominicana a la Anexión a los Estados Unidos," *BANDR* 4 (December, 1941) 395–407.

7891. Pierce, E. L. "A Senator's Fidelity Vindicated," *NAR* 127 (1878) 61–80.

Concerns Charles Sumner.

7892. Pinkett, H. T. "Efforts to Annex Santo Domingo to the United States, 1866–1871," *JNH* 26 (January, 1941) 12–45.

7893. Smith, T. C. "Expansion After the Civil War, 1865—1871," *PSQ* 16 (1901) 412–436.

7894. Sumner, C. *Charles Sumner, His Complete Works.* 20 vols., Boston, 1900.

Sumner was in part responsible for defeating the annexation treaty in the Senate.

7895. USCH. *Dominican Republic . . . Report of the Secretary of State Relative to the Dominican Republic* (41st Cong., 3d Sess., H. Ex. Doc. 42). Wash., 1871.

7896. USCS. *Copies of Correspondence with and Orders Issued to the Commander of Our Naval Squadron in the Waters of the Island of San Domingo Since the Commencement of the Late Negotiations* (41st Cong., 3d Sess., S. Ex. Doc. 34). Wash., 1871.

7897. ———. *Information Relative to the Proposed Annexation of the Dominican Portion of the Island of San Domingo* (41st Cong., 3d Sess., S. Ex. Doc. 17). Wash., 1871.

7898. ———. *Report of the Commission of Inquiry to the Island of Santo Domingo, April 5, 1871* (42d Cong., 1st Sess., S. Ex. Doc. 91). Wash., 1871.

7899. Walsh, R. "My Mission to San Domingo," *LIP* 7 (1871) 293–307.

XIV–L–3 cross references: 2094, 2112a, 7870, 7871, 7879.

4. UNITED STATES–DOMINICAN RELATIONS, 1905–1924

7900. Academia Colombiana. *Memorial de Protesta Contra la Arbitraria Ocupación Militar de la República Dominicana por Tropas de los Estados Unidos de Norte América, 1916.* Santo Domingo, 1916.

7901. Adams, R. G. "Santo Domingo: A Study in Benevolent Imperialism," *SAQ* 20 (1921) 10–24.

7902. Brown, P. M. "The Armed Intervention of Santo Domingo," *AJIL* 11 (1917) 394–399.

7903. Cestero, J. M. "El Problema Dominicana," *RSO* 16 (December, 1919) 222–238.

7904. ———. "Los Estados Unidos y la República Dominicana," *RSO* 8 (December, 1916) 74–103; 9 (1917) 66–112.

7905. Chapman, C. E. "The United States and the Dominican Republic," *HAHR* 7 (1927) 299–319.

7906. Dominican Republic. *Reconstrucción Financiera de la República Dominicana.* 2 vols., Santiago de los Caballeros, D.R., 1944.

The first volume covers 1903 to 1930; the second covers 1930 to 1944.

7907. Fairchild, F. R. "The Public Finance of Santo Domingo," *PSQ* 33 (1918) 461–481.

7908. Fiallo, F. *La Comisión Nacionalista Dominicana en Washington (1920–1921).* Cd. Trujillo, 1939.

This is a selection taken from item 7909.

7909. ———. *The Crime of Wilson in Santo Domingo.* Havana, 1940.

7910. ———. "The Evacuation of Santo Domingo," *CH* 14 (1921) 290–294.

7911. Franco-Franco, T. *La Situation Internationale de la République Dominicaine à Partir du 8 Février, 1907.* Paris, 1923.

A juridical analysis.

7912. González Arrili, B. *La República Dominicana y los Estados Unidos: La Soberanía de las Pequeñas Naciones.* B.A., 1919.

7913.   Henríquez Ureña, M. *Los Estados Unidos y la República Dominicana: La Verdad de los Hechos Comprobada por Datos y Documentos Oficiales.* Havana, 1919.

7914.   ———. *Los Yanquis en Santo Domingo.* Madrid, 1929.

7915.   Hoepelmann, A., and J. A. Senior (eds.). *Documentos Históricos que Refieren a la Intervención Armada de los Estados Unidos de Norte América y la Implantación de un Gobierno Militar Americano en la República Dominicana.* Santo Domingo, 1922.

7916.   Hollander, J. H. "The Convention of 1907 Between the United States and the Dominican Republic," *AJIL* 1 (1907) 287–297.

7917.   ———. *The Debt of Santo Domingo.* Wash., 1905.

7918.   ———. "The Financial Difficulties of Santo Domingo," *AAAPSS* 30 (1907) 93–103.

7919.   ———. "The Readjustment of Santo Domingo's Finances," *QJE* 21 (1907) 405–426.

7920.   Inman, S. G. *Through Santo Domingo and Haiti, a Cruise with the Marines: Report of a Visit to These Island Republics in the Summer of 1919.* N.Y., 1919.

7921.   Júarez, J. R. "United States Withdrawal from Santo Domingo," *HAHR* 42 (1962) 152–190.

7922.   Knight, M. M. *The Americans in Santo Domingo.* N.Y., 1928.
        Spanish ed., Cd. Trujillo, 1939. Expresses the anti-interventionist point of view.

7923.   Livingstone, N. P. "A Caribbean Derelict," *NAR* 195 (1912) 261–265.

7924.   Marvin, G. "Watchful Acting in Santo Domingo," *WW* 34 (June, 1917) 205–218.

7925.   Mejía, F. E. *Alrededor y en Contra del Plan Hughes–Peynado.* Santo Domingo, 1922.
        Concerns the plan for withdrawal of the marines negotiated in 1922.

7926.   Newlands, F. G. "The San Domingo Question," *NAR* 180 (1905) 885–898.

7927.   Phelan, J. D. *Santo Domingo Investigation: Copy of the Report, Findings, and Opinion of James D. Phelan, Commissioner Named by the Secretary of State, with the Approval of the President, to Investigate Charges Against United States Minister to the Dominican Republic, Charles H. Strong, Counsel.* Wash., 1916.

7928.   Rippy, J. F. "The Initiation of the Customs Receivership in the Dominican Republic," *HAHR* 17 (1937) 419–457.

7929.   Roig de Leuchsenring, E. *La Ocupación de la República Dominicana por los Estados Unidos y Derecho de las Pequeñas Nacionalidades de América.* Havana, 1919.
        Also appears in *RMDI* 2 (1920) 249–296.

7930.   Rosa, A. de la. "Les Finances de Saint-Domingue et le Contrôle Américain," *RGDIP* 18 (1912) 73–120.

7931.   Schoenrich, O. "The Present American Intervention in Santo Domingo and Haiti," *JIR* 10 (1920) 45–62.

7932.   Tolentino, R. C. (ed.). *La Información Frente a la Ocupación.* Santiago de los Caballeros, D.R., 1922.

7933.   Wright, T. P., Jr. "The United States and Latin American Dictatorship: The Case of the Dominican Republic," *JIA* 14, no. 2 (1960) 152–157.

XIV–L–4   cross references: *7118, 7638, 8085, 8092*

5. UNITED STATES–DOMINICAN RELATIONS SINCE 1924

7934.   Almoina, J. *Yo Fuí Secretario de Trujillo.* B.A., 1950.

7935.   Ariza, S. *Trujillo: The Man and His Country.* N.Y., 1939.
        Sympathetic biography.

7935a. Atkins, G. P. "The United States and the Dominican Republic during the Era of Trujillo," American U. Diss., 1966.

7936.   Balaguer, J. *Dominican Reality: Biographical Sketch of a Country and a Regime.* Mexico, 1949.

7937.   ——— (ed.). *El Pensamiento Vivo de Trujillo: Antología.* Cd. Trujillo, 1955.

7938.   Besault, L. de. *President Trujillo: His Work and the Dominican Republic.* Wash., 1936.
        A eulogistic treatment.

7939.   Bonilla Atiles, J. A. *Discursos y Conferencias Enjuiciando la Política del Presidente Trujillo, 1940–1946.* Cd. Trujillo, 1946.

7940. Bosch, J. *Trujillo: Causas de una Tiranía sin Ejemplo.* Caracas, 1959.

7940a. Calderón, T. R. *Tratados y Convenciones Internacionales Vigentes de la República Dominicana.* Santo Domingo, 1937.
Texts in Spanish.

7941. Castillo de Aza, Z. *Trujillo y Otras Benefactores de la Iglesia.* Cd. Trujillo, 1961.

7942. Chapman, C. E. "The United States and the Dominican Republic," *HAHR* 7 (1927) 84–91.

7943. Crawford, H. P. *Rights of Foreign Companies in the Dominican Republic.* Wash., 1937.

7944. Cruz, F. A. *Génesis, Evolución y Agonía del Partido Comunista Dominicano.* Cd. Trujillo, 1947.

7945. Díaz Ordóñez, V. *La Política Exterior de Trujillo.* Cd. Trujillo, 1955.

7946. Dominican Press Society. *Report on the National Assembly . . . December 7 and 8, 1957: Inter-American Press Association Interventionism Rejected.* Cd. Trujillo, 1958.

7947. Dominican Republic. Secretaría de Estado de Relaciones Exteriores. *Compilación Trujillo de Tratados y Convenciones de la República Dominicana.* 9 vols., Cd. Trujillo, 1958.

7948. ———. ———. *Boletín: Nos. 63, 64.* Cd. Trujillo, 1949.
Dominican response to invasion attempt, 1949.

7949. ———. ———. *Tratados, Convenciones y Acuerdos Vigentes en la República Dominicana el 1º de Julio de 1946.* Cd. Trujillo, 1946.

7950. ———. Secretaría del Interior. *Libro Blanco del Comunismo en la República Dominicana.* Cd. Trujillo, 1956.
English ed., Cd. Trujillo, 1958.

7951. Espaillat, A. *Trujillo: The Last Caesar.* Chicago, 1963.

7952. Figueres, J. "Mandato de las Naciones Unidas en la República Dominicana," *COMB* 1 (September, 1958) 67–70.

7953. Franco Ornes, P. *La Tragedia Dominicana: Análisis de la Tiranía de Trujillo.* Santiago, 1946.

7954. Galíndez, J. de. *La Era de Trujillo.* Cd. Trujillo, 1955.
The controversial book by the Spanish

exile who was subsequently murdered, reputedly on Trujillo's order.

7955. Gonzáles Herrera, J. *Trujillo: Genio Político.* Cd. Trujillo, 1956.
A laudatory biography.

7956. González-Blanco, P. *Trujillo, o la Restauración de un Pueblo.* Cd. Trujillo, 1946.

7957. Grullón, R. "Antecedentes y Perspectivas del Momento Político Dominicano," *CA* 21 (January, 1961) 221–252.

7958. Hardy, O. "Rafael Leonidas Trujillo Molina," *PHR* 15 (1946) 409–416.

7959. Henríquez, N. *La Verdad Sobre Trujillo: Capítulos que se le Olvidaron a Galíndez.* Havana, 1959.
Title refers to item 7954. Like the Galíndez work, this also is a bitter attack.

7960. Herráiz, I. *Trujillo Dentro de la Historia.* Madrid, 1957.

7961. Hicks, A. C. *Blood in the Streets.* N.Y., 1946.
A journalist's condemnation of the Trujillo regime.

7962. Hoepelmann, A. *Páginas Dominicanas de Historia Contemporánea.* Cd. Trujillo, 1951.

7962a. James, D. *Detrás de la Cortina de Azúcar.* Mexico, 1956.
Highly critical of Trujillo.

7963. Jiménez, R. E. *Biografía de Trujillo.* Cd. Trujillo, 1955.
A tribute to Trujillo.

7964. Jimenez Grullón, J. I. *Una Gestapo en América: Vida, Tortura, Agonía y Muerte de Presos Políticos bajo la Tiranía de Trujillo.* Havana, 1946.
Title is expressive of book's contents.

7965. Landestoy, C. *¡Yo También Acuso! Rafael Leonidas Trujillo Molina, Tirano de la República Dominicana, la Actual y Más Cruel e Inhumana Tiranía de América.* 2d ed., Havana, 1946.

7966. Marino Inchaustegui, J. *La República Dominicana de Hoy.* Cd. Trujillo, 1938.

7967. Mejía, F. A. *Vía Crucis de un Pueblo: Relato Sinóptico de la Tragedia Dominicana bajo la Férula de Trujillo.* Mexico, 1951.

7968. Mota M., F. A. *Un Estadista de América: Obra Socio-Política de Trujillo.* Cd. Trujillo, 1945.
Covers the period 1930 to 1944.

7969. Murray-Jacoby, H. *The Diplomacy of President Trujillo*. N.Y., 1943.

7970. Ornes, G. E. *Trujillo: Pequeño César del Caribe*. Caracas, 1958.
English ed., N.Y., 1958.

7971. Ornes, H. *Desembarco en Luperón: Episodio de la Lucha por la Democracia en la República Dominicana*. Mexico, 1956.
Concerns invasion attempt of June, 1949.

7972. Osorio Lizarazo, J. A. *El Bacilo de Marx*. Cd. Trujillo, 1959.

7973. ———. *Germen y Proceso del Antitrujillismo en América*. Santiago, 1956.
English ed., Madrid, 1958.

7974. ———. *La Isla Iluminada*. Santiago, 1947.
Catalogues the achievements of the regime.

7975. ———. *Portrait of Trujillo*. Madrid, 1958.

7976. Pagán Perdomo, D. *Porqué Lucha el Pueblo Dominicano: Análisis del Fenómeno Dictatorial en América Latina*. Caracas, 1959.
Critical of United States support of Trujillo.

7977. Pellerano Alfau, A. J. (ed.). *Ocho Años de Reconstrucción Nacional*. Cd. Trujillo, 1938.
Covers the years 1930–1938.

7978. Peña Batlle, M. A. *Política de Trujillo*. Cd. Trujillo, 1954.
Supports the regime.

7979. Pérez Leyba, S. A. *El Generalísimo Trujillo Molina, la Convención Dominico-Americana, y la Política de "Buen Vecino."* Cd. Trujillo, 1940.

7980. Rodríguez Demorizi, E. *Actos y Doctrina del Gobierno de la Restauración*. Santo Domingo, 1963.

7980a. ———. *Cronología de Trujillo*. 2 vols., Cd. Trujillo, 1955.

7981. Sánchez Lustrino, G. *Trujillo, el Constructor de una Nacionalidad*. Havana, 1938.

7982. Slater, J. "U.S., the OAS, and the Dominican Republic, 1961–63," *IO* 18 (Spring, 1964) 268–291.

7983. Stefanich, B. *Comunismo sin Máscara*. Cd. Trujillo, 1957.

7984. Thomson, C. A. "Dictatorship in the Dominican Republic," *FPAR* 12, no. 3 (1936)

7985. Tolentino Rojas, V. "Los Problemas de la Postguerra: La Situación de la República Dominicana en el Momento Actual y su Posición en el Futuro," *CDC* 2 (December, 1944) 15–45.

7986. Trujillo Molina, R. L. *Discursos, Mensajes y Proclamas*. 12 vols., Santiago, 1946–1957.

7987. ———. *Fundamentos y Política de un Régimen*. Cd. Trujillo, 1960.
English ed., Cd. Trujillo, 1960.

7988. ———. *Evolución de la Democracia en Santo Domingo*. Cd. Trujillo, 1950.
English ed., Cd. Trujillo, 1955.

7989. ———. *Reajuste de la Deuda Externa*. Cd. Trujillo, 1959.

7990. Unión Democrática Antinazista Dominicana. *América Contra Trujillo*. Havana, 1944.

7990a. Vega y Pagán, E. *La Era de Trujillo: 25 Años de Historia Dominicana*. 20 vols., Cd. Trujillo, 1955.
Especially relevant volumes are listed separately.

7991. ———. *Military Biography of Generalissimo Rafael Leonidas Trujillo Molina, Commander in Chief of the Armed Forces*. Cd. Trujillo, 1956.

7992. Vergés Vidal, P. L. *Trujillo, Prócer Anticomunista*. Cd. Trujillo, 1958.

7993. Viau, A. *La Era de Trujillo: Economía y Finanza*. Cd. Trujillo, 1950.

7994. Wiarda, H. J. "The Politics of Civil-Military Relations in the Dominican Republic," *JIAS* 7 (October, 1965) 465–484.

XIV–L–5 cross references: 7906, 7914

6. THE UNITED STATES INTERVENTION OF 1965

7994a. Amigo Jansen, G. "América Latina, los Estados Unidos y Santo Domingo, 1965," *RJA* (1965) 552–556.

7995. Bosch, J. *Crisis de la Democracia de América en la República Dominicana*. Mexico, 1965.

7995a. Brugal Alfau, D. *Tragedia en Santo Domingo: Documentos para la Historia*. Santo Domingo, 1966.
Over 100 speeches and pertinent documents.

7995b. Castillo, R. C. "The Dominican Crisis," *RIA* 16 (July, 1965) 11–12.

7995c. Connell-Smith, G. "The OAS and the Dominican Crisis," *WT* 21 (1965) 229–236.

7995d. Dorta-Duque, F. "La Tragedia de Juan Bosch," *ECA* 20 (July, 1965) 172–175.

7996. Draper, T. "Juan Bosch y el Comunismo," *CUA* 80 (January, 1964) 29–38.

7996a. Fenwick, C. G. "The Dominican Republic: Intervention or Collective Self-Defense," *AJIL* 60 (1966) 64–67.

7997. Institute for International Labor Research. *Dominican Republic: A Study in the New Imperialism.* N.Y., 1965.

7998. Johnson, L. B. "The Dominican Republic: A Target of Tyranny," *VS* 31 (May 15, 1965) 450–452.

7999. Kurzman, D. *Santo Domingo: Revolt of the Damned.* N.Y., 1965.
By the *Washington Post* correspondent.

8000. Mallin, J. *Caribbean Crisis: Subversion Fails in the Dominican Republic.* N.Y., 1965.
A defense of United States reaction.

8000a. Martin, J. B. *Overtaken by Events: The Dominican Crisis from the Fall of Trujillo to the Civil War.* Garden City, N.Y., 1966.
The United States ambassador defends the administration policy.

8000b. Niedergang, M. *La Révolution de Saint-Domingue.* Paris, 1966.
Condemnation of United States intervention by a *Le Monde* reporter.

8001. Silva Herzog, J. "La República Dominicana, Nación Mártir," *CA* 24 (July, 1965) 7–18.

8002. Szulc, T. *Dominican Diary.* N.Y., 1965.
Pb. ed., N.Y., 1966. An on-the-spot account by the *New York Times* correspondent.

8002b. Thomas, A. J., Jr., and A. Van Wynen Thomas. *The Dominican Republic Crisis, 1965.* Dobbs Ferry, N.Y., 1967.

8003. USCS. Committee on Foreign Relations. *Background Information Relating to the Dominican Republic* (86th Cong., 1st Sess.). Wash., 1965.

8004. Wells, H. "Turmoil in the Dominican Republic," *CH* 50 (January, 1966) 14–21.

8004a. Wilson, L. C. "The Monroe Doctrine, Cold War Anachronism: Cuba and the Dominican Republic," *JP* 28 (1966) 322–346.

M. THE UNITED STATES AND HAITI

1. UNITED STATES–HAITIAN RELATIONS: GENERAL WORKS

8005. Alexis, S. *Abrégé d'Histoire d'Haiti, 1492–1946: Cours Elémentaire et Moyen, à l'Usage du Candidats au Certificat d'Etudes Primaires.* 3d ed., Port-au-Prince, 1946.

8006. Bellegarde, D. *Haiti et son Peuple.* Paris, 1953.

8007. ———. *Histoire du Peuple Haitien, 1492–1952.* Port-au-Prince, 1953.

8008. ———. *La Nation Haitienne.* Paris, 1938.

8009. Benjamin, G. J. *Contribution à l'Histoire Diplomatique et Contemporaine.* Port-au-Prince, 1951.

8010. Davis, H. P. *Black Democracy: The Story of Haiti.* Rev. ed., N.Y., 1936.
Political history stressing the United States intervention.

8011. Dorsainvil, J. C. *Manuel d'Histoire d'Haiti.* Port-au-Prince, 1925.
Used as a text in the Haitian schools.

8012. Haiti. Secrétaire d'Etat des Relations Extérieures. *Recueil des Traités de la République d'Haiti.* 2 vols., Port-au-Prince, 1945–1951.
Official texts of treaties: vol. I, 1804–1904; vol. II, 1905–1921.

8013. Léger, J. N. *Haiti: Her History and Her Detractors.* N.Y., 1928.

8014. Leyburn, J. G. *The Haitian People.* New Haven, Conn., 1941.
Pb. ed., New Haven, Conn., 1966.

8015. Madion, T. *Histoire d'Haiti.* 4 vols., Port-au-Prince, 1847–1904.

8016. Massoni, P. *Haiti, Reine des Antilles.* Paris, 1955.
Surveys Haitian history since independence.

8017. Montague, L. L. *Haiti and the United States, 1714–1938.* Durham, N.C., 1940.

8018. Pierre-Audain, J. J. *La República de Haiti: Su Pasado—su Presente—su Porvenir.* Mexico, 1954.

8019. Rodman, S. *Haiti: The Black Republic.* N.Y., 1954.

8020. Turnier, A. *Les Etats-Unis et la Marché Haitien.* Wash., 1955.
Traces the development of commercial relations between the two countries.

2. UNITED STATES–HAITIAN RELATIONS: NINETEENTH CENTURY

8021. Alexis, S. *Black Liberator: The Life of Toussaint L'Ouverture.* London, 1949.

8022. An American. *The United States and Haiti, 1888–1889.* N.Y., 1889.

8023. Ardouin, B. *Etudes sur l'Histoire d'Haiti.* 11 vols., Paris, 1853.

8024. Baur, J. E. "Faustin Soulouque, Emperor of Haiti: His Character and His Reign," *TA* 6 (October, 1949) 131–166.

8025. ———. "The Presidency of Nicolas Geffrard of Haiti," *TA* 10 (April, 1954) 425–461.

8026. Boyd, W. D. "James Redpath and American Negro Colonization in Haiti, 1860–1862," *TA* 12 (October, 1955) 169–182.

8027. ———. "The Ôle à Voche Colonization Venture, 1862–1864," *TA* 16 (1959) 45–62.

8028. Capo, J. M. *Crónicas de la Revolución Francesa en Haiti: Tres Dictadores Negros.* Havana, 1944.

8029. Clark, B. C. *A Plea for Haiti, with a Glance at Her Relations with France, England and the United States for the Past Sixty Years.* 3d ed., Boston, 1853.

8030. ———. *Remarks upon United States Intervention in Hayti, with Comments upon the Correspondence Connected with It.* Boston, 1853.

8030a. Córdoba Bello, E. "La Revolución Haitiana y la Independencia Hispanoamericana," *RHC* 1 (April, 1961) 27–48.

8031. "Correspondencia Diplomática de Levasseur, de Moges, Barras, Años 1843 y 1844," *CL* 4 (1936) 39–45, 87–93, 120–123, 144–148, 194–196.
Correspondence published in French.

8032. Dalencour, F. S. R. *La Fondation de la République d'Haiti par Alexandre Pétion.* Port-au-Prince, 1944.

8033. Dewey, L. D. (ed.). *Correspondence Relative to the Emigration to Hayti of the Free People of Colour in the United States Together with the Instructions to the Agent Sent Out by President Boyer.* N.Y., 1824.

8033a. *Documents Diplomatiques, Relations Extérieures, Affaire Maunder.* 2 vols., Paris, 1882.

8034. Douglass, F. "Haiti and the United States: Inside History of the Negotiations for the Môle St. Nicholas," *NAR* 53 (1891) 337–345, 450–459.

8035. Firmin, A. *Une Défense: M. Stewart et les Finances Haitiennes.* Paris, 1892.

8036. Friend of Hayti and of the United States. *The United States and the Government of Gen. F. D. Legitime.* N.Y., 1889.

8037. Griggs, E. L., and C. H. Prator (eds.). *Henry Christophe and Thomas Clarkson: A Correspondence.* Berkeley, Calif., 1952.

8038. Haiti. Ministère des Relations Extérieures. *Documents Diplomatiques: Réclamations Pelletier et Lazare: Rapport du Secrétaire d'Etat des Etats-Unis, et Annexes.* Port-au-Prince, 1887.

8038a. Hill, A. C. "Revolution in Haiti, 1791 to 1820," *PAF* 20 (1958) 5–27.

8039. Justin, J. *Les Relations Extérieures d'Haiti: Etudes Historiques et Diplomatiques.* Paris, 1895.

8040. Korngold, R. *Citizen Toussaint.* Boston, 1944.
Pb. ed., N.Y., 1965.

8041. Laurent, G. M. *Coup d'Oeil sur la Politique de Toussaint L'Ouverture.* Port-au-Prince, 1949.

8042. Lecorps, M. *La Politique Extérieure de Toussaint-Louverture: Nos Premières Relations Politiques avec les Etats-Unis, Lettres de Toussaint-Louverture et d'Edward Stevens (1799–1800).* Port-au-Prince, 1935.

8043. Léger, A. N. *Histoire Diplomatique d'Haiti, 1804–1859.* Port-au-Prince, 1930.

8044. Léger, J. N. *La Politique Extérieure d'Haiti.* Paris, 1886.

8045. Logan, R. W. *The Diplomatic Relations of the United States with Haiti, 1776–1891.* Chapel Hill, N.C., 1941.

8046. Menos, S. *L'Affaire Luders.* Port-au-Prince, 1898.
Luders was a German investor in Haiti whose claims against the Haitian government led Germany to send two vessels to force collection.

8047. Metzger, J. D. *La Question Américaine en Haiti*. Port-au-Prince, 1891.
    English ed., Port-au-Prince, 1891.

8048. Montague, L. L. "Henry Everard Peck: Le Premier Ministre Résident des Etats-Unis à Port-au-Prince, 1862–1866," *RSHGH* 11, no. 35 (1939) 15–19.

8049. Moran, C. *Black Triumvirate: A Study of Louverture, Dessalines, Christophe—the Men Who Made Haiti*. N.Y., 1957.

8050. Nemours, A. *Haiti et la Guerre de l'Indépendance Américaine*. Port-au-Prince 1952.

8051. ———. *Histoire des Relations Internationales de Toussaint Louverture: Avec des Documents Inédits*. Port-au-Prince, 1945.

8052. Nichols, R. F. "Navassa: A Forgotten Acquisition," *AHR* 38 (1933) 505–510.
    Possession of the island was contested by the United States and Haiti.

8053. Paxson, F. L. "A Tripartite Intervention in Hayti, 1851," *USC* 1 (February, 1904) 323–330.

8054. Pradine, L., and E. Emmanuel (eds.). *Recueil Général des Lois et Actes du Gouvernment d'Haiti, Depuis la Proclamation de son Indépendance Jusqu'à nos Jours, 1804–1845*. 8 vols., Paris, 1851–1888.

8054a. Price, H. *The Haytian Question*. N.Y., 1891.
    Comments on United States–Haitian relations by the Haitian minister to Washington.

8055. Price-Mars, J. "La Diplomatie Haitienne et l'Indépendance Dominicaine, 1858–1867," *RSHGH* 10, no. 32 (1939) 1–72.

8056. ———. "La Diplomatie Haitienne et l'Indépendance Dominicaine: Les Données du Problème," *RSHGH* 15, no. 54 (1944) 7–19.

8057. ———. "Les Rélations Diplomatiques Entre les Etats-Unis et Haiti: Ce qu'elles Ont Eté dans le Passé, 1717–1804," *RSHGH* 15, no. 53 (1944) 1–14.

8058. Scharon, F. *Toussaint Louverture et la Révolution de St. Domingue*. Port-au-Prince, 1957–.

8059. Sears, L. M. "Frederick Douglass and the Mission to Haiti, 1889–1891," *HAHR* 21 (1941) 222–238.
    Discusses the abortive attempt to annex the Môle St. Nicholas.

8060. St. John, S. *Hayti, or the Black Republic*. London, 1884.
    Critical comments by the British minister to Haiti.

8061. Stoddard, T. L. *The French Revolution in Santo Domingo*. Boston, 1914.

8062. Volney-Nemours, P. L. *Conférence sur les Relations Diplomatiques et Commerciales d'Haiti avec Quelques Puissances Etrangères*. Paris, 1894.

8063. Waxman, P. *The Black Napoleon: The Story of Toussaint Louverture*. N.Y., 1931.

8064. Wesley, C. H. "The Struggle for the Recognition of Haiti and Liberia as Independent Republics," *JNH* 2 (1917) 369–383.

3. United States–Haitian Relations, 1900–1941

8065. Balch, E. G. (ed.). *Occupied Haiti*. N.Y., 1927.
    Treats the eleven years of occupation by the marines.

8065a. Bastien, R. "Jacques Roumain en el Décimo Anniversario de su Muerte," *CA* 74, no. 4 (1954) 243–251.
    Biographical sketch tracing career of Jacques Roumain (1907–1944), leader of the Communist party in Haiti.

8066. Beauvoir, V. *Le Contrôle Financier du Gouvernement des Etats-Unis d'Amérique sur la République d'Haiti*. Paris, 1930.
    A juridical analysis of the treaty rights given the United States.

8067. Bellegarde, D. *Haiti et les Etats-Unis Devant la Justice Internationale*. Paris, 1924.
    An anti-interventionist plea.

8068. ———. *L'Occupation Américaine d'Haiti: Ses Conséquences Morales et Economiques*. Port-au-Prince, 1929.

8069. ———. *La Résistance Haitienne: L'Occupation Américaine d'Haiti*. Montreal, 1937.

8070. ———. *Pour une Haiti Heureuse*. 2 vols., Port-au-Prince, 1928–1929.

8071. Blanchet, J. *Peint par Lui-Même ou la Résistance de Mr. Dantes Bellegarde*. Port-au-Prince, 1937.
    Critique of item 8069.

8072. Buell, R. L. "The American Occupation of Haiti," *FPAIS* 5 (1929) 327–392.

8073. Calixte, D. P. *Haiti: The Calvary of a Soldier*. N.Y., 1939.

A condemnation of the administration of Stenio Vincent (1930–1941).

8074. Chapman, C. E. "The Development of the Intervention in Haiti," *HAHR* 7 (1927) 299–319.

8075. Coffey, R. B. "A Brief History of the Intervention in Haiti," *USNIP* 48 (1922) 1325–1344.

8076. Cooper, D. B. "The Withdrawal of the United States from Haiti, 1928–1934," *JIAS* 5 (January, 1963) 83–101.

8077. Craige, J. H. *Black Bagdad*. N.Y., 1933.

Author was a United States Marine who was stationed in Haiti during the occupation.

8078. Danache, B. *Le Président Dartiguenave et les Américaines*. Port-au-Prince, 1950.

8079. Douglas, P. H. "American Occupation of Haiti," *PSQ* 52 (1927) 228–241.

8080. Editions l'Assaut. *La Voix de la Génération de l'Occupation*. Port-au-Prince, 1936.

8081. ———. *Vers les Etats-Unis du Nord*. Port-au-Prince, 1936.

8082. Firmin, A. *M. Roosevelt, Président des Etats-Unis et la République d'Haiti*. N.Y., Paris, 1905.

8083. Fletcher, H. P. "Quo Vadis Haiti?" *FA* 8 (1930) 533–548.

8084. Foreign Policy Association. *The Seizure of Haiti by the United States: A Report on the Military Occupation of the Republic of Haiti and the History of the Treaty Forced upon Her*. N.Y., 1922.

8084a. Fuller, R. N. "American Achievements in Haiti," *CH* 32 (April, 1930) 86–90.

8085. Gruening, E. H. "Conquest of Haiti and Santo Domingo," *CH* 15 (1922) 885–896.

8086. ———. "The Issue in Haiti," *FA* 11 (1933) 279–289.

8086a. Hackett, C. W. "Haiti's New Status," *CH* 32 (May, 1930) 347–352.

8087. Haiti. *Exposé Général de la Situation de la République d'Haiti*. Port-au-Prince, 1917.

8088. ———. Consulate General. *La République d'Haiti dans la Politique Interaméricaine. The Republic of Haiti in Interamerican Politics*. N.Y., 1939.

8089. ———. Ministère des Relations Ex-térieures. *Documents Diplomatiques: Affaires Diverses*. Port-au-Prince, 1921.

8089a. Holly, A. P. B. "Our Future Relations with Haiti," *AAAPSS* 156 (July, 1931) 110–115.

8090. Hudicourt, P. *Anexión de la República de Haiti por los Estados Unidos del Norte*. Santiago, Chile, 1923.

8091. Justin, J. *Les Réformes Nécessaires: Questions Haitiennes d'Actualité*. Port-au-Prince, 1915.

8092. Kelsey, C. "The American Intervention in Haiti and Santo Domingo," *AAAPSS* 100 (1922) 113–165.

8092a. Logan, R. W. "The United States Colonial Experiment in Haiti," *WT* 17 (October, 1961) 435–446.

8093. ———. "The United States Mission in Haiti, 1915–1952," *INAF* 6, no. 4 (1953) 18–28.

8094. MacCorkle, W. A. *The Monroe Doctrine in Its Relation to the Republic of Haiti*. N.Y., 1915.

8095. Malval, M. E. *La Politique Financière Extérieure de la République d'Haiti Depuis 1910: La Banque Nationale de la République d'Haiti ou Nos Emprunts Extérieurs*. Paris, 1932.

8096. McCrocklin, J. H. *Garde d'Haiti: Twenty Years of Organization and Training by the United States Marine Corps, 1915–1934*. Annapolis, Md., 1957.

8097. Millspaugh, A. C. *Haiti Under American Control, 1915–30*. Boston, 1931.

Balanced analysis of the occupation.

8098. ———. "Our Haitian Problem," *FA* 7 (1929) 556–570.

8099. Nicolas, H. *L'Occupation Américaine d'Haiti, la Revanche de l'Histoire*. Madrid, 1956.

8100. Posner, W. H. "American Marines in Haiti, 1915–1922," *TA* 20 (January, 1964) 231–266.

8101. Spector, R. M. "W. Cameron Forbes and the Hoover Commissions to Haiti," Boston U. Diss., 1961.

The commission recommended reforms but not immediate withdrawal.

8102. USCH. Committee on Foreign Affairs. *Policies of the United States in Haiti* (71st Cong., 2d Sess., H. Rept. 39). Wash., 1929.

8103. ———. ———. *Policies of the United*

States in Haiti (71st Cong., 2d Sess., H. Rept. 52). Wash., 1929.

8104. USCS. Select Committee on Haiti and Santo Domingo. *Inquiry into Occupation and Administration of Haiti and Santo Domingo: Hearings* (67th Cong., 1st and 2d Sess.). 2 vols., Wash., 1921–1922.

8105. USDS. *Haitianization of the Garde, Withdrawal of Military Forces from Haiti, and Financial Arrangement: Agreement Between the United States of America and Haiti.* Wash., 1933.

8106. ———. Commission for Study and Review of Conditions in Haiti. *Report.* Wash., 1930.

XIV–M–3   cross references: 7513, 7920

4. UNITED STATES–HAITIAN RELATIONS SINCE 1941

8107. Bellegarde, D. *Dessalines a Parlé.* Port-au-Prince, 1948.

8108. Bonhomme, C. *Révolution et Contre-révolution en Haiti de 1946 a 1957.* Port-au-Prince, 1957.

8109. Célestin, C. *Compilations pour l'Histoire.* 4 vols., Port-au-Prince, 1958–1960.

8110. Charles, H. L. *La Révolution Duvalieriste et la Compréhension des Masses.* Port-au-Prince, 1962.

8111. *Foreign Trade of Haiti: 1945–1950.* Wash., 1954.

8112. Haiti. Service d'Information de Presse et de Propagande. *Deux Ans au Service du Pays.* Port-au-Prince, 1953 (?).

8113. Herring, H. "Dictatorship in Haiti," *CH* 46 (January, 1964) 34–37.

8114. Magloire, J. *Dumarsais Estimé: Esquisse de Sa Vie Politique.* Port-au-Prince, 1950.

8115. Magloire, P. E. *Le Présidente Magloire Parle au Congrès Américain.* Port-au-Prince, 1955.

8116. Morre, O. E. "Is Haiti Next?" *YR* 51 (December, 1961) 254–263.

8117. *The Haiti Pilot Project: Phase One, 1947–1949.* Paris, 1951.
    Concerns the UNESCO Project in the Marbial Valley.

8118. UN. Mission to Haiti. *Report of the United Nations Mission of Technical Assistance to the Republic of Haiti.* Lake Success, N.Y., 1949.

8119. United States Tariff Commission. *Economic Controls and Commercial Policy in Haiti: One of a Series of Reports on Economic Controls and Commercial Policy in American Republics.* Wash., 1946.

XIV–M–4   cross references: 4185, 8093

Chapter XV   The United States and Colombia

A. UNITED STATES–COLOMBIAN RELATIONS: GENERAL WORKS AND SPECIAL STUDIES

8120. Arboleda, G. *Historia Contemporánea de Colombia.* 6 vols., Cali and Bogotá, 1918–1935.
The most detailed narrative political history; covers 1830–1860.

8120a. ———. *Manual de Historia de Colombia para los Colegios y Escuelas de la República.* Cali, 1934 (?).

8121. Arboleda Llorente, J. M. *Historia de Colombia.* Popayan, 1952.

8122. Bell, P. L. *Colombia: A Commercial and Industrial Handbook.* Wash., 1921.

8123. Bermúdez, J. A. *Compendio de la Historia de Colombia.* 4th ed., Bogotá, 1937.

8124. Beyer, R. C. "The Colombian Coffee Industry: Origins and Major Trends, 1740–1940," U. of Minnesota Diss., 1948.

8125. Cavelier, G. *La Política Internacional de Colombia.* 2d ed., 4 vols., Bogotá, 1959.
Covers the period since independence. Vol. I, 1820–1860; vol. II, 1860–1903; vol. III, 1903–1959; vol. IV, diplomatic asylum.

8126. Colombia. Ministerio de Relaciones Exteriores. *Anales Diplomáticos y Consulares de Colombia.* Bogotá, 1900–

8127. Cortés, E. *Los Tratados de Colombia con los Estados Unidos y Panamá.* London, 1909.

8128. Galbraith, W. O. *Colombia: A General Survey.* N.Y., 1953.
Rev. ed., N.Y., 1966.

8129. García Samudio, N. *Capítulos de Historia Diplomática.* Bogotá, 1925.

8130. Gibson, W. M. *The Constitutions of Colombia.* Durham, N.C., 1948.

8131. Gonzales Fernández, H. *Historia de Colombia.* Bogotá, 1944.

8132. Henao, J. M., and G. Arrubla. *Historia de Colombia para la Enseñanza Secundaria.* 7th ed., 2 vols. in one, Bogotá, 1952.
English ed., Chapel Hill, N.C., 1938.

8133. Humbert, J. *Histoire de la Colombie et du Vénézuela des Origines Jusqu'à Nos Jours.* Paris, 1921.

8134. Ortega Ricuarte, D. "Datos Sobre la Cronología de los Ex-Mandatarios de Colombia," *BHA* 48 (January, 1961) 36–61.
A list of Colombian heads of state and chief justices from 1819 to 1957.

8135. Osorio Lizarazo, J. A. *Colombia Donde los Andes se Disuelven.* Santiago, 1955.

8136. Ospina Vásquez, L. *Industria y Protección en Colombia, 1810–1930.* Bogotá, 1955.

8137. Parks, E. T. *Colombia and the United States, 1765–1934.* Durham, N.C., 1935.
The most comprehensive treatment of the subject in English.

8138. Pombo, M. A., and J. J. Guerra (eds.). *Constituciones de Colombia, Recopiladas y Precedidas de una Breve Reseña Histórica.* 2 vols., Bogotá, 1911.

8139. Puentes, M. *Historia del Partido Liberal Colombiano, 1810–1942.* Bogotá, 1942.
More a general history, from the liberal point of view, than the title suggests.

8140. Restrepo, J. M. *Historia de la Revolución de la República de Colombia en la América Meridional.* 5 vols., Bogotá, 1942–1945.

8141. Rippy, J. F. *The Capitalists and Colombia.* N.Y., 1931.
Emphasis on United States investments in Colombia.

8142. ———. "The Development of Public Utilities in Colombia," *HAHR* 25 (1945) 132–137.

8143. Rivas, R. *Historia Diplomática de Colombia, 1810–1934.* Bogotá, 1961.

8144. Romero Aquirre, A. *El Partido Conservador ante la Historia.* Bogotá, 1944.

Liberal analysis of conservative short-comings.

8145. Romoli, K. *Colombia: Gateway to South America.* N.Y., 1941.

8146. Uribe, A. J. (ed.). *Anales Diplomáticos y Consulares de Colombia.* 9 vols., Bogotá, 1900–1959.

8147. ———. *Colombia y los Estados Unidos: Colombia, Venezuela, Costa Rica, Ecuador, Brasil, Nicaragua y Panamá: Colombia y el Perú.* 3 vols., Bogotá, 1931.

8148. Uribe Echeverri, C. *Colombia y los Estados Unidos.* Bogotá, 1921.

XV–A   cross references:

a) For the role of the United States in attempting to mediate the boundary dispute with Costa Rica, see items 7271–7285.

b) See also items 1289, 1473.

B. THE UNITED STATES AND THE INDEPENDENCE OF GRAN COLOMBIA

8149. Academia Nacional de la Historia (ed.), *Archivo del General Miranda.* 24 vols.. Caracas and Havana, 1929–1950.

8150. *Archivo Santander.* 24 vols. in 20, Bogotá, 1913–1932.
Edited by E. Restrepo Tirado and others. See item 8206.

8151. Becerra, R. *Ensayo Histórico Documentado de la Vida de Don Francisco de Miranda.* 2 vols., Caracas, 1896.

8152. Belaúnde, V. A. *Bolívar y el Pensamiento Política de la Revolución Hispanoamericana.* New ed., Madrid, 1959.
English ed., Baltimore, 1938.

8153. Bierck, H. A., Jr. "The First Instance of U.S. Foreign Aid: Venezuelan Relief in 1812," *IEA* 9 (Summer, 1955) 47–59.

8154. ———. *Vida Pública de Don Pedro Gual.* Caracas, 1947.
Spanish version of the English, which first appeared in 1944 as a Ph.D. dissertation at U.C.L.A.

8155. Biggs, J. *The History of Don Francisco de Miranda's Attempt to Effect a Revolution in South America.* Boston, 1808.
Spanish ed., Caracas, 1950.

8156. Bingham, H. *The Journal of an Expedition Across Venezuela and Colombia in 1906–07: An Exploration of the Route of*

Bolívar's Celebrated March of 1819 and of the Battlefields of Boyaca and Carabobo. New Haven, Conn., 1909.

8157. Blanco, J. F., and R. Azpurúa (eds.). *Documentos para la Historia de la Vida del Libertador de Colombia, Perú y Bolivia.* 14 vols., Caracas, 1875–1878.
Supplements original edition, published in 22 volumes (Caracas, 1826–1828).

8157a. Blossom, T. *Nariño: Hero of Colombian Independence.* Tucson, Ariz., 1967.

8158. Bolívar, S. *Obras Completas: Compilación y Notas de Vicente Lecuna con la Colaboración de Esther Barret de Nazaris.* 2d ed., 3 vols., Havana, 1950.

8159. Brice, A. F. *Bolívar: Libertador y Estadista.* Caracas, 1953.

8160. Briceño Perozo, M. *Don Francisco de Miranda: Maestro de Libertadores.* Trujillo, Venezuela, 1950.

8161. Carbonell, D. *Sobre el Tablado.* Bogotá, 1935.
The author was a former rector of the University of Caracas.

8162. Carrasco, R. *Francisco de Miranda, Precursor de la Independencia Hispanoamericana, 1750–1792.* B.A., 1951.

8163. Clavery, E. "Antonio Nariño, Precursor Colombiano, ante las Críticas de Uno de sus Compatriotas," *BHA* 22 (1935) 353–362.

8164. Cortazar, R. (comp.). *Cartas y Mensajes del General Francisco de Paula Santander.* 10 vols., Bogotá, 1953–1956.

8165. Cova, J. A. *El Centauro: Vida del General José Antonio Páez, Caudillo Venezolano y Brigadier del Ejército Argentino.* B.A., 1937.

8166. Dalencour, F. *Francisco de Miranda et Alexandre Pétion: L'Expédition de Miranda, le Premier Effort de Libération Hispanoaméricaine, le Premier Vagissement du Panaméricanisme.* Port-au-Prince, 1955.
Concerns the *Leander* expedition of 1806.

8167. Dávila, V. *Biografía de Miranda.* Caracas, 1933.

8168. Delgado Nieto, C. *José Padilla: Estampa de un Almirante.* Bogotá, 1957.
Padilla was a naval officer in the independence movements.

8169. Dietrich, W. *Simón Bolívar y las Guerras de la Independencia Americana*. Santiago, 1940.

8170. Ducoudray Holstein, H. L. *Memoirs of Simón Bolívar, President Liberator of the Republic of Colombia*. Boston, 1829.
An anti-Bolivarian account by a disappointed office-seeker.

8171. Encina, F. A. *Bolívar y la Independencia de la América Española: El Imperio Hispano Hacia 1810 y la Génesis de su Emancipación*. Santiago, 1957.

8172. ———. *Independencia de Nueva Granada y Venezuela*. 2 vols., Santiago, 1961–1962.

8173. Estrada Monsalve, J. *Bolívar, su Pensamiento, su Vida, su Obra, su Lección*. Bogotá, 1944.

8174. Fosalba, R. J. "Trascendencia Económica y Política de las Acuñaciones Obsidionales y de Emergencia Durante la Revolución por la Independencia de Venezuela y Colombia," *RNC* 6 (January, 1944) 37–98; 6 (February, 1944) 29–91.
Treats fiscal policy and foreign trade.

8175. Frankel, B. A. "Venezuela and the United States 1810–1888," U. of S. California Diss., 1964.

8176. Gálvez, M. *Don Francisco de Miranda, el Más Universal de los Americanos: Biografía*. B.A., 1947.

8177. Gandía, E. de. *Bolívar y la Libertad*. B.A., 1957.

8178. García Ortíz, L. (ed.). *Bolívar y Santander: Correspondencia, 1819–1820*. Bogotá, 1940.

8179. García Samudio, N. "Relaciones Entre Colombia y los Estados Unidos: La Primera Nota de 1810," *BPAU* 55 (1922) 388–391.

8180. Giménez Silva, F. *La Independencia de Venezuela ante las Cancillerías Europeas*. Caracas, 1961.

8181. Graham, R. B. C. *José Antonio Páez, the "Father of Venezuela."* London, 1929.
Spanish ed., Caracas, 1958.

8182. Grases, P. *La Conspiración de Gual y España y el Ideario de la Independencia*. Caracas, 1949.

8183. ———. *Traducciones de Interés Político-Cultural en la Epoca de la Independencia de Venezuela*. Caracas, 1961.
Treats the impact of political ideology in the United States on the independence movements.

8184. Hanke, L. (ed.). "Baptis Irvine's Reports on Simón Bolívar," *HAHR* 16 (1936) 360–373.
Irvine was a United States agent who popularized the independence movement in the press.

8185. ——— (ed.). "Simón Bolívar and Neutral Rights," *HAHR* 21 (1941) 258–291.

8185a. "The Ill-Fated Expedition of Miranda, the Venezuelan Liberator," *PAM* 37 (September, 1924) 419–423.

8186. Instituto Panamericano de Geografía e Historia. Comisión de Historia. *Comité de Orígenes de la Emancipación: El 19 de Abril de 1810*. Caracas, 1957.

8187. Jos, E. "Notas Sobre Juan Vicente Bolívar y su Misión Diplomática en los Estados Unidos, 1810–1811," *RIN* 2 (April, 1941) 135–163.
Juan Vicente was the elder brother of Simón Bolívar.

8188. Lavretskii, I. R. *Bolívar*. Moscow, 1960.

8189. Lecuna, V. (ed.). *Colección de Cartas del Libertador*. 11 vols., Caracas and New York, 1929–1948.
A basic collection. Vol. 12 was edited by M. Pérez Vila (Caracas, 1959).

8190. ———. *Proclamas y Discursos del Libertador Mandados Publicar por el Gobierno de Venezuela Presidido por el General Eleazar López Contreras*. Caracas, 1939.

8191. ———, and H. Bierck (eds.). *Selected Writings of Bolívar*. 2 vols., N.Y., 1951.
Selected documents, translated by Lewis Bertrand. Vol. I covers 1810–1822; vol. II, 1823–1830.

8192. ———, and E. Barret de Nazaris (eds.). *Cartas de Santander*. 3 vols., Caracas, 1942.

8193. Lee López, A. (ed.). "Documentos Sobre Don Pedro Gual," *BHA* 50 (1963) 605–617.
Letters of 1815–1816, written while Gual was a patriot agent in the United States.

8194. Lloyd, T. *The Trials of William Stephens Smith and Samuel G. Ogden*. N.Y., 1807.
Smith and Ogden cooperated with Miranda in making preparations for the *Leander* expedition.

8195. Ludwig, E. *Bolivar: The Life of an Idealist*. London, 1947.

8196. Madariaga, S. de. *Bolívar*. 2 vols., Mexico. 1951.
　　　English ed., London, 1952.

8196a. "The Many-Sided Miranda: A Few Glimpses of his American and English Connections," *BPAU* 67 (1933) 497–511.

8197. Masur, G. *Simón Bolívar*. Albuquerque, N.M., 1948.
　　　Spanish ed., Mexico, 1960.

8198. Mendoza, C. L. *Las Primeras Misiones Diplomáticas de Venezuela*. 2 vols., Madrid, 1962.

8199. ———. "Las Primeras Relaciones Diplomáticas de Venezuela con los Estados Unidos," *BANHC* 27 (October, 1944) 346–373.
　　　Correspondence of Telésforo de Orea (1811–1812), a representative of the Caracas junta, in which Madison's Latin American policy is analyzed.

8200. ———. "Misiones de Juan Vicente Bolívar y Telésforo Orea à Washington," *BANHC* 18 (1935) 711–742.

8201. Naranjo Martínez, E. "Alejandro Macaulay: Un Héroe Norteamericano en la Liberación de Colombia," *BHA* 30 (April, 1943) 495–508.

8202. O'Leary, D. F. *Correspondencia de Extranjeros Notables con el Libertador*. 2 vols., Madrid, 1920.

8203. ———. *Memorias del General O'Leary, Publicados por su Hijo, Simón B. O'Leary*. 32 vols., Caracas, 1879–1888.

8204. ———. *Memorias del General Daniel Florencio O'Leary: Narración*. 3 vols., Caracas, 1952.

8205. Ortíz, S. E. *Franceses en la Independencia de la Gran Colombia*. Bogotá, 1949.

8206. Otero Muñoz, G. "Archivo Santander: Erratas Sustanciales en los Veinticuatro Tomos," *BHA* 30 (January, 1943) 1–222.
　　　Refers to item 8150.

8207. Páez, J. A. *Autobiografía del General José Antonio Páez*. 2 vols., N.Y., 1945.
　　　Reprint of the original edition (N.Y., 1869).

8208. Parra-Pérez, C. "La Diplomacia de Bolívar," *RIHGU* 2, no. 2 (1923) 863–895.

8209. ———. *Historia de la Primera República*. 2 vols., Caracas, 1939.
　　　Contains information on early Venezuelan agents in the United States.

8210. ———. "Miranda and the Revolution in Europe and America," *BPAU* 67 (1933) 452–466.

8211. Pereyra, C. *Bolívar y Washington: Un Paralelo Imposible*. Madrid, 1915.

8212. Pérez Vila, M. "Miranda en Filadélfia," *BANHC* 42 (July, 1959) 362–367.

8213. ———. *Vida de Daniel Florencio O'Leary*. Caracas, 1957.

8214. Picón-Salas, M. "D. Francisco Miranda y Jefferson," *IP* 4 (September, 1945) 47–52.

8215. Porras Troconis, G. "Relaciones Diplomáticas Entre Colombia y los Estados Unidos en la Guerra de Independencia," *AE* 4 (1936) 154–168.

8216. Rafter, M. *Memoirs of Gregor McGregor: Comprising a Sketch of the Revolution in New Granada and Venezuela, with Biographical Notices of Generals Miranda, Bolivar, Morillo, and Hore, and a Narrative of the Expeditions to Amelia Island, Porto Bello, and Rio de la Hache, Interspersed with Revolutionary Anecdotes*. London, 1820.

8217. Rangel Baez, C. "La Expedición de Miranda," *CV*, no. 57 (1924) 136–146; no. 58 (1924) 35–44.

8218. Reyes, V. *Páez: Venezolano Integral: Biografía: El Hombre—el Héroe—el Magistrado*. Caracas, 1957.

8219. Rippy, J. F. "Bolívar as Viewed by Contemporary Diplomats of the United States," *HAHR* 15 (1935) 287–297.
　　　Bolívar was not well thought of by United States diplomats.

8220. Rivas, R. *Relaciones Internacionales Entre Colombia y los Estados Unidos, 1810–1850*. Bogotá, 1915.
　　　A basic monograph from the Colombian point of view.

8221. Robertson, W. S. "Francisco de Miranda and the Revolutionizing of Spanish America," *AHAAR* (1907) Wash., 1909.
　　　Spanish ed., Bogotá, 1918.

8222. ———. *The Life of Miranda*. 2 vols., Chapel Hill, N.C., 1929.

8223. Rourke, T. *Man of Glory, Simón Bolívar*. N.Y., 1939.
　　　Pseudonym for D. J. Clinton.

8224. Rumazo González, A. *Simón Bolívar.* Caracas, 1955.

8225. Sheldon, F. "General Miranda's Expedition," *AM* 5 (1860) 589–602.

8226. Shepherd, W. R. "Bolívar and the United States," *HAHR* 1 (1918) 270–298.

8227. Sheridan, P. J. *Francisco de Miranda: Forerunner of Spanish-American Independence.* San Antonio, Texas, 1960.

8228. Sherman, J. W. *A General Account of Miranda's Expedition, Including the Trial and Execution of Ten of His Officers.* N.Y., 1808.

8229. Sherwell, G. A. *Antonio José de Sucre.* Wash., 1924.

8230. Smith, M. *History of the Adventures and Sufferings of Moses Smith During Five Years of His Life, Beginning of the Year 1806 When He Was Betrayed into the Miranda Expedition Until June 1811.* N.Y., 1812.

8231. Sparks, E. E. (ed.). "Diary and Letters of Henry Ingersoll, Prisoner at Carthagena, 1806–1809," *AHR* 3 (1898) 674–702.

8232. Sucre, A. J. de. *Cartas de Sucre al Libertador (1820–1830).* 2 vols., Madrid, 1919.

8233. Thorning, J. F. *Miranda, World Citizen.* Gainesville, Fla., 1952.

8234. Tisnés, J. R. M. *Movimientos Pre-Independientes Grancolombianos.* Bogotá, 1962.

8235. Trend, J. B. *Bolívar and the Independence of Spanish America.* London, 1946.

8236. Urdaneta, A. *Bolívar y Washington.* Caracas, 1865.

8237. Vasconcelos, J. *Simón Bolívar: Interpretación.* Mexico, 1939.

8238. Vergara y Velasco, F. J. *Guerra de Independencia, 1818.* 2d ed., Bogotá, 1960.

8239. Wilgus, A. C. "Francisco de Miranda in the United States," *BPAU* 67 (1933) 484–489.

8240. Ybarra, T. R. *Bolívar: The Passionate Warrior.* N.Y., 1929.

8241. Zubieta, P. A. *Apuntaciones Sobre las Primeras Misiones Diplomáticas de Colombia (1809–1830).* Bogotá, 1924.

XV–B   cross references:

For more general works on the role of the United States during the period of Latin American independence see items 1805–1896.

C. THE UNITED STATES AND GRAN COLOMBIA, 1819–1830

8242. Bache, R. *Notes on Colombia Taken in the Years 1822–1823, with an Itinerary of the Route from Caracas to Bogota, and an Appendix.* Phil., 1827.

8243. Bierck, H. A., Jr. "The Struggle for Abolition in Gran Colombia," *HAHR* 33 (1953) 365–386.

8244. Bowman, C. H., Jr. "Manuel Torres: Early Advocate of Inter-American Commerce," *IEA* 14 (Winter, 1960) 73–83.

The chargé d'affaires of Gran Colombia. He attempted to interest the United States in establishing trade ties with Latin America.

8245. Bushnell, D. *The Santander Regime in Gran Colombia.* Newark, Del., 1954.

8246. Cadena, P. I. *Anales Diplomáticos de Colombia.* Bogotá, 1878.

8247. Camacho Montoya, G. *Santander, el Hombre y el Mito.* Caracas, 1943.

8248. Duane, W. *A Visit to Colombia in the Years 1822 and 1823 by La Guayra and Caracas, over the Cordillera to Bogotá and Thence by the Magdalena to Cartagena.* Phil., 1826.

Duane, an influential U.S. journalist, had long supported the patriot cause in his Philadelphia *Aurora.*

8249. Grillo, M. "Santander en Venezuela," *BHA* 31 (May, 1944) 472–491.

8250. Harrison, W. H. *Remarks of General Harrison, Late Envoy Extraordinary and Minister Plenipotentiary of the United States to the Republic of Colombia, on Certain Charges Made Against Him by That Government.* Wash., 1830.

8251. Helguera, J. L. (ed.). "Francisco de Paula Santander: 1819–1836: Nuevos Materiales para su Biografía," *BHA* 48 (December, 1961) 113–122.

8252. Hernández Carillo, J. *Santander y la Gran Colombia.* Bogotá, 1940.

8253. Huck, E. R. "Colombian–United States Commercial Relations, 1821–1850," U. of Alabama Diss., 1963.

8254. Mendoza, D. "Estudios de Historia Diplomática: El Tratado de 1824 Entre Colombia y los Estados Unidos," *BHA* 2 (1904) 389–402, 458–476.

8255. Miramón, A. "Los Diplomáticos de la

Libertad," *BHA* 36 (April, 1949) 256–285.

Concerns Manuel Torres, Ignacio Sánchez de Tejada, and Pedro Gual.

8256. Mollien, G. *Voyage dans la République de Colombie en 1823.* 2 vols., Paris, 1824.

English ed., London, 1824. Mollien was a secret French agent in Colombia who tried to evoke anti–United States sentiment.

8257. Parks, E. T., and A. Tischendorf (eds.). "Cartagena to Bogotá, 1825–1826: The Diary of Richard Clough Anderson, Jr.," *HAHR* 42 (1962) 217–231.

Anderson was the first Colombian minister to the United States.

8258. Rivas, A. C. *Ensayos de Historia Política y Diplomática.* Madrid, 1916.

8259. Tischendorf, A., and E. T. Parks (eds.). *The Diary and Journal of Richard Clough Anderson, Jr.* Durham, N.C., 1964.

8260. Urrutia, F. J. *Política Internacional de la Gran Colombia.* Bogotá, 1941.

XV–C cross references: 2341, 2582, 8149, 8175, 8191, 8192, 8220, 8241

D. UNITED STATES–COLOMBIAN RELATIONS, 1830–1903

8261. Acosta de Samper, S. *Biografía del General Joaquín Acosta, Prócer de la Independencia, Historiador, Geógrafo, Hombre Científico y Filántropo.* Bogotá, 1901.

Joaquín Acosta was Colombia's minister to the United States in 1842.

8262. Aguilera, M. *Visión Política del Arzobispo Mosquera.* Bogotá, 1954.

8263. Arboleda Llorente, J. M. *Vida del Illmo. Señor Manuel José Mosquera, Arzobispo de Santa Fé de Bogotá.* 2 vols., Bogotá, 1956.

8264. Benedetti, C. *Historia de Colombia.* 2d ed., Lima, 1887.

8265. Bushnell, D. "Two Stages in Colombian Tariff Policy: The Radical Era and the Return to Protection (1861–1885)," *IEA* 9, no. 4 (1956) 3–23.

8266. Caballero, L. *Memoria de la Guerra de los Mil Días.* Bogotá, 1939.

8267. Cadena, P. I. *Colección de Tratados Públicos de los Estados Unidos de Colombia.* 2 vols., Bogotá, 1883–1884.

8268. Castillero Calvo, A. A. "Un Antecedente de la 'Tajada de Sandía,'" *L* 6 (August, 1961) 20–23.

Concerns United States relations with Panama in the 1850's.

8269. Castillo Mathieu, N. del. *Biografía de Rafael Núñez.* Bogotá, 1955.

8270. Colombia. *Nueva Granada i los Estados-Unidos de América: Final Controversia Diplomática con Relación a los Sucesos de Panamá, del Día 15 de Abril de 1856.* Bogotá, 1857.

8271. Galindo, A. *El Tratado de 14 de Enero de 1869 para la Escavación del Canal de Darién.* Bogotá, 1869.

8272. Grenville, J. A. S. "Great Britain and the Isthmian Canal, 1898–1901," *AHR* 61 (1955) 48–69.

8272a. Helguera, J. L. "The First Mosquera Administration in New Granada, 1845–1849," U. of North Carolina Diss., 1958.

Contains new documentation on the origins of the Mallarino-Bidlack Treaty of 1846.

8273. Hoyos, J. A. *Les Etats-Unis et la Colombie.* Paris, 1918.

8274. Liévano Aguirre, I. *Rafael Núñez.* 2d ed., Bogotá, 1944.

8275. McGregor, R. R. "The Treaty of 1846: Seventeen Years of American-Colombian Relations, 1830–1846," Clark U. Diss., 1929.

8276. Múnera, L. A. *Núñez y el Radicalismo.* Cartagena, 1944.

8277. Olney, R. *The Clayton-Bulwer Treaty: Memorandum.* Wash., 1900.

8278. Otero Muñoz, G. *Un Hombre y una Epoca: La Vida Azarosa de Rafael Núñez.* Bogotá, 1951.

8279. Patterson, R. S. "The New Granadan Draft of a Convention for the Settlement of the Panama Riot Claims," *HAHR* 27 (1947) 87–91.

8280. Restrepo, A. J. *Al Pueblo Colombiano, Replica a la Legación en Washington: Labor por la Paz: Cuestión Canal y Cuestión Constitucional, Peligros Imaginarios: La Paz: Intervención Personal.* Madrid, 1902.

8281. Restrepo, J. M. *Historia de la Nueva Granada.* 2 vols., Bogotá, 1942–1963.

8282. Rippy, J. F. "Dawn of the Railway Era in Colombia," *HAHR* 23 (1943) 650–663.

8283. Robinson, T. *Panama: A Personal Narrative of Forty-six Years, 1861–1907.* N.Y., 1907.

8284. Roldán, S. *Relaciones Comerciales Entre los Estados Unidos de América i los Estados Unidos de Colombia.* Bogotá, 1870.

8284a. Salazar, V. M. *Memorias de la Guerra (1899–1902).* Bogotá, 1943.
Refers to the "War of a Thousand Days."

8285. Salgar, E. *El Ministro Colombiano en Washington i la Adquisición del Vapor "Rayo."* Bogotá, 1867.
The steamship *Rayo* was purchased by the Colombian government in the 1860's but was detained by the United States.

8286. Shaw, C., Jr. "Church and State in Colombia as Observed by American Diplomats, 1834–1906," *HAHR* 21 (1941) 577–613.

8287. Stewart, J. *Bogotá in 1836–7: Being a Narrative of an Expedition to the Capital of New Granada, and a Residence There of Eleven Months.* N.Y., 1838.

8288. Tamayo, J. *Don Tomás Cipriano de Mosquera (1798–1878).* Bogotá, 1936.

8288a. ———. *La Revolución de 1899.* Bogotá, 1938.

8289. *The Panama Massacre: A Collection of Principal Evidence and Other Documents, Including the Report of Amos W. Corwine, Esq., U.S. Commissioner, the Official Statement of the Governor and Depositions Taken Before the Authorities, Relative to the Massacre of American Citizens at the Panama Railroad Station on the 15th of April, 1856.* Panama, 1857.

XV–D cross references: 2346, 2388, 8220, 8246, 8247, 8253

E. THE PANAMA DISPUTE

8290. Aldana, A. *The Panama Canal Question: A Plea for Colombia.* N.Y., 1904.

8291. Ameringer, C. D. "The Panama Canal Lobby of Philippe Bunau-Varilla and William Nelson Cromwell," *AHR* 68 (1963) 346–363.

8292. ———. "Philippe Bunau-Varilla and the Panama Canal," Fletcher School of Law and Diplomacy Diss., 1958.

8293. ———. "Philippe Bunau-Varilla: New Light on the Panama Canal Treaty," *HAHR* 46 (1966) 28–52.

8294. Arango, J. A. *Datos para la Historia de la Independencia del Istmo.* Panama, 1922.

8295. Arias, R., and P. Arosemena. *La Opinión Sensata de Panamá Tocante al Tratado Herrán–Hay.* Panama, 1903.

8296. Arosemena, P. *La Secesión de Panamá y sus Causas.* Panama, 1903.

8297. Biard, P. *Le Canal Interocéanique et son Régime Juridique.* Paris, 1902.

8298. Boyd, F. *The Secession of Panama.* Panama, 1911.

8299. Boyd, J. E. *Refutation of Bunau-Varilla's Book.* Panama, 1913.

8300. Brunet, G. *Le Procès de Panama.* Paris, 1904.

8301. Bunau-Varilla, P. *From Panama to Verdun: My Fight for France.* Phil., 1940.
Author was a French engineer and stockholder in the New Panama Canal Company.

8302. ———. *The Great Adventure of Panama.* N.Y., 1920.

8303. ———. *Panama: The Creation, Destruction, and Resurrection.* London, 1913.

8303a. ———. "La Question de Panama," *NR*, n.s., 37 (1904) 433–458.

8304. Calderón, C., *et al. La Questión de Panama.* Paris, 1903.

8305. *Canal de Panamá: Informes de las Comisiones Parlamentarias de Colombia.* Bogotá, 1903.

8306. Carles, R. D. *Horror y Paz en el Istmo, 1899–1902.* Panama, 1950.

8307. Castillero Reyes, E. J. de. *La Causa Inmediata de la Emancipación de Panamá: Historia de los Orígenes, la Formación y el Rechazo por el Senado Colombiano, del Tratado Herrán–Hay.* Panama, 1933.

8308. ———. *Episodios de la Independencia de Panamá.* Panama, 1958.

8309. Chaloner, W. H. "The Birth of the Panama Canal, 1869–1914," *HT* 9 (July, 1959) 482–492.

8310. Colombia. Ministerio de Relaciones Exteriores. *Canal de Panamá: Documentos Relativos a las Negociaciones para la Apertura de Esta Vía Interoceánica.* Bogotá, 1903.

8311. ———. ———. *Documentos Diplo-*

máticos Sobre el Canal y la Rebelión del Istmo de Panamá. Bogotá, 1904.

8312. Colombia. Ministerio de Relaciones Exteriores. *Protest of Colombia Against the Treaty Between Panama and the United States.* London, 1904.

8313. ———. Senate. *Canal de Panamá: Documentos Relacionados con Este Asunto.* Bogotá, 1903.

8314. Concha, J. V. *Las Negociaciones Diplomáticas del Canal de Panamá.* Bogotá, 1904.

8315. Dean, A. H. *William Nelson Cromwell, 1854–1948: An American Pioneer in Corporation, Comparative and International Law.* N.Y., 1958.

8315a. Dennis, W. C. "The Panama Situation in the Light of International Law," *ALRR* 52 (1904) 265–306.

8316. Diego-Fernández, S. *La Independencia de Panamá.* Mexico, 1904.

8316a. *La Doctrina Monroe y la Política Roosevelt en Panamá.* Santiago, 1913.

8317. "Documentos Importantes (1902): Canal Interoceánico de Panamá," *L* 6 (October, 1961) 45–53.

8317a. Dykes, D. O. "The Panama Canal and Treaty Rights," *JR* 24 (1913) 261–273.

8318. Escobar, F. (comp.). *"I Took the Isthmus": Ex-President Roosevelt's Confession, Colombia's Protest, and Editorial Comment by American Newspapers on "How the United States Acquired the Right to Build the Panama Canal."* N.Y., 1911.
   Author was the Colombian consul-general in New York.

8319. ———. "President Roosevelt's Message and the Isthmian Canal," *NAR* 178 (1904) 122–132.

8320. Esguerra, N. *El Canal de Panamá y la Verdadera Historia de la Prórroga.* Bogotá, 1903.

8321. Favell, T. R. "The Antecedents of Panama's Separation from Colombia: A Study in Colombian Politics," Fletcher School of Law and Diplomacy Diss., 1950.

8322. Fisher, G. J. B. "Bunau-Varilla, Protagonist of Panama," *USNIP* 59 (1933) 1313–1322.

8323. Fox, G. L. *President Roosevelt's Coup d'Etat: The Panama Affair in a Nutshell.* New Haven, Conn., 1904.

8324. Freehoff, J. C. *America and the Canal Title: Or, an Examination, Sifting and Interpretation of the Data Bearing on the Wresting of the Province of Panama from the Republic of Colombia by the Roosevelt Administration in 1903 in Order to Secure Title to the Canal Zone.* N.Y., 1916.

8325. Friedlander, R. A. "A Reassessment of Roosevelt's Role in the Panamanian Revolution of 1903," *WPQ* 14 (1961) 535–543.

8326. Gatell, F. O. "The Canal in Retrospect: Some Panamanian and Colombian Views," *TA* 15 (July, 1958) 23–36.

8327. Gonionskii, S. A. *Istoriia Panamskoi "Revoliutsii."* Moscow, 1958.
   History of the Panamanian "Revolution."

8328. González Valencia, J. M. *Separation of Panama from Colombia: Extracts of Letters Addressed by José M. González Valencia, Former Minister of Foreign Affairs of Colombia, to a Friend of Colombia in the United States.* Wash., 1916.

8329. ———. *Separation of Panama from Colombia: Refutation of the Misstatements and Erroneous Conceptions of Mr. Roosevelt in His Article Entitled "The Panama Blackmail Treaty."* Wash., 1916.

8330. Graell, C. A. *Historia de la Independencia de Panamá: Sus Antecedentes y sus Causas, 1821–1903.* Panama, 1933.

8331. Heilprin, A. *A Defense of the Panama Route.* Phil., 1902.

8332. Heinrich, J. *Kolumbien und der Nordamerikanische Imperialismus.* Munich, 1929.

8333. *La Honra Nacional y el Ex-Ministro Mendoza Pérez.* Bogotá, 1906.

8334. Hyde, C. C. "The Isthmian Canal Treaty," *HLR* 14 (1900) 52–58.

8335. Johnson, E. R. "The Panama Canal," *PSQ* 18 (1903) 197–215.

8336. Keasbey, L. M. "The National Canal Policy," *AHAAR* 1 (1902) 275–288. Wash., 1903.

8337. Latané, J. H. "The Neutralization Features of the Hay-Pauncefote Treaty," *AHAAR* 1 (1903) 289–303. Wash., 1903.

8338. ———. "The Principle of Neutralization Applied to Canals," *SAQ* 1 (1902) 310–325.

8339. ———. "The Treaty Relations of the United States and Colombia," *AAAPSS* 22 (1903) 115–126.

8340. Leduc, A. *Colombia, Estados Unidos y Canal de Panamá*. Mexico, 1904.

8341. Leigh, J. G. "The Republic of Colombia and the Panama Canal," *EMA* 26 (1903) 1–19.

8342. Lodge, H. C. *Panama* (67th Cong., 1st Sess., S. Doc. 37). Wash., 1921.

8342a. López, J. "Situación Política, Económica y Social de Colombia en el Período de las Negociones con los Estados Unidos para la Celebración del Tratado del Canal de Panamá," *CC* 10 (?) (1915) 224–239.

8343. Mahan, A. T. "Was Panama a Chapter of National Dishonor?" *NAR* 196 (1912) 549–568.

8344. Medina Planas, H. "Independencia de Panamá," *RABN* 7 (1928) 180–189.

8345. Mendoza, D. "El Canal Interoceánico y los Tratados," *AJ* 5, 5th ser. (1901) 1–281.

8346. Mills, J. S. *The Panama Canal: A History and Description of the Enterprise*. London, 1913.

8347. Miner, D. C. *The Fight for the Panama Route: The Story of the Spooner Act and the Hay–Herrán Treaty*. N.Y., 1940.

8348. Moore, J. B. *The Interoceanic Canal and the Hay-Pauncefote Treaty*. Wash., 1900.

8349. Morales, E. A. "The Political and Economical Situation of Colombia," *NAR* 175 (1902) 347–360.

8350. Mowat, R. B. *The Life of Lord Pauncefote, First Ambassador to the United States*. London, 1929.

8351. Mullon, M. C. "Diplomatic Relations Between the United States and Colombia About the Panama Canal," Fordham U. Diss., 1935.

8352. Nieto Caballero, L. E. *La Separación de Panamá: Conferencia*. Bogotá, 1928.

8353. Pasco, S. "The Isthmian Canal Question as Affected by Treaties and Concessions," *AAAPSS* 19 (1902) 24–45.

8354. Otero, L. A. *Panamá*. Bogotá, 1926.

8355. Patterson, J. "Latin-American Reactions to the Panama Revolution of 1903," *HAHR* 24 (1944) 342–351.

8356. Pérez, R. "The Treacherous Treaty: A Colombian Plea," *NAR* 177 (1903) 934–946.

8357. Pierce, C. *The Roosevelt Panama Libel Cases*. N.Y., 1959.
Refers to the Panama libel cases against the Pulitzer newspapers.

8358. Rebolledo, A. *Reseña Histórico-Político de la Comunicación Inter-Oceánica: Con Especial Referencia a la Seperación de Panamá y a los Arreglos Entre Los Estados Unidos y Colombia*. San Francisco, 1930.

8359. Reyes, R. *Escritos Varios*. Bogotá, 1920.
Reyes was the Colombian minister to the United States, 1903–1904.

8360. ———. *Misión Diplomática y Militar, 1903–1904*. Bogotá, 1904.

8361. ———. *The Two Americas*. N.Y., 1914.

8362. Rives, G. L. "Problems of an Inter-Oceanic Canal," *PSQ* 14 (1899) 189–210.

8363. Roosevelt, T. "How the United States Acquired the Right to Dig the Panama Canal," *O* 99 (1911) 314–318.

8364. Sauvé, M. "La Séparation de Panama," *QDC* 16 (1903) 780–787.

8365. Storey, M. *The Recognition of Panama*. Boston, 1904.

8366. Tavernier, E. *Etude du Canal Inter-océanique de l'Amérique Centrale, au Point de Vue Diplomatique, Juridique, et Economique*. Paris, 1906.

8367. Terán, O. *Del Tratado Herrán-Hay al Tratado Bunau-Varilla*. 2 vols., Bogotá, 1937.

8368. Uribe, A. J. *Colombia y los Estados Unidos de América: El Canal Inter-Océanico: La Separación de Panamá: Política Internacional Económica: La Cooperación*. Bogotá, 1931.

8369. Uribe Uribe, R. *La Separación de Panamá*. Bogotá, 1906.

8370. USCH. *The Story of Panama: Hearings on the Rainey Resolution Before the Committee on Foreign Affairs of the House of Representatives* (62d Cong.). Wash., 1913.

8371. USCS. *Canal Treaties: Executive Documents Presented to the United States Senate, Together with Proceedings by the Senate, Thereon Relative to the Panama Canal* (63d Cong., 2d Sess., S. Doc. 456) Wash., 1914.

8372. ———. *Diplomatic History of the Panama Canal: Documents* (63d Cong., 2d Sess., S. Doc. 474). Wash., 1914.

8373. ———. *The Panama Canal and Our Relations with Colombia: Papers Relating to the Acquisition of the Canal Zone* (63d

Cong., 2d Sess., S. Doc. 471). Wash., 1914.

8374. USCS. *Relations of the United States with Colombia and the Republic of Panama* (58th Cong., 2d Sess., S. Doc. 95). Wash., 1904.

8375. ———. *Use by the United States of a Military Force in the Internal Affairs of Colombia* (58th Cong., 2d Sess., S. Doc. 143). Wash., 1904.

8376. USDN. *Correspondence Relating to the Military Occupation of Bays of Panama and Colon, etc. . . . Copies of all Reports and of all Correspondence in the Navy Department with Naval or Other Officers of the United States on Duty in the Bays of Panama and Colon Since April, 1902, Which Relate to the Military Occupation of Said Bays and the Region Between Them, and the Cities of Colon and Panama, etc.* (58th Cong., Special Sess., 1903, S. Doc. 10). Wash., 1903.

8377. USDS. *History of Amendments Proposed to the Clayton-Bulwer Treaty.* Wash., 1911.

8378. U.S. Isthmian Canal Commission. *Report of the Isthmian Canal Commission, 1899–1901, Rear Admiral John G. Walker, United States Navy, President* (58th Cong., 2d Sess., S. Doc. 222). Wash., 1904.

The commission favored the Nicaraguan route.

8379. ———. *Supplementary Report of the Isthmian Canal Commission* (57th Cong., 1st Sess., S. Doc. 123). Wash., 1902.

Concerns the proposed sale of the New Panama Canal Company to the United States.

8380. Valdés, R. M. *La Independencia del Istmo de Panamá.* Panama, 1903.

English ed., Panama, 1903; French ed., Panama, 1904.

8381. Venable, A. L. "John T. Morgan, Father of the Inter-Oceanic Canal," *SSSQ* 19 (1939) 376–387.

8382. Viallate, A. *Essai d'Histoire Diplomatique Américaine: le Developpement Territorial des Etats Unis: le Canal Interocéanique: la Guerre Hispano-Américaine.* Paris, 1905.

XV–E   cross references:

a) For specialized works on the background of the Panama dispute, see items 2350, 2351,

2353, 2358, 2361, 2365, 2368, 2369, 2370, 2377, 2378, 2379, 2380, 2381, 2387, 2388, 2395, 2397, 2401, 2403, 2408, 2409, 2410, 2411, 2414, 2432, 2435, 2437, 2438, 2439, 2447, 2450, 2454, 2457, 2458.

b) For general accounts of the Theodore Roosevelt administration, see items 2984–3035.

c) See also items 2506, 8283, 8426.

F. UNITED STATES–COLOMBIAN RELATIONS, 1903–1948

8383. Andrade de Pombo, H. *Tres Godos en Aprietos.* Bogotá, 1956.

An eye-witness report of the Bogotá uprising of April 9, 1948.

8384. Bartholomew, W. H. *The Colombian Treaty.* N.Y., 1921.

Concerns the indemnification. See also items 8396, 8415, 8416, 8429.

8385. Burr, R. N. "Colombia and International Cooperation, 1920–30," U. of Pennsylvania Diss., 1949.

8386. Carreño, P. M. *Proceso Contra el Ex-Ministro de Estado, Doctor Pedro María Carreño.* Bogotá, 1939.

Carreño was a legal adviser to several U.S. corporations (including the United Fruit Company) as well as the foreign minister under Olaya Herrera (1933–1934). He was charged with conflict of interests.

8387. Colombia. *Proyecto de Ley por la Cual se Aprueba Un Convenio Comercial Entre la República de Colombia y los Estados Unidos de América.* Bogotá, 1935.

8388. ———. Congreso. Senado. Comisión de Relaciones Exteriores. *Informe de la Comisión de Relaciones Exteriores del Senado, Sobre el Proyecto de Ley "Que Aprueba las Modificaciones Introducidas por el Senado Norteamericano al Tratado de 6 de Abril de 1914" Entre Colombia y los Estados Unidos de América.* Bogotá, 1921.

8389. ———. ———. ———. ———. *Los Modificaciones al Tratado Entre Colombia y los EE. Unidos, Artículos y Discursos por el Doctor Antonio José Uribe.* Bogotá, 1921.

8390. ———. Ministerio de Relaciones Exteriores. *Exposición del Ministro de*

Relaciones Exteriores al Congreso Nacional, Acerca del Convenio de Comercio Celebrado en 1935 Entre la República de Colombia y los Estados Unidos de América. Bogotá, 1936.

8391. ————. ————. *Exposición que Presenta el Ministro de Relaciones Exteriores á la Honorable Asamblea Nacional Constituyente y Legislativa Sobre los Tratados Celebrados por la República de Colombia con las Repúblicas de los Estados Unidos y Panamá.* Bogotá, 1909.

8392. ————. Oficina de Longitudes y Fronteras. *Arreglo de Límites Entre la República de Colombia y la República de Panamá.* Bogotá, 1941.

8393. ————. Presidente. *Declaraciones Presidenciales: Abril de 1941 a Agosto de 1942.* 2 vols., Bogotá, 1942.

Contains texts of treaties as well as presidential speeches.

8394. ————. ————. *Mensajes del Presidente López al Congreso Nacional, 1934–1938.* Bogotá, 1939.

8395. Cox, I. J. "The Colombian Treaty: Retrospect and Prospect," *JIR* 11 (1921) 549–570.

See also items 8384, 8415, 8416, 8429.

8396. Du Bois, J. T. *Colombia's Claims and Rights.* Hallstead, Pa., 1914.

Author was a former minister to Colombia.

8397. ————, et al. *El Tratado de 6 de Abril ante al Senado y Pueblo de los Estados Unidos.* Bogotá (?), 1914.

8398. Eder, P. J. *Colombia.* London, 1913.

8399. Estrada Monsalve, J. *El 9 de Abril en Palacio: Horario de un Golpe de Estado.* 3d ed., Bogotá, 1948.

A treatment of the Bogotazo.

8400. Fandiño Silva, F. *La Penetración Soviética en América y el 9 de April.* Bogotá, 1949.

Discusses alleged communist influences in the Bogotazo.

8401. Faust, G. H. "Economic Relations of the U.S. and Colombia, 1920–1940," U. of Chicago Diss., 1946.

8402. Fitzgibbon, R. H. "Colombian Gadfly," *INA* 4 (February, 1945) 15–17.

Concerns Laureano Gómez.

8403. Fluharty, V. L. *Dance of the Millions: Military Rule and the Social Revolution in Colombia, 1930–1956.* Pittsburgh, 1957.

8404. García, A. *Gaitán y el Problema de la Revolución Colombiana.* Bogotá, 1955.

8405. García Samudio, N. (comp.). *Tratados y Convenios de Colombia, 1938–1948.* Bogotá, 1950.

A compilation of international agreements for the years indicated. For earlier agreements, see items 8146, vol. 6, and 8406.

8406. Guzmán Esponda, E. (comp.). *Tratados y Convenios de Colombia, 1919–1938.* Bogotá, 1939.

8407. Harding, E. "In Justice to the United States—a Settlement with Colombia," *JRD* 4 (1914) 427–442.

8408. Hoffman, H. T. "A History of Railway Concessions and Railway Development Policy in Colombia in 1943," American U. Diss., 1947.

8409. Knox, P. C. *Relations Between the United States and the Republic of Colombia* (62d Cong., 3d Sess., H. Doc. 1444). Wash., 1913.

8410. Lleras Camargo, A. *Un Año de Gobierno, 1945–1946: Discursos y Otros Documentos.* Bogotá, 1946.

Documents pertaining to Lleras' provisional presidency.

8411. López, A. *La Política Internacional: Discursos, Mensajes, Cablegramas y Otros Documentos del Presidente López Sobre Asuntos Internacionales.* Bogotá, 1938.

Documents from López's first administration, 1934–1938.

8412. López Michelsen, A. *Los Ultimos Días de López, y Cartas Intimas de Tres Campañas Politicas, 1929–1940–1958.* Bogotá, 1961.

8413. Martínez C., D. *On the Treaty Between United States and Colombia.* Wash., 1916.

8414. Martínez Zelada, E. *Colombia en el Llanto.* Mexico, 1948.

Concerns the Bogotazo of 1948.

8415. Mendoza, D. *El Canal Interoceánico.* Bogotá, 1930.

Concerns the indemnity treaty. See also items 8384, 8395, 8416, 8429.

8416. Nieto Caballero, L. E. *El Dolor de Colombia.* Bogotá, 1922.

Colombian response to the indemnity treaty. See also items 8384, 8395, 8415, 8429.

8417. Niño H., A. *Antecedentes y Secretos del 9 de Abril.* Bogotá, 1950.

Author, a former chief of the security police, builds a case for communist involvement in the Bogotazo.

8418. Orrego, G. *El 9 de Abril Fuera del Palacio*. Bogotá, 1949.

8419. Ortiz C., L. B. "El Comercio Internacional de Colombia," *COL* 1 (August, 1944) 170–189.

8420. Osorio Lizarazo, J. A. *Gaitán: Vida, Muerte, y Permanente Presencia*. B.A., 1952.

Biographical treatment of the liberal leader whose assassination touched off the Bogotazo in April, 1948.

8421. Ospina Pérez, M. *El Gobierno de Union Nacional: Un Programa en Acción Mensajes y Otros Documentos*. 2 vols., Bogotá, 1948.

Ospina was President of Colombia from 1946 to 1950.

8421a. Ospina, R. E. "Aspectos Económicos de la Explotación de Petróleo en Colombia," *RFO* 2 (October, 1939) 109–119.

8422. Parks, E. T. "The Colombian Treaty: A Triumph for Mr. Hull," *WA* 97 (March, 1934) 48–50.

8423. Peña, L. D. *Gaitán Intimo*. 2d ed., Bogotá, 1949.

A eulogistic biography.

8424. Petre, F. L. *The Republic of Colombia: An Account of the Country, Its People, Its Institutions and Its Resources*. London, 1906.

8425. Raisbeck, J. W. *Petróleos, Legislación y Jurisprudencia*. Bogotá, 1939.

8426. Rebolledo, A. *Reseña Histórico-Política de la Comunicación Interoceánica, con Especial Referencia a la Separación de Panamá y a los Arreglos Entre los Estados Unidos y Colombia*. San Francisco, 1930.

8426a. Restrepo, R. L. "Consideraciones Sobre un Canal Interoceánico por Territorio Colombiano," *UCB* 55, nos. 11–13 (1939) 166–176.

8427. Rippy, J. F. "The United States and Colombian Oil," *FPAIS* 5 (1929–1930) 19–36.

8428. Santos, E. *Las Etapas de la Vida Colombiana: Discursos y Mensajes, 1938–1942*. Bogotá, 1946.

Documents covering the years of Santos' presidency.

8429. Scott, J. B. "The Treaty Between Colombia and the United States," *AJIL* 15 (1921) 430–439.

See also items 8384, 8395, 8415, 8416.

8430. Stewart, W. "The Ratification of the Thomson-Urrutia Treaty," *SPSQ* 10 (1930) 416–428.

8431. Suárez, M. F. *Tratado Entre Colombia y los Estados Unidos*. Bogotá, 1914.

8432. Sullivan, W. W. "A Study in the Relations Between Colombia and the U.S., 1900–1924," U. of Illinois Diss., 1925.

8433. Taylor, H. *Why the Pending Treaty with Colombia Should Be Ratified*. Wash., 1914.

8434. Thomson, N. *Colombia and the United States*. London, 1915.

8435. USCS. *The Panama Canal and Our Relations with Colombia* (63d Cong., 2d Sess., S. Doc. 471). Wash., 1914.

8436. ———. *Settlement of Differences with Colombia: Diplomatic Correspondence and Documents Submitted to the Committee on Foreign Relations, United States Senate, 63d Cong., 3d Session* (65th Cong., Special Sess., S. Doc. 1). Wash., 1921.

8437. Uribe, A. J. *Cuestiones Internacionales, Económicas, Políticas, y Sociales*. Bogotá, 1925.

8438. ———. *Las Modificaciones al Tratado Entre Colombia y los Estados Unidos*. Bogotá, 1921.

8439. Yepes, J. M. "La Política Internacional de Colombia y el Panamericanismo," *RCDI* 1 (July, 1947) 38–60.

XV–F   cross references:

a) For a discussion of the Costa Rica–Panama (Colombia) boundary arbitration, see items 7271–7285.

b) See also items 2903, 3408, 4854, 7085, 7311, 7375, 8351, 8354, 8368.

G. THE LETICIA DISPUTE

8440. Cabeza de Vaca, M. *La Posición del Ecuador en el Conflicto Colomboperuano*. Quito, 1934.

8441. Cano, L. *Semblanzas y Editoriales*. Bogotá, 1936.

Analyzes the Leticia dispute from a Colombian point of view.

8442. Colombia. *El Conflicto de Leticia*. 2d ed., Bogotá, 1934.

8443. Colombian Legation [Washington]. *La Opinión Internacional y el Conflicto de Leticia*. Wash., 1933.
    English ed., Wash., 1933.

8444. Cooper, R. M. *American Consultation in World Affairs*, N.Y., 1934.

8445. Córdoba, D. L. *El Debate Sobre el Protocolo de Rio de Janeiro en la Cámara*. Bogotá, 1936.
    Treats the Leticia settlement.

8446. De Wilde, J. C. "South American Conflicts: The Chaco and Leticia," *FPAR* 9 (May, 1933) 58–80.

8447. Hubbard, U. P. "Peru–Colombia Dispute," *IC*, no. 329 (1937) 402–410.

8448. Jordan, A. *Leticia*. Quito, 1941.

8449. LN Council. *Dispute Between Colombia and Peru*. Geneva, 1933.

8450. López, J. *Los Tratados de Límites y la Paz Internacional Americana, el Tratado Secreto de 1922 Entre Colombia y el Perú*. N.Y., 1932.

8451. López, N. F. *Estudios Internacionales Sobre el Conflicto Colombo-Peruano*. Quito, 1934.

8452. Manjauze, C., and P. de la Pradell. "L'Affaire de Leticia," *RDISDP* 11 (1933) 235–371.

8453. Maúrtua, V. M. "La Conflit de Leticia et la Procédure de Conciliation," *RDISDP* 11 (1933) 172–184.

8453a. Pereira Vela, E. *La Sangrienta Sorpresa en Calderón*. Lima, 1959.
    Treats Peruvian military action in the dispute.

8454. Pérez Serrano, J. *El Tercero en la Discordia: La Actuación Internacional de Ecuador en el Conflicto de Leticia y Antecedentes Histórico-Diplomáticos de la Misma*. Quito, 1936.

8455. Reyes, A. *La Conferencia Colombo-Peruana para el Arreglo del Incidente de Leticia, Rio de Janeiro, 25 de Octubre de 1933 a 24 de Mayo de 1934*. Mexico, 1947.

8456. Romero, F. *Marinos en la Selva: Notas para una Historia de la Flotilla Fluvial de Guerra*. Lima, 1935.

8457. Thomas, D. Y. "The Settlement of the Leticia Dispute," *SSSQ* 15 (1934) 155–165.

8458. Woolsey, L. H. "Leticia Dispute Between Colombia and Peru," *AJIL* 27 (1933) ``7–324, 525–527.

8459. ————. "Leticia Dispute Between Colombia and Peru," *AJIL* 29 (1935) 94–99.

8460. Yepes, J. M. "L'Affaire de Leticia Entre la Colombie et le Pérou: Etude Historique et Juridique," *RDISDP* 11 (1933) 133–171.

8461. ————. *Le Conflit Entre la Colombie et le Pérou Devant le Droit International*. Paris, 1933.

XV–G cross references: 8760, 8779, 9120.

H. UNITED STATES–COLOMBIAN RELATIONS SINCE 1948

8462. "Anti-Americanism in Colombia," *RUA* 2 (June, 1959) 105–115.

8462a. Arciniegas, G. "La Dictadura en Colombia," *CA* 49 (January, 1950) 7–33.
    Concerns the elections of 1949.

8463. Barrington and Company. *Industrial Development of Colombia*. N.Y., 1961.
    Special study prepared for the Ministry of Development, the National Planning Council, the Government of Colombia, and the United States Operations Mission to Colombia (of the International Cooperation Administration, United States Government).

8464. Bunegina, I. A. *Kolumbiia: Ekonomika i Vneshniaia Torgovlia*. Moscow, 1959.
    Colombia: The Economy and Foreign Trade.

8465. Bushnell, D. "What Has Happened to Democracy in Colombia?" *CH* 24 (January, 1953) 38–42.

8466. Cabot, J. M. "United States–Colombian Cooperation," *USDSB* 37 (1957) 1038–1042.

8466a. Charry Samper, H. "La Beligerancia del Interamericanismo," *COMB* 3 (January, 1962) 33–38.

8467. Colombia. Ministerio de Relaciones Exteriores. *Política Internacional de Colombia*. Bogotá, 1961.

8468. Eder, P. J. *American-Colombian Private International Law*. N.Y., 1956.

8469. Foreign Area Studies Division. Special Operations Research Division. The American University. *Special Warfare Area Handbook for Colombia*. Wash., 1961.

8470. Forero Moralés, N. *Laureano Gómez: Un Hombre, un Partido, una Nación.* Bogotá, 1950.
       A sympathetic biography.

8471. Galindo, A. "Colombia's Five Year Plan," *APAU* 3 (July, 1951) 3–5, 41–44.

8472. Geithman, D. T. "Money and Income in Colombia, 1950–1960," U. of Florida Diss., 1964.

8473. Goering, T. J. "United States Agricultural Surplus Disposal in Colombia," Michigan State U. Diss., 1962.

8474. Helguera, J. L. "The Changing Role of the Military in Colombia," *JIAS* 3 (July, 1961) 351–358.

8475. Hernández B., E. *Colombia en Korea: Impresiones de un Tripulante del A.R.C. "Almirante Padilla" en su Viaje a Korea.* Bogotá, 1953.

8476. Holt, P. M. *Colombia Today—and Tomorrow.* N.Y., 1964.

8477. Hunter, J. M. *Emerging Colombia.* Wash., 1962.

8478. International Bank for Reconstruction and Development. *The Basis of a Development Program for Colombia: Report of a Mission Headed by Lauchlin Currie.* Wash., 1950.

8479. Lleras Camargo, A. *Addresses Delivered During His Visit to the United States, April, 1960.* N.p., 1960.

8480. ———. *El Primer Gobierno del Frente Nacional.* 2 vols., Bogotá, 1960.

8481. ———. *Sus Mejores Páginas: Selecciones por Alberto Zalamea.* Lima, 1960.

8482. Martz, J. D. *Colombia: A Contemporary Political Survey.* Chapel Hill, N.C., 1962.
       Emphasizes political developments since the Bogotazo.

8483. PAU. *A Statement of the Laws of Colombia in Matters Affecting Business.* Wash., 1961.

8484. Ruiz Novoa, A. *El Batallón Colombia en Korea, 1951–1954.* Bogotá, 1956.
       Ruiz Novoa was the commander of the Colombian forces in Korea.

8485. Sánchez Camacho, J. *El General Ospina: Biografía.* Bogotá, 1960.

8486. Torres Almeyda, P. E. *Colombia en la Guerra de Corea: Impressiones de un Combatiente.* Bogotá, 1960(?).

8487. Turbay Ayala, J. C. *Política Internacional de Colombia.* Bogotá, 1961.
       A collection of speeches by the foreign minister, 1958–1961.

8488. USDC. Office of International Trade. *Investment in Colombia: Conditions and Outlook for United States Investors.* Wash., 1953.

8489. Wilgus, A. C. (ed.). *The Caribbean: Contemporary Colombia.* Gainesville, Fla., 1962.

8490. Wurfel, S. W. *Foreign Enterprise in Colombia.* Chapel Hill, N.C., 1965.

XV–H cross references: 4152b, 4152e, 4152f, 4152g, 7221, 8413.

Chapter XVI   The United States and Venezuela

A. UNITED STATES–VENEZUELAN RELATIONS: GENERAL WORKS AND SPECIAL STUDIES

8491. Aguado, P. de. *Historia de Venezuela*. 2 vols., Madrid, 1918–1919.

8492. Arellano Moreno, A. *Guía de Historia de Venezuela, 1492–1945*. Caracas, 1955.

8493. Fergusson, E. *Venezuela*. N.Y., 1939.
       A popular history.

8494. Franco, J. L. *Documentos para la Historia de Venezuela, Compilados y Ordenados*. Havana, 1960.

8495. García Chuecos, H. *Relatos y Comentarios Sobre Temas de Historia Venezolana*. Caracas, 1957.

8496. Gil Fortuol, J. *Historia Constitucional de Venezuela*. 3 vols., rev. ed., Caracas, 1953–1955.

8497. González Guinán, F. *Historia Contemporánea de Venezuela*. 15 vols., Caracas, 1909–1925.

8498. Grases, P., and M. P. Vila (comps.). *Documentos que Hicieron Historia: Siglo y Medio de Vida Republicana, 1810–1961*. 2 vols., Caracas, 1962.

8499. Lieuwen, E. *Petroleum in Venezuela: A History*. Berkeley, Calif., 1954.

8500. ———. *Venezuela*. N.Y., 1961.
       Short summary history. In the Latin American series of the Royal Institute of International Affairs.

8501. Marsland, W. D., and A. L. Marsland. *Venezuela Through Its History*. N.Y., 1954.

8502. Morón, G. *A History of Venezuela*. N.Y., 1964.

8503. Oropesa, J. *Breve Historia de Venezuela*. Mexico, 1945.

8504. Parra, F. J. *Doctrinas de la Cancillería Venezolana*. 5 vols., N.Y., 1952–1960.
       Treats diplomatic relations in the nineteenth and twentieth centuries.

8505. Perera, A. *Historia Orgánica de Venezuela*. Caracas, 1943.

8506. Picón-Salas, M., *et al. Venezuela Independiente, 1810–1960*. Caracas, 1962.

8507. Pierson, W. W. "Foreign Influences on Venezuelan Political Thought, 1830–1930," *HAHR* 15 (1935) 3–42.

8508. Rayburn, J. C. "Development of Venezuela's Iron Ore Deposits," *IEA* 6, no. 1 (1952) 52–70.

8509. ———. "Rail Transportation in Venezuela, 1835–1955," *IEA* 10 (Spring, 1957) 23–46.

8510. ———. "United States Investments in Venezuelan Asphalt," *IEA* 7, no. 1 (1953) 20–36.

8511. Rodulfo C., S. *Antología Documental de Venezuela, 1492–1900: Materiales para Enseñanza de la Historia de Venezuela*. Caracas, 1960.

8512. Siso Martínez, J. M. *Historia de Venezuela*. 5th ed., Mexico, 1956.

8513. Ulric, J. *Venezuela*. Paris, 1961.

8514. Venezuela. Ministerio de Relaciones Exteriores. *Tratados Públicos y Acuerdos Internacionales de Venezuela*. 7 vols., Caracas, 1924–1945.
       Covers the period 1820–1944.

8514a. ———. Presidencia de la República. *150 Años de Vida Republicana: 1811–1961*. 2 vols., Caracas, 1963.
       Long essays on republican development.

8515. Watters, M. *A History of the Church in Venezuela, 1810–1930*. Chapel Hill, N.C., 1933.

XVI–A   cross references: 1473, 8133.

B. UNITED STATES–VENEZUELAN RELATIONS, 1830–1908.

8516. Academia Nacional de la Historia. *Biblioteca de la Academia Nacional de la Historia*. 44 vols., Caracas, 1959–1961.

8517.   Andrade, I. ¿ Por Qué Triunfó la Revolución Restauradora? Caracas, 1955.
Andrade was President, 1898–1899.

8518.   Bance, J. B. Defensa de la New York and
Bermúdez Company ante la Corte Federal
de Venezuela. Caracas, 1904.

8519.   Bonsal, S. "Castro: A Latin-American
Type," NAR 176 (1903) 747–757.
Refers to Cipriano Castro, President of
Venezuela, 1899–1908.

8520.   Brandt, C. Bajo la Tiranía de Cipriano
Castro. Caracas, 1952.

8521.   Briceño, M. de. A Memoir Justifying the
Conduct of the Venezuelan Government on
the Aves Island Question. Wash., 1858.
Spanish ed., Wash., 1858. The author
represented Venezuela in Washington
when this pamphlet appeared, and the
United States demanded his recall.

8522.   Camacho, S. Cosas de los Estados Unidos.
N.Y., 1864.
Impressions of a Venezuelan journalist
and diplomat.

8523.   Casanova, P. Reclamaciones Internacionales. Caracas, 1872.
Cites many nineteenth-century Venezuelan complaints against the United
States.

8524.   Castillo, D. B. Venezuela y el Monroeismo.
Caracas, 1905.

8525.   Clarke, R. F. "Castro, the Ungrateful,"
NAR 187 (1908) 567–577.

8526.   Commission to Arbitrate Claims of
Venezuela, Steam Transportation Com-
pany of New York Against Venezuela.
Final Report of Alexander Porter Morse,
Agent of the United States. Wash., 1895.

8527.   Cova, J. A. Guzmán Blanco, Su Vida y Su
Obra. Caracas, 1950.

8528.   Dallett, F. J. "Páez in Philadelphia,"
HAHR 40 (1960) 98–106.

8529.   Dennis, W. C. "The Orinoco Steamship Case Before the Hague Tribunal,"
AJIL 5 (1911) 35–64.

8530.   Eastwick, E. B. Venezuela or Sketches of
Life in a South American Republic.
London, 1868.
Spanish ed., Caracas, 1959. Comments
upon United States and British rivalry in
Venezuelan enterprises.

8531.   Fenton, P. F. "Diplomatic Relations of
the United States and Venezuela, 1880–
1915," HAHR 8 (1928) 330–356.

8531a.   Frankel, B. A. "Venezuela and the
United States, 1810–1888," U. of California Diss., 1964.

8532.   Grases, P., and M. Pérez Vila (comps.).
Pensamiento Político Venezolano del Siglo
XIX: Textos para su Estudio. 15 vols.,
Caracas, 1960–1962.

8533.   Gray, W. H. "American Diplomacy in
Venezuela, 1835–1865," HAHR 20
(1940) 551–574.
Surveys the diplomacy of the Páez
period.

8534.   ———. "The Diplomatic Relations
Between the U.S. and Venezuela, 1830–
1864," U. of Chicago Diss., 1937.

8535.   ———. "Steamboat Transportation on
the Orinoco," HAHR 25 (1945) 455–
469.

8536.   Grisanti, C. F. Affaire de the Orinoco
Steamship Company Limited. Paris, 1910.

8537.   Grummond, J. L. de (ed.): Caracas
Diary, 1835–1840: The Journal of John
G. A. Williamson, First Diplomatic
Representative of the United States to
Venezuela. Baton Rouge, La., 1954.

8538.   ———. Envoy to Caracas: The Story of
John G. A. Williamson, Nineteenth
Century Diplomat. Baton Rouge, La.,
1951.

8539.   ———. "The Jacob Idler Claim Against
Venezuela, 1817–1890," HAHR 34
(1954) 131–157.

8540.   Hanna, A. J., and K. A. Hanna. Confederate Exiles in Venezuela. Tuscaloosa,
Ala., 1960.

8541.   Hibbs, J. R. "The Caracas Awards of
1868 and Their Significance in the
Relations of Venezuela and the U.S.,
1865–1889," U. of Pennsylvania Diss.,
1941.

8542.   Jackson, C. G. "The Manoa Company,"
IEA 13 (Spring, 1960) 12–45.
Concerns U.S. land speculation in the
Orinoco Valley, 1883–1895.

8543.   Morris, R. C. "Our Controversy with
Venezuela," YLJ 18 (1909) 243–251.

8544.   Nava, J. "A Social History of Venezuela:
Guzmán Blanco," Harvard U. Diss.,
1955.

8545.   Núñez, E. B. Anales Diplomáticos de
Venezuela. 4 vols., Caracas, 1951.
Collection of nineteenth-century diplo-
matic documents.

8546. Picón-Salas, M. *Los Días de Cipriano Castro*. 2d ed., Braquisimeto, Venezuela, 1955.

8547. Pile, W. A. *A Plea for Justice: Venezuela's Appeal to the United States for Redress and Fair Play: The Conspiracy to Plunder Venezuela and Certain American Citizens: The Powers of Congress to Set Aside, for Cause, Awards of International Commissions*. Wash., 1878.

8548. *Protocoles des Séances de Tribunal d'Arbitrage Constitué en Exécution du Compromis Signé Entre les Etats-Unis d'Amérique et les Etats-Unis de Vénézuela le 13 Fevrier 1909; Différend au Sujet d'une Réclamation de la Compagnie des Bateaux à Vapeur "Orinoco."* The Hague, 1910.

8549. Rippy, J. F., and C. E. Hewitt. "Cipriano Castro, 'Man Without a Country,'" *AHR* 55 (1949) 36–53.

8550. Rondón Márquez, R. A. *Guzmán Blanco, el Autocrata Civilizador*. 2 vols., Madrid, 1952.

Stresses the accomplishments of the regime.

8551. Scelle, G. "L'Affaire de la Orinoco Steamship Company," *RGDIP* 58 (1911) 164–202.

8552. Seijas, R. F. *Prácticas del Ministerio Venezolano de Relaciones Exteriores*. Madrid, 1890.

8553. Thurber, O. E. *The Venezuelan Question: Castro and the Asphalt Trust from Official Records*. N.Y., 1907.

8554. United States. *The Case of the United States of America on Behalf of the Orinoco Steamship Company Against the United States of Venezuela*. Wash., 1910.

Appendix . . . , 2 vols., Wash., 1910. *The Counter Case of the United States*, Wash., 1910.

8555. USCS. *Correspondence Relating to Wrongs Done to American Citizens by the Government of Venezuela* (60th cong., 1st sess., S. Doc. 413). Wash., 1908.

8556. ———. *Orinoco Steamship Company . . . Papers . . . Showing the Settlement of the Controversies Which Existed with the Government of Venezuela with Respect to the Claims of the Orinoco Steamship Company Against That Government* (61st Cong., 1st Sess., S. Doc. 13). Wash., 1909.

8557. USDS. *In the Matter of the Claim of the Venezuela Steam Transportation Company Against the Government of Venezuela: Correspondence Between the Department of State of the United States and Counsel for the Claimant, 1879–1884*. N.Y.(?), 1884(?).

8558. Venezuela. Ministerio de Relaciones Exteriores. *Documentos Relativos á la Reclamación Intentada por la Legación de los Estados Unidos de América en Caracas, á Favor del Ciudadano Norte-Americano Hancox, ó de la Compañia de Transporte por Vapor de Venezuela*. Caracas, 1890.

8559. Villafañe, J. G. *Informe Dado al Gobierno Sobre los Actos de la Comisión Mixta*. Caracas, 1868.

8560. Villanueva Berrizbeitia, F. *Dieciseis Cancilleres de Venezuela*. Caracas, 1950.

Biographical sketches of sixteen Venezuelan foreign secretaries, 1810–1900.

8561. Wise, G. S. *Caudillo: A Portrait of Antonio Guzmán Blanco*. N.Y., 1951.

A study of the phenomenon of caudillismo as well as a biography of Guzmán Blanco.

XVI–B cross references:

a) For works on the Olney Corollary (1895), see items 2494–2515.

b) The role of the United States in the independence of Gran Colombia is treated in items 8149–8241.

c) See also items 8175, 8207, 8218, 8606, 8607, 8614.

C. THE VENEZUELAN–BRITISH GUIANA BOUNDARY CONTROVERSY

8562. Alverstone, Viscount. *Recollections of Bar and Bench*. London, 1914.

Lord Alverstone was the counsel for Great Britain in the arbitration of the boundary controversy.

8563. Baker, M. "The Anglo–Venezuelan Boundary Dispute," *NG* 11 (1900) 129–144.

8564. ———. *The Digest of Evidence Arranged According to Localities*. N.Y., 1899.

8565. ———. *Geographical Results of the Venezuela–British Guiana Dispute*. Berlin, 1900.

8566. ———. "The Venezuelan Boundary

Commission and Its Work," *NG* 8 (1897) 193–201.

8567. Baylen, J. O. "Valentine Chirol, Baron Von Holstein and the Venezuelan Crisis of 1895–96: An Unpublished Memorandum," *HIS* 27 (1965) 210–217.

8568. Burr, G. L. "The Guiana Boundary," *AHR* 6 (October, 1900) 49–64.

8569. ———. "The Search for the Venezuela–Guiana Boundary," *AHR* 4 (April, 1899) 470–477.

8570. Carnegie, A. "The Venezuelan Question," *NAR* 162 (1896) 129–144.

8571. Child, C. J. "The Venezuela–British Guiana Boundary Arbitration of 1899," *AJIL* 44 (1950) 682–693.

8572. Cleveland, G. *Venezuelan Boundary Dispute.* N.Y., 1907.
Also in *CE* 62 (1901) 283–297, 405–419.

8573. Davis, N. D. *Venezuelan International Law.* Georgetown(?), British Guiana, 1896.

8574. Dennis, W. C. "The Venezuela–British Guiana Boundary Arbitration of 1899," *AJIL* 44 (1950) 720–727.

8575. Fossum, P. R. "The Anglo–Venezuelan Boundary Controversy," *HAHR* 8 (1928) 299–329.

8576. Great Britain. *British Guiana Boundary Case, Appendix, Atlas, Counter Case, Appendix, Argument.* 7 vols., London, 1898.

8577. ———. *The Case (Appendix) on Behalf of the Government of Her Britannic Majesty.* 8 vols., London, 1898.

8578. ———. *The Counter-Case on Behalf of the Government of Her Britannic Majesty (and Appendix).* 2 vols., London, 1898.

8579. Hedrick, E. V. "The Diplomacy of the Venezuelan Boundary Controversy," U. of California Diss., 1942.

8580. Im Thurn, E. F. (comp.). *Venezuelan and British Guiana Boundary Arbitration: Synopsis of the Principal Events in Guiana (1498–1897), Arranged in Chronological Order, with Special Reference to the Documents Printed in the Appendices of the British and Venezuelan Governments.* N.p., 1897 (?).

8581. Jervey, T. D. "William Lindsay Scruggs, a Forgotten Diplomat," *SAQ* 27 (1928) 292–309.

U.S. envoy to Venezuela during the boundary dispute. See also items 8594–8596.

8582. Johnes, E. R. *The Anglo–Venezuelan Controversy and the Monroe Doctrine.* N.Y., 1888.

8583. Kulp, C. A. "Venezuela and the Monroe Doctrine," *PAM* 30 (1920) 131–140.

8584. Markham, C. R. "Boundaries of British Guiana: Evidence of Maps," *GJ* 7 (1896) 277–280.

8585. Mathews, J. J. "Informal Diplomacy in the Venezuelan Crisis of 1896," *MVHR* 50 (1963) 195–212.

8586. Morley, J. "Arbitration with America," *NC* 40 (1896) 320–337.

8587. Pariset, G. *Historique Sommaire du Conflit Anglo–Vénézuélien en Guyane: Des Origines au Traité d'Arbitrage, 1493–1897.* Paris, 1898.

8588. ———. *L'Arbitrage Anglo–Vénézuélien de Guyane.* Paris, 1900.

8589. Phillips, P. L. "Guiana and Venezuela Cartography," *AHAAR* (1897) 681–776. Wash., 1898.

8590. ———. "The Value of Maps in Boundary Disputes, Especially in Connection with Venezuela and British Guiana," *AHAAR* 1 (1896) 457–462. Wash., 1897.

8591. Rugg, R. *Anglo–American Boundary Question as Stated by Great Britain, Venezuela, and the United States, in Their Official Despatches.* London, 1896.

8592. Salter, W. M. *The Venezuelan Question.* Phil., 1896.

8593. Schoenrich, O. "The Venezuela–British Guiana Boundary Dispute," *AJIL* 43 (1949) 523–530.

8594. Scruggs, W. L. *The Colombian and Venezuelan Republics.* Boston, 1900.
Author was the U.S. minister to Venezuela, 1889–1893.

8595. ———. *Fallacies of the British Blue Book.* Wash., 1896.

8596. ———. *The Venezuelan Question.* Atlanta, 1896.

8597. Seijas, R. F. *British Boundaries of Guayana.* Paris, 1888.

8598. Silvestri, C. *La Questione Anglo–Venezuelana per la Delimitazione del Confini Territoriali Della Asserzioni del Geografo Prof. G. Cora Della R. Univ. di Torino.* Rome, 1896.

8599. U.S. Commission to Investigate and Report upon the True Divisional Line Between Venezuela and British Guiana. *Report and Accompanying Papers of the Comm. Appointed by the President of the United States "to Investigate and Report upon the True Divisional Line Between the Republic of Venezuela and British Guiana."* 9 vols., Wash., 1896–1897.

8600. USDS. *Correspondence in Relation to the Boundary Controversy Between Great Britain and Venezuela.* Wash., 1896.

8601. Venezuela. Ministerio de Relaciones Exteriores. *Acuerdo del Congreso de los Estados de Venezuela, Dictado el 9 de Marzo de 1896 como Expresión de Reconocimiento á los Altos Poderes de los Estados Unidos de América, por su Benéfica Interposición en el Asunto de los Límites de Guayana.* Caracas, 1896.

8602. ———. ———. *Correspondence Between the Venezuelan Government and H.B.M.'s Government About the Question of the Frontier.* Caracas, 1887.

8603. ———. ———. *Latest Correspondence on the Question of Limits of Guiana.* Caracas, 1887.

8604. ———. ———. *Venezuela y la Gran Bretaña; Cuestión Límites de Guayana: Estado en que la Halló el Gobierno Inaugurado el 19 de Marzo y su Situación Actual.* Caracas, 1890.

8604a. Villacrés Moscoso, J. W. "Eloy Alfaro y el Conflicto Anglo-Venezolano Guayana-Esequiva," *BANHC* 45 (January, 1962) 65–72.

8605. Webber, A. R. F. *Centenary History and Handbook of British Guiana.* Georgetown, British Guiana, 1931.

8605a. Wheelwright, J. T. "President Cleveland's Foresight: The Venezuela Message," *UM* 17 (December, 1918) 506–512.

XVI–C cross references:

a) For works on the Olney Corollary (1895), see items 2494–2515.

b) See also items 2112, 2112b, 2638.

D. THE VENEZUELAN DEBTS CONTROVERSY

8605b. Bohler, G. "La Question du Venezuela," *QDC* 15 (1903) 226–239.

8606. Bowen, H. W. "Queer Diplomacy With Castro," *NAR* 184 (1907) 577–580.

Bowen was the United States minister to Venezuela, 1901–1905, and a counsel for Venezuela at the Hague proceedings of 1903.

8607. ———. *Recollections, Diplomatic and Undiplomatic.* N.Y., 1926.

8608. ———. "Venezuela and The Hague," *IN* 61 (1906) 1472–1475.

8609. Dillon, R. "The Venezuela Arbitration Once More: Facts and Law," *ALR* 38 (1904) 648–661.

8610. Drago, L. M. *La República Argentina y el Caso de Venezuela: Documentos, Juicios, y Comentarios Relacionados con la Nota Pasada al Ministro Argentino en Washington.* B.A., 1903.

8611. Gaché, A. *Le Conflit Vénézuélien et l'Arbitrage de la Haye.* Paris, 1905.

8611a. Giménez Rodríguez, G. E. "Visión General del Bloque a Venezuela, 1902–1903," *FAV*, no. 163 (January, 1960) 60–63.

8612. Grisanti, C. F. *Los Estados Unidos de Venezuela y los Estados Unidos de América ante el Tribunal de la Corte Permanente de Arbitraje de la Haya . . . . Alegatos.* Caracas, 1909.

8612a. Hasenclever, A. "Zur Geschichte der Venezuela-Blockade, 1902 und 1903," *HV* 31 (1937) 107–118.

8612b. Hendrickson, E. J. "Root's Watchful Waiting and the Venezuelan Controversy," *TA* 23 (1966) 115–129.

8613. Hershey, A. S. "The Venezuelan Affair in the Light of International Law," *ALR* 51 (1903) 249–267.

8614. Hewitt, C. E. "Venezuela and the Great Powers, 1902–1909: A Study in International Investment and Diplomacy," U. of Chicago Diss., 1949.

8614a. Holland, T. E. "War sub Modo," *LQRE* 19 (1903) 133–135.

8615. Livermore, S. W. "Theodore Roosevelt, the American Navy, and the Venezuelan Crisis of 1902–1903," *AHR* 51 (1946) 452–471.

8616. MacVeagh, W. "The Value of the Venezuelan Arbitration," *NAR* 177 (1903) 801–811.

8616a. Pacheco, L. E. (ed.). "Cipriano Castro en

Estados Unidos," *BAHM* 3 (March, 1962) 25–83.

8617. Penfield, W. L. "The Anglo-German Intervention in Venezuela," *NAR* 177 (1903) 86–96.

8618. ———. "The Hague Tribunal," *IN* 55 (1903) 3001–3003.

8619. ———. "The Venezuelan Case at The Hague," *IN* 55 (1903) 2560–2562.

8619a. Platt, D. C. M. "The Allied Coercion of Venezuela, 1902–03: A Reassessment," *IEA* 15 (Spring, 1962) 3–28.

8620. Rippy, J. F. "The Venezuelan Claims Settlements of 1903–1905," *IEA* 7, no. 4 (1954) 65–77.

8621. Sageser, A. B. "Ex-President Cleveland Invited to Head the Counsel for the Venezuelan Arbitration," *AHR* 29 (1933) 78–81.

8622. Tello Mendoza, R. *Venezuela ante el Conflicto con las Potencias Aliadas, Alemania, Inglaterra é Italia en 1902 y 1903.* 2 vols., Caracas, 1905.

8623. "The Blockade of Venezuela, 1902," *HT* 15 (1965) 475–485.

8624. "The Venezuela Affair and the Monroe Doctrine," *NAR* 176 (1903) 321–335.

8625. USCS. *The Venezuelan Arbitration Before the Hague Tribunal, 1903: Proceedings of the Tribunal Under the Protocols Between Venezuela and Great Britain, Germany, Italy, United States, Belgium, France, Mexico, The Netherlands, Spain, Sweden, and Norway, Signed at Washington, May 7, 1903* (58th Cong., 3d Sess., S. Doc. 119). Wash., 1905.

8626. ———. *Venezuela Arbitrations of 1903, Including Protocols, Personnel and Rules of Commissions, Opinions, and Summary of Awards, with Appendix Containing Venezuelan Yellow Book of 1903, Bowen Pamphlet Entitled "Venezuelan Protocols," and "Preferential Questions," Hague Decision, with History of Recent Venezuelan Revolutions* (58th Cong., 2d Sess., S. Doc. 316). Wash., 1904.

8627. Venezuela. Ministerio de Relaciones Exteriores. *Asuntos Internacionales: Correspondencia del Ministerio de Relaciones Exteriores de los Estados Unidos de Venezuela con Algunas de la Legaciones Acreditadas en la República, 1900–1903.* Caracas, 1905.

E. UNITED STATES–VENEZUELAN RELATIONS, 1908–1948

8628. Arcaya, P. M. *The Gómez Régime in Venezuela and Its Background.* Wash., 1936.
Sympathetic treatment of the Venezuelan dictator (1908–1935). The author was the Venezuelan Minister to the United States.

8629. ———. *Venezuela y su Actual Régimen.* Baltimore, 1935.

8630. Arnold, R., *et al. The First Big Oil Hunt: Venezuela—1911–1916.* N.Y., 1960.

8631. Bell, P. L. *Venezuela: A Commercial and Industrial Handbook.* Wash., 1922.

8632. Betancourt, R. *Venezuela: Política y Petróleo.* Mexico, 1956.
Covers the period 1945–1956. Book was written while Betancourt was in exile during the Pérez Jiménez regime.

8633. ———. *Semblanza de un Político Popular, 1928–1948.* Caracas, 1948.
Collection of Betancourt's papers.

8634. Blanco Peñalver, P. L. *López Contreras ante la Historia.* Caracas, 1957.
López Contreras was President of Venezuela, 1935–1940.

8635. Carlisle, D. H. "The Organization for the Conduct of Foreign Relations in Venezuela, 1909–1935," U. of North Carolina Diss., 1951.

8636. Crawford, H. P. *Trading Under the Laws of Venezuela.* Wash., 1937.

8637. García Naranjo, N. *Venezuela and Its Ruler.* N.Y., 1927.
Concerns the Gómez regime.

8638. Lavin, J. *A Halo for Gómez.* N.Y., 1954.

8639. Lugo, F. A. *La Revolución Venezolana.* Caracas, 1937.
Treats the immediate post-Gómez period.

8640. Márquez Bustillos, V. *Semblanza del General Juan Vicente Gómez.* Caracas, 1919.
A favorable treatment.

8641. Matos Romero, M. *El Problema Petrolero en Venezuela.* Caracas, 1938.

8641a. Medina Angarita, I. *Cuatro Años de Democracia.* Caracas, 1963.
President Medina treats his own administration, 1941–1945.

8642. Pocaterra, J. R. *Gómez: The Shame of America.* Paris, 1929.

8643. Rourke, T. [pseudonym of D. J. Clinton]. *Gómez, Tyrant of the Andes.* N.Y., 1936.

8644. United States Tariff Commission. *Economic Controls and Commercial Policy in Venezuela.* Wash., 1945.

8645. Ybarra, T. R. *Young Man of Caracas.* N.Y., 1941.

XVI–E cross references: 8531.

F. UNITED STATES–VENEZUELAN RELATIONS SINCE 1948

8646. Alexander, R. *The Venezuelan Domestic Revolution: A Profile of the Regime of Romulo Betancourt.* New Brunswick, N.J., 1964.
Sympathetic examination of the social revolution under Betancourt.

8647. Beatty, W. D. "Venezuela: A New Era," *CH* 38 (March, 1960) 144–149.

8648. Betancourt, R. *The Hour of Decision.* Caracas, 1961.

8649. ———. *Posición y Doctrina.* 2d ed., Caracas, 1959.
Speeches and other public papers of Rómulo Betancourt.

8650. ———. *Tres Años de Gobierno Democrático: 1959–1962.* 3 vols., Caracas, 1962.

8651. Briceño-Iragorry, M. *Dimensión y Urgencia de la Idea Nacionalista: Pequeño Discurso Sobre Venezolanidad y Americanidad.* Madrid, 1953.

8652. Cárdenas, R. J. *La Insurrección Popular en Venezuela.* Caracas, 1961.
Concerned with anti-government activities in 1960.

8653. Groves, R. F. "Administrative Reform in Venezuela, 1958–1963," U. of Wisconsin Diss., 1965.

8654. Hauberg, C. A. "Venezuela Under Betancourt," *CH* 40 (1961) 232–240.

8655. International Bank for Reconstruction and Development. *The Economic Development of Venezuela: Report of a Mission Organized by the International Bank for Reconstruction and Development at the Request of the Government of Venezuela.* Baltimore, 1961.

8655a. Jankus, A. P., and N. M. Malloy. *Venezuela: Land of Opportunity.* N.Y., 1956.
Stresses business opportunities.

8655b. Kantor, H. "Rómulo Betancourt y Acción Democrática de Venezuela," *COMB* 1 (May, 1959) 3–12.

8656. ———. "The Development of Acción Democrática de Venezuela," *JIAS* 1 (April, 1959) 237–251.

8656a. Martz, J. D. *Acción Democrática: Evolution of a Modern Political Party.* Princeton, N.J., 1966.

8657. Maza Zavala, D. F. *Problemas de la Economía Exterior de Venezuela.* Caracas, 1962.

8658. Moore, J. R. "The Impact of Foreign Direct Investment on an Underdeveloped Economy: The Venezuelan Case," Cornell U. Diss., 1956.

8658a. Naranjo Ostty, R. *Breve Exégesis Sobre el Caso del General Marcos Pérez Jiménez, ex-Presidente de la República de Venezuela.* Caracas, 1964.
Pérez Jiménez' lawyer argues that his client's extradition from the United States was illegal.

8659. Pepper B., J. V. *Reconstrucción Integral de Venezuela.* Valencia, Spain, 1953.
Favorable to the Pérez Jiménez regime.

8660. Pérez-Castillo, J. P. "Some Aspects of the Economic Development of Venezuela During the Post–World War II Period: 1945–1960," Tulane U. Diss., 1963.

8661. Serxnes, S. J. *Acción Democrática of Venezuela: Its Origin and Development.* Gainesville, Fla., 1959.

8662. Shoup, C. S. *The Fiscal System of Venezuela: A Report.* Baltimore, 1959.

8663. Tarnoi, L. *El Nuevo Ideal Nacional de Venezuela: Vida y Obra de Marcos Pérez Jiménez.* Madrid, 1954.

8664. Taylor, W. C. *The Creole Petroleum Corporation in Venezuela.* Wash., 1955.
A sympathetic analysis of the company's activities.

8665. Umaña Bernal, J. (ed.). *Testimonio de la Revolución en Venezuela.* Caracas, 1958.
Concerns the revolution against Pérez Jiménez.

8666. U.S. Bureau of Foreign and Domestic Commerce. Office of International Trade. *Investment in Venezuela: Conditions and Outlook for United States Investors.* Wash., 1953.

8667. USDS. *Venezuela: Oil Transforms a Nation.* Wash., 1953.

8668.   Venezuela. *Alianza para el Progreso: Visita del Presidente Kennedy a Venezuela.* Caracas, 1962.

8669.   ————. Presidencia. *Venezuela y Cuba, Rompimiento de Relaciones: Respaldo Nacional.* Caracas, 1961.

8670.   Wilgus, A. C. (ed.). *The Caribbean: Venezuelan Development: A Case History.* Gainesville, Fla., 1963.

XVI–F cross references: 3844, 3873, 3888, 3896, 3897, 4119a, 4192, 4289, 8632.

Chapter XVII   The United States and Ecuador

A. UNITED STATES–ECUADORIAN RELATIONS: GENERAL WORKS AND SPECIAL STUDIES

8671. Beebe, W. *Galápagos: World's End.* N.Y., 1924.

8672. Benites Vinueza, L. *Ecuador: Drama y Paradoja.* Mexico, 1950.

8673. Blanksten, G. T. *Ecuador: Constitutions and Caudillos.* Berkeley, Calif., 1951.

8674. Bustamante Muñoz, A. *Lista de los Instrumentos Internacionales Concluidos por el Ecuador.* Quito, 1960.

8675. Conway, A., and F. Conway. *The Enchanted Islands [Galápagos].* N.Y., 1947.

8676. Ecuador. *Los Convenios Culturales del Ecuador.* Quito, 1956.

8677. ———. Ministerio de Relaciones Exteriores. *Exposición del Ministerio de Relaciones Exteriores del Ecuador a las Cancillerías de América.* 2d ed., Quito, 1941.

8678. ———. ———. *Informe del Ministro de Relaciones Exteriores.* Quito, 1839– .

8679. Eibl-Eibesfeldt, I. *Galapagos: The Noah's Ark of the Pacific.* Garden City, N.Y., 1961.

8680. Eichler, A. *Ecuador: Snow Peaks and Jungles.* N.Y., 1955.

8681. Enock, C. R. *Ecuador.* London, 1914.

8681a. Franklin, A. B. *Ecuador: Portrait of a People.* N.Y., 1943.

8682. Jaramillo Alvarado, P. *Estudios Históricos, Ensayos Sobre la Vida Interna e Internacional de la República.* Quito, 1934.

8683. Jaramillo Pérez, C. *Historia del Ecuador.* Quito, 1959.

8684. Linke, L. *Ecuador: Country of Contrasts.* 3d ed., N.Y., 1960.

8685. Morales y Eloy, J. *Ecuador, Nociones Históricas, Geografía, Física y Antrópica.* Guayaquil, 1938.

8686. Noboa, A. *Recopilación de Mensajes Diri-gidos por las Presidentes y Vice-Presidentes de la República a las Convenciones y Congresos Nacionales.* 5 vols., Guayaquil, 1900–1908.

8687. Orellana, J. G. *Resumen Histórico del Ecuador, 1830–1930.* 2 vols., Quito, 1947–1948.

8688. Pareja y Diezcanseco, A. *Historia del Ecuador.* 2 vols., Quito, 1958.

8689. Parks, E. T., and J. F. Rippy. "The Galápagos Islands: A Neglected Phase of American Strategic Diplomacy," *PHR* 9 (1940) 37–45.

8690. Pérez Concha, J. *Ensayo Histórico-Crítico de las Relaciones Diplomáticas del Ecuador con los Estados Limítrofes.* 2 vols., Quito, 1958.

8691. Reyes, O. E. *Breve Historia General del Ecuador.* 3d ed., Quito, 1949.

8692. Slevin, J. R. *The Galapagos Islands: A History of Their Exploration.* San Francisco, 1959.

8693. Von Hagen, V. W. *Ecuador and the Galapagos Islands.* Norman, Okla., 1949.

8694. ———. *Ecuador, The Unknown.* N.Y., 1940.

XVII–A   cross references: 1473

B. UNITED STATES–ECUADORIAN RELATIONS: NINETEENTH CENTURY

8695. Armijo Suárez, J. *Gabriel García Moreno, Presidente de la República del Ecuador y Monseñor José Ignacio Eyzaguirre Portales, Fundador del Pontificio Colegio Pío Latino Americano.* Quito, 1962.

8696. Agramonte y Pichardo, R. *Biografía del Dictador García Moreno.* Havana, 1935.

8697. Carrión, B. *García Moreno, el Santo del Patíbulo.* Mexico, 1959.

A biography employing psychoanalytic techniques.

8698. Cevellos, P. F. *Resumen de la Historia del Ecuador Desde su Origen Hasta 1845.* 6 vols., Guayaquil, 1886.

8698a. Crespo Toral, R. "García Moreno y un Episodio de la Cuestión Peruano-Ecuatoriana," *RCHGC* (April, 1939–August, 1940) 50–79.

8699. Gálvez, M. *Vida de Don Gabriel García Moreno.* B.A., 1942.

8700. González Suárez, F. *Historia General de la República del Ecuador.* 9 vols., Quito, 1890–1903.

8700a. Hassaurek, F. *Four Years Among Spanish Americans.* N.Y., 1868.

Author was United States resident minister to Ecuador from 1861 to 1865.

8700b. Loyola, M. "García Moreno of Ecuador," *TA* 1 (January, 1945) 317–319.

8701. Moncayo, P. *El Ecuador de 1824 a 1875: Sus Hombres, sus Instituciones y sus Leyes.* Quito, 1906.

8702. Orellana, J. G. *Resumen Histórico del Ecuador.* 2d ed., 2 vols., Quito, 1948.

8703. Pattee, R. *Gabriel García Moreno y el Ecuador de su Tiempo.* 2d ed., Mexico, 1944.

Portuguese ed., Petropolis, 1956.

8704. ———. "García Moreno y la Política Internacional Ecuatoriana," *BANHC* 17 (January, 1939) 185–208.

8705. Ponce Ribandeneira, A. *Quito: 1809–1812, Según los Documentos del Archivo Nacional de Madrid.* Madrid, 1960.

8706. Robalino Dávila, L. *Orígenes del Ecuador de Hoy: García Moreno.* Quito, 1949.

8707. Rocafuerte, V. *Colección Rocafuerte.* 19 vols., Quito, 1947.

Valuable collection for early-nineteenth-century history. See especially vol. III: *Rocafuerte y la Democracia.*

8708. Smith, P. H. "The Image of a Dictator: Gabriel García Moreno," *HAHR* 45 (1965) 1–24.

8709. Toscano, H. *El Ecuador Visto por los Extranjeros: Viajeros de los Siglos XVIII y XIX.* Puebla, Mexico, 1960.

XVII–B   cross references:

a) For the role of the United States in the independence of Gran Colombia, see items 8149–8241.

b) For the Flores expedition, see items 2339–2342.

c) For García Moreno's scheme to unite France and Ecuador, see items 2343, 2347.

d) See also item 2348.

C. UNITED STATES–ECUADORIAN RELATIONS: TWENTIETH CENTURY

8710. Adamson, W. "Ecuador in Transition: An Analysis of Persistent Problems and Current Progress," Fletcher School of Law and Diplomacy Diss., 1956.

8710a. Andrade y Pino, C. J. *Guía Consular y Comercial.* Quito, 1948.

Contains commercial treaties.

8711. Arroyo del Río, C. A. *Bajo el Imperio del Odio: Primera Parte.* 2 vols., Bogotá, 1946.

Treats the Ecuadorian revolution of 1944.

8712. Checci and Company. *Expanding Private Investment for Ecuador's Economic Growth: A Report and Recommendations.* Wash., 1961.

8713. Crespo Toral, J. *El Comunismo en el Ecuador.* Quito, 1958.

8714. Jaramillo Alvarado, P. *Estudios Históricos.* Quito, 1960.

8714a. Linke, L. "Ecuador's Politics: President Velasco's Fourth Exit," *WT* 18 (February, 1962) 57–69.

8714b. Parks, L. F., and G. A. Nuermberger. "The Sanitation of Guayaquil," *HAHR* 23 (1943) 197–221.

Discusses United States assistance in eliminating yellow fever and bubonic plague.

8714c. Quevedo, A. "Sobre Política Externa Ecuatoriana en el Post-Guerra," *AUCE* 72, no. 321 (1944) 8–94.

8715. Ralondo, C. A. *Conozca Usted lo que Fué el General Sr. Don Eloy Alfaro.* Guayaquil, 1958.

8716. Santamaría, J. H. *La Tragedia Internacional del Ecuador y sus Responsables.* Quito, 1945.

8717. Scholes, W., and M. V. Scholes. "The United States and Ecuador, 1909–1913," *TA* 19 (1963) 276–290.

8717a. U.S. Bureau of Foreign and Domestic Commerce. *Investment in Ecuador: Basic Information for United States Businessmen.* Wash., 1959.

8717b. United States Tariff Commission. *Economic Controls and Commercial Policy in Ecuador.* Wash., 1946.

8718. United States Trade Mission to Ecuador. *Report of the United States Trade Missions to Ecuador and to the Cities of Quito and Guayaquil, Ecuador, October 19–25, 1959.* Wash., 1959.

8719. Velasco Ibarra, J. M. *Cuarta Jornada: Significado y Proyecciones de la Gesta Incomparable de un Pueblo que se Afirma como Principio y Fin de Todo Poder.* Quito, 1961.

XVII–C cross references: 3224, 4109, 4150, 4673, 4850, 4855, 4988, 5259, 6212, 8702

D. ECUADORIAN–PERUVIAN BOUNDARY DISPUTE

8720. Acevedo, A. de. *Le Conflit Entre l'Equateur et la Pérou et ses Possibilités de Réglement Pacifique: L'Etat Actuel de Droit Panaméricain en ce qui Concerne la Solution des Conflits Internationaux.* Paris, 1950.

8721. Aguilera-Malta, D. "El Problema Limítrofe Ecuatoriano-Peruano," *CA* 20 (1961) 38–54.

8722. Alba, L. L. *La Campaña de 1941: La Agresión Peruana al Ecuador.* Quito, 1964.

8723. Alomía Garaicoa, T. *Sinopsis del Derecho Territorial Ecuatoriano.* Quayaquil, 1952.

8724. Alvarado, R. *La Elocuencia de las Cifras en el Problema Territorial Ecuatoriano-Peruano.* Quito, 1941.

8725. ———. *Memorándum Sobre el Problema Fronterizo Entre el Ecuador y el Perú en el Sector Lagartocochagüepí.* Quito, 1948.
Ecuadorian claims.

8726. Alvarado Garaicoa, T. *Sinopsis del Derecho Territorial Ecuatoriano.* Quayaquil, 1952.

8727. Arroyo, D. E. *Las Negociaciones Limítrofes Ecuatoriano-Peruanas en Washington, 1936–1938.* Quito, 1939.

8728. Banda, F. *Ecuador and Its Southern Boundary.* Quito, 1937.

8729. Barra, F. de la. *Tumbes, Jaén y Maynas: Estudio Integral de la Controversia Limítrofe Peruano-Ecuatoriana Hasta el Pacto de Rio de Janeiro y su Renuncia por el País del Norte, con Sinopsis Histórica de las Operaciones Militares en 1941.* Lima, 1961.

8730. Belaúnde, V. A. *Relaciones con el Ecuador: La Constitución Inicial del Perú ante el Derecho Internacional.* Lima, 1942.
First volume of *La Vida Internacional del Perú.*

8731. Bossano, L. *La Ultima Etapa de las Discusiones Limítrofes.* Quito, 1940.

8731a. *The Boundary Question Between Peru and Ecuador: Record and Present Status of the Matter.* N.Y., 1937.

8732. Bowman, I. "The Ecuador-Peru Boundary Dispute," *FA* 20 (1942) 757–761.

8732a. Cabeza de Vaca, M. *Aspectos Históricos y Jurídicos de la Cuestión Limítrofe: Las Negociaciones en Washington y los Desenvolvimientos Posteriores.* Quito, 1956.

8733. Canalejas y Méndez, J. *Limitas Entre las Repúblicas del Ecuador y del Perú.* Madrid, 1905.

8734. Chiriboga Villagómez, J. R. *El Ecuador Exhibe ante el Mundo la Justicia de su Causa.* Quito, 1960.
Author was the Ecuadorian foreign minister.

8735. Coral, L. *Conflicto Internacional Entre el Ecuador y el Perú.* Guayaquil, 1894.

8736. Cornejo, M. H., and F. de Osma. *Memoria del Perú en el Arbitraje Sobre sus Limites con el Ecuador Presentada a S.M. El Real Arbitro.* 4 vols., Madrid, 1905–1906.
A supplemental set is *Documentos Anexos* issued at the same time.

8737. Cornejo M., P. *El Ecuador y el Perú.* Quito, 1905.

8737a. Kojanec, G. "La Controversia sui Confini tra il Peru e L'Ecuador," *CIN* 16 (1961) 36–38.

8737b. *La Cuestión Peruano-Ecuatoriano de Límites y los Buenos Oficios de Argentina, Brazil y Estados Unidos.* Mexico, 1941.

8738. [Corpancho, M. N.]. *Perú y Ecuador, Cuestion Internacional.* Lima, 1861.

8739. Delgado, L. H. *Campaña del Ecuador.* Lima, 1944.

8740. Destruge, C. *El Ecuador y el Perú en su Cuestión de Límites.* Guayaquil, 1899.

8741. *Documentos Diplomáticos Referentes al Conflicto Equatoriano-Peruano.* 2d ed., Quito, 1910.

8742. Ecuador. *El Litigio Territorial Entre el*

Ecuador y el Perú: El Protocolo de Rio de Janeiro, su Origen y sus Consecuencias: Polémica Entre los Embajadores del Ecuador y del Perú. Caracas, 1953.

8743. Ecuador. *Memorandum Sobre Límites Entre el Ecuador y el Perú, Presentado a Pedido del Señor Ministro de Relaciones Exteriores.* Quito, 1936.

8744. ———. Cancillería Ecuatoriana. *Negociaciones Limítrofes Ecuatoriano-Peruanas: El Ecuador Insiste en su Proposición de Someter el Litigio al Arbitrage Total de Derecho: 30 de Agosto de 1938.* Quito, 1938.

8745. ———. Ministerio de Relaciones Exteriores. *Dictámenes Jurídicos Acerca del Problema Equatoriano-Peruano Dados por Ilustres Internacionalistas Americanos.* 2 vols., Quito, 1942.

8746. ———. ———. *Documentos Diplomáticos Referentes al Conflicto Ecuatoriano-Peruano.* Quito, 1910.

8747. ———. ———. *El Protocolo de Río de Janeiro de 1942 Es Nulo.* Quito, 1960.

8748. ———. ———. *Exposición del Ministro de Relaciones Exteriores del Ecuador a las Cancillerías de América.* 2d ed., Quito, 1941.

8749. ———. ———. *Las Negociaciones Ecuatoriano-Peruanos en Washington Septiembre 1936–Julio 1937.* Quito, 1937.

8750. ———. ———. *Resumen del Litigio Fronterizo Entre el Ecuador y el Perú.* Quito, 1938.

Appeared simultaneously with the English edition, Quito, 1938.

8751. *Ecuadorean-Peruvian Boundary Negotiations: Ecuador Insists upon Her Proposal to Submit the Entire Controversy to Arbitration Juris by the President of the United States of America: August 20, 1938.* Baltimore, 1938.

8752. Edman, V. R. "The Boundary Dispute Between Ecuador and Peru," Clark U. Diss., 1933.

8753. Eguiguren, L. A. *Apuntes Sobre la Cuestión Internacional Entre el Perú y Ecuador.* Lima, 1941.

8754. ———. *Invincible Jaén.* Lima, 1943.

8755. Elizalde, R. H. *Paz, pero Justicia en América.* Santiago, 1938.

From the Ecuadorian point of view.

8756. Fernández Prida, J. *Límites Entre las*

Repúblicas del Ecuador y del Perú. Madrid, 1905.

8757. Flores, P. "History of the Boundary Dispute Between Ecuador and Peru," Colombia U. Diss., 1921.

8758. Flores y Caamaño, A. *Ecuador and Peru: A Résumé of the Boundary Controversy.* Wash., 1910.

8759. Franco Chávez, M. *Cartilla Patria.* Quito, 1922.

Surveys the dispute historically.

8760. Gálvez, I. *International Conflicts: Peru Against Colombia, Ecuador, and Chile.* Santiago, 1920.

8761. García Velasco, R. "El Arbitraje de Límites Entre Ecuador y Perú, ante el Rey de España," *AUCE* 87, no. 342 (1958) 111–147.

8762. Herrera, P. *Límites Entre el Ecuador y el Perú: Alegato del Gobierno del Ecuador.* Quito, 1892.

8763. Latino, Américo. *La Cuestión de Límites Entre el Perú y el Ecuador.* B.A., 1910.

Pseudonym of Aníbal Mautua.

8764. Llerena, J. A. *Ecuador, Peril de su Progreso: Notas de Geografía Económica.* Quito, 1960.

8765. MacLean y Estenós, R. E. "Protocolo Peruano-Ecuatoriano de Paz, Amistad y Límites," *LL,* no. 21 (1942) 5–18.

Opposes the Rio settlement.

8766. Marín, R. *Ecuador, la Gran Mutilada.* Quito, 1959.

A passionate plea from the Ecuadorian side.

8767. Maura y Montaner, A. *Defensa de los Derechos de la República del Ecuador en su Contienda con la República del Perú Sobre Límites Territoriales de Ambas.* Madrid, 1906.

8768. Moncayo, P. *Cuestión de Límites Entre el Ecuador i el Perú.* Santiago, 1860.

8768a. Morales Padrón, F. "La Frontera Peruano-Ecuatoriana," *EA* 2 (September, 1950) 455–466.

8769. Muñoz, J. H. *La Campaña Internacional de 1941.* Quito, 1945.

8770. Murillo Ordóñez, E. *El Protocolo de Rio de Janeiro y sus Consecuencias en los Ríos Cenepa, Morona y Marañón.* Cuenca, Ecuador, 1953.

Claims that the protocol of Rio de Janeiro (1942) is invalid.

8771. Oliver y Esteller, B. *Determinación del Territorio de la República del Ecuador Confinante con el de la República del Perú.* Madrid, 1906.

8772. Pérez Concha, J. "El Proceso Arbitral Perú-Ecuatoriano ante S. M. el Rey de España," *CHA* 1, nos. 2–3 (December, 1951) 125–251.

8773. ———. *El Protocolo de Rio de Janeiro y los Problemas Derivados de su Ejecución.* Guayaquil, 1954.

8774. Peru. Ministerio de Relaciones Exteriores. *Cuestión de Límites Entre el Perú y el Ecuador: Exposición del Ministro de Relaciones Exteriores del Perú.* Lima, 1941.

8775. Peruvian Boundary Delegation. *The Question of the Borders Between Peru and Ecuador: A Historical Outline Covering the Period Since 1910.* Baltimore, 1936.

8776. ———. *The Question of the Boundaries Between Peru and Ecuador: Reply of the Peruvian Delegation to the Ecuadorian Document of August 9 [1937].* Baltimore, 1937.

8777. ———. *The Question of Boundaries Between Peru and Ecuador: Statement of the Peruvian Delegation to the Washington Conference.* Baltimore, 1937.

8778. Ponce, N. C. *Límites Entre el Ecuador y el Perú.* 3d ed., Wash., 1921.

8779. Pons Muzzo, G. *Las Fronteras del Perú: Historia de los Límites.* Lima, 1962.

8779a. *La Posición Jurídica Internacional del Perú en el Proceso de la Determinación de su Frontera con el Ecuador.* Lima, 1952.

8780. Puente, R. A. *La Agresión Peruana.* 2d ed., Quito, 1955.

8781. Rodríguez S., L. A. *La Agresión Peruana: La Campaña del Zarumilla.* Quito, 1948.
Concerns the Peruvian campaign of July, 1941, against Ecuador.

8782. Romero Terán, D. *Los Traidores al Ecuador: Apuntes para la Historia.* Quito, 1952.
The "traitors" are those who accepted the protocol of Rio de Janeiro.

8783. Santamaría, J. H. *La Tragedia Internacional de Ecuador y sus Responsables.* Quito, 1945.

8784. Santamaría de Paredes, V. *A Study of the Question of Boundaries Between the Republics of Peru and Ecuador.* Wash., 1910.
Photographed ed., Lima, 1936.

8785. Sociedad Bolivariana del Ecuador. *La Revisión del Protocolo de Rio.* Quito, 1949.

8786. Soria, F. de Paula. *Lacciones Graduados Sobre Límites del Ecuador con el Perú.* Quito, 1938.

8787. Tobar Donoso, J. *La Invasión Peruana y el Protocolo de Río.* Quito, 1945.

8788. ———, and A. Luna Tobar. *Derecho Territorial Ecuatoriano.* Quito, 1961.

8789. Tudela, F. *The Controversy Between Perú and Ecuador.* Lima, 1941.

8790. Ulloa Sotomayor, A. *Perú y Ecuador: Ultima Etapa del Problema de Límites (1941–1942).* Lima, 1942.

8791. Vacas Galindo, E. *Colección de Documentos Sobre Límites Ecuatoriano-Peruanos.* 3 vols., Quito, 1902–1903.

8792. ———. *Exposición Sobre los Límites Ecuatoriano-Peruanos.* Quito, 1903.

8793. ———. "Resumen de la Cuestión de Límites del Ecuador con Perú," *OD* 9 (1936) 171–178, 213–215, 266–267.

8794. Velasco, A. *Una Palabra Más Sobre la Cuestión de Límites Entre el Ecuador y el Perú.* Quito, 1894.

8795. Villacrés Moscoso, J. W. *La Responsabilidad de la Diplomacia Ecuatoriana en la Demarcación Fronteriza.* Guayaquil, 1945.

8796. Viteri Lafronte, H. *El Ecuador y su Salida Propia al Marañón.* Quito, 1952.

8797. Vittone, J. C. "La Cuestión de Límites Entre el Ecuador y el Perú," *RFCECP* 10 (May, 1941) 493–501.

8798. Yepes, J. M. *La Controversia Fronteriza Entre el Ecuador y el Perú.* Quito, 1960.

8799. Zook, D. H., Jr. "The Spanish Arbitration of the Ecuador-Peru Dispute," *TA* 20 (1964) 359–375.

8800. ———. *Zarumilla-Marañón: The Ecuador-Peru Dispute.* N.Y., 1964.
A comprehensive English-language survey.

XVII–D   cross references: *8690, 8813, 8954, 9120*

Chapter XVIII   The United States and Peru

A. UNITED STATES–PERUVIAN RELATIONS: GENERAL WORKS AND SPECIAL STUDIES

8800a. Alzamora Silva, L. *La Evolución Política y Constitucional del Perú Independiente.* Lima, 1942.

8801. Basadre, J. *Historia de la República del Peru.* 5th ed., 10 vols., Lima, 1961– .

8801a. Beals, C. *Fire on the Andes.* Phil., 1934.

8801b. Dávalos y Lissón, P. *Historia Republicana del Perú.* 10 vols., Lima, 1931–1939.

8801c. Delgado, L. H. *El Militarismo en el Perú, 1821–1930.* Lima, 1930.
    Favors the military point of view.

8802. Dunn, W. E. *Peru: A Commercial and Industrial Handbook.* Wash., 1925.

8803. García Salazar, A. *Guía Práctica para los Diplomáticos y Cónsules Peruanos.* 2 vols., Lima, 1918.

8804. ———. *Historia Diplomática del Perú.* Lima, 1930.

8805. Kauffmann Doig, F., *et al. Historia del Perú Desde sus Orígenes Hasta el Presente.* 3 vols., Lima, 1961.

8806. McQueen, C. A. *Peruvian Public Finance.* Wash., 1926.

8807. Owens, R. J. *Peru.* N.Y., 1963.
    General survey in the Royal Institute of International Affairs series.

8808. Peru. Ministerio de Relaciones Exteriores. *Memoria del Ministro de Relaciones Exteriores.* Lima, 1849– .

8809. ———. ———. *Boletín del Ministerio de Relaciones Exteriores.* Lima, 1902– .

8810. ———. Presidente. *Mensajes del Presidente de la República.* Lima, 1899– .

8811. Stuart, G. H. *The Governmental System of Peru.* Wash., 1925.

8812. Ugarteche, P. *El Perú en la Vida Internacional Americana.* Lima, 1927.

8813. Ulloa Sotomayor, A. *Posición Internacional del Peru.* Lima, 1941.
    Concludes that cool relations between Peru and the United States are attributable to U.S. positions on various Peruvian boundary disputes.

8814. Vargas, M. N. *Historia del Perú Independiente.* 8 vols., Lima, 1903–1917.

8815. Vargas Ugarte, R. *Historia del Perú.* Lima, 1939.

8816. Wiesse, C. *Historia del Perú.* 2d ed., 4 vols., Lima, 1937–1941.

8817. Zavala Oyague, C. *Historia del Perú: Frientes.* Lima, 1951.

XVIII–A   cross references:

a) For works on the Peruvian boundary controversy with Ecuador, see items 8720–8800.

b) See also item 1473.

B. UNITED STATES–PERUVIAN RELATIONS: NINETEENTH CENTURY

8818. Aranda, R. (ed.). *República del Perú: Colección de los Tratados, Convenciones, Capitulaciones, Armisticios, y Otros Actos Diplomáticos y Políticos Celebrados Desde la Independencia Hasta el Día....* 14 vols., Lima, 1890–1911.

8819. Barreda, F. L. *El Ministro del Perú en los Estados Unidos y su Calumniador.* Lima, 1867.

8820. Basadre, J. *Historia de la República: 1822–1899.* Lima, 1939.

8821. ———. "El Mariscal Don Ramón Castilla," *REMI* 19 (August, 1944) 583–592.

8821a. ———. "Ramón Castilla como Peruano y como Militar," *REMI* 17 (June, 1942) 493–504.

8822. ———. *La Iniciación de la República.* 2 vols., Lima, 1928–1929.

8823. Costa y Laurent, F. *Reseña Histórica de los Ferrocarriles del Perú.* Lima, 1908.

8824. Delgado, L. H. *Mariano Ignacio Prado,*

Caudillo y Prócer del Perú. Lima, 1952.

8825. Duffield, A. J. *Peru in the Guano Age*. London, 1877.

8826. ———. *The Prospects of Peru: The End of the Guano Age*. London, 1881.

8827. Dulanto Pinillos, J. *Castilla*. Lima, 1952.

8828. García Salazar, A. *Resumen de Historia Diplomática del Perú, 1820–1834*. Lima, 1928.

8829. García y García, J. A. *Correspondencia Diplomática Entre el Enviado Estraordinario y Ministro Plenipotenciaro del Perú en Washington y el Secretario de Estado de los Estados Unidos de América, Sobre la Cuestión de los Monitores Peruanos "Atahualpa" y "Manco-Capac," Anteriormente Llamados "Catawba" y "Oniota."* N.Y., 1868.

   English ed., N.Y., 1869.

8830. Humphreys, R. A. (ed.). "James Paroissien's Notes on the Liberating Expedition to Peru, 1820," *HAHR* 31 (1951) 253–273.

8830a. ——— (ed.). "Letters of William Miller, Lord Cochrane, and Basil Hall to James Paroissien, 1821–1823," *FRBN* 10 (1954) 203–234.

8831. ———. *Liberation in South America, 1806–1827: The Career of James Paroissien*. London, 1952.

8832. Izcue, J. A. de. *Los Peruanos y su Independencia*. Lima, 1906.

8833. López, J. *Manuel Pardo*. Lima, 1947.

   President of Peru, 1872–1876.

8834. Malinowski, E. *Ferrocarril Central Trasandino*. Lima, 1869.

8835. Mariátegui, J. C. *Obras Completas de José Carlos Mariátegui*. 10 vols., Lima, 1959.

8836. Markham, C. R. *A History of Peru*. Chicago, 1892.

8837. McNicoll, R. E. "Peruvian-American Relations in the Era of the Civilist Party," Duke U. Diss., 1938.

8838. Miller, J. (ed.). *Memoirs of General [William] Miller, in the Service of the Republic of Peru*. 2d ed., 2 vols., London, 1829.

8839. Mújica Gallo, M. *Soldado de la Ley*. Lima, 1959.

   A short biography of President Ramón Castilla.

8840. Nolan, L. C. "The Diplomatic and Commercial Relations of the U.S. and Peru, 1826–1875," Duke U. Diss., 1935.

8841. ———. "The Relations of the United States and Peru with Respect to Claims, 1822–1870," *HAHR* 17 (1937) 30–66.

8842. Odriozola, M. de. *Documentos Históricos del Perú*. 10 vols., Lima, 1863–1879.

8843. Paz Soldán, M. F. *Historia del Perú Independiente*. 3 vols., Lima, 1868–1874.

8844. Peru. Ministerio de Relaciones Exteriores. *Reclamación del Ciudadano Americano Victor H. MacCord: Alegatos y Documentos Justificativos*. Lima, 1899.

8844a. ———. ———. *Tratados, Convenciones y Acuerdos Vigentes Entre el Perú y Otras Estados: Instrumentos Multilaterales*. Lima, 1936.

8845. *Question Between the United States and Peru in Consequence of the Seizure and Confiscation of the Two American Vessels, "Lizzie Thompson" and "Georgiana": Diplomatic Correspondence*. Lima, 1861.

8846. Stewart, W. *Henry Meiggs, Yankee Pizarro*. Durham, N.C., 1946.

   Meiggs was a railroad-builder in Peru and Chile in the late nineteenth century.

8846a. ———. "El Ultimo Negocio de Meiggs en el Perú," *HL* 1 (July, 1943) 238–251.

8847. Torata, El Conde de (ed.). *Documentos para la Historia de la Guerra Separatista del Perú*. 5 vols., Madrid, 1894–1898.

8847a. Valdez de la Torre, E. "Enrique Meiggs, su Vida y Actuación en el Perú," *CEST* 2, no. 4 (1942) 103–150.

8848. Vargas Ugarte, R. *Historia del Perú: Emancipación (1809–1825)*. B.A., 1958.

8849. Vicuña Mackenna, B. *La Revolución de la Independencia del Perú Desde 1809 á 1819*. Lima, 1860.

XVIII–B cross references:

a) For accounts of the attempted Spanish reconquest of 1863–1866, see items 2203–2232.

b) See also items 9330, 9360.

C. WAR OF THE PACIFIC, 1879–1884

8850. Almada y Moreno, P. *Guerra del Pacífico*. 9 vols., Santiago, 1886.

8851. Barros Arana, D. *Historia de la Guerra del Pacífico*. 2 vols., Santiago, 1880–1881.

8851a. Basadre, J. "Cinco de Abril de 1879," *HL* 1 (September, 1943) 401–412.
Diplomatic background of the War of the Pacific.

8851b. ———. "La Correspondencia de los Diplomáticos Norteamericanos en Lima, Santiago y La Paz Durante los Primeros Meses de Guerra del Pacífico y la Gestión Pettis," *RDCP* 4, no. 3 (1940) 390–396.

8852. Beck, W. T. "Anglo–United States Relations with Chile During the War of the Pacific, 1879–1883: A Study in Diplomatic History," U. of Pittsburgh Diss., 1942.

8853. Blanlot Holley, A. *Historia de la Paz Entre Chile y el Perú, 1879–1884.* 3d ed., Santiago, 1919.

8854. Bolivia. Ministerio de Relaciones Exteriores. *Mediación de Estados Unidos en la Guerra del Pacífico.* La Paz, 1880.

8855. Boyd, R. N. *Sketches of Chili and the Chilians During the War, 1879–1880.* London, 1881.

8856. Bulnes, G. *Chile and Peru: The Causes of the War of 1879.* Santiago, 1920.
This work is a partial translation of item 8857.

8857. ———. *Guerra del Pacífico.* Rev. ed., 3 vols., Santiago, 1955–1956.

8858. Caivano, T. *Historia de la Guerra de América Entre Chile, Perú y Bolivia.* Florencia, 1882.

8859. Chile. Departamento de Relaciones Exteriores. *Las Conferencias en Arica: Documentos Relativos á la Mediación Ofrecida por el Gobierno de los Estados Unidos de Norte América para Poner Fin a la Guerra Entre Chile, Peru, i Bolivia.* Santiago, 1880.

8860. Crosby, K. W. "The Diplomacy of the U.S. in Relation to the War of the Pacific, 1879–1884," George Washington U. Diss., 1949.

8860a. Cruchaga Tocornal, M. "Actitud de Alemania Durante la Guerra del Pacífico," *BACH* 16, no. 40 (1944) 29–44.

8861. Errázuriz, I. *Hombres y Cosas Durante la Guerra.* Santiago, 1882.

8862. Espinosa Moraga, O. *La Postguerra del Pacífico y la Puna de Atacama (1884–1899).* Santiago, 1958.

8863. Gómez Sánchez, E. *Memorándum Sobre la Actitud del Gobierno de los Estados Unidos de Norte América en el Pacífico.* B.A., 1882.

8864. Gutiérrez, A. *La Guerra de 1879.* Paris, 1914.

8865. Gutiérrez, H. *Crónica de un Soldado de la Guerra del Pacífico.* Santiago, 1956.

8865a. Heredia, I. "Guerra del Pacífico," *RMP* (October, November, December, 1940) 319–323, 471–478, 659–665; (January, March, July, September, 1941) 89–96, 393–408, 419–430, 77–86.

8866. Jordán López, M. *Historia Diplomática de la Guerra del Pacífico.* Santiago, 1957.

8867. Kiernan, V. G. "Foreign Interests in the War of the Pacific," *HAHR* 35 (1955) 14–36.

8868. López, J. *Historia de la Guerra del Guano y el Salitre: O, Guerra del Pacífico Entre Chile, Bolivia y el Perú.* N.Y., 1931.

8869. Markham, C. R. *The War Between Peru and Chile, 1879–1882.* London, 1882.

8870. Mason, T. B. M. *War on the Pacific Coast of South America.* Wash., 1883.

8871. *Mediación de los Estados Unidos de Norte América en la Guerra del Pacífico: El Señor Doctor Don Cornelio A. Logan y el D. Francisco García Calderón.* B.A., 1884.

8872. Millington, H. *American Diplomacy and the War of the Pacific.* N.Y., 1948.

8873. Moreno, P. *Guerra del Pacífico.* 8 vols., Valparaiso, 1892.

8874. Oblitas Fernández, E. *La Geopolítica Chilena y la Guerra del Pacífico: Nuevos Datos para la Historia.* La Paz, 1959.

8875. Pacheco, R. *Episodios de la Guerra del Pacífico.* 20 vols., Santiago, 1936–1940.

8876. Sotó Cárdenas, A. *Guerra del Pacífico: Los Tribunales Arbitrales (1882–1888).* Santiago, 1950.

8877. USCS. *Correspondence Between That Department [State] and the Hon. William Trescot, Special Envoy Extraordinary to the Republics of Peru, Chili, and Bolivia, and Walker Blaine, Third Assistant Secretary of State* (47th Cong., 1st Sess., S. Ex. Doc. 181). Wash., 1882.

8878. USDS. *Papers Relating to the War in South America, and Attempts to Bring About a Peace, Submitted to the Senate, January 26 and 27, 1882, and to the House of Representatives, January 26 and February 17, 1882, in Reply to Resolutions* of *Those Bodies, Calling for Correspondence Touching the Efforts of This Government to Bring About Peace Between Chili and Peru and Bolivia, and Touching Claims Against or Contracts Respecting Either of the Belligerent Governments.* Wash., 1882.

8878a. *The War in South America and Attempts to Bring About a Peace.* Wash., 1882.

8879. Williams, H. *Guerra del Pacífico 1879: "Verdad, Sepultura de la Difamación": Respuesta a la Diatriba de Francisco A. Encina en el Tomo XVI de su Historia de Chile.* Valparaiso, 1955.

Refers to item 9282.

XVIII–C cross references: 2607, 2608, 8880

D. TACNA-ARICA DISPUTE

8880. Aldunate, L. *Los Tratados de 1883–1884.* Santiago, 1912.

8881. Alvarez, A. *El Libro de la Cancillería Chilena Sobre el Problema de Tacna y Arica.* Santiago, 1912.

8882. Alzamora, I. *La Cuestión Peruano-Chilena.* Paris, 1919.

8883. Angulo y Puente Arnao, J. *Historia de los Límites del Perú.* Lima, 1927.

Discusses the Tacna-Arica controversy from the Peruvian point of view.

8884. *Arbitraje Sobre Tacna y Arica.* 3 vols., Santiago, 1924.

8885. Artega, L. *Las Negociaciones de Washington.* Santiago, 1922.

The author was one of the Chilean commissioners.

8886. Baldivia, G. J. M. *Páginas Históricas: Tacna y Arica.* La Paz, 1919.

8887. ———. *Tacna, Arica y Cobija: Páginas Históricas.* 2d ed., La Paz, 1919.

8888. Barreto, J. M. *El Problema Peruano-Chileno (1883–1911).* Lima, 1912.

8889. Barros Borgono, L. *La Cuestión Chileno-Peruana: El Mensaje del Presidente Wilson, Discursos Pronunciados en la Cámara de Diputados por el Ministro de Relaciones Exteriores en las Sesiones del 12 y 13 de Diciembre 1918.* Santiago, 1919.

8890. Barros Jarpa, E. *Hacia la Solución.* Santiago, 1922.

The author was the Chilean foreign minister.

8891. Belaúnde, V. A. *Nuestra Cuestión con Chile.* Lima, 1919.

The majority of this work treats the Tacna-Arica question.

8892. ———. *The Treaty of Ancon in the Light of International Law.* Wash., 1923.

8893. Borchard, E. M. *Opinion on the Controversy Between Peru and Chile Known as the Question of the Pacific.* Wash., 1920.

8894. ———. "The Tacna-Arica Controversy," *FA* I (1922) 29–48.

8895. Brieba, E. *Memoria Sobre los Límites Entre Chile y Perú.* 3 vols., Santiago, 1931.

8896. Bulnes, G., and J. Vial Solar. *La Cuestión Tacna y Arica.* Lima, 1919.

8897. Calderón Cousiño, A. *La Cuestión Chileno-Peruano.* Santiago, 1919.

8898. Chile. *Tacna-Arica Arbitration: Notes on the Peruvian Case and Appendix, Submitted with the Counter Case of the Republic of Chile to the President of the United States as Arbitrator Under the Provisions of the Protocol and Supplementary Agreement Entered into Between Chile and Peru at Washington on July 20, 1922.* Wash., 1924.

Spanish ed., Wash., 1924.

8899. ———. *Tacna-Arica Arbitration: The Appendix to the Case of the Republic of Chile.* Wash., 1923.

8900. ———. *Tacna-Arica Arbitration: The Case of the Republic of Chile Submitted to the President of the United States as Arbitrator.* Wash., 1923.

Spanish ed., Santiago, 1924.

8901. ———. *Tacna-Arica Arbitration: The Countercase of the Republic of Chile, Submitted to the President of the United States as Arbitrator Under the Provisions of the Protocol and Supplementary Agreement Entered into Between Chile and Peru at Washington on July 20, 1922.* Wash., 1924.

Spanish ed., Santiago, 1924.

8902. ———. *Tacna-Arica: Fallo Arbitral.* Santiago, 1925.

8903. ———. Ministerio de Relaciones Exteriores. *Comunicaciones Cambiadas Entre las Cancillerías de Chile i el Perú i Algunos Antecedentes Sobre la Cuestión de Tacna i Arica 1905–1910.* Santiago, 1912.

8904. ———. ———. *Comunicaciones Cam-*

biadas Entre las Cancillerías de Chile y Perú Sobre la Cuestión de Tacna y Arica (1905–1908). Santiago, 1908.

8905. Deitrick, J. *What Price Tacna-Arica*. Lima, 1926.

Series of articles written for Peruvian newspapers.

8906. Dennis, W. J. *Documentary History of the Tacna-Arica Dispute*. Iowa City, Ia., 1927.

8907. ———. *Tacna and Arica: An Account of the Chile-Peru Boundary Dispute and of the Arbitrations by the United States*. New Haven, Conn., 1931.

A comprehensive treatment.

8908. Edwards Bello, J. *Tacna y Arica*. Santiago, 1926.

8909. Egaña, R. *La Cuestión de Tacna i Arica*. Santiago, 1900.

8910. Figueroa, P. P. *Cuestiones Internacionales: El Problema de Nuestras Fronteras del Norte: Tacna y Arica*. Santiago, 1900.

8911. James, H. G. "The Controversy over Tacna and Arica," *SPSQ* 1 (September, 1920) 155–169.

8912. Jane, C. "The Question of Tacna-Arica," *GST* 15 (1929) 93–119.

8913. Julio y Elizalde, J. J. *Los Chilenizadores de Tacna y Arica*. Callao, 1908.

8914. Lastra Bernales, J. de la. *Historia Diplomática de la Cuestión de Tacna y Arica*. Santiago, 1951.

8915. Maúrtua, V. M. *Sur le Pacifique du Sud*. Dijon, France, 1922.

From the Peruvian point of view.

8916. ———. *The Question of the Pacific*. N.Y., 1923.

8917. Montenegro, E. *La Cuestión Chileno-Peruano*. Santiago, 1919.

8918. Page, A. N. "United States Diplomacy in the Tacna-Arica Dispute, 1884–1929," U. of Okla. Diss., 1958.

8919. Paz Soldán, C. *Límites Entre Arica y Tarapacá*. Lima, 1904.

8920. Peru. *Arbitration Between Peru and Chile: Appendix to the Countercase of Peru in the Matter of the Controversy Arising Out of the Question of the Pacific*. Wash., 1924.

8921. ———. *Arbitration Between Peru and Chile: The Countercase of Peru*. Wash., 1923.

8922. ———. *Case of Peru in the Matter of the Controversy Arising Out of the Question of the Pacific*. Wash., 1923.

8923. ———. Ministerio de Relaciones Exteriores. *Circular Sobre la Cuestión Tacna y Arica*. Lima, 1901.

8923a. *El Problema de Tacna y Arica*. Santiago, 1919.

A collection of opinions.

8923b. *El Proceso de Tacna y Arica, 1925–1927*. Lima, 1927.

8924. Rios Gallardo, C. *Chile y Perú: Los Pactos de 1929*. Santiago, 1959.

8925. Risopatrón, L. *La Linea de Frontera en la Puna de Atacama*. Santiago, 1906.

8926. Stuart, G. H. "The Tacna-Arica Dispute," *WPFP* 10, no. 1 (1927).

8927. "The Tacna-Arica Settlement," *FA* 7 (1929) 656–657.

8928. USDS. *In the Matter of the Arbitration Between the Republic of Chile and the Republic of Peru . . . . Opinion and Award of the Arbitrator*. Wash., 1925.

8929. Varas, C. *Tacna y Arica bajo la Soberanía Chilena*. Santiago, 1922.

Discusses the progress of the area under Chilean administration.

8930. Vicuña Fuentes, C. *La Libertad de Opinar y el Problema de Tacna y Arica*. Santiago, 1921.

8931. Woolsey, L. H. "The Tacna-Arica Settlement," *AJIL* 23 (1929) 605–610.

8932. Yáñez, E. *Apuntes Sobre la Puna de Atacama*. Santiago, 1898.

XVIII–D cross references: 3214, 8760, 8804, 8862, 8966, 8972, 9425

E. UNITED STATES–PERUVIAN RELATIONS: TWENTIETH CENTURY

8933. A. D. Little, Inc. *A Program for the Industrial and Regional Development of Peru: A Report to the Government of Peru, 1960*. Cambridge, Mass., 1961.

8933a. Bailey Lembcke, J. *Recuerdos de un Diplomático Peruano, 1917–1954*. Lima, 1959.

8933b. Basadre, J. "En Torno al Perú de 1900 a 1939," *HL* 1 (March, 1943) 45–50.

8933c. ———. "Las Etapas de la Historia del Perú," *RMP* 41 (July, 1944) 19–30.

8934. Belaúnde, V. A. *La Realidad Nacional*. Paris, 1931.

Critical of the Leguía regime.

8935. ————. *La Vida Internacional del Perú.* Lima, 1942.

8935a. ————, *et al. Visión del Perú en el Siglo XX.* Lima, 1962.

8936. Belaúnde-Terry, F. *Peru's Own Conquest.* Lima, 1965.

8937. Benavides Correa, A. *Interpelación a la Cancillería.* Lima, 1958.
     Critical of Peru's economic dependence upon the United States.

8938. Bonilla, J. E. *El Siglo de Leguía.* Lima, 1928.
     A sympathetic interpretation.

8939. Burgess, E. W. *Casa Grace in Peru.* Wash., 1954.
     Refers to W. R. Grace and company.

8940. Capuñay, M. A. *Leguía, Vida y Obra del Constructor del Peru.* Lima, 1951.

8941. Carey, J. C. *Peru and the United States, 1900–1962.* Notre Dame, Ind., 1964.
     Considerable emphasis on U.S. investments.

8941a. Driver, T. T. "Relaciones Culturales Entre el Perú y los EE. UU.," *IP* 25 (May, 1954) 8–13.

8942. García Sayán, E. *Notas Sobre la Soberanía Marítima del Perú: Defensa de las 200 Millas de Mar Peruano ante las Recientes Transgresiones.* Lima, 1955.

8943. Gómez, M. A. "The Role of International Technical Cooperation in the Interregional Development of Peru," Ohio State U. Diss., 1963.

8944. Letts S., E. "Las Reuniones Interamericanas de México y Ciudad Trujillo en Relación con la Política Marítima del Perú," *RPDI* 16 (January, 1956) 3–9.

8944a. Lévano, C. "Por la Nacionalización del Petróleo," *TPP* 1 (May, 1960) 50–83.
     Favors nationalization.

8945. López, J. *La Caída del Gobierno Constitucional en el Perú.* N.Y., 1927.

8946. Martin, P. F. *Peru of the Twentieth Century.* London, 1911.

8946a. McNicoll, R. E. "Recent Political Developments in Peru," *IEA* 18 (Summer, 1964) 77–86.

8946b. Needler, M. "U.S. Recognition Policy and the Peruvian Case," *IEA* 16 (Spring, 1963) 61–75.

8946c. Oviedo, E. *La Gran Crisis del Perú Frente al Comunismo y la Democracia.* Lima, 1964.

8947. Partido Comunista del Peru. *Resoluciones del Primer Congreso Nacional del Partido Comunista del Perú: Lima, 29 de Septiembre al 5 de Octubre de 1942.* Lima, 1942.

8948. PAU. Division of Economic Research. *The Peruvian Economy.* Wash., 1950.

8949. Peru. Ministerio de Relaciones Exteriores. *Tratados, Convenciones y Acuerdos Vigentes Entre el Perú y Otros Estados.* 2 vols., Lima, 1936– .
     The first volume is devoted to bilateral treaties and the second to multilateral treaties.

8950. Peterson, H. C., and T. Unger. *Petróleo: Hora Cero.* Lima, 1964.

8950a. Rachitoff Infantas, L. *Viene el Comunismo.* Lima, 1965 (?).
     Author is a Peruvian Christian Democrat.

8950b. Ramírez Gaston, J. M. *Medio Siglo de la Política Económica y Financiera del Perú, 1915–1964.* Lima, 1964.

8951. Rodríguez, R. F. *Market for U.S. Products in Peru.* Wash., 1961.

8952. Root, E. *Visita al Perú del Secretario de Estado de los Estados Unidos Excmo. Sr. Elihu Root.* Lima, 1906.
     English edition was published simultaneously.

8953. Santillana, S. C. *Comercio Interior y Exterior.* Lima, 1939.

8954. Sayán Alvarez, C. *Política Nacional e Internacional del Perú.* Lima, 1943.
     The author was president of the Peruvian Chamber of Deputies.

8955. Stuart, G. H. *The Governmental System of Peru.* Wash., 1926.

8955a. Suárez-Miraval, M. "Perú: Trasfondo de una Tragedia," *CA* 15, no. 5 (1956) 36–63.
     Covers 1930–1956; is critical of Aprismo.

8956. Ugarteche, P. *Formación del Diplomático Peruano.* Lima, 1955.
     Essays treating the training of Peruvian diplomats.

8957. ————. *La Política Internacional Peruana Durante la Dictadura de Leguía.* Lima, 1930.
     Critical of the regime.

8958. United States. Resources and Trade Development Mission to Peru. *Seven Americans in Peru: Report . . . October 7–November 10, 1961.* Wash., 1961.

8959. United States Tariff Commission. *Economic Controls and Commercial Policy in Peru.* Wash., 1945.

8959a. Wagner de Reyna, A. *Historia Diplomática del Perú, 1900–1945.* 2 vols., Lima, 1964.

XVIII–E   cross references:

a) For works on the Leticia controversy, see items 8440–8461.

b) For works on Aprismo, see items 5446–5515a.

c) For works on the Nixon visit see items 3844, 3873, 3888, 3896, 3897.

d) See also items 3147, 3166, 3286, 4151c, 4673.

Chapter XIX   The United States and Bolivia

A. UNITED STATES–BOLIVIAN RELATIONS: GENERAL WORKS AND SPECIAL STUDIES

8960. Adams, A. A. *The Plateau Peoples of South America*. London, 1915.

8961. Almaraz, S. *Petróleo en Bolivia*. La Paz, 1958.
    A Marxist interpretation. The oil companies are held accountable for the Chaco War.

8962. Argüedas, A. *Historia General de Bolivia: El Proceso de la Nacionalidad, 1809–1921*. La Paz, 1922.

8963. Arnade, C. W. *The Emergence of the Republic of Bolivia*. Gainesville, Fla., 1957.
    A study of the independence movement and the early post-independence period by a leading Bolivian historian in the United States.

8964. ———. *La Historia de Bolivia y la de los Estados Unidos*. Potosí, 1962.
    A comparative study.

8965. *Bolivia en el Primer Centenario de su Independencia*. N.Y., 1925 (?).

8965a. Bolivia. Ministerio de Relaciones Exteriores. *Colección de Tratados Vigentes de la República de Bolivia*. 5 vols., La Paz, 1940–1942.
    Edited by Luis de Iturralde Chine.

8966. Bustamente, D. S. *Bolivia, su Estructura y sus Derechos en el Pacífico*. La Paz, 1919.
    Concerns Bolivia's claims for an outlet on the Pacific.

8967. Camacho, J. M. *Compendio de la Historia de Bolivia*. La Paz, 1943.

8968. Carrasco, B. *Hechos e Imágenes de Nuestra Historia*. La Paz, 1950.

8969. Cleven, N. A. *The Political Organization of Bolivia*. Wash., 1940.

8970. Díaz A., J. *Historia del Ejército de Bolivia, 1825–1932*. La Paz, 1940.

8970a. Díaz Machicao, P. *Historia de Bolivia*. 5 vols., La Paz, 1954–1958.

8971. Díez de Medina, E. *Apuntes Sobre Tópicos Internacionales*. La Paz, 1919.
    Series of essays on international subjects by a Bolivian diplomat.

8972. ———. *La Cuestión del Pacífico y la Política Internacional de Bolivia*. La Paz, 1923.

8973. Finot, E. *Nueva Historia de Bolivia: Ensayo de Interpretación Sociológica*. 2d ed., La Paz, 1954.
    Historical treatment from the pre-conquest period to the 1930's.

8974. Jordán Sandoval, S. *Registro de Tratados y Congresos Internacionales de la República de Bolivia, Convenios Multilaterales y Bilaterales*. La Paz, 1944.

8975. Leonard, O. E. *Bolivia: Land, People and Institutions*. Wash., 1952.

8976. McQueen, C. A. *Bolivian Public Finance*. Wash., 1925.

8977. Mercado M., M. *Historia Internacional de Bolivia, Cuestiones de Límites.* ... Cochabamba, 1915.

8978. Navarro, G. A. *Ensayos y Crítica: Revoluciones Bolivianas, Guerras Internacionales y Escritores*. La Paz, 1961.

8979. Osborne, H. *Bolivia: A Land Divided*. 2d ed., London, 1955.

8980. Pando Gutiérrez, J. *Bolivia y el Mundo*. La Paz, 1947.

8981. Peñaloza, L. *Historia Económica de Bolivia*. 2 vols., La Paz, 1953–1954.
    The coverage is of a more general nature than the title indicates.

8982. Quijarro, A. *Bolivia: Política Internacional*. B.A., 1887.

8983. René-Moreno, G. *Ultimas Días Coloniales en el Alto-Perú: Narración: Documentos Inéditos de 1808 y 1809*. 2 vols., Santiago, 1896–1901.

8984. Ruiz González, R. *Bolivia: El Prometeo de los Andes.* B.A., 1961.

Historical survey from a leftist point of view.

8985. Salinas Baldivieso, C. A. *Historia Diplomática de Bolivia.* Sucre, 1938.

8986. Sánchez de Velasco, M. *Memorias para la Historia de Bolivia Desde el Año 1808 a 1848.* Sucre, 1938.

8987. Urquidi, J. M. *Compendio de la Historia de Bolivia.* 4th ed., B.A., 1944.

8988. Vásquez-Machicado, H., *et al. Manual de Historia de Bolivia.* La Paz, 1958.

8989. Walle, P. *Bolivia: Its People and Its Resources....* London, 1914.

XIX–A cross references:

a) For works on the War of the Pacific, see items 8850–8879.

b) See also item 1473.

B. UNITED STATES–BOLIVIAN RELATIONS: TWENTIETH CENTURY

8990. Achá Alvarez, E., and M. H. Ramos y Ramos. *Unzaga: Mártir de América.* B.A., 1960.

Oscar Unzaga was the leader of the Bolivian Falange, which opposed the M.N.R.

8991. Alemán U., H. *Pretérito, Presente y Futuro del Petróleo Boliviano.* Potosí, 1960.

8992. Alexander, R. J. "La Significación de la Revolución Nacional Boliviana," *P* 3 (November, 1959) 64–77.

8993. ———. *The Bolivian National Revolution.* New Brunswick, N.J., 1958.

A sympathetic treatment of the revolution of 1952 and of achievements to date of publication.

8994. Almaraz, S., and R. Rocabado. *Petróleo: Soberanía o Dependencia. Bases para una Política Petrolera Nacional.* Cochabamba, 1958.

8995. Arnade, C. W. "Bolivia's Social Revolution, 1952–1959," *JIAS* 1 (1959) 341–352.

Short summary discussion and analysis of sources.

8996. Arze, J. A. "Aspectos de la Política Diplomática de Bolivia," *RJ* 12 (December, 1948) 121–142.

8997. Avila, F. *Bolivia en el Concierto del Plata.* Mexico, 1941.

The author proposes that Bolivia cooperate with other countries in southern South America to stop the growth of U.S. influence.

8998. Ayala Mercado, E. *Defensa de la Revolución de Abril.* La Paz, 1961.

8999. ———. *¿Qué Es la Revolución Boliviana?* La Paz, 1956.

9000. Balderrama G., A. *La Reforma Agraria y la Experiencia Boliviana.* La Paz, 1960.

9001. Barcelli, S. A. *Medio Siglo de Luchas Sindicales Revolucionarias en Bolivia, 1905–1955.* La Paz, 1956.

9002. Barrientos, R. *Significado de la Revolución de Noviembre: Declaraciones del Gral. René Barrientos Presidente de la Excma. Junta Militar de Bolivia.* N.p., 1964.

9002a. Bedregal, G. *La Revolución Boliviana.* La Paz, 1962.

9003. ———, and G. Broersma. *El Convenio Internacional del Estaño: Evolución y Tendencias de los Precios del Estaño.* La Paz, 1962.

9004. Candia G., A. *Bolivia: Un Experimento Comunista en la América.* La Paz, 195?.

A *falangista* interpretation of the revolution of 1952.

9005. Carrasco, B. *Hernando Siles.* La Paz, 1961.

9006. Céspedes, A. *El Dictador Suicida: 40 Años de Historia de Bolivia.* Santiago, 1956.

Although the title refers to German Busch (President, 1937–1939), this is actually a summary of Bolivian history from 1900 to 1940.

9007. Coimbra Ojopi, J. *Víctor Paz Estenssoro, Biografía Ilustrada.* La Paz, 1960.

9008. Comisión del III Congreso de la Confederación Interamericana de Defensa del Continente. *El Marxismo en Bolivia.* Santiago, 1957.

9009. Deheza, J. A. *El Proceso de las Defraudaciones de la Standard Oil Co. of Bolivia.* La Paz, 1938.

9010. Duin, J. *Bolivia y la Revolución de Liberación Nacional.* La Paz, 1953.

9011. Fellman Velarde, J. *Víctor Paz Estenssoro: El Hombre y la Revolución.* La Paz, 1954.

A sympathetic biography.

9012. Fernández Larraín, S. *El Comunismo en Bolivia.* Santiago, 1956.

9013. Finot, A. *Así Cayó Villaroel.* B.A., 1951.
Condemnation of the M.N.R.

9014. Francovich, G. *El Pensamiento Boliviano en el Siglo XX*. Mexico, 1956.

9015. García, A. *La Rebelión de los Pueblos Débiles: Nacionalismo Popular y Anti-Imperialismo*. La Paz, 1955.

9016. González, H. "The Domestic Political Effects of Foreign Aid. Case: The Failure in Bolivia," *IEA* 15 (Autumn, 1961) 77–88.

9017. Gutiérrez, M. R. *La Operación Panamericana y la Reintegración Marítima de Boliva*. La Paz, 1960.

9018. Guzmán Galarza, M. V. *El M[ovimiento] N[acionalista] R[evolucionario] y la Revolución Americana en Marcha*. La Paz, 1961.

9019. Hallowell, B. C. "Some Aspects of Tin Control as Applied in Bolivia, 1931–39," Princeton U. Diss., 1949.

9019a. Hartman, T. "Bolivian-American Relations: A Task for Intellectuals and Business Men," *BOL* (July, 1940) 6–8.

9020. Joint Bolivian–United States Labour Commission. *Labour Problems in Bolivia: Report*. Montreal, 1943.

9021. Jordán Sandoval, S. *Alternativa de Bolivia para Ingresar a la Zona de Libre Comercio*. La Paz, 1962.

9022. Klein, H. S. "David Toro and the Establishment of 'Military Socialism' in Bolivia," *HAHR* 45 (1965) 25–52.

9023. Lepawsky, A. "The Bolivian Operation," *IC*, no. 479 (March, 1952) 103–140.

9024. Libermann Z., Jr. (ed.). *Bolivia: 10 Años de Revolución*. La Paz, 1962.

9024a. Linke, L. *Viaje por una Revolución*. Quito, 1956.

9025. Llosa M., J. A. *Víctor Paz Estenssoro: Adalid de la Revolución Nacional*. La Paz, 1960.

9026. Marsh, M. C. *The Bankers in Bolivia: A Study in American Foreign Investment*. N.Y., 1928.

9027. Mendoza, S. *La Revolución Boliviana: Vista por la Prensa Extranjera*. Santiago, 1955.

9028. Ness, N. T. "The Movement of Capital into Bolivia," Harvard U. Diss., 1938.

9029. Olmos Saavedra, R. "La Política Nacional Boliviana Frente a la Política Internacional del Petróleo," *RJA* 53 (April, 1960) 169–181.

9030. Ostria Gutiérrez, A. *The Tragedy of Bolivia: A People Crucified*. N.Y., 1958.

A critical account of the 1952 revolution by a political exile. Spanish ed., Santiago, 1956.

9031. ———. *Una Obra y un Destino: La Política Internacional de Bolivia Después de la Guerra del Chaco*. B.A., 1946.

9032. Pardo Valle, N. *Calendario Histórico de la Revolución Nacional*. La Paz, 1957.

9032a. Partido Communista de Bolivia. Comité Central. *Primer Congreso Nacional: Documentos*. La Paz, 1958.

9032b. Patch, R. W. "Bolivia: Diez Años de Revolución Nacional," *CUA* 64 (September, 1962) 18–35.

9032c. ———. "Bolivia: U.S. Assistance in a Revolutionary Setting," in Adams, *et al. Social Change in Latin America Today*, 108–176.

See item 3976.

9033. Paz Estenssoro, V. *Discursos Parlamentarios*. La Paz, 1955.

9034. ———. *Discursos y Mensajes*. B.A., 1953.

9035. ———. *El Pensamiento Revolucionario de Víctor Paz Estenssoro*. La Paz, 1954.

9036. ———, *et al. Programa de Gobierno: Movimiento Nacionalista Revolucionario, 1960–1964*. La Paz, 1960.

9037. Peddar, R. V. "The Quarrel with Argentina and Bolivia," *NC* 136 (July, 1944) 27–34.

9038. Poirier, A. J. *Bolivia's Trade Problems*. Wash., 1944.

9039. Schurz, W. L. *Bolivia: A Commercial and Industrial Handbook*. Wash., 1921.

9040. Siles Salinas, J. *La Aventura y el Orden: Reflexiones Sobre la Revolución Boliviana*. Santiago, 1956.

A conservative interpretation by an opponent of the revolution.

9041. ———. *Lecciones de una Revolución: Bolivia, 1952–1959*. Santiago, 1959.

9042. Siles Zuazo, H. *Cuatro Años de Gobierno*. La Paz, 1960.

9043. Smith Arínez, E. *Veinte Años de Revolución en Bolivia*. Lima, 1960.

9044. Stokes, W. "The 'Revolución Nacional' and the MNR in Bolivia," *IEA* 12 (Spring, 1959) 28–53.

9045. Torres Calleja, M. "*La Ayuda Americana*": *Una Esperanza Frustrada*. La Paz, 1962.

9046. UN. Technical Assistance Administration. *Report of the United Nations Mission of Technical Assistance to Bolivia.* N.Y., 1951.

9047. United States Operations Mission to Bolivia. *Point Four in Bolivia, 1942–1960.* La Paz, 1961.

9048. United States Tariff Commission. *Economic Controls and Commercial Policy in Bolivia.* Wash., 1946.

XIX–B   cross references: 3213, 4857

C. THE CHACO WAR, 1932–1936

9049. Adorno Benítez, F. *Relato de Episodios de la Guerra del Paraguay con Bolivia, 1932–1935.* Asunción, 1963.

9050. Aguirre Acha, J. *La Zona de Arbitraje en el Litigio Boliviano-Paraguayo.* La Paz, 1929.

A review of the negotiations. English ed., La Paz, 1929.

9051. Alaiza, M. *Los Derechos de Bolivia Sobre el Oriente y el Chaco Boreal.* La Paz, 1928.

9052. Alvarez del Vayo, J. "El Conflicto del Chaco y su Fin," *TF* 1, no. 2 (1935) 25–43.

9053. Amendola de Tehaldi, H. *La Tragedia del Chaco Boreal.* B.A., 1935.

9054. Arbo, H. *La Cuestión del Chaco Boreal: Conferencia Pronunciada por el Ministro del Paraguay en el Uruguay.* Montevideo, 1931.

9055. Argentina. Ministerio de Relaciones Exteriores y Culto. *La Conferencia de Paz del Chaco, 1935–1939.* B.A., 1939.

9056. ———. ———. *La Política Argentina en la Guerra del Chaco.* 2 vols., B.A., 1937.

9057. Ayala, E. *Paraguay y Bolivia en el Chaco Boreal.* Asunción, 1929.

9058. Ayala Moreira, R. *Por qué no Ganamos la Guerra del Chaco.* La Paz, 1959.

The author, a military man, places the blame on the country's political leadership.

9059. Benítez, J. P. *Estigarribia: El Soldado del Chaco.* B.A., 1943.

Leader of the Paraguayan army who subsequently became the President.

9060. Bolivia. Ministerio de Relaciones Exteriores. *La Conferencia de Mendoza y el Conflicto del Chaco.* La Paz, 1933.

9061. ———. ———. *Conflicto Boliviano-Paraguayo: Violaciones a las Prácticas del Derecho Internacional.* La Paz, 1932.

9062. ———. ———. *Memoria Presentada al Congreso de 1932: Conflicto Del Chaco.* La Paz, 1934.

9062a. Braden, S. "Inter-American Commercial Arbitration and Goodwill: A Resume of the Role Played by Arbitration in the Chaco Dispute," *AJO* (October, 1938) 387–395.

9063. Cano de la Vega, F. *The Bolivia and Paraguay Boundary Dispute: Brief Survey of Bolivia's Case.* N.Y., 1929.

9064. Cardozo, E. *Aspectos de la Cuestión del Chaco.* Asunción, 1932.

9065. De Ronde, P. *Paraguay, A Gallant Little Nation: The Story of Paraguay's War with Bolivia.* N.Y., 1935.

Spanish ed., B.A., 1935.

9066. Domínguez, M. *El Chaco Boreal Fué, Es y Será del Paraguay.* Asunción, 1927.

9067. ———. *El Chaco Boreal: Informe del Miembro de la Comisión Asesora de Límites, que Arruina las Tesis Bolivianas y Expone los Títulos del Paraguay Sobre Dicha Zona.* Asunción, 1925.

9068. ———. *Seven Kings and Ten Viceroys Affirm the Rights of Paraguay over the Chaco.* Wash., 1937.

9068a. Faupel, W. "Uber Entstehung, Verlauf und Legren des Chaco-Krieges, 1932–1935," *WWE* 70 (1936) 31–56.

9069. Fernández, C. J. *La Guerra del Chaco.* 3 vols., B.A., 1955–1962.

A military history by a Paraguayan participant.

9070. Finot, E. *Nuevos Aspectos de la Cuestión del Chaco.* La Paz, 1931.

9071. ———. *The Chaco War and the United States.* N.Y., 1934.

Spanish ed., La Paz, 1935.

9072. Franco, A. de Nello. *Episódios de História Internacional Recente.* Rio, 1941.

Brazil's policy in the Chaco War is defended by the Brazilian minister of foreign affairs, 1930–1933.

9073. Gandía, E. de. *Los Derechos del Paraguay Sobre el Chaco Boreal.* B.A., 1935.

Author argues that Bolivia's claim is based on a misinterpretation of colonial documents.

9073a. González-Blanco, P. "El Conflicto Entre Bolivia y Paraguay," *RE* 10 (1935) 48–56.

9074. ———. *El Conflicto Beligero Boliviano-Paraguayo y la Cuestión Chaqueña.* Madrid, 1934.
A moderate Bolivian interpretation.

9075. ———. *Los Derechos Inobjectables de Bolivia al Chaco Boreal.* Madrid, 1934.

9076. Graham, H. D. "Bolivian-Paraguayan Claims to the Chaco," U. of Illinois Diss., 1948.

9076a. Grotewald, C. "Die Vorgeschichte des Konfliktes Zwischen Bolivien und Paraguay," *EG* 7 (1929) 417–429.

9076b. *La Guerra Del Chaco Boreal Vista en sus Aspectos Diplomático, Político y Militar a Través de las Crónicas de la Epoca.* 4 vols., Asunción, 1949.

9076c. Gutiérrez Guerra, J. "A Paraguayan Play for Sympathy in the United States," *BOL* 5, no. 2 (1935) 21–24.

9077. ———. "The Chaco Boundary Award," *BOL* 7 (November, 1938) 6–8.

9078. Islas, A. *Perfiles y Relatos de la Epopeya Chaqueña.* Asunción, 1949.
Memoirs of the war.

9079. Kain, R. S. "The Chaco Dispute and the Peace System," *PSQ* 50 (1935) 321–342.

9080. Kirkpatrick, H. *The Chaco Dispute, The League and Panamericanism.* Geneva, 1936.

9081. Klein, H. S. "The Impact of the Chaco War on Bolivian Society," U. of Chicago Diss., 1963.

9082. La Foy, M. *The Chaco Dispute and the League of Nations.* Ann Arbor, Mich., 1946.

9083. [La Pradelle, P. de]. "Le Conflit du Chaco," *RDISDP* 12 (1933) 297–322, 645–665.

9084. Maas, E. R. "The Role of Uruguay in the Mediation of the Chaco War," U. of Nebraska Diss., 1958.

9085. MacLeod, M. J. "Bolivia and Its Social Literature Before and After the Chaco War: A Historical Study of Social and Literary Revolution," U. of Florida Diss., 1963.

9086. Mercado Moreira, M. *El Chaco Boliviano.* Cochabamba, 1928.

9087. ———. *El Chaco Boreal.* La Paz, 1920.

9088. ———. *Titulos de Bolivia Sobre el Chaco Boreal.* La Paz, 1935.

9089. Mogro Moreno, A. *La Provincia del Paraguay y el Chaco.* La Paz, 1937.

9090. Mujía, R. *El Chaco.* Sucre, 1933.
Monograph and supporting documents published under the auspices of the Bolivian government.

9091. Nieto Pena, X. *El Conflicto del Chaco a la Luz de la Historia.* Madrid, 1933.

9092. Oliver, M. M. *La Guerra en el Chaco Boreal: Como se Defiende el Paraguay: Crónicas de la Linea de Fuego.* B.A., 1935.

9092a. "Paraguay and the League of Nations: Text of the Memorandum of the Bolivian Foreign Office Issued Following the Paraguayan Reply to the League of Nations," *BOL* 5, no. 2 (1935) 8–10, 31–33.

9093. *Paraguay-Bolivia: Aspectos de la Guerra del Chaco.* Asunción, 1934.

9094. Paraguay. [Ministerio de Guerra?]. *Los Partes del Conductor: Comunicados Oficiales Sobre la Guerra del Chaco.* Asunción, 1950.

9095. Pol, H. R. *La Campaña del Chaco: Glosas y Reflexiones Militares.* La Paz, 1945.
Treats Bolivia's military vulnerabilities.

9096. *Proceedings of the Commission of Inquiry and Conciliation: Bolivia and Paraguay.* Baltimore, 1929.

9097. Quinteros, J. S. "El Litigio de la Standard Oil con el Gobierno de Bolivia," *K* 1, no. 1 (1939) 44–50.

9098. Ramírez, A. *Position Juridique de Conflit du Chaco Boréal.* Paris, 1935.
A legalistic analysis.

9099. Ramírez, J. I. *Alrededor de la Cuestión Paraguayo-Boliviana.* Lima, 1930.

9100. ———. *El Panamericanismo, al Arbitraje y la Agresión Boliviana en el Chaco.* Santiago, 1933.

9101. ———. *La Paz del Chaco.* B.A., 1942.

9102. Ríos, A. F. *La Defensa del Chaco: Verdades y Mentiras de una Victoria.* B.A., 1950.
A military history by a Paraguayan military surgeon.

9103. Ríos, C. *Cuestión de Límites Entre el Paraguay y Bolivia.* B.A., 1925.

9104. Rivarola, V. *Memorias Diplomáticas.* 2 vols., Ayacucho, 1952–1955.
Paraguayan diplomat's observations. The first volume treats the Chaco War.

9105. Rodas Eguino, J. *La Guerra del Chaco.* B.A., 1938.
From the Bolivian point of view.

9106. Roemer, H. "Die Neue Grenze im Chaco Boreal," *IAA* 12 (1939) 470–475.
Summary of the peace settlement of 1938.

9107. Saavedra, B. *El Chaco y la Conferencia de Paz de Buenos Aires*. Santiago, 1939.
The author, a former president of Bolivia, was on his country's peace commission.

9108. Sampognaro, V. *Causas Geográficas de la Guerra del Chaco*. Leipzig, 1935.

9109. Sandelmann, H. *Die Diplomatische Vorgeschichte des Chaco-Konflikts*. Leiden, 1936.

9110. Santos, C. R. *Conflicto Paraguayo-Boliviano*. 2d ed., Asunción, 1932.

9111. Schurz, W. L. "The Chaco Dispute Between Bolivia and Paraguay," *FA* 7 (1929) 650–655.

9112. Stefanich, J. *La Diplomacia de la Revolución*. B.A., 1945.
The Paraguayan foreign minister defends his position.

9113. Tabera, R. F. *Picuiba: Apuntes para la Historia de la Guerra del Chaco*. La Paz, 1960.

9114. Toro Ruilova, D. *Mi Actuación en la Guerra del Chaco*. La Paz, 1941.
By a Bolivian officer who subsequently became President.

9115. Tovar Villa, R. *Campaña del Chaco: El General Hans Kundt, Comandante en Jefe del Ejército en Bolivia*. La Paz, 1961.
Concerns the German general who trained and commanded the Bolivian forces.

9116. USDS. *Chaco Peace Conference: Report of Delegation of United States to Peace Conference Held at Buenos Aires, July 1, 1935–January 23, 1939*. Wash., 1940.

9117. Vergara Vicuña, A. *Bernardino Balbao Rioja: Vida y Hechos*. La Paz, 1948.
A biography of a Bolivian hero of the war.

9118. ———. *Historia de la Guerra del Chaco*. 7 vols., La Paz, 1940–1945.

9119. Watkins, A. I. "The Chaco War," *CR* 147 (1935) 590–595.

9120. Wood, B. *The United States and Latin American Wars, 1932–1942*. N.Y., 1965.

9121. Woolsey, L. H. "The Chaco Dispute," *AJIL* 26 (1932) 796–801.

9122. Ynsfran, P. M. (ed.). *The Epic of the Chaco: Marshal Estigarribia's Memoirs of the Chaco War, 1932–1935*. Austin, Texas, 1950.

9123. Zook, D. H., Jr. *The Conduct of the Chaco War*. New Haven, Conn., 1961.

XIX–C cross references:

a) For works on Latin America and the League of Nations, see items 3210–3242.

b) See also items 8444, 8446, 9009, 9203.

Chapter XX The United States and Uruguay

A. UNITED STATES–URUGUAYAN RELATIONS: GENERAL WORKS AND SPECIAL STUDIES

9124. Abadie Soriano, R. *Historia del Uruguay*. Montevideo, 1936.

9125. Acevedo, E. *Anales Históricos del Uruguay*. 6 vols., Montevideo, 1933–1936.
A standard national history. Coverage to 1930.

9126. ————. *Manual de Historia Uruguaya*. Montevideo, 1942.
Covers independence through 1933.

9127. *Colección de Tratados, Convenciones, y Otros Pactos Internacionales de la República Oriental del Uruguay*. 3 vols., Montevideo, 1923–1925.

9128. Fitzgibbon, R. H. *Uruguay: Portrait of a Democracy*. New Brunswick, N.J., 1954.

9129. Koebel, W. H. *Uruguay*. London, 1911.

9130. Manini Rios, P. "Uruguay and Her International Relations," *IA* 9 (December, 1925) 141–148.

9131. Pendle, G. *Uruguay*. 3d ed., N.Y., 1963.

9132. Pintos, F. R. *Historia del Uruguay, 1851–1938: Ensayo de Interpretación Materialista*. Montevideo, 1946.

9133. Pivel Devoto, J. E. *Uruguay Independiente*. Barcelona, 1949.

9134. ————, and A. R. de Pivel Devoto. *Historia de la República Oriental del Uruguay (1830–1930)*. Montevideo, 1945.
Of greatest value for the nineteenth century.

9135. Polleri Carrió, F. *Tratados: Repertorio Analítico, Cronológico, Constitucional*. Montevideo, 1959.

9136. Schurmann Pacheco, M., and M. L. Coolighan Sanguinetti. *Historia del Uruguay Desde la Epoca Indígena Hasta Nuestros Días*. Montevideo, 1956.

9137. Traversoni, A. *Historia del Uruguay*. Montevideo, 1956.

9138. Zum Felde, A. *Evolución Histórica del Uruguay: Esquema de su Sociología, Comprende la Evolución Social y Política del País Desde los Orígenes Hasta el Presente*. 3d ed., Montevideo, 1945.

B. UNITED STATES–URUGUAYAN RELATIONS: NINETEENTH CENTURY

9139. Acevedo, E. *José Artigas: Su Obra Cívica: Alegato Histórico*. 3 vols., Montevideo, 1950.

9140. Antuña, J. G. *Un Caudillo, el General Fructuoso Rivera, Prócer del Uruguay*. Madrid, 1948.

9141. *Archivo Artigas*. 2 vols., Montevideo, 1950–1951.

9142. Asiaín Márquez, C. *Luis de Herrera: Una Epoca Oriental, 1825–1865: Noticia Biográfica y de una Epoca*. Montevideo, 1961.

9143. Bell, A. *Apuntes Biográficos de Rivera y su Intervención Histórica en el Uruguay*. Paysandú, 1937.

9144. Blanco Acevedo, P. *El Federalismo de Artigas y la Independencia Nacional*. 2d ed., Montevideo, 1950.

9144a. Dahl, V. C. "Uruguay Under Juan Idiarte Borda: An American Diplomat's Observations," *HAHR* 46 (1966) 60–77.
The diplomat was Granville Stuart, United States minister to Uruguay and Paraguay, 1894–1898.

9145. Demaría, I. *Compendio de la Historia de la República O. del Uruguay*. 6 vols., Montevideo, 1864–1902.

9146. Falcao Espalter, M. *Formación Histórica del Uruguay (1810–1852)*. Madrid, 1929.

9147. Fernández, A. *Primeras Relaciones Políticas y Sociales Entre la República Oriental del Uruguay y los Estados Unidos de América*. Montevideo, 1958.

9148. Genta, E. U. *Historia de Artigas:*

Homenaje al Héroe en el Primer Centenario de su Muerte, 1850–1950. Montevideo, 1950.

9149. González Calderón, J. A. *Artigas, Precursor del Federalismo Republicano.* Montevideo, 1963.

9150. Herrera, L. A. *La Diplomacia Oriental en el Paraguay.* 6 vols., Montevideo, 1896.

9151. Hudson, W. H. *The Purple Land.* London, 1885.

9152. Martin, P. A. "Artigas: The Founder of Uruguayan Nationality," *HAHR* 19 (1939) 2–15.

9153. Martínez, J. L. *Brigadier General Fructuoso Rivera y la Campaña de las Misiones: El Hombre, el Soldado, el Gobernante.* Montevideo, 1961.

9154. Páez Formoso, M. A. *Artigas, Ciudadano del Plata.* Montevideo, 1952.

9155. Palomeque, A. (ed.). *Correspondencia Diplomática del Doctor Don Manuel Herrera y Obes con los Principales Hombres Públicos Americanos y Europeos de 1847 a 1852.* 3 vols., Montevideo, 1901.

9156. Pivel Devoto, J. E., and R. Fonseca Muñoz (eds.). *La Diplomacia de la Patria Vieja, 1811–1820.* Montevideo, 1943.

9157. Riva-Zucchelli, P. *Historia de la Independencia de la República Oriental del Uruguay.* Montevideo, 1934.

9158. Street, J. *Artigas and the Emancipation of Uruguay.* Cambridge, 1959.

9159. Uruguay. Ministerio de Relaciones Exteriores. *Libro de Acuerdos é Instrucciones del Ministerio de Relaciones Exteriores.* 2 vols., Montevideo, 1939. Covers 1829–1851.

XX–B cross references:

a) For works on the Paraguayan War, see items 9232–9247.

b) See also items 2157, 9692.

C. UNITED STATES–URUGUAYAN RELATIONS: TWENTIETH CENTURY

9160. Arcas, J. A. *Historia del Siglo Veinte Uruguayo, 1897–1942.* Montevideo, 1950.

9161. Azarola Gil, L. E. *Ayer, 1882–1952.* Lausanne, 1953. Memoirs of a Uruguayan diplomat.

9162. Barros, H. V. de. *La Cláusula de la Nación Más Favorecida y la Política Comercial del Uruguay.* Montevideo, 1938.

9163. Batlle y Ordóñez, J. *Batlle: Su Vida, su Obra.* Montevideo, 1956.

9164. Buero, J. A. *El Uruguay en la Vida Internacional.* Montevideo, 1919. Speeches and articles by the minister of foreign affairs, 1914–1918.

9165. Castellanos, F. *Luis Alberto de Herrera, Monografía Histórico-Política.* Montevideo, 1922. Herrera was the Uruguayan representative in Washington, 1902–1903. See also items 9173 and 9174.

9166. Couture, E. J., and H. Barbagelata. *A Statement of the Laws of Uruguay in Matters Affecting Business.* 2d ed., Wash., 1952.

9167. Gómez, E. *Historia del Partido Comunista del Uruguay, Hasta el Año 1951.* Montevideo, 1961. The author was the secretary-general of the Uruguayan Communist party.

9168. ———. *Historia de una Traición.* Montevideo, 1960. The treason was the ouster of the author from the Communist party by the Trotsky faction.

9169. González Conzi, E., and R. B. Guidice. *Batlle y el Batllismo.* 2d ed., Montevideo, 1959.

9170. Grompone, A. M. *La Ideología de Batlle.* Montevideo, 1962.

9171. Hanson, S. G. *Utopia in Uruguay.* N.Y., 1938. Covers 1904–1934; is sympathetic to the "welfare state."

9172. ———. "State Ownership in Uruguay," *SSQ* 16 (1935) 14–32.

9173. Herrera, L. A. de. *Desde Washington— Correspondencias Enviadas a "El Día."* Montevideo, 1903.

9174. ———. *Labor Diplomática en Norteamérica.* Montevideo, 1905.

9175. Lacalle, C. (ed.). *El Partido Nacional y la Política Exterior del Uruguay.* Montevideo, 1947.

9176. Lacarte Muro, J. A. *Política Económica Exterior del Uruguay.* Montevideo, 1955. Contains chapters on trade with the United States.

9177. Manacorda, T. *Itinerario y Espíritu de Jacobo Varela.* Montevideo, 1950.
Varela was ambassador to the United States for fifteen years.

9178. Martin, P. A. "The Career of José Batlle y Ordóñez," *HAHR* 10 (1930) 413–428.

9179. Morta Otero, J. A. *Sentido Internacional del Uruguay.* Montevideo, 1938.

9180. Patterson, J. *Diplomatic Terminus: An Experience in Uruguay.* Cambridge, Mass., 1962.
By the U.S. ambassador to Uruguay, 1955–1957.

9181. Pintos, F. R. *Batlle y el Proceso Histórico.* Montevideo, 1938.

9181a. ———. "Vlianie Leninisma na Rabocheie Dvizhenie Urugvaia," *NNI* 2 (1960) 79–93.
"The Influence of Leninism on the Uruguayan Labor Movement."

9182. Pintos Diago, C. *Luis Alberto de Herrera, su Vida—sus Obras—sus Ideas.* Montevideo, 1930.

9183. Quijano, C. *El Tratado con los Estados Unidos.* Montevideo, 1950.
Analysis of the 1949 Treaty of Friendship, Commerce, and Economic Development.

9184. Rodríguez Fabregat, E. *Batlle y Ordóñez, el Reformador.* B.A., 1942.
Standard one-volume treatment.

9184a. Solari, A. E. "Consideraciones Sobre el Problema de los Partidos Políticos y las Clases Sociales en el Uruguay," *TU*, nos. 6–7 (November, 1958) 20–29.

9184b. Suárez, A. "¿Es Posible una Salida Progresista a la Crisis?" *EPEFC* 4 (June, 1959) 3–9.

9185. Taylor, P. B., Jr. *Government and Politics of Uruguay.* New Orleans, 1962.
Examination of political structure and practices in the twentieth century.

9186. USCH. Committee on Foreign Affairs. *Special Mission to Uruguay to Attend the Inauguration of His Excellency, President Andrés Martínez Trueba of Uruguay, March 1, 1951: Report by A. S. J. Carnahan and Donald L. Jackson* (82d Cong., 1st Sess.). Wash., 1951.

9187. Vanger, M. I. *José Batlle y Ordóñez of Uruguay: The Creator of His Times, 1902–1907.* Cambridge, Mass., 1963.

9188. Varela Acevedo, J. *Recuerdos de mi Actuación en el Ministerio de Relaciones Exteriores, 1907.* Montevideo, 1949.

9189. ———. "The Meaning of the Monroe Doctrine to the Republic of Uruguay," *AAAPSS* 111 suppl. (1924) 21–23.

9190. Yriart, J. F. "Uruguay and the Proposed Basic Agreement for Inter-American Economic Co-operation," in *Political, Economic, and Social Problems of the Latin American Nations of Southern South America.* Austin, Texas, 1949.

9191. Zavala Muniz, J. *Batlle, Héroe Civil.* Mexico, 1945.

XX–C cross references: 3676, 4154, 4849, 4867, 9084

Chapter XXI The United States and Paraguay

A. UNITED STATES–PARAGUAYAN RELATIONS: GENERAL WORKS AND SPECIAL STUDIES

9192. Azara, F. de. *Descripción é Historia del Paraguay y del Río de la Plata*. 2 vols., Madrid, 1847.
Reprint, B.A., 1943.

9193. Báez, C. *Historia Diplomática del Paraguay*. 2 vols., Asunción, 1931–1932.
Author was a minister to both France and Great Britain.

9194. ———. *Le Paraguay*. Paris, 1927.

9195. Cardozo, E. *Paraguay Independiente*. Barcelona, 1949.

9196. Chaves, J. C. *Compendio de Historia Paraguaya Adaptado al Nuevo Programa del Primer Curso del Ciclo Básico*. B.A., 1958.

9197. Gómez Ríos, E. *El Paraguay y su Historia*. Asunción, 1952.

9198. Koebel, W. H. *Paraguay*. London, 1917.

9199. Pendle, G. *Paraguay: A Riverside Nation*. 2d ed., London, 1956.
A volume in the Latin American series of the Royal Institute of International Affairs.

9200. Raine, P. *Paraguay*. New Brunswick, N.J., 1956.

9201. Riquelme, A. J. *Apuntes para la Historia Política y Diplomática del Paraguay*. 2 vols., Asunción, 1952–1958.

9202. Warren, H. G. *Paraguay: An Informal History*. Norman, Okla., 1949.

B. UNITED STATES–PARAGUAYAN RELATIONS: NINETEENTH CENTURY

9203. Aceval, B. *Chaco Paraguayo: Memoria Presentada al Arbitro por Benjamín Aceval, Ministro Plenipotenciario del Paraguay en Washington*. Asunción, 1896.

9204. Benítez, J. P. *Carlos Antonio López: Estructuración del Estado Paraguayo*. B.A., 1949.

9205. Bliss, P. C. *Historia Secreta de la Misión del Ciudadano Norte-Americano Charles A. Washburn Cerca del Gobierno de la República del Paraguay*. N.p., 1868.

9206. Bourgade la Dardye, E. de. *Paraguay: The Land and the People*. London, 1892.

9207. Bray, A. *Solano López, Soldado de la Gloria y del Infortunio*. B.A., 1945.

9208. Chaves, J. C. *El Supremo Dictador: Biografía de José Gaspar de Francia*. 3d ed., B.A., 1958.

9209. *Correspondencia Entre el Gobierno del Paraguay y la Legación de los Estados Unidos de América y el Cónsul de S. M. el Emperador de los Franceses, Publicada en "El Seminario" de la Asunción*. B.A., 1863.

9210. *Correspondencias Cambiadas Entre el Ministerio de Relaciones Exteriores de la República del Paraguay y el Señor Charles A. Washburn, Ministro Residente de los Estados Unidos de América, Sobre la Conspiración Fraguada Contra la Patria, y el Gobierno en Combinación con el Enemigo: y el Atentado de Asesinato á la Persona del Exmo. Señor Mariscal López por Nacionales y Extranjeros*. Luque, 1868.

9211. Cova, J. A. *Solano López y la Epopeya del Paraguay*. 4th ed., Caracas, 1956.

9212. Decoud, J. S. *Paraguay*. 2d ed., Wash., 1902.

9213. Garay, B. *La Revolución de la Independencia del Paraguay*. Madrid, 1897.

9214. González, J. N. *Solano López Diplomático*. Asunción, 1948.

9215. Graham, R. B. C. *Portrait of a Dictator: Francisco Solano López*. London, 1933.

9216. *Historia Documentada de las Cuestiones Entre el Gobierno del Paraguay y de los Estados Unidos*. Asunción, 1858.

9217. Hopkins, E. A. *Historico-Political Memorial upon the Regions of the Río de la Plata and Conterminous Countries, to James*

Buchanan, President of the United States. N.Y., 1858.

Author was a commercial agent and promoter in Paraguay, 1844 to 1854. He became consul in 1853 and was expelled in 1854. See also item 9221.

9218. Ibarra, A. *José Gaspar de Francia, el Supremo Defensor del Paraguay.* Asunción, 1961.

9219. Moreno, F. R. *Estudio Sobre la Independencia del Paraguay.* Asunción, 1911.

9220. Oddone, R. *Esquema Político del Paraguay.* B.A., 1948.
Covers the period 1811–1876.

9221. Peterson, H. F. "Edward A. Hopkins: A Pioneer Promoter in Paraguay," *HAHR* 22 (1942) 245–261.
See also item 9217.

9222. *Une Question du Droit des Gens: M. Washburn, Exministre des Etats-Unis à l'Assomption, et la Conspiration Paraguayenne.* Paris, 1868.

9223. Robertson, J. P., and W. P. Robertson. *Letters on Paraguay: Comprising an Account of a Four Years' Residence in That Republic, Under the Government of the Dictator Francia.* 2d ed., 3 vols., London, 1839.

9224. Sánchez Quell, H. *Política Internacional del Paraguay: La Junta de 1811, Francia y los López.* 2d ed., B.A., 1945.

9225. Schmitt, P. A. *Paraguay und Europa: Die Diplomatischen Beziehungen Unter Carlos Antonio López und Francisco Solano López, 1841–1870.* Berlin, 1963.

9226. Sodré, A. "Solano López, Emperador," *RIHGB* 182 (January, 1944) 105–115.

9227. Solano López, F. *Proclamas y Cartas del Mariscal López.* B.A., 1957.

9228. Vittone, L. *El Paraguay en la Lucha por su Independencia.* Asunción, 1960.
Emphasis is on independence from Buenos Aires rather than from Spain.

9229. Washburn, C. A. *The History of Paraguay, with Notes of Personal Observations, and Reminiscences of Diplomacy Under Difficulties.* 2 vols., Boston, 1871.
By the U.S. minister.

9230. Ynsfran, P. M. "Sam Ward's Bargain with President López of Paraguay," *HAHR* 34 (1954) 313–331.
Concerns the U.S. naval expedition of

1858–1859. For a more detailed account, see item 9231.

9231. ———. *La Expedición Norteamericana Contra el Paraguay, 1858–1859.* 2 vols., Mexico, 1954–1958.
Discusses the business activities of the United States and Paraguay Navigation Company and the punitive expedition (twenty ships) sent after the firing on the *Water Witch*.

XXI–B   cross references: 9144a, 9692

C. THE PARAGUAYAN WAR, 1864–1870

9232. Amarilla Fretes, E. *La Liquidación de la Guerra de la Triple Alianza Contra el Paraguay: Negociaciones Diplomáticas.* Asunción, 1941.

9233. Benites, G. *Anales Diplomática y Militar de la Guerra del Paraguay.* 2 vols., Asunción, 1902.

9234. Beverina, J. *La Guerra del Paraguay.* 7 vols., B.A., 1921–1933.

9235. Box, P. H. *The Origins of the Paraguayan War.* 2 vols., Urbana, Ill., 1929.
Spanish eds., Asunción, 1936, and B.A., 1958.

9236. Cárcano, R. *Guerra del Paraguay.* 3 vols., B.A., 1939–1941.

9237. Cardozo, E. *Vísperas de la Guerra del Paraguay.* B.A., 1954.

9238. Fragoso, A. T. *Historia da Guerra Entre a Tríplice Aliança e o Paraguai.* 5 vols., Rio, 1934.
The major Brazilian interpretation of the war.

9239. Kolinsky, C. J. *Independence or Death! The Story of the Paraguayan War.* Gainesville, Fla., 1965.

9240. Pereyra, C. *Francisco Solano López y la Guerra del Paraguay.* New ed., B. A., 1953.

9241. Peterson, H. F. "Efforts of the United States to Mediate in the Paraguayan War," *HAHR* 12 (1932) 2–17.

9242. Schneider, L. *A Guerra da Tríplice Aliança: (Império do Brasil, República Argentina e República Oriental do Uruguai) Contra o Govêrno da República do Paraguai, 1864–1870.* 2 vols., São Paulo, 1945.

9243. Soares, A. Teixeira. *O Drama da Tríplice Aliança, 1865–1876.* Rio, 1956.

9244. Talavera, N. *La Guerra del Paraguay: Correspondencias Publicadas en " El Seminario."* B.A., 1958.

Author was a Paraguayan journalist and patriot.

9245. Thompson, G. *War in Paraguay, with a Historical Sketch of the Country and Its People and Notes upon the Military Engineering of the War.* London, 1869.

9246. Vittone, L. *Guerra de la Triple Alianza Contra el Paraguay.* N.p., n.d.

9247. Warren, H. G. "The Paraguayan Image of the War of the Triple Alliance," *TA* 19 (1962) 3–20.

D. UNITED STATES–PARAGUAYAN RELATIONS: TWENTIETH CENTURY

9248. Dahl, V. O. "The Paraguayan 'Jewel Box,'" *TA* 21 (1965) 223–242.

Concerns the return of certain valuables held in the United States legation from the nineteenth century.

9249. González Merzario, A. *Política y Ejército: Consideraciones Sobre Problemas Político-Militares del Paraguay.* B.A., 1955.

9250. Mercado Alder, W. "Paraguay y el Plan Kennedy," *COMB* 3 (September, 1961) 26–32.

9250a. Pérez Uribe, O. and E. A. Lugo. *Colección de Tratados Históricos y Vigentes.* Asunción, 1934.

9251. Poumaillou, P. *Study on Investment and Planning in the Economic Development of Paraguay.* Asunción, 1962.

9252. Prieto, J. "El Problema del Paraguay Mediterráneo," *PA* 1 (December, 1946) 29–45.

Argues that Paraguay should remain aloof from all international conflicts.

9253. Riquelme García, B. *Cumbre en Soledad: Vida de Manuel Gondra.* B.A., 1951.

Biography of the Paraguayan statesman, drafter of the Gondra Doctrine, and minister to the United States.

9254. Schurz, W. L. *Paraguay: A Commercial Handbook.* Wash., 1920.

9255. Unión Nacional Paraguaya. *El Tirano Stroessner ante la Conciencia Democrática de América.* Formosa, Argentina, 1960.

9256. U.S. Bureau of Foreign Commerce. *Investment in Paraguay: Conditions and Outlook for United States Investors.* Wash., 1955.

9257. Villamayor, J. M. *Stroessner y su Claque: Vicisitudes de un Soldado.* Montevideo, 1957.

9258. Ynsfran, E. *La Irrupción Moscovita en la Marina Paraguay.* Asunción, 1947.

XXI–D   cross references:

a) For works on the Chaco War (1932–1936), see items 9049–9123.

b) See also item 3401.

Chapter XXII   The United States and Chile

A. UNITED STATES–CHILEAN RELATIONS: GENERAL WORKS AND SPECIAL STUDIES

9259. Alessandri, A. *Chile y su Historia.* 2 vols., Santiago, 1945.
Survey from earliest times to 1925.

9260. Aliaga Ibar, I. *La Economía de Chile y la Industria del Cobre.* Santiago, 1946.

9261. Alvarez, A. *Rasgos Generales de la Historia Diplomática de Chile, 1810–1910.* Santiago, 1911.

9262. Barros Arana, D. *Historia Jeneral de Chile.* 2d ed., 16 vols., Santiago, 1884–1902.

9263. Bertrand, A. *The Chilean Nitrate Industry.* Paris, 1920.

9264. Bustos Pérez, V. *Historia de Chile: Texto Aprobado por el Ministerio de Educación.* 21st ed., Santiago, 1939.

9265. Butland, G. J. *Chile: An Outline of Its Geography, Economics and Politics.* 3d ed., London, 1956.
In the Latin America series of the Royal Institute of International Affairs.

9266. Campos Harriet, F. *Manual de Historia Constitucional de Chile.* Santiago, 1951.

9267. Castedo, L. (ed.). *Resumen de la Historia de Chile de Francisco A. Encina.* 3 vols., Santiago, 1954–1955.
An abbreviated version, profusely illustrated and with appendices, of the Encina history in 20 volumes. See item 9282.

9268. Castro Ruiz, C. "The Monroe Doctrine and the Government of Chile," *APSR* 2 (1917) 231–238.

9269. Centner, C. W. "Great Britain and Chilean Mining, 1830–1914," *EHRE* 12 (1942) 76–82.

9270. Chile. *Tratados Origentes de Chile.* 6 vols., Santiago, 1936.

9271. ———. Senado. *Manual del Senado, 1810–1942.* Santiago, 1942.

Lists cabinet members and senators.

9272. ———. Ministerio de Relaciones Exteriores. Sección Tratados. *Indice General de las Ratificaciones, Adhesiones, y Reservas Correspondientes a las Convenciones Multilaterales en que Chile Es Parte.* Santiago, 1949.

9273. ———. ———. ———. *Indice General de los Tratados Bilaterales de Chile al 31 de Diciembre de 1949.* Santiago, 1949.

9274. Cruchaga Ossa, A. *Estudios de Historia Diplomática Chilena.* Santiago, 1962.

9275. Délano, L. E. *Pequeña Historia de Chile.* Mexico, 1944.

9276. Donald, M. B. "History of the Chile Nitrate Industry," *ASCI* 1 (1936) 29–47, 193–216.

9277. Donoso, R. *Breve Historia de Chile.* B.A., 1963.

9278. ———. *Desarrollo Político y Social de Chile Desde la Constitución de 1833.* 2d ed., Santiago, 1942.

9279. Edwards MacClure, A. *My Native Land.* London, 1928.

9280. Edwards Vives, A. *La Fronda Aristocrática: Historia Política de Chile.* Santiago, 1952.
Covers the period from independence to 1925.

9281. Elliot, G. F. S. *Chile: Its History and Development.* London, 1907.

9282. Encina, F. A. *Historia de Chile Desde la Prehistoria Hasta 1891.* 20 vols., Santiago, 1941–1952.
For a condensation in three volumes, see item 9267.

9283. Espinosa del Campo, J. *Figuras de la Política Chilena: Primera Serie.* Santiago, 1945.

9284. Evans, H. C., Jr. *Chile and Its Relations with the United States.* Durham, N.C., 1927.

9285. Fergusson, E. *Chile*. N.Y., 1943.

9286. Frías Valenzuela, F. *Historia de Chile*. 4 vols., Santiago, 1947–1949.

9287. Galdames, L. *Estudio de la Historia de Chile*. 2 vols., 1906.
English ed., Chapel Hill, N.C., 1941.

9288. ———. *Evolución Constitucional de Chile*. Santiago, 1925.

9289. Gil, F. G. *Genesis and Modernization of Political Parties in Chile*. Gainesville, Fla., 1962.

9290. Guilisasti Tagle, S. *Partidos Políticos Chilenos*. 2d ed., Santiago, 1964.

9291. Hillman, T., Jr. "A History of the Armed Forces of Chile from Independence to 1920," Syracuse U. Diss., 1963.

9292. Koebel, W. H. *Modern Chile*. London, 1913.

9293. Pena, L. *Histoire du Chile*. Paris, 1927.

9294. Pendle, G. *The Land and People of Chile*. London, 1960.

9295. Pfeiffer, J. B. "The Development of Manufacturing Industry in Chile, 1820–1940," U. of Chicago Diss., 1947.

9296. Pike, F. B. *Chile and the United States, 1880–1962: The Emergence of Chile's Social Crisis and the Challenge to United States Diplomacy*. Notre Dame, Ind., 1963.
The most comprehensive coverage of the subject.

9297. Pinto, A. *Historia de Chile*. 8th ed., Santiago, 1938.

9298. Ramírez Necochea, H. *Historia del Imperialismo en Chile*. Santiago, 1960.
A Marxist interpretation.

9299. *Recopilación de Tratados y Convenciones Celebrados Entre la República de Chile y las Potencias Extrangeras*. 5 vols., Santiago, 1894–1908.

9300. Rippy, J. F. "A Century of British Investments in Chile," *PHR* 21 (1952) 341–348.

9301. Rivas Vicuña, M. *Historia Política y Parlamentaria de Chile*. 3 vols., Santiago, 1964.

9302. Santelices, A. *El Imperialismo Yanqui y su Influencia en Chile*. Santiago, 1926.

9303. Sherman, W. R. *The Diplomatic and Commercial Relations of the United States and Chile, 1820–1914*. Boston, 1926.

9304. Talbott, R. D. "A History of the Chilean Boundaries," U. of Illinois Diss., 1959.

9305. Vera Vera, R. *Historia de la Deuda Externa de Chile*. Santiago, 1942.

9306. Vergara, I. *El Protestantismo en Chile*. Santiago, 1962.

XXII–A   cross references: 1474, 4275

B. THE UNITED STATES AND CHILEAN INDEPENDENCE

9307. Alvarez, A. *La Diplomacia de Chile Durante la Emancipación*. Santiago, 1916.

9308. Amunátegui, M. L. *Los Precursores de la Independencia de Chile*. 3 vols., Santiago, 1870.

9309. Amunátegui y Solar, D. *Nacimiento de la República de Chile*. Santiago, 1930.
Covers the years 1808–1833.

9310. *Archivo de Don Bernardo O'Higgins*. Santiago, 1946– .

9311. Barros Arana, D. "El Primer Cónsul Estranjero en Chile, Mr. Joel Roberts Poinsett," in *Obras Completas*, vol. 11. Santiago, 1911.

9312. ———. *Historia Jeneral de la Independencia de Chile*. 4 vols., Santiago, 1854–1858.

9313. Benavente, D. J. *Primeras Campañas de la Guerra de Independencia de Chile*. Santiago, 1856.

9314. Bianchi Barros, A. *Bosquejo Histórico de las Relaciones Chileno-Norteamericanas Durante la Independencia*. Santiago, 1946.

9315. Cabello Reyes, C. *Genio y Figura de Bernardo O'Higgins*. Santiago, 1944.

9316. Chandler, C. L. "La Vida de Joel Robert Poinsett," *RCHG* 77 (1935) 33–52; 88 (1940) 295–309.

9317. Chisholm, A. S. M. *The Independence of Chile*. Boston, 1911.

9318. Coffin, J. F. *Diario de un Joven Norte-Americano Detenido en Chile Durante el Período Revolucionario de 1817 a 1819*. Santiago, 1898.

9319. *Colección de Historiadores y de Documentos Relativos a la Independencia de Chile*. 34 vols., Santiago, 1900–1946.
For an index to this collection, see S. Villalobos, *Indice de la Colección de Historiadores y de Documentos Relativos a la Independencia de Chile* (Santiago, 1956).

9320. Collier, W. M., and G. Feliú Cruz. *La Primera Misión de los Estados Unidos de América en Chile*. Santiago, 1926.

Treats the relationship between Carrera and Poinsett (1811–1814). Collier served as U.S. Ambassador to Chile in the 1920's.

9321. Cox, H. B. "Reasons for Joel R. Poinsett's Refusal of a Second Mission to South America," *HAHR* 43 (1963) 405–408.
A letter by Poinsett.

9322. Cruz, E. de la (ed.). *Epistolario de Don Bernardo O'Higgins, Capitán General y Director Supremo de Chile.* 2 vols., Madrid, 1920.

9323. Cruz, J. M. de la. *Recuerdos de Don Bernardo O'Higgins.* Santiago, 1960.

9324. Edwards MacClure, A. *The Dawn (Being the History of the Birth and Consolidation of the Republic of Chile).* London, 1931.

9325. Eyzaguirre, J. *Ideario y Ruta de la Emancipación Chilena.* Santiago, 1957.

9326. ———. *O'Higgins.* 4th ed., Santiago, 1960.

9326a. Feliú Cruz, G. "Comprobaciones Históricas: Poinsett en Méjico y en Chile," *RCHG* 12 (1928) 37–46.

9327. Goebel, D. B. "British-American Rivalry in the Chilean Trade, 1817–20," *JEH* 2 (1942) 190–203.

9328. Hill, H. *Incidents in Chili, South America, 1817–1821.* Weymouth, Mass., 1895(?).
Henry Hill was the U.S. vice-consul in Chile.

9329. Johnson, J. J. "Early Relations of the United States with Chile," *PHR* 13 (1944) 260–270.
Covers the years 1790 to 1817.

9330. Johnston, S. *Diario de un Tipógrafo Yanqui en Chile y Perú Durante la Guerra de la Independencia.* Madrid, 1919.

9331. Lande, I. M. "War by the Pen: Some Intellectual and Propagandistic Aspects of the Chilean Struggle for Independence, 1808–1820," Northwestern U. Diss., 1956.

9332. *Message from the President ... Transmitting ... Report of Theodorick Bland, Esquire, on South America.* Wash., 1819.
Spanish ed., *AUCH* 4 (1926) 927–980; 5 (1927) 1–53.

9333. Montaner Bello, R. *Historia Diplomática de la Independencia de Chile.* Santiago, 1941.
2d ed., Santiago, 1961.

9334. Neumann, W. L. "The Role of the United States in the Chilean Wars of Independence," U. of Michigan Diss., 1948.

9335. ———. "United States Aid to the Chilean Wars of Independence," *HAHR* 27 (1947) 204–219.

9336. Orrego Vicuña, E. *O'Higgins, Vida y Tiempo.* B.A., 1946.

9337. Palma Zuñiga, L. *O'Higgins, Ciudadano de América.* Santiago, 1956.

9338. Pereira Salas, E. *La Actuación de los Oficiales Navales Norteamericanos en Nuestras Costas (1813–1840).* Santiago, 1935.

9339. ———. *Buques Norteamericanos en Chile a Fines de la Era Colonial: 1788–1810.* Santiago, 1935.
English ed., Santiago, 1940; trans. by E. G. Trueblood.

9340. ———. "Un Comerciante Norte-Americano en Nuestras Costas: Samuel Hill y sus Viajes, 1815–1822," *RCHG* 76 (1935) 390–416; 77 (1935) 74–97.

9341. ———. "Don Mateo Arnaldo Hoevel, 1773–1819," *RCHG* 89 (July, 1940) 57–93.
Hoevel was designated U.S. Vice-Consul in Chile.

9342. ———. "The First Chilean Students in the United States (1815–1819)," *BPAU* 69 (1935) 712–716.

9343. ———. "Henry Hill, Comerciante, Vice-Cónsul y Misionero," *RCHG* 87, no. 95 (1939) 5–30.

9344. ———. "Jeremías Robinson, Agente Norteamericano en Chile, 1818–1823," *RCHG* 82, no. 20 (1937) 210–236.
See also item 9350.

9345. ———. "La Misión Bland en Chile," *RCHG* 78 (1935) 80–103.

9346. ———. *La Misión Worthington en Chile, 1818–1819.* Santiago, 1936.

9347. ———. "El Primer Vice-Cónsul Extranjero en Valparaíso," *RCHG* 81, no. 89 (1936) 173–183.
The U.S. vice-consul was appointed in 1812.

9348. Pizarro, O. *El Primer Prócer de Chile.* Temuco, 1949.
Biography of O'Higgins.

9349. Porter, D. *Journal of a Cruise Made to the Pacific Ocean in the Years 1812, 1813, and 1814.* 2 vols., Phil., 1815.

Author was a naval commander sent to protect U.S. commerce during the War of 1812.

9350. Robinson, J. "Diario Personal, May–June 1818," *RCHG* 85, no. 93 (1938) 99–126.

See also item 9344.

9351. Stuardo Ortiz, C., and J. Eyzaguirre Escobar. *Santiago: Contribuyentes, Autoridades, Funcionarios, Agentes, Diplomáticos y Consulares, 1817–1819*. Santiago, 1952.

9352. Varas Velásquez, M. *Don José Miguel Carrera en los Estados Unidos*. Santiago, 1912.

Covers 1816–1818.

9353. Vicuña Mackenna, B. *Ostracismo de los Carreras*. Santiago, 1857.

Deals with José Miguel Carrera, one of the two revolutionary brothers.

9354. Worcester, D. E. *Seapower and Chilean Independence*. Gainesville, Fla., 1962.

XXII–B   cross references:

a) For more general works on the role of the United States in the Latin American independence movements, see items 1805–1896 and 1972–1988.

b) See also items 5604, 5616, 5619, 5620, 5621, 5626, 9545, 9566, 9569, 9576, 9577.

C. UNITED STATES–CHILEAN RELATIONS, 1823–1891

9355. Alessandri, A. *Revolución de 1891: Mi Actuación*. Santiago, 1950.

9356. Bañados Espinosa, J. *Balmaceda, Su Gobierno i la Revolución de 1891*. Paris, 1894.

9357. Barros Arana, D. *Un Decenio de la Historia de Chile, 1841–1851*. 2 vols., Santiago, 1905.–1906.

Covers the presidency of Manuel Montt.

9357a. Blakemore, H. "John Thomas North, the Nitrate King," *HT* 12 (1962) 467–475.

9358. Brown, J. R. "The Chilean Nitrate Industry in the Nineteenth Century," Louisiana State U. Diss., 1964.

9359. Bunster, E. *Chilenos en California*. Santiago, 1954.

Only one section deals with the subject indicated in the title.

9359a. Burr, R. N. *By Reason or Force: Chile and the Balancing of Power in South America, 1830–1905*. Berkeley, Calif., 1965.

9360. Calderón Cousiño, A. *Breve Historia Diplomática de las Relaciones Chileno-Peruanas, 1819–1879*. 2d ed., Santiago, 1919.

9361. Centner, C. W. "Relaciones Comerciales de Gran Bretaña con Chile, 1810–1830," *RCHG*, no. 103 (July, 1944) 96–107.

9362. Correa Bravo, A. *Los Extranjeros ante la Ley Chilena*. Santiago, 1894.

9363. Cox Méndez, R. *Recuerdos de 1891*. Santiago, 1944.

Attacks the Balmaceda administration.

9364. Cruchaga Ossa, A. "Don Joaquín Campina: First Chilean Minister to the United States, 1827," *PAM* 39 (May, 1926) 37–42.

9365. ———. "Impressions of the First Chilean Minister to Washington, 1827–1830," *PAM* 39 (May, 1926) 157–161.

9366. Díaz V., F. J. *La Guerra Civil de 1891: "La Campaña del Norte."* 2 vols., Santiago, 1942–1944.

9367. Eastman, V. *Balmaceda, Don José Manuel, Presidente de Chile, 1886–1891, y el Conflicto con el Congreso Nacional*. Latacunga, Ecuador, 1935.

9368. Edwards MacClure, A. *Cuatro Presidentes de Chile, 1841–1876*. 2 vols., Valparaiso, 1932.

9369. Edwards Vives, A. *El Gobierno de Don Manuel Montt, 1851–1861*. Santiago, 1932.

A sympathetic analysis of the Montt administration.

9370. ———. *La Organización Política de Chile, 1810–1833*. Santiago, 1943.

9371. Encina, F. A. *Portales: Introducción a la Historia de la Epoca de Diego Portales*. 2 vols., Santiago, 1935.

A standard treatment.

9372. ———. *La Presidencia de Balmaceda*. 2 vols. Santiago, 1952.

9373. Espinosa, J. *Don Manuel Montt: Uno de los Más Grandes Estadistas de América*. Santiago, 1944.

9374. Famin, S. M. C. *Historia de Chile, 1799–1853*. Barcelona, 1859.

9375. Fuenzalida Grandón, A. *Lastarria y su Tiempo (1817–1888): Su Vida, Obras e Influencia en el Desarrollo Político e*

Intelectual de Chile. 2 vols., Santiago, 1911.

A biography of José Victorino Lastarria.

9376. Gandarillas, P. N. *Contestación a la Demanda Presentada al Tribunal Arbitral por la "North and South American Construction Co." Contra el Fisco.* Santiago, 1890.

See also item 9389.

9377. Gay, C. *Historia Física y Política de Chile.* 26 vols., Paris, 1844–1854.

9378. Hancock, A. U. *A History of Chile.* Chicago, 1893.

9378a. Hardy, O. "Los Intereses Salitreros Ingleses y la Revolución de 1891," *RCHG*, no. 113 (January, 1949) 60–81.

English ed., *PHR* 17 (1948) 165–180.

9379. ———. "The U.S. and Chile: A Study in Diplomatic Relations, with Special Emphasis on the Period of the Chilean Civil War of 1891," U. of California Diss., 1925.

9380. ———. "The United States and Chile: An Account of the Early Relations Between the Two Young Republic [*sic*]," *C* 7, no. 40 (1929) 60–64, 151–152.

9381. Hernández Cornejo, R. *Los Chilenos en San Francisco de California (Recuerdos Históricos de la Emigración por los Descubrimientos del Oro, Iniciada en 1848).* 2 vols., Valparaiso, 1930.

9381a. Hervey, M. H. *Dark Days in Chile: An Account of the Revolution of 1891.* London, 1891–1892.

9382. Hunter, D. J. A. *A Sketch of Chili Expressly Prepared for the Use of Immigrants from the United States and Europe.* N.Y., 1866.

9383. Iglesias Meléndez, J. H. *Wheelwright, Servidor de la Civilización: Biografía.* Santiago, 1947.

Wheelwright was a railroad and steamship promoter.

9384. Johnson, J. J. *Pioneer Telegraphy in Chile, 1852–1876.* Stanford, Calif., 1948.

9384a. ———. "Talcahuano and Concepción as Seen by the Forty-Niners," *HAHR* 26 (1946) 251–262.

9385. Kinsbruner, J. "The Business Activities of William Wheelwright in Chile, 1829–1860," New York U. Diss., 1965.

9386. Letelier, V. (ed.). *Sesiones de los Cuerpos Legislativos de la República de Chile, 1811 á 1845.* 37 vols., Santiago, 1887–1908.

9387. McKechnie, F. "Chile: The Critical Years—The Regime of Diego Portales," Georgetown U. Diss., 1936.

9388. Merwin, G. B. *Chile Through American Spectacles.* N.Y., 1863.

9389. Montt, A. *Visita del Fiscal de la Corte Suprema, Recaída Sobre la Presentación de D. Juan A. Palazuelos a Fin de que se le Reconozca como Agentes de la "North and South American Construction Company."* Santiago, 1891.

See also item 9376.

9390. Montt, P. "La Mediación Diplomática en la Revolución de 1891," *RCHG*, no. 118 (July, 1951) 169–183.

9390a. Montt Montt, P. *Exposition of the Illegal Acts of Ex-President Balmaceda Which Caused the Chilean Civil War of 1891.* Wash., 1891.

Documentary sources compiled by the son of President Montt (1851–1861).

9391. *Oral Arguments in the District Court of the United States for the Southern District of California, Before Honorable E. M. Ross, District Judge, by Charles Page and Stephen M. White, Esquires, for Defendants and Claimants, and Oral Argument of William W. Goodrich, Esquire, for Compania Sud-Americana de Vapores.* San Francisco, 1891.

9391a. Orrego Vicuña, E. *Un Canciller de la Revolución.* Santiago, 1926.

Treats foreign relations during the civil war of 1891.

9391b. Pergler, C. "Early Diplomatic Relations of the United States and Chile," *NULR* 10 (1930) 65–79.

9391c. Ramírez Necochea, H. *La Guerra Civil de 1891: Antecedentes Económicos.* Santiago, 1951.

A Marxist interpretation.

9392. Rasmussen, W. D. "The United States Astronomical Expedition to Chile, 1849–1852," *HAHR* 34 (1954) 103–113.

9393. Ruschemberger, W. S. W. *Noticias de Chile (1831–1832), por un Oficial de la Marina de los EE. UU. de América.* Santiago, 1956.

9394. Sears, J. H. *The Chilean Revolution of 1891.* Wash., 1893.

9395.   Shaw, P. V. *The Early Constitutions of Chile, 1810–1833.* N.Y., 1931.

9396.   Sotomayor Valdés, R. *Historia de Chile bajo el Gobierno del General D. Joaquín Prieto.* 4 vols., Santiago, 1900–1903.

Prieto was President from 1831 to 1841.

9397.   Stewart, W. *Enrique Meiggs en Chile.* Santiago, 1938.

9398.   ———. "Meiggs y la Inauguración del Ferrocarril de Arequipa," *RCHG*, no. 104 (January, 1944) 264–283.

9399.   ———. "El Trabajador Chileno y los Ferrocarriles del Perú," *RCHG* 85 (July, 1938) 128–171.

Concerns Henry Meiggs.

9400.   Vicuña Mackenna, B. *Diez Meses de Misión a los Estados Unidos como Agente de Chile.* 2 vols., Santiago, 1867.

Author served as a special envoy to the United States in 1865.

9401.   ———. *Páginas de mi Diario Durante Tres Años de Viaje, 1853–1854–1855.* 2 vols., Santiago, 1936.

Author spent these three years in the United States, Mexico, and Europe.

9402.   Wheelwright, W. *Statements and Documents Relative to the Establishment of Steam Navigation in the Pacific.* London, 1838.

9402a. Wycoff, D. P. "The Chilean Civil War, 1891," *USNIP* 88 (1962) 58–63.

9403.   Yrarrazával Larraín, J. M. *La Administración de Balmaceda y el Salitre de Tarapacá.* Santiago, 1953.

9404.   ———. *La Política Económica del Presidente Balmaceda.* Santiago, 1963.

9405.   ———. *El Presidente Balmaceda.* 2 vols., Santiago, 1940.

XXII–C   cross references:

a)   For accounts of the attempted Spanish reconquest (1863–1866), see items 2203–2232.

b)   For works on the War of the Pacific (1879–1884), see items 8850–8879.

c)   See also items 2524, 2616, 9310, 9322, 9324, 9336, 9337, 9338, 9348, 9495, 9611, 9637, 9694.

D. THE *BALTIMORE* AFFAIR, 1891

9406.   Barros Franco, J. M. *El Caso del "Baltimore": Apuntes para la Historia Diplomática de Chile.* Santiago, 1950.

9407.   Chile. Ministerio de Relaciones Exteriores. *Estados Unidos i Chile: Notas Cambiadas Entre la Legación de Estados Unidos de Norte-América i el Ministro de Relaciones Exteriores de Chile, a Propósito de las Cuestiones Suscitadas Entre Ambos Países.* Santiago, 1891.

9408.   Evans, R. D. *A Sailor's Log: Recollections of Forty Years of Naval Life.* N.Y., 1901.

9409.   *An Examination of the Chilean Incident, by a Member of the Bar.* Boston, 1896.

The study was prepared by J. A. Gillis.

9410.   Falk, E. A. *Fighting Bob Evans.* N.Y., 1931.

9411.   Fetter, F. W. "The Chilean Debt Payment of 1891," *EH* 2 (1930–1933) 609–616.

9412.   Hardy, O. "The Itata Incident," *HAHR* 5 (1922) 195–226.

Preceded the *Baltimore* affair.

9413.   ———. "Was Patrick Egan a 'Blundering Minister'?" *HAHR* 8 (1928) 65–81.

Egan was U.S. minister at the time of the *Baltimore* affair.

9413a. Lindsell, H. *The Chilean-American Controversy of 1891–1892.* N.Y., 1943.

9414.   Matta, M. A. *Cuestiones Recientes con la Legación y el Gobierno de los Estados Unidos de Norte América.* Santiago, 1892.

Author was the Chilean minister of foreign affairs during the *Baltimore* incident.

9415.   Moore, J. B. "The Chilean Controversy," *PSQ* 8 (1893) 467–494.

9416.   USCH. *Message of the President of the United States Respecting the Relations with Chile* (52d Cong., 1st Sess., H. Ex. Doc. 91). Wash., 1892.

9417.   Vergara, M. *El Imperialismo Yankee en Chile: Resumen Histórico del Incidente del U.S.S. "Baltimore."* Santiago, 1945.

XXII–D   cross references:

a)   For additional works pertaining to the *Baltimore* affair, consult the histories of the revolution of 1891 and the biographies of José Balmaceda cited in the previous section.

b)   See also items 2803, 9379.

E. UNITED STATES–CHILEAN RELATIONS, 1891–1925

9417a. Alessandri, A. *Recuerdos de Gobierno: Administración, 1920–1925*. Santiago, 1952.

9417b. *The Alsop Claim: The Case of the United States of America for and in Behalf of the Original American Claimants in this Case . . . Versus the Republic of Chile Before His Majesty George V*. Wash., 1910.

9418. "Award Pronounced by His Majesty King George V as 'Amiable Compositeur' Between the United States and the Republic of Chile in the Matter of the Alsop Claim, London, July 5, 1911," *AJIL* 5 (1911) 1079–1107.

9419. Ballesteros, P. "Un Conflicto Yankee-Chileno: La Cuestión Alsop," *EM* 257 (1910) 89–102.

9419a. Brown, J. R. "Nitrate Crises, Combinations, and the Chilean Government in the Nitrate Age," *HAHR* 43 (1963) 230–246.

9419b. Chile. *The Alsop Claim: Case Presented by the Government of Chile to His Britannic Majesty King George V, in the Arbitration to Which the Government of Chile and of the United States Have Submitted the Matter of the Claim of Alsop & Co. by the Convention of the First Day of December, 1909*. London, 1910.

9419c. ———. *The Alsop Claim: Counter-Case Presented*. London, 1910.

9420. Donoso, R. *Alessandri, Agitador y Demoledor: Cincuenta Años de Historia Política de Chile*. 2 vols., Mexico, 1952–1954.
Although it is a critical biography of Arturo Alessandri, the work covers Chilean political history from 1890 to 1940.

9420a. Durán B., A. *El Estado Libre de El Teniente y la Vida Obrera de las Minas*. Santiago, 1919.
Critical of U.S. copper companies.

9421. Eyzaguirre, J. *Chile Durante el Gobierno de Errázuriz Echaurren, 1896–1901*. 2d ed., Santiago, 1957.

9422. Haring, C. H. "Chilean Politics, 1920–1928," *HAHR* 11 (1931) 1–26.

9423. Jefferson, M. S. W. *Recent Colonization in Chile*. N.Y., 1921.

9424. Latcham, R. *Chuquicamata, Estado Yankee: Visión de la Montaña Roja*. Santiago, 1920.

9425. Lira, A. *Memorias*. Santiago, 1950.
Memoirs of a Chilean diplomat.

9426. Mora, G. *La Democracia al Poder: Chile, 1889–1938*. Managua, 1938.

9427. Nunn, F. M. "Civil-Military Relations in Chile, 1891–1938," U. of New Mexico Diss., 1963.

9427a. Artúzar, A. *Informe Comercial del Consulado General en Estados Unidos*. Santiago, 1908.

9428. Reinsch, P. S. "Parliamentary Government in Chile," *APSR* 3 (1908–1909) 507–538.

9429. Rodríguez Mendoza, E. *Como si Fuera Ahora*. Santiago, 1929.
Memoirs of a distinguished diplomat.

9430. United States and Chilean Claims Commission. *Minutes of Proceedings*. Wash., 1894.
Concerns the Alsop claim. See also items 9419b and 9419c.

9431. ———. *1900–1901. Minutes of Commission*. Wash., 1901.

9432. ———. *Final Report of John Hoyt Perry, Agent and Counsel for United States*. Wash., 1901.

9433. Walker Martínez, C. *Política Internacional de la Administración Errázuriz en 1898*. Santiago, 1902.

9434. Young, J. M. "Chilean Parliamentary Government, 1891–1924," Princeton U. Diss., 1953.

XXII–E cross references:

a) For works relating to the Tacna-Arica dispute and settlement, see items 8880–8932.

b) See also items 2909, 3144, 3152, 3155, 3157, 3164, 3165, 3167, 3168, 3169, 3171, 3176, 4161, 4162, 5440, 6112, 6145, 9645a.

F. UNITED STATES–CHILEAN RELATIONS SINCE 1925

9435. Aldunate Carvallo, G. *Posibilidades de la Economía Chilena para los Capitales Extranjeros*. Santiago, 1949.

9436. Alexander, R. J. "Labor Relations in Chile," Columbia U. Diss., 1950.

9437. Allende, S. *La Contradicción de Chile:*

Régimen de Izquierda, Política Económica de Derecha. Santiago, 1943.

Author is the socialist senator who ran for the presidency unsuccessfully in 1952, 1958, and 1964.

9438. Almeyda Medina, C. *Reflexiones Políticas.* Santiago, 1958.

A collection of newspaper articles.

9439. Ballanoff, E. N. "Chile's Balance of Payments, Economic Developments, and Foreign Economic Policy," Ohio State Diss., 1959.

9440. Barrett, M. R. "A Multiple Exchange Rate System: An Appraisal of Chile's Experience, 1946–1955," Harvard U. Diss., 1961.

9441. Blasier, S. C. "Chile: A Communist Battleground," *PSQ* 65 (1950) 353–374.

9442. Bowers, C. G. *Chile Through Embassy Windows: 1939–1953.* N.Y., 1958.

Spanish ed., Santiago, 1957. By the United States ambassador in Santiago.

9443. ———. *My Life: The Memoirs of Claude Bowers.* N.Y., 1962.

9444. Bray, D. W. "Chilean Politics During the Second Ibáñez Government, 1952–58," Stanford U. Diss., 1962.

9444a. Cabero, A. *Recuerdos de Don Pedro Aguirre Cerda.* Santiago, 1948.

A sympathetic treatment.

9445. Carril Echevarri, J. *Nuestra Deuda Externa, Suspensión y Reanudación de sus Servicios.* Santiago, 1944.

9446. Casiello, J. *Lo que Ha Hecho el Comunismo.* Santiago, 1942.

9447. Castillo Velasco, J. *El Problema Comunista.* Santiago, 1955.

9448. Cohen, A. *Economic Change in Chile, 1929–1959.* Gainesville, Fla., 1960.

9449. Correa Prieto, L. *El Presidente Ibáñez: La Política y los Políticos: Apuntes para la Historia.* Santiago, 1962.

9450. Cruz Coke, E. "América en el Crisol.... Proyecciones de la Política y la Economía Chilenas en la Postguerra," *ETSS* 1 (November, 1944) 199–210.

9451. Ellsworth, P. T. *Chile: An Economy in Transition.* N.Y., 1945.

9452. Etcheberry Orthusteguy, A. *American-Chilean Private International Law.* N.Y., 1960.

9453. Federación de Estudiantes de Chile.

"Cartas Cruzadas Entre los Estudiantes Chilenos y el Presidente Eisenhower," *COMB* 2 (July, 1960) 58–69.

9454. Fernández C., J. F. *Pedro Aguirre Cerda y el Frente Popular Chileno.* Santiago, 1939.

President, 1938–1941. Candidate of the short-lived Popular Front.

9455. Frei Montalva, E. *Pensamiento y Acción.* Santiago, 1956.

Collection of speeches and writings prior to his presidential election in 1964.

9456. Halperin, E. *Nationalism and Communism in Chile.* Cambridge, Mass., 1965.

9457. Hanson, E. P. *Chile, Land of Progress.* N.Y., 1941.

9458. Haring, C. H. "Chile Moves Left," *FA* 17 (1939) 618–624.

Treats the Popular Front government.

9459. ———. "The Chilean Revolution of 1931," *HAHR* 13 (1933) 197–203.

Concerns the revolution that toppled Carlos Ibáñez del Campo.

9460. Horowitz, I. L. "The Life and Death of Project Camelot," *AMP* 21 (1966) 445–454.

9461. Houseman, P. J. "Chilean Nationalism, 1920–1952," Stanford U. Diss., 1961.

9461a. Hughes, T. L. "Scholars and Foreign Policy: Varieties of Research Experience," *AMP* 21 (1966) 471–478.

Considers Project Camelot.

9462. Huneeus Gana, A. *La Derrota Comunista.* Santiago, 1947.

9463. Inglesias, A. *Alessandri, una Etapa de la Democracia en América: Tiempo, Vida, Acción.* Santiago, 1960.

A sympathetic biography.

9464. Illanes Benítez, F. *La Economía Chilena y el Comercio Exterior.* Santiago, 1944.

9465. International Business Machine Corporation. *Vista del Excelentísimo Señor Don Gabriel González Videla, Presidente de la República de Chile, a los Estados Unidos de América, 12 de Abril–3 de Mayo de 1950: Documentos Históricos.* N.p., 1951.

9465a. Jiles Pizarro, J. *Partido Comunista de Chile.* Santiago, 1957.

9466. Labarca Vergara, S. *Algunos Aspectos del Comercio Internacional de Chile.* Santiago, 1949.

9467. Lafertte, E. *Como Triunfaremos en las Elecciones de 1941.* Santiago, 1941.

Author was a president of the Chilean Communist party.

9468. ———. *Vida de una Comunista: Páginas Autobiográficas*. Santiago, 1957.

9469. Mesa Seco, M. F. *El Comunismo ante la Ley Chilena*. Santiago, 1947.

9469a. Montero Moreno, R. *La Verdad Sobre Ibáñez*. Santiago, 1952.

9470. Olavarría Bravo, A. *Chile Entre Dos Alessandri: Memorias Políticas*. 2 vols., Santiago, 1962.

9471. *Outlook for Chile's Foreign Trade and Economic Growth, 1959–1965*. Santiago, 1959.

9472. Partido Comunista de Chile. *X S'ezd Kommunisticheskoi Partii Chili (Aprel, 1956 g.).* Moscow, 1957.
   The Tenth Congress of the Chilean Communist Party (April, 1956).

9472a. *El Partido Comunista de Chile y el Movimiento Comunista Internacional: Documentos e Informes Emanados de Plenos y Congresos del Partido Comunista de Chile.* Santiago, 1964.

9473. Pike, F. B., and D. W. Bray. "A Vista of Catastrophe: The Future of U.S.–Chilean Relations," *RP* 22 (1960) 393–418.
   Very critical of United States policy.

9474. Pinto Santa Cruz, A. *Hacia Nuestra Independencia Económica*. Santiago, 1953.
   Treats "independence" from U.S. economic domination.

9475. Ramírez Necochea, H. *Origen y Formación del Partido Comunista de Chile*. Santiago, 1965.

9476. *Recent Developments in the Foreign Trade of Chile*. Wash., 1945.

9477. Selna, J. M. "Inflation and Economic Development (A Case Study: The Chilean Experience, 1937–1950)," Harvard U. Diss., 1957.

9478. Skartvedt, E. W. *Industrial Development in Chile*. Wash., 1944.

9479. Stevenson, J. R. *The Chilean Popular Front*. Phil., 1942.
   Covers the 1920's and 1930's.

9480. Tarr, T. S. "Military Intervention and Civilian Reaction in Chile, 1924–1936," U. of Florida Diss., 1961.

9480a. "Testimony Before House Subcommittee on International Organizations and Movements of the Committee on Foreign Affairs, July 8, 1965, Washington, D.C.," *AMP* 21 (1966) 455–470.
   The testimony is on the Camelot Project.

9480b. Vallance, T. R. "Project Camelot: An Interim Postlude," *AMP* 21 (1966) 441–444.

9481. Videla Lira, H. *Desastrosos Efectos de la Acción Comunista en Chile: Discurso Pronunciado ... el Martes 21 de Enero de 1947*. Santiago, 1947.

9481a. Walsh, J. "Foreign Affairs Research: Review Process Rises on Ruins of Camelot," *AMP* 21 (1966) 438–440.
   Much of volume 21 is devoted to a discussion of the controversial Camelot Project.

9482. Ysita, E. "The International Trade of Chile," 1940–1944," *CPA* 14 (January, 1945) 1–69.

XXII–F cross references: 3408, 3409e, 4055, 4146a, 4673, 5235, 7674, 9420, 9422, 9426, 9427

Chapter XXIII   The United States and Argentina

A. UNITED STATES–ARGENTINE RELATIONS: GENERAL WORKS AND SPECIAL STUDIES

9483. Antokoletz, D. *Histoire de la Diplomatie Argentine*. B.A., 1914.

9484. Arce, J. "Tradición Internacional Argentina: El Arbitraje Amplio," *AACE* 3, no. 1 (1945) 5–34.

9485. Arenas Fraga, A. "Relación Histórica de las Misiones Diplomáticas Argentinas: Embajadas y Legaciones," *RBNA* 8, no. 25 (1943) 199–208; 8, no. 26 (1943) 471–480; 9, no. 27 (1943) 217–240; 9 (1943) 454–465.
Lists the heads of Argentine missions from 1810 to date of publication.

9486. Argentina. Ministerio de Relaciones Exteriores y Culto. *Apéndice: Servicios Prestados en la Carrera Diplomática y Administrativa, 1810–1910*. B.A., 1910.

9487. ———. ———. *Instrumentos Internacionales de Carácter Bilateral Suscriptos por la República Argentina (Hasta el 30 de Junio de 1948)*. 3 vols., B.A., 1950.
The first two volumes are devoted to the Americas.

9488. Best, F. *Historia de las Guerras Argentinas de la Independencia, Internacionales, Civiles y con el Indio*. 2 vols., B.A., 1960.

9489. Biblioteca de Mayo. *Colección de Obras y Documentos para la Historia Argentina*. 8 vols., B.A., 1960.
Basic sources on Argentine independence.

9490. Bosch, F. *Historia Naval Argentina*. B.A., 1962.

9491. Caillet-Bois, R. R. *Historia Naval Argentina*. B.A., 1944.

9492. Calderaro, J. D. *Los Presidentes Argentinos de Bernardino Rivadavia a Roberto M. Ortiz*. B.A., 1940.

9493. *Colección de Tratados por la República Argentina con las Naciones Extrangeras*. 3 vols., B.A., 1884.

9494. Cowles, F. *Bloody Precedent*. N.Y., 1952.
Comparison of the Rosas and Perón regimes.

9495. Dickens, P. D. "Argentine Arbitrations and Mediations with Reference to United States Participation Therein," *HAHR* 11 (1931) 464–484.
Treats the Chaco arbitration of 1867, the Chilean boundary arbitration of 1899, the Misiones Arbitration of 1892–1895, and the A.B.C. mediation of 1914–1915.

9496. Easum, D. B. "The British–Argentine–U.S. Triangle: A Case Study in International Relations," Princeton U. Diss., 1953.

9496a. Ermolaev, V. I., *et al.* (eds.). *Ocherki Istorii Argentiny*. Moscow, 1961.
Essays in Argentine History.

9497. Gandía, E. de. *Historia de la República Argentina en el Siglo XIX*. B.A., 1940.

9498. García Mata, C. *La Economía Algodonera Norteamericana y su Relación con la Situación Argentina*. B.A., 1937.
Discusses the role of cotton in the economic relations of the United States and Argentina.

9499. Haring, C. H. *Argentina and the United States*. Boston, 1941.
Spanish ed., Mexico, 1942.

9500. Kennedy, J. J. *Catholicism, Nationalism, and Democracy in Argentina*. Notre Dame, Ind., 1958.

9501. Kirkpatrick, F. A. *A History of the Argentine Republic*. Cambridge, 1931.

9502. Lafond, G. *Argentine*. Paris, 1948.

9503. Lascano, V. *América y la Política Argentina: Antecedentes Diplomáticos e Históricos*. B.A., 1938.
Emphasizes the period 1802–1923.

9504. Levene, R. *A History of Argentina*. Chapel Hill, N.C., 1937.
Translated by W. S. Robertson; a standard Argentine text.

9505. ———— (ed.). *Historia de la Nación Argentina*. 2d ed., 10 vols., B. A. 1936–1942.

9506. ———— (ed.). *Historia del Derecho Argentino*. 11 vols., B.A., 1945–1958.

9507. ————. *Lecciones de Historia Argentina*. 12th ed., 2 vols., B.A., 1929.

9508. Lewin, B. *De la Colonia a la Emancipación, 1810–1960*. Rosario, Argentina, 1960.

9509. López, V. F. *Historia de la República Argentina*. 10 vols., B.A., 1883–1893.
Reprinted in eight vols., 1957.

9510. Mabragana, H. (comp.). *Los Mensajes: Historia del Desenvolvimiento de la Nación Argentina, Redactada Cronologicamente por sus Gobernantes, 1810–1910*. 6 vols., B.A., n.d.

9511. Macdonald, A. F. *Government of the Argentine Republic*. N.Y., 1942.

9512. Moreno Quintana, L. M. *Política Internacional de la República Argentina*. B.A., 1948.
Survey of Argentine diplomatic history.

9513. Palacio, E. *Historia de la Argentina, 1515–1957*. 3d ed., 2 vols., B.A., 1960.

9514. Pelliza, M. A. *Historia Argentina*. 5 vols., B.A., 1888–1897.

9515. ————. *Historia de Argentina*. B.A., 1910.

9516. Pendle, G. *Argentina*. 3d ed., N.Y., 1963.
In the Latin American series of the Royal Institute of International Affairs.

9516a. Peterson, H. F. *Argentina and the United States, 1810–1960*. N.Y., 1962.

9517. Pinedo, F. *En Tiempo de la República*. 5 vols., B.A., 1946–1948.

9518. Piñero, N. *La Política Internacional Argentina*. B.A., 1924.
Covers independence to date of publication.

9518a. Prellwitz, J. von. "Die Argentinisch-Nordamerikanischen Beziehungen," *ZP* 4, no. 2 (1957) 132–152.
Critical analysis of United States–Argentine relations from 1810 to the present.

9519. Quesada, V. G. *Historia Diplomática Latino-Americana*. 3 vols., B.A., 1918–1920.
Author was minister to the United States, 1885–1892.

9520. Ramos, J. A. *Revolución y Contrarrevolución en la Argentina: Las Masas en Nuestra Historia*. 2d ed., B.A., 1961.

9521. Ramos Mejía, H. G. *Historia de la Nación Argentina*. 2 vols., B.A., 1945.

9522. Ravignani, E. *Historia Constitucional de la República Argentina*. 3 vols., B.A., 1926–1927.

9523. Rennie, Y. F. *The Argentine Republic*. N.Y., 1945.

9523a. Romero, J. L. *A History of Argentine Political Thought*. Stanford, Calif., 1963.
Translated by T. F. McGann.

9524. Rosa, J. M. "La Doctrina de Monroe y su Aplicación en la República Argentina," *RCJS* 9, no. 41 (1944) 5–29.

9525. Ruíz Moreno, I. *Historia de las Relaciones Exteriores Argentinas, 1810–1955*. B.A., 1961.

9526. Ruiz y Ruiz, R. A. *Historia General de la República Argentina*. 4 vols., Santa Fe, Argentina, 1945.

9527. Saldías, A. *Historia de la Confederación Argentina*. 9 vols., B.A., 1946.

9528. Sánchez Viamonte, C. *Historia Institucional de Argentina*. Mexico, 1948.

9529. Scobie, J. R. *Argentina: A City and a Nation*. N.Y., 1964.
An interpretive account with an excellent bibliography.

9530. Sierra, V. D. (ed.). *Historia de la Argentina*. B.A., 1956–
Four volumes completed by 1963; projected for ten volumes.

9531. *Tratados, Convenciones, Protocolos, y Otros Demás Actos Internacionales Vigentes Celebrados por la República Argentina*. 3 vols., B.A., 1901–1905.

9532. Vera y González, E. *Historia de la República Argentina*. 3 vols., B.A., 1926.

9533. Villanueva, C. A. *Historia de la República Argentina*. 2 vols., Paris, 1924.

9534. Whitaker, A. P. *The United States and Argentina*. Cambridge, Mass., 1954.
Spanish ed., B.A., 1956.

9535. White, J. W. *Argentina: The Life Story of a Nation*. N.Y., 1942.

XXIII–A   cross references: 1474

B. THE UNITED STATES AND ARGENTINE INDEPENDENCE

9536. Academia Nacional de la Historia. *Memorias del Almirante Brown: Publicación de la Comisión Nacional de Homenaje al Almirante Guillermo Brown en el Centenario de su Muerte.* B.A., 1957.

Brown was an Irish naval officer who participated in the wars of independence.

9537. Altamira, L. R. *San Martín: Sus Relaciones con Don Bernardino Rivadavia.* B.A., 1950.

9538. *Archivo General de la Nación: Partes Oficiales y Documentos Relativos á la Guerra de la Independencia Argentina.* 4 vols., B.A., 1900–1903.

9539. Barcia Trelles, A. *Antecedentes para Estudiar la Personalidad y la Obra de José de San Martín.* 5 vols., B.A., 1941–1945.

9540. Bealer, L. W. *Los Corsarios de Buenos Aires: Sus Actividades en las Guerras Hispano-Americanas de Independencia, 1815–1821.* B.A., 1937.

9541. Belgrano, M. *La Francia y la Monarquía en la Plata (1818–1820).* B.A., 1933.

9542. Bemis, S. F. *Early Diplomatic Missions from Buenos Aires to the United States, 1811–1824.* Worcester, Mass., 1940.

Concludes that United States assistance was more significant than British aid.

9543. Biedma, J. J. *Los Estados Unidos de América y la Independencia Argentina.* B.A., 1906.

9544. Brackenridge, H. M. *Voyage to Buenos Aires Performed in the Years 1817 and 1818 by Order of the American Government.* London, 1820.

9545. Caillet-Bois, T. "Brown-Cochrane: Un Paralelo," *AHA* (1941) 125–133.

A comparison of the contributions of William Brown and Thomas Cochrane to the independence of Latin America.

9546. Cané, M. *La Diplomacia de la Revolución: El Director Pueyrredón y el Emisario Le Moyne.* B.A., 1960.

Covers the years 1818–1820.

9547. Chandler, C. L. "La Influencia de los Estados Unidos de América en el Río de la Plata, 1799–1802," *RCE* 5 (September, 1917) 133–145.

9548. ———. "The River Plate Voyages, 1798–1800," *AHR* 23 (1918) 816–826.

9549. ———. "United States Merchant Ships in the Río de la Plata (1801–8), as Shown by Early Newspapers," *HAHR* 2 (1919) 26–54.

9550. ———. "United States Shipping in the La Plata Region, 1809–1810," *HAHR* 3 (1920) 159–176.

9551. Craine, E. R. *The United States and the Independence of Buenos Aires.* Hays, Kan., 1961.

9552. Currier, T. S. *Los Corsarios del Río de la Plata.* B.A., 1929.

Treats the influence of privateering on United States–Argentine relations.

9553. *Documentos del Archivo de Pueyrredón.* 4 vols., B.A., 1912.

Primarily letters between Pueyrredón and San Martín.

9554. *Documentos del Archivo de San Martín.* 12 vols., B.A., 1910–1911.

9555. Espil, C. L. de. "Belgrano and Washington: Their Collaboration in Immortality," *BPAU* 78 (1944) 64–69.

9556. Fúrlong, G. "The Influence of Benjamin Franklin in the River Plate Area Before 1810," *TA* 12 (January, 1956) 259–263.

9557. Gianello, L. *José de San Martín.* Santa Fe, Argentina, 1956.

9558. González Puebla, M. "El Origen de la Diplomacia Argentina," *BACH* 12, no. 32 (1945) 29–34.

9559. Keen, B. *David Curtis de Forest and the Revolution of Buenos Aires.* New Haven, Conn., 1947.

De Forest was a U.S. merchant in Buenos Aires at the time of the independence movement.

9560. Kenway, M. M. (ed.). "Correspondence Between General William Winder and President Monroe with Reference to Proposals Made by the United Provinces of South America," *HAHR* 12 (1932) 457–461.

9561. Levene, R. (ed.). *Ensayo Histórico Sobre la Revolución de Mayo y Mariano Moreno.* 2d ed., B.A., 1925.

9562. ———. *El Pensamiento Vivo de Mariano Moreno.* B.A., 1942.

9562a. Loudet, E. "Cesar Auguste Rodney, algo Sobre la Trascendencia de su Misión," *RHIST* 9 (1919) 514–520.

9563. ———. *El Primer Diplomático Norte-*

Americano en la República Argentina.
B.A., 1938.

A biographical sketch of Cesar A. Rodney.

9564. Medrano, S. W. *El Libertador José de San Martín.* B.A., 1950.

9565. Menéndez, J. M. *San Martín: Sus Ideas y su Acción en la Epopeya de la Libertad.* 3 vols., B.A., 1950.

9566. *Message from the President . . . February 2, 1819* (15th Cong., 2d Sess., H. Doc. 48). Wash., 1819.

Report on Argentina and Chile by T. Bland.

9567. Metford, J. C. J. *San Martín, the Liberator.* N.Y., 1950.

9568. Mitre, B. *Historia de Belgrano y de la Independencia Argentina.* 4 vols., B.A., 1858–1859.

9569. ———. *Historia de San Martín y de la Emancipación Sudamericana.* 3 vols., B.A., 1950.

By the President of Argentina. First published 1887–1888; condensed English edition by William Pilling (London, 1893).

9570. Museo Mitre. *Documentos del Archivo de Belgrano.* 7 vols., B.A., 1913–1917.

9571. Otero, J. P. *Historia del Libertador Don José de San Martín.* 4 vols., B.A., 1932.

9572. Palomeque, A. *Orígenes de la Diplomacia Arjentina: Misión Aguirre á Norte América.* 2 vols., B.A., 1905.

Covers the years 1817–1818. Aguirre was allowed to purchase several ships in the United States.

9573. Peterson, H. F. "Mariano Moreno: The Making of an Insurgent," *HAHR* 14 (1934) 450–476.

9574. Piccirilli, R. *Rivadavia y la Diplomacia.* B.A., 1945.

9575. Roberts, C. *Las Invasiones Inglesas del Río de la Plata (1806–1807) y la Influencia Inglesa en la Independencia y Organización de las Provincias del Río de la Plata.* B.A., 1938.

9576. Rojas, R. *San Martín, Knight of the Andes.* N.Y., 1945.

9577. Sarmiento, D. F. *Vida de San Martín.* B.A., 1950.

9577a. Stewart, W. "Activities of Early Argentine Agents in the United States," *SSSQ* 18 (1938) 353–362.

9578. ———. "The Diplomatic Service of John M. Forbes at Buenos Aires," *HAHR* 14 (1934) 202–218.

9579. ———. "Early U.S.–Argentine Diplomatic Relations," U. of Chicago Diss., 1928.

9580. ———. "The South American Commission, 1817–1818," *HAHR* 9 (1929) 31–59.

Describes the mission of Rodney, Graham, and Bland to the La Plata area.

9581. Zorraquín Becú, H. *De Aventurero Yanqui a Cónsul Porteño en los Estados Unidos.* B.A., 1943.

Concerns David C. De Forest, appointed United Province Consul-General in 1818, but not recognized by the United States.

XXIII–B   cross references:

For more general works on the role of the United States in Latin American independence, see items 1805–1896 and 1972–1988.

C. UNITED STATES–ARGENTINE RELATIONS, 1820–1852

9582. Angelis, P. de (ed.). *Archivo Americano y Espíritu de la Prensa del Mundo.* B.A., 1843–1851.

Contains diplomatic correspondence.

9583. Arana, E. *Juan Manuel de Rosas en la Historia Argentina: Creador y Sostén de la Unidad Nacional.* 3 vols., B.A., 1954–1955.

9584. Becker, G. B. "Rosas of Argentina: Patriot and Dictator: An Interpretation in the Light of New Evidence," U. of California Diss., 1942.

9585. Burgin, M. *The Economic Aspects of Argentine Federalism, 1820–1852.* Cambridge, Mass., 1946.

9586. Busaniche, J. L. *Rosas Visto por sus Contemporáneos.* B.A., 1955.

9587. Celesia, E. H. *Rosas: Aportes para su Historia.* B.A., 1954.

9588. Correa Luna, C. *Alvear y la Diplomacia de 1824–1825 en Inglaterra, Estados Unidos y Alto Perú con Canning, Monroe, Quincy Adams, Bolívar, y Sucre.* B.A., 1926.

A series of essays.

9589. Criscenti, J. T. "Argentine Constitutional History, 1810–1852: A Re-examination," *HAHR* 41 (1961) 367–412.

9590. Davis, T. B. *Carlos de Alvear: Man of Revolution.* Durham, N.C., 1955.
First Argentine minister to the United States.

9591. Delle Piane, A. *Rosas.* B.A., 1950.
Very critical of Rosas.

9591a. Dusenberry, W. "Halsey's Claim Against the Government of Buenos Aires, 1818–1859," *IEA* 13 (Spring, 1960) 95–107.

9592. ———. "Juan Manuel de Rosas as Viewed by Contemporary American Diplomats," *HAHR* 41 (1961) 495–514.

9593. ———. "The Service of William A. Harris at Buenos Aires, 1846–1851," *TA* 16 (1960) 251–270.
Harris was U.S. chargé d'affaires in Buenos Aires for the period 1846–1851.

9594. Ferns, H. S. *Britain and Argentina in the Nineteenth Century.* Oxford, 1960.

9595. Forbes, J. M. *Once Años en Buenos Aires, 1820–1831.* B.A., 1956.
Letters from the U.S. commercial agent and subsequently chargé to the secretary of state.

9596. Gallardo, G. *La Caída de Rosas y la Traición de Coe en el Relato de un Testigo.* B.A., 1960(?).

9597. Gálvez, M. *Vida de Don Manuel de Rosas.* B.A., 1963.

9598. Irazusta, J. *Vida Política de Juan Manuel de Rosas a Través de su Correspondencia.* 4 vols., B.A., 1941–1950.

9599. Izquierdo, J. *Juan Manuel de Rosas.* B.A., 1946.

9600. Kroeber, C. B. *The Growth of the Shipping Industry in the Rio de la Plata Region, 1794–1860.* Madison, Wis., 1957.

9601. McGill, M. "Diplomatic Relations Between the U.S. and Argentina, 1830–1860," U. of Texas Diss., 1936.

9602. Piccirilli, R. *Rivadavia y su Tiempo.* 2d ed., 3 vols., B.A., 1960.

9603. Pratt, E. J. "Anglo-American Commercial and Political Rivalry on the Plata, 1820–1830," *HAHR* 11 (1931) 302–335.

9604. Ravignani, E. (ed.). *Correspondencias Generales de la Provincia de Buenos Aires Relativas á Relaciones Exteriores (1820–1824).* B.A., 1921.

9605. Robertson, W. S. "Foreign Estimates of the Argentine Dictator, Juan Manuel de Rosas," *HAHR* 10 (1930) 125–137.

9606. Rodríguez, G. F. *Historia de Alvear.* 2 vols., B.A., 1913.

9607. Saldías, A. *Historia de la Confederación Argentina: Rosas y su Epoca.* 5 vols., B.A., 1892.

9608. Sarmiento, D. F. *Life in the Argentine Republic in the Days of the Tyrants: or Civilization and Barbarism.* N.Y., 1960.

9609. Stewart, W. "Argentina and the Monroe Doctrine, 1824–1828," *HAHR* 10 (1930) 26–32.

9610. ———. "United States–Argentine Commercial Negotiations of 1825," *HAHR* 13 (1933) 367–371.
Argentina was willing to grant the U.S. trading concessions similar to those granted England.

XXIII–C   cross references:

a) For the French and British interventions in the Rio de la Plata (1838–1850), see items 2150–2177.

b) See also items 2344, 9542, 9579, 9841, 9844, 9852.

D. UNITED STATES–ARGENTINE RELATIONS, 1853–1930

9610a. Academia Nacional de la Historia. *Historia Argentina Contemporánea, 1862–1930: Historia de las Presidencias.* 2 vols., B.A., 1963.
Contains a section on foreign relations for each president.

9611. Alberdi, J. B. *Mitre al Desnudo.* B.A., 1961.

9612. ———. *La Vida y los Trabajos Industriales de William Wheelwright en la América del Sud.* Paris, 1876.
Wheelwright was instrumental in the construction of the Argentine Central Railroad between Rosario and Córdoba.

9613. Aldao, C. A. *La Cuestión de Misiones ante el Presidente de los Estados Unidos de América.* N.Y., 1894.

9613a. Alem, L. *Mensaje y Destino.* 8 vols., B.A., 1955.

9614. Arbro, H. "El Cincuentenario del Fallo Arbitral del Presidente Hayes," *RDI* 15 (1929) 5–27.

9615. Argentina. *Documentos Oficiales, Mediación del Encargado de Negocios de los Estados Unidos de América, D. Benjamin Yancey, en la Cuestión de la Integridad Nacional y Proclama del Presidente de la Confederación Arjentina.* Montevideo, 1859.
Treats the attempted U.S. mediation of the Argentine capital controversy. Yancey was the United States minister resident in 1859.

9616. ———. Ministerio de Relaciones Exteriores. *Reciprocidad Comercial: Negociaciones Entre Estados Unidos y la República Argentina.* B.A., 1892.

9617. Bajarlía, J. J. *Mitre.* B.A., 1944.

9618. Baldrich, A. *La Rivalidad de las Potencias Imperialistas en Torno del Petróleo y sus Consecuencias para la Soberanía Argentina.* B.A., 1927.

9619. Barager, J. R. "Sarmiento and the United States," U. of Pennsylvania Diss., 1951.

9620. ———. "Sarmiento y los Estados Unidos," *HIST* 6 (April, 1961) 25–33.

9621. Barrett, R., and K. Barrett. *A Yankee in Patagonia, Edward Chace: His Thirty Years There, 1898–1928.* Cambridge, 1931.

9622. Baudon, H. R. *Urquiza y Mitre: Consolidan la Unidad y la Constitución Nacional.* B.A., 1956.

9623. Bengoa, J. L. *La Vida Gloriosa de Sarmiento.* B.A., 1938.

9624. Bessone, R. *Urquiza, Padre de la Constitución.* Rosario, Argentina, 1951.

9625. Bosch, B. "Urquiza y la Presidencia de Sarmiento," *HUM* 37, no. 2 (1961) 145–169.

9626. Brandt, N. "Don Yo in America: Domingo Faustino Sarmiento's Second Visit to the United States," *TA* 19 (1962) 21–49.

9627. Braun-Menéndez, A. *Mitre y la Cuestión Límites Argentino-Chilena.* B.A., 1957.

9628. Bunge, A. E. *La Economía Argentina.* 2 vols., B.A., 1928.

9629. Bunkley, A. W. *The Life of Sarmiento.* Princeton, N.J., 1952.
The major emphasis is on Sarmiento's literary contributions.

9629a. ———. "Sarmiento and Urquiza," *HAHR* 30 (1950) 176–194.

9630. Carilla, E. *El Embajador Sarmiento: Sarmiento y los Estados Unidos.* Rosario, Argentina, 1961.

9631. *Cartas Confidenciales de Sarmiento a M. R. García (1866–1872).* B.A., 1917.
Some of the letters were written while Sarmiento was in the United States.

9632. Cevedo, E. J. *Enrique B. Moreno: Un Gran Diplomático. Prólogo.* B.A., 1948.

9633. Correas, E. *Sarmiento and the United States.* Gainesville, Fla., 1961.

9634. Davis, H. E. "Hipólito Yrigoyen, 1852–1933: The Argentine Man of Mystery," *WA* 110 (Winter, 1947) 275–282.

9635. Denis, P. *The Argentine Republic: Its Development and Progress.* London, 1922.

9636. DeWitt, P. "The Commercial Relations Between the United States and Argentina," *SPSSQ* 11 (1930) 156–172.

9637. Dodge, J. W. *William Wheelwright, His Life and Work.* Newburyport, Mass, 1898.

9637a. Ferrer, J. "The Armed Forces in Argentine Politics to 1930," U. of New Mexico Diss., 1965.

9638. Gálvez, M. *Vida de Sarmiento, el Hombre de Autoridad.* B.A., 1945.

9639. García Mérou, M. *Apuntes Económicos e Industriales Sobre los Estados Unidos.* B.A., 1905.
Author was Argentine minister to the United States, 1890–1899 and 1901–1904.

9640. ———. *Estudios Americanos.* B.A., 1900.

9641. Giusto, R. F. "Sarmiento y los Estados Unidos," *IRB* 15 (1965) 11–126.

9642. Gollán, J. "Estados Unidos de Norte América Visto con Ojos Argentinos," *PUL*, no. 10 (1941) 7–25.
Primarily Sarmiento's impressions.

9643. González Arrili, B. *Sesenta Años de República: 1852–1912.* B.A., 1945.

9644. Hirst, W. A. *Argentina.* London, 1910.

9645. Hodge, J. E. "Carlos Pellegrini, Argentine Statesman," U. of Illinois Diss., 1963.

9645a. Holdich, T. H. *The Countries of the King's Award.* London, 1904.
Concerns the boundary conflict beween Argentina and Chile.

9645b. Ilisevich, R. D. "American Economic Failures in Argentina During the 1880's," *IEA* 11 (Winter, 1957) 49–60.

9646. Jeffrey, W. H. *Mitre and Argentina.* N.Y., 1952.

Sympathetic biography emphasizing his political career rather than his literary career.

9647. Jeffrey, W. H. *Mitre and Urquiza: A Chapter in the Unification of the Argentine Republic.* Madison, N.J., 1952.

9647a. Johnson, V. L. "Edward A. Hopkins and the Development of Argentine Transportation and Communication," *HAHR* 26 (1946) 19–37.

9648. Kamia, D. *Entre Yrigoyen e Ingenieros: Un Episodio de la Historia Argentina Contemporánea.* B.A., 1957.

9649. Kurtz, R. *La Argentina ante Estados Unidos.* B.A., 1928.
Contrasts the development of the two and analyzes Yankeephobia.

9650. Labougle, R. de. "Mitre y la Política Exterior Argentina," *M* 1 (May, 1960) 115–137.

9651. Leonard, I. "La Visita de Sarmiento a Norteamérica," *UNIV* 2 (April, 1961) 40–53.

9651a. Luiggi, A. H. *65 Valiants.* Gainesville, Fla., 1966.
Concerns U.S. women who went to Argentina to aid the school system.

9652. ——— (ed.). "Some Letters of Sarmiento and Mary Mann, 1863–1876," *HAHR* 32 (1952) 187–211, 347–375.

9653. Luna, F. *Yrigoyen, El Templario de la Libertad.* B.A., 1954.

9654. Manacorda, T. *Além: Un Caudillo: Una Epoca.* B.A., 1941.

9655. Márquez, N. P. *Mitre y la República.* B.A., 1956.

9656. Martínez Estrada, E. "Sarmiento y los Estados Unidos," *CA* 11 (May, 1952) 186–204.

9657. Mayer, J. M. *Alberdi y su Tiempo.* B.A., 1963.

9658. McGann, T. F. "Argentina and the U.S., 1880–1890: The Origins of a Hemispheric Rivalry," Harvard U. Diss., 1952.

9659. ———. *Argentina, the United States, and the Inter-American System, 1880–1914.* Cambridge, Mass., 1957.

9660. *Memorandum du Gouvernement de Buenos Aires sur les Traités Conclus par les Ministres de France, d'Angleterre, et des Etats-Unis avec le Général Justo José de Urquiza Touchant la Libre Navigation des Rivières le Parana et l'Uruguay.* B.A., 1853.

9661. Moreno Quintana, L. M. *La Diplomacia de Yrigoyen: Relación Técnica, Objetiva y Documentada de la Política Internacional Argentina Durante el Período de Gobierno, 1916–1922.* La Plata, 1928.

9662. Murray, L. A. *Pro y Contra de Alberdi.* B.A., 1960.

9663. Ortiz, R. M. *Historia Económica de la Argentina, 1850–1930.* 2 vols., B.A., 1961.
Marxist analysis.

9664. Palcos, A. *Sarmiento: La Vida, la Obra, las Ideas, el Genio.* B.A., 1929.

9665. Pelliza, M. A. *et al. Colección de Tratados Celebrados por la República Argentina con las Naciones Extrangeras.* 3 vols., B.A., 1884.

9666. Pereira Olazabal, R. *Mitre: Vocación y Destino.* B.A., 1955.

9667. Phelps, V. L. *The International Economic Position of Argentina.* Phil., 1938.
Treats United States–Argentine economic relations from 1914 to date of publication.

9668. Quesada, E. *La Epoca de Rosas.* B.A., 1923.

9669. Quesada, V. G. *Recuerdos de Mi Vida Diplomática: Misión en Estados Unidos (1885–1892).* B.A., 1904.

9670. Rippy, J. F. "Yankee Teachers and the Founding of Argentina's Elementary School System," *HAHR* 24 (1944) 166–169.

9671. Rodríguez, C. J. *Irigoyen: Su Revolución Política y Social.* B.A., 1943.
Collection of speeches and writings.

9672. Rohde, J. M. (ed.). *Tratados y Convenciones Vigentes en la Nación Argentina.* 2 vols., B.A., 1925–1926.

9673. Rojas, R. *El Profeta de la Pampa: Vida de Sarmiento.* B.A., 1945.

9674. Rowe, L. S. *The Federal System of the Argentine Republic.* Wash., 1921.
Author was president of the PAU.

9675. Ryan, R. *La Política Internacional y la Presidencia Yrigoyen.* B.A., 1921.

9676. Saavedra Lamas, C. *Por la Paz de las Américas.* B.A., 1937.
Covers 1916–1936.

9677. Sáenz-Hayes, R. *Ramón J. Cárcano en las Letras, el Gobierno y la Diplomacia (1860–1946).* B.A., 1960.

9678. Saenz Peña, R. *Escritos y Discursos*. 3 vols., B.A., 1914–1935.

Author was President of Argentina, 1910–1913, and also the Argentine delegate to a number of international conferences.

9678a. ———. *La Reforma Electoral*. B.A., 1952.

Considers United States' influences on Saenz Peña's electoral reforms.

9679. Sarmiento, D. F. *Obras*. 53 vols., Paris, 1889–1909.

The index to the works was published in Buenos Aires in 1903.

9680. Scobie, J. R. "A Chapter in the Formation of the Argentine Nation, 1860–1865," Harvard U. Diss., 1954.

9681. ———. *La Consolidación de la Nación Argentina, 1852–1862*. B.A., 1964.

9682. ———. "Evocación de la Personalidad de Sarmiento y de sus Visitas a los EE. UU.," *HUM* 37, no. 1 (1961) 289–304.

9683. ———. "Implications of the Argentine Wheat Economy, 1870–1915," *IEA* 14 (Autumn, 1960) 3–18.

9684. ———. "Los Representantes Británicos y Norteamericanos en la Argentina, 1852–1862," *HIST* 6 (April, 1961) 122–166; 6 (July, 1961) 85–128.

9685. ———. *Revolution on the Pampas: A Social History of Argentine Wheat, 1860–1910*. Austin, Texas, 1964.

9686. Sommi, L. V. *Hipólito Irigoyen, su Epoca y su Vida*. B.A., 1947.

9687. Stewart, W., and W. M. French. "The Influence of Horace Mann on the Educational Ideas of Domingo Faustino Sarmiento," *HAHR* 20 (1940) 12–31.

9688. Stimson, F. J. *My United States*. N.Y., 1931.

Contains comments on Stimson's ambassadorship to Argentina.

9689. Tamagno, R. *Sarmiento, los Liberales y el Imperialismo Inglés*. B.A., 1963.

9690. Tristan, L. *Yrigoyen y la Intransigencia Radical*. B.A., 1955.

9691. USCS. *Further Information Concerning Transactions in the Region of La Plata Affecting the Political Relations, etc.* (40th Cong., 1st Sess., S. Ex. Doc. 5, Pt. 2). Wash., 1869.

9692. ———. *Information Concerning Recent Transactions in the La Plata, Affecting the Political Relations of the United States with Paraguay, the Argentine Republic, Uruguay, and Brazil* (40th Cong., 3d Sess., S. Ex. Doc. 5). Wash., 1869.

9693. Walford, A. J. "Economic Aspects of the Argentine War of Secession (1852–1861)," *IEA* 1, no. 2 (1947) 70–96.

9694. Wheelwright, W. *Proposed Railway Route Across the Andes*. London, 1860.

9694a. Willis, B. *A Yanqui in Patagonia*. Stanford, Calif., 1941.

Covers the period 1911–1915. Willis was a consultant to the Argentine government.

9695. Yrigoyen, H. *Mi Vida y mi Doctrina*. B.A., 1957.

9695a. ———. *Pueblo y Gobierno*. 12 vols., B.A., 1956.

Collection of documents. Volumes 7–12 are particularly relevant to international relations.

9696. Yunque, A. *Leandro N. Alem: El Hombre de la Multitud*. B.A., 1953.

9697. Zeballos, E. S. *Argument for the Argentine Republic upon the Question with Brazil in Regard to the Territory of Misiones, Submitted to the Arbitration of the President of the United States, in Accordance with the Treaty of September 7, 1889*. Wash., 1894.

President Cleveland awarded the disputed territory to Brazil.

9698. ———. *International Law of Spanish America: Arbitration on Misiones: Statement Made by the Late Minister of Foreign Affairs of the Argentine Republic . . . to Refute Mistakes of Brazilian Origin and to Enlighten Public Opinion in South and North America*. B.A., 1893.

XXIII–D   cross references:

a) For works treating the Paraguayan war, see items 9232–9247.

b) See also items 2119, 2245, 2621, 2909, 3151, 3162, 3170, 3173a, 3176, 3211, 3236, 3286, 4531, 8610, 9594, 9601, 9803.

E. UNITED STATES–ARGENTINE RELATIONS SINCE 1930

9699. Acossano, B. *Eva Perón: Su Verdadera Vida*. B.A., 1955.

9700. Acuña, J. H., *et al. Argentina, 1930–1960*. B.A., 1961.

9701. Agosti, H. P. "A Crise Argentina," *RBR* 42 (July, 1962) 11–31.
Concerns the overthrow of Frondizi.

9702. Aldazábal, R. V. *Cartas a Presidentes Argentinos: Perón, Lonardi, Aramburu, Frondizi*. Santiago, 1958.

9703. Alexander, R. *The Peron Era*. N.Y., 1951.
Of particular value for the trade union movement.

9704. ———. "Peronism and Argentina's Quest for Leadership in Latin America," *JIA* 9 (1955) 47–55.

9705. Amadeo, M. *Ayer, Hoy, Mañana*. B.A., 1956.
Author was Lonardi's foreign minister (1955).

9706. Argentina. Ministerio de Relaciones Exteriores y Culto. *Política Internacional Argentina: Discursos Pronunciados por . . . Arturo Frondizi y el Señor Ministro de Relaciones Exteriores y Culto*. 2 vols., B.A., 1959.

9707. ———. ———. *Por la Cooperación y la Paz Mundial. 1: Declaración de . . . Juan Perón. 2: Nota a los Gobiernos de América de . . . Juan Atilio Bramuglia. 3: Proyecto de Paz Interior y Exterior, Propuesto a las Naciones de América por la República Argentina*. B.A., 1947.

9708. ———. ———. *La República Argentina ante el "Libro Azul."* B.A., 1946.
Treats the publication of the famous Argentine Blue Book during the ambassadorship of Spruille Braden.

9709. Bagú, S. *Argentina en el Mundo*. Mexico, 1961.

9710. Beals, C. "Argentina vs. The United States," *CH* 50 (July, 1939) 28–31.

9711. Berraz Montyn, C. *Ensayo Sobre el Justicialismo y la Unión Americana*. 2d ed., Santa Fe, Argentina, 1954.
A *Peronista* interpretation of inter-American relations.

9712. Beveraggi-Allende, W. M. "Argentine Foreign Trade Under Exchange Control," Harvard U. Diss., 1952.

9713. Blanksten, G. I. *Peron's Argentina*. Chicago, 1953.
Published prior to Perón's overthrow.

9714. Bledel, R. *La Economía Argentina (1952–*

1963): *Libre Empresa, Capitalismo Popular y Colonialismo: La Dinámica del Retroceso Económico*. B.A., 1963.

9715. Borthen, L. *Reise i Peróns Rike*. Oslo, 1952.
By a Norwegian press attaché.

9715a. Braden, S. "United States Foreign Policy and Argentina," *RRP* (June 1, 1945) 21–24.

9715b. Bravo, G. C. "Argentine–United States Trade, 1939–1950," *CAT* 30 (February, 1951) 21–31.

9716. Brignole, D. *E.U. de Norteamérica Contra la Argentina*. B.A., 1945.

9717. Bruce, J. *Those Perplexing Argentines*. N.Y., 1953.
The author was United States ambassador to Argentina, 1947–1948.

9717a. Bunge, C. A. "La Posición Argentina Frente a la Política Arancelaria Norteamericana," *HE* 17 (November, 1953) 199–211.

9718. Castelli, E. *Segunda Tiranía*. Mendoza, Argentina, 1955.
Concerns the Perón regime. The first tyranny was that of Juan Manuel Rosas.

9719. Chambers, E. J. "Argentina's Post-War Balance of Payments," U. of Nebraska Diss., 1953.

9720. Christensen, A. N. "Political Events and Governmental Changes in Argentina, 1943–1948," *PESP* (1949) 86–107.

9721. Cipolletti, E. D. *Ante los Ojos de América*. B.A., 1947.
Sympathetic account of the *Peronista* movement.

9721a. Ciria, A. *Partidos y Poder en la Argentina Moderna, 1930–1946*. B.A., 1964.

9722. Codovilla, V. *Batir al Nazi-Peronismo para Abrir una Era de Libertad y Progreso*. B.A., 1946.
Program of the Argentine Communist party.

9723. ———. *Trayectoria Histórica del Partido Comunista, Discurso de Apertura: Donde Desembocará la Situación Política Argentina*. B.A., 1946.

9724. Confalonieri, O. D. *Perón Contra Perón*. B.A., 1956.

9725. Conil Paz, A., and G. Ferrari. *Política Exterior Argentina, 1930–1962*. B.A., 1964.

9726. Cooke, J. I. *Acción Diplomática*. B.A., 1947.

Author was minister of foreign relations under President Farrell. Book discusses a wide array of topics, including the Argentine Blue Book controversy.

9727. ———. *Primeras Consideraciones Formuladas por el Ministro de Relaciones Exteriores y Culto de la Argentina, Juan I. Cooke, Sobre el Denominado "Libro Azul," Publicado el 12 de Febrero por la Secretaría de Estado Norteamericana*. B.A., 1946.

English ed., B.A., 1946.

9728. Culbertson, W. S. *Argentine-American Trade Relations*. N.Y., 1937.

9729. Cúneo, D. "La Política Exterior Argentina," *CA* 23 (March, 1964) 7–20.

Covers Frondizi's presidency.

9730. DeWilde, J. C., and B. Wood. "U.S. Trade Ties with Argentina," *FPAR* 17 (1941–1942) 222–233.

9731. Díaz Goitia, J. J. *La Riqueza Petrolífera Argentina en Peligro*. B.A., 1936.

Critical of the foreign oil corporations.

9731a. Dietze, G. "Der Peronismus: Ursachen und Grundzüge Seines Wesens," *ZP* 2, no. 2 (1955) 97–117.

9732. Domínguez, F. *El Apóstol de la Mentira: Juan Perón: Las Palabras y los Hechos de un Tiranía*. B.A., 1956.

9733. Duquenne, L., and P. Biondini. *L'Argentine de Perón*. Bordeaux, 1954.

A sympathetic view.

9734. Editors of *La Prensa*. *Defense of Freedom*. N.Y., 1952.

Treats Perón's suppression of the famous newspaper in 1951.

9735. Elasser, E. C. "Argentine Relations with the Export-Import Bank, 1934–45," *IEA* 8, no. 4 (1955) 87–93.

9736. Estéban, J. C. *Imperialismo y Desarrollo Económico: La Argentina Frente a Nuevas Relaciones de Dependencia*. B.A., 1961.

9736a. Ferrer, A. *The Argentine Economy*. Berkeley, Calif., 1967.

Lack of economic viability viewed within an historical framework.

9737. Fisk, Y. "Argentina: The Thirteen-Year Crisis," *FA* 22 (1944) 256–266.

Covers the period 1930 to 1943.

9738. Fitzgibbon, R. H. "Argentina After Eva Perón," *YR* 42, n.s. (Autumn, 1952) 32–45.

9739. Flores, M. *The Woman with the Whip: Eva Perón*. Garden City, N.Y., 1952.

Pseudonym of Mary Foster Main; anti-*Peronista* view.

9740. Florit, C. A. *Política Exterior Nacional*. B.A., 1960.

Author was minister of foreign relations early in the Frondizi administration.

9741. Frondizi, A. *La Argentina ante los Problemas Mundiales: Definición de una Política Exterior al Servicio de la Nación*. B.A., 1961.

9742. ———. *La Lucha Antiimperialista: Etapa Fundamental del Proceso Democrático en América Latina*. B.A., 1955.

A nationalistic analysis of the Argentine oil position.

9743. ———. *La Política Exterior Argentina: Ordenación y Prólogo de Dardo Cúneo*. B.A., 1962.

Collection of speeches and letters for the period 1958–1962.

9744. ———. *Ni Odio ni Miedo: Reconstruir el País* [*Discursos de Arturo Frondizi y Declaraciones de la Mesa Directiva del Comité Nacional de la Unión Cívica Radical del 17 de Junio de 1955 al 25 de Junio de 1956*]. B.A., 1956.

Collection of speeches made prior to his presidency.

9744a. ———. "President of Argentina Addresses Joint Session of Congress (January 21)," *USDSB* 40 (1959) 280–283.

9745. Frondizi, S. *La Crisis Política Argentina*. B.A., 1946.

9746. Fuchs, J. *La Penetración de los Trusts Yanquis en la Argentina*. 2d ed., B.A., 1959.

9747. Galíndez, B. *Apuntes de Tres Revoluciones: 1930, 1943, 1955*. B.A., 1956.

9748. García Mata, C. "Reflexiones Sobre Nuestras Exportaciones a los Estados Unidos," *REA* 36, no. 232 (1937) 276–280.

9749. Ghioldi, A. A. *El Mito de Eva Duarte*. Montevideo, 1952.

9750. Goldwert, M. "The Argentine Revolution of 1930: The Rise of Modern Militarism and Ultra-Nationalism in Argentina," U. of Texas Diss., 1962.

9751. Gollán, J. S. "Argentine Interregnum," *FA* 35 (1956) 84–94.

Treats the fall of Perón and the Lonardi presidency.

9752. Gondra, L. R. "Buena Vecindad y Buen Comercio," *PEC* 1 (April, 1942) 324–328.

Calls for a larger U.S. market for Argentine exports.

9753. Greenup, R., and L. Greenup. *Revolution Before Breakfast: Argentina, 1941–1946*. Chapel Hill, N.C., 1947.

9754. Griffis, S. *Lying in State*. Garden City, N.Y., 1952.

The author was the United States ambassador in Argentina for a short time during the Perón era.

9754a. Gutiérrez, E. "El Momento Político Interamericano: La Argentina y los Estados Unidos," *Y* (April, 1946) 7–28.

9755. Hechen, S. "La Política Exterior Argentina y el Desarrollo," *FI* 5 (April, 1965) 489–510.

Covers the period 1963 to 1965.

9756. Hernández Arregui, J. J. *La Formación de la Conciencia Nacional, 1930–1960*. B.A., 1960.

9757. Herring, H. "Our Argentine Policies," *FPAHS*, no. 65 (1947).

Summarizes relations from 1933 to 1946.

9757a. ———. "Wanted: An Argentine Policy," *INA* (October, 1946) 12–13, 34–35.

9758. Hoffmann, F. L. "Perón and After," *HAHR* 36 (1956) 510–528; 37 (1959) 212–233.

9759. Holmes, O. "Argentina and the Dream of Southern Union," *PESP* (1949) 43–57.

About union with Bolivia, Uruguay, Chile, and Peru.

9760. ———. "Argentina: Focus of Conflict in the Americas," *FPAR* 21 (1945–1946) 298–309.

9761. ———. "Peron's 'Greater Argentina' and the United States," *FPAR* 24 (December, 1948) 158–171.

9762. Irazusta, J. *Perón y la Crisis Argentina*. B.A., 1956.

9763. Jordan, D. C. "Argentina's Nationalist Movements and the Political Parties (1930–1963): A Study of Conflict," U. of Pennsylvania Diss., 1964.

9764. Josephs, R. *Argentine Diary*. N.Y., 1944.

Journalistic treatment of Argentina in 1943.

9764a. Leddy, J. M. "The United States Market for Argentine Exports," *CPA* (November, 1940) 292–321.

9765. Lerner, A. *El Peronismo y Nuestro Tiempo: Su Doctrina, a la Luz de las Ideas Progresistas del Mundo*. B.A., 1946.

9766. Lewis, I. S. *American Press Opinion of Argentina, 1939–1949*. Wash., 1951.

9767. Luelmo, J. "La Política Internacional de la República Argentina," *MAG* 7 (July, 1945) 211–227.

9768. Malagarriga, C. C. *En Favor del Retorno al Régimen de la Constitución*. B.A., 1945.

A protest against *Peronismo*.

9769. Malerga Pittaluga, A. *Verdad y Mentira de Perón*. B.A., 1955.

9770. Mallan, L. "Argentina: Postwar Threat to the Americas," *VQR* 20 (1944) 12–32.

9771. Manross, L. M. *United States Policy Toward Argentina: A Survey of Past and Present Policy*. Wash., 1947.

Covers 1942–1947.

9772. Marks, R. L. "A View of Argentina Under Perón," *YR* 38, n.s. (1949) 483–506.

9773. Martínez, R. *Grandezas y Miserias de Perón ¿ Debe Volver a Gobernar?* Mexico, 1957.

9774. Mayers, H. W. D. "United States–Argentine Commercial Relations: An Economic Nightmare," *QJIR* 1, no. 3 (1939) 120–132.

9775. Morales Loza, N. *Frondizi y la Verdad*. B.A., 1957.

A collection of Frondizi's writings.

9776. Moreno Quintana, L. M. "La Argentina Trabaja por la Paz Mundial," *AMA* 1 (1947) 177–217.

Analyzes Perón's "third position" in foreign policy.

9776a. Morris, S., Jr. "Argentina—Too Big to Spank," *AQU* (Autumn, 1947) 250–260.

9776b. Mufer, A. F. "Basic Principles in U.S.–Argentine Relations," *USDSB* 34 (1956) 839–840.

9777. Murkland, H. B. "The World Crisis Aids Perón," *CH* 20 (June, 1951) 326–329.

Perón profited from the cold war.

9777a. ———. "What Latin America Policy?" *INA* (May, 1946) 14–16, 33.

Refers to controversy with Argentina in 1946.

9778. Noel, C. M. *Principios y Orientaciones.* B.A., 1939.

By an Argentine congressman. Approximately half of the book is devoted to Argentine foreign policy.

9778a. Nolan, L. C. "Agriculture in the Argentine Trade Agreement," *FAG* (November, 1941) 445–468.

9779. Notta, J. *Crisis y Solución del Comercio Exterior Argentino.* B.A., 1962.

9780. Núñez Arca, P. *Perón: Man of America.* B.A., 1950.

A sympathetic biography.

9781. Olivari, R. E. *El Comercio Exterior Argentino: Reorientación Necesaria.* B.A., 1963.

9781a. Orfila Regnal, A. "Breve Historia y Examen del Peronismo," *CA* 14, no. 6 (1955) 7–37.

Emphasizes relations with the United States.

9782. Ortiz, D. *Eva Perón: La Inmortal.* Quito, 1952.

9783. Owen, F. *Perón: His Rise and Fall.* London, 1957.

9784. Paita, J. A. (ed.). *Argentina, 1930–1960.* B.A., 1961.

9785. Palacios, A. L. *En Defensa de la Libertad.* B.A., 1946.

Critical of the Perón regime.

9786. Pan, L. *Prensa Libre, Pueblo Libre.* B.A., 1950.

9787. Pastor, R. A. *Frente al Totalitarismo Peronista.* B.A., 1959.

Treats the period 1943–1945.

9788. ———. *La Otra Faz de la 2ª Dictadura.* B.A., 1960.

Denounces the Perón regime.

9789. Pattee, R. "The Argentine Question: The War Stage," *RP* 8 (1946) 475–500.

9790. PAU. *Desarrollo Económico y Social de la Argentina.* 2 vols., Wash., 1962.

9791. Peffer, E. L. "Cordell Hull's Argentine Policy and Britain's Meat Supply," *IEA* 10 (Autumn, 1956) 3–21.

9792. Pendle, G. "The Revolution in Argentina," *IAF* 32 (1956) 166–172.

9793. Pepper B., J. V. *I Accuse Braden.* 2d ed., Cd. Trujillo, 1947.

By a Venezuelan journalist.

9794. Perina, E. *Detrás de la Crisis.* B.A., 1960.

By a Brazilian journalist.

9795. Perón, E. *Mi Obra de Ayuda Social.* B.A., 1949.

9796. ———. *La Razón de Mi Vida.* B.A., 1951.

Ghost-written reminiscences of the wife of the dictator. English ed., N.Y., 1953.

9797. ———. *The Writings of Eva Perón.* B.A., 1950.

9798. Perón, J. D. *Doctrina Peronista.* B.A., 1949.

Collection of speeches.

9799. ———. *La Fuerza Es el Derecho de las Bestias: La Realidad de un Año de Tiranía.* Caracas, 1957.

Perón's interpretation of his overthrow.

9800. ———. *Habla Perón.* B.A.(?), 1948.

9801. ———. *El Pueblo Quiere Saber de Qué se Trata: Discursos.* B.A., 1946.

9802. ———. *The Voice of Perón.* B.A., 1950.

9803. Peters, H. E. *The Foreign Debt of the Argentine Republic.* Baltimore, 1934.

9804. Pons Lezica, C. *La Cuestión Internacional Argentina: La Verdad Frente a Sus Arbitrarias Deformaciones.* B.A., 1946.

Treats Argentine foreign policy, 1939–1946.

9805. Potash, R. A. "The Changing Role of the Military in Argentina," *JIAS* 3 (1961) 571–578.

9806. Rabinovitz, B. *Sucedió en la Argentina (1943–1946): Lo Que no se Dijo.* B.A., 1956.

9807. Ramos, J. A. *El Partido Comunista en la Política Argentina: Su Historia y Su Crítica.* B.A., 1962.

9808. Reiner, S. *Eva Perón.* Paris, 1960.

9809. "Representatives, Agents and Distributors for U.S. Companies Active in Argentina," *CAT* 38 (June, 1959) 8–183.

9810. Rodríguez, L. J. "A Comparison: United States Economic Relations with Argentina and Brazil, 1947–1960," Louisiana State U. Diss., 1963.

9811. Sammartino, E. E. *La Verdad Sobre la Situación Argentina.* 2d ed., Montevideo, 1951.

Anti-*Peronista* account.

9812. Setaro, R. "Some Real Trouble in South America: Truth About the Argentine Crisis," *HA* 188 (March, 1944) 377–384.

9813. Shaw, E. B. "Geographic Aspects of United States–Argentine Relations," *JG* 46 (1947) 136–146.

9814. Smith, O. E., Jr. *Yankee Diplomacy: U.S. Intervention in Argentina.* Dallas, 1953.
Criticism of United States–Argentine policy under Roosevelt and Truman.

9815. Solari, J. A. *Doce Años de Oprobio.* B.A., 1956.

9816. ———. *Examen y Responsabilidades de la Situación Argentina.* B.A., 1959.
Covers 1955–1958.

9817. ———. *En el Frente Democrático.* B.A., 1942.

9818. ———. *Socialismo y Demagogia: Etapas de la Crisis Moral y Política Argentina.* B.A., 1946.
Treats the rise of Perón.

9819. Tannenbaum, F. "Argentina, the Recalcitrant American State," *FA* 23 (1945) 271–283.

9820. "The Argentine–United States Exchange of Notes on the Subject of Argentine Foreign Policy," *RRP* (September 10, 1943) 13, 15, 17–18, 20.

9821. United States Tariff Commission. *Economic Controls and Commercial Policy in Argentina.* Wash., 1945.

9821a. USDD. Armed Forces Information and Education Office. "Argentina, Democracy or Dictatorship?" *FCTCW* 2, no. 2 (1962). Wash., 1962.

9821b. USDS. "Argentina Expresses Purpose to Promote International Cooperation: Exchange of Notes Between the Secretary of State (Marshall) and the Argentine Minister for Foreign Affairs and Worship (Bramuglia)," *USDSB* 16 (1947) 337–340.

9822. ———. *Consultation Among the American Republics with Respect to the Argentine Situation: Memorandum of the United States Government.* Wash., 1946.
The Blue Book.

9823. Urrutia, F. de. *Perón.* Madrid, 1946.
A eulogistic treatment.

9824. Valenzuela, R. G. *Para los Argentinos de Mañana: Justicia Social, Libertad, Económica y Soberanía Política.* B.A., 1950.

9825. Varsi, T. *Imperialismo en América, Antecedentes Históricos: La Unión Latinoamericana. Nuestra Sugestión a Favor de Bolivia en 1938.* B.A., 1945.

9826. Washington, S. W. *A Study of the Causes of Hostility Toward the United States in Latin America: Argentina.* Wash., 1957.

9827. Weil, F. J. *Argentine Riddle.* N.Y., 1944.

9828. ———. "Can Perón be Bought?" *IEA* 4 (Autumn, 1950) 27–36.

9829. Whitaker, A. P. *Argentine Upheaval: Peron's Fall and the New Regime.* N.Y., 1956.

9829a. ———. "Blue Book Blues," *CH* 10 (April, 1946) 289–297.

9829b. Woltman, H. R., Jr. "The Decline of Argentina's Agricultural Trade: Problems and Policies, 1929–1954," Stanford U. Diss., 1959.

9830. Zamboni, H. *Peronismo, Justicialismo, Juicio Crítico.* Córdoba, Argentina, 1956.
Denunciation of the Perón regime.

XXIII–E cross references: 3331, 3401, 3409c, 3681, 3683, 3684, 3688, 3694, 3695, 3696, 3698, 4086, 4113, 4848, 4852, 4856, 4861, 5233, 5234, 9037, 9056, 9667, 9676, 9677

F. THE MALVINAS (FALKLAND) ISLANDS DISPUTE

9831. Arce, J. *Las Malvinas: Las Pequeñas Islas que nos Fueron Arrebatadas.* Madrid, 1950.
English ed., Madrid, 1951.

9832. Areco, I. P. *Títulos de la Rep. Arg. a la Soberanía y Posesión de las Islas Malvinas.* B.A., 1885.

9833. Argentina. Cámara de Senadores. *Las Malvinas Han Sido, Son y Serán Argentinas: Publicación Dispuesta por el Honorable Senado el 23 de Junio de 1950.* B.A., 1951.

9834. ———. Ministerio de Relaciones Exteriores. *Papers Relative to the Origin and Present State of the Questions Pending with the United States of America, on the Subject of the Malvinas (Falkland Islands), Laid Before the Legislature of Buenos Ayres by the Government of the Province Charged with the Direction of the Foreign Relations of the Argentine Republic.* B.A., 1832.

9835. Barcia Trelles, C. *El Problema de las Islas Malvinas.* Madrid, 1943.

9836. Beltrán, J. G. *El Zarpazo Inglés a las Islas Malvinas.* B.A., 1934.

9837. Boyson, V. F. *The Falkland Islands.* Oxford, 1924.

9837a. Buenos Aires. Universidad Nacional. Instituto de Historia Argentina "Doctor Emilio Ravignani." *Colección de Documentos Relativos a la Historia de las Islas Malvinas.* B.A., 1957–   .

9838. Caillet-Bois, R. R. *Las Malvinas: Una Tierra Argentina.* 2d ed., B.A., 1952.

9839. Carrasco, R. "Actos y Documentos que Legitiman el Derecho Argentino Sobre las Islas Malvinas," *AAHC* 30 (January, 1948) 23–62.

9840. Comisión Nacional del Antártico. "Soberanía Argentina en las Islas Malvinas," *BMREC* 3 (January, 1948) 141–156.

9841. Corbazzon, A. P. "El Dictador Rosas y las Islas Malvinas," *A* 17 (January, 1943) 49–53.

9842. Corominas, E. V. *Cómo Defendí Malvinas.* B.A., 1950.
    Attempt to settle the dispute at the ninth Inter-American Conference.

9843. Díaz Molano, E., and E. Homet. *Tierras Australes Argentinas: Malvinas, Antártida.* B.A., 1948.
    Traces historical development of the dispute.

9844. Dickens, P. D. "The Falkland Islands Dispute Between the United States and Argentina," *HAHR* (1929) 471–487.

9845. Goebel, J., Jr. *The Struggle for the Falkland Islands: A Study in Legal and Diplomatic History.* New Haven, Conn., 1927.

9846. Groussac, P. *Las Islas Malvinas.* B.A., 1936.

9847. Hadfield, N. *Brazil, the River Plate, and the Falkland Islands.* London, 1854.

9848. Hernández, J. *Las Islas Malvinas: Lo que Escribió Hernández en 1869 Respecto a Este Territorio Argentino y las Noticias que Acerca de su Viaje a las Islas le Comunicó A. Lasserre.* B.A., 1952.

9849. "Islas Malvinas," *RBNA* 3, nos. 5–7 (1938) 141–192, 249–400, 401–624.

9850. "Islas Malvinas y Patagonia," *RBNA* 3, nos. 9–10 (1939) 5–176, 177–394.

9851. Leguizamón Pondal, M. "Derechos de la Argentina a las Islas Malvinas Basados en Autores Ingleses," *BANCC*, no. 39 (1956) 417–431.

9852. Levene, R. *La Política Internacional Argentina en 1833 ante la Invasión de las Islas Malvinas.* B.A., 1949.

9853. Martínez Moreno, R. S. *La Soberanía Argentina en las Islas Malvinas: Con un Apendice Conteniendo: 1. El Pleito Argentino en la IX Conferencia Internacional de Bogotá. 2. Documentación.* Tucumán, 1948.

9854. Molinari, D. L. *Orígenes de la Frontera Austral Argentino-Chilena, Patagonia, Islas Malvinas y Antártida.* B.A., 1961.

9855. Montarcé Lastra, A. *Redención de la Soberanía: Las Malvinas y el Diario de Doña María Sáez de Vernet.* B.A., 1946.

9856. Moreno, J. C. *Nuestras Malvinas y la Antártida.* 4th ed., B.A., 1948.

9857. Palacios, A. L. *Las Islas Malvinas, Archipiélago Argentino.* B.A., 1935.

9858. Pedrero, J. *América, las Malvinas y el Derecho Internacional.* B.A., 1954.

9859. Quesada, H. C. *Las Malvinas Son Argentinas: Recopilación de Antecedentes.* B.A., 1948.

9860. Ramos Giménez, L. *Las Islas Malvinas y la Antártida Argentina: Atlas Documental.* B.A., 1948.

9861. Ratto, H. R. "Hacia una Doctrina Argentina Sobre Malvinas," *BCN* 57 (September, 1938) 327–370.

9862. Sayán de Vidaurre, A. *Para la Inmediata Restitución de las Malvinas.* B.A., 1943.

XXIII–F   cross references: 2168, 4698, 6957

Chapter XXIV   The United States and Brazil

A. UNITED STATES–BRAZILIAN RELATIONS: GENERAL WORKS AND SPECIAL STUDIES

9863. Abranches C., D. de. *Brazil and the Monroe Doctrine*. Rio, 1915.

9864. ———. *Expansão Econômica e Comércio Exterior do Brasil*. Rio, 1915.

9865. "A Política do Brasil com os Estados Unidos," *CP* 3, no. 31 (1943) 77–84.

9866. Accioly, H. "O Reconhecimento da Independência do Brasil, a Doutrina de Monroe e Outros Aspectos do Entendimento Brasileiro-Americano," *MEN* 3 (1938) 441–448.

9866a. Almeida, A. G. de. *Trade Relations Between United States and Brazil*. Boston, 1913.

9867. Arruda Botelho, A. R. de. *Le Brésil et ses Relations Extérieures*. Paris, 1935.

9867a. Azevedo, F. de. *Brazilian Culture: An Introduction to the Study of Culture in Brazil*. N.Y., 1950.
Translated by W. R. Crawford.

9867b. Bailly, L. *Legislação Brasileira Sôbre Atos Internacionais*. Rio, 1940.
Foreign policy legislation covering the years 1889 to 1940.

9867c. Barros, J. de. "A Defesa Coletiva da América," *CP* 1, no. 3 (1941) 11–20.
An overview of Brazilian foreign policy.

9868. Barros, J. do Rêgo. *Do Baronato ao Estado Nôvo: Desfile de Entidades Históricas que Atuaram na Formação da Sociedade Brasileira, Onde Hoje Assenta o Estado Nôvo*. Rio, 1942.

9869. Basbaum, L. *História Sincera da República: Das Origens Até 1889*. Rio, 1957.

9870. Bello, J. M. "Cooperação Brasil–Estados Unidos," *MEN* 7 (1939) 359–366.
Survey relations from the time of independence.

9871. ———. *História da República*. São Paulo, 1959.
The English edition, *A History of Modern Brazil, 1889–1964*, has been translated by J. L. Taylor and brought up to date by R. E. Poppino (Stanford, Calif., 1966).

9872. Beltrán, J. G. *Historia del Brasil*. B.A., 1935.
A leading history in Spanish.

9873. Bittencourt, A. G. R. "Friendship Between Brazil and the United States," *BPAU* 78 (1944) 1–12.
Survey of relations by a Brazilian attaché in Washington.

9874. Bouças, V. F. *História da Vida Externa*. 2d ed., Rio, 1950.

9875. *Brasil–Estados Unidos: Factores de Amizade Entre as Duas Grandes Pátrias Americanas*. Rio, 1939.

9876. Brazil. Instituto Brasileiro de Administração. Divisão de Pesquisas. *Evolução do Ministério das Relações Exteriores*. Rio, 1954.

9877. Brito, J. do Nascimento. *Economia e Finanças do Brasil, 1822–1940*. Rio, 1945.

9877a. Burns, E. B. (ed.). *A Documentary History of Brazil*. N.Y., 1966.
Seventy documents covering the period 1494–1964.

9878. Calmon, P. *Brasil e América: História de uma Política*. 2d ed., Rio, 1944.
Brazilian views toward programs for hemispheric unity.

9879. ———. *História Diplomática do Brasil*. Belo Horizonte, 1941.

9880. ———. *História do Brasil*. Rev. ed., 7 vols., São Paulo(?), 1959–1960.

9881. ———. *História Social do Brasil*. 2 vols., São Paulo, 1937–1939.

9882. Calógeras, J. P. *A History of Brazil*. Chapel Hill, N.C., 1939.
Translated by P. A. Martin.

9883. Camacho, J. A. *Brazil: An Interim Assessment.* 2d ed., London, 1954.
A volume in the Latin American series of the Royal Institute of International Affairs.

9884. Campos, R. A. de. *Legislação Internacional do Brasil.* 2 vols., Rio, 1929.

9885. Carvalho, C. M. Delgado de. *História Diplomática do Brasil.* São Paulo, 1959.
Pertinent documents are appended to the chapters.

9886. *Constituições do Brasil.* Rio, 1948.
Covers period 1824–1946.

9887. Cortesão, J., and P. Calmon. *Brasil.* Barcelona, 1956.
Historical survey from colonial times to date of publication.

9888. *Documentos Históricos.* Rio, 1928–
More than 100 volumes of documentation; irregularly published.

9889. Ermolaev, V. I., *et al.* (eds.). *Ocherki Istorii Brazilii.* Moscow, 1962.
Essays in Brazilian History.

9890. Freyre, G. *Interpretação do Brasil: Aspectos da Formação Social Brasileira como Processo de Amalgamamento de Raças e Culturas.* Rio, 1947.
English ed., N.Y., 1945.

9891. ———. *The Masters and the Slaves.* 2d ed., N.Y., 1956.
Translated by Samuel Putnam. A study in Brazilian social history.

9892. ———. *New World in the Tropics: The Culture of Modern Brazil.* N.Y., 1959.

9893. Furino, K. *Brazilia e no Gohvakiu-nen: Monogatara Brazil Shi.* 2 vols., Tokyo, 1963.
Five Hundred Years to Brazilia: A Romantic History of Brazil.

9894. Furtado, C. *Formação Econômica do Brasil.* 2d ed., Rio, 1959.
Economic survey from colonial times. Spanish ed., Mexico, 1962; English ed., Berkeley, Calif., 1963.

9895. Galanti, R. M. *História do Brasil.* 5 vols., São Paulo, 1910–1913.

9896. Garland, P. G. *American-Brazilian Private International Law.* N.Y., 1959.

9897. Gonsálvez, R. B. *Proceso del Imperialismo del Brasil: De Tordesillas a Roboré.* La Paz, 1960.
A Bolivian diplomat's analysis of Brazil's territorial expansion.

9898. Harris, M. *Town and Country in Brazil.* N.Y., 1956.

9899. Hill, L. F. (ed.). *Brazil.* Berkeley, Calif., 1947.

9900. ———. *Diplomatic Relations Between the United States and Brazil.* Durham, N.C., 1932.

9901. Holanda, S. Buarque de (ed.). *História Geral da Civilização Brasileira.* São Paulo, 1962.

9902. Hunnicutt, B. M. *Brazil, World Frontier.* N.Y., 1949.

9903. James, H. G. *The Constitutional System of Brazil.* Wash., 1923.

9904. Lacombe, A. J. *Brazil: A Brief History.* Rio, 1954.
Translated by W. A. Richardson.

9905. Livermore, H. V. (ed.). *Portugal and Brazil: An Introduction.* Oxford, 1953.

9906. Lôbo, H. *Cousas Americanas e Brasileiras.* Rio, 1923.

9907. ———. *Cousas Diplomáticas.* Rio., 1918.
Part I deals with United States–Brazilian relations, 1822–1916.

9908. Lyra, H. *História Diplomática e Política Internacional: Ensaios.* Rio, 1941.
Survey of Brazilian diplomatic history from 1825 to date of publication.

9909. Magalhães, B. de. *História do Brasil.* Rio, 1942.

9910. Manchester, A. K. *British Preeminence in Brazil: Its Rise and Decline.* Chapel Hill, N.C., 1933.

9911. Maximiliano, C. (ed.). *Comentários à Constituição Brasileira.* 4th ed., 3 vols., Rio, 1948.

9912. Melo, R. Ferreira de. *Textos de Direito Internacional e de História Diplomática.* Rio, 1950.

9913. Mendonça, R. de. *Breve Historia del Brasil.* Madrid, 1950.

9914. ———. *Fronteira em Marcha: Ensaio de Geopolítica Brasileira.* Rio, 1956.

9915. ———. *Historia de la Política Exterior del Brasil.* Mexico, 1945.

9916. Moore, O. K. "The Brazilian Coffee Economy," U. of Florida Diss., 1962.

9917. Normano, J. F. *Brazil: A Study of Economic Types.* Chapel Hill, N.C., 1935.
Develops the thesis that the Brazilian economy follows cyclical patterns.

9918. ———. *Evolução Econômica do Brasil.* São Paulo, 1939.

9919. Oliveira, J. M. Cardoso de. *Atos Diplomáticos do Brasil.* 2 vols., Rio, 1912.
Covers 1493 to 1912.

9920. Peixoto, A. *História do Brasil.* Lisbon, 1940.

9921. Pierson, D. *Negroes in Brazil: A Study of Race Contact at Bahia.* Chicago, 1942.

9922. Pinto, A. Pereira. *Apontamentos para o Direito Internacional, ou Colleção Completa dos Tratados Celebrados Pelo Brasil com Diferentes Nações Estrangeiros: Acompanhada de uma Notícia Histórica e Documentada Sobre as Convenções mais Importantes.* 4 vols., Rio, 1864–1866.

9923. Pombo, J. F. da Rocha. *História do Brasil.* 10 vols., Rio, 1905.

9924. Ramos, A. *The Negro in Brazil.* Wash., 1939.

9925. Rodrigues, J. Honório. "The Foundations of Brazil's Foreign Policy," *IAF* 38 (1962) 324–338.

9926. ———. *A Pesquisa Histórica no Brasil: Sua Evolução e Problemas Atuais.* Rio, 1952.

9927. ———. *Teoria da História do Brasil: Introdução Metodológica.* 2d ed., 2 vols., São Paulo, 1957.

9928. Romero, M. *História da Organização Administrativa da Secretaria de Estado dos Negócios Estrangeiros e das Relações Exteriores, 1808–1951.* Rio, 1951.
A documented history of the Brazilian Ministry of Foreign Affairs.

9929. Schurz, W. L. *Brazil: The Infinite Country.* N.Y., 1961.
An informal general history.

9930. Sensabaugh, L. F. "The Coffee-Trust Question in United States–Brazilian Relations, 1912–1913," *HAHR* 26 (1946) 480–496.

9931. Serrano, J. *Resumen de la Historia del Brasil.* Rio, 1943.

9932. Smith, T. L. *Brazil: People and Institutions.* Rev. ed., Baton Rouge, La., 1954.

9933. ———, and A. Marchant (eds.). *Brazil: Portrait of Half a Continent.* N.Y., 1951.
Essays on history, government, law, and society.

9934. Sodré, N. Werneck. *Formação Histórica do Brasil.* N.p., 1962.

9935. ———. *Introdução à Revolução Brasileira.* Rio, 1958.
A Marxist interpretation.

9936. Tapajós, V. *História do Brasil.* 10th ed., São Paulo, 1960.

9937. Truda, P. de L. *O Brasil e a Doutrina de Monroe.* São Paulo, 1924.

9938. Vasconcelos, M. de Barros. *Motivos de História Diplomática do Brasil.* Rio, 1930.

9939. Vianna, F. J. de Oliveira. *Evolução do Povo Brasileiro.* 3d ed., São Paulo, 1938.

9940. Vianna, H. *História Diplomática do Brasil.* São Paulo, 1958(?).

9941. ———. *História do Brasil.* 2 vols., São Paulo, 1961.

9942. Wagley, C. *An Introduction to Brazil.* N.Y., 1963.
An interpretive account.

9943. Wilgus, A. C. *A Brief Survey of the Political Relations Between Brazil and the U.S.* Boston, n.d.

XXIV–A   cross references:

a) For works on Brazil and the inter-American system, see items 4869–4876.

b) See also items 1235, 1474.

B. THE UNITED STATES AND BRAZILIAN INDEPENDENCE

9944. Accioly, H. *O Reconhecimento da Independência do Brasil.* Rio, 1927.

9945. ———. *O Reconhecimento do Brasil pelos Estados Unidos da América.* São Paulo, 1936.

9946. Agan, J. "Corrêa da Serra," *PMH* 49 (1925) 1–43.
Concerns the minister of Portugal to Washington, 1816–1820.

9947. ———. *The Diplomatic Relations of the United States and Brazil: The Portuguese Court at Rio de Janeiro.* Paris, 1926.

9948. Alden, D. "Yankee Sperm Whalers in Brazilian Waters, and the Decline of the Portuguese Whale Fishery (1773–1801)," *TA* 20 (1952) 267–288.

9949. *Arquivos Diplomáticos da Independência.* 8 vols., Rio, 1922–1925.

9950. Chandler, C. L. "O Brasil e os Estados Unidos de 1774 a 1820," *RIBEU* 1 (September, 1943) 63–77.

9951. ———. "Commercial Relations Between the United States and Brazil, 1798–1812," *RIHGB* 1, special set (1925) 389–414.
The special set is entitled *Congresso*

Internacional de História da América (1922).

9952. ———. "List of United States Vessels in Brazil, 1792–1805," *HAHR* 26 (1946) 599–617.

9953. Freitas, C. de. *George Canning e o Brasil: Influência da Diplomacia Inglêsa na Formação Brasileira.* São Paulo, 1958.

9954. Lima, M. de Oliveira. *Dom João VI no Brasil, 1808–1821.* 2 vols., Rio, 1908.

9955. ———. *História Diplomática do Brasil: Reconhecimento do Império.* 2d ed., Rio, 1902.

9956. ———. *O Movimento da Independencia, 1821–1822.* São Paulo, 1922.

9957. Manchester, A. K. "The Recognition of Brazilian Independence," *HAHR* 31 (1951) 80–96.

9957a. Manning, W. R. "An Early Diplomatic Controversy Between the United States and Brazil," *AJIL* 12 (1918) 291–311; *HAHR* 1 (1918) 123–145.
The controversy was over recognition.

9958. Spalding, W. "Jefferson e o Brasil: Ensaio Histórico en Tôrno das Relações Políticas Entre o Brasil-Colônia e os Estados Unidos Independentes (1786–1789)," *RHIS* 11 (July, 1955) 355–386.

9959. Varnhagen, F. A. de. *História da Independência do Brasil: Até ao Reconhecimento pela Antiga Metrópole, Compreendendo, Separadamente, a dos Sucessos Occorridos em Algumas Províncias Até Essa Data.* 3d ed., São Paulo, 1957.

9960. Whitaker, A. P. "José Silvestre Rebello: The First Diplomatic Representative of Brazil in the United States," *HAHR* 20 (1940) 380–401.

XXIV–B cross references:

For more general works on the role of the United States in Latin American independence, see items 1805–1896, 1972–1988.

C. UNITED STATES–BRAZILIAN RELATIONS, 1824–1889

9961. Adams, J. E. "The Abolition of the Brazilian Slave Trade," *JNH* 10 (1925) 607–637.

9962. Alexander, H. B. "Brazilian and United States Slavery Compared," *JNH* 7 (1922) 349–364.

9963. Armitage, J. *The History of Brazil.* 2 vols., London, 1836.
Portuguese edition, Rio, 1943. Covers the period 1808 to 1831.

9964. Bastos, C. Tavares. "Brasil–Estados Unidos," *MEN* 4 (1938) 115–120.
Letters exchanged between A. C. Tavares Bastos and U.S. Minister James Watson Webb, 1861–1869.

9965. Bell, W. J., Jr. "The Relation of Herndon and Gibbon's Exploration of the Amazon to North American Slavery, 1850–1855," *HAHR* 19 (1943) 494–504.

9966. Besouchet, L. *Mauá e seu Tempo.* São Paulo, 1942.
Treats the Minister of Finance during the reign of Pedro II.

9967. Brown, F. "The Case of the *Canada*: A Chapter of Whaling and Diplomacy," *MHSP* 11 (1953–1957) 179–194.
Treats the incident which resulted in a brief rupture of United States–Brazilian relations in 1856.

9968. Brown, R. *American Emperor: Dom Pedro II of Brazil.* N.Y., 1945.

9969. Calmon, P. *Vida de D. Pedro I: O Rei Cavaleiro.* 3d ed., Porto, 1952.

9969a. Calógeras, J. P. *A Política Exterior do Império.* 3 vols., São Paulo, 1933.

9970. Cardozo, M. S. "Slavery in Brazil as Described by Americans, 1822–1888," *TA* 17 (January, 1961) 241–260.

9971. Carvalho, J. de. *O Marquez de Abrantes e a Diplomácia Brasileira.* Rio, 1935.

9972. Castro Rebello, E. de. *Mauá, Restaurando a Verdade.* Rio, 1932.

9973. Cleven, N. A. N. "James Watson Webb, United States Minister to Brazil, 1861–1869," *RIHGB* 1, special set (1925) 295–394.
This special set is entitled *Congresso Internacional de História da América (1922).*

9973a. ———. "Some Plans for Colonizing Liberated Negro Slaves in Hispanic America," *SPSSQ* 6 (1925) 151–166.

9974. *Correspondência Entre D. Pedro II e o Barão do Rio Branco.* São Paulo, 1957.

9975. Costa, S. Corrêa da. *As Quatro Coroas de D. Pedro I.* 2d ed., Rio, 1942.
Diplomatic history of the reign of Pedro I.

9976. Costa, S. Corrêa da. *Every Inch a King: A Biography of Dom Pedro I, First Emperor of Brazil*. N.Y., 1950.
Translated by Samuel Putnam.

9977. Dozer, D. M. "Matthew Fontaine Maury's Letter of Instruction to William Lewis Herndon," *HAHR* 28 (1948) 212–228.
Treats the naval exploring expedition to the Amazon, 1851–1852.

9978. Dunn, B. S. *Brazil, the Home for Southerners: Or a Practical Account of What the Author and Others ... Saw and Did While in That Empire*. New Orleans, 1866.

9979. Goldman, F. "Norte-Americanos e o 'Eldorado' Paulista no Século XIX," *ANH* 32 (November, 1958) 468–478.
Concerns the Confederate migration to Brazil.

9980. Graham, R. "Mauá and Anglo-Brazilian Diplomacy, 1862–1863," *HAHR* 42 (1962) 199–211.

9981. Guimarães, A. de Segadas Machado. *D. Pedro II nos Estados Unidos: As Reportagens de James O'Kelly e o Diário do Imperador*. Rio, 1961.
Concerns Pedro's visit to the United States in 1876.

9982. Hamilton, C. G. "English-Speaking Travelers in Brazil, 1851–1887," *HAHR* 40 (1960) 533–547.

9983. Haring, C. H. *Empire in Brazil: A New World Experiment with Monarchy*. Cambridge, Mass., 1958.
A political history of the empire.

9984. Harrell, W. A. "Brazil's Search for Government Under the Regents," U. of Florida Diss., 1964.

9985. Harrison, J. P. "Science and Politics: Origins and Objectives of Mid-Nineteenth Century Government Expeditions to Latin America," *HAHR* 35 (1955) 175–202.

9986. Herndon, W. L. *Exploration of the Valley of the Amazon*. N.Y., 1952.
Original publication, Wash., 1854 (L. Gibbon is listed as co-author).

9987. Hill, L. F. "The Abolition of the African Slave Trade to Brazil," *HAHR* 11 (1931) 169–197.

9988. ———. "Confederate Exiles to Brazil," *HAHR* 7 (1927) 192–210.

9989. ———. "The Confederate Exodus to Latin America," *SWQ* 39 (1935) 101–134; 40 (1936) 161–199, 309–326.

9990. "Imigração Norte-Americana para o Brasil," *RIC* 4 (June, 1943) 264–333.

9991. Javari, J. J. Dodsworth (ed.). *Organizações e Programas Ministeriais: Regime Parlamentar no Império*. 2d ed., Rio, 1962.

9992. Kienzl, F. *Kaiser von Brasilien: Herrschaft und Sturz Pedros I. und Pedros II.* Berlin, 1952.

9993. Lima, M. de Oliveira. *O Imperio Brasileiro, 1822–1889*. São Paulo, 1927.
A sympathetic view of the empire.

9994. Manchester, A. K. "The Paradoxical Pedro, First Emperor of Brazil," *HAHR* 12 (1932) 176–197.

9995. Marchant, A. "A New Portrait of Mauá, the Banker: A Man of Business in Nineteenth-Century Brazil," *HAHR* 30 (1950) 411–431.
Emphasizes the 1850's and 1860's.

9996. Martin, P. A. "The Influence of the United States on the Opening of the Amazon to the World's Commerce," *HAHR* 1 (1918) 146–162.

9997. ———. "Slavery and Abolition in Brazil," *HAHR* 13 (1933) 151–196.

9998. Mauá, I. E. de Sousa. *Autobiografia*. Rio, 1943.

9999. Mendonça, R. *Um Diplomata na Côrte de Inglaterra: O Barão do Penedo e sua Epoca*. São Paulo, 1942.
Barão do Penedo also was minister to Washington.

10000. Nabuco, J. *Um Estadista do Império: Nabuco de Araújo, sua Vida, suas Opiniões, sua Epoca*. 3 vols., Rio, 1897–1899.
New ed., 2 vols., Rio, 1936. José Tomas Nabuco de Araújo was a parliamentary leader during the regency.

10001. Nogueira, S. P. *A Mission of Friendship: José Silvestre Rebello in Washington, 1824*. Wash., 1964.

10002. *Pareceres do Conselho de Estado e do Consultor do Ministério dos Negócios Estrangeiros, 1841–1889*. Rio, 1942.

10003. Pereira, N. *O Período Regencial Brasileiro*. Recife, 1939.

10004. Pereira da Silva, J. M. *História da Fundação do Império Brasileiro*. 3 vols., Rio, 1870–1871.

10005. Reinhart, H. K. "A Political History of the Brazilian Regency, 1831–1840," U. of Illinois Diss., 1960.

10006. Sousa, O. Tarquínio de. *Diogo Antônio Feijó, 1784–1842*. Rio, 1942.
Father Feijó was one of the regents in the period 1831–1840.

10007. ———. *A Vida de D. Pedro I*. 2d ed., 3 vols., Rio, 1954.

10008. West, J. R. "The Foreigner in Brazilian Technology, 1808–1900," U. of Chicago Diss., 1950.

10009. Williams, M. W. *Dom Pedro the Magnanimous*. Chapel Hill, N.C., 1937.

10010. ———. "The Treatment of Negro Slaves in the Brazilian Empire: A Comparison with the United States of America," *JNH* 15 (1930) 315–336.

10010a. Woodcock, G. "The Brazilian Empire: An Experiment in Liberal Monarchy," *HT* 6 (1956) 404–413.

XXIV–C cross references:
a) For works treating the Paraguayan war, see items 9232–9247.
b) See also items 9692, 9947.

D. UNITED STATES–BRAZILIAN RELATIONS, 1890–1930

10011. Abranches, C. D. de. *Rio Branco e a Política Exterior do Brasil, 1902–1912*. 2 vols., Rio, 1945.
Covers the period during which Rio Branco was Minister of Foreign Relations.

10012. Amado, G. *Rio Branco*. Rio, 1947.

10013. Amaral, L. Gurgel do. *O Meu Velho Itamarati: De Amanuense a Secretário de Legação, 1905–1913*. Rio, 1947.
Treats the early career of Amaral, later the Ambassador to the United States, 1925–1931.

10013a. Araujo Jorge, A. G. de. *Ensaios de Historia Diplomática do Brazil no Regimen Republicano: I. Serie: 1889–1902*. Rio, 1912.

10014. Baleeiro, A. *Rui, um Estadista no Ministério da Fazenda*. Rio, 1952.

10015. Barbosa, M. de Lima. *Ruy Barbosa*. São Paulo, 1949.

10016. Barbosa, R. *Obras Completas*. Rio, 1951– .
Forty-six volumes were completed through 1956.

10017. ———. *A Questão Social e Política no Brasil*. Rio, 1951.

10018. Barroso, G. *História do Palácio Itamaraty*. Rio, 1956.
This work, in part, is a history of the Ministry of Foreign Affairs.

10019. Bastos, H. *Rui Barbosa: Ministro da Independência Econômica do Brasil*. Rio, 1949.

10020. Bello, J. M. "Política Diplomática e Econômica de Rodrigues Alves," *CP* 1 (May, 1941) 39–51.

10021. Besouchet, L. *José Ma. Paranhos Visconde do Rio Branco: Ensáio Histórico-Biográfico*. Rio, 1945.

10022. Burns, E. B. *The Unwritten Alliance: Rio Branco and Brazilian-American Relations*. N.Y., 1966.
Analysis of diplomatic relations, 1902–1912.

10023. Calógeras, J. P. *Rio Branco e a Política Exterior*. Rio, 1916.
An anecdotal biography.

10024. Carvalho, A. G. de. *Rio Branco*. Rio, 1945.

10025. Correia, O. Moraes. "Rio Branco e a Política Exterior do Brazil," *RIHGB* 187 (April, 1945) 163–172.

10026. Costa, S. Correa da. *A Diplomacia do Marechal: Intervenção Estrangera na Revolta da Armada*. Rio, 1945.
Concerns the naval revolt of 1893.

10027. Culbertson, W. S. "America's New Commercial Policy as Illustrated by Our Commercial Relations with Brazil," *QJE* 38 (1924) 352–357.

10028. Delgado, L. *Rui Barbosa, Tentativa de Compreensão e de Síntese*. São Paulo, 1945.
A sympathetic biographical treatment.

10029. Eça, R. d'. "Joaquim Nabuco nos Estados Unidos," *RIBEU* 7 (July, 1949) 43–61.
Nabuco was the ambassador to the United States, 1905–1910. For his own works, see item 10064.

10030. Elliott, L. E. *Brazil Today and Tomorrow*. N.Y., 1917.

10031. Fleiuss, M. *Rio Branco*. Rio, 1931.
A sympathetic biography.

10032. Fonseca Filho, H. da. *Pinheiro Machado: Uma Individualidade e Uma Epoca*. Rio, 1939.

10033. Funke, A. *Brasilien im 20-ten Jahrhundert*. Berlin, 1926.
Treats the German colonization.

10034. Gabáglia, L. Pessoa Raja. *Epitácio Pessoa, 1865–1942.* 2 vols., Rio, 1951.
President of Brazil, 1919–1922.

10035. Ganzert, F. W. "The Baron do Rio-Branco and Brazilian Foreign Relations," U. of California Diss., 1933.

10036. ———. "The Baron do Rio Branco, Joaquim Nabuco and the Growth of Brazilian-American Friendship, 1900–1910," *HAHR* 22 (1942) 432–451.

10037. Gauld, C. A. *The Last Titan, Percival Farquhar, American Entrepreneur in Latin America.* Stanford, Calif., 1964.
The life of a U.S. engineer in Latin America.

10038. Gonçalves, S. *A Aguia de Haia: Biografia de Rui Barbosa.* Rio, 1947.

10039. Graham, R. B. C. *A Brazilian Mystic: The Life and Miracles of Antonio Conselheiro.* London, 1920.
The leader of the Canudos revolt.

10040. Griscom, L. C. *Diplomatically Speaking.* Boston, 1940.

10041. Hilton, R. *Joaquim Nabuco e a Civilização Anglo-Americana.* Rio, 1949.

10042. ———. "Joaquim Nabuco e os Estados Unidos," *RIBEU* 7 (July, 1949) 26–43.

10043. Hutchinson, L. "Reciprocity with Brazil," *PSQ* 18 (1903) 282–312.

10044. James, H. G. *Brazil After a Century of Independence.* N.Y., 1925.

10045. Jorge, A. G. de Araújo. *Ensaios de História Diplomática do Brasil no Regímen Republicano, 1889–1902.* Rio, 1912.

10046. Kerbey, J. O. *An American Consul in Amazônia.* N.Y., 1911.
Concerns the consul at Pará, 1890–1891.

10047. Kravigny, F. W. *The Jungle Route.* N.Y., 1940.
By a U.S. engineer who worked on the Madeira–Mamore railroad.

10048. Lacerda, V. C. de (ed.). *Rui Barbosa: Escritos e Discursos Seletos em um Volumen.* Rio, 1960.

10049. ———, and R. Monteiro Real. *Rui Barbosa em Haia: Cinqüentenário da Segunda Conferência da Paz, 1907–1957.* Rio, 1957.

10050. Lacombe, A. J. *Rio Branco y Rui Barbosa.* Rio, 1955.
Spanish edition translated by J. Alarcón Fernández.

10051. LaFeber, W. "United States Depression Diplomacy and the Brazilian Revolution, 1893–1894," *HAHR* 40 (1960) 107–118.

10052. Lima, M. de Oliveira. *Nos Estados Unidos.* Leipzig, 1899.

10053. ———. *The Relations of Brazil with the United States.* N.Y., 1913.
International Conciliation Pamphlet No. 69.

10054. Lins, A. *Rio Branco (Barão de Rio Branco), 1845–1912.* 2 vols., Rio, 1945.
A balanced biography.

10055. Lôbo, H. *Brasilianos y Yankees.* Rio, 1926.

10056. ———. "As Relações Entre os Estados Unidos e o Brasil," *RAM* 7 (November, 1917) 79–102.

10057. Lopes, M. B. *Rui Barbosa e a Marinha.* Rio, 1953.

10057a. Lorin, H. "La Politique Américaine du Brésil," *QDC* 33 (1912) 95–105.

10058. Lyra Filho, J. *O Barão.* Rio, 1936.

10059. Mangabeira, J. *Rui, O Estadista da República.* Rio, 1943.
Sympathetic to Rui Barbosa.

10060. McCloskey, M. B. "The United States and the Brazilian Naval Revolt, 1893–1894," *TA* (January, 1946) 296–321.
Concludes that the United States intervention helped to assure the victory of the government forces.

10061. Melby, J. "Rubber River: An Account of the Rise and Collapse of the Amazon Boom," *HAHR* 22 (1942) 452–469.

10062. Mendonça, S. de. *A Situação Internacional do Brasil.* Rio, 1913(?).
The author was the Brazilian minister to the United States, 1891–1898. He is critical of Rio Branco.

10063. Nabuco, C. *A Vida de Joaquim Nabuco.* Rio, 1958.
English ed., Stanford Calif., 1950. A biography by Nabuco's daughter. Considerable emphasis on the ambassadorship to Washington.

10064. Nabuco, J. *Obras Completas.* São Paulo, 1947– .
Fourteen volumes through 1949.

10065. Napoleão, A. *Rio Branco e as Relações Entre o Brasil e os Estados Unidos.* Rio, 1947.

10066. Nash, R. *The Conquest of Brazil*. N.Y., 1926.

10067. Neves, J. *Rui Barbosa, Orador*. Rio, 1960.

10068. Nogueira, R. *História de Ruy Barbosa*. Salvador, 1954.

10069. O. N. B. *Brasil e Estados Unidos da América*. Rio, 1930.
Written by Otávio Nascimento Brito.

10070. Peixoto, S. *A Tormenta que Prudente de Moraes Venceu!* Curitiba, 1942.

10071. Pires, H. *Anglo-American Political Influences on Rui Barbosa*. Rio, 1949.

10072. Prado, E. *A Ilusão Americana*. 2d ed., Paris, 1895.
Spanish ed., Madrid, 1918 (?).

10073. Rêgo, A. M. *Nabuco*. Rio, 1951.

10074. Rio Branco, Barão de. *Brazil, the United States, and the Monroe Doctrine*. Rio, 1906.
A sympathetic evaluation not shared by most Latin American diplomats of the period.

10075. ———. *Obras*. 9 vols., Rio, 1945–1948.

10076. ———. *Relações Exteriores do Brazil Durante a Administração do Presidente Rodriguez Alves*. Rio, 1906.

10077. Rippy, J. F. "The United States and the Establishment of the Republic of Brazil," *SPSQ* 3 (1922) 39–53.

10078. Sandberg, H. O. "Mission of Dr. Lauro S. Müller to the United States," *BPAU* 37 (July, 1913) 1–31.
The Brazilian foreign minister visited the United States in 1913.

10078a. Sensabaugh, L. F. "The Coffee-Trust Question in United States–Brazilian Relations: 1912–1913," *HAHR* 26 (1946) 480–496.

10079. Silveira, A. B. da. *Barão do Rio Branco*. Rio, 1956.

10080. Soares, A. Teixeira. "O Barão do Rio Branco e a Diplomacia Brasileira," *RIHGB* 187 (April, 1945) 175–185.

10081. Soares, J. C. de Macedo. *Discursos: Rumos da Diplomacia Brasileira*. Rio, 1937.
Speeches of the foreign minister.

10082. Taunay, A. de E. *No Brasil República, 1906–1927*. 3 vols., Rio, 1941.

10083. Timm, C. A. "The Diplomatic Relations Between the United States and Brazil During the Naval Revolt of 1893," *SPSQ* 55 (1924) 119–137.

10084. Turner, C. W. *Ruy Barbosa: Brazilian Crusader for the Essential Freedoms*. Nashville, 1945.

10085. Vasconcelos, M. de Barros e. *O Barão do Rio Branco: Biografia*. Rio, 1954.

10086. Veiga, V. da. "A Missão Oswaldo Aranha e as Relações Comerciais Entre os Estados Unidos e o Brasil, do Princípio do Século Até Hoje," *MEN* 5 (1939) 281–284.

10087. Viana Filho, L. *A Vida de Rui Barbosa*. São Paulo, 1949.

10088. ———. *A Vida do Barão do Rio Branco*. Rio, 1959.
A balanced scholarly study.

XXIV–D cross references: *2909, 3143, 3146, 3149, 3150, 3163, 3229, 4672, 4675, 4871, 9697, 9698*

E. UNITED STATES–BRAZILIAN RELATIONS SINCE 1930

10089. Accioly, H. *Actos Internacionais Vigentes no Brasil*. 2 vols., Rio, 1936–1937.

10090. Acheson, D. G. "A Review of U.S.–Brazilian Relations," *USDSB* 27 (July, 1952) 47–51.

10091. Alexander, R. J. "Brazilian 'Tenentismo,'" *HAHR* 36 (1956) 229–242.

10092. Alvares, D. *Culpados sem Culpa*. Rio, 1947.
Treats terrorism under Getúlio Vargas.

10093. Amado, J. *O Cavalheiro da Esperança: Vida de Luiz Carlos Prestes*. 10th ed., Rio, 1956.
Biography of the leader of the Brazilian Communists. Spanish ed., B.A., 1942.

10094. Amaral, A. J. Azevedo. *Getúlio Vargas, Estadista*. Rio, 1941.
A sympathetic biography.

10094a. Amaral, I. M. Azevedo do. *Ensaio Sôbre a Revolução Brasileira: Contribuição para o Estudo dos Problemas da Brasilidade, 1931–1934*. Rio, 1963.

10094b. Amaral, L. G. do. *Cousas Idas e Vividas: Lembranças Intimas e da Carreira Diplomática*. Rio, 1959.

10095. Andrade, T. de. "O Brasil no Comércio dos Estados Unidos com a América Latina," *DNC* 7 (July, 1939) 689–693.

10096. Aranha, O. "The Commercial Relations Between the United States and Brazil," *BR* (February, 1936) 6–10.

10096a. Aranha, O. "Relações Diplomáticas com a União Soviética," *RBPI* 1 (June, 1958) 18–28.

10097. ———. *A Revolução e a América, o Presidente Getúlio Vargas e a Diplomacia (1930–1940): Discurso a Conferência Realizados no Palácio Tiradentes, no Dia 23 de Dezembro de 1940.* Rio, 1941.

10098. "Arrendamento de Contra-Torpedeiros Norte-Americanos," *RMB* 57 (1937) 233–250, 421–430.
Concerns leasing of U.S. destroyers to Brazil.

10099. Barbêdo, A. *O Fechamento do Partido Comunista do Brasil.* Rio, 1947.
About the outlawing of Brazil's Communist party.

10100. Barros, J. de. "A Política do Brasil na América," *CP* 1 (March, 1941) 34–41.

10101. ———. *A Política Exterior do Brasil (1930–1942).* 2d ed., Rio, 1943.

10102. ———. *Sete Anos de Política Exterior do Brasil: (Aspectos Principais), 1930–1937.* Rio, 1938.
Official account of foreign relations under Vargas.

10103. Bastos, H. *A Crise Comercial: Aspectos da Conjuntura do Comércio Exterior.* São Paulo, 1953.

10104. Bastos, R. *Getúlio Vargas o Reformador.* Rio, 1939.

10104a. Beals, C. "Cash for Brazil's Good-Will: The United States, with Hand Deep in Pocket, Leads the Race There for Trade and Influence," *CH* 50 (April, 1939) 37–39, 64.

10105. Bopp, R. *Notas de um Caderno Sôbre o Itamarati.* Rio, 1956.
Treats organizational problems of the Brazilian foreign office.

10106. Brandis, R. "Cotton Competition, U.S. and Brazil, 1929–1948," *JFE* 34 (1952) 67–82.

10107. Brasil. Embaixada. Presidência. Serviço de Documentação. *Resenha do Govêrno do Presidente Juscelino Kubitschek, 1956–1961.* 3 vols., Rio, 1960.

10108. ———. ———. *President Jânio Quadros' Message to the Congress of Brazil Covering Foreign Relations, March 15, 1961.* Wash., 1961.

10108a. ———. Ministério das Relações Ex- teriores. *Coleção de Atos Internacionais.* Rio, 1927– .
A treaty series.

10108b. Cabot, J. M. "The Growing Importance of U.S.–Brazil Cooperation," *USDSB* 41 (1959) 753–757.

10109. Caó, J. *Dutra: O Presidente e a Restauração Democrática.* São Paulo, 1949.

10110. Carrazzoni, A. *Getúlio Vargas.* Rio, 1939.

10111. Carvalho, A. G. de. *Raul Fernandes: Um Servidor do Brasil.* Rio, 1956.
A sympathetic biography of the minister of foreign relations and statesman under Dutra and Vargas.

10112. Carvalho, L. A. *As Realizações do Govêrno Getúlio Vargas no Campo do Direito.* Rio, 1942.

10113. Carvalho, N. R. *Operação Brasil, Ensaio Panamericano.* Belo Horizonte, 1959.

10114. Chaves, E. "A Visita do Presidente Eisenhower," *RBR* (March, 1960) 1–10.

10114a. "Comércio Brasil–Estados Unidos," *OEF* 14 (June, 1949) 7–10.
Covers 1911–1948.

10115. Cooke, M. L. *Brazil on the March: A Study in International Cooperation.* N.Y., 1944.
Author was the head of a U.S. technical mission to Brazil in 1942.

10115a. Costa, V. R. da. "O Comércio Brasil–Estados Unidos e a Conquista de Novos Mercados," *RSPU* 84 (September, 1959) 259–302.

10116. Cottam, H. R. *Point 4 in Brazil: Address Delivered Before the School of Economic and Administrative Science of the University of São Paulo at São Paulo, Brazil, on August 29, 1958.* Wash., 1959.

10117. Dale, W. B. *Brazil: Factors Affecting Foreign Investment.* Menlo Park, Calif., 1958.

10118. Dantas, M. *A Fôrça Nacionalizadora do Estado Nôvo.* Rio, 1942.
Apology for the Vargas regime.

10119. Diffie, B. W. "Some Foreign Influences in Contemporary Brazilian Politics," *HAHR* 20 (1940) 402–429.

10120. Dulles, John W. *Vargas of Brazil: a Political Biography.* Austin, Texas, 1967.

10120a. Efimov, A. V., *et al.* (eds.). *Braziliia.* Moscow, 1963.
Brasilia. Deals in part with Soviet-Brazilian relations.

10121. Fleury, J. G. *Getúlio Vargas, Président des Etats-Unis du Brésil*. Paris, 1939.
A sympathetic biography.

10122. Fonseca, G. da. *Assim Falou Julião*. São Paulo, 1962.
Speeches of the radical peasant organizer of the northeast drought area.

10123. Freyre, G. "Misconceptions of Brazil," *FA* 40 (1962) 453–462.

10124. Frischauer, P. *Presidente Vargas*. São Paulo, 1943.
A favorable biography.

10125. Galvão, F. *Diretrizes do Estado Nôvo*. Rio, 1942.

10126. Garrido Torres, J., and D. Nogueira. *Joint International Business Ventures in Brasil*. N.Y., 1959.

10127. Gentil, A. *As Idéias do Presidente Getúlio Vargas*. Rio, 1939.

10128. Giffin, D. W. "The Normal Years: Brazilian-American Relations, 1930–1939," Vanderbilt U. Diss., 1962.

10129. Glinkin, A. N. *Noveishaia Istoriia Brazilii (1939–1959)*. Moscow, 1961.
Contemporary History of Brazil (1939–1959).

10130. Godfrey, E. E. "The Influence of Economic Factors on U.S.–Brazilian Relations, 1940–1960," U. of Kentucky Diss., 1960.

10131. Gordon, L. "Relações dos Estados Unidos com a América Latina, Especialmente o Brasil," *RBPI* 4 (September, 1961) 13–30.
The author was United States ambassador to Brazil and subsequently assistant secretary of state for inter-American affairs.

10132. ———, and E. L. Grommers. *United States Manufacturing Investment in Brazil: The Impact of Brazilian Government Policies, 1946–1960*. Boston, 1962.

10133. Gouveia, O. *Que é o Estado Nôvo*. Rio, 1938.

10134. Haas, W. *Os Investimentos Estrangeiros no Brasil: Realização e Coordenação Desta Obra de Jean Bernet e Roland A. Bossart*. Rio, 1959.

10135. Haddad, J. A. *Revolução Cubana e Revolução Brasileira*. Rio, 1961.

10136. Haman, H. "Problemas Econômicos de Após-Guerra," *BMTIC* 11 (March, 1945) 163–190.

10137. Hanblock, E. "The New Régime in Brazil," *FA* 16 (1938) 484–493.
Concerns the Vargas regime.

10138. Hanson, S. G. "Brazilian-American Relations: Case Study in American Foreign Policy," *IEA* 4 (Spring, 1952) 3–35.

10139. Haring, C. H. "Vargas Returns in Brazil," *FA* 29 (1951) 308–314.

10140. Heare, G. E. *Brazil: Information for United States Businessmen*. Wash., 1961.

10141. Hechen, S. *Proyección Internacional de Brasil*. Santa Fe, Argentina, 1964.

10142. Henriques, A. *Vargas, O Maquiavélico*. São Paulo, 1961.

10143. Herring, H. "Brazil," *YR* 36 (1947) 304–319.
Concerns United States relations with Vargas.

10144. Hickey, J. "The Limits of Foreign Aid: Responsibility Without Authority: The Brazilian Drought," *IEA* 13 (Autumn, 1959) 3–19.

10145. Holmes, O. "Brazil: Rising Power in the Americas," *FPAR* 21, no. 15 (1945) 210–219.
Treats the period prior to the election of Dutra.

10146. Horowitz, I. L. *Revolution in Brazil: Politics and Society in a Developing Nation*. N.Y., 1964.
Concentrates on the Goulart period.

10146a. "How U.S. Industry Cooperates with Brasil," *BB* 39 (August, 1959) 20–33, 40–41.

10147. International Telephone and Telegraph Corporation. *The Expropriation of I.T.T. in Rio Grande do Sul, Brazil: A Threat to the Alliance for Progress*. N.Y., 1962.

10148. Jobim, D. *A Experiência Roosevelt e a Revolução Brasileira*. Rio, 1940.

10149. Johnson, J. J. "Potential in Brazil," *CH* 46 (January, 1964) 1–7.

10150. Joint Brazil–United States Economic Development Commission. *The Development of Brazil: Report*. Wash., 1954.

10151. Klinghoffer, H. *La Pensée Politique du Président Getúlio Vargas*. Rio, 1942.

10152. Kubitschek, J. *Discursos, 1957*. Rio, 1958.

10153. ———. *A Marcha do Amanhecer*. São Paulo, 1962.

10154. ———. *Three Years of Administration: President Juscelino Kubitschek de Oli-*

veira Speaks to the Brazilian People, on the Third Anniversary of His Government. Rio, 1959.

10155. Kuznets, S., *et al.* (eds.). *Economic Growth: Brazil, India, Japan.* Durham, N.C., 1955.

10156. Lakas, I. A. "The Effects of Brazil's Foreign Exchange Policy on the Value of Her Exports and on the Flow of Private Foreign Investment with Respect to Brazil's Economic Development: 1946–1960," Harvard U. Diss., 1962.

10157. Lima, C. de Araújo. *Mito e Realidade de Vargas.* Rio, 1955.

10158. Linhares, H. "O Comunismo no Brasil," *RBR* 25 (September, 1959) 146–166.

10159. Loeb, G. F. *Industrialization and Balanced Growth with Special Reference to Brazil.* Groningen, 1957.

10160. Loewenstein, K. *Brazil Under Vargas.* N.Y., 1942.

10161. Magalhães, J. P. de Almeida. *Controvérsia Brasileira Sôbre o Desenvolvimento Econômico.* Rio, 1961.

10162. ———. *Desenvolvimento Econômico.* Rio, 1962.

10163. Maia, J. "O Brasil e o Início da Política de 'Boa Vizinhança,'" *CP* 1 (April, 1941) 79–86.

10164. ———. *Um Decenio de Política Externa.* Rio, 1942.

10165. Marini, R. M. "Contradicciones y Conflictos en el Brasil Contemporáneo," *FI* 5 (1965) 511–546.
    Covers the 1950's and 1960's.

10166. Marshall, A. "Brazil: The Reawakening of the Giant," *WT* 17 (August, 1961) 336–344.

10167. McMillan, C., Jr., and R. González. *International Enterprise in a Developing Economy: A Study of U.S. Business in Brazil.* East Lansing, Mich., 1964.

10168. Montalvo, R. J. *Getúlio Vargas y la Unidad Brasileña.* B.A., 1939.

10169. Morel, E. *O Golpe Começou em Washington.* Rio, 1965.

10170. Moura, A. *Capitais Estrangeiros no Brasil.* 2d ed., São Paulo, 1960.

10171. Moura, P. Rolim de. *O Líder da América Latina.* São Paulo, 1960.
    A sympathetic treatment of Jânio Quadros.

10172. Mourão, M. M. *Dutra, História de um Govêrno.* Rio, 1955.
    Covers the period 1946–1951.

10172a. Nattier, F. E. Jr. "The United States Market for Brazilian Exports," *CPA* (February, 1941) 20–88.

10173. Neto, F. A. Gomes. *Da Luta Pela Autodeterminação.* São Paulo, 1962.
    Series of newspaper articles covering the years 1944–1948.

10174. Neto, M. *Brasil, Guerra-Quente na América Latina.* Rio, 1965.

10175. Oliveira, F. de. *Revolução e Contra-Revolução no Brasil.* Rio, 1962.
    Treats the Janio Quadros administration and the Punta del Este Conference.

10176. Onody, O. "Relações Comerciais do Brasil com o Bloco Soviético," *RBPI* 3 (1960) 38–74.

10177. Passos, G. de Rezende. *Nacionalismo.* São Paulo, 1959.

10178. Patric, A. *Toward the Winning Goal.* Rio, 1940.
    Treats Brazil during the Vargas period.

10179. Peixoto, A. Vargas do Amaral. *Getúlio Vargas, Meu Pai.* Rio, 1960.

10180. Peterson, P. J. "Brazilian Political Parties, Formation, Organization and Leadership, 1945–1959," U. of Michigan Diss., 1962.

10180a. Phillips, H. A. *Brazil: Bulwark of Inter-American Relations.* N.Y., 1945.

10181. Pimpão, H. *Getúlio Vargas e o Direito Social Trabalhista.* Rio, 1942.

10182. Pincus, J. "The Foreign Economic Policies of Brazil Since 1939," American U. Diss., 1953.

10183. Pinto, L. B. "A Política Exterior do Brasil na América Latina," *RBPI* 2 (December, 1959) 51–64.

10184. Pontes Sette, A. *A Verdade Sôbre a Deposição de Getúlio Vargas.* Juiz de Fora, 1947.

10185. Quadros, J. "Brazil's New Foreign Policy," *FA* 40 (1960) 19–27.

10186. Robock, S. H. *Brazil's Developing Northeast: A Study of Regional Planning and Foreign Aid.* Wash., 1963.

10187. Rocha, G. *País Espoliado.* Rio, 1949.

10188. Rocha Diniz, O. da. *O Brasil em Face dos Imperialismos Modernos.* São Paulo, 1940.
    Brazil is viewed as a victim of economic imperialism.

10189. Rodrigues, J. H. "The Foundations of Brazil's Foreign Policy," *IAF* 38 (July, 1962) 324–339.

10190. Sampaio, S. "Brasil–Estados Unidos: Duas Nações Irmãs," *RABL* 45 (May, 1943) 5–29.

10190a. San Tiago Dantas, F. C. *Política Externa Independente*. Rio, 1962.

Author was minister of foreign relations, 1961–1962.

10191. Sharp, W. R. "Brazil 1940—Whither the 'New State,'" *IAQ* 2 (October, 1940) 5–17.

10192. Sivolobov, A. M. *Agrarnye Otnosheniia v Sovremennoi Brazillii*. Moscow, 1959.

The Agrarian Situation in Contemporary Brazil.

10193. Souza, A. de. *O Brasil e a 3ª Guerra Mundial*. Rio, 1959.

10194. Storm, W. B., and B. G. Markey. *Technical Assistance in Public Administration. The Domestic Role. II: A Report on the Brazilian Program*. Los Angeles, 1959.

10195. Tavares de Sá, H. "Brasil em California," *TA* 2 (September, 1950) 22–23, 46.

Reports on a Stanford conference on Brazil.

10195a. Thomas, E. "The Reciprocal Trade Agreement Between Brazil and the United States," *BR* (December, 1935) 6–9.

10196. Thorning, J. P. "Brazilian-American Friendship: A Prize in Jeopardy," *WA* 113 (Winter, 1950) 106–108.

10197. USCS. Committee on Foreign Relations. *Brazil and U.S. Policies: Report*. Wash., 1962.

By Senator Mike Mansfield.

10198. "United States Cooperation in Meeting Brazilian Economic and Material Requirements," *BPAU* 25 (1951) 654–655.

10198a. "U.S.–Brazil Trade in Review," *CECO* 2 (March, 1955) 27–31.

10198b. USDD. Armed Forces Information and Education Office. "Brazil: Latin American Giant," *FCTCW* 1, no. 8 (1961).

10199. USDS. *Report of the Joint Brazil–United States Technical Commission*. Wash., 1949.

10200. Vargas, G. *A Nova Política do Brasil*. 7 vols., Rio, 1940.

A collection of speeches and writings.

10201. Wagley, C. "Brazil: Crisis and Change," *FPAHS*, no. 167 (1964).

10202. Washington, S. W. *A Study of the Causes of Hostility Toward the United States in Latin America: Brasil*. Wash., 1956.

10203. Wharton, C. R., Jr. "A Case Study of the Economic Impact of Technical Assistance: Capital and Technology in the Agricultural Development of Minas Gerais, Brazil," U. of Chicago Diss., 1959.

10204. Wrzos, C. *Juscelino Kubitschek: Estados Unidos–Europa: Diário da Viagem*. Rio, 1960.

10204a. Wylie, K. H. "What the Future Holds for U.S. Farm Markets in Brazil," *FAG* 20 (September, 1956) 6–7, 20.

10205. Wythe, G., *et al. Brazil: An Expanding Economy*. N.Y., 1949.

10205a. Young, J. M. *The Brazilian Revolution of 1930, and the Aftermath*. New Brunswick, N.J., 1967.

XXIV–E   cross references:

a) For the role of Brazil during World War II, see items 3709–3724.

b) See also items 3408, 3409c, 4106, 4107, 4136, 4152c, 4152d, 4158, 4171, 4180, 4289, 4348, 4870, 4871, 5423, 7701, 9072, 9810, 10086.

Index

Only items with identifiable authors are listed in this index. Each entry includes the author's name, followed by the serial number(s) assigned to his work(s) in the text. There are no entries for organizations like "Pan American Union" or "United States" or "United Nations," because in the editors' judgment they would be of little value. In such instances the detailed Table of Contents will be helpful in locating information on specific topics.

Arnolds, Alfonso, 1193
Arosemena, Juan D., 5191
Arosemena, Justo, 2369, 2432
Arosemena, Pablo, 7311, 8295, 8296
Arosemena Arias, C., 7389
Arosemena G., Diógenes, 7289
Arragon, Reginald F., 2565
Arraiz, Antonio, 1396
Arredondo, Harcio, 941
Arrocha, Angela, 6854
Arroniz, J. Joaquín, 2397a
Arroyo D., Enrique, 8727
Arroyo del Río, Carlos A., 8711
Arroyo Rivera, Alberto, 4597a
Arrubla, Gerardo, 8132
Arruda Botelho, A. Roberto de, 9867
Arrús, Oscar F., 3792
Artega, Luis, 8885
Arthur, Stanley C., 1897
Artiles Jérez, H., 4787a
Artúzar, Adolfo, 9427a
Arvelo, Perina, 7705
Arze, José A., 3670, 3793, 8996
Ashford, Gerald, 5637
Ashworth, Jessie, 6632
Asiaín Márquez, Carlos, 9142
Association of the Bar of the City of New York, 4364
Astigueta, Francisco B., 5317
Asturias, Francisco, 6930
Atkins, Edwin F., 2681, 7502, 7503
Atkins, George P., 7935a
Atkins, T. B., 2433
Atlantic and Pacific Ship Canal Company, 7040a
Atria R., Manuel, 5318
Auburn, Charles V., 6633
Auchmuty, James J., 1813
Aufricht, Hans, 30, 3524
Auguste, Barry L., 4673
Austin, Stephen F., 5638
Auten, John H., 4325
Auxier, George W., 2682, 2683, 2684
Avarina, V. I., 3980a, 4199a
Avila, Federico, 8997
Avila Camacho, Manuel, 3628, 3629, 3630, 3631, 3632, 3633, 3794
Ayala, Elías, 9057
Ayala, Eusebio, 4673a
Ayala, Segundo F., 5217
Ayala Mercado, Ernesto, 8998, 8999
Ayala Moreira, Rogelio, 9058
Ayón, Tomás, 7041
Azara, Félix de, 9192
Azarola Gil, Luis E., 942, 9161
Azcárate, Pablo de, 2623
Azcárraga Bustamante, L. de, 4674
Azevedo, Fernando de, 9867a
Azoy, Anastasio C., 2791, 2792
Azpurúa, Ramón, 1283

B

Babcock, Charles E., 151, 1082
Bacarisse, Charles A., 5639
Bach, F., 6392
Bache, Richard, 8242
Bacher, E. L., 5017
Baciu, Stefan, 7706
Backus, Richard C., 611
Bacon, Robert, 3037
Baerresen, D. W., 4325a
Báez, Cecilio, 9193, 9194
Baeza Flores, Alberto, 2685, 5447
Báez Camargo, Gonzalo, 6570
Bagaglia, A. C. R., 3145
Bagot, Josceline, 1990
Bagú, Sergio, 9709
Bailey, Helen M., 1403
Bailey, N. A., 3728a
Bailey, Stephen K., 3523
Bailey, Thomas A., 1546, 1571, 1572, 2808, 2865, 2984a, 3038, 3128, 4508, 7078
Bailey Lembcke, J., 8933a
Bailly, Luiza, 9867b
Bajarlía, Juan J., 9617
Baker, George W., Jr., 3039, 6855, 6979, 7079, 7224, 7311a, 7504
Baker, Marcus, 8563, 8564, 8565, 8566
Baker, Ray S., 3040, 3041
Balaguer, Joaquín, 7936, 7937
Balch, Emily G., 8065
Balderrama, Luis C., 6571
Balderrama G., Adalid, 9000
Baldivia G., José M., 8886, 8887
Baldrich, Alonso, 9618
Baldwin, E.F., 4598
Baldwin, Hanson W., 3608, 3609
Baldwin, Leland D., 1482
Baldwin, Simeon E., 990, 991
Baleeiro, Aliomar, 10014
Balen, Willem J. van, 1083
Balink, Albert, 6634
Ball, Eleanor E., 91
Ball, Mary M., 4396, 4599, 4755, 4755a
Ballanoff, Eric N., 9439
Ballesteros, Pío, 9419
Ballesteros Gaibrois, Manuel, 1483
Ballesteros y Beretta, Antonio, 1484
Ballivián, Adolfo, 6207
Ballivián Calderón, René, 3671
Ballón Benavides, Federico, 3547
Balseiro, José A., 5321
Bañados Espinosa, Julio, 9356
Bance, Juan B., 8518
Banco Central de Honduras, 6980
Banco de México, 4365, 6326
Bancroft, Frederic, 2058, 2059, 2236
Bancroft, Hubert H., 5518, 5519, 5640, 6672

Caldwell, Edward M., 5851
Caldwell, Robert G., 4567, 7441
Calero, Manuel, 6151
Calhoun, John C., 2065a
California State Library, Sutro Branch, 771
Calixte, Démosthènes P., 8073
Call, Tomme C., 6328
Callahan, James M., 2066, 2246, 5521, 5852, 7442, 7443
Callava, José, 1946
Callcott, Wilfred H., 2899, 5522, 5603, 5655
Calle, Manuel J., 1319
Calles, Plutarco E., 6271
Callorda, Pedro E., 3337
Calmon, Pedro, 9878, 9879, 9880, 9881, 9887, 9969
Calógeras, João P., 9882, 9969a, 10023
Calvo, Alejandro, 2067
Calvo, Carlos, 1087, 1827
Calvo, Joaquín B., 2462
Calvocoressi, Peter, 4788
Calzada Flores, Miguel, 4758
Calzadíaz Barrera, Alberto. 6016, 6229
Camacho, J. A., 9883
Camacho, José M., 8967
Camacho, Panfilo D., 7516
Camacho, Simón, 8522
Camacho Montoya, Guillermo, 8247
Cambon, Jules, 3244
Cameron, Duncan H., 7291a
Camín, Alfonso, 6230
Camp, Robert J. de, 3565
Campa, Miguel A., 7677a
Campa y Caraveda, Miguel A., 6718
Campbell, Alec, 2626
Campbell, A. E., 2810
Campbell, Charles S., Jr., 2811
Campo, Carlos del, 1263
Campobello, Nellie, 6231
Campos, Alfredo R., 3676
Campos, Francisco, 1320
Campos, Raul A. de, 1235, 9884
Campos, Roberto de O., 3732, 3985
Campos Harriet, Fernando, 9266
Campos Ponce, Xavier, 7095
Campos Salas, Octaviano, 4366
Campuzano, J. F., 7444
Canalejas y Méndez, José, 8733
Canales Salazar, Félix, 6983
Cañas, Juan J., 2463
Candamo, Victor G., 2690a
Candia G., Alfredo, 9004
Candioti, Luis A., 3944a
Cané, Miguel, 9546
Canelas O., Amado, 4100a
Canning, George, 7445
Cano, Luis, 8441
Cano de la Vega, Emeterio, 9063
Canterero, Luis A., 7096

Canyes, Manuel S., 4759, 5067, 5181j, 5236
Caó, José, 10109
Capdevila, Arturo, 3270
Capella y Pons, F., 2953
Capo, José M., 8028
Capó Rodríguez, Pedro, 4838
Capuñay, Manuel A., 8940
Capurro, A., 1370
Caraballo, Isa, 7678
Caraballo Sotolongo, Francisco, 2900
Caracas, Biblioteca Nacional, 955, 956, 957
Cararallo Setelengo, F., 7517
Carbajal, C., 5182
Carbajal, F., 5024a
Carballal, Rodolfo Z., 7518
Carbía, Rómulo D., 445, 446
Carbonell, Diego, 1935
Carbonell, José M., 7414
Carbonell, Miguel A., 7519
Carbonell, Néstor, 4405
Cárcano, Ramón, 9236
Carcovich, Luis, 2524
Cardenal, Luis G., 7097
Cárdenas, Lázaro, 6272, 6273, 6398, 6399
Cárdenas, Raúl F., 5237
Cárdenas, Rodolfo J., 8652
Cárdenas, Vicente, 2204
Cárdenas C., Antonio L., 1397
Cárdenas Ramírez, Julio, 1398
Cárdenas y Echarte, Raúl de, 1733, 2901, 7520
Cardon, Raúl L., 4653
Cardoza y Aragón, Luis, 6863, 6864
Cardozo, Efraím, 904, 9064, 9195, 9237
Cardozo, Manoel S., 508a, 9970
Cardozo, Michael H., 1656
Carey, James C., 8941
Carilla, Emilio, 9630
Carles, Rubén D., 8306
Carleton, William G., 3733
Carlisle, Calderón, 2691
Carlisle, Douglas H., 8635
Carlson, Evans F., 7098
Carlson, Fred A., 1088
Carlson, Oliver, 2692
Carman, Harry J., 345
Carmo, J. A. Pinto do, 509
Carmona, Antonio B., 1293
Carnegie, Andrew, 2872, 2873, 8570
Carnegie Endowment for International Peace, 5218
Carneiro, Octávio A., 4204
Carneiro, Virginia T., 3712
Carnero Checa, Genero, 3734
Carney, John P., 6594
Carnoy, Alan, 3986
Caron, P., 7
Carr, Albert Z., 2464
Carr, Edward H., 3185
Carr, P., 3526a

DeVries, Henry P., 4530
Dewart, Leslie, 7740
Dewey, Loring D., 8033
Dewhurst, W. W., 1951
DeWilde, John C., 3570, 3571, 8446, 9730
DeWitt, Paul, 9636
Díaz A., Julio, 1221, 8970
Díaz Cisneros, César, 3215, 3216
Díaz Doin, Guillermo, 4605, 4791
Díaz Dufoo, Carlos, 5951, 6410
Díaz Goitia, José J., 9731
Díaz Machicao, Porfirio, 8970a
Díaz Molano, Elías, 9843
Díaz Ordóñez, Virgilio, 7945
Díaz Rozzotto, Jaime, 6872
Díaz V., Francisco J., 9366
Díaz Versón, Salvador, 3650
Dickens, P. D., 9495, 9844
Dickey, John S., 1671
Dickmann, Enrique, 3678
Didapp, Juan P., 2629a, 6101
Diebold, William, Jr., 3572
Diego-Fernández, Salvador, 8316
Dienst, Alex, 788
Dietrich, Ethel B., 3573
Dietrich, Wolfram, 8169
Dietze, Gottfried, 9731a
Diez, William E., 2906, 6720
Díez de Medina, Eduardo, 8971, 8972
Diez de Medina, Raúl, 5155
Diffie, Bailey W., 5330, 10119
Difrieri, Horacio A., 1188
Dillon, Dorothy, 4062
Dillon, Emile J., 6023, 6280
Dillon, Richard H., 187, 187a
Dillon, Rudolf, 8609
Dimock, Marshall E., 7323
Dinegar, Caroline A., 1586
Diniz, Hilton, 4107
Dion, Marie B., 6873
Dios Bojórquez, Juan de, 6024, 6025
Divine, Robert A., 1553, 3468, 3469
Divinnie, Louis L., 6573
Dizard, Wilson P., 3737
Dmytryshyn, Basil, 1774
Doblado, Manuel, 6102
Dobles Segreda, Luis, 638, 1296
Dodd, William E., 2075, 3041
Dodds, Harold W., 7114, 7115
Dogee, John W., 9637
Domenech, Emmanuel, 2262
Domenech, Roberto, 6210
Domínguez, Francisco, 9732
Domínguez, Manuel, 9066, 9067, 9068
Domínguez Bordona, Jesús, 188
Domínguez Ferman, Serafín, 4833
Dominican Press Society, 7946
Domke, Martin, 3574

Donald, M. B., 9276
Donnan, Elizabeth, 1716
Donnell, Guy R., 6211
Donoso, Ricardo, 587, 1833, 9277, 9278, 9420
Donovan, Frank, 1775
Donovan, John, 4063
Donovan, Robert J., 3864
Dopp, Lloyd H., 6026
Dorfman, Adolfo, 4208
Dorland, Arthur G., 3715
Dorsainvil, Justin C., 8011
Dorta-Duque, Francisco, 7995d
Dorticós Torrado, Osvaldo, 7741, 7742
Doubleday, C. W., 7045
Douglas, Paul H., 8079
Douglass, Frederick, 8034
Downey, Fairfax, 5774
Downey, Joseph T., 5775
Downs, Robert B., 352, 1156, 1157
Doyle, George A., 4289
Doyle, Henry G., 4979
Doyle, John T., 6521
Dozer, Donald M., 1420, 2076, 2076a, 2994, 3186, 3996, 5203, 7867, 9977
Draghicescu, Dimitrie, 3217
Drago, Luis M., 2956a, 4531, 4606, 4607, 8610
Drago, Mariano J., 2162
Draper, Theodore, 7743, 7744, 7745, 7746, 7747, 7748, 7748a
Drascher, Wahrhold, 2907
Dreier, John C., 4108, 4791a, 4792, 4793, 5271a
Driver, T. T., 8941a
Dromundo, Baltasar, 6236
Drucker, Peter R., 4209
Drummond, Donald F., 3470
Drummond, Roscoe, 3865
Duane, William, 8248
DuBois, James T., 8396, 8397
Dubois, Jules, 4064, 7393, 7749
Ducassi Mendieta, Francisco, 5204
Ducoff, Louis J., 6769
Ducoudray Holstein, H. L., 8170
Dudden, Arthur P., 3053
Dudgeon, Lucile, 1131
Dueñas Van Severen, J. Ricardo, 7046
Duffield, Alexander J., 8825, 8826
Dugdale, E. T. S., 3085
Duggan, Lawrence, 3347, 3738, 5071
Duggan, Stephen P. H., 1421, 3218, 4733
Duin, Edgar C., 7868
Duin, Juan, 9010
Dulanto Pinillos, Jorge, 8827
Dulebohn, G. R., 2076b
Dulles, Eleanor L., 3865a
Dulles, Foster R., 1554, 2908, 3348
Dulles, John F., 6874, 7324
Dulles, John W. F., 6027, 10120
Dumont, René, 7750

Hill, N. L., 1680
Hill, Ricardo G., 6349
Hill, Roscoe R., 364, 365, 1102a, 1103, 1103a, 1257, 2354, 7126, 7127, 7128
Hillekamps, Carl H., 4069
Hiller, Harley E., 4437
Hillman, Tommie, Jr., 9291
Hilton, Ronald, 214, 1104, 10041, 10042
Hilton, Stanley E., 3683, 6575
Hinckley, Ted C., 6216
Hines, Calvin W., 6242a
Hinton, Harold B., 3359
Hirschman, Albert O., 3754, 4215, 4216
Hirschowicz, Erwin, 1105
Hirschberg, Herbert S., 366, 1024
Hirst, William A., 9644
Hispanic Society of America, 215, 216, 1106
Hitchman, James H., 661b, 7554
Hoar, George F., 2883
Hobbs, William H., 7555
Hoben, Katherine H., 7243
Hobson, Jane A., 2289
Hockett, Homer C., 3223
Hodge, John E., 9645
Hodges, Henry G., 4620
Hoepelman, Virgilio, 7856
Hoepelmann, Antonio, 7915, 7962
Hoffman, H. Theodore, 8408
Hoffmann, Fritz L., 9758
Hogan, William R., 5684
Hohmann, Janey E., 4176
Holanda, Sérgio B. de, 9901
Holdich, Thomas H., 9645a
Holland, H. F., 3879
Holland, T. E., 8614a
Hollander, Jacob H., 7916, 7917, 7918, 7919
Holleran, Mary P., 6820
Holley, H. A., 4202
Holls, Frederick W., 4689
Holly, A. P. B., 8089a
Holman, Donald A., 2726a
Holmes, Henry A., 6349a
Holmes, Lula T., 1107a
Holmes, Olive, 3953, 4217, 5242, 9759, 9760, 9761, 10145
Holmes, Ruth E. V., 522
Holmes, Vera L., 1502
Holst, Herman E. von, 2095
Holt, Pat M., 8476
Holt, W. Stull, 1681, 1756
Honduras, Biblioteca Nacional, 755
Hooker, Roberto M., 2185, 7129
Hoome, John G., 7556
Hoover, Herbert C., 3290, 3291, 3292, 3293, 3360, 3361
Hopkins, Edward A., 9217
Hopkins, John A. H., 6725
Horelick, A. L., 7771

Horn, Paul V., 4335
Horne, Bernardino C., 3588
Hornet, Esteban, 9843
Horowitz, Irving L., 9460, 10146
Hoskins, Halford L., 217, 1974, 2290
Houk, R. J., 7244
Houseman, Philip J., 9461
Houston, David F., 3059
Houston, John A., 4177, 4178
Houston, Sam, 5685
Houtart, François, 4008
Hovet, Thomas, Jr., 4179
Hovey, Harold A., 3953a
Howard, Harry N., 7334
Howard, John A., Jr., 4438
Howe, George F., 64a, 2096, 2343, 2384
Howe, Samuel G., 7889
Howland, Hewitt H., 6291
Howren, Alleine, 5686
Hoyo Algara, Francisco del, 4802
Hoyos, J. A., 8273
Huart, M. R. d'Artois, 2291
Hubbard, Harlan P., 65, 66
Hubbard, Ursula P., 8447
Hubbell, John G., 7739
Huberich, Charles H., 2355
Huberman, Leo, 7772
Huck, Eugene R., 8253
Hudicourt, Pierre, 8090
Hudson, Jerry E., 1849
Hudson, Manley O., 1717, 3224, 4658, 6727
Hudson, William H., 9151
Huebner, G. G., 7335
Huelin, David, 4369d
Huete Abella, Rodolfo, 7130
Hughes, Charles E., 3251, 3252, 3253, 3294, 3295, 3296, 5144
Hughes, Emmet J., 3880
Hughes, George W., 2385
Hughes, Thomas L., 9461a
Hughlett, Lloyd J., 4255
Hulen, Bertran D., 1682
Hull, Cordell, 3362, 5164
Hull, William I., 4690
Hulsey, Ramon H., 7773
Humbert, Jules, 8133
Hume, Edgar E., 7464
Humphrey, Hubert H., 3926
Humphrey, John P., 4738, 4884, 5221
Humphrey, Norman D., 6592
Humphreys, Robert A., 218, 1108, 1431, 1737, 1841, 1850, 1851, 1852, 1853, 1854, 3809, 4768, 6952, 6953, 8830, 8830a, 8831
Hundley, Norris, Jr., 6545, 6546
Huneeus Gana, Antonio, 9462
Hunnicutt, Benjamin M., 9902
Hunt, Gaillard, 1683, 1855
Hunt, Jay B., 4180

Jameson, J. Franklin, 1162
Jamison, James C., 7050
Jane, Cecil, 1433, 8912
Janes, Henry L., 7465
Jankus, Alfred P., 8655a
Jaramillo Alvarado, Pío, 3484, 8682, 8714
Jaramillo Pérez, César, 1503, 8683
Jaryc, M., 7
Jáuregui Rosquellas, Alfredo, 4857
Javari, Jorge J. D., 9991
Javits, Jacob K., 4369f
Jay, John, 2294
Jay, William, 5801
Jefferson, Mark S. W., 9423
Jefferson, Thomas, 1856
Jeffrey, William H., 9646, 9647
Jenkins, Myra E., 5974
Jenks, Leland H., 7559, 7560
Jensen, Amy E., 6821
Jervey, T. D., 8581
Jessup, Philip C., 3007, 3548, 4693, 5169
Jewell, Malcolm E., 1687
Jiles Pizarro, Jorge, 9465a
Jiménez, Ramón E., 7963
Jiménez de la Romera, Waldo, 2728
Jiménez Grullón, Juan I., 7857, 7964
Jiménez Montellano, Bernardo, 3298
Jiménez y Núñez, Victoriano, 4621
Jinesta, Ricardo, 2356, 2357, 4119, 7246
Jobim, Danton, 1782, 10148
Johannesson, Fredrik, 4442
Johnes, Edward R., 8582
Johnsen, Julia E., 4886
Johnson, Allen, 1163
Johnson, Claudius O., 3191
Johnson, Emory R., 1601, 7337, 8335
Johnson, Guion G., 2578
Johnson, Haynes, 7775
Johnson, John J., 3954, 3955, 4009, 4010, 4011, 9329, 9384, 9384a, 10149
Johnson, Kenneth F., 3755
Johnson, L. L., 4336
Johnson, Louis, 3617
Johnson, Lyndon B., 3941a, 7998
Johnson, Richard A., 5877, 5878
Johnson, Robert B., 6243
Johnson, Victor L., 9647a
Johnson, Walter, 1602
Johnson, Wayne E., 6996
Johnson, Willis F., 2358, 7425
Johnston, Samuel, 9330
Johnston, William D., 367
Joint Bolivian–United States Labour Commission, 9020
Joint Brazil–United States Economic Development Commission, 10150
Joint Publications Research Service, 4119a, 4294a
Jones, Alexander, 7466
Jones, Anson, 5687

Jones, Cecil K., 14, 15, 809, 810
Jones, Chester L., 1688, 2921, 2922, 6043, 6292, 6577, 6728, 6729, 6730, 6731, 6732, 6822, 7130a, 7247, 7247a, 7561
Jones, Clarence F., 1110, 3411
Jones, J. P., 3131
Jones, Joseph M., Jr., 3412, 6779
Jones, Robert C., 811
Jones, Tom B., 227, 1434, 1435
Jones, Willis K., 228
Jordan, Ancieto, 8448
Jordan, David C., 9763
Jordan, Donaldson, 2098
Jordan, H. D., 5688
Jordán López, Manuel, 8866
Jordán Sandoval, Santiago, 8974, 9021
Jorge, A. G. de Araujo, 10045
Jorrín, Miguel, 1535, 3756
Jos, Emiliano, 8187
Joseph, F. M., 1603
Josephs, Ray, 3881, 9764
Juárez, Benito P., 5879
Juarez, Joseph R., 7921
Juárez Muñoz, J. Fernando, 6955
Judson, Lyman S., 3553
Julien, Claude, 7776
Julio y Elizalde, Juan J., 8913
Junco, Alfonso, 6167
Justin, Joseph, 8039, 8091
Jústiz del Valle, Tomás, 5344
Justo, Liborio, 4012

K

Kagawa, Toshihiko, 3956
Kahle, Louis G., 4561, 6168
Kain, Ronald S., 5169a, 9079
Kaiser, Chester C., 4906, 5880, 5975
Kaiser, John B., 16
Kalb, Courtenay de, 872
Kalijarvi, Thorsten V., 6645
Kalugin, G. A., 4013
Kalvoda, Josef, 4071
Kamia, Delia, 9648
Kamman, William, 7131
Kane, Joseph N., 1164
Kantor, Harry, 229, 915, 3927, 5480, 5481, 7248, 8655b, 8656
Kaplan, Lawrence S., 1915
Kaplan, Louis, 368
Karnes, Thomas L., 6646
Katz, Friedrich, 3153, 6892
Kaufmann, Wilhelm, 7337a
Kaufmann, William W., 1857
Kauffmann Doig, Federico, 8805
Kearney, Thomas, 5802
Kearny, Ruth E., 5881

Ladas, S. P., 4693b
Ladd, E. F., 6294
Ladrón de Guevara, Matilde, 7778
LaFeber, Walter, 1857a, 2099b, 2099c, 2501, 2502, 2503, 2731, 10051
Laferrière, J., 2962
Lafertte, Elías, 9467, 9468
Lafond, Georges, 9502
La Foy, Margaret, 9082
Lagarrique, Juan E., 5433
Lagos Valenzuela, Enrique, 4660
Lakas, Ivan A., 10156
Lally, Frank E., 2296
Lamadrid, Lázaro, 731a
Lamas, Andrés, 452
Lamb, Dean I., 2476a
Lamont, Corliss, 7779
Lande, Irvin M., 9331
Landestoy, Carmita, 7965
Lane, Anne W., 3061
Lane, Franklin K., 6171
Lane, George B., Jr., 4713
Lane, Jack C., 2924a
Lane, Walter P., 5692
Lane, Wheaton J., 6683
Lang, Franz, 6420
Langer, Robert, 4694
Langer, William L., 1033, 2925, 3485, 3486
Langley, Lester D., 7342a
Lanning, John T., 1975
Lansing, Marion, 1858
Lansing, Robert, 3062, 6172
Lantz, Benne, 7780
Lanuza, Pedro J., 2178d
La Plata, Universidad Nacional, Biblioteca, 453, 454, 455, 456
La Pradelle, Paul de, 9083
Lara y Pardó, Luis, 1347, 6108
Larco Herrera, Rafael, 3958
Lardé y Arthés, Enrique, 6647
Larde y Larín, Jorge, 7211, 7212
Larin, N. S., 6580, 7132
Larkin, John D., 3414
Larned, Josephus, 370
La Rosa, Pascual, 5094a
Larraín Zañartu, José J., 1273
Larrainzar, Manuel, 2412, 2413
Larsen, K., 75
Larson, Cedric, 3133, 3159
Larson, David L., 7781
Lascano, Victor, 9503
Lasch, Christopher, 2884
Lascuraín y Osio, Angel, 6045
Lastarria, J. F., 2613
Lastra B., Jaime de la, 8914
Latané, John H., 1560, 1740, 1741, 2634, 2732, 2926, 3119, 3226a, 7343, 8337, 8338, 8339
Latcham, Ricardo, 9424

Latham, Earl, 3063
Latham, Harris L., 3811
Latin American Juridical Committee, 5222
Latin America Kyôkai, Tokyo, 1111b, 1438
Latino, Américo, 8763
Latorre y Setién, Germán, 4444
Latour, Arsène L., 1918
Latrille Urriola, Fernando, 4562
Latzina, Francisco, 1204, 1205
Lauerhass, Ludwig, Jr., 234
Laurent, Gerard M., 8041
Lauro, Faffaele di, 3487
Lauterpacht, Hersh, 4563
Laval, Ramón A., 592
LaValle, Juan B., 4938a
Lavalle Cobo, Jorge, 2168
Lavalle y Arias de Saavedra, José A. de, 1381
Lavender, David, 5805a
Laverde Amaya, Isidro, 625, 626
Laves, Walter H. C., 3488
Lavin, John, 8638
Lavín, José D., 6353, 6421
Lavretskii, Iosif R., 8188
Lavrov, N. M., 1858a, 5516a
Lawrence, T. J., 4695
Lawson, Leonard A., 2007
Lawson, Ruth C., 1035
Lay, Bennett, 5612
Lay, T. C., 1689
Lazcano Mazón, Andrés M., 4887
Lazitch, Branko, 4071a
League of Nations Association, 5038
Leard, Robert B., 7468
Leavitt, Joshua, 2100
Leavitt, Sturgis E., 235
Lebraud, Elie, 2834
Lecorps, Marceau, 8042
Lecuna, Vicente, 2536, 8189, 8190, 8191, 8192
Leddy, John M., 9764a
Leduc, Alberto, 1347, 8340
Lee, Fitzhugh, 2635
Lee, H. E., 5264a
Lee, Thomas F., 3415
Lee, W. S., 7343a
Leech, Margaret, 2636
Lee López, Alberto, 8193
Lefèvre, Eugène, 2297
Le Fur, Louis, 2835
Léger, Abel-Nicolas, 8043
Léger, Jacques N., 8013, 8044
Leggett, Aaron, 5806
Leguizamon, J. A., 236
Leguizamón Pondal, Martiniano, 9851
Lehmann, Richard, 7343b
Leidy, W. Philip, 371
Leigh, John G., 8341
Leighton, George R., 6015
Leite, Cleantho, 4262

Marchiori, Carlo, 1789
Marcus, Elliot A., 2616
Mariátegui, José C., 917a, 5482, 8835
María Tornel, José, 5614, 5698
María y Campos, Armando de, 6356
Mariluz Urquijo, José M., 2344
Marín, Rufino, 6959, 6960, 8766
Marinho, Ilmar P., 4772
Marini, Ruy M., 10165
Marino Pérez, Luis, 374, 7575c, 7576, 7576a
Maris, Gary L., 7426b
Maritano, Nino, 4126
Markey, Beatrice G., 10194
Markham, Clements R., 8584, 8836, 8869
Markov, Walter, 1439
Marks, R. L., 9772
Márquez, N. P., 9655
Márquez Bustillos, V., 8640
Márquez Camacho, Reinaldo, 4844
Márquez Montiel, Joaquín, 5576
Márquez Padilla, Tarsicio, 3814
Márquez Sterling, Carlos, 2738, 7427
Márquez Sterling, Manuel, 2739, 4950, 6111, 7577, 7578, 7579
Marrazzo, Javier, 1207
Marrero Aristy, Ramón, 7859
Marrero y Artiles, Leví, 1305
Marriott, J. A. R., 2013
Marsh, Margaret C., 9026
Marshall, Andrew, 10166
Marshall, C. B., 1607
Marshall, Thomas M., 1959, 5699
Marsland, Amy L., 8501
Marsland, William D., 8501
Martí, José, 2740, 2741, 2742, 2743, 2744, 2745
Martillo, Trinidad, 4072
Martin, Bernard L., 4338
Martín, Carlos, 2414
Martin, Charles E., 1608
Martin, John B., 3883, 8000a
Martin, Lawrence, 1112
Martin, Lawrence W., 1649
Martin, Michael R., 1113, 1168
Martin, P. F., 2300, 7213, 8946
Martin, Percy A., 1114, 1432, 3108, 9152, 9178, 9996, 9997
Martin, Thomas P., 239
Martín Artajo, Alberto D., 5351
Martínez, Enrique N., 2542
Martínez, Héctor P., 817
Martinez, John R., 6603
Martínez, José L., 9153
Martínez, Marcial, 4921
Martínez, Ricardo A., 4450
Martínez, Rodolfo, 9773
Martínez, Rufino, 1315
Martínez Alomía, Santiago, 6961
Martínez Arango, Felipe, 2639

Martínez C., Diego, 8413
Martínez Caro, Ramón, 5695
Martínez de la Torre, Ricardo, 3687, 5483
Martínez del Río, Ramón, 6357
Martínez Estrada, Ezequiel, 9656
Martínez Hague, Carlos, 5244
Martínez-López, R., 3532
Martínez Méndez, Nemisio, 4662, 4907
Martínez Moreno, A., 5133
Martínez Moreno, Raúl S., 5087, 9853
Martínez Ortiz, Rafael, 7580
Martínez Palafox, Luis, 6962
Martínez Zelada, Eliseo, 8414
Martino, John, 7785
Martins, Mário, 3718
Martín y Oñate, Cayetano, 2198
Martz, John D., 6686, 6782, 6897, 8482, 8656a
Marure, Alejandro, 6651, 6687
Marvaud, Angel, 6737
Marvin, George, 7924
Marx, Fritz M., 3492
Marzani, Carl, 7782
Maschke, Arturo, 4370
Masingill, Eugene F., 6112
Masini, José L., 457
Masis Rojas, T., 2478
Mason, Bruce B., 3961
Mason, Gregory, 2746
Mason, Theodorus B. M., 8870
Massa, Nicolas, 457a
Massad, Carlos, 4371
Massa Gil, B., 818
Massey, Vincent, 4888
Massó, José L., 7786
Massoni, Pierre, 8016
Masters, Ruth D., 1115
Masur, Gerhard, 8197
Mata, Luis I., 5979
Matá Gavidia, José, 6650
Matamoros, Luis, 7279
Mathews, John M., 3368
Mathews, Joseph J., 8585
Mathews, Sidney T., 2363
Mathieu, Beltran, 3157
Mathy, Leonard G., 3416
Matienzo, José N., 2617
Matos, Almir, 7789
Matos Romero, Manuel, 8641
Matta, Manuel A., 2220, 9414
Matta Vial, Enrique, 1274
Matteson, D. B., 1161
Matthews, Herbert L., 3762, 3883a, 7787, 7788
Matthews, Mary A., 375
Matijevic, Nicolás, 458
Mauá, Irineu E. de Sousa, 9998
Maudslay, A. P., 6841
Maudslay, Ann C., 6841
Maul, Carlos, 4873

Meyer, Michael C., 826, 6113, 6180a
Meyer Cosío, Lorenzo, 6439a
Meyer-Lindenberg, Hermann, 4542
Michel, Paul H., 3109, 3110
Middleton, Annie L., 5700, 5701
Mignone, A. Frederick, 6360
Migone, R. C., 1117
Mikesell, Raymond F., 4222, 4339, 4340, 4341
Mikhailov, S. S., 239a, 239b, 1863a
Mikoyan, Anastas I., 7794
Milk, Richard G., 4019
Millares Carlo, Agustín, 239c, 827, 828, 829
Miller, Alexander E., 2965
Miller, C. R., 2506
Miller, Carlos G., 4453
Miller, David H., 1720, 3230
Miller, Eugene H., 4889
Miller, Hugh G., 6738, 7352
Miller, John, 8838
Miller, Robert R., 2305, 5893, 5894, 5895
Miller, Warren, 7795
Millington, Herbert, 8872
Millis, Walter, 1612, 1613, 2642, 3887
Mills, Charles W., 4019a
Mills, C. Wright, 7796
Mills, J. Saxon, 8346
Millspaugh, Arthur C., 8097, 8098
Minelli, Pablo M., 3417, 3518
Miner, Dwight C., 8347
Minge, Ward A., 5702
Minger, Ralph E., 7397, 7586
Minor, Van L., 876
Mintz, Sidney W., 743
Miramón, Alberto, 8255
Miranda, Jorge, 7138
Miranda Arenas, Osvaldo E., 1538
Mirkin, Stanford M., 1038
Miró, Rodrigo, 7301
Miró Quesada, Antonio, 2643
Miró Quesada G., Alejandro, 4859
Mitani, Hiroshi, 1118
Mitchell, Broadus, 3192
Mitchell, Harold, 6739
Mitre, Bartolomé, 1864, 9568, 9569
Mock, James R., 3132, 3133, 3159
Moctezuma, Aquiles P., 6583
Mogro Moreno, Antonio, 9089
Molina, Felipe, 7251, 7252, 7276
Molina, Raul, 459
Molina Argüello, Carlos, 877, 878
Molina de Lines, María, 2480a
Molina Enríquez, Andrés, 6440
Molinari, Diego L., 9854
Mollien, Gaspard, 8256
Momsen, Richard P., 1208
Monaghan, Jay, 2107
Monahan, James, 7797
Moncada, José M., 7139

Moncada Sánchez, José A., 4223
Moncayo, Pedro, 8701, 8768
Monge Alfaro, Carlos, 1297, 7253
Monner Sans, Ricardo, 2750
Monroe, Keith, 6900
Monroy, Guadalupe, 830, 2306
Monsalve Martínez, Manuel, 1289
Monsegur, Sylla J., 460
Montague, Ludwell L., 8017, 8048
Montalvo, Ricardo J., 10168
Montaner Bello, Ricardo, 9333
Montarcé Lastra, Antonio, 9855
Monteagudo, Bernardo, 2545
Monteiro Real, Regina, 10049
Montenegro, Ernesto, 8917
Montero Barrantes, Francisco, 7254
Montero Moreno, René, 9469a
Montero Ríos, Eugenio, 2849
Montes, Arturo H., 6689
Monte y Tejada, Antonio del, 7874
Monticone, Charles R., 5404
Montiel Argüello, A., 7140
Montllor, Joseph J., 7890
Montt, Ambrosio, 9389
Montt, Luis, 461
Montt, Pedro, 9390, 9390a
Montúfar y Rivera Maestre, Lorenzo, 2481, 6690
Moody, William I., 4342
Moor, Carol C., 81
Moore, David R., 1441
Moore, Ernest R., 831
Moore, John B., 1614, 1615, 1616, 2107b, 2108, 2109,
    2506a, 2546, 2644, 2751, 2836, 2837, 2930, 3257,
    7280, 8348, 9415
Moore, John P., 2418, 7470
Moore, John R., 8658
Moore, Oscar K., 9916
Moore, R. Walton, 2016
Moorhead, Max L., 6842
Moos, Malcolm, 3860
Mora, Gaspar, 9426
Mora, José A., 4020, 4809
Moraes, João B. M. de, 3719
Moraes, Rubens Borba de, 533, 534
Morales, Eusebio A., 8349
Morales, Vicente, 5981
Morales Carrión, Arturo, 4130
Morales Jiménez, Alberto, 1353, 6051
Morales Loza, Néstor, 9775
Morales Morales, Minerva, 3418, 3931, 5184
Morales Padrón, Francisco, 1508, 6740, 8768a
Morales y Eloy, Juan, 8685
Morales y Morales, Vidal, 2645
Moral Pérez, Carlos R., 7302
Moran, Charles, 3656, 8049
Moran, W. T., 3592
Mora Valverde, Manuel, 3369
Moreau, Henry, 2307

Nance, Joseph M., 5704
Napoleão, Aluizio, 535, 10065
Naranjo, Francisco, 1354
Naranjo Martínez, Enrique, 8201
Naranjo Ostty, Rafael, 8658a
Nardone, Benito, 4074
Nasatir, Abraham P., 1403
Nash, Roy, 10066
Nathan, Paul, 6304, 6305
Nathan Associates, 7215
National Education Association, 243
National Planning Association, 4298
Nattier, Frank E., Jr., 10172a
Nava, Julian, 8544
Navarrete, Félix, 6584
Navarrete, George, 3309
Navarro, Gustavo A., 8978
Navarro Andrade, Ulpiano, 4455a
Navarro y Lamarca, Carlos, 1509
Navarro y Rodrigo, Carlos, 5578
Navas, José, 7588
Naylor, Robert A., 2389
Nazaris, Esther B. de, 8192
Neal, Marian, 4185
Neale, R. G., 2819
Nearing, Scott, 2933, 2934
Needler, Martin C., 1540, 1541, 8946b
Neel, Virginia P., 4875
Nehemkis, Peter, 3763
Nemours, Alfred, 8050, 8051
Nenclares, F. Carmona, 5351a
Nerval, Gaston, 1790, 3500, 5173
Nesbitt, Wallace, 7354
Ness, Norman T., 3831, 9028
Neto, Francisco A. G., 10173
Neto, Maia, 10174
Nettles, H. Edward, 4629
Neuberger, Otto, 595, 744, 756, 972
Neumann, William L., 4564, 9334, 9335
Neves, J., 10067
Nevins, Allan, 1867a, 2112, 2112a, 2112b, 2113, 2935, 3192a, 3193, 3371, 5816
Newbold, Stokes, 6903
Newell, Chester, 5705
New England Institute of Inter-American Affairs, 244
Newlands, Francis G., 7926
Newman, P. C., 7683
Newton, Walter H., 3307
Newton, Wesley P., 3194, 3194a
New York Public Library, 245, 246, 386, 387, 387a, 834
Nicaise, August, 2482
Nicaragua, Biblioteca Nacional, 879
Nichols, Egbert R., 3621
Nichols, Jeannette P., 2113a
Nichols, Madaline W., 9601a
Nichols, Roy F., 1868, 2114, 2483, 8052
Nicholson, Norman L., 4891

Nicolas, Hagar, 8099
Nicolau d'Olwer, Luis, 5817
Nicholson, Harold G., 6306
Niedergang, Marcel, 8000b
Niemeyer, Eberhardt V., 200, 6115
Nieto Caballero, Luis E., 8352, 8416
Nieto Navia, Rafael, 1791
Nieto Pena, Xesús, 9091
Nimmo, Joseph, Jr., 2444
Niño H., Alberto, 8417
Niosi, Jerome J., 5896
Nitze, Paul H., 3887a
Nixon, Lewis, 7355, 7356
Nixon, Richard M., 3888
Noboa, Alejandro, 8686
Noel, Carlos M., 9778
Noel, John V., 4924
Nogales y Méndez, Rafael de, 7151
Nogueira, D., 10126
Nogueira, Rubem, 10068
Nogueira, Sizinio P., 10001
Noguera, J. J., 1206
Nolan, Louis C., 8840, 8841, 9778a
Normano, João F., 3195, 3196, 3533, 5405, 9917, 9918
North, Joseph, 7800
Norton, H. D., 3310
Norton, Henry K., 3311, 6743, 6744
Notta, Julio, 9779
Notter, Harley, 3073, 3818
Novo y Colson, Pedro de, 2221
Nowell, Charles E., 2171
Nuermberger, Gustave A., 2618, 4456, 8714b
Nunes, Reginaldo, 4699
Núñez, Eduardo, 2547
Núñez, Enrique B., 2507, 8545
Núñez Arca, P., 9780
Núñez Ortega, Gabriel, 5706
Nunn, Frederick M., 9427
Nystrom, J. Warren, 4131c

O

Obaid, Antonio H., 4126
Oberlitner, Thomas B., 6307
Obermeyer, Charles, 5207
Oblitas Fernández, Edgar, 8874
Obregón Loría, Rafael, 2484, 7255
Obyden, Konstantin M., 4021
O'Connor, Harvey, 6441
O'Connor, James, 7801
O'Connor, Nancy L., 2648
O'Connor, R., 6247
O'Connor d'Arlach, Tomás, 1224
Octavio, Rodrigo, 4592
Oddone, Rafael, 9220
Odriozola, Manuel, 917, 8842
Offner, John L., 2755

Thomas, A. J., Jr., 4643, 4824, 4825, 8002a
Thomas, Alfred B., 1469, 4034
Thomas, Alfred D., 1967
Thomas, Ann Van Wynen, 4643, 4825, 8002a
Thomas, Benjamin P., 2044
Thomas, David Y., 1802, 2980, 5373, 8457
Thomas, D. H., 111
Thomas, E., 10195a
Thomas, Eugene P., 3600
Thomas, Lula, 6349a
Thompson, Arthur W., 345
Thompson, George, 9245
Thompson, George A., 6846
Thompson, Kenneth W., 1639, 1640
Thompson, Waddy, 5628
Thompson, Wallace, 1521, 6665, 6755
Thomson, Charles A., 5009, 5058, 6316, 6472, 7220,
    7629, 7690a, 7984
Thomson, Norman, 8434
Thord-Gray, I., 6138
Thorne, J. O., 1002
Thorning, Joseph F., 3902, 8233
Thorning, J. P., 10196
Thorpe, George C., 6509
Thorton, Everett W., 2943
Thurber, O. E., 8553
Thurston, Walter C., 3324
Tijerino, Toribio, 7179
Tilton, Eva M., 112
Timm, Charles A., 6563, 6564, 6565, 10083
Timmons, Bascom N., 3395
Timmons, Wilbert, 5585
Tingley, Donald F., 7630
Tischendorf, Alfred P., 5286a, 6003, 8257, 8259
Tisnés, J. Roberto M., 8234
Titherington, Richard H., 2805
Tobar Donoso, Julio, 8787, 8788
Tolentino R., César, 7932
Tolentino Rojas, Vicente, 7985
Tolley, H. R., 4296
Tomasek, Robert D., 6610
Tomic R., Radomiro, 3701
Tomlinson, Edward, 3781, 4035, 5059
Tompkins, Dorothy C., 403
Tompkins, Edwin B., 2944
Tompkins, Frank, 6255
Torata, El Conde de, 8847
Toribio Medina, José, 604, 605
Toriello Garrido, Guillermo, 6917
Toro, Alfonso, 6591
Toro, Gaspar, 4670
Toro, Josefina del, 302
Toro Ruilova, David, 9114
Torre Revello, José, 466, 467, 468, 469, 470, 471, 472,
    1139b
Torre Villar, Ernesto de la, 849, 1885, 2182, 7064
Torrea, Juan M., 5922, 6139, 6224
Torrente, Mariano, 1884, 7491

Torres, José G., 4379
Torres Almeyda, Pablo E., 8486
Torres Bodet, Jaime, 4487, 5097
Torres Caicedo, José M., 2562
Torres Calleja, Mario, 9045
Torres García, F., 4580
Torres Lanzas, Pedro, 303
Torres Manzo, Carlos, 6377
Torriente y Peraza, Cosme de la, 2663, 3663, 3664,
    3833, 3834, 4602, 4644, 7433, 7631, 7632, 7633, 7634,
    7665, 7666, 7667
Torriente y Peraza, Emilio de la, 7635
Toscano, Humberto, 8709
Toth, Jane, 749
Toulmin, Harry A., Jr., 6256
Toussaint, Manuel, 850
Tovar Villa, Raúl, 9115
Tower, Charlemagne, 7373
Tower, W. S., 3101
Townsend, William C., 6317, 6474
Toynbee, Arnold J., 4036, 4236
Tracy, D. W., 5060
Traphagen, Jeanne C., 3325
Trask, David F., 3139
Travernier, E., 7374
Traversoni, Alfredo, 9137
Travesi, Gonzalo G., 6140
Travis, Ira D., 2188, 2393
Travis, Martin B., 4488, 4826, 7406
Trelles y Govín, Carlos M., 671, 672, 673, 674, 675,
    676, 5586, 7636
Trembley, William A., 749, 1260
Trend, John B., 8235
Trescot, W. H., 7492, 7493, 7494
Treudley, Mary, 7880
Treviño, Ricardo, 6628
Trías, Vivian, 4142
Tristan, L., 9690
Troncoso, Jesús M., 7881
Trotter, Reginald G., 4902
Trübner, Nicolas, 556
Truda, P. de Leonardo, 9937
True, C. Allen, 5629
True, Marshall M., 2777a
Trueblood, Howard J., 3428, 3601, 3602, 3603, 3835,
    4747, 5211
Trujillo Molina, Rafael L., 6318, 7986, 7987, 7988,
    7989
Truman, Harry S., 3903, 3904, 3905
Tuchman, Barbara, 3172
Tucker, George F., 2140
Tucker, William P., 6378
Tudela, Francisco, 8789
Tudela, José, 304
Tugwell, Rexford G., 3396
Tumba Ortega, Alejandro, 933
Turbay Ayala, Julio C., 8487
Turlington, Edgar W., 1763, 4489, 5098, 6079